INTERNATIONAL FINANCE HANDBOOK

Volume 2

INTERNATIONAL FINANCE HANDBOOK

Volume 2

Edited by

ABRAHAM M. GEORGE

Multinational Computer Models, Inc.

IAN H. GIDDY

Columbia University

A Wiley-Interscience Publication

JOHN WILEY & SONS New York • Chichester • Brisbane • Toronto • Singapore

This publication is designed to provide accurate and authoritative information in regard to the subject matter covered. It is sold with the understanding that the publisher is not engaged in rendering legal, accounting, or other professional service. If legal advice or other expert assistance is required, the services of a competent professional person should be sought. *From a Declaration of Principles jointly adopted by a Committee of the American Bar Association and a Committee of Publishers.*

Library of Congress Cataloging in Publication Data:

Main entry under title:

International finance handbook.

"A Wiley-Interscience publication."
Includes bibliographies and indexes.
1. International finance—Handbooks, manuals, etc.
2. International business enterprises—Finance—Handbooks, manuals, etc. I. George, Abraham M.
II. Giddy, Ian H.
HG3881.I57633 1983 332′.042 82-23824
ISBN 0–471–09861–2 (set)

Printed in the United States of America

10 9 8 7 6 5 4 3 2 1

PREFACE

This *International Finance Handbook* is designed to deal directly with the practical problems of international finance. It is conceived along the lines of Wiley's *Accounting Handbook* and *Financial Handbook*, and is intended to bring together all the major tasks and tools of international financing, banking and investment.

The two volumes of which the book comprises amply supplies the need expressed by many for a single comprehensive and detailed reference source for the intelligent nonspecialist in the field of international finance. Moreover, we believe that not only does the book offer insights into the intricacies of international finance to the amateur in the field, it also throws light on the many specialized areas of the subject to the experienced international financial community.

The **Handbook** is divided into nine parts, each part self-contained and treated as a guide to a particular sub-field of international finance. Moreover, the reader gets the option to choose and read a chapter here, a chapter there, as the need arises to familiarize himself with a particular subject area.

The introductory chapter opens the reader to the world of international finance, followed by fourteen chapters in three parts that give a comprehensive view of the foreign exchange and eurocurrency markets. Part 4 describes seven national money and banking markets and also three regional surveys. Part 5 deals with the international bond markets, followed by an authoritative description of the world's major and a few minor equity markets. Part 7 contains four chapters on specialized international financing techniques, and the subsequent 12 chapters in Part 8 deal in a practical manner with the management of international finance.

Volume II of the Handbook concludes with two extensive appendices on information sources and on calculations of international finance, a glossary of terms and a detailed index. The authors have also selected a short list of references for further exploration on the subjects which are listed at the end of each chapter. The index given is intended to help the reader find explanations and applications of key concepts, words or institutions.

As editors, we have not sought to eliminate all repetition because we value the shift in perspective that is gained from different authorities' treatment of the same problem. On the other hand, we have sought clarity of exposition and the use of sub-headings and bold type for rapid reviews. While we do vouch for the authority of our authors, most of whom are at the top of their fields, erros will, of course have escaped our eagle eyes, and alert readers who bring these to our attention will have performed a valuable service.

This brings us to the thank-you notes: to our colleagues and friends who have put so much time and knowledge into the pages that follow; to Professor Robert Hawkins of New York University for his encouragement; to our assistants, who helped us to produce, and perfect (especially Zora Prochazda, Mary Townswick), and to Stephen Kippur, our editor, and the staff of John Wiley and Sons, Inc.

We trust you will find the book useful, and we hope you enjoy it.

Abraham M. George
Ian H. Giddy

Montclair, N.J.
New York, N.Y.
March 1983

CONTENTS

SECTION 6.3

THE U.K. EQUITY MARKETS

CONTENTS

SECTION 6.3

THE U.K. EQUITY MARKETS

Stuart Valentine

REGULATION OF SECURITIES TRADING

Unlike many countries in the world, the United Kingdom is relatively free from government or statutory involvement in securities trading. Ultimately a government department, the Department of Trade, is responsible for supervising the workings of the securities industry, but the day-to-day regulation is carried out by the Council of the Stock Exchange.

THE STATUTORY FRAMEWORK. The **statutory arrangements** administered by the **Department of Trade** provide a legal framework rather than a detailed system of regulating the markets. There are, however, two pieces of legislation that are of major concern to the securities industry.

The Companies Acts are primarily concerned with such matters as incorporation and capital structure, the requirements of prospectuses, and the relationships among shareholders, directors, and creditors. The Secretary of State for Trade has the power to appoint inspectors to inquire into a company's affairs under these acts. Since 1980, **insider dealing** (i.e., profiting through stock exchange dealings as a result of privileged information about a company) has been made a criminal offense.

The Prevention of Fraud (Investments) Act of 1958 is mainly concerned with **licensing** and the conduct of **dealers** in securities. All dealers in securities must obtain a license, unless specifically exempt. Because of the control over its members exercised by the stock exchange, all stock exchange members are in fact exempt from the licensing provisions of this act. The Secretary of State for Trade has the power to revoke a dealer's license and severe penalties can also be imposed on those who fraudulently induce people to invest their money.

THE REGULATORY ROLE OF THE STOCK EXCHANGE. In the field of **nonstatutory regulation**, supervision rests mainly with the stock exchange itself. In this role it has been assisted, since 1968, by the **Panel on Takeovers** and **Mergers**, the latter, as its title suggests, assisting in its own particular sphere of activities. This latter body is now a working arm of the **Council for the Securities Industry** (CSI), which was established in 1978 to play a more general role in the **nonstatutory** aspect of regulating the securities market. This new supervisory body is actively supported on its council

The author wishes to thank Cazenove and Co., members of the U.K. Stock Exchange, for permission to quote topics verbatim from their publication, *Investment Memoranda*, 1981–82.

by all the major city organizations having an interest in securities' dealing. These include the merchant banks, investment trusts, insurance companies, the banks, pension funds, and unit trusts. In addition the accountancy bodies, the Confederation of British Industry, and the **Council of the Stock Exchange** are fully represented. The chairman and deputy chairman of the CSI are appointed by the governor of the Bank of England, who also appoints three lay members to the council as representatives of the individual investor and the wider public interest.

The CSI is a voluntary body. Its authority stems from the commitment that its constituent bodies have to support its codes and implement its recommendations and rulings. The bodies recognize the CSI's right to make recommendations bearing on any aspect of their members' activities in relation to the securities industry. The force of these recommendations is effective because, although they are not binding in law, they cannot in practice be ignored by the participating institutions, given the close-knit nature of the U.K. securities industry.

The **CSI**'s objectives are to maintain the highest ethical standards in the conduct of business within the securities industry, to keep under review the evolution of practices in the market, to maintain the effectiveness of the existing forms of regulation, to make arrangements for the investigation of cases of alleged misconduct within the industry, and to initiate new policies and codes of conduct as necessary. The **CSI** also acts as a link between the statutory and the nonstatutory sides of regulation by considering the need for changes in legislation affecting the securities industry and by examining any proposals for the introduction of such legislation.

In carrying out its work, the CSI relies on the disciplinary mechanisms of its constituent organizations, including, most importantly, those of the stock exchange itself.

The rules of the stock exchange define the structure of the market, particularly the roles of the **jobbers** and **brokers**, which are discussed later in this section; they also define the basis on which members can deal with each other, with nonmembers (i.e., the general public), and with members of other stock exchanges. They aim to provide a system of professional ethics and business practice that will protect the interests of the investing public. The rules are continually amended to meet changing needs and circumstances.

Control over Members and Member Firms. Many of the rules relate to the standards of professional practice of members, and the maintenance of the separate capacities of **jobbers** and **brokers**. This is the disciplinary aspect of the **stock exchange's regulatory function** as it affects members, and is supervised by **its council**. In addition to rules and the Code of Dealing, the council issues "Notes of Guidance" with which it expects its members to conform. These notes include guidance for member firms acting as brokers to listed companies where a conflict of interest might arise between the brokers' duties to listed companies on the one hand and to their investing clients on the other.

A breach of any of the rules or the Code of Dealing leaves the member open to **disciplinary proceedings**. The council has powers in disciplining members that range from expulsion from membership, through various degrees of suspension from trading, to censure or reprimand.

The **Stock Exchange Council** also exercises **financial supervision over its members** by a regular monitoring of their financial position. More recently it has appointed an inspector with powers to carry out spot checks on the trading and financial position of any member firm. The U.K. Stock Exchange also maintains a **compensation fund** to protect those investors who lose money as a result of the failure of a stock exchange member firm.

Control over Listed Companies. The rules and regulations of the U.K. Stock Exchange cover the requirements for listing of a company on the stock exchange. These requirements are detailed in a publication, **"Admission of Securities to Listing"** (widely known as the "yellow book"). The sanction of the stock exchange for a refusal to comply with its listing requirements is to withhold the grant of a listing for the securities being offered. Sanction for a breach of the **listing agreement** by a company already listed is **suspension of dealings** in that company's shares. A suspension of dealing has the effect that no stock exchange member can deal in the suspended security. The stock exchange is aware of the effects of suspension on the interests of investors generally and makes use of this sanction only after very careful consideration. In recent years, these requirements have been progressively strengthened to require fuller **disclosure of information** relevant to potential investors. The disclosure requirements are more stringent than required by the law and are sometimes said to be a disincentive to a company considering listing, but they form an essential part of the **nonstatutory regulation** that has developed over the years for the protection of investors and the avoidance of fraud.

Control of Market Users. Users of the stock market deal subject to the rules and regulations of the stock exchange and thus accept the obligations imposed through their agents, the **brokers**. Many important users of the market are also regulated in that, through their professional bodies, they subscribe to the system of voluntary regulation. The U.K. Stock Exchange, through a **model code**, has imposed restrictions on dealing in securities by the **directors of listed companies**, while any stock broker is expected to question any deal that, by its unusual size or method of dealing, might arouse suspicion of insider dealing, market rigging, or other abuse. The U.K. Stock Exchange monitors all **share price movements** and can carry out an investigation if there is a suspicion of any of the above activities.

Where a takeover is involved, details from the stock exchange's own inquiries will be passed to the **Takeover Panel** for further investigation.

Prior to 1980, when **insider dealing** became a criminal offense under the **Companies Act**, the **U.K. Stock Exchange** and/or the **Takeover Panel** would carry out a full **investigation into share dealings** where suspicion of irregularity was involved, and would frequently publish their findings. Currently, after initial inquiries have been made, the findings are passed to the **Department of Trade** for further investigation and possible criminal proceedings.

Thus the system of regulation of securities trading in the United Kingdom remains a mixture of statutory and nonstatutory restraints. The **nonstatutory regulation** is constantly developing to meet changing situations and will call for the support of legal sanctions if, and when, it finds a problem beyond its own control. Recent changes in the regulation of **insider dealing** are an example of this development and cooperation.

The Stock Exchange Compensation Fund. In 1950, to protect the investor and promote confidence in the market, the London Stock Exchange set up, and now administers, a compensation fund to which all member firms contribute.

The compensation fund is available to investors who lose money or shares as a result of the failure of the business of their stock brokers. Payment from the fund is at the discretion of the Stock Exchange Council, which decides an appropriate course of action after taking into account all the circumstances relating to the claim. Although payment from the fund is discretionary, and applies only to stock exchange-related business, few claims are ever refused.

The fund is maintained at approximately £1.25 million, but as all member firms are liable to contribute to the fund to make up any deficit in the event of a failure of a member firm, the actual level of cash in the fund understates the real assets on which the fund can call to compensate investors.

THE STOCK EXCHANGE SYSTEM

The basic **function of any stock exchange** is to provide the method whereby an investment in capital (i.e., stocks and shares) can be bought and sold. Secondly, it is to provide a mechanism by which companies and governments can raise new capital by means of issuing new securities. The basic purpose of the market is to overcome the essential mismatch between the needs of the savers on the one hand and the raisers of capital on the other. Companies and governments wish to invest large amounts in long-term nonliquid assets, such as factories, warehouses, stores, plants, machinery, vehicles, and stocks, while savers, having relatively small amounts of money to invest, wish to have their savings in forms that they can readily convert back to cash when they choose to do so. The mechanism of the stock exchange allows the savers to sell their shareholdings in the market and thus get their cash back while companies retain the use of the capital for their business purposes.

THE STRUCTURE OF THE STOCK EXCHANGE. Since the **unification of the U.K. Stock Exchange in 1973,** it now covers the whole of the United Kingdom and the Republic of Ireland. The main trading floor is in London, but there are subsidiary floors in Birmingham, Dublin, Glasgow, and Liverpool. Altogether, including those who are not located close to any trading floor, there are brokers' offices in approximately 110 towns and cities throughout the United Kingdom and Ireland.

At the present time the U.K. Stock Exchange has around 4,100 **members**; 3,600 of these are **brokers** and 500 are **jobbers**. Individual members cannot trade as individually owned businesses, but must form themselves into partnerships or companies; there are approximately 230 firms of stock brokers and 17 of stock jobbers.

Member firms do business mainly as **partnerships**, but there are 15 **companies with unlimited liability** and 11 with **limited liability**, of which two jobbing companies have their own shares listed on the U.K. Stock Exchange. All principals, including the directors of these stock exchange limited companies, trade with unlimited liability (and in the event of the failure of their company, each of the partners or directors is liable to his or her clients to the full amount of any personal resources). Some broking firms, while carrying out normal broking business, also specialize in various aspects; some will concentrate on new issue work, others on arbitrage between different foreign centers and London, while others might seek to develop a retail broking business overseas, perhaps in North America or the Middle East.

Foreign brokers with offices in London are not part of the stock exchange mechanism, and therefore are not controlled by the Council of the Stock Exchange, but they compete with U.K. brokers in various activities. Similarly, there are dealers in securities who are licensed by the **Department of Trade** but are not members of the U.K. Stock Exchange. They are not, therefore, subject to its rules and regulations.

All members of the stock exchange are subject to the rules and regulations administered by the **council**, which consists of 46 members elected from among the membership.

The Jobbing System. The trading practices of the stock exchange in the United Kingdom are based upon the competitive jobbing system, the important aspect of which is a complete separation of the function of the brokers on the one hand and the jobbers on the other. The jobbers agree not to deal with nonmembers of the stock exchange (i.e., the brokers' clients), while the brokers agree to bring all their business to the marketplace and deal through the jobbers.

There is a complete **separation of capacity** in the stock exchange. No broking firm can act as a jobber and no jobbing firm can act as a broker or agent. Jobbers deal as principals for their own profit; brokers deal as agents and must deal to the best advantage of their clients. By bringing all of their business to the market, the brokers ensure the fairest possible price for each and every deal. Furthermore, investors can deal in the market without there being a matching order from another investor, since the jobbers are prepared to buy and sell shares at all times, thus providing a continuous and liquid market in which investors can always deal at times of their own choosing.

Stock Jobbers. The jobbing system is based on **competition between the jobbers.** In every security traded on the U.K. Stock Exchange floor there must be at least two jobbers prepared to make a market in that stock. Thus the brokers always have at least two jobbers whom they can approach to ask the price of a share when acting on their client's instructions.

The brokers will approach all the jobbers who deal in a particular security and ask their prices. The jobber will not know whether the broker wishes to buy or sell and so will make a **two-way price**. The lower price is that price at which the jobber will buy shares from the broker, the higher that at which he will sell shares to the broker. The broker then checks the price with other jobbers competing in the market in that particular share and goes to the jobber who offered the best price for the broker's client (i.e., the jobber who offered to sell at the lowest price, or the jobber who wanted to buy the shares at the highest price). Thus the client is certain of getting the best possible price in the market for the deal at that particular time.

As noted elsewhere, a deal can take place in any number of shares up to a maximum normal market size. This will vary from a few hundred shares in a small, infrequently traded issue to many thousands in a large active company. This does not mean that there is a maximum number of shares that can be traded in any one deal; it just means that if a larger deal is in mind, the jobber will have the right to quote different prices (should he or she wish) for such a deal. Such deals and the price at which they are struck are subject to skillful negotiation between the broker and the jobber. Even a very large deal, however, is unlikely to move the market price very much, so deep and adaptable is the market in most securities.

When a deal is struck between the broker and the jobber, the only people who know the details of the deal, the price and the amount of shares involved, are the jobber, the broker, and the client. In the **competitive jobbing system**, details of buying and selling orders would immediately open up the books of one jobber to rivals. It is, therefore, essential that this secrecy be maintained. There is no tape of transactions.

The **protection of investors**, which many markets help to maintain by the use of a tape, is given in the United Kingdom by the insistence of the stock exchange that the role of the broker and the jobber are kept separate. No member firm can control both a jobbing and a broking function; the broker will always act solely in an agency role, while the jobbers act wholly as principals.

Stock Brokers. The traditional role of the stock broker is to act as the agent for a client, whether that client be a savings institution or an individual investor. To attract business the broker has to offer certain services, the minimum of which will be an efficient **dealing** and **settlement service**. In addition to these basic services an **advisory service**, often backed by sophisticated research analysts in the case of larger firms, would also be offered. A broker can frequently act as an overall investment adviser, providing portfolio valuations and suggesting not only individual shares to buy or sell, but also an overall investment strategy, advice on taxation, and even alternative investments outside the stock exchange. The reward for these services is obtained by the **commission** on the business that the broker undertakes for the client, and not by any separate charges.

Banks, accountants, and lawyers can also act **as agents** between individual investors or trustees and the broker. Where such an agent is used, a separate scale of commission charges is laid down, as indicated in a later topic, "The Dealing and Settlement Process."

Price and News Dissemination. A principal requirement of an effective stock exchange is that company news and all other information relevant to the making of prices on the floor is quickly disseminated and available to all at one and the same time. It is a requirement of the listing agreement (which all listed companies must sign with the stock exchange) that all price-sensitive information is disclosed on the stock exchange at the same time as it is released by the company itself. The information is released to the market by the Company Announcements Office of the U.K. Stock Exchange and flashed on to news information screens on the market floor. The information is also sent by facsimile transmission to all other stock exchange floors around the country. **Exchange Telegraph**, a financial news distribution organization, sends such company information out on its financial news tape to newspapers and investment institutions around the country.

TOPIC and the Market Price Display Service. Information on the latest middle prices of shares on the floor of the exchange is collected by market price reporters and fed into a computer installation that transmits the information via a stock exchange television system, TOPIC, to subscribers, including brokers, investing institutions, and investment advisers. The prices of 1,500 securities are listed on TOPIC, which also contains company news items, traded options details, and other relevant information. TOPIC is now replacing an older system, **MPDS (Market Price Display Service)**, which carried around 750 share prices, details of traded options, and pages of company news items.

Prices are constantly updated and give a speedy up-to-the-minute view of how they are changing. The prices on TOPIC are middle market prices, and do not indicate the prices at which actual deals may have been completed.

The Stock Exchange Daily Official List. The *Stock Exchange Daily Official List* (SEDOL) is the authoritative journal of the Stock Exchange, showing closing **price quotations of the jobbers** and details of trading on the previous day. The details of completed trading simply give the price at which a deal, or deals, took place; they do not show either the quantities of shares involved, or whether the deal was a buying or a selling transaction. The importance of SEDOL is not only in giving a continuing, authentic record of the market, but also in providing a daily valuation of every security listed on the stock exchange forming the legal basis for valuation in any dispute or nonmarket transaction (e.g., valuations for probate purposes).

THE NEW ISSUES MARKET

THE STRUCTURE OF COMPANY FINANCE. The extent to which industrial and commercial companies in the United Kingdom have relied on **new stock exchange issues** as a source of new funds in recent years can be seen from Exhibit 1. Over the five years shown the percentage of new funds raised by means of stock market issues varied between a low of 2.8% in 1979 and a high of 5.1% in 1980, averaging just over 3.5% over the period as a whole.

As can be seen from Exhibit 1, U.K. companies over this period (which is quite typical), raised most of their new funds from internal sources, mainly by way of **profits retained** in the business and not distributed by way of interest or dividends. Around 66% came from this source. The existence of a well-developed stock market

EXHIBIT 1 INDUSTRIAL AND COMMERCIAL COMPANIES, SOURCES OF FUNDS 1976–80 (in millions of pounds sterling)

Income	1976	1977	1978	1979	1980
Internal					
Undistributed income	12,563	15,064	16,777	20,406	15,781
Other internal sources	595	478	1,044	2,699	861
Total	13,158	15,542	17,821	23,105	16,642
External					
Credit received	852	517	527	1,594	−226
Bank borrowing	2,398	2,966	2,890	4,903	6,642
Other loans and mortgages	426	38	386	662	726
Capital issues					
Ordinary shares	785	730	829	906	897
Debentures and preference shares	42	−67	−71	−22	423
Overseas capital issues	25	82	−43	−59	−15
Other overseas finance	1,218	1,189	744	469	995
Total	5,746	5,455	5,262	8,453	9,442
Overall total	18,904	20,997	23,083	31,558	26,084

helps companies to finance themselves through **retained profits**. Since the retentions remain a part of **shareholders' funds**, the retained earnings strengthen a company's financial position, a strengthening that can be reflected in the price of a company's shares on the market. Thus shareholders are willing to allow profits to be ploughed back, knowing that they can take advantage of them through an enhanced share price. For the company this is a cheaper and more efficient way of maintaining and enhancing the value of the business than the alternative of distributing profits and bidding for new funds by way of capital issues. Some observers of the stock market scene might alternatively suggest that the latter method would lead to a more efficient allocation of resources overall.

The money actually raised by means of **new issues of capital** is also dynamic money in the sense that, by increasing the capital base of a company, it also enlarges the company's short-term borrowing power (through the banks, for instance). New capital raised on a permanent basis from shareholders is a doubly important element in company finance.

FACTORS AFFECTING THE PATTERN OF NEW ISSUES. Exhibit 2 shows the type of securities that U.K. companies have favored in recent years when making new issues. As can be seen from the table, **equity issues**, most commonly by means of **rights issues**, have been by far the most popular method. It was not always so. In the 1960s and early 1970s, the majority of new money was raised by means of **long-term, fixed-interest debt issues**, not by new ordinary shares. The situation has changed for a number of reasons; first, in times of sharply fluctuating interest rates, investors have been less willing to commit their funds for long periods at rates that might turn out to be too low. Second, the U.K. government, in order to finance its annual

EXHIBIT 2 NEW ISSUES OF COMPANY SECURITIES IN THE UNITED KINGDOM (in millions of pounds sterling)

BY TYPE OF SECURITY

Year	Equity	Preference	Loans	Convertibles	Total
1978	1,324	49	10	1	1,384
1979	1,170	70	55	36	1,331
1980	1,098	255	2	222	1,577
1981	2,493	120	43	253	2,909

BY TYPE OF ISSUE

Year	Prospectus Offer for Sale or Placing	Rights Issues	Options and Other Offers	Total
1978	NA	NA	NA	1,384[a]
1979	179	974	178	1,331
1980	305	1,060	212	1,577
1981	735	1,972	202	2,909

[a]Subdivision not available.

borrowing requirement, has used the long-term bond market extensively. In doing so, it has had to offer rates of interest of up to 15.5% for long-term money, rates that companies could not afford. Thus companies have resorted to equity issues, by way of **rights** to existing shareholders as the major element of raising new money from investors.

Because of the instability of stock market prices, the ability to issue new equity at the time of the company's own choosing is restricted. At times, most particularly in the period 1973–74, when market prices were falling sharply, companies were unable to come to the market for long-term funds, and most of their external need for new funds was met by means of short-term bank borrowing. As the market improved in 1975, companies took the opportunity to restructure their balance sheets to a longer term basis. Since 1976, although there have been fluctuations in the market during the years, the flow of new issues over each year as a whole has been fairly steady.

THE STOCK EXCHANGE'S LISTING REQUIREMENTS. Before a company can achieve a full listing for its securities on the stock exchange it must fulfill certain requirements, and must agree to provide a further regular flow of information relating to its activities and trading position. The normal initial requirements for a listing on the U.K. Stock Exchange are:

1. The company must normally have been trading for at least five years and possess full records of its balance sheets and profit and loss accounts for that period.
2. The company must also have a market capitalization of at least £500,000, but while this is an initial requirement, a company is not automatically removed from listing if its market valuation subsequently falls below this level. In practice, the majority of companies approaching the U.K. Stock Exchange for a listing would be valued at a much higher level.
3. The proprietors of the company must normally agree to arrangements under which at least 25% of the company's equity capital is held by the public on the occasion of initial listing. This proportion is usually considered sufficient for marketability of the shares for investors.
4. A prospectus must be issued containing, among other things, a history of the business, describing the nature of the trade carried on and development in recent years under the present management, and a report by independent, qualified accountants on financial information, showing the level and trend of the company's business. This financial information includes the sales, cost of sales, pretax trading results, and other items for each of the last five years, together with a statement of the assets and liabilities at the beginning of the five-year period and at the end of each year reported upon.

The purposes of these listing requirements are, first, to enable the public to assess the worth of the business and to evaluate the future prospects at the date of the prospectus, and second, to enable subsequent investors, through the secondary market, to be confident that all listed companies have shown a certain minimum record of management.

Thus the U.K. Stock Exchange does not normally admit to listing a company that does not have an existing business. Equally, a company that sells its business for cash is not normally permitted to remain listed until its cash, or a substantial part of it, is once again employed in a business. However, the stock exchange does exercise flexibility in applying these requirements by not insisting on a record of five years' trading, so long as the prospectus demonstrates a record of activity of sufficient length to enable future profitability to be evaluated.

THE LISTING AGREEMENT. The main features associated with maintenance of the listing of a company's securities, however, are contained in the listing agreement, which takes the form of a resolution of the board of directors. The terms of this resolution lay down certain rules and procedures a company must fulfill if it wishes to continue to have its securities traded on the U.K. Stock Exchange. There are three main aspects in the listing agreement, of which the most important is the publication and dissemination of price-sensitive information. Thus any information that can affect the price of a company's securities must be given to the U.K. Stock Exchange immediately following a board decision or other corporate development. Timeliness of the communication with the stock exchange and the market is a paramount consideration. On receipt of information the U.K. Stock Exchange releases the news and the market price adjusts immediately and affects all users of the market at the same time, thus maintaining an orderly and efficient market.

The listing agreement extends protection to investors in any listed company by laying down procedures the company must follow if it wishes to expand its capital base. Further issues of equity for cash, other than by way of rights in proportion to existing holdings, cannot be made unless existing shareholders in a general meeting decide otherwise. In this way the proportion of an investor's stake in the company is protected.

Investor protection is also maintained by requiring the company to provide information relating to specific share transactions. The stock exchange, for example, must be informed of any transactions in its shares involving a director of the company. The **Companies Act** also requires that a company must inform the stock exchange if an investor buys or sells shares, thus altering his or her holding to or from any level comprising 5% or more of the company's shares.

SUPERVISION. As part of the U.K. Stock Exchange's supervision of the conduct of listed companies, they are required to present regular reports to investors. For example, under the **Companies Acts** companies must present an annual report and accounts to shareholders. The regular information required by the stock exchange to be given to investors goes beyond company law by requiring the company to present a semiannual report. Some companies also provide quarterly reports, but there is no obligation on the company to do this. If, on the other hand, a company were experiencing exceptional difficulties, the stock exchange would expect investors to be informed of this through the stock exchange mechanism. Annual and interim reports include figures previously decided upon by the directors, and so the stock exchange requires companies to announce their trading results as soon as the board reaches its decision and before the accounts or interim reports are printed. In this way the market price reflects the latest news and no one deals at a disadvantage.

There are other instances where the reporting **requirements of the U.K. Stock Exchange** are more stringent than required under the law. Under the **statutory requirements**, for instance, the shareholdings of directors on the balance sheet date must be included in the annual report. The U.K. Stock Exchange, however, states that this information must be more up-to-date and that the directors' shareholdings one month prior to the annual general meeting must be shown. The stock exchange also requires the company to submit copies of all circulars, notices, and announcements as they are issued. In many cases, the U.K. Stock Exchange will, as part of its requirements, have approved copies of notices of meetings and other information of direct concern to the shareholders before they are printed. The company must also provide any information that might affect the price of its securities and anyone, whether on the staff of the company or not, who is in possession of such information is under a statutory obligation not to take financial advantage of it. Any person in possession of price-sensitive information about the company falls under provisions on insider dealing in the Companies Act of 1980.

In the interests of a fair and open market, the U.K. Stock Exchange is concerned to ensure, so far as possible, that any information that might affect the price of the security is made available to all investors at the same time. It is continually **monitoring price movements** to ensure that no irregularities occur. If an untoward movement in the price of a security is noted, the jobbers dealing in the security will be approached for information on the basis of which a decision is reached as to whether or not there are grounds for further investigation. Should this be the case those firms of **brokers** who have dealt will be required to submit a return of their transactions. Information can also be sought from other sources and if, as a result of the investigation, it is felt there is evidence to justify further examination by the **Department of Trade** in accordance with the **insider dealing** provisions of the **Companies Act of 1980**, this will be submitted to the **Department of Trade** for them to decide whether to prosecute.

This is one area of regulation in the securities market that highlights the close working arrangement that exists between the **statutory and nonstatutory regulatory authorities**. The existence of a centralized market provides the nonstatutory authorities with a more effective policing of the activities of the users of the market. In doing so they do not act independently of the statutory authorities but maintain a close working relationship and complement their activities.

The results of the investigations into share price movements carried out by the stock exchange might or might not be published. The U.K. Stock Exchange is under no obligation to do this, but in the past announcements have been made in cases that have been of public concern. In future cases of a director of a company buying or selling company shares on the basis of privileged information, it will be for the Department of Trade to decide whether or not to prosecute the person concerned.

MODEL CODE FOR DIRECTORS. The U.K. Stock Exchange, however, regards it as highly desirable that directors of listed companies hold shares in their companies. In order to reduce any conflict that might arise through this desire and the need to prevent improper share dealings, the stock exchange has published guidelines for directors regarding dealings in the shares of their own companies. The guidelines are set out in the form of a model code and by following these a director can guard against criticism of his or her dealing. The model code recognizes that the directors will always be in possession of more information than is published at any one time and so restrictions are placed on directors' share transactions. Consequently a director would be prevented from dealing when there is price-sensitive information that the board has not yet published. A director should not deal in company securities on a short-term basis, and should not trade for a fixed period before publication of regular information (such as profits and divided announcements) or any other information that may be expected to influence the price of the shares—for example, takeover bid terms. A director should always notify the chairperson (or the chairperson notify the board) if he or she intends to buy or sell company securities.

The model code is not a rigid set of rules, but rather provides a set of guidelines that should be regarded as the minimum standard of good practice.

RAISING CAPITAL ON THE STOCK EXCHANGE. Most listed companies have an official relationship with a broking firm that acts formally on their behalf in communications with the stock exchange. Some member firms specialize in this role and will advise a company on the appropriate **source and type of finance**, taking account of the company's requirements and of the terms on which a new issue could be offered regarding market conditions. The size of a company, its credit rating, the nature of its assets, and its type of business will all help determine the sources of capital available to it.

Corporate capital can be broadly divided into two classes, loan capital and share capital. **Loan capital** covers many types of issue, such as mortgage debentures, unsecured loans, and convertible stocks, which are all borrowings repayable in the event of a liquidation before any distribution of surplus assets to shareholders. Share capital is the risk-bearing capital of the company and represents the members' participation in the fortunes of the enterprise.

Share Capital. The share capital of a company can basically be divided into two categories—preference capital and ordinary, or equity, capital.

Preference Capital. The main feature distinguishing preference capital from ordinary capital is that preference shares normally give a holder the right of a fixed dividend out of after-tax profits and, in any liquidation, priority over ordinary shareholders for the repayment of the amounts originally subscribed. Preference shares do not normally have a vote, except where there is a proposal to vary the rights attaching to them or if the dividend is in arrears. There are a number of variations on preference share issues.

1. Cumulative preference shares have the right to payment of arrears of accumulated dividends as soon as there are sufficient profits to pay them.
2. Redeemable preference shares are preference shares that the company has undertaken to repay on a specified date, sometimes at a premium on their nominal value.
3. Participating preference shares have the right to a fixed dividend before any payment is made to ordinary shareholders, and also have the right to a further distribution of profits related to the dividend payment made to ordinary shareholders.
4. Convertible preference shares carry a right of conversion into ordinary shares at specified future dates and at specified prices.

Equity Capital. Equity, or ordinary, shares are the risk capital of a business. Ordinary shares give holders rights of ownership in the company, which normally include the right to such dividends as the directors declare from time to time, the right to appoint and dismiss directors, and the right to have a share in any surplus of the company's assets in the event of dispersal once all the creditors have been paid. Again, equity capital can be subdivided into a number of categories.

1. *Ordinary shares.* In the United Kingdom, equity capital is usually referred to as "share capital," while fixed-interest securities are usually called "stocks." (There is here a difference in terminology between the U.K. and U.S. markets, but throughout this section the U.K. terminology is used.) The owners of ordinary shares in a company have all the proprietorial rights referred to above, including the right to vote in company meetings in proportion to the number of shares that they hold.
2. *Nonvoting or restricted voting shares.* A few companies issue a number of shares with no voting rights, or restrictions on the ability of shareholders to vote. For ease of reference these are usually referred to as "A" shares. These shares are becoming less popular among investors, and a number of companies, when they are in a position to do so, are tending to enfranchise these restricted voting shares.
3. *Deferred shares.* A variation on ordinary equity capital is the deferred share, which, while giving full voting rights and rights on liquidation as ordinary shares, does not rank for dividend until a specified date, or until the company's profits have reached a given level.
4. *Warrants.* Strictly speaking, a warrant is not a security as such, but a contract entered into by the company to issue shares to the holders of the warrants at specified dates in the future at given prices. They are often issued as part of a loan stock issue, which enables a lower rate of interest to be paid on the loan stock, but with the added attraction that shares can be purchased at favorable prices at future dates. Warrants as such attract no interest or dividend for the holder.

All of these types of securities have been issued by companies and are dealt in on the stock exchange in the United Kingdom.

UNLISTED COMPANIES. All companies that have their shares listed will have gone through a rigorous process of appraisal before the listing of their shares has been allowed by the stock exchange authorities. Within the last few years, however, there has been a demand for facilities to allow shares to be traded where a young and growing company perhaps did not have sufficient qualifications to be granted a listing by the stock exchange. In order to meet the needs of these companies, the stock exchange authorities have developed their practices to allow a market to develop in shares of companies that have not qualified for a listing.

Dealings in unlisted securities can take place under a number of stock exchange rules. For ease of identification these rules can be broadly subdivided into the rules dealing with the trading of overseas shares, which have a listing on a stock exchange other than in the United Kingdom, and those that relate to unlisted U.K. companies.

DEALING IN OVERSEAS SECURITIES. Under stock exchange Rule 163(1e) dealings can take place in securities that have a listing on a stock exchange other than that in the United Kingdom. To qualify for dealing under this rule any security must have a full listing on a recognized stock exchange overseas.

Under Rule 163(1f) the securities of certain overseas governments (United States, South Africa), any local authorities within those countries, the securities of U.S. federal agencies, and those of the World Bank can be traded. This rule also allows dealings in securities of U.S. banks that are members of the Federal Reserve System or of Canadian banks and U.S. and Canadian insurance and electric power companies. In addition, securities that are traded in the United States and Canada on their over-the-counter markets can be traded in London under this particular rule.

DEALING IN UNLISTED DOMESTIC SECURITIES. For many years the stock exchange rules allowed specific bargains to be made in the securities of companies that did not qualify for a listing, but in all these cases, each bargain had to carry specific permission to deal from the Council of the Stock Exchange before it could be carried out. Rule 163(2), the rule under which these dealings were allowed, was designed for occasional dealings in shares that did not have a listing and no trading market in these shares was permitted to develop. All dealings under this rule are done on a *caveat emptor, caveat vendor* basis, and any such contract note that a stock exchange member firm issues states that the security is not listed on the U.K. Stock Exchange. However, there are certain protections for anyone who buys and sells shares under this rule in that in the event of a failure of a member firm the full protection of the U.K. Stock Exchange's compensation fund is available.

Under Rule 163(3) the securities of public companies that are engaged in mineral exploration activities can be traded for a limited period without the prior consent of the Council, which is required under Rule 163(2). Rule 163(3) was introduced to help companies that were engaged in North Sea oil exploration to raise the capital they needed and to develop a market for their shares even if they were unable to produce the five-year trading record necessary before a listing could be granted.

THE UNLISTED SECURITIES MARKET. In recent years, as noted, much more attention has been paid to the facilities available to the small company that is unable to apply for a stock exchange listing. The dealings under Rule 163(2) had developed to such an extent that stock exchange authorities felt further facilities were needed for certain unlisted securities. Late in 1980, therefore, a new market, the unlisted securities market (USM), was introduced to allow securities of such companies to be actively traded. The objective of the market is to allow trading in unlisted securities to develop to help companies realize their full potential for development and allow them to make a positive contribution to the country's rate of economic growth. By the end of the first full year over 80 companies had their shares traded on the USM.

The criteria for allowing shares to be traded on the USM differ from those where a listing is involved. The major differences are

1. Companies wishing their securities to be traded on the USM need only show a three-year trading record, rather than the five-year record required for companies seeking a listing.
2. There is no minimum market capitalization requirement for a company wishing its shares to be traded on the USM, in comparison with the £500,000 minimum that is required for a listing.
3. When a company comes to the USM for the first time the advertising requirements for shares are less than those for a listed company. Only abbreviated details need be given, except where there is to be an active marketing

of the shares. This helps to reduce considerably the costs involved for a company seeking to widen its shareholder base through an active market in its shares.

4. Only 10% of a USM company's shares need to be available to the public through the market, compared with the 25% that the stock exchange lays down for the shares of a listed company.
5. A company coming to the USM pays a fee of £1,000 annually to the stock exchange authorities, compared with a listing fee, which varies according to market capitalization in the case of a company with a stock exchange listing.

All companies whose shares are traded on the USM must, however, comply with the stock exchange's requirements on the continuing disclosure of information, requirements that apply equally to companies on the USM and those with a listing.

The stock exchange trading market as it has now developed is, therefore, a threefold structure: (1) an official listing; (2) the USM for the securities of those unlisted companies that are prepared to accept a degree of regulation from the stock exchange, and in which an active market can be developed; and (3) a framework of rules in which brokers remain able to transact an occasional deal in unlisted securities, subject to the prior consent of the Council of the Stock Exchange.

THE TRADING MARKET

THE STRUCTURE OF THE MARKET: CAPITALIZATION AND TURNOVER. The Stock Exchange in the United Kingdom is one of the world's major stock exchanges. Relative size can be measured in a number of ways: number of securities listed, **capitalization**, turnover, and so forth. The measurement is further complicated in that the **U.K. government securities market** is housed within the stock exchange, not outside of it, as with most other government bond markets, and also by the measurement of turnover (the subject of a footnote to Exhibit 4).

Taking each of these measures in turn, the U.K. Stock Exchange lists the largest number of securities of any stock exchange in the world. Over 7,000 different securities are listed, covering both public and private sectors from the United Kingdom, Ireland (the Irish unit is a constituent member of the stock exchange despite the country's separate political, economic, financial, social and legal framework), and the rest of the world. As can be seen from Exhibit 7, almost 400 securities of non-U.K. and Irish bodies have a listing in London, plus many others with a listed Eurobond issue. Of these 7,000 securities, over 5,200 are securities of 2,600 U.K. companies. For comparison, at the end of 1980 the New York Stock Exchange (NYSE) listed the equity of 1,503 companies, Tokyo listed 1,402, Australia listed 1,067, and the American Stock Exchange (AMEX), 837. Internationally London also leads with 396 overseas companies with equity listed compared with 294 in Amsterdam and 83 in Copenhagen. The NYSE had just 37 and AMEX, 55.

In terms of **total market capitalization**, London ranked third in the world at the end of 1980, with £177.9 million. New York was the leader with over £733 million, and Tokyo second at £254.5 million.

Making allowances for the U.K. method of calculating turnover figures, the U.K. exchange (£98 million in 1980) ranks second in the world to New York (£162 million), with Tokyo third (£83.5 million). However, the figures from the United Kingdom are dominated by the turnover in the market in government and other public sector stocks, which account for some 80% of the total value of dealing.

Exhibit 3 shows the **market capitalization** of the company sector of the U.K. stock exchange at the end of December 1981, showing the split between U.K.-, Irish-, and overseas-registered securities, the division among some categories of companies and the division between the different types of capital, described following.

EXHIBIT 3 CAPITALIZATION OF THE U.K. STOCK EXCHANGE, AS OF 31 DECEMBER 1981 (in millions of pounds sterling)

Security	Loan		Ord. and Preference		Total	
	Number of Securities	Market Value	Number of Securities	Market Value	Number of Securities	Market Value
UNITED KINGDOM–REGISTERED SECURITIES						
Banks, discount houses, building societies	29	£ 247	64	£ 5,903	93	£ 6,150
Breweries, distilleries	140	278	79	3,256	219	3,534
Commercial, industrial	889	2,040	2,096	56,741	2,985	58,781
Financial trusts, land	44	131	84	1,171	128	1,302
Insurance	9	24	41	5,921	50	5,945
Investment and unit trusts	261	206	421	6,712	682	6,918
Mines	5	134	26	2,514	31	2,648
Oil	8	150	36	12,308	44	12,458
Plantations	4	2	59	879	63	881
Property	153	515	128	4,515	281	5,030
Shipping	3	3	28	619	31	622
Utilities	15	11	9	18	24	29
Waterworks	143	63	231	256	374	319
Railways	14	4	6	7	20	11
Finance for industry[a]	1	44	—	—	1	44
Total	1,718	£3,851	3,308	£100,820	5,026	£104,671
Eurobonds	76	£1,201	—	—	76	£ 1,201
IRISH-REGISTERED SECURITIES						
Banks	2	£ 14	4	£ 246	6	£ 260
Commercial, industrial	12	12	110	561	112	573
Total	14	£ 26	114	£ 807	118	£ 833
Eurobonds	6	£ 71	—	—	6	£ 71

EXHIBIT 3 *(Continued)*

Security	Loan		Ord. and Preference		Total	
	Number of Securities	Market Value	Number of Securities	Market Value	Number of Securities	Market Value
OVERSEAS-REGISTERED SECURITIES						
Banks, discount houses	1	£ 40	31	£ 18,931	32	£ 18,971
Breweries, distilleries	—	—	4	1,537	4	1,537
Commercial, industrial	5	28	200	134,721	205	134,749
Financial trusts, land	—	—	20	4,121	20	4,121
Insurance	—	—	9	3,087	9	3,087
Investment, unit trusts	—	—	20	2,475	20	2,475
Mines	4	58	120	18,759	124	18,817
Oil	1	42	24	32,248	25	32,290
Plantations	1	1	8	642	9	643
Property	—	—	2	142	2	142
Shipping	—	—	1	24	1	24
Utilities	10	11	14	5,087	24	5,098
Railways	1	13	7	1,386	8	1,399
Total	23	£ 193	460	£223,160	483	£223,353
Eurobonds	613	£16,100	—	—	613	£ 16,100

Total number of companies with listed securities at the end of December 1981

United Kingdom-registered	2,403
Ireland-registered	82
Overseas-registered	396
Total	2,881

For comparison, the total market valuation of public sector securities[b] listed at the end of December 1981 was

British- and Irish-registered	£ 76,628
Overseas-registered	477
Total	£ 77,105

Total market capitalization of all securities listed at the end of December 1981

Public sector	£ 77,105
Eurobonds	16,100
Company sector	328,854
Total	£422,059

[a]An organization sponsored by the U.K. government and the banks that helps provide finance to smaller companies.

[b]Includes government stocks, public boards, local authorities.

Turnover on the U.K. stock exchange for recent years is shown in Exhibit 4, in terms of the total value of dealings, the number of bargains (deals), and the average value for each deal. There are no published figures of the number of shares traded in the United Kingdom, so a deal can be a handful to many thousands of shares. The average price for each share in the United Kingdom is small (especially in relation to those of the United States), so the actual number of shares traded is believed to be very high.

EXHIBIT 4 TURNOVER ON THE U.K. STOCK EXCHANGE

	Public Sector		Company Sector: Fixed-Interest		Company Sector: Equity	
VALUE OF DEALINGS[a,b]						
Annual data						
1976	£ 90,846	85.4%	£1,425	1.3%	£14,163	13.3%
1977	150,808	87.0	2,358	1.5	20,168	11.6
1978	117.871	84.9	1,684	1.2	19.215	13.8
1979	143,068	84.7	1,763	1.0	24.106	14.3
1980	163,738	83.4	1,751	0.9	30,801	15.7
1981	156,806	82.2	1,474	0.8	32,387	17.0
Quarterly data—1981						
1st quarter	£ 42,419	83.3%	£ 407	0.7%	£ 8,087	15.9%
2nd quarter	36,876	79.4	374	0.8	9,183	19.8
3rd quarter	31,875	78.9	382	0.9	8,167	20.2
4th quarter	45,636	86.3	311	0.6	6,950	13.1
NUMBER OF BARGAINS[c]						
Annual data						
1976	£ 906.6	18.6%	£392.9	8.1%	£3,566.7	73.3%
1977	1,175.3	19.3	474.8	7.8	4,434.5	72.9
1978	932.7	17.0	427.1	7.8	4,130.0	75.2
1979	1,020.8	18.7	323.3	5.9	4,111.8	75.4
1980	1,139.0	20.0	338.3	5.9	4,230.7	74.1
1981	1,064.4	20.1	279.4	5.3	3,944.5	74.6
Quarterly data—1981						
1st quarter	£ 309.0	20.3%	£ 79.1	5.2%	£1,137.6	74.6%
2nd quarter	247.3	17.1	78.2	5.4	1,117.5	77.4
3rd quarter	249.3	20.4	66.9	5.5	908.1	74.2
4th quarter	258.8	23.6	55.2	5.0	781.3	71.3
AVERAGE VALUE EACH DEAL[a]						
Annual data						
1976	£100,205		£3,627		£3,970	
1977	128,314		4,966		4,548	
1978	126,376		3,943		4,652	
1979	140,153		3,453		5,863	

EXHIBIT 4 *(Continued)*

	Public Sector	Company Sector	
		Fixed-Interest	Equity
1980	143,756	5,176	7,280
1981	147,319	5,276	8,211
Quarterly data—1981			
1st quarter	£137,278	£5,145	£7,109
2nd quarter	149,114	4,783	8,217
3rd quarter	127,858	5,710	8,994
4th quarter	176,337	5,634	8,895

[a]An aggregate of purchases and sales. Turnover statistics in the United Kingdom are based on the brokers' dealings with the jobbers. Thus if broker A sells a given parcel of shares of Company B to the jobber at a total value of £10,000 and broker C buys those shares of Company B from the same jobber at £10,100, this will show in the statistics as two bargains with a total value of £20,100, even though it is the same parcel of shares.

[b]In millions of pounds sterling and percentages.

[c]In thousands and percentages.

[d]In pounds sterling.

Although this section is concerned primarily with the equity market, the figures of turnover in public sector securities are also given.

Exhibit 5 shows the leading 50 United Kingdom-registered companies in terms of market capitalization at the end of December 1981, with the leading 25 Irish companies shown in Exhibit 6.

The international spread of London's interests is reflected in Exhibits 7 and 8, which show, respectively, the division of the overseas-registered stocks by country of incorporation and the leading 50 overseas-registered companies by total market capitalization at the end of December 1981.

EXHIBIT 5 LEADING 50 U.K. COMPANIES IN TERMS OF MARKET CAPITALIZATION (in millions of pounds sterling)

Company	Position	Total Market Value
British Petroleum Co.	1	£5,747.9
General Electric Co.	2	4,526.8
Shell Transport & Trading Co.	3	4,425.3
Imperial Chemical Industries	4	1,724.9
Marks & Spencer	5	1,663.6
Beecham Group	6	1,417.3
Barclays Bank	7	1,266.6
Bat Industries	8	1,265.1
Rio Tinto-Zinc Corp.	9	1,239.2
Racal Electronics	10	1,155.6

EXHIBIT 5 *(Continued)*

Company	Position	Total Market Value
Unilever Ltd.	11	1,110.2
Great Universal Stores	12	1,067.4
Land Securities Investment Trust	13	1,020.1
Grand Metropolitan	14	1,003.0
National Westminster Bank	15	960.4
Consolidated Gold Fields	16	914.3
Thorn-EMI	17	898.1
Plessey Co.	18	868.3
Sainsbury (J.)	19	853.3
BTR	20	824.4
Lloyds Bank	21	736.3
Glaxo (holdings)	22	728.9
Boots Co.	23	709.4
Prudential Corp.	24	686.3
Bass	25	665.1
Hawker Siddeley Group	26	644.7
Royal Insurance Co.	27	630.8
Midland Bank	28	619.2
Distillers Co.	29	595.6
Standard Chartered Bank	30	584.0
Cable & Wireless	31	577.8
Blue Circle Industries	32	537.4
Ultramar Co.	33	534.6
BICC	34	532.1
Commercial Union Assurance Co.	35	530.9
General Accident Fire & Life Corp.	36	517.3
BOC International	37	513.4
Imperial Group	38	507.7
Associated British Foods	39	507.3
Sears (holdings)	40	485.8
Associated Dairies Group	41	482.8
Allied-Lyons	42	470.2
Guardian Royal Exchange Assurance	43	465.6
Trusthouse Forte	44	456.7
Pilkington Brothers	45	453.1
Eagle Star (holdings)	46	452.3
Royal Bank of Scotland Group	47	441.2
Harrisons & Crosfield	48	439.3
Standard Telephones & Cables	49	435.0
British Aerospace	50	416.0

EXHIBIT 6 LEADING 25 IRISH COMPANIES BY MARKET CAPITALIZATION (in millions of pounds sterling)

Company	Position	Market Valuation
Allied Irish Banks	1	£131.8
Cement-Roadstone (holdings)	2	129.4
Bank of Ireland	3	109.0
Smurfit (Jefferson) Group	4	99.1
Waterford Glass	5	45.8
Carroll Industries	6	33.0
Insurance Corporation of Ireland	7	31.6
Irish Distillers Group	8	21.9
Arnott & Co. Dublin	9	15.8
Rohan Group	10	14.0
Lyons Irish (holdings)	11	11.5
New Ireland Assurance Co.	12	10.2
Jones Group	13	10.0
Abbey	14	9.9
Independent Newspapers	15	9.8
Crean (James)	16	9.0
C.P.I. (holdings)	17	8.5
Readymix	18	8.1
Silvermines	19	8.1
Industrial Credit Co.	20	7.2
Fitzwilton	21	6.7
D.A.D. Properties	22	6.6
Clondalkin Group	23	5.1
Hall (R&H)	24	4.6
Unidare	25	4.6
Total Valuation		£751.3

THE DEALING AND SETTLEMENT PROCESS.

Buying a Security. When the broker has carried out a buying order on behalf of a client he or she will immediately provide the client with a **contract note** (see Exhibit 9), which details the title of the security, the amount of shares bought, the price at which the deal was made, and the total amount of money involved, together with additional charges such as the transfer stamp, contract stamp, commission, and value-added tax (VAT).

In the United Kingdom there is no distinction between round lot and odd lot prices. The **jobbing system** is flexible enough to allow odd amounts of shares to be bought and sold easily and without any differentiation in price.

Almost all **securities in the United Kingdom are registered**. This means that a central register of shareholders is maintained and any dividends or interest payable on the securities is paid on the due dates directly by the company, or its registrars, to those investors on the share register at a given time. Once a share purchase has been made, therefore, the broker will arrange for the new shareholder's name to be put

EXHIBIT 7 CLASSIFICATION OF ORDINARY STOCK OF OVERSEAS COMPANIES BY COUNTRY OF ORIGIN, 31 DECEMBER 1981
(in millions of pounds sterling)

Country of Origin	Number of Companies	Market Value
Australia	11	£ 4,911.0
Bahamas	1	46.0
Belgium	2	384.7
Bermuda	5	990.4
Brazil	2	2.9
Canada	22	13,301.4
Denmark	4	505.2
France	7	1,621.5
Hong Kong	1	2,074.7
India	2	5.3
Israel	4	406.9
Japan	7	10,474.2
Kenya	1	3.0
Liberia	1	23.6
Luxembourg	4	264.5
Malaysia	19	1,905.4
Malta	1	2.1
Netherlands Antilles	1	8,684.8
New Zealand	2	212.7
Norway	2	565.4
Panama	3	35.3
South Africa	103	16,952.1
Sweden	10	1,669.1
Switzerland	1	3.2
The Netherlands	12	9,518.0
Turkey	1	22.5
United States	139	141,651.4
West Germany	7	6,568.2
West Indies	1	0.4
Zambia	2	16.6
Zimbabwe	5	19.0
Total	383	£222,841.5

on the register, and a new certificate to be issued as evidence of the shareholder's title.

This all takes some time, however, and until the **certificate** is received the **contract note** is the evidence of the shareholder's entitlement to the security. It is also the evidence that the shareholder might have to produce (e.g., to the tax authorities) to show the details of the transaction. It is therefore important that the buyer of shares keeps the **contract note** safely. The buyer becomes entitled to all the benefits of the shares that have been purchased from the moment the transaction takes place. Thus the buyer can be entitled to a dividend that the company is about to pay, or to a

EXHIBIT 8 LEADING OVERSEAS SHARES LISTED ON THE U.K. STOCK EXCHANGE BY MARKET CAPITALIZATION (in millions of pounds sterling)

Company	Position	Country of Origin	Market Value
International Business Machines	1	United States	£18,227.3
Schlumberger	2	Netherlands Antilles	8,684.8
General Electric Co.	3	United States	6,943.9
General Motors Corp.	4	United States	6,035.6
Mobil Corp.	5	United States	5,529.6
Royal Dutch Petroleum Co.	6	The Netherlands	4,925.2
Texaco Inc.	7	United States	4,889.2
Gulf Oil Corp.	8	United States	4,163.1
Halliburton Co.	9	United States	3,241.2
Sun Co. Inc.	10	United States	3,233.4
Dow Chemical	11	United States	2,829.1
Sears Roebuck & Co.	12	United States	2,724.7
Caterpillar Tractor Co.	13	United States	2,596.2
General Telephone & Electronics	14	United States	2,574.9
Tenneco Inc.	15	United States	2,254.9
Sony Corp.	16	Japan	2,075.6
Hong Kong & Shanghai Banking Corp.	17	Hong Kong	2,074.7
Broken Hill Proprietary Co.	18	Australia	2,071.6
Pfizer Inc.	19	United States	2,031.2
Toshiba Corp.	20	Japan	2,011.0
Nippon Electric Co.	21	Japan	1,968.4
Dome Petroleum	22	Canada	1,966.3
Xerox Corp.	23	United States	1,925.8
Union Carbide Corp.	24	United States	1,913.3
Abbott Laboratories	25	United States	1,897.1
International Telephone & Telegraph	26	United States	1,794.6
Citicorp	27	United States	1,727.5
Bank America Corp.	28	United States	1,724.4
American Express Co.	29	United States	1,655.3
Fujitsu	30	Japan	1,649.1
Warner Communications	31	United States	1,615.4
Dart & Kraft Inc.	32	United States	1,577.9
Bell Canada	33	Canada	1,540.7
Anglo-American Corp. of S. Africa	34	South Africa	1,530.7
AMAX Inc.	35	United States	1,513.8
Hughes Tool	36	United States	1,484.1
Southern California Edison Co.	37	United States	1,450.8
Deutsche Bank A.G.	38	West Germany	1,433.4
United Technologies Corp.	39	United States	1,432.1
Honda Motor Co.	40	Japan	1,407.6
Monsanto Co.	41	United States	1,386.7
Pennzoil Co.	42	United States	1,377.1
Baker International Corp.	43	United States	1,348.8
Canadian Pacific	44	Canada	1,334.7
Flour Corp.	45	United States	1,294.1
De Beers Consolidated Mines	46	South Africa	1,284.4

EXHIBIT 8 *(Continued)*

Company	Position	Country of Origin	Market Value
BASF A.G.	47	West Germany	1,261.4
Rockwell International Corp.	48	United States	1,256.3
Robeco N.V.	49	The Netherlands	1,253.1
Bayer A.G.	50	West Germany	1,245.4

bonus issue of shares that it might be undertaking. If the buyer's name has not been registered, the broker will make sure that the new holder gets all the rights to which he or she is entitled, and the **contract note** will be the evidence on which entitlement to benefit will be decided.

In due course the shareholder will receive a **certificate** from the company's registrars, showing the number of shares held. An example of a typical share **certificate** is shown in Exhibit 10.

In due course the shareholder will become entitled to any **dividends** that the directors of the company declare. On the due date the shareholder will receive from the company a **dividend warrant**, together with a check for the due amount. An example of a dividend warrant and check are shown in Exhibit 11. As with the **contract note**, the **dividend warrant** is an important document for the shareholder to keep safe as it will be necessary to declare interest and dividends to the Inland Revenue when his or her tax is being calculated. As can be seen from Exhibit 11, the dividend warrant shows the number of shares held, the value of the dividend, whether it is an interim or a final, the tax credit that has been paid by the company to the Inland Revenue, and the amount of net dividend that is included in the check. The taxation of dividend income on shares is outlined under "Taxation of Dividends."

A company from time to time might wish to raise new capital. As detailed elsewhere in this section, the most common method of doing this in the United Kingdom is by way of a **rights issue** to existing shareholders in proportion to the amounts they already own. It is possible, therefore, that a shareholder who owns, for example, 1,000 shares in a company, will be offered the chance to buy additional shares at a favorable price. The offer might be one extra share for every four he or she already owns. In this case the shareholder would be asked, by means of a **letter of allotment**, if he or she wished to subscribe to another 250 shares. If the shareholder does so he or she will pay the required amount directly to the company's bankers, and in due course will get the new certificate for the additional shares. On the other hand, the shareholder might not wish to subscribe to extra shares and he or she can sell the letter of allotment received from the company through his or her broker on the stock exchange.

Selling a Security. When an investor decides to sell a security he or she will so instruct the broker. Again the shareholder will receive a contract note from the broker, showing the details of the transaction as before. The only significant difference between the "bought" and the "sold" **contract note** is that there is no transfer stamp duty payable on a selling transaction.

EXHIBIT 9

BOUGHT	BY ORDER OF	BARGAIN NUMBER	BARGAIN DATE & TAX PT.
		0024	5th Nov. 1980

Miss A. BUYER SAL 0024

A Public Company Ltd. £1 Ordinary Shares

AMOUNT	PRICE		CONSIDERATION	
500	£1.28		£640.00	
		TRANSFER STAMP	12.80	N
		CONTRACT STAMP	0.30	N
	1·5% on £640·00	COMMISSION	9.60	T
0·70221-5		V.A.T. 15%	1.44	
FOR SETTLEMENT	17th Nov. 1980	**TOTAL £**	664.14	

VAT SUB TOTALS:	TAXABLE ITEMS EXCLUDING V.A.T.	**9·60**	EXEMPT ITEMS	0	E. & O. E.

A. N. BROKER & CO.

99 THROGMORTON STREET - LONDON EC2X ABC

LONDON - CHICAGO - SYDNEY - HONG KONG

TELEGRAMS:	TELEPHONE:	TELEX:	V.A.T. REGISTRATION
INLAND: BROTHER, LONDON, TELEX	01-588 2355 (20 lines)	44259	NUMBER: 242 0024

PARTNERS

T. H. WOOD	**S. G. CORK**
A. B. JONES	**S. H. THUMB**
C. D. SMITH	**A. K. WOOD**
K. A. WIER	**B. G. OAK**
T. D. CHILD	**R. N. SWEEPER**

CONSULTANT

T. C. BOOTH

A. N. BROKER & CO.

CONTRACT STAMP **£0·30**

MEMBERS OF THE STOCK EXCHANGE

Subject to the rules and regulations including temporary regulations of The Stock Exchange

For Capital Gains and V.A.T. purposes this contract note should be retained

An asterisk means commission is shared with yourselves a member of the staff or an agent

V.A.T. Symbols; T = Taxable; E = Exempt: N = Outside the scope

EXHIBIT 10

CERTIFICATE No. TRANSFER No. DATE NUMBER OF SHARES

Lloyds Bank Limited

Incorporated under the Companies Act 1862.

This is to Certify that the undermentioned is/are the proprietor(s) of fully paid Shares of One Pound each in Lloyds Bank Limited *as shown herein subject to the Memorandum and Articles of Association of the Company.*

NAME(S) OF MEMBER(S) NUMBER OF SHARES OF £1 EACH

Given under the Common Seal of the Company

SPECIMEN

No transfer of any portion of this holding will be registered unless this certificate is deposited at the office of the Registrar, Lloyds Bank Limited, Goring-by-Sea, Worthing, West Sussex BN12 6DA.
In any correspondence to the Registrar please quote Reference No. 014.

L.B.L. Ex'd. R.

431964

Smith & Ouzman Ltd 3-11814 5/80

The seller will also receive from the broker a **TALISMAN sold transfer form** (see Exhibit 12), which he or she will be required to sign and return to the broker, along with the share certificate. This TALISMAN sold transfer form is then used to register the sale of the security and the transfer to another owner. Again the contract note should be kept safely, as evidence of the sale of the security, for production as necessary.

The Settlement System. In 1979 the U.K. Stock Exchange introduced a new method of settling business in equities, called "TALISMAN." TALISMAN is a computer-based system of settlement and any seller of securities transfers his or her holding into the name of **SEPON Ltd.**, a stock exchange nominee account, while any buyer of a security purchases it from SEPON. This new system, which also involves the registrars in transferring securities from one holder to another, has significantly improved the speed and efficiency of transfer of securities through the stock exchange in the United Kingdom.

The Dealing Account. Dealing in equity shares in the United Kingdom is normally done on a two-week dealing account basis, laid down in a stock exchange calendar. This usually runs from the Monday of week one to the Friday of week two (although sometimes the account might run for three weeks if public holidays occur during the period). The next dealing account then starts on the following Monday, and so on. Settlement of all business done in the first dealing account is made on the Monday of week four; all business done in account number two is settled on the Monday of week six, and so on, as shown in the following list.

Dealing Account Number	Which Covers Weeks	Settlement Day, Monday of Week
1	1 and 2	4
2	3 and 4	6
3	5 and 6	8
4	7 and 8	10
5	9 and 10	12

The result of this system is that all dealings within a single account are settled on one day. It is, therefore, possible to buy and sell securities within the account and receive (or pay) a balance check on **settlement day**. If an investor does deal within the account in this way, he or she will pay only one amount of stockbroker's commission on the combined deal. No investor trying to make a quick profit in this way, however, should forget that the share price might move contrary to expectations.

The account dealings system applies to the majority of equity shares. It does not apply in the gilt-edged market, nor does it apply to dealing in new issues, for which settlement is required the day following the deal.

Dealing in New Issues. When a company comes to the market for a listing for the first time, it must publish a full prospectus showing its management history and trading record, its financial accounts, and a large amount of further information relating to the company and the value of its shares. Some of the details of the information required at an initial listing are given elsewhere in this section. The **prospectus** for the issue is published, both in book form and by means of advertisement, in at least two national newspapers (unless the issue is of less than £3 million). Accompanying the prospectus must be an application form, which a person wanting to invest in the company will send to the company's bankers. If the subscriber's application is successful he or she will receive a **letter of allotment**, illustrated in Exhibit 13.

In any new issue the activity in the first few weeks of dealing is likely to be fairly substantial, and so the evidence of title to these shares passes by means of this letter of allotment. These **allotment letters** are essentially bearer documents; they can transfer ownership by delivery. They can thus be renounced by signature and passed on to a new holder; they can be split, transferring only part of the holding; or they can be consolidated, and a number of holdings amalgamated.

After about two months, the allotment letter ceases to be transferable; holders are then registered and future transfers are made in the usual way.

Stock Brokers' Commissions. Securities traded on the stock exchange are subject to minimum scales of commission, laid down by the Council of the Stock Exchange,

EXHIBIT 11

233

Lloyds Bank Limited

Security code: 0–521–103

28th August, 1981

I enclose a warrant for the interim dividend for the year ending 31st December, 1981, at 8·625p per share, on the shares of £1 each, fully paid up, registered in your name on 31st July, 1981. I certify that Advance Corporation Tax of an amount equal to that shown below as a Tax Credit will be accounted for to the Collector of Taxes.

D. H. DAVIES, *Secretary.*

Notice of change of address, quoting the name of the Company, the full name, address, and reference of the holder as shown on this form, and the new address, should be signed by the shareholder and sent to:—

THE REGISTRAR,
LLOYDS BANK LIMITED,
REGISTRAR'S DEPARTMENT,
GORING-BY-SEA,
WORTHING, WEST SUSSEX,
BN12 6DA

This voucher should be kept. It will be accepted by the Inland Revenue as evidence of Tax Credit in respect of which you may be entitled to claim payment or relief.

SPECIMEN

REFERENCE	SHAREHOLDING	TAX CREDIT	DIVIDEND PAYABLE
014/			

Lloyds Bank Limited
HEAD OFFICE, LONDON

30-00-00T

PAY *or Order* 28th August, 1981

This warrant should be presented for payment through a banker within six months, and if not, returned to the Registrar for verification.

SPECIMEN

& Co. NOT NEGOTIABLE

233

Smith & Ouzman Ltd
7-16484 6/81

035569 30 0002 1438846

to be charged by brokers to their clients. The scales for company debentures and bonds, equities, and U.S. and Canadian securities are as shown in Exhibit 14. When a deal is carried out by a broker through an agent, such as a bank, accountant, or lawyer, a slightly higher scale operates and is sometimes shared with that agent. In addition, on all deals over £5,000 a levy by the Council for the Securities Industry (**CSI levy**) of 60p (pence) is payable.

These scales are those in operation 31 December 1981. The scales are presently being revised by the Council of the Stock Exchange, but details are not yet available.

All of Exhibit 14 listings are subject to a minimum commission charge of £7 on a sale and £10 on a purchase, except in deals where the total consideration is less than £200, in which case the commission is at the broker's discretion.

EXHIBIT 12

TALISMAN SOLD TRANSFER

This transfer is pursuant to a Stock Exchange transaction, and is exempt from Transfer Stamp Duty.

Above this line for Registrar's use only

Bargain Reference No: *1764/12345*

Certificate lodged with Registrar

(*for completion by the Registrars/ Stock Exchange*)

Name of Undertaking: *A Public Company Limited*

Description of Security: *Ordinary Shares of £1 each fully paid*

Amount of Stock or number of Stock units or shares or other security in words: *Five hundred*

Figures: *500*

In the name(s) of

Thomas Harold Edward Seller
21, High Street,
Zellingham,
London, EC7Y CAB

Account Designation (if any)

Name(s) of registered holder(s) should be given in full; the address should be given where there is only one holder

If the transfer is not made by the registered holder(s) insert also the name(s) and capacity (e.g., Executor(s)) of the person(s) making the transfer

Specimen

I/We hereby transfer the above security out of the name(s) aforesaid into the name of SEPON LIMITED and request the necessary entries to be made in the register.

Bodies corporate should affix their common seal and each signatory should state his/her representative capacity (e.g. 'Company Secretary' 'Director') against his/her signature.

PLEASE SIGN HERE

1 J. H. E. Seller

2 ______

3 ______

4 ______

Balance Certificate Required for (amount or number in figures)

Stamp and Firm Code of Selling Broker

A. Broker, Sons & Co.,
Austin Friars Court,
London, EC2Y BAC.

Members of The Stock Exchange

Date

SEPON LIMITED is lodging this Transfer at the direction and on behalf of the Member Firm whose stamp appears herein ('the Original Lodging Agent') and does not in any manner or to any extent warrant or represent the validity or genuineness of the transfer instructions contained herein or the genuineness of the Transferor's signature. The Original Lodging Agent by delivering this Transfer to SEPON LIMITED authorises SEPON LIMITED to lodge this Transfer for registration and agrees to be deemed for all purposes to be the person(s) actually lodging this Transfer for registration.

Stock Exchange Operating Account Number (if applicable)

TAL 112/1

EXHIBIT 13

IMPORTANT.—THIS DOCUMENT IS OF VALUE AND IS NEGOTIABLE. THE OFFER EXPIRES AT 3 p.m. ON 10th APRIL, 1981. IF YOU ARE IN ANY DOUBT ABOUT IT OR IF, PRIOR TO RECEIVING IT, YOU HAVE SOLD ALL OR PART OF YOUR REGISTERED HOLDING OF EXISTING ORDINARY SHARES YOU SHOULD IMMEDIATELY CONSULT YOUR STOCKBROKER, BANK MANAGER, SOLICITOR, ACCOUNTANT OR OTHER PROFESSIONAL ADVISER. ALL ENQUIRIES CONCERNING THIS PROVISIONAL ALLOTMENT LETTER SHOULD BE ADDRESSED TO HILL SAMUEL REGISTRARS LIMITED, 6 GREENCOAT PLACE, LONDON, SW1P 1PL, QUOTING THIS NUMBER:—

The new Ordinary Shares now being issued have been admitted to the Official List by the Council of The Stock Exchange.

A copy of this document having attached thereto the circular letter to Ordinary Shareholders dated 20th March, 1981 has been delivered to the Registrar of Companies for registration.

IMI LIMITED

(Incorporated under the Companies Act 1948. Registered in England No. 714275)

Transfer Office: 6 Greencoat Place, London, SW1P 1PL
Registered Office: P.O. Box 216,
Witton,
Birmingham, B6 7BA

20th March, 1981.

At Lloyds Bank Limited, Registrar's Department, Goring-by-Sea, Worthing, West Sussex, BN12 6DA (by post) or Lloyds Bank Limited, Registrar's Department, Issue Section, 111 Old Broad Street, London EC2 (by hand)

Latest time for Acceptance and Payment .. .. 3 p.m. on 10th April, 1981

At Hill Samuel Registrars Limited
6 Greencoat Place, London, SW1P 1PL. (01-828 4321)

Latest times for:
Splitting:
Nil paid .. .. 3 p.m. on 8th April, 1981
Fully paid .. .. .. 3 p.m. on 27th May, 1981
Registration of Renunciation 3 p.m. on 29th May, 1981
Certificates ready .. .. .. 26th June, 1981

Rights Issue of 59,598,520 Ordinary Shares of 25p each at 48p per share payable in full upon acceptance not later than 3 p.m. on 10th April. 1981

PROVISIONAL ALLOTMENT LETTER

(1) Ordinary Shares registered in your name(s) at the close of business on 6th March, 1981	(2) Ordinary Shares provisionally allotted	(3) Amount payable at or before 3 p.m. on 10th April, 1981

Dear Sir or Madam,

PROVISIONAL ALLOTMENT.—In accordance with the terms of the circular letter to Ordinary Shareholders dated 20th March, 1981 you have been provisionally allotted, upon the terms contained in the circular letter and this letter and subject to the Memorandum and Articles of Association of the Company, the number of new Ordinary Shares of 25p each in the capital of the Company indicated in Column (2) above, being in the proportion of two new Ordinary Shares for every seven Ordinary Shares of 25p each held at the close of business on 6th March, 1981, fractions of a new share being disregarded. Fractional entitlements will be aggregated and sold in the market for the benefit of the Company.

The new Ordinary Shares will, when fully paid, rank *pari passu* with the existing Ordinary Shares save that they will not rank for the final dividend payable in respect of the year ended 31st December, 1980.

ACCEPTANCE AND PAYMENT. —**If you wish to accept the provisional allotment, this Allotment Letter must be forwarded to Lloyds Bank Limited, Registrar's Department, Goring-by-Sea, Worthing, West Sussex, BN12 6DA (by post) or Lloyds Bank Limited, Registrar's Department, Issue Section, 111 Old Broad Street, London EC2 (by hand), accompanied by a remittance in sterling for the amount shown in Column (3) above, so as to reach them not later than 3 p.m. on 10th April, 1981.** It will then be returned to the person lodging it and such payment will constitute acceptance of this provisional allotment upon the terms of this letter and the circular letter and subject to the Memorandum and Articles of Association of the Company.

Cheques should be made payable to **"Lloyds Bank Limited"** and crossed **"Not Negotiable"**. All payments must be made in pounds sterling drawn on a Bank in the United Kingdom. Residents of the Republic of Ireland should consult their professional adviser. No interest will be allowed on payments made before the due date.

If payment for the Ordinary Shares comprised in this letter is not made at or before 3 p.m. on 10th April, 1981 the provisional allotment will be deemed to have been declined. Those new Ordinary Shares provisionally allotted and not taken up which can thereafter be sold in the market at a premium over the total of the subscription price and expenses of sale (including any VAT thereon) by 3 p.m. on 15th April, 1981 will be sold and the net proceeds (after deducting expenses and the amounts payable on acceptance) will be distributed *pro rata* to the original allottees save that amounts of less than £1 will not be so distributed but will be retained for the benefit of the Company. Cheques for the amounts due will be despatched to such persons at their own risk to their registered addresses.

RENUNCIATION AND SPLITTING.—This letter may be renounced or split, in which case the instructions overleaf must be complied with.

REGISTRATION.—**If this letter has been renounced or split and your name does NOT appear in the box above, the Registration Application Form Y overleaf must be completed and this letter must be lodged at or before 3 p.m. on 29th May, 1981 with Hill Samuel Registrars Limited, 6, Greencoat Place, London, SW1P 1PL, who will acknowledge receipt to the person so lodging. After 3 p.m. on 29th May, 1981 renunciations will not be accepted and the shares comprised in this letter, if paid for, will be registered in the name(s) shown above and thereafter will only be transferable by transfer in the usual common form attracting stamp duty.**

SHARE CERTIFICATES.—**This Allotment Letter (when fully paid and if not renounced) should be carefully preserved and should be presented without further request on or after 26th June, 1981 to Hill Samuel Registrars Limited, 6, Greencoat Place, London, SW1P 1PL, to be exchanged for a share certificate. On 24th July, 1981 Allotment Letters will cease to be valid for any purpose whatsoever and Hill Samuel Registrars Limited will post any share certificates remaining in their hands to the (first) registered holder at his registered address at the risk of the holder(s).**

TRANSFERS.—After 29th May, 1981, and pending the issue of share certificates, Hill Samuel Registrars Limited will certify instruments of transfer against delivery of Allotment Letters and/or acknowledgements for renounced letters.

By Order of the Board,
J. METCALF
Secretary.

Exd.

Name and address of Paying Agent. (If this box is not completed this letter will be returned to the original allottee named above)	Received the amount payable on acceptance For Lloyds Bank Limited

EXHIBIT 13 *(Continued)*

INSTRUCTIONS FOR RENUNCIATION, SPLITTING AND CONSOLIDATION

RENUNCIATION. This allotment may be renounced in whole by completing Form X. Form Y must then be completed by or on behalf of the person(s) in whose favour the allotment is renounced and this letter (when fully paid) must be lodged at or before 3 p.m. on 29th May, 1981 with Hill Samuel Registrars Limited, 6, Greencoat Place, London, SW1P 1PL, who will acknowledge receipt. A share certificate in the name(s) of the renouncee(s) will be sent on or about 26th June, 1981 to the person(s) lodging this Allotment Letter for registration. After 3 p.m. on 29th May, 1981 renunciations will not be accepted.

SPLITTING.—This allotment cannot be renounced in part, but this letter may be split on application to Hill Samuel Registrars Limited, 6, Greencoat Place, London, SW1P 1PL, with Form X duly completed, at or before 3 p.m. on 8th April, 1981 (nil paid) or 3 p.m. on 27th May, 1981 (fully paid). The application should state the number of shares to be comprised in each split letter. Form X on split letters will be marked "Original duly renounced".

CONSOLIDATION.—The shares comprised in several renounced fully paid Allotment Letters may be registered in the name(s) of one holder or joint holders if Form Y and the Consolidation Listing Form are completed on one letter (referred to in the listing form as the Principal Letter) and all the letters are lodged together.

NOTE.—Surrender of this Allotment Letter with the Form of Renunciation X purporting to have been signed by the allottee(s) or marked "Original duly renounced" shall be conclusive evidence in favour of the Company of the right of the person(s) named in the Registration Application Form Y to be registered as the holder(s) of the shares comprised herein and of the title of the party or parties surrendering it to deal with the same and to receive split letters and/or an acknowledgement and/or a share certificate, as the case may be. When documents are received through the post they, or the documents to be issued in exchange, will be returned through the post at the risk of the person(s) entitled to them.

FORM X FORM OF RENUNCIATION

To the Directors of
IMI LIMITED.

I/We hereby renounce my/our right to the shares comprised in this Allotment Letter in favour of the person(s) named in the Registration Application Form Y relating to or including such shares.

Dated this *day of* , 1981.

Signature(s) of allottee(s)

(In the case of joint allottees ALL must sign.)
(A corporation must affix its seal.)

FORM Y REGISTRATION APPLICATION FORM

THIS FORM SHOULD NOT BE COMPLETED IN THE NAME(S) OF ORIGINAL ALLOTTEES

To the Directors of
IMI LIMITED.

FULL NAME(S) (Please state title, if any, or whether Mr., Mrs., or Miss) AND FULL POSTAL ADDRESS(ES) (including county and, if applicable, postal code) OF THE PERSON(S) IN WHOSE NAME(S) THE SHARES ARE TO BE REGISTERED.	**Please complete in typewriting or in block capitals**
REN.	

I/We request registration in the above name(s) of the shares specified in this Allotment Letter (‡*and in the several Allotment Letters attached hereto and amounting to* ☐ *shares in all, as shown in the Consolidation Listing Form*).

Stamp or name and address of person lodging this form

CONSOLIDATION LISTING FORM

SERIAL NUMBER	NUMBER OF SHARES
TOTAL	

NUMBER OF PRINCIPAL LETTER

‡Delete words in italics if not required. Where several Allotment Letters are consolidated the total number of shares included in the consolidation must be inserted.

LODGED FOR SHARE CERTIFICATE BY:

Greenaways London DC 5035-

EXHIBIT 14 EXTRACTS FROM THE STOCK EXCHANGE SCALES OF MINIMUM COMMISSIONS (in percentages)

Consideration	Not Shared with an Agent	Shared
COMPANY DEBENTURES AND BONDS		
Registered Stocks		
On the first £ 5,000	0.75	0.75
On the next £ 5,000	0.375	0.75
£ 40,000	0.375	0.50
£ 50,000	0.325	0.45
£150,000	0.300	0.375
£500,000	0.25	0.3125
£1 million	0.20	0.25
On the excess	0.125	0.1563
Bearer Stocks		
On the first £5,000	0.5	0.5
On the next £5,000	0.25	0.5
On the excess	0.25	0.3125
STOCKS AND SHARES		
On the first £ 7,000	1.5	1.5
On the next £ 3,000	0.5	1.25
£ 15,000	0.5	1.00
£ 25,000	0.5	0.75
£ 50,000	0.5	0.625
£ 20,000	0.4	0.625
£130,000	0.4	0.5
£500,000	0.3	0.4
£1 million	0.2	0.27
On the excess	0.125	0.17
Canadian and U.S. Shares		
On the first £ 5,000	0.9	0.9
On the next £ 5,000	0.4	0.9
£10,000	0.3	0.8
On the excess	0.3	0.375

TAXATION OF SECURITIES AND SECURITIES DEALING. There are a number of taxes and duties on dealing in securities in the United Kingdom. They can be divided into those that are imposed at the time of buying a share, those that are imposed at the time of sale or other disposal, and those that are levied on income arising from the holding of shares.

Taxes on the Purchase and Sale of Shares.

Transfer Stamp Duty. Any registered stock, shares, or marketable securities passing by transfer (except government stocks and company loan capital) attracts transfer stamp duty. In practice this means ordinary shares (except new issues), convertible shares, and anything other than straight fixed-interest stock is liable.

The rates of duty are 2% on consideration for U.K. residents and 1% for non-U.K. residents. In order to qualify for the reduced rate of duty for nonresidents, the following must apply.

1. The person acquiring the securities as beneficial owner must be resident outside the United Kingdom.
2. The transfer must be for full consideration in money or money's worth.
3. The instrument of transfer or bearer instrument (as the case might be) must bear a certificate by an authorized depositary that the above conditions are satisfied.

Bearer Stocks and Shares. All bearer instruments relating to stocks and shares expressed in currencies other than pounds sterling are free of stamp duty. In practice, sterling bearer issues will have been stamped when they were originally issued, and stamp duty is not payable on subsequent transfer.

Gifts. In the case of a gift of stock, the transfer must be stamped where appropriate with *ad valorem* conveyance duty on the market value of the stock, an exception being gifts made in consideration of marriage, when fixed duty of 50p if payable.

Contract Stamp. The contract stamp duty is levied both on the buyer and seller of a security.Where the value of the stock or marketable security

is £100 or less, the contract stamp is	Nil
exceeds £100 and does not exceed £500	10p
exceeds £500 and does not exceed £1,500	30p
exceeds £1,500	60p

Value-Added Tax. The value-added tax is levied on a stock broker's commission at the standard rate, currently 15%.

Taxation of Dividends. Any dividend received by the shareholder is subject to tax at the shareholder's marginal rate. The rates of income tax currently in operation in the United Kingdom are as follows.

Taxable Income*		Rate of Tax
first:	£12,800	30%
next:	2,300	40%
	4,000	45%
	6,200	50%
	6,200	55%
Above	£31,500	60%

Companies declare and pay **dividends** net, and pay to the British tax authorities an amount equivalent to the individual's basic rate of tax (i.e., 30% of a gross figure). This payment is called **advance corporation tax** (ACT) and must be paid to the Inland Revenue authorities shortly after the **dividend** payment is made to shareholders. The ACT can be offset against a company's total corporation tax liability on its profits when its main corporation tax liability falls due. The amount of ACT paid in respect of each individual dividend is shown as a tax credit on the dividend warrant form, as illustrated in Exhibit 11. An individual who does not pay tax can claim back the amount of this tax credit from the Inland Revenue authorities, but those who are liable to pay more than the basic rate of tax must later account for the additional amount.

Investment Income Surcharge. For those individuals who have a substantial amount of investment income, an additional tax payment, called the "investment income surcharge," is payable on interest and dividends received. The rates are presently nil for investment income up to £6,250, and 15% for investment income over £6,250.

Taxes on the Disposal of Securities. When a security is sold, the contract stamp is payable at the same levels as a purchase and the VAT is again levied on the stock broker's commission.

Capital Gains Tax. In addition, an individual can be liable to capital gains tax on any real profit made on the sale of securities. This applies to shares issued by U.K. and overseas companies, but not to disposals of government securities that have been held for more than one year. Capital gains tax is currently levied at a rate of 30% of the nominal gain made. However, to help small shareholders, gains of less than £3,000 annually are at present exempt from tax, and losses on qualifying assets can be offset against gains in order to arrive at the net taxable position. Allowances are made when computing the amount of gains for capitalization (scrip) issues, rights issues, reorganizations of a company's share capital, amalgamations, and mergers.

Capital Transfer Tax. Any gratuitous transfer of securities (and indeed other assets) from one person to another in the United Kingdom is chargeable to capital transfer tax (CTT). The first £55,000, however (accumulated over a period of 10 years), is charged at a nil rate and transfers between spouses are exempt.

The rate of tax varies from 15% on transfers of between £55,000 and £75,000, rising by stages to 50% on lifetime transfers of £2.50 million or more. Rates of CTT

*After personal allowances (£1,565 for a single person, £2,445 for a married man) and other tax allowances (e.g., mortgage interest payments).

on death (rather than lifetime transfers) are higher, ranging from 30% on amounts between £55,000 and £75,000 to 75% on amounts of £2.50 million, but as with lifetime transfers, the first £50,000 is exempt.

Tax Benefits to Shareholding. Generally there are no tax incentives to buy shares directly, but two exceptions should be noted.

Company Profit-sharing schemes. A company can establish a company profit-sharing scheme for its employees. Under these schemes, which were established under the Finance Act of 1978, up to £1,250 a year can be allocated to an employee by the issue of shares in his or her company. These shares must be held in trust for two years. If the employee sells all the shares after that period the calculated income benefit of the allocation is chargeable to income tax on a declining scale, depending upon how long the employee has held the allocation. If he or she sells the shares within four years of their first being allotted, the total amount of the chargeable benefit will be subject to tax at his or her marginal rate. If the employee holds on to the shares for seven years or more, there will be no tax payable at all. The declining scale is shown below.

Period of Holding	Percentage of Benefit Liable to Tax
0–2 years	holder cannot sell
2–4 years	100%
4–5 years	75%
5–6 years	50%
6–7 years	25%
over 7 years	nil

Share Option Schemes. There are two other types of schemes in operation under which employees can obtain shares in the company for which they work. The first of these is a **share option scheme**, open usually only to directors and certain senior key personnel, by which they can acquire the option to buy shares in the company at advantageous prices. Tax law in recent years has, however, rendered such schemes relatively unattractive.

More widely available are save-as-you-earn schemes, whereby employees can put aside up to £50 a month in National Savings or with a building society. On the maturity of the savings scheme (either five or seven years, at the saver's option), the capital sum can be used to purchase shares in the employee's company at a favorable price.

SPECIAL ARRANGEMENTS FOR OVERSEAS INVESTORS.

Stocks Free of Income Tax, and Other Tax Reductions, for Nonresidents. For this purpose nonresidents in the United Kingdom include all those residing outside England, Scotland, Wales, and Northern Ireland. It should be noted that residents of the Isle of Man and the Channel Islands are thus classified as nonresidents.

Interest. There are certain stocks on which the interest is free or partly free of U.K. income tax to nonresidents, except where it is deemed to form part of profits of a trade or business carried on in the United Kingdom.

Interest is paid without deduction of tax and for nonresident holders there is no subsequent U.K. tax liability on 3.5% War Loan stocks (which are free of tax even if forming part of a U.K. trade or business carried on by a nonresident), and International Bank for Reconstruction and Development stocks (all issues).

Interest on the following British government stocks is free of U.K. income tax to nonresidents (provided the stocks are held for at least one month) and arrangements can be made for the interest to be paid gross.

8.5 %	Treasury Loan 1980–82	14.5 %	Treasury Loan 1994
3 %	Treasury Stock 1982	9 %	Treasury Loan 1994
14 %	Treasury Stock 1982	12.75%	Treasury Loan 1995
12 %	Treasury Loan 1983	9 %	Treasury Loan 1992–96
5.5 %	Funding Loan 1982–84	15.25%	Treasury Loan 1996
8.5 %	Treasury Loan 1984–86	13.25%	Exchequer Loan 1996
6.5 %	Funding Loan 1985–87	13.25%	Treasury Loan 1997
7.75%	Treasury Loan 1985–88	8.75%	Treasury Loan 1997
13 %	Treasury Stock 1990	6.75%	Treasury Stock 1995–98
8.25%	Treasury Loan 1987–90	15.5 %	Treasury Loan 1998
5.75%	Funding Loan 1987–91	9.5 %	Treasury Loan 1999
12.75%	Treasury Loan 1992	8 %	Treasury Loan 2002–06
12.5 %	Treasury Loan 1993	5.5 %	Treasury Stock 2008–12
6 %	Funding Loan 1993	7.75%	Treasury Loan 2012–15
13.75%	Treasury Loan 1993		

Interest on sterling loans of British dominions, colonies, and foreign states is free of U.K. tax to residents abroad. This applies whether the loans carry a U.K. government guarantee or not. After certain simple formalities, the interest is paid without deduction of tax.

Nonresidents can also make arrangements with the U.K. tax authorities to have interest (and dividends) on foreign stocks paid and retained in London without deduction of U.K. tax. Such payments will, of course, not suffer U.K. tax where the paying agent transmits the monies directly abroad to a nonresident. Such payments will, however, be subject to the withholding taxes of other countries where relevant.

Under various **double-taxation agreements**, residents of certain overseas countries are sometimes able to receive interest on U.K. stocks free or partly free of the normal U.K. income tax deduction.

In the majority of cases, liability to tax on the interest in the country of residence is a prerequisite for obtaining relief from U.K. withholding tax. In some cases, however, the recipient need only be a resident in the country to which the agreement applies.

At present the following reduced rates of **U.K. withholding tax** on interest are in force in respect to payments of all types of interest in the countries specified. This list is not exhaustive, and includes only the main countries that might be of interest. A column showing those countries where there is no reduction and the full U.K. income tax applies is also included.

Nil	10%	12%	15%	Full Rate
Austria	Australia	Spain	Belgium	Hong Kong
Denmark	France		Canada	Italy
Ireland	Japan		Malaysia	New Zealand
Luxembourg	South Africa		Singapore	
Norway			Philippines	
Sweden				
Switzerland				
The Netherlands				
United States				
West Germany				

Residents of the Channel Islands and the Isle of Man can obtain a tax credit in the United Kingdom equal to the local tax suffered in the Channel Islands or Isle of Man on interest paid by U.K. companies. This leads to repayment in part of the U.K. tax deducted, such repayments of U.K. tax being liable to further local tax, which in turn can be reclaimed from the United Kingdom, and so on. In practice the total repayments will approximately equal the local tax liability.

For companies only, in order to simplify the procedure, there is an alternative method of claiming relief that involves only one claim on the U.K. tax authorities. Under this procedure, a company will, in most cases, be able to claim relief up to its effective rate of local tax on the net sum received from the United Kingdom.

British subjects, wherever they are resident, and residents of the Channel Islands and the Isle of Man, can obtain relief from U.K. tax in respect to their personal allowances in the proportion that their taxable U.K. income bears to their worldwide income. For this purpose U.K. income that bears tax at a reduced rate because of double-taxation relief arrangements is not counted as U.K. taxable income.

Dividends. The change to the imputation system of **corporation tax** in the United Kingdom in 1973 rendered obsolete the provisions of all existing **double-taxation agreements** insofar as they related to dividends paid by U.K. companies to residents of the countries concerned. A significant number of agreements have now been amended and shareholders resident in those countries qualify for both the net dividend and the tax credit to which a U.K. resident is entitled. Shareholders resident in other countries are entitled only to the net dividend and effectively suffer a 30% withholding tax.

At the present time, of the more important agreements, those with Australia, Canada, Denmark, Ireland, France, Japan, Luxembourg, Switzerland, and the United States have been amended. Shareholders of U.K. companies resident in these countries are entitled to the tax credit in respect to dividends and suffer withholding tax of only 15% on the total of net dividend and tax credit. In some cases, liability to tax on the dividend in the country of residence is a condition of relief.

Formalities for Gaining Exemption. In the case of War Loan and World Bank stocks, interest payments are automatically paid without deduction of U.K. tax.

The rest of the governmental free-of-tax stocks normally suffer U.K. tax by deduction at their source but on the completion of certain formalities arrangements can be made for the interest to be paid without deduction of U.K. tax. The formalities vary a little with each class of security, but the U.K. authorities will normally require a declaration containing

Name of beneficial owner
Address
If a married woman, husband's address
Previous and anticipated periods of residence in the United Kingdom
If a corporation, where the effective control and management takes place

The various procedures for obtaining relief on U.K. dividends and interest where this is provided under the terms of a double-taxation agreement are set out below. Regarding dividends, there are two ways in which relief is given. The first is that of the "G arrangement." Under this scheme, residents of certain countries (at present, of the most important countries, Australia, Canada, Denmark, Ireland, France, Malaysia, New Zealand, Norway, Singapore, Sweden, The Netherlands, and the United States qualify) are able, provided that the conditions of the double-taxation agreement are fulfilled, to obtain the sum of the net dividend and tax credit with the reduced withholding tax deductions specified by that agreement. There is no obligation on companies to operate the arrangement, however, and not all companies have agreed to do so, but the majority of those listed in London have agreed, and these are designated in the **Stock Exchange Daily Official List**. In order to obtain relief under this scheme, nonresident shareholders must transfer their holdings into the name of a nominee company that has been approved by the Inland Revenue for this purpose. The nominee company completes any necessary formalities with the Inland Revenue and pays the sum of the net dividend and tax credit less the appropriate rate of U.K. tax to the shareholder.

Second, shareholders resident in a country to which the G arrangement does not apply, or holding shares in a company that does not operate the arrangement, but who are, nevertheless, entitled to relief under the terms of a double-taxation agreement, will normally have to submit a claim to the Inland Revenue.

Regarding interest payments, where a **double-taxation agreement** provides for relief, arrangements can normally be made through the Inspector of Foreign Dividends to have the interest paid less the appropriate reduced rate of tax. The procedure is broadly similar to that outlined in connection with free-of-tax government stocks.

SHAREHOLDING IN THE UNITED KINGDOM. Over the years, the proportion of shares owned by individuals has been declining in the United Kingdom, while the proportion and amount held by savings institutions have been rising.

Some indication of the extent of the changes can be seen from the statistics in Exhibit 15, which show the earliest and the latest figures, relating to 1957 and 1975, respectively.

These figures are updated by statistics of the net acquisition and/or disposal of shares by some of the major groups. From the figures in Exhibit 15 it has been calculated that the proportion owned by the personal sector is now down to about 28% to 30%, with over 50% held by the institutions. However, a U.K. Stock Exchange survey of companies' annual reports for the end of 1980 showed the following results,

EXHIBIT 15 PERCENTAGE OF U.K. COMPANY SHARES HELD

Shareholder	1957	1975
Persons	65.8	37.6
Charities	1.9	2.3
Stock brokers, jobbers	0.9	0.4
Banks	0.9	0.7
Insurance companies	8.8	15.9
Pension funds	3.4	16.8
Unit trusts	0.5	4.1
Investment trusts	6.8	10.0
Industrial and commercial companies	2.7	3.0
Public sector	3.9	3.6
Overseas sector	4.4	5.6
Total	100	100

Source. The Ownership of Company Shares: Studies in Official Statistics, No. 34, Central Statistical Office, London. Available from HMSO, London, £2.50.

suggesting that the decline in the personal sector's holding had not been as great as originally thought.*

Percentage of U.K. Company Shares Held by	End of 1980
Persons	36
Insurance companies	18
Pension funds	18
Investment and unit trusts	13
Other institutions	15
Total	100

Because of the differences between this survey and other estimates, the stock exchange has recently announced that it is to carry out a full survey to assess the shareholding structure at the end of 1981.

Some idea of the savings institutions' net purchases and/or sales of company securities can be gauged from the following:

		Institutions			
Year	Personal Sector	Unit Trusts	Investment Trusts	Insurance Companies	Pension Funds
1977	−1,817	130	40	201	1,225
1978	−1,152	36	−59	84	979
1979	−2,105	18	−146	71	1,331
1980	−1,735	−26	−282	104	1,647

**Shareholder Analysis: A Supplement to the Stock Exchange Fact Book,* The Stock Exchange, Economics Department, London, EC2 (price £5).

Following the abolition of exchange control, the investment trusts, in particular, invested heavily in overseas assets, while pension funds remained substantial net buyers of U.K. company shares. The personal sector is shown as a substantial net seller of shares, but this is a residual figure and probably overstates the true position.

TRADED OPTIONS. Traded **call options** were first introduced on the floor of the London Stock Exchange in April 1978 following the success of similar markets elsewhere in the world. The major difference between ordinary and traded options is that the latter can themselves be traded on the market, so that instead of buying or selling the underlying shares that were subject to the option, or letting the option itself lapse, the holder can sell back the option into the market when he or she wishes, thus closing the position and taking a profit (or loss).

Like the ordinary option, a traded call option gives the buyer the right to buy a share close to today's market price at a specified future date. For this the buyer makes a payment, called a "premium," to the person granting the option (who is known as the "writer" of the option). In 1981 traded **put options** were introduced in London. Puts are the opposite of calls, in that a put option gives the buyer the right to sell the underlying securities at close to the current price at or before a specified future date.

At present there are 18 companies in whose shares a traded call option is available and 11 on which a traded put option can also be written.

Put and Call Options	Call Options Only
British Petroleum	Barclays Bank
Consolidated Gold Fields	Commercial Union Assurance
G.E.C. (General Electric)	Courtaulds
Grand Metropolitan	Land Securities Investment Trust
Imperial Chemical Industries	London and Scottish Marine Oil
Imperial Group	Marks & Spencer
Lonrho	P. & O.
Racal Electronics	
Rio Tinto-Zinc	
Shell Transport & Trading	
Vaal Reeds Exploration & Mining	

Class of Options. Options are available for up to three, six, and nine months ahead, and at any time there will be at least two different exercise prices in each option, one above the present market price of the underlying security and one below. As the price of the underlying share moves so new options with different exercise prices will be introduced. The different exercise prices and expiry dates in the options of each company's shares are together called a "class."

Option Expiry Dates. The expiry dates of traded options are arranged at intervals of three months, so that on any day in the year there are always three possible expiry dates from which to choose. On some stocks the traded options are on the January, April, July, and October cycle, while on others the options expire in February, May,

August, and November. There will always be traded options for the next three dates ahead in the cycle and when an expiry date is reached a new range of options is introduced with an expiry date nine months ahead.

Series. All options that have the same expiry date and exercise price in a given class of options are called a "series." For example, if a traded call option was introduced in company A in late February with its shares standing at 200p, there would be six different series available for trading.

Expiry Date	Exercise Prices
May	190–210
August	190–210
November	190–210

At the outset, therefore, these six series constitute the class of options in company A, but if the share price of that company rises above 210 for a period of four consecutive days, three new series of options at 220p would be introduced, one for each of the current expiry dates. At this stage, therefore, there would be nine series of options in this particular class. As the share price continues to move, so more series of options can be introduced.

Premium. The price paid by the buyer of an option and received by the writer is called the **option premium**. It is quoted as an amount for each option on a single share of the underlying security. Because the exercise price, the expiry date, and the number of shares are all fixed under a traded options contract, this premium is the only variable factor. The premiums at which the different series of options can be traded will vary widely. As a general rule the later the expiry date and the lower the exercise price of a call option, the higher the premium will be, and vice versa.

Contract. In London the minimum unit of trading is one contract, which represents the option on 1,000 shares of the underlying security, although this figure can vary in particular circumstances if there has been a share capitalization, rights issue, or other factor introduced into the equation since the beginning of the option contract. The buyer of an option contract can trade in any number of contracts, but not in fractions of a contract.

OTHER STOCK BROKER SERVICES. Brokers now offer a much wider range of services than simply advice, dealing, and settlement. Among other services, stock brokers provide the following to their clients.

Management of Clients' Funds. Some brokers operate their own in-house unit trusts to meet the needs of their smaller individual investors. Stock brokers often manage investment funds on behalf of major individual or institutional clients on a discretionary basis. They might also run investment trusts or occupational pension schemes.

Overseas Markets Expertise. Some broking firms now provide research and dealing expertise in overseas markets for institutional and international clients, especially since the ending of exchange control in 1979. Around a dozen brokers have overseas offices and many have correspondents in other centers. These brokers also offer readily available expertise to the overseas investor wishing to invest in the London market, and other markets, as well as to U.K. clients on their overseas investments.

Corporate Finance. Some broking firms run an active corporate finance department, which advises its clients on their financing needs. In this respect, these brokers operate like merchant banks, helping companies to raise the finance they need, whether from investors or from other sources. Many brokers act as a channel of communication between the stock exchange and their listed company clients, making sure that U.K. Stock Exchange requirements are followed and discussing company requirements for new securities issues with the stock exchange authorities. The company's stock broker is the recognized channel when the stock exchange authorities need to communicate with listed companies.

Sterling Broking. Some brokers will compete with other sterling money brokers in the banking world in placing clients' short-term sterling funds with local authorities and banks.

Money Broking. Six stock exchange brokers are recognized as money brokers by the Bank of England. These brokers help to finance the jobbing system by acting as a channel for the lending of stock or money as required. Such a role is needed since the jobber, as a principal bidding for and offering shares, must be prepared to sell shares he or she does not already own and to purchase shares for which a buyer has not yet been found. In order to settle deals the jobber can borrow either money against the securities held, or securities in order to fulfill sold bargains. This facility enables the market to be much more liquid than would otherwise be the case.

Traditional Options. A few members provide facilities for clients or other brokers to take out an option in a particular security for a period of three months ahead. This facility has been offered in the London market for many years, and recently has been supplemented by the establishment of the traded options market, discussed earlier in this section. Traditional options can be taken in a wide range of listed securities, but cannot be traded.

SECTION 6.4

FRANKFURT: EQUITY MARKETS

CONTENTS

SECTION **6.4**

FRANKFURT: EQUITY MARKETS

Rolf E. Breuer

DEVELOPMENT AND SURVEY

HISTORICAL BACKGROUND. In the Federal Republic of Germany the history of the stock exchange, using the term in a somewhat broader sense than usual, goes back to the early Middle Ages. The commercial activities associated with the trade fairs led to the appearance of exchange booths at an early date (e.g., in 1402 in Frankfurt). Up until the early sixteenth century money and capital movements were mainly associated with trade in goods. In the following decades they started to become independent of trade, to develop a role of their own.

At the end of the sixteenth century the Frankfurt Stock Exchange was founded. Whereas initially there was a substantial volume of transactions in bills of exchange, by the end of the eighteenth century trading in bonds and borrowers' notes had become the standard form of business. In Frankfurt they were joined by shares for the first time at the beginning of the nineteenth century.

With the introduction of shares, the way was paved for the Industrial Revolution. By accumulating numerous, even relatively small or medium-sized, sums of capital and documenting them in the form of shares, it was possible to make large investments that the individual private investor could not finance alone. Parallel to this, a large number of new technical inventions was appearing (e.g., in the electrical field, the chemical industry, and mechanical engineering). The large companies set up in the second half of the nineteenth century—Siemens, AEG, BASF, Bayer, Hoechst, Deutsche Bank, to name but a few—owe their existence to the financing power of shares. Those decades have, rightly, come to be known as the *Gründerzeit*, the founding years.

At the same time, the share has made it possible for the person who has provided capital to dispose of holdings via the stock market and to place these funds elsewhere. Capital permanently available to the enterprise on the one hand, and a liquid investment for the investor on the other (thanks to the possibility of selling at any time at the price quoted on the stock exchange), characterize shares as a financing and investment instrument. Only an efficient stock market guarantees that they perform their full function.

TYPICAL FEATURES OF THE VARIOUS TYPES OF SECURITY. As customary elsewhere, fixed-interest securities and a number of other types of paper are also traded on the West German stock exchanges in addition to shares. The following provides a brief introduction.

Ordinary Shares. A good 95% of all West German shares are ordinary shares; they participate in the assets and growth of the AG (*Aktiengesellschaft,* a joint stock corporation) and carry voting rights.

Preference Shares. Preference shares make up the remaining 5% of West German shares. In contrast to other countries, where the rights conferred by preference shares can vary greatly (e.g., possibility of redemption, fixed coupon, right of exchange), under West German law they are all largely similar: the shares participate in the company's assets and earnings, like ordinary shares, but are nonvoting; instead they have a preferential right to dividend (higher and/or guaranteed dividend, generally with an obligation to fully pay any arrears). They are, on the whole, a by-product of the relatively high proportion of industrial share capital held by families and other large shareholders (to retain existing voting majorities where possible).

Trades on the Market for Fixed-Interest Securities

Bonds. Today, bonds are almost entirely public sector issues (government, federal railways, federal post office, Reconstruction Loan Corporation, Equalization of Burdens Fund, etc.). There is a good market, with price supports, for bonds.

Special Types of Public Sector Issues. Special types of public sector issues are usually those of the government: government bonds, federal savings bonds, and financing bonds. Generally, they may only be purchased by residents. Not all are listed on the stock exchange.

Mortgage Bonds. Issued by public or private mortgage banks, mortgage bonds include terms that can be very individually structured. Proceeds are used for housing construction; mortgages on real estate serve as security for the mortgage bonds issued.

Communal Bonds. Communal bonds are technically similar to mortgage bonds. The proceeds from their sale are used to finance communal or public sector projects. Security is provided by the public sector.

Industrial Bonds. Industrial financing has become much less important than it used to be because of its tax aspects and financing costs.

Hybrid Forms (Share and Bond Features)

Convertible Bonds. In addition to regular interest payments, convertible bonds carry the right of conversion into shares of the company concerned. Because of this share link, interest is generally somewhat lower than on straight bonds. To guarantee conversion rights, the issuer creates conditional capital equivalent to the value of the convertible paper. The bearer can wait for a favorable moment to convert the bonds. The advantage for the issuer rests in relatively low interest and capital increase at a conversion price appreciably above par (a high premium).

Bonds with Warrants. Bonds with warrants give the bearer the right—documented separately in the warrants—to purchase shares of the company in question at the option price, fixed in advance. After a certain period the issue is divided into three types of paper: (1) bond cum (a bond with warrant); (2) bond ex (a bond without warrant); and (3) warrant. The warrants are traded separately on the stock market. They offer the holder or buyer the opportunity to purchase shares of the particular company at the fixed option price at any time within a fairly long period, or to take advantage of the rise in the price of the warrant itself. After selling the warrant or exercising the option, the buyer of a bond cum—as opposed to a convertible bond—still retains the bond ex bearing regular interest. Again because of the share link, the interest is generally not quite as high as on straight bonds, so for the issuer there is a cost advantage similar to that provided by convertible bonds.

Special Securities on the West German Stock Market

Genussscheine. Genussscheine (**dividend rights certificates**) are only occasionally available. They allow the owner to participate in certain profits, but without capital participation represented by shares (e.g., the Audi-NSU Genussschein, issued by resolution of the annual general meeting (AGM) on 26 April 1969, grants the right to share in part of the license income from the production of Wankel engines). The Audi-NSU Genussschein is a paper with no par value and no real asset base. It becomes worthless on the expiratory date (31 December 1983).

Partizipationsscheine. In principle, partizipationsscheine (**participation certificates**) are a type of Genussschein. They are more common in Switzerland, and are not represented on the West German stock exchanges at present. They document rights to assets, but not membership rights.

Investment Fund Shares. Shares in securities funds (share funds, bond funds, and mixed funds) are not traded on stock exchanges in the Federal Republic of Germany (open-end funds). Prices are calculated by the companies operating the funds on each stock exchange trading day. But the dispositions of the fund managers, who buy and sell the securities for their funds on the stock exchange, are frequently an important market factor. The shares are sold through the fund companies' custodian and partner banks.

CHARACTERISTICS OF THE WEST GERMAN SHARE MARKET. In West Germany, in contrast to other countries, especially the United States, shares of industrial, banking, and transport companies are bearer shares. Since with this legal construction the person in possession of the share is entitled to the rights it confers, ownership is transferred when the share changes hands. There is no need to amend the share register. Each bearer share has a dividend coupon sheet; each dividend coupon is individually numbered. The dividend is paid to the person who presents the coupon, or is credited to holders who keep their shares in safe custody at a bank. This bearer share tradition (most bonds are also bearer paper) was only interrupted briefly after World War II, at the instigation of the Allies, in favor of registered shares (sometimes without coupon sheets).

But there has always been an exception to the general principle of bearer shares, namely, insurance shares. This is because the capital of insurance companies in West

Germany is often not fully paid, and, depending on the development of business, the companies may ask the holders of partly paid shares to pay more, or the full amount, in accordance with the conditions laid down in the company's articles of association. The shares are in the names of the current owners so that the insurance company knows to whom it can turn for payment. The dividend, however, is paid in the same way as for industrial shares, namely against coupons (dividend coupon sheets).

For stock market trading, and especially the technical side (transfer, delivery, etc.), which is geared entirely to bearer shares, the registered share is not a foreign body, in that it is now general practice to provide such shares with a blank endorsement. If, however, the owner does wish his or her name to be inserted, this can easily be done at the bank. Quite independent of this, the names of the shareholders are entered in the share register of the company.

There is an even more restricted form of share, the *vinkulierte Aktie* (a share with limited transferability). This type of share is found most frequently in insurance companies, but also occasionally in other sectors. It goes a step further than the registered share in that not only must any change of ownership be recorded in the share register, but the transfer is subject to the consent of the company.

THE STOCK EXCHANGE SCENE IN THE FEDERAL REPUBLIC TODAY. At first glance the West German stock exchange system would appear to be quite decentralized, which it is if one considers that the Federal Republic of Germany, as a relatively small country, has seven stock exchanges, with the one in Berlin as the eighth West German bourse. There are historical reasons for this. When, at the end of World War II, Berlin lost its preeminent position as economic, financial—and hence also stock market—center, the greater part of its role passed to Federal Republic territory. But in the course of time, as a result of the way business developed, and especially because of old traditions, new centers emerged. This applied particularly to Frankfurt, today by far the largest West German stock exchange. It is followed by the Rheinisch-Westfälische Börse in Düsseldorf, then Hamburg and Munich.

A further reason for greater concentration in stock market business came with the increased use of electronic data processing. Computerization made it necessary to expand the major centers and to work closely with the smaller exchanges.

The link uniting the eight West German stock exchanges is the Arbeitsgemeinschaft der deutschen Wertpapierbörsen (Association of German Stock Exchanges), which devotes its attention to standardizing stock exchange conditions, for instance, and coordinating questions of settlement and the like. This arrangement ensures that the West German stock exchanges all function in the same manner. The individual centers are thus practically combined, by common principles, into one joint stock market.

THE WEST GERMAN STOCK MARKET

GENERAL CHARACTERISTICS

The Joint Stock Corporation as Financing Instrument and Investment Opportunity. In the Federal Republic the heyday of the Aktiengesellschaft, or AG, as a means of obtaining financing for new companies is over. Today, there is still a large volume of capital increases, which provide new shares, and some smaller companies have been introduced to the stock exchange in recent years. But the most important type of share business now is the trade in shares among shareholders. So, in its present form, the West German share market must be termed a secondary market. Primary market business (i.e., the placing of new shares, mostly from capital increases), is effected between the banks and their customers directly. Subscription rights, however, are traded officially on the stock exchange.

For the investor the West German stock market represents an opportunity to invest in many different sectors and companies. A mix of shares from a wide spread of sources permits risks to be well balanced, even though shares from a number of sectors, those that are only traded on foreign exchanges, such as raw materials shares, gold mine shares, shares of the tobacco industry, are not available on the market in West Germany.

In the Federal Republic of Germany there are somewhat more than 2,000 joint stock corporations with nominal capital of DM92 billion (as of the end of 1980). If unofficial dealing is included shares of about 600 of these companies are traded on the stock exchange. They represent nominal capital of over DM45 billion, and a market value of more than DM150 billion. The difference between the total number of joint stock corporations and the number listed on the stock exchange reflects the relatively high number of family enterprises, of wholly owned subsidiaries, and of West German subsidiaries of foreign groups to be found in the Federal Republic of Germany.

For traditional reasons, too, the proportion of West German share capital in the hands of firms is relatively high. A holding may actually date back to the time the company was founded, if, in addition to a number of outside shareholders, a family happened to be involved in setting up the new company. In other cases majority holdings have resulted from measures to streamline a company, or from mergers. Agreements on cooperation between companies also frequently led to assistance in the form of capital.

Finally, share packages have also arisen through the involvement of banks in cases where corporations required support. But holdings of this kind are not very extensive, and as the study commission on fundamental questions concerning banking (the Gessler Commission) reported in 1979, they do not have any detrimental effect on competition in the sectors concerned. The commission also found no evidence to bear out the criticism that the banks restricted the independence and freedom of action of the companies through their shareholdings.

All in all, it is estimated that almost 66% of the share capital of German joint stock corporations is in the hands of firms.

Main Areas of Business on the West German Stock Market. The West German share market presents a fairly accurate picture of the country's economy. The main emphasis is on shares of manufacturing industries, while—in line with the natural resource situation of the Federal Republic of Germany—shares of raw materials industries, as already mentioned, are hardly represented at all.

According to figures from the federal Statistical Office, the nominal capital listed on the stock exchange is divided among the various sectors as shown in Exhibit 1. The high proportion of chemical shares is a characteristic feature of the West German share market. Chemical shares make up more than 20% of West German listed nominal capital. They are followed by the energy sector, commercial banks, iron and steel, the automotive industry, electricals, and mechanical engineering.

EXHIBIT 1 CAPITAL LISTED ON THE WEST GERMAN STOCK EXCHANGE

Sector	Nominal Capital (in DM millions)	Share (in Percentage)
Large chemicals	6,687	14.3
Other chemicals	3,241	6.9
Chemicals, total	(9,928)	(21.2)
Energy sector	5,862	12.5
Commercial banks	4,835	10.3
Iron and steel	4,429	9.5
Automotive industry	4,343	9.3
Electricals	3,772	8.1
Mechanical engineering	2,472	5.3
Insurance	1,366	2.9
Transport (road, rail, air)	1,217	2.6
Department stores	1,077	2.3
Nonferrous metals	689	1.5
Breweries	651	1.4
Mortgage banks	579	1.2
Fine ceramics, glass	579	1.2
Construction, quarries	575	1.2
Trade (excluding department stores)	473	1.0
Leather, textiles	448	1.0
Paper, printing	304	0.7
Shipping	259	0.6
Food, drink, tobacco	181	0.4
Miscellaneous	2,709	5.8
Total	46,748	100.0

Growing Importance of Foreign Shares. The introduction of foreign stocks has brought a welcome addition to the range of sectors represented by domestic companies on the West German stock market. In practice foreign stocks were introduced with the full liberalization of the West German capital market vis-à-vis other countries in the late 1950s, but they attained their greatest momentum in the 1960s and 1970s. As the following figures show, foreign shares have meanwhile caught up strongly to domestic stocks in importance. In Frankfurt, for example, more than 180 foreign companies are today officially quoted, alongside 225 domestic companies. In addition, shares of numerous foreign issuers are traded in unofficial dealing.

Shares of foreign issuers are most often traded in the form of fiduciary certificates. The original share certificates are held blocked in the respective home countries. In recent years trade in book shares (giro-transferable entries) of the West German *Auslandskassenvereine* (foreign security clearing associations) has become increasingly prevalent. Here again, the original share certificates on which the giro trading is based are generally held blocked in the country of the issuer. Finally, and to a lesser extent, foreign share certificates are also physically deliverable in Germany.

Size of the West German Share Market. Although the West German share market offers a wide variety of investment opportunities, for the foreign investor especially, its size and special features should not be overlooked. In terms of turnover in 1980 the West German share market ranked fifth among the world's markets: after New York, Tokyo, London, Canada and West Germany.

According to the statistics of Deutsche Bundesbank, shares with a market value of DM33 billion changed hands on the West German stock exchanges (excluding Berlin) in 1980; shares of foreign issuers accounted for a good DM5 billion of this amount. In the first half of 1981 share turnover totalled almost DM17 billion, with DM2.5 billion in foreign shares. For the sake of comparison, turnover in bonds on West German stock exchanges is larger in size than shares. Total turnover in 1980 came to DM50.3 billion, of which almost DM10 billion was in foreign bonds.

Another difference between the share market and the bond market is that, according to the business conditions of the banks, investors' orders to buy and sell shares are passed to the stock exchange dealer unless otherwise indicated in the order, so that practically all customer orders relating to shares are transacted on the stock exchange. Taking the total volume of turnover, the situation is different. The banks' direct dealings (with institutional investors, both domestic and, above all, foreign) then play a much greater part. It is estimated that at least half, and probably even more, of total share turnover stems from direct transactions between the banks and large-scale investors.

Because of the structure of the bond market, the corresponding figures there differ somewhat. With bonds the proportion of issuing business, and hence of direct business, is many times higher than with shares. This is particularly true of business in mortgage bonds, communal bonds, and other debt instruments, whereas in the case of public sector issues (apart from the initial placement) a greater proportion of business is handled by the dealers in the secondary market. Issuing business, however, is generally conducted by the banks with large-scale investors directly with insurance companies, large concerns, pension funds, investment funds, and other institutional investors making up the largest contingent. It is estimated that, depending on the type of security, about 80% to 90% of bond turnover is handled directly by the banks.

Since the turnover figures mentioned earlier only refer to shares and bonds traded on the stock exchange, the total volume of turnover in securities in West Germany must be put considerably higher.

Average Dividend, Average Yield. In summer 1981 the average dividend rate at West German companies whose shares are officially listed on the stock exchange was 12.83%. The dividend yield on these shares at that time was 3.41%. For domestic holders of West German shares the rates are improved substantially by certain tax arrangements. Following the amendment of the Corporation Tax Act, which has been in force since 1977, domestic taxpayers also receive a tax credit in proportion to the profit distributed, which is included in the shareholder's tax return. When this tax benefit is included the corresponding rates are as follows:

Average dividend	20.04%
Average yield	5.33% (including tax credit)

There are plans to give foreign investors some tax relief via double-taxation conventions (for details see "Taxation of Capital Gains and/or Losses," this section).

Who Holds West German Shares? The national financing accounts of Deutsche Bundesbank provide very interesting information as to which categories of investors hold West German shares. They cover the shares of all companies whether listed on the stock exchange or not, but the proportions can also give useful indications as to stock exchange business.

According to these statistics the largest portion of West German shares (almost 40%) is held by nonfinancial companies (i.e., the corporate sector, excluding banks). Their share has risen markedly since 1970 (to over 33%). In second place come foreign investors, who account altogether for a good 20% of the shares, after 16.5% 10 years ago. Households in West Germany own about 18%; their holdings have shrunk over the past years (28% in 1970), probably mainly as a result of the increasing popularity of saving through investment funds. The latter attract a large proportion of private demand for shares, especially among small investors, and then appear on the market as buyers. By contrast—for the sake of comparison—the share of households in the bond market rose substantially (recently under the influence of the high interest rate level). The statistics give the proportion of total share volume held by the public sector as 8% (10% in 1970), banks, 10% (8% in 1970), and insurance companies, 5% (4% in 1970).

FUNCTIONAL ASPECTS OF THE WEST GERMAN SHARE MARKET

Basic Setup

Products Traded. Official dealing forms the basis of trading on the West German stock exchanges. Only securities that have been officially introduced after a special investigation procedure may be traded in official dealing.

There is also unofficial dealing and dealing by telephone. Stocks of smaller companies, companies with only regional significance, or companies whose management does not consider official listing important are traded in both these ways. (For further information about the three methods of trading see "Forms of Trading," this section.)

Which shares are traded most on the stock exchange? On the Frankfurt Stock Exchange, whose turnover has excellent public coverage and which is probably typical of all the West German exchanges, Siemens, Deutsche Bank, and BASF were the favorites in terms of turnover in the first half of 1981, as Exhibit 2 shows.

Market Participants. Who is allowed to deal on the West German stock exchanges? There are two large groups of market participants: (1) the banks as stock exchange dealers, and (2) the brokers, who operate independently, balancing supply and demand.

Banks and other persons admitted to the stock exchange. Altogether there are more than 1,500 persons admitted to the Frankfurt Stock Exchange (banks and their dealers, brokers, backroom staff, and the press).

Private individuals are not permitted to deal on the stock exchange in West Germany. This stipulation also protects the private investor. He or she is advised by the banks and they execute the investor's orders on the exchange.

The banks are admitted to the stock exchange and are represented by members of staff who conduct business on their behalf. In addition to the banks, some West German investment funds are admitted to the stock exchange, but they do not act as dealers.

There are detailed admission regulations. Certain persons, specified in the Stock

EXHIBIT 2 HIGHEST TURNOVERS, FRANKFURT STOCK EXCHANGE (in millions of deutsche marks)

Favorites	Turnover First Half, 1981
Siemens	582.8
Deutsche Bank	414.9
BASF	308.3
Hoechst	299.1
Bayer	282.3
Daimler Benz	270.9
Volkswagenwerk	245.8
Dresdner Bank	245.6
RWE, ordinary and preferred	235.6
Preussag	146.8
Kali und Salz	144.8
Veba	131.3

Exchange Act, are excluded (this is to prevent dubious elements from gaining access to stock exchange operations). The details are laid down in the rules of the eight West German stock exchanges. Banks wishing to be admitted to the exchange must, when applying, name three sponsors, who themselves are already members. The sponsors must give the Stock Exchange Board their opinion on the personal, professional, and financial qualifications of the applicant. Admission is granted by the Stock Exchange Board.

Position and duties of the Makler. The *Makler* is a West German creation and there is no one in other countries to whom this individual can really be likened. These "brokers" mediate between the buyers and sellers of securities (i.e., the banks and bank representatives admitted to the stock exchange). The Makler collates orders (i.e., oversees supply and demand), and from the limits indicated by the buyers and sellers works out the price at which the greatest volume of turnover can be achieved. Thus the price calculated is economically fair and is binding for the maximum quantity of shares.

Basically, the stipulations for admission to the stock exchange as Makler are the same as for the other market participants. The person must supply the appropriate stock exchange authorities with proof of professional qualifications. The Makler is appointed by the government of the particular Land (state), which also supervises his or her activities and, if necessary, removes the Makler from office. Qualifying persons have to deposit security on taking up this position.

The *Kursmakler* (official broker) is a commercial broker as defined by the German Commercial Code. The code stipulates the Kursmakler's rights and duties in detail. For instance, a Kursmakler must issue to each of the parties to any transaction that he or she has arranged a contract note, setting out the details of the deal, immediately upon conclusion of the transaction. The Kursmakler has to keep daily account of the deals he or she concludes. In return for services as intermediary the Kursmakler receives a commission or brokerage fee amounting to 1% of the market value of the shares bought and sold (the fee for bonds is 0.75% to 0.075% of the market value, depending on the volume of turnover).

Only the Kursmakler is authorized to establish official quotations in official dealing. Investors who buy shares in official dealing are entitled to have the deals transacted at the official quotation. These prices are published in the stock exchange's official list so that the investor is able to check and raise objections.

The brokers in unofficial dealing, the *Börsenmakler*, can only arrange transactions outside official dealing.

During trading hours the official brokers take their place in a type of ring, the layout of which differs according to the design of the individual exchange. The bank representatives come to them to conduct their business. The official brokers (the Frankfurt Stock Exchange, for example, has 24) each specialize in particular market sectors (chemicals, steels, banks, etc.). There has been a parallel development among the banks' dealers, so the individual types of shares are the responsibility of certain brokers and certain dealers.

Quotation. The banks' stock exchange dealers note down investors' orders in a list, which they bring to the stock exchange session (11:30 A.M. to 1:30 P.M., Monday through Friday), where they contact the appropriate Makler. They pass orders for smaller amounts (amounts of less than 50 shares employ the single quotation market; for details see "Single Quotation, Continuous Quotation," this section) to the Makler for inclusion in price determination, and for recording in the order book. With orders for 50 or more shares—in other words, on amounts for which quotations are determined several times during the session (variable or continuous quotation) the Makler can wait to observe the trend, and if prices are rising, for instance, he or she will hold back a selling order for a time.

The Makler determines the quotation for a particular share on the basis of the buying and selling orders received. He or she is bound here by strict regulations. The Stock Exchange Act (Section 29.3) contains provisions, for example, to ensure that the quotation "corresponds with the true state of business on the stock exchange." Before being admitted to the exchange, Kursmaklers take an oath that they will "faithfully perform their duties" (Stock Exchange Act, Section 30.1). The Kursmaklers are supervised by the Chamber of Brokers, their representative body. In certain cases the Stock Exchange Board is also consulted.

In addition to the number of shares to be bought or sold, the order also contains any special details of how the transaction is to be executed and settled. A purchase order, for example, must indicate whether the shares are to be bought at bottom, or whether a certain maximum price (limit) is not to be exceeded. A selling order stipulates either at-best or a minimum price (limit).

Example of how a single quotation is reached. The Kursmakler begins to establish the quotation for shares being traded in the single quotation market at 12:00 noon. For the purposes of this example the Kursmakler has received the following orders for the shares of one company.

Buy (Number)	Limit Price		Sell (Number)	Limit Price	
25	at bottom	(25)	20	at best	(20)
12	143	(37)	10	140	(30)
13	142	(50)	15	141	(45)
10	141	(60)	10	142	(55)

Buy (Number)	Limit Price		Sell (Number)	Limit Price	
6	140	(66)	7	143	(62)
5	139	(71)	8	144	(70)

The figures in parentheses show the running total of shares to be bought or sold at the respective limits. They are shown to simplify matters. In practice the Kursmakler does not use this aid and limits are often shown to one place after the decimal point (i.e., the spread of limits is narrower, something that has been disregarded in this example).

From the orders noted the Makler finds that supply and demand would be balanced at a price of DM142, if he or she could obtain a purchase order for five shares with a limit of DM142. The Makler informs the market parties accordingly and tries to find the order required. If he or she is successful the quotation can be set at DM142, with turnover of 55 shares. At any other price, the turnover would be markedly lower.

If the Makler does not manage to find a suitable order, as assumed above, he or she can balance the order book personally. The Makler is authorized to do so if it is necessary for execution of the orders issued to him or her (Stock Exchange Act, Section 32.2). As a rule, the Makler reserves the right to name the party to the contract later (the seller's—or buyer's—name to follow). If the Makler does not find a partner the next day, he or she has to perform the contract personally. If a partner is found, but at less favorable conditions, the Makler has to cover the difference. Because of the risk involved, a special permit is required from the Stock Exchange Board to operate as a name-to-follow broker (the broker has to put up security).

To inform the interested public about the circumstances under which a quotation was reached, the official lists display the following symbols beside the price.

b	*bezahlt* (paid; all orders were executed)
bG	*bezahlt Geld* (paid and bid; not all orders were executed, surplus demand)
bB	*bezahlt Brief* (paid and paper; not all orders were executed, surplus supply)
ebG	*etwas bezahlt Geld* (some paid and bid; only a small portion of the orders to buy were executed)
ebB	*etwas bezahlt Brief* (some paid and paper; only a small portion of the orders to sell were executed)
ratG	*rationiert Geld* (scaled down and bid; orders to buy at or above the fixed price and unlimited orders to buy could only be partially executed, by allotment)
ratB	*rationiert Brief* (scaled down and paper; orders to sell at or below the fixed price and unlimited orders to sell could only be partially executed, by allotment)
*	small amounts without turnover

The following symbols indicate whether orders to buy and sell at the fixed price were in fact executed.

G	*Geld* (bid; at this price demand only)
B	*Brief* (paper; at this price supply only)
—	*gestrichen* (cancelled; it was not possible to determine a price)
-G	*gestrichen Geld* (it was not possible to determine a price as demand predominated)
-B	*gestrichen Brief* (it was not possible to determine a price as supply predominated)
-T	*gestrichen Taxe* (it was not possible to fix a quotation; the price was estimated)

To complete the picture, there are some symbols used in special circumstances.

exD	ex dividend
exBr	ex subscription right

The variable quotation is also determined by the Makler in a similar manner. Quotations are fixed a number of times during the day.

If there are significant changes in the price, the Makler has to consult the member of the Stock Exchange Board on duty before determining the quotation. He or she must do so if the price of a share deviates by more than 5% from the previous day's quotation. The board must also be consulted whenever the orders on hand have to be scaled down for execution. Any larger deviations, upward or downward, have also to be indicated on the quotation boards (by a plus or minus sign). If the deviation is expected to be larger than 10%, the quotation is preceded by double plus or double minus signs.

The West German Share Market: Special Features

Forms of Trading. On the West German stock exchanges a distinction is made among three different methods of trading: (1) official dealing; (2) regulated unofficial dealing; and (3) dealing by telephone. All of these are found on both the share and the bond market.

Official dealing. In order to protect the investor by ensuring that all shares traded on the stock exchange are in companies of sound standing and enterprises that can be expected to continue to develop steadily, a special Listing Commission was set up at the end of the nineteenth century. Securities are introduced to the stock exchange after a listing procedure in which the company, or the share, is subjected to careful investigation. Figures from the company's accounts have to be submitted to a special commission, and a number of other requirements (the reporting of turnover, general reputation, etc.), have to be fulfilled (for details see "Introduction of New Shares to Official Trading," this section). The investigation is based on the listing prospectus in which the company has to give the details of its organization and development, and, above all, figures from the balance sheet and profit and loss account. The company also has to report on current business, and the regulations that this information must be up-to-date are strict. The prospectus is declared binding by the commission, which consists of both banks and representatives of local industry.

Under the Stock Exchange Act, the listing prospectus entails special liability. The banks and representatives of the business community involved in compiling the listing prospectus are liable for the accuracy of the information in the prospectus, if they have been, or—through gross negligence—should have been, aware of its incorrectness. The right to claim compensation lapses five years after admission of the securities. This arrangement ensures that only shares of companies that offer the basis required for sound, steady development are admitted to the stock exchange.

The company must also satisfy certain regular reporting requirements (by publishing the annual report, giving notification of important company developments). Many companies publish interim reports regularly. If all the requirements are fulfilled the listing application is approved.

The listing procedure on the bond market is basically the same as that of the shares market. Public sector issues are exempted from presentation of a prospectus. In the case of mortgage banks, the applications for the listing of the individual series of mortgage bonds are approved in a simplified procedure.

All major joint stock corporations with sufficient available share capital consider it important to have their shares officially listed, as official stock market dealing gives their shares a certain stamp of recognition. The fact that their shares become better known also makes it easier for the companies to raise capital by issuing new shares. The benefit to the company's advertising in general from becoming known through stock exchange trading should not be underestimated.

For the investor the advantage of official stock exchange dealing lies in the breadth of the market, which stems from the concentration of a large number of securities orders and therefore guarantees a reasonable price. On top of this, the public is kept informed by the press of the prices published on the stock exchange. Besides being published in the official stock exchange price lists, the quotations, or a selection of them, appear in the business press and in most daily newspapers. Radio and television also report on the stock market. The investor is entitled to have an order executed at the price quoted in official dealing and published in the official price lists.

Regulated unofficial dealing. The volume of regulated unofficial dealing, which could be said to occupy a position midway between official dealing and dealing by telephone, is relatively small, on share and bond market alike. Admission of securities to regulated unofficial dealing is also subject to an investigation, but the regulations are not as strict and detailed as for official dealing. For example, only an exposé about the company has to be submitted; unlike the listing prospectus required for official dealing it is not published. Some shares of regional importance are traded in official dealing on their local stock exchange and in regulated unofficial dealing on others.

In some cases, inclusion in regulated unofficial dealing is used to test public interest in the shares prior to filing an application for official listing.

Unlike official dealing, which is supervised by the Stock Exchange Board and a number of other stock exchange bodies, trading in regulated unofficial dealing is entirely in the hands of the banks and the börsenmaklers (independent brokers). It is governed by a code of practice established by the Standing Commission at the Federal Association of German Banks for matters relating to trade in securities not officially listed. At each stock exchange there is a committee that publishes the prices in regulated unofficial dealing. They appear in a supplement to the official list.

Whereas the quotations published for official dealing give the prices at which business was transacted in the respective shares, the prices for regulated unofficial dealing and dealing by telephone indicate the margin between the lower bid price and the higher asked price. The actual trading price lies somewhere between. It does not always have to be in the middle. In any one type of share there may be several transactions at different prices. In regulated unofficial dealing—unlike official dealing—the investor cannot demand that an order be executed at a certain quoted price.

Dealing by telephone (unregulated unofficial dealing). Dealing by telephone covers various types of business: those trades in securities not officially listed and not included in regulated unofficial dealing, and all the interbank dealing by telephone outside the stock exchange—including, therefore, trade in officially listed paper (the banks' own account dealing, direct trade, business before and after stock exchange hours).

Unregulated unofficial dealing is not tied to stock exchange hours; deals are concluded between banks by telephone or telex. There is no supervision or listing procedure, nor are principals entitled to have orders executed or to demand that any general code of practice be observed. Prices (bid and asked) are published daily for a number of securities traded by telephone, for example, in Frankfurt in the list "Bid and Asked Prices for Securities Not Listed in Frankfurt" (which also appears as a supplement to the official price list), issued by the Association of Frankfurt Securities Dealers.

Trading outside hours. Since there is also demand among domestic and foreign banks, and the independent brokers, for share trading outside regular stock exchange hours, a market has also evolved in West Germany prior to and after the stock exchange session. But this market consists primarily of banks' own-accounts trading; few customer orders are executed.

One of the main reasons for the emergence of this form of trading was the time difference between stock exchange business hours in West Germany and abroad. In addition, professional traders at times deal outside stock exchange hours to even up positions, or to take on new commitments if new developments have become known before the stock exchange reopens. Some of the prices reached in trading outside stock exchange hours are published in the press. They can provide the interested investor with an indication of possible changes in the trend.

Dealing as per issue. Unregulated unofficial dealing (trading by telephone) is particularly important in dealing as per issue, that is, dealing in securities for which deliverable certificates have not yet been issued, such as new shares from a capital increase, or newly floated bonds. The printing of new certificates generally takes some time, and, although demand is already there, the security cannot be included in official dealing until the certificates are available. In recent years, however, there has been a growing tendency to deposit a global certificate for new issues with the respective security clearing associations, as a basis for giro delivery.

Settlement Procedure

Share Deals for Customers

Cash bargain, forward bargain (option trading). Since forward trading was terminated by decree in 1931 during the world economic crisis, all trading on West German stock exchanges has been settled for cash, that is, the securities are delivered on payment. But, for practical reasons, all contracts concluded on West German stock exchanges must be performed on the second trading day after contract day. Option business—introduced on West German stock exchanges in 1970—is an exception. It has certain characteristics in common with the forward bargains of the past, which link it with those traditions, but the settlement procedure is very different.

The essence of option business is that by buying a **call option** the buyer secures the right to purchase a certain number of shares from a counterpart (option seller) within a certain period (two, three, or six months). Or, by buying a **put option,** the investor acquires the right to sell shares to the option seller within the mentioned periods. In both cases a binding price is agreed before the contract is concluded. The option can be exercised at any time during the set period, so the buyer or seller is able to wait for a favorable time for the transaction. (For further details, see "Option Business," this section.)

The role of the contract note. A special relationship based on trust has evolved between the Maklers and bank representatives on the West German stock exchanges. It is essential in view of the speed with which transactions have to be settled and the large quantities often traded. Orders to buy and sell—unless given to the Makler in writing (at the single quotation)—are only issued orally. The deals between bank representatives themselves on the stock exchange are also only concluded orally. To save time, a type of shorthand has been developed. When the Makler calls out the price he or she usually only says the last figure ("Siemens 6 bid" is a purchase order for Siemens at DM226). If the number of shares is not called out, 50 shares will change hands.

The deals concluded orally during stock exchange hours are only confirmed in writing after the session, in the form of a contract note. The contract note, formerly handwritten by the Makler and now issued by computer, is sent to each of the banks that is party to the deal. The contract note is needed for settlement between the banks and between each bank and its customer.

Commission business, own-account business. Under general business conditions a bank executes its customers' orders to buy and sell securities officially listed on the stock exchange as commission agent (in the bank's own name for third-party account) with the right to act as contracting party without the special notification required under the Commercial Code, Section 405. The bank buys or sells for its customer.

In own-account business, on the other hand, the bank concludes deals in its own name and for its own account. Securities not officially listed are traded in this way. Also, deals concluded outside stock exchange hours—on the telephone directly from bank to bank, or from bank to institutional investor—in officially listed paper are own-account transactions. New shares, for instance, are placed in own-account trading.

In commission business, the expenses incurred (brokerage, the bank's commission, and stock exchange turnover tax) are charged separately against the gross. In own-account trading the bank generally settles deals net, that is, the expenses are not shown separately; they are included in the contracting parties' price calculation. Thus own-account business is frequently referred to as net price business.

Single quotation, continuous quotation. As the name suggests, the single quotation, or cash quotation, means that only one quotation was determined for the security in question during stock exchange trading hours. On the West German stock exchanges the term "cash quotation" has also come into general usage for the single quotation.

In order to be taken into account in the determination of the single quotation, orders have to be submitted to the official broker by a certain time—in Frankfurt, by 12:00 noon.

Securities of a certain importance are included in continuous trading on the West German stock exchanges. A special permit is required for inclusion and is normally granted with the general admission to trading. In continuous trading, changes in the tendency during the stock exchange session are taken into account and—depending on the orders to buy and sell—deals may be concluded a number of times during the day. The need to be able to conclude deals at different times is due partly to the contact with other stock exchanges and partly to the reaction of customers. This type of trading frequently follows the announcement of political or economic news that has an influence on the tendency.

Securities that are included in continuous trading are either shown separately in the **Official Price Lists** or are specially marked.

The minimum quantity of shares that may be dealt in continuous trading is 50 or a multiple thereof. There can be any number of deals between the opening price and the closing price.

To enable smaller investors with fewer shares to deal in the large shares admitted to continuous trading, a single quotation—that is, for transactions involving fewer than 50 shares—is also determined for shares in continuous trading. When more than 50 shares are to be bought or sold, a deal is concluded for 50 shares or a multiple thereof, and the remainder is traded at the single quotation.

Transfer of ownership. In the case of the bearer shares customary on West German stock exchanges, ownership is transferred upon surrender of the security (in legal terminology "by agreement and surrender"). To transfer registered shares (e.g., insurance shares) an assignment (endorsement) must be affixed to the share (for details see "Characteristics of the West German Share Market," this section). If the buyer of shares is also a customer for whom the bank holds securities in custody, surrender is effected and ownership transferred by placing the shares acquired in the customer's **jacket deposit.** The bank sends the buyer a list of the shares purchased. The transfer takes place when this list, containing all the necessary details (type of share, nominal amount, serial numbers, and other features), is mailed.

If the shares are delivered for giro-transferable collective custody, co-ownership of the collective holding is transferred by a book transfer of the corresponding amount. The bank informs the purchaser as soon as transfer has been effected. This is generally done by indicating on the settlement note that the securities have been entered "to the credit of giro-transferable collective custody." Registered shares are not eligible for this type of custody.

In the case of registered shares the transfer of title requires the seller's endorsement (assignment) in addition to the above procedure. Similarly, the new buyer must sign his or her name. To simplify trading, registered shares are as a rule provided with a blank endorsement.

The technical handling of stock exchange orders. Settlement of stock exchange orders is today largely handled by electronic data processing. At the larger banks orders from the branch network are channeled directly to a central computer (direct ordering), stored there, edited, and delivered in batches to each dealer, according to his or her market sector. Only the heart of stock exchange business, the determination of the price, is still carried out in traditional form. The remainder of the settlement procedure is performed by electronic data processing.

Once the rate has been established the dealer enters it on a slip containing the other information required, which is then fed back into the computer. From that point on, settlement is automatic; that is, the settlement note for the customer and the instructions for the custody account entries and for disposition over the shares are obtained automatically from the computer system.

Electronic data processing is also involved in drawing up the contract note, in this case at the stock exchanges' central data bank, a legal entity in its own right, in Frankfurt. Furthermore, the data bank records settlement for the banks so that in many cases it also gives the instructions for the book transfers of the securities at the security clearing association (collective security deposit). Besides this, the central data bank uses the information available on turnover and prices to compile comprehensive statistics for the stock exchanges (index, turnover, etc.).

Kassenvereine as a technical component of stock exchange business. In seven of the West German cities where there is a stock exchange the collective security deposit banks (security clearing associations, or *Kassenvereine*) have not only taken over the custody of securities, they also make it possible to simplify the transfer of securities considerably. They are specialized institutes, without which a modern system of handling and settling stock exchange business would be unthinkable.

Whereas securities in jacket deposit are kept separately and are identified on the jacket as the property of the individual depositor, in giro-transferable collective custody the securities of one issuer are kept in custody as one unit at the security clearing association. Here the depositor loses individual ownership of specific numbered certificates, but obtains instead fractional co-ownership of the respective association's total stock of the type of security in question. The advantages of collective deposit are obvious. Portions of the total stock held in co-ownership can be transferred by giro from one owner to another without the actual certificates having to be physically moved. Banks use security checks (special instruction vouchers) to transfer holdings. The collective security deposit banks are members of the Arbeitsgemeinschaft deutscher Kassenvereine (Association of German Kassenvereine), which ensures standardized technical arrangements and a uniform contractual basis.

Buyers of securities must indicate in their purchase order which form of deposit they want. They can choose between jacket deposit (individual deposit of the actual certificates) and giro-transferable collective deposit (share in total stock). As a rule there is no question of the buyer looking after the certificates personally. Not all types of securities traded on the West German stock exchanges are suitable for collective deposit. One notable exception is bonds that are to be redeemed, for example, through drawing by lots.

For the investor, one of the main criteria in deciding between jacket deposit and collective deposit is the question of cost. The cost of collective deposit is half that of jacket deposit (e.g., for private customers on shares with a market value of less than DM200 the jacket deposit is 1.2% annually; collective deposit 0.6%).

The collective security deposit banks are also involved in the financial clearing of stock exchange transactions. The claims and liabilities arising from deals are balanced against each other in a cashless procedure among the firms participating in settlement (balances are calculated daily and settled via the participants' accounts).

In order to be able to have the advantages of dealing without physical certificates in foreign business as well, the West German collective security deposit banks set up the German Foreign Security Clearing Association several years ago. It manages the West German security owner's claims to delivery of foreign securities against the foreign custodians. In addition, it is becoming increasingly involved as trustee when foreign shares are admitted to official trading on the stock exchange; in these cases it issues fiduciary certificates for the securities it holds abroad.

Customer costs of share dealing. The expenses incurred in buying and selling are standard on all West German stock exchanges. For deals concluded in official trading, that is, for which settlement is on a gross basis, three items appear on the customer's settlement note.

Brokerage	For shares 1% of the value of the deal
Banks' commission	For shares 1% of the value of the deal (for customers; between banks the rate is halved)
Stock exchange turnover tax	For domestic private customers 2.5%. If the order is received from a nonresident and from abroad, the rate is halved. Interbank deals are exempt from stock exchange turnover tax.

If the deal is concluded net, the above expenses (with the exception of the stock exchange turnover tax) are incorporated into the price; they are not specified on the settlement note.

Special Forms of Share Business

Arbitrage. In arbitrage, a form of business between banks in different stock exchange centers, advantage is taken of the price differences that can emerge from one exchange to another. Although, with modern communications technology, the price differences in high-turnover paper are as a rule not now as pronounced as formerly, some banks do still engage in arbitrage. However, as a proportion of total stock exchange business it is not very large.

Option business. Option business consists of two parts: (1) purchase of the option; (2) exercise of the option (i.e., purchase or sale of securities). By contrast, in the forward market, which existed until 1930, it was possible to buy or sell securities immediately, with payment or delivery deferred until a later date. Another major difference is that in the old type of forward business the date of performance was fixed (end of month, middle of month), whereas the holder of an option today is able to observe the market for the entire term of the option and to buy or sell the respective securities at the agreed price at a time he or she considers favorable.

On the Frankfurt Stock Exchange the shares of more than 40 West German companies and more than 10 foreign companies are admitted to option trading.

There are call options and put options. The buyer of a call option gains the right to purchase a certain number of shares (50 or a multiple thereof) at the price agreed that day (striking price) at any time he or she chooses within a fixed period. The buyer buys the shares at the agreed price if and when the market rate rises appreciably beyond it. By buying a put option the buyer acquires the right to sell a certain number of shares within a fixed period at the agreed striking price. The buyer exercises the put option when the market price falls.

In both cases the other party to the transaction is the option seller. At the agreed terms, the option seller is willing to await the option buyer's decision, that is, to deliver the shares when called in the case of a call option, and to take up the securities in the case of a put option. For his or her services the option seller receives the option money paid by the buyer. The option seller has to provide certain collateral.

An option may be concluded for a period of two, three, or six months. The option money payable for both call options and put options for these periods is determined daily in regulated unofficial dealing and is published in the supplement to the *Official Price List*. The amount of option money is determined, like any regular stock exchange quotation, by supply and demand and bears a certain relationship to the share price. With some exceptions it is equivalent to between 3% and 10% or more of the share price, depending on the type of share involved and the option period. Generally speaking, the longer the option period, the higher the option money.

Option deals are for the minimum number of shares required for continuous quotation, that is, 50 West German shares, or a multiple thereof. The end of the option period is standardized for technical reasons; it may fall on day 5, 15, or 25 of the respective month. Special allowance is made for mark downs for dividends or subscription rights during the option period.

The purchase, or sale, of options is settled in regulated unofficial dealing (i.e., net). The option is exercised (the securities are bought or sold) in official trading, so settlement is gross, but no brokerage is incurred as the deal is not handled by the Makler.

Large-lot dealing. Large-lot dealing refers to the purchase or sale of a large number of shares, or of a holding. Such dealing is handled by the banks in own-account trading as the volume of shares involved would put too great a strain on stock exchange trading and would push the quotation in either direction. Large-lot dealing—which does not occur frequently—is not stock market business in the true sense, since it is generally not intended as a normal investment, but as the purchase or sale of an industrial holding represented by shares.

The price in large-lot dealing is agreed directly between the trading partners, or the banks involved, and is based, of course, on the stock exchange quotation. Depending on the business situation of the company in question, the buyer may be asked to pay a premium since he or she obtains a large number of shares, which the buyer could otherwise only purchase bit by bit over a long period on the stock exchange. Similarly, a markdown will be expected from a seller of a holding that is less favorably assessed, since the transaction enables the seller to dispose of a holding in one lot without having to make great efforts elsewhere.

Over-the-counter trading. The term "over-the-counter trading" means the purchase or sale of shares or other securities over the banks' counters. Although the proportion of total securities business transacted in this way is not especially large, over-the-counter trading is important for certain purposes. Only actual certificates can be bought or sold. The securities are generally sold by the banks from their own holdings, or bought for them. The securities requested in over-the-counter trading are sometimes obtained by banks on the stock exchange.

The securities are delivered and paid in one operation at the counter. Prices are based on the stock exchange quotations. The investor always pays in cash, for then the investor does not have to give the bank his or her name.

An investor might buy securities over the counter if, for example, he or she does not have an account or custody account with the bank concerned or does not want the transaction booked to an account. Buyers who want to pass securities on as a present also buy them over the counter. Securities bought over the counter are kept in the owner's possession. Besides bonds, shares of investment funds are the type of security most frequently bought in this manner.

Price regulation. Price regulation, an activity of the banks, is not the result of investor initiative; it is banking relations with the issuer, that is, the respective joint stock corporation, that are most important here. The company instructs a bank to observe the movement of its share quotation on the stock exchange and to intervene as buyer, for example, if the quotation threatens to fall markedly or if a slightly upward trend is wanted.

The company will only instruct the bank (generally its house bank) to support the quotation for particular reasons. This might, for example, be the case if the capital is to be increased and the company is interested in starting off with a good share price basis. The share price and a sound price development are important considerations for the shareholder, or new investor, in deciding whether or not to subscribe to the new shares, and thereby help the company obtain the necessary new capital. Similarly, before a company is taken over, it might—with the fixing of the take over price in mind—be interested in achieving a relatively high stock exchange valuation for its shares.

Naturally it is also conceivable—though rare—to have the opposite situation, in which a company is interested in a lower quotation for its shares and the bank puts pressure on the price by selling. The paper would then have to be made available to the bank, or purchased by it beforehand in the market.

Prices can only be regulated for a certain time and in clearly defined ways in line with the stock exchange tendency since, in the longer term, the laws of the market always prevail. The Deutsche Bundesbank engages in large-scale market regulating operations for public sector bond issues. The central bank influences the movement of interest rates by large daily purchases and sales. But its scope, too, is restricted by developments on the market.

Banks' Own-Account Business. Apart from their direct activities with investors in securities the banks also operate extensively for their own accounts on the capital market. The main field is new issue business, that is, the floatation of new securities (from capital increases, bond issues, etc.). (For details see "New Issue Business in Shares," this section.) Trading outside the stock exchange (deals between banks, or between a bank and a large investor, which are not channeled via the broker) also forms part of the banks' own-account business. The areas treated above—arbitrage business, large-lot dealing, over-the-counter business, price regulation—also come under this heading.

The banks' own-account trading is very varied. In all cases, however, the bank takes securities it has purchased into its own holdings, or sells securities out of its own holdings. These transactions may be concluded at the stock exchange session, but the securities usually pass through certain sales channels, partly via syndicates or existing business relationships at home and abroad. These deals are therefore mostly settled net at a fixed price (i.e., the subscription price for new shares), or at a firm price at which trading by telephone takes place.

The reason for banks' own-account trading may lie outside the bank, for example, when it is approached regarding capital increases or new bond issues, or in dispositions decided by the bank's own management. This may be the case, for instance, if a bank buys certain shares for its own account initially in anticipation of a more favorable development. Own-account trading makes up a substantial proportion of the banks' total securities dealings. As mentioned previously, own-account trading makes up about 50% of total trading volume in shares and about 80% to 90% of trading in fixed-interest securities. Naturally certain tax points have to be taken into consideration in own-account trading. Under certain circumstances, for example, the difference between purchase price and selling price plays a role in the calculation of corporation tax.

Protection against Manipulation. In the Federal Republic the banks, stock exchanges, and central associations of trade and industry have agreed on a procedure to prevent misuse of information acquired in stock exchange or banking business (inside information). This is laid out in the Insider Rules and the Rules for Traders and Advisers that came into force early in 1970. Insiders and third parties treated as such—that is, people who have obtained advance information about certain business developments—may not at any time or in any way conclude or cause to be concluded for their own benefit or for the benefit of third parties transactions in insider securities using inside information that they have obtained as a result of their position.

The basic principle of the Rules for Traders and Advisers is that no securities transactions may be concluded for reasons that are not in the customer's interest; in particular, no recommendations may be made for the purpose of reducing or increasing the bank's own holdings, those of its managers or employees engaged in securities trading, or in professional investment counseling, or for the purpose of causing prices to move in a certain direction for the sake of own-account transactions. Furthermore, it is not permissible, on the basis of a customer's instructions to purchase or sell securities, to effect any own-account transactions that would result in price-related disadvantages for that customer. If investment advisers act in breach of the rules, the Association of German Stock Exchanges can cause them to be struck from the list. All employees active in banking or stock exchange business or in the companies concerned have acknowledged these regulations by their signature.

A special Investigation Commission has been appointed to examine such cases involving insiders. If it is found that the insider rules have been infringed the party concerned has to bear the costs of the proceedings and, regardless of further civil-law sanctions, he or she has to pay over to the company the financial gains deriving from these infringements. So far, there have rarely been proceedings under the insider rules. The regulations are generally accepted.

NEW ISSUE BUSINESS IN SHARES

Capital Increase against Contributions in Cash by Shareholders. New issue business in shares forms a large part of the banks' own-account trading. Because of the different structures of the two markets the volume is smaller than that of new fixed-interest securities, but in absolute figures it is still an important business sector. In 1980 new shares placed amounted to DM6.7 billion (market value) as compared with DM137 billion gross, or DM45 billion net, of fixed-interest securities.

Syndicated Business. As a general rule, new shares from capital increases are sold (placed) via a syndicate, that is, a group of banks formed especially for this purpose, which takes up the new shares from the company and arranges the placement. The quota allotted to each of the banks is fixed in advance. There are frequent examples of fixed syndicates with fixed quotas for specific companies. The placing of new shares through the intermediary of a syndicate ensures that they are sold quickly, using all possible sales outlets. Only where a small company wishes to increase its capital is the forming of a syndicate eliminated; in this case the house bank handles the issue. In contrast to the syndication method described herein (third-party issue), mortgage banks act as issuer in the sale of their own paper.

A syndicate is formed on the basis of a special contract (syndicate agreement), which defines the rights and obligations of the individual members and the size of their quotas. Syndicates are in the form of a civil-law association. The syndicate remuneration (as a rule the difference between the price at which the shares were underwritten and the selling price) is distributed among the individual members according to their allotment, the lead manager receiving the largest share.

Syndicates as described above bear the full risk for the placement of the shares. Compared with this form of syndicate, known as an "underwriting syndicate," which is now most common, the *Begebungskonsortium* (issue syndicate) has lost much of its importance. The latter type of consortium only acts as selling agent in return for a fixed fee.

Subscription to New Shares. Syndicates have to take the new securities to be placed from the issuing company (in the case of fixed-interest securities this may be a public authority) and place them with the investing public. Only syndicates can handle such large volumes of securities as frequently occur in new issue business.

Whereas fixed-interest securities may be sold to all interested investors at the time of placement, new shares from capital increases must be offered to all the existing shareholders, as the Joint Stock Corporation Act (Section 182) grants them a preemptive right to the shares. This legal provision aims to prevent the percentage of capital owned by the individual shareholders from being diluted against their will.

Since the company for its part is interested in having, as far as possible, a permanent circle of shareholders, it helps its shareholders subscribe to new shares by fixing an issue price suitably lower than the quotation for the old shares. The syndicate banks act as advisers to ensure that the requirements of the capital market are also taken into consideration. Besides the issue price, which the syndicate has to set, the dividend entitlement of new shares also plays a role at the time of issue. Depending on whether the capital increase takes place at the beginning of the year or more toward the middle, the company will give the new shares entitlement to either the full dividend for the current year or only part of it. As a positive gesture toward its shareholders, the company can, of course, make the new shares entitled to the full dividend for the current year even if the year is already far advanced.

The direct subscription right system is difficult to apply in practice as every shareholder must be approached and it is effective only after shares have been fully taken up. For practical reasons, another way of handling subscription rights has evolved on the West German capital market: they are offered indirectly, which also satisfies fully the criteria established by the Joint Stock Corporation Act. In this case the syndicate takes over the new shares to be placed, with the obligation to offer them to shareholders on the stipulated terms. For this procedure the preemptive subscription right to which each shareholder is entitled by law must be excluded.

The subscription to new shares from a capital increase of a domestic company is regarded as an initial acquisition and is therefore generally exempt from stock exchange turnover tax. This also applies to indirect subscription if the issuing company reserves the right of disposition over unsold shares and has provided the bank syndicate with an assurance that it will exercise this right.

Trading in Subscription Rights. If a joint stock corporation intends to raise its capital to increase its financial flexibility or to consolidate its balance sheet ratios, it requires a resolution of the general meeting. This resolution must be passed with at least a 75% majority of the capital represented at the general meeting.

After resolution and notification of a capital increase the banks then use electronic data processing to send those shareholders of the company in question who have deposited their shares with them for safekeeping a subscription notice containing all the necessary details (e.g., resolution of the general meeting; amount of the capital increase; subscription ratio; issue price; number of new shares that can be subscribed in that particular case; and dividend entitlement of the new shares). The shareholder must inform the bank of a certain deadline whether he or she wishes to exercise subscription rights and, if so, whether in full, in part, or by purchasing additional subscription rights. The customer can also choose not to reply, thus waiving the subscription opportunity.

From the incoming replies, the bank is able to see to what extent the subscription right is being exercised, which shares are unplaced, and how many additional new shares are required. To balance supply and demand among the individual banks, trading in subscription rights takes place on the stock exchange.

The subscription right is traded and quoted as an independent right—mainly in official trading—during almost the whole of the subscription period, with the exception of a few days set aside for the settlement of technicalities (trading as a rule takes place for eight to 10 stock exchange days).

Subscription rights trading ensures that a balance is achieved between the banks where either too many or too few new shares have been ordered. The price of the subscription right is established only once during the stock exchange session. As with other paper, the price is reached according to supply and demand, with the stock exchange assessment being the arithmetical value or above or below it (i.e., the right will be assessed on its conditions, either more or less favorably in accordance with the assessment of the company). The arithmetical value or par value is the theoretical value of the subscription right resulting from the relationship of the price of the old shares to the price of the new shares, taking into account the subscription ratio (number of old shares to the number of new shares) and dividend entitlement (i.e., the different dividend entitlements).

Expressed as a formula, the value of the subscription right can be calculated as follows:

$$p = \frac{(a - d) - e}{q + 1}$$

where

p = par value of the subscription right
a = market price of the old share
d = dividend advantage of the old share
e = issue price of the new share
q = subscription ratio

$$p = \frac{(180 - 9) - 100}{\frac{6}{1}} + 1 = \frac{71}{7} = 10.14$$

The above example is based on the assumption that the market price of the old share is DM180, the issue price of the new share DM100. Since the new shares are only entitled to one fourth of the dividend and the old shares receive a dividend of DM12, the advantage of the old share comes to DM9, which must be subtracted. The subscription ratio is 6:1, that is, for every six old shares, the shareholder may buy one new share.

With the 1977 Reform of the Corporation Tax Act an important amendment with respect to dividend payments came into force for domestic taxpayers. The West German shareholder receives a tax credit, which is offset against income tax liability, for the company corporation tax apportionable to his or her dividend. The tax credit amounts to 56.25% of the dividend distributed. This ruling does not yet apply to nonresident owners of West German shares. There are plans to alleviate the situation by revising double-taxation conventions. (For details see "Nonresidents," this section.)

The arithmetical value of the subscription right can give an indication of what the stock exchange price is more or less likely to be, but one must always remember that extraordinary market conditions cannot be taken into account. Furthermore, the arithmetical value of the subscription right provides information as to whether it is worthwhile for an outside interested party who does not possess any old shares to buy new shares by acquiring subscription rights. This will be the case if the stock exchange quotation is below the arithmetical value.

Discretionary sale of shares. Apart from the above-mentioned subscription right, another method of selling shares on West German stock exxchanges, albeit rare, is discretionary selling. Generally speaking a certain volume of shares of a joint stock corporation not yet listed on the stock exchange is put up for sale. The banks taking over these shares than offer them to their customers. Official admission to the stock exchange usually follows at a later date.

Another form of discretionary selling takes place when banks or syndicates bring certain amounts not placed during capital increases on to the market successively. Some joint stock corporations keep a smallish amount aside for such discretionary selling when raising capital. One underlying consideration here is that through such discretionary selling on the stock exchange, it is possible to achieve a price higher than the issue price.

Authorized capital. Apart from the capital increase resolved ad hoc by the general shareholders' meeting, and usually carried out shortly afterward, West German company law also has the instrument of authorized capital. In this case the board of managing directors is authorized by the general meeting—again with at least a 75% majority of the capital represented at the meeting—to raise capital up to a specific amount within a maximum period of five years. This resolution is precautionary. Within the stipulated period the board of managing directors can put through the capital increase at a time it deems favorable without requiring a further resolution of the general meeting.

When creating authorized capital, the general meeting can also exclude the subscription right, with the result that the board of managing directors is in a position to sell (dispose of) the new shares on the stock exchange at its discretion.

Introduction of New Shares to Official Trading. So as to place shares from a capital increase on an equal footing with old shares, the new ones are also introduced to official trading. The introduction of new shares on the stock exchange is carried out by the syndicate that handled the placement. The syndicate submits an admission application to the Listing Commission of the stock exchange concerned.

New shares can be listed either by inclusion in the price of the old shares (i.e., when a dividend difference no longer exists between the old and the new share), or by quotation separately in official trading until such time as dividend parity is achieved (i.e., both kinds of shares are entitled to dividend from the same point onward). Generally speaking the new shares are listed shortly after the capital increase. But there can be a time lag during which the new shares are traded over the telephone.

The syndicate submitting the listing application for the new shares must provide the Listing Commission with a series of documents. The keystone of the procedure is the listing prospectus. The total nominal amount of the securities to be listed must be at least DM500,000. The securities must be fully paid up, with the exception of registered shares (shares of insurance companies). The securities must be produced according to uniform printing regulations (as security against forgery). Further documents to be submitted include evidence of the legal basis of the issue, a certified excerpt from the *Commercial Register* showing the company's current status, the articles of association, annual reports for the past three years, specimens of the shares, name of the payment, and depositary office at the stock exchange location, and the like.

The listing prospectus must contain, *inter alia,* the following details: development of the company; purpose or business of the enterprise; development of the share capital; composition of the board of managing directors and the supervisory board; provisions in the articles of association concerning voting rights; business year of the company; publication of company announcements; appropriation of profits; last statement of accounts or consolidated statement of accounts, which should not as a rule be more than 13 months old (if the statement is more than nine months old, an up-to-date status report is required); explanatory notes on the most important balance sheet items; description of the company's property and business premises; turnover; and statements on the development of business and prospects. The Listing Commission gives official notification of the submitted application (through publication in newspapers authorized to publish official stock exchange announcements). At the Frankfurt Stock Exchange, the decision of the commission is as a rule given in writing.

The listing application is turned down if essential information required by law is not provided or if there are misgivings for local reasons or important economic doubts. Revocation of the listing is considered particularly in the event of financial deterioration or dissolution of the company as well as in the event of nonfulfillment of obligations assumed in connection with the admission. Revocation of the listing is as a general rule preceded by suspension or cessation of quotation by the stock exchange board.

Capital Increase Out of the Company's Reserves: Scrip Shares. Unlike the regular capital increase, where new capital flows into the joint stock corporation, with the capital increase out of company reserves, portions of published reserves are converted into liable funds (i.e., share capital). This form of capital increase (capital adjustment) was introduced in the Federal Republic of Germany in 1959–60. The main objective at that time was to bring the share capital of companies, very cautiously calculated after the currency reform, into line with the rapid expansion in business volume and to establish a balanced relationship between the latter and reserves without triggering off tax repercussions. Even today this form of capital increase/conversion is still used, though to a lesser extent than the regular form of capital increase. In 1980, the inflow of capital as a result of capital adjustments totalled a nominal DM0.7 billion as opposed to a nominal DM3.7 billion for cash capital increases.

In the event of a capital increase out of company reserves, the bank informs shareholders how many new shares they are entitled to have. When issuing scrip shares, an allocation ratio (e.g., 1:5, or one new share for five old shares) is established just as with regular subscription rights. But for balancing purposes there is only settlement of fractional amounts; that is, with amounts that do not make up a full share, the customer can request that they be rounded up or down to the next full share. However, there is no rights trading and therefore no possibility of acquiring additional shares, as is the case with regular capital increases. The settlement of the fractional amounts is carried out at the day's quotation for the old share.

A further difference between this form and the capital increase against cash contribution is that the new shares from the capital increase out of company reserves are admitted to offical trading by law, without a special listing procedure.

TAXATION

Taxation of Income on Shares. In the Federal Republic, dividends of domestic joint stock corporations are subject to a 25% capital yield tax, which must be deducted on payment of the dividend at source, as withholding tax, by the dividend payer (the joint stock corporation).

Residents. The domestic shareholder liable to income tax or corporation tax on the dividend also has the right to a tax credit of 56.25% of the gross dividend, which corresponds to the corporation tax payable by the joint stock corporation on the dividend amount.

Capital yield tax and tax credit have practically the same effect as advance payments of income or corporation tax. If the shareholder is assessed for income tax, the capital yield tax and the tax credit are imputed against income tax (corporation tax) or reimbursed in the event of overpayment. Thus the amount of tax finally levied on the total earnings deriving from the share (dividend plus tax credit) depends, in the final analysis, on the shareholder's personal income/corporation tax rate.

In the case of nonassessable domestic wage earners, the capital yield tax and the tax credit can, in specific cases, be credited with the dividend.

Nonresidents. Nonresident shareholders are not entitled to imputation or reimbursement of the tax credit, unless their shares are held by a domestic subsidiary. Also excluded from the tax credit are domestic corporations exempt from corporation tax (including exempted banks and pension funds, corporations, associations and trusts serving charitable, benevolent, or religious purposes, non-profit-making housing and settlement companies, trade unions and other professional associations) insofar as they do not conduct business operations, as well as public-law legal persons (in particular the federal government, the Länder, municipalities, churches) insofar as they do not conduct business on a commercial basis.

The nonentitlement of the above-mentioned shareholders reflects the general principle that a tax credit may only be enjoyed if income (e.g., dividends) subject to otherwise imputable corporation tax is included in the assessment basis for domestic tax. The meaning and purpose of the imputation procedure is the avoidance of double taxation of distributed profit through corporation tax levied on the company distributing the dividend and through income tax (or corporation tax) on the shareholder. However, the distributed profit should not be exempted from all taxation. Such an eventuality could arise if the corporation tax on the dividend were imputed to the shareholder, although the shareholder's corresponding income is either not subject to taxation at all or at least is not included in the assessment.

Nonresident shareholders' nonentitlement to imputation has been discussed in detail—also bearing in mind competition and investment policy aspects—by the West German Bundestag and expressly approved in a resolution of 10 June 1976. According to the wording of the resolution, the capital yield tax burden should, however, be examined within its present framework for reasons of competition in view of the fact that the capital yield tax to be retained on dividends paid to nonresident shareholders is extensively governed by **double-taxation conventions (DTCs).** In the course of the renegotiation of DTCs instigated as a result of this resolution and in some cases already concluded, there are indications that there will be a general reduction of capital yield tax also for intercompany reduced-tax dividends to 15%, the rate already generally valid for small holdings (the current DTC rate is still 25% in most cases).

Irrespective of these DTC reductions in the rate of taxation, West German capital yield tax on dividend payments is always withheld at a rate of 25% and only any excess amount withheld is refunded on submission of a special refund application.

The final rates of capital yield tax payable as a rule as of October 1981 by nonresident small shareholders under the various DTCs are listed in Exhibit 3.

An exception to the general principle that shareholders with no entitlement to imputation have no right to the tax credit is the so-called corporation tax increment. A corporation tax increment arises when a company pays a dividend using profit portions originating from abroad, which have remained exempt from domestic taxation or are taxed at less than 36% as well as in cases where the dividend payment contains profit portions originating from reserves created prior to 1 January 1977 (when amendments were made to the West German corporation tax system). The corporation tax increment is refunded to shareholders by the federal tax office on special application; the capital yield tax payable on the amount refunded is deducted at the source, where applicable, taking into account any capital yield tax reductions under DTCs.

EXHIBIT 3 CAPITAL YIELD TAX PAYABLE

Shareholder's Country of Residence	Of the 25% Capital Yield Tax Withheld on Dividends	
	Percentage Refunded on Application	Percentage Finally Retained in the Federal Republic
Argentina	10	15
Australia	10	15
Austria	—	25
Belgium	10	15
Brazil	10	15
Canada	—	25
Cyprus	10	15
Denmark	10	15
Egypt	10	15
Finland	—	25
France	10	15
Great Britain	10	15
Greece	—	25
Hungary	10	15
Iceland	10	15
India	—	25
Indonesia	10	15
Iran	5	20
Ireland	10	15
Israel	—	25
Italy	—	25
Jamaica	10	15
Japan	10	15
Kenya	10	15
Korea (South)	10	15
Liberia	10	15
Luxembourg	10	15
Malaysia	10	15
Malta	10	15
Mauritius	10	15
Morocco	10	15
New Zealand	10	15
The Netherlands	10	15
Norway	10	15
Pakistan	—	25
Poland	10	15
Romania	10	15
Singapore	10	15
South Africa	10	15
Spain	10	15
Sri Lanka (Ceylon)	—	25
Sweden	10	15
Switzerland	10	15
Thailand	5	20
Trinidad and Tobago	5	20
Tunisia	10	15
United States	10	15
Zambia	10	15

Taxation of Subscription Rights. The right of subscription to new shares does not represent a profit distribution on the part of the company nor does the sale of the subscription right as part of private property as a rule result in taxable earnings. The subscription right, allocated on the basis of the original right, is split from the old share; it is to be regarded as a part of real assets given concrete and independent form by the resolution to increase capital. After the split, the shareholder's interest is no longer represented by one share only, but by an old share and a subscription right. The granting of a right of subscription to new shares does not therefore increase wealth; it is merely a rearrangement of existing wealth with no effect on taxation.

If a domestic corporation grants its shareholders bonus shares, these are in principle taxable for the shareholders. An exception does, however, exist in some cases where the company increases its nominal capital by converting reserves into share capital (capital adjustment). The acquisition by the shareholder of the new shares (scrip shares) originating from this conversion is exempt from income and corporation tax. Bonus shares issued by nonresident limited companies and comparable with West German scrip shares may be acquired tax-free.

If scrip shares are acquired by a company, the purchase price of the old share and the scrip shares deriving from it is considered to be the purchase price of the old share apportioned between the old share and the scrip shares in the ratio of the nominal amounts.

Taxation of Capital Gains and/or Losses. As opposed to the tax legislation in numerous foreign countries, West German tax legislation does not have a special speculation or capital gains tax. Insofar as capital gains are liable to income tax at all as speculative profits, they form part of general income and are likewise subject to income tax. Together with the taxation of profits deriving from the sale of shares from a substantial holding (a direct or indirect holding of more than 25%), the taxation of speculative profits represents the exception to the general principle that in the sphere of private property—as opposed to company assets—capital gains are not liable to tax.

For residents, profits from the sale of privately owned shares are liable to tax as profits from speculative transactions, if the period between purchase and sale does not exceed six months or the sale of the shares ensues prior to their acquisition (so-called short selling). Profits remain exempt from tax if the total profit made from speculative transactions is less than DM1,000 in any one calendar year. Losses deriving from speculative transactions can only be offset against tax up to the amount of the speculative profits made in the same calendar year.

Private persons residing abroad are not subject to tax in the Federal Republic on speculative profits from the sale of shares. However, private persons residing abroad are subject to tax in the Federal Republic on profits or losses deriving from the sale of shares from a substantial holding if the sale concerns shares in a limited company domiciled in the Federal Republic.

A tax liability on capital gains also exists for profits deriving from the whole or partial sale of privately owned shares in limited companies (e.g., joint stock corporations) in the case of substantial holdings. Under certain conditions a tax-free allowance can be deducted from the capital gain. The remaining capital gain is then, on application, taxed as extraordinary earnings at a lower rate of tax equivalent to half the average rate of income tax. Capital losses on a substantial holding can, in principle, be offset against other income.

THE SIGNIFICANCE AND FUTURE PROSPECTS OF THE WEST GERMAN SHARE MARKET

The share is not only very important for joint stock corporations as a means of acquiring capital but is also of great significance to investors for wealth formation. By investing even modest amounts, the owner of shares can purchase a stake in an industrial company, a bank, or an insurance company and participate in the company's growth and earnings. Thus the share offers a welcome alternative to investment in fixed-interest securities, which, apart from the interest payment, only offer the right to repayment of the face value, thus remaining a cash claim.

For this this reason the purchase of shares has been promoted by various bodies. Complementing the work of the competent sections of the Federal Ministry for Economic Affairs, the Working Group for the Promotion of the Share, a joint venture among banks in the Federal Republic, attracts investors by drawing attention to the significance of the share as a capital investment and for wealth formation through publications, lectures, and other informative material.

Similar considerations also prompted the denationalization of various large companies at the beginning of the 1960s. In 1959, 1961, and 1965, for example, the state instigated the transfer of Preussag, Volkswagenwerk, and Veba from public sector to private ownership and the shares were broadly dispersed. Numerous joint stock corporations have in the meantime issued staff shares to enhance the financial situation of their staff and also, in a certain sense, to create a bond with the company. Generally speaking, too, the share has gained considerable importance as an element of wealth formation. It is, to touch on a social component, also suited for the creation of co-ownership.

Even though the shares issued in this form are mostly blocked for a certain period, a central institution for the exchange of paper, the stock exchange, is still needed. Looking at the West German stock market, it can be said that it performs its tasks well and in an orderly manner. The stock exchange establishes a link between industry and banks. Issuers welcome it as an aid to the acquisition of capital; investors esteem it as an aid to wealth formation.

The publicity work carried out by the stock exchange is considerable. Every day, visitors from home and abroad can observe stock exchange activities from special visitors' galleries. Last year the Frankfurt Stock Exchange welcomed 43,000 guests.

The popularity of the share was substantially enhanced by the conversion of its nominal value from DM100 to DM50 at the beginning of the 1960s and thus the introduction of trading at this small denomination. Thus the share has become more accessible: it can also be bought by the smaller investor. The conversion to a quotation at a nominal DM50 was a substantial step toward stimulating share business.

Nevertheless, certain qualifying remarks are necessary. Unlike foreign exchanges, the West German stock exchanges are not issuing markets. The West German capital market needs new blood. The first steps have already been taken to introduce new capital. In the last few years the shares of several small- and medium-sized companies have been admitted to official trading. There is a whole row of further potential candidates. But the path is a long one and requires perseverance.

SECTION **6.5**

PARIS: EQUITY MARKETS

CONTENTS

SECTION 6.5

PARIS: EQUITY MARKETS

Bertrand Jacquillat

Although the French equity market is the largest in continental Europe, it is much smaller than its counterparts in London, Tokyo, or New York in regard to its size and the volume of trading. Total market capitalization of French stocks in French francs (FrF) is FrF 260 billion and about 1,200 companies are traded on all the French exchanges, with 285 of these being foreign. Each security can be quoted on only one of the seven French stock exchanges but Paris stands by far as the largest since it represents over 98% of market capitalization and transactions. As a result, French securities traded on a national or international scale are quoted in Paris together with all foreign securities; securities issued by regional companies are traded on the appropriate regional exchange.

The French securities markets are organized on one fundamental principle: an exclusive monopoly granted by law to the *agents de change* (brokerage firms) for the trading of stocks. This monopoly covers officially listed as well as unlisted securities. The latter are traded on the *marché hors-cote* (over-the-counter market), while the former are traded on either the *marché à terme* (forward market) or the *marché au comptant* (spot market).

The equity markets of the world are categorized into three kinds of organization: the private type of organization that is characteristic of the U.K. and U.S. markets, the banking type of organization in which the market is very much controlled by the banking system—a representative of which could be the West German market—and the state-controlled markets, to which belong the Latin stock markets. The French equity market belongs clearly to this last category.

As they have such close links with French private savings, the securities markets are closely watched by the authorities, and the stock exchanges are under the supervision of the Secretary of the Treasury. The Commission des Opérations de Bourse (COB) (whose chairman and members are appointed by the government for four years) also acts in a supervisory capacity. Set up in 1967, the COB has a purpose and objectives similar to the U.S. Securities and Exchange Commission (SEC).

INSTITUTIONAL FRAMEWORK

SUPERVISING BODIES. The French securities markets are located in seven cities: Paris, Lille, Nancy, Lyon, Marseille, Bordeaux, and Nantes. However, the Paris Stock Exchange is by far the largest since it represents over 98% of total market

EXHIBIT 1 TRANSACTION VOLUMES ON THE 1980 FRENCH EQUITY MARKET (billion francs)

	Paris Market			Regional Markets			Total
	Official Market	Over-the-Counter Market	Total	Official Market	Over-the-Counter Market	Total	Paris and Regional Markets
Forward market	35.4	—	35.4	0.2	—	0.2	35.6
Spot market	22.1	1.8	23.9	0.5	0.3	0.8	24.7
Total	57.5	1.8	59.3	0.7	0.3	1.0	60.3
French listings	43.5	1.3	44.8	0.7	0.3	1.0	45.8
Franc zone listings	0.7	—	0.7	—	—	—	0.7
Foreign listings	13.3	0.5	13.8	—	—	—	13.8
Total	57.5	1.8	59.3	0.7	0.3	1.0	60.3

Source. Compagnie des Agents de Change, *L'Annee Boursiere*, 1980.

capitalization and transactions in both stocks and bonds. Exhibit 1 indicates the preeminence of the Paris Stock Exchange.

Role of the Public Authorities. The primary responsibilities of the COB are the following: (1) to make sure that listed companies disclose all legally required information in due time; (2) to prevent corporate insiders from using confidential information for their own purposes; and (3) to register any complaints from shareholders and process them.

The COB can suggest modifications to the rules governing stock exchange organization and procedures. It also decides on the admission of securities to the official list on the advice of the Chambre Syndicale.

THE INTERMEDIARIES

Agents de Change. The *agents de change* are *officiers ministériels* (sworn officials) and are appointed by the Secretary of the Treasury after passing professional examinations and being admitted by all the agents de change in general assembly. Their number is around 80; whether they are limited partnerships or corporations, their firms remain strictly private. They are regrouped within 60 brokerage firms. The main function of the agents de change is collecting all buying and selling orders, either from their own clients or from the banks and institutions. They then bring the orders into the floor to be traded between the different brokerage firms acting on behalf of the buyers and sellers.

Although the agents de change may not act as market makers as do jobbers (in the United Kingdom) or specialists (in the United States), they are now allowed to make deals directly with large institutional clients, provided they obey the following specific rules.

1. They may make such deals outside the official trading hours.
2. Such deals must be carried out on the basis of the latest price quoted on the market minus (or plus) a commission if the agents de change are buying (or selling).

3. The agents de change must resell any securities they have bought or buy any they have sold on the market as soon as possible. Since brokerage firms are not allowed to own securities, they cannot carry inventories of shares for too long a period of time.

The objective of such rules is to preserve the unity of the market.

The agents de change can also advise their clients or manage portfolios for them; they ensure the safekeeping of securities, dividend collection, and so forth. Also, the agents de change are pledged unconditionally to complete a transaction even if their clients default; they are all jointly responsible for completion. Their collective liability is guaranteed by a fund that is the property of the agents de change.

Chambre Syndicale des Agents de Change. All the agents de change must belong to the Compagnie des Agents de Change (CAC, National Brokers' Association). This association, although a private entity, provides a service that is officially recognized. Consequently, the association rules (Règlement Général de la Compagnie des Agents de Change) that govern the seven exchanges are legally endorsed by the Secretary of the Treasury. The French equity market is state controlled, although it also has a corporative ingredient.

The Chambre Syndicale des Agents de Change is the executive body of the Compagnie des Agents de Change and is elected annually by the members. It is made up of a chairman, called "Syndic," and seven governors. The main duties of the Chambre Syndicale are (1) to make all the necessary decisions required to ensure the smooth running of the market; (2) to enforce the regulations that govern the activities of members; (3) to grant arbitrage when necessary among its members; and (4) to manage the guarantee fund.

An administrative staff of about 500, headed by the general secretary, assists the Chambre Syndicale in carrying out its duties, which include examining all the documents that must be filed by a company when applying for listing; publishing the daily official list of share prices; and supplying information about the market with the help of a large computer center.

Banks. It has been estimated that over 80% of all orders are transmitted via banks. The banks play an important role as intermediaries between clients and brokers in France since they have an especially dense network of branches with the large French commercial banks throughout the national territory. Their role is, however, confined to that of intermediaries transmitting orders from clients to brokers as agents of their clients. In addition, the banks provide the usual services connected with investment—advising clients, holding securities, managing portfolios and mutuals funds (the SICAV, Sociētē d'Investissement ā Capital Variable).

TYPES OF MARKETS. The Paris Stock Exchange is open from Monday through Friday, from 11:30 A.M. to 12:30 P.M. for dealings in most public bonds and private debentures, and from 12:30 P.M. to 2:30 P.M. for dealings in shares, convertible bonds traded on the official market, and all the securities traded on the over-the-counter market.

Foreign securities that are traded on the forward market from 12:30 to 2:30 P.M. are quoted again during a later session that coincides with the first hour of trading on the New York Stock Exchange.

Official Market. The official market is itself divided into two main markets: (1) the marché au comptant, the spot market, and (2) the marché à terme, the forward market.

All officially listed securities are negotiable on the spot market, where they can be bought and sold in any quantity (odd lots) for immediate payment and delivery.

In addition, 250 or so of the most active French and foreign securities are also negotiable on the forward market. On this market, bargains are firm in price and quantity on the day they are negotiated but payment and delivery only take place on the next settlement day (i.e., seven working days before the end of the month in which the transaction is made). On the forward market, securities can only be traded in round lots of 10, 25, 50, or 100 shares. The appropriate lot for each security is decided by the Chambre Syndicale by reference to its price.

When making commitments on the forward market, clients must provide a cover (margin), which is a percentage of the amount of their position. These percentage margins are indicated in Exhibit 2 and may change from time to time.

Exhibit 3 gives a detailed breakdown of the number of both French and foreign companies traded on the spot and forward Paris and regional markets.

The Marché des Reports. On the French **forward market,** all transactions must be settled by both buyers and sellers on the next settlement day, as indicated in Exhibit 4. However, they can carry over their positions to the following settlement day on the *marché des reports* (contango market). This market operates once a month on the day of the settlement and allows buyers (bulls) to sell their share at a fixed price and to buy them back again at the same price on the settlement day of the following month. Sellers (bears) buy their shares and resell them on the settlement day of the following month.

As the buying position usually exceeds the selling position, the market fixes a backwardation rate to be paid by the bears.

Over-the-Counter Market. Unlisted securities are traded on the *marché hors-cote* (over-the-counter market) under the supervision and control of the Compagnie des Agents de Change on behalf of clients, as is done on the official market. Securities traded on this over-the-counter market are divided into two sections:

1. The special section (*Compartiment Spécial*) comprises companies that have committed themselves to disclose all the information normally required from companies listed on the official market and to apply for the listing of their shares within three years at the latest.

EXHIBIT 2 PERCENTAGE MARGIN REQUIREMENT FOR FORWARD MARKET TRANSACTIONS

Type of Assets for Cover	Percentage of Margin Required
Cash or Treasury bonds	20
French fixed-yield securities	25
Gold	25
Other securities	40

EXHIBIT 3 NUMBER OF COMPANIES TRADED ON THE FRENCH EQUITY MARKETS

Listings	Forward and Spot Markets	Spot Market Exclusively	Total Listings	Total Markets
Paris	238	737		975
French	178	500	678	
Zone franc	—	14	14	
Foreign	60	223	283	
Regional markets	1	235		236
French	1	230	231	
Zone franc	—	5	5	
Total			1,211	

Source. Compagnie des Agents de Change, *L'Annee Boursiere,* 1980.

2. The ordinary section covers all other securities. Transactions are carried out for cash and the agents de change are only responsible for the prices quoted and their publication, not for the validity of the securities traded.

Options Market. Most of the securities traded on the forward market can also be traded on the options market (*marchés conditionnels*). On the marchés conditionnels, two types of financial assets are traded, the primes and the options. The principal differences between primes and options are the following:

1. Option trades operate in both directions, buying (call) and selling (put). Primes involve only the buying side (like a call).
2. Primes and options are of the European type. However, options have nine possible expiration dates and the person who acquires the option may exercise it at any one of the nine expiration dates. Primes have three monthly expiration dates and the buyer of the prime can only exercise it at one of the three monthly expiration dates.
3. In the case of options, the seller acquires the premium, whatever the outcome, at the settlement day (see Exhibit 4) that follows the contract. In the case of primes, the seller receives the premium of the contract only if the deal is not exercised by the buyer, at the terminal period of the contract.

EXHIBIT 4 SETTLEMENT SCHEDULE

Declaration Day	First Day	Second Day	Third Day	Fourth Day and Fifth Day	Sixth Day	Seventh Day
Buyers of prime and options dealings make their decision	Settlement day	Contango day (first day of the new account)	Sellers deliver registered certificates	Clearing between brokerage firms	Sellers deliver bearer certificates	Last trading day of the month: payment

The options market, created in 1964 after the former over-the-counter (OTC) options market in the United States, has not developed as much as its founders had hoped. In practice, the options are very unevenly divided among the nine monthly expiration dates. The longer ones are far more used than the first three. For the first three expiration dates, clients prefer the more traditional primes. Call options are a lot more numerous than put options.

Premiums for put options are markedly lower than those for call options, because they are less popular, thus giving interesting arbitrage opportunities. However, because of the absence of a secondary market, the scope of the marchés conditionnels is very limited; it represented only FrF3.5 billion (about US$750 million) in 1980. As a consequence, the arbitrage opportunities one can see on paper might not necessarily be possible to pursue.

OWNERSHIP STRUCTURE. French institutional and individual investors as well as foreign residents are active on the Paris Bourse (stock exchange).

Institutional Ownership. Institutional ownership represents 45% of the ownership structure. It is usually divided into two areas: the institutional investor per se on the one hand, and the banks and corporations on the other.

Institutional investors include insurance companies, pension funds, the Caisse des Dépôts et Consignations, which manages all the deposits of the savings and loans, and mutual funds: the SICAV and the newly created Fonds Communs de Placement (FCP). As indicated in Exhibit 5, the ownership share of institutional investors in France is low compared with that of other countries (60% in the United Kingdom and 35% in the United States and Japan). This phenomenon has at least three causes: life insurance is less developed in France than in the other major countries; the retirement system in France is not based on capitalization but repartition of the contributions of the employers and the employees; and mutual fund management is relatively new.

Banks and industrial corporations own close to 30% of French listed stocks but represent only 10% of volume.

Foreign investors own 15% of French listed companies. This plus the fact that

EXHIBIT 5 OWNERSHIP STRUCTURE OF FRENCH EQUITIES (in percentages)

Institutions	%
Institutional investors	
Insurance companies	10
Pension funds	2
Caisse des dépôts	3
SICAV and FCP	3
Total	18
Banks and industrial corporations	28
Total	46
Individual Investors	39
Foreign Investors	15
Total	100

Source. La Bourse—Pourquoi? Comment? Qui? Compagnie des Agents de Change, 1979.

over 30 French companies are also listed on foreign stock markets and over 230 foreign companies are listed on the French exchange illustrate its international dimension.

Individual Investors. Close to 4 million French individual investors own 40% of French equity either directly (1.5 million) or through shares in an investment club (45,000), a SICAV (1.5 million), or a Fonds Communs de Placement (2.5 million).

THE PRIMARY SECURITIES MARKET

This section investigates the way securities, both French and foreign, get traded on the equity market and the means by which companies pursue secondary offerings in France.

LISTING REQUIREMENTS AND PROCEDURES ON THE NEW ISSUES MARKET. As has been indicated, shares can be traded either on the official market or the OTC market.

The Official Market

Listing Requirements. The French procedure for companies to go public on the official market is the auction procedure. The French new issue auction procedure is a modification of a competitive auction; it represents one of the major existing alternatives to the underwriting-distribution system used in the U.S. capital market.

Security auctions may be organized by bidding and pricing rules in two forms: price discrimination and the classic competitive auction. The French auction pricing procedure for unseasoned equity issues is a modified competitive auction, similar in some respects to the offer for sale by tender used infrequently for new issues in the United Kingdom.

The French new issue auction represents a modification of the classic competitive auction. One of the Paris banks acts as an adviser and consultant to the issuing company in preparing an application to the COB and to the CAC two to six months prior to the offering.

Before going public on the official market, companies must file an application to the CAC and the COB, which must approve all new listings. The only explicit requirements set up by the CAC for listing on the official exchange are that the company has paid a cash dividend in each of the three years prior to the listing, has a minimum of 300,000 shares outstanding for application on the Paris Bourse, and 80,000 on a regional exchange, with a total par value of US$5 million or more, and that the company's original stockholders agree to sell at least 25% of existing shares to the investing public.

The applicant company must send to the authorities (CAC and COB) a letter requesting admission of its securities to quotation, with a preliminary prospectus (*note d'information*) that must address the following topics: information on the issue (amount of shares, issue price, etc.); general information on the company (name of company, nationality, brief outline of the company's objects, company's financial year); information on the capital, the directors, management, and organization; auditor's report on the activity of the company; description on its subsidiaries and financial interests; earnings and financial situation over the last five years.

Notice of the intended issue must be inserted in the *Bulletin des Annonces Légales Obligatoires*. The preliminary prospectus drawn up by the company is eventually given a visa number by the COB, if approved by it and the CAC, and is distributed to the investing public by brokerage firms, banks, and other financial institutions. Finally a notice is published by the CAC itemizing the terms and conditions of the issue.

Auction Procedure. Several weeks before the offering, the minimum price (*prix d'offre*) acceptable to the company is announced. The issue is not underwritten, as the stockholders of the company bear the price risk as well as the very small risk that the issue cannot be sold at the minimum price. The minimum price and auction date are then published by the CAC in financial newspapers. The day before the auction, banks and brokers gather the bids specifying price and quantity from individual and institutional investors and transmit them to the CAC. The bids are ranked by price and the resulting confidential list is used by a committee—comprising several company directors, their banking and brokerage firms, and officials of the CAC—in setting the offering price (*cours d'introduction*) on the morning of the introduction day.

In order to obtain wide distribution of shares, the pricing committee generally allocates shares by partially filling bid quantities, a process that bidders obviously attempt to anticipate in setting their bid quantities.

The following example illustrates the listing procedure for one prominent French new issue, Carrefour, a major retail distribution company that went public with a US$20 million stock offering in June 1970. As announced several weeks before the offering date, the minimum price acceptable to the company on the issue of approximately 100,000 shares was FrF850 (approximately US$170 at the then and May 1981 prevailing exchange rate). Based on this demand curve of actual bids, the apparent competitive auction clearing price was approximately FrF1,180 a share. The committee regarded this price as too high in terms of their expectation of market price in the aftermarket, and decided upon FrF1,025 as the offering price. Bids at FrF1,500 or more totaling 4,000 shares were rejected as disguised market orders (market orders are forbidden when placing an order for a new issue). Bids between FrF1,350 and FrF1,500 a share were accepted in full quantity and 32,000 shares of the issue were allocated. Bids between FrF1,120 and FrF1,350 were 25% accepted at 50% of the quantity requested and 43,000 shares were allocated; bids between FrF1,025 and FrF1,350 were filled with 25,000 shares—a total issue of 100,000 shares allocated at the common offering price of FrF1,025.

In setting the offering price, the committee generally appears to treat the schedule of bids as a useful but upwardly biased reflection of the quantities demanded for the stock.

Once shares on new issues are traded, the bank that acted as a consultant to the company may attempt to stabilize the price of the security in the market by standing ready to make purchases or sales of the security. Such pegging may continue up to six months, according to industry sources. By the very nature of the procedure, which is not a firm commitment like most of the underwriting arrangements for secondary issues in the United States, the bank has no direct interest, except in keeping the good faith of the company for future banking relationships.

Performance of the Procedure. Since its existence in 1964, around 120 companies have come to the official market under the procedure outlined. Only on rare occasions have banks intervened to stabilize prices of new issues, since prices set by the committee tend to fall slightly below the average price of the shares when trading opens; the premium between the average opening of trade price and the issue price has historically been around 5% of the issue price, with a low variance around that mean. In this respect, issue costs to the original shareholders appear very low; several studies made on the new issues market through underwriting have shown this premium to be slightly above 20% in the United States. Direct costs for listing include printing costs, audit, information searches, and advertising. They amount to US$150,000 to US$750,000, depending on the size of the issue.

The OTC Market. No condition is required for companies to be listed on the ordinary section of the OTC market by the COB. For the price quoted to be published, the CAC requires companies to send its bylaws and the two most recent annual balance sheets and income statements.

Before allowing shares to be traded on the special section of the OTC market (as of 1981, shares of 10 companies were traded in the recently created special section of the Paris and regional exchanges), the COB examines the bylaws of the company that asked for such listing, its three most recent annual reports, and a short note giving information about the company. The COB examines in particular the chances that the company can fulfill within three years at the latest all the necessary requirements to be listed on the official market.

LISTING REQUIREMENTS AND PROCEDURES FOR FOREIGN COMPANIES. The requirements for the listing of foreign companies on one of the exchanges (for all practical matters, foreign companies are listed only in Paris) are the same as those presented for French companies. In addition, and prior to any formal application to the exchange or the COB, foreign companies must get an authorization to be listed from the French Secretary of the Treasury. Also application for listing in France requires the following additional conditions.

1. The company must be listed on the exchange of the country representing the nationality of the foreign company.
2. Management of the company must clearly show its intentions that French residents hold shares.
3. The company must obey the same disclosure laws as those required for any listed French company. In particular, it must translate to French and make available to the investing public documents distributed at the shareholders' meetings.

Of course, first (and subsequent) share prices of foreign companies in France are not fixed by auction but by simple arbitrage with the price existing on the foreign stock market.

RIGHTS ISSUES. In France, all secondary offerings of common stock are made through a rights issue—a preemptive right to subscribe to new offerings, which simply reinforces the fact shareholders are owners of the business; as such, they have a priority before any other investors to anything of value that the firm might distribute, including the potentially valuable opportunity to buy new issues of securities. Except the fact that a rights offering is the only means a listed company has to raise equity money, there is nothing special in the French procedure vis-à-vis other countries where it is used. Therefore, the interested reader is referred elsewhere for further details (e.g., Brealey and Myers, 1981).

THE SECONDARY SECURITIES MARKET

TRADING PROCEDURES

Placing of Orders. Orders by institutional investors or the investing public must include the following stipulations on price, length of time for which the order is valid, and type of market on which it should be executed.

1. Price can be stipulated in different ways. *Les ordres au mieux* (at best or at market price) means that the order, if received before the beginning of the session, will be carried out at the opening price. If the order arrives after the quotation of the opening price, it will be carried out at the first price quoted after the order has reached the floor. *Les ordres à cours limité* (limit order) are those in which the investor specifies the highest price above which he or she will not buy or the lowest price below which he or she will not sell. *Les ordres premier ou dernier cours* (opening or closing price) are carried out at the opening or at the closing price, depending on their nature. If an opening price order is received during the session, it may only be carried out if it is still possible to do so; closing price orders can only be given on the forward market. *Les ordres sans forcer ou soignant* (carefully executed orders) are given on thin markets to avoid too wide price variations. The agents de change carry such orders in small quantities spread over the session or over several sessions if the order so indicates, according to the state of the market. *Les ordres stop* (stop orders) are given by clients wanting to buy when the price goes above a fixed limit. Whenever the price reaches this limit, the stop order becomes a market order to be carried out at the next price quoted.
2. Validity, that is, the length of time for which the order is valid, is stipulated in two ways: *les ordres jour seulement* (orders that are valid only for that day), in which the order can only be carried out during the session that immediately follows receipt and lapses if it is not carried out; or *les ordres à révocation* (orders that are good until cancelled), which are given without a time limit and stay valid until either they are executed or they are cancelled. On the cash market, these are valid until the last day of the month; on the forward market, they remain valid until the next settlement day.
3. For securities traded on both the cash and forward markets, the market must be stipulated on which the order is to be carried out. If there is no stipulation, the order will be carried out on the cash market.

Execution of Orders and Quotation. In France, shares as well as convertible bonds, floating-rate and indexed bonds, and bonds issued in foreign currencies are quoted in francs and centimes. The minimum fluctuations in prices are FrF0.01 for securities up to FrF5, FrF0.05 for securities from FrF5 to FrF100, FrF0.10 for securities from

FrF100 to FrF500, F1 for securities from FrF500 to FrF5,000, and and FrF10 for securities above FrF5,000.

On French exchanges, only one price is quoted for any given security at any given moment. This price is binding for both buyers and sellers. Therefore, the agents de change and the other floor traders match up their overall holdings of buying and selling orders in each security; they then establish the balancing or market price according to the total number of shares bid and offered. The quoted price is that at which the greatest number of shares are exchanged since it is the price at which all market orders on both the buying and the selling sides, all buying orders whose limits are higher, and all selling orders whose limits are lower can be carried out. These principles are illustrated in Exhibit 6.

Three methods of quotation exist: *par casiers, à la criée,* and *par opposition.* The par casiers (pigeonholes) quotation method is used on the cash market. One casier exists per security; fixed blocks of casiers are assigned to different brokerage firms (they are the specialists on the securities they are assigned) and each firm is responsible for collecting all orders that belong to its block. A clerk (representing the specialist brokerage firm) stands at an appointed place on the floor. At the beginning of each session, he or she receives all the orders from the other brokerage firms, together with those from his or her own firm. The clerk then summarizes the buying and selling orders on a special form, as in the example in Exhibit 6. The clerk thus establishes the price at FrF487, which represents the fairest balance between the total number of shares offered and bid, as this is the price at which the greatest number of shares will be traded, 425 (therefore, 25 of the 50 shares offered at FrF 487 remain unsold orders at this price; they are called "*ordres à cours touche*" and can be only partly carried out).

The à la criée quotation method, in contrast with the previous method, is purely oral and explains the exceptionally noisy character of the Paris Bourse during trading sessions (as opposed to the U.K. market, for example, which is called a "whisper market"). The à la criée method is an auction, but the principle is exactly the same as that of the par casiers method. Securities are assigned to six auction groups: the Corbeille, where all the agents de change gather and quote the most prestigious securities, and five other groups, each arranged in circles, which quote all the other

EXHIBIT 6 THE PARIS STOCK EXCHANGE

Number of Shares Bid at Each Limit	Total at Each Limit	Limits in French Francs	Total at Each Limit	Number of Shares Offered at Each Limit
225 =	225	bid at best	—	—
+ 25 =	250	495	775	= 200+
+100 =	350	490	575	= 125+
+ 75 =	425	487	450	= 50+
+150 =	575	485	400	= 75+
+125 =	700	484	325	= 125+
+100 =	800	482	200	= 75+
+ 75 =	875	480	125	= 50+
+150 =	1,025	477	75	= 0+
—	—	offered at best	75	= 75+

securities. An auctioneer (appointed by the Chambre Syndicale) and a representative of each brokerage firm stand in each group. Each group always deals in the same securities, which are always called for dealing in the same order.

Continuing the example of Exhibit 6, what actually happens when the representatives of each brokerage firm gather together with their orderbooks in hand is that the clerk of the Chambre Syndicale calls out the closing price of the last trading session, for example, 482. Brokers proceed to try to complete transactions with one another. Those with orders to buy at that price indicate the number of shares they wish to buy. Those with orders to sell do likewise. Some deals are made at this point, but as Exhibit 6 shows, 800 shares might be demanded against 200 supplied at that price. When trading dies down, a number of brokers would then be calling buy orders and none will stand ready to sell to them. The auctioneer, seeing that the price was too low, would cry out a different price, for example, 484, and the same phenomenon would repeat itself: there would be too much demand. The auctioneer would raise the price until he reached the balancing price (i.e., 487), where there are relatively few unsatisfied brokers, and then he would put that price on the board. When new orders are brought onto the floor, further transactions would be settled at a second price and so on, until the closing price is reached.

Quotations on the cash market for securities traded on the forward market are fixed in accordance with a procedure called "par opposition," whose purpose is to make sure that the gap between cash and forward prices is limited to a maximum of 2%.

Settlement and Delivery. The method of settlement in force in France is similar in spirit to the one in force in futures and options markets. Although brokers deal with each other bilaterally, the fictitious presence of a third party is introduced to simplify settlement, namely, the Chambre Syndicale, which acts as a clearing house. This means that instead of brokers settling with each other bilaterally, settlement is centralized. Each broker is assumed to have bought or sold the shares in any given transaction fictitiously from or to the Chambre Syndicale, thus ending up with a single debit or credit balance with the latter. The centralized system of accounts is computerized.

CONTROLS, REGULATIONS, AND DISCLOSURE RULES. The Chambre Syndicale des Agents de Change is responsible for insuring controls and regulations relating to some financial operations. Also the Commission des Opérations de Bourse has the primary responsibility of making sure that companies and investors obey the disclosure rules it has set up.

Control Over Prices. All prices quoted on both the official and OTC markets must be endorsed by the Chambre Syndicale. On the cash market, the Chambre Syndicale does not allow the opening prices for French shares to differ by more than 4.5% from the close of the previous day. If the disparity between supply and demand is such that the opening price will exceed this limit, the Chambre Syndicale sets a fixed price for that day with a spread of 4%. Supply and demand are then balanced by reducing buying or selling orders (depending on which side is in excess) at the price set. In the daily official list of prices, an R (for reduced) is shown next to the price of the security concerned. If fewer than 20% to 25% of buying and selling orders can be carried out at the price set, trading is suspended for the day and the following indications follow the price set in the *Daily Official List:* off for offered (offer in excess) or dem for demanded (demand in excess of offer).

On the forward market, if the opening price of a security differs by more than 8% from its previous closing price, trading is suspended so that traders may have time to confirm or cancel their orders. Trading is then resumed in the same session.

Prices of foreign securities are, however, free to move with those of their home market.

Publication of Prices. The Chambre Syndicale publishes the *Bulletin de la Côte Officielle* (*Daily Official List*) on each working day. It shows, for each security, the opening price as well as the highest, lowest, and closing prices.

Decisions and notices from the Chambre Syndicale relating to takeover bids, mergers, block trading, and so forth are included in the *Daily Official List*. A supplement shows prices at which unlisted securities have been traded in the OTC market.

Special Operations. So as to ensure the fairness of the market, all shareholders of a company, whatever the number of shares they hold, must be given a chance to participate on equal terms in any special operation that may affect their rights. This is achieved through the takeover and block-trading procedures.

Takeover Bids. On behalf of the offeror, one or several banks can submit an offer for approval by the Chambre Syndicale. The offeror's application must contain the following information.

1. The minimum and, if any, maximum number of shares the offeror wishes to buy.
2. The offering price and means of payment. (If the offer is for cash, it is called "*offre publique d'achat*"—OPA. If the offer is for exchange of securities, it is called "*offre publique d'échange*"—*OPE.)*

With a few exceptions, an offer is not admissible if it involves less than 10% of the capital of the offeree company. Furthermore, the Secretary of the Treasury can veto any offer within three days.

If the offer is approved, a notice is published by the Chambre Syndicale in the *Daily Official List* with full details of the offer, which must remain open for a minimum of one month. An offer is conditional upon acceptances being received for a minimum number of shares. If a maximum number of shares is fixed by the offeror, acceptances will be dealt on a pro rata basis according to the total number of acceptances received. Shareholders in the offeree company may withdraw their acceptances at any time up to, but not later than, 10 days before the expiration of the offer. Only if there is a competing offer can the offeror cancel the offer. In addition, while an offer remains open, a 100% margin must be provided with any order for shares in the offeree company on the forward market; primes and option dealings are not allowed during that time.

Block Trading. Before block trading can be undertaken, the Chambre Syndicale decides whether this could give the buyers a controlling interest in the company concerned. If so, the buyer must either make a takeover bid or get permission from the Chambre Syndicale to acquire the block, providing: that (1) a notice is published in the *Daily Official List* showing who is buying and who is selling the block, together with the date and price of the transaction and the number of shares exchanged; and (2) the buyer agrees to purchase, at the same price, every share offered for sale during the 15 following sessions.

ECONOMICS OF THE FRENCH EQUITY MARKET

THE FISCAL REGIME AND OTHER PROVISIONS APPLICABLE TO NONRESIDENTS. Nonresidents can purchase or sell freely all French and foreign securities listed on both the official and OTC markets as well as on the spot and forward markets. However, they are not allowed to hold more than 20% of the capital of any listed French company without price authorization of the Secretary of the Treasury. Financing for such operations must be provided by either: (1) selling foreign currencies on the French currency market (the equivalent in French francs of these foreign currencies is then credited to a foreign account, called "*compte étranger en Francs*"); or (2) using French francs already credited to a foreign account.

French and foreign securities purchased by nonresidents must be held in **foreign portfolios** (*dossiers étrangers*) opened in the buyer's name by a financial intermediary, either a bank or a brokerage firm. Securities (either bearer or registered) can be transferred at any time to any country. The amount in francs credited to a foreign account can be used to buy other securities, to cover any expenditures incurred in France, or to buy any foreign currency on the French currency market for repatriation.

The fiscal regime for equity investment applicable to nonresidents is different from the one facing French residents. In general, dividends and interest from French securities are subject to a withholding tax of 25%. This withholding tax exempts nonresidents from any further income tax if they have no other tax liability in France; in case they have any other taxable income in France, the withholding tax in dividends is deductible from the tax payable (but not the withholding tax on bond or debenture interest).

The withholding tax can either be reduced to a lower rate (usually 15% for dividends) or abolished in accordance with the reciprocal tax agreements that exist between France and over 70 countries. There is no withholding tax on income from foreign securities.

In order to lessen the effects of the double taxation on dividends, an *avoir fiscal* was set up in the late 1960s. The avoir fiscal is a tax credit equal to 50% of the amount of the dividends paid to shareholders. Private individuals who hold shares in French companies are granted the avoir fiscal if they are a resident of West Germany, Austria, Belgium, Brazil, the United Kingdom, Sweden, Switzerland, or Spain.

Similarly foreign corporate organizations (with the exception of Belgium) are granted the avoir fiscal. However, in certain countries, corporate entities are no longer granted this tax credit when the percentage of capital they hold in a French company is greater than 5% (The Netherlands); 10% (the United States and the United Kingdom); 20% (Switzerland); 25% (West Germany and Luxemburg).

Finally, as far as capital gains are concerned, nonresidents are not liable for any capital gains tax on securities.

THE EFFICIENCY OF THE FRENCH EQUITY MARKET. The efficient market concept is from the financial economist's point of view an extension of the zero-profit competitive equilibrium condition from the certainty world of classical price theory to the dynamic behavior of prices in speculative markets under conditions of uncertainty. This hypothesis has been tested and, with very few exceptions, found consistent with the data of a wide variety of markets.

Although some light is shed on the efficiency of the French equity market understood in that context, this discussion considers this concept on both a much broader and more practical level. It takes the point of view of foreign assets managers and tries to answer the following questions: Is the market sufficiently competitive and efficient so that without special information on French companies one can be sure to be able to buy them at a fair price? How important are the transaction costs of dealing in French stock? Does the liquidity of the market allow large transactions in single securities?

Size and Liquidity of the French Equity Market. The French equity market ranks as about the fifth largest equity market of the world with West Germany and Switzerland and after the United States, Japan, Canada, and the United Kingdom. Exact figures and the relative size of major equity in terms of total market capitalization are indicated on Exhibit 7.

Two measures allow focus on the liquidity of the French market. The first is the annual transactions volume as a percentage of total equity capitalization, which is reproduced on a comparative basis with other markets for 1980 in Exhibit 8. On such a measure the French equity market ranks third after Japan and Hong Kong. The second is the market capitalization of the 10 largest companies as a percentage of

EXHIBIT 7 COMPARATIVE SIZE OF MAJOR EQUITY MARKETS, 1980

Country	Equity Capitalization ($ billion)	Percentage of Total
France	55	3.0
United States	820	45.5
Japan	350	10.0
Canada	165	9.0
Australia	25	1.0
United Kingdom	120	7.0
West Germany	70	4.0
Belgium	10	0.5
Switzerland	60	3.0
The Netherlands	25	1.5
Italy	16	1.0
Denmark	2	—
South Africa	30	1.5
Other markets	70	4.0
Total	1,318	100.0

Source. Capital International Perspective, 1981, Geneva, Switzerland.

EXHIBIT 8 COMPARATIVE LIQUIDITY OF EQUITY MARKETS, 1980

Market	Annual Transaction Volume as a Percentage of Total Equity Capitalization
France	28.1
Japan	52.6
United States	24.5
Canada	18.6
United Kingdom	16.9
West Germany	23.4
Hong Kong	39.4
Belgium	10.6
The Netherlands	21.4
Italy	25.7
Average	26.1

Source. Capital International Perspective, 1981, Geneva, Switzerland.

total equities capitalization. The higher this ratio, the more concentrated the liquidity of the corresponding market is on a few companies. With a ratio as low as 24% (see Exhibit 9), France appears again as a market where liquidity exists on a large number of companies.

Exhibit 10 is a list of the 25 most active stocks in 1980 with their average daily transaction volume.

EXHIBIT 9 MARKET CAPITALIZATION OF THE 10 LARGEST COMPANIES AS A PERCENTAGE OF TOTAL EQUITIES CAPITALIZATION, 1980

Market	Market Capitalization as a Percentage of Total Equities Capitalization
France	24
Japan	15
United States	20
Canada	23
Australia	27
United Kingdom	28
West Germany	41
Hong Kong	48
Belgium	59
Switzerland	64
The Netherlands	75

Source. Capital International Perspective, 1981, Geneva, Switzerland.

EXHIBIT 10 AVERAGE DAILY TRANSACTIONS ON THE 25 MOST ACTIVE STOCKS (US$ hundred thousand)

Companies	Transactions
Elf–Aquitaine	2,500
Matra	1,500
Francaise des Pétroles	1,100
Air Liquide	1,100
CSF-Thomson CSF	880
BSN-Gervais Danone	700
Financière de Paris et des Pays-bas	600
Suez	600
Hachette	500
Carrefour	500
Pechiney Ugine Kuhlmann	500
Rhône Poulenc	500
Saint-Gobain	450
Michelin	400
Beghin Say	400
Compagnie Générale d'Électricité	400
Bouygues	400
L'Oréal	400
Thomson Brandt	350
Moët-Hennessy	350
Eaux (Compagnie Générale des)	350
Pernod-Ricard	350
Perrier (Source)	350
Midi (Compagnie du)	350
Lafarge	350

Source. Compagnie des Agents de Change, *L'annee Boursiere,* 1980.

Transactions Costs. Brokerage commissions are indicated in Exhibit 11. Fiscal charges are levied on top of the brokerage commission; they include the *impôrt de bourse* (stamp duty), which is payable on securities except those traded on regional exchanges. Its rate is 0.30% of transactions up to FrF1 million and 0.15% thereafter; on contango dealing, the rate is 0.15%. Another fiscal charge is that of the value added tax, the rate of which is 17.6% of the brokerage commission.

Efficiency of the Market. As has been shown, many reforms related to the French financial market have taken place in the last 15 years. Those regarding information and disclosure rules and the functioning of the market have contributed to a greater efficiency of the market in the sense that it is probably more difficult today to make economic profits by trading on the basis of a certain set of information than it used to be in the past. Therefore one should look with reservations on any empirical study on the efficiency of the French equity market made with old data.

All studies, including the less recent, conclude to the efficiency of the market, at least at the weak-form level. At this level, when the only information available for consideration is based on past prices, an almost instaneous adjustment of prices was

EXHIBIT 11 BROKERAGE COMMISSION STRUCTURE[a]

	Percentage Rate for an Amount of French Francs			
French Equity Market	Up to 600,000	From 600,000 to 1,100,000	From 1,100,000 to 2,200,000	Over 2,200,000
Bonds and debentures	0.50	0.33	0.25	0.165
Convertible bonds, shares, and rights	0.65	0.43	0.325	0.215
Paris Stock Exchange	0.75	0.50	0.375	0.25
Regional stock exchanges				
Primes and options				
if given up				
if taken up				

[a]The commission is 4% of the premium on the prime and the option. The commission is based on the full amount of the transaction at the usual rate (see above for shares).

Source: Côte Officielle, Compagnie des Agents de Change.

established. The coefficients of serial correlation were significantly different from zero, but still too weak to allow trading profits after transaction costs.

At the semi-strong form of efficiency level, when all the publicly available information is taken into consideration (earnings and dividends, announcements, splits, rights issues, etc.), the results are confusing and mixed, although after allowing for transaction costs, it does not seem that trading on the basis of this information would make significant economic profits.

Finally, no recent study exists on the strong form of efficiency level, in which all privileged information is taken into account. A study by McDonald (1974) demonstrates the superiority of investment strategies by certain mutual funds (SICAV). The banks that manage SICAVs generally have substantial advantages in access to information for investment analysis. McDonald (1974) findings, based on 1965–71 data, that most of the SICAVs achieved superior performance in French securities, suggest that the Paris Stock Exchange is not as efficient as some other markets in the strong-form sense.

RISK AND RETURN, THE PAST AND THE FUTURE

The Record. Holding period returns on any market very much depend on the precise period during which returns are measured. Exhibit 12 indicates the holding period returns from 1959 to 1981 on the French equity market. Periods of calculation go from one year to 22 years, with every holding period between these two numbers. The returns are real returns; they include dividends but are adjusted for the inflation rate of the holding period. The diagonal of Exhibit 12 indicates yearly real holding period returns; they are positive for 13 years, with the highest return 48.8% in 1978, and negative for 9 years, with the lowest return, 25.9% in 1974.

The Future. Risk and return are the two key features of investment strategy. A simple but powerful description of the relationship between risk and return is provided by the **security market line (SML),** where all securities and porfolios lie theoretically.

EXHIBIT 12 HOLDING PERIOD RETURNS ON THE FRENCH EQUITY MARKET, 1959 TO 1981 (in percentages)

Buying in January	1959	1960	1961	1962	1963	1964	1965	1966	1967	1968	1969	1970	1971	1972	1973	1974	1975	1976	1977	1978	1979	1980
Selling in January																						
1960	30.0																					
1961	21.1	12.8																				
1962	17.4	11.6	10.4																			
1963	12.9	7.7	5.2	0.2																		
1964	7.1	2.1	−1.3	−6.6	−13.0																	
1965	3.7	−0.9	−4.1	−8.5	−12.5	−12.0																
1966	3.3	−0.6	−3.0	−6.1	−8.2	−5.6	1.2															
1967	0.5	−3.1	−5.5	−8.4	−10.5	−9.6	−8.4	−17.0														
1968	0.9	−2.2	−4.2	−6.5	−7.8	−6.4	−4.4	−7.2	3.9													
1969	1.8	−0.9	−2.5	−4.2	−4.3	−3.2	−0.9	−1.6	7.2	10.6												
1970	3.9	1.6	0.4	−0.7	−0.9	1.3	4.2	5.0	13.5	18.6	27.2											
1971	2.9	0.7	−0.4	−1.5	−1.7	0.0	2.2	2.4	7.9	9.2	8.5	−7.5										
1972	2.1	0.0	−1.1	−2.1	−2.4	−1.0	0.7	0.6	4.6	4.8	2.9	−7.5	−7.5									
1973	3.1	1.3	0.4	−0.5	−0.6	0.9	2.7	2.9	6.7	7.2	6.4	0.2	4.3	17.6								
1974	2.4	0.8	−0.1	−0.9	−1.0	0.3	1.7	1.7	4.8	4.9	3.8	−1.3	0.9	5.3	−5.7							
1975	0.4	−1.3	−2.2	−3.1	−3.4	−2.5	−1.5	−1.8	−0.4	−0.2	−1.9	−6.8	−6.6	−6.4	−16.5	−25.9						
1976	1.3	−0.3	−1.1	−1.9	−2.0	−1.0	0.0	−0.1	2.0	1.8	0.5	−3.3	−2.5	−1.2	−6.7	−7.3	16.1					
1977	0.2	−1.3	−2.1	−2.9	−3.1	−2.3	−1.5	−1.7	0.0	−0.5	−1.8	−5.3	−5.0	−4.4	−9.3	−10.4	−1.5	−16.5				
1978	−0.6	−2.1	−2.9	−3.6	−3.9	−3.2	−2.5	−2.8	−1.4	−1.9	−3.2	−6.4	−6.3	−6.1	−10.2	−11.3	−5.8	−15.2	−13.8			
1979	1.5	0.1	−0.5	−1.1	−1.2	−0.4	0.5	0.5	2.1	1.9	1.1	−1.5	−0.7	0.3	−2.3	−1.6	5.6	2.3	13.2	48.8		
1980	1.6	0.4	−0.2	−0.8	−0.8	−0.0	0.8	0.8	2.3	2.2	1.5	−0.8	0.0	0.9	−1.3	−0.5	5.6	3.1	10.6	25.2	5.4	
1981	1.6	0.4	−0.2	−0.7	−0.8	−0.0	0.8	0.8	2.2	2.0	1.4	−0.7	0.0	0.9	−1.1	−0.4	4.7	2.5	7.9	16.3	2.9	0.3

Source. *Economie et Statistique*, I.N.S.E.E. (Institut National de la Statistiques et des Études économiques), 133 May, 1981.

Such an SML is provided in Exhibit 13 for the French market as of August 1981. It indicates both high inflation expectations (above 15% a year) and an underaverage reward for risk taking.

REFORM PROJECTS. In 1979, the Secretary of the Treasury commissioned M. Perouse, Managing Director of the Caisse des Dépôts et Consignations, to head a committee of six members and make recommendations to modernize the functioning of the equity market. These were presented and accepted in March 1981.

Although the preamble to the Perouse report underlines some positive aspects in the evolution of the French equity market since World War II, the report criticizes the functioning of the Paris Bourse in essentially two respects. Even considering the improvements implemented during the last decade (some of which were the recommendations of another commission, which published a report—the Baumgartner report—in 1971), the stock market and particularly the equity market plays a too minor role in the strategic planning and corporate finance of most French companies (see section 4.5, "France: Banking, Money, and Bond Markets"). The second criticism pertains to all the technical weaknesses of the stock market itself in its structure, techniques, organization, and the attitudes of savers and borrowers.

The recommendations of the commission were grouped in three areas: the modernization and simplification of the different forms of securities; the establishment of a continuous and modernized market; and a drastic change in the commissions structure.

As far as the modernization of securities is concerned, the commission recom-

EXHIBIT 13 FRENCH SECURITY MARKET LINE, AUGUST 1981

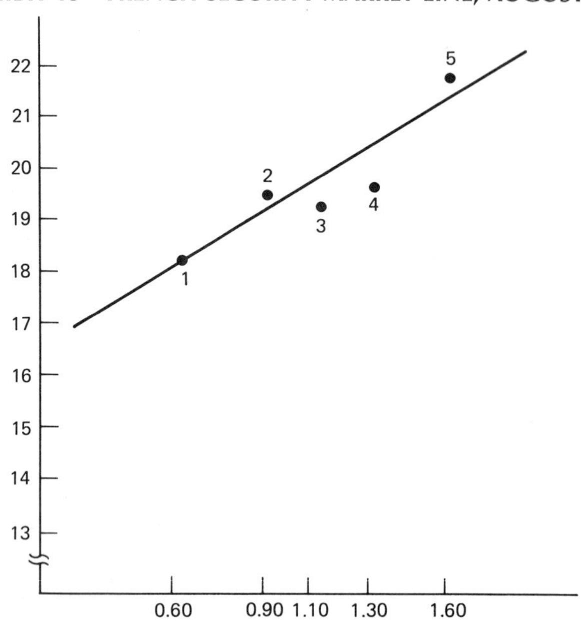

Source. Associes en Finance, Service Droite de Marche.

mended that methods of holding securities be unified, and bearer and registered securities be eliminated and replaced by SICOVAM-like accounts, in which the owners of securities would have the choice between a single collective organization such as SICOVAM to deposit securities or one of several financial intermediaries. In any case, anonymity would be preserved. In a second phase, such a simplification would be extended to securities traded on the unofficial market.

As far as the establishment of a continuous and modernized market is concerned, the commission confirmed the monopoly of the agents de change on trading and the fact that securities should continue to be traded and quoted either on the Paris Stock Exchange or on the regional stock markets, but not both. The commission recommended:

1. The quotations methods should be unified.
2. Trades should not be concentrated on the first price quoted.
3. The forward market should be enlarged to 350 securities to be traded exclusively on this market. This measure would lead to an integration of the spot and forward markets.
4. The trading hours should be greatly extended beyond the present two midday hours.
5. The system of placing orders should be partly computerized; orders whould be accompanied by information to be processed by a central system. This information would include at least price and quantity of securities and would be available to the intermediaries in the market as well as to the general public.

As far as the commission structure is concerned, the commission officially recognized that it is maintained by a public decree at too low a level for the securities industry to be profitable and to have enough muscle to develop (see Exhibit 14 for an international comparison of the commission structures).

EXHIBIT 14 INTERNATIONAL COMPARISON OF COMMISSION STRUCTURES[a]

	Commissions on Amount of Transaction (in FrF)			Commissions and Taxes (in FrF)		
Stock Exchange	50,000	500,000	5,000,000	50,000	500,000	5,000,000
Paris	325	3,250	12,135	532	5,322	23,270
Buyers	325	3,250	12,135	532	5,322	23,270
Sellers						
London	300	3,500	21,000	2,000	15,000	130,000
Buyers	800	3,500	21,000	900	4,000	22,000
Sellers						
New York	1,500	4,000	32,000	1,600	4,000	32,000
Buyers	1,500	4,000	32,000	1,700	5,500	44,000
Sellers						

[a]US$1 = FrF5.8; US$1 = £.5.

Source. Adapted from *U.K. Stock Exchange: Evidence to the Committee to Review the Functioning of Financial Institutions.*

As a consequence, the report recommended that the stock market tax of 3% on transactions be abolished for orders whose value is less than FrF1 million and reduced to 1.5% for orders above this limit. Also recommended was that the level of commission on equities should be raised to a proportional fee of 1% thereafter. Finally the commission recommended degressive commissions. If implemented, these changes in the commission structure would bring the Paris market in line with the other major markets.

In addition to these reforms, the commission strongly recommended new extensions to the market. While this plan should be implemented in several phases, the last phase should correspond to the creation in Paris of a negotiable options market such as exists in Chicago, London, or Amsterdam. Ultimately a market for options on an index might be created.

Although making recommendations for far-reaching reforms, the Perouse report is an interesting compromise between the needs for a modernization of the market on the one hand and its traditions, both corporate and environmental, on the other.

September 1981

BIBLIOGRAPHY

TECHNICAL PUBLICATIONS. These publications are mainly those of the CAC and by the COB. They include the following:

Bulletin Officiel de la Côte is the *Official Daily List*. It supplies stock prices quoted on Paris and regional exchanges on all types of markets and for all securities.

Bulletin des Indices de Cours (index of French stocks). The daily bulletin includes the general index of common stocks (market value weighted CAC index of approximately 350 French stocks), and indices on industrial stocks, nine sectors, and 35 subsectors. In addition, the weekly supplement indicates the index of the 68 constituent sections, each subsector being a constituent section in itself or containing two or several constituent sections.

Graphiques de la Bourse de Paris (Paris Stock Exchange charts). This booklet, issued every two weeks, shows an up-to-date chart of price and volume of transactions for each French stock quoted on the forward market and for 50 of the most active stocks quoted on the cash market only. Each chart includes (1) the price quoted during a period of 8 to 12 months; (2) the moving average based on 200 days; (3) the volume of transactions during a period of 8 to 12 months; (4) a yearly range chart giving latest, highest, and lowest prices since 1962.

Statistiques Mensuelles de la Bourse de Paris (monthly statistics). This booklet contains all market statistics concerning activity and prices, with emphasis on the forward market and for the 50 most active stocks of the cash market.

L'Année Boursière (annual report). This report is published by the Chambre Syndicale des Agents de Change, as are the preceding publications. Published since 1962, it contains all the figures, statistics, and graphs concerning the activity of the market during the year and for all types of securities (including the bond and gold markets).

La Bourse—Pourquoi, Comment, Qui? A booklet on the Paris Bourse, this publication provides market organization, structure, purpose, and activity information.

Annual Report to the President of the Republic is published by the Commission des Opérations de Bourse. It reports market activity under its supervisory capacity during the previous year and compliance to its regulations. The COB has other, nonregular publications. A translation of the general introduction and the summary of the report is available in English.

Le Marché des Options is the report presented to the Minister of Finance by the commission entrusted to study the stock market and its fluctuations. It is this report, the Baumgartner report, that recommended to enlarge the development and the role of the French equity market.

The Perouse Report, *La Modernisation du Marché des Valeurs Mobilières* (modernization of the Paris stock market). A synthesis in English of the recommendations of the Perouse report can be found in *Reforming the Paris Stock Market*, by P. Stonham, an investment analyst. Also one may read on this subject the special issue of *Banque*, May (1981).

GENERAL PUBLICATIONS. For a general overview of the French stock market, the following are recommended.

Les Marchés Financiers et la Geston de Portefeuille, by Bertrand Jacquillat and Bruno Solnik (Paris: Dunod, 1981), is a book on modern portfolio theory with special emphasis on its application to the French and European stock markets.

"The Pricing of Initial Equity Issues: The French Sealed-Bid Auction," *Journal of Business*, 47, January, 1974, by J. McDonald and B. Jacquillat, contains a detailed description of the French auction for new issues. A later article by the same authors and J. Rolfo, "French Auctions of Common Stock New Issues 1966–74," *Journal of Banking and Finance*, 2, 1978, gives empirical results of aftermarket performance of new issues.

Principles of Corporate Finance, by R. Brealey and S. Myers (New York: McGraw-Hill, 1981), gives hindsight on some of the institutional differences among the United States, the United Kingdom, and continental securities markets (see in particular Chapter 15 on how corporations issue securities).

L'Efficience du Marché de Paris, by H. Jousset (Paris: C. Jousset, 1974), and J. Hamon, *L'Efficience des marchés Boursiers: Étude du Marché parisien*. Thèse pour le doctorat d'Etat es Sciences de Gestion, Université de Rennes, 1978, discusses the operation of French stock markets, particularly the Paris Bourse. This, and B. Solnik's "Note on the Validity of the Random Walk for European Prices," *Journal of Finance*, December (1973), present evidence on the efficiency of the Paris and other European markets.

See also J. McDonald, "French Mutual Fund Performance: Evaluation of Internationally Diversified Portfolios," *Journal of Finance*, December (1973).

INFORMATION ABOUT COMPANIES. The following organizations provide security analyses pertinent to companies listed in the French exchanges.

DAFSA (Société de Documentation et d'Analyses Financières, 125 rue Montmartre, 75081 Paris Cedex 02) publishes a series of documents and analyses on French companies (600), French groups (80), and the industrial sector (50). The DAFSA has pioneered the application of the European method of security analysis, which makes possible the comparison of companies registered in different European countries despite differences in national accounting procedures and standards.

SAFE (Société d'Analyses Financières et Economiques) is one of the most well-recognized research outfits on the Paris Bourse. It is a subsidiary of Paribas, with about 30 financial analysts.

Associes en Finance is an independent organization that publishes measures of expected return and risk on companies and convertible bonds.

NEWSPAPERS AND PERIODICALS. Principal daily financial and economic newspapers are l'Agence Economique et Financière, and *Le Nouveau Journal.*

Principal economic and financial weeklies are

Le Nouvel Economiste, and *La Vie Française.*

Principal periodical publications are

L'Expansion (bimonthly); *Banque* (monthly); and *Analyse Financière* (quarterly, published by the French Federation of Security Analysts).

SECTION **6.6**

SWITZERLAND: EQUITY MARKETS

CONTENTS

SECTION **6.6**

SWITZERLAND: EQUITY MARKETS

Alexander Galli

The international importance of the Swiss financial market is the result of a variety of factors. For the origin of this international financial center, one need look back no further than three decades. After World War II, Switzerland was one of the few countries in Europe with a normally functioning banking system. In addition, it was a banking system that already had been very open to all kinds of national and international banking business. On these foundations, and supported by a relatively stable fiscal and monetary policy, the Swiss financial center was developed.

The favorable development of the Swiss economy in the 1950s and 1960s and the well-organized banking system attracted foreign investors as well as companies. Thus, the Swiss financial market gained an international reputation beyond all proportion to the small size of Switzerland's economy. For example, in 1981 its national income reached only 3.3% of the U.S. national income. On the other hand, since the beginning of the 1960s Switzerland's share in worldwide issues of traditional foreign bonds increased from 5% to more than 40%.

Despite the international reputation of the Swiss financial sector, the Swiss equity market is not particularly broad. Even though the number of joint stock companies was growing relatively fast in the 1970s, in 1980 their total share capital reached the amount of only SF67 billion (see Exhibit 1). This is a relatively small figure, since in 1980 the gross capital formation was SF45 billion.

As of 1980, only 5% of the total number of joint stock companies had a share capital of more than SF1 billion. This partly explains why the Swiss equity market is not very broad. Furthermore, the figures in Exhibit 1 demonstrate that there is still some potential within the Swiss capital market to absorb new share and bond issues.

ISSUE OF SHARES

Usually, shares are issued by a private company that has recently been established as a joint stock company, or are issued by an existing company that plans to increase its share capital. Such a decision implies that the company knows which method of placement should be used (i.e., whether a public issue or a private placing is preferable). Furthermore, it has to be determined whether the supply of new shares is offered to new shareholders, old shareholders, or a combination of those two groups.

EXHIBIT 1 THE DEVELOPMENT OF SWISS JOINT STOCK COMPANIES

Year	Joint Stock Companies (Number)	Total Share Capital (Billion Swiss Francs)
1950	20,326	8.6
1955	25,614	10.2
1960	33,441	14.6
1965	48,149	25.0
1970	64,379	36.4
1975	91,723	56.6
1980	108,834	67.0

Source. Federal Office of Statistics, *Statistical Yearbook of Switzerland*, 1980.

In the primary market the banks usually function as the middleman, whereas the stock exchange (discussed later) is the trading place for securities already issued. The following describes some of the placement methods for shares and the volume of domestic issue of shares in Switzerland.

DIFFERENT METHODS OF ISSUING SHARES. It is required by law that an increase of the share capital has to be approved by the meeting of shareholders in two steps. In the first meeting the shareholders have to agree upon the increase of the share capital. In a second meeting, after the issue of the shares, the shareholders confirm the submittance of the subscription forms and the payment of the new share capital. Such a procedure is relatively inflexible, takes a lot of time, and is expensive.

For these reasons, the decision to increase the share capital and the confirmation of the share issue takes place at the same meeting of shareholders. However, such a proceeding presupposes that somebody has already made the payment for the shares to be issued. In Switzerland the banks usually make the payment for the total increase in the share capital (firm underwriting). After the approval by the meeting of shareholders the new shares are offered to the old shareholders and the public at a fixed price. The old shareholder has a subscription right that he or she can use to buy new shares or can sell to somebody else.

Firm underwriting is the most frequently used procedure for the issue of shares in Switzerland. Besides this method of placement, companies also have the possibility of direct placement. Under direct placement, companies themselves raise the new share capital instead of through a bank and they also bear the risk of the issue. Companies do not know in advance whether total new capital needed can be raised on the market. These uncertainties and risks discourage companies from using this method when issuing new shares. The banks, however, which are already endowed with the know-how for the issue of shares, usually apply the method of direct placement.

A company might bear the risk of the issue of shares but the placing is carried out by banks. In such instances, the bank or a group of banks (a syndicate) receives a commission for the number of subscription forms collected by them. This placement on a commission basis is a way of saving the underwriting commission. Even so a majority of companies refrain from using this method. The risk of failing in the marketplace and a lack of experience are the main reasons preventing companies from using this method.

The three **methods of placement** described are used for public issues. Companies do not always make press announcements about the increase of share capital in the newspapers; they might mail out the prospectus to the clients of banks. In this case there is a private placement. A listing on the stock exchange is not always desirable and at times is not possible, since the listing on the stock exchange requires the publication of a prospectus. Nonpublic issue of shares means that the bank sells the securities to a very select part of their clientele. The method of private placement is used only to a very limited extent by rather small companies. The lack of publicity makes this kind of share unattractive to investors.

For the shareholders the differentiation between **bearer** and **registered shares** might be of some importance. Bearer shares are negotiable without any restriction. As a financing instrument they are preferred by big companies that are well known to the public. Registered shares, on the other hand, cannot be sold to anybody without the permission of the company. Companies that want to limit the number of shareholders prefer this type of share. In this case the shareowner's name is printed on the face of the security and recorded in the company's register of shareholders.

In Switzerland, bearer shares and registered shares are very common. A majority of banks, companies, and trusts have a share capital that consists of both bearer and registered shares.

VOLUME OF SHARE ISSUES. The issue of shares depends on the economic conditions and the legal stipulations applying to joint stock companies. Even though changes in the legislation for joint stock companies have occurred in the past, these did not have any significant impact on the issue of new shares. More important was the liquidity situation in the capital market, the level of interest rate, and the economic activity.

In Exhibit 2 the development of the domestic issue of shares and bonds since 1960 is presented. Even though the total issue of shares increased from about SF1 billion in 1960 to around SF3 billion at the beginning of the 1980s, the growth of bond issues was much faster. In the same period of time the volume of bond issues climbed from SF1.8 billion in 1960 to SF25 billion in 1981. The market share of the issue of shares thus fell from approximately 35% to 10% (see Exhibit 3).

The relatively small increase of share issues in the Swiss capital market is due to the fact that in recent years a great number of foreign borrowers raised capital in Switzerland by bond issues. As a result, the market share of the issue of shares fell to 10%. If the issue of foreign bonds is excluded, this market share is cut from about 50% to 20%.

The reduced importance of shares on the capital market is expressed in the above figures. In the 1970s many companies had difficulties or failed in placing new shares on the market. The average investor did not want to trade in securities but wanted to put the high-yielding bonds into a portfolio. As a consequence of such behavior, losses on shares were fairly common. Such an experience discouraged investors even further from buying new shares.

The companies had to look for new financing instruments. For the investor, bonds are attractive substitutes for shares because bonds yield a fixed income. Therefore, companies started to raise money by issuing different types of bonds. In the 1970s the degree of indebtedness of companies thus increased due not only to the old crisis but to changes in the portfolio selection of investors.

Currently on the Swiss capital market, securities such as bonds, convertible bonds,

EXHIBIT 2 DOMESTIC ISSUE OF SHARES AND BONDS
(in million Swiss francs)

Year	Shares Public Issues	Shares Private Placings	Total Shares	Total Bonds	Domestic Bonds	Foreign Bonds	Total Bonds and Shares
1960	193.3	727.2	920.5	1,814.5	955.7	770.8	2,735.0
1961	372.6	864.0	1,236.6	2,384.9	1,268.5	1,116.4	3,621.5
1962	661.6	1,157.1	1,818.7	2,158.9	1,453.9	705.0	3,977.6
1963	524.0	1,028.1	1,552.1	3,240.4	2,628.3	628.1	4,792.5
1964	567.8	981.4	1,549.2	3,417.9	3,017.3	400.6	4,967.1
1965	281.6	1,327.9	1,609.5	3,389.2	3,011.7	378.5	4,998.7
1966	257.8	1,020.9	1,278.7	3,898.3	3,415.4	482.9	5,177.0
1967	321.5	1,023.7	1,345.2	4,240.8	3,521.5	719.3	5,586.0
1968	502.5	1,432.5	1,935.0	4,261.7	3,114.2	1,147.5	6,196.7
1969	820.0	1,637.5	2,457.5	4,610.7	3,600.7	1,010.0	7,068.2
1970	544.2	1,963.0	2,507.2	5,201.9	4,180.5	1,021.4	7,709.1
1971	998.5	2,026.4	3,024.9	9,027.7	6,026.7	3,001.0	12,052.6
1972	1,018.8	2,118.0	3,136.8	9,259.2	5,727.2	3,532.0	12,396.0
1973	911.6	2,006.1	2,917.7	10,722.5	5,978.5	4,744.0	13,640.2
1974	615.8	2,554.9	3,170.7	8,440.3	5,643.0	2,797.3	11,611.0
1975	1,089.9	1,603.2	2,693.1	18,094.6	9,109.0	3,985.6	20,787.7
1976	1,535.0	1,654.2	3,189.2	23,778.5	10,367.0	13,411.5	26,967.7
1977	741.7	1,987.2	2,728.9	18,791.2	7,135.2	11,656.0	21,520.1
1978	1,090.5	1,484.9	2,575.4	22,639.1	9,872.9	12,766.2	25,214.5
1979	1,349.2			25,456.9	10,020.2	15,436.7	
1980	2,267.1			22,022.3	9,601.8	12,420.5	
1981	2,043.2			24,994.0	8,613.9	16,375.1	

Source. Swiss National Bank, *Monthly Bulletin;* OECD, *Financial Statistics.*

straight bonds, subordinated bonds, and bonds with floating interest rates are found. Convertible bonds or notes and subordinated bonds or loans have been created just to avoid new issues of shares. In Exhibit 4 the relative market shares in the 1960s and 1970s are shown.

As mentioned, the issue of shares is also dependent on money market conditions. In Exhibit 5 the volume of share issues, the growth rate of the money supply M_1 (currency in circulation and demand deposits of the private nonbanking sector), and the yield on long-term government bonds are shown.

In the period 1960–78 there is a significant positive correlation between the volume of share issues and the growth rate of M_1 and a negative correlation between the interest rate and the share issue. This result is to be expected, because a high growth rate of M_1 means usually easy capital market conditions and therefore induces companies to raise funds. On the other hand, high capital market interest rates make it less attractive for investors to buy shares and thus it is not a preferable time for placing shares on the market. The empirical evidence supports such a hypothesis for the period up to 1978–79.

After 1978–79, despite the increase in interest rates and the reduction of the growth rate of money, the volume of share issues increased. This result is even more surprising in that the trading in shares at the stock exchange during these years was not

EXHIBIT 3 PERCENTAGE DISTRIBUTION BETWEEN SHARE AND BOND ISSUES

Year	Share Issues (in Percentage of Total Bond and Total Share Issues)	Total Share Issues (in Percentage of Domestic Bond and Total Share Issues)	Private Issues (in Percentage of Total Share Issues)
1960	33.6	49.0	79.0
1961	34.1	49.3	69.8
1962	45.7	55.5	63.6
1963	32.3	37.1	66.2
1964	31.1	33.9	63.3
1965	32.1	34.8	82.5
1966	24.6	27.2	79.8
1967	24.0	27.6	76.1
1968	31.2	38.8	74.0
1969	34.7	40.5	66.6
1970	32.5	37.4	78.2
1971	25.0	33.4	66.9
1972	25.3	35.3	67.5
1973	21.3	32.7	68.7
1974	27.3	35.9	80.5
1975	12.9	22.8	59.5
1976	11.8	23.5	51.8
1977	12.6	27.6	72.8
1978	10.2	20.6	57.6

Source. Swiss National Bank, *Monthly Bulletin;* OECD, *Financial Statistics.*

overwhelming. There are three reasons for such a development: first, up to 1980 the economic activity in Switzerland was relatively high; many new companies were established during this period. Second, the capital market was still liquid as a consequence of the money creation by the Swiss National Bank in October 1978 in order to dampen the revaluation of the Swiss franc. Third, a growing number of companies are issuing shares by public issues. Therefore, a shift from private to public issues is registered.

Of some interest is the question: To what extent can the Swiss capital market absorb share issues? Following the statistics published by the Swiss National Bank, total issues of bonds, notes, and shares reached a volume of SF28 billion. This total includes traditional foreign issues of bonds of SF15 billion.

ORGANIZATION OF THE SECONDARY EQUITY MARKET

In Switzerland purchase and sale transactions of shares can take place on different markets. Most important, and also most efficient, is the stock exchange. In addition, there are different forms of over-the-counter trading.

STOCK EXCHANGE TRADING. Unlike other principal European stock exchanges, the Swiss stock exchanges were established only relatively late in the nineteenth

EXHIBIT 4 DISTRIBUTION OF THE ISSUE OF SHARES AND BONDS IN SWITZERLAND (total share issues as percentages of total bond and share issues)

Average 1960–64

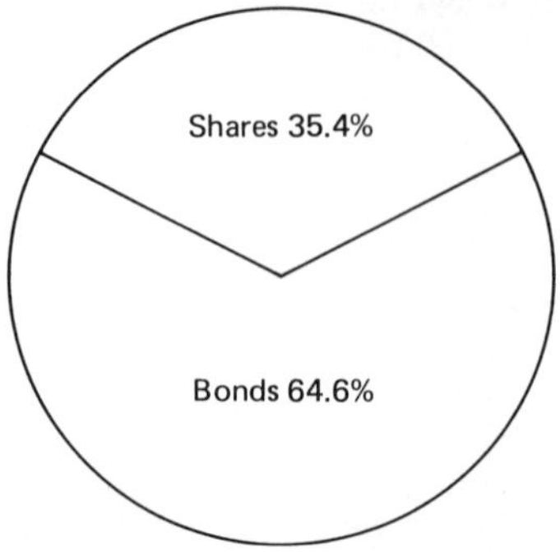

Average 1975–78

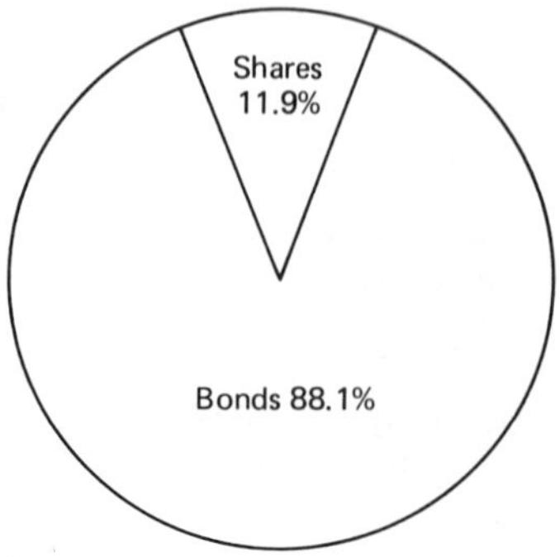

Source. Swiss Nationalbank, *Monthly Bulletin.*

century. The first Swiss stock exchange was founded in Geneva in 1850. Other stock exchanges were founded more than 20 years later, the latest at the end of the nineteenth century in Sankt Gallen.

The relatively slow industrialization of the country and the fact that a large part of the companies existing at that time were privately owned by individuals or families were the main reasons for the late development of the Swiss stock exchanges. Only at the beginning of the twentieth century did trading at the stock exchanges expand. However, the Swiss stock exchanges did not have any international reputation before World War II. With the development and expansion of the Swiss financial market in the 1950s and 1960s the Swiss stock exchange expanded too and today it is one of the leading stock exchanges in Europe.

The Swiss stock exchange is divided into eight different marketplaces, Zurich, Basle, Geneva, Lausanne, Berne, Sankt Gallen, Chur, and Neuchâtel. Only the stock exchanges in Zurich, Basle, and Geneva have an international character. All the other stock exchanges are of solely local importance. The organization and functioning of the Zurich, Basle, and Geneva stock exchanges differ only slightly. There-

EXHIBIT 5 PUBLIC ISSUES OF SHARES (in millions of Swiss francs), INTEREST RATES (in annual percentages), MONEY STOCK, M_1 (annual growth rate)

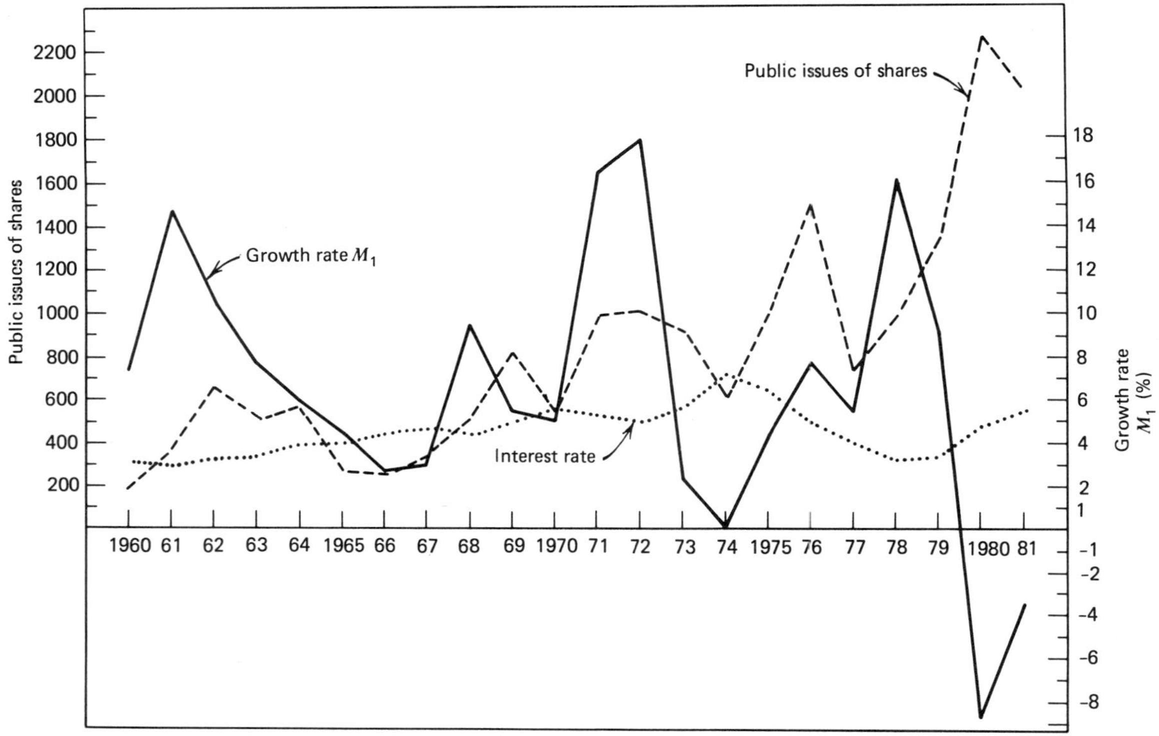

Source. Swiss Nationalbank, *Monthly Bulletin.*

fore, unless otherwise indicated, in the following, reference is made to the Zurich Stock Exchange, which is the most important one.

Originally set up as independent bodies, the stock exchanges of Zurich, Basle, and Geneva are public institutions subject to the legislation of the cantons in which they are located. There is no direct control by the federal government. The stock exchanges in the other towns are independent, private institutions.

OVER-THE-COUNTER TRADING. Not all shares fulfill the conditions for admittance at the stock exchanges. This is certainly true when a company does not publish a statement of accounts or an annual report, or when shares have been issued by a private placing. Sometimes companies for tax reasons do not apply for listing. The shares of smaller and medium-sized companies are usually traded over the counter. Sometimes listed shares are also traded over the counter.

Trading Outside Official Trading Hours. Before the official trading at the stock exchange starts, a "pre–stock exchange trading" takes place, usually at the same building. Sometimes securities are traded after the official trading hours. The volume of shares traded in such a manner often is considerable but not as voluminous as on the official stock exchange. Since there is no official price list for this market, some of the banks specializing in over-the-counter trading publish price lists on a regular basis.

Trading Within the Banking System. Shares that are not traded at some special trading place can be traded by telephone. Banks with some knowledge of the market can trade shares that are only very limited in number or are in demand by investors only from time to time. This market is not very efficient and for that reason offer and bid prices can differ considerably. The market prices of such shares sometimes fluctuate considerably.

To some extent there exists also a form of **over-the-counter trading** in which the bank acts like the stock exchange. This means that the bank compensates purchases and sales of shares ordered by its own clientele. This kind of share trading is common among bigger banks. In this case the stock exchange is used as a clearing place for the shares not available from a client's portfolio within the bank.

THE ZURICH STOCK EXCHANGE

The Zurich Stock Exchange is the most important market for the trading of shares in Switzerland. In 1981 about 62% of the total securities traded at this stock exchange were shares. Exhibit 6 shows that in no other European country is the trading of shares as important for the stock exchange as in Switzerland.

MEMBERS AND AGENTS OF THE STOCK EXCHANGE. At present the Zurich Stock Exchange has 24 members, which are banks or brokerage firms (among them also is one foreign—U.S.—institution) authorized to deal. At the same time over-the-counter dealers have reached a total of 163. Only the 24 members of the Zurich Stock Exchange are allowed to trade securities at the stock exchange. They are the only recognized and authorized stock brokers.

The members of the Zurich Stock Exchange are appointed by the cantonal gov-

EXHIBIT 6 SECURITIES TRADED AT THE ZURICH STOCK EXCHANGE IN 1981

Stock Exchange	Value of Securities Traded (in million U.S.$)	Sales	
		Shares (in Percentages)	Bonds (in Percentages)
London	223,039	15.7	84.3
Zurich	35,038	61.9	38.1
Paris	25,524	48.1	51.9
Frankfurt	19,146	36.3	63.7
Amsterdam	11,176	42.6	57.4

Source. The Zurich Stock Exchange, *Annual Report*, 1981.

ernment with the advice of the Cantonal Advisory Commission on Securities Trading, the Cantonal Securities Trading Commission, and the Executive Committee of the Members of the Zurich Stock Exchange. The task of the members of the Zurich Stock Exchange is to draw up stock exchange rules as well as the regulation and conditions for listing. The Executive Committee is responsible for the running of the daily business.

The Executive Committee, which is composed of seven members, decides on the listing of shares subject to a veto of the cantonal government. The Court of Arbitration consists of several members of the stock exchange and is presided over by a judge appointed by the cantonal government. Disputes arising between members of the stock exchange have to be settled by the Court of Arbitration. The supervision and the functioning of the stock exchange are controlled by the cantonal Securities Trading Commission. Its members are public officials appointed by the cantonal government. The Cantonal Advisory Commission on Securities Trading is appointed by the cantonal government and has exclusively advisory functions.

At the stock exchange only its members can trade shares. Since these members are exclusively banks or brokerage firms, they must appoint their own representatives, who have access to the floor with a special permit. Stock exchange dealers can effect transactions in their own name. To become a stock exchange member, the applicant is not required to have special qualifications besides integrity, full enjoyment of civil rights, Swiss citizenship, and sufficient professional qualification with several years' experience in banking or stockbroking in Switzerland.

As already mentioned, in Zurich there exists also an over-the-counter market. On this market unlisted shares are traded. This market often has the function of a testing ground for shares prior to their introduction on the official market. A growing number of dealers (163 in 1981), among whom are domestic and foreign banks and private dealers, have access to trading on that market (see Exhibit 7).

FUNCTIONING OF THE STOCK EXCHANGE. On the stock exchange both cash as well as forward transactions are effected. However, there is no separation of the security trading according to these different types of transactions. Both types of transactions are effected at the same time. The largest share of the trading at the stock exchanges is effected as a **cash transaction** with settlement on the next working day following the transaction for registered securities and delivery of securities within the fifth stock exchange session following the transaction for bearer securities.

EXHIBIT 7 MEMBERS OF THE ZURICH STOCK EXCHANGE

Year	Members	Representatives	Over-the-Counter Dealers
1884	13	—	—
1902	16	—	30
1930	34	119	32
1950	22	102	45
1960	25	128	59
1970	26	140	105
1980	24	176	157
1981	24	175	163

Source. Zurich Stock Exchange, *Annual Report.*, 1981.

Forward transactions are mainly effected in domestic and foreign shares. Usually delivery and settlement of the shares are at the end of the month in accordance with the stock exchange calendar.

A third type of transaction is that of **option contracts.** In an option contract the buyer pays a premium that gives the right to withdraw from the purchase at no other cost but the premium. There are, however, no standardized option contracts like on foreign stock exchanges.

Different kinds of securities are traded at the stock exchange. As can be seen in Exhibit 8, domestic as well as foreign securities are listed. Even though the number of domestic shares is considerably smaller than the number of domestic bonds, the market value of domestic shares is about the same as the market value of domestic bonds. For the different bonds and shares, minimum amounts for stock exchange transactions are fixed by the members of the stock exchange.

Orders are given "at best," "at limited prices," or in the customer's best interest, and are executed either at a single price or at prices obtained during the session following the time at which the order was given. If validity of the order is not indicated, the order is valid for one session only. Orders given at limited prices are executed gross of brokerage commission.

At the stock exchange prices are fixed exclusively by calling out—a stock exchange official calls out the name of a share or a bond. Immediately after calling out the stock exchange dealer makes a bid on the basis of the transactions he or she handles. This can give rise to several prices, which are automatically registered by stock exchange officials and entered on the official list. The list is published daily by the Cantonal Securities Trading Commission after one of its members has ascertained that the prices have been determined conscientiously in accordance with the law of the security market.

The published list gives information about the bond and share prices. It contains information about all the prices established during the stock exchange session, like the bid and offer prices, the prices of the previous day, and high and low prices of the current year. It further gives details of the nominal value of shares and the amount of dividend for the last three years expressed as a percentage. Prices are marked by special symbols to indicate the type of transactions made (i.e., cash transactions or future delivery contracts). In the list are also printed the bid and offer prices of

EXHIBIT 8 NUMBER AND MARKET VALUE OF LISTED SECURITIES 1977–81
(in million Swiss francs)

	Bonds					Shares				
Year	Domestic	Market Value	Foreign	Market Value	Total	Domestic	Market Value	Foreign	Market Shares	Total
1877	34		1		35	42		6	48	83
1890	41		23		64	65		8	73	137
1900	93		24		117	69		13	82	199
1910	202		76		278	102		34	136	414
1920	337		89		426	80		40	120	546
1930					482			152	634	
1940	329		103		432	92		41	133	565
1950	276		95		371	87		38	125	469
1960	398		137		535	98		60	158	693
1970	971		253		1,224	130		91	221	1,445
1975	1,454	56.3	350	19.4	1,804	153	43.2	136	289	2,093
1976	1,541	62.2	376	24.1	1,917	156	49.4	138	294	2,211
1977	1,556	71.5	390	26.4	1,946	167	59.3	153	320	2,266
1978	1,454	69.2	385	26.7	1,839	167	61.3	160	327	2,166
1979	1,348	64.1	356	25.1	1,704	171	68.8	163	334	2,038
1980	1,412	68.1	397	27.3	1,809	176	75.6	166	342	2,151
1981	1,464	70.3	460	31.3	1,924	183	67.8	168	351	2,275

Source. The Zurich Stock Exchange, *Annual Report*, 1981.

foreign currencies, the list of declared dividends, and any notice of the Executive Committee of the stock exchange.

LISTING OF SHARES. Prior to official listing on the stock exchange, the shares and all the other securities have to fulfill certain conditions that are laid down in the listing rules of the Zurich Stock Exchange. The following procedure must be followed when applying for listing of domestic shares.

The application must be submitted to the Executive Committee. The introductory prospectus should include all the information that is needed to evaluate the share in question. It must be clear if the shares involved are in their definitive form or whether provisional certificates have been issued. The names and numbers of the newspapers in which the prospectus was published have to be known as well as the undertaking by the company to supply the Executive Committee regularly with the annual report. The company has to make announcements available to its shareholders. The listing takes place only if it can be assured that a permanent trading of the share involved is possible.

On the basis of the required information the Executive Committee proceeds with the examination of the application. When approved by the Executive Committee the application is displayed on the floor of the stock exchange for four days. If no objection is raised within that term by members of the stock exchange and if the cantonal government has not availed itself of its veto, the security will be officially listed.

When a foreign company applies for the listing of its shares, nearly the same preliminary conditions as those for domestic securities have to be fulfilled, except that the total nominal value of the shares for which the listing is requested should reach at least SF1 million. The application must be accompanied by a declaration of the Swiss National Bank stating that the bank does not object to the listing of the foreign securities on the stock exchange.

The decision on the listing of foreign equities is taken by an organization that is composed of members of the important stock exchanges in Switzerland as well as representatives of the federal government. This federal committee and the Swiss National Bank guarantee that all relevant economic factors affecting the future value of the company issuing the shares to be listed have been checked. The decision of these two bodies, if unfavorable, binds all Swiss stock exchanges. However, if the decision is favorable, the Executive Committee of the stock exchange is not bound to approve the listing and still has to examine the application. In particular cases the federal committee has the power to decide to list a foreign equity.

INVESTORS IN THE STOCK EXCHANGE. Contrary to regulations in other countries, Swiss residents are completely free to purchase foreign securities, whether they are listed on Swiss stock exchanges or not. This is one of the reasons why foreign companies raise funds in Switzerland and list their shares on the Swiss stock exchange.

In principle, foreign residents have the same rights regarding purchase and sale transactions at the stock exchange or on the Swiss capital market outside the stock exchange. However, in the past, during the fixed exchange rate period and as a result of the economic situation, the purchase of Swiss securities by foreigners has been severely restricted by the Swiss National Bank. Within the foreseeable future the imposition of a similar regulation does not seem very likely.

The dealers and the officials working on the stock exchange have to be paid. The floor, the offices, and all the technical equipment of the stock exchange have to be financed. Therefore, a brokerage fee is charged to customers. New brokerage rates came into force at the beginning of March 1982. Since that date the following basic commission rates are charged on Swiss stock exchanges.

Bonds	Domestic, 0.375% of market value and accrued interest
	Foreign, 0.5% of market value and accrued interest
Shares	Domestic and foreign up to SF150 a share, 1% of market value
	Exceeding SF150 a share, 0.625% of market value
	Minimum brokerage fee, SF10 for each transaction

Federal and cantonal stamp duty and stock exchange commission fee

Domestic bonds and shares, SF0.90 for each SF1,000
Foreign bonds and shares, SF1.65 for each SF1,000

As can be seen from the different commission fees, the rates on domestic securities are slightly lower than on foreign securities.

All income from capital invested in Switzerland (dividends on shares, interest payments, etc.) are subject to a 35% withholding tax, which can be offset by Swiss residents against their tax liabilities. Residents of countries having a double-taxation agreement with Switzerland can claim back at least a portion of this tax (see Exhibit 9). All other foreign residents have to pay this tax.

In the case of incorporation or in the case of new issues of shares, a stamp tax must be paid, for which companies have the right of partial or total recovery from shareholders. Furthermore, when a bank or a syndicate of banks makes a firm commitment for the purchase of issued shares a federal tax is paid on the amount of the transaction.

DEVELOPMENT OF THE SWISS EQUITY MARKET

There are no broad statistics available on the Swiss equity market. The data published by the Swiss National Bank refer only to new public issues of shares and to some new private placings. A further source of information can be found in the publications of the stock exchange. Each stock exchange in its annual report publishes figures on trading volume, share prices, listed securities, and the like. However, trading of shares outside the stock exchange is completely unknown. Despite this unsatisfactory situation the following focuses on two main points: the Swiss market volume and price movements.

VOLUME OF THE EQUITY MARKET. To demonstrate the importance of the Swiss financial market in an international comparison, people very often use the trading volume at the Zurich Stock Exchange. However, the trading volume as calculated at the Zurich Stock Exchange can be misleading. First, the trading volume is not separated by types of securities; therefore, the trading volume of shares can be estimated only with the help of the number of quotations.

Second, the trading volume published by the Zurich Stock Exchange overesti-

EXHIBIT 9 RELIEF FROM SWISS WITHHOLDING TAX (35%) APPLICABLE TO NONRESIDENTS

Country with Double-Taxation Agreement	Dividends on shares		Interest payments	
	Relief[a] (in Percentage)	Net Tax[b] (in Percentage)	Relief[a] (in Percentage)	Net Tax[b] (in Percentage)
Australia	20.0	15.0	25.0	10.0
Austria	30.0	5.0	30.0	5.0
Belgium	20.0	15.0	25.0	10.0
Canada	20.0	15.0	20.0	15.0
Denmark	35.0	0.0	35.0	0.0
Finland	25.0	10.0	35.0	0.0
France	30.0	5.0	25.0	10.0
Great Britain	20.0	15.0	35.0	0.0
Ireland	25.0	10.0	35.0	0.0
Italy	20.0	15.0	22.5	12.5
Japan	20.0	15.0	25.0	10.0
Norway	30.0	5.0	30.0	5.0
South Africa	27.5	7.5	0.0	35.0
Spain	20.0	15.0	25.0	10.0
Sweden	30.0	5.0	30.0	5.0
The Netherlands	20.0	15.0	30.0	5.0
United States	20.0	15.0	30.0	5.0
West Germany	20.0	15.0	35.0	0.0

[a]A claim for tax refund must be filed with the tax authorities at the taxpayer's place of residence.
[b]The remainder is allowed against local income tax in a majority of countries listed.

mates the volume of the market. It is not the trading volume of the stock exchange exclusively, but also all securities on the Canton Zurich capital market on which a cantonal stamp duty has to be paid. This means that each transaction on which a cantonal stamp duty has to be paid, even when it takes place outside the stock exchange, is included in the trading volume of the Zurich Stock Exchange. But this is not the full story; each transaction is counted twice because cantonal stamp duties have to be paid on purchase as well as on sale transactions. Stamp duties have to be paid also on new issues of shares, which in recent years have been quite numerous.

Despite these negative influences on the statistics, the trading volume is used to discuss some aspects of the equity market. To eliminate double counting the published trading volume is divided into two parts. It is assumed that only about 60% of the total trading volume is transactions in shares. This figure is taken from the number of quoted domestic and foreign shares on the stock exchange (see Exhibit 10).

The estimated volume of the equity market rose from SF6 billion in 1960 to about SF44 billion in 1981, nearly eight times larger than that of 20 years ago. Noteworthy is the increase since 1970. In this period the volume climbed from about SF11 billion to SF44 billion. This considerable expansion of the volume of the equity market was possible because in the period under observation the total monetary sector was also growing fast. Total assets of all banks in Switzerland rose from SF60 billion in 1960

EXHIBIT 10 TRADING VOLUME OF SHARES, 1960–81 (in million Swiss francs)

Year	Total Trading Volume of Shares and Bonds (Official Statistics)	Estimated Trading Volume of Shares
1960	19,483	5,845
1961	23,943	7,182
1962	21,343	6,403
1963	19,022	5,706
1964	19,993	5,998
1965	19,045	5,713
1966	20,342	6,102
1967	25,951	7,785
1968	41,450	12,435
1969	42,242	12,672
1970	35,702	10,710
1971	54,516	16,354
1972	74,003	22,201
1973	65,407	19,622
1974	58,583	17,575
1975	82,941	24,882
1976	105,476	31,642
1977	111,995	33,598
1978	99,220	29,766
1979	115,553	34,666
1980	132,597	39,779
1981	147,104	44,131

Source. Zurich Stock Exchange, *Annual Report*, 1981.

to SF490 billion in 1980. This means that the security market was increasing at the same rate as the banking sector.

Of some interest is the annual growth of the equity market. As can be seen in Exhibit 11, the growth rate of the equity market fluctuated quite heavily. However, this was more or less in line with the liquidity situation in Switzerland as well as with the economic development. But Exhibit 11 also shows that even during periods of liquidity squeeze and economic slowdown, the market grew at a high rate. This is mainly due to a more frequent issuing of shares, which had a strong impact on the share market.

As is already well known, on the Swiss equity market a relatively large share of traded equities is of foreign origin. In recent years about 60% of total quoted shares at the Zurich Stock Exchange were foreign shares. In the 1960s and early 1970s this ratio of foreign shares was even higher. The most important countries in the Swiss equity market are the United States, Canada, West Germany, and The Netherlands. Domestic shares traded on the Swiss equity market originate from different business sectors. However, most important are the equities of industrial and transportation companies (see Exhibit 12).

EXHIBIT 11 GROWTH OF THE EQUITY MARKET, 1960–81

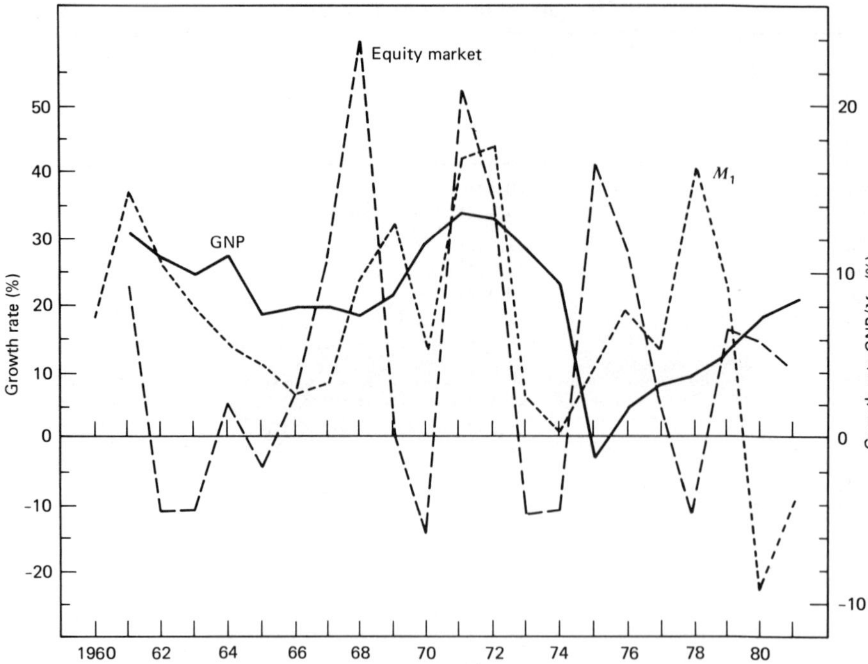

Sources. Swiss Nationalbank, *Monthly Bulletin*; Federal Office of Statistics, *National Income Statistics*; The Zurich Stock Exchange, Annual Report.

Note. GNP = gross national product (at current prices); M_1 = money stock.

EXHIBIT 12 NUMBER OF QUOTED SHARES AT THE ZURICH STOCK EXCHANGE

Sector and Country	1980	1981	Percentage Distribution, Average (1980–81)
Domestic shares	71,611	66,193	39.2
Banks	11,845	12,324	6.9
Finance companies	20,235	17,766	10.8
Insurance	6,550	6,648	3.8
Industrial transportation	29,041	25,564	15.5
Trusts	3,940	3,891	2.2
Foreign shares	112,810	101,072	60.8
United States, Canada	77,180	72,374	42.6
West Germany	7,890	7,090	4.3
Other countries	27,740	21,608	13.9
Total	184,421	167,265	100

Source. Zurich Stock Exchange, *Annual Report*, 1981.

DEVELOPMENT OF THE STOCK PRICE INDEX. Stock price indices are the most commonly used economic indicators. Therefore, there not only exists widespread literature about stock price indices, but there are also different kinds of indices available. Switzerland, which is a rather small economy, uses three different related indices. They are composed of a different selection of equities and calculated by different computation methods. The existing indices are examined first and afterward the stock price index of recent years is discussed.

Selection of a Representative Stock Price Index. The Swiss National Bank (SNB) publishes a stock price index every week that is computed on a movable base. At the end of 1981 the SNB index included the market prices of 121 different shares, which are listed at each of the Swiss stock exchanges. The aggregate index is subdivided into six partial indices. The total industrial share price index, which includes 49 names, is divided into five partial industrial share price indices.

Credit Suisse also supplies the capital market with a stock price index. This index is published daily and is computed on a movable base. The Credit Suisse stock price index includes 25 different shares only. From time to time the weights of the individual shares in the index are adjusted. A breakdown of the index according to individual business sectors is also computed.

The stock price index of the Swiss National Bank and that of Credit Suisse are not used very often in security trading. More important seems to be the stock price index computed by the *Swiss Bank Corporation Scheizerischer Bankverein (SBV)*. This so-called SBV index covers the prices of 90 different equities. In the index each individual share has the weight of the market value of the company. Apart from the aggregate index, the Swiss Bank Corporation works out a share price index for the banking sector, the insurance companies, the engineering sector, the chemical industry, the consumer sector, and power plants.

The index computed by the Swiss National Bank dates from 1966. Thus comparison of the three indices is possible only for the period since 1966. The development of the three indices can be found in Exhibit 13. Although each index has its own characteristics, they show nearly the same picture. The upward and downward movements are almost uniform and the turning points in the share price developments are indicated similarly. However, the intensity of the individual swings can differ, because of the various methods of computation.

Stock Prices in Recent Years. Sometimes stock market price trends are used as indicators of economic activity. Some argue that stock market price fluctuations are dominated by noneconomic factors, especially psychological influences. On the other hand, nobody would deny that economic factors might have a strong impact on the pattern of share price movements. Thus, it should be possible to formulate a hypothesis as to how economic effects influence the stock market. This has been done for Switzerland and some of those factors have in fact been identified through empirical tests. Some of the effects causing variations in the stock price index are discussed below.

Generally, the market value of a share (and consequently also the stock price index) is the result of expected future profits of the company. However, expected future profits are difficult to work out. One could argue that the share price index depends on expected future economic conditions. Factors affecting expectations about the future business environment thus have to be taken into consideration.

EXHIBIT 13 STOCK MARKET INDICES FOR SWITZERLAND, 1966–81 (end 1966 = 100)

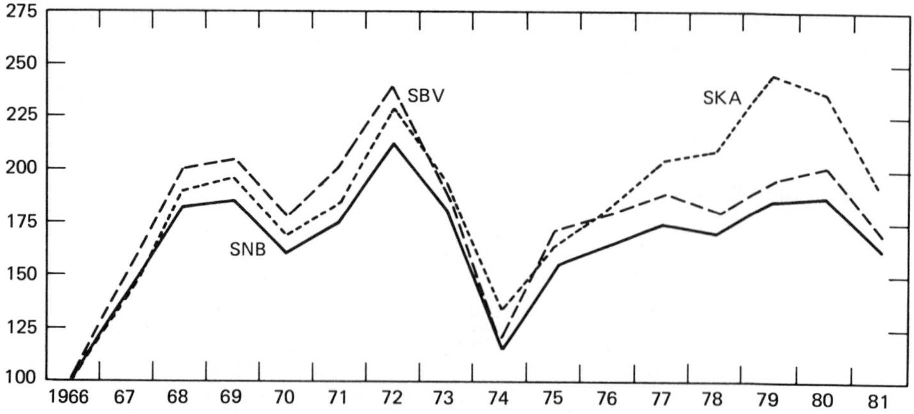

Source. Zurich Stock Exchange, *Annual Report*.

Note. SNB = Swiss Nationalbank; SKA = Crédit Suisse; SBV = Swiss Bank Corporation.

Variables to focus on are the growth rate of the gross national product, the variations of the money supply M_1—currency in circulation and demand deposits with banks of the private nonbanking sector—the fluctuations in interest rates, price level increases, and inflationary expectations. Influences on the Swiss equity market are identified in Exhibit 14 (see Rutz, 1973).

Not every variable listed in Exhibit 14 has a direct impact on the stock market index. As pointed out in an empirical study, statistically significant influences can be found only for the gross national product (GNP) growth rate, the variation of the money supply (M_1), and the U.S. share price index (Dow Jones Industrials). Interest rate and inflation rate changes also have influences on the share price index, but these effects are already included in the growth of the money supply (see Rutz and Zehnder, 1977).

Exhibits 15, 16, and 17 show the performance of the Swiss stock price index and some of the variables influencing the equity market. Exhibit 15 demonstrates the

EXHIBIT 14

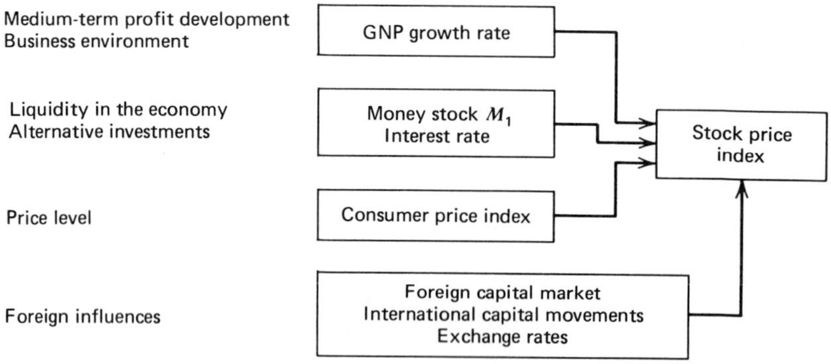

EXHIBIT 15 INTERNATIONAL COMPARISON OF THE STOCK MARKET INDICES, 1966–81 (end 1966 = 100)

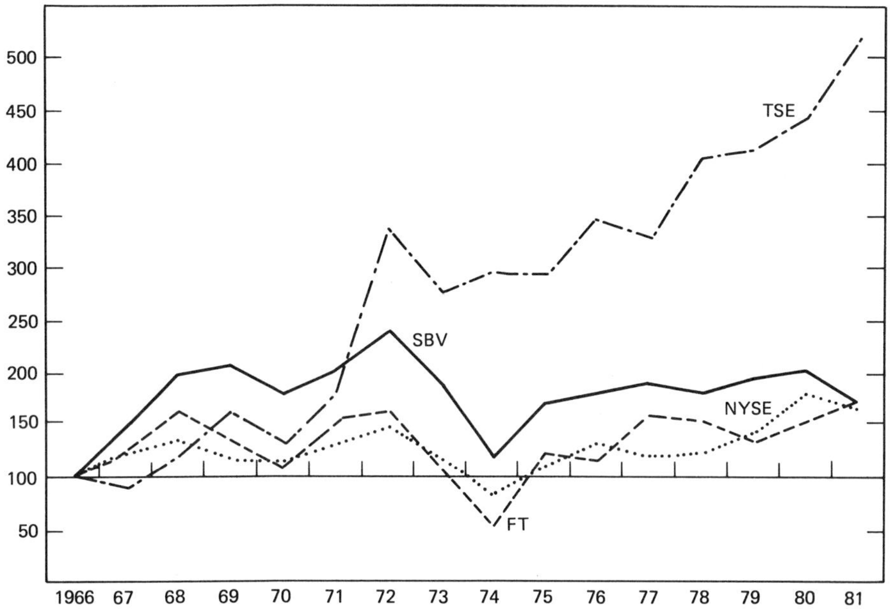

Source. Zurich Stock Exchange, *Annual Reports*.

Note. SBV = Zurich Stock Exchange; NYSE = New York Stock Exchange; FT = London Stock Exchange, Financial Time Index; TSE = Tokyo Stock Exchange.

performance of the Swiss stock price index in comparison to some of the world's leading stock exchanges. With the exception of the Tokyo Stock Exchange, since 1966 the various stock price indices had about the same pattern. Nevertheless, during the 1960s share prices in Switzerland followed a more favorable development than at the three other centers.

At the beginning of the 1970s, when the Bretton Woods monetary system suffered its first shock, stock price indices all over the world reached new heights. But as can be seen in the chart, this upswing did not last very long. On the contrary, the final breakdown of the Bretton Woods monetary system in 1973 and the first oil price hike not only struck the real economies of the Western Hemisphere but also had a strong effect on the stock market. In Switzerland the SBV index fell from 406 at the end of 1972 to 203 at the end of 1974. Thus there was a reduction of the share prices of exactly 50% within two years. Only the stock markets in London and Australia suffered the same or an even sharper drop than that in Zurich.

After the 1974–75 crisis the stock market regained its vitality. However, with the exception of the Tokyo Stock Exchange, none of the leading European or U.S. indices reached the same height as at the beginning of the 1970s. The excellent performance of the Japanese economy during the 1970s is the main reason for the extraordinary development of the Japanese share prices.

Exhibit 16 illustrates the relatively strong influences of the business cycle on the share price index. It also demonstrates that the SBV index is a leading indicator with

EXHIBIT 16 THE STOCK MARKET INDEX (SBV Index), ECONOMIC ACTIVITY IN SWITZERLAND (real GNP growth rate), AND U.S. INDUSTRIAL SHARE PRICES (Dow Jones), 1960–81

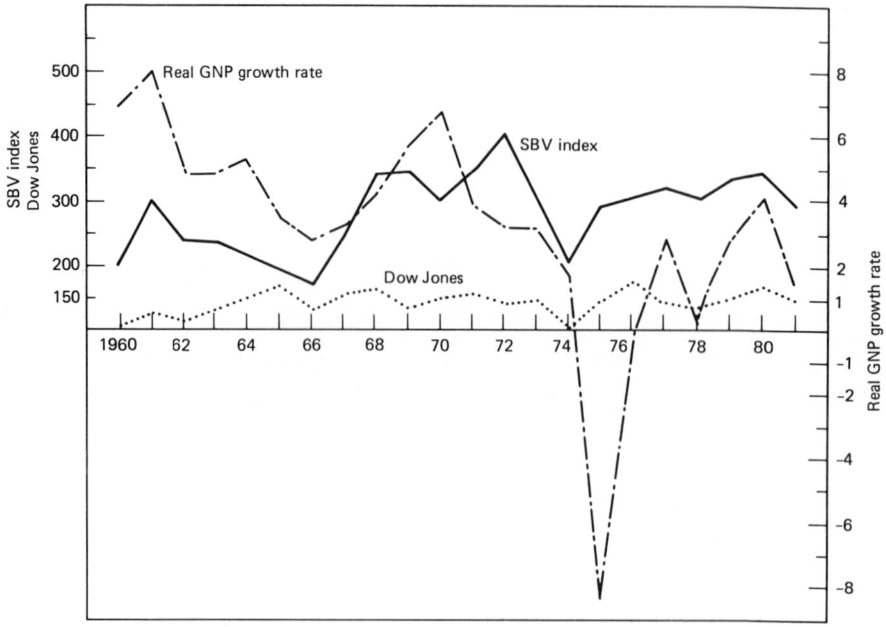

Sources. Zurich Stock Exchange, *Annual Report*; Federal Office of Statistics, *National Income Statistics*.

respect to economic growth. Not clear is the influence of the Dow Jones index. It seems, however, that some of the peaks and troughs in the Swiss share price index have been accentuated through the movement on the U.S. stock market. However, in the long run, the New York Stock Exchange does not seem to have significant influence on the Swiss stock market.

More interesting is the short-term influence of the New York Stock Exchange on the Swiss share prices. The daily fluctuation at the New York Stock Exchange has a very strong impact on price movements in Switzerland. Very often those effects are caused by certain somewhat unclear expectations about the economic future, inflation, or expected monetary policy. Exhibit 17 shows the relationship between these two indices in the last three years. The connection between the two is somewhat stronger than in the long-term comparison.

A dominant influence on the stock market results from the variation in the money supply (M_1). The supply of liquidity through the Swiss National Bank is crucial for the development in the capital market and therefore also the equity market.

Most remarkable is the downward movement of the SNB index in fhe period 1961 to 1966. (See Exhibit 18.) This was in line with the reduction of the growth rate of the real gross national product and money supply. Because during the period of fixed exchange rates fluctuation in the money stock was dominated by international capital movements, the reduction of the stock price index was also under the influence of

EXHIBIT 17 SHORT-TERM MOVEMENTS OF THE SWISS AND U.S. SHARE PRICE INDICES, 1979–81 (1958 = 100)

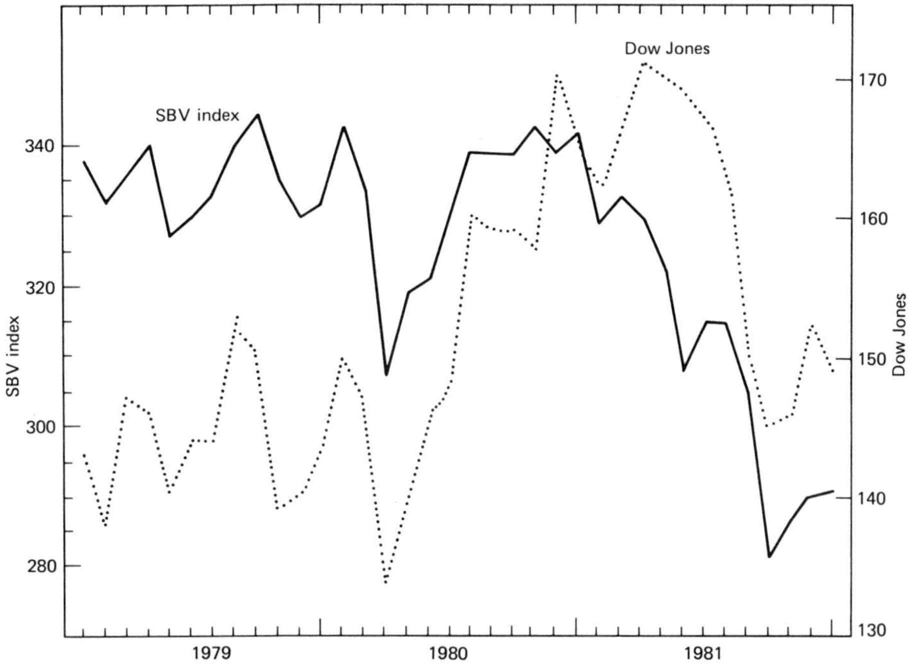

Source. Zurich Stock Exchange, *Annual Report.*

foreign factors. Actually the spring of 1962 saw the start of the downward movement of the SBV index; several crises in the international monetary system reinforced the uncertainty in the stock market.

In 1966 a strong cyclical upswing of business activity began in the United States. This had positive effects on the world economy and therefore also on the stock markets. The Swiss stock price index rose from 170 points in 1966 to 406 in 1972. In this year as well as in 1971 the money supply was excessive. As in former years a huge capital import in 1971–72 was the cause of this situation. At this time the exchange markets as well as the capital markets were highly volatile. In August 1971 the president of the United States suspended the obligation of the United States to convert gold into dollars. This was the beginning of the demonetization of gold and the start of a new international monetary system.

Huge capital inflows caused an economic upswing, especially in the housing construction sector, creating an excess demand leading to an acceleration in the rate of inflation. Inflation at the end of 1973 reached its highest level (11.4% annually) since World War II.

The oil price shock in 1973, the high inflation rates, and the restrictive monetary policy caused one of the most severe recessions in Switzerland. In 1975 the real GNP fell by 7.7%. It is quite clear that during these years the equity market too suffered under precarious economic conditions.

EXHIBIT 18 STOCK MARKET INDEX (SBV) AND THE GROWTH OF THE MONEY STOCK M_1, 1960–81

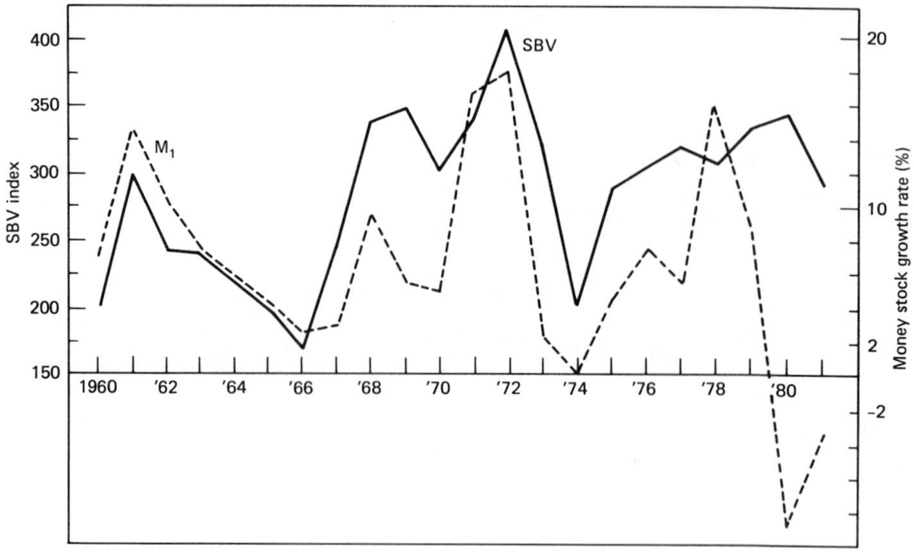

Sources. Swiss Nationalbank, *Monthly Bulletin*; Zurich Stock Exchange, *Annual Report*.

From 1975 to 1979 the stock market moved upward again. Especially in 1975, the price development contrasted with the slumps in previous years, which was very much to the liking of investors and traders. During 1975 the stock price index rose from 203 at the beginning of the year to 289 at year-end. This rise of 42% was the highest since 1967. However, the index was still considerably below the peak of 406 at the end of 1972.

In 1975 some modifications of the Swiss stock market took place. The "big three" banks issued new restrictedly transferable registered shares. Unlike most other Swiss companies, these banks previously had only bearer shares outstanding. The Swiss federal government recommended that they issue registered shares, in order to enable the banks to maintain control of their ownership.

The battle against inflationary price movements turned out to be successful in 1976. The inflation rate fell from 11% to 1.3%. The low interest rate stimulated the capital market and thus the trading at the Zurich Stock Exchange reached an unprecedented volume of more than SF100 billion. Stock prices were not subject to extreme fluctuations. At the end of the year, the stock price index was only 5% higher than it was 12 months earlier.

In 1977 money and capital markets were characterized by low interest rates, increasing volatility of the Swiss franc exchange rate, and by the Credit Suisse Chiasso affair. Nevertheless, the relatively good condition of the Swiss economy had positive effects on the stock market. The trading volume increased again considerably and the stock price index rose once more by 5%. In this year the Zurich Stock Exchange celebrated its centennial.

Unfortunately, 1978 was a rather bad year for the stock exchange. Not only did the trading volume fall by 12% and stock prices decline by 3.4%, but for the first time since 1950 the number of securities listed on the Zurich Stock Exchange declined in the course of the year. The main reason for this development was the revaluation of the Swiss franc. As the Swiss franc exchange rate against the U.S. dollar reached SF1.80 late in February 1978, the Swiss National Bank, together with the federal government, imposed a ban on investment in Swiss securities by persons living outside the country.

Regulations were very stringent. Foreigners selling Swiss shares or bonds were not allowed to reinvest this capital in the stock market. Since they were not allowed to have a banking account in Switzerland, the only possibility was to export the capital. The investment ban was relaxed on two occasions during 1978 and lifted in January 1979.

The investment ban had significant effects on the equity market but completely missed the main objective, namely, the stabilization of the Swiss franc exchange rate. Therefore, the Swiss National Bank had to intervene very heavily in the exchange market, though the growth rate of the money supply (M_1) reached 16.2% (year average) instead of 5%, the goal set for 1978. But, despite the excessive liquidity supply, the equity market's performance was, due to the investment ban, rather less encouraging.

After the setback in 1978 there was a new start in 1979. Due to satisfactory economic conditions as well as optimistic forecasts, the excessive liquidity in the banking system, and the abrogation of the investment ban in January, the year 1979 was quite favorable for the stock market. The stock price index rose by 7.8% until the end of the year. However, the index reached its peak of 350 points in early October, which was a six-year high. Although the 8% price increase was a good result, it was not overwhelming, considering that the liquidity situation and economic prospects should have allowed a much better performance.

Switzerland's economy performed unexpectedly well during 1980. However, the inflation rate that had already by 1979 started to climb rose to 7.5% in the course of 1981. The second oil price hike in 1979 and the excess supply of liquidity caused this price development. As a consequence, the Swiss National Bank and the central banks in other countries introduced restrictive monetary policies. Thus short-term as well as long-term interest rates started to climb to new heights. However, there was not only a rise in interest rates but they also became extremely volatile in the years 1980 and 1981. In the United States the prime rate climbed to 21.5% at the beginning of 1981. Although Swiss interest rates also rose during this period, there was still a considerable difference between Swiss and U.S. interest rates. Thus during both years there was a substantial capital outflow from Switzerland into dollar-denominated instruments.

The increase in interest rates and in inflation rates, the restrictive monetary policy, and the first signs of a worldwide economic recession had negative impacts on the equity markets. Although security trading on the Zurich Stock Exchange reached a new peak in 1981, the performance of the price index was discouraging. After the small increase of 3.4% in 1980, the stock price index dropped by 15% in 1981. Only in France and in Australia were the setbacks deeper than in Switzerland. However, with the exception of Canada, Tokyo, and Brussels, all leading stock exchanges suffered considerable price drops in 1981.

CONCLUSION

In Switzerland, as well as in several other countries, the equity market is no longer the number one financing instrument for companies. Additionally, in periods of high and volatile interest rates investors have preferred short-term time deposits to equities. Such a development certainly is not good for industry because lending costs become extremely high, and this in turn reduces the incentives to make new investment. After the experience of the 1970s one can hope that central banks will try to fight inflation and follow a stable monetary policy. In the longer perspective, this is in the best interest of companies as well as investors in the capital market. It also guarantees foreign borrowers and investors in Switzerland that exchange rates will not fluctuate unduly.

REFERENCES

Rutz A., "Der Kurs schweizerischer Aktien im letzten Jahrzehnt: Regressionstechnische Bestimmung möglicher Einflussgrössen," *Schweizerische Zeitschrift für Volkswirtschaft und Statistik,* July (1973).

Rutz, A. and R. Zehnder, "Eine spektraltechnische Schätzung zum Kursverlauf der Schweizer Aktien," Universität Basel Discussion Paper 14, 1977.

SECTION **6.7**

JAPAN: EQUITY MARKETS

CONTENTS

SECTION 6.7

JAPAN: EQUITY MARKETS

Paul H. Aron
Laurie J. Aron

Soon after its establishment in 1868, the Meiji government recognized the need for a securities exchange to provide a secondary market for the government bonds issued to commute feudal stipends. The initial attempt to establish a securities market in 1873 on the model of the London Stock Exchange was stillborn; brokers who had already emerged objected to the proposed British-style jobbers' monopoly of trading for their own account and urged rules permitting greater speculation. During the Tokugawa Shogunate there were exchanges for gold and silver and commodities such as rice. The rice exchanges provided the model for the Stock Exchange Regulations issued by the government in 1878, on the basis of which a group of dealers who had already organized group trading in a sugar warehouse established the **Tokyo Stock Exchange (TSE)** at Kabuto-cho, its present location. The TSE was a private, profit-making joint stock company. Government bonds were traded daily and equities twice monthly. Initially, only four equities were traded: the First National Bank, two rice exchanges, and the TSE, which, incidentally, remained a trading favorite until 1943. By 1886, five additional exchanges were founded under these regulations.

In the first 10 years of existence, the TSE was dominated by bond trading—at first only in government bonds, and later railway bonds too. The first Japanese joint stock companies were primarily banks, which constituted 69% of total capital in 1884 and 36% in 1893. Beginning in 1880 joint stock firms were established in industry and commerce and the volume of shares traded rose from 11,798 in 1879 to 1,278,579 in 1887.

After the Sino-Japanese War of 1894–1895 and the Russo-Japanese War of 1904–1905 Japan experienced the classic Industrial Revolution. The Zaibatsu, the privately owned holding companies, dominated large sectors of industry and derived their capital either by internal growth or by bank loans without the medium of a stock exchange. The Japanese stock market was dominated by highly speculatiye trading in a few issues and it served only in a limited way as a source of industrial capital. From 1896 to 1914 the number of joint stock companies rose from 2,577 to 7,053 and the amount of paid-up capital rose from Y357 million to Y1,770 million. Public offerings were usually heavily oversubscribed; the 99,000 shares of the South Manchurian Railway offered to the public were 1,077 times oversubscribed.

In 1893 the government's new Exchange Law resulted in a mushrooming number of exchanges. By 1891 there were 137 exchanges, almost all private, profit-making, joint stock companies. By 1899, the government decided to halt this expansion and approved no new stock exchanges, a policy that continued until 1939. In addition, by raising the minimum capitalization and by administrative guidance, the government reduced the number of securities markets to 10 by the end of 1914. Speculative abuses, especially corners, were countered by government action to regulate dealers more strictly and to order timely publication of official quotations and volume. The TSE received almost half of the brokers' commission; in exchange, the TSE guaranteed transactions and had to pay damages for broken contracts.

From 1904 to 1914 the number of stock issues on the TSE rose from 108 to 227, while their capitalization rose from Y442 to Y961 million. From 1914 to 1921 the number of business corporations in Japan increased from 7,000 to 18,000 and capital increased even more, but less than 700 companies raised capital on the TSE. The number of new issues rose from five in 1914 to 235 in 1919; dividends almost doubled and reserves increased 40%. The price of a TSE share, a good market barometer, increased 354% from June 1914 to January 1920, the peak of prices. Volume on the TSE rose from 9.27 million shares in 1914 to 48.86 million in 1921. During this period the corporate dealer emerged and between 1914 and 1920 the number of dealers on the TSE rose from 10 to 50 on the TSE. Commission rates increased, while the brokers' share of commissions rose from 20% to 80%.

The boom in Japan created by World War I changed it from a debtor to a creditor nation; however, it gave way in 1920 to a protracted depression. The Western nations' concentration on the war cut off Japan from foreign manufactured goods and stimulated the development of heavy and chemical industry. At the same time it provided Japan with an opportunity to supply Asian and other markets.

After World War I, despite the loss of markets, the decrease in exports, and an adverse balance of trade, the Japanese tried to maintain and even expand their wartime production level. Bank loans exceeded deposits and money became tight. A stock market crash took place in 1920, but this was merely the beginning of a succession of crises: the bank panic of 1922, the Great Kanto Earthquake of 1923, the financial panic of 1927, and the arrival of the Great Depression from 1929 to 1931. Small recoveries took place between the crises, but Japan remained in a chronic depression. During the 1920s the stock market gradually expanded and the paid-in capital of listed companies grew from Y1, 800 million to Y8, 100 million. The stock market began to supply equity capital, but mainly to the smaller corporations. The long period of stagnation led to further concentration and amalgamation and the Zaibatsu extended its domination of the Japanese economy. The Zaibatsu companies rarely offered their stock for public subscription and instead raised their capital by bank borrowing. As a consequence, market transactions continued to be highly speculative, short-term, and concentrated on a few small issues.

The equity market was by no means unaffected by the quasi-wartime and then wartime economy that emerged after the invasion of Manchuria in 1931, further developed with the war in China beginning in 1937 and the Japanese plunge into World War II. The military industries required capital, and from 1931 to 1937 the equity markets were vital in providing additional capital. In addition, the Zaibatsu companies began to make public offerings, mostly to meet new capital needs and partly to build political support in an atmosphere that was becoming dominated by antibusiness militarists. The New Zaibatsu, companies more closely associated with the militarists and dedicated to arms industries, used the equity market to raise capital, too.

But the outbreak of the China War in 1937 created a need for capital far exceeding the ability of the ordinary capital markets to supply it. The government provided an increasing amount of capital and soon began to regulate and control the flow of funds.

Beginning in 1937 the government established a succession of quasi-public firms to maintain stock prices by purchasing shares in the market. This organization, the Japan Cooperatiye Securities Company, as it was ultimately called, was absorbed by the Wartime Finance Bank. In April 1942 the Wartime Finance Bank was established and largely funded by the government to finance industrial expansion and maintain share price stability. In 1943 all the Japanese stock exchanges were abolished and merged into the Japan Securities Exchange, primarily a government agency. At the same time, the securities companies established so-called investment trusts without any provision for redemption; therefore, they served primarily as a form of compulsory savings. The Wartime Finance Bank continued until June 1945 to buy securities while the Japanese military position was clearly deteriorating.

In order to allocate more labor to military industries, in 1943 the government forced substantial reductions in the number of brokers and their staffs. The members of the TSE declined to the lowest number since 1907. Securities dealers in Tokyo were reduced from 157 to 29 in 1943, while only five underwriters remained by merger—those who today constitute the "Big Four" brokers and the Industrial Bank of Japan. Ultimately, the entire securities community was reduced to a mere arm of government.

The end of the war and the U.S. occupation drastically changed the character of the Japanese stock market. The Holding Company Liquidation Commission (HCLC) received the stock from 30 big holding companies (including the four major Zaibatsu—Mitsui, Mitsubishi, Sumitomo, and Yasuda) and 53 individual members of Zaibatsu families. An additional 50 holding companies were permitted to continue only after divestment had changed their character as holding companies. A study by HCLC indicated that in 1945 the four Zaibatsu held 24.5% of all paidup capital, 49.7% of finance, and 32.4% of heayy industries (the corresponding statistics in 1937 were 10.4%, 22.5% and 14.6%). This prompted a fear of concentration and in 1948 a law excluded members of Zaibatsu families from holding any official positions in Zaibatsu companies.

In 1947 the Securities Liquidation Coordinating Council (SLCC) was established to dispose of the stock that had been transferred to the HCLC and to other liquidating commissions, stock that by this time constituted 40% of all Japanese securities. As part of the Securities Democratization Movement shares were sold first to employees, then to inhabitants of the areas in which the plants were located; the balance was sold on the securities market.

This process was complicated by the absence of an organized securities market in the years immediately after the end of the war. The stock exchanges were closed on 9 August 1945 and SCAP (the Allied occupying authority) forbade their reopening. Over-the-counter trading resumed almost immediately after the war. Public stock offerings were resumed in April 1946. By the end of 1948 group trading within a single room was organized in Tokyo and spread to six other major financial centers within less than a year. In the immediate postwar years, however, over-the-counter trading, group trading, and sales of new issues were quite modest.

The securities markets were completely reorganized under the Securities and Exchange Law (SEL), enacted in May 1948 and largely patterned on U.S. law, partly by SCAP insistence. The SCAP demanded a limited membership, nonprofit stock exchange, to which the Japanese acquiesced. Banks and trust banks were forbidden to offer or underwrite securities except for riskless government and municipal bonds; the securities firms, which in prewar times had served primarily as subcontractors in bond emission, now received an opportunity to change substantially the character of Japan's financial patterns. The independent Securities Commission, established to enforce the law, was transferred to the Ministry of Finance in 1952 after the peace treaty.

The Tokyo Stock Exchange was established in 1949 but it was not permitted to reopen until the body accepted SCAP's Three Principles of Market Operations, which became the basis of Japan's postwar securities market: (1) all transactions must be recorded in time sequence; (2) all transactions of listed securities must be conducted on the exchange, with a few minor exceptions; and (3) trading in futures is not permitted. On 16 May 1949 the first trading session began in the TSE, with a volume of 1,500,660 shares. By April 1950 nine stock exchanges were operating in Japan, one of which, Kobe, was subsequently shut down.

After the resumption of trading stock market activity stagnated until the outbreak of the Korean War in June 1950. The Nikkei Dow Jones Average (NDJA) fell from 176.21 at the time of the TSE's reopening to 86.17 by June 1950. Over-the-counter transactions, often of a highly speculative character, exceeded TSE transactions. Investment in equities (which had gained some popularity as a hedge in the highly inflationary postwar atmosphere) declined as the Dodge Line, a strong fiscal deflationary policy, was adopted in 1949.

During the Korean War, Japanese industry achieved its pre–World War II level and on 28 April 1952 the Allied occupation, after six years and eight months, ended. The bull market that developed during the Korean War came to an end as the war halted and Japan's role as an Allied procurement base likewise ended. The wartime boom was further sparked by the introduction in 1951 of a U.S. style of margin trading and the introduction of investment trusts, both of which helped to enhance the demand for equities. Foreign investment in Japanese stocks was made possible by a law permitting repatriation of profits after a two-year waiting period, but the amount remained a modest $1 or $2 million annually.

In 1955 the Japanese economy, now fully rehabilitated from wartime destruction, entered a period of successive booms until 1961. The NDJA rose from a 1955 average of 374 to a 1961 average of 1,519, and total annual stock transactions rose from 3.8 billion shares in 1955 to 48.3 billion shares in 1961. The capital increases for listed companies rose about nine times during the same period. Investment trusts provided the dynamic variable as their assets rose to Y1,026.8 billion in 1961 (a 1,700% increase since 1955). The explosive expansion of the investment trusts contributed to the ease of capital increases and the growth of trading and turnover; the latter exceeded 100% of market capitalization from 1959 to 1961, a growth of three to four times since 1955. During this boom the three major stock exchanges established second sections for less seasoned and smaller stocks.

The successive economic booms of the late 1950s were followed by a period of depression in the economy. Lethargy in the stock market dominated the period from 1961 to 1968. The heated expansion had created an enormous thirst for capital, resulting in a credit strigency. Companies continued to try to raise capital by new issues, increasing the supply of stocks just as the public investor began to lose interest. Beginning in the spring of 1963 investors began to redeem their holdings, forcing investment trusts to liquidate their assets. Hopes for foreign investment were dashed by the U.S. adoption in 1963 of the Interest Equalization Tax, which levied a high tax of 18.75% on new U.S. investment abroad.

To absorb the oversupply of stocks and to stabilize stock prices, the securities companies and banks helped establish the Japan Joint Securities Corporation in January 1964, which received significant loans from the Bank of Japan. Just a year later, the securities companies, with the aid of the Bank of Japan, founded the Japan Securities Holding Association, whose purpose was to purchase excess stocks held by securities companies and investment trusts. The government did not hesitate to take strong action to enable the securities market to weather the storm. Major securities companies faced bankruptcy, and in May 1965 the Bank of Japan had to extend emergency loans to Yamaichi, one of the Big Four securities companies. New capital issues were forbidden. Investment trust maturities were allowed to be extended when their present market value declined below the original offering price. Probably the most significant action that the government took in 1966 was to improve corporate disclosure and to assure its reliability by reforming the accounting system. Although the economy began to turn upward (the Izanagi boom began in November 1965 and lasted until August 1970), the equities market required several more years to recover from its lethargy.

During 1968 the stock market began an ascent that, with two relatively brief interruptions in 1970 and in 1971, continued until January 1973. The business expansion reflected in favorable corporate financial reports and the sharp improvement in the balance of trade fueled the stock market boom. Foreign investors began to make significant purchases in Japanese stock, and U.S. investors, led by the Dreyfuss Fund in 1969, braved the Interest Equalization Tax, now reduced to 11.25%, to invest in the TSE. The boom provided a great opportunity to dispose of the frozen stocks held by the Japan Securities Holding Association and the Japan Joint Securities Corporation, which were dissolved in 1969 and 1971 respectively. The boom was interrupted in April 1970 as some badly managed foreign investment funds such as Investors Overseas Service (IOS) liquidated their Japanese holdings. A second sharp decline took place in August 1971 (known in Japan as the "Nixon Shock") when the United States attempted to strengthen the dollar by (among other things) imposing a 10% import surchange. However, the currency realignment strengthening the yen (from Y360 to Y300 to the dollar) and economic recovery sent the market booming again. The NDJA doubled from November 1971 to January 1973 while, in an easy money atmosphere, trading volume increased to 300 million shares daily and Japanese institutional investors substantially increased their equity holdings. The favorable market atmosphere made possible new capital issues at market price.

In 1973 mounting inflationary pressure became evident worldwide. Seeking to curb the trend of rising prices, the Japanese government curtailed aggregate demand, gradually tightened the credit market, and raised the official discount rate from 4.25% to a new postwar high of 9%. In the midst of this attempt to curb inflation Japan was subjected in the fall of 1973 to the first oil shock, which rocked the very foundations of the country, a country that had to import most of its energy. The government reacted with still tougher measures to reduce aggregate demand. Real gross national product (GNP) declined in 1974 after years of expansion, during which it averaged a double-digit rate. The Japanese stock market declined precipitously from January 1973 almost to the end of 1974.

Although economic recovery became evident in 1975 as the government pursued a four-step reduction of the discount rate from 9% to 6.5%, the market remained listless. This stagnation was partly the result of bond issues to finance government deficits that had been caused by declining tax revenues and by the government's stimulative economic policy.

The stock market recovered very slowly and only in 1978 did the NDJA finally reach the 1973 high. By the end of 1978 the NDJA, exceeding even the most bullish predictions, reached the heights of Y6,000. In 1979 the stock market oscillated within a narrow range as Japan was struck by the second oil shock and fears of uncontrolled inflation loomed large. The ability of the Japanese to copy swiftly with this crisis encouraged investors, especially foreigners, and the NDJA rose until August 1981 to Y8,019.14.

The investors in Japanese stock soon discovered that Japan was not immune to the world economy: Japan could not score huge gains in output while the rest of the world suffered from a recession. The Japanese market was among the last of the world markets to react to the economic decline, but the reaction was sharp and the market, with some oscillation, moved steeply downward for the remainder of 1981. However, the government and society, aware of the international problems confronting Japan, have continued their economic approach—to reduce inputs for each unit of output and thus to make the economy as efficient as possible. The future of the TSE rests upon Japan's ability to develop its internal market and to improve international trade.

THE PRIMARY SECURITIES MARKETS

Companies in Japan have three major objectives in raising capital, as seen in Exhibit 1.

Debt repayment emerged as a double-digit figure only in fiscal year 1977. Although the relative share of plant and equipment funds declined, the total amount used for that purpose was actually higher in 1980 than in 1970.

Corporations also seek to raise new capital for other reasons. A corporation might issue new shares and allocate them to another corporation as part of a planned capital tie-up. A corporation can try to prevent a takeover by issuing new shares and offering them to a third party or to the public. Sometimes a corporation issues new shares to enable it to be listed on a stock exchange or to expand its ability to issue bonds.

Corporations can issue new shares to increase capital by four different methods. The most common is to issue new shares for a consideration, usually a cash payment.

EXHIBIT 1 USE OF PROCEEDS FROM NEW SHARE ISSUES

New Issues	Fiscal Year 1970	Fiscal Year 1980
Plant and equipment	64.6%	56.7%
Operating funds	28.8%	33.1%
Debt repayment	3.8%	12.1%
Total (Y100 billion)	10,997	15,974

Source: Japan Securities Market Research Institute, *Securities Market in Japan*, Tokyo, 1982.

Three methods of subscription are used: allotment to shareholders, allotment to third parties, or public offering. Corporations can select one of three prices for new issues: par value (usually Y50), market price, or a price between the two.

The **par value issue** for allotment to shareholders had been the most popular method; prior to 1971 it exceeded 80% of paid subscriptions. The shareholder receives the right to buy a number of shares proportionate to his or her holding as of a fixed date. The shareholder need not subscribe but can sell the rights. (In American Depositary Receipts—ADR—issues not registered under Section 1 with the Securities and Exchange Commission, the U.S. depositary bank will usually sell these rights by auction on behalf of the stockholders, since they are not permitted by U.S. law to exercise the rights.)

Subscription rights can also be granted to selected persons, but if prices are substantially below market the issue requires the approval of a genral stockholders' meeting. Use of this method sharply increased in 1971 and 1972 but afterward declined until 1977. To meet the higher criteria required to avoid delisting, a growing number of listed corporations issued new shares to third parties to increase their capital or to reduce the ratio of excess liabilities.

Since 1971, all listed firms have raised more capital by public offering at market price than by rights offerings, reaching 72% of total capital increases for a consideration in fiscal 1980. Only when markets are weak or stagnating, such as in 1974 to 1975, does capital raised by rights issues exceed capital raised by market price issues.

The longstanding practice of determining the dividend rate on the basis of par value aroused criticism that after a market price issue profit was not being fully redistributed to shareholders. In 1973 the underwriters developed a series of guidelines for market price issues, which they have continuously sought to establish as a standard practice. The guidelines include minimum quality standards: Y5 dividends and Y10 earnings a share based on par value of Y50; new shares not to exceed 15% of total shares; and no issuance of new shares within one year of the preceding issue. The guidelines establish alternative methods of returning profits to shareholders—a specified pay-out ratio, a range of pay-out ratios with 20% of the premium of the preceding issue to be returned before a new stock issue, or a return of 20% of the premium of the preceeding issue with a return of 10% of the accumulated premium at the end of each accounting period. In the 10 year period of 1968 to 1978, over 23% of the aggregate premiums were returned to shareholders.

New shares can be issued without consideration by either a stock split or a stock divident. The board of directors can issue additional shares to the shareholders by capitalizing part of the legal reserve, capital surplus reserve, or earned surplus reserve. Since the company does not change its dividend rate after the issuance of these new shares, the shareholder actually receives an increase in dividends. This is particularly important, since the dividend rate based on par value tends to be identical within a single industry. The stock dividend method capitalizes earnings that would have been distributed as dividends and requires a special resolution of the general shareholders' meeting.

The fourth method to increase capital is the simltaneous but separate issues of new shares, one with consideration and one without.

According to the **Commercial Code of 1950**, the articles of incorporation establish the number of authorized shares. A corporation might begin operations with a minimum of 25% subscription of authorized shares and the board of directors can issue new shares from time to time. An increase in authorized shares requires approval of a general shareholders' meeting. Securities companies underwrite new shares only in a public offering.

Another source of new shares is the issuance of convertible bonds. In 1981 the 138 issues included 36 convertible debentures issued domestically, 99 convertibles issued overseas, and three bonds issued domestically with warrants attached (see Exhibits 2 and 3).

STOCK PRICE INDEXES. Many different stock price indexes are calculated and published, but the **Nikkei Dow Jones Average** (NDJA) of 225 stocks, though not the most accurate, remains the most popular. The NDJA, adopted during postwar re-opening of the stock market, was originally formulated by Dow Jones & Company to correct the defects in the old Arithmetic Tokyo Stock Exchange Average.

The NDJA adjusts for rights issues by using a divisor that is revised for each rights issue. The formula for the NDJA is as follows.

$$D = \frac{A}{N}$$

where D = NDJA on final day with rights
A = aggregate total of 225 issues on final day with rights
N = the divisor

On the initial ex-rights day

$$\frac{A}{N} = \frac{A - P}{Z}$$

where P = decline in price due to ex-rights
Z = new divisor

In solving for Z,

$$Z = \frac{N\,(A - P)}{A}$$

Thus

$$D' = \frac{A'}{Z} = \frac{A'}{N(A - P)/A}$$

where A' = aggregate total of 225 issues on the initial ex-rights day
D' = NDJA on the initial ex-rights day

The NDJA has several major weaknesses. First, it uses only 225 issues, less than 25% of the total listed First Section issues. Second, the average is merely an unweighted arithmetic average, and does not take into consideration the number of shares issued by each constituent. Thus a high-priced, thinly traded, and therefore highly volatile stock exerts a disproportionate impact on the NDJA. Finally, by the end of December 1980, as a result of capital increases, the 225 individual shares had

EXHIBIT 2 FINANCING BY LISTED COMPANIES
(in billion yen)

	Number of Cases		Amount Raised		Premium	
	1961	1981	1961	1981	1961	1981
Offering to shareholders	381	54	613	484	—	15
Public offering	191	210	77	1,331	55	1,173
Private placement	3	16	1	33	—	28
Total	575	281	691	1,848	55	1,214
Straight bonds	—	123	—	1,219	—	—
Convertible bonds	1	138	2	1,129	—	—

Source: Daiwa Securities Company Ltd., *Tokyo Stock Market Quarterly Review*, various issues, 1982.

EXHIBIT 3 SOURCES OF INCREASE IN OUTSTANDING SHARES OF LISTED COMPANIES, 1981 (in thousands)

Number of shares outstanding	222,500,386
New increase for year	14,061,080
New listings	356,792
Capital increases	13,800,262
Rights offering	5,533,626
Public offering	2,270,341
Private placement	84,160
Converted stocks	2,531,180
Stock split or gratis shares	3,217,525
Stock dividends	56,738
Mergers	106,690
Reduction in capital	−4,000
Removals	−92,008

Source: Daiwa Securities Company Ltd., *Tokyo Stock Market Quarterly Review*, various issues, 1981.

grown 20-fold and thus a Y1 rise on the Arithmetic Stock Price Average created a Y20 increase in the NDJA.

To correct these defects, in July 1969 the TSE introduced the **TSE Index**. The base day of 4 January 1968 was selected and its market level was defined as 100. Each day's index equals the total market value of that day divided by the base day's total market value and multiplied by 100. The TSE Index adjusts for changes in market value resulting from nonmarket factors such as capital increases, listings, or delistings by revising the base day's total market value. Thus

$$B' = B\left(\frac{A + P}{A}\right)$$

where A = total market value on the day before revision
B = base day's total market value on the day before revision
P = total capital increase or decrease
B' = base day's total market value following revision

Thus the base value is constantly changed to permit accurate comparison. The TSE Index better reflects the market than the NDJA because it includes all First Section–listed stocks. By weighing each issue according to the number of shares outstanding, it avoids the bias that high-priced volatile stocks exert on the NDJA. The TSE Index has been calculated historically to the postwar reopening of the TSE on 16 May 1949. Several group indexes are also published—one each for large, medium, and small stocks (defined as capital stocks exceeding Y10 billion, exceeding Y3 billion, and under Y3 billion) and also for 28 different industry sectors. These subgroups indexes are only available from the base date 4 January 1969. A composite index of 300 selected issues listed in the Second Section has been computed back to its establishment on 2 October 1961.

The TSE also issues other stock price indexes. The TSE publishes the total market value of the First and Second sections and also data useful in analyzing macroeconomic issues (such as the significance of the TSE to the capital market and the importance of the TSE in comparison to other national stock markets). There are pitfalls in using these data, since any new listing increases its value even though the other shares have not increased in value. The Arithmetic Stock Price Average is a simple total of each stock price divided by the number of issues. Its weakness, like the NDJA, is in its failure to consider the number of shares listed. The **Weighted Stock Price Average** is computed by dividing the total market value by the stated capital of all stock listed and multiplying the quotient by 50. This compensates for the arithmetic average's failure to consider the number of shares; however, the weighted average fails to make adjustments for price declines as a result of rights issues, depriving it of continuity.

The TSE also provides two averages for yield. The **average yield** is equal to 100 times the average dividend divided by the arithmetic stock price average. This average is available both for all issues and for dividend-paying companies only. The **weighted-average yield** is equal to 100 times the total amount of dividends divided by tbe market value. (See Exhibit 4.)

STOCK EXCHANGE: ORGANIZATION AND MEMBERSHIP. After World War II, nine stock exchanges were established: Tokyo, Osaka, and Nagoya on 16 May 1949; Kyoto, Hiroshima, Fukuoka, Nigata, and Kobe on 4 July 1949; and Sapporo on 1 April 1950. The Kobe Stock Exchange was dissolved on 31 October 1967 and its business was taken over by the nearby Osaka Stock Exchange. The Tokyo Stock Exchange is clearly the dominant exchange; of the others only Osaka and Nagoya have significant trading volumes. The smaller stock exchanges are important primarily for regional stocks. (See Exhibits 5 and 6.)

The stock exchanges are nonprofit membership organizations with four types of members. Regular members are broker-dealers buying and selling either for investors or for their own accounts. Certain members, called **"saitori"** (Nakadachi members

EXHIBIT 4 AVERAGE YIELDS AND DIVIDENDS

	First Section		Second Section	
	1971	1981	1961	1981
Arithmetic stock price	184.70	405.36	166.24	393.23
Average dividend (in yen)	Y6.18	Y5.91	Y6.87	Y5.23
Average yield (in percentage)	5.57%	1.46%	4.21%	1.33%
Weighted average yield (in percentage)	4.01%	1.65%	3.67%	1.26%
Number of listed companies	771	960	532	442
Number of dividend-paying companies				
Average dividend of dividend-paying companies (in yen)	Y6.56	Y6.63	Y7.06	Y6.45
Average yield of dividend-paying companies (in percentage)				

Source: Tokyo Stock Exchange, *Annual Statistics Report*, Tokyo, 1981.

EXHIBIT 5 TRANSACTIONS ON STOCK EXCHANGE (in percentages)

	1950 Volume	1960 Value	1960 Volume	1971 Volume	1981 Volume	1981 Value
Tokyo	56.24%	55.18%	62.84%	74.68%	83.82%	84.03%
Osaka	28.16	27.57	28.82	21.79	11.58	11.97
Nagoya	5.82	6.68	4.16	2.44	3.76	3.30
Kyoto	2.62	2.82	1.05	0.31	0.14	0.12
Hiroshima	1.16	1.47	0.77	0.28	0.31	0.25
Fukuoka	1.49	1.29	1.22	0.11	0.10	0.09
Nigata	0.78	0.95	0.12	0.24	0.23	0.19
Sapporo	0.72	0.73	0.11	0.11	0.06	0.05
Kobe	2.95	3.32	0.91	—	—	—

Source: Japan Securities Market Research Institute, *Securities Market in Japan*, Tokyo, 1982.

in Osaka), act only as intermediaries between regular members and cannot trade for their own accounts. Tokyo has 12 saitori, Osaka five, and Nagoya three; the other exchanges have none. A special member, Nikon Kyoei Securities, consummates trade in Tokyo and Osaka for the six regional exchanges in which it is a special member. Finally, the Tokyo and Osaka stock exchanges each have one member to receive orders from nonmember securities companies that are its shareholders. Stock exchanges each regulate the number of members; TSE allows 83 regular members and 12 saitori.

The general meeting of members in each stock exchange is the supreme decision-making body; in the TSE for example, it elects or approves 23 governors (23 member

EXHIBIT 6 STOCK EXCHANGE MEMBERSHIP (1 October 1981)

	At Date of Reestablishment		Regular Members of Stock Exchange	
	Principal Office Members	Branch Office Members	Principal Office Members	Branch Office Members
Tokyo	126	3	71	12
Osaka	86	10	30	21
Nagoya	44	6	13	19
Hiroshima	27	5	2	13
Nigata	25	4	6	9
Fukuota	21	8	1	17
Kyoto	37	8	6	11
Sapporo	11	5	2	10
Kobe	28	6	—	—
Total	385	55	131	112

Source: Japan Securities Market Research Institute, *Securities Market in Japan*, Tokyo, 1982.

governors and 10 nonmembers representing the public interest). The president, elected by the governors, is the chief executive officer. While in office, the president cannot engage in the securities business. The president is assisted by both standing and special advisory committees, as well as other executives. The auditing body—two member and one nonmember auditors—audit stock exchange accounts and operations.

In accordance with the **Securities and Exchange Law**, the stock exchanges issue numerous rules and regulations and enjoy considerable authority to limit excessive speculation and to eliminate unfair trading. The exchanges have the right to punish members who disregard or violate their rules.

STOCK TRADING. Each customer's order is sent by the broker-dealer to the floor clerk by either order slip, telephone, or through real time on-line systems. In the TSE First Section the 14 U-shaped trading posts, each for a different industry sector, are manned by the saitori's clerks, who receive the order from the broker-dealer's clerk and enter it into a book (actually a white pasteboard sheet). One unnumbered post trades specially designated stocks without saitori intermediation. When purchases and sales are matched, the saitori sends the order to an exchange employee, who posts the official quotation board. At the same time the trade is transmitted to the relevant broker-dealers and to the news service. The saitori prepares a trade confirmation sheet to be sent to the computing center, which prepares the necessary documents.

Except for a few specified stocks (which are discussed later), the opening prices are determined by the price that allows the maximum trading volume. All orders reaching the floor before the opening of trading are considered to have arrived simultaneously. After the opening price is set, the auction begins, with priority given to the lowest price when selling, the highest price when buying, and the earlier order at the same price. A group of about 12 stocks specified for their high volume are traded at the separate unnumbered post, where a group auction fixes the opening and closing prices.

METHOD OF TRADING IN STOCKS. There are four kinds of stock transactions, each depending upon the time lag between contract and settlement. Over 99% are "regular way" transactions; settlement is on the third business day following the day of contract. A cash transaction is settled either on the day of the contract or by agreement one day later. The special agreement transaction permitting settlement within 14 days was originally established for remote customers, but is rarely used now. The "when issued" transaction applies to new capital increase shares as yet unissued.

The unit of stock trading is 1,000 shares for Y50 par value and 100 shares for Y500 par value. High-priced stocks, even with a par value of Y50, if specially designated by the stock exchange, can trade in 100-share units. Foreign shares listed on the TSE trade in four different units—10, 50, 100, or 1,000 shares, depending on the price. The government has recently arranged for stock certificates to be issued after October 1982 for a minimum of Y50,000. This will not affect trading in stocks since it conforms with round lots. (However, this might produce an impact on rights issues and stock dividends where the corporation issues less than 1,000 shares.)

BLOCK TRANSACTION SYSTEM. In view of the growing presence of institutional investors and the concomitant increase in the size of orders, the TSE developed three systems to handle blocks: the **on-floor block sales**, the **on-floor block purchases**, and the **off-floor distributions**. The on-floor block sales (or purchases), established in February 1968, has not yet been used. Normally if a customer's order is too large, the TSE member would divide the order to avoid severe price fluctuation. On-floor block sales or purchases provide for the prompt execution of the block by crossing orders at market price. The sellers of the blocks pay a regular commission and an acceptance fee of up to 30% of the regular commission; the buyers pay 70% of the commission.

The off-floor distributions are regulated and require approval by the TSE. Generally the TSE grants permission when such an action is considered to be in the interest of the customer. In this method the member can solicit orders off the floor—a customer's order has first priority, while a securities company's own account has second priority. The price must be at least 90% of the closing price on the day of approval; announcement is made after the trading session and execution takes place the following day. The seller pays the standard commission and an acceptance fee up to 1.25% of the distributing price; the buying customer pays no commission.

The **commission rates** in Exhibit 7 were put into effect on 1 April 1977 by Japanese stock exchanges. The rates are based on the value of the transactions and apply to stock transactions and subscription warrants. Commissions on odd lot transactions follow the same schedule, except that for transactions of less than Y200,000 the commission is 2%, with a maximum of Y2,500.

In addition, a transfer tax amounting to 0.55% of the proceeds is levied on stocks at the time of the sale. United States investors in Japanese stock do not pay a capital gains tax in Japan, but dividends are subject to a 15% withholding tax according to tax treaty. For investment from country where no tax treaty has been negotiated, 20% of the dividend payment is withheld.

MARGIN TRADING. The **margin selling system**, first introduced in 1951 and modeled on the U.S. method, is designed to provide supply and demand temporarily to stabilize against excessive price fluctuation. Only stocks listed on the First Section are eligible for margin transactions; only regular way transactions can be used; and the customer must settle margin trades with the securities company within six months of the date of the contract. Incidentally, no foreigner can buy Japanese equities on margin.

EXHIBIT 7 COMMISSION SCHEDULE

Value of Transaction	Commission[a]
Less than Y200,000	Y2,500
Y200,000 to Y1 million	1.25%
Over Y1 million to Y3 million	1.05% plus Y2,000
Over Y3 million to Y5 million	0.95% plus Y5,000
Over Y5 million to Y10 million	0.85% plus Y10,000
Over Y10 million to Y30 million	0.75% plus Y20,000
Over Y30 million to Y50 million	0.65% plus Y50,000
Over Y50 million to Y100 million	0.60% plus Y75,000
Over Y100 million	0.55% plus Y125,000

[a]Fractional yen amounts disregarded.
Source: Daiwa Securities Company Ltd.

The margin customer must deposit a portion of the value of the transaction with the securities company, usually the higher of Y300,000 or 30% of the value in cash. Where securities are used instead of cash, the value of the securities is usually assessed at 70%. The Ministry of Finance can tighten or relax margin requirements and has done so to discourage or encourage trading. In addition, since January 1978, the TSE has published the margin transaction balances of 50 listed issues weekly. To discourage excessive margin trading in an issue, the balance of margin trading is published daily for an issue under observance, that is, an issue whose margin trading exceeds the guidelines.

The **margin transaction** includes several charges, such as an interest charge to the buyer on margin and a lesser interest payment to the lender. The seller is also responsible for any stock borrowing fee.

A special margin system introduced in October 1978 exists for the designated issues; these highly marketable stocks include—but are not restricted to—the specified stocks, those that are traded by group auction in the unnumbered post. The special terms, allowed only for trades of 5,000 or more of these issues, require a three-month settlement but provide for only 60% of the regular commission and a higher interest rate to the seller.

In 1981, margin transactions constituted 25% of trading in value and 23.4% in volume. In the last 20 years, margin transaction as a proportion of total trading value reached a high of 37.6% in 1971 and a low of 16.4% in 1961.

Securities companies obtain the cash and stocks necessary for the massive margin transactions in one of three ways. They can match a buying order and selling order in the same issue, lending the seller's payment to the buyer and the buyer's stock certificates to the seller. They can lend cash or stocks provided by the securities companies themselves, or from financial institutions other than the securities finance companies. They can lend stock or money borrowed from one of the three securities finance companies—the Japan Securities Finance Company for Tokyo and three other stock exchanges, the Osaka Securities Finance Compnay for Osaka and two other exchanges, and the Chubu Securities Finance Company. Until 1956, a separate securities finance company existed for each of the nine exchanges. Consolidation was adopted to strengthen this area. Funds for loan transactions are borrowed by these securities finance companies from the Bank of Japan (regular call) and the call money market (free call).

PRICE STABILIZATION. During a public offering, a temporarily excessive supply of stock can upset the supply and demand relationship and drive prices down. To prevent this, governmental regulation and self-regulation by the stock exchanges and the Securities Dealers Association permits securities companies to stabilize prices within a limited time period provided that full disclosure is made. When companies issue subscription rights, price stabilization efforts begin a few days before opening of the subscription and are permitted for 20 days until the closing of the subscription period. When a public offering is made, price stabilization is allowed prior to the subscription closing for 21 days when the price is set and for 10 days when no price is set.

BOOK ENTRY CLEARING SYSTEM. The stock exchanges adopted the **book entry clearing system** in 1967, and it is not yet fully developed. This system is superior to the physical transfer of stock certificates—it eliminates the transportation of stock certificates and the possible loss of stock certificates. The TSE owns one such body, the Japan Securities Clearing Corporation. The securities companies still withdraw the deposited share certificates at the end of the accounting period of the issuer. The system, though still not fully used, is playing a greater role, as shown in Exhibit 8.

LISTING OF STOCKS. The stock exchanges establish the criteria for listing and delisting securities, but Ministry of Finance approval is required to carry out listing or delisting a security. The three most important stock exchanges, Tokyo, Osaka, and Nagoya, each haye two sections, and newly listed stocks, even where they meet the more stringent First Section listing criteria, are required to spend some time on the Second Section.

Criteria for listing on the TSE First Section are as follows:

1. There must be Y500 million in capital stock and 10 million shares. (This is doubled for a corporation whose main business is located outside the Greater Tokyo area.) Falling below Y500 million or below 10 million shares causes delisting.
2. The company must have at least 2,000 floating shareholders (defined as holders of 500 to 50,000 shares). Falling below 1,000 floating shareholders causes delisting.
3. For companies with less than 20 million shares, floating shares must constitute at least 25% of the shares but not less than 3 million. For companies with 20 million to 60 million shares, floating shares must make up at least 1 million shares plus 20% of the total shares. For companies with over 60 million shares, floating shares must number 8.2 million shares plus 8.2% of the total shares, with a maximum of 16 million shares. A company with less than 60 million shares is delisted if floating shares fall below 10% of listed shares of 1.5 million shares. A company with over 60 million shares can be delisted if the floating shares fall below 3.6 million shares plus 4% of the total listed shares, except where a company maintains 8 million floating shares.
4. The company must have net tangible assets of Y1,500 million in total and of Y100 a share.
5. There must be a minimum pretax profit for the last three years of Y200 million the first year, Y300 million the second year, and Y400 million the third year.

EXHIBIT 8 USE OF BOOK ENTRY CLEARING SYSTEM (in percentages)

Usage	1972	1980
Spot share for both delivery and receipt	68.9%	30.6%
Spot share for delivery and accounting for receipt	15.0	21.6
Spot share for receipt and accounting for delivery	13.3	26.5
Accounting for delivery and receipt	3.7	21.3

Source: Japan Securities Market Research Institute, *Securities Market in Japan*, Tokyo, 1982.

Pretax profits for each share must be Y15 for the last three years and Y20 for the last year.

6. Dividends of Y5 a share for the last three years must have been announced, and there must be an expectation of maintaining this minimum dividend after listing. The company can be delisted if it has paid no dividend in the last five years or if liabilities exceeded assets in the last three years.
7. The company can be delisted if the monthly average trading volume for the last six months falls below 10,000 or if no transactions have taken place in the last three months. No action is taken, however, if a company effects a share redistribution within three months of the announcements of its proposed delisting.
8. The company must have been incorporated for at least five years.
9. The company can be delisted for filing false financial reports or for violating the listing agreement.

The exchange examines the periodic company reports submitted in accordance with the Securities and Exchange Law. Listed companies are required to inform the exchange of imporatant corporate decisions, such as new share issues and dividends. Likewise, the listed company must provide the exchange with immediate notice of any change in major corporate activity, such as suspension of its bank account, dishonoring a check or bill, suspension of business activity, or drastic change in the nature of business. The exchange can also request information from the listed corporation and require it to make prompt disclosures of information.

OVER-THE-COUNTER MARKET. The **over-the-counter** is a very small, unorganized market. The establishment of the Second Section in Tokyo, Osaka, and Nagoya inOctober 1961 provided an organized trading market for securities that had been previously traded over the counter. In 1980 the Tokyo OTC market totaled 121 stocks, including 30 delisted stocks, known as "sub-registered" stocks, and 91 registered stocks. The Securities Dealers Association of Japan regulates the OTC stocks and publishes quotations on the registered stocks. Trading is done by private negotiation within the securities companies' offices. The Japan Over-the-Counter Trading Co.was established in June 1978 to stimulate OTC trading. A special transaction of the OTC market is the tender offer, which by law requires advance notice to the Ministry of Finance and disclosure of the proposal.

SECURITIES COMPANIES. The number of registered securities companies declined sharply from 1,152 at the end of 1949 to 251 at the end of 1981. (Five foreign securities firms are registered and one has two branches.) The number of branch offices, excluding head offices, declined from 2,300 in 1963 to 1,566 as of 30 September 1969 in response to the market decline during this period. However, when the market boomed after 1969 the government, using the licensing system that replaced registration in 1968, limited the growth of branches and by 30 September 1980 the number of branches had grown to only 1,816.

The government also sets **minimum capital requirements** for securities companies. The 12 integrated securities companies that can act as managing underwriters and engage in business other than underwriting are required to have a minimal capitalization of Y3 billion. The minimum capital for a firm that specializes in underwriting and acts as a syndicate manager is Y1 billion; the minimum for an underwriter who will not act as a syndicate manager is Y200 million. The minimum for a regular exchange member is Y100 million for Tokyo or Osaka, Y50 million for Nagoya, and Y30 million for the other five stock exchanges. The minimum for a nonmember company is Y30 million in Tokyo and Osaka and Y20 million elsewhere. A securities company dealing only with other securities companies requires a minimum capital of Y4 million in Tokyo and Osaka and Y1 million elsewhere. The above requirements were set in 1963, but in November 1980 the Ministry of Finance indicated the desirability of doubling them and urged the securities firms to meet the new standards in two to three years.

Four large integrated firms—Nomura, Nikko, Daiwa, and Yamaichi—play a major role in the securities business, involving a higher degree of concentration than is characteristic of the securities business in other countries. Their relationship is typically Japanese—they are nonadversaries in matters of common interest but intensely competitive otherwise. Unlike their U.S. colleagues, the Japanese registered representatives, investment analysts, and portfolio managers tend to remain within the same securities firm for their lifetime.

As of June 1980, the number of people employed in the securities business was 86,529—36,452 back-office workers and 49,359 registered representatives.

Securities firms in Japan are engaged in a variety of businesses. The stock business generates the largest revenues and more than 70% of these revenues are from brokerage, of which margin trading represents about 30%. Other stock activities include dealing in stocks for their own account and underwriting new shares. Securities companies also engage in underwriting bonds and in bond dealing.

Since 1973 the ecurities companies have been organized into a single **Securities Dealers Association (SDA)** with 10 district offices. Previously many separate associations had existed. The securities salesmen are required to register with the Ministry of Finance (MOF). They are also required to pass the association's qualification examination, which is held two to four times annually at local SDA offices. The self-regulation of the SDA is supplemented by over 200 MOF securities inspectors.

STOCKHOLDERS. The structure of Japanese stock holding has changed significantly since the reestablishment of the stock exchanges in 1949, as shown in Exhibit 9.

The last 30 years have been characterized by the decline of the role of the individual stockholder and the growth of corporate ownership, financial and nonfinancial. The dissolution of the Zaibatsu holdings after World War II was accompanied by the sale of stock to individuals. By 1950, 61.3% of all listed stock was owned by Japanese individuals. Since that time, individuals have not purchased the same proportion of new issues. Often individuals have been net sellers. The decline of yields from 4% and 5% to about 1.5% has discouraged individuals who invest for income. The increasing sale of new issues at market price rather than par value has not been attractive to individuals.

When the rights issue at par was the normal method of raising capital, the individual subscribed because the additional stock really increased the total dividends received. Taxes on dividends were withheld—20% on annual dividends of less than Y100,000 paid by one corporation and 30% on less than Y500,000; dividends in excess of this amount were treated as ordinary income with a tax credit of 10% for less than Y10 million. In contrast, beginning in 1963, the government exempted from taxation interest from small savings, at first defined as Y500,000, but since 1973 defined as

EXHIBIT 9 CHANGES IN STOCK HOLDING OF ALL LISTED STOCKS ON ALL STOCK EXCHANGES (in percentages)

Stockholder	1950	1955	1960	1965	1970	1975	1980
Government and municipal corporations	3.1%	0.4%	0.2%	0.3%	0.3%	0.2%	0.2%
Financial institutions	12.6	19.5	23.1	23.4	30.9	34.4	37.3
Domestic corporations	11.0	13.2	17.8	18.4	23.1	26.3	26.0
Securities companies	11.9	7.9	3.7	5.8	1.2	1.4	1.7
Investment trusts	—	4.1	7.5	5.6	1.4	1.6	1.5
Individuals (Japanese)	61.3	53.1	46.6	45.0	40.1	33.5	29.3
Foreign corporations	—	1.5	1.1	1.6	3.0	2.5	4.0
Foreign individuals	—	0.3	0.3	0.2	0.2	0.1	0.1

Source: Japan Securities Market Research Institute, *Securities Market in Japan*, Tokyo, 1982.

Y3 million. This exemption was extended separately to each member of a family and to several types of accounts—ordinary savings, loan trusts and money in trust, postal savings, and new or recent government bonds.

Individual investors are oriented toward capital gains. The government encourages this by exempting from taxation the capital gains on the first 49 trades annually. Only people engaged in 50 or more transactions involving a minimum of 200,000 shares are subject to capital gains taxation. As a result, the individuals, who as a group hold less than 30% of the stock, are responsible for over 70% of the trading volume.

The other domestic source of substantial trading is **investment trusts**, two types of which exist in Japan. The unit trust, started in 1951, is similar to a U.S. closed-end fund, while the open trust fund, initiated in 1952, is similar to a U.S. open-end mutual fund. In the stock market boom (1955–1961) investment trusts played a significant role in the equity market, but this role has since diminished. In 1960 funds held 7.5% of all stock; by 1980 the total was only 1.5%. Investment trusts often faced net redemption; in the last several years the bias toward investing in bonds and money market instruments has grown.

The **corporations**, both financial and nonfinancial, are the largest stockholders in the equity market. They are often known as "stable stockholders," because they do not normally sell their stock except at the request of the issuing corporation. Banks and insurance companies own stock to promote their interests in the issuing companies. This is also true of domestic corporations that buy the shares of their suppliers or distributors. The members of the Keiretsu, a group of closely associated companies either of Zaibatsu origin (Mitsubishi, Mitsui, Sumitomo, Yasuda) or bank-led (Fuji, Dai-Ichi Kangyo, Sanwa), often own stock of fellow members. The practice of retaining substantial ownership in an affiliate but offering the balance for sale has become quite common and has been an important source for raising capital. The Keiretse companies differ from the old Zaibatsu—they are publicly held and no single controlling holding company exists for the group. Keiretsu ties are not as close as the old Zaibatsu; some companies belong to as many as three different Keiretsu.

Some **foreign corporations** hold stock in joint ventures and could be considered stable stockholders. But foreign investors also include foreign investment companies that actively buy and sell stock. Foreign holdings, though small, are quite volatile and strongly influence Japanese investors who become aggressive on news of increased foreign investment. Since almost 70% of the Japanese stock is held by stable stockholders, the injection of foreign investment can exert a strong impact on the supply and demand relationship. In like manner, foreign disinvestment in Japanese stock can exercise a disproportionately heavy influence.

CORPORATE DISCLOSURE. According to the **Securities and Exchange Law**, a public offering of Y100 million or more by a corporation requires a registration statement to be filed with the MOF, while a public offering of less than Y100 million requires only a notification statement to the MOF. The purpose of this disclosure is to provide the general public, including potential investors, with the necessary information to make an investment decision. The MOF ordinance specifies the data to be submitted, including audited, operational, and financial conditions, as well as a comparison of the last two accounting periods. False entries in the registration statement are liable to a lengthy suspension order and other penalties. Solicitation can begin upon the MOF's receipt of the registration statement, but sales can be made only when the registration becomes effective (usually after 30 days) and must be preceded or accompanied by a prospectus.

Companies listed on the stock exchange or registered for OTC trading with the Securities Dealers Association are required to file a securities report similar to the securities registration statement within three months after the end of each accounting period. Since 1971, companies that issue annual reports (now most of the listed corporations) must also file a semiannual report that includes audited financial statements. In contrast, U.S. companies report quarterly, but except for the annual reports they are unaudited. Some Japanese companies that are traded on the New York Stock Exchange (such as Sony and Honda) are issue unaudited quarterlies. In addition, companies are required to issue current reports after any event that significantly affects their business (*e.g.*, an overseas public offering, a capital increase by allotment to third parties, a change in major shareholders, or a major accident).

Tender offers, whereby a company offers to buy shares of another company outside the stock market by public announcement of the price and number of shares to be purchased within a time period, were made possible by a revision of the SEL in 1971. Thus far only two tender offers have been made—one by Bendix Corporation (of the United States) in March 1972 to purchase controlling interest in an automotive parts manufacturer and one in December 1975 by Okinawa Power Company to purchase the shares of five power-distributing companies in Okinawa.

There are three sources of accounting for corporate disclosure: the **Commercial Code**, the **Financial Accounting Standards** and the **regulations of the MOF** (based upon the SEL), and tax legislation. The existence of two systems of disclosure—the Commercial Code, enforced by the Ministry of Justice, and the SEL, enforced by the MOF— has created some confusion and over the years legislation has been introduced to harmonize the two systems. The Commercial Code covers all joint stock companies and limited companies; the SEL covers only listed securities and registered OTC securities. The primary objective of the Commercial Code is to protect creditors; that of the SEL is to protect investors. The SEL requires far more detailed information than does the Commercial. The Commercial Code requires audited statements only from large companies, originally defined as less than Y500 million in capitalization. Until 1 December 1982 companies capitalized at less than Y1,000 million and not subject to the SEL are not required to file audited statements, but afterward, joint stock companies with debts exceeding Y20 billion will be required to file audited statements. The MOF issues regulations to enforce the Financial Accounting Standards set by its Business Deliberation Council. Three such sets of standards have been issued—those for business enterprises, consolidated financial statements, and interimte statements.

The tax laws necessarily exert a significant influence on corporate financial statements. By defining taxable income, fiscal legislation determines accounting standards. In Japan, unlike in the United States, only one set of accounts is permitted—the reports to stockholders must conform to tax legislation. In the United States, a company can use accelerated depreciation for the tax report and straight-line depreciation for the shareholders' report; thus the U.S. corporation can minimize taxes and maximize earnings for each share. In Japan the company must use accelerated depreciation in its report to stockholders if this method is used in its tax reports. The difference is significant in comparing earnings per share (EPS) in the United States and Japan and is reflected in the considerably higher cash flow of the reported average Japanese company compared to the reported average U.S. company. This difference in treatment of depreciation is estimated to result in an average understatement of Japanese-reported EPS by 20% compared to that in the United States.

The **tax conformity** of Japanese accounting is reflected in other understatements. The Japanese rarely capitalize organizational, start-up, and research and development costs, since a corporation cannot deduct them for tax purposes unless it has carried them as expenses on the books. Japanese tax law, which provides for a reduction in the tax bill for an increase in research and development expenditures, provides a disincentive for their capitalization. Japanese corporations rapidly expenses intangible assets since the tax code provides for the tax deductibility of goodwill arising from a merger. In the United States goodwill acquired before 21 October 1970 need not be written off, and goodwill acquired after that date is to be written off over a period of 40 years.

Japanese corporations are also entitled to deduct from taxable income a wide variety of reserves that vary in character and size. The special reserves change quite regularly in accordance with government industrial policy. These special reserves (such as the reserve for special extradepreciation) are often repayable beginning in the sixth year in five equal annual payments. At times companies establish reserves in excess of the legally deductible limits. In such a case reported pretax income is lower than taxable income. The *Daiwa Analysts Guide* indicates that net reserves increased 36% for 1,301 listed companies in fiscal 1980. (The Japanese legal reserve is not included, as it is not a true reserve but a deduction from retained income.) In 1980, according to Japanese accounting principles, the reported net income of Tokio Marine, the largest casualty insurer in Japan, was understated by 96% compared to its net income computation by U. S. general accounting principles, largely as a result of differences in the treatment of reserves. By omitting the net addition to reserves after taxation, Japanese EPS in fiscal 1980 are estimated to be understated by 20% in comparison with American EPS.

Since 1977, **consolidated accounting** has become the Japanese standard, but the Japanese version differs substantially from U.S. practice. Both the U.S. and Japanese corporations consolidate all subsidiaries in which parent ownership exceeds 50% of the voting stock; for those subsidiaries in which the parent owns 20% to 50% of the voting stock its equity share in undistributed profit is consolidated accordingly in U.S. reports. The Japanese use this equity accounting but are not required to do so until fiscal 1983 and very few corporations presently do so.

Moreover, many Japanese corporations have limited their ownership of affiliates to less than 50%; effective control, however, is easily exercised because the parent, despite its minority holding, is often joined by its other subsidiaries and its lead banks and together they own more than 50% of the voting stock. Most Japanese listed companies now report consolidated results without equity accounting, usually later than parent-only results. Some 17 Japanese companies that are registered under Section 1 of the SEC do use the equity method and in fiscal 1979 their consolidated EPS were on an average 29% higher than parent EPS. It has been estimated that the absence of equity accounting causes an understatement of 20% to 29% in Japanese EPS compared to that in the United States.

Financial statements are reviewed by company statutory auditors. The statutory auditor post is usually an honorific one reserved for retired directors. However, the SEL requires in addition an independent audit. In 1984, a Certified Public Accountant Law was established on the U.S. model. However, the bankruptcy or liquidation of several corporations in 1964 and 1965 exposed a series of accounting irregularities and the system was strengthened to provide greater regulation by the Japan Institute of Certified Public Accounts (JICPA), and to establish a system of audit corporations instead of individual accounting practitioners.

The JICPA uses a series of three very strict examinations to select its members. The first examination is waived for college graduates. The second test, a test of accounting and auditing theory, is a high hurdle. Only 5% to 8% of the people who take the exam pass. After passing this examination, a candidate for the third test—a combination of theory and practice, both written and oral—must have had at least one year of on-the-job training and two years of actual experience. The number of certified public accountants (CPAs) in Japan at the end of 1980 was just above 6,000, and about 300 become CPAs annually. The United States, with about double Japan's population and gross national product, has over 150,000 CPAs, with about 80% in practice.

The basic principles of **Japanese accounting standards** are similar to those of the United States, including the principles of truth, clarity, and consistency. Income standards include the principles of matching income, accrual, and realization. The basis of valuation is the lower of cost or market price.

Using the lower cost or market price has substantially understated stockholder equity on two counts. Landed property is held by corporations at a value far below its market price and in a cyclical business downturn companies have sold some land at high prices. In addition, companies often own large portfolios of stock that includes (often been acquired on issuance) large, unrealized profits. These hidden assets could explain in part the willingness of banks to make substantial loans to companies with a seemingly low equity/debt ratio.

Despite the similarity of principles, some of the practices, in addition to those already mentioned, do differ. The Japanese, except some listed firms in the United States, did not accept Statement of Financial Accounting Standards (SFAS) 8, but instead charged or credited to assets or liabilities translation differences in the foreign currency balance sheets (similar to SFAS 52). Employees' retirement benefits differ sharply from those in the United States. In Japan many employees, upon mandatory retirement (usually 55 to 60 years of age) or upon earlier voluntary severance, are entitled to payment based upon the latest wage and length of service (usually one month's pay for each year of service). The retirement fund is not separately funded but is established as a tax-deductible reserve equal to 50% of the amount required if all employees voluntarily terminated employment as of the balance sheet date. Bonuses to directors (usually the senior managers) and statutory auditors are appropriated from retained earnings on approval at the shareholders' meeting.

All registration statements and required reports to the MOF are available at the issuing companies, the MOF, and the stock exchanges.

These reports are printed in Japanese, but an increasing number of Japanese companies are issuing English language annual reports for foreign shareholders and potential investors.

SECURITIES ADMINISTRATION. The **Securities and Exchange Law**, patterned after the 1933 Securities Act and the 1934 Securities Act of the United States, and enforced beginning in 1948, provides for overall regulation of the primary and secondary securities markets. The SEL has been revised constantly, notably in 1965 to provide greater control over securities companies, and in 1971 to improve corporate disclosure. The SEL provides for the registration of securities and the necessary disclosure, the regulation of securities trading, and the supervision of all institutions involved in the securities market, such as securities companies, stock exchanges, securities dealers associations, and securities finance companies. Furthermore, the SEL provides for the Minister of Finance to mediate disputes regarding securities transactions, authorizes the Securities Exchange Council (which is described later), and provides penalties for violation of the regulations.

The organization of the Securities Administration has often been changed. An independent Securities Exchange Commission existed as a separate extradepartmental body for a short period of time (from 1948 to 1952). Since 1952 the MOF includes the Securities Bureau, which is the chief administrative body, headed by a director general. The director general is assisted by two deputies, one of whom serves as comptroller of the TSE. The central administration has several major divisions:

- Coordination Division
- Securities Companies Division, which licenses and supervises securities companies
- (Securities) Inspection Division, which audits securities companies
- Trading Market Division, which licenses and supervises stock exchanges and insures a fair and equitable market
- Capital Market Division, which makes policy and coordinates the capital market
- Corporate Finance Division, which accepts and investigates periodic corporate reports and governs the certified public accountant system

Other units of the MOF work closely with the Securities Bureau, including the Business Accounting Deliberation Council (the body that sets accounting standards) and the Certified Public Accountant Examination Commission. Local supervision is exercised by 10 finance bureaus and 41 finance departments. Stock exchange controllers work under the Finance Bureau directors. The Securities Exchange Council, appointed by the Minister of Finance and consisting of 13 members, is associated with the business and financial communities and studies problems related to the securities market; the council makes considerable use of academics in its research and deliberations. This organization has been the major source of changes in the SEL.

INTERNATIONALIZATION. The **internationalization** of the equities markets began only in 1960 and proceeded slowly during the next two decades. In June 1960 the import of foreign capital into Japan was liberalized and foreigners began to acquire Japanese shares. To ease investment the Japanese arranged for foreign depositary receipts; one receipt usually represented as many as 40 Japanese shares, usually held by a foreign bank branch located in Japan. The dividends are payable in the foreign currency but they are merely translations of the current yen dividend. In 1961 Sony issued the first American Depositary Receipt for a Japanese company, 2 million Japanese shares. By the autumn of 1963 nine ADRs were issued, but the introduction of the Kennedy interest equalization tax (IET), which placed a tax of 18.75% on U.S. capital exports, halted this development. This tax was successfully lowered and finally abolished a decade later. The lowering of the IET was complicated in the first Nixon Administration by the Federal Reserve guideline that limited investment in foreign securities to its current level. A U.S. resident desiring to purchase Japanese stock could only do so by selling Japanese stock that he already owned or by buying from a U.S. owner.

The decline of foreign investment in Japan was closely related to the stock market stagnation in Japan until 1968. Thus one LDR (London Depositary Receipt) was issued in 1964 and no more were issued until 1969. The rising Japanese stock market after 1968 revived depositary receipts, not only the ADR but also the EDR (European Depositary Receipt), CDR (Curacao or Continental Depositary Receipt), the HKDR (Hong Kong Depositary Receipt) and DRS (Depositary Receipt of Singapore), which joined the market in 1980. (See Exhibit 10.) During the 1974–1975 oil shock foreign investment in Japanese stock again stagnated, but after Japanese recovery in the late 1970s foreign investment grew substantially. Japanese securities are now listed in markets all over the world.

To facilitate **foreign investment** the MOF in December 1980 set up a new system, changing its practice from prohibition in principle to freedom in principle. To purchase less than 10% of the stock of any Japanese company (excepting 11 companies, for which is discussed later) for portfolio investment requires no advance notice if the acquisition is made through one of the 26 leading Japanese securities companies.

EXHIBIT 10 ISSUE OF DEPOSITARY RECEIPTS
(in millions of U.S. dollars)

1968	$ 5.9
1969	49.3
1970	5.0
1971	0
1972	5.1
1973	6.5
1974	0
1975	74.5
1976	312.9
1977	222.7
1978	68.0
1979	65.7
1980	503.9

Source: Japan Securities Market Research Institute, *Securities Market in Japan*, Tokyo, 1982.

Acquisition of over 10% of the shares of a single company requires 30 days advance notice to the MOF, though the MOF can shorten or lengthen the period. The MOF can reject the application if it imperils national security, adversely affects the economy, or creates problems regarding international reciprocity. Previously, the MOF had limited foreign ownership to about 25%, which could be and was raised on request of the company. A group of 11 stocks (including five oil companies) are exceptions to the new regulation; for each of these a specific foreign ownership ratio is established, ranging from 25% to 50%. In such companies the prospective purchaser must inquire from the MOF whether a purchase would violate the ratio. The MOF reserves the right to include other companies in this category and it is believed that 25% might be the upper limit for foreign ownership unless a company requests a higher ratio. In March 1981, the TSE asked companies to report when foreign ownership reached 20%.

JAPANESE INVESTMENT IN FOREIGN SECURITIES. The MOF was very slow to permit Japanese investment in foreign securities. In April 1970 investment trusts were permitted to buy up to $100 million of stock and bonds listed on eight major foreign stock exchanges. In January 1971 this permission was extended to insurance companies. In July 1971 this limitation was abolished and for the first time the Japanese individual investor was permitted to purchase foreign stocks. In November 1972 the MOF permitted sale of foreign open-end mutual funds in Japan and in early 1973 Daiwa Securities offered Dreyfus Fund shares, the first U.S. mutual fund to be sold in Japan. By October 1981 19 foreign mutual funds, mostly registered in Luxembourg, were distributed in Japan. Partly as a result of the interest rate differential, the Japanese tended to focus upon purchases of foreign bonds.

In 1972 General Telephone and Electronics (GTE) made a public offering in Japan of 750,000 shares, worth approximately $21 million, the first public offering of a foreign stock in Japan. The issue aroused considerable interest for some practices relatively new to Japan—the issue at market price on the day of the offering at almost nine times par value, individual underwriter responsibility for its share of the issue without joint responsibility, and postponement of the payment upon agreement of the issuer and management. Other public offerings followed: an International Utilities issue of 300,000 shares in 1973 and a Pan Am issue of 400,000 shares in 1976 concurrent with an offer of 6.6 million shares in the United States. (See Exhibit 11.)

To be listed on the TSE, a foreign stock must be listed in its home country or be

EXHIBIT 11 FOREIGN STOCKS TRADED ON THE TOKYO STOCK EXCHANGE

Year	Number of Shares	Value (Million Yen)
1977	1,234,840	15,040
1978	846,660	9,097
1979	1,477,990	20,226
1980	670,110	7,949
1981	594,900	6,352

Source: Tokyo Stock Exchange, *Annual Statistics Report*, Tokyo, 1981.

a continuously traded OTC stock, listed on an exchange other than in its own country. Listing also requires a certain number of stockholders in Japan and minimum net assets, net profits, and dividends.

Transaction of foreign stocks are conducted in the Foreign Section of the TSE in cash and regular way transactions. The trading session lasts for 30 minutes, starting at 10:30 A.M. and 2:30 P.M. Physical delivery of the stock is eliminated since all trades are handled through the Central Depository Clearance System.

Japanese securities firms have been active overseas. Originally their business was derived primarily from representing foreign investors in Japanese securities. Their activity has greatly diversified to include brokerage for Japanese investors in foreign securities and mutual funds and underwriting Japanese convertible debt issues overseas. At the end of 1980 Japanese securities companies had 84 branches or subsidiaries of various types in 22 cities in 16 countries.

The MOF has granted licenses to five brokers to open branches in Japan. These branches have the same scope of business as Japanese securities companies. Their major business has been brokerage for sale of foreign stock to Japanese investors and Japanese stock to foreign investors. As of the end of 1981 no foreign securities firm had yet become a member of any Japanese stock exchange. The relatively high cost of a seat on the TSE might inhibit but not make impossible such an application. As of 20 November 1981 Merrill Lynch had two branches (one in Tokyo founded in 1972, and one in Osaka founded in 1978); Bache Halsey Stuart and Smith Barney Harris Upham, from the United States, one each; Vickers da Costa, from the United Kingdom, and Jardine Fleming (of Hong Kong) one branch office each in Tokyo. Some 66 foreign companies have representative offices in Japan; their major activity is to collect and dispense information on the market.

SECURITY ANALYSTS. The *Security Analysts Association of Japan* (SAAJ) was established in 1962 as a nonprofit professional organization to improve the level of competence of its members. The SAAJ trains security analysts and provides information useful for security analysis. As of September 1981 the SAAJ had a total membership of 1,195, including 249 institutional members, 19 associate members, and 927 individual members. Institutional membership is unique to Japan—it includes securities firms, investment trust management and advisory firms, banks, and insurance companies. Institutional membership allows two representatives to be individual members. Associate members are securities-related firms. These two categories provide strong financial support to the SAAJ. Individual members must belong to an institutional or associate firm and are required to have three years of experience in investment analysis or portfolio management. The SAAJ makes an exception for employees of governments, universities, or public research institutions who have sufficient knowledge and experience in investment analysis.

Education plays a major role in SAAJ activity. Since 1971, the SAAJ has conducted seminars in Tokyo and Osaka. In 1977, SAAJ began offering nationwide correspondence courses. The first-level course, which lasts 10 months, includes security analysis, economics, and financial accounting. The number of first-level students in the last four years was 4,460. After completion of the first-level course, the student must take an examination. Some individuals can be exempted from the level one examinations.

In August 1980 the SAAJ instituted the eight-month level two correspondence course, from which no exemption is granted. A candidate who passes the level two examination and who has the minimum of three years experience in investment analysis and/or portfolio management receives the title of Chartered Member (CMA). Of the 600 who began the initial level two course in August 1980, only 245 finally passed (72% of those who actually sat for the examination). An additional 750 are attending the second level two course, which began in August 1981.

In addition to this training activity SAAJ sponsors company presentations and talks by Japanese and foreign specialists on a broad range of topics. The SAAJ also publishes monthly the *Security Analysts Journal*, with a circulation of about 2,000; this publication encompasses a broad range of investment topics, including the latest developments in investment analysis abroad. The SAAJ has been active in international activities—it belongs to the International Coordinating Committee, which promotes cooperation between financial analysts' societies in the world. The SAAJ is also a charter member of the Asian Securities' Analysts Council (ASAC), which promotes cooperation among the Pacific rim security analysts' societies. Japanese analysts, under the leadership of the SAAJ, participate actively in the annual meetings of the Financial Analysts Federation (of the United States and Canada) and the European Federation of Financial Analysts Societies. Unlike their counterparts, the board of directors of the SAAJ has the top financial executives as its chairperson and three vice chairs. The present chairperson is T. Yamauchi, who until recently was chairman of Daiwa Securities. The SAAJ's staff is headed by an executive managing director, M. Yoshino. Not all securities analysts are members of the SAAJ. The SAAJ is a highly regarded representative for the profession, which probably exceeds 2,000 security analysts.

Some limitations on security analysts unique to Japan should be noted. The Japanese technique of rotating jobs meant that security analysts often did not remain long in that occupation before being shifted, often to a totally different department. Only during the 1970s did the securities companies begin to maintain at least some of the security analysts or portfolio managers for a longer tenure. This was partly a response to the growing international interest in Japanese investors, since foreign investors were accustomed to more highly professional analysts. Brokerage firms established separate research institutes, which at least provides longer tenure for analysts by providing for promotion within the research institute. The second limitation on security analysis is the limited number of types of securities—usually common stock, bonds, convertible debentures, and subscription rights for new shares. Preferred stocks are legal but none have been issued. Warrants have just appeared and options have no place yet in the Japanese equities market.

Technical analysis has been and remains popular in Japan. A rich variety of chart books, including point and figure charts, are published regularly. A wide variety of technical indicators are also available, including 200-day moving averages, the ratio of short sales to the volume of market trading, and the margin balance—the ratio of shares bought on margin to short sales. Until 1970 the investment analyst tended to pay more attention to dividend and yield based on par value, although investment analysis based on PER or earnings growth were known. The entry of foreign investors into the TSE in the late 1960s helped to reinforce and expand the trend toward U.S. security analysis methods.

The Japanese have been aware of the research done on the efficient market hypothesis (EMH) and have, in fact, applied this analysis to the Japanese market. Many securities firms provide extensive data on alphas, betas, and sigmas for all listed TSE securities, usually based on five years of data.

The *Japanese Securities Institute* has published many tests of the EMH. The results of these initial studies are summarized as follows:

1. Prices in Japan seem to move in a less random fashion and prices tend to persist for one or two days.
2. Prices do not react instantaneously to news announcements. Thus after the announcement of a free distribution, prices rise but continue the upward trend toward the ex-distribution date and tend to drift downward after the ex-distribution date. Thus inefficiency can be the result of a step-up in broker activity after a free distribution announcement and a decline in promotional activity after the ex-distribution date.
3. Stock price decline on the ex-dividend date represents only a minor fraction of the actual dividend paid. Unlike in the United States the amount of the dividend is not determined until long after the announcement of the ex-dividend date, and payment is usually two to three months after that date.
4. Beta and the return on stocks are not related in a linear manner and risk is not necessarily related positively to return.

APPENDIX A. COMPONENTS OF NOMINAL GROSS NATIONAL PRODUCT (in billion yen)

Year	Private Consumption Expenditure	Public Spending	Private Fixed Investment
1945	—	—	48
1946	333	55	48
1947	915	102	117
1948	1,741	282	258
1949	2,261	394	324
1950	2,397	437	450
1951	3,018	552	681
1952	3,861.9	668.9	886.2
1953	4,664.7	780.1	1,065.8
1954	5,162.0	860.4	1,155.2
1955	5,529.2	894.0	1,143.8
1956	6,012.0	936.1	1,682.2
1957	6,596.9	1,008.6	2,223.2
1958	7,056.8	1,104.6	2,121.6
1959	7,722.1	1,209.4	2,477.2
1960	8,823.0	1,382.0	3,526.4
1961	10,105.6	1,606.5	4,889.6
1962	11,746.5	1,864.4	5,171.1
1963	13,768.5	2,200.1	5,600.5
1964	16,038.5	2,554.0	6,892.9
1965	19,122.9	2,690.0	6,999.4
1966	22,000.8	3,054.3	8,121.6
1967	25,241.8	3,410.3	10,582.8
1968	28,851.3	3,943.2	13,192.5
1969	33,252.3	4,558.4	16,535.9
1970	38,272.4	5,455.3	20,152.7
1971	43,160.4	6,421.4	20,437.7
1972	49,812.8	7,536.8	22,650.3
1973	60,229.2	9,336.4	30,108.2
1974	72,836.9	12,240.3	34,613.8
1975	84,568.0	14,890.2	34,599.1

APPENDIX A. (*Continued*)

Year	Private Consumption Expenditure	Public Spending	Private Fixed Investment
1976	95,148.8	16,417.2	37,320.5
1977	105,789.0	18,243.2	39,338.7
1978	115,909.6	19,752.5	42,284.5
1979	127,066.3	21,486.2	48,242.1
1980	136,779.2	23,531.8	52,273.4
1981	143,920.6	25,325.6	52,716.4

Year	Increase in Inventory	Export of Goods and Services	Import of Goods and Services
1945	—	—	—
1946	28	5	24
1947	83	28	82
1948	236	81	191
1949	208	217	327
1950	368	469	364
1951	570	908	699
1952	385.9	788.9	720.4
1953	141.7	788.9	870.3
1954	139.5	853.6	882.2
1955	421.3	978.9	904.4
1956	506.7	1,189.0	1,208.0
1957	739.7	1,338.4	1,549.0
1958	251.7	1,318.1	1,149.9
1959	418.2	1,531.3	1,389.9
1960	551.3	1,773.9	1,713.3
1961	1,381.7	1,859.9	2,198.5
1962	458.9	2,141.6	2,148.2
1963	884.3	2,349.4	2,613.4
1964	1,082.5	2,889.4	3,036.4
1965	694.9	3,562.8	3,196.5
1966	815.0	4,165.9	3,665.8
1967	1,527.7	4,466.8	4,471.2
1968	1,909.9	5,527.4	5,087.0
1969	1,938.4	6,818.3	5,989.7
1970	2,573.2	8,272.7	7,488.5
1971	1,214.6	9,895.0	7,806.4
1972	1,298.8	10,377.5	8,236.8
1973	1,885.3	12,132.5	12,081.0
1974	3,395.9	19,447.0	20,693.2
1975	493.9	20,254.4	20,349.2
1976	1,072.8	23,839.1	22,660.3
1977	1,210.6	25,561.3	22,612.9
1978	1,037.3	24,104.8	20,479.8
1979	1,816.6	27,903.6	29,627.0
1980	1,595.1	35,706.7	37,933.7
1981	842.0	41,724.4	40,228.5

APPENDIX A. (*Continued*)

Year	Total Gross National Product Amount	Per Capital (in U.S. Dollars)
1945	—	—
1946	475	—
1947	1,309	—
1948	2,665	—
1949	3,376	—
1950	3,946	—
1951	5,442	$178.3
1952	6,263.1	202.1
1953	7,054.6	224.8
1954	7,831.1	246.0
1955	8,623.6	267.7
1956	9,726.0	300.0
1957	11,080.3	338.6
1958	11,521.9	348.9
1959	12,926.3	387.6
1960	15,499.2	461.0
1961	19,125.5	561.7
1962	21,199.2	617.3
1963	24,464.0	703.8
1964	28,931.7	822.5
1965	32,656.5	919.2
1966	37,931.9	1,057.0
1967	44,462.8	1,225.3
1968	52,702.7	1,442.5
1969	62,018.4	1,687.8
1970	73,128.2	1,951.3
1971	80,522.3	2,181.7
1972	92,312.8	2,830.0
1973	112,440.9	3,793.1
1974	133,921.7	4,146.7
1975	147,873.8	4,451.0
1976	165,694.7	5,517.5
1977	184,368.2	6,015.0
1978	202,707.9	8,363.5
1979	218,894.1	8,601.2
1980	234,871.8	8,848.8
1981	248,533.7	9,556.0

Source: Daiwa Securities Company Ltd., Tokyo , Bank of Japan, Tokyo.

APPENDIX B. COMPONENTS OF REAL GROSS NATIONAL PRODUCT (in billion yen)

Year	Private Consumption Expenditure	Public Spending	Private Fixed Investment
1945	—	—	—
1946	6,826	1,123	1,645
1947	7,410	828	1,576
1948	8,391	1,360	1,734
1949	9,297	1,619	1,605
1950	10,077	1,838	1,777
1951	11,040	2,022	1,929
1952	8,237.9	2,742.1	1,487.1
1953	9,269.3	2,782.2	1,679.4
1954	9,727.0	2,848.2	1,789.4
1955	10,495.7	2,834.9	1,798.8
1956	11,312.6	2,823.5	2,372.8
1957	12,021.9	2,807.1	2,871.0
1958	12,888.2	2,934.8	2,851.1
1959	13,891.6	3,088.1	3,254.9
1960	15,280.9	3,226.9	4,476.8
1961	16,571.0	3,423.5	5,837.5
1962	18,148.2	3,712.0	6,157.5
1963	19,890.5	4,036.4	6,676.6
1964	22,202.4	4,276.6	8,120.9
1965	42,135.0	8,777.7	12,741.7
1966	46,234.6	9,285.7	14,208.9
1967	50,617.6	9,726.0	17,743.0
1968	54,818.2	10,284.3	21,598.2
1969	60,350.8	10,805.2	26,418.7
1970	64,530.4	11,418.3	31,084.3
1971	68,319.0	12,030.6	30,973.6
1972	74,829.7	12,661.0	33,271.2
1973	81,820.1	13,289.5	38,607.6
1974	81,254.1	13,750.8	35,762.4
1975	84,546.3	14,680.3	34,618.7
1976	87,383.3	15,282.6	35,695.0
1977	90,693.4	15,878.2	36,491.8
1978	94,967.8	16,680.4	38,906.2
1979	100,606.3	17,392.0	41,919.5
1980	101,238.4	17,783.3	42,690.6
1981	101,889.8	18,417.0	43,090.6

Year	Increase in Inventory	Export of Goods and Services	Import of Goods and Services
1945	—	—	—
1946	812	102	534
1947	1,273	247	757

APPENDIX B. (*Continued*)

Year	Increase in Inventory	Export of Goods and Services	Import of Goods and Services
1948	1,734	352	889
1949	1,230	753	1,186
1950	1,277	1,614	1,307
1951	2,009	2,187	1,757
1952	388.3	897.4	610.6
1953	54.8	897.9	816.6
1954	176.7	961.2	857.9
1955	610.2	1,098.8	867.1
1956	533.9	1,293.1	1,139.4
1957	727.7	1,466.6	1,456.8
1958	311.7	1,562.0	1,221.9
1959	493.3	1,758.5	1,516.3
1960	619.5	2,022.9	1,889.1
1961	1,481.7	2,164.1	2,408.3
1962	417.2	2,523.5	2,414.9
1963	945.8	2,710.2	2,850.6
1964	1,161.1	3,270.8	3,273.5
1965	1,213.9	5,632.2	7,010.7
1966	1,468.9	6,501.8	7,859.7
1967	2,571.8	6,884.7	9,698.8
1968	3,204.2	8,436.1	10,790.5
1969	3,034.0	10,148.9	12,224.6
1970	3,744.9	11,886.6	14,819.6
1971	1,781.6	13,912.3	15,508.0
1972	1,848.8	14,797.2	16,983.3
1973	2,449.0	16,023.5	21,040.0
1974	3,528.2	19,590.2	22,530.3
1975	493.9	20,311.4	20,416.8
1976	1,050.8	23,872.2	21,549.3
1977	1,153.2	26,596.2	22,426.6
1978	965.7	26,649.5	23,878.0
1979	1,809.4	28,396.4	27,390.0
1980	1,845.2	33,710.0	26,285.0
1981	771.9	39,231.0	27,785.0

Year	Total Gross National Product Amount	Per Capita (in U.S. Dollars)
1945	—	—
1946	10,874	—
1947	11,966	—
1948	13,921	—
1949	14,469	—
1950	16,240	—
1951	18,430	—
1952	13,808.8	$445.7

APPENDIX B. (*Continued*)

Year	Total Gross National Product Amount	Per Capita (in U.S. Dollars)
1953	14,662.2	467.2
1954	15,529.6	487.8
1955	16,900.6	524.7
1956	18,131.9	558.8
1957	19,478.4	595.3
1958	20,575.4	623.1
1959	11,403.0	671.8
1960	25,407.5	755.7
1961	29,065.9	853.6
1962	31,100.2	905.6
1963	34,345.6	988.1
1964	38,894.3	1,105.7
1965	68,991.9	1,942.0
1966	76,324.9	2,126.9
1967	84,567.0	2,330.6
1968	95,318.5	2,609.0
1969	107,034.5	2,912.8
1970	117,591.4	3,137.7
1971	123,104.0	3,335.4
1972	134,147.3	4,112.5
1973	145,976.9	4,924.4
1974	144,166.5	4,463.9
1975	147,654.7	4,444.4
1976	155,501.8	5,178.1
1977	163,751.7	5,342.4
1978	172,133.4	7,102.0
1979	181,136.8	7,117.5
1980	188,733.6	7,110.6
1981	194,218.4	7,470.1

Source: Daiwa Securities Company Ltd., Tokyo. Bank of Japan, Tokyo.

APPENDIX C. VALUE OF JAPANESE EXPORTS AND IMPORTS BY COUNTRY IN 1981 (in millions of U.S. dollars)

Rank	Exports To	Amount	Rank	Imports From	Amount
1	United States	$38,608.754	1	United States	$25,297.077
2	West Germany	5,967.541	2	Indonesia	13,305.297
3	Saudi Arabia	5,876.433	3	Saudi Arabia	21,482.081
4	Korea	5,657.863	4	United Arab Emirates	8,835.997
	Taiwan	5,404.570			
5			5	Australia	7,419.287

APPENDIX C. (*Continued*)

MAJOR COMMODITIES

Rank	Goods	Amount	Rank	Goods	Amount
1	Machinery and equipments	$100,162.627	1	Mineral fuels	$72,562.720
2	Metals	22,455.619	2	Foodstuffs	15,913.446
3	Textiles	7,173.590	3	Raw materials	10,347.075
4	Chemicals	6,840.677	4	Machinery and equipments	10,240.060
5	Nonmetallic mineral manufacturers	2,122.482	5	Metal ores and scrap	7,284.355

Source: Ministry of Finance, Tokyo, Japan.

APPENDIX D. INTERNATIONAL COMPARISON OF OVERSEAS DEPENDENCE ON KEY RESOURCES, 1979 (in percentage)

Resource	Japan	United States	West Germany	United Kingdom	France
All energy sources	87.0%	20.6%	57.7%	9.3%	80.3%
Coal	79.2	−9.6	−8.7	1.6	57.0
Oil	99.8	42.3	95.8	18.9	99.0
Natural gas	88.7	5.8	65.8	19.5	68.8
Iron ore	98.6	29.7	96.9	80.7	44.4
Copper	95.6	33.5	99.9	100.0	99.9
Lead	82.4	59.9	90.9	99.3	86.0
Zinc	68.7	70.6	71.9	100.0	87.2
Tin	97.7	100.0	100.0	81.8	100.0
Aluminum	100.0	63.6	100.0	100.0	−230.5
Nickel	100.0	93.0	100.0	100.0	100.0
Lumber	69.2	3.8	20.7	72.9	16.0
Wool	100.0	23.2	92.3	51.4	73.3
Cotton	100.0	−84.4	100.0	100.0	100.0
Soybeans	95.4	−51.2	100.0	100.0	97.2
Corn	100.0	−42.9	79.1	100.0	−30.0
Wheat	93.0	−147.1	−0.8	25.4	−80.2

Source. Ministry of International Trade and Industry, Tokyo, Japan.

Note. Negative numbers mean that no only is domestic demand met from domestic supplies but that exports occur as well; −100% implies exports are as large as domestic demand. Metals data are for ores and concentrates, not refined metals, except in the case of tin.

APPENDIX E. NIKKEI DOW JONES AVERAGE

Year	Open	High	Date	Low	Date	Close	Year Average
1949	176.21	176.88	9.01	98.50	12.14	109.91	149.05
1950	108.56	114.99	8.21	85.25	7.06	101.91	101.86
1951	102.10	170.32	10.27	102.10	1.04	166.06	136.33
1952	167.80	370.55	12.15	167.80	1.04	362.64	245.87
1953	364.89	474.43	2.04	295.18	4.01	377.95	390.11
1954	362.88	377.27	1.11	314.08	3.22	356.09	340.64
1955	361.10	425.69	12.28	345.89	4.27	425.69	373.81
1956	428.59	566.30	12.06	420.14	1.25	549.14	485.28
1957	549.45	595.46	5.04	471.53	12.27	474.55	534.86
1958	475.20	666.54	12.27	475.20	1.04	666.54	572.38
1959	671.28	976.93	11.30	664.69	1.09	874.88	822.84
1960	869.34	1,356.71	12.28	869.34	1.04	1,356.71	1,116.50
1961	1,366.74	1,829.74	7.18	1,258.00	12.19	1,432.60	1,551.82
1962	1,425.30	1,589.76	2.14	1,216.04	10.29	1,420.43	1,418.01
1963	1,418.25	1,634.37	4.05	1,200.64	12.18	1,225.10	1,441.20
1964	1,204.40	1,369.00	7.03	1,202.69	11.09	1,216.55	1,263.69
1965	1,227.11	1,417.83	12.28	1,020.49	7.12	1,417.83	1,200.28
1966	1,430.13	1,588.73	4.01	1,364.34	12.05	1,452.10	1,480.10
1967	1,441.35	1,506.27	3.01	1,250.14	12.11	1,283.47	1,412.66
1968	1,266.27	1,851.49	10.02	1,266.27	1.04	1,714.89	1,546.30
1969	1,733.64	2,358.96	12.27	1,733.64	1.04	2,358.96	1,956.63
1970	2,407.85	2,534.45	4.06	1,929.64	5.27	1,987.14	2,191.86
1971	2,001.34	2,740.98	8.14	1,981.74	1.06	2,713.74	2,390.88
1972	2,712.31	5,207.94	12.28	2,712.31	1.04	5,207.94	3,753.48
1973	5,232.86	5,359.74	1.24	3,958.57	12.18	4,306.80	4,759.56
1974	4,259.20	4,787.54	6.01	3,355.13	10.09	3,817.22	4,277.70
1975	3,777.40	4,564.52	5.12	3,627.04	1.10	4,358.60	4,248.53
1976	4,403.06	4,990.85	12.28	4,403.06	1.05	4,990.85	4,653.23
1977	4,998.85	5,287.65	9.05	4,597.26	11.24	4,865.60	5,030.35
1978	4,867.91	6,097.26	12.13	4,867.91	1.04	6,001.85	5,539.86
1979	6,041.57	6,590.69	9.29	5,925.87	4.10	6,569.47	6,273.69
1980	6,560.16	7,188.28	11.06	6,475.93	3.28	7,116.38	6,869.14
1981	7,150.95	8,019.14	8.17	6,956.52	3.13	7,681.84	7,516.18

Source. Daiwa Securities Company Ltd., Tokyo.

APPENDIX F: TOKYO STOCK EXCHANGE INDEX

Year	Open	High	Date	Low	Date	Close	Year Average
1949	22.06	22.06	5.16	11.95	12.14	12.85	16.86
1950	12.66	13.24	8.21	9.59	7.03	11.57	11.51
1951	11.58	17.11	10.20	11.58	1.04	16.94	14.60
1952	17.09	33.55	11.22	17.07	1.08	33.35	23.82
1953	33.54	42.18	2.04	28.46	4.01	33.30	34.68
1954	32.19	33.22	1.11	26.79	11.13	30.27	29.30
1955	30.64	39.06	12.28	30.00	3.28	39.06	32.97
1956	39.40	52.95	12.06	38.81	1.25	51.21	44.85
1957	51.42	54.82	1.21	43.18	12.27	43.40	49.19
1958	43.48	60.95	12.27	43.48	1.04	60.95	51.70
1959	61.46	90.14	11.30	61.11	1.09	80.00	75.49
1960	79.46	112.53	11.15	79.46	1.04	109.18	97.35
1961	109.97	126.59	7.14	90.86	12.19	101.66	112.10
1962	101.34	111.45	2.14	83.39	10.30	99.67	98.59
1963	100.11	122.96	5.10	91.21	12.18	92.87	108.20
1964	91.61	103.77	7.03	87.94	11.11	90.68	95.56
1965	91.30	105.68	12.28	81.29	7.15	105.68	91.68
1966	106.49	114.51	3.24	105.21	1.19	111.41	109.88
1967	111.23	117.60	5.31	99.17	12.11	100.89	110.48
1968	100.00	142.95	10.02	100.00	1.04	131.31	118.91
1969	132.62	179.30	12.27	132.62	1.04	179.30	151.05
1970	182.63	185.70	4.08	147.08	12.09	148.35	163.48
1971	149.02	209.00	8.14	148.05	1.06	199.45	179.62
1972	199.93	401.70	12.28	199.93	1.04	401.70	282.42
1973	403.92	422.48	1.24	284.69	12.18	306.44	362.46
1974	304.12	342.47	6.05	251.96	10.09	278.34	307.21
1975	276.04	333.11	7.02	268.24	1.10	323.43	312.06
1976	326.28	383.88	12.28	326.28	1.05	383.88	347.51
1977	384.14	390.33	9.29	350.49	11.24	364.08	376.78
1978	364.04	452.60	12.13	364.04	1.04	449.55	415.41
1979	452.85	465.24	9.29	435.13	7.13	459.61	449.88
1980	458.80	497.96	10.20	449.01	3.10	494.10	474.00
1981	495.79	603.92	8.17	495.79	1.05	570.31	552.29

Source. Daiwa Securities Company Ltd., Tokyo.

APPENDIX G. TOKYO STOCK EXCHANGE VOLUME (in thousand shares)

Year	Total	Daily Average	Turn over	Most Active Day	Date	Least Active Day	Date
1949	255,934	1,333	18.37	2,656	8.26	653	11.26
1950	512,109	1,701	25.64	9,444	7.17	516	2.04
1951	821,258	2,738	30.42	6,933	1.31	923	1.04
1952	2,002,637	6,653	52.37	15,541	11.24	1,448	3.29
1953	2,091,539	6,995	36.55	22,533	2.02	1,904	7.04
1954	1,238.494	4,128	15.77	13,564	12.24	1,521	8.07
1955	2,505,297	8,351	26.02	27,253	2.09	2,207	5.28
1956	6,692,411	22,015	52.17	89,249	11.02	5,288	1.28
1957	7,691,636	25,469	45.48	80,488	1.17	8,801	11.16
1958	11,684,473	38,948	58.52	121,324	10.07	7,710	1.04
1959	21,200,964	70,906	89.79	189,952	12.02	21,519	4.25
1960	27,230,260	90,166	92.41	226,459	930	20,409	1.04
1961	31,089,058	103,286	77.50	252,893	4.11	20,285	10.28
1962	33,134,838	109,718	63.69	339,646	11.08	38,271	3.03
1963	39,375,685	130,383	65.64	594,510	4.01	31,176	7.27
1964	28,578,364	94,945	41.87	370,974	1.14	30,085	9.19
1965	33,952,288	112,798	45.99	685,634	1.21	23.697	6.12
1966	34,466,410	115,659	45.38	323,851	3.03	39,996	10.17
1967	27,697,777	92,635	34.78	430,655	2.02	22,545	11.18
1968	45,105,495	149,356	53.18	574,268	10.01	29,086	1.04
1969	48,246,516	162,446	52.28	346,650	5.30	31,918	8.23
1970	41,043,709	138,194	40.27	419,314	1.06	50,824	5.23
1971	59,033,469	197,436	52.70	552,402	12.22	58,889	10.23
1972	97,346,763	327,767	80.73	1,066,524	11.14	87,816	4.22
1973	57,883,985	201,686	44.40	1,055,828	1.18	45,207	9.10
1974	49,791,968	174,709	35.50	562,909	5.17	46,559	9.28
1975	50,753,161	178,708	33.41	397,454	2.28	59,711	8.23
1976	67,286,861	235,268	41.16	640,337	1.12	83,542	7.31
1977	68,474,445	239,421	39.60	912,242	8.31	90,837	5.28
1978	93,221,823	327,094	51.48	838,461	12.08	137,537	5.27
1979	94,963,891	332,042	50.62	903,729	5.11	124,991	6.09
1980	100,219,563	351,648	51.30	930,759	2.15	132,592	6.09
1981	105,930,325	371,685	51.24	1,384,877	4.08	110,639	12.26

Source. Daiwa Securities Company Ltd., Tokyo.

APPENDIX H. STOCK INDEXES

End of Period	Number of Listed Companies	Total Market Value	Trading Volume				Turnover Ratio	Tokyo Stock Price Index			Dow Jones Average, 225 Stocks			Outstanding Margin Transactions (Billion Yen)		PER	PBR 225 Stocks	Dividend Yield
			Billion Yen		Million Shares													
		Billion Yen	Total	Daily Average	Total	Daily Average	Percentage	High	Low	Close	High	Low	Close	Shares Sold Short	Shares Bought on Margin			Percentage
1971	771	Y21,500	Y13,505	45.2	59,033	197.4	62.8%	209.00	148.05	199.45	2,740.98	1,981.74	2,713.74	—	—	13.84	—	3.37%
1972	806	45,950	20,612	69.4	97,347	327.8	44.9	401.70	199.93	401.70	5,207.94	2,712.31	5,207.94	—	—	23.24	3.00	2.21
1973	849	36,507	14,532	50.6	57,884	201.7	39.8	422.48	284.69	306.44	5,359.74	3,958.57	4,306.80	Y75	Y568	13.06	2.21	1.96
1974	881	34,420	12,080	42.4	49,792	174.7	35.1	342.47	251.96	278.34	4,787.54	3,355.13	3,817.22	103	548	12.53	1.75	2.41
1975	901	41,468	15,182	53.5	50,753	178.7	36.6	333.11	268.24	323.43	4,564.52	3,627.04	4,358.60	134	645	19.95	1.94	2.24
1976	914	50,751	22,670	79.3	67,287	235.3	44.7	383.88	326.28	383.88	4,990.85	4,403.06	4,990.85	130	884	27.40	2.16	1.80
1977	926	49,350	20,650	72.2	68,474	239.4	41.8	390.93	350.49	364.08	5,287.65	4,597.26	4,865.60	179	967	20.35	2.05	1.68
1978	936	62,704	30,309	106.3	93,222	327.1	48.3	452.60	364.04	449.55	6,097.26	4,867.91	6,001.85	125	1,126	26.80	2.38	1.48
1979	950	65,909	33,448	117.0	94,964	332.0	50.7	465.24	435.13	459.61	6,590.69	5,925.87	6,569.47	132	1,322	21.09	2.39	1.42
1980	960	73,221	35,407	124.2	100,218	351.6	48.4	497.96	449.01	494.10	7,188.28	6,475.93	7,116.38	164	1,394	19.94	2.34	1.48
1981	974	87,978	48,297	169.5	105,930	371.7	54.9	603.92	495.79	570.31	8,019.14	6,956.52	7,681.84	246	1,783	20.36	2.22	1.46
1981 Jan.	960	75,737	3,149	143.1	8,362	380.1	4.2	510.06	495.79	510.06	7,315.33	7,137.59	7,284.15	189	1,456	20.76	2.39	1.42
Feb.	961	75,550	2,612	118.7	5,310	241.4	3.5	511.94	501.51	507.73	7,322.06	7,095.26	7,149.57	190	1,445	20.66	2.33	1.40
Mar.	962	79,206	4,356	174.3	9,772	390.8	5.5	530.17	502.80	530.17	7,334.31	6,956.52	7,334.31	257	1,604	20.63	2.37	1.42
Apr.	963	84,029	5,880	245.0	15,482	645.1	7.0	560.86	533.65	560.86	7,674.19	7,388.89	7,674.19	231	1,663	20.51	2.44	1.44
May	963	84,195	5,546	241.1	11,438	497.3	6.6	561.65	540.01	560.24	7,576.18	7,264.01	7,558.65	238	1,641	20.11	2.35	1.46
Jun.	966	88,270	5,112	204.5	10,017	400.6	5.8	586.15	546.42	586.15	7,867.42	7,334.97	7,867.42	236	1,688	21.16	2.42	1.45
Jul.	968	89,621	4,679	180.0	8,780	337.7	5.2	595.10	581.85	592.15	7,927.59	7,717.07	7,828.26	223	1,710	20.76	2.33	1.42
Aug.	969	89,765	4,717	188.7	9,564	382.5	5.3	603.92	584.54	589.44	8,019.14	7,726.59	7,815.78	179	1,725	20.48	2.31	1.43
Sep.	970	84,080	2,728	118.6	6,376	277.2	3.2	582.47	546.37	550.27	7,735.71	7,037.12	7,455.50	143	1,736	19.60	2.16	1.51
Oct.	972	84,794	3,408	136.3	7,953	318.1	4.0	561.24	526.75	552.62	7,587.80	7,076.65	7,499.42	241	1,837	19.89	2.17	1.54
Nov.	972	85,315	3,372	153.3	6,940	315.5	4.0	566.16	551.74	554.45	7,674.92	7,489.28	7,549.33	279	1,894	20.18	2.18	1.50
Dec.	974	87,978	2,738	119.0	5,937	258.1	3.1	573.43	552.92	570.31	7,789.16	7,521.73	7,681.84	246	1,783	20.36	2.22	1.50

Source. Daiwa Securities Company Ltd., *Tokyo Stock Market Quarterly Review*, various issues, 1982.

SECTION **6.8**

CANADA: EQUITY MARKETS

CONTENTS

SECTION **6.8**

CANADA: EQUITY MARKETS

Roger Hubley

Any company that wishes to raise money by selling stocks or bonds to the public in Canada must be legally incorporated under either provincial or federal legislation. A company incorporated under Canadian law is treated as an individual person and thus can enter into contracts, purchase or sell property, sue or be sued, and so forth. Virtually all incorporated companies in Canada raise capital financing either by selling shares or bonds or both. This section is concerned with the buying and selling of equity shares in Canada. Much of the material here is based on Canadian Securities Institute publications, particularly the *Canadian Securities Course,* 1980 and *How to Invest in Canadian Securities,* 1978. (Most of the features of stock trading in Canada duplicate those that occur in the United States.)

An indication of the importance of corporate equity financing in Canada is given in Exhibit 1, which shows the net new security issues by the Canadian federal government, the 10 provincial governments, municipal governments, and corporations for the period 1976–1981. Aggregate new financing increased at an annual average rate of 15.9% over this period. The annual average growth rate in net new security financing would have been even greater except for the sharp 24.4% decline in 1979. In 1981 the Canadian federal government accounted for 34.9% of total net new issues; the provincial governments 33.6%; the municipal government 1.0%; and the corporate sector 32.2%. Compared to the year 1976, the corporate sector increased its share of net new security financing at the expense of provincial and municipal governments. The corporate sector is a major borrower, ranking behind only the federal government in Canadian net new security financing in 1981. A breakdown in net new corporate security issues between bonds and common and preferred shares is also given in Exhibit 1. For the six-year period shown, corporate net new financing was evenly split between bond issues and common and preferred shares.

TYPES OF EQUITIES AND EQUITY CHARACTERISTICS

COMMON STOCK. When the investor purchases a common stock, he receives a **share certificate** as evidence of legal ownership. This certificate normally states the number of shares purchased, their par value, if any, and usually the owner's name

EXHIBIT 1 NET NEW ISSUES OF SECURITIES PLACED IN CANADA AND ABROAD, 1976–1981 (in millions)

Year	Government of Canada					Corporations		Total
	Bonds	Treasury Bills	Provincial	Municipal	Other	Bonds	Common and Preferred Stocks	
1976	C$2,588	C$1,645	C$9,261	C$1,238	C$15	C$3,992	C$1,275	C$20,014
1977	5,536	2,470	7,514	1,201	78	5,072	3,143	25,014
1978	7,670	2,820	7,207	636	3	4,648	6,980	29,963
1979	6,159	2,125	6,473	587	−8	2,807	4,506	22,649
1980	5,913	5,975	8,640	439	215	3,718	5,352	29,752
1981	12,784	−35	12,601	361	42	6,292	5,927	37,971

Source. *Bank of Canada Review*, November 1982.

and transfer agent. A **street certificate** is a share certificate that is made out in the name of the investment dealer or a stock broker. When the common stock is sold, the seller's broker or dealer normally has the former shareholder's certificate canceled and reregistered in the name of the new buyer (or new broker or dealer in the case of street certificates). Thereafter, all dividend payments and company reports are sent to the name appearing on the certificate.

There are certain advantages to being a common shareholder in Canada, including

1. The right to dispose of share holdings. The common shareholder has the right to sell common shares whenever he so desires if a buyer can be found. When the issuing company first offers its common shares for sale, the proceeds of such sales belong to the company. Thereafter, when the outstanding shares are traded the sale proceeds go to the seller of the shares, not to the company.
2. Limited liability. If the company goes bankrupt, the financial liability of common shareholders is limited to the purchase price of the shares. Common shareholders are not liable for any amount of money beyond their initial investment to the creditors of a bankrupt company.
3. The right to vote. Each share of common stock gives the investor one vote in the election of the board of directors for the company and for and against major issues at stockholders' meetings. The common shareholder can vote by proxy, designating a named person, usually part of management, to vote the shares of the proxy signer at the shareholders' meetings.
4. Ownership of an irredeemable security. A share of common stock is an irredeemable security. The company cannot redeem a common share by call, although companies can purchase their own outstanding shares for cancellation from investors who are willing to sell.
5. Right to share in earnings. Common shareholders, as part owners of a company, share in the net earnings of the company in the form of dividends. Dividends on common shares are not paid automatically, but must be declared by the board of directors. Dividend payments are made directly to the named investor on the share certificate. Dividends are paid annually, semiannually, quarterly, or not at all, at the option of the board of directors. The board of directors can decide to pay the dividend in the form of additional stock rather than cash. Stock dividends are made in exact proportion to the number of shares held by the individual shareholder.

In Canada a company can engage in stock splits (with the approval of its shareholders) in order to lower the market value of its stock and achieve a wider distribution. In most cases a company will merely issue additional certificates to carry out the stock split. For example, on a four-for-one split, the company will send the investor holding one share a certificate for three additional shares. Alternatively, the company could split the stock by calling in its old outstanding shares in exchange for new share certificates. The stock split reduces the market price for each share in proportion to the split. For example, after a four-for-one split, a $100 stock would sell for $25. Conversely, a company in Canada can also engage in reverse stock splits, offering one new share for four old and as a result the market value of each common share will increase in proportion.

PREFERRED SHARES. In Canada, as in the United States, preferred stockholders have a prior claim ahead of common shareholders in the event of liquidation to a company's after-tax earnings in the form of dividends and to the company's assets. However, the claims of debt creditors and bondholders rank ahead of both preferred and common shareholders.

Preferred shareholders are entitled to a fixed dividend payment, expressed either as a percentage of par value or as a stated amount in dollars. These dividend payments, unlike bond interest, are received only if they are declared by a company's board of directors. However, no dividends can be paid on common stock unless the preferred shareholders have received all dividend payments to which they are entitled.

Preferred shares are usually **nonvoting** although it is a common characteristic that the nonvoting cumulative preferred does receive a voting privilege if the preferred dividends are missed for a stated length of time. The preferred shares have or do not have the following features.

1. Cumulative or noncumulative preferred shares. In the case of **cumulative preferred shares,** a dividend must be ultimately paid to the stockholder, whether the company earns it or not. Dividends that have not been paid (or passed) pile up or cumulate in the form of arrears. These cumulative dividends or arrears must be paid in a later period before any dividends on common stock can be paid. On **noncumulative** preferred stock, the shareholder receives a specified dividend payment only when such dividends are declared. If they are not declared, the dividends do not accrue.
2. Participating or nonparticipating preferred shares. If the preferred stock is **participating,** the stockholder is entitled to a share in the company's earnings over and above the specified dividend rate. For example, the preferred stockholder might be entitled to a specified dividend rate of 5% annually plus an additional equal share in earnings to common stockholders once the common shareholders have been paid $1.00 a share. A **nonparticipating** preferred receives a specified dividend only.
3. Redeemable preferred shares. The preferred shares are callable if the issuing company has the right to redeem them. Callable preferred shares will generally state the price at which these shares can be redeemed. This call price usually provides for a small premium that is paid above the par value of the stock and its regular dividend. The call price acts as a ceiling price for the market value of the preferred shares, as no investor would be willing to pay a price higher than the call price.

   Many Canadian callable preferred shares have either an annual sinking fund or a purchase fund for their gradual retirement. The company sets aside a specified percentage of its net earnings or a fixed sum annually in these funds in order to retire a portion of its outstanding preferred stock by calling in the preferred shares or by buying them on the market, if the market price is less than the call price.
4. Convertible preferred shares. The issuing company can grant the preferred shareholder the right to convert his shares into some other class of shares. There are many versions of this conversion privilege; generally, the preferred shareholder is given the option of converting preferred shares to the company's common stock on the basis of a given number of common stocks for each preferred within a specified time period.

RIGHTS AND WARRANTS. A Canadian corporation can give its existing shareholders the right to acquire additional shares in any new stock issues. The company can offer each shareholder the right to buy shares in direct proportion to the number of shares the investor already owns. For example, the company might give the shareholders the right to buy one additional share for each 10 shares held. These new shares are offered to the existing shareholder at a price below the current market price of the old shares.

Generally, the company grants rights to the shareholder in the same way that it pays dividends to the investor. Normally a company will issue one right for each common share outstanding. The shareholder can then combine these rights into the multiples required for purchasing one or more shares in any new share issue. The shareholder pays no commission when these rights are used to buy new shares.

Rights have market value, since they are transferrable and the rights holder can purchase additional common shares of the issuing company at a price below the current market price. Investors can buy additional rights or sell surplus rights on the stock exchanges. A rights holder need not be an existing shareholder to buy the common shares of the issuing company. Normally, however, the investor can trade rights or exercise these rights to buy common shares only for a stated period of time (usually four to six weeks), after which the rights expire and become worthless. Generally, the stock exchanges will automatically list the rights for trading if the common shares of the issuing company are listed on the exchange.

When issuing bonds or preferred shares a company in Canada sometimes also grants the investor an option to buy the company's common shares at a stated price, which is generally below the current market price. This option (which is evidenced by a certificate known as a **warrant**) is transferrable and thus such options are actively traded. Warrants, like rights, also expire after a specified period of time; but, unlike rights, the time period is normally measured in years, not weeks.

EQUITY MARKET PARTICIPANTS AND INSTITUTIONS

INVESTMENT DEALERS AND BROKERS. When purchasing or selling a security in Canada, the investor normally goes to an investment firm, that acts as a dealer or broker or an underwriter of a new security issue. An investment dealer buys a security at one price and sells it to clients at another price. The dealer's profit is the difference between the buying and the selling price. At some point in the transaction the dealer personally will own the securities traded. An investment broker, in contrast, normally brings together the buyers and sellers of equities, for which service the broker receives a commission. The broker buys and sells on behalf of a client and normally does not own the shares traded at any stage of the transaction. As an underwriter, the investment firm purchases a new issue of securities from a particular company, an issue that it hopes to resell to the public at a higher price. The major financial firms in Canada generally engage in all these activities—dealing, brokerage, and underwriting.

These financial firms are generally incorporated as limited companies, although some are organized as partnerships and sole proprietorships. Most of the major investment firms have memberships in one or more of the stock exchanges in Canada. As investment dealers these firms can act as financial advisors to a particular company wishing to raise capital. An investment firm can advise a company about the type of financing required, the amount of financing that the market can absorb, the timing of new security issues, and the characteristics and price at which the security should be sold.

To conduct business in Canada, an investment firm must be registered with the appropriate provincial Securities Commission and must be a member of the Investment Dealers Association of Canada.

THE INVESTMENT DEALERS ASSOCIATION OF CANADA. The Investment Dealers Association (IDA), originally founded in 1916, is a national nonprofit professional organization whose membership consists of about 80 investment firms in Canada. The IDA is a self-policing body that has considerable regulatory and disciplinary powers over its members. It engages in numerous activities to encourage saving and investment in Canada. It has established many bylaws and regulations for its members to prevent fraudulent practices and to protect the well-being of both investors and its members. The IDA works closely with each provincial Securities Commission and the provincial and federal governments to establish security industry regulations and legislation. As a self-regulatory body the IDA is responsible for educational standards, the adequacy of member firm capital, maintaining the orderly marketing and trading of securities, maintaining high ethical standards for its members, providing statistical data, and the like. The IDA can impose fines, and suspend and expel members for any infraction of its bylaws or regulations.

THE CANADIAN SECURITIES INSTITUTE. The Canadian Securities Institute is a nonprofit educational organization cosponsored by the IDA and the organized stock exchanges in Canada. The institute offers basic and advanced correspondence courses on buying and selling financial securities and prepares and administers the qualifying examinations for investment dealers and brokers. The provincial securities regulatory bodies, the IDA, and the stock exchanges in Canada require security salespersons to complete successfully the basic Canadian securities course offered by the Canadian Securities Institute. The address of the Canadian Securities Institute is 380 Bay Street, Toronto, Ontario, Canada.

BUYING AND SELLING EQUITIES

An investor can purchase or sell common and preferred shares on either the over-the-counter (OTC) market or through the facilities of one of the organized stock exchanges in Canada. Information on stock exchange membership, regulations, and listing requirements is also available in Forbes and Johnson, 1980.

OVER–THE–COUNTER MARKET. The over-the-counter market is located primarily in Toronto, Montreal, and Vancouver. The OTC market, however, does not have a central location for trading securities. The investment dealers engaged in this market are not necessarily members of an organized stock exchange and thus are not subject to the direct regulation of the organized exchanges. Most bond trading is done in this market, but the dealers-brokers also trade the common and preferred shares of companies that are not listed on an organized stock exchange.

The type of shares traded in OTC markets varies greatly, and includes speculative mining and oil shares, new industrial stocks not yet listed on an organized exchange, and the shares of mature companies who have decided not to list their stock offerings.

In OTC trading, the small investor normally purchases an unlisted common stock or preferred share directly from the inventory of such securities held by the investment dealer. If the investment dealer does not have the requested equity in inventory, the dealer can attempt to purchase the shares from another dealer. The investment dealers-brokers arrange trades directly with one another in OTC markets using modern telecommunication systems rather than meeting on the floor of a stock exchange. The price of the traded security is reached through negotiation between the dealer-brokers rather than auction bidding in organized exchanges. When buying unlisted equities, the investor must normally pay the quoted price for the security, but generally no commissions are charged on OTC stock trading.

The size of the OTC market for equity trading in Canada cannot be measured precisely, since complete statistics are not available for this market. The Investment Dealers Association does provide some OTC trading information for unlisted equities in Ontario. The Montreal Stock Exchange gathers and distributes some OTC equity trading information in Quebec. The financial press in Canada sometimes prints the bid and ask price quotations for selected unlisted shares.

STOCK EXCHANGES. Most of the trading in common and preferred shares in Canada on the organized stock exchanges. There are five organized stock exchanges in Canada located in Toronto, Montreal, Vancouver, Calgary, and Winnipeg. The stock exchanges are competitive auction markets in which the prices for the traded securities are determined by the economic forces of supply and demand. Trading occurs on the floor of the exchanges as brokers buy and sell preferred shares, common shares, rights, and warrants. Generally, only listed securities are bought and sold on the exchanges. Moreover, a company's shares can be traded on more than one exchange, including stock exchanges in the United States. The Canadian stock exchanges are private institutions, with their own rules and regulations governed by their own members under the overall preview of the appropriate provincial regulatory body. The major exchanges are

Toronto Stock Exchange
234 Bay Street
Toronto, Ontario, Canada M5J 1R1
(416)-868-5100

The Montreal Stock Exchange
P.O. Box 61, Tour de la Bourse
Montreal, Quebec, Canada H4Z 1A9
(514)-871-2424

Vancouver Stock Exchange
536 Howe Street
Vancouver, British Columbia, Canada V6C 2E1

The Alberta Stock Exchange
3rd Floor, 300 Fifth Avenue S.W.
Calgary, Alberta, Canada T2P 3C4
(403)-262-7791

Winnipeg Stock Exchange
303–167 Lombard Avenue
Winnipeg, Manitoba, Canada R3B OT6
(204)-942-8431

A comparison of the share volume and dollar value of the listed security trading on Canada's organized stock exchanges is given in Exhibit 2. In terms of value of shares traded, the Toronto Stock Exchange is clearly dominant. In 1981 the value of shares traded on the five Canadian exchanges amounted to \$33.6 billion, of which the Toronto Stock Exchange accounted for nearly 80%. The Vancouver Stock Exchange is the largest exchange in terms of volume and the second largest in terms of value. The other major Canadian exchange, the Montreal Stock Exchange, accounted for only 9.9% of the total dollar value of transactions. The remaining western exchanges, which make up the balance, specialize in the trading of local mining and oil and gas company shares.

Exchange Membership. Only members of the stock exchanges can trade listed securities on the floor of the exchange. Initially, when a particular exchange was founded, membership seats were sold to different individuals. To become a new member, a broker generally must buy a seat from an existing member who is willing to sell, and then make a written application to the board of governors of the exchange. The market price of an exchange seat varies over time in response to the demand and the available number of seats to be sold.

Seats on the exchanges can be purchased and held for investment reasons. Consequently, the number of exchange seats normally exceeds the number of active members. For example, in 1981 there were 126 seats on the Toronto Stock Exchange, but only 78 member firms. Nonetheless, despite the number of seats held, each exchange member is limited to one vote.

The majority of the seats on Canadian exchanges are held by the partners and directors of large Canadian investment firms. Moreover, many of these brokerage firms hold membership in more than one stock exchange in Canada and even in the United States.

To be eligible for a seat on a Canadian stock exchange, the potential member

EXHIBIT 2 TOTAL SHARE VOLUME AND DOLLAR VALUE OF TRANSACTIONS FOR ALL STOCK EXCHANGES IN CANADA, 1981

Exchange	Share Volumes (in hundreds)	Percentage	Dollar Values of Transactions (in hundreds of Canadian dollars)	Percentage
Toronto	1,510,273	43.9%	C\$25,940,255	77.3%
Montreal	204,592	5.9	3,328,231	9.9
Vancouver	1,585,952	45.6	3,859,216	11.5
Alberta	178,670	5.1	426,806	1.3
Winnipeg	914	0.9	967	0.0
Total	3,480,401	100.0%	C\$33,555,475	100.0%

Source. Toronto Stock Exchange.

must satisfy certain criteria as to experience, financial status, and ethical responsibility. To become a member, the applicant must be elected in a secret ballot by the majority of existing exchange members. Once a broker-dealer becomes a member, he must observe the regulations and bylaws of the respective stock exchange. Among these many regulations the following are generally included.

1. The investment firm must agree to annual audits, and occasional, surprise audits by the stock exchange's own examining staff. Moreover, the investment firms must meet certain requirements for the segregation of each customer's securities.
2. Client orders must be executed as given. Trading on the exchange floor is limited to open outcry during regular trading hours to prevent security trades at secret prices.
3. The client's order must always be given priority when it competes at the same price with that of an employee of the member firm.
4. The investment firm must agree to the severe penalties imposed for making a fictitious exchange transaction, accepting orders where no real change in share ownership takes place, or making trades that abnormally disturb the market.

Listing Requirements. For a company's securities to be traded on Canadian stock markets they must be accepted by the appropriate stock exchange's board of governors as listed for trading. To obtain a listing for its securities, the company must make a formal application to the particular stock exchange, revealing all relevant facts about the company's operations. The company must provide, in support of its application, copies of the company's charter, any current security prospectus, financial statements (including five years of profit and loss statements), annual reports, and other relevant documents.

In general, companies must show that they have a reputable management and that they have sufficient financial resources to carry on the company's business for the foreseeable future. To do this they must show that they have a good earnings performance over the previous three to five years. In the case of mining and oil companies, the companies must also demonstrate that they have acceptable plans and financial resources to cover a one-year exploration and development program and that they possess working capital substantially above the cost of current exploration and development projects. The stock exchanges also generally require that the company shares be widely distributed, with at least 25% of the issued shares in the hands of 150 to 300 shareholders. This last requirement assures the liquidity of the shares and helps prevent stock market manipulation by any large individual shareholders.

Once a company's securities are accepted for listing, the company must comply with certain stock exchange regulations to maintain its listing. In particular, the listed company must release quickly to the public any news or information that might materially affect the market for its securities. For example, the company must submit annual reports to its shareholders and the stock exchange; it must publish quarterly financial statements; it must notify the stock exchange promptly about dividends and the allotment of rights and warrants; it must abide by the stock exchange requirements governing options, underwriting, sale or issue of shares; and the company must notify the stock exchange of any proposed change in the business or financial state of the company. Many of these prompt and full disclosure regulations of the stock exchanges are aimed at preventing unusual market activity or substantial price changes in the company's stock due to certain investors having inside information.

To protect investors, the stock exchange can temporarily or permanently suspend trading in the listed shares of a particular company or even delist these shares if the company fails to comply with the terms of its listing agreement with the stock exchange or if the company violates the exchange's bylaws and regulations.

Trading Units. To facilitate floor trading in Canada, the stock exchanges have specified board lots, which contain a certain quantity of shares in various price ranges (see following).

Occasionally the exchanges specify different quantities as "special board lots" for particular stock issues. Moreover, the stock exchanges permit stock trading in odd lot or broken lot units, which refer to a block of shares having a smaller quantity than board lots.

Share Price	Board Lot
Shares selling under C$0.10	1,000 shares
Shares selling at C$0.10 and under C$1.00	500 shares
Shares selling at C$1.00 and under C$100	100 shares
Shares selling at $100 and over	10 shares

Commission Rates. The stock exchanges in Canada require members to impose standardized commission rates on executing buy and sell orders. The schedule of commission rates provides for two distinct types of orders—those with values of $5,000 or less and those in excess of $5,000. (See Exhibit 3.) Member firms and their employees are generally prohibited from attempting, either directly or indirectly, to obtain listed business from investors by offering any rebates or discounts from these minimum commission rates, except as allowed under stock exchange regulations.

EXHIBIT 3 SCHEDULE OF COMMISSION RATES

ORDERS OF C$5,000 OR LESS

Price for Each Share	Base Commission Rate
C$0.005 to C$4.99	3%

Example: The commission on 100 shares sold at C$4 a share would be 3% of (100 × C$4) = C$12

Price for Each Share	Base Commission Rate
C$5 to C$14.99	2% plus C$0.05 a share

Example: The commission on 100 shares sold at C$10.00 a share is

2% of (100 × C$10) =	$20
plus 100 × C$0.05 =	5
	$25

EXHIBIT 3 (*Continued*)

Price for Each Share	Base Commission Rate
C$15 and above	1% plus C$0.20 a share

Example: The commission on 100 shares sold at $20 a share is

$$\begin{aligned} 1\% \text{ of } (100 \times \text{C\$}20) &= \text{C\$}20 \\ \text{plus } 100 \times \text{C\$}0.20 &= \underline{\quad 20} \\ &\quad \underline{\underline{\text{C\$}40}} \end{aligned}$$

ORDERS OVER C$5,000 AND UP TO C$500,000

The following tapering schedule can be applied to the base commission on any order valued over C$5,000 up to and including C$500,000.

For the First C$40,000 of the Order:

Money Involved	Tapering Schedule
On first C$5,000	100% of base commission
On next C$15,000	90% of base commission
On next C$20,000	80% of base commission

For Portion Over C$40,000 and Up to $500,000
The following commission charge applies to each share in the portion of the order over C$40,000 in value.

Where the Average Order Price (of Canadian Transactions Is	The Charge for Each Share Associated with the Portion of the Order Over $40,000 Is
Under C$10 a share	Average order price (of Canadian transactions) ÷ 100
C$10 or above	C$0.10

In determining the tapering schedule applicable to an order, only the portion of the order executed on a stock exchange in Canada shall be considered.

Source. Canadian Securities Institute: *How to Invest in Canadian Securities.*

Types of Buy and Sell Orders. An investor can choose between several options when placing buy and sell orders on either the organized stock exchange or the over-the-counter market.

Market Order. The investor simply orders that a specified number of shares be bought or sold at the best possible price as soon as the order reaches the stock exchange trading floor. The investor does not specify a price for the trade, which means that he will be accepting the offer price when selling or paying the bid price when buying. Normally the broker on the floor will try to obtain a higher bid price when selling or a lower offer price when buying than that prevailing on the floor if possible. This type of order is the most common and is carried out the most rapidly since no price is specified.

Limit Order. The investor specifies a maximum price that he will pay when buying and a minimum price that he will accept when selling. If the broker cannot obtain the limit price for the investor, no security trade is made.

Limit Order with Price Discretion. The investor gives a limit order but allows the floor broker some limited price discretion in executing the transaction.

Day Order. A day order is an investor order to buy or sell that is good only for the day that it is given to the broker. All orders are considered to be day orders unless otherwise specified. There are also week and month orders.

Open, or Good till Canceled, Orders. An open, or good till canceled (GTC), order is an investor order that normally involves a specific price, but remains in effect indefinitely until the order is either executed or canceled. Normally most brokers limit a GTC order for a specified time period (e.g., 60 to 90 days) and then, if not executed, request the client to either reconfirm or cancel the GTC order.

Stop Orders. A stop order is an investor order designed to reduce the amount of loss that might be incurred or protect the profit that might be earned by the investor. A stop loss order is a selling order that becomes effective as a market order when the price of a stock falls to or below a specified limit price. For example, if an investor had purchased a particular stock for C$80 and the current market price is C$100, the investor has earned a paper profit of C$20 a share. If the investor expects that the market price will fall, he or she might give a stop loss order to sell at C$90. The order to sell can be carried out at a price below the C$90 as the broker attempts to obtain the best possible price available for the client. A stop buy order, which is the opposite of a stop loss order, can be given by an investor who has sold shares short in an attempt to reduce loss or protect profit if the market price should rise unexpectedly.

Contingent Order. A contingent order is an investor order to buy one security, and simultaneously, to sell another security. These two orders can be given (1) at the market price, (2) at the same price, (3) at a certain price spread, (4) at a share ratio (e.g., 100 shares of one company and 200 shares of another company). With a contingent order, however, one transaction cannot be executed without the other.

Switch Order. A switch order is an investor order to sell one security and to use the proceeds to buy another security.

Delayed Delivery Order. A delayed delivery order is an investor order that involves a security trade in which there is a clear understanding that the delivery of the securities will be delayed beyond the normal settlement period.

Either/Or Order. An either/or order is placed when an investor order to buy or sell one security is given when orders for other securities are still to be executed; as soon as the broker executes any one of these either/or orders the other order is automatically canceled.

All-or-None Order. An all-or-none order is an investor order in which the broker must buy or sell a specified number of shares before the client will accept the order as being executed. Generally the all-on-none order will specify the minimum number of shares to be traded.

Any-Part Order. An any-part order is an order for which the investor indicates a willingness to accept stock shares in odd, broken, or board lots up to the full amount of the order.

Fill or Kill Order. A fill or kill order is an order that specifies that as soon as a part of an ordered trade is completed, the remaining portion of the trade, which is not executed, is canceled.

Good-through Order. Any buy or sell order that is good for a specified number of days and then is canceled if the order has not been executed is a good-through order.

Opening Order. An opening order is a buy or sell order that is to be executed at the best available price at the market opening.

Pro Order. A pro order is a professional (an employee of the member firm or a member of the immediate family of an employee) or nonclient order that must be executed only after a client's order if both orders compete at the same price for the same security.

Cancel or Change Former Order. An investor order that cancels or changes a current outstanding order to the broker is a cancel or change former order.

Margin Orders. With a margin order an investor can purchase shares that have a market price of C$1.50 or higher on margin. The investor must put up 50% of the purchase price; the remainder can be borrowed from an investment broker. Daily interest is charged by the broker for the duration of the loan. Generally, the investment firm requires the margin buyer to complete a margin agreement form, which gives the broker wide powers to manage the margin account.

Short Sales. With short sales the investor sells a stock that the investor does not yet own, one that is borrowed from a broker. The short seller must maintain a cash position with the broker in excess of the market value of the stock sold short (usually 150% of market value) as security for the sale. The investor's broker will normally borrow the stock sold short from a third party for delivery to the purchaser. Ultimately the investor must buy back the stock sold short and cover the original sale by returning the stock to the lender. An investor sells short to make an expected speculative profit if the investor expects the market price to fall.

The Contract Note and Delivery. If an investor's buy or sell order is not executed on the day it is placed, the investment firm sends the investor confirmation of an outstanding order. If the buy or sell order is executed, the broker will send the client a contract note confirming the purchase or sale. The contract note specifies both the date the order was executed and the settlement date—normally the fifth business day after the transaction date. Complete payment for securities purchased (or delivery of securities sold) must be made by the settlement date.

REGULATING THE SECURITIES MARKET

In addition to the numerous rules and regulations of the Investment Dealers Association of Canada and the various organized stock exchanges, all the provincial governments of Canada have enacted various laws to regulate the underwriting, distribution, and sale of securities. These Securities Acts are enforced by a provincial Securities Commission, which is normally a government department under the responsibility of the attorney general for each province. Most provincial Securities Acts are modeled on the Ontario Securities Act (last amended in 1980), although various features of the provincial legislations are different from one province to another.

Generally, the various provincial Securities Acts in Canada are based on the principal of full, true, and plain disclosure of all relevant facts related to new security issues and trade in outstanding issues. Security issuers must fully disclose all information about their operations and financial health that might affect the value of their securities. A company cannot issue securities for public sale unless all relevant information has been fully disclosed to the satisfaction of the provincial Securities Commission. Securities regulation is centered around three main areas: registration, disclosure, and investigation-prosecution.

REGISTRATION. No one in Canada can legally sell securities to the public or advise investors unless registered with the respective provincial Securities Commission. These commissions can suspend or cancel the registrations of existing dealer-brokers if it is in the public interest to do so.

Every financial firm that sells securities or underwrites new security issues must be registered in the province where the securities are sold. All investment dealers and brokers employed by an investment firm must also be registered with the appropriate provincial Securities Commission. These registrations must be renewed annually. Applicants for registrations must provide all relevant personal, employment, and educational background information, including bankruptcies, criminal records, or outstanding criminal charges or judgments. The individual dealer-broker must complete either the Canadian securities course or the Canadian Mutual Funds Association's course. All individuals must be registered as either salespersons, or partners, or officers and must, in turn, be associated with a firm that is registered separately with the appropriate provincial regulatory body.

The provincial Securities Acts, following the lead of Ontario, generally classify investment firms as dealers, advisers, or underwriters. A dealer is defined to be a person or company who trades in securities as a principal or as an agent, while an adviser is a person or company who advises investors in the buying and selling of securities. An underwriter is a person or company who as principal or as agent distributes to the public securities issued by some other company.

The provincial Securities Commission also controls the establishment and practices of the provincial stock exchanges. All stock exchanges must be registered with the appropriate Securities Commission and they must operate in accordance with all orders and rulings made by these regulatory bodies.

DISCLOSURE. The Securities Commission in each province requires all companies that sell new security issues to the public to file with the appropriate Securities Commission and deliver to the purchaser of a new issue a prospectus containing all relevant information about the company's operations and financial health that might affect the issue's market value. The mailing or delivery of the prospectus must be made before midnight on the second business day after a purchase contract has been agreed. In its prospectus a company must generally include in a narrative format the following information.

1. Complete details on the securities being offered for sale, including the offering price to the public, the proceeds to the issuer, and the underwriting discount on a unit and total basis.
2. Details of the company's history, its present and planned operations, and its real property assets.
3. The estimated net proceeds of the issue, as well as the principal uses to which the proceeds will be put.
4. All purchases and sales of shares or property assets by the issuing company and its subsidiaries over the two previous years and the impact of these transactions on the company's financial position.
5. Financial statements, including detailed notes and an auditor's report. Companies are generally required to provide an income statement covering the previous five years (or since the company's incorporation), a retained earnings statement, and a changes in financial position statement for the same period, a balance sheet no older than 120 days before the date of the prospectus, and a pro forma statement showing the company's capitalization as it will appear after the security issue financing has been completed.
6. A description of any pending legal proceeding in which the securities issuer is involved.

Each provincial Securities Commission has also established certain rules requiring continuous disclosure by a reporting security issuer. In particular, a reporting company issuing securities must release and file with the Securities Commission a press statement as soon as a material change occurs in the company's business, operations, or capital structure—any change that can reasonably be expected to have a significant effect on the market price or value of the company's securities. Moreover, companies whose common and preferred shares are traded on the recognized stock exchanges must file with the appropriate provincial Securities Commission annual and interim audited financial statements. Most provincial regulatory bodies also require the companies to provide their shareholders with audited annual and interim financial statements.

The provincial Securities Acts also generally require a company's management to solicit proxy votes from shareholders whenever management calls a shareholders' meeting. At the same time, management must provide shareholders with an information circular. The information circular must state whether or not the person or company giving the proxy can revoke it and whether or not the solicitation is on behalf of the management.

Provincial securities legislation requires that insiders of public companies report their buying and selling of company securities. Insiders include the directors, senior officers, and any person controlling or directing more than 10% of the voting rights attached to all outstanding equity shares of the company. Whenever a person or company becomes an insider, a report must be filed with the appropriate provincial Securities Commission. These reports must state the extent of the insider's ownership or control or direction over the company's security issues. Thereafter, an insider must report any change in holdings of the company's securities. These insider reports are made public. In Ontario, Quebec, and the western provinces, any insider or any of the insider's associates who has knowledge of a material fact or change in the company, one that has not been generally publicly disclosed, is liable for damages to the other person in a securities trade and perhaps also to the issuer of the security.

The various provincial Securities Acts have set out certain rules governing the takeover of one company by another. The takeover bid legislation is normally designed to protect the interests of the target company's shareholders by ensuring that each of these shareholders has the opportunity and full information to assess the takeover bid. In general, a takeover bid is defined as an offer to purchase a target company's voting securities in sufficient amount to give the bidding company 20% or more of the outstanding voting securities of the target company. Normally takeover bids must comply with certain informational requirements.

1. The bidding company must provide the shareholders of the target company a takeover bid circular setting out the details about the bid, the bidding company's holdings in the target company, and its relation to the target company's management.
2. A director's circular must be sent to the target company's shareholders in which the target company's directors recommend the acceptance or rejection of the takeover bid.
3. The takeover bid must be sent to all investors in the respective province who hold the voting securities being sought and those securities that are convertible into the desired class of securities.

Takeover bids made through the Toronto or Montreal or Vancouver stock exchanges are exempt from these takeover bid informational circular requirements but must satisfy the bylaws and regulations of the appropriate stock exchange under the provincial Securities Acts. If the bidding company knowingly omits or misrepresents material facts in the takeover bid circulars, the target company's shareholders can seek legal damages from the bidding company, the directors of the bidding company, and anyone who filed reports, opinions, or statements related to the takeover bid with the respective provincial Securities Commission.

INVESTIGATION AND PROSECUTION. A provincial Securities Commission has the power to make investigations and undertake prosecutions for violations of the Securities Acts. Under the authority of the appropriate provincial attorney general, the Securities Commission can seize documents, take evidence under oath, and compel witnesses to attend hearings. As a result of any prosecution, the Securities Commission can suspend or cancel registrations, order the cessation of security trading, or impose other severe penalties for fraud, misrepresentation, or the intentional omission of relevant information in the underwriting, distribution, or sale of securities. The Securities Commission cannot interfere with internal shareholder disputes or compel the restitution of monies paid. However, the Securities Commission can recommend that criminal charges resulting in fines or imprisonment be imposed against offending parties.

FOREIGN INVESTMENT REVIEW AGENCY. The Foreign Investment Review Agency (FIRA) was established by the federal government of Canada to screen foreign direct investment in Canada in order to determine whether such investments were likely to be of significant benefit to Canada (Langford, 1979). The FIRA legislation deals with two forms of foreign direct investment: the acquisition of control of a Canadian business enterprise by foreign residents, corporations, or governments and the establishment of new business in Canada, either by foreign residents who do not already have an existing business in Canada, or by expanding existing foreign resident–controlled companies in Canada.

Several aspects of the FIRA legislation should be emphasized. First, FIRA is concerned with the acquisition of control of Canadian-owned business, not with the purchase of company shares or assets where the purchase does not give the foreign buyer control. Second, FIRA is not concerned with foreign investors purchasing land or other real estate in Canada. Third, FIRA does not discriminate among foreign resident investors on the basis of nationality. Fourth, FIRA applies to foreign direct investment in all sectors of the Canadian economy. Fifth, FIRA is not retroactive. It does not review or regulate foreign resident direct investment made before the establishment of FIRA. Finally, the acquisition of the foreign parent of a Canadian subsidiary company constitutes obtaining control of the Canadian subsidiary and thus is subject to FIRA review.

In general terms, the FIRA legislation defines control in terms of two different kinds of acquisitions. First, foreign control is achieved whenever a foreign resident or group or corporation acquires more than 50% of a Canadian company's voting shares, unless the foreign resident or corporation purchasing the shares already had effective control of the Canadian company. Second, foreign de facto control is presumed to be acquired whenever a foreign resident or group or corporation purchases 5% of the voting shares of a Canadian company whose shares are publicly traded or when the foreign resident purchases 20% of the voting shares of a Canadian company whose shares are not publicly traded. In the second case, the presumption as to foreign control is subject to review on submission to FIRA and the responsible minister.

The Foreign Investment Review Agency screens foreign direct investment using the criteria of "significant benefit to Canada" in terms of

The effect of the foreign direct investment on overall economic activity in Canada, including the impact on employment, on resource processing, on the use of Canadian-produced goods and services, and on exports from Canada.

The degree and significance of participation by Canadian residents in the company and the industry sector to which the company belongs.

The impact on productivity, industrial efficiency, and scientific and technological development and research in Canada.

The effect on industry and overall economic competition in Canada.

The compatibility of the foreign direct investment with Canadian industrial, economic, and regional development policies.

The relative weight given to these and other factors when determining "significant benefit to Canada" varies in time and across industries and regions. The

Foreign Investment Review Agency assesses the proposed foreign direct investment in terms of the "significant benefit to Canada" and advises the Federal Minister of Industry, Trade and Commerce whether or not the foreign direct investment should be allowed. The Federal Minister, on the basis of FIRA's assessment, can then allow or disallow the proposed foreign direct investment.

TAXATION OF EQUITY INCOME

The following presents a brief outline of the major features of the taxing of dividend income and capital gains on equities in Canada (*Canadian Master Tax Guide 1981*, 1981). However, the tax laws are fairly complex and are amended and changed on a continuous basis. For any major tax problem, the interested investor is advised to consult a tax lawyer or accountant.

THE TAX ENVIRONMENT. In Canada, both the federal and the provincial governments have the constitutional power to impose taxes. However, the taxing power of the federal government is unlimited, while the provincial governments are limited to direct taxation within each province. Only the federal government can levy indirect taxes (a direct tax is supposedly one that is imposed on the person intended to pay it). In general economic terms, an indirect tax would be a tax that is the major determinant of the market price of a good of service. However, the courts have decided that the provincial retail sales tax is a direct tax on the basis that it is collected by retailers from consumers. Income taxes are considered to be direct taxes in Canada.

The principal taxes levied by the federal government include individual income taxes, corporate income taxes, customs duties and excise taxes, and manufacturer (or wholesaler) sales taxes.

The provincial governments impose individual income taxes, corporate income taxes, succession duties and gift taxes (in Quebec only), retail sales taxes, and natural resource royalties.

The federal government collects all provincial income taxes (except in the province of Quebec) and corporate income taxes (except in Ontario). Quebec administers its own income tax on both individuals and corporation, while Ontario collects its own corporate income tax.

Canada imposes income tax on the gross income of Canadian residents, regardless of the country of origin, and on the Canadian source of income of nonresidents. Income is broken down into four different categories, each of which is taxed differently: (1) income from employment (salaries and commissions); (2) income from property (rents, royalties, dividends, and interest); (3) income from business (profits); and (4) capital gains on the sales of real estate, stocks, bonds, and so forth.

All individual taxpayers must calculate their incomes and tax by calendar year. Corporations can choose any fiscal year to calculate their income and tax payments, but must report consistently on the same fiscal year basis.

To calculate the income tax payable, the Canadian taxpayer applies standard graduated tax rates to net taxable income. Once the gross tax payable is determined, certain tax credits are deducted to calculate the net tax payable. Canadian individual taxpayers receive a dividend tax credit for dividend income from Canadian corporations (described below) and a foreign tax credit, which applies to foreign source income.

EQUITY TAXATION FOR CANADIAN RESIDENT INVESTORS. Both corporations and individual investors must pay income tax on the capital gains earned from selling securities. However, only half of the capital gains is taxed, and both corporations and individual investors can deduct half of any capital losses incurred to reduce the taxable capital gains realized in the same year. Moreover, for both individual Canadian investors and corporations any remaining net capital losses can be deducted from taxable capital gains in the immediately preceding year and in future years until the net capital losses are fully absorbed. Individual investors resident in Canada, however, can also deduct any remaining capital losses from other types of income in the same year up to an annual maximum of $2,000. Moreover, the Canadian individual investor can deduct any remaining net capital losses up to a maximum of $2,000 annually from taxable income in the preceding year and in future years until the net capital losses are fully absorbed.

Capital gains are not taxed at a special rate, but are included in taxpayer income and taxed at normal graduated rates, the actual rate depending on a taxpayer's total income. The capital gains on the sale of company shares are normally calculated by deducting the adjusted cost of the shares (including commissions paid) from the proceeds of the sale. When identical shares are sold but were originally purchased at different prices, the identical shares are given a cost price calculated as an average price of the original prices paid.

Canadian resident taxpayers must report dividends on the shares held in Canadian and foreign resident companies as part of their taxable income. However, investment in Canadian securities is encouraged by allowing individual taxpayers, whether resident or nonresident, to deduct the first $1,000 of net investment income from taxable income. Moreover, individual taxpayers receive a preferential tax treatment in the form of a gross-up method of calculating dividend income from taxable Canadian corporations.

The gross-up method increases the dividend income received for tax purposes by 50%. The federal income tax is then imposed on the grossed-up dividend income and not on the actual dividend income received. Then a federal tax credit equal to 75% of the gross-up is applied to the federal tax. The net result of this procedure reduces the amount of tax the investor must pay on dividend income from Canadian corporations below that payable by applying the federal tax rate directly to the actual dividend income.

In all provinces (except Quebec) the provincial tax payable is calculated by applying the provincial tax rate to the gross federal tax payable on the dividend income. Then a provincial tax credit equal to the provincial tax rate times the federal tax credit is deducted to determine the provincial tax payable. For Quebec residents, the net federal tax payable is reduced by a standard federal tax abatement, while both the Quebec income tax and the Quebec standard dividend tax credit are applied to the grossed-up dividend income rather than the federal tax credit.

EQUITY TAXATION FOR FOREIGN RESIDENT INVESTORS. A foreign nonresident investor must pay income tax on any net capital gains or dividend income earned. In terms of capital gains, however, the rule that half of capital gains are included in income and that half of capital losses are allowed as deductions also applies for individual nonresident investors and nonresident corporations. The taxable capital gains and the deductable capital losses are combined with the nonresident investor's income from other Canadian sources and then taxed at the appropriate graduated individual or corporate rates.

Canada imposes a withholding tax on the dividend and other income of foreign investors. Generally, under bilateral tax agreements with other countries, the rate of withholding tax is 15%, although the legislated rate can be as high as 25%. The rate of withholding tax for foreign investors in companies with a specified degree of Canadian ownership, however, is 5% lower than the normal rates.

Canada has entered into bilateral tax agreements with some 30 countries (including the United States and the United Kingdom) to avoid double taxation of incomes and to prevent tax evasion. Generally under these agreements, nonresidents must still pay Canadian income tax and withholding tax on Canadian sources of income.

For example, under the Canada–United States Tax Convention of 1980, the withholding tax rate is limited to 15% on Canadian sources of income for U.S. resident investors or U.S. corporations having no permanent establishment in Canada. A U.S. resident individual investor or corporation having no permanent establishment in Canada is exempt from capital gains taxes in the United States from the sale of capital assets in Canada. Conversely, a Canadian resident investor or corporation having no permanent establishment in the United States is exempt from Canadian capital gains taxation on the sale of capital assets in the United States. Dividends and interest paid by a Canadian corporation to a U.S. resident investor or corporation are exempt from U.S. income taxes. Conversely, the dividends and interest paid to Canadian resident investors or corporation by U.S. resident corporations are exempt from Canadian income taxes.

SOURCES OF INFORMATION

The following list in not exhaustive, but can be used as an initial starting point for the interested investor.

Investment Houses and the Stock Exchanges. Most of the leading investment houses in Canada have research departments that provide stock market information, and analyses of specific markets and industries and the overall economy to their clients. Some of the leading broker-dealers in Canada with head offices in Toronto, Ontario include

Ames (A.E.) & Company Ltd.
Dominion Securities Ltd.
Greenshields Inc.
MacLeod, Young, Weir Ltd.
Merrill Lynch, Royal Securities Ltd.
Nesbitt, Thomson, Bonguard Ltd.
Pitfield McKay Ross Ltd.
Richardson Securities of Canada Ltd.

In addition, the Toronto, Montreal, and Vancouver exchanges publish monthly reviews that give price and sales volume information on the listed stocks plus supplementary data on dividends, stock splits, and membership. Listing statements, filing statements, and pamphlets describing the stock exchanges are also made available to the public upon request. Both the Toronto and Montreal stock exchanges compile and publish indexes of common stock prices. The Toronto Stock Exchange (TSE) 300 composite Index covers 300 companies divided into 14 major industry subgroups. The base year for all TSE indexes is 1975, with a base value of 100 for the 300 Composite Index. The Montreal Stock Exchange (MSE) produces an industrial index covering 65 companies and a composite index of 85 companies.

The Financial Press. These publications are written on a regular basis for a national audience of knowledgeable investors. They report economic and political developments on a national and international basis. They also carry detailed articles about individual industries and firms in Canada, as well as volume data on the securities traded on the organized stock exchanges, commodity markets, bond markets, and the foreign exchange markets in both Canada and the United States.

The Financial Post (weekly)
481 University Avenue
Toronto, Ontario, Canada M5W 1A7

The Financial Times (weekly)
Suite 500, 920 Yonge Street
Toronto, Ontario, Canada M4W 3L5

The Globe and Mail (daily)
444 Front Street West
Toronto, Ontario, Canada M5V 2S9

Investors Digest of Canada (bimonthly)
481 University Avenue
Toronto, Ontario, Canada M5W 1A7

The Business Quarterly
School of Business Administration
University of Western Ontario
London, Ontario, Canada N6A 5B9

Business Life (monthly)
Suite 100, 3016 19th Street N.E.
Calgary, Alberta, Canada T2E 6Y9

Canadian Business (monthly)
CB Media Limited, 70 The Esplanade
Toronto, Ontario, Canada M5E 1R2

The Canadian Business Review (quarterly)
The Conference Board of Canada
Suite 100, 25 McArthur Road
Ottawa, Ontario, Canada K1L 6R3

Executive (monthly)
1450 Don Mills Road
Don Mills, Ontario, Canada M3B 2X7

Books

Canadian Securities Course, Canadian Securities Institute, 1980.

How to Invest in Canadian Securities, Canadian Securities Institute, 1978.

Canadian Master Tax Guide 1981, CCH Canadian, Don Mills, Ontario, 1981.

Forbes, R.E. and D.L. Johnson, *Canadian Companies and the Stock Exchanges,* CCH Canadian, Don Mills, Ontario, 1980.

Langford, J.A., *Canadian Foreign Investment Controls,* 2nd ed., CCH Canadian, Don Mills, Ontario, 1979.

SECTION 6.9

THE ASIAN EQUITIES MARKETS

CONTENTS

SECTION 6.9

THE ASIAN EQUITIES MARKETS

Paul H. Aron
Laurie J. Aron

Several markets in the Asian Pacific area have reached sufficient size and development that they have attracted international investment. Japan has the largest market capitalization—it represents about 75% of the total of the entire Asian Pacific area. Japan, likewise, has the most liquid stock exchanges—representing over 82% of the value of all trading turnover in the Asian Pacific region. Australia, Hong Kong, and Singapore-Malaysia have smaller stock exchanges with less liquidity, but they have achieved considerable international importance. These markets have produced higher returns than Tokyo, as measured in U.S. dollars over a five-year period, but were less attractive in 1981. The other stock exchanges in the area are better classified as Third World equity markets—small in size and often highly illiquid, especially in market downturns.

AUSTRALIA

Australia's population of nearly 15 million is relatively small compared to the vast expanse of its territory—7.7 million square kilometers—and its rich resources. Australia's gross domestic product (GDP) for the fiscal year ending 30 June 1981 was Aus$130,119 million and GDP per capita was US$10,070. Exports equal 17% of the GDP, of which foodstuffs are over 34% and metals and coal almost 25%. Australia's major trading partners are the United States and Japan, the former representing 22% of Australia's imports and 11.2% of its exports, and the latter representing 19.1% of its imports and 27.2% of its exports.

Traditionally, Australia had been an agricultural country that experienced periodic gold rushes. From the end of World War II until 1973 Australia completed its transformation into an industrialized nation. Although agriculture, forestry, and fishing constitute less than 7% of its GDP, Australia remains the world's largest wool producer, its leading meat exporter, and a major producer of grains, dairy products, and sugar cane.

Australia's transformation was based upon its extremely rich mineral and energy resources. It accounts for 20% of world trade in iron ore and 25% in coal. Its relatively inexpensive electric power has stimulated the processing of bauxite into aluminum, for which Australia holds a 23% share of the world's output. Australia now provides about 66% of its oil requirements from domestic fields, and it is expected that in the coming decade the vast recoverable reserves of energy fuels—coal, natural gas, and uranium—will be further developed. The scale of capital requirements indicates that Australia's substantial dependence on overseas investments will probably continue.

In the 1950s and 1960s Australian manufacturing, protected from competition by barriers of distance and tariffs, expanded to supply the domestic market. In the 1970s, manufacturing growth decelerated, partly because of foreign competition and partly because of Australia's small population, whose annual growth had slowed to 1.2% from an average of 3% in 1953 to 1961. In addition, Australia was compelled to provide markets for the countries that imported its products. The tertiary (or service) sector, growing faster than the other two sectors, now employs over 50% of the labor force.

The great postwar expansion, fueled by overseas capital and immigration, slowed down sharply in the 1970s. Initially this was seen as a consequence of the brief stay in power of the Labor Party, with its nationalistic program of "buying back Australia for the Australians" and restricting immigration to a few professionals. The slowdown in expansion, however, was a worldwide phenomenon that spread after the rapid rise of oil prices.

Although the Labor party lost political power at the end of 1975, the economy grew very slowly and real per capita income in 1980 to 1981 was substantially lower than in 1973 to 1974. The Labor party guidelines for foreign investment continue: all foreign investment proposals are reviewed by the Treasurer, who is assisted by a Foreign Investment Review Borad (FIRB), and are permitted if not contrary to "the national interest." To purchase shares in an Australian company that is 15% owned by a single overseas interest or 40% owned by several overseas interests requires consultation with the FIRB. Foreign ownership is limited to below 10% in banks and is closely scrutinized in other financial and insurance firms. Foreign holdings are restricted to 25% in uranium mining, 20% in broadcasting, and 15% in television. New mining and rural industry ventures generally require a 50% minimum Australian interest. In other areas, foreign portfolios are generally unrestricted except for compliance with stock exchange regulations. No exchange control restricts the purchase of shares, and capital and income can be freely repatriated. Australian bankers have the general authority from the Reserve Bank to buy and sell securities on behalf of nonresidents. Dividends are subject to a 15% withholding for citizens of countries that have a tax treaty with Australia, such as the United States. For countries without such a treaty 30% of dividends are withheld. Offshore money is practically free from the capital gains tax; on the other hand, the profits of Australians who sell property within 12 months of acquisition are added to their taxable income.

Australia is a federal commonwealth of seven states. Discovered by the Dutch in 1606, it became a British colony in 1788. All people but about 10,000 aborigines are of European descent. As the country became more industrialized the federal government increased in power, but the individual states still retain considerable authority.

Thus, for example, the securities industry, formerly regulated by the states, is now federally supervised by the National Companies and Securities Commission (since 1 July 1981). This was made possible by an act of the commonwealth and of the various Australian states. Three regulatory codes came into force at that time, and the Companies Code, formerly the Companies Act, became operative on 1 January 1982.

The investment required to fuel Australia's economic expansion led to greater regulation of the securities industry and enhanced the drive to a single unified equities

EXHIBIT 1 AUSTRALIAN ECONOMY

Year[a]	Private Consumption Expenditure	Public Spending	Private Fixed Investment	Increase in Stock	Export of Goods and Services	Import of Goods and Services	Statistical Discrepancy	Total	
								Amount	Per capita (US$
GROSS DOMESTIC PRODUCT, AT CURRENT PRICE (AUS$000,000)									
1970–1971	20,408	7,144	5,839	460	5,032	5,092	43[b]	33,748	2,922
1971–1972	22,686	8.084	6,331	20	5,578	5,218	211	37,692	3,341
1972–1973	25,449	8,929	6,685	293[b]	6,918	5,353	537	42,872	4,105
1973–1974	30,092	10,820	7,772	1,209	7,784	7,782	1,549	51,444	5,575
1974–1975	36,569	14,855	8,534	1,094	9,889	10,247	1,074	61,768	6,129
1975–1976	43,605	18,155	10,322	50	10,982	10,837	431	73,708	6,586
1976–1977	49,830	20,510	11,859	1,152	13,190	13,784	419	83,176	6,778
1977–1978	55,390	23,075	12,707	417[b]	13,991	15,021	550	90,275	7,146
1978–1979	62,122	24,997	14,917	1,058	16,513	17,892	52[b]	101,663	8,007
1979–1980	69,834	27,567	16,330	674	21,625	20,915	767[b]	114,348	8,715
1980–1981	78,352	31,841	21,309	242	22,272	24,840	943	130,119	10,070
GROSS DOMESTIC PRODUCT, AT 1974–1975 PRICE									
1970–1971	30,526	12,323	9,290	461	8,864	7,841	54[b]	53,569	4,637
1971–1972	31,786	12,642	9,411	102[b]	9,481	7,552	316	55,982	4,963
1972–1973	33,545	12,809	9,346	530[b]	9,673	7,660	750	57,933	5,547
1973–1974	35,403	13,419	9,591	1,482	9,083	9,985	1,905	60,898	6,599
1974–1975	36,569	14,855	8,534	1,094	9,889	10,247	1,074	61,768	6,129
1975–1976	37,718	15,780	8,888	72	10,213	9,755	406	63,322	5,736
1976–1977	38,642	15,946	9,099	925	11,026	10,711	359	65,286	5,320
1977–1978	39,228	16,627	8,850	543	11,223	10,282	415	65,518	5,186
1978–1979	40,345	16,9a7	9,640	1,216	11,472	11,169	5[b]	68,426	5,392
1979–1980	4,325	16,908	9,610	250	13,143	11,107	428[b]	69,701	5,313
1980–1981	42,635	17,333	11,327	16[b]	12,113	12,183	529	71,738	5,552

Source: Reserve Bank of Australia Bulletin.

Note: Year refers to the period from July through June.

EXHIBIT 1 (CONTINUED)

EXTERNAL TRADE (1980–1981)

Major Trading Partners

Rank	Exports to	Amount (AUS$)	Percentage of Total	Imports From	Amount (AUS$)	Percentage of Total
1	Japan	5,223	27.2	United States	4,169	22.0
2	United States	2,149	11.2	Japan	3,628	19.1
3	New Zealand	916	4.8	United Kingdom	1,586	8.4
4	United Kingdom	717	3.7	West Germany	1,079	5.7
5	People's Republic of China	671	3.5	Saudi Arabia	1,032	5.4

Major Goods (Millions)

	Exports			Imports		
Rank	Goods	Amount (AUS$)	Percentage of Total	Goods	Amount (AUS$)	Percentage of Total
1	Food, beverages, and tobacco	4,065	21.2	Machinery other than transport equipment	5,597	29.5
2	Agricultural products	2,498	13.0	Chemicals and petroleum	2,649	14.0
3	Basic metals	2,865	14.9	Transport equipment	2,219	11.7
4	Textiles	1,989	10.4	Oil and gas	1,491	7.9
5	Coal	1,917	10.0	Textiles	965	5.1

Other Key Statistics

Fiscal Year	GDP Growth Current Market Price	Inflation: Consumer Price Index	Inflation: GDP Deflator	Money Supply[b] M_1	Money Supply[b] M_2	Money Supply[b] M_3	Short-Term Interest Rate[c]	Exchange Rate (per U.S.$)[d] Year End	Exchange Rate (per U.S.$)[d] Average
1970–1971	10.6%	6.0%	5.2%	6.6%	6.3%	6.8%	5.44%	0.8873	0.8929
1971–1972	11.7	6.0	7.0	9.1	11.4	10.5	5.44	0.8396	0.8561
1972–1973	13.8	9.4	9.9	26.3	29.5	25.7	6.37	0.7057	0.7806
1973–1974	20.0	15.1	13.9	2.3	18.0	14.5	17.26	0.6720	0.6786
1974–1975	20.3	15.1	18.5	12.6	17.2	15.4	9.27	0.7541	0.7318
1975–1976	17.7	13.5	14.8	14.1	13.3	14.4	10.15	0.8091	0.7933
1976–1977	14.4	12.3	10.9	8.4	11.4	11.0	10.51	0.8961	0.8719
1977–1978	8.9	7.9	8.2	8.6	6.1	8.0	10.16	0.8715	0.8866
1978–1979	11.8	9.1	7.8	16.7	13.3	11.8	9.84	0.8920	0.8804
1979–1980	11.2	10.1	10.4	12.9	16.5	12.3	13.23	0.8639	0.8977
1980–1981	12.2	9.3	10.5	12.0	15.2	12.7	15.01	0.8711	0.8701

Source: *Reserve Bank of Australia Bulletin*, 1982; *Reserve Bank Occasional Paper*, No. 8A, 1982

[a]Year refers to period from July to June.

[b]Money supply figures are as at year end.

[c]Short-term interest rate refers to weighted average issue yield of certificates of deposit.

[d]Average exchange rate figures are from international financial statistics. Thus they may not conform with year-end figures provided by the Reserve Bank.

market. At present, six state capitals have their own stock exchanges: Sydney, Melbourne, Adelaide, Brisbane, Perth, and Hobart. The Australian Associated Stock Exchanges (AASE), which dates back to 1937, has become the policy-making body for the six exchanges. Its council of 13 members includes three each from the two major exchanges, Sydney and Melbourne, and two from the others, except for Hobart, which has just one. The AASE has recently made huge strides toward unification by establishing, in 1979, a single code of listing requirements and by computing the Australian Stock Exchange share price indexes since January 1980.

Unification is not easy, since all six exchanges have long histories and have developed organizations and local interests. In the 1830s, some 50 years after the founding of the Australian colony, stock brokers in Sydney began trading in Australian shares. The Sydney Exchange was founded in 1871 and charged a membership fee of about $10. In those early days, speculative mining stocks provided the main activity of the stock market. Finally, in 1964, the exchange was organized into a nonprofit, limited-liability company, the Sydney Stock Exchange Limited. A committee of 10 members elected by the membership governs the exchange, which is managed by a general manager and staff. Members are elected by the committee, not by the membership as a whole, a typical Australian stock exchange practice.

The **Stock Exchange of Melbourne,** the other important Australian exchange, was formed in 1859, but it was incorporated as a limited nonprofit company only in 1970. A committee of nine to 12 members, elected by the membership, approves new members and governs the exchange. The other stock exchanges generally date back to the gold mining boom of the 1880s.

LISTING REQUIREMENTS. The AASE listing requirements primarily cover capitalization and share distribution. The minimum paid-up value of the class being offered is Aus$200,000 (or Aus$300,000 if at a premium) for an industrial company, Aus$300,000 and Aus$500,000 respectively for a mining company, and Aus$500,000 for a management company. A foreign company has no minimal capitalization requirement.

The listing also requires a minimum number of holders of such shares, 300 in the case of industrial and mining companies and 200 for a management company or a foreign company. In addition, the public owners must have a minimum percentage of the total capital and a minimum number of shares, which vary with the company's type and size. The minimum (200,000 shares required for a foreign company) can be reduced by the exchange on which it is listed.

As of 31 December 1981, 1,024 companies (1,003 domestic and 21 foreign, including Dart & Kraft Inc. and Bougainvelle Copper) were listed on the AASE. Each of these stocks had a home exchange; as of 30 June 1980 these home exchange figures were as follows:

Home Exchange	Number
Adelaide	90
Brisbane	91
Hobart	23
Melbourne	275
Perth	121
Sydney	480

Melbourne and Sydney dominate the stock market. The 111 member firms (with a total of 476 members) belong to the six exchanges, as follows:

Exchange	Number of Firms
Sydney	43
Melbourne	30
Adelaide	15
Brisbane	12
Perth	8
Hobart	3

In terms of raising new capital, the Melbourne and Sydney exchanges also dominate the market (see Exhibit 2).

The AASE has not raised substantial equity capital, but the total has been rising swiftly.

Year to 30 June	Equity Raised (in millions)	Total Capital Raised (in millions)
1977	Aus$154.5	Aus$ 872.7
1978	Aus$158.9	Aus$1,094.7
1979	Aus$300.2	Aus$1,651.3
1980	Aus$762.5	Aus$2,476.6

The Australian share markets can often become illiquid, especially during periods of falling prices. During price declines, sales of large quantities of shares, even in companies with very high market capitalizations, are very difficult.

Turnover as a percentage of market capitalization from 1977 to 1979 did not exceed 10%; even in the boom year of 1980 turnover did not exceed 15% (see Exhibit 3). Industrials represented better than 66% of the turnover, and resources less than 33% from 1977 to 1979; in 1980 resources represented just over 50% of all turnover value. Equities were traded significantly on just two exchanges, Sydney and Melbourne, representing in fiscal 1978, for example, 42.6% and 46.7% respectively, or almost 90% of all equity trading. Of the other exchanges at that time Brisbane (5.6%) was most active and Hobart (0.5%) least active; Adelaide and Perth each represented about 2% of turnover value.

STOCK EXCHANGE PROCEDURE. The AASE has some national peculiarities. The size of a round lot, or "marketable parcel," depends on the equity price, as follows:

Security Price	Marketable Parcel
Aus$0.01–0.25	2,000 shares
0.26–0.50	1,000
0.51–1.00	500
1.01–10.00	100
10.01 and over	50

EXHIBIT 2 CAPITAL UNDERWRITING BY MEMBERS, YEAR ENDING 30 JUNE 1980 (in millions of Australian dollars)

	Equities	Total Capital
Adelaide	3.8	Aus$3.8
Brisbane	4.7	4.7
Hobart	—	7.3
Melbourne	470.4	1,459.8
Perth	56.3	67.7
Sydney	227.3	933.3
Total	Aus$762.5	Aus$2,476.6

Marketable parcels of rights issues likewise depend on price, ranging from 100 shares where the price does not exceed Aus$5.00 to five shares where the price exceeds Aus$50.00. Smaller quantities, according to stock exchange uniform regulations, must be traded through the odd lot broker and involve an additional charge.

The AASE quotes prices in cents, not in eighths, and minimum bids or spreads are specified based on the following amounts (in Australian dollars).

Price of Stock	Spread (Minimum Bid)
up to Aus$0.10	Aus$0.005
over 0.10 up to 5.00	0.01
over 5.00 and up to 10.00	0.02
over 10.00 and up to 20.00	0.05
over 20.00 and up to 50.00	0.10
over 50.00	0.20

Thus a stock selling at Aus$6.00 could have a bid or offer of Aus$6.02 or Aus$6.04, but not Aus$6.01 or Aus$6.03. Similarly, a stock selling at Aus$11.50 could be offered or bid at Aus$11.55 or Aus$11.45, but not at Aus$11.51 or Aus$11.49. There is no restriction on daily price moves.

EXHIBIT 3 TURNOVER OF SIX EXCHANGES (in millions of Australian dollars)

	Value of Turnover					
To 30 June	Mining	Oil	Industrial	Total Equities	Total Market Capitalization	Turnover as Percentage of Market Capitalization
1977	418.7		1,044.5	1,463.2	19,227.0	7.6%
1978	361.7	119.4	1,326.0	1,807.1	21,399.0	8.4
1979	674.8	155.2	1,679.9	2,509.9	26,485.0	9.5
1980	2,400.5	1,059.8	3,288.0	6,748.3	45,666.0	14.8

The AASE has two trading sessions daily, five days a week, from 10:00 A.M. to 12:00 noon and from 2:00 P.M. to 3:00 P.M. Posts open progressively at 10:00 A.M. and the post cleark, who enters the prices on the post with chalk (hence the name "chalker," or "chalkie"), enters the highest bid and the lowest offer with the broker's identifying number alongside. If several brokers offer the same price, all their numbers appear on the post. A broker listed on the post must sell at least one marketable parcel of that particular security. Once the selling brokers' sale is completed, the clerk removes the brokers' offer and identifying number. A post can remain only bid or only offer. During the trading session, the bids or offer prices can be changed by the broker's floor operator, who advises the clerk of a higher bid or lower offer. The board also includes indicators to notify brokers of telephone calls, a column for stocks by computer code (a yellow background if the stock is ex-dividend), and a column for stock status indicated by symbol and color (a green background with $\overset{\text{X}}{\text{B}}$ is ex-bonus and with $\overset{\text{X}}{\text{R}}$ is ex-rights). Additional columns show first sale, daily high and low, last sale, and column for the broker's number of the odd lot (or half-parcel) trader. A visual display ticker above the board shows the price, number of shares, and exchange for the trades.

On the completion of a sale, the selling operator fills the sales slip and forwards it to the exchange's data processing center, which flashes details of the sale across the visual display ticker and uses the slip for accounting records. If one or both operators have filled their orders, they advise the clerk to remove their bid or offer. The post system is essentially a double auction, as buyers raise bids and sellers reduce offers until the two prices coincide and a sale is effected.

Based upon the computer, the AASE issues a trading summary at the close of the morning and for the entire day at the close of the afternoon session. Volume is not printed, but a computer printout is available for each stock, including details such as the size of each parcel traded, the price, and the identifying numbers of the buying and selling brokers.

After the official market close the brokers can conduct after-hours transactions known as "off room" sales, which they must report immediately to the AASE. Sales by an Australian broker outside of Australia must be reported to the exchange. An overseas sale made on the exchange during official hours, even though for overseas clients, is not reported as overseas sales. A list of all overseas and overnight sales are published by the exchange during the morning trading session.

Brokerage rates in Australia are as follows, in addition to which a nominal Aus$5.00 is added.

on the first Aus$5,000	2.5%
on the next Aus$10,000	2.0%
on the next Aus$35,000	1.5%
on the next Aus$200,000	1.0%
on the next Aus$500,000	0.75%
in excess of Aus$500,000	0.5%

Concessionary rates for reselling and repurchasing within one month are Aus$5.00 plus one half of the percentages aforementioned. For members of recognized overseas stock exchanges without an Australian branch or associated office minimum rates are as follows:

on the first Aus$250,000	1.0%
on the next Aus$250.000	0.75%
in excess of Aus$500,000	0.5%

In addition to the commission, a state government stamp duty is payable by both buyers and sellers at the rate of 0.3%.

INDEXES. Prior to 1980, indexes were issued by the individual stock exchanges. Sydney and Melbourne each developed their own series of group indexes, while Brisbane offered the Oil Index.

Sydney organized 16 industry groups, and also provided five general indexes: one each for group 21, the "all ordinaries" (i.e., common stocks, the most comprehensive, and those generally used by most non-Australians; group 22, the nonfinancial groups; group 23, the secondary sector; group 24, ordinaries without the metals and minerals; and group 25, the ordinaries without metals, minerals, steel and engineering. All groups used the base years 1936 to 1939 as 100 except group 25, whose base date was 1 April 1966. Because it had no oil stocks, Sydney used the Brisbane Oil Index, whose base of 100 was the first quarter of 1961. A more comprehensive index, the Statex Actuaries, used 31 December 1971 as its base, with 500 for its price index and 1,000 for its accumulation index (gains/losses plus dividends).

The **Melbourne Share Price Index** covered 17 industry groups, including a small oil and gas group not covered by its Sydney counterpart. Melbourne offered five group indexes: all ordinaries, which covered about 85% of all equities listed in Melbourne; all ordinaries, excluding metals, minerals, oil, and gas; the 50 leading ordinaries; all ordinaries, excluding the aforementioned 50; and preference shares, that is, preferred shares. As Melbourne and Sydney developed closer collaboration and as natural resources became even more important, the necessity of a single index for all Australia became evident.

The AASE Indexes, introduced in January 1980, replaced the existing Sydney and Melbourne indexes, which were phased out during that year. The new indexes are based on the share prices on the joint trading floors of the Melbourne and Sydney exchanges and incorporate data from other exchanges as computer banks are established. The indexes are on an on-line computer system and are available continuously, not just at the close of the morning and afternoon sessions. Twenty-four separate industry groups are published, as shown in Exhibit 4. Besides the industry groups, five other indexes are available: metals and minerals (groups 1 and 2); all resources (groups 1 to 3 plus two conglomerates, BHP and CSR); all industrials (groups 4 to 23 less BHP and CSR); all ordinaries (groups 1 to 24); and the 50 leaders. The AASE indexes were set at 500 on 1 January 1980. To reduce the influence of companies with a high proportion of listed shares held by another company in the same base index, an adjusting factor has been introduced. A set of accumulation indexes has also been computed; these include income as well as capital gains or losses. On 30 June 1980 the AASE all ordinaries had a market capitalization of Aus$35.3 billion, compared to total market capitalization of equity securities of Aus$45.7 billion.

The indexes cover as much as 88% of Australian market capitalization, and sector coverages range from 80% for textiles and clothing to 98% for banks. The basic formula is as follows:

$$PT = (\mathrm{PT} - 1)\left(\frac{VT}{VT - 1}\right)$$

where PT = today's ASE price index
$PT - 1$ = previous day's index
VT = today's aggregate market value
$VT - 1$ = previous day's aggregate market value

The *Australian Stock Exchange Journal* now reports only the AASE Share Price Indexes, both monthly averages and daily closing values. The aggregate market value includes only the Australian registered shares of companies domiciled overseas, in addition to all shares of Australian-based companies.

EXHIBIT 4 BREAKDOWN OF THE AUSTRALIAN STOCK EXCHANGE INDEXES BY INDUSTRY GROUP

Number Group		Number of Companies	31 Dec 1979 (Percentage)	30 Nov 1981 (Percentage)	31 Dec 1981 (Percentage)
1	Metals	32	24.7%	18.3	17.1%
2	Solid fuels	18	7.7	4.6	4.5
27	*Metals and minerals*	50	32.4	22.9	21.6
24	Diversified resources (BHP and CSR)	2	14.4	12.7	12.6
3	Oil and gas	20	6.2	8.6	9.7
28	*All resources*	72	53.0	44.2	43.9
4	Developers and contractors	8	1.5	1.8	1.9
5	Building materials	22	6.1	8.0	7.9
6	Electrical hardware and durables	7	0.8	1.0	1.0
7	Alcohol and tobacco	9	3.3	3.6	3.7
8	Food, household goods	21	3.6	3.2	3.3
9	Textiles, clothing	7	0.6	0.5	0.5
10	Automotive	8	1.1	1.2	1.2
11	Chemicals	7	2.2	2.0	2.2
12	Light engineering	9	1.6	1.4	1.4
13	Heavy engineering	15	2.2	2.9	2.8
14	Paper and packaging	7	2.1	2.2	2.2
15	Banks and finance	10	7.0	8.9	8.7
16	Insurance	7	0.7	0.7	0.7
17	Retail	10	3.8	3.8	3.7
18	Merchants and agents	5	1.1	1.5	1.6
19	Transport	4	1.9	2.4	2.4
20	Media	9	2.2	2.4	2.5
21	Property trusts	6	1.3	2.0	2.0
22	Other services	15	2.3	3.4	3.5
23	Diversified and miscellanous industrial	8	1.6	2.9	2.9
29	*All industrials*	194	47.0	55.8	56.1
30	*All ordinaries*	266	100.0	100.0	200.0

Source. Daiwa Securities Company Ltd., Tokyo.

EXHIBIT 5 AUSTRALIAN EQUITY MARKET KEY STATISTICS

Year	Number of Companies Listed As of June 30	Market Capitalization As of June 30	Value Turnover, Year Ending in June[a]	Composite Index, Yearly Average	PER Year End (X)	(Percentage) Dividend Yield Year End
1970	1,043	NA	1,903	385.1	20.3	2.8
1971	1,136	18,846	1,182	321.6	19.0	3.0
1972	1,551	23,165	689	386.6	20.8	2.7
1973	1,510	22,752	836	361.5	11.9	4.7
1974	1,451	16,539	648	268.2	6.4	8.0
1975	1,408	15,839	475	252.2	11..5	5.1
1976	1,321	19,573	586	312.2	11.4	4.7
1977	1,255	19,227	58 1	299.4	9.3	5.4
1978	1,184	21,399	787	339.3	10.8	4.8
1979	1,110	26,485	1,126	417.8	10.6	4.2
1980	1,081	45,666	3,021	624.1	12.1	3.6
1981	1,073	51,372	4,217	650.0	9.9	4.9

Source. Daiwa Securities Company Ltd., Tokyo.

[a]In millions of Australian dollars (Aus$).

EXHIBIT 6 TWENTY TOP STOCKS BY MARKET CAPITALIZATION (as of 8 June 1982)

Rank	Name	Value Turnover[a]
1	BHP	Aus$3,312
2	MIM	1,362
3	CSR	1,224
4	CRA	1,179
5	Bank NSW	1,166
6	Santos	997
7	WMC	987
8	ANZ Bank	969
9	Hamersley	849
10	National Bank	707
11	AGC	608
12	ACI	596
13	Comalco	587
14	ERA	584
15	Woodside	565
16	TNT	548
17	Coles	497
18	Bougainville	489
19	APM	463
20	EZ Indust	444

Source. Sydney Stock Exchange; Reserve Bank of Australia, *International Capital Perspective*

[a]In hundred thousands of Australian dollars (Aus$000,000).

EXHIBIT 7 AUSTRALIAN PRICE PERFORMANCES—ALL ORDINARIES

Year	High	Low	Closing	Average
1970	448.2	320.2	348.7	385.1
1971	350.3	273.6	340.8	321.6
1972	431.9	331.1	408.6	386.6
1973	429.9	287.2	297.5	361.5
1974	362.1	173.5	201.6	268.2
1075	299.3	195.8	299.3	252.2
1976	353.0	273.5	291.4	312.2
1977	322.4	283.5	322.3	299.4
1978	382.9	298.0	366.1	339.3
1979	500.0	369.1	500.0	417.8
1980	746.2	513.5	713.5	624.1
1981	737.4	546.1	595.5	650.0

Source. Daiwa Securities Company Ltd., Tokyo.

SECURITY ANALYSIS AND ANALYSTS. The security analysts of Australia have a professional organization, the **Securities Institute of Australia** (SIA), founded in 1966, which in 1975 merged with the Australian Society of Security Analysts. As of October 1980, its membership numbered 1,516. The institute provides training for analysts through a one-year diploma course for college business school graduates, which permits full membership to the SIA. The SIA also offers a certificate course and

EXHIBIT 8 TWENTY MOST ACTIVELY TRADED STOCKS IN AUSTRALIA, 1981

Rank	Name	Value Turnover[a]
1	BHP	Aus$235.9
2	Tooth & Co	144.7
3	Woodside Pet.	111.8
4	CSR	100.9
5	Strata Oil	100.2
6	W MC	91.1
7	Ampol Pet.	81.8
8	Santos	68.4
9	Pan Continental	58.2
10	MIM	55.7
11	TNT	48.2
12	Pako Wallsend	46.3
13	Bank of NSW	41.6
14	CRA	35.1
15	CBC	31.9
16	CN Gold	29.9
17	Pioneer Concrete	29.6
18	Howard Smith	29.6
19	Bridge Oil	29.2
20	Sthn Pacific Pet.	27.6

Source. Daiwa Securities Company Ltd., Tokyo.

[a]In hundred thousands of Australian dollars (Aus$000,000).

EXHIBIT 9 AUSTRALIAN SUBINDEXES

Year	Oil and Gas	Minerals and Metals	All Industrials	Metals	Solid Fuels	Developers and Contractors	Banks and Finance
1970	157.7	467.3	328.1	—	—	—	—
	N.A.	526.9	355.8	—	—	—	—
1971	143.4	301.9	365.4	—	—	—	—
	N.A.	344.0	323.8	—	—	—	—
1972	229.0	281.6	505.1	—	—	—	—
	198.2	310.9	446.6	—	—	—	—
1973	133.1	196.9	374.4	—	—	—	—
	169.1	268.2	447.4	—	—	—	—
1974	75.9	163.9	230.4	—	—	—	—
	99.2	195.0	320.0	—	—	—	—
1975	138.4	203.3	365.9	—	—	—	—
	89.2	181.7	298.4	—	—	—	—
1976	113.1	247.4	328.7	—	—	—	—
	109.0	237.4	368.3	—	—	—	—
1977	124.4	217.2	403.5	—	—	—	—
	104.7	243.1	351.2	—	—	—	—
1978	156.6	281.5	424.6	—	—	—	—
	142.6	243.2	409.9	—	—	—	—
1979	500.0	500.0	500.0	500.0	500.0	500.0	500.0
	254.5	357.2	455.1	—	—	—	—
1980	943.7	724.6	660.9	682.1	901.0	705.5	580.3
	663.4	650.2	576.3	633.9	721.4	627.5	545.2
1981	685.8	424.1	741.2	531.8	634.5	862.4	837.5
	801.4	549.5	711.9	411.6	486.1	880.8	719.8

Source. Daiwa Securities Company Ltd., Tokyo.

Note. Upper figures are end-of-the-year and lower ones are averages.

individual subjects ranging from mining investment analysis, behavior of security prices, and applied portfolio management. A quarterly journal of the SIA, *JASSA*, publishes articles on investment theory and practice.

The Australians, especially the academics, have displayed an intense interest in the efficient market hypothesis and the capital asset pricing model. They have conducted extensive experiments, and have published highly sophisticated analyses. Major articles have been collected in *Share Markets and Portfolio Theory*, edited by the leading Australian efficient market theorists R. Ball, P. Brown, F. Finn, and R. Officer. Their conclusions have not gone unchallenged, and lively exchanges have appeared in the professional journals. The relatively large number of Australian security analysts and their extensive professional training assures a fairly high level of analysis. In addition, their efforts are supplemented by U.K., U.S., and Japanese analysts while stationed in Australia and overseas.

DISCLOSURE. Information on listed Australian companies is readily available. The stock exchanges regularly publish summaries of pertinent information. Statex, another stock exchange service, provides the most detailed company historical statistics. Commercial services provide a wide range of chart books, while Australian and overseas brokers provide analytic reports. The monthly *Australian Stock Exchange Journal* publishes timely statistical data.

The federal and state governments have endorsed a program of uniform regulation of companies and the securities industry. Listed companies are required to file three reports: a semiannual report, a preliminary final report, and an annual report. The semiannual report is filed with the stock exchange, and the results are usually published in the financial press. The report includes turnover, investment income, profit, tax, minority interest, and such. The preliminary final statement, also submitted to the exchange, includes the aforementioned data as well as operating profit as a percentage of turnover and of issued capital. The annual report, due within four months of the end of the fiscal year, includes additional information, such as the maximum contingent liability for severance benefits, a statement of sources and uses of funds, a statement of each director's interest in the capital and material contracts involving directors, the class distribution of shareholders, and a list of the 20 largest shareholders. Companies usually announce an interim and final dividend.

Although Australian companies provide considerable information, the accounting system, largely of British origin but now somewhat influenced by U.S. standards, has several deficiencies that limit security analysis. The absence of segmented accounting is a major shortcoming, since many Australian companies are diversified. While most accounts use historical cost, fixed assets are sometimes revalued, while properties are often not depreciated. Surplus and losses on the realization of fixed assets are concluded both above and below the line.

SINGAPORE AND MALAYSIA

Singapore and Malaysia have long been intertwined historically. Late in the 18th century, the British began to penetrate the Malay peninsula. In 1819 Singapore was founded by the East India Company. During the 19th century British rule was gradually extended over the entire peninsula and the area was known as the "Straits Settlements." During this time, tin was discovered on the peninsula, and the rubber industry was developed; Chinese and Indians migrated to work the tin mines and rubber estates. Singapore provided port and financial services to the resource-rich interior. The Japanese invasion swept out the British in 1942. After the war, the British came to terms with local nationalism. In 1957, the Federation of Malaya, led by the United Malay National Organization, became independent, but the political situation was complicated. The indigenous Malay Moslems constituted a narrow majority; the Chinese represented better than 33% and the Indians about 10% of the population. In 1959 Singapore, about 75% of whose population was Chinese, became self-governing under the leadership of the People's Action party. In 1963, after a brief 19 days of independence, Singapore joined the Federation of Malaysia, a new state that included Malaya and two states, Sabah and Sarawak, which were located on Borneo adjacent to Indonesia. In 1965 Singapore left the Federation of Malaysia and became independent again.

At present Singapore is an independent, self-governing republic and a member of the British Commonwealth. It is a city-state located on an island with an area of 616.3 square kilometers. It has a unicameral parliamentary system and is still led by its founders, Prime Minister Lee Kuan Yew and the People's Action party. Its population of about 2.4 million is 76% Chinese, 15% Malay, and 7% South Asian.

The Malaysian Federation, with an area of 332,952 square kilometers, is a constitutional monarchy, with a king elected for five years from one of the rulers of the nine Malay states. The king selects the governors of the four non-Malay states and each serves for four years. The bicameral legislature (the upper house selected by the king and the 13 popularly elected state legislative bodies, and the lower house, which is popularly elected) is led by the National Front, a coalition of the various nationalities. The population of about 13 million is made up of Malays and other indigenous peoples (56%), Chinese (34%), Indians (9%), and others (1%). (For a statistical comparison of the Singapore and Malaysian economies, see Exhibit 10.)

Just as their political and economic history is intertwined, the histories of the stock exchanges in Singapore and Malaysia are likewise connected. Although the Singapore Stock Brokers' Association was founded only in 1930, trading in securities has had a long history in this area. Fraser and Company, the oldest stockbrokerage firm in the Far East, was established in 1873 by a Scotsman, John Fraser, an original partner in a local beverage firm, Fraser and Neave. (Both, incidentally, are still in business, and the Fraser indexes remain among the most popular measurements of the contemporary Singapore and Malaysian stock exchanges.) Trading became relatively active in the late 1880s as stock brokers located in the major urban centers of the Straits Settlements traded both through London brokers and also in locally owned British stocks. Until quite recently, most of the shares traded were those of largely British-owned and British-controlled tin mining and plantation companies listed on the London Stock Exchange. A few of these companies are still traded more actively in London than locally.

No central marketplace existed until the great rubber boom of 1910, when a bar in an arcade and the pavement outside, policed by a single European constable, became the scene of hectic trading. The decline in demand for rubber in 1912 brought the inevitable bust, and many brokerage firms disappeared. Trading continued, although the brokers changed streets from time to time. The great boom of the 1920s brought many foreign firms, mainly U.S. firms, to Singapore. In 1930, primarily to establish a closed shop, and partly in response to the Crash of 1929, 15 local firms organized the Singapore Stock Brokers Association under the Securities Ordinance of the Straits Settlements for the declared purpose of regulating trading in the interest of the public.

The market was still dispersed, and every morning each broker, dressed in a tutup—an all-white jacket buttoned from top to bottom with five heavy, highly polished silver buttons—climbed into a single-seater rickshaw armed with telegrams from London and visited clients. At 4:00 P.M. the brokers would congregate and mark the prices for the day to be published in the press. The venerable Fraser and Company clearly dominated the scene. In 1938 the association changed its name to the Malayan Share Brokers Association (MSBA) and admitted members from the non-Singapore areas. After World War II the MSBA was reestablished.

In 1960, the **Malayan Stock Exchange** was founded by 19 firms (10 from Singapore), largely under the leadership of the Sydney Stock Exchange chairman. In 1961 trading rooms were set up in Kuala Lumpur, now the federal capital, and Singapore. When Singapore joined the Federation of Malaysia, the exchange changed its name to the Stock Exchange of Malaysia (SEM). When Singapore separated from the federation, the exchange continued to act as a single unit, with two telephone-linked trading rooms. Only the name was changed, in 1965, to the Stock Exchange of Malaysia and Singapore (SEMS). The SEMS had regulations, but no enforcement policy. As

EXHIBIT 10

GROSS DOMESTIC PRODUCT, AT CURRENT PRICE (S$000,000)

Year	Private Consumption Expenditure	Government Consumption Expenditure	Gross Domestic Fixed Capital Formation	Increase in Stock	Export of Goods and Services	Import of Goods and Services	Statistical Discrepancy	Total	
								Amount	Per Capita(US$)
1971	4,531.5	860.8	2,473.4	270.7	1,484.2		171.1	6,823.3	3,229
1972	5,071.2	990.2	3,054.3	300.1	1,378.2		118.2	8,155.8	3,789
1973	6,340.1	1,117.7	3,561.1	438.9	1,041.0		211.7	10,205.1	4,653
1974	7,657.6	1,298.4	4,694.8	897.2	2,132.8		128.0	12,543.2	5,625
1975	8,120.7	1,423.0	4,698.4	336.2	1,508.1		302.8	13,373.0	5,910
1976	8,605.9	1,541.5	6,149.1	343.1	1,185.2		120.8	14,575.2	6,356
1977	9,392.1	1,716.3	5,282.8	55.7	489.4		11.4	15,968.9	6,867
1978	10,402.0	1,989.5	5,926.7	417.0	1,119.4		42.2	17,658.0	7,503
1979	11,674.5	2,060.6	6,922.0	928.1	1,648.5		134.1	20,070.8	8,421
1980	13,547.7	2,483.4	9,111.1	904.1	2,634.4		100.2	23,512.1	9,740
1981(p)	15,433.3	2,785.1	11,158.1	394.4	2,692.3		200.9	27,279.5	11,165

GROSS DOMESTIC PRODUCT, AT 1968 PRICE (S$000,000)

Year	Private Consumption Expenditure	Government Consumption Expenditure	Gross Domestic Fixed Capital Formation	Increase in Stock	Export of Goods and Services	Import of Goods and Services	Statistical Discrepancy	Total	
								Amount	Per Capita (US$)
1971	4,330.1	786.3	2,101.8	235.2	1,343.2		166.5	6,276.7	982
1972	4,722.6	891.2	2,411.2	191.1	1,241.6		145.1	7,119.7	1,177
1973	5,100.0	940.1	2,614.5	181.7	828.2		— 66.8	7,941.3	1,482
1974	5,436.1	941.1	2,884.1	483.6	1,359.3		59.6	8,445.2	1,554
1975	5,628.1	966.9	2,766.3	184.8	941.2		185.3	8,790.3	1,638
1976	5,982.5	1,015.3	2,908.6	190.2	728.0		78.8	9,447.4	1,667
1977	6,373.2	1,108.9	2,952.2	30.9	288.8		16.8	10,193.2	1,797
1978	6,861.8	1,252.4	3,261.8	229.7	597.6		65.9	11,074.0	2,070
1979	7,383.6	1,234.9	3,601.2	441.2	604.4		57.2	12,114.1	2,336
1980	8,025.9	1,357.5	4,289.0	357.5	569.4		—103.1	13,357.4	2,585
1981	8,700.1	1,415.9	4,816.1	152.9	420.1		20.8	14,685.7	2,845

Source. Daiwa Securities Co. Ltd., Tokyo.

EXHIBIT 10 (CONTINUED)

EXTERNAL TRADE

Major Trading Partners

Rank	Exports To	Amount[a]	Percentage of Total	Imports From	Amount[a]	Percentage of Total
1	Malaysia	6,907	15.6	Japan	10,957	18.8
2	United States	5,849	13.2	Saudi Arabia	10,772	18.5
3	Japan	4,488	10.1	United States	7,356	12.6
4	Hong Kong	3,881	8.8	Malaysia	7,210	12.4
5	Thailand	1,865	4.2	Kuwait	1,995	3.4

Major Goods

Rank	Exported Goods	Amount[a]	Percentage of Total	Imported Goods	Amount[a]	Percentage of Total
1	Mineral fuels	14,176	32.0	Mineral fuels	19,831	34.0
2	Rubber	2,455	5.5	Food	3,271	5.6
3	Television and radio	2,444	5.5	Electronic components	2,989	5.1
4	Electronic components	2,415	5.5	Chemicals	2,756	4.7
5	Food	2,125	4.8	Iron and steel	2,361	4.1

Source. Daiwa Securities Company, Ltd., Tokyo.

[a]In millions of Singapore dollars.

a consequence fraud and manipulation ran rampant in this highly speculative stock market.

In 1973, when the market had soared to a high point, the Malaysian authorities precipated a split in the exchange by terminating the interchangeability of Malaysian and Singapore currencies. In 1973 two separate exchanges were incorporated, the **Stock Exchange of Singapore Ltd. (SES)** and the **Kuala Lumpur Stock Exchange Bhd. (KLSE).** Shares originally listed on the unified exchange (SEMS) continue to be listed on both separate exchanges but newly listed shares can appear on only one exchange. Volume is greater in Singapore, even for Malaysian companies (excepting some tin and plantation companies). Brokers deal in both markets, and shares purchased in Kuala Lumpur can be delivered in Singapore (and vice versa). (For a comparison of the Singapore and Malaysian markets, see the statistics in Exhibits 11 and 12.)

After the two exchanges separated, the Singapore government enacted the Securities Industry Act of 1973 to regulate the industry and began to enforce the Singapore Code on Takeovers and Mergers, patterned on British law.

Both countries encourage foreign investment and expect it to grow; they plan to continue free movement of capital and relatively stable exchange rates. However, nationalism has influenced policy; foreign holdings of sensitive stocks in Malaysia (such as banks) are restricted to 20%. More important, the Malaysian New Economic

EXHIBIT 11 MALAYSIAN ECONOMY AND STOCK MARKET

MALAYSIAN EQUITY MARKET, KEY STATISTICS

Year	Number of Companies Listed, Year End	Market Capitalization	Value Turnover[a]	KLSE[b] Index, Yearly Average
1970	—	—	—	—
1971	—	—	—	—
1972	—	—	—	—
1973	262	13,288.3	(936.7)	(338.3)
1974	264	8,085.1	722.7	227.2
1975	268	11,747.8	1,305.7	211.4
1976	264	12,680.1	1,010.8	232.0
1977	256	13,735.5	1,047.5	221.5
1978	253	23,073.5	2,539.0	293.3
1979	253	24,627.6	1,641.2	338.1
1980	248	43,095.3	5,600.2	464.0
1981	251	55,414.7	8,059.4	612.8

SHARE PRICE PERFORMANCE, KLSE INDEX

Year	Opening	High	Low	Closing	Average
1970	—	—	—	—	—
1971	—	—	—	—	—
1972	—	—	—	—	—
1973	460.6	414.6	243.3	268.9	338.3
1974	260.7	301.5	143.5	147.6	227.2
1975	149.4	269.0	144.2	218.3	211.4
1976	215.5	263.1	209.6	229.8	232.0
1977	230.3	285.9	203.6	227.0	221.5
1978	227.6	398.4	221.8	306.9	293.3
1979	305.5	376.9	304.6	376.9	338.1
1980	380.2	547.2	375.3	536.0	464.0
1981	535.8	823.1	458.8	572.4	612.8

KLSE SUBINDEXES

Year	Industries and Commerce	Finance	Hotels	Property	Mining	Plantations
1970	—	—	—	—	—	—
1971	—	—	—	—	—	—
1972	—	—	—	—	—	—
1973[c]	338.29	570.96	322.07	491.09	142.17	312.99
1974	227.22	352.48	253.63	267.83	122.21	246.23
1975	211.37	358.79	244.21	252.79	109.58	223.12
1976	231.97	453.58	226.54	216.40	113.39	224.64

EXHIBIT 11 (CONTINUED)

KLSE SUBINDEXES

Year	Industries and Commerce	Finance	Hotels	Property	Mining	Plantations
1977	221.46	383.69	229.88	200.49	163.83	253.36
1978	293.34	444.47	274.10	254.02	208.29	411.81
1979	338.14	543.90	332.26	303.85	225.70	561.59
1980	464.01	829.02	442.72	644.89	334.04	788.30
1981	612.77	1,354.13	634.12	1,374.17	351.02	871.50

GROSS DOMESTIC PRODUCT, AT CURRENT PRICE (M $000,000)

Year	Private Consumption Expenditure	Government Consumption Expenditure	Gross Domestic Fixed Capital Formation	Increase in Stock	Export of Goods and Services	Import of Goods and Services	Total: Amount	Total: Per Capita (US $)
1971	7,911	2,170	2,701	— 13	5,242	5,056	12,955	419.7
1972	8,609	2,738	3,324	—150	5,111	5,412	14,220	458.8
1973	10,450	2,919	4,136	86	7,766	6,735	18,622	671.5
1974	12,776	3,516	5,798	714	11,043	10,989	22,858	851.4
1975	13,086	3,924	5,602	—381	10,172	10,071	22,332	723.6
1976	14,715	4,301	6,206	— 71	14,554	11,620	28,085	905.4
1977	16,798	5,388	7,343	243	16,279	13,711	32,340	1,087.3
1978	19,450	5,786	8,627	571	18,592	16,405	36,272	1,274.3
1979	22,367	6,717	11,291	596	26,029	21,556	44,252	1,526.4
1980	26,213	8,904	15,336	619	30,791	29,249	51,376	1,736.9

GROSS DOMESTIC PRODUCT, AT 1970 CONSTANT PRICE (M $000,000)

Year	Private Consumption Expenditure	Government Consumption expenditure	Gross Domestic Fixed Capital Formation	Increase in Stock	Export of Goods and Services	Import of Goods and Services	Total: Amount	Total: Per Capita (US $)
1971	7,731	2,078	2,609	— 26	5,480	4,856	13,016	421.7
1972	8,128	2,429	3,088	—200	5,581	4,788	14,238	459.4
1973	8,918	2,540	3,508	67	6,384	6,513	15,904	573.5
1974	9,822	2,919	4,252	450	7,401	7,517	17,227	641.7
1975	9,651	3,117	3,936	—266	7,179	6,232	17,365	562.7
1976	10,304	3,382	4,133	— 38	8,397	6,805	19,373	624.5
1977	11,268	3,714	4,677	271	8,779	7,834	20,875	701.8
1978	12,389	3,931	5,011	308	9,430	8,805	22,264	782.2
1979	13,615	4,461	5,952	— 41	10,750	10,566	24,171	833.8
1980	15,108	5,159	7,043	— 57	11,144	12,279	26,118	883.0

EXHIBIT 11 (CONTINUED)

GROSS DOMESTIC PRODUCT, AT CONSTANT 1970 MARKET PRICE, BY INDUSTRY (in percentages)

Year	Agriculture, Forestry, Fishing	Mining	Manufacturing	Electricity and Water	Construction	Transport and Communication	Wholesale and Retail	Financial and Business Services	Other Services	Imputed Bank Service Charge
1971	29.9	6.5	14.4	1.8	4.2	4.9	12.3	8.7	14.1	1.1
1972	29.4	6.3	14.5	2.0	4.1	5.1	12.1	8.6	14.9	1.1
1973	29.1	5.4	15.8	1.9	4.1	5.2	12.8	8.2	14.4	1.1
1974	28.8	4.6	16.1	2.0	4.2	5.5	12.8	8.1	14.6	1.1
1975	27.7	4.6	16.4	2.1	3.8	6.2	12.8	8.5	15.6	1.2
1976	27.8	4.9	17.4	2.1	3.7	6.0	12.4	8.0	15.2	1.1
1977	26.4	4.6	17.9	2.1	3.8	6.2	12.4	8.0	15.7	1.2
1978	25.2	4.7	18.3	2.2	4.1	6.4	12.7	8.2	15.4	1.2
1979	24.6	5.0	18.7	2.3	4.3	6.4	12.6	8.1	15.2	1.2
1980	23.6	4.6	19.4	2.3	4.6	6.4	12.5	8.1	15.6	1.3

EXTERNAL TRADE

Major trading partners (1980)

Rank	Exports To	Amount[a]	Percentage of Total	Imports From	Amount[a]	Percentage of Total
1	Japan	6,447.7	22.9	Japan	5,373.1	22.8
2	Singapore	5,393.7	19.0	United States	3,556.6	15.1
3	United States	4,609.1	16.3	Singapore	2,750.2	11.7
4	The Netherlands	1,691.7	6.0	Australia	1,289.9	5.5
5	West Germany	1,017.4	3.6	West Germany	1,276.1	5.4

Major Goods (1980)

Rank	Exported Goods	Amount[a]	Percentage of Total	Imported Goods	Amount[a]	Percentage of Total
1	Crude material, inedible	9,128	32.4	Machinery and transport equipment	9,081	38.6
2	Mineral fuel	6,906	24.5			
3	Manufactured goods classified by materials	3,688	13.1	Manufactured goods classified by materials	3,911	16.6
4	Machinery and transport equipment	3,238	11.5	Mineral fuel	3,539	15.0
5	Animal and vegetable oils and fats	3,131	11.5	Food, beverages, and tobacco	2,671	11.3
				Chemical	2,035	8.6

Source. Daiwa Securities Company, Ltd., Tokyo.

[a]In millions of Malaysian dollars.

[b]Kuala Lumpur Stock Exchange.

[c]Yearly average from May to December.

EXHIBIT 12 SINGAPORE ECONOMY

SINGAPORE EQUITY MARKET, KEY STATISTICS

Year	Number of Companies Listed at Year End	S $Million Market Capitalization[a]	Value Turnover[a]	SES Index, Yearly Average	Price; Earnings Ratio at Year End[c]	Year End Dividend Yield (in percentages)
1970	256		746.9	100.4	N.A.	N.A.
1971	260		934.0	125.6	N.A.	N.A.
1972	264		2,162.9	260.0	54.7	1.0
1973	277	13,353.1	2,436.3	380.4	25.4	2.1
1974	263	8,250.1	1,123.5	215.4	8.7	5.3
1975	269	14,051.6	1,829.9	209.8	13.7	3.4
1976	269	16,283.1	1,928.4	237.2	17.8	2.8
1977	258	20,291.2	1,157.6	226.2	15.5	3.3
1978	266	22,708.0	3,382.9	300.6	17.0	2.8
1979	264	29,383.4	2,308.9	346.8	17.9	2.6
1980	261	51,118.9	7,806.1	489.6	16.1	1.9
1981	270	71,292.9	13,419.1	737.1	22.1	2.0

TWENTY TOP STOCKS BY MARKET CAPITALIZATION, 1981 YEAR END

Rank	Name	Market Capitalization[a]
1	Hong Kong Land	10,427.7
2	Overseas Chinese Banking Corporation	3,411.8
3	Sime Darby	2,143.4
4	Development Bank of Singapore	1,908.1
5	United Overseas Bank	1,751.5
6	Algemene Bank Nederland	1,720.2
7	Malaysia Mining Corporation	1,575.4
8	Malayan United Industry	1,387.5
9	Malayan Banking	1,350.0
10	Genting	1,206.5
11	Straits Trading	1,068.0
12	Overseas Union Bank	1,056.4
13	Consolidated Plantations	923.6
14	Promet	858.2
15	Bander Raya	815.2
16	Selangor Properties	784.8
17	Singapore Land	776.1
18	Goodwood Park Hotel	769.5
19	Keppel Shipyard	756.0
20	Highlands and Lowlands	740.3

EXHIBIT 12 (CONTINUED)

SHARE PRICE PERFORMANCE, SES INDUSTRIALS

Year	Opening	High	Low	Closing	Average
1970	108.0	108.7	89.1	96.3	100.4
1971	98.7	164.5	98.7	164.5	125.6
1972	166.6	433.8	164.7	433.8	260.0
1973	460.6	666.4	243.2	262.6	380.4
1974	254.5	289.0	123.1	126.8	215.4
1975	129.3	273.5	128.6	218.2	209.8
1976	216.4	272.9	208.0	227.9	237.2
1977	228.9	243.0	207.9	232.1	226.2
1978	230.5	411.7	228.2	314.9	300.6
1979	314.9	384.9	314.3	384.9	346.8
1980	385.8	627.6	379.8	597.5	489.6
1981	595.4	993.3	525.0	682.0	737.1

SES SUBINDEXES

Year	Industry and Commerce	Finance	Hotels	Property	Mining	Plantations
1970	100.4	99.0	100.2	99.3	99.6	100.5
1971	125.6	128.8	96.9	119.5	113.4	107.0
1972	260.0	300.8	172.1	278.3	147.4	186.1
1973	380.4	642.2	343.1	571.9	154.4	326.8
1974	215.4	312.7	193.4	273.1	126.3	250.8
1975	209.8	339.4	224.7	252.6	114.6	222.2
1976	237.2	426.9	211.9	213.4	109.2	228.1
1977	226.2	366.8	216.8	200.0	162.9	258.0
1978	300.6	422.4	314.2	251.1	213.0	394.6
1979	346.8	523.2	425.7	306.2	232.4	514.7
1980	489.6	769.9	727.6	621.4	358.7	684.6
1981	737.1	1,228.5	1,584.0	1,247.5	395.7	704.5

Policy (1970–1990) provides the Bumiputra (native Malaysian) ownership in the corporate sector will grow to 30% by 1990.

It is planned that other Malaysians will hold 40% and foreigners 30% of corporate stock. It is possible that in the exhaustible resources (tin, oil) the 30% policy will be enforced before 1990. Singapore, lacking in natural resources, has no such policy.

PRIMARY MARKET. A Singapore company's board of directors must receive approval of the general stockholders' meeting to increase its capital and, if listed, approval of the SES is necessary as well. New shares for a consideration are usually alloted to existing shareholders at less than market price. Private placements and public offerings are infrequent, except when a company issues new shares in order to go public. A company can issue new shares without consideration to stockholders in proportion to their holdings by capitalizing the earned surplus, capital reserve, or asset revaluation reserve. Public issues require a complete prospectus to be filed with the Registrar of Companies, but a stockholder allotment necessitates only a simplified prospectus.

Without a systematic **over-the-counter market** in Singapore, going public is inseparable from listing. The complete prospectus must include the company's capital, an outline of its business, its directors and their interests in the issuer, and audited financial statements for the past six months. If the company has a subsidiary, either a consolidated financial statement or a statement of the subsidiary is also required. To encourage listing of foreign companies on the SES, the Registrar of Companies can give consideration to the accounting system of the home country. When a company goes public a merchant bank or stock trader is usually the underwriter. Standby commitments are most popular. Firm commitments are used, but best-efforts and all-or-none underwriting are seldom used. The underwriting commission is set at the lower of less than 10% or that provided by the company's articles of association. Underwriting syndicates are common.

The **primary market** is slightly different in Malaysia in view of the government's Bumiputra policy. Companies can allot new stock to existing stockholders, but public offerings have been increased to promote Malay stock ownership. The Capital Issues Committee, established in 1968, consists of government and local financial and commercial representatives, including the KLSE, and it screens companies applying for new issues. The issue price is determined by negotiation. A premium issue is permitted, and the premium can be placed into an account used to issue shares without consideration. In the primary market, banks—rather than securities companies—are engaged in underwriting. The Malaysian Industrial Development Finance Bhd., in which the government owns a large stake, enjoys a very large share in underwriting.

STRUCTURE AND MANAGEMENT. As of 31 December 1980 the **Stock Exchange of Singapore (SES)** had 21 member companies, comprising 89 stock broker members. The SES is a joint stock company, not for profit, with an authorized capital of 2,000 shares of S$1.00 each. Each SES member owns one share at S$1.00 par value, but the market price is much higher. In 1979 one securities company paid S$2 million for its one share. Membership is limited to securities companies with dealer's licenses issued by the Registrar of Companies. A stockholder of a member company must be at least 21 years old, and either a native Singaporean or a resident of Singapore for more than five years. Thus no foreign securities companies can become members. Trading in the SES is also handled by dealers and dealers' representatives (*remisiers*) attached to member firms. In 1979 there were 37 dealers and 266 remisiers. Remisiers are not employees of firms to which they are attached. The receive 40% of the brokerage for buying and selling only on behalf of their own clients. Dealers are attached to stockbroking firms and buy and sell for their own and their firm's clients, receiving a combination of fixed salary plus commissions. Dealers and remisiers are required to pass either the dealer's representative examination given by the SES or hold a part one diploma in investment analysis, sponsored by the Securities Research Institute (which is described later).

The General Meeting of the Members, the SES's supreme decision-making body, elects a committee of five members to administer the exchange, including listing, delisting, and admitting new members. The SES secretary general and staff conduct the day-to-day business.

The **Kuala Lumpur Stock Exchange** is a limited joint stock, nondividend-paying company approved by the Malaysian Minister of Finance under the Securities Act of 1973. A committee administers the exchange. This committee consists of seven exchange members elected by the General Meeting of the Members. Applicants for members must meet several qualifications, among which are a minimum age of 21 years, Malaysian citizenship or five years' residency, securities experience (a minimum of three to five years), and a security license from the Minister of Finance. The committee can reject an applicant, even if qualified, and can designate in which one of the several federal states the member can do business. Both exchanges are self-regulatory bodies conducting their own affairs in the securities industry, but each exchange is closely monitored by its own Ministry of Finance and by the Monetary Authority in Singapore and the Central Bank (Bank Negara) in Malaysia. Both governments, acutely aware of the importance of a properly regulated equity market in economic development, proclaim their desire to avoid market excesses.

SINGAPORE SECURITIES MARKET REGULATIONS. The Singapore government enacted the **Securities Industry Act of 1973,** establishing government regulations over the SES. The ordinance under which the stock brokers' association and stock exchanges had previously operated provided for little or no effective government control. The only protection for investors was the Companies Act, which by the late 1960s was considered inadequate. Concern was expressed about the ease with which inexperienced and unqualified persons could set themselves up as securities dealers or as representatives of stock exchange members. The self-regulatory function was deemed insufficiently effective when two important listed companies collapsed. Securities regulation was an outgrowth of excessive speculation and public criticisms of manipulating and rigging that took place in the SEMS during the rapid succession of booms and busts—the new issue mania of 1963, the 1966 run after Indonesia ended its confrontation policy against Malaysia, and the second new issue mania of 1968. The bear market of 1969–1970 was followed by a merger and takeover euphoria from July 1971 to February 1973, sparked by the Slater-Walker acquisition of Haw Par Brothers. To safeguard the interests of public investors and to insure the availability of investable funds for economic expansion, the government adopted strong steps to prevent fraud and price manipulation in the stock exchange.

In 1969 the government appointed George Ferris, a governor of the New York Stock Exchange, to prepare a report, based on which the Securities Industry Act was enacted in 1970. But the Singapore government delayed legal enforcement in the hope of receiving Malaysian government approval for its application to the SEMS. With the split of the SEMS, Singapore repealed the act of 1970, and adopted a stronger Securities Industry Act in 1973.

The Minister of Finance has the authority to regulate the establishment and operation of stock markets, and to regulate the conduct of persons engaged in the securities market. The Securities Industry Council (SIC), set up under the Securities Industry Act of 1973, consists of representatives of the Monetary Authority of Singapore, business, and government, all appointed by the Minister of Finance. The SIC has five major functions.

To advise the Minister of Finance on matters of investor protection and control of the securities industry

To advise the committee of the SES on the administration of trading and on listing and delisting

To advise the Registrar of Companies on subject companies

To control company takeovers and mergers in accordance with the Singapore Code on Takeovers and Mergers established in 1974. The code established a set of general principles and rules but also asserted that detailed rules could not be devised to cover all circumstances. The SIC has the power to interpret the code; its rulings are final and not subject to challenge in the courts.

To approve application by companies seeking to raise capital by a public issue

LISTINGS. At the end of 1981, 270 stocks were listed on the SES and 251 on the KLSE. As shown in Exhibit 13, 217 companies are dually listed, out of a total of 304 companies listed on either one of the exchanges. Those stocks already listed on the SEMS when it split in 1973 were dually listed on the new, independent SES and KLSE.

A company seeking **listing** must receive the approval in Singapore of the SIC and the SES, and in Malaysia of the Capital Issues Committee and the KLSE. The major requirements are as follows:

Minimum paid-in capital of S$4 million in Singapore and M$2 million in Malaysia

Minimum public ownership (defined as a holding of 500 to 10,000 shares) of at least S$1.5 million in Singapore and M$750,000 in Malaysia or 25% of the issued and paid-up capital, whichever is greater, in the hands of at least 500 shareholders

EXHIBIT 13 LISTED COMPANIES BY INDUSTRY, YEAR END 1981

	Singapore				Malaysia			
Industry	S[a]	M[b]	O[c]	Total	S[a]	M[b]	O[c]	Total
Industrial and commerical	65	90	3	158	31	110	1	142
Finance	15	7	1	23	7	7	0	14
Hotels	15	1	0	16	9	1	0	10
Property	8	6	1	15	7	7	0	14
Plantations	0	32	1	22	0	39	2	41
Mining	0	21	4	25	0	22	8	30
Total	103	157	10	270	54	186	11	251

TOTAL SINGAPORE AND MALAYSIA

Listed	S[a]	M[b]	O[c]	Total
SES only	49	0	4	53
KLSE only	0	29	5	34
Dually	54	157	6	217
Total	103	186	15	304

Source. Daiwa Securities Company Ltd., Tokyo.

[a]Companies incorporated in Singapore.

[b]Companies incorporated in Malaysia.

[c]Companies incorporated in other countries.

In the case of Singapore, an applicant files a listing application with the exchange through a securities company or a merchant bank. The application must include the articles of association, financial statements for the past five years, and the business outlook for the coming three years. If the listing involves a public offering, the applicant is required to submit a tentative prospectus, which can be distributed publicly only after receipt of the exchange's approval.

In Malaysia, the process of listing is more difficult. The applicant must first pass a preliminary investigation by the Capital Issues Committee, which requires more detailed information than the Singapore process. Acceptance by that committee is only the first step; the KLSE committee has final say on the listing of the applicant.

Foreign companies also can be more easily listed in Singapore, where listing is at the discretion of the SES committee, which has been quite liberal in an effort to attract listings and replace Hong Kong as the South Pacific financial center. In Malaysia the foreign companies must meet the requirements imposed on domestic companies, and, in addition, maintain a share register in Malaysia and agree to obey the Companies Act whenever applicable. Ten of the 11 companies listed on the KLSE that are incorporated overseas are British plantation and mining companies. The numbers of such British-owned companies are declining, as Malaysian investment institutions are taking them over. The SES includes a variety of companies incorporated also in The Netherlands, Hong Kong, and Japan.

The Malaysian Securities Industry Act, which became operative in December 1976, provides for greater government control of the securities industry, and greater protection of the investors. The Capital Issues Committee, consisting of representatives of the Central Bank and the KLSE, controls all new share issues.

CAPITAL MARKET POLICY. Since their independence, both Malaysia and Singapore have encouraged foreign investment, but at the same time have taken steps to enhance local share ownership and local control. Malaysia has been more direct. It has curbed foreign participation to 20% in sensitive sectors such as banking. In addition the government has adopted the Bumiputra policy already described. The government expects that by 1990, foreign corporate investment will grow from M$3.2 billion to M$13.95 billion out of a total share ownership of M$41.65 billion. Bumiputra ownership has risen very slowly, from 2.6% in 1971 to 3.6% in 1978. In an effort to hasten the process, the government established a Bumiputra fund and an investment company to acquire shares from companies and deliver them to Malaysians.

British-owned companies have sold shares to the fund, possibly to gain local support for their activities. Overseas Chinese, however, have avoided going public, and tend to depend on loans from banks with whom they maintain close personal relations.

Singapore has been more active than Malaysia in encouraging foreign capital. Lacking the rich resources of its neighbor, the Singapore government has promoted the city-state as a manufacturing center and even more as a financial center, challenging Hong Kong. Singapore maintains a free market in securities and foreign exchange—foreigners can invest freely in Singapore securities and Singaporeans can invest freely abroad. To encourage foreign investment, the SES has rapidly incorporated improved regulatory practices and operations; the Securities Research Institute, the introduction of the Second Section, the combined computing and clearing operation, and finally, in 1980, membership in the International Federation of Stock Exchanges (FIBV) have all been part of that effort.

TRADING. The KLSE has only one section, while the SES has since, January 1975, two sections. To be assigned to the First Section, a company must meet certain minimum requirements: S$5 million in paid-up capital, 500 shareholders, turnover at 5% of paid-up capital, and a 5% annual dividend. The SES committee can exempt a stock from any of these criteria. All other listed stocks are on the Second Section. Second Section stocks, numbering about 33% of the listed stocks, can be traded on a "ready delivery" basis only—delivery is two days after the date of the contract. First Section stocks can be sold on a ready delivery basis or on a settlement contract basis, with delivery usually at the end of the month. The KLSE has three kinds of trading—immediate bargain, settled on the following day; ready bargain, settled on the fourth day; and time bargain, settled in a month.

About 90% of the trades in the SES First Section are on a settlement contract basis. Where issues are traded on both bases, the trading is done separately and the commission rate for a settlement contract is somewhat higher.

The minimum unit of trading, called a "board lot," is usually 1,000 shares. For stock priced over S$10 or M$10, lots of 100 or 500 can also be traded. This is true of both exchanges, but active issues on the SES, generally called the "big board," are traded in lots of 3,000 shares.

Trading is conducted in both exchanges from 9:30 A.M. to 12:30 P.M. (with a 15 minute break at 11:00 A.M.) and 2:30 P.M. to 4:30 P.M. Monday through Friday.

Trading clerks of the member companies do the trading on the floor. Exchange clerks receive bids and offers from the trading clerks by voice or hand signals and enter them on the boards. Transactions are done by individual auction, with a recognition of preference for time and price. After the conclusion of the contract, the selling broker prepares a confirmation in triplicate—one for the buyer, one for the exchange, and one for personal use. Transactions and other information—such as dividends—are included on the boards. The stocks are divided into six sectors: commercial and industrial, finance, hotels, properties, plantations, and mining.

Both exchanges have almost the same scale for spreads (minimum bids).

Price	Spread
up to $1	.5¢
up to $3	1. ¢
up to $5	2. ¢
up to $10	5. ¢
up to $25	10. ¢
up to $100	50 ¢

For prices above $100 the SES spread is still 50¢ but the KLSE is S$1.00.

In Singapore, settlement is done through the Securities Clearing and Computer Service (SCCS), whose first stage was established on 1 January 1978. The SCCS offsets each member's buying and selling of the same issue and notifies each member of the balance due in shares or value. Ultimately, the SCCS expects to eliminate all physical delivery of stock certificates.

Commission rates in both Malaysian and Singapore dollars (shown here in Singapore dollars) are as follows:

Share Price	Ready (SES and KLSE)	Time (KLSE)	Settlement (SES)
Less than S$0.50	S$0.005	S$0.0075	S$0.0075
S$0.50 to S$0.99	S$0.01	S$0.015	S$0.0125
S$1.00 and more or stocks in foreign currency	1%	1.5%	1.25%

The minimum commission for stocks is (M or S) $5.00.

In Singapore and Malaysia, the ad valorem stamp duty, payable by both buyer and seller, is M or S$1.00 for each M or S$1,000, or part thereof. The transfer stamp payable by the seller is 0.2% of the contract price in Singapore only and M$0.30 for every M$100 or part thereof in Malaysia. Incidentally, neither country has a capital gains tax, but they both impose a 40% withholding tax on dividends. In Malaysia, since 1968, a company designated as a pioneer industry by the government is exempt from withholding on dividends from two to five years.

INDEXES. There are many indexes for SES and KLSE stocks, some only for a single exchange with a companion for the other exchange, and some covering both exchanges.

The **Straits Times Index (STI),** begun in July 1948, initially consisted of three indexes, with April 1948 as their base period. The STI now has separate indexes for six SES groups, each with its own base period. The Straits Times Industrial Index (STII), the unweighted-average market prices of 30 industrials and probably the most commonly quoted, is published daily in the local newspaper, The Straits Times. The New Straits Times Index (NSTI) provides a similar set of six indexes for the KLSE. The New Straits Times Industrial Index (NSTII) is probably the most popular KLSE index. Incidentally, the STII and the NSTII share 25 of their 30 stocks; the other five are predominantly Singaporean (STI) or predominantly Malaysian (NSTI).

The most comprehensive index is the **Stock Exchange of Singapore Index (SESI)**—not a composite index, but a set of six weighted indexes: industrial and commercial, finance, hotels, properties, mining, and plantations. No index is provided for oil palms. Six separate indexes were constructed because of the belief that distinct forces shape the share prices in each of these groups. The construction of the SES Industrial and Commercial Index was the most difficult because, unlike the other sectors, it had a large number of stocks (88). For the other five sectors, almost all stocks were included in the appropriate index and covered 90% of the paid-up capital (as seen in Exhibit 14). Thirty high-volume industrial stocks were selected to represent the different sizes of paid-up capital. In addition, 10 industry subgroups were proportionately represented as far as possible by the 30 stocks. Over the years the exact percentage of coverage for each of the six indexes has changed as a result of new listings, delistings, and bonus issues. Exhibit 14 shows the coverage when the SES Index was established and eight years later.

The **SES Index** is the percentage of current aggregate market value to the base aggregate market value. The latter is the average daily aggregate market value for the year 1970; this is superior to the choice of a single day as the base, which could subject the index to short-term abnormal influences. The formula can be expressed as follows:

EXHIBIT 14 NUMBER OF COMPANIES AND PAID-UP CAPITAL BY INDUSTRY GROUP

Group	Number of Companies		Paid-Up Capital[a]		
	Total	Index	Total	Index	Percentage
As of 1 January 1970					
Industrial and commercial	88	30	S$1,063,984	S$409,974	38.5 %
Finance	15	11	266,397	240,294	90.2
Hotels	15	14	196,102	192,602	98.2
Properties	13	12	164,155	157,155	95.7
Mining (tins)	23	19	107,503	103,281	96.1
Plantations (rubber)	27	22	112,714	108,394	96.2
As of 28 February 1978					
Industrial and commercial	147	33	S$7,607,760	S$1,020,024	13.41%
Finance	16	11	687,912	650,057	94.50
Hotels	15	14	455,162	430,651	92.42
Properties	14	12	1,596,530	361,246	22.64
Mining (tins)	29	18	164,908	129,302	78.41
Plantations (rubber)	24	16	541,518	229,600	42.41

Source. Saw & Limb, *Investment Analysis in Singapore*, Singapore University Press, Singapore.
[a]In hundreds of Singapore dollars.

$$\text{SES Index} = \frac{(P_i)(Q_i}{(P_0)(Q_0)} \times 100$$

where P_i = current market price
P_0 = base market price
Q_i = current number of listed shares
Q_0 = base number of listed shares

The formulae adjusting the aggregate market value (AMV) for changes are as follows:

1. For rights issue $\text{AMV} = \text{old base AMV} \times \dfrac{\text{old current AMV} + \text{payment for rights}}{\text{old current AMV}}$

2. For new listing $\text{AMV} = \text{old base AMV} \times \dfrac{\text{new current AMV, including new listings}}{\text{new current AMV, excluding new listing}}$

3. For delisting $\text{AMV} = \text{old base AMV} \times \dfrac{\text{old current AMV, excluding delisting}}{\text{old current AMV, including delisting}}$

The six indexes of the SES are calculated daily at the end of morning and afternoon sessions, broadcast over radio and television, and published daily in the press. Analysts and chartists use them for in-depth studies (usually published in the *Singapore Stock Exchange Journal* and the *Securities Industry Review*), but the indexes do not yet seem to have gripped the popular imagination as the STII or Fraser's Singapore Industrial Index have.

The **KLSE Index,** like the **SES Index,** has no composite index but has six separate indexes. The number of the KLSE constituents are as follows:

Industrials	30
Finance	13
Hotels	10
Property	11
Mining	17
Plantations	24

The **Business Times Index** (BT Index) is an average of the 10 most active stocks, and therefore its components vary each day.

The **Kay Hian Geometric Indexes** are the only ones that separate the stocks from the First and Second Section of the SES, and are the only ones calculated on a geometric basis. A geometric index weighs each stock equally and a given percentage increase in the market price of any stock has an identical effect on the average.

The **OCBC Index** was developed by the Overseas Chinese Banking Corporation with the assistance of Capital International S.A. of Geneva. It is a composite index of 40 stocks, representing not only the industrial-commercial sector, but all the other sectors—property, hotel, finance, tin and rubber—as well as oil palms. The index is constructed and adjusted on the same basis as the SES indexes, but it uses as its base one day, 1 January 1970, which is given the value of 100.

Fraser and Company, the oldest Singapore stock broker, has computed indexes since 1958, but has published them only since 1970. They are printed daily by Reuters Service and weekly by the highly influential *Far Eastern Economic Review*. There are five indexes: **Singapore Industrial Index, Malaysian Industrial Index, Plantation Index, Hotel and Property Index,** and **Tin Index.** On 31 December 1958 (the base date for all the indexes), the Singapore Index contained eight components, the Malaysian Index only four. To be incorporated in the index a company must be incorporated in Singapore or Malaysia and should be reasonably marketable. Exceptions, however, are made—some firms are incorporated in the United Kingdom and the tin and plantation shares are at best thinly traded. Fraser gives preference to trustee stocks, companies with paid-in capital of $5 million and five years of continuous dividends. Fraser seeks a wide variety, but avoids quoted subsidiaries of larger groups. The components of the indexes are weighted by their respective market capitalizations. To obtain basic market capitalization, the number of shares of each component is multiplied by its closing price. The products are added together and become the base market capitalization, assigned a value of 100. Current market capitalization is calculated the same way, and divided by basic market capitalization with the quotient multiplied by 100 to reach the current index. The basic market capitalization is adjusted for rights issues, listings, and delistings.

At the end of 1978 the Singapore Industrial Index had 20 issues, all trustee stocks, including several major banks. It included Cold Storage, incorporated in the United Kingdom, but the rest were incorporated in Singapore. It did not include Sime Darby, one of the most active stocks. The Malaysia Industrial Index comprises 23 Malaysian incorporated stocks (except Sime Darby)—all trustee stocks—but only one bank. Prices are computed in Malaysian currency, although all these stocks are also listed on the SES and can be more actively traded there. The Hotel and Property Index includes 20 stocks, incorporated in Singapore or Malaysia, only six of which are trustee stocks. The Plantation Index comprises 36 plantation stocks, all incorporated in Malaysia and computed in Malaysian currency prices, of which 17 are trustee stocks. The Tin Index, computed in Malaysian currency prices, includes 28 tin stocks, four incorporated in the United Kingdom and 24 in Malaysia. Eleven companies are trustee stocks, only one of which is from the United Kingdom.

USE AND LIMITATION OF THE INDEXES. The SES can be evaluated by seven different indexes, but only one, **the OCBC Index,** is both composite and market weighted. It represents more accurately market price movements as a whole than the weighted SES Industrial, Fraser's Singapore Industrial Index, and the unweighted **ST Industrial,** all of which cover only one sector of the market. For movements in individual sectors the SES, Fraser's, and the STI provide individual group indexes. The weighted indexes—the SES Index and Fraser's—give greater influence to the large capitalization stocks, while in the unweighted STI, the high-price stocks receive undue influence. The STI suffers from a major weakness as a stock dividend or stock split reduces the stock price; the SES and OCBC indexes are unaffected since the aggregate value on which they are based is unchanged after a stock split or stock dividend. Both of the last two indexes are also adjusted for rights offerings.

All the indexes except the BT Index include inactive and suspended stocks among their constituents. The daily index includes the last price of the inactive stock, which sometimes remains unchanged for a month. The next trade, possibly a month later at a sharp decrease in price, reduces the index significantly. Another weakness of all indexes is the problem of double counting, as many companies own shares of other companies and both are included in the index.

In the KLSE, the two major stock market indexes each incorporate their own biases: the unweighted NSTI is sensitive to sharp price fluctuations among its higher-priced constituents, while the KLSE moves in concert with the large capitalization issues.

SINGAPORE SECURITY ANALYSIS. The center of security analysis in Singapore is the Singapore **Securiteis Research Institute** (SSRI), founded in December 1974 as a subsidiary of the SES. In the absence of a professional society, the SSRI has undertaken the obligation of both research and training and is an associate member of the Asian Security Analysts Council (ASAC). Since 1975 it has published twice annually the *Securities Industry Review,* which includes the research of the SSRI staff, the stock brokers, and the universities. In 1979 the SSRI produced a 546-page book, *Investment Analysis in Singapore,* a collection of 66 articles by Singaporean analysts and investment researchers. In 1977 SSRI launched a diploma program to train security analysts. The program is in two parts, the first on stock exchange practices, interpretation of financial reports and business statistics, and the second on business law, investment analysis and management, and business finance. By the end of 1981, about 100 students had received the diploma.

A reading of *Investment Analysis in Singapore* and other Singapore publications like the *Securities Industry Review* and the *Singapore Stock Exchange Journal* indicates a fairly extensive knowledge of charts, including point and figure technical analysis, fundamental analysis, and efficient market theory. A study of random walk in *Investment Analysis in Singapore* found "a tendency for persistence of price movements in the same direction," and suggested that "in a small exchange, stocks are not so actively traded, and prices may be subject to manipulation by large traders." A study of betas in Singapore concluded that betas seemed "quite stationary for large portfolios, less stationary for smaller portfolios, and unpredictable for individual securities" and that "there seemed to be a greater tendency for error as beta values move away from the mean."

MALAYSIAN SECURITY ANALYSIS. Malaysia has no securities analysts association and no research center for securities research. It is not a member of the **Asian Security Analysts Council,** but the KLSE has sent an observer to some of the ASAC meetings. The *Kuala Lumpur Stock Exchange Gazette,* a monthly publication, contains a few relatively unsophisticated articles and reports. However, the presence in Singapore of far more mature analysts and investment managers assures a regular flow of analytic data.

SHAREHOLDERS. The ownership of shares listed on the SES and KLSE is difficult to determine with certainty. The SSRI conducted a share ownership survey of Singapore-registered companies, excluding mining and plantation stocks, in 1975, and of Malaysian companies listed on the SES in 1977. The result of the 1975 survey is as shown on Exhibit 15.

While individuals made up 93% of the corporate shareholders, they owned just 29.4% of the stock, with a rather insignificant average holding of 3,299 shares. Individual investors constituted less than 3% of Singapore's population. Firms owned

EXHIBIT 15 PERCENTAGE DISTRIBUTION OF SHAREHOLDERS AND SHARES BY CLASS, 1975

Class	Shareholders	Shares	Average Number of Shares for Each Shareholder
Individuals	93.0	29.4%	3,299
Nominees and trustees	2.1	22.4	112,013
Corporate firms	3.2	38.5	126,084
Institutions	0.7	8.4	127,772
Others	1.0	1.3	12,758
Total	100.0%	100.0%	10,424

Source. Daiwa Securities Company Ltd., Tokyo.

38.5% and institutions owned 8.4% of all stock, and both of their holdings were large, over 125,000 shares. Nominees and trustees holding 22.4% refers to the shareholders whose stocks were registered in the names of banks, stockbrokerage firms, financial institutions, and trusts. The number of foreigners included is not precisely known. However, the study indicated that of all SES-listed stock, 62.9% was owned by residents of Singapore, 21.8% by residents in Malaysia, and 15.3% by foreign owners, which seems to indicate that a majority of nominee and trustee stock is held by foreigners.

BROKERAGE INSTITUTIONS. The brokerage community in Singapore has not grown significantly in the last decade from its high point of 1760 employees in 1973 to 1,887 in 1980, as shown in Exhibit 16.

In Malaysia, the small brokerage community is concentrated in a few states—14 member firms in Kuala Lumpur, and six each in Ipoh and Penang. Two other states have three member firms and six states have one member firm only.

In Singapore, however, the securities community is strengthened by many foreign brokerage, merchant banking, and investment management firms. The British have traditionally been located in Singapore since colonial days, but the community has been enlarged by other foreigners, including U.S. nationals and Japanese.

DISCLOSURES. Both the SES and KLSE require companies to issue an unaudited semiannual statement of pretax profits, sales volume, and information about any unusual factor that could affect the company's earning capacity. Incidentally, mining companies are required to issue data on production and development. When the semiannual statement is issued, companies can declare an interim dividend.

From three to six months after the end of the fiscal year, the company issues audited preliminary profits and announces a final dividend. In about two to three weeks, a final annual report is published; and it must be sent to stockholders at least 21 days before the regular annual meeting that it announces.

Although company law in both countries requires fully consolidated accounts for all companies except banks, the accounting treatment of affiliates is not rigidly prescribed. While Singapore adheres to the international accounting standards of the International Accounting Standards Committee, a study of company accounts reveals varying practices that have a material effect on reported results. These include such accounts as depreciation, valuation of inventory and work in progress, conversion of foreign currencies, warranties, valuation of intangibles, and research and development costs. The financial statements usually disclose the barest minimum required

EXHIBIT 16 BROKERAGE EMPLOYEES, 1973 AND 1980

	1973	1980
Member firm's staff	1,310	1,329
Exchange staff	55	61
Members	70	89
Dealers	29	40
Remisiers	297	368
Total	1,760	1,887

Source. Daiwa Securities Company, Ltd., Tokyo.

by the Companies Act. Some confusion also exists on the definitions of extraordinary profits and prior period items, so ordinary net earnings often include extraordinary elements.

These accounting problems are magnified by the nature of Singaporean and Malaysian companies, many of which, especially the larger companies, are holding companies in the most widely diversified activities—production ownership and/or management, trading, property development, leasing, services, and the like. Even production within a single company can range from auto assembly to saw milling, from oil field services to property development. The leading banks in the area offer the widest range of services, from retail banking to international finance, and often participate in joint ventures involving property development and management.

Stock exchange requirements do somewhat increase required disclosure. Thus the prospectus must include the basis for fixed assets valuation when the annual report fails to publish sufficient data. Companies must publicly disclose details of any acquisition or disposal that involves over 5% of assets, capital, or profits and, if over 20%, this action requires stockholder approval. The exchange also requires disclosure of any transaction involving the interests of directors or significant stockholders, past or present. While it does not have the force of law, violation of the Takeover Code can lead to the removal of the offender's quotation.

These accounting procedures, as well as tax regulations, do affect investment analysis. Thus the price/earnings ratio is complicated by the fact that in addition to the 40% corporate tax payable in both countries, Malaysian companies pay a 5% development tax, and an excess profits tax if return on share owners' funds exceeds 25%. Therefore, Malaysian companies can pay an effective tax rate of 50%. The price/earnings ratio (PER) is further complicated by pioneer status. Finally, interim reports disclose only pretax earnings. Dividend policy is also complicated, since to the extent that corporate profits are distributed net of the basic 40% tax, the tax is receivable by the shareholder in the form of a credit. Residents of Singapore and Malaysia receive a dividend voucher that records the gross dividend, tax payable, and net dividend. This voucher can be used to offset personal taxes when they are exceeded by the 40% rate. Dividends of foreign shareholders are taxed at a rate of 40% and relief can be obtained when a double-taxation relief agreement is in force. As of the end of 1981, the United States had no such agreement with Singapore or Malaysia. Local investors generally calculate share earnings on a pretax basis after deduction for minority holdings, while dividends usually published are gross dividends. However, foreign investment managers resident in Singapore generally publish pretax and net share earnings and gross and net dividends.

HONG KONG

Hong Kong was acquired by the British in three stages: Hong Kong Island (32 square miles) was acquired in 1842, and Kowloon Peninsula and Stonecutter's Island (3.75 square miles) in 1860 (both theoretically belonging to Britain in perpetuity); the New Territories (365 square miles consisting of the mainland bordering Kowloon and 235 islands) were leased for 99 years, a lease that terminates in 1997.

Although officially a colony, Hong Kong is widely regarded as Chinese territory under British administration and the British usually refer to the city-state as a territory, not a colony. The survival of the area after the return of the New Territories in 1997 is considered economically infeasible and despite repeated Chinese government reassurance that investors have nothing to fear, the Chinese refusal to state when and how they plan to reintegrate Hong Kong does contribute an element of uncertainty. As the only safe deep-sea anchorage between Shanghai and the southern Chinese border, Hong Kong served as a commercial entrepôt for the China trade from the 1840s to the 1950s, except for the period of Japanese occupation. British trading companies (*hongs*) dominated the economy, while the population, now about 5 million, was and is overwhelmingly Chinese. After the end of the civil war in China and the Korean War, Hong Kong's role as a trading center was largely diminished until the late 1960s and the 1970s, and the city began to turn toward manufacturing and finance. Although known for a reputation of laissez-faire, the Hong Kong government has been active (however insufficiently, according to some opinions) in providing low-cost housing and low-cost transportation, without which labor-intensive industries might not have been developed.

While stock trading dates back at least to 1866 in Hong Kong, formal, systematic trading began only in 1891, with the establishment of the Association of Stockholders—renamed, in 1914, the Hong Kong Stock Exchange. Members gathered together twice daily to trade—at 10:00 A.M. and 2:30 P.M. In 1921, a second stock exchange, the Hong Kong Stockholders' Association, was formed, but during the post–World War II reorganization the two stock exchanges merged to become the Hong Kong Stock Exchange (HKSE).

Hong Kong did not develop a significant capital market until late in the 1960s, and that market was highly speculative, with share prices fluctuating violently. Until that time, no large industry had developed in Hong Kong, and local capital tended to be invested overseas. The anticipation of a Chinese occupation in Hong Kong limited interest in local investment. The Hang Seng Index (HSI) which is described later, was set at 100 for 31 July 1964, but fear of the territorial ambitions stirred by the Chinese Cultural Revolution plunged the HSI to 58.61 on 31 August 1964, its record low. As the Cultural Revolution ebbed, the Chinese interest in the immediate reversion of Hong Kong disappeared. In addition, the gradual restoration of relations between China and the United States stimulated the belief that Hong Kong might reemerge as the traditional entrepôt of the China trade. Foreigners began to invest in Hong Kong—some to initiate labor-intensive manufacturing to take advantage of the colony's low wages and laissez-faire policy, and some to establish commercial and financial operations to service the potential China trade. These activities, in turn, led to a sharp upsurge in Hong Kong real estate prices, enhanced by the limited amount of land available for residential and commercial construction.

In this expansive economic atmosphere the unwillingness of the British-oriented HKSE to admit new members on the grounds of insufficient securities business aroused the dissatisfaction of a group of Chinese businessmen, who in December 1969 established the Far Eastern Stock Exchange (FESE). This not only attracted new money into the stock market, but stimulated other groups of businessmen to take advantage of Hong Kong's laissez-faire policy and establish stock exchanges. In March 1971 the merchants of the Chinese Gold and Silver Exchange established the Kam Ngan Stock Exchange, and in January 1972 the Kowloon Stock Exchange was formed. At this stage, the government finally acted to prevent the establishment of yet other stock exchanges, several of which were then in the process of formation. It did, however, recognize the Kowloon Stock Exchange by the end of 1972.

By the time these new exchanges were formed, stock prices were soaring upward, led by the real estate–related issues. The market became extremely speculative and volatile—at one point, Hong Kong Land sold at 300 times its earnings. The establishment of the additional exchanges made it possible to process the rapidly increasing volume. By 8 March 1973 the HSI skyrocketed to 1,774.96 points. By the second half of 1973 the boom collapsed, and on 12 October 1974 the HSI, overwhelmed by the oil crisis, plunged to a low of 150.11.

In the aftermath of the 1973–1974 boom and bust, the government abandoned its laissez-faire policy toward securities. In 1974 it promulgated the Securities Ordinance, providing tighter controls in securities sales and trading and establishing a regulatory Securities Commission. At the same time, the government imposed some coordination between the four stock exchanges, and the Hong Kong Federation of Stock Exchanges was established. In 1977 the government made additional efforts to regulate the securities industry—the Companies Ordinance required disclosure of consolidated accounts, and the four exchanges agreed to common listing requirements. In 1977 the four exchanges agreed to the formation of a single exchange, but by the end of 1981 a unified exchange has not yet emerged. The government also introduced a code regulating takeovers and mergers, modeled on London regulations, but without any clear definition of insider dealing, which was to create severe criticism during the merger wave of 1980–1981.

From 1974 to 1978 the stock market gradually recovered. However, the value of turnover reached a nadir in 1977, and only in 1980 did it exceed the 1972 and 1973 levels. In the boom years the value of turnover approached 50% of total market capitalization, but during the collapse, liquidity became very tight—in 1974 only 9% and in 1977 11% of market capitalization turned over.

From 1979 to 1981, the Hong Kong market boomed again—the HSI exceeded its 1973 historic high and reached 1,810.20—and then declined sharply, but not as catastrophically as in 1974, reaching a low of 1,113.77, and closing in 1981 at 1,405.82.

By the end of September 1981, Hong Kong had absorbed HK$7.5 billion of new shares, equal to about 10% of the market's capitalization. The gap between high interest and low dividends encouraged companies, especially in property, to issue stock as a cheap financing method. The boom was intensified by a merger mania with record takeover bids.

The takeover battle was fueled by a growing rivalry between the traditional British-oriented hongs and the Chinese entrepreneurs, enriched by investments in shipping and property development. The nonbinding takeover code was flaunted by avoiding 50% ownership, which required a general offer at the price paid to acquire control. In a swift dawn raid rival groups acquired 40% to 49% of the ownership, which effectively permitted control. In September 1981, Hong Kong's Commissioner of Securities reqigned after a contested takeover battle in which his office acknowledged an error in judgment. This climaxed several years of frustration to regulate the securities industry without sufficient authority. The confidence in an early decline of U.S. interest rates proved to be unfounded, and the Hong Kong market joined the international decline of equity markets in the fall of 1981.

Like its 1972–1973 predecessor, the 1979–1981 boom was also fueled by soaring prices for land and real estate-related stocks. The boom was also escalated by highly optimistic estimates of Hong Kong's trade possibilities with China and its export potential as a low-cost, labor-intensive producer. Reexports to China in 1981 represented about 35% of Hong Kong's exports. China has followed a pragmatic policy toward Hong Kong; it owns banks, trading companies, property companies, and reportedly stockbrokerage firms in Hong Kong. The general world recession, combined with the increased use of automated machinery in Japan, dampened Hong Kong's rising export expectations. Singapore, its rival city-state, also challenged Hong Kong's financial leadership in the Pacific. The evident scaling down of China's economic program compelled a reexamination of the potential of the Chinese market. These changed expectations were reflected in a decline of land prices and commercial rentals. The role of Hong Kong as a newly industrialized country and as a commercial and financial center still augers well for the future, but the tempo of its realization could be less rapid than had been anticipated. (For economic statistics, see Exhibit 17.)

EXHIBIT 17 HONG KONG ECONOMY

HONG KONG EQUITY MARKET, KEY STATISTICS

Year	Number of Companies Listed at Year End	Market Capitalization at Year End[a]	Value Turnover[a]	Composite Index (Far East Index), Yearly Average	Price/Earnings Ratio, Yearly Average (×)	Dividend Yield, Yearly Average (percentage)
1970	—	—	5,989	—	—	—
1971	85	22,827	14,793	1,329.62	18.64	3.82
1972	159	81,445	43,758	2,270.32	25.43	2.61
1973	217	88,037	48,217	3,885.24	35.51	2.05
1974	213	124,145	11,246	1,523.46	11.51	6.00
1975	211	45,373	10,335	1,463.27	12.97	4.92
1976	209	58,699	13,156	2,047.20	17.16	3.36
1977	205	55,682	6,127	2,090.41	12.89	4.39
1978	193	67,221	27,419	2,458.19	12.7	4.64
1979	191	114,347	25,633	2,783.74	11.85	4.91
1980	191	209,697	95,684	5,359.43	16.76	3.51
1981	204	231,560	105,618	7,593.12	17.58	3.55

TWENTY TOP STOCKS BY MARKET CAPITALIZATION, 1981 YEAR END

Rank	Company	Market Capitalization[a]	Rank	Company	Market Capitalization[a]
1	Hong Kong Bank	22,775	11	New World Development	4,371
2	Hong Kong Land	19,969	12	Hong Kong Hotel	4,234
3	Hang Seng Bang	18,047	13	Carrian Investment	3,921
4	Hutchison Whampoa	8,048	14	International City	3,920
5	Cheung Kong	7,877	15	Swire Pacific	3,857
6	Hong Kong & Kowloon Wharf	7,682	16	Bank of East Asia	3,746
7	Jardine Matheson	6,916	17	Swire Properties	3,685
8	China Light	6,384	18	Henderson Land	3,525
9	Hong Kong Electric	6,065	19	Sino Realty	3,381
10	Sun Hung Kai Properties	4,337	20	World International	3,085

EXHIBIT 17 (CONTINUED)

TWENTY MOST ACTIVELY TRADED STOCKS, 1981

Rank	Company	Value Turnover[a]	Rank	Company	Value Turnover[a]
1	Carrian Investment	3,536	11	Hong Kong & Kowloon Wharf	642
2	Cheung Kong	2,038	12	Wheelock Marden (A and B)	635
3	Hong Kong Land	1,309	13	Hong Kong Electric	539
4	Hutchison Whampoa	1,229	14	Eda Investment	455
5	Hongkong and Shanghai Bank	923	15	Overseas Union Realty	454
6	Trafalgar Housing	826	16	Swire Properties	424
7	New World Development	735	17	International City	419
8	Swire Pacific (A and B)	697	18	Far East Cosnortium	377
9	Jardine Matheson	678	19	Tai Cheung Properties	374
10	Sun Hung Kai Properties	653	20	Hang Seng Bank	351

PRICE PERFORMANCE, HANG SENG INDEX

Year	Opening	High	Low	Closing	Average
1970	155.38	211.91	154.75	211.64	185.24
1971	213.26	406.32	201.07	341.36	275.73
1972	346.81	843.40	323.95	843.40	466.53
1973	869.14	1,774.96	400.01	433.68	799.82
1974	432.78	481.86	150.11	171.11	317.80
1975	167.11	352.94	160.42	350.00	293.87
1976	354.53	465.33	354.53	447.67	409.62
1977	451.00	452.17	404.02	404.02	429.69
1978	393.74	707.79	383.44	495.51	519.53
1979	493.83	879.38	493.83	879.38	600.06
1980	889.13	1,654.57	738.92	1,473.59	1,081.81
1981	1,524.86	1,810.20	1,113.77	1,405.82	1,510.54

GROSS DOMESTIC PRODUCT, AT CURRENT PRICE (HK$000,000)

Year	Private Consumption Expenditure	Government Consumption Expenditure	Gross Domestic Fixed Capital Formation	Increase in Stock[b]	Export of Goods and Services	Import of Goods and Services	Total	
							Amount	Per Capita (US$)
1971	15,622	1,230	4,777	—	17,104	20,287	21,873	905
1972	17,525	1,534	5,365	—	19,400	21,788	25,854	1,117
1973	23,912	1,912	6,698	303	25,999	29,049	33,964	1,566
1974	27,216	2,438	7,743	678	30,036	34,142	38,786	1,782
1975	28,427	2,646	7,850	731	29,833	33,532	40,574	1,868
1976	31,857	3,047	9,698	2,979	41,557	43,520	51,973	2,396
1977	39,126	3,675	13,016	1,702	44,833	48,796	59,615	2,837
1978	48,541	4,454	16,838	2,067	53,908	63,263	69,557	3,232
1979	58,902	5,568	24,218	3,252	75,934	86,339	89,473	3,667
1980	75,188	7,294	31,042	3,035	98,242	111,794	111,114	4,439
1981	92,475	19,396	38,196	2,632	122,163	139,246	135,346	4,928

EXHIBIT 17 (CONTINUED)

GROSS DOMESTIC PRODUCT, AT 1973 PRICE (HK$000,000)

Year	Private Consumption Expenditure	Government Consumption Expenditure	Gross Domestic Fixed Capital Formation	Increase in Stock[b]	Export of Goods and Services	Import of Goods and Services	Total Amount	Total Per Capita (US$)
1971	19,001	1,571	5,513	—	21,673	25,355	26,612	1,101
1972	20,188	1,701	5,788	—	23,154	26,247	29,190	1,261
1973	23,785	1,912	6,698	303	25,999	29,049	33,964	1,566
1974	23,527	2,106	6,490	469	24,373	26,068	34,574	1,588
1975	24,005	2,213	6,578	713	25,161	27,046	35,349	1,627
1976	26,119	2,392	7,681	2,415	32,215	33,743	42,005	1,936
1977	30,626	2,690	9,683	1,313	33,853	36,424	46,281	2,203
1978	35,984	3,033	11,287	1,572	38,517	44,244	51,052	2,373
1979	39,389	3,356	13,372	1,974	46,030	51,281	57,565	2,359
1980	44,273	3,612	15,570	1,957	54,192	60,832	63,179	2,524
1981	48,689	4,504	17,578	1,526	61,066	67,864	69,732	2,539

EXTERNAL TRADE, 1981

Major Trading Partners

Rank	Exported To[c]	Amount[a]	Percentage of Total	Imported From	Amount[a]	Percentage of Total
1	United States	29,200	36.3	Japan	32,130	23.2
2	United Kingdom	7,710	9.6	China	29,510	21.3
3	West Germany	7,048	8.8	United States	14,442	10.4
4	Japan	2,940	3.7	Taiwan	10,762	7.8
5	Australia	2,710	3.4	Singapore	10,627	7.7

Major Goods

Rank	Exports[c]	Amount[a]	Percentage of Total	Imports	Amount[a]	Percentage of Total
1	Apparels & Clothings	28,288	35.2	Manufactured Goods Classified by Material	40,149	29.0
2	Watches & Clocks	7,104	8.8	Machinery & Transport Equipment	32,298	23.3
3	Toys & Dolls	6,685	8.3	Foodstuffs	13,993	10.1
4	Textile Fabrics	4,116	5.1	Mineral Fuels	10,966	7.9
5	Radio Receivers	2,815	3.5	Chemicals & Related Products	9,059	6.5

[a] In millions of Hong Kong dollars.
[b] "Increase in Stock" first appeared in 1973.
[c] Domestic exports exclusive of reexports.

PRIMARY MARKET. The issuance of new shares for a consideration is the usual form of a capital increase, and their allotment to stockholders, though not an obligation of the company, is the most general method, with the price set at par. The public offering of new shares is rare, but on the occasion of listing, new shares can be sold to the public at a price set by the exchange in order to meet listing requirements. Private placements are infrequent, and they are generally set at prices fairly below market prices. Companies can allot stock options to employees at prices well below market, but such action requires approval of a general shareholders' meeting and must conform to stock exchange regulations. The company can also issue new shares without consideration (i.e., a stock dividend). A general stockholders' meeting can grant the board of directors the power to issue up to 10% of the number of outstanding shares unconditionally, but such permission is effective only until the next general stockholders' meeting.

THE STOCK EXCHANGE. The four Hong Kong stock exchanges have a current membership totaling 1,084, including 15 overseas members.

Exchange	Members	Overseas Members
Hong Kong	134	12
Far Eastern	425	2
Kam Ngan	350	1
Kowloon	175	0
Total	1,084	15

The Far Eastern and Kam Ngan exchanges have outstripped the HKSE, doing over 80% of the total trading. In 1970 the FESE almost equalled, and in 1971 it surpassed, the trading volume of the HKSE. The **Kam Ngan Stock Exchange** equalled HKSE trading volume in 1973 and surpassed it in 1974. The Kowloon Stock Exchange represented about half of the total trading in its first two years of existence, 1972 and 1973, but it swiftly declined and now its share is minuscule. In 1981 turnover was as follows:

Exchange	HK$ Millions	Percentage of Total
Hong Kong	HK$17.451	16.5%
Far Eastern	50.804	47.9
Kam Ngan	37.545	35.4
Kowloon	0.186	0.2
Total	HK$105,896	100.0%

The HKSE still retains some of its traditional British flavor and is more foreign-oriented. It has the largest number of overseas members (seven British, four Japanese, and one Canadian) and the largest number (16) and market value of foreign equities.

Companies can be listed on more than one exchange, and most major issues are listed on all four. No single individual can be a member of more than one stock exchange; however, a husband is often a member of one exchange while his wife is a member of another. Corporate brokerage houses have members on each of the four exchanges.

Since the four exchanges are quite similar, the HKSE is a good example to use to explain the structure and function of all exchanges. The stock exchanges are limited private companies, and their members, individual and corporate, are the stockholders, limited in number. Foreign members must also be members of the stock exchange of their home countries; they are permitted access to the floor, but only for information, and must place their trades through local brokers.

The general meeting of the stock exchange members is its decision-making body; it also elects its executive body, the Stock Exchange Committee (nine members in the case of the HKSE). New members must obtain approval of the committee before purchasing a seat from an outgoing member. Fees are quite low—the entrance fee is HK$5,000 and the monthly fee is about HK$200. Bank employees cannot be members; female members have been permitted since 1970, corporate members since 1977. Birth in Hong Kong or residence for five of the last seven years is required for membership (excepting foreign members).

All four stock exchanges trade stock by auction at the trading board. In the HKSE the hall is 6,000 square feet and the board, slightly curved for better vision, is 120 square feet long. The members' seats are arranged in rows across the hall facing the trading board. Each member can have two authorized clerks to conclude trades, and runners to assist in the trading (who cannot conclude trades). Each member has a board initial that appears on the member's seat and on red armbands of the authorized clerks. Multiple television cameras are installed on the floor and from his or her seat a member can monitor different parts of the board. The Far Eastern and Kam Ngan exchanges have similar monitors, and the floors of the exchanges have television monitors for the floors of other exchanges. Similar monitors are installed in securities houses and in other financial institutions.

Members who wish to buy or to sell securities write the price on the securities trading board. The stocks then can be purchased or sold by any person in the trading hall at the price marked on the board. All trades, except for special or odd lots, must be done on the board. Microphones assist communications between members or their clerks. Trading takes place Monday through Friday in two sessions—10:00 A.M. to 12:30 P.M. and 2:30 P.M. to 3:30 P.M. All securities are traded in board lots, which vary from 20 to 12,000 shares, with 1,000 and 2,000 the most common number. Odd lots, defined as less than a board lot, are generally sold at a modest discount from board lot prices. Share prices can move within a limited range, known as a spread, whose size is determined by the stock price, as shown in the following schedule.

Market Value	Spread
under HK$2.00	HK$0.02
above HK$2.00 and under HK$5.00	HK$0.025
above HK$5.00 and under HK$10.00	HK$0.05
above HK$10.00 and under HK$30.00	HK$0.10
above HK$30.00 and under HK$50.00	HK$0.25

above HK$50.00 and under HK$100	HK$0.50
above HK$100 and under HK$200	HK$1.00
above HK$200	HK$2.00

A **buying price** for a board lot might not be four spreads less than the last sale and vice versa for a selling price. However, at the opening a buyer or seller can set any price that he or she cares to fix. In actual practice some of the larger brokers make a market in the popular stocks.

Settlement, which until 1925 was done on a monthly basis, now takes place with delivery of the share certificates and attached transfer deeds by 2:45 P.M. on the trading day following the day of the conclusion of the sale. Since registration normally takes six weeks in Hong Kong, overseas customers must register their stock as soon as possible in the nominee companies of Hong Kong banks. The buying broker can exercise the right to buy in.

The board on the floor is divided into two sections, a wider upper section for active issues, and a narrower lower section for the inactive issues. The company board shows the name of the company and the latest financial data, such as dividends, the size of the board lot and the spread, and buying price, and the selling price. Below each of the prices are two columns, one column with initials of buyers willing to purchase at the buying price and one column for those willing to buy at one spread lower. Two similar columns exist for the sellers, except that the second column for selling is at one spread higher. The day's trades are all recorded on the board, including interexchange transactions between HKSE members and a member of one of the other three exchanges. At the bottom of the board are shown bids and offers for odd or special lots.

A member with an order that can be fulfilled by the quotes on the board touches the appropriate quote with a finger. The displays on the board only list the broker's initials, without mention of the size of the order. The basis is first come, first served. Since the size of the order is not posted, the member there first contacts the broker who initialed the price and arranges the transaction with three copies of the contract—one each for the buyer, seller, and market. The price, volume, and members' initials then appear on the company board list of trades.

Brokerage commission is negotiable, with a minimum of HK$25.00 and a 1% ad valorem upper limit. The minimum and actually effective rate is 0.5%, reducible to 0.25% for overseas members of the HKSE and members of other Hong Kong stock exchanges. Members of overseas exchanges can charge commissions at a rate that they deem appropriate. Buyer and seller must pay an ad valorem stamp duty of 0.03%. Only the seller must pay a transfer stamp of HK$5.00.

Licensed banks (all charging similar fees) provide custodial services, and some brokerage houses do so without charge in return for the opportunity to execute orders. Nominee services are also available at some other establishments. The fee schedule, established by the Hong Kong Association of Banks, provides for transaction charges, safe custody charges, dividend collection charges, and handling commissions.

The Hong Kong government still maintains primarily a laissez-faire attitude toward equities. There is no capital gains tax, no tax on dividends, and no foreign exchange control—money can and does flow freely in and out of Hong Kong.

LISTED SECURITIES. In the absence of a real over-the-counter market, a company must be listed on a stock exchange to go public. To do so, the company must submit a prospectus to the Registrar of Companies in accordance with the revised Companies Ordinance of 1972. Afterward, the company publishes the prospectus in the local newspapers and submits this prospectus in its listing application. Listing requirements are ostensibly quite similar for all four exchanges, but there is considerable discretion for each. The listing is essentially a result of private negotiations with the applicant. The HKSE is regarded as most rigorous in its examination as compared to the other three exchanges.

An applicant company must have a minimum paid-up capital of HK$20 million and the public offer must have a minimum value of HK$5 million. A foreign applicant must conform only to the last requirement. A domestic company must publically offer a total of 25% of the outstanding securities at a price approved by the stock exchange committee. A foreign applicant need not conform to the 25% rule, but it must be listed on its home country's stock exchange. In addition, up to 10% of the shares offered can be allotted to the company's own employees or affiliated companies.

At the end of 1981, the HKSE listed 188 stocks, including 16 foreign stocks (11 Japanese, two Dutch, two Singaporean, and one Malaysian); the FESE listed 204 companies, of which four were foreign (three Philippine and one Japanese). The market capitalization of the FESE at year-end 1981 was HK$105,618 million (about US$18,860 million).

In 1972, a boom year, HK$1,990 million was raised on the HKSE. The total capital increase is slightly more because a few new capital issues were listed on other exchanges, but not on the HKSE. The issues were mainly from small companies, many of which were highly speculative. From 1973 to 1977 capital increases declined, reaching a total of about HK$6,000 million. In the 1981 bull market about HK$4,500 million was raised, but most of this sum was concentrated in existing big companies and only five new issues of significance appeared. At the end of 1977, the FESE listed about 74% of the total of 277 listed companies. As indicated in Exhibit 17, the number of FESE-listed securities reached a high point in 1973 of 217, and declined steadily so that at year-end 1980, it had dropped to 191. The year 1981 saw the first increase, to 204. The contraction of listed securities reflects a combination of some reversion to private companies and merger and acquisition activity. On the FESE the 10 leading stocks represent 46.7% and the 20 leading stocks 62.5% of total market capitalization. Thus the stock markets in Hong Kong are rather highly concentrated in a few stocks.

The market is not divided into sectors, but at least 70% of listed stocks are for companies involved in property, the traditional Chinese investment vehicle. The major stocks are primarily banks, such as Hongkong and Shanghai and Hang Seng; the trading houses, or hongs, such as Jardine Matheson; shipowners, such as Cheung Kong; and property-holding and development companies, such as Hong Kong Land. Both domestic and foreign investors follow the leading stocks, and these stocks are quite liquid. Stock exchanges report daily total value of transactions but do not issue daily turnover of shares by number. During a boom period turnover can be exceptionally high. In the 1972–1973 period, daily turnover averaged HK$400 million and peaked at HK$784 million; during the ensuing bust period turnover dried up, falling to HK$10 million to HK$20 million daily in late 1975. Exhibit 17 indicates that the FESE market capitalization turns over about 50% during boom periods and about 10% during busts. The turnover of the floating shares is quite considerable, since a large percentage of the shares are still in the hands of the original family owners, especially in the smaller issues.

Little data is available on the nature of the holders of Hong Kong stock. In the

1972–1973 boom, an estimated 19% of Hong Kong's 4.2 million people participated in the market. Investment management companies thrive in Hong Kong, and pension funds and insurance companies are growing, but the decisive role in market trading is played by private investment syndicates and the big trading houses. Foreign money, especially from "overseas" Chinese, has been important in Hong Kong. English merchant bankers and brokers have also been quite active in Hong Kong; Japanese and U.S. securities companies have taken an increasing role. Nonetheless, at this stage the local Hong Kong investors still dominate the market. Their activities are often motivated not so much by sophisticated investment analysis, but by sentiment, often no more than rumor (sometimes referred to a "teashop whisper"). It should be noted that many, if not a majority, of stock exchange members trade only for their own account and do not serve as brokers for others.

INDEXES. Three indexes are popular in Hong Kong: the Hang Seng Index (HSI), the Far East Index (FEI), and the Kam Ngan Index (KNI). The Hang Seng Index, the oldest and most popular, is usually the only one cited in foreign publications. Many changes have taken place in the HSI since its introduction in 1969, and the present 33 constituent stocks represent about 70% of total turnover. The base date, given the value of 100, is 31 July 1964. The HSI is compiled on an arithmetic basis, weighted by market capitalization. The formula for the index is as follows:

$$\text{HSI} = \frac{P_t \times Q_0}{P_0 \times Q_0}$$

where P_t = market price on current day t

P_0 = market price on base day 0

Q_0 = number of shares outstanding of on base day 0

High capitalization stocks such as the Hongkong and Shanghai Bank and Hong Kong Land exercise great influence on the HSI.

The FEI is more useful. The FESE releases yields and price/earnings ratios, as well as price indexes by industrial sector consistent with the index. The FEI has a base day of 1 April 1971, and thus it lacks the historical depth of the HSI. The FEI includes 52 stocks, each weighted according to the number of shares traded in the most recent five years. There are nine subindexes. The number of stocks in the indexes are shown in Exhibit 18; the two indexes not shown are docks—one stock and investment; investment services, three stocks. The subindexes reveal that growth has centered in the banks, land and construction, and hotels. The Commercial and Industrial Subindex ended in 1981 about the same level as in 1973, but the annual average in 1981 was about double that of 1973. Utilities have moved more rapidly, but a significant part of this movement is related to the property holding of the utility companies. Shipping and textiles have experienced far less growth than the property companies.

The exchanges publish daily reports on transactions, weekly summaries, a monthly review that also includes company news, and a yearbook that provides extensive earnings, dividends, and price data for each listed stock.

SECURITY ANALYSIS. The Hong Kong Society of Security Analysts, founded in 1974, has 150 members. It beongs both to the International Coordinating Committee (ICC) and the Asian Securities Analysts Council (ASAC). It has been active in seeking greater disclosure of company data, but until sufficient accounting data are made

EXHIBIT 18 SUBINDEXES: FAR EAST CLASSIFIED INDEXES

Year	Banks (4)	Utilities (6)	Land and Construction (14)	Commercial and Industrials (9)	Hotels (4)	Shipping (5)	Textiles (6)
1971	1,543.86	1,634.75	1,915.50	1,725.39	1,056.32	—	981.99
	1,364.13	1,479.60	1,633.05	1,385.02	1,040.39	—	983.75
1972	2,444.40	2,501.70	6,876.26	5,595.58	3,118.62	—	2,214.22
	1,754.65	1,844.00	3,308.89	2,692.33	1,532.81	—	1,601.48
1973	2,184.52	1,207.66	2,686.72	2,769.51	1,396.16	—	1,747.12
	2,738.97	2,261.04	6,190.83	5,341.79	2,791.31	—	1,815.58
1974	829.04	585.31	1,224.90	861.21	542.25	—	762.00
	1,629.64	907.21	2,007.93	1,920.49	939.46	—	1,346.72
1975	2,130.49	947.16	2,260.79	1,684.55	1,007.63	—	902.00
	1,702.22	822.70	1,947.99	1,558.84	812.93	—	751.52
1976	2,649.22	1,844.00	2,512.66	2,026.17	1,512.49	—	1,133.55
	2,441.40	1,432.52	2,317.98	1,913.47	1,369.71	—	1,141.78
1977	2,453.33	1,790.39	2,070.87	1,507.97	1,684.64	814.30	1,034.85
	2,524.14	1,878.90	2,227.27	1,801.16	1,689.64	994.53	1,087.79
1978	2,713.52	2,241.31	2,526.97	1,678.92	2,085.98	842.02	1,775.52
	2,701.68	2,373.58	2,943.07	2,007.62	2,084.67	887.36	1,498.81
1979	4,460.97	2,995.87	5,204.31	3,058.13	4,459.59	1,267.25	2,137.27
	3,194.13	2,336.22	3,238.86	2,043.85	2,771.90	959.61	1,791.26
1980	8,117.57	3,864.24	10,949.13	5,266.70	7,330.60	1,255.07	2,944.82
	6,070.79	3,151.80	7,138.38	3,652.25	5,568.97	1,178.82	2,234.62
1981	7,194.52	4,106.33	10,682.19	5,132.97	8,972.11	860.95	2,132.46
	7,774.90	3,984.88	11,818.60	5,451.41	8,621.63	1,106.55	2,581.82

Source. Daiwa Securities Company Ltd., Tokyo.

Note. Upper figures are as of the end of the year, and lower ones are average. Numbers in parentheses in column heads represent the number of companies in each classification.

available, security analysis will continue to be relatively unsophisticated. Foreign investment analysts and managers resident in Hong Kong are often well trained, but investment reports, especially from local Hong Kong brokers, often lack depth.

SECURITIES ADMINISTRATION. Until 1972 the government exercised neither control nor supervision over the equities market. The stock market boom and the subsequent swift collapse compelled the government to exercise some control over the stock exchanges and brokers to protect the investor from abuses. In 1972 companies were first required to submit prospectuses to the Registrar of Companies. In 1974 the Securities Ordinance was promulgated, creating four institutions.

1. The Securities Commission controls securities issuance and trading. The effectiveness of its investigatory staff is still questioned.
2. The Securities Supervisory Board registers those engaged in securities trading, and requires an annual audited financial statement and a security deposit from them (through their exchange).
3. The Hong Kong Federation of Stock Exchanges assists the Securities Commission and plans for a single stock exchange.
4. The Compensation Fund is prepared to compensate up to HK$1 million any stockholder who sustains a pecuniary loss due to default. Each exchange has to deposit with the Securities Commission HK$25,000 and a guarantee for an equal amount for each of its members for this fund.

DISCLOSURE AND ACCOUNTING. Fourteen days prior to the annual stockholders' meeting a company is required by the stock exchanges to publish an annual report, audited by accountants in accordance with the Hong Kong Companies Ordinance. Most companies announce one interim dividend a year and issue an interim statement, but do not publish semiannual profit accounts, although an increasing number of them are doing so. The final dividend is announced any time between one and six months after the end of the company's fiscal year and is accompanied by a preliminary profit figure.

Company financial reporting in Hong Kong leaves much to be desired, although gradual improvements have been noticed recently. International accounting standards, established by the International Accounting Standards Committee, have won greater acceptance, especially in prospectuses issued by major Hong Kong companies to raise capital in international markets. Thus major companies have offered disclosure of semiannual profits and sources and applications of funds. Equity accounting is not widely practiced, but public companies have provided greater detail in a more standardized accounting format.

A report of the Hong Kong Society of Security Analysts issued in September 1978 reveals the limitations of Hong Kong accounting. The report set up two sets of recommendations, one listed as "noncontentious" and relatively minor, which could be adopted at once, and one "more controversial," and therefore requiring prolonged debate. The noncontroversial recommendations include

A fuller chairman's statement to include current and future prospects

Concrete detail of actual interest in subsidiaries, instead of merely issuing a list of names

Detailed information on acquisitions and disposals

Publication of parent financial accounts, instead of just consolidated accounts

Depreciation of all fixed assets, as at present some investment properties are not depreciated

Classification of inventory by type, not just an inventory total

Segmentation of turnover, net profit, and assets according to type of activity and, if possible, geographic area (at present, turnover is an "amalgam of different types of business calculated in various different ways" and cost of sales is seldom disclosed)

The "more controversial" but equally desirable recommendations include the following:

1. Disclosure of details of nonrecurring items is recommended. The profits and/or losses arising from sales of fixed assets held originally for investment purposes are usually classified as extraordinary, and shown below the line in the profit and loss account in view of the absence of a capital gains tax in Hong Kong.
2. Disclosure should be made of accounting methods for foreign transactions and translations.
3. Premiums issued instead of cash dividends should be credited to the share premium account, not to distributable reserves. In the extreme, this practice could amount to a distribution of capital.
4. Disclosure of the amount of interest capitalized that is due to fellow group companies is recommended.
5. Earnings of property companies should be separately classified into developmental and rental.
6. Disclosure should be made of the directors' interests, since "a large number of quoted companies are effectively family and/or director controlled," and the directors' dealing often represents the making of a market "where otherwise no effective market would exist."
7. Disclosure is desirable of material interests at a 10% level, including some provision for parties acting in concert to prevent evasion of the recommendation's spirit.
8. Disclosure of interest rates on loans from a company to a fellow group company is recommended.

The criticism by the Hong Kong Society of Security Analysts indicates that accounting in Hong Kong requires substantial improvement.

DEVELOPMENT OF A SINGLE STOCK EXCHANGE. The amalgamation of the four stock exchanges is probably one of the biggest problems facing the Hong Kong securities industry. In 1973 the government acted and limited the number of exchanges to four, and legislated the Hong Kong Federation of Stock Exchanges in order to enhance uniform regulation. The planned merger, having made little progress in the 1970s because of the intense opposition by the members, was finally legislated, but with a lengthy preparatory period. The merger has several advantages: It allows avoidance of possible deterioration of listing requirements arising from competition among the exchanges, it provides more effective and economical operation, and it contributes to greater size and liquidity. All of this is a necessary prerequisite to an improved foreign image of the Hong Kong market and an increased capital inflow from abroad. The merger problems, however, are significant. To accomodate all the members of the four stock exchanges on one trading floor requires a large amount of space, which has been difficult to obtain in Hong Kong. Furthermore, if members of all four exchanges are treated as equals, the Kowloon members, whose seats are much less in value than the others, receive an unfair advantage. The time preference system, based on priority in touching the posted quotes on the board, will have to be changed if total chaos is not to reign on the single trading floor. The greatest fear of the members, however, is whether capital requirements will be increased, which could ultimately eliminate many. This is of particular importance to members who use their seats primarily, if not exclusively, to trade for their own account. An additional factor is the opposition of many local brokers to the admission of foreign brokers as exchange members. Thus the merger of the exchanges might still require some time before a successful completion.

BIBLIOGRAPHY

General

Asian Wall Street Journal, daily in Far East and weekly in the United States.

Daiwa Securities Company Ltd., Daiwa Securities Research Institute Asia-Pacific, 1982.

Far Eastern Economic Review, weekly journal.

Far Eastern Economic Review, Asia 1982 Yearbook.

Financial Times, especially their periodic surveys of Asian areas.

Oriental Economist, regular reports from stock exchanges, brokerage firms, governmental agencies.

Security Analysts Association of Japan (with the cooperation of the Tokyo Stock Exchange), *Securities Market in Asia*, October (1981).

World Bank, *Atlas*, 1981.

Hong Kong

Far Eastern Exchange, *The Year Book*.

Hong Kong Stock Exchange, *Year Book* and *Monthly Gazette*.

Kam Ngan Stock Exchange, *Monthly Bulletin*.

Singapore and Malaysia

The Kuala Lumpur Stock Exchange Gazette, monthly.

Swee-Hock, S., *The Securities Market in Singapore*, Singapore Securities Research Institute, Singapore, 1980.

Swee-Hock, S. and L. Choo Peng, (Eds.), *Investment Analysis in Singapore*, Singapore University Press, Singapore, 1979.

Securities Industry Review, Singapore Securities Research Institute, semiannual, Singapore, 1982.

Singapore Stock Exchange Journal, monthly, Singapore, 1982.

Daiwa Securities Company Ltd., *Daiwa Manual 1981: 200 Singapore and Malaysia Stocks*, Tokyo, 1982.

APPENDIX A. ASIAN EQUITIES MARKET SIZE (end of 1981 or year 1981)

Country	Market Capitalization (in Millions)		Value Turnover (in Millions)		Number of Companies Listed
	In Local Currency	In U.S. Dollars	In Local Currency	In U.S. Dollars	
Australia	Aus$48.213	$54,380	Aus$7,117	$8,180	1,024
Hong Kong[a]	HK$231,560	41,350	HK$105,618	19,819	204
Korea	W2,959,100	4,224	W2,534,200	3,721	343
Malaysia	M$55,415	24,717	M$8,059	3,585	251
Singapore	S$71,293	34,814	S$13,419	6,352	270
Taiwan	NT$201,331	5,321	NT$209,217	5,678	107
Indonesia	Rp45,220	72	Rp4,055	6	8
New Zealand	—	—	NZ$550	479	292
Philippines[b]	P14,255	1,738	P607	74	164
Thailand	B22,798	991	B2,120	97	75[e]
Japan[c]	Y91,905,691	417,943	Y49,364,571	$223,845	1,412
World[d]	—	$2,267,000	—	—	—

Source. Daiwa Securities Company Ltd., *Tokyo Stock Exchange Quarterly Review*, various issues, 1982.

[a]Market capitalization is that of the Far East Exchange. Value turnover is the combined amount of the four Hong Kong exchanges.

[b]The Manila Stock Exchange only.

[c]The Tokyo Stock Exchange only.

[d]The total in the international capital perspective plus Korea, Malaysia, Taiwan, Indonesia, New Zealand, the Philippines, and Thailand.

[e]As of the end of November 1981.

APPENDIX B. KEY INDICATORS

	Reference Period	Unit	Australia	Hong Kong	Indonesia	South Korea	Malaysia	New Zealand	Philippines	Singapore	Taiwan	Thailand	Japan
Currency			Aus$	HK$	Rupiah (Rp)	Won (W)	M$	NZ$	Peso (P)	S$	NT$	Baht (B)	Yen (Y)
For each U.S. dollar	End 1981		0.8866	5.600	631.8	700.5	2.242	1.213	8.200	2.048	37.84	23.00	219.9
For each U.S. dollar	End 1971		0.8396	5.710	414.9	373.2	2.886	0.837	6.435	2.900	40.05	20.93	314.8
GNP, current price	1981/1981	US$ millions	149,545	25,397	64,590	63,367	21,985	22,759[a]	39,693	12,491	46,235	36,016	1,127,084
Per capita		US$	10,070	4,928	425	1,629	1,636	7,341	820	5,113	2,573	775	9,583
GNP, constant price	1972/1981	%	3.0	(D)	(D)	7.9	(D)	2.6[a]	6.3	(D)	8.8	(D)	4.7
Annual compound growth				9.0	7.0		8.0[a]			8.9		7.2	
Exports, annual compound growth rate	1972/1981	%	16.2	25.3	37.7[a]	34.9	18.0	18.3	22.3[a]	23.5	27.7	24.2	20.3
Price rise, CPI, annual compound rate	1972/1981	%	10.7	10.1	18.4	16.2	6.7	13.0	13.4	8.9	11.8	11.0	8.9
Money supply growth, annual compound rate	1972/1981	%	15.0	18.7	33.3	30.6	21.4	21.9	20.0	16.7	25.2	20.0[a]	13.2
Per capita M_2	End 1981	US$	2,697	4,828	85	592	1,074	2,097	164	3,932	1,667	247	8,972
Population	Mid-1981	Million	14.85	5.15	151.89[a]	38.90	13.44[a]	3.10[a]	48.40[a]	2.44	17.97	46.46[a]	117.61

Source. Daiwa Securities Company Ltd., *Tokyo Stock Market Quarterly Review*, various issues, 1982.

[a]Statistics from 1980. Growth rates associated with these figures are for nine years.

(D) means GDP.

APPENDIX C: WORLD STOCK MARKETS PERFORMANCE

City of Exchange	Market Value billions of dollars	Return in Each Currency (Percentage) 3 months	1 year	5 years①	Currency Valuation (Percentage) 3 months	1 year	5 years②	Return in U.S. Dollars (Percentage) 3 months	1 year	5 years③	Sigma (σ) ①	②	③	Beta (β)	Correlation NY	Tky	Lon	Tor	Fra	Syd	Par	Zrh	HK	Mln	Ams	Sin
New York	1,139.8	5.5	−9.7	2.7	0.0	0.0	0.0	5.5	−9.7	2.7	4.2	0.0	4.2	1.06	1.00	0.08	0.32	0.76	0.24	0.46	0.26	0.31	0.28	0.19	0.31	0.30
Tokyo	897.6	3.6	15.4	8.2	6.0	−7.6	5.9	9.9	6.6	14.7	2.3	3.9	4.5	0.59		1.00	0.36	0.20	0.42	0.41	0.22	0.40	0.39	0.28	0.37	0.30
London	166.5	11.6	11.8	8.4	5.8	−19.9	2.4	18.1	−10.4	11.0	6.1	3.3	6.9	1.23			1.00	0.52	0.41	0.47	0.25	0.43	0.32	0.45	0.32	0.20
Toronto	105.4	3.8	−13.9	14.1	1.8	0.7	−3.2	5.6	−13.3	10.4	5.4	1.4	6.0	1.41				1.00	0.36	0.59	0.25	0.36	0.36	0.31	0.32	0.30
Frankfurt	62.8	−0.4	−1.2	−1.5	3.4	−12.0	1.0	3.0	−13.1	−0.5	2.8	3.8	5.0	0.73					1.00	0.31	0.26	0.81	0.29	0.08	0.68	0.30
Sydney	52.4	3.9	−16.5	15.4	−1.3	−4.5	0.8	2.6	−20.3	16.3	5.2	1.4	5.8	1.04						1.00	0.16	0.34	0.40	0.35	0.36	0.30
Paris	37.9	0.0	−21.0	7.1	−2.5	−20.4	−2.7	−2.5	−37.1	4.1	7.2	11.0	14.4	1.61							1.00	0.34	0.04	0.14	0.03	0.09
Zurich	40.0	2.4	−13.7	−1.9	10.4	0.0	6.5	13.1	−13.7	4.4	3.5	4.7	5.4	0.86								1.00	0.35	0.14	0.68	0.33
Hong Kong	34.1	9.8	−4.6	25.7	8.2	−10.3	−3.7	18.8	−14.4	21.1	9.1	1.6	9.6	1.27									1.00	0.40	0.42	0.57
Milan	22.4	−1.5	13.2	21.1	−1.3	−22.0	−6.0	−2.8	−11.7	13.8	3.6	2.6	8.3	0.86										1.00	0.26	0.23
Amsterdam	17.6	−1.4	2.4	−5.4	5.2	−12.7	0.0	3.7	−10.6	−5.4	4.5	3.6	5.4	0.78											1.00	0.13
Singapore	30.5	20.3	18.2	25.1	3.4	1.7	3.7	24.4	20.2	29.8	7.1	1.7	7.8	0.98												1.00
Total	2,107.1							7.6	−7.7	6.6			3.5													

Source. Daiwa Securities Company Ltd., *Tokyo Stock Market Quarterly Review*, December (1981).

NOTE. Market value estimate is for the end of December 1982. The return in each currency is derived solely based upon each market's stock price index (dividends are not included) for the periods ending on the last trading date of the latest quarter. Five-year data are shown in the annual compound rate. Stock price indexes referred to are S &P500, Tokyo Stock Price Index, FT industrial, Toronto composite, Commerzbank general index, Sydney Stock Exchange all ordinaries, CAC industrial, Swiss Bank Corporation general index, Hang Seng Bank index, Banca Commerciale Italiana index, ANP-CBS industrial, and Straits Times industrial.

Currency valuation is the rate of change of each currency's value in U.S. dollar terms (New York market) for the corresponding periods. Five-year data are shown in the annual compound rate. The return in U.S. dollars is the return of each market in U.S. dollar terms. Five-year data are shown in the annual compound rate.

① : Standard deviation of each market's return in each currency terms, calculated from the most recent 60 monthly returns.
② : Standard deviation of each currency's value in U.S. dollar terms, calculated from the most recent 60 monthly rate of change.
③ : Standard deviation of each market's return in U.S. dollar terms, calculated from the most recent 60 monthly returns.

Sensitivity of each market return relative to the world market, derived with the assumption of no restriction on international investment activities; calculated from the most recent 60 monthly returns in U.S. dollar terms and world market return averaged by weighting each market return with each market value of each month.

The correlation is the correlation coefficient between each stock market return in U.S. dollar terms, calculated from the most recent 60 monthly returns.

SECTION 6.10

SECURITIES MARKETS IN DEVELOPING COUNTRIES

CONTENTS

SECTION 6.10

SECURITIES MARKETS IN DEVELOPING COUNTRIES

Antoine W. van Agtmael

THE ROLE OF A STOCK MARKET

When a small company is founded, **capital** is typically provided by the entrepreneur-manager, relatives, and friends. Larger projects are sometimes financed by industrial groups or wealthy families, frequently in a joint venture with foreign partners. The government might also become a major shareholder, especially in basic industries. And finally, in the United States and a few other countries, specialized venture capital companies play a major role in raising equity for new firms. Their principal function is to invest in new, high-technology-oriented companies and to assist them in their difficult first years. Unfortunately, few venture capital firms are found in the developing world.

Why do companies need capital? Doing business requires finance—for short-term working capital and long-term fixed assets. Companies must invest money in order to start their business and, even after start-up, internally generated cash flow is usually not sufficient, especially when a company is expanding rapidly. Moreover, bankers are not willing to extend loans without the entrepreneur putting his or her own money on the line. From the banker's point of view, capital is a cushion against the variability of earnings and even possible losses. It is a permanent source of funds that does not require fixed-interest payments or repayments. Without equity, a company might not be able to serve its debt properly in case results fall short of expectations. Equity is **risk capital** in that its return is **variable**, depending on how well the company prospers. If the company is dissolved, it is paid back last—and only after all loans have been repaid.

While capital provides comfort to the banker, from the entrepreneur's point of view capital does not only present a downside risk but is also the means through which rewards are reaped for the initiative in starting and running a business. If the company is successful, the entrepreneur's return from dividends and from the increased value of the stock (reflected in capital gains upon selling out) is much higher than the interest the banker receives on a loan.

This material is adapted from "Investment Banking in Emerging Securities Markets," (Euromoney Publications).

As companies grow larger, the need for additional capital often exceeds the resources of the original shareholders. At the same time, such a company builds a tangible performance record that, in turn, makes it more attractive to outside shareholders who are not intimately involved. An effective mechanism is needed to attract a wider group of investors so that existing shareholders can sell their shares to new investors or increase a company's capital through a public offering or private placement. Thus, the need for a **securities exchange** arises.

1. Without an active market place where shares can be bought and sold continuously, the new shareholders are likely to have reservations about the **liquidity** of their investment.
2. A stock exchange is an efficient mechanism for putting a daily **price** tag on the value of companies. This is important for both old and new shareholders and helps to establish a framework for the pricing of new issues.
3. Through a stock exchange, the **original shareholders** are able to sell some of their shares at attractive prices. Thus they are rewarded for their initiative and risk taking and are able to free their capital for new ventures.
4. A securities exchange enables new shareholders to participate in the growth of more than one company at the same time and thus to **spread their risk**.
5. From a societal point of view, a stock market assists in more widely **distributing wealth and ownership** by including the emerging middle class (and through pension plans many others) among those who benefit from a country's economic growth.
6. Indirectly, the need for improved accounting and auditing standards—which are needed to provide adequate disclosure to outside shareholders—increases **financial professionalism** in the corporate world and helps, in the long run, in an equitable collection of corporate taxes.

TWO CONTRASTING EXAMPLES

In a number of developing countries, including several with a colonial past, stock markets developed many years ago. For example, the Egyptian stock market is nearly a century old, the Hong Kong Stock Exchange was established in 1891, and the Mexican Bolsa in 1895; Korean brokers formed a stock exchange in 1920. Other examples of long-established exchanges are those in Argentina, Brazil, and Chile.

However, many of these securities markets led a dormant existence until the 1960s. During the past two decades, other new markets were also established. Some stock markets developed spontaneously, while elsewhere promotional efforts by government authorities induced the creation of stock exchanges and active trading.

As an example of the first type, Chinese brokers in **Hong Kong** formed their own market, the Far East Stock Exchange Limited, in 1969 because of restrictions on new members of the traditional Hong Kong Stock Exchange. Two more exchanges were established and the three new trading floors quickly assumed a dominant position, with 75% of the trading volume. Prices began to rise, new underwritings were many times oversubscribed, and overnight profits attracted new issuers, underwriters, and investors, from businesspersons to manual laborers. Of course, this sudden speculative boom in 1972–73 did not last. The share price index that had jumped in a few years from 200 to 1,775 dropped back to 150 in little over a year. It took the Hong Kong markets until 1978 to recover and find renewed interest in trading and new issues.

In contrast, the **Korean** example is one of careful government nurturing and less violent fluctuations in trading volume and prices. Despite a long—but sleepy—history, the limited supply of securities was a serious constraint on the development of the market until late 1968, when the goyernment enacted special legislation to encourage listings and trading through tax concessions. In later years, other carrot-and-stick inducements followed, favoring public corporations by making taxation more onerous and financing more difficult for private companies. As a result, the number of companies listed grew from 15 to 350, with a total market capitalization of $4.2 billion (at year-end 1981) and trading increased steadily from a low of $10 million (in 1965), to $3.7 billion in 1981.

REQUIREMENTS FOR A SUCCESSFUL STOCK EXCHANGE

There are several **basic prerequisites** for the establishment and continued success of a stock exchange: (1) a stable political environment and growing economy; (2) a favorable government attitude and an economic structure in which private enterprise is allowed to take a significant role; (3) a sufficient demand for and supply of stocks; (4) at least equal tax treatment of investment in shares in comparison with other investment alternatives, or special tax and other incentives; (5) reasonably well developed accounting and auditing standards; and (6) adequate protection of outside investors through securities legislation and enforcement of such legislation. Without these elements, a stock market is doomed to fail, to remain dormant, or to be subject to excessive speculation. It is obvious that several of these factors are closely related to the level of economic development that a country has achieved and the type of development path it has chosen.

POLITICAL AND ECONOMIC ENVIRONMENT. Investors are very sensitive to political uncertainty. In countries that are in turmoil domestically, engaged in major border conflicts, or involved in a war, there is little interest in establishing a stock market. If a market exists, trading activity and prices are usually in a decline. One reason is that investors need a psychological sense of security. Another reason is that political disruption nearly always affects economic activity because companies postpone investments and scale down their growth projections. In such an environment, new share issues are neither needed (because companies are not expanding) nor well received by investors.

In contrast, rapid economic growth leads to a sense of confidence among investors and entrepreneurs. Concurrently, it opens up new markets, providing companies with a strong inducement to expand their operations. Thus their need for finance, including share capital, grows.

Further, those economies dominated by government enterprises (as is the case, for example, in many socialist countries and a number of African economies) or those that have a scarcity of entrepreneurial experience are not likely candidates for the establishment of a stock market. This is not true, however, for cases where the government has made a conscious decision to change course and sell its stake in government corporations in order to allow them to be run as private enterprises.

DEMAND FOR STOCKS. Demand for stocks depends on a variety of different factors.

Individual Demand. The first important factor in the demand for stocks is the number of individuals who have both money (enabling them to purchase shares) and financial sophistication. This number is usually difficult to estimate in a country without a stock market. The size of the population, particularly the city population, and the level of per capita income give rough indications. A better approximation can be derived from estimating the numbers of businesspeople, professionals (doctors, engineers, and higher level employees in companies), and senior civil servants. If such data are not available, the number of car owners, bank depositors, or holders of government bonds can serve as useful proxies. In their early stages, stock markets cater to as few as 10,000 shareholders, of whom only several hundred might be active traders.

Institutional Demand. In some markets demand from insurance companies, pension or provident funds, and mutual funds is negligible, while elsewhere their presence plays an important role. Regulations governing the obligatory reserves of insurance companies have a major impact on their investment activities. Government-controlled pension and social security funds are sometimes not fully funded or can invest only in government securities, while private pension or provident funds are usually more active buyers of shares, depending on rules pertaining to their fiduciary responsibility. Both private parties and government authorities interested in the development of a stock market should be well aware of the potential importance of institutional investment and do everything possible to promote it, as otherwise the risk of a market dominated by individual speculators becomes great. On the other hand, a market controlled by institutional investment can be lifeless or move on the basis of the preferences of a few money managers.

Investment Alternatives. The attractiveness of shares in comparison with other investment alternatives is crucial to both individual and institutional investors. Rational investors look at overall return, risk, liquidity, and tax treatment in determining where and how to invest their money. In theory, they should evaluate future expectations regarding these factors, but in reality most investors—and especially the less sophisticated speculators—look for performance in the most recent past. For example, hopes for capital gains play a major role in buying decisions when prices are soaring but are easily ignored when a stock exchange does not yet exist or prices have not moved for some time. In the case of shares, overall return (or yield) on investment includes both dividends and capital gains. This combination must be higher than the interest yield that the investor receives from bank deposits or bonds because most investors look upon shares as being more risky.

Taxes and related incentives or exemptions are important factors in after-tax yield to the investor and thus government measures to improve the tax treatment of shares can have a major impact. (See discussion following "Incentives and Other Inducements".) Liquidity—or the ability of the investor to sell shares quickly without affecting the market price—is also of importance when investors compare the after-tax yields of shares and bonds or deposits. A comparison of potential capital gains (including their tax treatment) becomes especially relevant in situations where land or real estate is appreciating rapidly.

Information. Public awareness of the existence of a stock market and of shares as an investment medium is essential. Promotion campaigns on television and radio as well as regular coverage of stock market activities in the newspapers are helpful in educating the public.

The potential number of investors can only be estimated within a broad range. Demand for stocks is quite flexible, as the close relationship between stock market volume and ups and downs of stock indices shows. Many people who would not have dreamed of investing might suddenly start to buy shares when their friends and relatives are pocketing substantial capital gains, while investors can disappear in droves when prices are collapsing.

SUPPLY OF STOCKS. The availability of a sufficient number of shares for trading is often a greater constraint in the development of an active stock market than the number of investors. A too-limited number of shares might at first deter investors to enter the market at all and in later stages, when trading is active, such limitation leads to a situation where too many people are chasing too few stocks, creating violent price movements.

Another potential problem frequently encountered in developing stock markets is the lack of float, the percentage of the capital of a company that is available for trading on the stock market to outside investors rather than being held by the major existing owners, such as a family, an industrial group, a bank, or a foreign company.

Before a stock market can start, at least 20 companies, each with a float of about 25% of their capital, should be available for trading. Stock markets like those in Korea, Thailand, and Jordan initially started with such a relatively small number. Active markets (such as those in Mexico, Hong Kong, Brazil) now have 300 or more listed shares, of which on average at least 25 to 50 are traded on a daily basis.

The following facilities influence the **supply** of securities.

Size. The size of the economy, its level of development and growth rate, its location close to major export markets, and its free enterprise orientation largely determine the number of sizable corporations that are likely to be available for listing their shares on the stock exchange.

Attitude. The attitude of existing owners toward allowing outsiders into the company and opening up their books is important. This attitude usually depends on whether the companies are still managed by the original owners or by professional managers. In the latter case existing shareholders are more likely to be willing to list their companies on a stock exchange and sell some of their shares, especially if they can make a good profit in the process.

Need. A major factor inducing companies to go public is the need for a sizable amount of additional capital. Such a need exists when the company is growing so rapidly that internally generated cash flow or the owner's resources are outstripped by the capital requirements of major expansions. This is frequently the case in a rapidly growing economy. In such an environment, other investment opportunities are also ample to provide new horizons for the original owners, while bank credits might be in short supply and companies already overleveraged.

Tax and Other Incentives. Tax incentives can provide an additional or even a key reason for existing owners to sell their shares to the public rather than to transfer ownership to their progeny.

Legislation. Of course, no incentives can overcome the obstacle of unrealistically low or artificially determined prices. In many countries where there are outdated regulations the prices at which companies can be sold to the public are determined by government authorities on the basis of par or book value instead of being evaluated by underwriters on the basis of their professional judgment of the earnings potential of the company, combined with the expected demand for an issue given current market conditions.

Government Participations. In some countries governments are in a position to substantially increase the supply of stocks available for trading by selling portions of their interest in government-owned corporations that are profitable and professionally managed. But in most countries, the size of the corporate sector and the outlook (modern or traditional) of the existing private owners are the major determinants.

A Securities Industry. An active securities market cannot exist without underwriters, dealers, and brokers. During later stages, mutual funds, money management firms, securities finance institutions, financial information firms and central custodians of share certificates often play important roles.

INCENTIVES AND OTHER INDUCEMENTS. A flexible and positive government attitude toward the establishment and continued success of a stock market is essential. At the time stock exchanges are established, most countries have outdated laws for companies and a less-than-favorable tax treatment of dividends and capital gains. Moreover, companies might be afraid to go public because they fear that the tax authorities could catch them more easily at tax evasion, which is a widespread practice among privately held companies in many countries. Tax incentives are designed partially to counter such fears and partially to provide a positive inducement for owners to sell, for companies to go public, and for investors to buy shares:

1. Tax exemptions for **capital gains** on shares of public companies induce investors to buy shares.
2. Tax exemptions (or partial tax exemptions up to a certain amount) for **dividends** benefit the market. Corporate income usually is already taxed and a withholding tax on dividends or their inclusion in taxable income would amount to double taxation; this can have the effect of deterring owners of private companies to let their companies go public; it can also result in unequal tax treatment in comparison with bank deposits or bonds, which are often officially or de facto tax exempt.
3. A lower **corporate income tax** is a tax incentive for public companies in comparison with private companies when corporate tax rates are reduced; this differential should be sufficient (at least 10% to 20%) to negate the customary tax evasion of privately held companies. An insufficient differential or no differential would be a deterrent rather than an incentive.
4. **Special tax credits or deductions** for individuals (and possibly companies) investing in shares of publicly held companies also provide investment incen-

tives. France, Mexico, Brazil, and Egypt all have various forms of such incentives, sometimes for investment in new issues or mutual funds only, in other cases for all investment in shares of public companies; usually there is a requirement that such shares must be held for a minimum period of, for example, two years. These tax advantages can take the form of a tax deduction from taxable income or a straight tax credit and are usually limited to a specific amount or a percentage of taxable income.

5. Tax exempt retirement accounts stimulate long-term savings and investment. Special tax deduction benefits may be given for funds committed until retirement age for investment in shares, bonds, and possibly other instruments. In addition, dividends and capital gains on such investments are sometimes exempt from taxation until paid after retirement.
6. Also of benefit to stock markets is a **tax on the transfer** of shares by an owner in a private company while any capital gains related to the sale of shares after the company goes public are tax exempt; this constitutes a tax disincentive to remain private.

Other measures to induce companies to go public (which have been used, for example, in Korea) are special investigations by the tax authorities of companies that have been identified as being potential public companies but have chosen not to go public, and limitations on the amount of or conditions for bank credit applying to private companies but not to public companies (such as the Korean Public Corporations Inducement Act of December 1972). Such a carrot-and-stick approach has proved to be very successful in several countries in inducing a large number of corporations to go public within a short time.

PROTECTION OF OUTSIDE INVESTORS. Outside investors need to be protected against stock manipulation by insiders (major shareholders, directors, and management) and the ability of those same insiders to skim off profits before they ever reach the hands of the small investors. Other aspects of investor protection are the need to establish high standards for professional conduct by brokers and underwriters and the need to avoid excessive speculation caused by market rumors and overly easy availability of margin loans. Without some form of investor protection, investors are likely to lose confidence sooner or later as a result of a stock scandal or swindle or the bursting of a speculative bubble. Such protection can be exercised by a securities commission or another type of government watchdog, the stock exchange itself, or through self-regulation by an association of stock brokers and underwriters. Usually all three types of protection are found, but the brunt of the effort is in most cases in the hands of one of these three. In securities markets based on the U.S. model, the securities commission, armed with extensive securities legislation, plays the major role (e.g., in Korea or Mexico), while in securities markets based on the U.K. model (such as in Hong Kong or Singapore) self-regulation is the dominant factor. A third model—that of a combined securities exchange and commission—has been chosen in several new, small markets such as Thailand and Jordan.

The following measures are typical of those protecting the small investor.

1. **Disclosure and financial reporting requirements** provide outside investors the wherewithall to be able to form an informed judgment regarding the operations of a company, its profitability, financial health, growth, and prospects. Even if the final investor does not study the financial information carefully, this

enables his or her broker or investment adviser to do so. Without being forced to open their books, companies are usually reluctant to do so. Thus it is important that disclosure requirements for public companies should also be applicable to private companies that have attained a reasonable size. In most cases, this requires changes in state regulations. Disclosure should cover not only the need for a prospectus at the time of a new issue, but also regular publication of financial information afterward through annual reports, quarterly earnings reports to the stock market, and the like.

2. Financial information cannot be accurate or comparable from company to company without the adoption and enforcement of **accounting and auditing standards** that are generally accepted. Such standards go hand in hand with the need for a strong auditing profession that is adequately remunerated and plays an independent role.
3. Independent of the disclosure requirements of a securities commission, a stock exchange can set specific **listing requirements** before company stock can be traded. Typical requirements are those for minimum capital, a minimum number of shareholders, minimum float and a free transfer of shares.
4. **Insider trading**, manipulation by directors or management who are in a better position to know the prospects of the company than outsiders, is not uncommon without regulation. Insiders can be asked to disclose their sales and purchases of the company's stock on a periodic basis or they can be otherwise restricted. Legislation and regulations in this area are usually very controversial and it might be necessary or desirable to control insider trading on an informal basis during the early days of an exchange and formalize regulations only later.
5. Without some general guidance, brokers have a tendency to overextend **margin loans** to customers, endangering not only their own financial health but also fueling speculation. Desirable limitations include a list of shares that are acceptable as collateral for margin finance; rules requiring brokers to know their customer through detailed account information; specific margin limits and margin calls; margin loan contracts between brokers and clients; and stringent collateral arrangements.
6. The supervision of **trading floor procedures** protects small investors. Collusion between brokers, fraud by trading floor personnel, and purchases by brokers for their own account before purchases and/or sales are made for clients are common problems in the absence of regulation. Some stock exchanges set daily limits on price changes in order to control speculation in the short run, but such measures are usually not effective.
7. Professional standards for brokers and underwriters can be established by legislation or through self-regulation in broking and underwriting associations. Incorporation of brokers with a minimum capital is often desirable. Brokers and securities analysts can be asked to undergo exams before they are qualified to deal with the public or analyze corporate statements for prospectuses.

Obviously, it is often politically impossible and perhaps not even desirable to introduce too many rules or too much legislation at the same time because overkill can strangle a stock market during its early stages. Each of the above measures can be introduced in distinct stages. On the other hand, too gradual an approach should be avoided because it leads to uncertainty and confusion.

ATTITUDE TOWARD FOREIGN INVESTMENT. Most developing countries have foreign investment laws that resulted from a fear of foreign domination and a desire to protect domestic entrepreneurs. Unfortunately, these laws do not discriminate between direct and portfolio investment by foreigners. Portfolio investment is by its nature minority investment and is aimed at an attractive economic return rather than control.

Foreign portfolio investment can play a significant role in the development of a stock market, either directly or through mutual funds, not only by adding to the demand for stocks but also by introducing a new group of sophisticated investors to the market who may be more inclined than local investors to require securities analyses. Thus such investment indirectly increases the level of sophistication in the market.

If a country is hesitant to allow direct investment but has no objections against portfolio investment, it can use several methods to limit foreign participation:

A ceiling on foreign shareholders in all companies through B shares, in certain companies, or in certain strategic industries

A requirement for a minimum period of investment before proceeds (including capital gains) can be remitted

Limitation of foreign investment through mutual funds controlled by local authorities only

Separation of the economic (dividends and capital gains) and voting aspects of ownership through a trustee arrangement whereby the trustee exercises voting rights (a method used in the Mexico Fund)

Government authorities and parties interested in the development of the stock market sometimes overlook a potentially very important source of demand for stocks—the savings of nationals working abroad who regularly send home remittances. Special mutual funds with blue chip management can be set up to capture such remittances.

STAGES IN THE DEVELOPMENT OF A STOCK MARKET

The development of two stock markets is not exactly alike. Nevertheless, five distinct stages can usually be observed: the dormant stage, manipulation, speculation, consolidation (or crash), and maturity. During the **dormant** stage only few people are aware of the existence of the stock market, trading is slow, few companies are listed, and prices remain close to par. As time goes by, shares become undervalued, especially in a dynamic economic environment. Inevitably, brokers or individuals discover that dividend yield—even excluding potential capital gains—exceeds the yield on other investment alternatives and they begin to buy shares, cautiously at first, and actively later.

The **manipulation** begins when some market participants discover that the small supply of stocks— and thus limited liquidity—makes it possible to drive up the price of one or more stocks with even minor purchases. As soon as prices soar, this demonstration effect encourages others to buy, enabling the manipulators to get out of the market with quick profits. The start of more active trading can also be induced by government measures making investment in stocks more attractive. In some other cases, a sudden, dramatic upturn in the fortune of a country or company starts the buying fever.

As soon as some people begin to make substantial capital gains and proudly tell their friends of their overnight profits (realized or not), a wider group of speculators is attracted. Businesspeople, doctors, government officials, even taxi drivers get caught up. A **speculative** stage begins, during which prices are driven beyond their fundamental values and trading volume soars. New issues are so heavily oversubscribed that many companies go public, broadening the supply of available stocks, because the original owners see attractive opportunities to sell out. Responsible government action, such as an increase in margin requirements, higher brokerage commissions, selling by institutional investors controlled by the government, increases in board lots, activation of new underwriting of major companies, and so forth, can dampen this speculation but it is probably not possible to avoid it altogether.

At some point, the amount of new money available for investment dries up, new issues become less oversubscribed, and the more cool-headed among the investors begin to realize that prices have been driven up so high that they no longer bear any relation to their underlying value. Quite suddenly, stock prices and the market index begin to waver and then prices begin to drop. Depending on the extent of the boom during the speculative stage, prices either decline gradually or tumble deeply. The **consolidation** stage (or **crash**) begins.

It might take investors from several months to a few years to regain confidence in the stock market after such a price decline. Much depends on the extent of the price drop as well as on interest rates, yields on other investment alternatives, new incentives to restimulate buying, and the behavior of institutional investors. During this consolidation stage, many speculators become, out of necessity, investors. Unwilling to sell their shares at a loss, they hold on to them for long-term investment in the hope that prices will improve again in the future. With a more cautious group of individual investors, joined by new groups of investors who did not get hurt during the first price decline and—often—an enlarged presence of institutional investors, a new stage of **maturity** can begin. Trading volume is more consistent, investors are more sophisticated, the supply of shares is broader, and thus liquidity is greater. Prices will continue to fluctuate but the swings are generally less violent and, it is hoped, are on a long-term rising trend as the economy and corporate earnings continue to grow.

SECTION 7.1

INTERNATIONAL TRADE FINANCING TECHNIQUES

CONTENTS

SECTION 7.1

INTERNATIONAL TRADE FINANCING TECHNIQUES

Ian H. Giddy
Mona A. Ismael

THE FINANCING OF INTERNATIONAL TRADE

Financing international trade is a complex process, involving many variables, ranging from corporate policy and marketing strategy to exchange risk and general borrowing conditions. The reason behind this complexity is that trade involves two countries with **different currencies** and **jurisdictions.** In addition, payments must be made **at a distance** and **across time,** so the exporter, the importer, or both need credit during part or all of the period from the initial manufacture of goods by the exporting firm to the time of the final sale and collection by the importer. The main objective of a good corporate export financing policy should be financing the greatest possible amount of sales with the greatest possible management simplicity and with minimal risk.

International trade financing, one of the oldest functions of international business, is also one of the least glamorous. Nevertheless, for the majority of firms engaged in international business, export financing forms the core of international finance. While the techniques are standardized, the range of applications is as varied as the content and destinations of a nation's exports, and things can easily go wrong. Among the potential problems are that of **exchange risk,** the problem of **inadequate information** regarding financial strength of foreign customers, and the problem of **special financing sources** and costs. In addition, many of the less-developed nations have strict and sometimes unpredictable **exchange controls** on remittance and convertibility of hard currencies. The export financing manager must develop experience in handling all of these details in addition to the extensive, often tedious, documentation needed for the transfer of goods and payments internationally.

These obstacles aside, the exporter can count on readily available support and expertise from major commercial banks. Moreover, it is almost every government's policy to promote exports in order to improve the balance of payments and increase employment. Various countries have programs to assist the exporter, whether in the

The authors wish to acknowledge the cooperation of the First National Bank of Chicago, by whose permission certain passages and exhibits have been reproduced from *International Trade Finance Services,* published by the bank's International Banking Department.

EXHIBIT 1 BANK SERVICES TO EXPORTERS

Collecting drafts (outgoing and incoming)
Granting advances to exporters
Discounting drafts
Opening credit lines
Opening letters of credit (for importers)
Confirming letters of credit (acting for foreign banks)
Negotiating letters of credit
Creating bankers' acceptances
Collecting payments for creditors from foreign debtors
Opening accounts for customers in foreign branches or banks abroad in which export proceeds can be collected (e.g., Eurodollar accounts)
Buying and selling foreign currencies and making foreign remittances
Extending loans against merchandise in warehouses or in transit
Providing credit information on foreign buyers
Providing services incidental to export transactions, such as on customs, interest rates, and collection experience

financing of the trade or in managing the different risks involved. The U.S. government is no exception. There are several U.S. programs available to promote exports, whether directly or indirectly through supporting the private sector by extending the needed credits and insurances.

From the point of view of a bank, export-import financing can be one of the most profitable of the bank's international activities, especially when foreign exchange transactions are involved. Exhibit 1 provides a list of typical **export-related services** provided by commercial banks.

FINANCING BY THE EXPORTER

There are various methods by which the exporter can finance a transaction; the method chosen will depend on the familiarity and trust that the exporting firm has in the importing firm, and the relative ability of the exporter to extend credit as an element in the firm's marketing policy.

SHIPMENT ON AN OPEN-BOOK ACCOUNT. In an open-account transaction, the arrangement provides for future payments but with no definite maturities and without any negotiable instrument evidencing the obligation between buyer and seller. Such an arrangement is extremely advantageous to the importer because it permits the importer to receive the goods and even sell them before making payments. The exporter runs the risk that in time of stress the importer might give preference to pressing domestic obligations, and efforts to collect by legal proceedings can prove difficult and expensive. In some countries where exchange controls are in effect importers' applications for dollar drafts take precedence over applications for open-account payments.

Even though open-account transactions permit greater flexibility, involve less cost, and offer a tool to meet competition, they involve a considerable amount of risk. For this reason open-account settlements are used in cases where there is an established relationship over the years between seller and buyer, a nearby or established market, or where exchange controls are minimal or nonexistent. Sales to foreign branches or subsidiaries are often made on an open account basis. Banks might be willing to grant exporters loans on evidence of the sales contract and shipment of the goods.

TIME CREDITS. This method, similar to open-account sales, incorporates a definite maturity period. The importer agrees to pay either on a regular scheduled basis or after a specified period. Generally, periods granted are up to 180 days for short-term credits, up to five years for medium-term credits, and over five years for long-term credits.

CONSIGNMENTS. The exporter can ship goods to a branch, agency, or resident salesman abroad and order the sale of goods while they are in transit or upon arrival at a fixed price or at the best obtainable price. Under a consignment agreement, no payment is due to the **consigner** (exporter) until the goods are sold by the **consignee** (importer). The goods remain the legal possession of the consigner until the sale is made. The exporter thus ties up funds until the goods are sold and purchased. In addition, the exporter assumes the exchange risk for foreign currency–invoiced sales. This method is rarely used for the sale of goods to unrelated foreign firms because of the obvious risks. Banks are reluctant to finance consignments.

COLLECTION DRAFTS. When the exporter perceives some risk in consignments, which are rather open-ended methods, the most widely used technique of arranging for the payment and financing of an export is often an alternative: the **bill of exchange,** or **draft.** A draft is essentially a **request for payment** to the exporter (**drawer**) by the importer (**drawee**). An exporter **draws a draft** on the importer at the time of shipment. The draft becomes a legally accepted obligation when the importer acknowledges the debt by **accepting** the draft. There are two broad classifications of collection drafts, **documentary** drafts and **clean** drafts. Each can be either **sight** (see Exhibit 2) or **time** drafts. Exhibits 3, 4, and 5 show specimens of time drafts.

Collection drafts are typically used when the exporter considers the purchaser a good credit risk. In general, an exporting firm will use collections with clients with whom it has prior experience. In the absence of substantial evidence of creditworthiness, a new exporter would be well advised to seek a more secure method, such as letters of credit (which are explained later). Nonetheless, if collections are the customary terms of trade for the commodity involved, then the exporter will, more likely than not, have to assume the buyer's commercial risk to acquire the account. Furthermore, letters of credit are so expensive in some countries (particularly in South America and the Middle East) that an importer cannot afford them. Time drafts, as previously noted, are riskier than sight drafts. The decision to use a collection draft rather than a letter of credit is simply one of risk versus return. A letter of credit is clearly less risky, yet insisting upon one might cause the exporter to lose the sale.

Documentary drafts are accompanied by documents conveying title to goods. The exporter delivers the documents to the collecting bank with instructions regarding when to deliver them to the importer, depending on the agreed terms, which can be **DP** (documents against payments) or **DA** (documents against acceptance). The exporter retains control of the goods when a documentary draft is employed, because

EXHIBIT 2 SIGHT DRAFT (payable at presentation)

FORM 8050-3-AB

No. .001 U. S. A. August 1, 19--

Exchange for $100,000.00

At ------------------------------ Sight of this **FIRST** of Exchange (Second being unpaid)

Pay to the order of Exporter for Profit, Inc.

the sum of ONE HUNDRED THOUSAND U.S. DOLLARS

Drawn under Letter of Credit No. 700000 Dated July 1, 19--

Issued by The First National Bank of Chicago

Value received and charge to the account of

To The First National Bank of Chicago — Exporter for Profit, Inc.

Chicago, Illinois — By: (Authorized Signature)

the importer cannot obtain shipping documents from the collecting bank until the draft is paid or accepted. The accepted draft—called **trade acceptance**—becomes a **clean bill.** Under a **clean draft** the seller sends all documents to the buyer and only the draft to the collecting bank. This, of course, involves a considerable amount of risk, since the merchandise is surrendered to the buyer regardless of payment or acceptance of the draft. This method is generally used in cases where there is a considerable amount of faith between the seller and the buyer or in cases where the sale is to an affiliate or a subsidiary.

Whether the draft is documentary or clean it can be either a **sight** or a **time** draft. Under a documentary **sight draft** documents are delivered to the buyer only after payment of the draft. This method is advantageous to the seller since the seller retains title and control until payment is made. The buyer is not required to pay until the documents are received.

Under a **time draft** documents are delivered to the buyer upon acceptance only. Once the buyer accepts the draft the buyer obtains control of goods and is not required to pay until a certain number of days after sight or date. This method favors the buyer, since after obtaining documents there is no requirement to pay immediately.

EXHIBIT 3 DAYS AFTER SIGHT DRAFT
(payable a specific number of days after presentation)

FORM 8050-3-AB

No. .002 U. S. A. August 1, 19--

Exchange for $100,000.00

At ---90 Days----------------- Sight of this **FIRST** of Exchange (Second being unpaid)

Pay to the order of Exporter for Profit, Inc.

the sum of ONE HUNDRED THOUSAND U.S. DOLLARS

Drawn under Letter of Credit No. 700001 Dated July 1, 19--

Issued by The First National Bank of Chicago

Value received and charge to the account of

To The First National Bank of Chicago — Exporter for Profit, Inc.

Chicago, Illinois — By: (Authorized Signature)

EXHIBIT 4 DAYS DATE DRAFT
(payable a specific number of days after date appearing on draft)

Corresponds to
(Bill of Lading Date)

FORM 8050-3-AB
No. .003 U. S. A. August 1, 19--

Exchange for $100,000.00

At ---60 days---Date---------- ~~Sight~~ of this FIRST of Exchange (Second being unpaid)

Pay to the order of Exporter for Profit, Inc.

the sum of ONE HUNDRED THOUSAND U.S. DOLLARS

Drawn under Letter of Credit No. 700002 Dated July 1, 19--

Issued by The First National Bank of Chicago

Value received and charge to the account of

To The First National Bank of Chicago
Chicago, Illinois

Exporter for Profit, Inc.
By:
(Authorized Signature)

The selling firm is at a disadvantage since it is relying entirely on the ability and willingness of the buyer to pay.

The Role of the Bank in Exporter-Financed Trade. A bank that undertakes the service of collection must receive detailed **instructions from the exporter** (drawer) so that the bank can protect its client's interests in accordance with the sales contract. The instructions are given on a printed form supplied by the bank (see Exhibits 6 and 7). The instructions given in each instance are determined by the sales contract, the policy of the exporter, and any special requirements of the moment. Since the bank must follow instructions explicitly, it is advisable that the exporter designate a representation located near the importer (drawee), with instructions "in case of need, refer to." This **local representative** knows the exporter's policies, and reference to him or her implies that the representative can be trusted by the bank to modify original instructions to meet emergencies.

The exporter's bank forwards the draft and documents with the exporter's instructions to its branch or correspondent bank in the country of the importer. Upon receipt of payment from the importer the foreign bank remits the funds to the ex-

EXHIBIT 5 FIXED-MATURITY DRAFT (payable at the maturity date on the draft)

FORM 8050-3-AB
No. .004 U. S. A. August 1, 19--

Exchange for $100,000.00

At November 29, 19-- ~~Sight~~ of this FIRST of Exchange (Second being unpaid)

Pay to the order of Exporter for Profit, Inc.

the sum of ONE HUNDRED THOUSAND U.S. DOLLARS

Drawn under Letter of Credit No. 700003 Dated July 1, 19--

Issued by The First National Bank of Chicago

Value received and charge to the account of

To The First National Bank of Chicago
Chicago, Illinois

Exporter for Profit, Inc.
By:
(Authorized Signature)

EXHIBIT 6 EXPORTER'S LETTER OF INSTRUCTION—SIGHT DRAFT BASIS

Exchange for

$ 687.50 US CHICAGO, ILLINOIS U.S.A., NOVEMBER 13 198-

* * * * * * * * AT SIGHT * * * * * * * * * * of this ***FIRST*** of Exchange

(Second being unpaid) pay to the order of The First National Bank of Chicago

the sum of SIX HUNDRED EIGHTY SEVEN AND 50/100 UNITED STATES Dollars

IN LAWFUL MONEY OF THE UNITED STATES OF AMERICA

Value received and charge the same to the account of

EXPORTER FOR PROFIT, INC.
CHICAGO, ILLINOIS

To FOREIGN BUYER LTD.
PARIS, FRANCE

No. 101

The First National Bank of Chicago
INTERNATIONAL BANKING DEPARTMENT
Chicago, Illinois 60670

Date NOVEMBER 13, 198-

We enclose for ~~DISCOUNT~~ COLLECTION

Please follow instructions prefixed "X"

DRAFT No. 101 AMOUNT $687.50 TENOR AT SIGHT

DRAWN ON FOREIGN BUYER LTD. AT PARIS, FRANCE

The following documents marked with the letter "X" are attached.

BILLS OF LADING 1	2	3	Copies	INVOICES Comml.	Consular	INSURANCE CERTIFICATE	CTF. OF ORIGIN	MAIL RECEIPT	MISCELLANEOUS
		X		3/3	-	2/2 Copies	2/2	-	2/2 PACKING LIST

X Deliver documents against Payment.
___ Deliver documents against Acceptance.
___ All collection charges are for account of Drawer.
X All collection charges are for acount of Drawee.
X Airmail expenses for forwarding documents for account of drawee.

X Do Not Protest.
___ Protest for ___ Non-Acceptance ___ Non-Payment.
X Cable advice of ___ Non-Acceptance X Non-Payment.
___ Have Proceeds Remitted by Cable.
X Waive charges if refused by Drawee.
___ Hold draft for arrival of goods.

X Allow drawee discount of $ 13.75 IF PAID UPON FIRST PRESENTATION
___ Interest to be collected at ___ % per annum from ___ to ___
X In case of need refer to SMITH, JONES & CIE., 99, RUE DES ACHETEURS, PARIS, FRANCE
___ We have instructed ___ to deliver
(Name of forwarder or Steamship Company delivering documents)
controlling documents to your correspondent First Chicago International Banking Corporation, 1290 Avenue of the Americas, New York, N.Y. 10019. Complete attached draft for $ ___ plus ___

Special Instructions PRESENT DOCUMENTS THROUGH BUYERS BANK LTD., PARIS, FRANCE. SMITH, JONES & CIE. ARE AUTHORIZED TO ASSIST IN COLLECTION BUT MAY NOT ALTER ANY INSTRUCTIONS.

X Credit our Account with Proceeds. ___ Please Remit Check.

FORM 8370-6-AD (REV. 10-74)

From EXPORTERS FOR PROFIT INC.
Address 111 N. NORTH
City CHICAGO, ILLINOIS
By ___

EXHIBIT 7 EXPORTER'S LETTER OF INSTRUCTION—TIME DRAFT BASIS

Exchange for

$ 687.50 US CHICAGO, ILLINOIS U.S.A., NOVEMBER 13 198-

* * NINETY DAYS AFTER SIGHT * * * * * * * of this **FIRST** of Exchange (Second being unpaid) pay to the order of The First National Bank of Chicago

the sum of SIX HUNDRED EIGHTY SEVEN AND 50/100 UNITED STATES Dollars

IN LAWFUL MONEY OF THE UNITED STATES OF AMERICA

Value received and charge the same to the account of

EXPORTER FOR PROFIT, INC.
CHICAGO, ILLINOIS

To FOREIGN BUYER LTD.
PARIS, FRANCE

No. 102

The First National Bank of Chicago
INTERNATIONAL BANKING DEPARTMENT
Chicago, Illinois 60670

Date NOVEMBER 13, 198-

We enclose for ~~DISCOUNT~~ COLLECTION

Please follow instructions prefixed "X"

DRAFT No. 102 AMOUNT $687.50 TENOR 90 D/S

DRAWN ON FOREIGN BUYER LTD. AT PARIS, FRANCE

The following documents marked with the letter "X" are attached.

BILLS OF LADING				INVOICES		INSURANCE CERTIFICATE	CTF. OF ORIGIN	MAIL RECEIPT	MISCELLANEOUS
1	2	3	Copies	Comml.	Consular				
		X		3/3	-	2/2 Copies	-	-	2/2 PACKING LIST

___ Deliver documents against Payment.
X Deliver documents against Acceptance.
X All collection charges are for account of Drawer.
___ All collection charges are for acount of Drawee.
___ Airmail expenses for forwarding documents for account of drawee.

X Do Not Protest.
___ Protest for ___ Non-Acceptance ___ Non-Payment.
X Cable advice of X Non-Acceptance ___ Non-Payment.
___ Have Proceeds Remitted by Cable.
___ Waive charges if refused by Drawee.
___ Hold draft for arrival of goods.

___ Allow drawee discount of $___

___ Interest to be collected at ___ % per annum from ___ to ___

X In case of need refer to SMITH, JONES & CIE., 99 RUE DES ACHETEURS, PARIS, FRANCE

___ We have instructed ___ to deliver
(Name of forwarder or Steamship Company delivering documents)
controlling documents to your correspondent First Chicago International Banking Corporation, 1290 Avenue of the Americas, New York, N.Y. 10019. Complete attached draft for $___ plus ___

Special Instructions
PRESENT DOCUMENTS THROUGH BUYERS BANK LTD., PARIS, FRANCE.
SMITH, JONES & CIE. ARE AUTHORIZED TO ASSIST IN COLLECTION BUT MEY NOT ALTER ANY INSTRUCTIONS.

X Credit our Account with Proceeds. ___ Please Remit Check.

FORM 8370-6-AD (REV. 10-74)

From EXPORTER FOR PROFIT, INC.
Address 111 N. NORTH
City CHICAGO, ILLINOIS
By ___

porter's bank, which in turn makes them available to the exporter. In case of a DA draft, the **correspondent bank** will hand over the documents to the importer upon the importer's acceptance of the draft. On the due date, the correspondent bank presents the acceptance to the importer, and when it is paid remits the amount to the exporter's bank. Although the exporter's bank selects the correspondent abroad, the latter acts as the agent of the exporter and not of the bank. Should the correspondent bank become insolvent or bankrupt before it has remitted the collected funds to the exporter's bank, the loss will be borne by the exporter.

FINANCING BY THE IMPORTER

Although the burden of financing international trade does not normally fall on the importer, the latter may sometimes be forced to finance production or shipment, particularly when the commodity or equipment involved is specially designed. In addition, an importing firm might choose to finance an import if it is in a strong financial position and can use this strength to negotiate a favorable price. The importer has three principal means for financing operations.

PAYMENT WITH ORDER. Payment with order means that the importer must pay for the goods at the time the order is placed with the exporter. To effect the payment, the importing firm might pay its bank, which would provide a draft (essentially a check) drawn on a bank located in the city of the exporter, or in the financial center of the exporter's country. Sales on such terms are rarely encountered in foreign trade, except when the credit standing of the importer is unsatisfactory or not known. The exporting firm receives payment before it ships the goods, often even before they are manufactured. The importer thus not only finances the entire transaction and assumes the foreign exchange risk involved, but pays cash without security, except for the credit standing of the exporter. Should the order not be filled, or should the goods be unduly delayed or prove to be of inferior quality, the importer's only redress is to bring legal action on the basis of the sales contract unless the exporter makes an adjustment voluntarily.

PARTIAL PAYMENT IN ADVANCE. To protect itself against the contingency that goods ordered by importers might be rejected on delivery, an exporting firm might stipulate in the sales contract that importers must remit in advance a partial payment on the order as evidence of good faith and intention to pay the balance as agreed. Such provision is usually made when the order is for specialized equipment, or when the goods involved cannot be satisfactorily disposed in the country of destination if the importer fails to take them as agreed. The partial payment by the importer should suffice to cover the cost of freight out and back, insurance, and other expenses incidental to the shipment of goods abroad.

PAYMENT ON DOCUMENTS. When the contract stipulates payment on documents, the importer must provide funds in the exporter's country to pay for the shipment on the day the exporter turns over to a designated bank documents evidencing shipment of the goods ordered. The importer thus raises the funds, converts them into the currency of the country of the exporter (unless invoiced in local currency), and carries the financing burden while the commodities are in transit.

FINANCING BY BANKS

The best-known method of international trade financing is through a **commercial bank**—either that of the exporter or that of the importer. The most common way to assure such financing is to obtain a **letter of credit** (LC). The letter of credit, however, is not a financing instrument in itself; it merely assures the exporter of payment under specified conditions.

Indeed, bank financing can be done without a letter of credit, where **commercial risk** is not a major factor. Typical non-LC bank financing arrangements include advances on drafts, discounts of the drafts themselves, and refinancing bills.

ADVANCE ON DRAFTS. Under advances on drafts, the financing is done jointly by the exporter and the exporter's bank. An exporter who is unwilling to have funds tied up while the goods are en route to the importer can borrow from the bank a percentage of the amount of the draft. The draft on the importer and pertinent shipping documents, turned over by the exporter to the bank for collection, constitute **collateral** for the advance. In case the drawee (importer) fails to pay the draft when due, the bank has recourse against the drawer, whether the draft is made out to the order of the drawer (exporter) and endorsed by the drawer to the bank, or to the order of the bank. Thus the credit risk rests on the exporter just as when the draft is handed to the bank for collection only. After the draft has been paid by the drawee, the bank retains the amount of the advance plus interest and collection fees, crediting the balance to the exporter. The amount that an exporter can borrow on foreign drafts depends on the financial responsibility of exporter and importer, and the collateral behind the draft. The **character of the merchandise** shipped determines its value as collateral. Staple commodities not subject to rapid deterioration (cotton, wheat, wool) and traded on organized markets are obviously better collateral than perishable goods or manufactured articles requiring expert selling to be settled without loss.

DISCOUNT OF DRAFTS. The bank can discount the draft drawn by the exporter on the importer when the credit standing of the exporter is high, and particularly if the exporter already has a line of credit. The exporter then receives the face amount of the draft, less interest and collection charges, unless custom requires the drawee to absorb all charges.

REFINANCING BILL. Under a refinancing bill, an exporter hands over to the bank the draft and documents for collection, and the bank allows the exporter to draw on itself a time draft of a maturity identical with that of the draft upon the importer. The bank **accepts the draft** on itself, and this refinancing bill becomes a **banker's acceptance** that the exporter can sell in the open market at a very low rate of discount. When the original draft has been paid by the importer abroad, the bank uses the funds to pay off its own acceptance at maturity.

FORFAITING. Forfaiting is the discounting at a fixed rate without recourse of medium-term export receivables denominated in fully convertible currencies (e.g., U.S. dollars, Swiss francs, West German deutsche marks). The discount is based on the prevailing interest rate (such as 1.25% above LIBOR, the London interbank offered rate).

Forfaiting is used by, among others, the socialist countries. There, government-owned enterprises frequently import capital goods, often in the form of turnkey plants, from suppliers in industrialized countries on extended payment terms related to the life of the project. Such maturities, which may range anywhere from three to 12 years, cannot be handled through the institutions that undertake traditional export financing. From the point of view of the exporters who can finance such transactions by borrowing in the markets this would be too costly. More important, technologically oriented capital goods manufacturers feel very uncomfortable with the economic and political risks associated with loans to foreign political entities. Forfaiting solves the exporter's problems and it is also advantageous to the borrower (i.e., the importer). A typical transaction involves four parties: besides the exporter and the importer, there are the importer's bank, which tends to be government entity too, and the forfaiter, usually a special-purpose subsidiary of one of the large Swiss, West German, or Austrian banks that have innovated this financing technique.

When an exporter's negotiations with the importing organization are about to reach a decisive state, the exporter obtains a **commitment** from the forfaiter to finance the transaction at a firm interest cost. This cost is represented by the discount at which the forfaiter will purchase at the time the deal is completed. For this commitment the forfaiter charges a **fee** that will be compensation for the cost of assuring availability of funds, which might involve the forfaiter's borrowing funds on a long-term basis and reinvesting on a short-term basis during the commitment period.

When the export transaction is completed, the exporter receives from the importing organization a series of promissory notes with maturities staggered according to the repayment terms, usually in six-month intervals reflecting the installments. Most important, these promissory notes are endorsed guaranteed by the importer's bank, which becomes the **primary obligor** in the transactions, just as in the case of a banker's acceptance.

The forfaiter will purchase the total bundle from the exporter **without recourse,** taking on the risk of the state-owned bank and, ultimately, the government of the importer's country. The essence of forfaiting involves the shifting of the country risk to an institution that specializes in assessing such risks. But the forfaiter is also an international market specialist. Usually the package of notes is broken up and sold to various investors who differ in terms of maturity preference. The forfaiter endorses the notes, thus collecting the risk premium in addition to the difference in yield between the sum of the individual note and the discount that the forfaiter obtained when the package was bought.

COMMERCIAL LETTERS OF CREDIT. A letter of credit is a document issued by a bank at the buyer's (importer's) request in which that bank promises to pay the seller upon presentation of documents as specified in the terms of the credit. The basic function is to **reduce the commercial risk to the seller.** Also, because the seller cannot receive payment until the required documents are relinquished, the **buyer** receives some (but not total) assurance that the seller will comply with the negotiated terms of the sale.

In summary, a commercial letter of credit can be defined as a notification issued by a bank to an individual or firm authorizing the latter to draw on the bank, its branch, or a correspondent bank, for amounts up to a specified sum and guaranteeing acceptance and payment of the drafts if drawn in accordance with the terms in the letter. A letter of credit can be either an **import** or **export letter of credit** (there is no difference between the two, only a matter of perspective).

Parties to the Letter of Credit. The basic parties are the buyer (the applicant), the buyer's bank (the **issuing bank**), the issuing bank's foreign correspondent (the **advising bank,** or **confirming bank**) and the seller (beneficiary).

Issuing Bank

The relationship between the buyer and the issuing bank is governed by the terms of the application and agreement for the letter of credit.

Advising/Negotiating Bank

The relationship between the advising bank and the seller is strictly defined by the terms of the letter of credit. The advising bank acts only as an intermediary.

Buyer —— The relationship between the buyer and the seller is governed by the sales contract. —— Seller

The beneficiary might wish to have the advising bank add its **irrevocable promise to pay** to that of the issuing bank. If the advising bank agrees to do so, it becomes the **confirming bank.** An advising bank that has confirmed a letter of credit is legally obligated to pay the beneficiary upon compliance with the terms of the letter of credit. On an **unconfirmed letter of credit,** an advising bank will pay the seller only if there are sufficient funds on deposit in the issuing bank's account.

Contents of the Letter of Credit. Banks normally issue letters of credit on forms that clearly indicate the bank's name and the extent of the bank's obligation under the credit. In general, letters of credit contain the following information.

Name of the seller, who is also known as the **beneficiary**

Name of the buyer, who is also known as the **applicant**

Amount of credit, which should be the value of the merchandise plus any other charges to be paid under the credit

Trade terms, such as FOB vessel, CIF Antwerp

Tenor of the draft, which is normally dependent upon the terms of the sales contract

Expiry date, which specifies the latest date for shipment and presentation of documents (in this manner, or by including a latest shipping date, the applicant can exercise control over the date of shipment)

Documents required, which will normally include commercial invoices, consular or customs invoices, insurance policies or certificates if the insurance is to be effected by the beneficiary, and original bills of lading

General description of the merchandise, which briefly and in a general manner only describes the merchandise covered by the letter of credit

The letter of credit should not be excessively detailed. Some buyers believe that they can ensure performance by the seller under the sales contract by asking their banks to include numerous details and a lengthy description of the merchandise in the letter of credit. The insertion of these details, however, serves only to impede and hamper the effectiveness of the letter of credit. It will not prevent a beneficiary from invoicing goods as ordered in the credit and shipping material of an entirely different nature. As the conditions become more numerous and complex, the likelihood of trivial discrepancies increases, resulting in annoyances, cable expenses, and the like, with resulting delays to both the buyer and the seller.

Letter-of-Credit Cycle. The letter-of-credit cycle merely involves the exchange of documents (and money) through intermediaries. The following steps are the basic steps needed to complete a letter-of-credit cycle (see Exhibits 8 and 9).

Step 1. The buyer and seller agree upon the terms of sale. The sales contract dictates that a letter of credit is to be used to finance the transaction.

Step 2. The buyer completes an application for a letter of credit (see Exhibit 9) and forwards it to the bank that will issue the letter of credit.

Step 3. The issuing bank then forwards the letter of credit to a correspondent bank in the seller's country.

Step 4. The advising bank relays the letter of credit to the seller.

Step 5. Having received assurance of payment, the seller makes the necessary shipping arrangements.

Step 6. The seller prepares the documents required under the letter of credit and delivers them to the advising bank.

Step 7. The advising bank negotiates the documents. If it finds them in order,

EXHIBIT 8 IMPORT LETTER OF CREDIT CYCLE

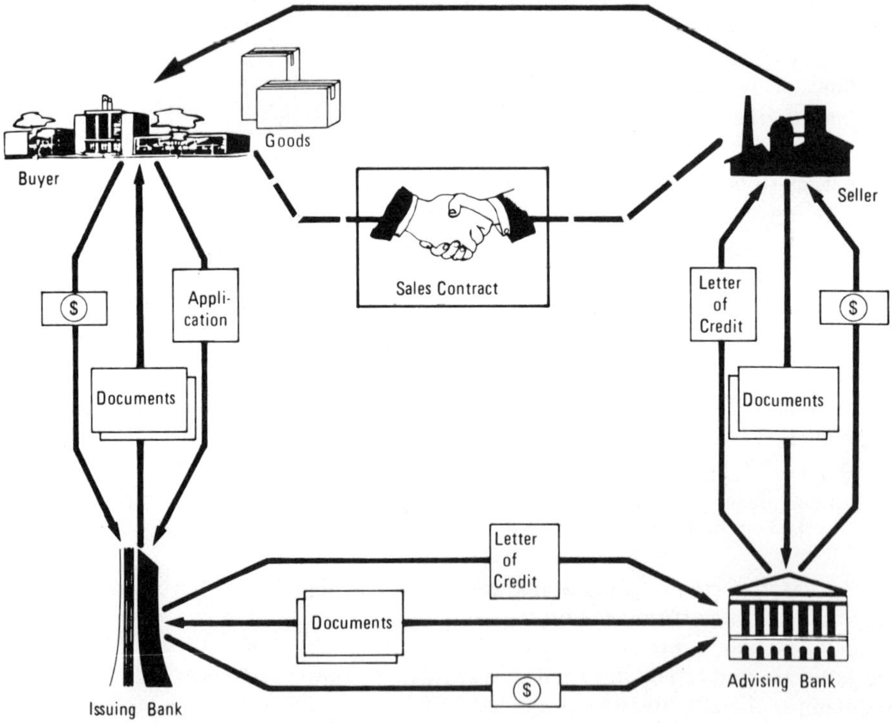

EXHIBIT 9 APPLICATION FOR IRREVOCABLE COMMERCIAL LETTER OF CREDIT

The First National Bank of Chicago
International Banking Department/Import Letter of Credit Unit
Two First National Plaza, Chicago, Illinois 60670

F.N.B.C. No. GC 1234 (FOR BANK USE ONLY)

Date February 13, 198–

Please issue an irrevocable Letter of Credit substantially as set forth below and forward same to your correspondent by:

☒ Airmail ☐ Airmail, with short preliminary cable advice ☐ Full Cable, for delivery to the beneficiary

In issuing the credit you are expressly authorized to make such changes from the terms of this application as you, in your sole discretion, may deem advisable provided no such changes shall vary the principal terms hereof.

	FOR ACCOUNT OF (APPLICANT)
Foreign Bank, Ltd. Nagoya, Japan	Importer for Profit, Inc. Chicago, IL
IN FAVOR OF (BENEFICIARY)	AMOUNT
Foreign Seller Ltd. P.O. Box 514 Nagoya, Japan	US$10,000 Ten Thousand U.S. Dollars Drafts must be presented for negotiation or presented to Drawee on or before (Expiry Date) September 30, 198-

Available by drafts at sight drawn, at your option, on you or your correspondent for 100 % of the Invoice value.

When accompanied by the following documents, as checked:

CHECK DOCUMENTS REQUIRED

☒ Commercial Invoice (4) ☐ Packing List
☒ Customs Invoice (4) ☐
☐ Marine and War Risk Insurance Policy and/or Certificate
☐ Other
(If other insurance is required, please state risks)
☐ Other documents
☐ Air Waybill consigned to
☒ ON BOARD Original Ocean Bill of Lading (if more than one original has been issued all are required)
issued to order of: Shipper, blank endorsed
marked: NOTIFY ABC Forwarding Co., 38 S. Dearborn St., Chicago Freight: ~~Collect~~/Paid

COVERING: Merchandise described in the invoice as: (Mention commodity only in generic terms omitting details as to grade, quality, etc.) General merchandise in accordance with buyer's purchase order no. 8524.

Check one: ☐ FAS ☐ FOB ☒ C&F ☐ CIF ☐ C&I Chicago, Illinois

Shipment from: Japan ☒ Partial Shipments Prohibited
To: Chicago, Illinois via the Great Lakes ☒ Transshipments Prohibited

☒ Documents must be presented to negotiating or paying bank within 10 days after the date of issuance of documents evidencing shipment or dispatch or taken in charge (shipping documents) but within validity of letter of credit.

☒ Insurance effected by applicant. Applicant agrees to keep insurance coverage in force until this transaction is completed.
Please instruct the negotiating or Drawee Bank to forward one set of negotiable documents to our Customs House Broker.
ABC Forwarding Co., 38 South Dearborn Street, Chicago, Illinois

Other Instructions: Discount charges are for ☐ Applicant ☐ Beneficiary

Unless otherwise instructed, documents shall be forwarded to you in one airmail.

PLEASE DATE AND OFFICIALLY SIGN THIS AGREEMENT ON THE REVERSE SIDE OF THIS APPLICATION

FOR BANK USE ONLY: Liabilities outstanding:	Approved by:	COMMISSION
Contingent Acceptances Accept. not under L/C Accept. by other banks Standby Loans Total	AUTHORIZED SIGNATURE Group:	RATE ___ % MIN. APPROVED

FORM 8270-7-AA (REV. 4-77)

The credit will be subject to the Uniform Customs and Practice for Documentary Credits of the International Chamber of Commerce, presently in effect.

it sends them to the issuing bank, and, if named the paying bank, the advising bank pays the seller in accordance with the terms of the letter of credit.

Step 8. The issuing bank, having received the documents, examines them. If they are in order, the issuing bank will charge the buyer's account and send the documents on to the buyer. The issuing bank also will reimburse the advising bank.

Step 9. The buyer receives the documents and picks up the merchandise from the shipper (carrier).

A letter of credit (see Exhibit 10) not only shifts the burden of financing to a bank or the money market, but also gives the exporter a bank guarantee that the exporting firm will receive cash or a bank acceptance, once the goods ordered are turned over to a common carrier for shipment to the importer, in accordance with the letter of credit. An importer supplying a letter of credit is usually able to buy at somewhat lower prices than those quoted to open-book-account customers, since the exporter neither carries the burden of financing nor assumes the credit risk. But there are two key points that must be emphasized. First, a letter of credit guarantees payments to the seller only if the seller complies exactly with the terms of the letter of credit. Second, since banks deal with documents and not merchandise, they can only guarantee to buyers that all the required documents in the letter of credit are in order—banks cannot insure that what is shipped is what the documents describe.

Import and Export Letters of Credit. United States banks usually distinguish between and handle separately import and export letters of credit. When a U.S. bank, on the application of a U.S. importer, issues a commercial letter of credit in favor of an exporter located abroad, it is termed "an import letter of credit." An export letter of credit is one issued by a foreign bank in favor of a U.S. exporter for the account of an importer abroad buying goods in the United States.

Revocable and Irrevocable Letters of Credit. A revocable letter of credit can be canceled by the importer's bank before drafts drawn by the exporter under the letter of credit have been negotiated by the correspondent bank. Banks do not favor revocable letters of credit; some banks refuse to issue them because the banks can become involved in resulting litigation. The correspondent bank, acting as agent for the importer's bank (the credit-issuing bank), assumes no obligation. An irrevocable letter of credit cannot be canceled by the importer's bank for the period specified without the consent of the beneficiary. Exporters generally insist upon irrevocable letters of credit.

Confirmed and Unconfirmed Letters of Credit. When a **correspondent bank** located in the country of the exporter confirms a letter of credit to the exporter by obligating itself to pay or accept the exporter's drafts, the instrument is called a **confirmed letter of credit.** The confirmation binds the correspondent bank to honor drafts drawn under the credit even if the importer's (issuing) bank should refuse or be unable to meet its obligation. An **unconfirmed letter of credit** does not give the exporter this additional security.

Exporters insist on confirmed letters of credit when the foreign issuing bank is not well known. It is obvious that the correspondent bank will confirm only irrevocable letters of credit, since a bank would not guarantee an agreement that might be canceled at will by the issuing bank.

Revolving and Installment Letters of Credit. If an importer maintains a continuous business relation with an exporter and receives repeated shipments of goods, a revolving credit in favor of the exporter is often used. A **revolving letter of credit** assures automatic renewal of the amount of credit when it becomes exhausted at certain specified intervals. The buyer (importer) should be very cautious before

EXHIBIT 10

FIRST CHICAGO
The First National Bank of Chicago

Cable address: NATIONAL CHICAGO
Telex number: 2-53801
19-121-0
IRREVOCABLE NEGOTIABLE CREDIT

WORLDWIDE BANKING DEPARTMENT
INTERNATIONAL TRADE SERVICES GROUP

Two First National Plaza/Chicago, Illinois 60670

DATE: FEBRUARY 14, 198-

MAIL

ADVISING BANK
FOREIGN BANK, LTD.

NAGOYA, JAPAN

ALL DRAFTS DRAWN MUST BE MARKED
FNBC: 1552-00001234
OPENER'S REFERENCE NO: GC 1234
ADVISING BANK REF. NO.

GENTLEMEN:

BY THE ORDER OF IMPORTER FOR PROFIT, INC. CHICAGO, ILL. 60670, WE HEREBY ISSUE THROUGH YOU IN FAVOR OF:

FOREIGN SELLER, LTD.
P.O. BOX 514
NAGOYA, JAPAN

OUR IRREVOCABLE CREDIT FOR THE ACCOUNT OF IMPORTER FOR PROFIT, INC. FOR AN AMOUNT NOT TO EXCEED IN THE AGGREGATE US DOLLARS 10,000.00 AVAILABLE BY YOUR DRAFTS AT SIGHT ON THE FIRST NATIONAL BANK OF CHICAGO, CHICAGO, IL. U.S.A. EFFECTIVE FEBRUARY 14, 198- AND EXPIRING ON SEPTEMBER 30, 198-.

THIS CREDIT IS SUBJECT TO THE FOLLOWING:

TRANS SHIPMENT NOT ALLOWED.
SHIP FROM: JAPAN

PARTIAL SHIPMENT NOT ALLOWED.
SHIP TO: CHICAGO, ILL. VIA GREAT LAKES.

1. COMMERCIAL INVOICE–ORIGINAL AND 3 COPIES
2. CUSTOMS INVOICE–ORIGINAL AND 3 COPIES
3. FULL SET OCEAN CARRIERS CLEAN BILLS OF LADING DATED ON BOARD ISSUED IN TWO ORIGINALS, PLUS ONE NON-NEGOTIABLE COPY TO ORDER OF: SHIPPER, BLANK ENDORSED MARKED: FREIGHT PAID AND NOTIFY: ABC FORWARDING CO., 38 SOUTH DEARBORN STREET, CHICAGO, ILLINOIS.

COVERING SHIPMENT OF: GENERAL MERCHANDISE IN ACCORDANCE WITH BUYER'S PURCHASE ORDER NO. 8524. TERMS: C&F CHICAGO, ILLINOIS

INSURANCE EFFECTED BY BUYER.

NEGOTIATING BANK MUST AIRMAIL ONE ORIGINAL COMMERCIAL INVOICE. CUSTOMS INVOICE AND BILL OF LADING TO ABC FORWARDING CO., 38 SOUTH DEARBORN STREET, CHICAGO, ILLINOIS FOR OUR ACCOUNT AND A CERTIFICATE TO THIS EFFECT MUST BE SUBMITTED WITH THE REMAINING DOCUMENTS.

WE HEREBY ENGAGE WITH THE DRAWERS, ENDORSERS AND BONAFIDE HOLDERS THAT EACH DRAFT DRAWN UNDER, HAD IN COMPLIANCE WITH, THE TERMS OF THE SAID CREDIT, WILL BE DULY HONORED IF PRESENTED FOR NEGOTIATION ON OR BEFORE THE EXPIRY DATE.

THE AMOUNT OF EACH DRAFT MUST BE ENDORSED ON THE REVERSE OF THIS CREDIT BY THE NEGOTIATING BANK.

THIS CREDIT IS SUBJECT TO THE UNIFORM CUSTOMS AND PRACTICE FOR DOCUMENT CREDITS (1974 REVISION), INTERNATIONAL CHAMBER OF COMMERCE–PUBLICATION 290.

VERY TRULY YOURS,

THE FIRST NATIONAL BANK OF CHICAGO

AUTHORIZED SIGNATURE(S)

ADVISING BANK'S NOTIFICATION

PLACE, DATE, NAME AND SIGNATURE

providing the seller (exporter) with a revolving letter of credit. The maximum exposure of the buyer (importer) under a revolving letter of credit is not the amount of credit, but the amount of credit multiplied by the number of periods the credit is to revolve. The revolving letter of credit can be issued in irrevocable and revocable form. Revolving letters of credit can be **commulative** or **noncommulative.** In a **commulative letter of credit** the beneficiary is allowed to carry over any amount not drawn upon in previous periods. On the other hand a **noncommulative letter of credit** does not allow the beneficiary to draw amounts during a later period that were not drawn in previous periods. Nearly all revolving letters of credit are noncommulative. Revolving letters of credit are used by companies with repetitive sales or purchases. The most common users are retailers. For example, the importer of sweaters might sell up to $5,000 each month. The importer uses a revolving letter of credit for the amount of $5,000 to revolve monthly. This means that he or she will never have to pay for more than $5,000 a month.

The **installment letter of credit** is similar to a revolving noncommulative letter of credit with one exception, which is that once the seller misses a shipment the credit ceases to be in effect and a new one needs to be opened, or the existing credit reinstated by an amendment. This gives the buyer some control.

Transfers/Assignments of Letters of Credit. All or part of the proceeds of a letter of credit can be assigned to a third party at the instructions of the beneficiary. **Assignment** can be made against any letter of credit, and is often done by importers who maintain representatives abroad. An assignable letter of credit can itself be issued in favor of the foreign representative, who is ordered to buy the goods specified by the importer. When the representative has contracted for the goods on the stipulated terms, he or she assigns the letter of credit to the seller (exporter).

The **rights** of a letter of credit can be **transferred** only if the letter is expressly designated as transferable. The transferee then becomes responsible for complying with the letter's terms to acquire payment.

Standby Letters of Credit. A standby letter of credit does not typically involve direct purchase of merchandise or the presentation of title document. If the beneficiary submits documents in accordance with the terms of the letter of credit the bank must pay regardless of any circumstances. The applicant is legally bound to reimburse the bank. This type of letter of credit is used for (1) payments for merchandise shipped on **open account;** (2) **bid and performance bonds;** (3) **advance payment guarantees;** (4) other financial obligations.

The use of standby letters of credit as bid and performance bonds has increased in recent years, in particular for trade and projects in the Middle East. A clean standby letter of credit is initiated by the seller to guarantee goods or service at the bid price. This letter of credit guarantees the price and specifications of a signed contract and is payable simply against a draft. A standby letter of credit can be used to assure the return of any advance payments, if a contract is terminated, and it serves as a warranty to certify that a project works, once it is completed. This instrument is preferred by buyers to insurance company bonds since it is payable on demand. A standby letter of credit is extremely risky for the seller, since the seller places his or her own money as a guarantee and, at any time, the buyer can cash the standby LC. In addition, standby letters of credit can damage a company's credit rating if the company has too many outstanding, since banks look at this as an impairment of credit. In certain areas of the world, particularly for large projects, standby letters of credit are a condition for bidding or contracting for work by an international firm, and there are no other choices but to use them or lose the business.

Why Use Letters of Credit? Letters of credit are used in a wide variety of circumstances. Certain countries, particularly in the Far East, require that all export trade be conducted on a letter-of-credit basis. Some sellers will sell goods only on a letter-of-credit basis. The key advantage to the seller is that a letter of credit **reduces commercial risk.** Whereas a collection requires assuming the commercial risk associated with the buyer, a letter of credit requires assuming only the commercial risk associated with the issuing bank. In both cases, the beneficiary assumes foreign **political risk.** If the letter of credit is confirmed, the relevant commercial risk is that of the confirming bank, and the political risk is domestic. The buyer under a letter of credit also receives some protection. Having the banks examine the documents increases the likelihood of detecting errors. However, it does not insure that the goods actually shipped are of a sufficient quantity or of satisfactory quality as described in the documents.

Another important reason for a buyer without experience in international trade to use a letter of credit is to eliminate delays involved in establishing the buyer's own **credibility.** In fact, this credibility is so important that new importers are generally required to obtain letters of credit because suppliers will not be willing to sell on more liberal terms.

It must be reemphasized that neither a letter of credit nor a collection is a total substitute for good credit judgment. The buyer must trust the seller; a letter of credit will not prevent an exporter from invoicing goods as called for in the credit and shipping goods of a different nature. In addition, the seller needs to understand the political situation in the buyer's country, particularly in the area of foreign exchange.

The key reason exporters ask for **confirmation** of a letter of credit is to reduce political risk. Another common reason is that the beneficiary is not willing to assume the overseas bank's commercial risk. Finally, if the advising bank is not designated as the paying bank, the beneficiary will not receive funds until the issuing bank has approved the documents. If a domestic bank confirms the credit, however, payment will be made upon approval of the documents at the domestic bank.

AUTHORITY TO PURCHASE. The authority to purchase (**AP**), or **authority to negotiate,** is a letter or cable sent by the importer's bank to its branch, agent, or correspondent abroad, instructing the agent to buy an exporter's draft drawn on an importer. The authority to purchase, used mainly in Far Eastern trade, shifts the burden of financing from the exporter to the importer's bank. Its operation is illustrated by the following example.

An importer in Asia has bought goods from an exporter in San Francisco, the contract stipulating payment by a 90-day draft on the importer with an authority to purchase. The importer applies to the bank for an authority to purchase, specifying the amount, expiration date, shipping documents, and other conditions. When the bank approves the application, the importer signs a **letter of guarantee,** in which the importer is obligated to accept and pay the draft, pledging the documents conveying title to the goods as collateral security. The bank then instructs its agent in San Francisco to buy the exporter's draft drawn in compliance with the stated conditions. The San Francisco agent sends a notice (advice of authority to purchase) to the exporter, listing the terms on which the draft on the importer will be purchased. After the exporter has delivered the goods to the shipping company, the draft is presented with the required documents to the agent and payment is received. The authority to purchase thus enables the exporter to sell the draft immediately without using up a portion of the line of credit at the bank.

In contrast to the letter of credit, which gives rise to **bankers' acceptances,** the authority to purchase gives rise to a **trade acceptance,** with the importer as accepter. Although under both methods the exporter is only secondarily liable, that is, only if the accepter should fail to pay, it is obvious that an exporter is less likely to be called on to pay a dishonored bank acceptance than a trade acceptance. The exporter may, however, be relieved from liability by being authorized to endorse the draft on the importer with the words "without recourse." Thus, if the importer (drawee) refuses to accept or pay the draft, the exporter (drawer) cannot be called on to refund the money received from its sale. But authorities to purchase authorizing the exporter to endorse without recourse are rarely issued.

The authority to purchase can be revocable or irrevocable. In a revocable authority to purchase, the issuing bank has the right to cancel the authorization given to its agent to buy the exporter's draft. In such circumstance the agent's advice of authority to purchase contains a clause stipulating that the authority can be canceled by giving notice to the exporter.

BANKERS' ACCEPTANCES. When a time draft or bill of exchange is drawn and accepted by a bank, it becomes a **banker's acceptance** (see Exhibit 11). It is an obligation to pay a specified amount of money at a specified future date. The accepting bank agrees unconditionally to pay the face value of the draft at maturity to the holder. The key feature of a banker's acceptance is the ability of the holder to raise funds by **discounting** the accepted drafts in the marketplace before the day on which they mature. The fact that bankers' acceptances are discountable instruments that are negotiable and marketable creates for them a very active secondary market. The use of acceptance financing for export and import transactions has expanded considerably; for example, the volume of acceptances outstanding in the United States grew from $3.4 billion in 1965 to approximately $40 billion in 1979.

Traditionally, the most common use of bankers' acceptances has been in financing import and export transactions. The rapid expansion in the use of acceptance financing has largely paralleled the boom in U.S. and world trade. While U.S. bankers' acceptances are frequently associated with trade to and from the United States, it should be noted that in recent years the most dramatic increase in the use of acceptance financing has taken place in bills created to finance trade between foreign countries as well as to finance goods stored in nations abroad. These acceptances are known as **third-country bills.**

EXHIBIT 11

DEL. 1653

The transaction which gives rise to this instrument is the:
□□ IMPORTATION/EXPORTATION
□□ DOMESTIC SHIPMENT – Accompanied by shipping documents
□ STORAGE/WAREHOUSING – Secured at the time of acceptance by independent warehouse, terminal, or other similar receipt conveying title, stored in:

OF

FROM ______ TO ______

ACCEPTED
Date ______ No. ______
Payable at our office in Chicago – or if desired at
CHEMICAL BANK, NEW YORK, NEW YORK
THE FIRST NATIONAL BANK OF CHICAGO
Authorized Signature

NO. ______
Date ______
U.S. $ ______

AT ______ Pay to the Order of THE FIRST NATIONAL BANK OF CHICAGO
______ U.S. DOLLARS
Value Received and Charge to Our Account

To:
FIRST CHICAGO
The First National Bank of Chicago
Chicago, Illinois 60670

2-1/710

SPECIMEN
Authorized Signature(s)

Third-country bills presently represent the single largest category of acceptances outstanding. The actual outstandings figure is about six times larger than the volume of third-country bills outstanding at the end of 1970. This recent surge of offshore bills primarily reflects increased utilization of the U.S. acceptance market by Asian borrowers. In particular, a large portion of Asian foreign trade—even that with non-U.S. trading partners—is denominated and settled in U.S. dollars, thus leading Asian traders to utilize the U.S. acceptance markets extensively.

Types of Bankers' Acceptances. The following represent the five basic types of transactions that normally underlie a banker's acceptance financing:

Acceptances created under letters of credit to finance the movement of goods between the United States and a foreign country or between two foreign countries

Acceptances not under letters of credit created to finance the movement and/or storage of goods involving the United States and a foreign country or foreign countries only

Acceptances covering shipments of merchandise within the United States

Acceptances created to cover the storage of readily marketable staples in the United States as well as abroad

Dollar-exchange acceptances

One of the unique aspects of banker's acceptance financing is that in all cases, with the exception of dollar-exchange acceptances, the nature of the financing is **self-liquidating.** This means that the transaction being financed will, in and of itself, generate funds that will liquidate the acceptance liability.

Dollar-exchange acceptances are unique in that they are designed to alleviate seasonal shortages of dollars for payment of external obligations of certain nations, particularly those in Latin America, which typically rely on a limited number of crops for their foreign exchange earnings. These instruments anticipate proceeds from exports forthcoming within 90 days from the creation of the banker's acceptance and usually apply for the use of foreign central banks. The creation of dollar-exchange acceptances has been restricted by the Federal Reserve Act, since only certain countries are eligible for this form of credit.

Mechanics of the Secondary Market for Bankers' Acceptances. Bankers' acceptances are different from most forms of bank lending. One unique attribute of this type of financing is that a banker's acceptance is a discountable instrument. When discounted, the number of dollars extended to the drawer of an accepted draft is less than the face amount of the draft, usually by the market discount rate plus the bank's acceptance commission. Specific examples of the cost of borrowing under bankers' acceptances are presented later.

Unlike a conventional bank loan, an acceptance is a negotiable and marketable instrument for which a well-established and active secondary market exists. The drawer of a draft has the option to hold that draft until maturity or to obtain funds immediately by discounting the instrument. The drawer normally discounts the draft with the accepting bank. The bank can then choose to hold the discounted draft in its own portfolio or to sell it in the secondary market. Only when an acceptance-creating bank purchases (discounts) the acceptance from the seller of goods in a trade transaction, and thus extends credit, does a bank tie up funds for its own account. Acceptances created at banks generally are either sold in the acceptance market through special dealers or kept in the bank's portfolio and funded from the common pool of funds.

There are approximately 10 to 15 dealers in this secondary market, many with nationwide branches. The bankers' acceptances market is an over-the-counter market, and many of the firms dealing in these instruments also deal in a variety of other marketable obligations. Acceptance trading often constitutes only one part of their overall activities. Participants in the market, in addition to these dealers, are the accepting banks, Edge Act corporations, investors of all types (from individuals to foreign central banks), and the Federal Reserve System. Trading in this market is done on a negotiated basis, with bid and ask rates normally published for informational purposes only.

How Are Bankers' Acceptances Created? Bankers' acceptances can originate under commercial letters of credit or can be arranged by separate agreement. The following discusses both methods.

Bankers' Acceptances under Letters of Credit. Commercial letters of credit might require **time (usance) drafts** covering shipments whose terms comply with the conditions of eligibility discussed previously. The beneficiary of a letter of credit requiring a time draft drawn on a U.S. bank can receive funds through discounting the draft without using personally available credit lines, since the accepting bank will look to the issuing bank of the letter of credit for payment of draft at maturity.

When the terms of the letter of credit indicate that discount charges are for the account of the buyer, the seller will receive the face amount of the draft upon presentation of the documents to the accepting bank. If, however, the charges are for the account of the seller, then the seller will receive the face amount of the draft less discount charges for the applicable acceptances-financing period. If the buyer (the applicant of a letter of credit) wishes to obtain acceptance financing pursuant to a trade transaction, financing can be obtained in one of two ways. One alternative would be to apply for a letter of credit, with time drafts drawn on a U.S. bank, which stipulates that discount charges are for the buyer's account. Another means of obtaining acceptance financing to cover purchases would be under a sight letter of credit with drawings thereunder to be refinanced by bankers' acceptances under agreement. Regardless of the method employed, the buyer (applicant) must have an **approved credit facility** for letters of credit and bankers' acceptances at the bank.

Documentary requirements for bankers' acceptances created under letters of credit are virtually automatic since the bank creating the acceptance can obtain all pertinent details regarding the underlying trade transaction from the letter-of-credit documentation.

Bankers' Acceptances under Agreement (Clean Acceptances). Acceptance financing is also available for shipments not involving letters of credit. Under these circumstances, the customer must have an acceptance agreement with the bank. The acceptance agreement can cover one specific transaction or a series of transactions over a period of time. The latter type is commonly referred to as a **continuing agreement.**

Clean acceptances do not require presentation of shipping documents to the accepting bank.

Acceptances not under letters of credit are initiated when drafts, without a letter of credit, are drawn by a foreign bank or a large corporation on a U.S. bank. The drafts are accompanied by a statement describing (1) the value of the merchandise shipped and to be financed; (2) a general description of the merchandise; (3) the country of exportation and the country of importation; (4) the date of shipment; (5) a certification attesting that the shipment is not being financed by any other means.

Costs Associated with Financing via Bankers' Acceptances. A banker's acceptance usually compares favorably in cost to interest costs associated with other forms of bank credit. This is because lenders typically require conventional borrowers to maintain compensating balances to support borrowings under lines of credit. Thus the effective cost of borrowing is frequently higher than the nominal or stated interest rate.

When accepting a draft, a bank charges an **acceptance commission** as compensation for its assumption of credit risk and to cover the administrative costs associated with the transaction. When the bank discounts an acceptance, thus advancing funds against the time draft, it provides the funds at a rate that is determined by conditions present in the money markets at the time of discounting. While interest and other fees are most often collected in arrears under other forms of financing, the acceptance commission and discount charges on bankers' acceptances are collected from the borrower at the time of acceptance and disbursement. These fees are generally combined and quoted as an **"all-in" rate.** The effective cost of acceptance financing can be calculated as follows:

$$\frac{\text{all-in rate}}{1 - \dfrac{\text{tenor}}{360} \times \text{all-in rate}} \times 100 = \text{effective annual interest rate}$$

As an example, for a \$60,000 draft drawn at 90 days sight, the all-in rate is 10%. The effective cost is calculated as follows:

$$\frac{0.10}{1 - \dfrac{90}{360} \times 0.10} \times 100 = \frac{0.10}{1 - 0.025} = 10.26\%$$

In verification of this answer, the net proceeds from discounting the acceptance are \$60,000 − (90/360) × 10% × \$60,000, or \$58,000 for 90 days at 10.26% is \$60,000—the face amount of the acceptance.

FINANCING BY A THIRD PARTY

There are several sources of financing and assistance available to both the exporter and the importer. These sources are either public or private and they share both the risk and the financing burden.

PUBLIC SOURCES OF TRADE FINANCING. In this section public sources of trade financing are discussed briefly; more details are found in the next section, "Sources of International Trade Financing."

To promote employment and to improve the balance of payments, governments developed assistance programs to export and import trade. The programs range from financing and insurance to information gathering. The United States, like other countries, actively supports international trade activities by providing through public sources the following types of assistance.

Participating with private sources in supplying the capital requirement for some major projects that are so large that private financing alone is not possible.

Guaranteeing credits to private sources, who without these guarantees would not extend credit to traders.

Acting as a source of refinancing of loans made by private sources. The government endorses certain bonds, making them higher in rating.

Providing various assistance programs that involve supplying information regarding markets and general trade counseling.

Providing insurance services, alone or in cooperation with private sources (insurance can cover a wide range of export-related risks, including political risks)

Export-Import Bank of the United States. The Export-Import Bank of the United States (Eximbank), a corporation wholly owned by the U.S. government, has been an important source of export financing since its creation in 1934. Created by a Presidential Executive Order, the bank was established on a statutory basis in 1945 with the passage of the Export-Import Bank Act.

Since its establishment, Eximbank programs have assisted thousands of U.S. exporters, ranging from some of the world's largest and most experienced multinational corporations to small firms just beginning to pursue opportunities for foreign trade. Today, a growing variety of Eximbank financial services support a broad cross-section of U.S. products and projects—from industrial raw materials and farm products, computers and farm machinery, to cement plants, power generating plants, and commercial jet aircraft.

Eximbank's services are generally broken down into two financing areas. The first is the buyer credit or project financing area, which provides direct loans at fixed interest rates and extended terms of repayment, as well as financial guarantees for loans from private sources for heavy capital equipment and capital-intensive projects. The second area is that of supplier credit, which offers assistance through the Cooperative Financing Facility (an established network of foreign banks that work with Eximbank) to discount loans and offer medium-term commercial bank guarantees.

Meeting foreign government competition is also an important statutory requirement for Eximbank. The bank has been authorized to offer financing at rates and terms that are competitive with official foreign export credit agencies. Recent legislation has stressed this policy.

One unique feature of Eximbank is that it will **guarantee political risks,** which include inconvertibility of foreign currency into dollars, cancellation of export and import licenses, or other governmental actions preventing importation of goods, including war, civil strife, and expropriation or confiscation by government action.

The World Bank Group. The World Bank Group consists of three institutions—the International Bank for Reconstruction and Development (IBRD), the International Development Association (IDA), and the International Finance Corporation (IFC). (The IBRD is also known as the World Bank.) The common objective of these institutions is to help raise standards of living in developing countries by channeling financial resources from developed countries to the developing world.

The **World Bank,** established in 1945, is owned by the governments of 132 countries. The bank, whose capital is subscribed by its member countries, finances its lending operations primarily from its own borrowings in the world capital markets. A substantial contribution to the World Bank's resources also comes from its retained earnings and the flow of repayments on its loans. Bank loans generally have a grace period of five years and are repayable over 20 years or less. They are directed toward developing countries at more advanced stages of economic and social growth. The interest rate the World Bank charges on its loans is calculated in accordance with a formula related to its cost of borrowing.

The **International Development Association** (IDA) was established in 1960 to provide assistance similar to that of the World Bank, but primarily in the poorer developing countries on terms that would bear less heavily on their balance of payments than World Bank loans. Assistance from the IDA is, therefore, concentrated in the very poor countries—mainly those with an annual per capita gross national product of less than $520 (in 1975 dollars). More than 50 countries are eligible under this criterion.

Membership in IDA is open to all members of the World Bank, and 120 of them have joined to date. The funds used by IDA, called "credits" to distinguish them from World Bank loans, come mostly in the form of subscriptions, general replenishments from the more industrialized and developed members, special contributions by its richer members, and transfers from the net earnings of the World Bank. The terms of IDA credits, which are made to governments only, are 10-year grace periods, 50-year maturities, and no interest, but there is an annual service charge of 0.75% on the disbursed portion of each credit. Although legally and financially distinct from the World Bank, IDA is administered by the same staff.

The **International Finance Corporation** (IFC) was established in 1956. Its function is to assist the economic development of less-developed countries by promoting growth in the private sector of their economies and helping to mobilize domestic and foreign capital for this purpose. Membership in the World Bank is a prerequisite for membership in the IFC, which totals 109 countries. Legally and financially, the IFC and the World Bank are separate entities. The IFC has its own operating and legal staff, but draws upon the World Bank for administrative and other services.

While the World Bank Group has traditionally financed all kinds of capital infrastructure, such as roads and railways, telecommunications, and ports and power facilities, its present developmental strategy places a greatly increased emphasis on investments that can directly affect the well-being of the masses of poor people of developing countries by making them more productive and by integrating them as active partners in the development process. This strategy is increasingly evident in the agriculture and rural development projects that the World Bank and IDA help finance. It is also evident in projects for education, family planning, and nutrition, in projects designed to increase the productivity of small industries, and in the World Bank's concern for the urban poor, who benefit from projects designed to develop water and sewerage facilities as well as low-cost core housing. At the same time, lending for traditional projects continues, although it is being redirected to be more responsive to the new strategy of deliberately focusing on the poorest segments of society in the developing countries.

PRIVATE SOURCES AND TECHNIQUES. Private sources of export-import financing are **commercial banks, private finance firms,** and **international factors.** Commercial banks concentrate traditionally on short-term financing; they grant advances to exporters, discount drafts, confirm letters of credit, and create bankers' acceptances in addition to various other services that assist export-import activities.

Private commercial finance firms provide similar services to those of the banks but usually at a higher price. In addition, finance houses can arrange for inspection, check documents, and initiate credit investigations. An international factor concentrates on discounting and collection of drafts and foreign accounts receivable.

Domestic International Sales Corporation. A domestic international sales corporation (DISC) is a U.S. corporation established for tax purposes and devoted almost exclusively to the export of U.S. products. A DISC does not pay income tax on qualified export income. Its shareholders, however, are taxed on a portion of that income, regardless of whether it is actually distributed. A DISC can function as a commission agent or as an export sales company. Because DISCs are often owned by a related supplier, the Internal Revenue Code provides special safe-haven transfer pricing rules. Hence the DISC and related supplier need not concern themselves with the arm's-length pricing requirement of the Code. Because of the tax deferral provisions, a DISC can also be advantageous for an exporter dealing with unrelated suppliers.

A key feature of the DISC legislation is the provision for producer's loans. Basically, this allows the DISC to lend its tax-deferred earnings to the owners interest-free. These producer's loans are limited to the borrower's increase in U.S. productive facilities used for export.

The Foreign Credit Insurance Association. The Foreign Credit Insurance Association (FCIA) is a joint enterprise of a number of private U.S. insurance firms. It works with Eximbank to provide coverage of the following kinds: short-term comprehensive risk, medium-term comprehensive risk, all-term comprehensive master policies, catastrophe policies, small-business policies, and political risk policies.

The Private Export Funding Corporation. The Private Export Funding Corporation (PEFCO), established in 1970, provides private funding, guaranteed by Eximbank, to finance U.S. exports. Typically, PEFCO provides middle-maturity financing (five to 12 years) in a financial package of substantial size where one or more commercial banks take the shortest maturities and Eximbank the longest.

EXPORT AND IMPORT DOCUMENTS

In international trade, documents are important; they are instrumental in obtaining payment and transferring title, and are also required to clear the merchandise through customs and ports of entry and exit. The documents necessary in any transaction should be specified in the sales contract.

Trade Terms. The duties and responsibilities of both the buyer and the seller with respect to point of delivery and assumption of costs and risks must be completely clear, understood by both parties, and specified in the sales contract.

The Draft. A draft is a negotiable instrument containing an order to pay. The party requesting payment is called the **drawer** and is the **originator** of the draft. The party responsible for paying (honoring) the draft is known as the **drawee.** To be negotiable, a draft must (1) be signed by the drawer; (2) contain an unconditional order to pay a definite amount; (3) be payable on demand or at a specific time; and (4) be payable to the bearer or to order.

Commercial Invoices. The commercial invoice is the seller's bill addressed to the buyer; it clearly describes the merchandise and indicates the total cost of the merchandise sold. In many countries the commercial invoice is required to clear the merchandise through customs; the specific requirements for such countries should be considered. In this regard, the information given in the invoice must not be inconsistent with that in other documents accompanying the invoice.

Bills of Lading. The bill of lading, a signed document, acknowledges receipt of and conveys title to the merchandise specified therein. It is issued by a common carrier who agrees to transport the merchandise to a specified destination.

Ocean Bills of Lading. The ocean bill of lading is issued by a steamship company (or its agent) and indicates the terms and conditions of the contract with the shipper. The ocean bill of lading is normally issued in three originals, unless requested otherwise. The presentation of any original, properly endorsed (if endorsement is required), is sufficient to obtain the merchandise at the point of destination.

Beyond its provision for the transportation of merchandise, one of the most important aspects of the bill of lading is how and when title is transferred to the purchaser of the merchandise. Depending upon the means of consignment of the merchandise, a bill of lading can be considered a **straight bill of lading** or a **to-order bill of lading.** A straight bill of lading is not negotiable and the merchandise covered by it is normally consigned directly to the buyer. With this type of bill of lading the buyer can take delivery of the merchandise from the carrier upon identification and without presentation and surrender of the bill of lading. Thus control of merchandise passes at the time the bill of lading is issued.

The to-order bill of lading is a negotiable document normally consigned simply "to order" or "to order of shipper." Title to the merchandise remains with the shipper until the shipper chooses to relinquish title by endorsing it on the back, either in blank or to a specified party.

Airway Bills. Airlines typically issue airway bills or air consignment notes, which are straight bills of lading. These are subject to the same conditions as straight ocean bills of lading insofar as title is concerned.

Insurance Policy or Certificate. The risks of transportation range from slight damage to total loss of merchandise. Most exporters feel that the insurance coverage provided by common carriers up to the port of exit is sufficient. Because ocean carriers disclaim any responsibility for losses in transportation except those attributed to their negligence, some form of marine insurance to protect the interest of the buyer and seller should be arranged. The coverage available under marine policies ranges from limited coverage, such as fire, collision, and sinking, to the broad coverage of "all risks." Even in its broadest form many risks, such as those of war, strikes, riots, and civil commotion are included only upon special endorsement.

Other Documents. Other documents might be required by the buyer or might be necessary in clearing merchandise through ports of entry or exit. For example, most foreign shipments require an **export declaration** to be filed by the exporter at the port of exit in the United States. Some merchandise can be exported only under license. The buyer might also request specific documents, such as packing lists, certificates of inspection or quality, and certificates of weight. Certain countries require special **consular invoices,** or they require that documents such as the bill of lading, commercial invoice, or certificate of origin bear a consular visa before merchandise can enter into that country.

EXPORT AND IMPORT RISK AND RISK-ALLOCATION TECHNIQUES

One of the major tasks of a firm involved in international trade is to identify and manage several risks that might accompany a particular financing instrument. Management of risk can make the difference between success and failure in trade activity, since it can result in a total loss of the deal or erosion of profit margins. The allocation of risks is summarized in Exhibit 12. The chief risks follow.

Credit Risk. Credit risk arises from the provision of loans or guarantees between any of the parties involved in the trade. A major consideration when assessing credit risk, when a third party is involved other than the buyer and the seller, is whether that party has a recourse condition and to whom it can claim recourse.

Currency Risk. Currency risk arises when the proceeds of the sale are denominated in a foreign currency and are provided at a delayed time. The currency risk has become one of the major factors in international trade. Starting in the early 1970s, dollar devaluation, coupled with free fluctuation of the major currencies against the dollar, has led to serious worries for exporters and importers. Exchange rate fluctuations, if not handled properly, can often eliminate profits or even turn the sale into a loss. If the sale is denominated in a foreign currency and provides for delayed payment, the exporter has to cover the exchange risk for the period between the date of sale and the date of payment. If the exporter holds a time draft until maturity, the exporter can use a **foreign exchange hedge** by entering a forward exchange or futures contract. On the other hand, if a draft is negotiated with a bank, the bank will buy the draft at the rate of exchange prevailing for delivery at maturity (i.e., the rate quoted in the **forward market**). In general, whether the exporter or the importer finances the transaction, the party that expects to pay or to receive funds in a foreign currency over a period of time is the party at risk and should proceed with caution.

Interest Rate Risk. An interest rate risk arises when the seller or the bank holds an asset such as discounted acceptance until the maturity date without having a corresponding fixed-interest liability of the same maturity—since any interest rate fluctuation alters the market value of a fixed-interest instrument.

EXHIBIT 12 RISK ALLOCATION IN INTERNATIONAL TRADE

FINANCING METHOD		Credit risk	Interest rate risk	Collateral risk	Convertability risk
Shipment on open book account		Exporter			Exporter
Time credits		Exporter			Exporter
Consignments		Exporter			Exporter
Collections drafts:	Document Sight	Exporter			
	Documentary Time	Exporter			Exporter
	Clean	Exporter			Exporter
Payment with order		Importer			
Partial payment in advance		Importer/Exporter			
Payment on documents					
Advance on drafts		Exporter/Bank		Bank	Exporter
Discount of drafts		Exporter/Bank		Bank	Exporter/Bank
Refinancing bill		Exporter/Bank	Holder of acceptance		Exporter/Bank
Letters of Credit:	Revocable L/C	Exporter(s)			Exporter
	Irrevocable L/C	Issuing Bank			Exporter
	Confirmed L/C	Confirming Bank/ Issuing Bank			Confirming Bank
	Unconfirmed L/C	Issuing Bank			Exporter
	Revolving/Installement L/C	Issuing Bank/ Importer			Exporter
	Stand-by L/C	Exporter/issuer			Exporter
Authority to Purchase		Exporter/Bank			Exporter
Bankers acceptance		Accepting Bank	Holder of acceptance		Accepting Bank
Export/Import Bank		Eximbank			Eximbank
FCIA		FCIA			Eximbank
PEFCO		Eximbank			Eximbank

Collateral Risk. Since export financing is normally collateralized by goods being shipped, collateral risk arises from the possibility that the bank financing itself will incur expense and difficulty trying to sell the goods in the market, with which it has little familiarity. The collateral risk can be shifted back to the exporter by discounting an acceptance with recourse.

Convertibility Risk. A convertibility risk arises when the foreign government imposes exchange controls to prevent outflow of foreign currency.

Risk management involves tradeoffs between risk and expenses of increased protection. In general, various public and private sources of trade financing and services were created to share the risk involved in trade. With careful management, a firm can reduce the risk involved by using the services of these organizations.

BIBLIOGRAPHY

Bayalis, A.E., "The Documentation Dilemma in International Trade," *Columbia Journal of World Business*, Spring (1976).

Bloch, H.S., "Export Financing Emerging as Major Policy Problem," *Columbia Journal of World Business*, Fall (1976).

Business International, *Financing Foreign Operations*, various issues.

Chown, J.F., *Taxation and Multinational Enterprise*. Longman, New York, 1974.

Eiteman, D.K., and A.I. Stonehill, *Multinational Business Finance*, 2nd ed., Addison-Wesley, Reading, Mass., 1979.

First National Bank of Chicago, Worldwide Banking Department, *International Trade Financing Services*.

Greene, J., *Organizing for Exporting*. National Industrial Conference Board, Business Policy Study Number 26, New York, 1968.

Harfield, H., *Bank Credits and Acceptances*, 5th ed., Ronald Press, New York, 1974.

Harrington, J.A., *Specifics on Commercial Letters of Credit and Bankers' Acceptances*, Scott Printing, Jersey City, N.J., 1974.

Mathis, F.J., (Ed.), *Offshore Lending by U.S. Commercial Banks*, Robert Morris Associates, 1975.

Riehl, H., and R.M. Rodriguez, *Foreign Exchange Markets*, McGraw-Hill, New York, 1977.

Rodriguez, R., and E. Carter, *International Financial Management*, 2nd ed., Prentice-Hall, Englewood Cliffs, N.J., 1979.

Schneider, G.W., *Export-Import Financing*, Ronald Press, New York, 1974.

Shapiro, A.C., *Multinational Financial Management*, Allyn & Bacon, Boston, 1982.

Shaw, E.D., *Practical Aspects of Letters of Credit*, Irving Trust, New York, 1963.

Weston, J.F., and B.W. Sorge, *International Managerial Finance*, Richard D. Irwin, Homewood, Ill., 1972.

SECTION 7.2

SOURCES OF INTERNATIONAL TRADE FINANCING

CONTENTS

SECTION 7.2

SOURCES OF INTERNATIONAL TRADE FINANCING

J. Stuart Lemle

With the creation of sovereign borders and the passage of goods and services across them, increasingly complex means of financing trade evolved. Bankers first venturing into the international sphere supplemented the basic commercial practices of cash in advance and cash on delivery with loans to exporters and to importers, as advances against intended shipments. With more sophisticated trade patterns and the requirement that flexible credit facilities be available, bankers began offering a broad variety of both short- and long-term financing and insurance vehicles. Those alternatives—ranging from a simple bank draft to a cofinanced World Bank–export credit package—now have become an established component of international commercial activity.

This section, in conjunction with the previous one and those dealing with the Eurocurrency and international securities markets, describes the principal sources of such financing and risk protection. It is intended to provide practical information regarding the programs available to firms exploring or conducting international trade transactions. While it has been written primarily for the benefit of U.S. firms, most of the principles and organizations are similar in each of the major trading nations.

Given the range of factual circumstances of individual corporations, the appropriate balance among alternative sources must be determined on a case-by-case basis. Guidance concerning this blending decision can be obtained from the Bibliography, from organizations listed in the Appendix, and from consultation with international finance counsel.

TRADE FINANCING TECHNIQUES AND INSTRUMENTS

While a sizable number of methods have developed to handle payment for export sales, three have become particularly prevalent—drafts of foreign buyers, letters of credit, and bankers' acceptances. Advice on these and such other methods as prepayment, open-account sales, and consignment sales can be obtained from the international department of a commercial bank.

DRAFTS. A draft is simply a negotiable instrument directing the drawee to pay a specified sum of money and serving as a means of extending temporary credit to a customer. Two basic varieties are available, **sight** and **time drafts**. Under the sight draft, the seller's draft is drawn "at sight" of the buyer and, through his or her commercial bank (and its foreign correspondents), to the attention of the buyer. The bank is required to deliver the shipping documents (which authorize release of the goods) only after receiving the buyer's payment of the draft. By this means, title to the goods is passed to the buyer only upon payment for them.

A time draft authorizes the foreign bank to deliver the documents, but with payment on the draft deferred a certain stipulated number of days. Title to the goods normally passes upon delivery to the buyer and thus the seller must depend for payment upon the buyer's reliability.

For each type of draft there is a degree of trust required; parties who are unfamiliar with each other would be advised to use a less risky method of payment, such as a letter of credit.

LETTERS OF CREDIT. The basic letter of credit, as described in the previous section, is a bank-issued instrument promising its agreement to make payment to a seller when the buyer satisfies certain stipulated conditions. When those conditions are fulfilled, the advising bank is obligated to pay the seller to the extent that there are funds in the issuing bank's account. While not a negotiable instrument, the letter of credit shifts the risk of nonpayment for goods delivered from the seller to a respected financial institution.

Letters of credit are available in either **revocable** or **irrevocable** form. Revocable credit can be modified or cancelled at the sole discretion of the buyer and thus rarely is used except between related entities. Irrevocable credit requires the consent of all parties in order to have its terms modified and it is widely recommended, particularly for new buyers. As with drafts, letters of credit can stipulate payment on a sight or a time basis.

Additional protection for the seller can be obtained by having the advising (paying) bank agree to confirm an irrevocable letter of credit so as to be obliged to pay the seller once he satisfies his presentation obligations, regardless of whether there are sufficient funds in the buyer's bank account.

While use of letters of credit is considerable, particularly regarding transactions involving East Asia, they can be quite expensive for the buyer who must advance funds to the bank well before gaining title to or receiving the goods. The other major drawback is that the advising bank has no means of establishing the veracity of the seller's assertion that the goods shipped meet the specifications of those ordered. As described below, the **Overseas Private Investment Corporation (OPIC)** offers some protection by issuing insurance coverage against arbitrary drawings on letters of credit where they are required to be posted for bid, performance, or advance payment guarantees.

Letters of credit have developed a variety of forms. For example, they can be issued on a revolving or installment basis such that the seller in a repetitive sales situation can draw on a replenished sum at specified intervals. In another form, the seller can stipulate that the proceeds of a letter of credit be transferable or assignable to third parties who may have an interest in the transaction.

Standby letters of credit are essentially a form of guarantee against nonperformance of an obligation and are used in such instances as payments for merchandise shipped on open account, requirements for bid and performance bonds, and advance payment guarantees. Since only a draft and a certificate of nonperformance need be presented in order to require payment by the advising bank, standby letters of credit pose some risk to the creating party.

BANKERS' ACCEPTANCES. Bankers' acceptances are time drafts or bills of exchange drawn on, and accepted by the importer's bank (drawee bank). By accepting the draft the drawee bank assumes an unconditional obligation to pay a specified (face) amount at the draft's maturity to a bona fide holder. In effect, bankers' acceptances at the draft's maturity are guarantees of the debt by the importer's bank. Bankers' acceptances are negotiable instruments and, since the bank's name backs the instrument, they are discountable. These features allow the exporter who receives a bankers' acceptance in lieu of immediate payment to realize cash on the sale immediately by selling the acceptance, at a discount, to either the drawee or any other bank. Or, if the exporter does not need cash immediately, the acceptance can be held until the maturity date and then presented to the drawee bank for payment.

Bankers' acceptances can be created under a letter of credit, in which case a number of shipping documents must be submitted by the exporter to the drawee bank. There are also so-called clean acceptances, which do not require a presentation of the shipping documents to the accepting bank; in this instance the importer must have an acceptance agreement with the bank, which entitles the importer to request the issuance of bankers' acceptances.

TRADE ACCEPTANCES. Trade acceptances are similar to bankers' acceptances but instead of being drawn on and accepted by the importer's bank they are drawn on and accepted by the importer, who, by this acceptance, promises to pay to the holder in due course the face amount of the acceptance at the specified maturity date. Trade acceptances and bankers' acceptances are negotiable. They cannot, however, be discountable if the importer on whom it is drawn is not well known and regarded in the market.

RELATED SHIPPING DOCUMENTS. Firms engaged in international trade must deal with a number of shipping documents including:

Commercial Invoice. A bill from the seller to the buyer describing the goods sold and their price; it is often important for customs (tariff) purposes.

Insurance Certificate. A statement of the extent of insurance coverage for the risks involved in transporting the goods.

Bill of Lading. Documentary evidence prepared by a transportation agent for the receipt of, and transfer of title to, a specified quantity of goods; it indicates the terms regarding shipment and the point at which transfer of title to the buyer can occur.

Validated Export License. Authorization by a governmental authority to export certain regulated merchandise to specified countries.

UNITED STATES GOVERNMENTAL SOURCES

EXPORT-IMPORT BANK OF THE UNITED STATES. The Export-Import Bank of the United States, **Eximbank**, is an independent agency of the federal government with the sole purpose of assisting the financing of U.S. export sales. Currently, it has in excess of $27 billion in outstanding loan guarantee and insurance commitments. First created by Presidential Executive Order in 1934 and incorporated by Congress with a charter in 1945 (the Eximbank's legislative authority can be found in Title 12 of the *United States Code*, Section 635; its regulations are contained in Title 12 of the *Code of Federal Regulations*, parts 400–407), it has become a primary means for U.S. exporters to finance sales in an international business environment in which virtually every major Western nation offers even more attractive programs to its exporters. Those programs have similar objectives but vary considerably in the costs and risks assumed by the sponsoring government.

As defined by its original legislative authorization and reaffirmed in its most recent renewal in 1978, the Eximbank's activities are guided by several basic policy considerations. In order to make full use of its programs, it is important to be aware of those considerations.

Guidelines for Eximbank Programs

Relationship with Private Sources of Capital. Crucial to continuing support from the commercial banking community, the Eximbank has been directed by Congress to "supplement and encourage, and not compete with, private capital" in assisting U.S. export transactions. This conforms with its requirement to establish lending terms taking into consideration the average cost of money to the Bank as well as the Bank's mandate to support U.S. exports at rates and on terms and conditions that are competitive with exports of other countries. Often, a cooperative arrangement is structured whereby one or more commercial banks lend a portion of the credit without Eximbank participation (and have a priority in the amortization schedule) and the Eximbank then offers the remainder required by the exporter. The balance between the two sources varies with each transaction and is determined largely by the creditworthiness of the exporter and the type of financing available to foreign firms competing in the same market with the U.S. firm.

Domestic Impact. Private industries' concern that the federal government would become a major financial force in international trade transactions to their detriment led Congress in 1968 to require the Eximbank, in its consideration of program applications, to review any serious adverse effect of each contemplated loan or guarantee on the competitive position of the U.S. industry, the availability of materials that are in short supply in the United States, and employment in the United States.

With the expansion of foreign manufacture of goods that also are produced in the United States, Eximbank readily could find itself financing the creation of competition for domestic industry. Some forces in Congress sought a prohibition on Eximbank involvement in any project where the product was of a type found in excess in the United States and could be reexported back to this country. Instead, the 1968 legislative guideline was clarified with a 1979 amendment that focused on Eximbank financing of the manufacture of a product in surplus in the world as a whole and permits it only where Eximbank's directors determine that damage to the domestic industry is of less consequence than the overall benefits of the project to industry and employment generally in the United States. In practice, the balance is viewed as that between jobs likely to be gained and lost due to the contemplated project. Little attention has been paid to the short supply criterion for authorizing Eximbank participation in trade projects.

Creditworthiness of Exporter. In order to protect the U.S. Treasury while providing a service otherwise unavailable in the capital markets, the Eximbank is mandated to apply a somewhat more liberal lending standard than would commercial banks, namely, a "reasonable assurance of repayment." That policy apparently has struck a successful balance in that it has been estimated that the Eximbank now supports nearly 20% of the exports of U.S. manufactured products while less than 0.02% of its loans have defaulted and over $3 billion has been earned on its loans.

The routine procedure is for each loan application to be presented to Eximbank's Board of Directors by a staff committee. The presentation consists of a determination of other sources of financing domestically and competitive sources abroad, as well as more typical considerations, such as the details of the particular project and the creditworthiness of the debtor. In the 1978 renewal of Eximbank's charter, Congress directed it to consider applications only on their commercial merits unless, in particular cases, the president should deem otherwise.

Status of Foreign Government Competition. The Bank's charter further requires its board to structure its financing programs so as to be offered at rates and on terms and other conditions that are competitive "with the government-supported rates and terms and other conditions available for the financing of exports from the principal countries whose exporters compete with United States exporters." In order to assist Eximbank in satisfying that standard without compromising any of the others noted above, the United States has advocated an international understanding among exporting nations. A partial success was achieved with the 1978 International Arrangement on Officially Supported Export Credits, signed by 21 major trading countries. While it set minimum credit terms (though different levels were permitted based on the borrower's relative wealth) and thereby decreased the likelihood of an export credit war, the arrangement did not establish clear standards regarding the permissible extent of government subsidies. The arrangement was substantially improved in mid-1982 with an agreement among its signatories to raise minimum credit terms up to 10%–12.4% (depending on the borrower's GNP per capita). The United States viewed this agreement as only a transitional step to a system that was more permanent, enforceable, and in the interest of the United States (i.e., lower subsidies and therefore higher lending rates).

Among other consequences, the foreign competition in the trade financing area periodically subsidizes exports to the United States so as to enable those products to be sold at prices considerably below what a domestic manufacturer can match. In addition to the antidumping procedures that can be initiated against the offending country, the Eximbank since 1978 has been able to finance manufacturers' sales in the domestic U.S. market to the extent of the subsidy provided to its foreign competitor.

Public Policy Considerations. Congress has placed additional constraints on the Eximbank's flexibility by requiring it to take into account policy positions regarding such issues as nuclear proliferation, environmental protection, antiterrorism, and human rights. For instance, a recent Presidential Executive Order requires the preparation of an environmental impact statement prior to Eximbank involvement in certain projects whose only relationship to the United States is Eximbank's participation. (see Executive Order 12114, 4 January 1979, and Title 12 of the *Code of Federal Regulations*, part 408).

The Jackson-Vanik Amendment to the Trade Act of 1974 prohibits Eximbank financing of any project in a nonmarket economy country that restricts free emigration of its citizens, unless the president should affirmatively waive the restriction based on the receipt of assurances from that country that it permits free emigration. Through the end of 1981, waivers had been granted (and renewed each year) for Romania, Hungary, and the People's Republic of China. (Yugoslavia and Poland had been exempted from coverage by the original legislation.)

More generally, a 1978 amendment to the Eximbank charter provided that only in cases where the president determines that such action would clearly and importantly advance U.S. policy in such areas as international terrorism, nuclear proliferation, environmental protection, and human rights should Eximbank deny applications for credit for nonfinancial or noncommercial considerations.

Programs Sponsored or Administered by the Eximbank. The Eximbank's sole objective of providing financing to facilitate the export of U.S. products is accomplished through a number of programs. In addition to the use of its own funds for the provision of export credits, guarantees, and insurance, the Bank cooperates with two private associations—the **Foreign Credit Insurance Association (FCIA)** (a consortium of approximately 50 major insurance firms involved in providing commercial risk coverage) and the Private Export Funding Corporation (PEFCO), comprised of 54 banks, seven industrial corporations, and an investment banking firm interested in providing me- medium- and long-term financing for the purchase of U.S. exports. Either singly or in some combination, these three sources of capital have assumed a major role in assisting the competitive position of U.S. exports in the world market. The various options available to the exporter are described below and summarized in Exhibit 1.

Short-Term Programs. While no Eximbank programs are available for export-related projects involving repayment periods of less than 181 days, FCIA does provide insurance coverage for foreign accounts receivable. With such protection, the exporter normally can obtain reasonable financing terms through conventional commercial bank avenues (often by assigning FCIA policy proceeds to the bank). The exporter also will be in a position to extend more credit and on more liberal terms to its customers since it will have that much more working capital. The FCIA will handle coverage for either goods or services and for either commercial risks or political risks, or both. Examples of covered commercial risks include insolvency or protracted default due to natural disasters, competitive pressures, shifts in demand, obsolescence of technology, and the like. Examples of covered political risks include war, civil disturbance, expropriation, currency inconvertibility, and cancellation of a U.S. export license under circumstances beyond the exporter's control. Generally, FCIA will insure a portion of the risks and then the Eximbank will provide coverage for the balance.

The FCIA programs include: (1) the short-term comprehensive policy, which covers both commercial and political risks on a blanket basis (i.e., essentially all of an exporter's short-term sales); (2) the master policy, which covers all of an exporter's eligible short- and medium-term sales with payment terms of up to five years and permits the exporter to determine the extent of insured credit for each of its buyers; and (3) a services policy for exporters of U.S. personnel (e.g., architects, consultants, engineers) whereby insurance is provided against the failure of the foreign contractor to make required payments for services rendered. Detailed information and applications for FCIA programs can be obtained from one of the agency's regional offices (see Appendix).

EXHIBIT 1 EXIMBANK AND FOREIGN CREDIT INSURANCE ASSOCIATION (FCIA) PROGRAMS

Product Examples	Appropriate Eximbank, FCIA Program
SHORT–TERM (UP TO 180 DAYS)	
Consumables Small manufactured items Spare parts Raw materials Farm products	FCIA policies only
MEDIUM–TERM (181 DAYS TO FIVE YEARS)	
Mining and refining equipment Construction equipment Agricultural equipment General aviation aircraft Manufacturing equipment Communications equipment Planning and feasibility studies	FCIA policies Commercial bank guarantees Cooperative financing facility Discount loans Bank-to-bank guarantee lines
LONG–TERM (MORE THAN FIVE YEARS)	
Cement plants Chemical plants Power plants (hydro, thermal, nuclear) LNG and gas processing Commercial jet aircraft Locomotives Other expensive heavy capital goods	Commercial bank loan combined with direct Eximbank loan Financial guarantee to commercial bank by Eximbank Direct loans Private Export Funding Corporation (PEFCO) loans

Source. Export-Import Bank of the United States.

Medium-Term Programs. The Eximbank administers several programs to facilitate medium-term export sales (i.e., those with repayment schedules of from one-half to five years): (1) FCIA policies, (2) the U.S. Commercial Bank Guarantee Program, (3) bank-to-bank guarantees, and (4) discount loans to commercial banks.

1. The FCIA and U.S. Commercial Bank Guarantee Program both provide insurance against commercial and political risks for periods of up to five years, depending on the contract value. The exporter must either self-finance the transaction or else get separate commercial bank financing; FCIA or Eximbank then guarantees its repayment.
2. FCIA medium-term insurance policies provide coverage for credit sales of capital and quasi-capital goods on an individual buyer basis (either for a single

sale or repetitive sales to a specified buyer). Under a separate program, sales to foreign dealers and distributors can be protected for inventory and accounts receivable financing. The master policy and services policy described earlier also are available for medium-term sales. Finally, FCIA provides a policy to insure against preshipment risks (e.g., those entailed during the manufacture of the goods for which contracts have been concluded) and political risks for goods shipped abroad on consignment.

3. Bank-to-bank guarantees involve the Eximbank's guarantee of a revolving credit line provided by a U.S. bank to an eligible financial institution in a nonindustrialized country in the context of the latter's financing of capital goods purchases from the United States. Guidelines for its operation parallel those of the Commercial Bank Guarantee Program.
4. The Discount Loan Program for U.S. commercial banks provides Eximbank financing for fixed-rate, medium-term export sales that the participating commercial bank would not otherwise finance. The Eximbank will issue advance commitments to lend to, or purchase fixed notes from, eligible commercial banks (including Edge Act corporations and U.S. branches of certain foreign banks) for up to 100% of a note's value. Applications for advance commitments must be made prior to shipment of the goods and are a prerequisite for subsequently gaining eligibility for the Discount Loan Program or a guarantee of notes under this program.

Eximbank purchase of notes also is available for "switch cover" transactions to encourage sales of U.S. equipment already in the inventory of foreign dealers (i.e., sales to end buyers). In order to be eligible, the contract value of the transaction must exceed $25,000 and Eximbank must have been involved in financing the original export sale to the dealer.

Long-Term Programs. Long-term programs involving direct loans and financial guarantees are the primary Eximbank facilities for the promotion of U.S. exports of capital goods and services. The bank can provide either a direct loan for a portion of the financing or financial guarantees of private financing or both. Repayment terms for the financed portion generally extend from five to 10 years and Eximbank often will agree to being repaid after the private sector financing institution.

Typically, the foreign buyer must make a cash payment of at least 15% of the contract price; a commitment fee of 0.5% annually is levied on the undisbursed portion of a direct loan; a guarantee fee is charged on outstanding balances of a guaranteed loan; and a 0.125% annual commitment fee is assessed on the undisbursed portion of a guaranteed loan. The basic interest rate is fixed at the inception of Eximbank's commitment and usually is paid (along with principal) in equal semiannual installments beginning six months after the date of shipment or project completion.

At no fee, the Eximbank can provide **preliminary commitments** describing the terms and conditions it is prepared to make available for its programs. With this assurance, the U.S. exporter has enhanced ability to structure its bid on foreign projects and otherwise plan its export activities. An application for a preliminary commitment is made directly to Eximbank by the prospective borrower, the U.S. exporter, or its bank in the form of a letter describing the following details of the transaction.

- Description of the borrower and its operations, including financial statements
- Purpose of the requested financing and its relationship to the entire project's costs (including other possible financing sources)
- Description of the goods and services to be purchased and the exporter, if known
- Copy of bid document, if any
- Whether a guarantee of the proposed financing is available from the host country's government, one of its banks, or some other source
- The borrower's projected financial data for the next five years or the project's construction period, whichever is longer
- Engineering and marketing data demonstrating the economic and technical feasibility of the transaction
- Information regarding known foreign competition for the contemplated sale, including availability of similar products and their financing terms
- A description of the effect of the sale on the U.S. exporter's labor force, as well as major subcontractors and small and minority-owned firms, if known
- Results of efforts to gain similar support from other sources (generally, commercial banks)

Should the exporter, importer, or participating bank not have sufficient information to apply for a preliminary commitment, it can seek a **letter of interest** from the Eximbank based on what data it does have available. This letter provides an informal indication of the bank's general attitude and the type of additional material it will need in order to make a formal commitment for financial assistance. The bank will not provide even tentative terms and conditions for its involvement except in the context of a preliminary or final commitment review.

The actual application for the direct loan must be made by the prospective buyer (i.e., the foreign importer). Essentially the same type of information noted above as required for a preliminary commitment is pertinent at this stage and it must be presented in considerable detail.

Additional Activities

Private Export Funding Corporation. Created in 1970 at the initiative of the Bankers' Association for Foreign Trade, PEFCO provides private capital to supplement Eximbank export promotion programs. It primarily purchases debt obligations of foreign importers of U.S. goods or services and receives 100% Eximbank guarantees on them. Typically, where PEFCO is involved in a transaction, the Eximbank and one or more commercial banks will also participate. PEFCO normally will purchase the medium-term notes in excess of $1 million, but it has the flexibility to accept any length of maturities of an Eximbank-approved credit.

Funds for PEFCO are raised by its sale of debt obligations secured through a pledge of its Eximbank guaranteed loans; interest on secured obligations is guaranteed directly by the Eximbank. It also sells short-term unsecured notes.

The corporation is entirely private and its stock is held by approximately 54 commercial banks, seven industrial corporations, and one investment bank. Firms interested in obtaining PEFCO assistance should contact the agency or one of the shareholder banks, a list of which can be obtained from PEFCO at 280 Park Avenue, New York, New York 10017; (212) 557-3100.

Small business assistance programs. While the Eximbank recently has been criticized for the extent of its commitments to a few major industries and firms (three corporations—Boeing, Westinghouse, and General Electric—are the beneficiaries of more than 25% of the current outstanding Eximbank credit commitment of approximately $27 billion), it is making an effort to assist small business exporters. While principal programs are available to any U.S. exporter, regardless of size, it provides several special services to small businesses, including seminars and in-house training. Further information can be obtained from the Advisory Service for Small Business, Export-Import Bank of the United States, 811 Vermont Avenue, NW, Washington, D.C. 20571; (202) 566-8883.

Feasibility studies. The Eximbank will make available FCIA insurance, commercial bank guarantees, and CFF programs for the domestic costs of feasibility studies. If the project is actually implemented, those costs can be refinanced, but Eximbank assumes no obligation to do so. Its evaluation of applications for feasibility study support is based on the creditworthiness of the foreign client and not of the underlying project itself.

Credit information. For the benefit of U.S. exporters and financial institutions (regardless of whether they are customers), the Eximbank maintains a public file with credit information on thousands of foreign firms and financial institutions.

Orientation programs. In addition to the counseling available by telephone, by correspondence, or in person from Eximbank staff members, they will conduct in-house orientation programs of one or two days to familiarize the business community with its programs. Details can be obtained from the Public Affairs Office, Export-Import Bank of the United States, 811 Vermont Avenue, NW, Washington, D.C. 20572; (202) 566-8990.

OVERSEAS PRIVATE INVESTMENT CORPORATION. The Overseas Private Investment Corporation (OPIC) was created by Congress in 1969 and most recently reauthorized in 1981 with the stated objective "to mobilize and facilitate the participation of United States private capital and skills in the economic and social development of less developed friendly countries and areas, thereby complementing the development assistance objectives of the United States." (OPIC's legislative authority can be found in Title 22 of the *United States Code*, Section 2191; its regulations are contained in Title 22 of the *Code of Federal Regulations*, parts 705–710.) In fulfilling that mandate, OPIC has established two programs: (1) insurance of U.S. private investment in developing countries against such political risks as inconvertibility of currency and losses due to expropriation or war, and (2) financing for the identification and promotion of investment projects by U.S. investors in those countries. Though wholly owned by the U.S. government, the agency is required to operate on a self-sustaining basis and thus charges fees and premiums for its services.

Programs under OPIC are available to U.S. citizens, businesses substantially owned by U.S. citizens and wholly owned foreign subsidiaries of such U.S. firms. Special consideration is provided to small businesses. The foreign investment for which assistance is sought must be in one of the more than 95 less-developed friendly countries with which the United States has concluded a bilateral agreement for this purpose. (These countries are listed in Exhibit 2) If that country's average per capita income exceeds $2,950 (in 1979 dollars), however, OPIC's program options are restricted to small business-sponsored projects, energy or mineral exploration in a non-OPEC country, special contractor guarantee coverage, projects reinsured by OPIC, and projects approved on a case-by-case basis by the OPIC Board of Directors.

Broad flexibility is employed in determining the eligibility of a particular investment since it is OPIC's purpose to encourage investments to the extent possible. It primarily is interested in new projects, though it will consider investments for the purpose of modernization, expansion, or buy-outs. For these purposes, Congress defined "investment" in OPIC's authorizing legislation to include

EXHIBIT 2 COUNTRIES FOR WHICH OPIC WILL OFFER SERVICES

Afghanistan	Guatemala	Paraguay
Antigua	Guinea	Peru
Argentina	Guyana	Philippines
Bangladesh	Haiti	Portugal
Barbados	Honduras	Romania
Belize	India	Rwanda
Benin	Indonesia	St. Kitts–Nevis
Bolivia	Israel[a]	St. Lucia
Botswana	Ivory Coast	St. Vincent
Brazil	Jamaica	Saudi Arabia[a]
Burundi	Jordan	Senegal
Cameroon	Kenya	Sierra Leone
Central African Republic	Korea	Singapore[a]
Chad	Lebanon	Somali Republic
Chile	Lesotho	Sri Lanka
China, People's Republic of	Liberia	Sudan
Colombia	Madagascar	Swaziland
Congo, People's Republic of	Malawi	Syria
Costa Rica	Malaysia	Taiwan
Cyprus	Mali	Tanzania
Dominica	Malta	Thailand
Dominican Republic	Mauritania	Togo
Ecuador	Mauritius	Trinidad-Tobago[a]
Egypt	Morocco	Tunisia
El Salvador	Nepal	Turkey
Ethiopia	Netherlands Antilles	Uganda
Fiji	Nicaragua	Upper Volta
Gabon[a]	Niger	Venezuela[a]
Gambia	Nigeria	Western Samoa
Ghana	Oman[a]	Yemen Arab Republic
Greece[a]	Pakistan	Yugoslavia
Grenada	Panama	Zaire
	Papua New Guinea	Zambia
		Zimbabwe (pending)

[a]Coverage by OPIC is limited because of relatively higher per capita income.

> any contribution of funds, commodities, services, patents, processes, or techniques, in the form of (1) a loan or loans to an approved project, (2) the purchase of a share of ownership of any such project, (3) participation in royalties, earnings, or profits of any such project, and (4) the furnishing of commodities or services pursuant to a lease or other contract.

Equivalent breadth is applied to the definition of an eligible project as long as it satisfies the basic criterion of having a positive development impact. OPIC also must determine that the project would not have any significant adverse effects on the U.S. economy, balance of payments, or employment. Other guidelines require the agency to foster private initiative and competition and discourage monopolistic practices (including discriminatory treatment by the host government), comply with all local (and possibly U.S.) environmental laws, and satisfy human rights considerations described previously regarding Eximbank activities. As a result of the 1981 legislation that reauthorized OPIC, the agency has the additional obligations to emphasize projects having positive trade benefits for the United States and reject projects subject to "performance requirements" (e.g., minimum export or local content standards) which would substantially reduce such positive trade benefits.

Insurance Programs. Insurance coverage by OPIC is solely for the political risks of inconvertibility, expropriation, and war, revolution, or insurrection and civil strife (as a result of the 1981 legislation). Coverage is not available for normal commercial risks.

The **inconvertibility** coverage is intended to ensure that such payments as earnings, principal, royalties, and contractual remittances can continue to be transferred into U.S. dollars to the same extent permitted when the insurance was issued. Thus, it is designed to protect against exchange control changes, hard currency shortages, or discriminatory treatment—but not devaluation actions.

Expropriation coverage is available in the event of nationalization of an enterprise or property or less drastic governmental action that continues for over one year. The action must further have had such effects as restricting receipt of remittances due the investor or limiting the investor's rights as a shareholder or creditor (unless it is a result of lawful official action reasonably related to a governmental objective, it was provoked by the investor or enterprise, or several other factors). Compensation by OPIC under this program is calculated based on the original amount of the insured investment, adjusted for retained earnings (or losses) and any prior recoveries of investment as of the date of the expropriation. Normally in such cases, OPIC will require that the investor's equity interest in the property be assigned to the agency, thereby denying the investor the ability to obtain reimbursement for previous losses or reduced investment values, while retaining the possibility of receiving future gains from the investment.

Coverage is available to protect against **war, revolution, or insurrection,** regardless of whether a formal declaration of war has been declared. Equity and debt investments and construction contracts are covered to the proportionate extent of the insured's interest. Continued defaults on scheduled payments of principal or interest as well as loss of a physical asset are covered.

Application for OPIC insurance is made by filing a request for a registration letter prior to the applicant's irrevocable commitment to the investment. The request can be made on OPIC Form 50 and must contain the following information.

Identity of the investor

Citizenship eligibility of the investor

Country or territory in which the investment is to be made

Brief description of the project

Statement that the investment has not yet been made nor irrevocably committed

Type of investment contemplated (e.g., equity or loan), kind of insurance coverages desired, and estimates of the amount under each coverage which can later be altered by the applicant)

OPIC usually responds within a few days, but if it issues a registration letter, that only is intended to establish the timeliness of the application and is not a binder or commitment to issue insurance. Once registered, the investor will receive a formal application from OPIC and should file it as soon as the final dimensions of the investment are reasonably clear. Among other data, the filing requires a showing that the applicant has obtained approval for the project and for OPIC participation from the host government.

General inquiries regarding OPIC's insurance programs and requests for registration letters should be addressed to the Application Officer, Overseas Private Investment Corporation, 1129 20th Street, NW, Washington, D.C. 20527; (202) 653-2962.

Financing Programs. The OPIC finance program uses a variety of loan and loan guarantee vehicles in a type of project-financing manner to assist participation by U.S. firms in overseas investments. The principal programs involve (1) direct loans, (2) loan guarantees issued to private U.S. financial institutions, and (3) feasibility survey assistance. Usually a combination of these services is utilized.

In order to be eligible for one of the programs, the project must be commercially and financially sound; OPIC does not offer concessionary terms. The host country must approve both the project and OPIC's participation. The project must make a meaningful contribution to the host country, such as increased availability of goods and services of better quality or at lower cost; creation of employment opportunities and development of skills through training; transfer of technology and managerial skills; increases in foreign exchange earnings or savings; increases in host country tax revenues; or stimulation of other local enterprises.

The extent of OPIC's participation varies, based on the project's likely contribution to the host country's development, the project's financial requirements, and the relative extent of risk shared by investors and lenders (a ratio of 40% equity to 60% debt is usually satisfactory). Typically, OPIC will support between 35% and 45% of a new project's costs, but never more than 50%. The proceeds of OPIC financing should be spent for capital goods and services in the United States, the host country, or in other developing countries; if substantial portions are to be spent in industrialized countries, OPIC expects that amount to be financed elsewhere.

Direct Loans. The program of direct loans is essentially limited to private sector projects sponsored by small businesses or cooperatives and, in 1982, was authorized at 10 million. Through this vehicle, OPIC will bear the commercial as well as the political risks. While OPIC cannot take an equity interest in the venture, it does make loans in the form of convertible notes with profit participation features. Those notes often are later sold to local investors, thereby expanding the domestic capital market.

Repayment schedules are flexible so as to respond to the purpose of the loan and the borrower's early ability to generate sufficient cash flows—usual terms involve a grace period followed by semiannual payments for five to 12 years. Interest rates also vary, depending on OPIC's assessment of the risks and its opportunity to share in the venture's ultimate success.

Guaranteed Loans. For financing requirements of up to $50 million, OPIC can provide a guarantee to a U.S. financial institution (including insurance companies and pension funds) prepared to lend funds for an OPIC-approved venture. The guarantee is an irrevocable OPIC commitment, backed by its cash reserve and the full faith and credit of the government, that it will make good on any defaults in the payment of principal or interest by the borrower. The agency's commitment is unconditional; regardless of the reason for the borrower's default or whether the lender has pursued other remedies against the borrower, OPIC will provide prompt payment. In recent years, OPIC has provided close to $200 million annually in such guarantees.

Interest rates on guaranteed loans must be comparable to those of other government-guaranteed issues and must be approved by OPIC. As well, OPIC assesses the borrower a guarantee fee on the outstanding principal, ranging from 1.75% to 2.5% a year, depending on the agency's commercial and political assessment of the venture.

Firms interested in applying for OPIC financing or guarantees should provide the following preliminary information in summary form in order to establish general eligibility.

Name, location, and business of the proposed project

Identity, background, and financial statements of the principal sponsors

Planned sources of supply, anticipated output and market, distribution channels, and the basis for projecting market share

Summary of costs and sources of procurement of capital goods and services

Proposed financing plan, including the amount of OPIC participation anticipated and financial projections

Brief statement of the contribution the business is expected to make to local economic and social development.

Based on this information, the OPIC staff will undertake a preliminary review and possibly request further specifics in a formal application for financing. Normally, OPIC requires from one to six months to process the formal application, largely depending on the completeness of the information provided to it and the time required to handle all the ancillary negotiations.

Feasibility Surveys. On a cost-sharing basis with private firms, OPIC will sponsor a study of the feasibility of an identified foreign investment. Small businesses can apply for such assistance for any country in which OPIC operates; firms in the Fortune 1,000 category can only apply when the study is proposed in a country with a per capita income of or below $680 (in 1979 dollars).

The basic eligibility criterion is that the sponsoring company must have a sound operating record, and, if the project proves feasible, have the ability to implement it and the intention to do so. As well, the project must appear economically viable for the sponsor, the host country, and the United States. Normally, OPIC will fund the lesser of $50,000 or 50% of the budgeted study costs. If an investment results from a study in which OPIC participates, its costs are included in the overall project financing.

Applications for feasibility financing should contain the following data to permit OPIC to make a preliminary determination of eligibility.

- Location and business of the proposed project
- Identity, background, and financial statements of the principals, in a form sufficient to establish their financial and managerial ability to undertake an eventual project
- Nature and results of preliminary or reconnaissance studies
- Scope of the survey, outlining in detail the factors to be studied
- Preliminary budget for the survey, indicating the members of the study team
- Tentative estimate of total project costs should the results be positive, and the applicant's contemplated investment in the project
- Brief statement of the contribution the project can be expected to make to local economic and social development

Should OPIC be preliminarily interested in participating in the feasibility study based on this information, it will work with the sponsor to prepare final scope of work and budget documentation, including the extent of OPIC involvement.

Preliminary applications and questions regarding OPIC financing of loans, guarantees, or feasibility studies for specific projects should be addressed to the Vice President for Finance, Overseas Private Investment Corporation, 1129 29th Street, NW, Washington, D.C. 20527; (202) 653-2870.

COMMODITY CREDIT CORPORATION. The Commodity Credit Corporation (CCC) was created by the U.S. Department of Agriculture to finance all of its dealings with the public in the sale of commodities. The export support programs that it administers include Public Law 480 (PL 480), Export Credit Sales Program (GSM 5), Noncommercial Risk Assurance Program (GSM 101), and Export Credit Guarantee Program (GSM 102).

Public Law 480. The 1954 statute creating Public Law 480 established a concessionary aid program to sell food to developing countries, originally with the objective of diminishing U.S. agricultural surpluses and now also for humanitarian and development purposes. It provides the CCC with the capability to negotiate agreements with such countries for their purchase of U.S. commodities. The agreements are negotiated yearly and typically provide for 20- to 40-year repayment periods, with interest set at approximately 3% annually.

Once an agreement is concluded, the terms are published and approved exporters can bid through the CCC. (Approval is obtained by having exported previously through the program or by posting a specified performance bond.) The importing government selects one of the bids, based on price and reputation of the bidder. The CCC can finance the entire transaction or can require the importing government to handle a portion, but in either case a letter of credit is opened in favor of the exporter and the exporter is assured of payment in full prior to shipping the commodities.

Export Credit Sales Program. The Export Credit Sales Program provides for CCC-subsidized interest rates for the financing of export sales of certain agricultural products (primarily cotton, tobacco, and rice), breeding swine, and cattle. Once an exporting firm identifies a possible contract opportunity, it seeks a CCC determination that funds will be available at the discounted interest rate if it obtains the award. Negotiations take place directly between the exporting and the importing firm. If the exporting firm is the successful bidder, it will be paid by the CCC upon shipment of the goods and assignment to the CCC of the commodity accounts receivable, even though the importing firm can defer payment for up to three years.

Noncommercial Risk Assurance Program. Under this program, CCC serves as an insurer against such noncommercial risks as war, civil disturbance, expropriation, and inconvertibility of funds. Its facilities are made available by the Department of Agriculture on a periodic basis regarding the export of particular commodities to specified countries. Interested exporters must negotiate a contract with a foreign buyer and obtain a deferred payment letter of credit from the buyer's bank. The exporter then can apply to the CCC for an assurance agreement, which essentially guarantees payment by the foreign issuing bank.

Export Credit Guarantee Program. The Export Credit Guarantee Program is designed to use guarantees to protect the exporter of commodities against loss from defaults in payment due to either commercial or noncommercial risks. Subsequent to the sale of the goods and the opening of a letter of credit by the foreign importer, the exporter can apply to the CCC for a payment guarantee. Once approved and the guarantee fee paid (which varies in amount based on length and risk), the CCC will reimburse the exporter for the amount due under the contract in the event that the foreign bank fails to remit it to the exporter.

Further information regarding any of the CCC programs can be obtained from the Export Programs Division, Foreign Agricultural Service, United States Department of Agriculture, 14th and Independence Avenue, SW, Washington, D.C. 20250; (202) 447-6225.

NON-U.S. EXPORT FINANCING AND INSURANCE PROGRAMS

As Exhibit 3 indicates, each of the major industrialized nations has comparable and often superior programs to that of the Eximbank and OPIC. Each offers two major categories of programs—insurance against the importer's default and insurance coupled with subsidized credit to enable the exporter or its banker to offer the buyer deferred payment terms or straight credit on preferential terms. The principal European agencies primarily provide guarantees (rather than loans) and thus are able to participate in considerably more export transactions than their U.S. counterpart.

While the Eximbank estimates that its programs affect 7% of U.S. exports (others estimate that figure at 20%), it approximates its competitors have assisted 39% of Japan's exports, 35% of the United Kingdom's, 33% of France's, and 11% of West Germany's. Interestingly, two of the dominant exporters—Japan and West Germany—sponsor quite disparate export support programs and two of the heaviest financial supporters of their country's exports—Great Britain and France—have had relatively little success with their programs. Though the true impact of these efforts is unclear, the respective governments continue to emphasize their importance.

What follows is a general overview of several of the principal non-U.S. agencies involved in assisting their country's exports (see Exhibit 4). Details can be obtained from the governments or the OECD or Library of Congress volumes listed in the Bibliography at the end of this section.

UNITED KINGDOM. The U.K. Export Credits Guarantee Department (ECGD) offers the largest variety, though not the most concessionary, services of any national export credit organization. Unique among such organizations, it is an arm of the government and refinances certain export-related loans on behalf of the Bank of England as well as provides insurance and official credit support to commercial banks.

In the insurance area, ECGD will provide coverage to exporters and lending banks for up to 95% of both commercial and political risks (100% where it has provided a buyer credit guarantee to the bank). The ECGD's guarantee program enables U.K. banks to make available both supplier and buyer credits up to 85% of the value of the U.K. content of the contract (and up to 30% of the European Economic Community content). Interest subsidies are made available in pounds sterling as well as certain foreign currencies. The credit term can range up to 10 or 12 years after completion of the supplier's obligations and the interest rate is expressed as consistent with the international arrangement, as is the case with each of the major trading nations. Among its other programs, ECGD will provide insurance against exchange risks (to protect against currency fluctuations) and cost escalation risks (to protect against unavoidable cost increases involved in the sale of capital goods with a long delivery period).

FRANCE. The French export system is comprised of two distinct entities, La Compagnie Française d'Assurance pour le Commerce Extérieur (COFACE) and La Banque Française du Commerce Extérieur (BFCE). Export credit insurance is provided by COFACE for commercial and political risks (up to 90% of the financed amount for the French content and 40% of the European Economic Community content) and the agency must provide such insurance in the context of transactions receiving preferential financing where the repayment terms exceed three years. The basic preferential financing program (i.e., discounted export credits) is offered directly by the Bank of France (where repayment is scheduled from 18 months to seven years). Longer term credits are provided by BFCE, either directly or by discounting credits provided by commercial banks.

The French program has been viewed as the broadest and most concessionary. A 1978 Library of Congress study found that French firms are able to receive mixed credits (official export credits plus loans for exports to developing countries) at as low as 3% interest and 25-year repayment periods. Private banks that make medium-term, fixed-rate export loans can borrow against them with attractive refinancing arrangements from the French Central Bank. As with the U.K. program, COFACE will provide insurance against exchange and inflation risks. Occasionally, BFCE will extend credits to foreign buyers for the local costs associated with a French export project.

FEDERAL REPUBLIC OF GERMANY. The principal West German institutions in the export financing field are Hermes Kreditversicherungs-AG (Hermes), which handles insurance, Ausfuhrkredit GmbH (AKA), which is a commercial bank consortium offering export credits, and Kreditanstalt für Wiederaufbau (KfW), which is a government-operated development bank.

EXHIBIT 3

Technique	Canada	France	Italy	Japan
Direct suppliers' credits		85% long-term (7+ years); earlier maturities funded by refinancing facility (below)		50% of contract, 15% to 20% down, the rest financed privately
Direct buyers' credits	60% of contract, end maturities, long-term only, 15% to 20% down, rest private financing with earlier maturities	Same as direct suppliers' credits		Same as direct suppliers' credits
Refinancing facilities		Government refinances 60% to 72% private low-interest credits, with guarantee, at rates attractive to private banks	Rare; some interest rate subsidies for 85% private buyer or seller credits;	Refinancing of short-term credits at normal rates through central bank
Government loans to private banks				
Export insurance	90% of contract for short-term loans; 90% to 100% of contract for medium-term loans; rates based on risk; tailored policies	90% to 95% of contract; all goods, short-term; capital, goods, medium-term; LDC capital goods, long-term; risk-related rates	75% to 90% or less of contract on limited bases; for medium- and long-term; risk-related terms	60% to 90% contract, risk-related but generally low rates

The Netherlands	Switzerland	United Kingdom	West Germany	United States
			45% of long-term low-cost credits, mostly to LDCs; late maturities, private banks take earlier maturities	
		Foreign governments if competition merits, for medium and long-term credits		Average 42% long-term credits, capital goods, end maturities; private banks; early maturities USDA credits
Central bank refinancing for certain bank credits, discount rates; limited		85% of special rate bank credits, refinanced or subsidized at rates attractive to private banks; now emphasizes supporting foreign currency denomination loans	80% of certain low-rate, medium-term suppliers' credits discountable at central bank at attractive rate	Rediscounts some medium-term bank loans to foreign buyers; lines of credit to facilitate private export lending
Central bank loans, medium-term, using private credits as security				Medium-term CFF loans to foreign banks for 50% of their loans for U.S. exports
Some official reinsurance of private export insurance, at commercial rates	80% to 90% of contract insurable, short- and medium-term, risk-related rates	90% to 95% comprehensive insurance, short-term; 90% to 100%, for some medium-term capital goods; risk-related rates	Government reinsurance for some private insurance covering 85% to 90% of the export contract	Reinsures some private FCIA insurance, for 90% to 95% contract; of the market terms

EXHIBIT 3

Technique	Canada	France	Italy	Japan
Export loan guarantees	Rare	80% to 85% loan; heavy capital goods for long-term; light capital goods for medium-term guarantees		80% commercial risk on private bank loans
Mixed credits	Rare	For LDCs, 50% of contract loaned at low-interest, long-term (25-year) discount rate		For LDCs, mix of aid credits with export credits to yield low-rate (4% to 6.5%) long-term (25-year) loan
Special insurance programs		Exchange rate flux insurance; inflation indemnity insurance; heavily subsidized rates	Exchange rate flux insurance planned	Exchange rate flux insurance; performance bond insurance

Source. Library of Congress, *Export Stimulation Programs in the Major Industrial Countries*, U.S. Government Printing Office, Washington, D.C., 1978.

As has been noted, the official West German export-financing program is among the leanest of the trading countries. Hermes, a private insurance firm having the obligation to offer export insurance, will cover 85% of commercial risks and up to 90% of political risks, but such coverage is not a prerequisite to obtaining export credits. Preferential financing of export credits, however, is quite limited and essentially is handled by the private banking community. Hermes also will provide exchange rate risk insurance. Some funds are available through AKA for local cost supports, supplier credit refinancing, and buyer credits, but it basically is a private source of assistance, offering credits at market interest rates.

The largest West German program to assist exports is operated through KfW, the government's development agency. It provides medium- and long-term credits at concessional interest rates to West German exporters to developing countries or their foreign buyers for 45% of the project.

JAPAN. The Japanese have achieved major successes in a number of foreign markets, in large part due to the extensive assistance offered by official export assistance programs. Its principal agency, the Export-Import Bank of Japan (EXIM) was modeled after its namesake in the United States and has as its objective the promotion of Japanese exports by supplementing and encouraging commercial bank financing.

(Continued)

The Netherlands	Switzerland	United Kingdom	West Germany	United States
		90% to 95% in some cases; 100% for medium-term loans for capital goods, lines of credit, subsidized credits (above)		Guarantees bank loans associated with long-term, 100% medium-term credits
			See direct export credits	
		Inflation indemnity insurance; performance bond guarantees; both limited	Exchange rate flux insurance, commercially related rates	

study prepared for the House Committee on International Relations, 95th Congress, 2nd session,

More recently, in response to a large balance of payments surplus and a need for funds for natural resource development, EXIM also began providing financing for imports.

Suppliers' credits, particularly for heavy machinery and related services, are offered for up to 85% of the export value. Also available are long-term funds for foreign direct investment by Japanese firms and for foreign corporations to allow them to enter into joint ventures with Japanese firms. Buyers' credits can be loaned directly to foreign governments or financial institutions (including development banks) by EXIM to assist in the purchase of Japanese goods and services. Finally, EXIM is empowered to provide guarantees for import, export, and foreign direct investment credits provided by financial instutions, although both EXIM and the borrowers have preferred direct credits to guarantees.

Japan also has an extensive Export Insurance Scheme relating to credits provided by private banks as well as EXIM. Over 40% of Japanese exports are covered by one or more of the nine components of the scheme: offering insurance in the following areas: preexport finance insurance, performance and bid bonds, general exports, export proceeds, export bills, exchange rate fluctuation, consignment exports, overseas investments, and overseas advertisement.

In sum, then, even within the guidelines of the international arrangement, there

EXHIBIT 4 PRINCIPAL AGENCIES PROVIDING FOREIGN INVESTMENT INSURANCE[a]

Country	Agency	Acronym
Australia	Export Finance and Insurance Corporation	(EFIC)
Austria	Osterreichische Kontrollbank A.G.	(OKB)
Belgium	Office National du Ducroire	(OND)
Canada	Export Development Corporation	(EDC)
France	Compagnie Française d'Assurance pour le Commerce Extérieur	(COFACE)
	Banque Française du Commerce Extérieur	(BFCE)
Federal Republic of Germany	Treuarbeit Aktiengesellschaft	(TREUARBEIT)
India	Export Credit & Guarantee Corporation Limited	(ECGC)
Israel	The Israel Foreign Trade Risks Insurance Corporation Limited	(IFTRIC)
Japan	Export Insurance Division, Ministry of International Trade and Industry	(EID/MITI)
Korea	The Export-Import Bank of Korea	(EIBK)
New Zealand	Export Guarantee Office	(EXGO)
Norway	Garanti-Instituttet for Eksportkreditt	(GIEK)
South Africa	Credit Guarantee Insurance Corporation of Africa Limited	(CGIC)
Sweden	Exportkreditnamnden	(EKN)
Switzerland	Geschaftsstelle fur die Exportrisikogarantie	(GERG)
The Netherlands	Nederlandsche Credietverzekering Maatschappij NV	(NCM)
United Kingdom	Export Credits Guarantee Department	(ECGD)
United States	Overseas Private Investment Corporation	(OPIC)

[a]These agencies are members of the Investment Insurance Committee of the International Union of Credit and Investment Insurers (Berne Union).

is considerable diversity of export assistance programs among the major trading nations, and the United States is among the least active in the area. The Eximbank concentrates on direct loans and the discounting of export obligations held by commercial banks, while its competitors stress insurance and bank guarantees that enable support funds to be applied more widely. Most of the Eximbank's credits are long-term, whereas those of others are primarily short- and medium-term. In general, the European and Japanese programs offer a substantial reduction in the average cost of financing exports, thus providing them with a competitive edge even with the 1982 international arrangement revisions regarding minimum credit terms.

ASSISTANCE PROGRAMS OF THE INTERNATIONAL FINANCIAL INSTITUTIONS

The international financial institutions can be divided into two basic groups: the fully international agencies, comprised of the International Monetary Fund (IMF) and the World Bank Group—the International Bank for Reconstruction and Development

(IBRD, often referred to as the "World Bank"), the International Development Association (IDA), and the International Finance Corporation (IFC)—and the regional development banks. Since the objectives and many of the programs of the major regional banks (which have been established for Asia, the Caribbean Latin America, and Africa) are similar to those of the World Bank Group, they are not discussed separately here. The activities of the IMF also are not discussed as its primary purpose is not trade finance but correcting the balance of payments problems that may have been caused by disproportionate trade patterns. Details regarding IMF and World Bank Group activities and those of the agencies described briefly below can be obtained from their respective headquarters, which are listed in the Appendix of this section.

Technically, the **World Bank** is in the business of financing international development, not trade—and certainly not trade by the industrialized countries. Nevertheless, given the more than $12 billion that it annually makes available to international borrowers, it has an enormous impact on the financing of trade among nations. Exporters are encouraged to bid on contracts offered by the World Bank Group borrowers and occasionally by the Bank itself; success virtually assures prompt, uncomplicated payment to the exporter for the goods and services delivered. Careful monitoring of tender is required in order for an exporter to file a competitive bid.

The Bank also indirectly supports export activity by assisting infrastructure growth, which can be expected to lead to expanded export potential by the recipient developing country.

INTERNATIONAL BANK FOR RECONSTRUCTION AND DEVELOPMENT. Since its inception at the 1944 Bretton Woods Conference, the World Bank's objective has been "to help raise standards of living in developing countries by channeling financial resources from developed countries to the developing world." That goal has been pursued by a large variety of means, all involving loans dedicated to advancing either economic infrastructure or social service programs in member countries. Recently, the emphasis has shifted to concentrate bank activities on the poorest segments of society in developing countries. Thus, such capital infrastructure sectors as roads, railways, telecommunications, and power facilities, as well as programs to improve education, family planning, and nutrition, have been focused on aiding the "poorest of the poor". Since its inception, the World Bank has approved loan commitments for more than $80 billion.

The Bank is owned by the governments of its approximately 135 member countries and finances its activities from its own borrowings in the world capital markets, retained earnings (dividends are never paid), and repayments on prior loans. In contrast to the International Development Agency, World Bank lending activity is intended to benefit developing countries that are at relatively higher stages of economic and social growth. As such, the interest rate on its loans is only slightly above its own cost of obtaining the funds and the repayment period is set at a maximum of 20 years.

The basic operating rules for the Bank's programs are detailed in its charter:

1. Loans must be for productive purposes and intended to stimulate economic growth.
2. Consideration must be provided to the prospects of repayment and also the availability of alternative sources of funds (it is noteworthy that there never has been a default on a World Bank loan).

3. A government must be the debtor or the guarantor of every loan.
4. Loan proceeds cannot be restricted to purchases in any particular country.
5. Ultimate decisions must be based solely on economic considerations.

Recently, the Bank has sought to increase its effectiveness by participating directly with other finance sources in specific projects. This concept of **cofinancing** associates the Bank with one or more partners: (1) official sources, including governments, their agencies, and multilateral financial institutions; (2) export credit institutions such as those described in this section; and 3) private financial institutions, including commercial banks, insurance companies, and pension funds. In fiscal year 1980, the Bank cofinanced 93 projects (40% of its total), involving in excess of $6 billion. Cofinancing with export credit agencies was undertaken with regard to 23 projects that resulted in loans totaling $2.3 billion.

The principal instances in which the Bank has cofinanced loans with export credit agencies have involved imports of substantial quantities of equipment in the industrial, public utilities, and transportation sectors. While the Bank formerly administered the competitive bidding among export credit agencies, that function now has been assumed by the borrower. The Bank's role is limited to appraising and supervising the project and assisting the borrower in negotiating with the credit agencies and suppliers. Hence, an exporter with an opportunity to market goods in a developing country where the World Bank has shown interest in a project can be doubly benefited from the availability of Bank funds in addition to those of an export credit facility.

INTERNATIONAL DEVELOPMENT AGENCY. The International Development Agency (IDA) is an affiliate of the World Bank established in 1960 to provide special attention to the financial needs of the poorest countries. It makes available credits (in contrast to the World Bank's loans) with repayment periods of up to 50 years, without interest (although an administrative fee of 0.75% is charged on the disbursed portion of each credit). The IDA programs, which essentially parallel in type those of the World Bank, are limited to countries with annual per capita gross national products of less than $625 (in 1978 dollars). Under that standard, more than 50 countries presently qualify. Approximately 120 nations are members of IDA. The IDA's outstanding commitment of credits exceeds $20 billion, a sum that is derived from three sources: (1) primarily special capital contributions (replenishments) from wealthier IDA members; (2) capital subscriptions from all members; and (3) transfers from the World Bank's net earnings on its portfolio.

Through procedures parallel to those described regarding the World Bank, IDA participates in the cofinancing of projects with export credit agencies, as well as with other governmental entities and private financial institutions. In fiscal year 1980, for example, IDA committed in excess of $1.6 billion to cofinanced ventures.

The opportunity for firms to obtain export financing as a consequence of IDA programs is similar to that described regarding the IBRD.

INTERNATIONAL FINANCE CORPORATION. Unlike its affiliates in the World Bank Group, the International Finance Corporation (IFC) pursues both equity and debt relationships with the countries it serves. Established in 1956, its stated function is to assist the economic development of less-developed countries "by promoting growth in the private sector of their economies and helping to mobilize domestic and foreign capital for this purpose." While it can operate in any of its member countries, of which there are approximately 122, it is mandated by its charter to concentrate in the less developed countries.

The IFC's flexibility in pursuing its objective is limited only by the conditions that a project in which it participates (a) be a "productive private enterprise", (b) contribute to the growth of the host country's private sector, that it have a strong prospect of being profitable (i.e., that there is an apparent market for its goods and services), and (a) be properly engineered, managed, and financed. Prior to participation, the IFC also will determine whether alternative sources of financing are available at reasonable terms, since its purpose as a "lender of last resort" is to supplement rather than compete with private sources.

The agency will not assume an equity stake in excess of 50% and it rarely will seek to exercise its stockholder voting rights. The agency will only participate in ventures in which local investors have the ability initially or in a secondary market to purchase shares—and the IFC charter mandates a sale of its stock i.e., "revolving of funds", after the venture is well established. As a matter of practice, the IFC's investment for its own account usually ranges between \$1 and \$30 million in any single project and is intended to be long-term in nature.

The basic IFC participation model involves a conventional loan and occasionally a direct subscription to equity. It has the ability, however, to lend funds without a right of conversion to equity. In whatever form the IFC's participation might assume, it will work with the project managers to obtain equity and debt participations from other institutional investors. Additionally, the technical expertise of its staff and that of the World Bank is available to assist the creation and operation of the private enterprises that meet its criteria for investment.

Activities of the IFC include direct underwriting international bond issues by major companies in developing countries, establishing joint ventures with foreign partners in a specific private project, acceptance of standby or underwriting commitments involving public or private stock offerings for subsequent resale, support of capital markets in developing countries to promote domestic savings and indigenous securities markets, and strengthening of regional and local development finance companies that perform a role similar to that of the IFC on smaller projects.

As with the other international financial institutions, the relationship of the IFC to export financing, although indirect, is substantial. While a firm cannot seek financing from the IFC for its exporting activities, it can profit as a result of IFC operations in a way similar to the activities of other members of the World Bank Group.

BIBLIOGRAPHY

Annual Report of the Export-Import Bank of the United States.

Annual Report of the Overseas Private Investment Corporation.

Comptroller General of the United States, *Report to Congress: Financial and Other Constraints Prevent Eximbank from Consistently Offering Competitive Financing for U.S. Exports*, U.S. Government Printing Office, Washington, D.C., 1980.

Exporters Financial and Marketing Handbook, Noyes Data Corporation, Park Ridge, N.J., 1973.

Finance Handbook, Overseas Private Investment Corporation, 1980.

Financing International Operations, American Management Association, New York, 1979.

International Investment: A Guide for Executives of Smaller Companies, Overseas Private Investment Corporation, Washington, D.C., 1978.

Investment Insurance Handbook, Overseas Private Investment Corporation, Washington, D.C., 1980.

Library of Congress, *Export Stimulation Programs in the Major Industrial Countries*, study prepared for the House Committee on International Relations, 95th Congress, 2nd session, U.S. Government Printing Office, Washington, D.C., 1978.

Organization for Economic Co-operation and Development, *The Export Credit Financing Systems in OECD Member Countries*, OECD, Paris, 1976.

Rendell, R. S. (Ed.), *International Financial Law*, Euromoney Publications, London, 1980.

Samuelson, R. J., "The Export Credit Subsidy Game: If You Can't Lick 'em, Join 'em," *National Journal*, April 1979.

Small Business Administration, *Export Marketing for Smaller Firms*, U.S. Government Printing Office, Washington, D.C., 1979.

United States Department of Commerce, *A Basic Guide to Exporting*, U.S. Government Printing Office, Washington, D.C.

Zenoff, D. and J. Zwick, *International Financial Management*, Prentice-Hall, Englewood Cliffs, N.J., 1969.

APPENDIX. DIRECTORY: SOURCES OF INFORMATION

ORGANIZATIONS (UNITED STATES)

Commodity Procurement Program
Office of Small Business
Agency for International Development
Washington, D.C. 20523
(202) 235-9155

Export-Import Bank of the United States
811 Vermont Avenue, N.W.
Washington, D.C. 20571
(202) 566-2117

Export Programs Division
Foreign Agricultural Service
Department of Agriculture
14th and Independence Avenues, S.W.
Washington, D.C. 20250
(202) 447-6225

Foreign Credit Insurance Association
Central Office
One World Trade Center, 9th Floor
New York, New York 10048
(212) 432-6200

FOREIGN CREDIT INSURANCE ASSOCIATION REGIONAL OFFICES

707 Wilshire Boulevard, Suite 3080
Los Angeles, California 90017
(213) 624-8412

1210 S. Omni International
Atlanta, Georgia 30303
(404) 522-2780

One World Trade Center
Ninth Floor
New York, New York 10048
(212) 432-6300

1425 H Street, NW, Suite 336
Washington, D.C. 20005
(202) 638-5028

20 N. Clark Street, Suite 804
Chicago, Illinois 60602
(312) 641-1915

55 Public Square, Suite 1300
Cleveland, Ohio 44113
(216) 523-1520

One Houston Center, Suite 1210
Houston, Texas 77002
(713) 759-1114

700 N. Water Street, Suite 1200
Milwaukee, Wisconsin 53202
(414) 224-0240

National Association of Export Management Companies
65 Liberty Street
New York, New York 10005
(212) 561-2025

Overseas Private Investment Corporation
1129 20th Street, N.W.
Washington, D.C. 20527
(800) 424-6742 or (202) 653-2800

Private Export Funding Corporation
280 Park Avenue
New York, New York 10017
(212) 557-3100

INTERNATIONAL AND REGIONAL DEVELOPMENT INSTITUTIONS

African Development Bank
B.P. 1387
Abidjan 01
Ivory Coast

Asian Development Bank
P.O. Box 789
Metro Manila
Philippines

Inter-American Development Bank
808 17th Street, N.W.
Washington, D.C. 20577
(202) 634-8000

International Bank for Reconstruction & Development
International Development Agency
International Finance Corporation
1818 H Street, N.W.
Washington, D.C. 20433
(202) 477-1234

International Monetary Fund
700 19th Street, N.W.
Washington, N.W. 20431
(202) 477-7000

SECTION 7.3

INTERNATIONAL PROJECT FINANCE

CONTENTS

SECTION 7.3

INTERNATIONAL PROJECT FINANCE

Larry Wynant

OVERVIEW OF PROJECT FINANCING

Project financing, a popular vehicle for funding large-scale international projects, is defined as the financing of an economic entity in which lenders look primarily to the earnings and assets of the entity to service the debt obligations. Capital needs for mining and energy ventures have escalated dramatically in the recent past; consequently, these industries have led in the development of project financing techniques. However, project financing is now finding widespread application in other industrial sectors, including transportation, power, chemicals, forestry products, and agribusiness. The project-financing approach can be useful for almost any venture where the company views the capital needs or risks to be too substantial to fund the project from its general resources.

Segregation of the project and its financing needs from the sponsoring company is the unique characteristic of project financing that sets it apart from traditional financing methods. Lending on a project basis contrasts with traditional lending in which a borrower's total resources are available as a source of repayment. In practice, definitions of project financing run the gamut, depending on the particular objectives or advantages that the financing package is designed to achieve and the degree of recourse that the project's lenders have to the sponsoring company. Pure project financings, those in which the lenders have no recourse to the project's shareholders, are rare. Most project loans require some credit support from the sponsors, and these support arrangements can range from limited recourse agreements to complete loan guarantees. Despite the varied interpretation and uses of the term, project-financing structures generally have important common characteristics.

1. The project is established as a **separate legal entity** and **finances a large proportion,** generally 65% to 75%, of its capital requirements with debt.
2. The borrowings are **direct obligations** of the project and and guarantees provided by the sponsor(s) are **limited.**
3. **Commitments by third parties** (suppliers, customers, and government agencies) provide vital elements of credit support for the lenders.
4. The project's debt arrangements are engineered to have a **minimum impact** on the parents' balance sheet and credit capacity.

DEVELOPMENT OF THE PROJECT-FINANCING CONCEPT. The basic notion underlying project financing, namely, linking the loan to the asset being developed, is not a new concept. Nonrecourse lending originated in the United States in the 1920s with the need to exploit oil reserves in Texas. Since most developers had very limited equity to support their borrowing requests, banks began to look carefully at the value of the reserves in place and the security of agreements by large refiners to purchase the crude. Other variants of the project-financing approach emerged. Captive finance companies, borrowings arranged directly by a subsidiary rather than through its parent, and the financing of start-up situations could all be considered forms of project financing.

However, project financing received increased attention over the past 20 years as **large international ventures** began to require new and imaginative financing approaches. The challenge of raising huge sums of money for projects, sometimes located in remote areas and often entailing considerable technical, business, and political risks, forced further development and refinement of project-financing techniques. Three factors in particular contributed to the growth of project financing.

1. The **capital needs** of certain industries burgeoned under the pressure of inflation and technological needs.
2. **Governments and international funding agencies** became more involved in funding international projects.
3. The **major lending institutions** developed the capacity to analyze and assume project risks.

Numerous recent projects have consumed capital in amounts that are massive by historical standards. A combination of **inflation,** a need for **complex and innovative technology,** and considerations of the **economies of scale** have generated costs for new or increased capacity that strain the financial capabilities of even the largest multinational companies. In addition, the developmental nature and political uncertainties of many of these projects involve dollar risks of such magnitude that the project's failure could spell disaster for the sponsoring firm. The mining and energy industries have been hit particularly hard by escalating costs. Exhibits 1 and 2 indicate the types of financing pressures faced by firms in those industries. A new mining venture costing \$100 to \$200 million would have been considered enormous only a decade ago. Today, projects are calling for expenditures of several billions of dollars and capital needs will likely continue to mushroom. Current projections for the energy industries (shown in Exhibit 2), for example, suggest that capital pressures will continue to mount over the coming decade. Forecasted expenditures for mining, forest products, transportation, and chemical projects around the world display very similar trends.

Financing such large expenditures has been difficult, if not impossible, for many corporations. These capital requirements have risen at a time when the **flexibility** of many companies to raise external financing has also declined. Corporate treasurers over the past 15 years have used debt financing much more heavily than new equity to fund capital needs. Exhibit 3 illustrates the increased reliance that corporations have placed on leverage. By the 1970s, the ability of many industries to finance new projects through an expanding debt/equity ratio became questionable. At the same time, the attractiveness of raising new equity had been dampened by a generally inactive and depressed new issues market.

EXHIBIT 1 SURVEYS OF NEW MINING PROJECTS FOR SELECTED COMMODITIES, 1966–81

Estimated Capital Costs ($ millions)	Number of Projects 1966	1971	1981
ALUMINUM			
0– 100	23	21	1
101– 500	9	17	21
501–1000	—	—	16
1001–2000	—	—	5
Over 2 billion	—	—	2
Largest reported project	(375)	(400)	(2,500)
COPPER			
0– 100	55	38	21
101– 500	6	8	18
501–1000	—	—	2
Over 1 billion	—	—	10
Largest reported project	(208)	(418)	(1,500)
LEAD AND ZINC			
0–100	9	15	9
101–500	—	—	10
Largest reported project	(68)	(70)	(500)
IRON ORE			
0– 100	15	17	2
101– 500	—	12	6
501–1000	—	1	3
1001–2000	—	—	—
Over 2 billion	—	—	1
Largest reported project	(100)	(550)	(3,600)
OIL AND SHALE AND SANDS			
0– 100	NA	NA	3
101– 500	NA	NA	3
501–1000	NA	NA	1
1001–2000	NA	NA	2
Over 2 billion	NA	NA	9
Largest reported project	NA	NA	(8,000)

Source. Engineering and Mining Journal, 1966, 1971, 1981.

Note. Based on McGraw-Hill Publications Company annual surveys of mine and plant expansions in progress or at a proposal stage. Only those projects for which capital costs estimates were provided are included.

EXHIBIT 2 ACTUAL AND FORECAST CAPITAL REQUIREMENTS FOR THE ENERGY INDUSTRIES (in billions of current dollars)

	Fixed Capital Spending		
Industry	1979	1980	1981–90
Oil and gas	34.2	40.9	893.8
Alternative fuels	3.5	3.6	74.3
Electric utility	35.3	35.3	611.7
Nuclear fuel cycle	1.9	2.4	70.9
Gas utility	4.2	5.2	109.8
Total energy industries	79.4	87.9	1,850.8

Source. *Iron Age,* March 1981.

Capital-intensive industries, therefore, have been forced to search out new funding vehicles and sources. This need, combined with an increased willingness by government funding agencies and private lenders to lend on a project basis, has given rise to the popularity of project financing.

Governments of the industrialized nations have stepped up their financing activities for international projects. Most of these nations now offer **direct financing** and **loan guarantees** to stimulate exports, facilitate foreign investment by domestic firms, and in some instances, to help local companies compete for markets and access to raw materials. Financing support can be arranged directly by a project and on attractive terms.

Over the past 10 to 15 years, the large international lending institutions, primarily the **commercial banks,** have been more willing to lend on a project-financing basis. These institutions have developed an in-house capacity to recognize and assess project risks and to assume certain risks in return for higher loan spreads or other forms of compensation.

EXHIBIT 3 USE OF LEVERAGE IN SELECTED U.S. INDUSTRIES, 1960–80

	Ratio of Total Debt to Total Assets			
Industry	1960	1970	1975	1980
All manufacturing	0.35	0.46	0.51	0.50
Chemicals	0.32	0.44	0.45	0.47
Machinery	0.38	0.46	0.43	0.48
Paper and allied products	0.31	0.48	0.47	0.47
Petroleum refining[a]	0.25	0.38	0.38	0.48
Primary metals	0.32	0.47	0.47	0.54
Rubber and plastic products	0.38	0.51	0.49	0.53

Source. U.S. Federal Trade Commission, *Quarterly Financial Report for Manufacturing, Mining and Trade Corporations,* for the particular years, 1960–1980.

[a]Ratios are not strictly comparable because of changes in the industry's definition over the period.

ARRANGING PROJECT FINANCING. The widespread use of project financing, then, is in large part a forced consequence of the escalating costs of international projects. Many new undertakings simply cannot be accommodated through traditional, direct financing by the sponsor. But in addition to being a creation of necessity, project financing can serve as a means of achieving **financial** and **strategic** objectives. The ultimate in project financing to the sponsor is to arrange a maximum amount of debt for the project and on a totally nonrecourse basis to the developing company. A project financing would enable the sponsor to achieve certain important objectives: (1) to finance most of the project's needs with **external debt financing;** (2) to reduce the sponsor's exposure to project failure by **transferring risks** to other parties; (3) to arrange a financing that is **off the balance sheet** and has a minimum impact on the sponsor's financial flexibility.

A host of other factors can be important in financing a new project, such as **tax considerations** and relations between the project and its parent or the parties in a **joint venture.** However, the sponsor's concerns with securing debt financing, reducing risks, and achieving a favorable balance sheet impact are the major motives underlying most project financings.

Commercial lenders, on the other hand, are only prepared to accept **normal credit risks.** They are not equity risk takers. Lenders will insist that the financing be well secured by either the earnings strength of the project, the general resources of the sponsor, or commitments by the third parties.

Achieving a high degree of leverage with limited recourse to the project sponsors, while maintaining an acceptable level of credit risk for the project loans, constitutes the **complexity and innovativeness** of the project-financing approach. The **key** to a successful project financing is **laying off** the major project risks to the equity owners or other third parties to the extent that they are unacceptable to private lenders. Exhibit 4 sketches the major considerations and activities that are at play in arranging a project financing. The financing package will differ for each project depending on its risks, capital requirements, and the funding groups that might be interested in participating in the venture. However, there are a number of major steps that a company and its financial advisors will have to follow in structuring a project financing: (1) carefully assessing the project's overall feasibility and major risks; (2) identifying the funding sources available to the project, the risks that they are prepared to assume, and the costs attached to the borrowed funds; (3) transferring or reducing project risks through lenders or by securing commitments from other third parties; and (4) structuring the ownership and credit arrangements to maintain the sponsor's financial flexibility.

RISK EVALUATION OF INTERNATIONAL PROJECTS

Large international resource projects face considerable risks of failure. Many of these projects require a long lead time for construction and development (as long as five to 10 years for mining ventures), are located in less advantageous areas, and depend on new technology for success. Offshore gas wells, for example, are now in deeper and colder waters and oil refineries are located farther from sources of equipment and skilled labor. Mining industries are also developing ore bodies with lower grades and situated in more remote locations. Once the project reaches an operating stage, uncertainties and risks associated with **operating costs, market prices,** and

EXHIBIT 4. STRUCTURING A PROJECT FINANCING

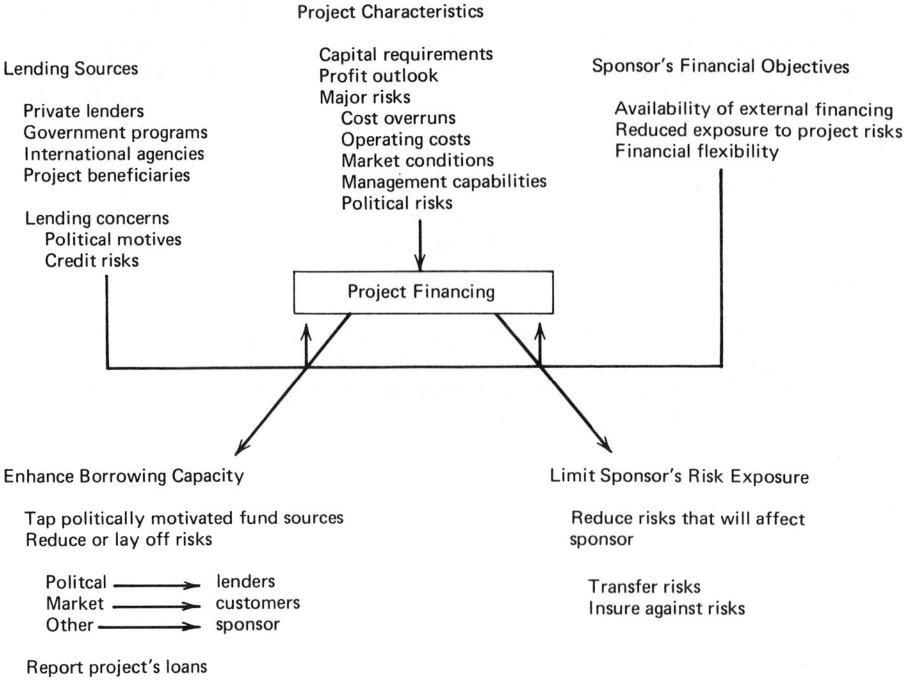

political developments will continue to threaten the project's viability. It is not surprising then to find that many resource projects have failed. A study undertaken at the Chemical Bank exaxined the major reasons for project failure for a sample of mining ventures initiated in the 1960s and 1970s. These causes are summarized in Exhibit 5.

Failure of a major project could have a tremendous impact on the parent, depending on the equity investment at stake, the company's commitments to lenders, and the general importance of the project in the company's overall operations. A critical first stage in deciding to develop a new project and to explore financing options is a careful assessment of the project's feasibility. Since lenders are asked to accept project risks in a nonrecourse or limited resource financing, they will independently subject the project to careful economic security.

EVALUATING PROJECT VIABILITY. The general characteristics of the project and its overall feasibility should be thoroughly investigated. The sponsor and lenders must be convinced that the project can be completed and operated as planned, that there is an assured market for the output, and that the profitability of the project will be sufficient to meet debt repayments and provide an attractive return on the equity invested. Staff professionals such as engineers and geologists, often supplemented by independent consultants, should assess the technical aspects of the projects—the quality and quantity of ore or oil reserves, the facilities and technological process required to produce output, and the fixed capital costs of the project. Analyzing the project's cash flows is a more difficult task since operating costs, market prices, and

EXHIBIT 5 TYPICAL CAUSES OF PROJECT FAILURES OR PROBLEMS

Construction delays and cost overruns
- Inflation
- Improperly designed or engineered facilities
- Disruptions in receipt of construction materials and equipment
- Labor difficulties
- Bankruptcy of the contractor

Operating and market problems
- Reserve miscalculations
- Inappropriate process design
- Increases in energy and raw material costs
- Lack of skilled labor, strikes, boycotts
- Increases in labor rates
- Volatile market prices
- Violations of sales agreements

Management difficulties
- Inexperience of project sponsor
- Disagreements among partners in joint ventures

Financial costs
- Increased capital costs because of capitalized interest charges
- Higher interest rates
- Inability to refinance debt
- Foreign exchange losses

Political developments
- Expropriation
- Increased taxes and royalties
- Imposition of import duties on raw materials needed for the project
- Delays in completion caused by the time needed to obtain import licenses or required parts
- Currency inconvertibility and foreign exchange restrictions
- Restrictions on dividends
- War and social unrest

political interference can sharply affect profitability and are often difficult to predict with any degree of confidence.

Most large companies use **discounted cash flow (DCF)** techniques for evaluating a project's profitability. The DCF analysis requires an estimate of the project's cash flows using the company's best guess of future output levels, operating costs, market prices, and loan payments. Lenders will normally test the project's profitability under more conservative assumptions to ensure that the project can withstand some adverse developments and still generate sufficient revenues to service its loans.

The DCF technique is particularly appropriate for projects, such as oil and industrial projects, that have relatively short construction times, stable market conditions, and quick repayment periods. The DCF is more difficult to use as an evaluation approach for mining projects with long lead times, longer lives, volatile market prices, and huge profits when prices are at cyclical peaks. These uncertainties make a cash flow projection subject to large errors and therefore, of less usefulness. However, the DCF approach enables the sponsor or lender to alter key assumptions and to gauge the impact of such changes on the project's profits and cash flows. **Sensitivity analysis** is extremely important and requires that multiple forecasts be prepared or a simulation technique be used to produce probability distributions of the project's cash flows. Computerized financial packages are now available that enable an in-depth sensitivity analysis of the project's assumptions and forecasts. Sensitivity analysis can provide insights into those risks or uncertainties that are central to the project's success and, therefore, require further investigation.

The uncertainties inherent in long-term forecasts have led many companies to an alternative method of evaluating projects—comparing the **project's cost position** to that of competitors. If a mine, for example, is a low-cost producer relative to other suppliers of the mineral, then the project is given a go-ahead regardless of the current world metal prices. Advocates of this approach argue that demand and supply conditions will always adjust to permit a low-cost producer to be profitable over the life of a project.

Both the DCF technique and the relative cost position approaches are helpful in evaluating a project's feasibility. However, sizing up the project's attractiveness requires a judgment based not only on technical studies and cash flow projections but also on an assessment of the more general characteristics of the project and the risks that are likely to affect it.

TECHNICAL AND CONSTRUCTION RISKS. The long start-up period and complex technology required for large new ventures suggest that some projects will not be physically completed or will involve construction costs that destroy the economics of the venture. Many recent projects have entailed **cost overruns** as high as 100% of the original cost estimates. In some instances, unanticipated capital costs have been severe enough to cause the sponsors to abandon the project. The trans-Alaska pipeline, completed in the 1970s, is perhaps one of the most publicized examples of massive cost overruns. Capital costs for that project escalated by roughly 400% before the pipeline was fully operational. However, studies by Grover Castle (1975) and Richard Radez (1978) also found large overruns for new projects in six different industries. These overruns ranged between 5% and 300% and averaged nearly 100%.

Three major factors can contribute to the construction and technical risks of a project: (1) the **physical or logistical difficulties** associated with the project's location; (2) the **type of technology** required; (3) the **skills and experience** of the sponsors, the design engineers, and general contractors.

The location of the project will affect construction costs as well as operating expenses. A mining venture located high on a rugged mountainside or an oil exploration project in the Arctic will entail more sophisticated technology, often unproven, and therefore run the risks of project failure or cost overruns. Transportation of materials, supplies, and output to and from a remote location might also entail unexpected costs.

A project that requires new or untested technology will pose greater risks for the sponsors and lenders. Design changes at the application stages can cause serious completion delays and additional capital costs because of capitalized interest charges.

The likelihood of a project's being completed at a cost close to planned expenditures will be affected by the experience of the project sponsor, the design engineers, and the general contractor. A project developer lacking the experience to undertake a joint venture will often need to acquire the required skills through a joint venture with another company. The design engineers and contractor should have an established track record and worldwide reputation if the project is major. A contractor should also have adequate financial resources for completing large-scale ventures.

Construction and technical risks need careful assessment. A breakdown of estimated capital costs into major categories, such as engineering, equipment, labor, interest charges, and construction materials, should permit the sponsor to identify areas that are most vulnerable to overruns and technical difficulties.

OPERATING AND MARKET RISKS. A project's profitability and cash flows will depend on **output levels, operating costs,** and **market prices** for the product. The risks surrounding each of these profit components are numerous and depend to a large extent on the location and nature of the project. However, the major risks should be identified and built into the feasibility and DCF analysis.

Output capacity for a new venture can usually be forecast with a reasonably high level of confidence. Estimates of reserves and grades are often very precise for mining and oil and gas ventures. And production levels for an industrial project can be predicted accurately if the sponsor is using an established process. Output risks are greatest in those cases where (1) the process involves new technology and design and output specifications might be inaccurate; (2) energy and raw material sources are critical to the project and could be interrupted because of location or political factors; (3) the supply of skilled labor is inadequate or could be affected by strikes, social unrest, and the like.

Incorrect estimates of operating costs can also destroy a project's profitability. Several areas require close attention to determine the likelihood of problems.

1. The **cost of energy** can increase dramatically. This risk is particularly important when the project is energy-intensive and local energy sources are nonexistent or minimal.
2. Rapid **inflation** in the country can cause labor rates and energy or raw material costs in excess of planned levels.

A $400 million mining venture in Australia in the mid-70s, for example, used oil as a fuel source and the price of that commodity soared. Increased fuel costs, combined with other unexpected hikes in operating expenses, caused the sponsors to eventually write off their equity investment in the venture.

Future market prices and demand for the output of some projects are very difficult to forecast. The prices of metals and forest products, in particular, have demonstrated considerable volatility in past cycles, as shown in Exhibit 6. The best-guess market prices calculated during the planning stages and used in the DCF analysis might never be achieved. A copper project, for example, that can only tolerate a 10% decline from current market prices before the break-even point is reached will be subject to high risks given that copper prices have traditionally fluctuated over a much larger range. Sponsors can use several approaches to **minimize market risks.** One strategy that has already been noted is to ensure that the project is a low-cost

EXHIBIT 6 SELECTED COMMODITY PRICES

Year	Copper (U.S. Cents per Pound)	Nickel (U.S. Cents per Pound)	Lead (U.S. Cents per Pound)	Pulp (US$ per Metric Ton)
1970	58.1	129.1	15.7	154.18
1971	51.5	133.0	13.9	158.66
1972	51.3	139.7	15.4	153.65
1973	59.4	153.0	16.4	184.37
1974	77.0	173.5	22.3	298.48
1975	64.5	205.8	21.6	373.04
1976	68.8	225.6	23.0	371.75
1977	65.8	236.0	30.7	347.50
1978	65.5	209.1	33.8	292.62
1979	92.3	271.5	53.0	380.21
1980	101.4	338.8	43.5	470.20
1981 fourth quarter	79.9	336.7	35.7	476.43

Source. International Financial Statistics.

producer by world standards. However, this technique can leave the sponsor and lenders feeling quite uncomfortable when the market price of copper is $0.98 a pound and the market price needed to justify the venture on a DCF basis is $1.25. Another common approach is to sell the project's output under **long-term contracts** calling for prices that are fixed or allowed to escalate with increases in costs or future market prices. However, even with a floor price protection, there remains some likelihood that customers will force renegotiation of the price terms or evoke escape clauses to reduce their contract commitments in the event of a major decline in world market prices. Australian iron ore mines, for example, negotiated sales contracts that required Japanese steel mills to purchase contracted amounts, within plus or minus 10%, at prices to be renegotiated every two years. A subsequent slump in the steel industry and iron ore prices led the steel makers to cut their purchases by considerably more than 10%.

MANAGEMENT RISKS. A **sponsor's ability** to develop and operate the project is of critical importance to the success of the venture. Lenders will usually view management capability as the key factor in determining whether or not the project is viable. Several factors will receive close attention in that assessment:

1. The sponsor's **past experience** with similar projects is very important. The chances of success are greater if the proposed project is an extension of the sponsor's business than if it is a complete departure from its usual activities. The developers track record in successfully constructing and operating large international projects must be considered. The sponsor's technical and engineering skills, ability to negotiate supply and output contracts, importance in the industry, and proven willingness to stand by projects that have run into technical or financial difficulties all signal the likelihood that the new project will be a success.

2. The **importance of the project** to the sponsor is a determining factor in success. Lenders will be more confident of the sponsor's commitment to the project if it is a critical source of raw material supply to the overall company or if the sponsor is prepared to make a substantial investment, either through direct equity or credit guarantees, in the project. The sponsor's equity, in the lender's view, ideally should be an investment of cash resources as opposed to soft dollars (such as capitalized management fees or development expenses that are really sunk costs to the sponsor).

If the developer lacks the experience or resources to undertake the project, then a joint venture partner to contribute the necessary skills is essential.

FINANCIAL RISKS. The **financial structure** of the project will seriously affect profits and cash flows. Three financial aspects are particularly important: (1) the amount of leverage used; (2) the maturity structure of borrowings and proportion of fixed- versus floating-rate debt negotiated for the project; (3) the project's currency risk exposure.

Negotiating the amount of debt financing and the borrowing terms for a project is covered in detail later in this chapter. At this point, however, it is important to note that the risks of deficit cash flows rise as the project relies more heavily on leverage. A project's financial risks also increase if the debt financing has a short maturity or consists largely of floating-rate borrowings. Prime rates quoted by the banks and interest rates based on LIBOR (the London interbank offered rate) have displayed considerable volatility in recent years, as shown in Exhibit 7. A sudden increase in interest rates can cause the profit projections for a venture financed by floating-rate credit to be substantially off-target. Financings that call for loan repayment after three to five years will also pose serious refinancing risks if the project experiences long delays in construction and start up.

A project's exposure to currency fluctuations has to be carefully managed. Revenues, operating expenses, and borrowings denominated in different currencies could

EXHIBIT 7 VARIATIONS IN EURODOLLAR INTEREST RATES (rates for three-month deposits, in percentages)

Year	Monthly High	Monthly Low	Yearly Average
1970	10.0	7.2	8.5
1971	8.5	5.1	6.6
1972	6.0	4.9	5.5
1973	11.1	6.2	9.2
1974	13.6	8.5	11.0
1975	8.6	6.1	7.0
1976	6.2	5.4	5.6
1977	7.1	5.1	6.0
1978	11.6	7.3	8.7
1979	15.0	10.5	12.0
1980	19.9	9.8	14.4
1981	18.8	12.0	16.5

Source. International Financial Statistics, International Monetary Fund, Washington, D.C., 1981.

impair the project's success if there are substantial changes in the parities of currencies. **Hedging techniques** and denominating borrowing and sales contracts in the same currencies can alleviate much of the project's foreign exchange risks. However, many projects must still contend with the potential for rapid inflation in local inputs not being fully offset by changes in the official or market rates of exchange for the local currency.

POLITICAL CONSIDERATIONS. When a project is located in a country other than that of the sponsor or lenders, the **political risks** must be assessed. The risks surrounding foreign projects have become very serious during the past decade as the less-developed countries (LDCs) and industrialized nations alike have adopted more hostile postures toward foreign investments. The most extreme political risk is the possibility of **expropriation** of the project without fair compensation. A successful political revolution might result in a disavowal of the debts, guarantees, or agreements by the overthrown government. The threat of such political developments (often called **sovereign risks**) are very real for some projects. Instances of outright expropriation by the LDCs, such as in Peru, Chile, and Cuba, as well as industrialized nations, such as Canada's nationalization of the potash industry, have been well publicized. However, there are a number of other political developments that could destroy or at least reduce the project's economic viability: (1) war or political instability that cause disruptions in the supply of vital raw materials or delivery of the finished product; (2) foreign exchange or export restrictions; (3) currency inconvertibility; (4) increases in local taxes, royalties, or government-controlled input costs; (5) demands by the host government for management or equity participations.

Companies can adopt several tactics to minimize the political risks in undertaking a foreign venture. Participation by a **prominent local business or investor group** in the project or an **equity involvement by the host government** will reduce the chances of government actions that impair the project's profitability. **Insurance** can also be purchased to cover some sovereign risks. Finally, the project financing can be structured to transfer political risks to lenders or other third parties or to reduce the chances of adverse political development through a careful **composition of the lending group** or structuring of the lending agreements. Arranging the debt sources for the project and managing the sponsor's and project's risk exposures are treated in the material following.

SOURCES OF FINANCING FOR INTERNATIONAL PROJECTS

A large project financing will often require several lending groups and a multinational source of credits. Depending on the nature and location of the project, there are several sources of potential financing, including private lenders, export credits, development banks and institutions, international funding agencies, and the project's beneficiaries.

INTERNATIONAL LENDING INSTITUTIONS. **International commercial banks** are the major source of project financing. Loans from commercial banks are available through their participation in export credit programs as well as on the strength of the project's repayment capacity. Other institutions, such as insurance companies, are involved in project financings; however, their participation is more restricted to lending under government guarantee programs and purchasing long-term bond issues once the project is operational.

The leading commercial banks have dominated project financing because of their massive financial resources and the expertise they have developed to analyze and assume project risks. Commercial banks have established technical staffs of engineers and geologists who can work closely with project developers to assess the feasibility and risks of a new venture. The largest banks have also gained considerable experience and contacts in the worldwide placement of large and complex financings.

Over the past 10 years, most of the larger banks around the world have created a project-financing group or department. Project financing was until recently almost solely the **domain of North American banks,** largely because of their long experience in working with petroleum and mining companies in the United States and Canada. However, the North Sea development encouraged European institutions to broaden their worldwide involvement in project financing and to compete with U.S. and Canadian banks.

A **relatively small number of banks still dominate** the field, although many banks claim experience in project financing. That experience is often based on their participation in lending syndicates. A commercial bank's reputation for project financing is established by the number of projects in which the bank has taken the lead as manager or comanager in structuring the financing package. To successfully manage a project financing, a commercial bank must have the skills and experience to assess the project and to have its judgment accepted as credible within the international financial community from which a lending syndicate will be organized.

A lack of public data on many large projects and their financings makes it difficult to rank the project financing capabilities of the commercial banks. However, recent surveys of project-financing activities (in *The Banker, Euromoney,* and the *Institutional Investor*) point to roughly two dozen banking institutions that have managed project financings or are frequently associated with the project-financing field. Exhibit 8 lists these institutions. Many banking institutions have developed a broadly based project-financing capability, whereas other banks have concentrated on particular industries or geographic areas in which they have acquired expertise. Some of the Texas-based banks, for example, have specialized in oil and gas project financings.

Project loans from commercial banks generally carry repayment terms of five to 10 years, depending on the productive life of the project. Bank loans are typically priced on a floating-interest-rate basis, generally at an increment over LIBOR or bank prime rates in a major money center. However, some portion of the commercial bank funding might be through a government guarantee program that will offer the borrower subsidized interest rates, fixed for the maturity of the loan.

EXPORT CREDITS. Most of the industrialized nations around the world have established **export credit programs.** In the United States, the **Export-Import Bank** (Eximbank) grants long-term financing and guarantees loans by private institutions to stimulate the exports of U.S. manufacturers. The Eximbank also works with the **Private Export Funding Corporation** (PEFCO), which provides intermediate-term financing of U.S. exports. Similar programs are available from other government agencies around the world, such as the Export Development Corporation in Canada, the Export Credit Guarantee Department in Great Britain, and the Export Insurance Division in Japan.

The costs and terms of export financing are generally very attractive. Loans are

EXHIBIT 8 COMMERCIAL BANKS ACTIVELY INVOLVED IN PROJECT FINANCINGS AND EURODOLLAR PREDICTIONS

U.S. BANKS

Citibank	Manufacturers Hanover Trust
Chase Manhattan Bank	Bankers Trust
Morgan Guaranty Trust	Chicago First National Bank
Bank of America	Boston First National Bank
Continental Illinois	Republic National Bank of Dallas
Wells Fargo Bank	Chemical Bank

CANADIAN BANKS

Royal Bank of Canada	Bank of Montreal
Canadian Imperial Bank of Commerce	Toronto Dominion Bank

EUROPEAN BANKS

Lloyd's Bank	Credit Lyonnais
Barclays Bank	Amsterdam-Rotterdam Bank

usually provided with long maturities (from eight to 10 years) and at fixed-interest rates lower than commercial rates. In 1978, the 22 members of the OECD agreed to match repayment terms, down payment requirements, and interest rates offered by their export credit agencies. Rates ranging between 7.5% and 8.75% were established for projects located in one of three categories of nations (rich, intermediate, and poor). But the agencies of some industrialized countries, particularly France, Great Britain and Japan, have offered more competitive rates through mixed credits that combine concessionary aid lending with the normal export credit facilities. A recent Japanese credit in Malaysia, for example, carried an interest rate of 4% and a repayment period of 25 years.

Export programs can provide an important source of project loans; however, the export credit agencies have traditionally required very strong credits as borrowers and guarantors. The U.S. Eximbank has developed the capacity to appraise a project's feasibility and credit risks. Many of the European export agencies, on the other hand, are not equipped to undertake a detailed analysis of the project and will often require guarantees from the sponsor, a commercial bank, or the government of the country where the project is located. There are indications, however, that certain official export credit agencies are increasingly prepared to lend on a nonrecourse basis if the project has been analyzed and financed by major international banks and the exports in question are important to the supplying nation.

DEVELOPMENT BANKS AND INSTITUTIONS. Many nations have created **development banks** or equivalent institutions to encourage direct foreign investment in particular countries around the world.

In the United States, the **Overseas Private Investment Corporation** (OPIC) provides **insurance** against political risks of expropriation, currency unconvertibility, and war damage for investments by U.S. firms in friendly developing nations. Political risk insurance is available for the sponsor's equity investment or for loans by U.S. financial institutions. Insurance against total political risk costs roughly 1.5% to 2% of the insured amount. Also OPIC will guarantee **commercial risks** for medium- and long-term loans by U.S. lenders. The insurance charge varies between 1.75% and 3%, depending on risk.

Development banks and insurance institutions can be an important source of credit support for nonrecourse project loans. The objective underlying most of these programs has been to encourage investment in the LDCs. Some of the government institutions, however, have expanded their financing programs to help local companies compete for markets and access to raw materials. The West German and Japanese governments, for example, have guaranteed loans to foreign projects where the output was sold under contract to firms in West Germany and Japan.

INTERNATIONAL FINANCING AGENCIES. Several international financing agencies will provide funding for industrial projects located in particular regions of the world. The International Finance Corporation of the World Bank Group, the European Investment Bank, the African Development Bank, the Asian Development Bank, and the Inter-American Development Bank will fund development projects in third-world countries. These agencies offer long-term financing (seven to 15 years) on a nonrecourse basis with loan rates fixed at prevailing interest rates. The agencies also make concessional loans in situations where the project makes important contributions to the economic betterment of the host country and the venture involves large infrastructure needs.

PROJECT BENEFICIARIES. Certain of the **project's beneficiaries,** in addition to the sponsor, can be a source of project loans. **Customer credits** are frequently an important component in a project financing, particularly if the products or services produced by the project are in short supply and users are anxious to lock in long-term sources. It is increasingly common for utility companies, for example, to finance exploration and development through advance payments to oil companies in order to secure sources of future gas or petroleum. Similarly, market conditions for nickel, copper, iron ore, and other metals have forced Japanese and West German companies to seek long-term sources of supply. For projects located in Indonesia, Australia, or South America, for example, these companies were willing to provide financing directly or to solicit support from their own government's funding agencies.

PROJECT FINANCING AND THE ALLOCATION OF RISKS

NONRECOURSE FINANCING. It is not uncommon for a mining or energy company to undertake one or two projects where the capital investment at stake exceeds the parent's total assets. The failure of such a large project would have dire consequences for the sponsor's profitability as well as its financial flexibility to undertake any new ventures. A major motive underlying most project financings, then, is to reduce the sponsor's risks in undertaking the project. By minimizing its equity investment and limiting any guarantees or commitments for the project's loans, the sponsor can escape many of the hazards that the project might encounter.

A **pure** or **nonrecourse,** project financing reduces the sponsor's risk exposure to the maximum degree possible. However, pure project financings are arranged very infrequently. Private lenders will only assume reasonable credit risks and unless the project's earnings prospects are virtually certain, the lenders will insist that project risks be absorbed by either the sponsor or some third party with strong financial capacity.

Although a project financing might not permit the sponsor to completely avoid all financial responsibility for the project, carefully structured project loans can transfer significant risks to parties other than the equity owners, or lower the project's overall riskiness.

SHARING PROJECT RISKS. The previous discussion of financing sources available to large international projects indicates three primary groups that are prepared to **share project risks** with sponsors: governments and international financing agencies, the project's customers, and private lenders.

Export credits and loans from public sector institutions can be obtained on a nonrecourse basis and essentially transfer all commercial and political risks associated with that financing to government institutions. Political and credit risk insurance can also be purchased by the sponsor to cover the equity investment or to guarantee private loans to the project.

The sponsor might also arrange for customers to assume the marketing risks, particularly if the output is in short supply and there is a premium placed by the market on a long-term, dependable source of supply. **Floor prices** and **price-escalation provisions** in purchase agreements will enable the sponsor to shift the risks of price fluctuations to the project's offtakers. And direct **financial participation** by customers in the project, either as a joint venture partner or as a lender, reduces the other element of market risk, namely, the possibility that sales agreements will not be honored in the future.

The large international banks are also prepared to accept certain project risks. As the banks have developed their capacity to analyze project risks, they have also been increasingly willing to take on more project risks, essentially having stretched the definition of normal credit risks used in the banking community. Commercial banks have been willing to take on the **political risks** for many foreign ventures. Through their balance of payments loans to developing nations, the banks are experienced in appraising sovereign risks. The large international banks would argue that they have a **comparative advantage** in taking on political risks. Through its diversified loan portfolio, a bank can minimize and better manage political risks than could the sponsor, with its assets concentrated in a few geographical locations. A bank can also use its bargaining strength and other measures to reduce political hazards to tolerable levels.

Commercial banks have been prepared to accept the **commercial risks** and, on occasion, some of the **technical risks** associated with a new project. The level of risk exposure that lenders in a project financing will tolerate varies over time, depending on the general economic outlook, the success or failure record of recent large projects, and the competitive activity among banks for new project financings. For example, banks have generally been **unwilling** to accept the technical and cost overrun risks during the start-up phrase of a project and have demanded strong financial commitments by sponsors to guarantee borrowings until the project is operational. However, the enthusiasm of banks in the late 1960s and early 1970s to participate in international project lending resulted in recourse agreements that provided ineffective protection against unanticipated capital expenditures. Massive cost overruns subsequently occurred and caused the banks to tighten their completion and recourse agreements. In the early 1980s, stepped-up competition among the banks for project financing has produced completion agreements that limit the sponsors' financial responsibility to only a portion of the project loans should the venture become noneconomic and not be completed. There are signs, however, that the banks were reverting to a more cautious posture in early 1982. A sponsor's ability to arrange a limited-recourse financing therefore varies over time, depending on the prevailing mood in the banking community.

REDUCING POLITICAL RISKS. Linking the financing to the fortunes of the project can **reduce,** as well as shift, project risks. The likelihood that the host government will take actions that jeopardize the project's success is lessened if the project is financed on a largely nonrecourse basis and the lending group consists of institutions that are important in the international financial markets.

In the event of nationalization or expropriation, nonrecourse project loans will more likely be regarded as legitimate debts as opposed to being viewed by the government as a substitute for equity and, therefore, of questionable status. Interest payments on project loans are also less likely to be curtailed by foreign exchange restrictions. Interest on loans extended by the sponsor to the project are occasionally regarded as dividends and treated more unfavorably.

The **ties between governments and the commercial banks** are close because of foreign trade financing needs. Any difficulties arising in a nonrecourse financing because of the government's actions can likely be negotiated by the banks in a wider and, therefore, more effective context than would be possible by the project's sponsor. If the lenders are the major international banks, the host government will likely be cautious in carrying out an expropriation or in imposing tax and royalty measures that jeopardize the project's success and thereby risk alienating an important segment of the international credit market. An interesting example of this type of development unfolded when Peru requested a $300 million balance of payments loan from a syndicate of U.S. banks in 1976. Preconditions of the loan were satisfactory settlements of government interference incidents with two local projects undertaken by U.S. firms.

The involvement of an **international financing agency** such as the World Bank in a project financing further lessens political risks. In a cofinancing, where the commercial banks supplement the long-term fixed-rate funding provided by an international agency or an export credit program, lenders are typically tied together through **cross-default clauses.** The commercial banks believe that the host government is less likely to cause the project to default when it is funded by a major international agency.

STRUCTURING PROJECT FINANCING

COMPLEXITY OF THE FINANCING PACKAGE. Negotiating a project financing that calls for a large amount of debt financing with limited recourse to the project's sponsor is a complex task. Private lenders might be prepared to accept some commercial and political risks facing the venture. However, if these risks are excessive, then the sponsor or other third parties will have to protect the banks' positions. In addition, there are technical and marketing risks that the banks are unprepared to absorb and these, in turn, will have to be laid off to other parties interested in the project. Arranging a project financing under these circumstances can require multiple funds sources, an international sourcing of the credits, and complicated legal agreements.

Engineering a complex project financing calls for **considerable skill and experience.** Many of the multinational mining and energy companies have assembled in-house project financing specialists. The larger construction and consulting engineering firms are now adding financial experts to their bidding teams for complex and costly projects as an adjunct to selling their basic engineering services. However, **international banking institutions** still play the key role in designing a project financing package.

Two groups of banks offer project-financing advice. The **largest international banks** (see Exhibit 8) seek to advise projects while at the same time retaining the possibility of lending their own money to the project. **United States investment banks** with international capacity and **U.K. merchant banks** also offer financial engineering services. The U.K. merchant banks have focused their activities around U.K. and international credit export programs. A handful of U.S. investment banks, led by First Boston Corporation and Morgan Stanley, have an international project-financing capability. They have concentrated their efforts on joint venture projects, where legal, tax, and accounting matters are particularly important, and projects that are capable of being financed through the U.S. capital markets.

ACCOUNTING CONSIDERATIONS. While the sponsor ideally prefers nonrecourse borrowings, most project financings will require that the sponsor provide some credit support for the project's loans. The sponsor's support arrangements for the project's loans should be structured to minimize their impact on the parent's credit standing and balance sheet. The **off–balance sheet nature** of project financing is promoted as an important benefit for the sponsoring company. It is often claimed that off–balance sheet financing will have a favorable impact on the parent's overall borrowing capacity for several reasons—institutional lenders and the rating agencies look on limited-recourse obligations more favorably than would be the case for direct debt; project financings typically fall outside the debt restrictions in existing loan agreements; and many investment and credit analysts, particularly smaller institutions and private investors, are likely not aware of off–balance sheet liabilities or do not incorporate such obligations fully into their evaluation of the company's financial position.

The sponsors and financial advisors will pay close attention to the **accounting treatment** of project loans. Their goal is not to hide or conceal these obligations, although this has clearly been an objective in some past project financings. The primary objective is to segregate the sponsor's project obligations so that creditors, rating agencies, and stockholders can better appraise the limited nature of the sponsor's commitment for the project's debts.

A direct financing of the project or a full guarantee by the sponsor of the project's borrowings will result in the project loans being shown on the **face of the sponsor's balance sheet.** However, the reporting of project loans might be relegated to a **footnote or not disclosed** at all in the sponsor's financial statements, depending on the extent of the sponsor's ownership in the project and the types of guarantees provided. Accounting treatment varies from country to country. The **U.S. Financial Accounting Standards Board** (FASB) has recently paid close attention to the disclosure of indirect liabilities and project-financing arrangements in particular. Consequently, U.S. reporting conventions can likely be used as a guide to the maximum reporting and disclosure that will result for project-financing obligations.

For U.S. financial accounting purposes, a subsidiary more than 50% controlled is consolidated on the parents' statements on a line-by-line basis, while for a less-than-majority-owned subsidiary, only the parent's investment is reported in the assets section of its balance sheet. Therefore, for many joint ventures, project loans are **not incorporated into the liabilities sections** of their sponsors' financial statements. In addition, a company can use several forms of **nominee corporations,** technically owned by third parties, such as the financial advisor, to avoid consolidation of a majority-ownership position in a project.

A sponsor's guarantee of project loans, particularly if limited, can be structured to avoid a direct debt obligation being shown on the balance sheet. Accounting terms such as **"contingent liability," "indirect liability," "deferred liability,"** and **"advance payment"** can be used to allow the sponsor some scope in positioning project-financing obligations in its financial statements. Recent changes to FASB principles, however, require that the amount, timing, and nature of indirect guarantees and commitments arising from a project financing be disclosed in **footnote** form.

Most project-financing obligations fall outside of the debt restrictions in loan agreements and bond indentures. However, financial institutions are becoming increasingly aware of off–balance sheet commitments and the financial burdens that they might place on a sponsor. Standard and Poor's Corporation, for example, changed Shell Oil's triple-A rating to a double-A plus in 1980 as a result of the $3.4 billion Belridge oil field financing. Despite the nonrecourse nature of much of the financing, the rating agency took the view that Shell could not walk away from an investment of that size and importance.

TAX AND LEGAL FACTORS. There are a variety of other factors that must be considered in the choice of a financing strategy for a new venture. The increasing frequency of **joint ventures,** for example, provides the stimulus for project financing. Although joint ownership allows a sharing of expertise, capital, and risks, it also entails limited control by any particular sponsor over the future performance of the project. A company's desire to avoid responsibility for problems created by its partners can be an important incentive for a project-financing structure with carefully defined recourse agreements rather than a decision to fund the company's pro rata share of the project's needs directly.

Tax considerations are also key in structuring a project financing. **Maximizing the tax benefits** accruing to the sponsor from the project requires careful consideration of the tax provisions in the country where the project is located and the tax relationship between the project and its parents. In the United States, for example, the flow of a project's profits and losses to the sponsor for tax purposes depends on the ownership structure used for the venture and the sponsor's proportion of equity ownership in the project. A **partnership** or **joint venture** does not pay tax and allows a transfer of the project's revenues, deductions, and tax credits to the sponsors. (A joint venture resembles a partnership except that the parties contract among themselves rather than enter into a partnership agreement. The Alaska pipeline project is probably the most famous example of a joint venture.) A **corporation** is often not a satisfactory way to structure a joint project financing because a sponsor cannot file a consolidated federal income tax return with the project if the sponsor's ownership is less than 80%.

The project financing should be structured to fully utilize the tax benefits from investment tax credits, depreciation, depletion deductions, interest charges, and other noncapital start-up expenses. Since the project entity often does not have taxes to shelter in its early years of operation, it is important to **shift available tax benefits** to the parties that can make maximum use of them. These tax shifts can be accomplished through the ownership arrangements as well as the types of financing vehicles used. **Leveraged leases, industrial** or **municipal bond financings,** and **drilling funds** can offer unique tax advantages. **Production payments** used to finance intangible expenses in developing a new mineral source can also provide the sponsor with greater flexibility in timing its tax obligations. (Common project financing vehicles are described in Exhibits 9 and 10.) There are a myriad of possible tax maneuvers available, depending on the specific tax provisions applicable to the project and its sponsors. The importance of tax considerations for a new venture underscores **the need for tax and legal expertise** in engineering the project-financing package.

SPONSOR'S GUARANTEES AND COMMITMENTS. The sponsor in a project financing will often contract to cover those risks that the commercial lenders do not have the capacity to analyze or accept. These risks most often relate to the **technical problems** that might occur during the construction stage and **market uncertainties** once the project begins producing. The sponsor will attempt to appease the banks' concerns and at the same time limit the scope of its own liability.

Completion Guarantees. A major risk from the lender's point of view is that the project might never be completed due to engineering or technical problems or cost overruns that are serious enough to cause the sponsor to abandon the project. Lenders view completion risks as particularly high when the technical aspects or production techniques are novel. The sponsors, on the other hand, have more confidence in their technical skills or the project would not have been undertaken.

Bankers, therefore, generally ask that the project's owners provide **formal assurances** that the project will be completed. Completion is not defined to mean an obligation to construct the installation, since this would be unnecessary and unreasonable should the project become uneconomic. The traditional form of a **completion agreement** is essentially a financial guarantee by the developer up to the time of the project's completion. The sponsors usually provide the lenders with several assurances of completion: (1) to physically complete the project (measured by technical and engineering specifications); (2) to have the project meet tests of technical per-

EXHIBIT 9 PURCHASE COMMITMENTS USED IN PROJECT FINANCINGS

Sales contracts: The project's customers contract to purchase the output at specified prices, typically over an extended time period.

Take-and-pay contracts: The customer (often the sponsor) agrees to purchase the product or service, if it is available and delivered, at prices sufficient to pay operating costs and service the project's debts. A take-or-pay or a hell-or-high-water contract requires payment even if the product is not available. Examples include

- **Through-put agreements:** Pipelines and refineries
- **Transportation agreements:** Ships
- **Tolling agreements:** Metal processing
- **Processing agreements:** Industrial projects

EXHIBIT 10 TYPICAL PROJECT FINANCING ARRANGEMENTS

Asset-based financing arrangements

Production payments: An interest in a share of production, or the proceeds from production, of minerals or oil and gas in the ground is sold to a corporation with nominal equity. The purchase price is refinanced by pledging the production payment as collateral on a loan. Production payments are reported on the balance sheet as a deferred liability. Examples include

Reserved production payment: To finance purchase of an oil or mineral property

Carved-out production payment: To finance a producing oil, gas, or mineral property

Development carve-outs: To raise capital to develop an oil, gas, or mining property

Advanced Sales: Advanced sales are similar to a production payment for oil or gas except that future production itself is sold rather than an interest in that production. The advance payment is usually obtained from a customer in return for a future supply of oil or gas.

Indirect loan guarantees: Indirect loan guarantees are undertakings used by a sponsor to indirectly guarantee the project's loans. Common examples are

Deficiency agreements

Cost company arrangements

Working capital or debt-to-equity maintenance agreements

---

formance (this essentially means that the project must achieve a certain level of output at less than a specified percentage of operating costs during a test period); (3) to provide overrun financing.

Depending on the technical risks of the project and the confidence that the lenders have in the sponsors, the provisions of a completion guarantee can be limited or relaxed. One form of partial completion guarantee is to loosen the completion test definition—completion might be provided in stages or the definition of technical completion might be relaxed to permit lower output levels. The lenders might also agree to provide for overrun financing up to a specified percentage (currently around 20% of the projected capital costs) and additional funds will then have to be provided by the sponsor. The sponsor's contractual agreement to finance overruns is crucial for the lenders; without such a commitment, the lenders would find themselves holding the largest financial stake in an uncompleted project and, therefore, in a weak bargaining position to require more equity input from the project's owners. In the early 1970s, banks were placed in the unfortunate position of lending to projects that encountered exceptional overruns without formal overrun financing agreements by the owners. The final form of a partial completion guarantee is to arrange some portion of the bank financing as nonrecourse from the outset of the project. Recent large oil financings have negotiated part of the project loans to be on a nonrecourse basis. The amount of the nonrecourse loan is generally set by the banks to allow sufficient security to cover the risks. For example, banks will often require that the nonrecourse loan not exceed 40% to 50% of the discounted cash flow of the project.

A sponsor's ability to negotiate a partial completion agreement, as was noted earlier, depends on the mood and attitudes prevailing at the time in the banking community. Once the completion agreement is fulfilled, the sponsor's liability is automatically released. The project loans are nonrecourse and lenders can look to the cash flow of the project only to service the debt.

Purchase Commitments. Lenders might not be prepared to accept the market risks for a new project, particularly if market conditions are highly volatile or uncertain.

If the project cannot lock in third-party customers or if the project was undertaken primarily as a supply source for its sponsors, then the owners will have to make **purchase commitments** that essentially remove most market uncertainties. If the project is generally of high risk in the lenders' view, project loans will likely be obtained only if the sponsor offers an **overall guarantee** of the project's debt-servicing capacity.

A host of **indirect guarantees and commitments** allow a sponsor to provide the credit support necessary for the project and still achieve favorable balance sheet treatment of the project obligations. These credit support mechanisms consist of three basic types: **purchase agreements, asset-based financings,** and **indirect loan guarantees.**

Long-term contracts by a sponsor to buy the project's output are commonly used to assure lenders of inflows sufficient to pay off the project's debts. The contract might be an unconditional guarantee to buy an agreed amount of a product or service, whether or not it is delivered. These agreements are frequently called **"take-or-pay" contracts** or **"hell-or-high-water" contracts.** A **take-and-pay contract,** on the other hand, requires the customer to purchase the output or service only if it is produced and delivered. Purchase contracts vary by industry and are described in Exhibit 9.

A host of financing arrangements have been developed that **link loans to specific assets** and thereby permit the obligations to be shown as other than direct debt on the company's balance sheet. **Leasing** is a typical example. **Production payments** and **advance sale** financings are common in the petroleum and mining industries and are highly specialized methods of financing whereby a loan is amortized out of the proceeds for the sale of the mineral or oil as, if, and when produced. These financings are usually reported on the balance sheet as **deferred liabilities.** Exhibit 10 describes typical production payment and advanced sales arrangements.

A sponsor can enter into other undertakings that indirectly provide lenders with guarantees of the project's debts. Commonly used agreements include the following:

Deficiency Guarantees. The sponsor provides a guarantee limited in amount to the deficiency suffered by a creditor in the event of default, repossession, and resale.

Cost Company Agreements. The sponsors agree to share, on a pro rata basis, all costs incurred by the project, including debt-servicing requirements.

Working Capital Maintenance Agreements. The parent agrees to maintain the project's working capital at a specified level. This agreement effectively becomes a full guarantee of project loans since they become a current liability if the project defaults on its obligations.

COSTS OF PROJECT FINANCING. Project financing can be a **costly financing vehicle.** Many project-financing proposals are ultimately abandoned or financed on a traditional basis because the costs and time required to arrange project financing are considered excessive by the sponsor. Most new projects are financed by their shareholders or sponsored from internal sources, supplemented by export credits and bank loans guaranteed directly and unconditionally by the sponsors themselves.

A project financing takes a large amount of **time and effort** to arrange. The sponsor and its financial advisors will have to search out financing sources, usually around the world, negotiate commitments from banks, government agencies, customers, and the sponsor, arrange a lending syndicate, and prepare numerous legal agreements. These negotiations and approvals often require several years to complete and involve high **front-end fees.** A management fee of 0.5% to 1% of the financing is typically charged by the financial advisor to the project.

The process of sharing and/or reducing risks to produce a limited recourse financing entails other costs. Bank loans to the project will carry **higher interest rates** than the sponsor typically pays for its own credit lines, particularly if the company enjoys a high credit rating. Private lenders will charge a higher interest spread to accept sovereign and commercial risks in a project financing. The extra rate for the sovereign risks will be at least equal to the rate differential charged by banks for balance of payments loans to the foreign country. Obtaining financial and purchase commitments from customers can also be costly, particularly if weak market conditions for the project's output places the sponsor in an unfavorable bargaining position. Customer participation might require substantial **price concessions and other restrictions** on the project's flexibility.

In developing.a large international venture, project financing can offer a sponsor the benefits of reduced risks and improved financial flexibility. However, the sponsor will have to weigh those benefits against the additional complexity and costs of engineering a complex project financing.

BIBLIOGRAPHY

Angelini, A., M. Eng and F.A. Lees, *International Lending, Risk and Euromarkets*, Macmillan, New York, 1979.

Benson, R.N., "Project Financing—Banking's Response to a New Environment," *The Canadian Banker and ICB Review*, December (1980).

Clarke, P. and S. Martin, "The Big Swing to Project Financing," *Euromoney*, October (1980).

Davis, R.S., "New Developments in Project Financing," *The Bankers' Magazine*, February (1981).

Eiteman, D.K. and A.I. Stonehill, *Multinational Business Finance*, 2nd ed., Addison-Wesley, Reading, Mass., 1979.

Fowler, T.V., "International Project Finance: Big Business for the Banks," *The Banker*, December (1977).

Hayes, D.A., *Bank Lending Policies: Domestic and International*, 2nd ed., University of Michigan Press, Ann Arbor, 1977.

Leeper, R., "Perspectives on Project Financing," *The Banker*, September (1979).

Mathias, F.J., Ed., *Offshore Lending by U.S. Commercial Banks*, Robert Morris Associates, Philadelphia, 1975.

Nevitt, P.K., *Project Financing*, Euromoney, London, 1979.

Ricks, D.A., *International Dimensions of Corporate Finance*, Prentice-Hall, Englewood Cliffs, N.J., 1978.

Rose, P.S. and T.W. Cooper, "Oil and Gas Financing: An Appraisal of Current Methods," *World Oil*, October (1977).

Sarmet, M., "Recent Trends in International Project Financing," *The Banker*, September (1981).

Wells, L.J. Jr. and D.N. Smith, *Negotiating Third World Mineral Agreements: Promises as Prologue*, Ballinger, Cambridge, Mass., 1976.

Weston, J.F. and B.W. Sorge, *Guide to International Financial Management*, McGraw-Hill, New York, 1977.

Wynant, L., "Project Financing for Extractive Ventures: Impact of Reporting Practices on a Firm's Borrowing Capacity," *Management Accounting*, October (1978).

Wynant, L., "Essential Elements of Project Financing," *Harvard Business Review*, May/June (1980).

REFERENCES

Castle, G.R., "Project Financing—Guidelines for the Commercial Banker," *Journal of Commercial Bank Lending*, April (1975).

Radaz, R.E., "Opportunities in Project Financing," *The Banker*, August (1978).

SECTION 7.4

LEASING IN AN INTERNATIONAL CONTEXT

CONTENTS

SECTION 7.4

LEASING IN AN INTERNATIONAL CONTEXT

Gernot Reiners

INTRODUCTION

Many transactions, both in a purely domestic and in an international context, are labeled "leases." Only a fraction of these transactions are the subject of this section. Leasing in its **broadest definition is an arrangement providing the use of an asset without its legal ownership.** The use of the asset can be provided for a few hours, days, or weeks, or for a period covering many years.

OPERATING LEASES. Short-term leases are usually further characterized by the fact that the owner (the lessor) remains responsible for maintenance, insurance, property taxes, and similar attributes of ownership. In many leases personnel supplied by the owner rather than the user will be responsible for operating the equipment. Typical examples are "wet" leases of aircraft or vessels or contract drilling. Such leases are called **operating leases.** Operating leases are not a means of financing. Their objective is to provide the user with the asset for a period considerably shorter than the useful life of the asset. The user generally is not interested in acquiring ownership of the asset and is willing to pay a significant premium for the flexibility to return the asset when it is no longer needed. Using operating leases as a financing alternative would be very costly. Imagine paying daily rental rates to achieve long-term financing of an automobile. Since the only concern herein is with leasing as a financing method, operating leases will not be covered.

FINANCING LEASES. Leases that are not operating leases but are contracted to provide financing are generally called **"financing leases."** They are mainly but not always full pay-out leases. Full pay-out leases are leases where the sum of the lease rentals, tax benefits of ownership (if any), and the anticipated (or contractual) proceeds from disposition of the asset at the end of the primary lease term amortize the original acquisition cost of the asset to the lessor and provide the lessor with a desired rate of return. If the lessor needs to realize more than 25% of the original purchase price by selling the asset at the end of the lease to recover the investment and realize an anticipated rate of return, the transaction would generally not be considered a full pay-out lease. In the United States, national banks are not permitted to enter into leasing transactions if the assumed residual value is in excess of 25% of original cost.

If the anticipated residual value is guaranteed by a third party, such as the manufacturer or an insurance company, these rules do not apply and the lease would be considered a full pay-out lease. This discussion of leasing is restricted to full pay-out leases. Full pay-out leases can be divided into two groups: money-over-money leases and tax leases.

Money-over-Money Leases. Money-over-money leases are structured so that the sum of the lease rental payments plus any additional obligation the lessee might have upon termination of the primary lease term—such as the obligation to make up any shortfall between the expected sales proceeds upon disposition of the asset by the lessor and actual realization—will amortize the original cost of the asset in full and give the lessor an interest rate of return in excess of funding costs. The lessee will usually have the right to purchase the asset at the end of the lease term for a nominal amount or for an amount substantially below the market value of the asset. In many cases the lessor is also able to put the asset to the lessee for the unamortized balance of the original purchase price or for the value of the asset as shown in the lessor's books. Ownership for tax purposes in **money-over-money leases** can be either with the lessor or the lessee. If it is with the lessor, the rentals do not reflect any tax benefits of ownership that the lessor might have. The term "money-over-money lease" always implies that the lessor is **earning a positive spread** on funds employed in the lease irrespective of how the lease is treated for tax purposes. In some countries, Belgium, France, Mexico, and Brazil, for example, a lessor might be the owner of the leased asset for income tax purposes but cannot derive any benefit from this, because local tax laws will not permit depreciation in excess of the principal portion of the lease rentals received. In most cases, however, the lessee is considered the owner for tax purposes.

The lessors view this type of transaction strictly as a **spread lending** business, mainly at fixed but recently increasingly at floating rates of interest. The lessors themselves borrow their funds, mainly from banks, and as a result their leases are more expensive than bank loans for comparable amounts and terms. As a general rule money-over-money leases are an expensive financing alternative. They are, however, a convenient way of obtaining 100% financing for real assets and, since the leasing companies are frequently willing to take greater risks or have a better understanding of collateral values than banks, they are for many small or highly leveraged companies the only financing alternative available.

For all purposes, money-over-money leases are **secured term loans** and should be evaluated as such. There is little about them to make them different from secured loans, domestic or international, and they will not be discussed any further here.

Tax Leases. Tax leases are **full pay-out leases** where the lessor is considered the owner of the asset for tax purposes and where the tax benefits of ownership permit the lessor to offer leases at a pretax cost that is lower than that of loans for the same amount and the same maturity. Whether or not the after-tax cost of such a lease is also lower depends on the tax position of the lessee.

The balance of this section is devoted to a detailed discussion of full pay-out tax leases in the international context. A lease is international in nature if the lessor and the lessee are domiciled in different countries, with the location of the asset being of secondary importance.

OBJECTIVES OF INTERNATIONAL LEASE FINANCINGS

Bank of America, in a 1978 publication entitled *Direct Leasing,* lists 26 reasons why companies might want to enter into a domestic leasing transaction. Few of these arguments for leasing hold up under close scrutiny.

The most convincing reason is either a **lower after-tax cost** or comparable cost with a significant **improvement in the timing of cash outflows.** Existing convenants prohibiting other kinds of financing without restricting leasing might be sufficient reason to lease even at a slightly higher cost, but unless the prospective lessee is in desperate financial shape, renegotiation of the covenants is usually preferable to leasing at a substantially higher cost.

Other arguments, like off–balance sheet financing, 100% financing, or improved reported earnings as opposed to improved economics, should be carefully analyzed. Such reasons are usually catchy buzzwords of leasing company salespersons rather than an indication of sound financial management. The hidden cost of such leases is a deterioration in the quality of a company's reported earnings or balance sheet. In addition to the more traditional reasons for entering into domestic leases, companies will enter into cross-border leases for a number of other reasons.

REASONS FOR CROSS–BORDER LEASING

Reduction of Political Risk. Company A wants to drill for oil in a developing country that is characterized by a rather uncertain political environment. To the extent that some of the needed equipment can be obtained locally, leasing it from a local leasing company might be an attractive way of financing it.

Unfortunately, the local leasing markets are generally not well developed in countries where leasing might be advisable even at a significantly higher cost to avoid the political risk. Leasing should be used to the extent possible, since it is less likely that a government hostile to foreign investment will expropriate equipment owned by an indigeneous leasing company. Should problems arise, it is much easier for a lessee to suspend payments to a local financial institution than to a major international bank.

Company B is building a very expensive capital asset to be used in the territorial waters or within a country that has repeatedly stated that it plans to expropriate foreign-owned assets or is generally hostile to foreign corporations. Rather than owning the asset outright, company B decides to lease it from an international consortium of major banks. The lease agreement provides that the lessee bears the **risk of expropriation.** What is the lessee's rationale for leasing?

The lessee is convinced that the host government will be much more reluctant to antagonize a group of multinational lenders—which presumably are providing a significant portion of the country's funds—than a corporation that might have outlived its usefulness as far as the government of the host country is concerned.

Company B simply thinks that the lessors are in a much stronger negotiating position than the lessee and that the mere fact that the asset or facility is leased from these specific lessors might prevent trouble in the first place. Many lessees feel that their experience in Iran confirms this view—not because many of the assets used by foreign corporations in Iran were leased, but because these lessees are convinced that banks were able to settle their claims with Iran in full and much faster than corporations.

Company C, a tough negotiator and a very desirable lessee, is successful in getting the lessor to assume some of the **political risks** under the terms of the lease agreement. The lessor, for example, might have accepted a local subsidiary as lessee, with or without a maintenance of ownership, keepwell, or similar undertaking by the lessee's parent (a triple-A-rated multinational). In addition, the lessor has accepted the risk that the local subsidiary will be able to convert local currency into dollars or some other major currency in which the lease is denominated. The lessor, in pricing the lease, might have assumed a certain residual value. The lease provides only that the lessee has to make the asset available to the lessor in the local country when the lease matures. The lessor has assumed the risk that the asset might not be recoverable for sale to a purchaser in another country.

All of these aspects can be considered part of the political risk associated with foreign operations, and if a lessor can be found to take some of this risk, this might be sufficient reason for leasing. While this section only deals with **tax leases,** it should be noted that the shifting of political risk can be an objective for other types of cross-border leases as well.

Group Profitability Improvement. **Cross-border leases** between companies belonging to the same group can be used as an effective means of **transfer pricing,** with the objective of shifting earnings from a high tax rate environment to one with lower taxes. It is much easier for the tax authorities to determine whether the interest rate on a loan is at a market rate than to decide whether the rental payments under a lease are arm's length rental payments. Rents on short-term operating leases are usually high, and there is little to prevent a parent company from leasing an asset with a useful life of 10 years to a foreign subsidiary for a three-year term at rentals comparable to other three-year leases in the market. At the end of the three-year period, the lease can be extended for another relatively short-term period at a high rent, or the subsidiary can purchase the asset at a price that gives credit for only a small portion of the rentals already paid. **Intercompany leases** are also an effective way of utilizing **tax benefits** that would otherwise have to be carried forward or might be lost altogether.

If parent company X is a sizable taxpayer in its home country and the home country is a suitable base for cross-border leasing, and if company X has a foreign subsidiary Y engaged in a major capital investment program, and as a result, Y is not currently paying any taxes and is not expected to be a taxpayer for the foreseeable future, then rather than have Y purchase major capital assets that generate tax benefits that Y cannot utilize, X purchases the assets and leases them to Y. Lease rentals are tailored—within permissible limits—to suit Y's tax position (i.e., they are lower in the early years and increase in later years, when Y is projected to become taxable). The net result is a significant improvement in the cash flow of the group.

FINDING A SUITABLE LESSOR COUNTRY

Previous discussion centered upon the reasons why it might make sense to lease certain assets rather than to purchase them. One can also assume that the circumstances of a capital investment are such that a **cross-border lease** might make sense. Which country might enable the lessor to write a lease that meets the lessor's objectives?

THE UNITED STATES. United States tax law permits the writing of cross-border leases, since a U.S. lessor can depreciate assets located overseas. In certain circumstances **offshore assets** will even qualify for an **Investment Tax Credit (ITC),** and then a cross-border lease from the United States really becomes interesting. The **Economic Recovery Tax Act,** signed by President Reagan on 14 August 1981, has completely changed the rules for domestic leases. A good comparison between the old and the new rules can be found in Volume 5, number 4 of the *Equipment Financing Journal,* July–August (1981). The article is entitled "Effects of the Economic Recovery Tax Act upon Leasing," and was written by Peter K. Nevitt, President, Bankamerilease. The new rules apply only if the asset would be Section 38 property (i.e., qualify for ITC) in the hands of the lessee. No property owned by a foreign person qualifies for **ITC** and the new rules therefore do not apply to **cross-border leases.** The Internal Revenue Service (IRS) will address this point in to-be-published permanent regulations interpreting the new Section 168 of the Tax Code. To date, the IRS has only published temporary regulations that do not cover this point at all. It remains to be seen whether a foreign lessee could take advantage of the new rules by setting up a U.S. subsidiary that would lease from a U.S. lessor and then pass on the benefits of this lease to the foreign parent through a sublease. This author suspects that the regulations will address this point and will define lessee as the lessee who is also the user of the asset. It must be assumed therefore that the new rules do not cover cross-border leases and that these leases continue to be governed by the old rules. The IRS has published guidelines (*Rev. Proc.* 75–21 and *Rev. Proc.* 75–28) to determine whether a lease will be considered a true lease for federal corporate income taxes or not. Leases not meeting these guidelines can still be true leases, but the IRS is under no obligation to issue a ruling on leases not meeting the guidelines, and the risk that the IRS will try to disqualify such leases from being true leases upon audit is considerable. The key provisions of the IRS guidelines for true leases follow.

Minimum Investment Rule. The lessor must have made a minimum unconditional at-risk investment in the property (the minimum investment) when the lease begins, must maintain such minimum investment throughout the entire lease term, and such minimum investment must remain at the end of the lease term.

The minimum investment must remain equal to at least 20% of the cost of the property at all times throughout the entire lease term.

Residual Investment. The lessor must represent and demonstrate that an amount equal to at least 20% of the original cost of the property is a reasonable estimate of what the fair market value of the property will be at the end of the lease term.

Fair Market Value Rule. No member of the lessee group can have a contractual right to purchase the property from the lessor at a price less than its fair market value at the time the right is exercised.

Other Requirements. No part of the cost of the property can be furnished by any member of the lessee group.

No member of the lessee group can lend to the lessor any of the funds necessary to acquire the property, or guarantee any indebtedness created in connection with the acquisition of the property by the lessor.

The IRS ordinarily will not raise any question about prepaid or deferred rent if the annual rent for any year is not more than 10% above or below the amount calculated by dividing the total rent payable over the lease term by the number of years in such term.

Implications for Lessor. If the lease meets these conditions, the lessor will be regarded by the IRS as the owner of the asset for U.S. tax purposes. This means first, that the lessor can depreciate the asset. The depreciable life is the class life (the mid-range of the ADR guidelines) of the asset. The lessor can use the double declining balance method of depreciation, switching to the sum of the years' digits method when this becomes more advantageous (usually in the third year of the lease).

In the exceptional cases where the asset qualifies for ITC as well (see second point, below) the depreciable life is not the class life, but is either three, five, or 10 years, in accordance with the accelerated cost recovery system (ACRS) provisions of the Economic Recovery Tax Act. The so-called safe harbor lease rules of the act (Section 168f8), however, do not apply.

Second, the lessor can claim 10% investment tax credit on new (not used) assets if they meet one of the criteria listed in Section 48a2B; for example, any aircraft that is registered by the administrator of the Federal Aviation Agency (FAA) and is operated to and from the United States or is operated under contract with the United States. This provision was designed to clarify that aircrafts owned and operated by U.S. airlines on their international routes and civilian aircraft carrying out flights for the U.S. government (mainly the military) qualify for ITC. The provision can, however, be interpreted more broadly and the U.S. leasing industry uses this provision to have a U.S. lessor purchase the aircraft, register it with the FAA, and lease it to foreign airlines for their flights to and from the United States.

Since only U.S. persons (individuals and corporations) can register aircraft with the FAA, this is the only way in which foreign airlines can take advantage of this provision. In a private ruling the IRS indicated that it will consider an aircraft landing in the United States once every two weeks as "being operated to and from the United States."

Several foreign airlines have since taken advantage of this provision and arranged very attractive financings, among them Air France, UTA, KLM, SAS, China Air (Taiwan), Philippine Airlines, and CAAC (People's Republic of China).

Another criterion for claiming ITC applies to rolling stock of a domestic railroad corporation subject to Part One of the Interstate Commerce Act, which is used within and without the United States. This provision clarifies that U.S. railroads that are interstate commerce can claim ITC on rolling stock, even if it is used outside the United States (i.e., Canada and Mexico) some or most of the time.

A few ITC leases have been drawn for Canadian railroads as well. Such transactions do not qualify for ITC on the basis of the above provision, but because the rolling stock is being used predominantly (i.e., over 50% of the time) in the United States.

An additional criterion includes any vessel documented under the laws of the United States that is operated in the foreign or domestic commerce of the United States. This provision covers U.S.-registered vessels (regardless where they were built) that fly the U.S. flag and have a U.S. crew. This provision is important for U.S. corporations that cannot meet certain citizenship requirements for registering vessels in the United States because of their foreign shareholders. Standard Oil of Ohio and Shell Oil are well-publicized examples.

A fourth criterion for ITC is that of any motor vehicle of a U.S. person as defined in Section 7701a30 that is operated to and from the United States. This provision is comparable to the provision for railroad rolling stock and covers automobiles operated into Canada or Mexico for business purposes.

Any container of a U.S. person that is used in the transportation of property to and from the United States is eligible for an investment tax credit. This provision has never been interpreted by the IRS. The prevailing view in the U.S. container industry is that a container that enters a U.S. port at least once during the course of a year will qualify for ITC. The U.S. container industry also seems to take the view that it is sufficient if a container fleet touches a U.S. port once a year in the aggregate rather than each individual container. If one container, for example, enters U.S. ports seven times a year, while six other containers never get there, the requirement (according to this view) has been met.

The author's own discussions with the IRS lead him to believe that the IRS would probably insist on more than one annual landing and would certainly require that each container meet the test rather than a container fleet in the aggregate. Most container companies, because of the capital-intensive nature of the business, do not pay U.S. taxes and have leased a large portion of their fleet. Many of these lease agreements provide an indemnity for the lessor, in the event the IRS should disallow the ITC. The container industry is a very young industry, not more than 20 years old, and during these years the IRS has never questioned the industry practice of claiming ITC on oceangoing containers. Should the IRS attack this practice today and disallow the ITC retroactively, most of the U.S. container companies would be facing severe financial difficulties or worse.

The U.S. container industry is therefore increasingly taking the attitude that it must not happen, therefore it cannot happen. While it cannot be ruled out that the IRS will take steps to significantly limit the availability of ITC on containers, this author doubts very much that any such action will be made retroactive, since the IRS has condoned the practice for so long.

Another criterion for ITC covers any property that is owned by a domestic corporation (other than a corporation that has an election in effect under Section 936 or is entitled to the benefits of Section 934b) or by a U.S. citizen (other than a citizen entitled to the benefits of Section 931, 932, 933, or 934c) and that is used predominantly in a possession of the United States by such a corporation or such a citizen, or by a corporation created or organized in, or under the law of, a possession of the United States. This provision makes ITC available to certain corporations doing business in U.S. possessions, provided the assets are used predominantly in a U.S. possession or the user is a corporation created or organized under the laws of a U.S. possession. Because of the other provisions of the Tax Code this condition is of limited practical relevance.

Any communications satellite, as defined in Section 103(3) of the Communications Satellite Act of 1962, 47 *U.S.C.* 702(3), or any interest therein of a U.S. person is a criterion for ITC. Although the IRS has never ruled on this provision, the wording seems to qualify the lessor of **communications satellites**—even those not made in the United States—for ITC, regardless whether the lessee is a U.S. or a foreign entity.

This point was not relevant when the provision was enacted, since at that time only the Soviet Union and the United States had the technical capabilities of launching satellites and it was not very likely that the Soviets would try to take advantage of this provision by leasing their satellites. A special provision to make satellites eligible for ITC was needed. Satellites are outside of U.S. air space and orbit the earth, so it was hard to argue that they were predominantly used within the United States.

In subsequent years, other nations, among them France and Great Britain, developed the capability to build and launch communications satellites, and competition among the manufacturers became intense. Satellites can now also be put into stationary orbit, which means that their relative position to the ground does not change. This opened up the possibility of financing a French-built satellite in stationary orbit over, for example, Africa, through a U.S. tax lease. To date, this concept has not been tested in practice, mainly because of the dominant position of the U.S. manufacturers. In spite of the attractive cost, even U.S.-made satellites sold overseas have so far not been lease-financed. Lease proposals have been made, but they were turned down, not because they lacked economic attractiveness, but because the government of the importing country felt that national pride required ownership of the satellites.

Provisions for ITC eligibility also include any cable, or any interest therein, of a domestic corporation engaged in furnishing **telephone service** to which Section 46c3B (iii) applies (or of a wholly owned domestic subsidiary of such a corporation), if such cable is part of a submarine cable system that constitutes part of a communication link exclusively between the United States and one or more foreign countries. To the author's knowledge, this provision has not been used to provide lease financing. The provision itself is self-explanatory.

Finally, two remaining criteria for ITC exist, namely, any property (other than a vessel or an aircraft) of a U.S. person, one that is used for the purpose of exploring for, developing, removing, or transporting resources from the outer continental shelf (within the meaning of Section 2 of the Outer Continental Shelf Lands Act, as amended and supplemented), and second, any property of a U.S. person (other than a vessel or an aircraft) that is used in international or territorial waters within the northern portion of the Western Hemisphere for the purpose of exploring for, developing, removing, or transporting resources from ocean waters or deposits under such waters.

For the purposes of clause, the phrase "northern portion of the Western Hemisphere" means the area lying west of the 30th meridian west of Greenwich, east of the international dateline, and north of the equator, but not including any foreign country that is a country of South America.

The author once asked counsel to research the legislative history of these provisions to see whether the clause covering exploring, developing, removing, or transporting resources from the outer continental shelf and it appears that this is not the case. Thus the former clause is essentially redundant. The latter clause is of significant relevance for the leasing industry, since it covers Canadian and Mexican waters in addition to U.S. waters. The provision has, for example, made it possible for Pemex, the Mexican national oil company, to finance most of its offshore oil exploration equipment through U.S. tax leases at very attractive rates.

These provisions form the basis for cross-border leasing from the United States. Leases of assets not qualifying for ITC, that is, leases not covered by one of the exceptions listed in Section 48a2B of the Tax Code, are only marginally attractive to the lessee. The accelerated depreciation available to the lessor will permit a reduction in the interest cost of the lease—when compared to a secured loan for the same amount and maturity—by 2% to 4% annually, depending on lease term, type of asset, and overall level of interest rates. The drawback is that the lessee can acquire the asset at the end of the lease term only at the then–fair market value. As a rule of thumb, the break-even residual value on depreciation-only cross-border leases from the United States is between 40% and 70% of the original cost of the asset. The break-even residual value compares the cost of the lease to the lessee with the cost of having purchased the asset instead. It is found by solving through trial and error for the residual value (or purchase price at the end of the lease), which will produce the same internal rate of return (or present value) for the cash flows from the lease, including the residual value, as from a purchase of the asset. It would go beyond the scope of this section to embark on a detailed discussion of a lease-versus-buy analysis. Suffice it to say that the analysis has to be done on an after-tax basis and that the discount rate, if a present value method is used, should at least be the after-tax cost of borrowing funds for the term of the lease rather than the cost of the capital, the reason being that the decision to acquire the the asset has already been made, so the lease-versus-buy analysis is a financing decision and not an investment decision. Care should be taken to remember that the after-tax cost of borrowing (i.e., the discount rate) for a company that is not paying taxes is equal to its pretax cost of borrowing.

In addition to depreciating the asset and claiming ITC, the lessor can deduct the funding cost, including any interest expense on nonrecourse debt, if the lease meets the conditions pertinent to asset ownership for U.S. tax purposes. (See "Funding the Cross-Border Lease," following.)

Finally, lease rentals received are taxable income to the lessor.

Foreign Source Income Considerations. The tax benefit of leasing is derived largely from the income-deferring effect of accelerated depreciation. In the early years of the transaction accelerated depreciation (a noncash charge) exceeds lease income. The lessor can use these losses to offset other taxable income, thus reducing current taxes payable and deferring these tax liabilities to the future. If the asset is located offshore the resulting losses are of a foreign source in nature, (i.e., they can only be taken if a lessor has no foreign tax credits or if the U.S. tax liability on foreign-source income after taking foreign tax credits into account is at least equal to the after-tax effect of the losses produced by the lease).

The tax position of most U.S. lessors is such that it does not permit them to write cross-border leases, at least not on competitive terms. Most bank-affiliated lessors do not have this problem and they have dominated the cross-border leasing market in recent years. Some industrial lessors have been active as well. Identification of those lessors who have the tax capacity to write cross-border leases from the United States has been a profitable and at times frustrating business for lease brokers and other intermediaries.

THE UNITED KINGDOM. The IRS tries to look at the economic substance of a transaction to decide who is the owner of an asset for U.S. tax purposes. Inland Revenue in the United Kingdom takes a more formalistic approach to distinguish whether a transaction is a conditional sale (the U.K. equivalent term is "hire purchase") or a true lease for U.K. tax purposes. If the lessee has a purchase option of any kind, the transaction is a hire purchase and the lessee will be considered the owner for U.K. tax purposes. Recently, however, some U.K. lessors and their tax advisors have taken the view that a purchase option at the asset's fair market value will not transfer tax ownership from the lessor to the lessee and they are willing to write leases on this basis without indemnity.

If the lease does not contain a purchase option, the lessor will be considered owner for U.K. tax purposes, even though other provisions transfer essentially all of the economic benefits of ownership (at least by U.S. standards) to the lessee. It is, for example, quite common for U.K. leases to provide that at the end of the primary lease term the lessee will be entitled to 95% to 99% of the sales proceeds of the asset as a "rebate of rentals" as long as this sum does not exceed the total of all rentals paid. In addition or as an alternative the lessee might have the option to renew the lease at secondary annual rentals as low as 0.25% of the original equipment cost for a few years and then dropping to as little as 0.10% for the remaining useful life of the asset. While the lease agreement might not provide for a purchase option, it is standard practice for U.K. lessees to make an offer to purchase the equipment at the end of the primary lease term. Since the lessee is entitled to most of the sales proceeds, it is not likely that any stiff competition in bidding for the asset will be encountered.

The U.K. leasing market is highly developed and in terms of size and sophistication is second only to the U.S. market. At the end of 1980 the book value of all leases written by members of the U.K. Equipment Lessors' Association was in excess of £4 billion and it is estimated that 15% to 20% of all capital expenditures in the United Kingdom are financed through leasing.

The U.K. tax benefits transferred through leasing are very generous. The buyer of plant and machinery (roughly equivalent to personal property as opposed to real estate in U.S. terminology) located in the United Kingdom is entitled to depreciate the asset 100% in the year it is acquired. Whether or not the asset is new or used is irrelevant as long as the person claiming the depreciation (capital allowance) is acquiring the asset in an arm's length transaction from an unrelated party. If the transaction is a sale/leaseback, the purchaser (lessor) can only claim allowances on the 25% declining balance basis.

If the assets are located outside the United Kingdom, capital allowances can be claimed on the 25% declining balance basis. This rule was introduced by the 1980 Finance Act. The rule was necessitated by the removal of exchange controls in the United Kingdom in 1979. Prior to the enactment of the 1980 Finance Act, the U.K. owner of an asset could depreciate the asset 100% in the year of acquisition, irrespective of the location of the asset. In theory this situation would have permitted U.K. lessors to lease assets irrespective of origin anywhere in the world at great cost to the U.K. taxpayer. In practice, as long as exchange controls were in effect, any cross-border lease involving a U.K. lessor had to be approved by the Bank of England. The Bank of England did not approve any such cross-border transactions unless a tangible benefit to the U.K. economy and the balance of payments could be demonstrated. This meant that approval was essentially only given for leases involving the export of British-made goods. In view of the very attractive British export financing available from ECGD and a rule prohibiting double subsidies through a combination of export financing and leasing (see "Double Subsidy" following), very few U.K.-based cross-border leases were actually done prior to the removal of exchange controls and the passing of the 1980 Finance Act.

The authors of the 1980 Finance Act and many members of the U.K. leasing industry believed that reducing the availability of depreciation from 100% in the first year to 25% on a declining balance basis for cross-border leases would make such transactions economically unattractive. Little did they know about the creativity and resilience of the leasing industry. The traditional U.K. leasing market—using 100% of the first year's depreciation—writes primarily leases with terms of five to seven years. Using the 25% declining balance method of depreciation, the undepreciated balance of an asset is 23.73% after five years and 13.35% after seven years. The rentals over the same period return 100% of the original cost of the asset plus interest, and rentals received are fully taxable income to the lessor. The lessor's tax deferral in the early years of a five- to seven-year lease is therefore minor and in later years the taxable income exceeds the annual depreciation by a significant margin. The authors of the 1980 Finance Act were therefore quite right in assuming that the 25% allowance would not make five- to seven-year cross-border leases attractive.

Long-Term Leases. A very different picture emerges when the lease term is extended to 12 or 15 years. Here the depreciation provides a significant deferral of tax payments for the lessor. Rather than paying taxes immediately, the lessor can invest the funds earmarked for current tax payments until the time when those taxes will actually become payable. This permits the lessor to offer lease financing at a rate below the cost of a loan for the same amount and term to a customer of comparable credit standing. The lessor is in effect sharing the benefit of the tax deferral with the lessee through a reduction in the cost of the lease as an inducement for the lessee to enter into the lease. What portion of the total benefit is retained by the lessor and how much is passed on to the lessee is determined by the market and can vary considerably over time. The 1980 Finance Act therefore created several problems for the U.K. leasing industry, which had to be resolved before cross-border leases could be written.

Problems for U.K. Leasing. Problems for U.K. leasing have included:

1. The U.K. leasing market is mainly a five- to seven-year market, yet cross-border leases from the U.K. are only attractive for terms of 12 years or longer.
2. The U.K. leasing market is primarily a fixed-rate market and leases are denominated in pounds sterling.
3. Long-term fixed-rate funding in pounds sterling is not readily available for U.K. lessors and writing leases in currencies other than pounds sterling presents two problems for a U.K. lessor. First, the lessor faces a currency exposure risk, as the depreciation benefits are sterling-denominated; the underlying liability incurred to fund the lease would be U.S. dollar-denominated. Second, the currency exposure also gives rise to a tax problem. It is assumed that the U.K. lessor would fund a U.S. dollar lease with a U.S. dollar borrowing. If the U.S. dollar/pound exchange rate changes, the U.K. lessor will record gains and/or losses on rental income, which will, on a pretax basis, be offset by matching gains and/or losses on the U.S. dollar borrowing. Unfortunately, the gains and/or losses on the rental income will represent ordinary items for U.K. tax purposes, whereas the gains and/or losses on the U.S. dollar borrowing will represent capital items, which are neither assessable nor deductible for U.K. tax purposes.

These problems required fairly creative solutions, if cross-border leasing from the United Kingdom was to offer a viable financing alternative. Initially, the major U.K. lessors offered 12- and 15-year floating-rate leases at rates of 1.5% to 2.5% below the London interbank offered rate (LIBOR). This solved the funding problem but not the foreign exchange exposure problem; it also met some resistance from potential lessees who had a preference for fixed-rate funding.

Attempts to solve the exchange exposure through **long-dated forward exchange contracts** failed because of practical difficulties in closing the lease and the currency hedge simultaneously. The lessee wanted to know the dollar cost of the lease in advance, but the dollar/pound relationship tends to change quickly and no lessee wanted to commit to the currency hedge without being certain that the lease could be closed on the anticipated terms and conditions. Conversely, no lessee was willing to sign a lease without knowing whether an acceptable currency hedge could be arranged. Forward exchange contracts for dollar/pound exposures are not readily available for terms in excess of five years, certainly not for large amounts and as many as 60 quarterly rental payments with different maturities. Therefore, the idea of hedging the dollar/pound exposure in the forward exchange markets was discarded as impractical. Other solutions, such as purchase by the lessee of a portfolio of U.K. government securities (gilts) matching each future rental obligation under the lease, were also not practical, both because gilts in the right amounts and for the right maturities are not always available and, more important, because of the doubling-up effect such a solution would have on the lessee's balance sheet.

Contrary to traditional U.S. leasing rules, the **U.K. permits funding of the lessor by the lessee.** This possibility offered a solution to the problems connected with cross-border leases from the United Kingdom. The lessee makes a pounds sterling deposit with the U.K. lessor or an affiliate of the U.K. lessor. The lessee funds this deposit in the preferred currency and in a preferred market, short-term or long-term, at fixed or at floating rates of interest. The lessor uses this deposit to fund the lease, or the group of companies of which the lessor is a member can use the deposit to eliminate the **interest rate exposure** resulting from the fixed-rate lease written by the lessor. Interest payments on the deposit and repayment of the deposit are set in such a fashion that these payments exactly match each periodic rental payment under the lease. The amount of the deposit required equals the purchase price of the asset less the present value of the tax benefits that the lessor is willing to pass on to the lessee. This structure is very similar to the **"wash" leases** that are now prevalent in the U.S. as a result of the safe **harbor leasing rules** under the Economic Recovery Tax Act. Any ballooning of the lessee's balance sheet under the U.K. deposit lease structure is avoided by giving the lessee the right to discontinue rental payments if the payments on the deposit are not received. This permits the lessee to net the lease obligations against the deposit.

This structure was successfully used to write in excess of $1 billion U.K. cross-border leases in late 1980 and during 1981. As a result, the U.K. Treasury became quite concerned about the impact of these transactions on revenues and the ultimate cost to the British taxpayer. The initial inclination on part of the U.K. Treasury was to limit the availability of U.K. capital allowances in cross-border leases to U.K. manufactured goods, but this would have been a discriminating trade practice under the GATT and European Economic Community treaties. Rather than taking legislative action the U.K. Treasury, in a series of meetings with the **Equipment Lessor's Association** (ELA), worked out a voluntary restraint program. Under this agreement, members of ELA will only write cross-border leases using U.K. capital allowances if the leases provide an ultimate benefit to the U.K. balance of payment. This is clearly subject to intepretation and it remains to be seen what type of lease will ultimately be permitted. It appears that if leases of U.K. goods are acceptable, the same should be true of leases written at a positive spread over the lessor's cost of funds before taking the tax benefits into account. Whether leases of assets employed by foreign subsidiaries of U.K. corporations will qualify is dubious.

At least in theory, lessors that are not members of ELA—many industrial lessors are in this position—are not bound by the voluntary restraint agreement. Whether they will abide by the rules remains to be seen; most likely they will insist on being indemnified against any adverse tax consequences and this will probably make such transactions unacceptable to potential lessees.

The 1982 Finance Act effectively eliminates the U.K. as a lessor country for cross-border leases. The Act has reduced the depreciation from 25% declining balance to 10% declining balance and has prohibited other tax-deferring devices such as low–high rentals as well. Cross-border leases from the U.K. are available but provide no cost advantages.

Special rules, incidentially, make vessels, aircrafts, and containers eligible for 100% first-year depreciation, if the operation of such assets is effectively controlled by a bona fide U.K. corporation. This offers interesting leasing possibilities for non-U.K. shipping and container leasing companies with U.K. subsidiaries.

OTHER COUNTRIES

West Germany. West Germany used to be a fairly attractive base for cross-border leases. The West German leasing market is dominated by the leasing subsidiaries of the large West German commercial banks and savings banks (*Girozentralen*). This leasing market is, however, not tax-oriented and essentially all leases written by these institutions are money-over-money leases.

Tax leasing does exist in West Germany, but it is not known under this name. Instead it is called *Abschreibungsgesellschaft* (literally, a company with the objective of depreciation) or *Fond* (fund). These entities are usually structured as partnerships, with one general partner (usually a corporation with limited liability) and hundreds of limited partners (usually wealthy individuals such as doctors, lawyers, dentists, and corporate executives). Partnership shares are sold to the limited partners through a public offering that is governed by rules less stringent than those governing similar offerings in the United States.

The partnership puts up a portion of the cost of the asset to be acquired and borrows the balance. In the 1960s and early 1970s this was done on a nonrecourse basis. In recent years the West German tax authorities have disallowed losses in excess of the capital contribution made by the limited partner (e.g., depreciation was limited to the at-risk investment of the taxpayer). This limitation can be overcome through a provision in the lease under which the limited partner has to advance additional funds—up to the maximum tax loss claimed during the life of the transaction—if necessary (*Nachschusspflicht*). The nonrecourse debt is now effectively with full recourse, since the additional obligations of the limited partners—if enforced—would provide sufficient funds in the aggregate to pay off the entire debt. In practice, as long as the lessee meets contracted obligations under the lease, the limited partners will never be called upon to advance additional funds. While previously the credit standing of the lessee was of no great concern to the limited partners, who could not lose more than their initial investment and recovered most of it from the West German Treasury even if the lessee defaulted, West German tax leases are now only available for lessees of the highest credit standing.

The West German tax authorities have in recent years pretty much limited depreciation to the straight-line method, certainly for cross-border type transactions with individuals as limited partners. This has reduced the interest cost advantage of these transactions from about 3% to 3.5% annually to between 75 and 150 basis points. Considering the management time required, the legal costs involved, and the considerable uncertainty whether the transaction can be successfully consummated, it is not surprising that few cross-border leases using West Germany as the lessor country have been completed in recent years. Philippine Airlines was successful in financing two Airbus A-300s through a 12-year West German tax lease using a limited partnership of individuals as lessors during 1980.

A similar structure, using West German corporations rather than individuals as the limited partners, will probably be less harshly scrutinized by the West German tax authorities. The problem with this approach is that few West German corporations are willing to enter into such transactions to shelter taxes.

West German tax accounting follows shareholder accounting (*Massgeblichkeitsprinzip*). This means that a West German corporation that wants to create tax losses through accelerated depreciation has to report the same losses to its shareholders and, more important since West German companies are usually undercapitalized, to its creditors. Tax shelter transactions have, therefore, limited appeal to West German corporations and they will only consider them if profits in a particular year are exceptionally high or if it is deemed prudent to show reduced profits because of imminent labor negotiations.

For example, in 1979, KLM successfully completed the sale/leaseback of a used Boeing 747 using a limited partnership of several large West German banks as lessor. (The debt portion of this lease, incidentally, was funded in Dutch guilders.) The interest cost of the lease to KLM is reportedly below 7% annually at a time when the cost of the longer term guilder financing was between 9% and 10% annually. The place of business for the limited partnership was Bermuda, eliminating the West German trade tax on the funding of the lease. Funding West German leases in foreign currencies does not present any tax problems and was done routinely during the early 1970s, the boom period for West German cross-border leases, when a fair portion of oil drilling ventures in the British sector of the North Sea were financed in this fashion.

Australia. Leveraged leasing, which had been in its infancy and rather dormant in Australia for many years, suddenly sprang to life over the last 18 months, when first Qantas and then the Australian subsidiary of General Motors arranged Australian tax-based leveraged leases in excess of $200 million each.

The Australian leasing market is dominated by the five large Australian Trading Banks and their finance company subsidiaries. The banks and their finance companies compete with each other for leasing business and have to be considered as separate sources of equity, because the concept of consolidation for tax purposes or profit and loss–pooling arrangements are foreign to Australian tax law. The sudden interest in acting as lessors on the part of the major Australian financial institutions was triggered by exceptionally good profits in recent years.

The Qantas transaction, involving assets used predominantly outside Australia, prompted interest in using Australian equity to fund cross-border leases for aircraft and vessels. The first to succeed was Air New Zealand, which completed an Australian leveraged lease for several Boeing 747s during 1981. This was quickly followed by transactions for Singapore Airlines and Cathay Pacific. While several other potential lessees are reportedly interested in the structure, available equity has become very scarce in Australia and it is doubtful that further large transactions can be successfully completed. So far the Australian Treasury, surprisingly, has done nothing to stop the practice. This is particularly intriguing since Qantas is government-owned, has been losing money, and the main beneficiaries of the largesse of the Australian Treasury are some of Qantas' toughest competitors.

The Australian aircraft leases are typically for 12 years, with interest rate savings in the range of 3.0% to 3.5% annually. Residual value is not really a problem and the lessee can acquire the aircraft at the end of the lease term for the unamortized loan balance, usually in the form of a balloon rental payment equal to approximately 20% of original cost. This is what happens economically, although the legal structure to achieve this result is rather convoluted.

The debt portion of an Australian lease can be funded in foreign currencies. Assets used predominantly outside Australia do not qualify for an investment allowance, but only for accelerated depreciation. The rate of depreciation varies greatly with the specific assets involved. This author is aware of only one Australian tax lease for vessels; it is unlikely that, apart from the aircraft deals, assets located outside of Australia have been financed through an Australian tax lease.

France. The type of lease financing usually encountered in France is called **creditbail** and is a money-over-money lease in U.S. terminology. This market is dominated by the leasing subsidiaries of the large French banks. Lease terms are three to five years, rates are mainly fixed, and the cost of these leases is quite high when compared to other financing alternatives. There is a special law governing creditbail leases and the transactions are structured accordingly.

However, as in West Germany, there is a different type of lease in France, one that does not follow the creditbail rules. These transactions are arranged by the merchant banking departments of the French commercial banks and by the French investment banks. The legal form used is known as a **groupement d' interet economique**, or GIE, and would be considered a partnership in the United States. The GIE puts up a portion of the funds, borrows the balance on a nonrecourse basis, and takes accelerated depreciation on the full purchase price of the asset. The members (partners) of a GIE are typically French banks, investment banks, or corporations. Usinor's large steel complex in Fos (near Marseille) was financed in this fashion. Ships and aircraft have also been financed through this structure. The GIE could be used to structure cross-border leases as well; however, its practical usefulness appears quite limited, since any such transaction would require French government approval. Most likely, only French-built vessels and possibly the Airbus are potential candidates for this kind of financing.

Japan. The concept of tax leasing is not known in Japan. All leases written by the leading Japanese leasing companies, such as Orient Leasing, Japan Lease, General Lease, and Pacific Lease, are money-over-money leases. Some of these leases, primarily those for vessels, are booked in offshore subsidiaries of the Japanese leasing companies located in tax havens (for shipping income) such as Hongkong or Singapore. Their sole purpose is to protect the earnings of these leasing operations from taxation in Japan and no benefits are passed back to the lessees through lower rates.

The so-called Samurai leases, which were offered by Japanese leasing companies, banks, and trading companies in 1978, while very attractive to the lessees, were money-over-money leases. The funding of these leases was subsidized by the Japanese government and some of these benefits were passed on to the lessees. The purpose of the program was to reduce the imbalance in Japanese trade by having

Japanese lessors purchase large capital assets, thus creating imports. The typical term of these transactions was 10 years, with 20 equal rental payments semiannually in arrears. The interest cost to the lessees was set by the Japanese government at a uniform 8.25% annually. The transactions were denominated in U.S. dollars. Presently the introduction of a similar program is under discussion in Japan.

Disadvantageous Countries. No other country is useful as a lessor country for cross-border leases. Some of the other English-speaking countries, such as Canada, Nigeria, Singapore, South Africa, and Ireland, have a domestic tax-based leasing industry, but for a variety of reasons they are not viable as lessor countries.

The Canadian government effectively killed the Canadian tax-leasing industry when it limited the tax deductibility of losses created through leasing to the taxable income generated through the leasing activity. This helped the established Canadian leasing companies whose maturing lease portfolios were generating some taxable income as the booking of new leasing business slowed down and made *de novo* entry into the tax-oriented sector for the Canadian leasing industry impossible. The few Canadian lessors who get some tax benefit from their mature lease portfolios face so little competition that they can afford to retain most of the tax benefits themselves. As a result, it is very difficult to write large leases providing meaningful savings to the lessee even in the domestic Canadian leasing market. The author is not aware of any cross-border leases using a lessor with a Canadian tax base.

Both Nigeria and Singapore permit tax-based leasing. The tax laws in both countries are not very specific when it comes to leasing and one cannot rely on the future viability of current interpretations. While smallish transactions might be permitted by the tax authorities, it is a virtual certainty that any large transactions with a significant impact on Treasury revenues would be attacked. This holds particularly true for any cross-border transactions that might be attempted.

South Africa has a well-developed domestic leasing industry and the available tax benefits, a 20% investment allowance, and generous accelerated depreciation permit a significant reduction in the interest cost of the lease to the lessee. The availability of these tax benefits in cross-border leases is, however, limited to assets manufactured in South Africa. Since South Africa is not a major exporter of large capital assets, the practical value of cross-border leases using a lessor with a tax base in South Africa is negligible.

The leasing industry in the Republic of Ireland is very much tailored after the British leasing industry. While Ireland might have some relevance to money-over-money lessors as a tax haven, permitting them to shelter the earnings from their leasing activities from taxation, the tax base of the Irish lessors is so limited that they are not a significant factor in cross-border leasing.

The continental European countries, other than France and West Germany, either do not have any structure that would be suitable for cross-border tax leasing (Austria, Belgium, Italy, Spain, Switzerland) or the tax base of potential lessors is so limited that they cannot even accommodate domestic demand (The Netherlands and Denmark are examples).

Leasing in Latin America is not tax-oriented. To the extent that the local leasing industry is well developed (as in Brazil, Mexico, and Venezuela) it provides much-needed liquidity at a comparatively high cost. In both Brazil and Mexico essentially the entire leasing market is linked to the U.S. dollar and refinanced offshore in dollars. The leases are usually fixed-rate leases and for terms of three to five years. They are money-over-money leases.

It is quite remarkable that almost all of the viable tax-leasing markets, with the limited exceptions of France and West Germany, are English-speaking countries. The main reason for the highly developed tax-leasing industries in the English-speaking countries and the lack of a similar development in the rest of the world lies in a basic difference in **accounting rules**. United States and U.K. accounting rules permit the lessor to report the earnings from a lease for shareholder reporting purposes in relation to the actual cash the lessor has at risk in the transaction and only during the period when this cash is still being recovered. During this same period the lessor usually reports heavy losses for tax purposes. In other words, the lessor gets all the benefits of tax losses and is reporting profits to the shareholders at the same time. Continental European accounting standards and countries whose accounting conventions were heavily influenced by continental European countries (such as Japan and the Latin American countries) use their reports to shareholders as the basis for their tax returns. In order to take losses for tax purposes, those same losses have to be reported to shareholders and, more important, to the creditors. Only well-capitalized and very profitable companies can afford to do this. It would be an interesting research project to explore how these different accounting standards have affected the quality of reported earnings in the English-speaking world as opposed to continental Europe and Japan.

DOUBLE LEASING

The criteria that make the lessor or the lessee owner of the leased asset for tax purposes tend to vary significantly from country to country.

Sometimes it is possible to take advantage of these different definitions of tax ownership to structure transactions in which both the lessor and the lessee are considered owners of the asset for tax purposes in their respective countries. Such transactions are known as **double (depreciation) leases**, or **double dipping**.

As discussed previously, in the United States the IRS looks at the economic substance of a transaction. A lease that transfers essentially all the risks and rewards of ownership to the lessee is not a true lease for U.S. tax purposes and the lessee is entitled to the tax benefits of ownership.

In the United Kingdom the Inland Revenue takes a more formalistic approach. A U.K. lessor will not lose the ownership position for U.K. tax purposes if the lease contains a renewal option at a nominal rental (**a peppercorn renewal option**) or if the lease agreement provides that the lessee is entitled to most of the proceeds from the sale of the asset upon termination of the primary lease period.

Both a peppercorn renewal option or the right to substantially all (98% to 99%) of the residual value of the asset are considered by the IRS as transferring the risks and rewards of ownership to the lessee.

It is therefore possible to have a U.K. lessor lease an asset qualifying for 25% declining balance depreciation to a U.S. lessee and have the U.S. lessee in turn claim ITC and depreciation in the United States.

If the U.S. lessee is not in a tax-paying position and therefore unable to utilize the U.S. tax benefits of ownership, it is even possible to have the U.K. lessor lease to a U.S. leasing company, which in turn subleases to the U.S. lessee.

With the recent changes in U.S. leasing rules as a result of the Economic Recovery Tax Act, it is also possible for the U.S. lessee to lease from a U.K. lessor and then sell the ITC and depreciation to another U.S. corporation within three months from the date on which the asset was first placed in service.

All three structures are viable and have been successfully used by U.S. lessees. As a result of the recent restrictions imposed in the U.K. through the voluntary restraint agreement between the U.K. Treasury and the members of the Equipment Lessor Association, the practical applicability of U.K.-U.S. **double leases** has been much reduced.

Reversing the roles by having a U.S. lessor lease to a U.K. lessee, incidentally, does not work, since the U.S. lessor would have to insist on a fair market purchase option and the Inland Revenue has indicated that a purchase option at fair market will not necessarily transfer ownership for U.K. tax purposes to the lessee.

But double leasing is not limited to U.K.-U.S. leases. A true U.K. lease with a **peppercorn renewal option** and a provision giving the lessee a substantial share in the residual value would be considered as a conditional sale, with the tax ownership resting with the lessee in West Germany, Hong Kong, the Netherlands, and Singapore and there is a better than even chance that the tax authorities in Australia and Canada would reach the same conclusions.

West Germany is another interesting country for double leasing. The West German tax authorities have published tables to establish the life of assets for tax-depreciation purposes similar to the U.S. asset depreciation range (ADR) tables. These West German tax-depreciation tables are called AfA tables (*Absetzung für Abnuetzung*, write-off for depreciation). The West German tax authorities have also ruled that in a lease with a term in excess of 90% of the useful economic life of the asset the lessee will be considered the owner for West German tax purposes. The useful economic life of the asset is defined as the AfA life of the asset.

It so happens that the West German AfA lives for most assets are quite short. The AfA life of ships or aircrafts, for example, is 12 years, and a fair amount of manufacturing equipment has an AfA life of about six years. United States ship leases routinely run for 20 to 25 years and aircraft leases run for 15 to 18 years. Industrial equipment can easily be leased for 10 years. In each case the lease term clearly exceeds 90% of the AfA life, with the result that a West German lessee would be considered owner of the asset for West German tax purposes. The same holds true for leases from other countries into West Germany, provided the leasing rules of the other country permit a sufficiently long lease term without jeopardizing the tax ownership position of the lessor.

Several U.S.–West German double-depreciation leases have been successfully completed.

The Netherlands considers the lessee the owner for tax purposes if the lease term is equal to the economic life of the asset. The primary lease term of a true lease for U.S. tax purposes cannot exceed 80% of the estimated useful life of the asset. The useful economic life of an asset is a rather subjective matter and at least one Dutch lessee has been very successful in convincing the Dutch tax authorities that U.S. leases are for the useful economic life of the assets, thus entitling the lessee to the tax benefits of ownership in The Netherlands.

This author is convinced that there are other countries offering similar possibilities. In many cases the rules are not very specific or subject to change. In those cases it may be too risky to attempt double leases with third parties, but within the same group of companies they might be worthwhile to pursue. If successful, the group could gain considerably and, if not, the group is usually no worse off than if it had not tried.

COMMON TAX PROBLEMS IN CROSS-BORDER LEASES

There are three common tax problems in cross-border leases that need to be resolved before such leases can be successfully concluded.

1. Will the lease cause the lessor to have created a **permanent establishment** in the lessee country in the eyes of the tax authorities there?
2. Will the purchase of the asset or the lease rentals be subject to **value-added tax** (VAT) or some other kind of turnover tax?
3. Will the lessee country subject the lease rentals or a portion of the lease rentals to **withholding taxes**?

PERMANENT ESTABLISHMENT. With a lessor who already has a permanent establishment in the lessee country because of other activities, a problem does not arise. Lease income derived from the lessee country will be treated as other income and taxed accordingly. The lessor simply has to decide whether a cross-border lease that is taxable to the lessor in the lessee country is economically sensible. This will largely depend on how taxes paid in the lessee country are treated for tax purposes in the lessor country, whether they are a credit, a deduction, or irrelevant for domestic tax purposes. If they are creditable or deductible it then depends on whether the lessor can use the tax credits or deductions.

If the lessor does not have a permanent establishment in the lessee country, it is important to explore whether the lease itself might create such a permanent establishment. This is a question of local law and of the tax treaty, if any, between the two countries.

A single cross-border lease will not normally create a **permanent establishment** in the lessee country. A large number of such leases might change the picture. Also certain sales finance, or "wet" leases, which are accompanied by significant operating or maintenance services on the part of the lessor, could create a permanent establishment. From the lessee's point of view it is important to avoid having to indemnify the lessor against taxes from such a permanent establishment. This issue is usually subject to intensive negotiations in cross-border leases.

VALUE-ADDED TAX. A value-added tax, turnover tax, or sales tax might be triggered by a lessee bringing an asset into its home country. This should not be an issue, since it is a tax for which the lessee would also be liable if it had purchased the asset.

However, payments of lease rentals might be considered services for VAT purposes, subjecting the lessee to VAT, unless existing tax treaties provide relief.

Lease rentals between EEC countries, for example, are considered exports and are, therefore, zero-rated. While the question needs to be addressed to avoid unpleasant surprises, VAT can usually be avoided.

WITHHOLDING TAX. Many countries subject lease rentals paid overseas to withholding taxes. Since lease rentals on **full-pay-out financial leases** consist in effect of principal plus interest, this would make cross-border leases very expensive, unless ways can be found to eliminate or minimize the impact of withholding taxes. Some countries, such as Saudi Arabia and Mexico, do not apply the withholding taxes to the lease rentals paid, but impute a profit to the lessor and apply the withholding tax to the imputed profit. Brazil applies a 25% withholding tax to lease rentals, but upon application this tax can be reduced or zero-rated if the Brazilian authorities decide that the lease provides an economic benefit to the Brazilian economy. No reduction in the rate will be granted on intercompany leases into Brazil.

In some countries it is not clear whether lease rentals are subject to withholding taxes and if so at what rate. This is so because many tax treaties do not address the question. Article 12 of the OECD Model Tax Treaty defines lease payments as royalties. Countries that have adopted the OECD model treaty treat lease payments as royalty payments, subject to the same withholding tax rates.

Under the treaties of Belgium, France, West Germany, and the United States the withholding tax on royalties is frequently zero-rated. Lease rentals paid from The Netherlands, Switzerland, and the United Kingdom for movable equipment (as opposed to real estate) are not subject to withholding taxes. The Canadian withholding tax on lease rentals paid to treaty countries is 15%, otherwise it is 25%. The Japanese rate is 40% for nontreaty countries and can be as low as 10% for treaty countries like the United States.

Lessors are usually very reluctant to absorb withholding taxes, at least during the early period of the lease, when the transaction is generating tax losses in the lessor country. In later years, when the lessor has run out of depreciation and incurs a significant tax liability on the lease rentals received, a lessor in a country permitting a tax credit for foreign withholding taxes paid (such as the United States) might be agreeable to absorbing withholding taxes to the extent that they are creditable.

If a withholding tax applies and a lessor willing to absorb it cannot be found, structures have to be designed that will eliminate or minimize the impact of withholding taxes.

THIRD COUNTRY AS CONDUIT. One such structure, which can also be used to eliminate VAT, is to run a cross-border lease through a third country with a favorable tax treaty. A suitable conduit country might be The Netherlands, the Dutch Antilles, or Switzerland. These countries might have a tax treaty with the lessee country eliminating withholding taxes (or VAT) and they do not impose a withholding tax on rentals paid to a lessor in the third country. The additional cost of going through an intermediary might be small when compared with the benefit of the lease and the cost of paying the withholding taxes. Depending on the circumstances and the particular anti-avoidance provisions of the countries involved, the intermediary can be a subsidiary of the lessor, of the lessee, or an independent third party, such as a friendly bank.

In some countries (Canada is an example) banks are exempt from withholding taxes and it might be possible to have a lessor lease to a bank that will then on-lease to the ultimate lessee.

A third structure, which has been successfully employed by U.S. lessors and might have broader application, is to set up a trust in the lessee country—the trust could or could not be beneficially owned by the lessor—and have the trust borrow the nonrecourse debt of the leveraged lease.

If the lenders are domiciled in the lessee country, the lease is structured in such a fashion that all rental payments during the tax-loss-producing phase of the lease are applied to service the debt. Rentals are paid to the trust and are remitted as debt service to the lenders in the lessee country, without crossing the border. In later years, after the lease has started producing taxable income to the lessor, the tax liability from the lease itself will usually be more than sufficient to permit the lessor to absorb the withholding taxes.

The same structure could work even if the lenders are located outside the lessee country, provided the lessee country levies withholding taxes only on rental payments but not on long-term loans. An example is Canada, where interest payments on corporate loans are exempt from withholding taxes, provided the term of the loan is at least five years and not more than 25% of the principal amount of the loan is amortized during the first five years of the loan.

In such a situation, the trust or a corporation make debt service payments across the border, relying on the withholding tax exemption for qualifying loans.

FUNDING THE CROSS-BORDER LEASE

There is a difference between **direct,** or **single investor, leases** and **leveraged leases**.

In a **direct,** or **single investor, lease** the lessor puts up 100% of the purchase price of the asset. In a **leveraged** lease the lessor puts up only a portion of the purchase price (in the United States usually between 20% and 40% of asset cost) and borrows the balance. These borrowings can be either without recourse to the lessor (the United States, for example) or they can be with full recourse (as in the United Kingdom). If the borrowings are with full recourse, the lease is not truly a leveraged lease. The lessor has only identified a specific source of funds for the lease rather than using general corporate funds. This might help the lessor's economic analysis of the lease but is of little additional relevance.

If the borrowings are without recourse to the lessor then the lenders are lending only against the collateral value of the equipment and are relying on the lessee to meet the lease rental obligations. Usually these rental payments are assigned to the lenders. The lenders are basing their credit decision on the credit standing of the lessee, not the lessor. The credit standing of the lessor is almost irrelevant—almost, but not quite. Should the lessee default, the only chance for the lessor to get the money back is to take over the asset. In order to do this, the lessor has to keep the lenders whole. If the lessor does not do this, the lenders will repossess the asset and sell it to the first buyer who is willing to buy it for the outstanding loan balance. If this happens, the lessor has lost the unrecovered equity investment. All things being equal, lenders will, therefore, prefer a strong lessor.

LEVERAGED VERSUS DIRECT LEASE: LESSOR'S VIEW. When would a lessor want to write a leveraged lease as opposed to a direct lease?

When the total cost of the asset exceeds the resources a lessor is willing or able to commit—diversification of risk.

When the credit standing of the lessee is equal to or better than that of the lessor. The lessor can borrow at lower cost, using the lessee's credit, and need not charge a spread to the lessee.

When the lessee has better access to a particular debt market, irrespective of credit standing. A Dutch lessee has better access to the long-term fixed-rate Dutch guilder market and a U.S. lessee has better access to the U.S. private placement market than a foreign lessor. The fact that technically the lessor is the borrower is usually not relevant.

When the lessor is unwilling to lend at a fixed rate of interest or is not willing to lend for the full term of the lease (different lending criteria).

One common misconception about leveraged leasing is that the structure is inherently cheaper than that for a direct lease. This is not so. No element of the structure itself reduces the cost to the lessee. The fact that the interest cost on the nonrecourse debt is deductible for tax purposes does not make the lease any cheaper, since the interest paid to the lenders comes out of the lease rentals received. The interest payments are an actual cash outflow and the rentals received are taxable income. Also, a lessor who funds 100% of the asset cost itself will usually borrow these funds and can deduct the associated interest expense.

If the lessor can borrow at a lower interest rate than the lessee and if the lessor is willing to lend the debt portion of the leveraged lease to the lessee at the same rate as other lenders, the lessor should consider writing a direct lease as opposed to a leveraged lease. The lessor might even be able to charge a slight premium, since the management time and the documentation expense for a direct lease is (or should be) considerably less than for a leveraged lease.

The Financial Accounting Standards Board (FASB) of the United States, in SFAS 13 has, however, decreed that the lessor in a leveraged lease can take the earnings from a leveraged lease into income over the net investment period, which can be as short as 18 months in a 15-year lease for shareholder-reporting purposes.

The lessor in a direct lease written on identical terms will realize the same economic return as the lessor in a leveraged lease. However, the lessor has to report these earnings for shareholder reporting purposes over the full 15-year life of the lease in relation to the declining investment in the lease. This does not make it very attractive for certain lessors to write direct leases. This is another example of how lease accounting tends to effect the quality of reported earnings.

As more and more leases are written at floating rather than fixed rates of interest, because the lessees feel that fixed interest rates are too high or because fixed-rate loans are simply not available, it becomes more and more worthwhile to ask for both direct and leveraged lease quotes and to discuss the economic thinking behind each offer with the lessor. All the more so since most cross-border lessors are bank-affiliated and the banks are the typical lenders of floating-rate debt in leveraged leases.

Once the lessee has decided in favor of a leveraged lease, the best funding sources of the debt portion for such a lease have to be carefully evaluated. First, it should be explored as to whether subsidized funding from some government agency in the country where the assets are being manufactured is available, or if such sources in the lessee country are available. Subsidized funding by the manufacturer can also be an alternative. This is more fully discussed in the following, "Export Leasing."

Second, the lessee has to decide whether to arrange fixed- or floating-rate funding. If the lessee is convinced that interest rates are headed lower, most lessors will be willing to permit refunding of the debt portion of the leveraged lease at any time without penalty, provided the refunding provisions are structured in such a fashion that they will not trigger adverse tax consequences for the lessor. This can usually be avoided.

Third, the lessee has to decide in which currency to fund the debt portion of the lease.

In most jurisdictions, with the notable exception of the United Kingdom, which does not grant tax relief on currency losses, it is not difficult to structure a lease with the equity in local currency and the debt portion in foreign currency. Such transactions have been drawn involving West German, U.S., and Australian lessors. Funding the debt portion of the lease in the preferred currency is usually the cheapest and most effective way for the lessee to hedge against currency exposure.

Finally, the lessee has to decide whether to raise the debt from banks, institutional lenders, such as the private placement market in the U.S., or through a public offering.

Few leveraged leases have been contracted using the public debt market, mainly because of the complexity of leveraged leases, timing difficulties, and the fairly stringent disclosure requirements. It is also difficult to renegotiate the lease later on, if the agreement of the public debt holders to the new terms is required.

EXPORT LEASING

The exporter of major capital assets usually has two objectives: (1) to offer the asset with a competitive financing package in order to get the order, and (2) to get the full sales price for the asset in cash in home currency as soon as possible. The importer usually wants to be able to finance the purchase price of the asset at the lowest possible cost over the longest possible term in the currency of choice.

Export leasing can frequently be a convenient way of meeting most or all of these objectives. Unfortunately, many exporters have developed three misconceptions about export leasing that cause them to waste a lot of their own time and money, as well as that of the leasing industry, by chasing the impossible. The first misconception is that the leasing industry applies less stringent credit criteria than traditional lenders. While it is true that the domestic leasing industry might be willing to take greater credit risks than traditional lenders, this is strictly a result of the lessors' ability to better assess and to realize the collateral value of leased assets. No exporter should, however, expect a cross-border lessor to take the same attitude. Cross-border leasing is essentially unsecured lending, except maybe for aircraft and ship leases. Anybody who does not believe this should try to repossess a container with an original cost of $2,000 leased by a U.S. lessor to an offshore container-leasing company that in turn has leased the container to a West German shipping company using the container on a vessel registered in Panama, while the vessel is docking in Japan. This example, while realistic, might be extreme, but it does make the point. Jurisdictional conflicts, language problems, and legal expenses make it virtually impractical to try to repossess most smaller assets. A well-known lawyer in a developing country, when asked what the lessor's rights under the lease were in his country, replied, "For $1,000 I will give you my opinion of the law; for $10,000 I will get that law changed."

The first rule for export leasing is, therefore: Do not waste anybody's time pursuing very creative lease structures if the importer is not creditworthy in the first place. The few people who really know something about cross-border leasing have better things to do.

The second misconception about export leasing is that the lessor might be willing to write the lease at less than market rates. Lessors are very profit conscious and they are not interested in subsidizing somebody else's export sale. The cost of an export lease is strictly the result of the funding cost of the lease, including the funding cost of the debt portion of a leveraged lease, plus the available tax benefits. Any subsidies to reduce the cost of the lease further have to come from the manufacturer, either by replacing the credit standing of the lessee (the importer) with that of the manufacturer through a guarantee, or by having the manufacturer make the debt portion of the lease available at subsidized rates. Once this is pointed out to the exporter, most "hot" export leases die a sudden death.

The third misconception is that lessors are happy to provide exporters with lease quotes because of the "do good" this generates with the exporter and because it gives the lessor firm a unique opportunity to get its name in front of the importer. Nothing could be further from the truth. Employees of an exporter asking for lease quotes are usually sales finance managers who are under heavy pressure from the sales force to come up with a financing package, often because the salesmen have made promises to the importers to clinch the deal. No "do good" is created by giving lease quotes to sales finance people, because they are generally in no position to influence the relationship between their employer and the financial institution providing the lease quote.

Getting a lease quote in front of the importer is even worse. All the importing firm will do is use it as a benchmark when shopping for better quotes from those financial institutions it normally deals with. The sophisticated lessor company does not waste time with exporters—it deals only with the importer. Remember, the exporter can always lose the deal to a competitor, but if one works with the importing firm and it likes the lease proposal, the financing is confirmed, no matter who gets the order.

Many governments provide export financing through special government entities, either in the form of direct loans or through guarantees. Examples are the U.S. Eximbank, ECGD in the United Kingdom, COFACE in France, EDC in Canada.

To the extent a lessor can access these export-financing programs to fund the debt portion of a leveraged lease, this will usually provide the cheapest source of funds. Few transactions have actually been completed using this technique and the reason is twofold: (1) subsidized export financing is governed by fairly stringent requirements set by the various export agencies resulting from international agreements; (2) some export agencies take the view that a combination of export financing and leasing constitutes a double subsidy and will therefore not permit it.

INTERNATIONAL AGREEMENTS. In order to limit competition between the export agencies of various countries at the expense of their respective taxpayers, the OECD countries (which include most of the major trading nations) have signed an agreement that sets maximum terms and minimum interest rates for most export items other than aircraft. A similar but less formal agreement—the so-called Geneva Stand Still Agreement—exists between the major producers of commercial aircraft.

The provisions in these agreements that create a problem for export leases from the United States are the maximum-term provisions, which are, for example, eight years for ships and 12 years for aircraft leases (10 years for aircraft loans). United States lessors can only write export leases with purchase options at fair market value. Leases of ships or commercial aircraft for terms of eight or 12 years respectively will rarely be economical for the lessee when the likely cost of the purchase or renewal option is included in an analysis. While is it technically possible to fund a 15-year leveraged aircraft lease with 12-year debt or to write a 10- or 12-year lease with fixed renewal options for a couple of years, switching to a fair market option later, the U.S. Eximbank so far has not agreed to participate in a lease, if the term of the lease, including any renewal options, exeeds the limits established in the various agreements. Eximbank, incidentally, will not as a matter of policy lend the debt portion of a lease, but will provide its guarantee. This policy is an outcome of the double-subsidy argument.

DOUBLE SUBSIDY. All export agencies providing subsidized export loans, such as the Eximbank, ECGD, and COFACE, are reluctant to provide the debt portion of leveraged leases on the theory that the lessee would obtain a double subsidy from the taxpayer, through the tax benefits provided by the lease and through the subsidized loan itself. Eximbank, as noted above, will support leases only through its guarantee, and that has been rarely used. ECGD, which does not have a guarantee program, will not fund a lessor if the interest cost of the lease drops below the rate on the ECGD loan. This can still be attractive, since it permits the lessor to absorb legal expense and fees and to provide the equity portion of the lease (the funds not provided by ECGD) as the same rate as the ECGD loan. Both West Germany and France have provided subsidized export loans for the debt portion of a leveraged lease for Airbuses, but this is a somewhat special situation and most of these aircraft were leased through a U.S. tax-based lease, and therefore did not involve a double subsidy by the West German and French taxpayer.

If the importer is of sufficient credit standing and a viable lease structure can be found, leasing is a very attractive means of export financing. The exporter gets full payment in cash in home currency upon delivery of the asset and the importer (lessee) gets long-term financing, frequently at a fixed rate of interest, at a low cost. This is especially true if the lease can be partially funded through subsidized export loans.

GUIDELINES FOR CROSS-BORDER LEASING

The leasing specialist of a major multinational oil company that has probably closed more cross-border leases for its own account than any other company once said that even a complex domestic leveraged lease is "plain vanilla" compared to a cross-border lease. How true! Therefore, a few rules need to be followed when embarking upon cross-border leasing.

Lead times. Cross-border leases should not be entered under time pressure, because mistakes can be costly. It is advisable to leave plenty of lead time and to talk to several competent lessors, and, if possible, to some experienced lessees on an informal basis.

Competent advisor. Once it looks as though cross-border leasing might provide a viable alternative, the prospective lessee should appoint an exclusive advisor with a competent representation in both the lessor and the lessee country. Good leasing advice tends to be expensive, but it will more than pay for itself, mainly in three areas.

1. A competent advisor should be able to provide the best possible access to all major sources of equity in the lessor country.
2. The advisor should reduce significantly the amount of time that management will have to devote to the transaction.

3. The advisor should be able to cut documentation expenses by keeping the lawyers under control. The advisor can do this, if he or she is intimately familiar with similar lease documents, knows the major issues, and knows how they have been resolved before.

Large Transaction. One should not even consider a cross-border tax lease unless the amount involved is at least $10 to $20 million. Smaller transactions should only be considered if they can be tailored after a prior successful transaction and involve the same lessor and, if possible, counsel. In smaller transactions, the management time required and the travel and legal expenses tend to offset whatever interest cost savings the transaction might provide.

Local Counsel. While the lessee might want to have regular counsel coordinate the overall documentation process, it is imperative that the lessee use competent local counsel in the lessor country and give this counsel the greatest possible freedom. Legal expenses—within a reasonable range—should be agreed upon at the outset.

Cross-border tax leasing can be very exciting and provide a low-cost financing alternative under the right circumstances. But it is a financing venture that should only be entered with the most competent professional advice available.

Detailed Term Sheet. The prospective lessee, together with an advisor, should prepare a very detailed term sheet to be sent to all prospective lessors. This, if properly drawn, should prevent unpleasant surprises six or eight weeks into the documentation, which might kill the transaction at great cost to all involved. If at all possible, the lessee should have counsel prepare the first draft of the documents, on the grounds that the lessee's counsel is more familiar with the specifics of the transaction—but this is a point that few lessors will concede.

CONCLUSION

Leasing is an arrangement providing the use of an asset without its legal ownership. It is the financial technique by which the lessor (usually a financial institution) obtains funds from the capital market and acquires title to the asset. The lessor then provides the lessee with the "use value" of the asset, while keeping the asset's residual value (if any) in exchange for a series of lease payments as prescribed by the lease agreement.

Although cross-border leasing has become an increasingly important source of financing in recent years, many of the reasons offered for its use are of dubious validity. The most convincing reason for any lease, domestic or cross-border, is either a lower after-tax cost or a comparable cost with a significant improvement in the timing of cash flows. Cross-border leases generally should be used as an effective means of transfer pricing or to take advantage of tax rate differences. And even when these criteria are met, a cross-border lease is likely to be cost-effective only if of sufficient size, and given sufficient lead time, and assisted by competent home and foreign advisors.

SECTION **8.1**

EXCHANGE RATE FORECASTING TECHNIQUES

CONTENTS

SECTION **8.1**

EXCHANGE RATE FORECASTING TECHNIQUES

Richard M. Levich

The introduction of floating exchange rates in the early 1970s marked a major systematic change for international financial markets. With the exception of the Canadian experiment (1950–62), a pegged but adjustable exchange rate system as specified under the Bretton Woods agreement dominated the post–World War II experience of all industrialized countries. Exchange rate behavior under the Bretton Woods system was characterized by relatively large, discrete and infrequent exchange rate changes. Consequently, market analysts (i.e., real world practitioners and economists) focused their attention on balance of payments data and international reserves. A sustained payments imbalance along with substantial shifts in international reserve holdings would increase the probability that a central bank could no longer support the pegged rate. Since these pressures are slow to accumulate, analysts could be certain of the direction of exchange rate change. The magnitude of exchange rate change (i.e., the amount required to restore payments balance and to halt international reserve flows) could be estimated from a **purchasing power parity** (PPP) model or from other data. However, the ultimate decision to change the peg was fundamentally a political decision, and economic analysis was of little use in picking the breaking points of political officials.

Exchange rate behavior under the **floating-rate system** is characterized by relatively small exchange rate changes that occur continuously as new information is received. Under the current system, private market assessment of demand and supply factors is the primary determinant of currency values. Government (i.e., central banks) continues to play a role, but one whose scope and impact is difficult to assess (see "Forecasting Exchange Rates: Economic Models," this section). In this environment, forecasting a bilateral exchange rate (e.g., US$/DM or US$/Mex$) requires the analyst to assess the relative demand and supply factors for both currencies. In the early 1970s, currency traders and analysts were poorly prepared to meet this requirement.

Research conducted over the last 10 years has shed much light on two key issues: (1) What are the fundamental determinants of exchange rates? (2) What are the best ways to forecast exchange rates? As might have been expected, this research has led to both good news and bad news.

The good news is that the understanding of exchange rate behavior has increased dramatically. Economists have been fairly successful in constructing models to explain cross-sectional exchange rate differences (e.g., why the U.S. dollar exchanges for roughly Lit1,300—Italian lire—but only DM2) and to explain time series exchange rate developments (e.g., quarter-to-quarter or year-to-year rate changes). Analysts are also more clear on the fundamental economic variables that drive exchange rates (e.g., money supply, national income, expected inflation, real interest rates, current account balances, etc.), the channels through which these variables act, and the directional impact of each variable. Drawing on the **efficient market principle,** the forward rate should be an accurate reflection of information concerning these economic variables and their interrelationships. Assuming there are no **risk premiums** in the forward market (an important point to be discussed under "Forecasting and Exchange Market Efficiency,") the forward rate would be an unbiased predictor of the future spot rate. Unbiased prediction would make the forward rate an excellent forecaster for many purposes, although not necessarily the best forecast by other criteria.

Each of the above points also suggests some bad news. While economists have had some success in explaining quarterly or yearly exchange rate changes, the ability to explain day-to-day or week-to-week changes is much more limited. In part, this is because many of the variables that play an important role in popular exchange rate models cannot be measured daily (e.g., the money supply or national income), while other variables by their very nature (e.g., expected money growth, expected inflation) cannot be observed directly. Furthermore, an economic theory that concludes that the spot rate is a function of some set of variables ($X_1, X_2, \ldots X_n$) does not solve the forecasting problem even if the theory is true. It only forces an analyst to forecast $X_1, X_2, \ldots X_n$, which raises its own difficulties. Finally, a major corollary of the **asset view of exchange rates** and the **efficient market principle** is that exchange rate changes are the result of unanticipated economic events, that is, news. By definition it is impossible to forecast news. The implication here is that forecasters cannot expect to be successful in predicting exchange rate movements relative to their anticipated trend. In this case, even forecasts that were very accurate might not help one to take profitable positions because other financial market prices (i.e., forward rates) were free to adjust to reflect the same information.

Research reported in the last year strongly suggests that foreign exchange forecasts are available that outperform forward rates. Some of these forecasts start with the forward rate and adjust for other public information (e.g., lagged forecast errors) or build a **composite forecast** based on current spot and forward rates. Other forecasts that appear to do well are from professional forecasting services that use a variety of techniques.

In the current environment, characterized by volatile exchange rates, it is clear that better exchange rate forecasts will improve the financial performance of multinational firms. Numerous models can be used to forecast exchange rates. The questions of import are

1. Can exchange rate forecasts be produced that are better than the forward rate or some other easily available public forecast?
2. If the answer to the above is yes, is the margin of superiority of the forecasts too large to be the result of chance?
3. If the answer to the above is yes, are the profits earned by following the forecasts large relative to the extra risks and transaction costs incurred?

These seem to be the important issues. Conclusions must be based on empirical analysis that covers a relatively short time period. For example, nine years of floating rates translate into only 36 independent (i.e., nonoverlapping) three-month forward rate forecasts. Given a period this short, afflicted by sporadic government intervention and structural changes, one might be skeptical about any strongly held empirical conclusions.

Nevertheless, current research supports a positive answer to questions 1 and 2. However, an answer to question 3 continues to be elusive. The benefits of using currency forecasts are closely related to the issue of active currency exposure management.

WHAT TO EXPECT FROM FORECASTING: THE USER'S VIEWPOINT

For the multinational firm, exchange rate forecasts play a role in a wide variety of decisions. Obviously, any foreign borrowing or investment decision requires a forecast of future exchange rates so that future foreign cash flows can be converted into units of domestic currency and a comparable domestic cost of funds or return on investment can be computed. A currency forecast is generally required for the firm to manage its **currency exposure** which results from current and planned holdings of foreign currency. Currency forecasts can play a role in marketing, specifically with respect to pricing decisions. If a Japanese automobile that sells for Y1.2 million in Japan is priced at \$6,000 in the United States when the exchange rate stands at Y200/\$, and if the yen appreciates to Y180/\$, each U.S. auto sale will earn only \$6,000 × Y180/\$ = Y1.08 million. The Japanese firm is now worse off and it is clear that their decision to raise U.S. prices will depend upon many factors, including the future yen-dollar exchange rate. From this example one can also see that assessing subsidiary performance will also require exchange rate projections. Finally, exchange rate forecasts can be valuable for long-range or strategic planning. If the real exchange rate is expected to change the U.S. firm can maximize its dollar profits (revenues/costs) by incurring costs in those countries where the currency has depreciated below its PPP level (so that the real value of production costs is lower) and by earning revenues in those countries where the currency has appreciated above its PPP level (so that the real value of revenues is higher).

The forecasting process itself is associated with other benefits. Most forecasting services provide an extensive discussion of macroeconomic conditions for each country. These reports are a convenient way to see the broad trends in money markets, labor markets, and the markets for goods and services. Several services offer extensive computer libraries of macroeconomic data. The analytical exercise of generating a currency forecast allows the user to see how the fundamental variables interact to affect currency variables.

Forecasting services also enable users to judge the likely range of currency values and to quantify the risks in maintaining open currency positions. Some services include a forecast range as part of their regular reporting. When a forecast range is not provided, users can estimate their own by allowing fundamental variables to vary over some likely range, thus generating a range of likely minimum and maximum currency values. The ability to specify a range for future exchange rates is an important part of many exposure management models that use a payoff-matrix approach, as described by Kohlhagen (1978b).

Another way to judge the range for future exchange rates is to analyze a group of forecasts from several forecasting services or several forecasting models. These forecasts will reflect both different assumptions on future economic variables and different ways for modeling exchange rates. As will be argued under "Forecasting Exchange Rates: Pure Forecasting Approaches," a **composite forecasting model** that combines diverse views of the future offers an efficient procedure for generating better forecasts.

Users should be advised that the available forecasting models have not overcome several important problem issues. First, most forecasting models, especially those that are formalized, assume that past economic data and relationships will remain relevant for the future. This can be a dangerous procedure in a world economy prone to frequent structural shocks. For example, **technical forecasters** often assume that past support and resistance levels will apply in the future. Econometric forecasters assume that regression equations estimated using in-sample data are valid for post-sample predictions. These procedures fail when there is a fundamental or structural economic change. Until the structural change is recognized and the model is modified, a formal model will lead to biased predictions.

A second problem concerns long-term exchange rate forecasting. Typically, forecasting services produce nominal exchange rate forecasts. But for long-term investment decisions, the **real exchange rate** is the more relevant variable. For example, the current dollar/deutsche mark rate is \$0.50 and the Consumer Price Index (CPI) in both the United States and West Germany is 100. It is forecast that in five years the exchange rate will be \$0.75/DM, roughly a 8.5% U.S. dollar depreciation for each year in nominal terms. On the surface, this forecast predicts a weak dollar, which might be taken as good news for U.S. exporting firms and bad news for importers. But looking more closely, if U.S. inflation outpaces West German inflation by 8.5% a year (as it would according to purchasing power parity theory) then the real exchange rate between U.S. goods and West German goods is unchanged, and there would be no change in the competitiveness of U.S. goods. Only if U.S. inflation exceeds West German inflation by less than 8.5% does the traditional result hold. This corresponds to a depreciating U.S. dollar in real terms and naturally this would encourage U.S. exports. On the other hand, if U.S. inflation exceeded West German inflation by more than 8.5%, the exchange rate change would not be sufficient to keep U.S. exporters from losing customers. The point is that a nominal exchange rate forecast can be completely accurate, and yet provide no information on the future real exchange rate. And it is the real exchange rate that influences both consumers' and producers' decisions concerning real goods and services.

The final problem with most forecasting approaches is that they forecast and provide exposure management advice on a currency-by-currency basis. This approach is deficient, first, because it ignores the increase in estimation efficiency that results from using a composite forecasting approach, and, second, because it ignores the reduction in risk associated with a portfolio risk management approach. For firms with exposure concentrated in only one or two currencies or with severe exposure management constraints, this currency-by-currency approach might not impose many costs. The advantages of composite forecasting and portfolio management are described in more detail later in this section.

FORECASTING AND EXCHANGE MARKET EFFICIENCY

Tests of the **efficiency** of asset markets as processors of information began in the 1950s and gained increasing popularity and significance during the 1960s. With the establishment of floating exchange rates in the early 1970s (presumably dominated by free-market behavior), it was natural to begin the investigation of foreign exchange market efficiency. The evidence on foreign exchange market efficiency is important for several reasons. First, macroeconomic models typically include price variables under the assumption that prices fairly aggregate bits of information that are dispersed throughout the economy. Economic agents who make decisions on the basis of observed prices will insure an efficient allocation of resources. Second, if the foreign exchange market is judged inefficient, some corrective actions might be required. These might include increased profit-motivated private speculation, increased distribution of accurate market information, or central bank intervention. Finally, tests of market efficiency can influence financial management strategies. In an efficient market, managers tend to favor passive hedging strategies in order to minimize transaction costs and maximize diversification gains. However, if the market is not efficient, selective hedging strategies to exploit available profit opportunities might be preferred.

DEFINITION. The classic definition of capital market efficiency was formalized by Fama (1970). A definition of capital market efficiency can be compressed into one sentence: A market is efficient if market prices *fully reflect available information*. The key words are in italics. The expression "fully reflect" implies the existence of an equilibrium model. But one model, which concludes that $2.25 is the fair spot price of pounds sterling, might not agree with another model, which draws a different conclusion. Similarly, one forecaster, who uses only public information, might conclude that $2.30 is the fair spot price for pounds sterling, while another forecaster, with inside information, might disagree strongly, even though both forecasters use the same framework for predicting exchange rates.

These arguments have been refined in two important directions. First, when information itself is costly to collect, market participants, in their own self-interest, will never choose to be completely informed. As a result, market prices will never reflect all information, although they still may reflect available information. Furthermore, if investors are heterogeneous in terms of their wealth, expectations, forecasting accuracy, and risk aversion, actual market prices will reflect a mixture of diverse opinions. However this mixture will correspond to investors' dollar votes rather than a set of optimal weights.

In economic jargon, the above implies that tests of market efficiency are testing a joint hypothesis. Any investigation that rejects market efficiency might be explained in two ways: (1) profit-seeking private investors had information that they could have used to earn unusual profits, but they failed to do so (i.e., in reality, the market is inefficient); or (2) the empirical tests are in error—a false measure of fair value has been used. That is, it was assumed that the investor used information that, in fact, was not available, and the costs of learning about or exploiting these profit opportunities was not included. Naturally, in a market populated with thousands of sophisticated, profit-seeking investors who can transact at low cost, the second explanation seems more reasonable. This takes one dangerously close to the **efficient**

market tautology: Any free market must be efficient. But since there is little agreement on what constitutes the true or fair value of foreign exchange, tests of market efficiency are both difficult to formulate and difficult to interpret.

IMPLICATIONS FOR FORECASTING. If foreign exchange markets are efficient, then all available information, including information on the future spot exchange rate, is fully reflected in market prices. The question now is one of specifics: Where does a user or analyst look to discover the market's implicit exchange rate forecast? As is shown later under "Forecasting and the Forward Rate," most economic models identify the market's implicit exchange rate forecast as the forward rate (equivalent to the interest rate differential under the interest rate parity theory) or the forward rate plus a risk premium. In the later case, forecasters would be required to estimate the risk premium.

If markets are efficient, then a forecast superior to the market's implicit forecast must be based either on new information or on superior analysis of available information. This process is costly and suggests that the production of information will be limited to the point where the marginal cost and marginal benefit from an additional unit of information are equalized. While information might be costly to generate, there are enormous economies of scale in the distribution of existing information (e.g., via newspapers, television, or news wires). An implication of the above is that investors can earn the competitive rate of return on their investment in information only if they have monopolistic access to the information. Once the information is publicly available (i.e., a public good), it is reflected in prices and is of no further value. Markets are once again efficient. This is the ultimate predicament for forecasters. If their forecasts are correct, use of these forecasts will move market prices to eliminate any profit opportunities associated with the forecasts.

As is examined in detail later, market efficiency criteria influence performance evaluation criteria. If markets are efficient and there is no risk premium, then forecasters can be judged vis-à-vis the forward rate. If markets are efficient and there is a risk premium, then it is expected that forecasters will outperform the forward rate. In this case, forecasters should be judged vis-à-vis the risk premium–adjusted forward rate. If markets are not efficient, then the forward rate is not an appropriate criterion for assessing forecasting performance, because it does not reflect the market's implicit forecast, although, in this case, there is no unambiguous formula to determine this implicit forecast.

EMPIRICAL EVIDENCE. The literature on foreign exchange market efficiency developed quickly over the last 10 years. Surveys of this literature have been prepared by Kohlhagen (1978a) and by Levich (1978). Three aspects of this evidence are briefly discussed below.

Tests of **covered interest arbitrage** have clearly established that the market efficiently polices risk-free profit opportunities in the Eurocurrency markets. Studies of arbitrage between traditional or on-shore securities (e.g., U.S. and U.K. Treasury bills) suggest that covered differentials do appear in the market. However, the evidence is unclear whether these differentials are the result of known costs (e.g., transaction costs, exchange controls, taxes, and other barriers), perceived risks (e.g., future controls and taxes), or an actual market failure to exploit risk-free arbitrage profits.

Tests of spot market efficiency began by analyzing the time series properties of spot rates. Several studies examined the hypothesis that changes in spot exchange rates are serially uncorrelated (i.e., the **random walk hypothesis**). For a number of reasons (including that exchange rates are driven by economic factors that themselves might be serially correlated) random walk exchange rate behavior first, is not necessary for spot exchange market efficiency, and second, is not sufficient to prove spot exchange market efficiency.

Other studies of the spot foreign exchange market have analyzed the performance of investment strategies that use a filter rule as a guide for picking speculative positions. These filter rules are in many ways similar to commercial technical services that are discussed later in this section. A filter rule is a mathematical rule that can be applied mechanically to produce buy signals and sell signals. For example, if the dollar/deutsche mark rate rises 1% above a previous low, this could be interpreted as a buy signal, under the assumption that momentum will carry the dollar/deutsche mark rate still higher. However, if international financial markets are efficient, Eurodeposit traders should also recognize the expected momentum in the exchange market. As a result, Eurodeposit traders would set relatively low deutsche mark interest rates and high dollar interest rates that would tend to offset the anticipated exchange rate change. This summarizes the efficient market process—Eurodeposit interest rate differentials should exactly offset the expected exchange rate change, so there are no expected profits from the filter rule strategy.

The results of empirical studies of filter rules are mixed. Some academic studies have concluded that simple filter rule strategies could have been profitable, especially during periods of exchange rate volatility. Studies of commercial technical or momentum advisory services have also suggested that their predictions could have led to profitable results. However, none of these studies has suggested that their trading profits are risk-free. On the contrary, investors who seek to profit from market timing lose the time diversification associated with maintaining a steady portfolio over time. It is therefore unclear whether filter rule profits are unusually large relative to the risk involved.

Tests of forward market efficiency have focused on the relationship between the current n period forward rate ($F_{t,n}$), the expected future spot rate ($E(\tilde{S}_{t+n})$), and the actual future spot rate (S_{t+n}). Market efficiency requires that market agents are able to process available information and form reasonable expectations—that is, $E(\tilde{S}_{t+n}) = S_{t+n}$. However, market efficiency allows for the possibility that investors might demand a risk premium on forward contracts, much the same as long-term interest rates might reflect liquidity premiums rather than simply pure interest rate expectations. Therefore, market efficiency does not require that $F_{t,n} = E(\tilde{S}_{t+n})$. As a result, the relationship between the current forward rate ($F_{t,n}$) and the actual future spot rate (S_{t+n}) is ambiguous, even in an efficient market.

To restate these points, what might be called the "simple efficiency hypothesis" is that

$$F_{t,n} = E(\tilde{S}_{t+n}) \qquad \text{and} \qquad E(\tilde{S}_{t+n}) = S_{t+n} \tag{1}$$

If this hypothesis is true, then deviations between $F_{t,n}$ and S_{t+n} should have mean zero and zero serial correlation. In a regression of the form

$$S_{t+n} = A + BF_{t,n} + CX_t + e_t \tag{2}$$

the null hypothesis, given simple efficiency, is that $A = 0$, $B = 1$, and the coefficient of any other variable, $C = 0$. The residuals, e_t, should of course be free of serial correlation.

A more general efficiency hypothesis that allows for a risk premium (RP) would presume

$$F_{t,n} = E(\tilde{S}_{t+n}) + \text{RP}_{t,n} \quad \text{and} \quad E(\tilde{S}_{t+n}) = S_{t+n} \tag{3}$$

We can clearly see that in this case, the equality between $F_{t,n}$ and $E(\tilde{S}_{t+n})$ is broken. Regression equations (such as 2) that reject the $(A,B,C) = (0,1,0)$ hypothesis are subject to two interpretations. In one, the simple efficiency hypothesis is rejected. The forward market is inefficient in reflecting exchange rate expectations. Expected profit opportunities through forward speculation exist. In the second, the general efficiency hypothesis cannot be rejected. A new forecast $S_{t+n} = A + BF_{t,n} + CX_t$ can be constructed that will be superior to the forward rate forecast. However, the profits earned through forward speculation will only reflect the fair risk premium for the additional risk incurred.

Unfortunately, unless the variable X_t is a good proxy for risk (rather than lagged forecast errors or lagged forward rates) one is not on solid ground accepting the second interpretation—and that is approximately where the frontier of research in this area stands today. Two thoroughly prepared studies, one by Hansen and Hodrick (1980) and the other by Hsieh (1982), are able to reject the simple efficiency hypothesis. But because they have not modeled the risk premium, they cannot discern whether the forward market is inefficient or is simply following the second interpretation.

Numerous empirical tests of the relationship between today's forward rate ($F_{t,1}$) and the future spot rate (S_{t+1}) have been published over the last five years. Some of the econometric tests are too technical for the purposes of this discussion and some of the details of the analyses might be disputed, but the general thrust of this literature is as follows:

1. In early studies, the forward rate was shown to be an unbiased predictor of the future spot rate. In more recent studies using more advanced econometric techniques, this view has been rejected. Nonetheless, there is a close association between the level of the forward rate and the level of the future spot rate. In a linear regression, variation in F_t generally explains more than 90% of the variation in S_{t+1}.
2. Similarly, in early studies the forward premium $(F - S)/S$ was shown to be an unbiased predictor of the future exchange rate change, $(S_{t+1} - S_t)/S_t$. Later studies reversed this view. However, all studies confirm that the forward premium is a poor predictor in the following sense: In a linear regression, variation in $(F - S)/S$ generally explains less than 10% of the variation in $(S_{t+1} - S_t)/S_t$. This suggests that the bulk of the short-run exchange rate changes are dominated by unanticipated events (i.e., news) and that the forward premium sits roughly in the middle of a wide distribution of exchange

EXHIBIT 1 MONTHLY PERCENTAGE CHANGES OF THE U.S./GERMAN CONSUMER PRICE INDICES, OF THE $US/DM EXCHANGE RATE, AND MONTHLY FORWARD PREMIUM, JULY 1973–FEBRUARY 1979

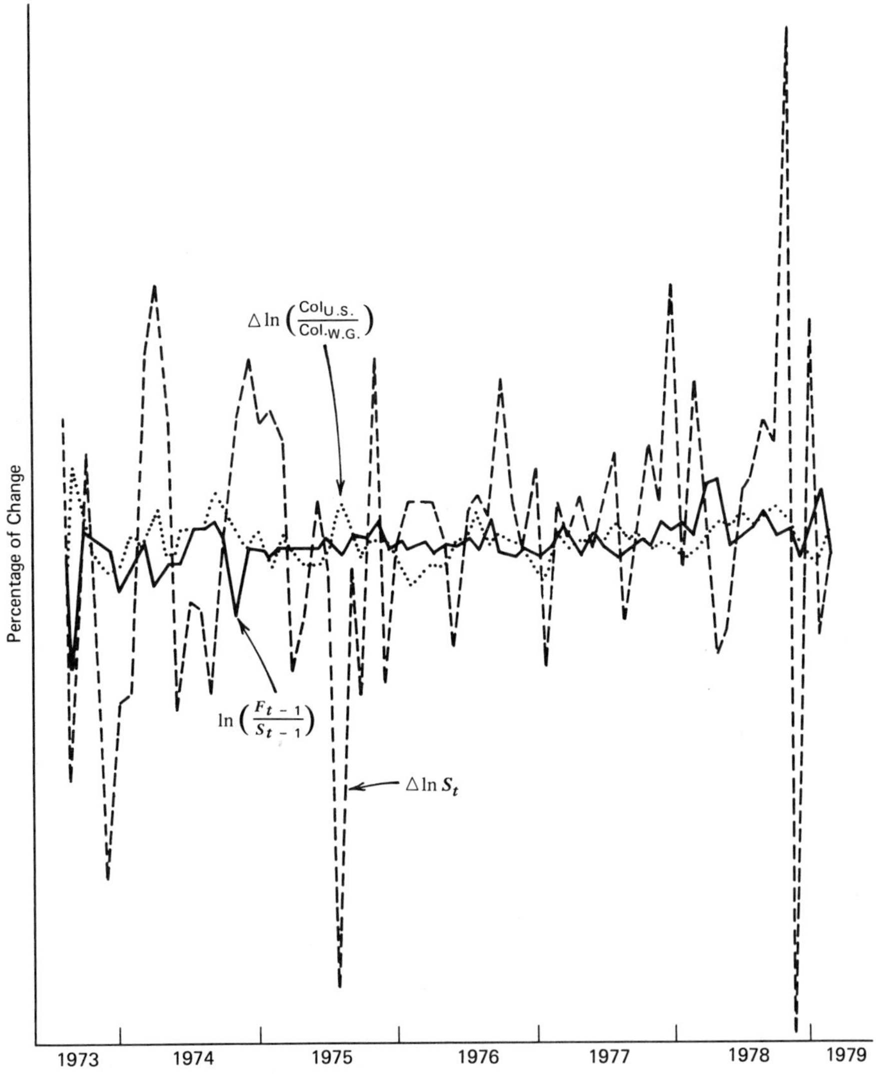

rate expectations. Exhibit 1 illustrates the wide variation in exchange rate changes relative to the forward premium for the deutsche mark.

3. Empirical studies showing a forward rate bias do not support the existence of a positive risk premium in forward contracts. This may be because (a) the premium actually is zero; (b) the premium is too small to measure in the limited history of floating; or (c) the premium changes signs and averages near zero.

4. Adding variables beyond the current forward rate might improve the ability to fit a regression equation explaining S_{t+1}. But in postsample comparisons, the forward rate by itself has often exhibited better predictive ability.

These results of early studies suggest that the foreign exchange market is fairly efficient and that the forward rate can offer stiff competition to other forecasters. More recent studies challenge this view. They suggest that other forecasts can beat the forward rate without concluding that the forward exchange market is inefficient.

FORECASTING AND THE FORWARD RATE

An interest in the forward rate as a forecaster of the future spot exchange rate is linked closely with the efficient market hypothesis, which states that market prices reflect available information. Since investors' expectations of the future spot rate are part of the available information set, and since these expectations should be reflected in market prices, under certain strict assumptions (which were outlined previously in the discussion of forward market efficiency) it is correct to argue that today's forward exchange rate is (1) the single market price that represents all investor expectations of the future spot rate, and (2) an unbiased forecast of the future spot rate. If these assumptions are met, then many multinational firms would view the forward rate as a very attractive forecast to use—first, because it represents the collective wisdom of many well-informed, profit-seeking traders; second, because the forward rate will be revised quickly as new information becomes available; and third, because the forward rate is a very inexpensive forecast to use.

Before going further, attention must be addressed to the assertion that forward rates reflect international interest rate differentials rather than exchange rate expectations. The first part of this statement summarizes the **interest rate parity theory.** The empirical surveys cited under "Forecasting and Exchange Market Efficiency" concluded that covered arbitrage profits are quickly eliminated so that

$$\frac{F_t - S_t}{S_t} = \frac{i - i^*}{1 + i^*} \tag{4}$$

where i and i^* are domestic currency and foreign currency Euromarket interest rates. But it has long been recognized that nominal interest rates in a free market can be decomposed into terms representing the anticipated real interest rate and anticipated inflation. Under the assumption that real interest rates in different countries tend to equalization, the interest rate differential, $i - i^*$, is a proxy for the difference in anticipated inflation rates. As a result, $i - i^*$ measures the market's expected exchange rate change under a **purchasing power parity** scenario. Consequently, a forward rate that simultaneously removes covered arbitrage profits and also reflects exchange rate expectations is a reasonable model to entertain.

THEORETICAL BACKGROUND. The fundamental question regarding theoretical background is the relationship between today's forward exchange rate for delivery in n days (called $F_{t,n}$) and the spot exchange rate n days in the future (S_{t+n}). Now consider the error term $e_{t,n}$ where

$$e_{t,n} = S_{t+n} - F_{t,n} \tag{5}$$

One interpretation of $e_{t,n}$ is that it is the **forecast error,** in which the forward rate forecasts the future spot rate. Another interpretation of $e_{t,n}$ is that it represents the speculative profit for investors who buy forward contracts outright at $F_{t,n}$ and then sell their matured contracts in the spot markets at price S_{t+n}.

Since $e_{t,n}$ can be interpreted as a speculative profit, it is unlikely that $e_{t,n}$ would be consistently large and positive. The reason is that consistently large profits would attract forward speculators. Their purchase of forward contracts would increase $F_{t,n}$ and decrease $e_{t,n}$, thus removing profits. Similarly, it is unlikely that $e_{t,n}$ would be consistently large and negative. In this case, forward speculators would sell forward contracts; $F_{t,n}$ would decrease and $e_{t,n}$ would increase, thus removing losses.

A credible story seems to be that $e_{t,n}$ will be negative at some times and positive at others. In repeated trials over long periods of time, the average value of $e_{t,n}$ should be a small number near zero. Furthermore, the time series of $e_{t,n}$ should not exhibit predictable patterns of positive and negative values. If patterns could be uncovered, speculators could use this information to make unusually large profits.

As a technical matter, when the average value of $e_{t,n}$ is small and not statistically different from zero, the forward rate is considered an unbiased forecaster of the future spot rate.

As stressed earlier in "Forecasting and Exchange Market Efficiency," the above discussion hides an important subtlety for this analysis. Equation 5 really represents a joint hypothesis: first, that the forward rate (at time t) represents the market's expectation (held at time t) about the future spot rate conditional upon the information set ($I^m{}_t$) used by the market

$$F_{t,n} = E(\tilde{S}_{t+n} \mid I^m{}_t) \tag{6}$$

and second, that the market's expectation is equal to the true expectation that would be formed using all relevant information (I_t), so that

$$E(\tilde{S}_{t+n} \mid I^m{}_t) = E(\tilde{S}_{t+n} \mid I_t) \tag{7}$$

The logical argument for the forward rate as an unbiased forecaster thus requires two steps: first, market participants must be able to form expectations that reflect underlying economic realities (expression 7) and, second, market participants must, in turn, set the forward rate equal to their expectation (expression 6). Expression 7 might not hold because investors lack knowledge of fundamental economic variables or structural relationships. If this knowledge were generally available, then violation of 7 would indicate market inefficiency in processing information. Expression 6 might not hold because the forward rate can reflect investor attitudes toward risk, transaction costs, or other factors not related to exchange rate expectations. Violation of expression 6 for these reasons does not suggest a market inefficiency.

If either 6 or 7 is false, then the simple and direct link between the forward rate and the future spot rate is broken and then the error series in 5 need not have a zero mean. Therefore, whether or not the forward rate is an unbiased forecast depends on underlying economic factors; it is not an inherent property of any economic system, even one that is in equilibrium and processes information efficiently.

FORECASTING BIAS. The special interest in unbiased forecasts is twofold. First, if the forward rate is unbiased, then on average, it is an accurate predictor of the future spot rate; no transformation of the forward rate is required to construct a forecast. Second, if the forward rate is unbiased, then any strategy for hedging foreign exchange risk or for speculating in forward contracts has the same long-run expected profit, namely, zero.

An interest in unbiased forecasts should not be construed to mean that this is the only property that matters for evaluating forecasts. For example, one unbiased forecaster might produce a series of +1% and −1% errors and a second unbiased forecaster might produce a series of +2% and −2% errors. If users are risk-averse, they will prefer the first forecaster because the magnitude of errors is smaller. A standard econometric treatment of this issue often assumes that users have a quadratic utility function so that investors desire lower average forecast errors and lower variance of forecast errors. In this setting, users choose the model that minimizes the mean-squared forecasting error (MSE), even if it happens to be a biased forecast. (The MSE is the summation of all e^2_{t+n} divided by the number of observations.)

In summary then, if users are concerned about the variance, skewness, or other characteristics of the forecast error (in addition to the mean error), then the variance or skewness of the forecast error series ($e_{t,n}$) is also important for selecting a forecasting model. These issues are discussed further under "Techniques for Evaluating Forecasting Performances."

Notwithstanding the above discussion, forward rate forecasting bias remains a fundamental property to analyze—especially for investors who seek only to maximize their expected profits without regard to variability. Some of the theoretical arguments for and against forecasting bias are now briefly outlined.

A Case for Bias. A theoretical case for forward rates as biased forecasters of future spot rates can be based on four arguments.

Risk Premium. The risk premium argument is the most critical because under a pure floating-rate system with no government intervention, small transaction costs, and efficient information processing, only the risk premium argument survives to explain a forward rate bias. Consequently, there has been renewed research interest in this topic. In the **modern theory of foreign exchange** (Grubel, 1966) investors are assumed to be risk-averse. The **speculative demand** for forward contracts is not infinitely elastic.

Speculators will bear foreign exchange risk only if they are compensated with risk premium. Therefore, expression 6 will not hold; the forward rate reflects factors in addition to expectations and a forecasting bias results.

In **portfolio theories of foreign exchange risk** the concept of risk and the sources of risk are somewhat different than in the modern theory. In the models described in Fama and Farber (1979) and Dornbusch (1980) exchange rates are set in a **purchasing power parity** framework, but investors take risk into account. If two countries have the same trend in rate of inflation, 10%, but one country has a smaller variance of inflation (2%) compared with the other country (5%), then investors will prefer the first country's currency. Because there is less purchasing power risk associated with the first country's currency, investors should pay a premium for it on the forward market. The smaller variance in inflation might be the result of greater monetary discipline, or less exposure to real disturbances. This framework suggests a risk premium that could change signs over the short run.

Another model by Solnik (1973) relates the foreign exchange risk premium to relative international investment positions. For example, U.S. investors might hold a net asset position in U.K. assets (i.e., U.S. investors might own more U.K. assets than U.K. investors own of U.S. assets). If U.S. investors are risk-averse, they might wish to hedge the returns on their investment consistently—even at forward rates less favorable than the expected future spot rate.

For example, assume there is a U.S. firm in London that plans to repatriate a £1 million dividend in 90 days, when the exchange rate is expected to be \$2.00/£. Unless there is a U.K. firm that wishes to repatriate \$2 million from New York to London in 90 days, the U.S. firm must locate someone who currently is in portfolio balance, yet who may be induced to exchange pounds sterling for U.S. dollars in 90 days. The supplier of the forward dollars might demand compensation for altering his or her currency portfolio and the U.S. firm, assuming risk aversion, will be willing to pay it. In this case, the U.S. firm can sell its pounds sterling at \$1.98 even though it expects the price to be \$2.00 in 90 days. The \$0.02 for each pound sterling is the compensation paid to the supplier of forward dollars for altering the initial currency portfolio and taking on additional risk. This **hedging pressure** leads to a **forward bias** because expression 6 will not hold. This framework seems less likely to lead to a risk premium that changes from positive to negative in the short run.

Government Intervention. If the central bank is a large actor in the foreign exchange market and it is not motivated by accounting profits, the forward rate can be supported at a rate bearing no relationship to the future spot rate. Alternatively, the central bank can use monetary policy to influence domestic interest rates. If covered interest arbitrage is active between domestic assets, the forward rate will reflect domestic monetary controls as well as exchange rate expectations. While both of these arguments are most applicable for the short run, it also seems that central banks hold a habitual desire to affect the foreign exchange value of their currency.

Expectations. From expression 7 it is clear that expectations play a central role for the **forecasting bias** issue. If expectations are conservative or slow to form, or if expectations overreact, then expression 7 need not hold.

Transaction Costs. When transaction costs are positive, they represent another cost that must be covered by speculators and these costs drive a wedge between $F_{t,n}$ and S_{t+n}. Positive transaction costs suggest that the forward rate will very likely underestimate (or overestimate) the future spot rate when the spot rate is rising (or falling). If the spot rate has a nonzero trend for rate of growth, transaction costs will lead to a measurable bias.

A Case against Bias. In response to the above arguments, the following counterarguments can be raised.

Risk Premium. Even though open positions in foreign currency might entail nondiversifiable risk, if any investors are risk-neutral, then any expected **speculative profit** will be exploited regardless of the risk involved. Even though individuals are typically assumed to be risk-averse, corporations are often assumed to follow a profit maximization criterion. These corporate decisions should be the same as under risk-neutral behavior. This process keeps the forward rate and the market's expected future spot rate very nearly equal and therefore, no risk premium exists. Expression 6 will hold.

On the other hand, it can be that foreign exchange risk is primarily diversifiable. Assuming that foreign exchange risk can be diversified away, no premium need be paid for holding it. Again, this keeps the forward rate and the market's expected future spot rate nearly equal.

Government Intervention. Even though governments might occasionally intervene, if risk-neutral investors are present, they will exploit expected speculative profits at the expense of the central bank. This argument has more force if intervention is expected to be short-run.

Expectations. Expectations are not likely to be consistently wrong. Incorrect expectations lead to speculative losses; investors either successfully revise their expectations or leave the marketplace.

Transaction Costs. Transaction costs certainly exist and can lead to forecast errors, but this is a rational response by investors. Any measurable bias should be smaller than transaction costs.

It thus appears that there are reasonable arguments on both sides of the **forecasting bias** issue, so the matter is not likely to be settled by theoretical debate.

EMPIRICAL EVIDENCE—ONCE AGAIN. Early empirical studies could not reject the unbiased prediction (or simple efficiency) hypothesis. These early studies were based on relatively small samples. Given the high volatility of exchange rates, the statistical tests were not powerful enough to detect a small bias even if it existed.

Subsequent testing analyzed the forward premium, $(F - S)/S$, as a predictor of the exchange rate change, $(S_{t+1} - S_t)/S_t$. This simple transformation of the data changed our inferences dramatically. The forward premium appeared to be a very poor predictor of rate changes.

Econometric techniques are now available to increase the available sample size and increase econometric estimation efficiency. Recent studies by Hansen and Hodrick (1980), Hsieh (1982), and Bilson (1981) argue that the forward rate is a biased predictor. As a result, these studies suggest that a forecast capable of beating the forward rate can be produced from readily available data.

FORECASTING EXCHANGE RATES: ECONOMIC MODELS

Among the alternative forecasting approaches, it is convenient to distinguish two broad categories—econometric forecasting and judgmental forecasting. This distinction is somewhat artificial since the decision to accept one forecasting equation and reject all the others clearly involves judgment. The most obvious difference between the two broad categories is that econometric forecasts are generated from an explicit numerical formula. The econometric forecaster's list of important driving variables and their weights is clearly stated. Also, some judgmental forecasters might consider econometric estimates of important (and quantifiable) variables (e.g., the money supply, trade balance, inflation rate, etc.). However, economic factors that are difficult to quantify (e.g., currency expectations, changes in capital controls or tax policy), along with other factors (e.g., political elections and appointments), are also considered. All of these factors are combined in some unspecified way to determine a judgmental forecast.

As emphasized earlier, the judgmental approach offers the potential advantage of shifting quickly when structural change occurs. To be sure, there is a cost since judgment can be wrong. Econometric forecasts, on the other hand, try to account for the systematic impact of variables on the exchange rate. But these relationships must be estimated from historic data, and structural relationships in the future are subject to change.

Econometric forecasts are very often based on a single-equation model, and most of these appear to be inspired by purchasing power parity or monetary models, with additional variables added to taste. For example, the money supply, inflation rate, national income, industrial production, and interest rates are typical explanatory variables. The advantage of this approach is simplicity and the ability of the user to easily simulate other scenarios. In fact, several companies offer this simulation facility on an interactive computer basis. The disadvantage of the single-equation approach is that the simple equation might not adequately represent the real world. Forecast errors can result even when the right-hand variables are known with some confidence.

Other econometric advisory services prepare their forecasts using models based on 50 to 900 equations, sometimes allowing for interaction and feedback between economic regions. These complex models attempt to be a better reflection of the real world. But more regression coefficients and variables have to be estimated, so forecasting performance need not improve beyond the simple models. In fact, some large econometric services add judgment factors to the pure econometric forecast. It is important for a user to be able to isolate these judgment factors in order to evaluate the pure econometric model.

PURCHASING POWER PARITY THEORY. Perhaps the most popular and intuitive model for exchange rate behavior is represented by the theory of purchasing power parity. The main thrust of purchasing power parity is that nominal exchange rates are set so that the real purchasing power of currencies tends to equalize. As a result, PPP suggests that in the long run, nominal bilateral exchange rate changes will tend to equal the differential in inflation rates between countries. The term "purchasing power parity" is associated with Gustav Cassel, who studied alternative approaches for selecting official exchange rates at the end of World War I and the resumption of international trade. As Frenkel (1978) has recently pointed out, the intellectual origins of purchasing power parity can be traced to the early 19th century and the writings of Wheatley and Ricardo. Economists have long debated whether the PPP doctrine applies to the short run or to the long run and whether the relevant inflation rate is describing a narrow class of goods (e.g., traded goods) or a broad class of goods (e.g., all traded and nontraded goods in a consumer price index). Frenkel has argued that much of the controversy over the usefulness of the PPP doctrine results from the fact that PPP specifies a final equilibrium relationship between exchange rates and prices without specifying the precise linkages and details of the process. If in the world, economy prices and exchange rates are determined by many other variables, then PPP represents an equilibrium relationship more than a precise theory of exchange rate determination.

The many writings on purchasing power parity have been surveyed by Officer (1976). The following discussion of PPP draws on a recent book by McKinnon (1979).

To implement PPP as a forecasting model, one must first select a time period (t) and domestic and foreign price indices (P and P^*) so that PPP is satisfied.

$$S_t = \frac{cP_t}{P_t^*} \tag{8}$$

The constant term c scales the price indices to equal the exchange rate S_t. In a later period, if PPP remains true, the exchange rate in period $t + n$ will be

$$S_{t+n} = \frac{cP_{t+n}}{P_{t+n}^*} \tag{9}$$

Dividing expression 9 by 8 results in

$$\frac{S_{t+n}}{S_t} = \frac{P_{t+n}/P_{t+n}^*}{P_t/P_t^*} \quad \text{or} \quad S_{t+n} = S_t \frac{P_{t+n}/P_{t+n}^*}{P_t/P_t^*} \tag{10}$$

Expression 10 suggests that the future exchange rate is equal to the current exchange rate adjusted for future domestic price changes relative to future foreign price changes. To take an example, S_t = \$0.50/DM and $P_t = P_t^* = 100$. If one thinks that over the next three years, U.S. inflation will be about 8% a year while West German inflation will be roughly 3% a year, then estimates of future price indices are $\hat{P}_{t+n} = 125.97$ and $\hat{P}_{t+n}^* = 109.27$, where the circumflex denotes a forecast. From expression 10 it follows that

$$\hat{S}_{t+n} = \$0.50 \times \frac{125.97/109.27}{100.00/100.00} = \$0.5764 \tag{11}$$

From the example, it is clear that two critical assumptions have been made. First, the exchange rate forecast depends on accurate forecasts of both price indices. As argued previously, this problem would persist even if PPP were known to be the true model of exchange rate determination. Second, it was assumed that exchange rates were determined in accordance with PPP. Put another way, it was assumed that factor c in expressions 8 and 9 was in fact constant.

The empirical evidence on PPP is mixed. Moreover, the evidence might be sensitive to the countries, time periods, and price indexes that are selected. Over long time periods and during periods of hyperinflation (when monetary factors swamp real changes), PPP offers a fairly good description of exchange rate behavior. However, over shorter time periods, such as three to 12 months, it has not been uncommon to observe substantial exchange rate changes, 10% to 20%, which are unrelated to commodity price changes. McKinnon (1979) concluded, "Substantial and continually changing deviations from PPP are commonplace. For individual tradable commodities, violations in the 'law of one price' can be striking."

The last statement refers to a study by Isard (1977) that compared the movement of the dollar prices of West German goods relative to their U.S. equivalents for specific goods selected at the two- and three-digit levels of the Standard Industrial

Trade Classificiation (SITC). The results implied persistent violations of the law of one price. In part, Isard concluded, "In reality the law of one price is flagrantly and systematically violated by empirical data.. . . Moreover, these relative price effects seem to persist for at least several years and cannot be shrugged off as transitory."

These arguments notwithstanding, McKinnon concluded, "Until a more robust theory replaces it, I shall assume that purchasing power parity among tradable goods tends to hold in the long run in the absence of overt impediments to trade among countries with convertible currencies. But . . . because commodity arbitrage is so imperfect in the short run, it cannot be relied on to contain nominal exchange rate movements within the predictable and narrow limits suggested by the law of one price."

As a consequence, economists have turned to monetary and portfolio balance models of exchange rate determination, which are discussed below.

MONETARY THEORY AND EXCHANGE RATES. It is perhaps trivial to observe that whenever a voluntary foreign exchange transaction occurs, for example, between U.S. dollars and deutsche marks, it represents an excess demand for one currency (e.g., deutsche marks) and an excess supply of the other currency (in this case, U.S. dollars). If the sources of this excess demand for deutsche marks can be identified (perhaps these sources include a transaction demand or a speculative demand for currency, or perhaps deutsche mark balances offer a more reliable store of real purchasing power), the basis for a **monetary theory of exchange rates** exists. The basic monetary approach to exchange rate determination is a direct outgrowth of purchasing power parity theory in combination with the **quantity theory of money.** While PPP concludes that the exchange rate is the relative price of goods in two countries, monetary theory suggests that the exchange rate is the relative price of two moneys. In this context, it follows that the exchange rate represents the relative demand for two moneys.

Economists commonly represent the demand for real money balances (M/P) as some function L of real income Y, interest rates i, and other factors K.

$$M/P = L(Y, i, K) \tag{12}$$

The relationship between real income and real money balances is direct since an increase in income raises the demand for transaction balances. The relationship between interest rates and real money balances is inverse since an increase in interest rates raises the opportunity cost of holding balances and therefore lowers demand. Other factors K are included since, given Y and i, increasing sophistication among banking and financial institutions can increase the velocity of money, and lower money demand.

According to the monetary theory of exchange rates, factors that lead to an increase in the demand for domestic currency (i.e., the U.S. dollar) should lead to an increase in the price of domestic currency on the foreign exchange market. As the preceeding argued, two factors that would increase the demand for domestic currency balances are an increase in U.S. income and a fall in U.S. dollar interest rates. Correspondingly, monetary theory predicts that these factors should cause the U.S. dollar to appreciate on the foreign exchange market. Notably, these predictions are contrary to more standard theories of trade and capital flows.

Trade models correctly argue that higher U.S. income will lead to greater demand for imports, and in turn an increased demand for foreign currency and a depreciation of the U.S. dollar. But capital flows would also respond to an increase in U.S. income, and monetary theory suggests that the net effect of higher U.S. income should be a U.S. dollar appreciation. **Capital flow models** correctly argue that high *real* U.S. interest rates should attract foreign capital that, in turn, acts to appreciate the U.S. dollar. **Monetary theory** however, emphasizes that high *nominal* U.S. interest rates that incorporate a large inflation premium actually imply low real interest rates. The data strongly confirm that currencies with high interest rates (e.g., Brazil and Argentina) generally have been characterized by depreciation, while currencies with low interest rates (e.g., West Germany and Switzerland) generally have been characterized by appreciation.

To implement **monetary theory** as a **forecasting model** one must first specify an explicit money demand function in place of equation 12. A popular specification is

$$\frac{M}{P} = K \cdot Y^{\eta} \cdot e^{-\epsilon i} \tag{13}$$

where η is the income elasticity of demand for real money balances and ϵ is the interest rate semielasticity of demand. (A time subscript, t, is suppressed.) If terms are rearranged in equation 13 to isolate the price level, we have

$$P = \frac{M}{K \cdot Y^{\eta} \cdot e^{-\epsilon i}} \tag{14}$$

Assumimg that the same specification of money demand also applies in the foreign country,

$$P^* = \frac{M^*}{K^* \cdot Y^{*\eta} \cdot e^{-\epsilon i^*}} \tag{15}$$

where as before, an asterisk indicates the foreign country. For simplicity only we assume the elasticities are identical in both countries. We now draw on **purchasing power parity** theory, substituting expressions 14 and 15 into 8, resulting in

$$S = \frac{M}{M^*} \cdot \left(\frac{Y^*}{Y}\right)^{\eta} \cdot \frac{K^*}{K} \cdot e^{\epsilon(i - i^*)} \tag{16}$$

In the context of equation 16, a forecast of the future spot rate ($\hat{S}_{t+n}$) would require forecasts of all the right-hand-side variables, plus estimates of η and ϵ. The estimates could be taken from outside sources or from a regression analysis of equation 16. In order to run a linear regression, we would take logorithms of equation 16 to get

$$s = (m - m^*) + \eta\,(y^* - y) + (k^* - k) + \epsilon(i - i^*) \tag{17}$$

where we use the convention that a lowercase letter represents the logarithm of a capital letter (e.g., $s = \ln S$).

Empirical estimates of equations similar to equation 17 have been reported by

Bilson (1977) Dornbusch (1980), and Frankel (1979). As with **PPP** models, **monetary exchange rate models** perform best when monetary disturbances are large and dominate economic aggregates, such as during hyperinflation. Monetary models can explain a significant fraction of quarter-to-quarter exchange rate movements during the 1970s. But their explanation is far from complete, suggesting that other models that incorporate other variables might account for the unexplained part of exchange rate behavior. In addition, it should be noted that models such as 17 do not explain short-run exchange rate changes very well, even though the marginal impact of each variable might be as predicted. Finally, it should be added that most published empirical studies address the issue of how well equations like 17 fit past data, rather than their use for forecasting future exchange rates.

PORTFOLIO BALANCE THEORY. An extension of this framework argues that investors' excess demand is not for currency as currency; rather, investors desire to shift from one set of financial assets (e.g., dollar-denominated assets) into another set (e.g., deutsche mark–denominated financial assets). In the **portfolio balance model,** demand in the foreign exchange market for currencies is derived largely from demand for financial assets. As a consequence, if wealth accumulates (e.g., via current account surpluses) in a country that traditionally prefers deutsche mark assets, it is likely that the value of the deutsche mark will increase. To take another example, if the spending patterns of a country shift (e.g., the United States changes its taste toward West German products) or if a country (e.g., Saudi Arabia) accumulates a substantial amount of financial wealth, prudent risk management principles suggest that investors in these countries diversify their asset portfolios. And in the examples given, diversification is away from dollar assets and toward deutsche mark assets.

The **portfolio balance approach** is appealing because it links the exchange rate to the distribution (across currencies) of financial wealth, while allowing a role for the current account, that is, flow changes in wealth. On the other hand, empirical tests of this model have not met with great success. In large part, this might simply be the result of data problems; it is very difficult to track the holdings of financial assets broken down by currency of denomination. Another problem is that the demand function for assets denominated in a particular currency is difficult to specify. Nonetheless, the broad themes of the portfolio balance approach seem to be applicable and they should be useful to incorporate when making exchange rate forecasts.

THE ASSET APPROACH. The **monetary** and **portfolio balance** approaches reviewed suggest that the demand for currency depends on its qualities as a durable asset. If a currency is expected to continue offering services as a medium of exchange (i.e., transaction services) and as a store of value and unit of account (i.e., the choice for denominating portfolio wealth), then the currency will continue to be demanded. One property of financial assets that is associated with stocks and bonds is that their prices are forward-looking, depending on future discounted cash flows. The same forward-looking property is true of exchange rate pricing and it can be helpful in forecasting.

In equation 17, the interest rate differential term, $\epsilon(i - i^*)$ appears. If **covered interest parity** holds, $(i - i^*) = f_t - s_t$, and forward rates are assumed equal to expected future spot rates, $f = E(s_{t+1})$, equation 17 can now be written as

$$s_t = z_t + \epsilon[E(s_{t+1}) - s_t] \tag{18}$$

where

$$z_t = (m - m^*) + \eta\,(y^* - y) + (k^* - k) \tag{19}$$

If we collect terms, we have

$$s_t = \frac{1}{1 + \epsilon} z_t + \epsilon E(s_{t+1}) \tag{19}$$

Expression 19 shows that the log of today's spot rate depends on today's economic variables (the z_t) plus an expectation of the spot rate in the next period. But from expression 18, one can see that $E(s_{t+1})$ will depend on $E(s_{t+2})$—and $E(s_{t+2})$ will depend on $E(s_{t+3})$, and so forth. By this process of forward iteration, one can show

$$s_t = \frac{1}{1+\epsilon}\sum_{k=0}^{\infty}\left(\frac{\epsilon}{1+\epsilon}\right)^k E(z_{t+k}) \tag{20}$$

In other words, the current spot rate depends on the current expectation of all important driving variables (the zs), from now into the indefinite future. The analogy to a security whose current price represents the discounted value of all future cash flows should be clear.

To put expression 20 as simply as possible, the current exchange rate reflects what is known or expected about the future. Without a model for the zs, this relationship is not useful for forecasting. However, the other implication of equation 20 is that exchange rates change only in response to unanticipated events.

THE ROLE OF NEWS. The implication of the asset market approach is that deviations between the forward rate and the future spot rate are the result of news, assuming no exchange risk premium. In a regression format, one would write

$$s_t = a + b \cdot f_{t-1} + \text{``news''} + w_t \tag{21}$$

Clearly, news could be modeled in a variety of ways. Frenkel (1981) allows unanticipated changes in the term structure of interest rates to play the role of news, and he finds a significant relationship in the context of expression 21. Dornbusch (1980) looks at news in terms of unanticipated current account balances and unanticipated cyclical income movements, as well as unanticipated interest rate changes. Again, the empirical results confirm that unanticipated changes in these important variables are significantly related to forward rate forecasting errors.

The implication of these results is that analysts who can forecast one or two key variables better than the market as a whole might be able to outperform the forward rate forecast.

FORECASTING EXCHANGE RATES: PURE FORECASTING APPROACHES

The term "pure forecasting approaches" is used to describe techniques that are not built on a particular economic model of exchange rates. Pure forecasting approaches are sometimes characterized as "black-box" approaches in that users are given a set of forecasts or forecasting procedures, but the economic structure or rationale for why these forecasts should work is not always clear. The advantage of a pure forecasting model is that it is selected because it produces good forecasts. The disadvantage is that to the extent that the approach is ad hoc, the approach can suddenly produce very bad forecasts. Surely, econometric forecasts can be bad when there is a change in structure, but the forecaster can try to be alert for these changes and to adjust the model accordingly. The pure forecaster who works without a clear underlying model might also try to account for changes in economic structure, but the linkages between the forecasts and the structure will be less clear.

TECHNICAL FORECASTING. Some forecasting companies specialize in very short-run forecasts. These so-called technical or momentum services advise their customers primarily on the direction of exchange rate movements in the very short run and correspondingly whether customers should hold long or short positions in particular currencies. These **directional forecasts** are typically based on a statistical analysis of recent exchange rate behavior, although judgment can play an equally large role.

Some aspects of the technical approach can be grounded in solid economic principles. For example, analysts might believe that the demand for deutsche marks will shift from D to D', as in Exhibit 2*a*. Information on this shift might leak out slowly, or, because the information is uncertain, only the least risk-averse traders will be attracted at first. If this information is later verified, the exchange rate will have moved from \$0.50 to \$0.54 and this early trend following will have paid off.

Many technicians speak of support points and resistance points when making exchange rate predictions. Exhibit 2*b* illustrates a case where the demand and supply curves are highly elastic over the range Q_1 Q_2. These particular demand and supply curves could be the result of expected central bank behavior, or many private participants who feel strongly about these particular values. A shift in the demand curve to D' will initially meet price resistance at \$0.52. A shift to D'' will clear away the elastic supply of deutsche mark sellers and the deutsche mark price will quickly rise.

More traditional economic analysis raises two major arguments against the technical approach. First, the dollar/deutsche mark exchange rate has no mystical affinity toward the \$0.50 range any more than the \$0.25 or \$1.25 range. The spot rate could move toward any value if economic policies are set in the appropriate manner. The exchange rate does not "know" whether it is supposed to move back toward \$0.50 and it would not care if it moved toward \$1.25. Exhibit 2 refers to the shaping and shifting demand curves, but technical analysis never considers the fundamental economic factors to know whether these shapes and shifts are indeed justified.

In response, technicians often return to a fundamental principle—that price changes reflect information. If one observes that price has changed from \$0.50 to \$0.52, technicians assume that demand has shifted and that regardless of the underlying explanation, they can make a prediction about future price changes.

Second, traditional economists raise the efficient market argument. If the path of

EXHIBIT 2 ECONOMICS OF TECHNICAL ANALYSIS

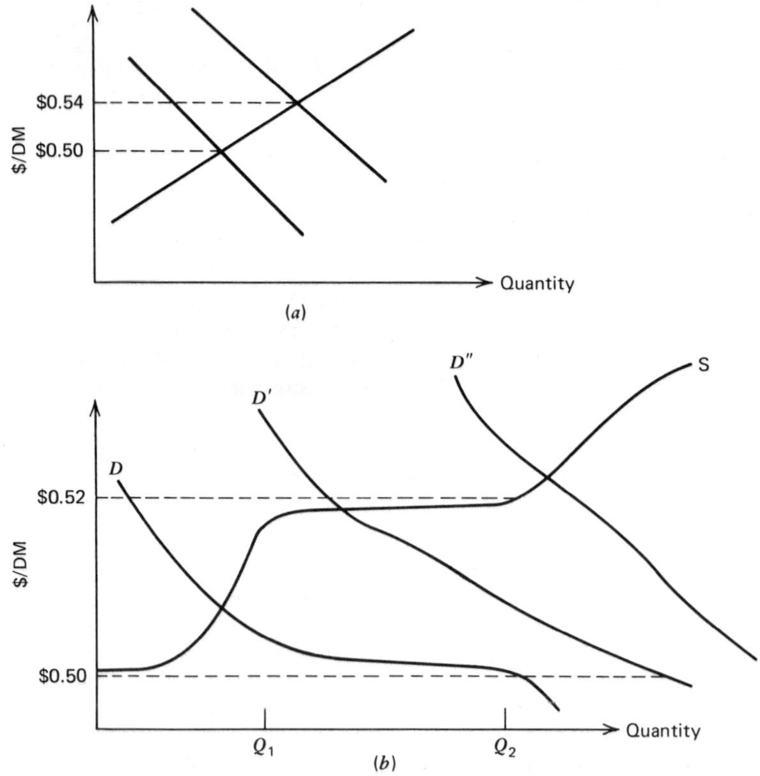

exchange rates leaves a readable signal about future exchange rates, why do not interest rates adjust to negate expected speculative profits from taking positions based on these forecasts? In response, technical analysts seem to argue that the market is inefficient, largely because of institutional constraints. A recent paper by Rosenberg (1981) summarizes many of these arguments and suggests that the market is inefficient because of a shortage of speculative capital. As an institutional matter, the large international banks and multinational corporations are permitted to hold small speculative positions relative to the enormous flow of foreign exchange trading (perhaps $200 billion a day). As a result, risky profit opportunities predicted by technical analysis are not quickly bid away.

The empirical studies cited earlier in this section on "Forecasting and Exchange Market Efficiency" have not ruled out the possibility that technical trading profits are simply the fair return for extra risks incurred. However, the two most recent studies, that of filter rules by Dooley and Shafer (1982) and that of professional technical services by Goodman (1981), strongly suggest a favorable risk/return ratio.

COMPOSITE FORECASTING. It has long been hypothesized that two heads are better than one. The composite forecasting approach builds on this principle. If two forecasts, $\hat{S}_1$ and $\hat{S}_2$, capture or reflect different information, it will be possible to construct a new, composite forecast that is superior to either forecast individually. One way to construct the composite forecast is through a linear regression,

$$\hat{S}_c = w_1 \hat{S}_1 + w_2 \hat{S}_2 \tag{22}$$

If "superior" is defined to mean minimum variance forecasters, than w_1 and w_2 are ordinary least squares regression coefficients. Noting that w_1 and w_2 are estimated from historical forecast data, one must assume that these weights remain applicable in a true forecast period. Expression 22 can easily be extended to a case where there are more than two forecasters.

The theoretical foundations of composite forecasting rest on two key points. First, it is assumed that different forecasters possess different information and different forecasting abilities. Market prices reflect this information only to the extent that investors have actually bought or sold foreign exchange based on these forecasts. The composite approach seeks to combine available information in a more efficient manner.

Second, the risk diversification principle suggests that single securities are risky, while diversified portfolios earn the market rate of return at minimum risk. By analogy, a portfolio of forecasters reduces the risk of large forecast errors and improves forecasting accuracy relative to the record of an individual forecaster.

The composite approach appears in this discussion of pure forecasting approaches because there are not obvious structural reasons why two forecasters should maintain a particular pattern of forecast errors. For example, if forecaster one's errors are generally twice as large and of opposite size than those of forecaster two (e.g., 2% vs. −1%; 4% vs. −2%; −3% vs. 1.5%) this would imply optimal weights $w_1 = 1/3$ and $w_2 = 2/3$ for unbiased forecasting. If either forecaster improves his or her accuracy, this weighting system will no longer produce unbiased forecasts.

Diversification gains through composite forecasting are possible in three directions—across currencies, across horizons, and across forecasting services. A recent study by Bilson (1981) attempts to exploit all of these. Bilson notes that exchange rate changes are imperfectly correlated across currencies and horizons and exchange rate forecasts from various services are also imperfectly correlated. Each dimension represents an avenue to diversify away the risks of forecast errors. Bilson's study examines five currencies, three horizons, and two forecasts (i.e., the current spot rate, S_t, and the current forward rate, F_t). His results offer strong evidence that the composite technique, combined with a portfolio currency exposure management system, can lead to significant profits.

In a related study, Levich (1981a) constructs composite forecasts based on 11 professional forecasting services. Again, these results indicate that the composite forecasts are generally more accurate and more reliable than the best individual forecasts.

TECHNIQUES FOR EVALUATING FORECASTING PERFORMANCES

How can one evaluate and choose among alternative currency forecasts? As in other similar problems (such as evaluating the performance of mutual fund managers or of individual subsidiaries or profit centers within a firm), evaluating foreign exchange forecasting performance is a tricky procedure. Basically, one must establish a standard of performance and then calculate how a forecast compares to the standard.

By definition, users select a forecast on the basis of qualities that they value. Suppose there are two forecasts—S_1 has made errors that average zero with 9% variance and S_2 has made errors that average zero with 16% variance. If the user is concerned only about average errors (i.e., only average errors appears in the user's utility function—the user is risk-neutral), then that user would be indifferent between the two forecasts. He or she might actually select the one that is cheaper. But if the user is concerned about the variability of forecast errors (i.e., the user is risk-averse), then that user would prefer forecast one, assuming the costs were identical. The possibility of buying both forecasts and building a **composite forecast** is considered later in this section.

If it is supposed instead that a firm has net ongoing cash flows in deutsche marks and that the firm's policy is either to sell the deutsche marks forward or to sell them on the spot market at the end of the quarter when they are repatriated, then this firm would not take a longer deutsche mark position if it forecast the future spot rate higher than F_t; it would not take a short deutsche mark position if it forecast the future spot rate lower than F_t. This firm might only be concerned with the forecaster's ability to predict depreciation in deutsche marks relative to F_t since the firm's only decision is whether to sell deutsche marks on the forward market. The firm might also be unconcerned about the magnitude of forecast errors because it is making a lump sum decision.

STATISTICAL ANALYSIS OF FORECAST ERRORS. There are two general approaches for analyzing the performance of an individual forecaster. The first general approach concentrates on the forecast error (forecast error equals predicted exchange rate minus actual exchange rate) and its various statistical properties. One desirable property of a forecast is that its forecast errors be small. However, even this simple criterion needs qualification. For example, if today's forward rate is \$2.00 and two alternative forecasts of the future spot rate are S_1 = \$1.99 and S_2 = 2.08, if the actual spot rate turns out to be \$2.02, the forecast error associated with S_1 (−\$.03) is smaller than the forecast error associated with S_2 (+\$0.06). However, forecast S_2 is superior because it leads investors to take long and profitable forward positions in pounds sterling—that is, forecast S_2 leads to a correct decision.

As a further qualification, a third forecast, S_3 = \$2.14, might also exist. Even though its forecast error is +\$0.12, it does not follow that this forecast is twice as bad as forecast S_2. If, for example, the firm is remitting a dividend from its U.S. parent and the firm is considering an all-or-nothing hedging decision, it will make the same decision using either S_2 or S_3 as a guide, and so there is no additional cost associated with S_3's larger forecast error. On the other hand, forecast S_3 might be more than twice as bad as forecast S_2. If the firm is considering investing a variable amount in U.K. bonds, based on the substantial appreciation predicted by S_3 the firm might invest 10 times as much in the U.K. bonds as it would based on forecast S_2. As a consequence, the firm foregoes other profitable investments; these opportunity costs of using S_2 might exceed twice the costs of using S_3.

Therefore one can conclude that there is no simple and unique relationship between the magnitude of forecast errors and the cost of forecast errors for investors. The implication of this statement is that there is no unique statistic for evaluating or ranking forecasters that will be correct for all investors. An all-or-nothing hedger will only be concerned that the forecast tells the correct direction, regardless of the magnitude of the forecast error. Investors who feel that exchange gains and losses are proportional to the forecast error will rank forecasters on the basis of mean absolute errors. Investors who feel that exchange gains and losses are proportional to the squared forecast error will rank forecasters on the basis of mean-squared errors. It is an empirical question whether these criteria will rank forecasters in similar order.

If the magnitude of forecast errors is ignored, one can evaluate a forecast by calculating the fraction of periods where the forecast correctly predicts only the direction of exchange rate movement. "Direction" is defined relative to the current forward rate or some other decision variable (e.g., the forward rate plus a risk premium). For example, in the earlier example, S_2 and S_3 were correct forecasts (relative to the forward rate), while S_1 was incorrect. If the fraction of correct forecasts is unusually high, then one can conclude that the forecast advisory service has expertise.

A numerical example helps to illustrate the above procedure. In a sample of 100 observations (n) there are 60 correct forecasts (r), or a 60% track record. Is this an unusually good track record that demonstrates expertise or is it simply the result of a sequence of lucky guesses? The question is analogous to another basic statistics problem: If a fair coin is tossed 100 times, what is the probability that it will land on heads 60 or more times? The answer is, this event would occur with roughly 2.3% probability. There are two ways to interpret this track record.

1. The forecaster does not have any special expertise in picking the direction of currency movements. A fairly rare event happened—the forecaster guessed correctly on 60 or 100 trials.
2. The forecaster does have special expertise. His or her track record for picking the direction of currency movements correctly is close to 60%, significantly greater than 50% (which would result from simply guessing).

In the case above, interpretation 2 would be more likely to be chosen. The track record appears too high to be the result of just guessing.

This **percentage-correct methodology** was used by Levich (1980, 1981b). In a sample of 12 forecasting services and nine currencies Levich concluded that there were too many forecasters with a high percentage of correct track records to be the result of chance. In this sense, the forecasters appeared to demonstrate expertise relative to the forward rate.

The second general approach for evaluating forecasting performance is to calculate the stream of returns that an investor could earn by following the forecast. One would conclude that the advisory service has expertise and that the forecasts are useful if the stream of investment returns (adjusting for risk) is high relative to alternative investments. Again, this straightforward evaluation procedure raises two difficult questions.

First, how does an investor translate a set of currency forecasts into a set of investment decisions? The investor recognizes that forecasts are seldom perfect. If the forward rate stands at \$2.00, the investor might not be willing to buy forward contracts unless the forecast is \$2.02, \$2.06, or perhaps higher. Furthermore, the investor is free to increase the number of forward contracts purchased as his or her expected profits, and the confidence in those profits, increases. These issues are often handled by assuming that the investor uses the forecast to determine a lump sum investment rather than an investment that increases with the expected returns predicted by the forecast or decreases with the expected variance of returns.

The second difficult question is how one should measure the risk associated with currency investment. This calculation is necessary so that an investor can determine if the return on currency investment is high relative to the risk incurred. Since the measurement of this risk factor is somewhat controversial, many analyses simply compare the returns from selective currency investments based on a forecast with returns from (1) always holding U.S. dollar assets, or (2) always holding foreign currency assets. These latter alternatives correspond to the (1) always-hedge-foreign-exchange risk strategy and (2) never-hedge-foreign-exchange risk strategy, both of which are simple rules of thumb for comparison.

In summary, a distinction is made between **correct forecasts** (those that correctly predict the direction of change relative to the forward rate) and **accurate forecasts** (those with low mean-squared forecast errors). Earlier it was noted that many exchange rate changes are very large and most are unanticipated by the market. Therefore, including these as large forecast errors might bias (upwardly) an estimate of forecasting inaccuracy and an estimate of the potential for profits. In this sense, calculating the percentage-correct forecast might offer a more meaningful measure of forecasting expertise.

EVALUATION IN A COMPOSITE MODEL. The suggestions given evaluate each forecast separately. However, the traditional concept of economic value implies that one should measure the marginal contribution of a forecast to optimal decision making. Evaluation procedures that focus on forecasters individually might not measure their true economic value. For example, a composite forecast based on the current spot rate and the current forward rate

$$S^{c}_{t+1} = w_1 S_t + w_2 F_t \tag{23}$$

can represent an optimal forecast based on public information. A professional forecast might rate well by itself, but in the context of equation 23, the new forecast might add very little. On the other hand, a poor individual forecast might be significant in the context of equation 23 if it reflects information not captured in the other forecasts. A forecast will be valuable if it brings new information that can be incorporated with existing forecasts.

SUMMARY AND CONCLUSIONS

Are exchange rate forecasts a necessary part of corporate operations? Are useful forecasts available through public information (e.g., forward rates and other variables) or private professional forecasters? Have forecasters demonstrated significant expertise and economic value in exposure management?

The evidence herein puts a mostly favorable light on exchange rate forecasting. Several models of exchange rate determination are offered that seem to explain the broad movements in currency values. Recent models focusing on the role of **news** suggest that superior forecasts of a few important variables could significantly improve forecasts relative to the forward rate. Several recent studies, by Bilson (1981),

Goodman (1981), and Levich (1981b), suggest that several forecasting approaches are useful and can lead to profits.

On the other hand, this section also notes reasons to be skeptical or cautious about forecasting and risk taking. While empirical studies indicate that forecasts can lead to profits, these profits are not risk-free. It is conceivable that the profits are only fair compensation for the extra risks of open foreign exchange positions. Risk here is difficult to quantify since potential overnight changes of 20% to 30% can wipe out a large string of earlier gains. The efficient market principle is also pertinent. Models that worked in the past supply valuable information that is incorporated into forward rates, making it harder to beat the forward rate in the future. Finally, there is the prospect of structural change. Governments can alter their monetary, fiscal, and intervention policies. Private agents can change their currency and asset-demand preferences. If these events happen, forecasting models that worked in the past need not work in the future.

REFERENCES

Bilson, J.F.O., "The Deutsche Mark/Dollar Exchange Rate—A Monetary Analysis," in Brunner, K. and Meltzer, A. (Eds.), *Policies for Employment, Prices and Exchange Rates*, Vol. 2, Carnegie-Rochester Conference, 1979.

Bilson, J.F.O., "The 'Speculative Efficiency' Hypothesis," *Journal of Business*, Vol. 54, July (1981).

Dooley, M.P. and J.R. Shafer, "Analysis of Short-Run Exchange Rate Behavior: March 1973 to November 1981," International Monetary Fund, Departmental Memorandum 82-22, April 1982.

Dornbusch, R., "Exchange Rate Economics: Where Do We Stand?" *Brookings Papers on Economic Activity*, No. 1 (1980).

Fama, E.F., "Efficient Capital Markets: A Review of Theory and Empirical Work," *Journal of Finance*, Vol. 25, May (1970).

Fama, E.F. and A. Farber, "Money, Bonds and Foreign Exchange," *American Economic Review*, Vol. 69, September (1979).

Frankel, J.A., "On the Mark: A Theory of Floating Exchange Rates Based on Real Interest Differentials," *American Economic Review*, Vol. 69, September (1979).

Frenkel, J.A., "Purchasing Power Parity: Doctrinal Perspectives and Evidence from the 1920s," *Journal of International Economics*, Vol. 8, May (1978).

Frenkel, J.A., "Flexible Exchange Rates, Prices and the Role of 'News': Lessons from the 1970s," *Journal of Political Economy*, Vol. 89, August (1981).

Goodman, S., "Technical Analysis Still Beats Econometrics," *Euromoney*, August (1981).

Grubel, H. G., *Forward Exchange, Speculation and the International Flow of Capital*, Stanford University Press, Stanford California, 1966.

Hansen, L.P. and R.J. Hodrick, "Forward Exchange Rates as Optimal Predictors of Future Spot Rates: An Econometric Analysis," *Journal of Political Economy*, Vol. 88, October (1980).

Hsieh, D.A., "Tests of Rational Expectations and No Risk Premium in Forward Exchange Markets," *National Bureau of Economic Research Working Paper*, No. 843, January (1982).

Isard, P., "How Far Can We Push the Law of One Price?" *American Economic Review*, Vol. 67, December (1977).

Kohlhagen, S.W., *The Behavior of Foreign Exchange Markets—A Critical Survey of the Empirical Literature*. New York University (Monograph Series in Finance and Economics, Salomon Brothers Center), New York, 1978a.

Kohlhagen, S.W., "A Model of Optional Foreign Exchange Hedging without Exchange Rate Projections," *Journal of International Business Studies*, Vol. 9, Fall (1978b).

Levich, R.M., "Further Results on the Efficiency of Markets for Foreign Exchange," in *Managed Exchange-Rate Flexibility: The Recent Experience*, Federal Reserve Bank of Boston (Conference Series No. 20), Boston, 1978.

Levich, R.M., "Analyzing the Accuracy of Foreign Exchange Advisory Services: Theory and Evidence," in Levich, R. and Wihlborg, C. (Eds.), *Exchange Risk, and Exposure*, Heath, Lexington, Mass., 1980.

Levich, R.M., "Maximizing the Return on Forex Services," *Euromoney Currency Report*, February (1981). (a)

Levich, R.M., "How to Compare Chance with Forecasting Expertise," *Euromoney*, August (1981). (b)

McKinnon, R.I., *Money in International Exchange*, Oxford University Press, New York, 1979.

Officer, L.H., "The Purchasing-Power-Parity Theory of Exchange Rates: A Review Article," *International Monetary Fund Staff Papers*, Vol. 23, March (1976).

Rosenberg, M.R., "Is Technical Analysis Right for Currency Forecasting?" *Euromoney*, June (1981).

Solnik, B.H., *European Capital Markets*, Heath, Lexington, Mass., 1973.

SECTION **8.2**

PRINCIPLES OF INTERNATIONAL PORTFOLIO SELECTION

CONTENTS

SECTION 8.2

PRINCIPLES OF INTERNATIONAL PORTFOLIO SELECTION

Donald Lessard

The logic of diversifying a portfolio across countries is no different than that of diversifying along any other dimension—whenever returns on different assets are not subject to exactly the same risks, the risks of a diversified portfolio can be less than the risks of the typical individual security. However, international diversification is of special interest for two reasons. First, empirical evidence suggests that it may represent one of the most powerful dimensions for risk reduction through diversification. Second, it is subject to a number of obstacles, including currency and political risks, additional taxes and transaction costs, less efficient markets, and, in some cases, outright barriers. Thus, international portfolio selection involves complex tradeoffs between the potential for reducing investment risk through diversification and the costs and risks unique to international investment. As a result, the ideal internationally diversified portfolio is likely to differ for investors with different preferences, different tax situations, and different beliefs about their ability to "beat the market" on one or another dimension.

This section reviews the logical evidence regarding international diversification, then explores the actual or perceived obstacles to cross-border investment and their implications for portfolio selection. A discussion of passive and active international investment strategies concludes. The emphasis is on equities, where diversification gains have been shown to be greatest, but discussion also encompasses international diversification of bonds and money market holdings.

GAINS FROM INTERNATIONAL DIVERSIFICATION

THE LOGIC OF DIVERSIFICATION. It is generally accepted that investors should and can expect higher rates of return on risky investments than they can earn on less risky investments. Thus the required **expected rate of return** on a particular investment will consist of the interest rate, reflecting time preference as well as a premium for inflation, and a risk premium.

$$R_j = r + \text{risk premium}$$

where R_j is the required rate of return on security j, a project, firm, or security issued by a firm, and r is the nominal interest rate on a riskless security.

As long as returns from different assets are not subject to exactly the same risks, the risk of a portfolio of these assets will be less than the risk of a typical security in the portfolio. This implies that the risk of an asset in the context of a well-diversified portfolio, termed its "systematic risk," will be less than its total risk. Recognizing this, risk-averse investors will hold diversified portfolios of assets. As a result, in equilibrium (when all investors have the same information and can adjust their portfolios without cost) the premiums that individuals demand for bearing risks will reflect only systematic risk, that portion of a risk that cannot be diversified away within an economy. The relationship between total risk, non-diversifiable risk and diversifiable risk, and the extent of risk reduction possible through diversification is illustrated in Exhibit 1.

THE MAGNITUDE OF RISK REDUCTION THROUGH DIVERSIFICATION. The proportion of total risk that is systematic depends on the degree of correlation among the outcomes of the various securities. For the United States, the degree of **correlation** between returns on shares of individual firms and the completely diversified portfolio, the market aggregate of all risky securities, typically is around .5. This means that on average, the systematic risk of a security is 50% of its total risk. Figures for a variety of other countries are presented in Exhibit 2.

In general, the proportion of risk of securities that is systematic in other countries is higher than in the United States. This reflects the fact that these countries typically have a less diverse industrial base than the United States and, in some cases, a more volatile political environment. This is particularly true for less-developed countries where there is little room for risk reduction through domestic diversification.

When **diversification** is extended across national boundaries, a substantial proportion of the risk that is systematic within each country can be averaged out. Exhibit 3 illustrates this, comparing the risk reduction through diversification within the

EXHIBIT 1 RISK REDUCTION THROUGH DIVERSIFICATION: THE DOMESTIC CASE

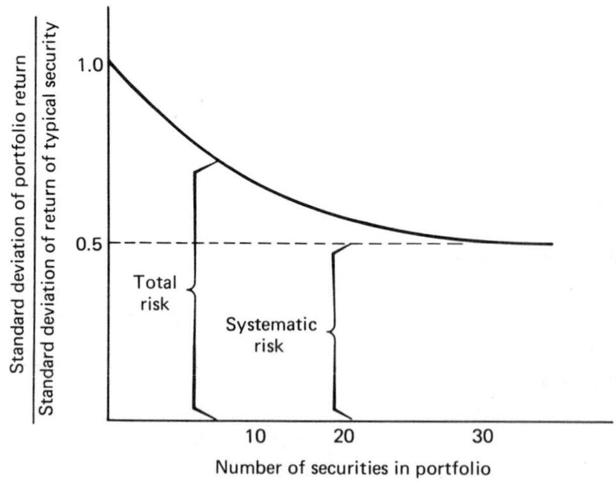

EXHIBIT 2 RISK REDUCTION THROUGH DOMESTIC DIVERSION

	Standard Deviation of Market Portfolio Divided by Standard Deviation of Typical Stock		
Country	Solnik (1967–73)	Lessard (1969–73)	Lessard (1958–68)
Argentina	—	—	.81
Brazil	—	—	.69
Chile	—	—	.71
Colombia	—	—	.69
France	.57	.68	—
Japan	—	.52	—
Switzerland	.66	.71	—
The Netherlands	.49	.63	—
United Kingdom	.59	.61	—
United States	.52	—	—
West Germany	.66	.66	—

Source. B.H. Solnik, "Why Not Diversify Internationally?" *Financial Analysis Journal*, July–August (1974); D.R. Lessard, "World, National, and Industry Factors through International Diversification," *Financial Analysis Journal*, January–February (1976); and D.R. Lessard, "International Portfolio Diversification: A Multivariate Analysis for a Group of Latin American Countries," *Journal of Finance*, June (1973).

United States to that obtainable through international diversification. In the international case, portfolio risk drops to 33% of that of the typical stock, one third less than the U.S. figure.

The reason for this additional diversification is that returns on diversified single-country portfolios display considerable independence. This can be seen by examining the correlations between returns on the stock markets of seven major countries and the United States for different periods of time, reported in Exhibit 4. In interpreting

EXHIBIT 3 RISK REDUCTION THROUGH NATIONAL AND INTERNATIONAL DIVERSIFICATION

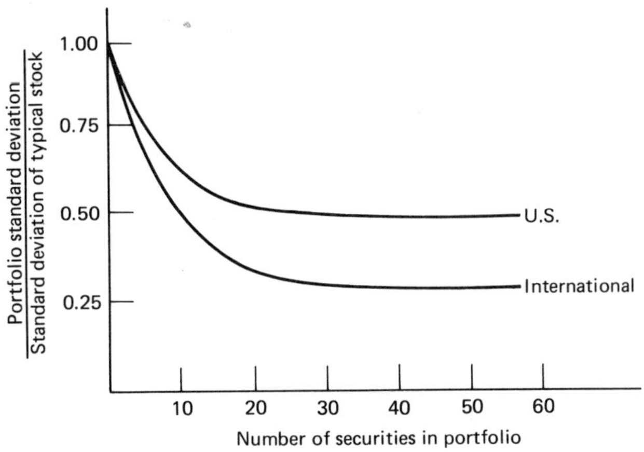

EXHIBIT 4 CORRELATIONS OF MAJOR WORLD EQUITY MARKETS WITH THE UNITED STATES[a]

Country	1959–63	1964–68	1969–73	1973–74	1975–79
France	.45	.02	.20	.37	.32
Japan	.02	.07	.42	.39	.36
Switzerland	.52	.35	.49	.49	.45
The Netherlands	.67	.60	.54	.37	.50
United Kingdom	.29	.19	.41	.08	.34
West Germany	.48	.12	.41	.52	.38

[a]All returns measured in U.S. dollars, based on stock market data reported by *Capital International Perspective,* Capital International S.A., Geneva, Switzerland.

these correlations, it should be kept in mind that each of these single-market portfolios is completely diversified within the country, reflecting only 50% to 70% of the risk of the individual securities that it includes. As a result, a useful benchmark for comparison is the typical correlation between well-diversified portfolios such as mutual funds in the United States and the overall U.S. market portfolio. These correlations average around .9.

EXPECTED RETURNS, THE OTHER PART OF THE EQUATION. Risk reduction is nice, but it is only part of what an investor seeks by diversifying across national boundaries. The investor is interested in enhanced **risk-adjusted returns,** not in risk reduction per se. In an idealized, perfectly integrated, efficient world capital market, there would be no question that a world portfolio would dominate all single-country portfolios. In such a market, all securities would be priced to yield future total returns in line with their contribution to the risk of the world portfolio and any subportfolio not perfectly correlated with the world portfolio would be inferior in terms of the ratio of expected return to risk. In such a setting, the relation of the U.S. portfolio to the world portfolio would be much like that of a portfolio of, for example, Texas-based firms or firms in a single industry, such as utilities, to the U.S. market. No investor would hold such a portfolio unless they expected overwhelming returns on it relative to the overall market.

Of course, the world capital market does not match the ideal. There are barriers to cross-border investment and there is no proof that various national markets are always priced properly in relation to each other. Thus, investors must consider the returns they are likely to earn in each market in relation to the risk that these investments contribute to their portfolios.

Logue and Rogalski (1979) distinguish between two types of gains from international diversification—**beta gains** and **alpha gains.** Beta gains are those outlined in the previous securities—gains due to the fact that a significant fraction of those risks that cannot be diversified within a single country are diversifiable internationally. These gains exist whether or not shares in various countries are properly priced. Alpha gains, in contrast, arise when securities in one market are mispriced relative to others and are likely to provide unusually high returns. Of course, an alpha gain to, for example, a U.S. investor in European securities is an alpha loss to a European investor in U.S. securities. In order to identify potential alpha gains, investors can turn to two types of data: (1) returns that have been earned in the past, and (2) expectations for future returns based on fundamental analysis.

Historical returns over the last two decades generally are favorable to international diversification from a U.S. perspective. Solnik and Noetzlin (1982) show that realized returns on equities in all major countries but Italy and Spain exceeded those for the United States from 1970 to 1980. The Capital International EAFE (Europe, Australia, Far East) Index for example, which is capitalization weighted within and across countries and hence a good proxy for the non-U.S. equity market, posted an annualized 13.4% U.S. dollar total return over this period compared to 6.8% for the United States. Hanna (1980) and Solnik and Noetzlin (1982) obtain similar results for bonds. From 1970 to 1980, total bond returns for all countries with well-developed bond markets except Canada exceeded those of the United States, typically at least doubling the 5.7% U.S. returns.

These high realized returns on foreign securities, though, do not represent a sound basis for estimating future returns for two reasons. First, in the case of equities, they cover a period of major opening of the international economy, which most benefited trading nations such as Japan and West Germany, as well as of the integration of the European economy, which certainly benefited those economies relative to others in the world system. While structural changes are likely over the next 10 years, they are unlikely to reoccur in the same pattern. In the case of bond returns, a large part of the higher foreign returns is attributable to the drop in the dollar. This event is unlikely to be repeated since this period covers the major transition from the dollar as a currency whose value was actively supported by such devices as the interest equalization tax, the temporary import surcharges, and constraints on capital movements, to one whose value is determined primarily by market forces. Second, and probably more important, if all investors believed that these situations would persist, everyone would try to tilt their portfolios toward non-U.S. securities. This, of course, would bid up these share and bond prices (lower bond interest rates) relative to U.S. secutiries until the expected returns fell into line with the relative riskiness of each market.

Given the low likelihood that realized returns will provide reliable estimates of future returns, many analysts favor examining various fundamental indicators in order to estimate growth rates for various economies. The track record of such forecasting, however, is spotty. Further, even if reliable growth estimates can be obtained, it does not follow that the fast-growing countries represent more attractive investment options. The key question is whether or not the growth prospects for a country are properly reflected in the price of the shares of stocks from these countries. Thus, fundamental projections regarding economic performance will be relevant only to the extent that they are substantially different from the consensus projections regarding individual economies. Projections in line with the consensus will be fully discounted in securities' prices.

Other analysts focus on comparative **price earnings ratios** or apply dividend discount models to determine if shares in different markets are appropriately priced relative to each other. Since earnings typically are not comparable across countries due to differences in accounting practices and in rates of inflation, those comparisons are complex. While some analysts might be able to use them to identify alpha gains, there are no credible statistical demonstrations of this ability to date.

For these reasons, most economists prefer to emphasize beta gains as the basis for international investment. In so doing, they focus on the returns that investors could logically expect to earn if they all were to agree on future prospects and select portfolios accordingly. Under the simplifying assumptions that there are no barriers to cross-border investment in the form of additional costs or risks and that no investors have special forecasting skills, all investors would choose to hold the (world) market portfolio. Given that there are some barriers to international investment, though, the equilibrium structure of returns will not necessarily imply that all investors should hold the world market portfolio. With this more complex situation, different investors would choose to hold different portfolios. This point is also covered below when the effects of various obstacles to international investment are discussed.

IS THE HOME BIAS OF U.S. INVESTORS JUSTIFIED? If the logic of capital market equilibrium is accepted, it is very hard to explain why U.S. investors have diversified so little overseas. In a recent study of U.S. pension funds, Ehrlich (1981) found that less than 2% of all U.S. assets were invested abroad—a far cry from the roughly 50% of world capitalization represented by non-U.S. markets. Investors of other countries also display strong home biases in their portfolio holdings. This implies that investors in aggregate bear much more risk than is necessary. In an example developed to illustrate required returns from a U.S. perspective, Lessard (1976) suggests that the expected annualized returns on U.S. holdings would have to exceed expectations on foreign securities by more than 3% to justify this extreme degree of home bias.

While some investors might forecast such a divergence based on their own estimates of future returns, there is no evidence that a significant proportion of investors possess this degree of forecasting skill. Incremental costs or risks, of course, might justify a home bias, but it is unlikely that they add up to 3% annually if investments are made over anything other than the shortest time periods.

An examination follows of the various incremental costs and risks associated with cross-border investments, costs and risks that are perceived by investors as obstacles to international diversification and that might explain some of the home bias.

OBSTACLES TO INTERNATIONAL INVESTMENT

CURRENCY RISK. The prime motivation for diversifying a portfolio internationally is to improve the reward-to-risk tradeoff by taking advantage of the relatively low correlation among returns on assets of different countries. However, since international investment implies investing in assets that provide returns in a variety of currencies whose relative values can fluctuate, it involves taking **foreign exchange risks.** A key question facing the investor, then, is whether these exchange risks are so large as to offset the benefits of international diversification. A related question is, what—if any—special strategies should be followed to reduce the impact of foreign exchange risk?

There is no question that the volatility of currency movements has increased in recent years and that it is significant relative to the volatility of equity markets. Exhibit 5 shows the volatility of equity returns in local currency, the volatility of exchange rate changes, and the volatility of returns in dollars (standard deviation) for the major equity markets from 1970 to 1980.

EXHIBIT 5 EQUITY AND CURRENCY VOLATILITY, 1970–80

Country	Return Volatility in Local Currency	Volatility of Exchange Rate	Return Volatility in US$
Australia	24.6	9.2	27.2
Belgium	13.3	11.0	18.8
Canada	18.9	4.2	20.3
France	22.0	10.2	25.8
Hong Kong	48.0	5.6	45.8
Italy	24.2	8.6	26.2
Japan	16.4	10.4	19.6
Singapore	35.8	6.5	36.0
Spain	16.7	9.1	20.3
Switzerland	16.8	14.7	21.4
The Netherlands	16.4	11.0	18.9
United Kingdom	28.9	8.9	31.6
United States	16.0	—	16.0
West Germany	13.9	11.9	18.4

Source. Solnik, B.H. and B. Noetzlin, "Optimal International Asset Allocation: Lessons from the Past," *Journal of Portfolio Management*, 1981.

In all cases, the dollar returns are more volatile than the local currency returns, although often by a very small margin relative to the volatility of the exchange rate. The reason for this is that the volatility of dollar returns depends not only on the volatility of local currency returns and exchange rate changes, but on the correlation between the two as well.* If local currency returns are independent of the exchange rate—in which case the share could be characterized as an instrument "denominated" in the local currency—the volatility of dollar returns would be substantially less than the sum of the underlying volatilities.† For West Germany, it would be 18.3, for Japan 19.4, for The Netherlands 19.8, for Switzerland 22.3, and for the United Kingdom 30.2. Most of the actual dollar volatilities are slightly lower than these figures, showing that local currency returns are slightly negatively related to movements in the currency. In the case of Hong Kong, though, dollar volatility is less than volatility in local terms, suggesting that returns on local shares can be more aptly characterized as "dollar-denominated" than as "denominated" in the local currency. (For the 1973–77 period, Lessard, 1979, identified several cases where the dollar volatility of share returns was less than the volatility measured in the local currency.)

This result has important implications. To the extent that local currency share prices are negatively correlated with the exchange rate, the exchange risk faced by the foreign investor is reduced. By the same token, the local investor is exposed to some exchange risk.

There are two other aspects of currency risk that must be taken into account. One is that currency risk as measured above is a valid concept only if investors judge

*Formally, $\sigma^2(R\$) = \sigma^2(R_L) + \sigma^2(R_S) + \rho(R_L, R_S)$, where R_S is the dollar return, R_L the local currency equity return, and R_S the change in the exchange rate.

†From the above formula, $\sigma^2(R_\$) = \sigma^2(R_L) + \sigma^2(R_S)$ when R_L and R_S are uncorrelated.

risk and return in nominal terms in their local currency. Given the substantial volatility of inflation in most economies, this is unrealistic. A pension fund, for example, should judge returns after adjustment for inflation. If this adjustment is made, exchange risk typically will be reduced and domestic securities will be viewed as having significant inflation risk. The choice of perspectives, however, does not make too much difference in the estimation of gains from diversification across equity markets, since the variance of stock prices is largely unrelated to changes in exchange rates or inflation. With bonds or money market instruments, though, which are less volatile in nominal terms but which bear a closer relationship to changes in purchasing power of the local currency, the choice of the appropriate perspective is critical.

Another consideration is that currency risks can be hedged by borrowing in the local currency or selling it forward. Thus, the benefits of international equity investment can be obtained without any significant currency exposure. (Here reference is made solely to the risk of fluctuations in exchange rates, not to the possibility of foreign exchange controls. The latter are discussed under "Political or Sovereign Risk," this section.)

The expected **cost of hedging** in the case of borrowing is the difference between the interest differential of the two currencies and the expected percentage change in the exchange rate. The cost of hedging through forward contracts is the difference between the forward discount or premium and the expected percentage change in the exchange rate. Barring controls on capital flows or on access to forward markets, these two costs will be identical through the interest rate parity relationship.

The cost of hedging is often incorrectly defined as the interest differential itself or the forward discount or premium, with no consideration of the expected change in exchange rates. This incorrect definition often leads to statements that hedging is prohibitively expensive and rests on the implicit assumption that foreign exchange markets are inefficient and do not reflect anticipations regarding a currency's future.

The incorrect definition of the cost of hedging is often accompanied by a view that shares in countries with strong currencies are good investments, while those in countries with weak currencies are poor ones. If the strength of weakness of a currency is generally recognized, it will be reflected in interest rates and forward rates as well as in equity prices and hence will have no bearing on the attractiveness of the investment.

In summary, **currency risk** is not a significant obstacle to international investment(see Lessard and Stulz, 1982, for a more extensive discussion). First, shares are not denominated in the local currency and hence are not necessarily more risky in a foreign reference currency than in the local currency. Second, currency risk should be considered in light of its effect on real (i.e., constant purchasing power) returns to the investor. From this perspective, currency risk typically is smaller than when returns are viewed in nominal terms. Third, regardless of the first two points, currency risk can be isolated through hedging and the risk-reducing benefits of international equity diversification can be obtained without significant currency exposure. (Since the local currency value of shares is volatile, currency exposure cannot be completely hedged. However, with frequent revisions in hedge positions, most of this volatility can be eliminated.) Finally, expected currency movements that are reflected in interest rates and forward rates have no bearing on investment decisions. The same arguments apply to bond and money market investment. However, when hedged, foreign money market investments become dollar money market instruments and bonds become much less volatile. Thus, when viewed properly, currency risks can reduce the attractiveness of money market and bond diversification much more than is the case for equities.

POLITICAL OR SOVEREIGN RISK. Political or sovereign risk is viewed by many as a major obstacle to international investment. Clearly, **political factors** are a major determinant of the attractiveness for investment in any country. Countries viewed as likely candidates for internal political upheaval or with a pronounced trend toward elimination of the private sector will be unattractive to all investors, foreign and domestic alike. As a result, securities of these countries should be priced accordingly, and little new private real investment will take place. The general question of the impact of political risk on international investment strategies can be broken down into three specific questions: (1) Are political risks properly reflected in securities' prices? (2) Do they differ from the perspectives of foreign and domestic investors? (3) If so, what does this imply about international investment strategies? There is little research relating to any of these questions. Most research on sovereign risk focuses on the conflict between host governments and firms with direct investment; little has been directed at portfolio investment. Further, what little has been done relates primarily to bank loans to developing countries.

In judging whether political risks are properly reflected in prices, the only available evidence is that relating to the overall efficiency of markets. This evidence suggests that information is reflected rapidly in major markets, and that realized returns, in general, bear a reasonable relationship to the risks taken.

The key consideration is that local investors as well as foreign investors typically are affected by these risks. There is no reason to believe that local investors will be systematically optimistic regarding their country's future. When political risks increase significantly, such investors will attempt to diversify from the home market as rapidly as will foreigners. As a result, prices will fall until someone will be satisfied to hold the securities of a risky country. One case where this will not be true, and where foreign investors might be able to shift political losses to local investors, is when domestic investors are prevented from liquidating their domestic holdings or from purchasing foreign assets by national regulations or moral suasion. In such cases, the market prices may not reflect generally shared views of the political situation. Of course, if foreign investors are constrained by the same regulations, then all investors lose. A careful evaluation of the relative flexibility of domestic and foreign investment, therefore, is a key element in determining whether political risks jeopardize cross-border holdings. The risk of currency controls is one of the few political risks that is borne primarily by foreign investors.

In some cases, political risks might even favor foreign investors relative to domestic investors. This is because risks are domestic phenomena that can be diversified away internationally. As a result they will have a greater impact on the risk of a domestic investor whose portfolio is concentrated in home assets than an internationally diversified investor. Accordingly, domestic shares might well be more attractive to foreign than domestic investors in periods of perceived high political risk.

LIMITED SIZE AND DEPTH OF FOREIGN MARKETS. A recurrent objection to international diversification is that the practical **scope** for foreign investing is limited. Many markets are perceived to be small, less liquid, and less efficient than those of the United States. Some investors question whether foreign markets are large enough and active enough to allow them to accumulate meaningful positions and realize

EXHIBIT 6 PERCENTAGE BREAKDOWN OF WORLD STOCK MARKET CAPITALIZATION

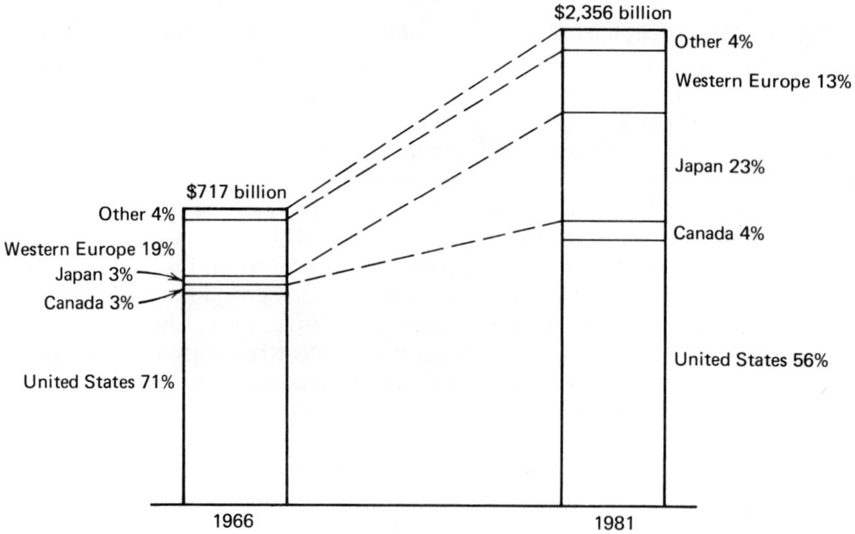

Source. *Capital International Perspective*, March 1976 and March 1981.

EXHIBIT 7 PERCENTAGE BREAKDOWN OF WORLD SHARE TURNOVER

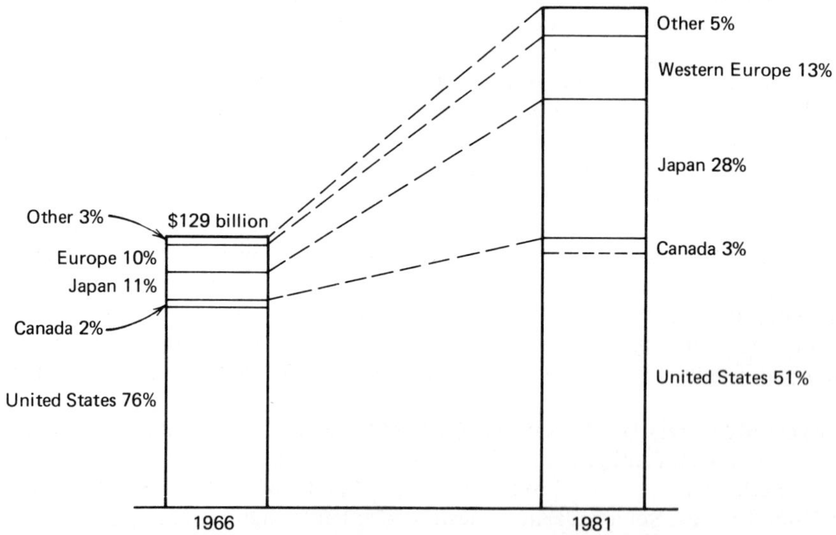

Source. *Capital International Perspective*, March 1976 and March 1981.

profits from them. The fact is that foreign markets have come of age. Exhibits 6 and 7 illustrate the growth of these markets since 1966 in terms of capitalization and turnover. The growth of turnover in foreign markets is especially striking—increasing from 24% of the world total in 1966 to 46% in 1980. This view is further reinforced by an examination of the number of companies with market capitalizations in excess of $2 billion, as shown in Exhibit 8. There are 65 such firms outside of North America, compared with 93 in the United States and nine in Canada (*Capital International Perspective*, 1981).

Undoubtedly, there are many foreign stocks whose total capitalization and turnover are too limited for them to be of interest to most U.S. institutional investors. Further, in many markets—particularly the Japanese and West German—market capitalizations are often misleading indicators of an issue's marketability because a large proportion of the shares might be owned by banks, holding companies, or other concerns. However, these considerations do not necessarily imply that these markets are less attractive to foreign institutional investors than to local investors. In fact, just the opposite might be the case. Domestic investors who depend primarily on their own market for liquidity and diversification are likely to be more constrained by these limitations than international investors who, through diversification, can virtually eliminate the nonmarket risk unique to individual companies even if they hold only a small number of shares in each market. International investors also do not have to rely on any single market for liquidity and, as a result, can take a longer view in regard to each market and security, even though they will wish to realize profits within a reasonable period in each market and currency.

The constraints on diversification within a single market become apparent when one considers the degree of concentration within various markets. In many markets, such as Belgium, The Netherlands, and Switzerland, as well as in West Germany, a small number of shares account for a major portion of the value of all shares in most smaller markets. Considering that 30 or more issues in about equal proportions are necessary to diversity away most of the specific (nonmarket) risk within a single national market, even a moderate-sized domestic fund will find it difficult to achieve a high degree of diversification in such markets. This fact implies that domestic investors in such markets will want to hold foreign assets and that a substantial

EXHIBIT 8 NATIONALITY OF FIRMS WITH CAPITALIZATION IN EXCESS OF $2 BILLION

United States	93
Japan	35
United Kingdom	9
Canada	9
West Germany	9
Switzerland	5
South Africa	3
Hong Kong	2
Australia	1
France	1
Italy	1
The Netherlands	1

Source. Capital International Perspective, Geneva, Switzerland, 1981.

proportion of the shares of the dominant countries should be held by foreigners even if the systematic risk component of returns in the local economy is closely related to the world market index.

RELATIVE EFFICIENCY OF FOREIGN MARKETS. A closely related concern is that of **market efficiency.** Although less efficiency can be desirable from an active investment manager's perspective because it implies that superior performance is possible, it also puts the international investor at a disadvantage relative to the domestic investor, who has greater knowledge and better information.

An efficient market is one where new information is quickly reflected in securities' prices and hence it is unlikely that any single investor will beat the market. Various types of tests can be performed to judge the degree of efficiency of a market. Three degrees of efficiency have typically been distinguished by researchers: (1) weak-form efficiency, where no useful information can be defined from the past sequence of stock prices, (2) semistrong efficiency, where it is impossible to exploit publicly available information to beat the market, and (3) strong-form efficiency, where all information is fully reflected in prices and no one can beat the market.

Most empirical research has focused on testing for the weak form of efficiency—whether sequences of price changes are related. The usual criterion of efficiency is whether share prices follow a random walk or martingale process (random walk with a trend). If so, momentum models (a type of technical analysis) are of no value. Researchers have performed some tests of the major European markets, and recently these same tests have been extended to the major Asian markets. The studies find that price changes show greater serial correlation in foreign markets than in the U.S. market. However, the magnitude of these departures from randomness typically is not sufficient to yield gains from trading strategies based on past prices.

Tests of the semistrong form of efficiency are substantially more complex. Since most tests involve comparing the results of a particular strategy with some benchmark portfolio, they involve joint tests of a particular equilibrium risk–return relationship and the ability to outperform the standard implied by that relationship. This is a difficult problem even within a single country and most tests for superior performance in the United States have been called into question by Roll (1977) and others. For internationally diversified portfolios, the problem is even more difficult. The benchmark is undefined and it is difficult to attribute the performance to various testable aspects, such as country selection, stock selection within countries, and currency selection, because of the interaction among the three. Since most managed European portfolios include some foreign securities, the problem applies to tests of efficiency in these markets as well.

In order to be valid, tests of performance must compare portfolio results with benchmark results for the same universe of securities. If a study shows that domestically managed funds outperform the market index, care must be taken to ensure that their performance does not reflect foreign holdings or domestic securities not included in the benchmark index. Taking this into account, there appear to be no credible studies that show consistently superior performance by managed funds in many foreign markets. Since many European funds contain shares listed outside the base country, foreign shares listed on the local exchange, and bonds, tests of efficiency for any single market are extremely difficult.

In summary, studies of foreign markets suggest that they generally can be considered to be efficient in the sense that prices adjust rapidly to new information and relationships between risk and return are consistent with those predicted by capital market theory. Whether they are efficient to the extent that most professional managers are unable to consistently outperform appropriate market benchmarks remains an open question. However, the results available suggest that the ability to consistently outperform the market is, at best, uncommon.

TAXES, RESTRICTIONS ON OWNERSHIP, AND OTHER INSTITUTIONAL OBSTACLES. There are several **institutional obstacles** that can make international investing costly, undesirable, or, in some cases, impossible. They include formal barriers to international transactions, such as exchange controls that do not allow investors in one country to invest overseas or that limit overseas investment to a fixed pool (such as those applied in the United Kingdom through 1979),* double taxation of portfolio income for certain investors in particular countries,† and restrictions on ownership of securities according to the nationality of the investor. These obstacles also include informal barriers, such as the difficulty of obtaining information about a market, differences in reporting practices that make international comparisons difficult, and, perhaps most important, subtle impediments to foreign investment based on traditional practice.

Few research studies have been conducted on the impact of these institutional and governmental obstacles on either appropriate investment strategies or portfolio performance. One study of U.K. investment trusts found that they benefited little from international diversification and attributed this to the costs imposed by the U.S. foreign investment controls (Guy, 1978). Whether these costs were necessary or whether they reflected unnecessary trading remains an open question. The U.S. interest equalization tax clearly hindered overseas investment by U.S. individual and institutional investors and, undoubtedly, the difficulty of buying into the Japanese market in the mid-1960s meant that its subsequent performance was academic to most U.S. investors.

A major implication of the existence of such obstacles is that even if one assumes an integrated, efficient world capital market, investors with different **legal domiciles** or **tax situations** might want to hold different portfolios. However, it is difficult to determine by how much such optimal portfolios should differ from the world market portfolio. This would depend on the balancing of the effect of the obstacles against the gains from more complete diversification. This is an area of active research and at least two theoretical studies that have explicitly introduced barriers into models of world capital market equilibrium show that investors should not hold the world market portfolio (Black, 1974, and Stulz, 1981a). Instead, investors should hold relatively high proportions of their home market portfolios and should select foreign assets least like assets from their home market. More research, both in terms of quantifying specific obstacles and ascertaining their impact on capital market equi-

*Under this system, U.K. investors seeking to invest abroad were required to purchase currency from an investment currency pool. As a result, the pound/dollar exchange rate paid to invest abroad rose to an often substantial premium relative to the regular exchange rate. Further, on liquidation, a portion of the proceeds had to be converted at the regular, typically less favorable, exchange rate. See Brealey and Cooper (1981) for an insightful analysis.

†United States pension funds, for example, might have to pay a withholding tax on income from some foreign countries but have no U.S. tax against which it can be credited. This problem is exacerbated by the movement of European countries toward the imputation of corporate taxes, which results in a different tax on foreign investors.

librium, is required before optimum international portfolios can be specified for particular investors.

CONCLUSIONS REGARDING OBSTACLES TO INTERNATIONAL INVESTMENT. When examined closely, many of the obstacles to international investment are less serious than commonly thought. This does not mean that there are no difficulties, but it does appear that the advantages of diversification, when properly pursued, outweigh the drawbacks.

Regarding the major specific areas of concern, currency risks do not appear to reduce significantly the gains from broadly based diversification. There is little reason to believe that political risks are systematically ignored by local investors or that they weigh more heavily on foreign investors. Finally, major foreign markets are not as narrow or inefficient as might generally be perceived.

CONCLUSIONS

Evidence suggests that the potential for risk reduction through international diversification is large, but that investors exploit it only to a limited extent. The examination of various potential obstacles to international investment explaining this home bias suggests that currency risk should not be a large factor, the size or efficiency of foreign markets should have little bearing, and political risks should matter only to the extent that foreign investors can be singled out effectively for discriminatory treatment. The primary remaining explanations are explicit barriers to international investment in the form of discriminatory taxation, controls on inward or outward foreign investments, local regulation of institutional investors, or simply tradition. While barriers undoubtedly do exist, theoretical models suggest that it is hard to attribute to them the full degree of homeward bias. Thus, investors who overcome the traditional resistance to international investment should be able to expect a significantly superior risk-adjusted performance than investors who restrict themselves to their home markets.

Because of barriers and currency considerations, investors pursuing **passive strategies**—strategies that do not depend on forecasting skills—will not necessarily want to invest in the world market portfolio or even in a portfolio such as that represented by Capital International's EAFE Index for their foreign holdings. In any market where they face higher costs or higher taxes than local investors, or where local investors are restricted from investing abroad, foreign investors should buy the securities least like those available in markets where they have relatively favorable access. For example, they should purchase shares of major multinationals at home and in other markets fully open to them and concentrate on domestically oriented firms in more restricted markets. To the extent that the foreign currency positions implicit in the resulting portfolio differ from their desired currency positions, they should adjust that dimension through borrowing or forward contracts.

Investors who believe that they can forecast along one or more dimensions will pursue **active strategies.** The key element in designing effective active strategies is to be sure that bets are actually placed on the dimension of returns for which the investor disagrees with the general expectations embedded in market prices. For example, if an investor believes that the Dutch economy will perform much better than generally expected, he or she should not simply add more Dutch shares to the portfolio. Many of these shares are of multinationals that depend only to a small extent on the state of the home economy and might even be negatively affected by a strong local economy. Similarly, if the investor wishes to place a currency bet, to do so by shifting equity holdings is both costly and inefficient. Equity market transition costs far exceed those in money markets and although equity returns do have an implicit currency component, they carry many other risks as well.

These considerations make it clear that both the theory and practice of international investing are in their infancy and that the rewards to developing more refined passive and active strategies should be substantial.

REFERENCES

Black, F., "International Capital Market Equilibrium with Investment Barriers," *Journal of Financial Economics* (1974).

Ehrlich, E.E., "International Diversification by United States Pension Funds," *Federal Reserve Bank of New York Quarterly*, Autumn (1981).

Guy, J.R.F., "The Performance of the British Investment Trust Industry," *Journal of Finance*, May (1978).

Hanna, J., "Why Americans Should Have Diversified," *Euromoney*, March (1980).

Lessard, D.R., "World, Country, and Industry Relationships in Equity Returns: Implications for Risk Reduction through International Diversification," *Financial Analysts Journal*, January–February (1976).

Lessard, D.R. and R. Stulz, "Currency Considerations in International Equity Investment," Unpublished working paper, Massachusetts Institute of Technology Sloan School (1982).

Logue, D.E. and R.J. Rogalski, "Offshore Alphas: Picking Countries Instead of Stocks," *Journal of Portfolio Management*, Winter (1979).

Roll, R., A Critique of the Asset Pricing Theory Tests, *Journal of Financial Economics*, Vol. 4, (1977).

Stulz, R.M., "On the Effects of Barriers to International Investment," *Journal of Finance*, September (1981). (a)

BIBLIOGRAPHY

CORRELATIONS OF RETURNS AND GAINS FROM INTERNATIONAL DIVERSIFICATION

Bergstrom, G.L., "A New Route to Higher Returns and Lower Risk," *Journal of Portfolio Management*, Fall (1975).

First National Bank of Chicago, *International Fixed-Income Portfolios*, Chicago, 1980.

Grubel, H.G., "Internationally Diversified Portfolios: Welfare Gains and Capital Flows," *American Economic Review*, December (1968).

Jacquillat, B. and B.H. Solnik, "Multinationals are Poor Tools for Diversification," *Journal of Portfolio Management*, Winter (1978).

Levy, H. and M. Sarnat, "International Diversification of Investment Portfolios," *American Economic Review*, September (1970).

Maldonado, R. and A. Saunders, "International Portfolio Diversification and the Stability of International Stock Market Relationships, 1957–1980," *Financial Management*, Autumn (1981).

Morgan Guaranty Trust, *Investing Internationally: The Role of Foreign Bonds in U.S. Dollar-Based Portfolios,* New York, 1981.

Ripley, D.M., "Systematic Elements in the Linkage of National Stock Market Indices," *Review of Economics and Statistics,* September (1973).

Solnik, B.H., "Why Not Diversify Internationally Rather than Domestically?" *Financial Analysts Journal,* July–August (1974).

Solnik, B.H. and B. Noetzlin, "Optimal International Asset Allocation: Lessons from the Past," *Journal of Portfolio Management,* 1981.

ON CURRENCY RISKS

Cornell, B., "Spot Rates, Forward Rates and Exchange Market Efficiency," *Journal of Financial Economics,* December (1977).

Giddy, I., "An Integrated Theory of Exchange Rate Equilibrium," *Journal of Financial and Quantitative Analysis,* November (1976).

Kohlhagen, S., *The Behavior of Foreign Exchange Markets—A Critical Survey of the Empirical Literature,* Solomon Brothers Monograph Number, 3, New York University, New York, 1978.

Levich, B.N., "On the Efficiency of Foreign Exchange Markets: Review and Extension," in D.R. Lessard (Ed.), *International Financial Management,* John Wiley and Sons, New York, 1982.

Oldfield, G.C. and D.E. Logue, "What's So Special about the Foreign Exchange Market?" *Journal of Portfolio Management,* Spring (1977).

Solnik, B. and B. Noetzlin, "Optimal International Asset Allocations: Lessons from the Past," *Journal of Portfolio Management* (forthcoming).

PRICING OF SECURITIES IN AN INTERNATIONAL CONTEXT

Grauer, F.L.A., R.H. Litzenberger, and R.E. Stehle, "Sharing Rules and Equilibrium in an International Capital Market under Uncertainty," *Journal of Financial Economics,* Vol. 3 (1976).

Solnik, B.H., *European Capital Markets,* Heath, Lexington, Mass., 1972.

Solnik, B.H., "The International Pricing of Risk: An Empirical Investigation of the World Capital Market Structure," *Journal of Finance,* May (1974).

Solnik, B.H. "Testing International Asset Pricing: Some Pessimistic Views," *Journal of Finance,* May (1977).

Stehle, R., "An Empirical Test of the Alternative Hypotheses of National and International Pricing of Risky Assets," *Journal of Finance,* May (1977).

Stulz, R.M., "A Model of International Asset Pricing," *Journal of Financial Economics,* Vol. 9 (1981). (b)

THE EFFICIENCY OF FOREIGN MARKETS

Guy, J.R.F., "The German Stock Exchange," *Journal of Banking and Finance,* June (1977).

Lau, S.L., S.T. Quay, and C.M. Ramsey, "The Tokyo Stock Exchange and the Capital Asset Pricing Model," *Journal of Finance,* May (1974).

Solnik, B.H., "A Note on the Validity of the Random Walk for European Stock Prices," *Journal of Finance,* December (1973).

ON THE PERFORMANCE OF INTERNATIONALLY DIVERSIFIED PORTFOLIOS

Farber, A.L., "Performance of Internationally Diversified Mutual Funds," in E.J. Elton and M.H. Gruber (Eds.), *International Capital Markets,* American Elsevier, New York 1975.

Guy, J.R.F., "An Examination of the Effects of International Diversification from the British

Viewpoint on Both Hypothetical and Real Portfolios," *Journal of Finance*, December (1978).

McDonald, J.B., "French Mutual Fund Performance: Evaluation of Internationally Diversified Portfolios," *Journal of Finance*, December (1973).

Corner, D.C. and Stafford, D.C., *Open-End Investment Funds in the EEC and Switzerland*, Westview Press, Boulder, 1977.

UNITED STATES INTEREST IN INTERNATIONAL INVESTMENT

Bergstrom, G.L., "Spreading the Risk—Investors Do Better to Broaden Their Universe," *Barron's*, February 24 (1975).

Hertzberg, D., "Pension Managers Invest More Overseas, Aware of Risks, but Hopeful about People," *Wall Street Journal*, July 2 (1981).

Richards, T.M., "International Diversification for U.S. Pension Funds," *Pension World*, June (1978).

SECTION 8.3

INTERNATIONAL PORTFOLIO DIVERSIFICATION: RISKS AND RETURNS

CONTENTS

SECTION 8.3

INTERNATIONAL PORTFOLIO DIVERSIFICATION: RISKS AND RETURNS

Abraham M. George
Vinita M. Ittoop

The early 1970s witnessed numerous changes of great significance to the international monetary order. Persistent U.S. balance of payments deficits eventually compelled the general abrogation, in December 1971, of the Bretton Woods accord on the par value system and a move toward greater flexibility in exchange rates. From the perspective of the international investor, the Smithsonian Agreement on floating exchange rates introduced an additional element in the management of internationally diversified portfolios—the element of foreign exchange risk.

Unquestionably, the experience of an international monetary system with flexible exchange rates indicates great volatility in foreign currency prices. This would suggest that the management of exchange risk is crucial in meeting investment objectives in relation to the risk-return trade-off.

A variety of options are available in managing **currency exposure.** They range from the entire elimination of currency exposure through hedging tactics to the other extreme of maintaining a totally open speculative stance. Obviously, the final rates of return realized and the total risk experienced will greatly depend, in part, on the nature of the strategy adopted in dealing with currency exposures.

This section evaluates the performance of the **equity** and **money** markets in terms of their net yield and volatility, in four major countries—**the United States, the United Kingdom, West Germany,** and **Japan**—from the perspective of a resident investor of each of the four countries. It accounts for the impact of currency movements appropriate for each resident investor on the overall risk and return realized in each of the markets.

As discussed, the net yield obtained on and the total risk associated with international investments vary with the strategy selected to handle currency exposure. Therefore, for the investigation reported here, it is necessary to specify the foreign exchange strategy employed. This study focuses on two polar cases. In one case, the entire portfolio is **completely hedged** in the forward market to eliminate currency risk, but the additional cost of assuming forward contracts is involved. In the other case, a **speculative posture** is assumed and the full impact of currency movements is included. These two polar cases capture the essence and the range of currency risk and the impact of exchange rate movements on net yields.

DEFINITIONS AND METHODOLOGY

In general terms, **net yield** is defined as the rate of return in domestic currency units on domestic or international investments. Therefore, it is necessary to identify not only the country of investment, but also the resident investor. For the case where these investments are fully covered through forward contracts, the nominal yield in the foreign currency must be adjusted for domestic currency premiums or discounts in the forward market as of the date of investment. If a speculative position is held, the nominal yield in foreign currency is adjusted for actual changes in the value of the domestic currency, in relation to the foreign currency, over the period of investment. When the country of investment and that of the resident investor coincide, no currency adjustment exists.

For the purpose of analysis, all investments are presumed to be held for a constant one-year period. For example, a purchase of assets denominated in deutsche marks by U.S. residents at the going deutsche mark/dollar exchange rate at the end of March 1976 is held to the end of March 1977. If a covered position is taken for the year, a one-year forward purchase of the U.S. dollar is contracted at the end of March 1976 and the translation to the U.S. dollar is conducted at the forward DM/US$ rate. If a speculative position is maintained, the translation to the U.S. dollar is executed at the DM/US$ rate as of the end of March 1977.

Yield calculations of investments in the international bond markets must take into account the impact of currency movements on the principal amount and on the accumulated interest. Covered positions will include the principal amount and the known interest receivable. Capital gains or losses on bonds are ignored, for data on bond price movements are unavailable for a general index of bonds. Yield calculations on speculative positions in the equity markets reflect the full impact of currency movements on both the initial investment amount and on the realized capital gains or losses. However, covered positions in the international equity markets do not include the portion of capital gains or losses realized through changes in equity prices, as such movements are not known with certainty at the time of investment. In other words, the premium or discount on forward currency contracts is not applied to capital gains or losses resulting from changes in equity prices. In practice, predictions of equity price changes are made continuously and the related currency risk can be removed or adjusted through hedging during the investment period.

Dividend yield is ignored in the computation of net equity yields across markets due to the lack of consistent information on average dividend yield for all markets. This shortcoming has no adverse impact on the attempt to measure the contribution of exchange rate movements on net yield and its volatility. But it is hoped that this bias in the estimation of total yields is not significant.

The above discussion on the measurement of net yields in the international bond and equity markets is summarized in the following arithmetic statements.

$$\text{Net speculative bond yield to resident investor of Country A in Country B} = I_b + E_{a/b} + \frac{I_b E_{a/b}}{100}$$

Net covered bond yield to resident investor of Country A in Country B $= I_b + F_{a/b} + \dfrac{I_b F_{a/b}}{100}$

Net speculative equity yield to resident investor of Country A in Country B $= S_b + E_{a/b} + \dfrac{S_b E_{a/b}}{100}$

Net covered equity yield to resident investor of Country A in Country B $= S_b + F_{a/b}$

where I_b = The annual long-term corporate bond yield of Country B
S_b = The annual percentage change in the share price index of Country B
$E_{a/b}$ = The annual percentage change in the exchange rate of the currency of Country A against the currency of Country B. The exchange rate is defined as the number of units of Currency A for one unit of Currency B
$F_{a/b}$ = The one-year forward premium of Currency B vis-à-vis Currency A

The **net speculative bond yield** to the resident of Country A consists of three components—the interest yield, I_b, the exchange factor, $E_{a/b}$, and the interest adjustment factor, $(I_b E_{a/b})/100$. The interest yield is merely the annual interest rate of Country B. The exchange factor is positive in case of a favorable movement in the exchange rate—an appreciation of currency B vis-à-vis currency A. Finally, the interest adjustment factor captures the impact of exchange rate movements on accumulated interest denominated in the foreign currency. The covered bond yield to resident investor of Country A consists of the interest yield, I_b, the forward premium of currency B, $F_{a/b}$, and the covered adjustment of interest earnings, $(I_b F_{a/b})/100$.

The **net speculative equity yield** to the resident investor of Country A comprises three components—the annual percentage change in the equity price index, S_b, the exchange factor $E_{a/b}$, and the currency adjustment factor for capital gains or losses denominated in currency B, $(S_b E_{a/b})/100$. The covered equity yield consists of capital gains or losses incurred in the equity market of Country B and the forward premium or discount.

The time span of this investigation is the decade of the 1970s under flexible exchange rates, 1971–1981. The analysis is conducted on a monthly basis with the starting investment date of January 1971. All investments are held for a one-year period and the final date of investment is December 1980. Data on exchange rates, equity share prices, and long-term corporate bond yields are obtained from the IFS tables published by the International Monetary Fund. For the period of January 1971 to November 1975, data on forward rates, or their proxy—the differential in Eurointerest rates—are not available for all currencies. For the remaining time span, data on forward exchange rates are obtained from market sources, as provided by Multinational Computer Models, Inc.

The following is divided into five sections. The first four are devoted to a cross-sectional study of markets from the perspective of each of the four resident investors; the final one reviews the general conclusions and emphasizes their implications for the management of international portfolios.

For each resident investor, there are four national market choices—the domestic market and the remaining three international markets. Market behavior is gauged in terms of the cross-sectional yield performances and their volatility. Comparsions of net returns are based on summary statistics such as the range and the average yield.

Time breakdowns are also useful to detect shifts in the overall pattern of associations among markets. The contribution of the exchange factor in determining net returns is also assessed. Volatility of net returns, a measurement of market risk, is evaluated using two summary statistics—the standard deviation and the coefficient of variation.

Finally, the possibility of reducing total portfolio risk through **market diversification** is analyzed. A strong, consistently negative correlation between returns in different markets would support the hypothesis that diversification along the various international markets would reduce the total portfolio risk. Strong, consistently positive correlations would suggest the alternate conclusion that diversification would accentuate the overall portfolio risk, and poor correlations would refute both of the above propositions in favor of a neutral, independent behavior of markets. In the last case, diversification would not aid in either escalating or diminishing the total portfolio risk.

The **notations** listed below conform to the scheme following in both text discussion and exhibits.

Net speculative bond (NB) yield realized in Country B by the resident in Country A	= NB—Country B—Country A
Covered bond (CB) yield realized in Country B by the resident in Country A	= CB—Country B—Country A
Domestic bond yield (BY) in Country A	= BY—Country A—Country A
Net speculative equity (NE) yield realized in Country B by the resident in Country A	= NE—Country B—Country A
Covered equity (CE) yield realized in Country B by the resident in Country A	= CE—Country B—Country A
Domestic equity yield (EY) in Country A	= EY—Country A—Country A
The exchange factor (EX) associated with investments in Country B by the resident in Country A	= EX—Country B—Country A

For example, net speculative equity yield (adjusted for the exchange rate factor) in West Germany for the U.K. resident is denoted as NE—DM—UK.

OBSERVATIONS BY UNITED STATES RESIDENT INVESTORS

EQUITY MARKETS. A general survey of **net speculative equity yields** (see Exhibit 1) reveals that Japan recorded the highest average yield for the entire period, followed by the United Kingdom. Average yields for the Japanese and the U.K. equity markets are 20.77% and 9.73% respectively. Japan manifested the highest yield (112.84%) and interestingly, the United Kingdom recorded the lowest yield (−57.39%) for a 12-month period within the entire time span.

On closer examination it is clear that the strong performance of the Japanese equity markets is augmented by the strong appreciation of the yen against the dollar. (see Exhibits 3, 4, and 5). The average 13.89% annual increase in the equity index of Japan and the average 5.42% Japanese exchange factor are the largest for the entire period. The appreciation of the Japanese yen (42.32% during a 12-month period against the dollar) is the highest for this period and the deutsche mark registered the largest annual depreciation (27.67% against the dollar). However, the U.K. equity market index recorded the greatest movement on an annual basis. The advance of the U.K. equity index of 140.65% and its reduction of 56.81% are by far the largest for this time period.

A breakdown of the entire framework into two segments (see Exhibit 1) reveals that, during the earlier period, from January 1971 to November 1975, Japan maintained the highest average yield due to dominant rise in its domestic share prices. Despite a mere 3.35% average contribution by the Japanese exchange factor, the mean yield of 23.56% is the highest due to an average increase in the equity index of 18.03%. From December 1975 to December 1980, however, the average return from investments in the Japanese equity markets dropped to 18.07% due to a slowdown in the increase on equity prices to 9.89% on the average. The United Kingdom recorded the highest mean yield, 18.51%, in this period, despite a mere 2.97% average annual appreciation of the pound against the dollar. The United Kingdom also recorded the lowest net return in both time segments, a yield of −57.39% in the first half and −25.13% in the last half.

A comparison of yields (see Exhibits 6, 7, 8, 9, and 10) realized on **covered investments** in the international equity markets and the domestic U.S. equity market indicates that Japan again provided the highest average return. The mean Japanese covered yield of 13.45% is much larger than the average U.S. return of 5.63%. The United States manifests the lowest yield (−13.75%) and the United Kingdom furnishes the highest (65.03%) for any 12-month period. Further, a comparison with speculative yields for the period December 1975 to December 1980 reveals that, with the exception of West Germany, covered investments render a lower mean rate of return.

The volatility of the rates of return on investments is extremely crucial in assessing their associated **risks.** An overview of speculative equity yields (see Exhibit 1) suggests that markets rendering the highest average return are not necessarily the most volatile. For instance, the Japanese equity market provided the largest average rate of return for the entire period, but the speculative yields realized in the U.K. equity market exhibited the largest volatility (as measured by the standard eviation of 33.27). Using the criterion of the coefficient of variation, which is a measure of the standard

EXHIBIT 1 BASIC STATISTICS OF SPECULATIVE EQUITY YIELDS AND THEIR COMPONENTS, U.S. RESIDENT

	January 1971–December 1980					January 1971–November 1975					December 1975–December 1980				
Variable	Mean	SD	Coef. of Var.	Max	Min	Mean	SD	Coef. of Var.	Max	Min	Mean	SD	Coef. of Var.	Max	Min
EY_US_US	4.065	15.29	376.6	34.77	−37.14	2.45	18.02	735.5	34.77	−37.14	5.63	12.04	213.8	33.58	−13.75
NE_UK_US	9.732	33.27	342.8	107.44	−57.39	0.66	38.61	5850.0	107.44	−57.39	18.51	24.41	131.9	105.69	−25.13
NE_JY_US	20.77	32.25	155.27	112.84	−31.69	23.56	41.31	175.3	112.84	−31.69	18.07	19.95	110.4	60.41	−22.07
NE_DM_US	5.92	15.11	253.95	34.61	−23.69	9.52	14.22	149.4	30.25	−22.89	2.45	15.24	622.0	34.61	−23.85
EY_US_US	4.065	15.29	376.6	34.77	−37.14	2.45	18.02	735.5	34.77	−37.14	5.63	12.04	213.8	33.58	−13.75
EY_UK_UK	11.544	32.61	282.5	140.65	−56.81	7.59	43.22	569.4	140.65	−56.81	15.37	16.56	107.7	80.32	−10.82
EY_JY_JY	13.89	23.37	168.25	98.79	−24.20	18.03	32.31	179.2	98.79	−24.20	9.89	6.42	64.9	25.99	− 1.40
EY_DM_DM	1.03	11.28	1095.1	30.20	−23.98	2.81	14.50	516.0	30.20	−23.98	−0.70	6.55	935.7	10.94	−13.53
EX_UK_US	−1.20	11.26	938.3	23.97	−24.26	−5.51	8.40	152.5	8.23	−23.68	2.97	12.13	408.4	23.97	−24.26
EX_JY_US	5.42	13.07	241.1	42.32	−23.01	3.35	8.89	265.4	18.69	−12.36	7.42	15.94	214.8	42.32	−23.01
EX_DM_US	5.16	12.31	238.6	34.99	−27.67	7.23	11.32	156.5	34.99	−10.92	3.17	12.99	409.7	22.66	−27.67

EXHIBIT 2

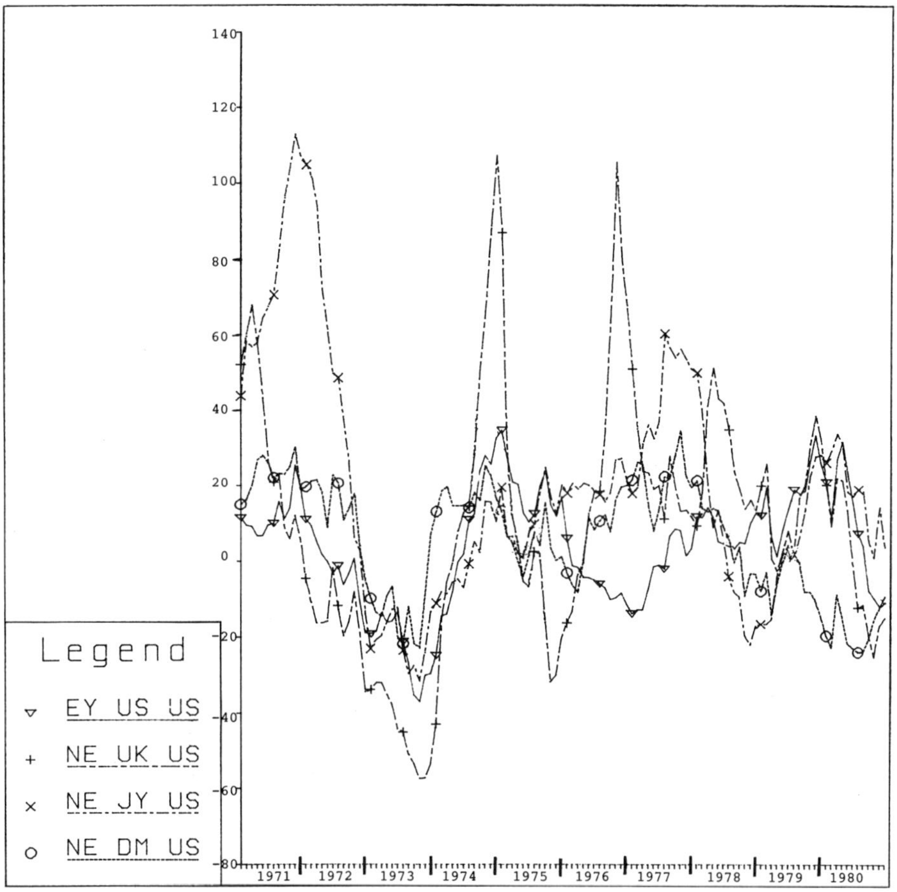

deviation relative to the mean, U.K. speculative equity yields were not the most volatile. Interestingly enough, the U.S. equity market manifested the highest coefficient of variation (376.60%).

The volatility of the **exchange factor** associated with a national currency is used in measuring foreign exchange risk. As suggested by the standard deviation, the Japanese yen is the most volatile and the U.K. pound sterling is the least volatile. But this conclusion is not upheld using the criterion of the coefficient of variation. The pound sterling, with a coefficient of variation of 938.30%, possesses the largest foreign exchange risk for the U.S. investor, followed by the yen, with a coefficient of variation of 241.10%.

A breakdown of the decade into halves indicates that there are shifts in the variability of net speculative equity yields. During the first half of the decade, the Japanese net yields exhibited the greatest volatility, as indicated by the highest standard deviation of 41.31; the United Kingdom topped the list with a coefficient of variation of 5,850.00%. However, this pattern is not repeated in its entirety in the

EXHIBIT 3

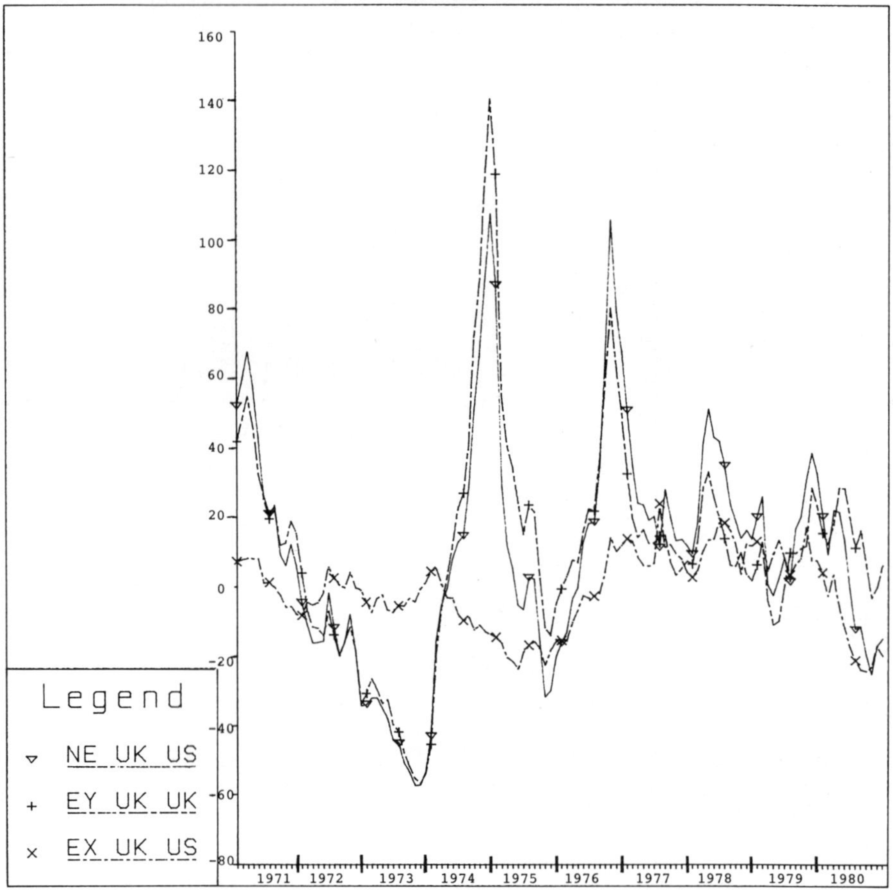

last half of the decade. The U.K. net yields depict the greatest volatility, but by a different criterion; the standard deviation of 24.41 is the largest, but as dictated by the coefficient of variation (622.0,%), deutsche mark net yields possess the greatest variability. The last result is a consequence of the low average net yield of 2.40% registered in the West German equity market.

The **foreign exchange risk,** as measured by the standard deviation, is higher during the last half of the decade compared to the first half. This conclusion is upheld for the pound and the mark when risk is measured by the coefficient of variation. In the case of the yen, the variability is greater as measured by the standard deviation in the last half and lower as dictated by the coefficient of variation.

A cursory survey of the **correlation matrix** of net speculative equity yields (see Exhibit 3) for the entire period does not indicate any strong associations. None of the correlation coefficients is above 0.60 and none is negative. This would suggest that diversification among different markets is not effective in reducing total portfolio

EXHIBIT 4

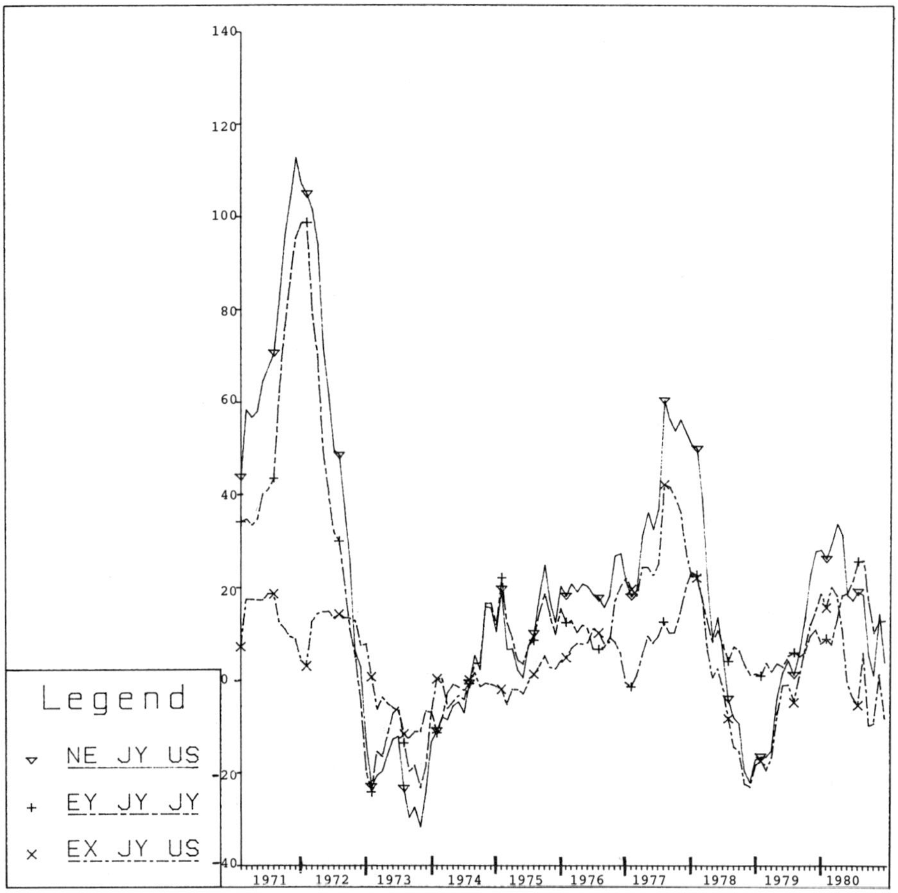

risk. Further, as these coefficients are not very large, it is also difficult to subscribe to the proposition that diversification could in fact increase portfolio risk.

The largest coefficient of correlation (0.59) is noted between Japanese and West German net speculative equity yields. On closer observation, an almost similar degree of association of 0.55 exists between movements in the domestic equity markets of West Germany and Japan. The changes in the equity price indexes of the United States and United Kingdom, however, show a stronger linkage, with a correlation coefficient of 0.62.

A time breakdown of the correlations indicate significant shifts in the pattern of associations. During the first half of the decade, the correlation coefficients between all net equity yields and changes in equity indexes are much higher than those obtained in the last half. For instance, during the first half, the largest coefficient of 0.78, between net speculative equity yields of the United Kingdom and the United States, supported by a 0.85 correlation coefficient between movements in the do-

EXHIBIT 5

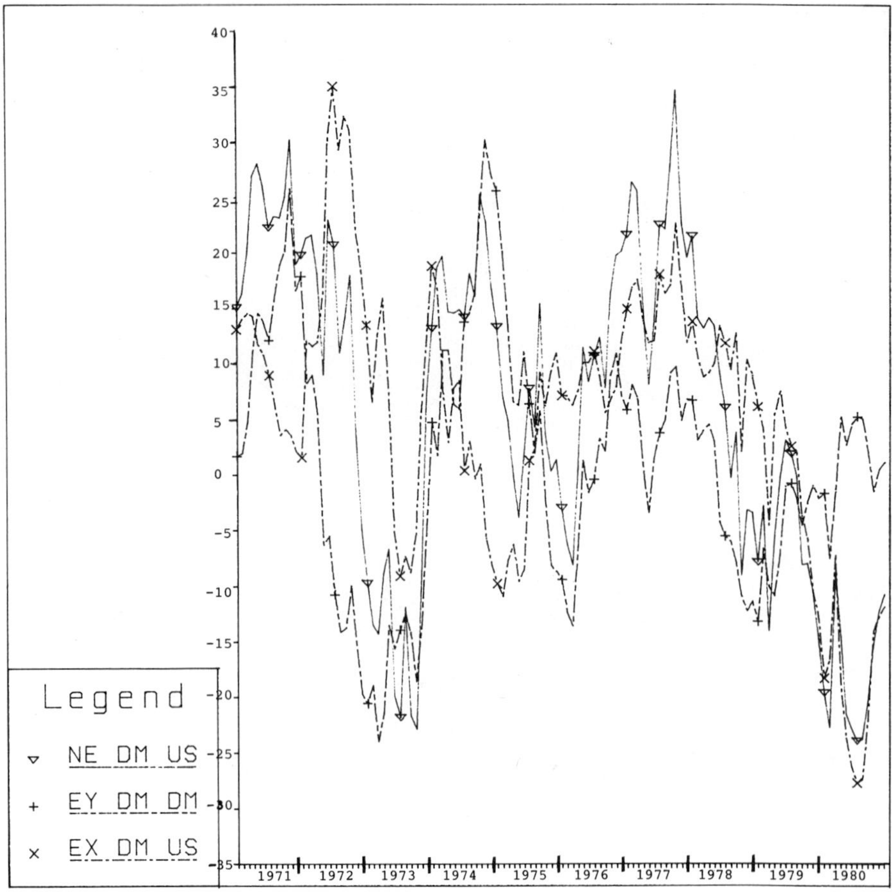

EXHIBIT 6 BASIC STATISTICS OF COVERED EQUITY YIELDS, U.S. RESIDENT

Variable	Mean	SD	Coef. of Var.	Max	Min
EY_US_US	5.63	12.04	213.8	33.58	−13.75
CE_UK_US	12.63	14.25	112.8	65.03	−11.42
CE_JY_US	13.54	6.63	48.96	29.9	− 1.37
CE_DM_US	3.35	5.79	172.8	13.15	−10.36

EXHIBIT 7

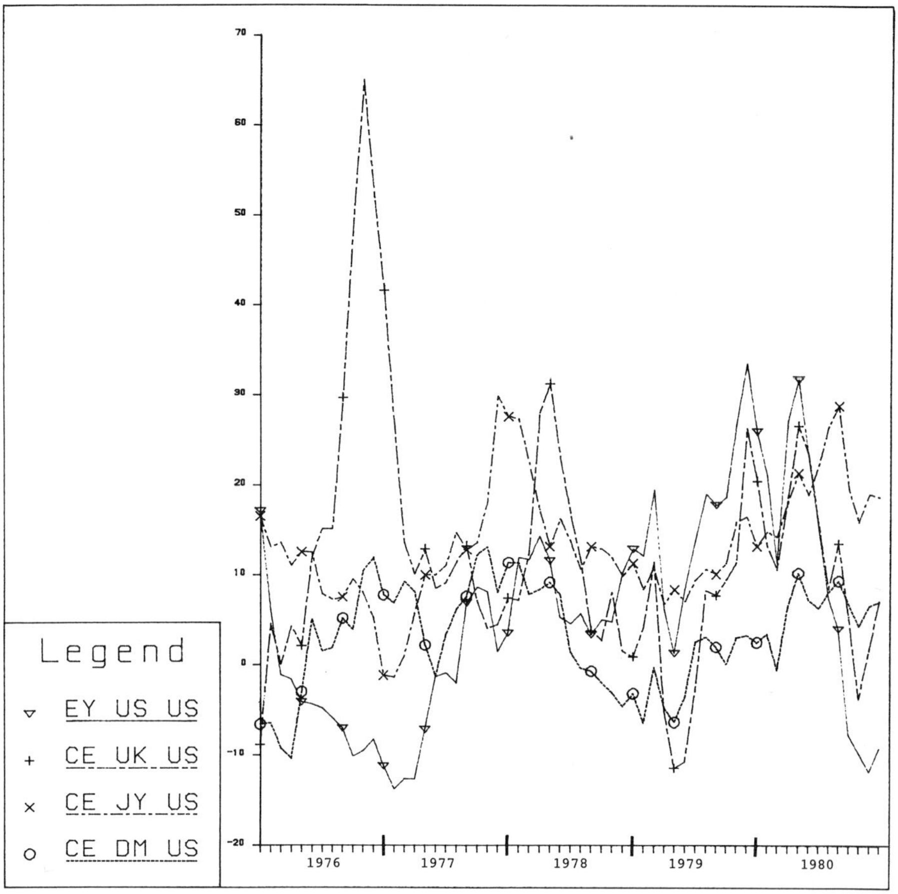

mestic equity prices of the United States and the United Kingdom, was not upheld in the last half of the decade. There is a significant drop to −0.08 in the correlation between the net speculative equity yields of the United Kingdom and the United States during the last half, confirmed by a low −0.18 correlation between changes in U.K. and U.S. domestic share prices. The largest correlation coefficient, 0.49, achieved in the last half of the decade between net speculative equity yields of the United Kingdom and West Germany, compares to the 0.64 correlation obtained between these respective yields during the first half of the time period. Interestingly, there has been a change in the sign of the correlation coefficients as well between the two time periods. In contrast to the earlier half, all international net equity yields are negatively associated with the U.S. equity yield during the later half, albeit these coefficients are small and close to zero.

The correlations between currency movements also indicate a decrease in their association over time. For the entire period the highest correlation coefficient (0.52) is noted between changes in the dollar–deutsche mark exchange rate and changes in

EXHIBIT 8

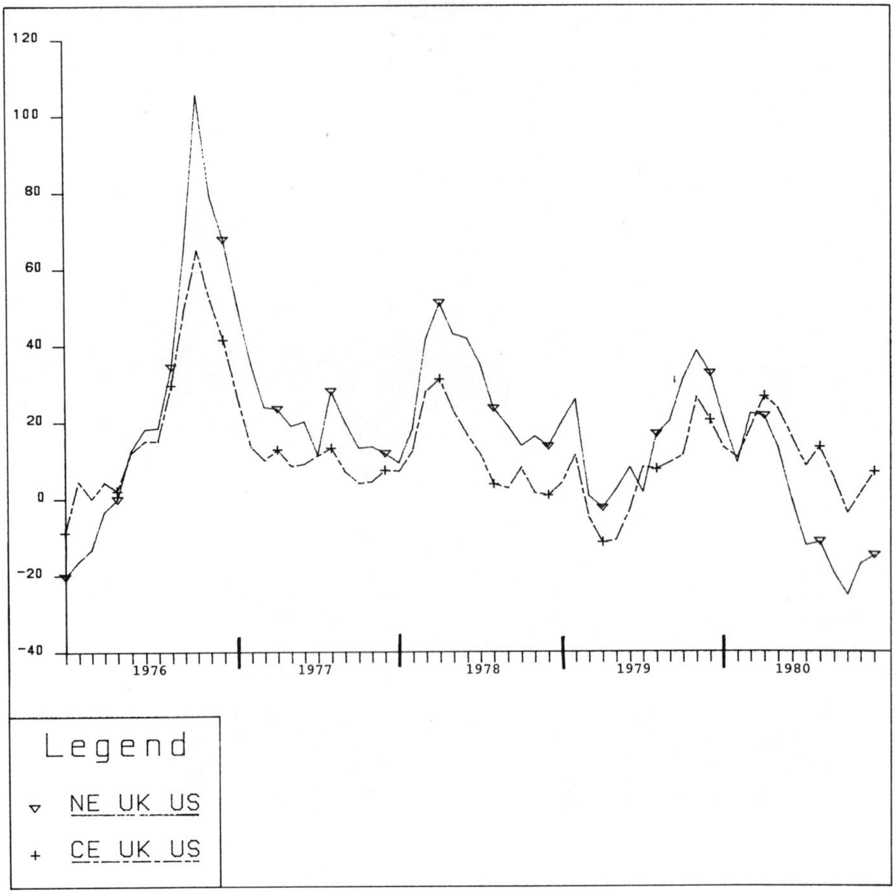

the dollar–pound exchange rate. This result is true for both time halves of the decade, despite the fact that the coefficient declines from 0.66 in the first half to 0.63 in the second half of the time period.

In **summary,** equity investments in Japan by U.S. residents displayed the highest overall average net return on both a covered and a speculative basis. However, the volatility (as measured by the standard deviation of net yields) is also practically the highest for Japan. The net average speculative yield of investments in Japan is considerably higher than their net average covered yield. But exchange rate movements did not have a deciding role in achieving the highest average net yield for Japan; the performance of its domestic equity market accounts mainly for the overall performance.

The correlation between markets is not large enough or consistent enough to support the argument that internationalization of portfolios will reduce risk. Neither does it confirm that it would increase risk.

EXHIBIT 9

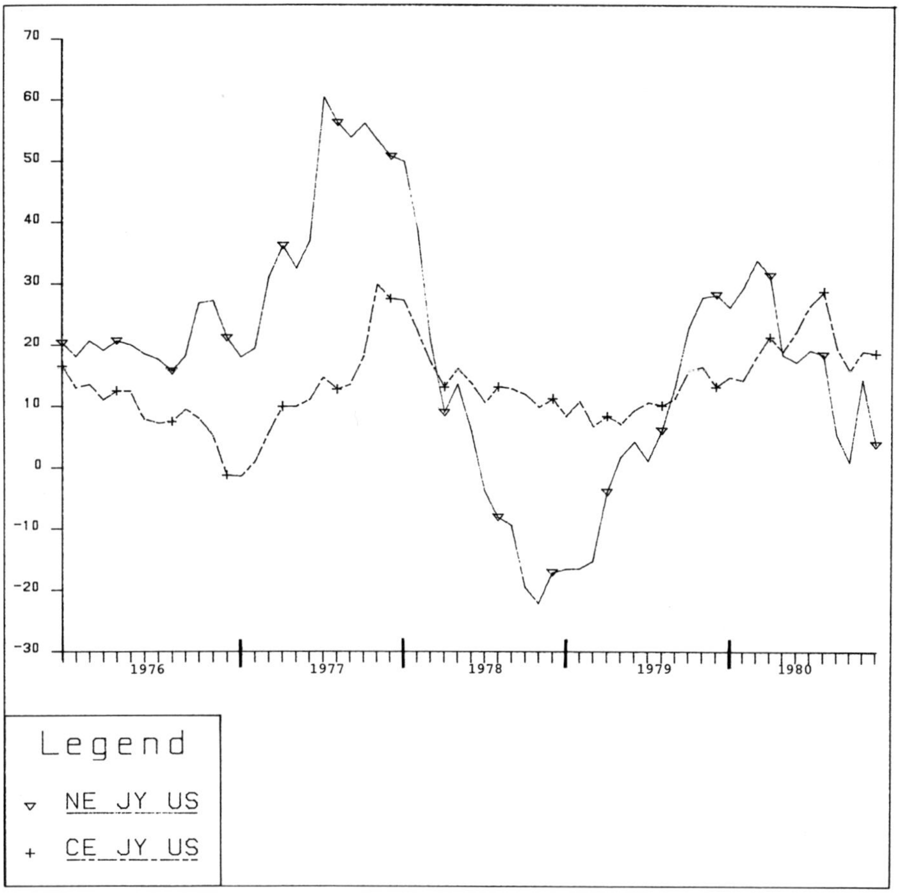

BOND MARKETS. **Speculative bond yields** (see Exhibits 12 and 13) across all markets indicate that Japan recorded both the largest average net bond yield as well as the highest net yield for any 12-month period. The mean Japanese yield of 13.44% is the largest recorded, while the 8.02% mean yield achieved in the domestic U.S. market is the lowest. The highest Japanese net bond yield (51.42%) compares with the lowest net yield (−21.95%), realized in the West German bond market.

The exchange factor for Japan has been a crucial determinant in producing this high average return (see Exhibits 14, 15, and 16). The Japanese mean bond rate of 7.87% is the lowest in comparison to all markets. Despite this fact, the mean annual appreciation of the yen against the dollar, 5.42%, which is the largest, is chiefly responsible for generating an average net yield of 13.44%. The U.K. average bond rate of 12.41% is the highest, but is unable to produce a comparable net yield to the U.S. investor due to a mean annual depreciation of 1.20% for the pound against the dollar.

EXHIBIT 10

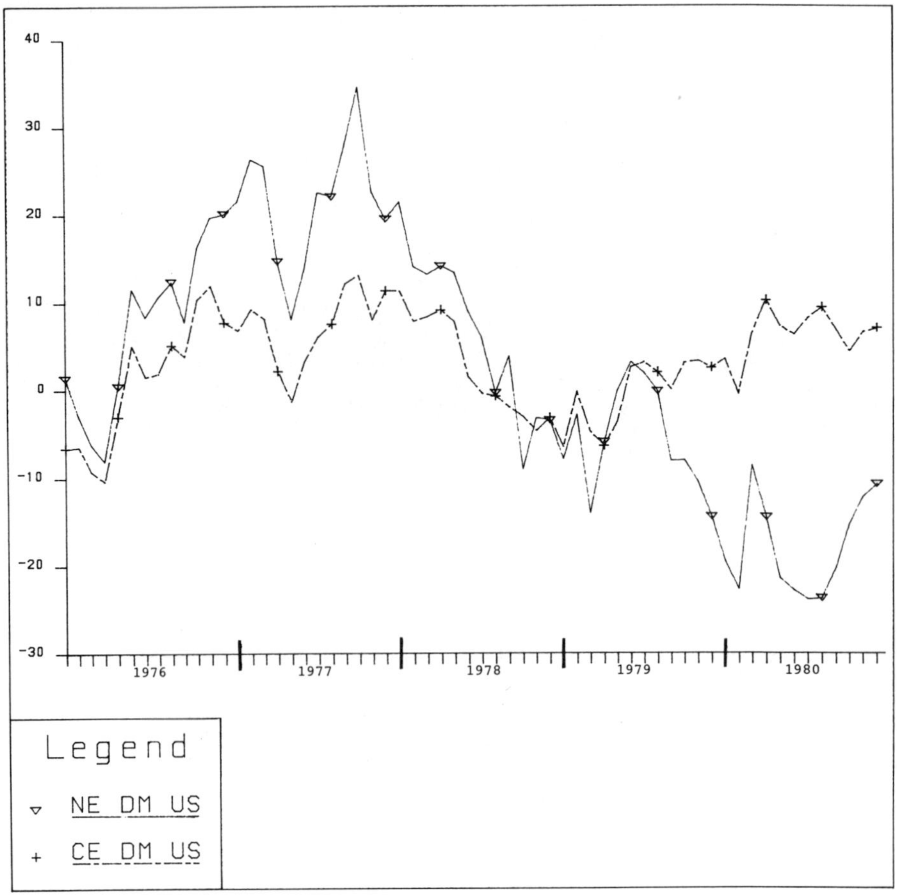

An analysis of the performance of the bond market during the first half of the decade indicates that the strong appreciation of the deutsche mark against the dollar helped generate a mean net West German bond yield that is well above those realized in the other bond markets. The average annual West German exchange factor of 7.23% accounts for nearly half of the average net yield of 16.58%. In the last half of the decade, however, net U.K. bond yields scored the highest average return of 16.50%, despite a mean annual appreciation of the pound of only 2.97%; the average U.K. interest rate of 13.30% is chiefly responsible for this result.

On a **covered basis** (see Exhibit 5) the U.S. domestic market fares poorly relative to other international markets. The U.S. bond yield of 8.94% is below those realized, on a covered basis, in Japan, West Germany, and the United Kingdom of 11.64%, 11.39%, and 10.01% respectively. In comparison to speculative yields, with the exception of West Germany, the covered yields are consistently below speculative rates of return.

EXHIBIT 11 CORRELATION MATRIX OF SPECULATIVE EQUITY YIELDS FOR THE U.S. RESIDENT

	January 1971–December 1980					January 1971–November 1975					December 1975–December 1980			
	(1)	(2)	(3)	(4)		(1)	(2)	(3)	(4)		(1)	(2)	(3)	(4)
(1) EY_US_US	1.0				(1)	1.0				(1)	1.0			
(2) NE_UK_US	0.522	1.0			(2)	0.78	1.0			(2)	−0.08	1.0		
(3) NE_JY_US	0.365	0.267	1.0		(3)	0.519	0.362	1.0		(3)	−0.031	0.123	1.0	
(4) NE_DM_US	0.147	0.462	0.591	1.0	(4)	0.615	0.644	0.72	1.0	(4)	−0.401	0.489	0.471	1.0
(1) EY_US_US	1.0				(1)	1.0				(1)	1.0			
(2) EY_UK_UK	0.622	1.0			(2)	0.85	1.0			(2)	−0.18	1.0		
(3) EY_JY_JY	0.439	0.237	1.0		(3)	0.55	0.30	1.0		(3)	0.18	−0.07	1.0	
(4) EY_DM_DM	0.517	0.717	0.554	1.0	(4)	0.79	0.79	0.57	1.0	(4)	−0.21	0.54	0.38	1.0
(1) EX_UK_US	1.0				(1)	1.0				(1)	1.0			
(2) EX_JY_US	0.303	1.0			(2)	0.449	1.0			(2)	0.2	1.0		
(3) EX_DM_US	0.52	0.369	1.0		(3)	0.658	0.61	1.0		(3)	0.633	0.32	1.0	

EXHIBIT 12 BASIC STATISTICS OF SPECULATIVE BOND YIELDS AND THEIR COMPONENTS, U.S. RESIDENT

	January 1971–December 1980					January 1971–November 1975					December 1975–December 1980				
Variable	Mean	SD	Coef. of Var.	Max	Min	Mean	SD	Coef. of Var.	Max	Min	Mean	SD	Coef. of Var.	Max	Min
BY_US_US	8.02	1.53	19.1	12.49	5.79	7.08	0.957	13.5	8.60	5.79	8.94	1.44	16.1	12.49	7.30
NB_UK_US	10.94	12.42	113.53	33.62	−14.12	5.19	8.09	155.9	19.47	−12.59	16.50	13.38	81.1	33.62	−14.12
NB_JY_US	13.44	14.0	104.17	51.42	−18.31	11.38	9.02	79.3	27.37	− 5.85	15.44	17.37	112.5	51.42	−18.31
NB_DM_US	13.41	12.76	95.15	45.78	−21.95	16.58	11.79	71.1	45.78	− 3.07	10.34	13.00	125.7	29.65	−21.95
BY_UK_UK	12.41	2.26	18.21	17.18	7.79	11.48	2.72	23.7	17.18	7.79	13.3	1.13	8.49	16.03	10.98
BY_JY_JY	7.87	1.18	14.99	10.30	5.96	7.92	1.13	14.3	9.70	6.39	7.83	1.23	15.71	10.3	5.96
BY_DM_DM	7.97	1.36	17.06	10.70	5.20	8.82	1.02	11.56	10.70	7.30	7.15	1.14	15.94	9.4	5.2
BY_US_US	8.02	1.53	19.1	12.49	5.79	7.08	0.957	13.5	8.6	5.79	8.94	1.44	16.1	12.49	7.3

EXHIBIT 13

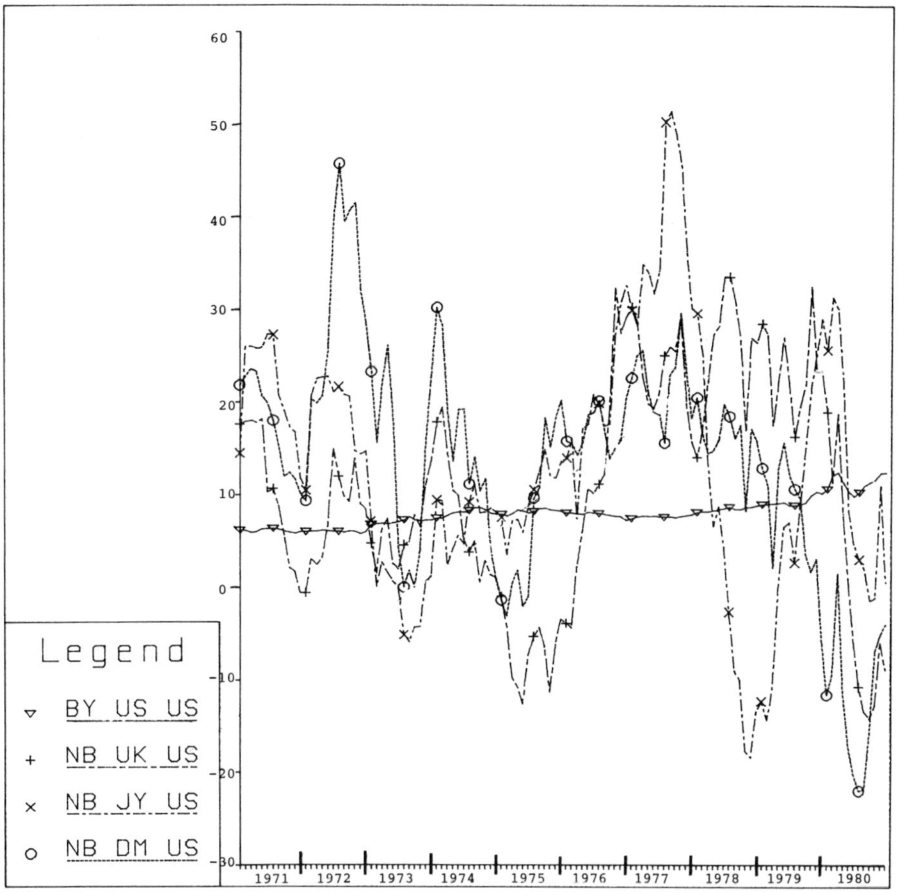

An analysis of the **volatility** of net bond yields (see Exhibits 17, 18, 19, and 20) indicates that their variability is dominated by the variability in the exchange factor. As the individual domestic bond yields have smaller standard deviations and coefficients of variation, the higher variability of their corresponding net yields reflects the volatility of currency movements. A general correspondence is noted between the orderings of the standard deviation of the exchange factor and the orderings of the standard deviations of net bond yields.

The Japanese net speculative bond yields, which registered the highest average rate of return for the entire period, also possess the largest standard deviation (14.0) and the second-largest coefficient of variation (104.17%). West German net bond yields, which outperformed all the other markets on the average in the first half, manifest the highest standard deviation (11.79) and the second largest coefficient of variation (71.10%). In the last half, Japanese net yields demonstrated the greatest variability, as measured by a standard deviation of 17.37, West German net yields exhibited the largest volatility, as indicated by a coefficient of variation of 125.70%.

EXHIBIT 14

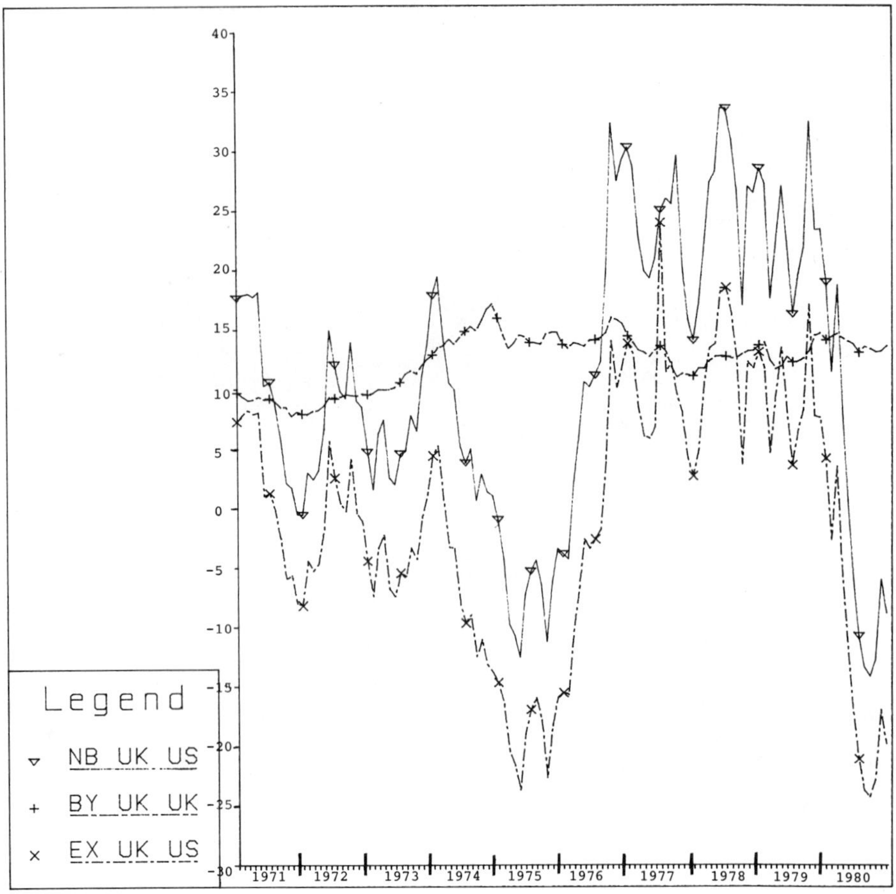

On covered yields (see Exhibit 21), as expected, the standard deviation and coefficient of variation drop significantly relative to those of speculative returns. But in comparison to the variability of the U.S. domestic bond yields, international covered bond yields demonstrate a larger volatility when measured either by the standard deviation or by the coefficient of variation.

In attempting to assess the possibility of **diversification** as a means of reducing portfolio risk, the observed behavior of net bond yields over the entire time period reveals few opportunities and at least one strong possibility (see Exhibit 22). A large negative correlation of -0.70 exists between net West German bond yields and the U.S. bond yields. This negative association is consistent over time; in fact, the negativity is accentuated toward the last half of the decade as the correlation coefficient increases from -0.54 in the first half to -0.83 in the second half.

The negative association noted earlier between international net speculative equity yields and the U.S. domestic equity yields is more predominant in its consistency and magnitude in the bond market. Negative correlations are observed in both halves of the decade and in the overall coefficients for bonds. However, a positive correlation

EXHIBIT 15

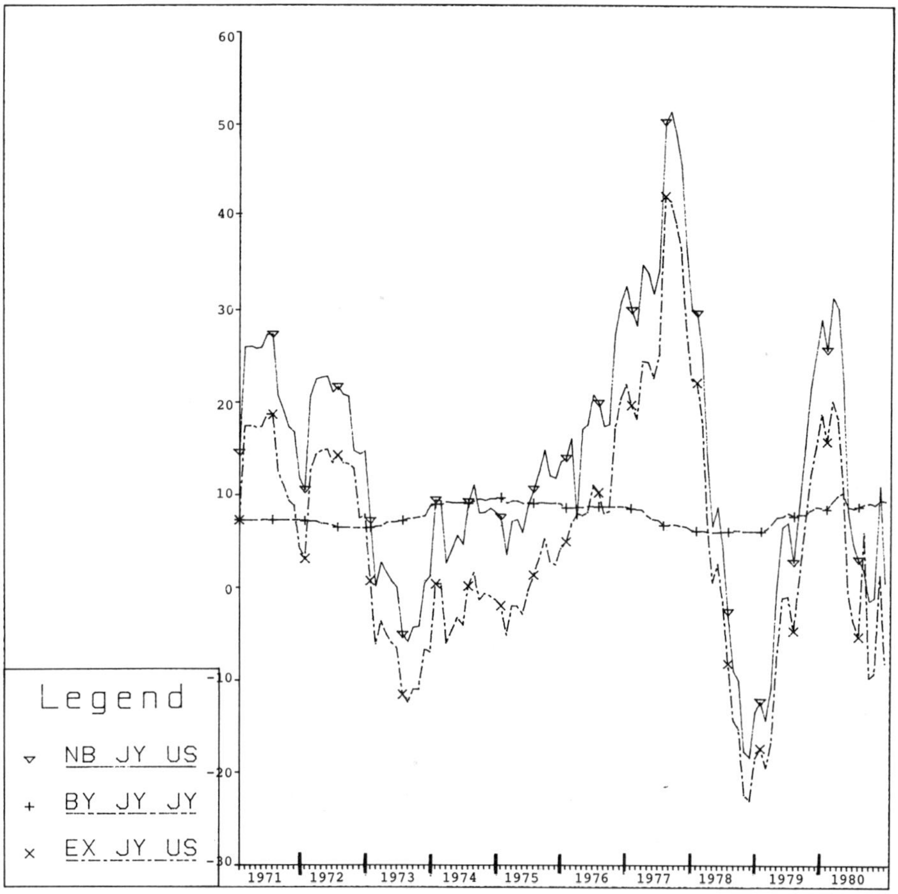

of 0.61 is noted in the last half of the time period between net bond yields of West Germany and the United Kingdom to the U.S. investor, suggesting the possibility of escalating portfolio risk in case of diversification in these two markets.

On a covered basis (see Exhibit 23), as expected, a stronger degree of association exists between covered international bond yields and domestic U.S. bond yields. The highest correlation (0.82) is observed between covered West German and Japanese bond yields, and the lowest correlation (0.59) is noted between covered U.K. and U.S. bond yields.

In **summary,** Japan fared best on both a speculative and a covered basis, and was considerably superior to the U.S. domestic bond market. Exchange rate movements played a significant role in determining net speculative yields. However, there is also a one-to-one correspondence between the orderings of average net yields and their respective volatility as measured by the standard deviation.

The correlation between markets is higher in bond markets than in equity markets. Consistently negative correlations in net yields between U.S. and other bond markets suggest the possibility of portfolio diversification to reduce risk.

EXHIBIT 16

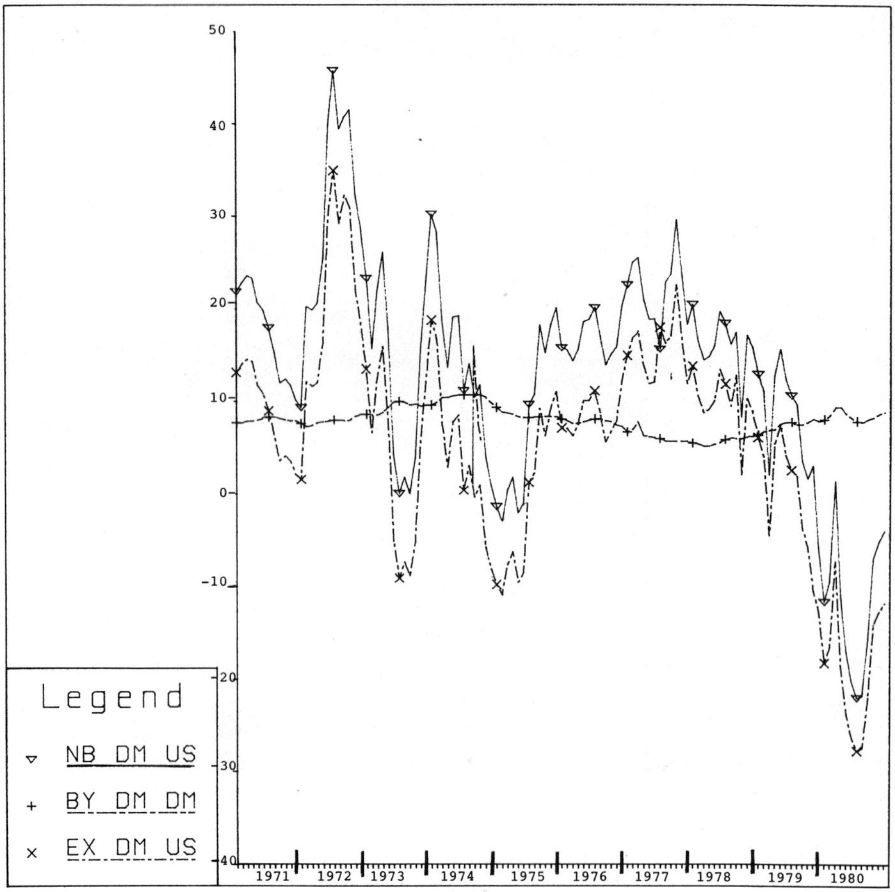
50
40
30
20
10
0
-10
-20
-30
-40
1971
1972
1973
1974
1975
1976
1977
1978
1979
1980
Legend
NB DM US
BY DM DM
EX DM US

EXHIBIT 17

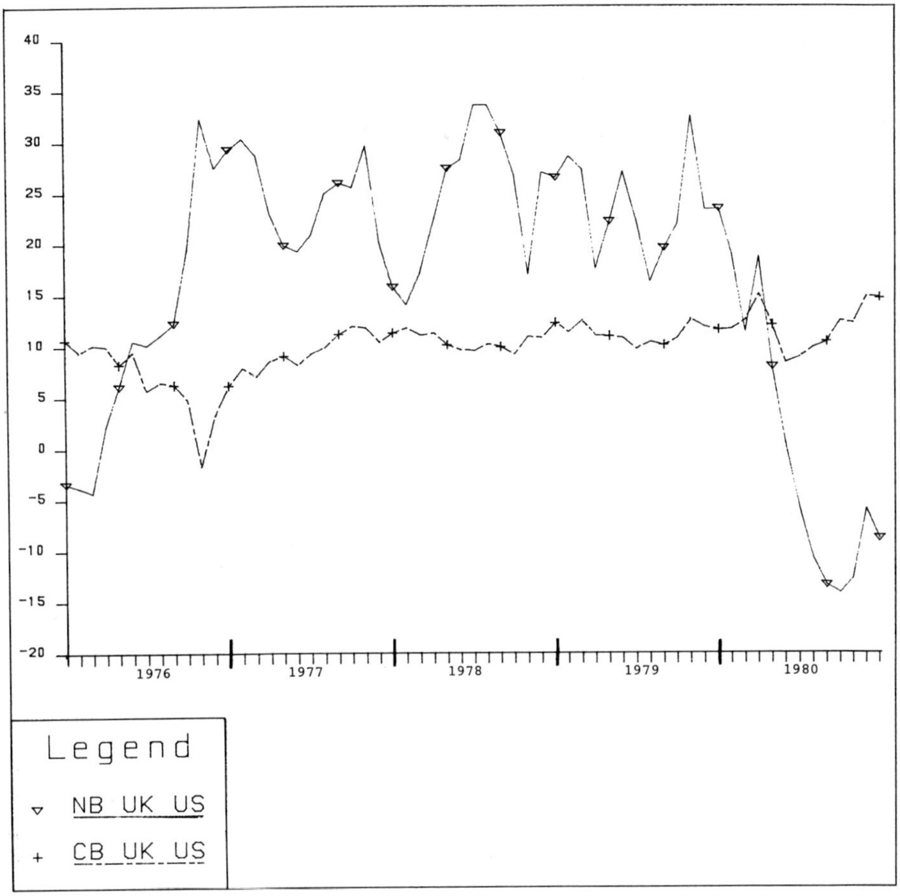

40
35
30
25
20
15
10
5
0
-5
-10
-15
-20
1976
1977
1978
1979
1980
Legend
NB UK US
CB UK US

EXHIBIT 18

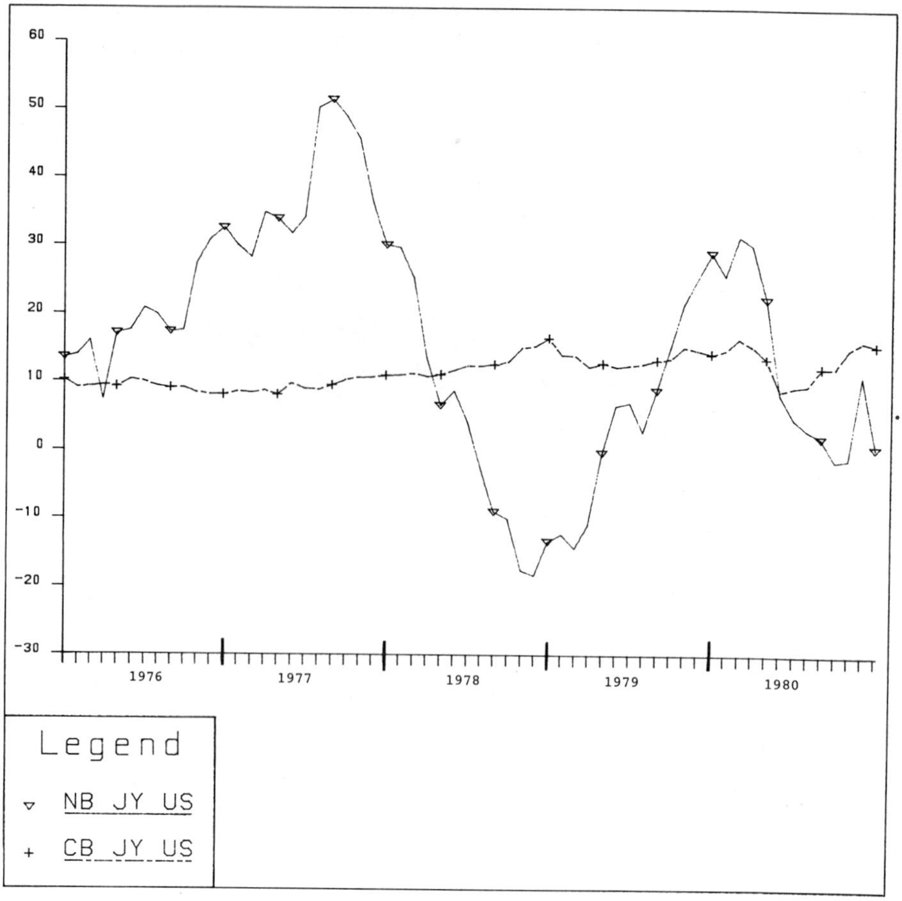
60
50
40
30
20
10
0
-10
-20
-30
1976
1977
1978
1979
1980
Legend
NB JY US
CB JY US

EXHIBIT 19

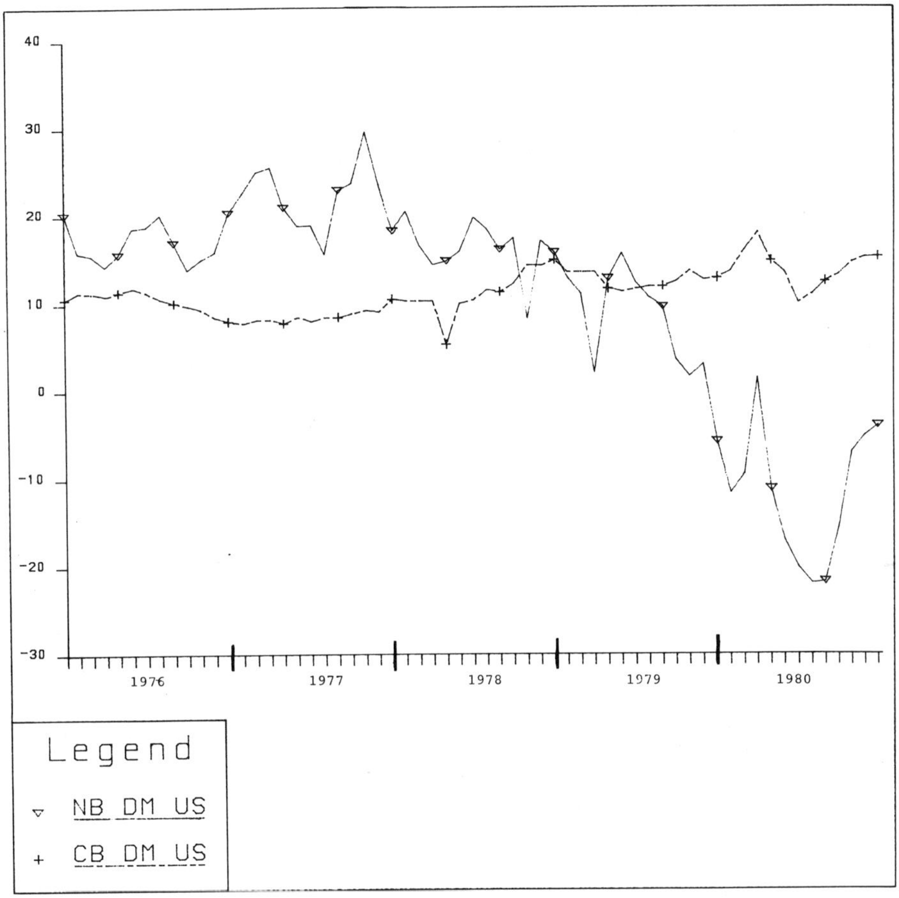
40
30
20
10
0
-10
-20
-30
1976
1977
1978
1979
1980
Legend
NB DM US
CB DM US

EXHIBIT 20

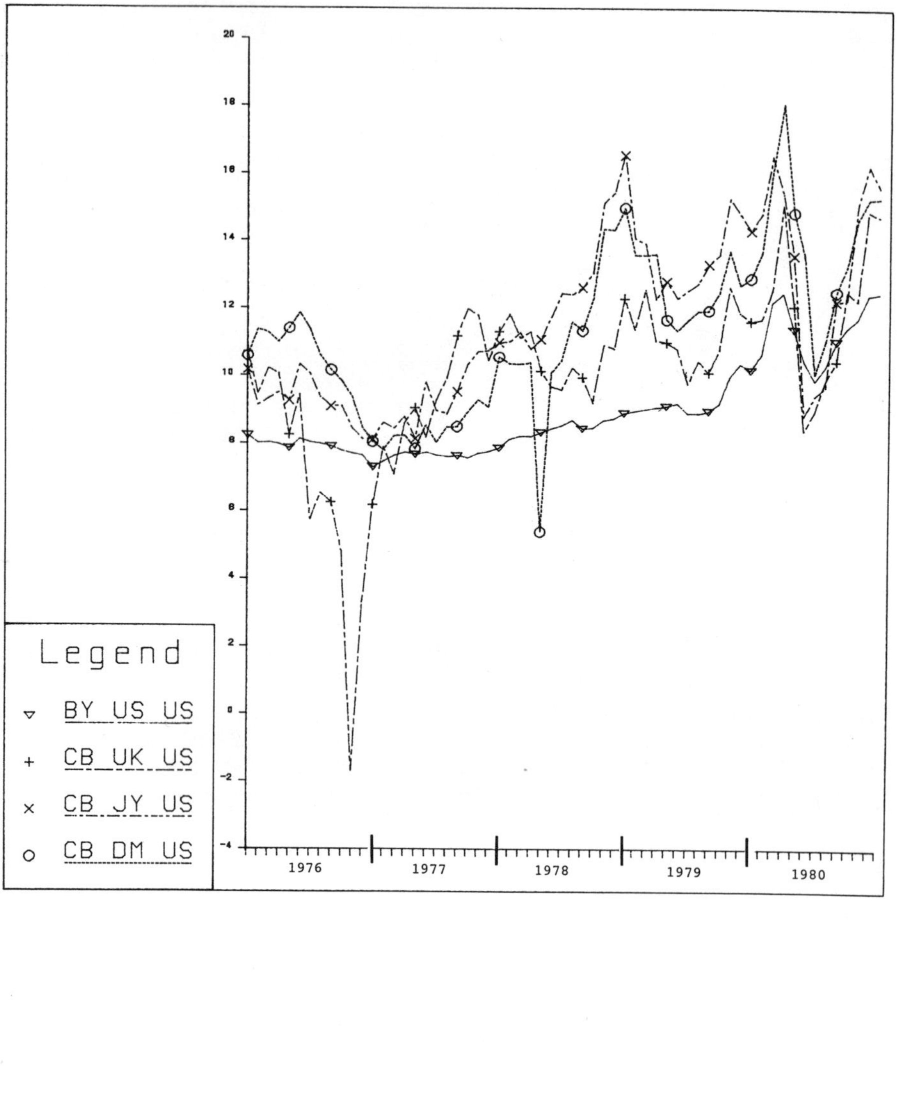

EXHIBIT 21 BASIC STATISTICS OF COVERED BOND YIELDS, U.S. RESIDENT

Variable	Mean	SD	Coef. of Var.	Max	Min
BY_US_US	8.94	1.44	16.10	12.49	7.30
CB_UK_US	10.01	2.72	27.14	15.10	−1.70
CB_JY_US	11.64	2.5	21.47	16.56	8.13
CB_DM_US	11.39	2.46	21.59	18.09	5.39

EXHIBIT 22 CORRELATION MATRIX OF SPECULATIVE BOND YIELDS AND THEIR COMPONENTS, U.S. RESIDENT

	January 1971–December 1980					January 1971–November 1975					December 1975–December 1980			
	(1)	(2)	(3)	(4)		(1)	(2)	(3)	(4)		(1)	(2)	(3)	(4)
(1) BY_US_US	1.0				(1)	1.0				(1)	1.0			
(2) NB_UK_US	−0.078	1.0			(2)	−0.52	1.0			(2)	−0.497	1.0		
(3) NB_JY_US	−0.192	0.249	1.0		(3)	−0.56	0.29	1.0		(3)	−0.29	0.18	1.0	
(4) NB_DM_US	−0.703	0.407	0.304	1.0	(4)	−0.54	0.63	0.51	1.0	(4)	−0.83	0.61	0.30	1.0
(1) BY_US_US	1.0				(1)	1.0				(1)	1.0			
(2) BY_UK_US	0.621	1.0			(2)	0.926	1.0			(2)	0.15	1.0		
(3) BY_JY_US	0.472	0.674	1.0		(3)	0.89	0.92	1.0		(3)	0.48	0.64	1.0	
(4) BY_DM_DM	0.02	0.178	0.633	1.0	(4)	0.67	0.68	0.58	1.0	(4)	0.61	0.61	0.92	1.0

EXHIBIT 23 CORRELATIONS BETWEEN COVERED AND DOMESTIC BOND YIELDS, U.S. RESIDENTS

	(1)	(2)	(3)	(4)
(1) BY_US_US	1.00			
(2) CB_UK_US	0.59	1.00		
(3) CB_JY_US	0.71	0.70	1.00	
(4) CB_DM_US	0.795	0.56	0.82	1.00

OBSERVATIONS BY UNITED KINGDOM RESIDENT INVESTORS

EQUITY MARKETS. An overview of **net speculative equity yields** from the perspective of the U.K. resident (see Exhibit 24) for the entire time span indicates that Japan offered the highest average rate of return, followed by the domestic U.K. equity market. Japan achieved an average net equity yield of 23.43% and the United Kingdom realized an average net yield of 11.54%. The highest and the lowest net yields recorded on a 12-month basis (140.65% and −56.81%, respectively) are both in the U.K. equity market.

A more detailed analysis reveals that the highest average net yield obtained in the Japanese equity market was due to the combined effect of a strong performance of the Japanese equity market and a large average increase in the value of the yen against the pound. The average rise in the Japanese equity index, 13.89%, and the mean annual appreciation of the yen against the pound, 7.68%, are the highest for the entire time period. It is of interest to note that the yen also manifested the highest depreciation, on an annual basis, against the pound—31.4%.

A breakdown of the time span into two segments discloses that Japan maintained its lead, in terms of average net yield, in the time period from January 1971 to November 1975, and achieved practically the highest average net yield in the second time frame also. In the earlier time period, the combination of a dominant mean increase in the Japanese equity index, 18.03% on an annual basis, and a strong mean appreciation of the yen, 10.06% against the pound, was responsible in achieving the highest average net return, 31.76%. In the last half, however, despite an average exchange factor of 5.39%, the highest in this period, the slowdown in equity price increases to an average of 9.89% resulted in a lower mean net yield of 15.36%. This reduction in net yield noted on Japanese equities in the last half versus the first half is true for all international net equity returns.

A comparison of **covered equity yields** (see Exhibit 25) reveals that Japan continues to dominate all other markets in terms of average return. Japan scored the highest mean covered return (16.31%) relative to the domestic and all international equity markets. The United Kingdom recorded the highest covered return, 80.32%, and the United States offered the lowest covered yield, −13.22%, for a 12-month period.

An examination of standard deviations for the entire time span (Exhibit 24) suggests that, on a speculative basis, Japanese net equity yields exhibited the highest volatility. The standard deviation of 34.54 on Japanese net returns is the highest, followed by the standard deviation on U.K. equity yields of 32.61. Despite the fact that the average net U.S. equity yield of 7.22% is the lowest, the volatility of its net

EXHIBIT 24 BASIC STATISTICS OF SPECULATIVE EQUITY YIELDS AND COMPONENTS, U.K. RESIDENT

	January 1971–December 1980					January 1971–November 1975					December 1975–December 1980				
Variable	Mean	SD	Coef. of Var.	Max	Min	Mean	SD	Coef. of Var.	Max	Min	Mean	SD	Coef. of Var.	Max	Min
EY_UK_UK	11.54	32.61	282.6	140.65	−56.81	7.59	43.22	569.4	140.65	−56.81	15.37	16.55	107.7	80.32	−10.82
NE_US_UK	7.22	21.72	300.5	57.91	−34.3	10.17	26.13	256.9	57.91	−34.3	4.37	16.09	368.2	39.75	−24.25
NE_JY_UK	23.43	34.54	147.4	130.03	−30.62	31.76	41.85	131.76	130.03	−28.61	15.36	23.22	151.0	55.33	−30.62
NE_DM_UK	8.12	16.72	205.9	41.4	−22.79	16.54	16.57	100.2	41.4	−19.41	0.091	12.42	13,648.0	22.83	−22.79
EY_UK_UK	11.54	32.61	282.5	140.65	−56.81	7.59	43.22	569.4	140.65	−56.81	15.37	16.56	107.7	80.32	−10.82
EY_US_US	4.07	15.29	376.6	34.77	−37.14	2.45	18.02	735.5	34.77	−37.14	5.63	12.04	213.8	33.58	−13.75
EY_JY_JY	13.89	23.37	168.5	98.79	−24.2	18.03	32.31	179.2	98.79	−24.2	9.89	6.42	64.9	25.99	−1.4
EY_DM_DM	1.03	11.28	1095.1	30.2	−23.98	2.81	14.5	516.0	30.2	−23.98	−0.7	6.55	935.7	10.94	−13.53
EX_US_UK	2.76	12.3	445.6	32.02	−15.62	6.83	10.16	148.8	31.03	−7.6	−1.18	12.98	1,100.0	32.02	−15.62
EX_JY_UK	7.68	14.31	186.3	32.81	−31.4	10.06	10.32	102.6	32.81	−7.96	5.39	17.10	317.3	27.29	−31.4
EX_DM_UK	7.21	12.21	169.3	37.31	−21.52	13.86	9.39	67.7	37.31	−5.61	0.78	11.19	1,434.6	31.93	−21.52

EXHIBIT 25 BASIC STATISTICS OF COVERED EQUITY YIELDS, U.K. RESIDENT

Variable	Mean	SD	Coef. of Var.	Max	Min
EY_UK_UK	15.37	16.55	107.7	80.32	−10.82
CE_US_UK	8.48	11.13	131.3	35.91	−13.32
CE_JY_UK	16.31	5.54	33.98	24.49	− 2.42
CE_DM_UK	6.32	6.6	104.4	25.75	− 6.48

returns is not the lowest. As measured by the coefficient of variation, U.S. net yields manifest the biggest coefficient, 300.50%, due to the low average net yield.

Currency risk, as measured by the standard deviation, is again highest for the Japanese yen for the entire time period. The standard deviation of annual changes in the value of the yen against the pound is 14.31 and its coefficient of variation of 186.30% is the second largest. The largest coefficient of variation of 445.60% is attributed to the U.S. dollar, mainly due to its low average depreciation of 2.76% against the pound.

A comparison of volatility of currency movements between the two time segments reveals that currency risks, whether dictated by the standard deviation or the coefficient of variation, increased over time. The Japanese yen continues to exhibit the highest variability in both time frames when measured by the standard deviation. The standard deviations of 10.32 and 17.10 for the Japanese exchange factor in the first and second halves of the decade respectively are the highest in each of the corresponding time frames.

The increase in currency volatility over time would tend to suggest that the risks associated with international speculative equity investments would consequently increase. Surprisingly this is not so, at least when risk is measured by the standard deviation of net speculative yields. There is a definite decrease in the standard deviation of net equity yields during the last half of the decade versus the first half, due to the reduction in the variability of equity price charges. The highest standard deviations in the first (41.85) and second (23.22) time segments for the Japanese net equity yields exhibit a considerable fall in volatility. As indicated by the coefficient of variation, however, this time trend of the risks in international investments is reversed.

On covered equity investments (see Exhibit 25) Japan manifests the lowest standard deviation and coefficient of variation despite the fact its average covered yield is the highest. The domestic U.K. equity market demonstrates the highest volatility as measured by a standard deviation of 16.55; U.S. covered yields possess the largest coefficient of variation, 131.30%.

A study of the **correlation** matrix of net speculative equity yields (see Exhibit 26) for the total time period does not indicate any strong associations. The largest correlation (0.65) is noted between West German and Japanese net yields. This observation is supported by a correlation of 0.55 between West German and Japanese equity price changes.

A time breakdown of the correlation matrix to detect changes in associations indicates shifts of considerable magnitude. In absolute terms, the correlation coefficients during the early half of the time span are much larger than those of the later

EXHIBIT 26 CORRELATION MATRIX OF SPECULATIVE EQUITY YIELDS AND THEIR COMPONENTS, U.K. RESIDENT

	January 1971–December 1980					January 1971–November 1975					December 1975–December 1980			
	(1)	(2)	(3)	(4)		(1)	(2)	(3)	(4)		(1)	(2)	(3)	(4)
(1) EY_UK_UK	1.0				(1)	1.0				(1)	1.0			
(2) NE_US_UK	0.51	1.0			(2)	0.74	1.0			(2)	−0.277	1.0		
(3) NE_JY_UK	0.24	0.49	1.0		(3)	0.35	0.48	1.0		(3)	−0.04	0.441	1.0	
(4) NE_DM_UK	0.4	0.49	0.65	1.0	(4)	0.71	0.83	0.66	1.0	(4)	0.04	−0.20	0.572	1.0
(1) EY_UK_UK	1.0				(1)	1.0				(1)	1.0			
(2) EY_US_US	0.62	1.0			(2)	0.85	1.0			(2)	−0.18	1.0		
(3) EY_JY_JY	0.24	0.44	1.0		(3)	0.3	0.55	1.0		(3)	−0.07	0.18	1.0	
(4) EY_DM_DM	0.72	0.52	0.55	1.0	(4)	0.79	0.79	0.57	1.0	(4)	0.54	−0.21	0.38	1.0
(1) EX_US_UK	1.0				(1)	1.0				(1)	1.0			
(2) EX_JY_UK	0.58	1.0			(2)	0.6	1.0			(2)	0.551	1.0		
(3) EX_DM_UK	0.43	0.46	1.0		(3)	0.29	0.56	1.0		(3)	0.34	0.41	1.0	

half. For example, during the first half, the largest coefficient (0.83), between West German and Japanese net yields, explained by a correlation of 0.79 between changes in West German and Japanese equity prices, drops to −0.20 in the second half due to the reduction in the correlation between their respective indexes to 0.54.

Other strong degrees of association noted in the first part of the time period between domestic U.K. equity yields and the U.S. and West German net yields are reduced to insignificance in the second half. The largest correlation (0.57) noted in the last half of the decade is between West German and Japanese net yields.

In summary, equity investments in Japan performed best on both a speculative and a covered basis for U.K. investors. The exchange factor for Japan contributed substantially to the overall performance of this market. However, the volatility of net speculative yields was also the highest, particularly due to the volatility of the yen. In contrast, Japan had the highest covered yield with the lowest volatility of any market. No significant positive or negative correlations were observed between markets, reflecting the neutral character of risk in portfolio diversification.

BOND MARKETS. **Net speculative yields** in the bond market are determined to the greatest extent by the relative performances of their respective exchange factors. In other words, the ranking of average returns, the standard deviations, and the coefficients of variation of net bond yields correspond to their respective orderings of the exchange factor.

For the entire time period (see Exhibit 27) net Japanese bond yields offered the highest average return, 16.22%, and correspondingly, the average exchange factor for Japan (7.87%) is the highest. The lowest mean net return of 10.87% in the U.S. bond market possesses the lowest exchange factor of 2.76%. The highest (48.82%) and the lowest (−15.12) net rate of return for the entire time frame occur in the West German bond market. There is again a one-to-one correspondence to the highest and lowest exchange factors recorded in the 10-year period (37.31% and −21.52% respectively) for the deutsche mark.

A time breakdown of bond yields reveals the consistency of the above pattern. In the first half of the decade, net West German bond yields recorded the highest average net return of 23.74% and correspondingly the West German exchange factor of 13.86% is the largest. In the second half, Japanese bonds registered the highest average net yield of 13.75%; the Japanese exchange factor of 5.39% is the largest, as expected.

A comparison of **covered bond yields** with the U.K. domestic market reveals (see Exhibit 12) that both the West German and Japanese net yields outperformed the domestic market on the average. The mean net yields of 14.57% and 14.56% in the West German and Japanese markets respectively are higher than the U.K. average yield of 13.30%.

The volatility of **net speculative bond yields** (see Exhibit 27) follows closely the variability of the exchange factor. Japanese bond yields consistently manifest the highest volatility as measured by the standard deviation in both time frames and the United States demonstrates the largest coefficient of variation (125.2%) in the overall time period, due to the low U.S. average yield. As anticipated, the uniform rise in the currency risk from the first half of the decade to the second increases the variability of international bond yields in the second half. For instance, the highest standard deviation of 11.50 in the first time period for net Japanese bond yields

EXHIBIT 27 BASIC STATISTICS OF SPECULATIVE BOND YIELDS AND THEIR COMPONENTS, U.K. RESIDENT

	January 1971–December 1980					January 1971–November 1975					December 1975–December 1980				
Variable	Mean	SD	Coef. of Var.	Max	Min	Mean	SD	Coef. of Var.	Max	Min	Mean	SD	Coef. of Var.	Max	Min
BY_UK_UK	12.41	2.26	18.2	17.18	7.79	11.48	2.72	23.7	17.18	7.79	13.30	1.13	8.5	16.03	10.98
NB_US_UK	10.87	13.61	125.2	47.26	−10.94	14.19	11.51	81.1	41.79	−2.11	7.65	14.77	193.1	47.26	−10.94
NB_JY_UK	16.22	15.92	98.2	44.88	−27.21	18.77	11.5	61.3	44.88	−0.96	13.75	19.03	138.4	37.71	−27.21
NB_DM_UK	15.75	13.43	85.3	48.82	−15.12	23.74	9.73	40.98	48.82	3.45	5.15	17.49	339.6	42.87	−15.12
BY_US_US	8.02	1.53	19.1	12.49	5.79	7.08	0.96	13.5	8.6	5.79	8.94	1.44	16.1	12.49	7.3
BY_UK_UK	12.41	2.26	18.2	17.18	7.79	11.48	2.72	23.7	17.18	7.79	13.3	1.13	8.49	16.03	10.98
BY_JY_JY	7.87	1.18	14.99	10.3	5.96	7.92	1.13	14.3	9.7	6.39	7.83	1.23	15.71	10.3	5.96
BY_DM_DM	7.97	1.36	17.06	10.7	5.2	8.82	1.02	11.56	10.7	7.3	7.15	1.14	15.94	9.4	5.2

advances to 19.03 in the second time segment, and the largest coefficient of variation of U.S. net yields, 81.10% increases to 193.00% in the second half of the time period.

Among covered bond yields (see Exhibit 28), the market that records the largest average yield also manifests the highest variability as dictated by the criteria of standard deviation. Covered West German bond yields offer the highest average return and reveal a standard deviation of 2.99, which is the largest. All covered yields possess standard deviations of similar magnitude, but as expected, the domestic U.K. bond rates indicate the lowest variability.

An examination of the **correlations** between speculative net returns (see Exhibit 29) for the entire time period reveals a poor degree of association between different markets. The highest correlation coefficient (0.60) is observed between Japanese and U.S. net yields. Further, no negative correlations of any suggestive magnitude are detectable.

A general trend of reductions in the correlation coefficients from the first half to the second half of the time period is identifiable. An exception to this pattern is the increase in the magnitude of the correlation between net West German and Japanese yields, from 0.51 in the early time segment, to −0.80 in the last half of the decade. A negative association between net West German yields and other net yields is recognizable during the second half of the time period.

A survey of the correlation between covered yields and the domestic bond rate (see Exhibit 30) suggests a much stronger degree of association. The largest correlation, 0.84, is noted between the U.K. and covered U.S. returns, and the lowest coefficient, 0.58, is observed between the domestic rate and Japanese net return. As anticipated, none of these correlations is negative in sign.

In summary, the rankings of the average yields of the different markets match the rankings of their respective average exchange factors. Similarly, the rankings of the volatility of the net yields also match the rankings of their respective volatility for the exchange factors. For the U.K. resident, this confirms that both returns and risks for the different bond markets directly correspond to the performance of their respective currencies. The negative association between net West German yields and all other market yields as seen in the last half of the time period suggests the possibility of portfolio diversification to reduce risk.

EXHIBIT 28 BASIC STATISTICS OF COVERED BOND YIELDS, U.K. RESIDENT

Variable	Mean	SD	Coef. of Var.	Max	Min
BY_UK_UK	13.30	1.13	8.49	16.03	10.98
CB_US_UK	12.07	2.90	24.03	24.16	6.54
CB_JY_UK	14.56	2.85	19.57	25.06	4.85
CB_DM_UK	14.57	2.99	20.52	25.85	8.50

EXHIBIT 29 CORRELATION MATRIX OF SPECULATIVE BOND YIELDS AND THEIR COMPONENTS, U.K. RESIDENT

	January 1971–December 1980					January 1971–November 1980					December 1975–December 1980			
	(1)	(2)	(3)	(4)		(1)	(2)	(3)	(4)		(1)	(2)	(3)	(4)
(1) BY_UK_UK	1.0				(1)	1.0				(1)	1.0			
(2) NB_US_UK	0.29	1.0			(2)	0.67	1.0			(2)	0.18	1.0		
(3) NB_JY_UK	0.09	0.595	1.0		(3)	0.22	0.64	1.0		(3)	0.21	0.56	1.0	
(4) NB_DM_UK	−0.20	0.40	0.45	1.0	(4)	0.11	0.30	0.51	1.0	(4)	−0.2	−0.33	−0.8	1.0
(1) BY_UK_UK	1.0				(1)	1.0				(1)	1.0			
(2) BY_US_US	0.62	1.0			(2)	0.93	1.0			(2)	0.15	1.0		
(3) BY_JY_JY	0.67	0.47	1.0		(3)	0.92	0.89	1.0		(3)	0.64	0.48	1.0	
(4) BY_DM_DM	0.18	0.02	0.63	1.0	(4)	0.68	0.67	0.58	1.0	(4)	0.61	0.61	0.92	1.0

EXHIBIT 30 CORRELATIONS BETWEEN COVERED AND DOMESTIC BOND YIELDS, U.K. RESIDENT

	(1)	(2)	(3)	(4)
(1) BY_UK_UK	1.00			
(2) CB_US_UK	0.84	1.00		
(3) CB_JY_UK	0.58	0.68	1.00	
(4) CB_DM_UK	0.81	0.88	0.82	1.00

OBSERVATIONS BY WEST GERMAN RESIDENT INVESTORS

EQUITY MARKETS. The general survey of **net speculative equity yields** (see Exhibit 31) indicates that the Japanese equity market performs the best for the West German investor. A consistently better performance of the Japanese exchange factor in combination with a relatively strong appreciation of its equity prices produces an average yield that is larger than those realized in other markets.

The overall average net yield of 16.07% on Japanese equities is by far the largest. United Kingdom equities follow with a much smaller net return of 6.19%. The U.K. equity market also displays the highest and the lowest net yields, on a 12-month basis, 125.70% and −59.48% respectively.

A closer look for the total time period reveals that the high average net yield on investments in Japanese equities is partly a consequence of the average annual appreciation of the yen of 1.16% against the deutsche mark, when all other currencies registered an average annual depreciation. Furthermore, Japan displayed an average increase in equity prices of 13.89%, the largest for this time period. It is noted that the yen manifested the largest annual appreciation and depreciation against the deutsche mark, 43.97% and −30.22% respectively, during the entire time span.

A breakdown of the time span into two segments discloses that Japan continued to lead, in terms of average net yields, during the time period January 1971 to November 1975, and achieved practically the highest net yield also in the second period. The mean net yield of 16.05% in the early time segment is much larger than the domestic average yield of 2.81%. All other international markets provided negative average yields.

In the first time segment, Japanese equity markets registered the highest average annual increase in its price index, 18.03%. The yen recorded an average annual depreciation of 2.94% against the deutsche mark, and this compares to a 11.40% depreciation of the pound and a 5.32% decrease of the dollar, both against the deutsche mark.

In the last time segment, however, despite an average exchange factor of 5.13% for the yen, the highest in this period, the slowdown in the rise of the Japanese equity price index to an average of 9.89% effected a decrease in the mean net yield to 16.10%. This is marginally below the U.K. net yield of 16.51%, the largest for this time period.

An examination of **covered equity yields** reveals (see Exhibit 32) that again Japan continues to be the dominant performer. Japan achieved the highest mean covered return (9.38%) relative to all international markets and this compares to the domestic equity market return of −0.70%. However, the United Kingdom recorded the highest

EXHIBIT 31 BASIC STATISTICS OF SPECULATIVE EQUITY YIELDS AND THEIR COMPONENTS, WEST GERMAN RESIDENT

	January 1971–December 1980					January 1971–November 1975					December 1975–December 1980				
Variable	Mean	SD	Coef. of Var.	Max	Min	Mean	SD	Coef. of Var.	Max	Min	Mean	SD	Coef. of Var.	Max	Min
EY_DM_DM	1.03	11.28	1,095.1	30.2	−23.98	2.81	14.50	517.8	30.2	−23.98	−0.698	6.56	950.7	10.94	−13.53
NE_US_DM	0.84	22.92	2,728.6	63.60	−37.21	−3.17	22.45	708.2	49.33	−37.21	4.72	22.9	487.2	63.6	−25.74
NE_UK_DM	6.19	34.53	557.8	125.7	−59.48	−4.47	41.09	919.2	125.7	−59.48	16.51	22.64	137.1	92.65	−28.19
NE_JY_DM	16.07	31.47	195.8	105.75	−32.74	16.05	38.08	237.3	105.75	−32.74	16.1	23.72	147.2	64.76	−29.43
EY_DM_DM	1.03	11.28	1,095.1	30.20	−23.98	2.81	14.5	516.0	30.2	−23.98	−0.7	6.55	935.7	10.94	−13.53
EY_US_US	4.065	15.29	376.6	34.77	−37.14	2.45	18.02	735.5	34.77	−37.14	5.63	12.04	213.8	33.58	−13.75
EY_UK_UK	11.54	32.61	282.5	140.65	−56.81	7.59	43.22	569.4	140.65	−56.87	15.37	16.56	107.7	80.32	−10.82
EY_JY_JY	13.89	23.37	168.5	98.79	−24.2	18.03	32.31	179.2	98.79	−24.2	9.89	6.42	64.9	25.99	− 1.4
EX_US_DM	−3.30	12.58	381.2	38.26	−25.92	−5.32	10.0	187.9	12.29	−25.92	−1.35	14.48	1,072.6	38.26	−18.47
EX_UK_DM	−5.44	11.04	202.9	27.42	−27.17	−11.49	7.16	62.3	5.94	−27.17	0.41	11.02	2,687.8	27.42	−24.20
EX_JY_DM	1.16	14.32	1,234.5	43.97	−30.22	−2.94	8.13	276.5	8.93	−18.14	5.13	17.62	343.1	43.97	−30.22

EXHIBIT 32 BASIC STATISTICS OF COVERED EQUITY YIELDS, WEST GERMAN RESIDENT

Variable	Mean	SD	Coef. of Var.	Max	Min
EY_DM_DM	−0.70	6.55	935.70	10.94	−13.53
CE_US_DM	2.06	11.21	544.20	29.31	−17.88
CE_UK_DM	8.14	15.06	185.00	63.57	−15.82
CE_JY_DM	9.38	6.09	64.90	24.49	− 2.42

covered return of 63.57% and the United States registered the lowest covered return of −17.88% for any 12-month period.

An examination of standard deviations for the entire time period (see Exhibit 31) indicates that Japanese equities, despite their high average net return, did not exhibit the highest **volatility.** The standard deviation of 31.47 for net speculative Japanese yields follows the highest standard deviation of U.K. net yields, 34.53. In fact, the coefficient of variation of Japanese net yields, 195.80%, is the lowest, while that of U.S. net returns, 2,728.00% is the highest.

In the overall time period, **currency risk** as measured by the standard deyiation is the highest for the yen and lowest for the pound. The standard deviation of 14.37 for the yen's movements against the deutsche mark is the largest, and that for the pound, 11.04, is the smallest.

A comparison of the volatility of currency fluctuations between the two time segments reveals that currency risk, whether measured by the criteria of the standard deviation or the coefficient of variation, increased with time. The pound, during the first half of the time period, exhibited the largest variability, with a standard deviation of 10.00; the yen demonstrated the largest volatility in the last half of the time span, with a standard deviation of 17.62.

To a large extent the variability in currency movements is reflected in the volatility of net yields. In the first half of the time period net U.K. yields possess the largest standard deviation (41.09) and in the second half of the time span Japanese net returns manifest the highest standard deviation (23.72).

On covered investments (see Exhibit 32), the volatility of the rate of return is greatly determined by the variability of their respective national equity markets. Japanese covered yields exhibit the lowest variability, with a standard deviation of 6.09 and a coefficient of variation of 64.90%, due to the low volatility of Japanese equity price movements. United Kingdom covered returns demonstrate the largest volatility, measured by a standard deviation of 15.06, as the fluctuations of its equity price index manifest the largest variability.

A study of the **correlation matrix** of net speculative equity yields (see Exhibit 33) for the entire time period reveals three overall coefficients that imply a moderate degree of association. In all three cases, the correlation between net yields captures the relatively closer association that exists between changes in their respective national equity price indexes. The correlation between West German yields and net speculative yields of the United Kingdom and Japan, 0.62 and 0.61 respectively, reflects the correlation of 0.72 and 0.55 between the movements of their respective national equity prices. The coefficient of 0.62 between U.S. and U.K. net yields

EXHIBIT 33 CORRELATION MATRIX OF SPECULATIVE EQUITY YIELDS AND THEIR COMPONENTS, WEST GERMAN RESIDENT

	January 1971–December 1980					January 1971–November 1975					December 1975–December 1980			
	(1)	(2)	(3)	(4)		(1)	(2)	(3)	(4)		(1)	(2)	(3)	(4)
(1) EY_DM_DM	1.0				(1)	1.0				(1)	1.0			
(2) NE_US_DM	0.44	1.0			(2)	0.80	1.0			(2)	−0.06	1.0		
(3) NE_UK_DM	0.62	0.62	1.0		(3)	0.80	0.81	1.0		(3)	0.40	0.34	1.0	
(4) NE_JY_DM	0.61	0.51	0.35	1.0	(4)	0.65	0.49	0.40	1.0	(4)	0.517	0.60	0.29	1.0
(1) EY_DM_DM	1.0				(1)	1.0				(1)	1.0			
(2) EY_US_US	0.517	1.0			(2)	0.79	1.0			(2)	−0.21	1.0		
(3) EY_UK_UK	0.72	0.62	1.0		(3)	0.79	0.85	1.0		(3)	0.54	−0.18	1.0	
(4) EY_JY_JY	0.55	0.44	0.24	1.0	(4)	0.57	0.55	0.3	1.0	(4)	0.38	0.18	−0.07	1.0
(1) EX_US_DM	1.0				(1)	1.0				(1)	1.0			
(2) EX_UK_DM	0.52	1.0			(2)	0.57	1.0			(2)	0.51	1.0		
(3) EX_JY_DM	0.61	0.43	1.0		(3)	0.60	0.34	1.0		(3)	0.61	0.36	1.0	

reveals a coefficient of similar magnitude between changes in their national equity prices.

A breakdown of the time span suggests shifts in association of much significance. The West German domestic yield and net international returns reveal reasonably high correlations that diminish considerably in the last half of the decade. The highest correlation of 0.81, seen in the first time segment between U.K. and U.S. net yields, falls to 0.34 in the second time segment. In only one case is a rise in the correlation coefficient noted; a correlation of 0.49 in the first part of the time period between Japanese and U.S. net returns increases to 0.60 in the second part of the time span.

Interestingly, the correlation between currency movements remains more or less constant over time. Therefore, the shifts in the degree of association between net yields (discussed above) reflect, to a large extent, the changes in the correlation between movements in national equity prices.

In summary, the smallest average depreciation among all currencies, that of the yen against the mark, contributed to the highest net speculative yield for West German investors in Japan. Although the yen demonstrated the highest volatility, the net yield of the Japanese equity market was not the riskiest. Furthermore, Japanese covered yields had the highest return and the lowest risk. No correlations of any significance were noticed.

BOND MARKETS. On an overall basis, Japanese bonds provided the largest average **speculative net yield** to the West German investor, due to the overall positive contribution of the Japanese exchange factor (see Exhibit 34). The domestic average West German bond rate of 7.97% is marginally higher than the mean Japanese rate of 7.87%, but the average annual appreciation of the yen (1.16%) against the deutsche mark generated a final net yield of 9.25%. The average U.K. bond rate is consistently the highest among all markets, but the poor performance of the pound against the deutsche mark, on the average, especially in the first half of the decade, diminished its relative attractiveness on a net basis.

In the first half of the time span the domestic market offered the highest mean return of 8.82%, as all currencies registered average annual depreciations against the deutsche mark to warrant a lower net return. Among the international money markets, Japanese bonds provided the highest average return of 4.89%. The yen had a mean annual depreciation of 2.94%, the lowest, against the deutsche mark.

In the second half, however, the predominance of the internal U.K. bond rate effected an average net yield of 13.76% despite the small mean contribution of the U.K. exchange factor, 0.41%. Japan followed with a mean net return of 13.48%, propelled by the average annual appreciation for the yen of 5.13% against the deutsche mark.

Among **covered yields** Japanese bonds once again provided the highest average yield, 7.27%, and the highest net yield, 10.17% (see Exhibit 35). The domestic bond rate of 7.17% follows second, while the covered U.S. yield of −6.64% is the lowest return recorded among all markets.

The **volatility** of net bond yields (see Exhibit 34) was dictated by the volatility of their respective exchange factors. Therefore, the ordering of standard deviations of net bond yields and the exchange factors resemble each other precisely. Japanese bonds, in the overall time frame, provide the largest average net return, but they are also the most volatile, as measured by the standard deviation of 15.97, the largest among international speculative investments.

EXHIBIT 34 BASIC STATISTICS OF SPECULATIVE BOND YIELDS AND THEIR COMPONENTS, WEST GERMAN RESIDENTS

	January 1971–December 1980					January 1971–November 1975					December 1975–December 1980				
Variable	Mean	SD	Coef. of Var.	Max	Min	Mean	SD	Coef. of Var.	Max	Min	Mean	SD	Coef. of Var.	Max	Min
BY_DM_DM	7.97	1.36	17.06	10.7	5.2	8.82	1.02	11.56	10.7	7.3	7.15	1.14	15.94	9.4	5.2
NB_US_DM	4.35	14.8	34.0	52.97	−21.47	0.92	11.0	1,195.6	20.91	−21.47	7.68	17.17	223.6	52.97	−12.11
NB_UK_DM	6.45	12.99	201.4	45.48	−17.45	−1.11	8.06	726.1	20.42	−17.45	13.76	12.71	92.37	45.48	−12.98
NB_JY_DM	9.25	15.97	172.65	57.38	−25.96	4.89	9.00	184.0	19.23	−12.38	13.48	19.76	146.6	57.38	−25.96
BY_DM_DM	7.97	1.36	17.06	10.7	5.2	8.82	1.02	11.56	10.7	7.3	7.15	1.14	15.94	9.4	5.2
BY_US_US	8.02	1.53	19.1	12.49	5.79	7.08	0.96	13.5	8.6	5.79	8.94	1.44	16.1	12.49	7.3
BY_UK_UK	12.41	2.26	18.21	17.18	7.79	11.48	2.72	23.7	17.18	7.79	13.3	1.13	8.49	16.03	10.98
BY_JY_JY	7.87	1.18	14.99	10.3	5.96	7.92	1.13	14.3	9.7	6.39	7.83	1.23	15.71	10.3	5.96

EXHIBIT 35 BASIC STATISTICS OF COVERED BOND YIELDS, WEST GERMAN RESIDENT

Variable	Mean	SD	Coef. of Var.	Max	Min
BY_DM_DM	7.15	1.14	15.94	9.4	5.2
CB_US_DM	4.42	2.17	49.1	7.97	−6.64
CB_UK_DM	5.45	2.05	37.6	8.58	−3.4
CB_JY_DM	7.27	1.17	16.09	10.17	3.96

There was a general trend of rising **volatility** of net bond yields from the first half of the time span to the second, as measured by the standard deviation; this was exactly the pattern noted in their currency risks. The risk effect is in fact reinforced by the increasing variability observed in the various national bond markets. The largest standard deviation of 11.00, noted for net U.S. yields in the first part of the time period, compares to the largest standard deviation of 19.76 for net Japanese yields in the second half.

Covered yields, as expected, definitely demonstrated lower volatility than speculative rates of return (see Exhibit 35). But interestingly, the market that offered the highest average covered return, the Japanese money market, also exhibited a rather low volatility. The standard deviation and the coefficient of variation of Japanese covered returns, 1.17 and 16.09% respectively, are marginally above their comparable counterparts in the West German domestic market. The standard deviation and coefficient of variation (1.14 and 15.95%) for the West German bond rates are the smallest among all markets.

An examination of the **correlation** between net speculative bond yields does not indicate any close associations (see Exhibit 36). This conclusion is generally true for the entire time frame as well as the first and second halves of the decade separately. However, a general pattern of decreasing coefficients of correlation with time is evident for a majority of the markets.

For the entire time span, the largest correlation (0.64) is noted between the Japanese and U.S. net yields. Correlation coefficients of almost similar magnitude are observed in the first and second half of the decade. The largest correlation, 0.62, in the second half of the time period, is noted between West German and U.S. net yields and between U.S. and Japanese net yields.

The correlations between domestic and covered rates of return, contrary to expectations, do not display a high degree of association (see Exhibit 37). The largest coefficient of correlation, 0.47, is observed between West Germany rates and covered U.S. yields, and the smallest coefficient, 0.02, is noted between the domestic rates and U.K. covered returns.

In summary, the low negative exchange factor contributed to the best overall speculative performance of the Japanese bond market for West German investors. However, the Japanese market was also the riskiest; all markets displayed an increasing volatility over time. Average covered bond yields for Japan were again the highest, but among covered investments, they also had the lowest volatility. No significant correlations between markets were noticed for both speculative and covered investments.

EXHIBIT 36 CORRELATION MATRIX OF SPECULATIVE BOND YIELDS AND THEIR COMPONENTS, WEST GERMAN RESIDENT

	January 1971–December 1980					January 1971–November 1975					December 1975–December 1980			
	(1)	(2)	(3)	(4)		(1)	(2)	(3)	(4)		(1)	(2)	(3)	(4)
(1) BY_DM_DM	1.0				(1)	1.0				(1)	1.0			
(2) NB_US_DM	0.28	1.0			(2)	0.44	1.0			(2)	0.62	1.0		
(3) NB_UK_DM	−0.15	0.58	1.0		(3)	0.54	0.68	1.0		(3)	0.19	0.52	1.0	
(4) NB_JY_DM	0.06	0.64	0.45	1.0	(4)	0.14	0.61	0.40	1.0	(4)	0.49	0.62	0.38	1.0
(1) BY_DM_DM	1.0				(1)	1.0				(1)	1.0			
(2) BY_US_US	0.02	1.0			(2)	0.67	1.0			(2)	0.61	1.0		
(3) BY_UK_UK	0.18	0.62	1.0		(3)	0.68	0.93	1.0		(3)	0.61	0.15	1.0	
(4) BY_JY_JY	0.13	0.47	0.67	1.0	(4)	0.58	0.89	0.92	1.0	(4)	0.92	0.48	0.64	1.0

EXHIBIT 37 CORRELATION BETWEEN COVERED AND DOMESTIC BOND YIELDS, WEST GERMAN RESIDENT

	(1)	(2)	(3)	(4)
(1) BY_DM_DM	1.0			
(2) CB_US_DM	0.47	1.0		
(3) CB_UK_DM	0.02	0.28	1.0	
(4) CB_JY_DM	0.35	0.13	0.25	1.0

OBSERVATIONS BY JAPANESE RESIDENT INVESTORS

EQUITY MARKETS. A comprehensive view of markets from the standpoint of the Japanese investor for the entire time span uncovers no international equity market in favor of the domestic market (see Exhibit 38). The average yield in domestic equities (13.89%) is much larger than the highest average international net return (4.85%) observed in the U.K. equity market.

A more detailed analysis discloses that the strong appreciation of the yen against most of the currencies was responsible for producing low average **speculative net returns** on international investments. The average annual depreciation of the pound (5.17%) and the dollar (3.61%) against the yen diminished the overall average net return in the U.K. and the U.S. equity markets to 4.85% and 0.10% respectively. The deutsche mark, however, displayed an average annual appreciation of 0.90%, but the small average annual rise in West German share prices of 1.03% consequently provided a low net return on West German equities of 1.35%.

In the first half of the decade, the domestic equity market remained the predominant choice for the Japanese investor. The domestic mean return of 18.03% is much higher than the largest international average net yield of 6.23% in the West German market. The United Kingdom offers the lowest average net return of −3.44%, due to an annual mean rate of depreciation of the pound of 8.32% against the yen and a low average increase in the U.K. equity prices of 7.59%.

In the second half of the decade, however, despite a continued depreciation of the pound at a slower rate of 2.12% against the yen, the mean advance of the U.K. equity price index of 15.37% generated a final net average speculative return that was higher than the domestic yield. The net U.K. average yield of 12.87%, the largest, now compares to the mean Japanese rate of return of 9.89%. The contribution of all exchange factors to net yield in this time segment is negative, thereby diminishing the net return on international investments.

A comparison of **covered yields** to net speculative yields (see Exhibit 39) discloses that covered investments do not necessarily offer higher returns despite the influence of negative exchange factors on net speculative yields. The domestic market offered by far the highest yield and the United Kingdom provided the largest return of 8.91% on covered investments.

The ranking of **volatility** of net speculative yields (see Exhibit 38), when measured by the standard deviation, bears a one-to-one correspondence to the ordering of the volatility of individual equity markets. The U.K. equity price movements display the largest standard deviation of the entire time period and also in the separate time segments. Consequently, net U.K. equity yields demonstrate the highest standard

EXHIBIT 38 BASIC STATISTICS OF SPECULATIVE EQUITY YIELDS AND THEIR COMPONENTS, JAPANESE RESIDENT

	January 1971–December 1980					January 1971–November 1975					December 1975–December 1980				
Variable	Mean	SD	Coef. of Var.	Max	Min	Mean	SD	Coef. of Var.	Max	Min	Mean	SD	Coef. of Var.	Max	Min
EY_JY_JY	13.89	23.37	168.3	98.79	−24.2	18.03	32.31	179.2	98.79	−24.2	9.89	6.42	64.9	25.99	− 1.4
NE_US_JY	0.10	185.58	18580.0	48.46	−29.84	−0.83	17.06	2055.0	37.41	−29.36	0.996	20.05	2013.0	48.46	−29.84
NE_UK_JY	4.85	31.75	654.6	110.29	−54.09	−3.44	36.53	1062.0	110.29	−54.09	12.87	24.02	186.6	75.56	−23.5
NE_DM_JY	1.35	13.06	967.4	27.44	−35.79	6.23	10.39	166.7	27.44	−14.24	−3.37	13.70	406.5	25.82	−35.79
EY_JY_JY	13.89	23.37	168.3	98.79	−24.2	18.03	32.31	179.2	98.79	−24.2	9.89	6.42	64.9	25.99	− 1.4
EY_US_US	4.07	15.29	376.6	34.77	−37.14	2.45	18.02	735.5	34.77	−37.14	5.63	12.04	213.8	33.58	−13.75
EY_UK_UK	11.54	32.61	282.5	140.65	−56.81	7.59	43.22	569.4	140.65	−56.81	15.37	16.56	107.7	80.32	−10.82
EY_DM_DM	1.03	11.28	1,095.1	30.2	−23.98	2.81	14.5	516.0	30.2	−23.98	−0.7	6.55	935.7	10.94	−13.53
EX_US_JY	−3.61	11.95	331.0	29.89	−24.71	−2.65	8.41	317.3	14.1	−15.75	−4.53	14.59	322.0	29.89	−29.46
EX_UK_JY	−5.17	14.97	289.5	45.77	−24.71	−8.32	8.82	106.0	8.65	−24.71	−2.12	18.72	883.0	45.77	−21.44
EX_DM_JY	0.9	14.11	1,567.7	43.31	−30.54	4.02	9.27	230.6	25.52	−24.71	−2.12	17.11	807.1	43.31	−30.54

EXHIBIT 39 BASIC STATISTICS OF COVERED EQUITY YIELDS, JAPANESE RESIDENT

Variable	Mean	SD	Coef. of Var.	Max	Min
EY_JY_JY	9.89	6.42	64.9	25.99	− 1.4
CE_US_JY	2.06	11.06	536.9	28.83	−17.97
CE_UK_JY	8.91	15.59	175.2	65.32	−16.22
CE_DM_JY	−0.08	6.93	8,662.0	12.54	−13.91

deviation throughout the decade. Further, the exchange factor for the United Kingdom also manifests the highest standard deviation for the entire time period and in the individual time segments.

A time break of standard deviations indicates that from the first half of the decade to the second, in the case of U.S. and West German net yields, there is an increase in variability, and for the United Kingdom and Japan, a decrease in variability. This pattern is not observed in the standard deviations of the exchange factor; the general trend is one of increasing currency risk as measured either by the standard deviation or the coefficient of variation.

The volatility of covered yields is much below the variability of their respective net speculative yields, as measured by the standard deviation. The U.K. equity market again exhibits the highest standard deviation of 15.59, followed by the U.S. equity market, with a standard deviation of 11.06 on a covered basis. These compared to the standard deviation on Japanese equity returns of 6.42.

The correlation matrix of net speculative equity yields reveals very poor degrees of association between markets (see Exhibit 40). In the overall time frame, the highest correlation, 0.55, is observed between the U.K. and U.S. net returns.

A time breakdown discloses a marked reduction in the magnitude of most correlations from the first half of the decade to the second. The largest correlation noted in the last half of the decade, 0.58, is between West German and U.S. net returns. This compares to the largest coefficient observed between U.K. and U.S. net returns (0.74) in the first half of the time span.

The **correlations** between the different exchange factors facing the Japanese investor manifest a contrary pattern. They tend to increase in magnitude toward the last half of the decade and maintain relatively larger coefficients in the overall time frame. The largest correlation for the entire time period (0.72) is noted between the West German and the U.K. exchange factors, followed by a 0.68 coefficient between U.K. and U.S. exchange factors.

In the first half of the time segment, the largest correlation (0.59) is observed between the movements in the deutsche mark and the pound; it increases to 0.85 in the second half. Interestingly enough, no negative correlations exist in any of the time frames.

In summary, the poor performance of the other three currencies against the yen caused domestic Japanese investments to perform better than any international investment. In fact, on a speculative basis, the average domestic yield was nearly 300% better than the highest international yield. On a covered basis also, no international market returns could compete with the Japanese domestic market. The

EXHIBIT 40 CORRELATION MATRIX OF SPECULATIVE EQUITY YIELDS AND THEIR COMPONENTS, JAPANESE RESIDENT

	January 1971–December 1980					January 1971–November 1975					December 1975–December 1980			
	(1)	(2)	(3)	(4)		(1)	(2)	(3)	(4)		(1)	(2)	(3)	(4)
(1) EY_JY_JY	1.0				(1)	1.0				(1)	1.0			
(2) NE_US_JY	0.14	1.0			(2)	0.26	1.0			(2)	−0.113	1.0		
(3) NE_UK_JY	0.08	0.55	1.0		(3)	0.23	0.74	1.0		(3)	−0.54	0.37	1.0	
(4) NE_DM_JY	0.16	0.32	0.39	1.0	(4)	0.31	0.48	0.56	1.0	(4)	−0.49	0.29	0.58	1.0
(1) EY_JY_JY	1.0				(1)	1.0				(1)	1.0			
(2) EY_US_US	0.439	1.0			(2)	0.55	1.0			(2)	0.18	1.0		
(3) EY_UK_UK	0.237	0.622	1.0		(3)	0.3	0.85	1.0		(3)	−0.07	−0.18	1.0	
(4) EY_DM_DM	0.554	0.52	0.72	1.0	(4)	0.57	0.79	0.79	1.0	(4)	0.38	−0.21	0.54	1.0
(1) EX_US_JY	1.0				(1)	1.0				(1)	1.0			
(2) EX_UK_JY	0.68	1.0			(2)	0.54	1.0			(2)	0.762	1.0		
(3) EX_DM_JY	0.61	0.72	1.0		(3)	0.27	0.59	1.0		(3)	0.709	0.85	1.0	

volatility of Japanese equity returns, as measured by the standard deviation, was relatively high but was only second to U.K. speculative yields. No correlations of any significance were observed in yields between markets.

BOND MARKETS. A survey of net **speculative bond yields** reveals that the exchange factor is crucial in determining the ordering of average net yields (see Exhibit 41). As the divergences between the various average bond rates are not large, the exchange component is an important constituent of net returns.

For the entire time period, West German bond yields offered the highest average return, 8.78%; as expected, the average exchange factor of 0.90% for West Germany is the highest. The United Kingdom recorded the highest average bond rate of 12.41%, but the exchange factor of −5.17% for the pound, the lowest for the time period, diminished the mean net yield for U.K. bonds to 6.71%. The highest net yield observed in the entire decade, 64.83%, is for the U.K. money market, and the largest corresponding exchange factor of 45.77% is noted for the pound sterling. The lowest net yield of −24.16% in the total time period is recorded for the U.S. bond market.

A time breakdown reveals that West German net bond yields provided the largest average net return in the first half of the decade, due to a relatively dominant average appreciation of the deutsche mark against the yen on an annual basis, while all other currencies registered an average depreciation. The average West German yield of 8.82% in this time segment is below the average U.K. yield of 11.48%, but the mean West German exchange factor of 4.02% is successful in raising the West German net average yield to 12.54%. The U.K. exchange factor of −8.32% reduced the net yield for the U.K. money market to an average of 2.24%.

In the second half of the decade the annual depreciation of the pound slowed to 2.12% and the dominant mean U.K. bond yield of 13.30% permitted an average net return of 11.03% to the Japanese investor, the highest in this time segment. The Japanese domestic money market was second, with an average return of 7.83%.

A comparison of **covered bond yields** and the domestic Japanese market (see Exhibit 42) indicates that the latter offers a higher return than international money markets. The Japanese average bond rate of 7.83% is larger than the highest international yield of 7.69% in the West German bond market, on a covered basis.

An analysis of the **volatility** of net bond yields (see Exhibit 41) suggests that the standard deviations of net yields primarily reflect the standard deviation of currency movements, or in other words, the currency risk. The rankings of the standard deviations of net yields resemble the orderings of the standard deviations of the exchange factor.

An overview of the entire time period indicates that the domestic money market offers the lowest risk, as measured by the standard deviation and the coefficient of variation of 1.18 and 14.99% respectively. The highest volatility as dictated by the standard deviation is recorded for net U.K. yields. The movements of the pound sterling exhibit the highest standard deviation of 14.97 and consequently the U.K. net yields are the most volatile, with a standard deviation of 16.97.

In the first half of the time frame, the deutsche mark manifests the highest variability, with a standard deviation of 9.27, and as expected, net West German yields are the most volatile, with a standard deviation of 9.98. In the second half, annual fluctuations of the pound sterling display the largest variability, and consequently U.K. net yields are the most volatile, as measured by the standard deviation of 20.9.

EXHIBIT 41 BASIC STATISTICS OF SPECULATIVE BOND YIELDS AND THEIR COMPONENTS, JAPANESE RESIDENT

Variable	January 1971–December 1980					January 1971–November 1975					December 1975–December 1980				
	Mean	SD	Coef. of Var.	Max	Min	Mean	SD	Coef. of Var.	Max	Min	Mean	SD	Coef. of Var.	Max	Min
BY_JY_JY	7.87	1.18	14.99	10.3	5.96	7.92	1.13	14.3	9.7	6.39	7.83	1.23	15.71	10.3	5.96
NB_US_JY	4.21	13.36	317.3	41.24	−24.16	4.31	9.57	222.04	22.79	−10.37	4.11	16.28	396.11	41.24	−24.16
NB_UK_JY	6.71	16.97	252.9	64.83	−13.65	2.24	9.94	443.7	22.23	−13.65	11.03	20.9	189.5	64.88	−11.12
NB_DM_JY	8.78	14.71	167.5	53.96	−23.66	12.54	9.98	79.58	32.9	− 0.67	5.15	17.49	339.6	53.96	−23.66
BY_JY_JY	7.87	1.18	14.99	10.3	5.96	7.92	1.13	14.3	9.7	6.39	7.83	1.23	15.71	10.3	5.96
BY_US_US	8.02	1.53	19.1	12.49	5.79	7.08	0.96	13.5	8.6	5.79	8.94	1.44	16.1	12.49	7.3
BY_UK_UK	12.41	2.26	18.21	17.18	7.79	11.48	2.72	23.7	17.18	7.79	13.3	1.13	8.49	16.03	10.98
BY_DM_DM	7.97	1.36	17.06	10.7	5.2	8.82	1.02	11.56	10.7	7.3	7.15	1.14	15.94	9.4	5.2

Further, a general pattern of increased currency risk from the first half of the time period to the second half is observed. This trend is reflected in the magnitude of the standard deviations, but is not conclusively proved when the measure of the coefficient of variation is utilized.

The volatility of covered returns is, as anticipated, much lower than the variability of speculative net yields (see Exhibit 42), but is still high in comparison to the volatility of the domestic money market. The highest observed standard deviation (2.67) and the coefficient of variation (52.9%) of U.S. covered bond yields are more than double their comparable counterparts in the Japanese markets.

A **correlation matrix** of net speculative yields (see Exhibit 43) for the entire time span indicates that net returns between the United Kingdom and the United States and between the United Kingdom and West Germany have a reasonably close degree of association. A correlation of 0.69 exists between U.K. and U.S. net yields and a coefficient of 0.66 is noted between U.K. and West German net returns. A time breakdown confirms that the above correlations have in fact increased with time. A coefficient of 0.64 and 0.59 observed between U.K. and U.S. and between U.K. and West German net returns respectively in the first half of the time period advanced to 0.74 and 0.83 respectively for these markets in the second half.

In the second half of the time period other correlations of some importance are the negative associations observed between domestic market returns and the U.K. and West German net yields. Despite the fact that the magnitude of the correlations is not large (−0.57 for Japanese and U.K. net yields, −0.56 for Japanese and West German net yields), the increases in their absolute values from the first half of the time period to the second are noteworthy.

The correlation between international covered yields and the domestic market is high, with the exception of net U.K. money market returns (see Exhibit 44). The low correlation coefficient of 0.48 observed between U.K. covered yields and Japanese bond rates, contrary to expectations, is of some significance.

In summary, the West German bond market performed best for Japanese investors on a speculative basis due to a small average appreciation of the mark against the yen. However, on a covered basis, the Japanese market had the highest average yield. Japan also offered the lowest risk on both speculative and covered investments. No correlation of any significance was observed between markets.

EXHIBIT 42 BASIC STATISTICS OF COVERED BOND YIELDS, JAPANESE RESIDENT

Variable	Mean	SD	Coef. of Var.	Max	Min
BY_JY_JY	7.83	1.23	15.71	10.3	5.96
CB_US_JY	5.05	2.67	52.9	10.3	−1.84
CB_UK_JY	6.08	2.37	38.98	9.48	−1.37
CB_DM_JY	7.69	2.23	28.99	13.48	4.53

EXHIBIT 43 CORRELATION MATRIX OF SPECULATIVE BOND YIELDS AND THEIR COMPONENTS, JAPANESE RESIDENT

	January 1971–December 1980					January 1971–November 1975					December 1975–December 1980			
	(1)	(2)	(3)	(4)		(1)	(2)	(3)	(4)		(1)	(2)	(3)	(4)
(1) BY_JY_JY	1.0				(1)	1.0				(1)	1.0			
(2) NB_US_JY	0.04	1.0			(2)	0.48	1.0			(2)	−0.19	1.0		
(3) NB_UK_JY	−0.36	0.69	1.0		(3)	0.05	0.64	1.0		(3)	−0.57	0.74	1.0	
(4) NB_DM_JY	−0.39	0.56	0.66	1.0	(4)	−0.15	0.27	0.59	1.0	(4)	−0.56	0.68	0.83	1.0
(1) BY_JY_JY	1.0				(1)	1.0				(1)	1.0			
(2) BY_US_US	0.47	1.0			(2)	0.89	1.0			(2)	0.48	1.0		
(3) BY_UK_UK	0.67	0.62	1.0		(3)	0.92	0.93	1.0		(3)	0.64	0.15	1.0	
(4) BY_DM_DM	0.63	0.02	0.18	1.0	(4)	0.58	0.67	0.68	1.0	(4)	0.92	0.61	0.61	1.0

EXHIBIT 44 CORRELATION BETWEEN COVERED AND DOMESTIC BOND YIELDS, JAPANESE RESIDENT

	(1)	(2)	(3)	(4)
(1) BY_JY_JY	1.0			
(2) CB_US_JY	0.79	1.0		
(3) CB_UK_JY	0.48	0.62	1.0	
(4) CB_DM_JY	0.87	0.84	0.49	1.0

CONCLUDING REMARKS

The objective of this study is to evaluate the performance of equity and money markets of four major countries—the United States, the United Kingdom, West Germany, and Japan—from the perspective of the resident investor of each of the four countries. The empirical results for the decade of the 1970s will, it is hoped, shed some light on the crucial issue of risk-return trade-offs and the influence of cross-currency movements on international portfolios.

The overall results clearly show that across all markets and for all residents, equity and bond investments in Japan offered the highest average yields for the time span under study. This conclusion is true for purely speculative as well as fully covered investments.

The dramatic and consistently superior performance of investments in Japan can be attributed to a number of factors. In the case of speculative equity yields, a combination of the best average performance of the Japanese equity market and an exceptionally strong yen in relation to all other currencies contributed to the final outcome. In spite of relatively low interest rates on Japanese bonds, net yields for non-Japanese resident investors benefited from a strong yen; for the Japanese investor, however, the negative currency factor diminished the attractiveness of foreign investments.

Covered equity and bond investments in Japan were particularly desirable to the foreign investor as the forward currency market offered the yen at a premium, due to relatively low Japanese interest rates. Other currencies were generally at a smaller premium or at a discount in the forward market, thereby reducing the attractiveness of alternate investments relative to those in Japan.

A suggestive measure of the contribution of currency movements is the ratio of the exchange factor to net yields. In the case of speculative equity investments, this ratio ranged from a high of 32.78% for the U.K. resident investor in Japan to a low of 7.22% for the West German resident investor in Japan. In the bond market, on the other hand, the contribution of the yen exchange factor ranged from 47.35% for the U.K. resident to 12.54% for the West German resident. In several cases, the exchange factor caused net yields to turn negative, verifying the key role of currency movements on overall yield performance.

A **comparison of speculative and covered yields** across residents reveals no consistent pattern about net average returns to investors. For the U.K. resident investor, for instance, covered yields were higher than speculative yields in both equity and bond markets. In contrast, for the West German resident investor covered investments produced lower net returns than speculative investments in equity and bond markets. The results were mixed in other cases.

In a great majority of cases, international investments had greater variability than purely domestic investments. This is true for both bond and equity markets, on a covered as well as speculative basis. As expected, the variability of covered yields is generally far less than that for speculative yields.

The market that offers the highest average return also has practically the highest volatility on speculative investments. This relationship does not necessarily hold good for covered investments; in fact, U.K. and West German covered equity investments in Japan have the lowest volatility and the highest returns.

The **contribution of currency risk** to overall risk is substantial in most cases, especially in the bond market. Currency variability as measured by the standard deviation was the highest for the yen for all residents. The impact of currency risk to total risk on Japanese investments, for example, as measured by the ratio of the standard deviations of the exchange factor and net yields, ranged from 89.70% on investments in the bond market by the West German resident to 40.50% on equity investments in Japan by the U.S. resident.

The correlation between yields in different markets for a given resident is poor. There is also a noticeable shift over time toward a decreasing degree of closeness between yield performances. This pattern is generally true for both equity and bond markets, and is best reflected in the correlations between performances of individual national markets. However, the correlations between exchange factors do not suggest conclusively a decreasing degree of association over time.

In conclusion, international investments offer opportunities for achieving higher yields; the choice of the investment country must be dictated by both the likely performance of the national market as well as that of its currency. Portfolio risk reduction was possible through partial and selective covering of exchange risk, but diversification across national markets by itself was generally not seen to be affective for the reduction of post folio risk for a given level of return. The latter conclusion is contrary to a generally accepted notion that portfolio risk can be reduced through internationalization. Finally, shifts in relationships between yields of various markets over time must be continuously examined and anticipated to improve the overall performance of international portfolios.

SECTION **8.4**

PORTFOLIO DECISIONS OF CENTRAL BANKS

CONTENTS

SECTION **8.4**

PORTFOLIO DECISIONS OF CENTRAL BANKS

Alan Teck
William B. Johns

The past decade has presented the international financial system with some of the most difficult problems and most profitable opportunities in recent memory. This section discusses how one member of this system, central banks, have managed their **foreign exchange reserves** during this period. There are particular references to a number of trends that are likely to become even more widespread in the years ahead.

For purposes of this section, foreign exchange reserves are defined as officially reported foreign exchange held by central banks, currency boards, exchange stabilization funds, and some government treasury departments. This component of total reserves, which also includes special drawing rights (SDRs), reserve positions in the International Monetary Fund, and gold, conforms with the definition and data in the *International Financial Statistics* of the International Monetary Fund. Gold, which also plays a crucial role in the international reserves of most central banks, is discussed separately.

Although monetary authorities do not release information about the specific composition of their international investments, aggregate data about central bank reserves and related activities are published by international organizations such as the International Monetary Fund (IMF), the Bank for International Settlements (BIS), and the Organization for Economic Cooperation and Development (OECD). However, the most important contributions about this sensitive topic were provided by central bankers from over a dozen industrialized and developing nations, other central bank specialists, and a number of commercial and investment bankers.

GROWTH OF RESERVES

As Exhibit 1 shows, one of the most significant developments in the international reserves of central banks has been their very rapid growth in recent years. Of the four components of international reserves, foreign exchange and gold are the most

While the people interviewed for this section provided information off the record, the authors would like to express appreciation for the helpful contributions of Geoffrey Bell, Mahesh Kotecha, and David Willey. None of these people would necessarily agree with the contents of the entire section, for which the authors alone are responsible.

EXHIBIT 1 OFFICIAL HOLDINGS OF RESERVE ASSETS, 1973–80
(in billions of special drawing rights)

Countries	Foreign Exchange			Special Drawing Rights			Reserve Positions in the Fund			Gold in Millions of Ounces			Gold[a] Valued at London Market Price		
	1973	1980	Percentage	1973	1980	Percentage	1973	1980	Percentage	1973	1980	Percentage	1973	1980	Percentage
Industrial	65.7	164.2	14.0	7.1	8.9	3.3	4.9	10.7	11.8	874	788	−1.5	81.3	364.2	23.9
Oil-exporting	10.2	67.1	30.9	0.3	1.2	21.9	0.3	4.1	45.3	34	40	2.3	3.1	18.5	29.1
Non-oil developing	24.8	60.2	13.5	1.4	1.7	2.8	0.9	2.1	12.9	109	107	−0.3	10.1	49.5	25.5
Total	101.5	293.3	16.4	8.8	11.8	4.3	6.2	16.8	15.3	1,018	938	−1.1	94.7	433.5	24.3

Source. International Monetary Fund, *Annual Report, 1981* and *International Financial Statistics*.

Note. Percentage change compounded annually.

[a]Gold valued at London price, afternoon fixing on the last day of the year.

significant. When valued in SDRs, foreign exchange accounted for 293 billion in 1980—almost 40% of total reserves. Gold, valued at market prices, accounted for over 57%. Although the amount of gold declined in terms of the number of ounces held from 1973 to 1980, it was the fastest growing component of world reserves. It expanded at a 24% compound annual rate when valued at market prices during the period. The foreign exchange component had the second-fastest rate of growth, increasing at an average annual rate of 16% in terms of the SDR. Importantly, these officially reported reserves do not include special funds that many central banks maintain with other government agencies and with private commercial banks in their own countries as an added cushion to be used as required. Some central bank specialists estimate that these unofficial reserves are almost 20% to 30% of the officially reported amounts in some countries.

Exhibit 2 indicates the rapid growth of central bank foreign exchange reserves among major regions. From 1972 (after the collapse of the Bretton Woods system and before the first major increase in oil prices) through 1980, the most rapid expansion was among the oil-exporting nations. These countries posted an average annual advance of 35.5% when reserves are measured in SDRs. As Exhibit 2 indicates, significant increases (at annual rates of between 20% to 23%) were also reported by the oil-importing nations of Asia, the Middle East, and the Western Hemisphere. Moreover, although the annualized growth rate was only 13.6% in the industrialized countries as a group, these nations experienced the largest absolute gain. The growth of 97 billion SDRs in their foreign exchange reserves accounted for nearly half of the total worldwide advance.

DIVERSITY AMONG NATIONS. Within the general pattern, there are very wide disparities among nations, not only in the growth rates of official assets but also in the way international reserves have been invested. For example, some countries, such as West Germany, have a policy of placing almost all of their foreign exchange reserves into **dollar-denominated assets**. Other nations, while holding most of their international reserves in dollar-denominated investments, also place significant amounts in other currencies. A dramatic example is the Saudi Arabian Monetary Agency's widely publicized movements into deutsche mark-denominated and yen-denominated deposits and securities. Other central banks, particularly in developing countries, have moved in the direction of diversifying their international reserves into currencies that approximate their trade or borrowing patterns with other countries. Still other nations hold reserves in a basket of currencies, approximating the SDR in some cases. Others have large holdings in the currency of a country to which they have strong political or economic ties. Examples of the latter are found in the French franc reserves of African nations that have historical ties with France.

With respect to **liquidity**, most central banks have traditionally kept most of their official reserves in very short term deposits, largely to have funds available if needed for intervention purposes. These deposits are usually held to maturity, and then reinvested in similar short-term assets. Portfolios with average maturities of 90 days or less have been most common throughout the post-1945 period, although some central banks have more recently started to move somewhat larger portions of their reserves into intermediate and longer-term deposits and government securities.

Many central banks are also expanding and diversifying their range of acceptable credit risks. In addition to placing more funds into time deposits and certificates of deposit (CDs) in the domestic and Euromarkets, using a widening range of world

EXHIBIT 2 FOREIGN EXCHANGE RESERVES OF GOVERNMENT MONETARY AUTHORITIES[a]
(in billions of special drawing rights)

	1972	1980	Compounded Annual Growth in Percentage
World	95	293	17.5
Industrial countries	67	164	13.6
Developing countries			
Oil-exporting	8	67	35.5
Oil-importing	19	61	18.1
Africa	2	4	10.4
Asia	5	21	22.7
Europe	3	5	7.6
Middle East	2	8	21.9
Western Hemisphere	6	23	21.2

Source. International Monetary Fund, *International Financial Statistics Yearbook.*

[a]Government monetary authorities include central banks, currency boards, exchange stabilization funds, and some government treasuries.

class banks, they are making short-term investments in government and, to a lesser extent, in government-guaranteed securities. Moreover, some monetary authorities now invest in bonds and equities of private companies with top credit ratings, although these investments are usually made through managed funds and are not included in the officially reported reserves.

The point is clear—although this section discusses general trends in the investments of official monetary organizations, each central bank faces unique conditions that affect its individual policies and practices, including the currencies in which its investments are denominated, the maturity structure, and selection of assets.

Furthermore, there are a number of reasons for holding official reserves and most monetary authorities pursue a number of objectives concurrently. The demand for foreign exchange reserves as a medium of exchange and a standard of value is determined by the need for working balances for international trade, debt repayment, and intervention. This requires that the primary and secondary markets for official assets have sufficient depth and breadth to assure liquidity as required. Official reserves also serve as a store of value. The safety of principal should be assured and the yields sufficient to at least maintain relative purchasing power. On the supply side, the currencies held in official assets are to an important extent dependent upon the willingness of nations to permit their currencies to be used as international reserves.

It is apparent that central banks as a group are now investing in a wider range of assets with longer maturities and denominated in a broader range of currencies than in previous years. In addition, there is a more active management of foreign exchange reserves and an increasing use of services provided by the private sector. These and other trends have significant implications for the future of the international monetary system. The foreign exchange reserves held by central banks have become so large that they represent a significant source of income and risk, and a potentially important force for stability or instability in the currency markets.

EARLY POSTWAR DEVELOPMENTS

In the years immediately following World War II, pounds sterling and the U.S. dollar were the dominant currencies in which international reserves were denominated. The important role of pounds sterling developed as a result of trade and financial patterns in the prewar period. During that time, the Bank of England managed numerous official sterling accounts under the directions of many central banks and other government agencies around the world, and this continued as pounds sterling accounts were generally blocked during the war. These funds were placed almost entirely into short-term, sterling-denominated deposits and high-quality government securities. Subsequently, a number of developments occurred that resulted in a reduced role for pounds sterling as the U.S. dollar became the predominant currency of international trade, investment, and official foreign exchange reserves.

Almost immediately after the war, there was a massive movement of dollars into foreign hands as the United States provided funds to war-torn countries and subsequently experienced persistently increasing balance of payments deficits. Until the mid-1950s, however, there was no significant offshore market for these dollars.

A number of changes occurred in 1957 that caused the U. S. dollars deposited abroad to be relent to foreign organizations and individuals. These developments signaled the start of the Eurodollar market, into which a very large portion of official foreign exchange reserves were, and still are, deposited by central banks throughout the world.

The sterling crisis of 1957, which resulted in severe limitations on the use of that currency to finance foreign trade, contributed to the use of the dollar as the main international reserve currency and the emergence of the Eurodollar market. British banks attempted to overcome these restrictions by using U.S. dollars for their foreign trade financings, thereby creating a substantial additional demand for dollar deposits in Europe.

At the same time, U.S. commercial banks were prohibited by Regulation Q from paying interest on demand deposits with maturities under 90 days. In addition, the domestic deposits had reserve requirements that did not apply to the Eurodeposits of foreign banks and offshore branches of U.S. banks. There was, therefore, a willingness among the foreign entities to accept narrower interest rate spreads between loans and deposits in the Eurodollar markets. Additional impetus was given to the growth of Eurodollar activity by the subsequent relaxation of exchange controls throughout Western Europe and the continual increase in U.S. balance of payments deficits.

During this period, the United Kingdom actively encouraged the phasing out of pounds sterling as an international reserve currency. Monetary officials wanted to reduce or eliminate the persistent conflict between domestic economic objectives, which often called for lower interest rates, and the perceived obligation to maintain the relative value of pounds sterling so that investors would not experience losses in international purchasing power. By the time the pound was forced to devalue in

1967, most central bankers throughout the world had already been aggressively reducing their sterling-denominated reserves.

By the mid-1960s, the proportion of foreign exchange reserves that central banks held in dollar-denominated assets had risen to an average of approximately 80% worldwide. About two-thirds of these assets were invested on behalf of these central banks by the Federal Reserve Bank of New York. Virtually all of these investments were placed according to the directions of the foreign central banks into short-term government securities and to a lesser extent into time deposits and CDs at large U.S. commercial banks. The remaining third of the dollar-denominated reserves was placed directly into short- and intermediate-term Eurodollar deposits either by the central banks themselves or on their behalf by the Bank for International Settlements.

In the mid-1960s, nearly all central bank reserves were managed conservatively. Average maturities were generally less than 30 days, deposits and securities were almost always held to maturity, and assets were placed either in short-term government securities or into time deposits or CDs with the largest and safest commercial banks.

THE ROLE OF GOLD

Gold reserves that central banks reported to the International Monetary Fund were 938 million ounces at the end of 1980, down almost 10% from 1018 million ounces reported in1973, as shown in Exhibit 1. This decrease is largely attributable to European Monetary System members that shifted about 20% of their gold reserves from the IMF to the European Monetary Cooperation Fund in exchange for **European Currency Units (ECUs)**.

When gold is measured at current market rates, as in Exhibit 1, this portion of central bank reserves is by far the largest, comprising 57.4% of the total reserves, despite the drop in the number of ounces held. It is also the fastest growing component when measured in terms of market prices, expanding at a 24.3% average compounded rate from 1973 to 1980. Whereas the changes in gold reserves measured in terms of either ounces or market prices were comparatively even among the major country groups, the proportion to total reserves varies considerably among the groupings. For example, gold valued at market prices in 1980 makes up 66.5% of reserves in the industrial countries, 20.4% in the oil-exporting countries, and 43.6% in non-oil developing countries. Furthermore, there are indications of large purchases of gold by monetary authorities going either unreported or being made indirectly through other government agencies.

Although central bankers generally indicate that they do not foresee an important role for gold in either the international or domestic monetary systems, they continue to hold the metal as a component of their reserve portfolios. A primary objective of official reserve management is the preservation of capital, and gold, rightly or wrongly, has historically been considered a good store of financial value.

Other central bank investment objectives, flexibility and secrecy, are also met by holding gold. As a financial commodity, gold is beyond national restrictions. Being without sovereign risk, gold adds strength and security to a government reserve portfolio. Secrecy in trading gold can be obtained by dealing through the extensive dealer network. Finally, central banks are not profit-maximizing institutions and can accept more readily than can private institutions the opportunity costs of holding gold. A possible drawback that establishes limits to the amount of gold that can be maintained in official reserve is a lack of liquidity if large amounts have to be sold quickly without seriously reducing market prices.

RECENT DEVELOPMENTS

In the late 1960s and through the 1970s, changes in both the international financial system and the asset preferences of central banks substantially altered the composition and manner in which many central banks invested their foreign exchange reserves. The following sections discuss four major trends: the lengthening maturity structures, a marginal shift from the dollar-denominated assets into investments in other currencies, the dramatic redistribution of international reserves to oil-exporting nations following the sharp increase in oil prices, and diversification of investments among a widening range of assets.

LENGTHENING MATURITY STRUCTURES. Short-term interest rates in the U.S. and Eurodollar money markets were extremely volatile during the past decade. They averaged less than 5% in 1971–72, rose sharply to just under 10% in 1973, and advanced into double digits in 1974. They then declined to an average of less than 6% for the next three years, and abruptly soared back into double figures by the end of the decade. Similar patterns generally occurred for yields in intermediate-term and long-term maturities.

At the beginning of the decade, virtually all central banks held most of their foreign exchange reserves in U.S. government securities and short-term U.S. and Eurodollar deposits. As interest rates rose, an ever-increasing number of monetary authorities began to invest idle funds more aggressively in overnight and short-term markets. Moreover, with long-term yields usually well above those for shorter term maturities, many central bankers shifted a portion of their assets into intermediate-term and longer-term deposits and securities. They wanted to obtain the higher rates and, in some cases, to match the maturity of assets with the maturity of long-term liabilities. According to one survey, the portion of international reserves invested in dollar-denominated assets with maturities exceeding one year rose to 50% by the close of the decade, from about 33% in 1974 (Kotecha, 1979). To many central bankers, investment in longer-term assets seemed to be a risk-free way to increase income.

This practice was to have serious opportunity costs, however, when interest rates continued to advance after funds had been locked in and when the yield curves became inverted, with short-term rates rising above long-term rates for many consecutive months. These developments initiated yet another phase of investment strategy involving the need for increased flexibility in portfolio management. At this stage of discussion, however, it is sufficient to note that the rising and generally upward-sloping yield curves in the early 1970s induced many central bankers to shift part of their official reserves into longer maturities.

DIVERSIFICATION AMONG CURRENCIES. By the late 1960s, about 80% of all official foreign exchange reserves were invested in dollar-denominated assets. By that time the dollar had become the main international trading currency, and persistent U.S. balance of payments deficits had shifted many billions of dollars to private and official organizations throughout the world. The depth and breadth of the U.S. and Eurodollar capital markets made that currency the most practical vehicle for holding large and rapidly growing central bank reserves. In addition, the dollar was generally considered to be a strong currency and a safe haven for preserving the international purchasing power of assets. This was in contrast to the perceived weakness of pounds sterling and many other currencies.

Throughout the 1970s, it is estimated that between 70% to 85% of the dollar-denominated central bank reserves were placed directly into the U.S. capital markets either by the Federal Reserve Bank of New York or by commercial and investment banks acting according to instructions from the foreign central banks. The remaining dollar-denominated funds were placed directly in the Eurodollar market or were deposited with the Bank for International Settlements, which, in turn, placed them into Eurodollar deposits. Deliberations of the Committee of Reform of the IMF (the Committee of Twenty) led to a proposal in 1974 to limit the placement of official reserves into the Eurocurrency market, and this was supported by similar understandings reached in 1971 and again in 1979 by the central bankers of the Group of Ten plus Switzerland. Although the IMF proposal was never formally adopted and the Group of Ten recommendations were never enforced, some central bankers accepted these pronouncements as a de facto restraint on their Eurocurrency activities.

The image that the dollar had persistent strength was shattered in 1971 and again in 1973 when that currency was devalued against gold by 7.9% and 10%, respectively. Moreover, currency values started to fluctuate widely after exchange rates began to float in early 1973, and the relative value of the U.S. unit began to move sharply in both directions. Changes of between 10% to 25% for each quarter were not uncommon in the cross-rates between the dollar and many other currencies.

Although there was no massive shift out of dollar-denominated assets by the monetary authorities, as no other currency could absorb a large inflow of investable funds, many central bankers did start to diversify their currency risks by moving at least some of their international reserves into deposits and securities denominated in other currencies. As Exhibit 3 indicates, U.S. dollar-denominated assets in terms of the SDR grew to 157 billion in 1980 from 75 billion in 1972, a 9.8% average annual increase. Meanwhile, pounds sterling investments actually declined, but funds held in deutsche marks, French francs, other European currencies, and European Currency Units grew very rapidly as a result of their perceived ability to maintain their international purchasing power and to provide diversification of currency risk. Some central bankers merely acquired more assets in currencies considered to be stronger; others began to match their reserves more systematically with their trade patterns; others diversified their currency risks still further by investing in **SDR-denominated assets** and other currency baskets.

Throughout the 1970s, the dollar remained the dominant reserve currency, declining only slightly from more than 80% to about 75% of total foreign exchange reserves. As Exhibits 4 and 5 indicate, however, there were some dramatic differences between the industrial and nonindustrial nations.

For the industrial countries, which often require dollars for intervention purposes, the dollar-denominated portion of reserves declined only six percentage points to 79% of total holdings. The deutsche mark rose to 11% as that unit's role expanded as an intervention currency, primarily among European countries.

In the nonindustrialized countries, by contrast, the dollar portion started and ended the decade at about 57% to 59%. At the same time, the proportions declined

EXHIBIT 3 OFFICIAL HOLDINGS OF FOREIGN EXCHANGE BY TYPE OF CURRENCY
(end of years 1972 and 1980, in billions of special drawing rights)

Official Holdings	1972	1980	Percentage Compound Annual Change
U.S. dollar	74.7	157.5	9.8
Pound sterling	8.1	6.9	−2.0
Deutsche mark	1.4	32.2	48.0
French franc	1.0	2.9	14.2
European Currency Units	—	47.5	—
Other[a]	10.9	46.3	19.8
Total	96.1	293.3	15.0

Source. International Monetary Fund, *Annual Report*, 1978 and 1981.
[a]Includes other Eurocurrency and reporting discrepancies.

for pounds sterling and advanced for the deutsche mark, Swiss franc, and yen. These changes partially reflect the fact that nonindustrial countries are less involved with intervention and more concerned with matching their foreign exchange reserves with their trade and borrowing patterns.

RESERVES OF OIL-EXPORTING NATIONS. Another significant development that affected central bank investment practices was the sharp increase in oil prices and the redistribution of international reserves that started in 1973–74. Oil-exporting nations, primarily in the Mideast, accumulated reserves so quickly and in such large

EXHIBIT 4 PERCENTAGE COMPOSITION OF FOREIGN EXCHANGE RESERVES IN INDUSTRIAL COUNTRIES
(valued in special drawing rights)

Year End	U.S. Dollar	U.K. Pound	Deutsche Mark	Yen	Swiss Franc
1970	85	5	2	0	1
1971	82	4	2	0	1
1972	86	4	3	0	1
1973	86	3	3	0	1
1974	87	2	3	0	1
1975	88	1	4	0	1
1976	84	1	3	0	1
1977	89	1	4	0	1
1978	86	1	6	0	1
1979	84	1	6	2	3
1980	79	1	11	2	3
1981[a]	79	1	11	2	2

Source. Group of Thirty, *How Central Banks Manage Their Reserves*, New York, 1982.
[a]First quarter.

EXHIBIT 5 PERCENTAGE COMPOSITION OF FOREIGN EXCHANGE RESERVES IN NONINDUSTRIAL COUNTRIES (valued in special drawing rights)

Year End	U.S. Dollar	U.K. Pound	Deutsche Mark	Yen	French Franc	Swiss Franc	Guilder
1970	57	20	2	0	3	0	0
1971	42	18	5	0	4	1	0
1972	55	12	14	0	5	2	0
1973	47	9	25	0	5	4	1
1974	67	11	10	0	2	2	1
1975	70	7	9	1	2	2	1
1976	73	3	10	2	2	2	1
1977	69	3	12	2	2	3	1
1978	61	3	14	4	2	3	1
1979	62	3	16	4	2	3	1
1980	58	5	15	5	2	5	1
1981[a]	59	5	15	5	2	5	1

Source. Group of Thirty, *How Central Banks Manage Their Reserves*, New York, 1982.
[a]First quarter.

amounts that it initially seemed most prudent, given the limited investment experience and expertise in those countries at that time, to place the funds almost entirely into very short-term dollar-denominated deposits with well-known banks in major money centers. Indeed, considering the magnitude and rapid growth of the official reserves acquired by the oil-producing nations, there was no immediately viable alternative to recycling the bulk of the funds into dollar-denominated assets. This is reflected in Exhibit 5 in the short-lived increase in the dollar portion of the official reserves held by nonindustrial nations.

As these countries became more knowledgeable (partially by retaining experienced financial advisors), at least two investment trends developed that highlighted to central banks in other parts of the world the possibility of using other strategies.

First, because large amounts of recently acquired funds were not required for immediate use, and as long-term interest rates exceeded short-term rates, the range of acceptable maturities was lengthened. This augmented the shift occurring in the central banks of other nations from the traditional short-term deposits and government securities into longer-term maturities. As Exhibit 6 shows, the short-term investments in the United States by the Organization of Petroleum Exporting Countries (OPEC) nations fell by 47% between 1974 and 1980, while long-term investments in the United States rose by 36%. The exhibit also indicates that the movement into longer-term assets was significantly greater than into the shorter maturities for non-dollar assets.

Second, the central banks of many oil-exporting nations began to diversify their foreign exchange reserves into investments denominated in currencies other than the dollar. This partially reflected a desire to spread the currency risk and partially a planned political strategy. Saudi Arabia, for example, acquired large amounts of deutsche mark- and yen-denominated securities, with annual purchases reaching the equivalent of $5 billion in 1980. The significance of this change in investment strategy becomes even more apparent when the increased purchase of nondollar securities is measured against incremental flows rather than against the entire size of Saudi Arabia's total reserves. Saudi authorities explained this diversification as a natural evolution reflecting their desire to have a stake in the West German and Japanese economies, from which they were purchasing increasing amounts of food and industrial supplies. It also reflected the desire for greater balance in their portfolio and an interest in placing at least a portion of their funds outside U.S. jurisdiction, a shift that was given some rationale by the freeze of Iranian assets during the Carter administration. Exhibit 6 shows that for all OPEC nations the growth of official assets held in currencies of industrial nations, excluding the United States and the United Kingdom, rose by 19% and 32% in short- and long-term investments, respectively.

DIVERSIFICATION OF INVESTMENTS. Another significant development in the 1970s was the shift by a growing number of central bankers into investments that had higher credit risks than those that dominated the portfolios in previous years. In the 1950s and early 1960s, virtually all incremental international reserves were placed into U.S. Treasury bills by the Federal Reserve Bank of New York, acting on behalf of the foreign central banks, into deposits with the Bank of International Settlements, or directly into U.S. deposits and Eurodeposits in the largest and safest world-class banks.

Although maintaining credit quality remained of prime importance, the range of acceptable credit risks was greatly expanded. Monetary authorities in the Mideast and elsewhere began investing in a broader range of domestic bonds, Eurobonds, and U.S. bonds, including those of the federal government, federally sponsored agencies, and major private corporations. In addition to investing in time deposits

EXHIBIT 6 ESTIMATED DEPLOYMENT OF OPEC COUNTRIES' INVESTABLE SURPLUS (in billions of U.S. dollars)[a]

Investments	1974	1980	Percentage of Compound Annual Change
Short-term	36.6	42.5	2.5
United States	9.4	0.2	−47.4
United Kingdom	18.2	16.1	−2.0
Eurocurrency deposits	(13.8)	(14.8)	1.2
Other industrial countries	9.0	26.2	19.5
Long-term	16.6	44.5	17.9
United States	2.3	14.3	35.6
United Kingdom	2.8	2.0	−5.5
Industrial countries	3.1	16.7	32.4
IBRD and IMF	3.5	4.9	5.8
Developing countries	4.9	6.6	5.1
Total	53.2	87.0	8.5

Source. Bank of England.

[a]Difference between current account position and identified foreign investment. (OPEC, Organization of Petroleum Exporting Countries; IMF, International Monetary Fund; IBRD, International Bank for Reconstruction and Development.

and CDs, bankers' acceptances were also included in the portfolios. Moreover, some monetary authorities began placing funds into the equities of top-quality private corporations. Indeed, when the portfolio of a merchant banklike institution that manages much of Kuwait's international reserves was improperly revealed to the public by a major U.S. newspaper, the equity section reflected holdings that looked like a cross-section of U.S. industry, much like the assets one would expect to find in a private trust or pension fund, (*The Washington Post*, 1981).

EMERGING TRENDS

During recent decades, most central banks adapted their investment practices to the opportunities presented by an increasingly challenging financial environment. This process, though not universal, resulted in several trends that can be expected to become even more widespread in the future.

First, central banks are investing their international reserves in a constantly **widening range of assets, maturities,** and **currencies.** There is a continuing attempt to increase income while preserving acceptable credit standards and reducing currency risks through currency diversification. Although the majority of reserves are still placed into high-quality government securities and short-term deposits, the range of acceptable investments for many central banks now permits the purchase of a wider range of government and government-guaranteed securities as well as bonds and equities of the private sector. At the same time, most central banks have lengthened the average maturity on their official assets by placing funds into longer term securities whenever it appears that attractive yields can be locked in without endangering appropriate liquidity standards. There has also been a secular diversification from dollar-denominated assets, particularly by the developing nations, with deutsche marks replacing pounds sterling as the second major currency of investment, followed by pounds sterling, yen, Swiss francs, and guilders.

Second, foreign exchange reserves are being more **actively managed** and the techniques of modern portfolio management are being applied more aggressively. Although a recent newspaper headline, "Central Banks Turn to Speculating" (*Financial Times* 1981), is probably a dramatic overstatement, many of these institutions have made important advancements in their quest for a more desirable relationship between higher income and acceptable risks. Virtually all central banks are aggressively investing overnight and short-term funds that previously remained idle. There is more switching among assets that were previously held to maturity in an attempt to maximize income when relative interest rates change significantly. Modern theories of portfolio management related to forecasting yields, evaluating the variances of expected returns, and finding ways to offset the variances are being more widely applied, although not yet to the same extent as they are in the private sector. In a few cases, monetary authorities are starting to use interest rate futures to lock in yields at attractive levels. An increasing number of central bankers in industrialized as well as developing nations are using outside portfolio managers, with discretionary and nondiscretionary relationships, to learn new techniques and as a benchmark against which to measure the performance of their internal investment officers. It must be noted, however, that these developments are still in the earlier stages of acceptance.

Third, private investment counselors are playing a progressively more active role in providing services for central bankers. In addition to various brokerage, custodial, and management services, a number of commercial, merchant, and investment banks provide advisory and educational services. Specialties extend from some of the more standard foreign exchange advisory services through personalized consulting tailored to the unique requirements of each client. In addition, a number of U.S. and European commercial banks regularly provide seminars specifically for foreign central bankers, usually to increase broker-dealer, investment management, and other types of business. As the private sector provides an ever-widening range of services to compete more effectively for fees and trading profits, central bankers are being made progressively more aware of their investment alternatives and the more advanced techniques of portfolio management. With the broader participation and services of the private sector, the role of public institutions is changing. The Federal Reserve Bank of New York, for example, provides an important safekeeping function for securities purchased through the private sector.

Fourth, many central banks, especially those in a number of developing countries, are devoting more attention to the relationship between their rapidly expanding official liabilities on the one hand and their international reserves on the other hand. Integrating the strategies of asset and liability management is becoming increasingly important, especially for almost a dozen nations in Latin America and Asia that borrowed heavily to finance their balance of payment deficits. Several investment banks in the United States, the United Kingdom, and France have provided some of these developing nations with counseling on debt restructuring as well as liability and asset management. This broader concept of viewing both sides of the balance sheet as an integrated unit will undoubtedly spread to other central banks as knowledge and experience expand.

Finally, computer technology is being used increasingly to provide fast and accurate information, to maintain accounting records, and to monitor and manage growing and increasingly diverse investment portfolios. Programs available on a time-sharing as well as a proprietary basis are being used to simulate alternatives for reaching the desired balance among yields, liquidity, and safety in a rapidly changing financial environment. This increased use of computerized portfolio management systems will continue to support and reinforce the continually widening application of the other trends mentioned in this section.

REFERENCES

"Central Banks Turn to Speculating," *Financial Times*, 23 April 1981.

International Monetary Fund, *International Financial Statistics*, Washington, D.C.

Kotecha, M.K., "Central Banks: A New Growth Market for Portfolio Advisors," *The Money Manager*, May (1979).

The Washington Post, 31 May 1981.

BIBLIOGRAPHY

Bank for International Settlements, *Annual Report*.

deKock, M.H., *Central Banking*, 4th ed., St. Martins Press, New York; 1974.

Group of Thirty, *How Central Banks Manage Their Reserves*, Group of Thirty, New York, 1982.

Group of Thirty, *Reserve Currencies in Transition*, Group of Thirty, New York, 1982.

Heller, H. R. and M. Knight, "Reserve Currency Preferences of Central Banks," *Princeton Essays in International Finance 131*, December (1978).

International Monetary Fund, *Annual Report*, Washington, D.C.

SECTION 8.5

INTERNATIONAL CAPITAL BUDGETING

CONTENTS

SECTION **8.5**

INTERNATIONAL CAPITAL BUDGETING

E. Eugene Carter
Rita M. Rodriguez

DEFINITION

Capital budgeting is a process of analyzing the financial benefits and costs of a potential investment in order to determine its overall profitability to the investing firm. Investment strategies vary widely from company to company; once a firm makes the strategic decision to undertake a certain type of investment, it then uses capital budgeting to determine whether a given project should be adopted or rejected. Capital budgeting is a purely financial tool that distills all the outlays on and earnings from a project into a single number that summarizes that project's contribution to the value of the investing firm.

There are several capital budgeting techniques described below. The two techniques used most frequently and generally considered to yield the most accurate estimate of a project's true profitability are the **net present value** method and the **internal rate of return** method. Both of these methods are based on comparing the cash investment required with the subsequent case flows generated by the project over its lifetime; these cash flows are then discounted by an appropriate discount rate to give recognition to the time value of money. The project is accepted if its net present value is positive or if its internal rate of return exceeds the firm's cost of capital.

Capital budgeting for international projects uses the same budgeting techniques. However the analysis of an investment is made more difficult by a number of additional factors which complicate the determination of the net cash flow figures and the calculation of the appropriate discount rate.

CAPITAL BUDGETING TECHNIQUES

Several decades ago, managers often relied exclusively on techniques such as **payback** and the **accounting rate of return** to measure the desirability of investment. Payback

---

This chapter is drawn in large part from the authors' book, *International Financial Management* (Prentice-Hall, Englewood Cliffs, N.J., 1979).

calculated the cash flow from an investment and the number of years until the investment would be recovered. Presumably, a quicker return of the investment was more desirable than a slower return. The accounting rate of return technique appeared in various forms; perhaps the most common approach was to calculate the average income over the life of the investment. Both of these techniques ignored the pattern of the cash flows, in that they considered a dollar of cash flows equally desirable in the first year of the project as in the last year. These methods had other shortcomings as well, among them the inability to take into account different levels of risk. In recent years firms have moved toward using two other measures of economic merit, both of which involve the concept of discounted cash flow (DCF): the net present value (NPV) method and the internal rate of return (IRR) method.

These two methods focus on two key variables: cash flow and discount rate. It is cash flow rather than income that is used for the calculations, since suppliers, labor creditors, shareholders, and other claimants upon a firm want cash, not profits. Profit is an accounting accrual concept that has value in other situations but, especially in the short run, does not measure cash flow per se. Since an investment requires cash, it is its ability to generate cash that must be analyzed. The second of the two variables is the cost of capital, or the minimum rate of return a project must earn in order to be profitable. If the rate of return from the project were lower, it would not pay the investing firm to go ahead with the project; the firm would be better off investing funds somewhere else, where the required rate of return could be earned.

NET PRESENT VALUE METHOD. According to Carter (1974), if one invests X dollars (e.g., \$10.00) at the cost of capital r (discount rate) of 10% in this example, then at the end of one year the value of the holding (Y_1) will be

$$Y_1 = X(1 + r)$$
$$Y_1 = \$10(1 + 0.10) = \$11.00$$

At the end of two years the value, Y_2, will be

$$Y_2 = Y_1(1 + r = X(1 + r)^2$$
$$Y_2 = \$10(1 + 0.10)^2 = \$12.10$$

Y_2 represents the **terminal value** of investment X at the end of the second year compounded annually at the rate r. One can reverse the procedure and find the amount (X) that has to be invested today at rate r in order to yield the desired amount Y_2 at the end of two years.

$$X = \frac{Y_2}{(1 + r)^2}$$
$$X = \frac{\$12.10}{(1 + 0.10)^2} = \$10$$

The present value of Y_2 is X.

In capital budgeting one must estimate the Y values (yearly net cash flows from the investment). This can be sometimes very difficult since the net cash flow figure should include all cash flows caused by the project, even those affecting other segments of the firm. Another complicating factor is the need to quantify nonmoney items, which necessarily involves a great deal of subjective judgment. These are then discounted by a discount rate that equals the opportunity cost of funds to the firm (the cost of capital), r (see "Traditional Cost of Capital," below). Then X, the net present value of the stream of cash flows, can be computed. This stream of cash flows includes the initial investment, Y_0, which is negative since it represents a cash outflow, and all the other future cash flows, which can be negative or positive, depending on whether in a given period the project generates or uses up cash when all the transactions for the period are added. Thus X, or the NPV, of the project, equals

$$X = Y_0 + \frac{Y_1}{(1 + r)} + \frac{Y_2}{(1 + r)^2} + \ldots + \frac{Y_n}{(1 + r)^n}$$

If this present value is positive, ($X > 0$), then the investment is considered desirable because it covers the cost of funds to the firm.

INTERNAL RATE OF RETURN. The rate of return is also called the "discounted rate of return," "internal rate of return" (IRR), or "return on investment" (ROI). It is the rate by which the future cash flows are discounted to equal the initial investment. It is obtained by using the same equation, but with a slightly different analysis. Instead of determining a discount rate (r) and then solving for X, the present value of the investment, the IRR approach sets X equal to 0 and solves the equation for r.

$$0 = Y_0 + \frac{Y_1}{(1 + r)} + \frac{Y_2}{(1 + r)} + \ldots \frac{Y_n}{(1 + r)^n}$$

Y_0 is negative, representing the cash investment by the firm in the project. These two standards will not always rank projects in the same way. Further, it is possible for a project to have more than one rate of return (this can happen mathematically when, during the project's life, some of the anticipated cash flows, in addition to the initial investment, are negative). One difficult assumption is that the project cash flows evaluated under a rate of return (ROR) calculation are presumed to continue to earn at that rate when reinvested (see "Terminal Rate of Return," below).

THE COST OF CAPITAL

TRADITIONAL COST OF CAPITAL. The cost of capital is the required rate a project must earn to be worthwhile. The cost of capital usually refers to the average cost of any funds (debt plus equity) used by a firm, and the project must yield at least that return to be considered a contribution to the value of the firm.

The cost of capital of a firm depends on the relative proportions and cost of debt and equity. The cost of capital declines as the cheaper debt is substituted for the more expensive equity, as shown in Exhibit 1. Later, the steadily increasing equity cost combined with the increasing cost of debt causes the cost of capital to level off or to rise. There can be one point or a band of points at which the cost of capital

EXHIBIT 1 THE COST OF CAPITAL

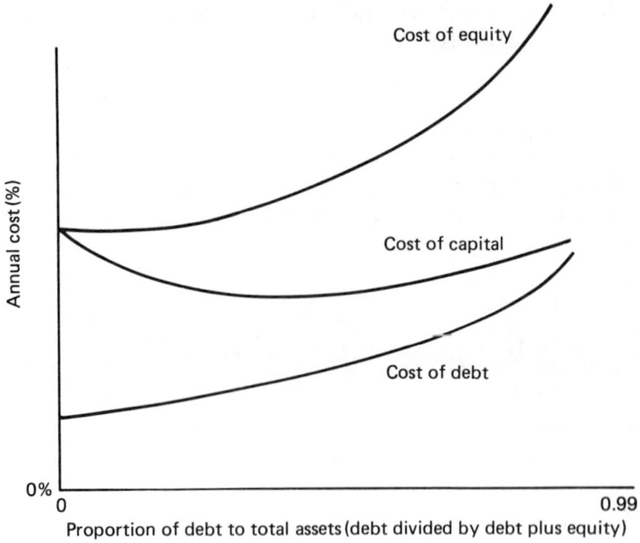

curve is lowest. This curve differs for different industries (dissimilar business risks) as well as for more involved financial structures, including warrants, leases, preferred stock, and so on. (For those readers interested in the assumptions behind this analysis and for additional references, see an introductory text such as Weston and Brigham, 1975, or Van Horne, 1981.)

The cost of capital to the firm is clearly related to the return and risk of the underlying projects. What is the appropriate cost of capital for projects of different risks? One can focus on the **cost of capital for this project.** When the corporation is a holding company, it can be viewed in effect as an investor owning separate corporations. The **weighted cost of capital** can be computed for each of these businesses either by noting how a local market evaluates publicly traded competitors of those units (i.e., what return it demands for that particular level of risk) or by discussing with lenders and investors the appropriate capital structure of these entities.

Internationally there are segmented capital markets, there is disequilibrium in the markets, and there are special financing arrangements unique to many projects, depending on their national location. When these imperfections in the markets exist, the determination of the lowest cost of capital is not possible theoretically. The manager still must find a discount rate by which to accept or reject projects in foreign countries. The way that local investors react to similar projects provides guidance in this endeavor.

An alternative to the concept of the average cost of capital is the concept of **return to equity,** one of the components of the total cost of capital. This approach can be particularly useful when special financing arrangements are attached to the specific project.

Sometimes management looks only at the return on equity, such as in a mining venture financed by a host government. In this case, the return to the equity holders is a function of the cost of the mine, the revenues and operating expenses, and the timing of the particular financing scheme offered by the national government.

PORTFOLIO ISSUES IN THE COST OF CAPITAL. There are often portfolio issues involved as well. Thus, a firm might invest in a project that will have spillover benefits (often called "joint effects") for other projects. Furthermore, there is an element of **diversification** involved in the investment in different geographic sectors, or different product lines, or different products altogether. For example, a natural resource company might invest in its home country, France, or elsewhere. The firm's managers know that if French duties on imports are increased, the returns from the firm's domestic mines will be more valuable, selling in a protected market that effectively reduces the supplies and thus raises the price. On the other hand, if tariffs are reduced and imports can profitably be sold in the market, the firm's domestic losses in part will be offset by greater profitability of its foreign operations. Essentially, demand for mineral products from any producer outside France who can economically ship to France has been increased by opening the French market to these imports. Thus the management and the shareholders of the mineral firm are somewhat hedged with a rare diversification—a downturn in one product from this cause (tariffs) is a direct stimulus to another product.

In general, as long as the investments are less than perfectly correlated with each other, there is a benefit from diversification, in that the total risk of the sum of the investments is less than the sum of the individual risks. (Correlation is a measure of how two variables move with each other, and ranges from +1 to −1. The standard deviation is a measure of the dispersion of one variable. The covariance, the product of the correlation times the standard deviations of each of the variables, is a measure of the joint dispersion of the two variables.) However, it is very important to note that the shareholders can diversify on their own in many cases. They can buy shares in a domestic firm and in a firm whose mines are outside France. Thus, in general, they might not be willing to pay the manager of the firm to diversify for them by having mines in various locations, unless such diversification results in a return to the shareholders that exceeds the return they themselves could realize. A major outgrowth of this view of shareholder diversification is the **capital asset pricing model** (CAPM) used in the area of capital budgeting for determining what returns the investors should expect (see Appendix). The model is based on the idea that investors must be compensated for the risk that is implicit in their investment; the return they expect is a function of the general level of interest rates and of the project's risk vis-à-vis the risk of investing into a well-diversified market portfolio.

FOREIGN DIRECT INVESTMENT

MOTIVES FOR FOREIGN DIRECT INVESTMENT. There are a multitude of reasons a firm might have for investing abroad; however, all of them have the common thread of seeking to contribute to the value of the firm. Profitability of foreign direct investment (FDI) is made possible by the imperfections existing in the international markets that the investing firms exploit.

A firm's motives for foreign direct investment can be divided into two categories: offensive and defensive. The first category consists of the cases when foreign direct investment is aimed at assuring the firm an advantage over its competitors, the other in preventing the competitors from gaining an advantage over the firm.

Comparative Advantage. Perhaps the most obvious reason for investing abroad is to capitalize on the existence of disparities in the relative cost of factors of production (labor, capital, technological know-how) in different countries. If a firm produces a very labor-intensive product and the cost of labor in the other (host) country is substantially lower than in the home country, then it benefits from producing abroad. On the other hand, if its product requires a large amount of capital, then lower wages become less important in making the investment decision.

Market Penetration. A firm might invest abroad in order to establish a presence in the host country, which enables it to gain knowledge of that market and to maintain visibility that will enable the firm to successfully compete in the market.

Reducing Costs of Distribution and Transportation. Foreign investment might be made in order to make a firm more competitive on price and/or delivery by enabling it to produce closer to the final destination for the product. An example would be a U.S. firm setting up a production facility in the United Kingdom to serve the whole European market.

Monopoly. Another reason why a firm would invest abroad is the erection of barriers against possible future entrants into the market. This can be done by taking control of the supplies (e.g., as in the case of an aluminum producer developing and operating a bauxite mine), or of technological innovation (when a company prefers to produce by itself rather than license its process), or of a distribution network (as in the case of an oil company controlling gasoline stations in the host country).

Among the defensive investment strategies can be included the following.

Preservation of Market Share. The product life cycle theory, a popular theory of foreign direct investment, states that firms regard foreign markets as extensions of the domestic market for their product. As the domestic market matures and approaches saturation, the foreign markets gain increasing importance if the overall market share and the accompanying economies of scale are to be preserved. The theory further describes the evolution of the firm's involvement in the foreign market from exporting to the eventual production on location as the foreign market grows to the extent where local production is not only feasible but also desirable in order to preserve the quality of the product and service, and efficiency and scale of distribution.

Operational Constraints. Some raw materials are available only in a few countries, and these sources may require location of the plant nearby if it is not economically feasible to transport the supplies to the home country.

Political Considerations. A firm might be forced to make an investment in a country as a condition of being allowed to operate in that country. The government of the host country might mandate a certain level of investment in return for granting the firm a business license, or it might simply make it very difficult for the firm to carry on its business in any other form but via direct investment.

Tariffs. Some countries impose high tariffs on imports and it is more profitable for a firm to set up local production rather than absorb the tariffs if it wants to maintain competitive products.

Market Structure. When there is limited product differentiation in a certain market, and a small number of sellers benefiting from economies of scale, an oligopolistic market structure induces a follow-the-leader strategy among competitors. To prevent one firm from dominating local or world markets, the other firms in the industry are compelled to match the first company's expansion.

Taxation and Investment Incentives. The management of a company has as its major goal the maximization of shareholders' returns, therefore, countries with very low corporate taxes are attractive for foreign direct investment. In addition to lower absolute tax rates, some countries have a more liberal definition of what constitutes taxable income, which again translates into a better return to the investors. Finally, some countries have very low taxes on receipt of dividends and/or low tax applied to dividends and interest payments that are remitted abroad. Such a country is ideal for setting up a financing subsidiary that receives dividends from one group of operating subsidiaries and remits payments to the other members of the company group.

Diversification. Another reason for investing abroad is the diversification of risk by diversifying sources of supplies, products, outlets for the products, and economic and political conditions, in order to lessen the firm's dependence on the outcome of a single investment.

SPECIAL ADVANTAGES OF MULTINATIONAL FIRMS

To summarize the above motivations, much of international direct investment occurs in response to imperfections in markets—ones that the firm can circumvent through **internalization**, the process of gaining control over foreign production or marketing. The other side of the coin, however, is the **ability** of firms to compete and profit in foreign markets. This ability is the subject of the following discussion. Success in foreign markets depends on the firm's having some advantage over other firms, particularly local ones.

In the hypothetical case of a perfectly competitive market for factors of production, host country firms would be able to purchase any technology, patent, or other advantage possessed by foreign firms, and because of the local firms' inherent cost advantage, foreign investors would never be able to compete profitably. Foreign investors must, if they are to succeed, possess some special or monopolistic advantage that cannot be purchased by actual or potential local competitors. The term "monopolistic advantage" is intended to suggest that a firm has some degree of monopoly control over its special asset.

Any firm that does not have, or loses, a competitive advantage over other firms must seek to create one. It must erect barriers to direct competition, and these barriers must be ones that are effective in many national markets—not just the domestic one. This means that firms whose dominant market position depends on country-specific barriers, such as control over retail outlets or state regulation, are not likely to be successful multinationals despite their size—witness certain European computer and aircraft firms.

Multinational firms tend to be oligopolies because of their ability to create and defend barriers to entry in world markets, but being an oligopolist does not insure a firm success as a multinational.

The **product life cycle model** describes changing barriers to entry facing firms looking abroad; the more general **industrial organization approach** argues that all forms of international investment are the result of the application abroad of barriers to entry in product and factor markets. Different multinational firms depend on different forms of barriers to entry, and although all forms tend eventually to erode, only some do so in accordance with the life cycle sequence.

Some international oligopolies are based on innovation, some on product differentiation, some on control of supplies or markets, and some on cartels, collusion, or mutual understandings. The behavior of these firms, particularly in response to competitive threats, differs accordingly. The common objective seems to be to avoid, wherever possible, markets in which perfect competition, or something like it, prevails. Three broad categories typify many multinationals.

INNOVATION-BASED OLIGOPOLIES. Firms such as Kodak (United States), Siemens (West Germany), and Matsushita (Japan) create barriers to entry through continuous introductions of new products and aggressive differentiation of existing ones, both at home and abroad.

Firms in this category behave most nearly in accord with the **product cycle pattern.** Their monopolistic advantages lie in their skill in bringing new products or new variations to the market, and so production location follows the product life cycle as domestic competition grows. But the decision to invest abroad depends not only on the need to protect and prolong an innovational lead but also on factor costs, scale economies, and transportation costs and tariffs.

Once innovational advantages have been dissipated, classical international trade and locational forces can reassert themselves. Many multinationals that can be characterized as skill intensive on the basis of their principal product line nevertheless retain a substantial proportion of standardized lines. If economies of scale or marketing have become important, they replace the innovation factor as a barrier to entry; the industry becomes a mature oligopoly.

MATURE OLIGOPOLIES. Industries in the mature oligopoly category remain concentrated long after their innovational leads have been eroded and the product standardized. They include the automobile, copper, and pulp and paper industries. The firms are able to share markets in the true oligopolistic tradition and fend off new entrants through economies of scale in production, transportation, or marketing, or through the economies of the experience curve. The latter concept argues that accumulated production confers cost advantages on a firm, although at a diminishing rate.

Because of the high fixed costs on which the mature oligopolists rely for barriers to entry, a major part of the manufacturing or marketing process operates at low marginal cost. Since this can generate instability when demand slackens in one country, members of the international oligopoly tend to seek strategies regarded as stabilizing for the industry. These include follow-the-leader behavior in entering new countries or product lines; pricing conventions; mutual hostages ("I'll have a subsidiary in your country and will tolerate your presence in mine"); mutual alliances (jointly producing subsidiaries, long-term contracts).

SENESCENT OLIGOPOLIES. All barriers to entry eventually fade, and, when they do, the firm must find new sources of differential advantage or be driven from the market.

What do large multinational firms do when standardization and decline in their product lines set in? The longer the oligopoly has been sustained, the harder it is to develop new products to replace old ones or to quit the industry. One way to prolong the equilibrium is to seek newer markets where pockets of imperfect competition remain. Some try to differentiate their products and brand names, while others enter into implicit cartels. However, market-sharing agreements are inherently unstable in the face of declining demand, and product differentiation, while requiring capital, is by no means an insurmountable barrier and cannot insure stability for market leaders.

When senescence sets in, multinational firms can respond in one of two ways. They can move production to low-cost locations. This can be done by contracting with third parties, but where control is important and barriers to foreigners not severe, firms have a strong incentive to internalize, and the result is a rationalized, integrated worldwide production system whose chief purpose is to minimize costs and hence prices.

The second and more common choice is to **drop the product**. Firms whose source of strength is product or technical innovation will do this readily and be standing by with new products to replace the old. But where the position of a firm in host countries is predicated on an obsolete advantage, entrophy sets in. In each host country, there tends to be a cycle from monopoly to oligopoly to effective competition by domestic firms. When oligopoly fades, so does the dominance of multinationals. If the foreign investor is unable to effect a strategy of continuous product rollover, or if its monopolistic advantages prove nontransferable to new industries, withdrawal must result.

HISTORY OF U.S. FOREIGN DIRECT INVESTMENT

Before World War I, most U.S. foreign direct investment was in mining ventures, and in the Western Hemisphere. (This material draws upon calculations based on Wilkins, 1974, and Schlotterbeck, 1938.) Over 33% of the investment was in Mexico, Cuba, and the West Indies, and 25% of the investment was associated with utility, agricultural, and railroad projects.

Foreign investment in manufacturing rose to 24% of the total by 1929. Along with the growth in petroleum and utility projects, the percentage loss was absorbed by railroads and mining ventures. These declines are relative, except for a few nationalizations, reflecting fewer new investments in mining and railroads. Mexico's early relative importance was replaced by greater investments elsewhere in Latin America. In the Great Depression, the book value of foreign investment declined from $7.6 billion to $7 billion, reflecting write-offs of assets. In addition, Mexico nationalized all U.S. petroleum investments in 1938. From 1950 to 1970 there was a 10.5% compounded growth in foreign investment in the first half and 9.5% in the last half. Investment moved sharply to the areas of manufacturing and sales, together accounting for nearly half of all direct investment by 1970. Utilities diminished in importance, and certainly by the late 1970s petroleum had also declined because of nationalization. Europe became the dominant location for U.S. investors, reflecting the booming markets after World War II, coupled with a desire of U.S. firms to take advantage of lower tariffs among European Economic Community countries for internally manufactured goods after the Common Market emerged.

DETERMINING THE INTERNATIONAL CASH FLOWS

When evaluating a project in another country, several issues alter the analysis from the traditional one outlined above. The following discussion focuses on the changes in the cash flows; in the next, the determination of the discount rate is addressed.

The key factor in evaluating the cost of the investment itself is to consider the cash foregone. In the simplest case, there is an investment of equipment and working capital that involves so many U.S. dollars. Thus, conversion rates, favorable government subsidies on duties, additional tariffs, and the like ultimately translate into so many dollars. However, the issue becomes slightly more complex when the U.S. parent, for example, contributes equipment that it already owns. The foreign government might permit a high valuation of the equipment for the sake of future depreciation charges against the income, reducing local income taxes in later years. Or the government can value the equipment at a low level, permitting lower import duties to be assessed; in either case, the local government is attempting to provide a subsidy. More important, neither valuation is relevant for decision-making purposes in the determination of the investment. Likewise, the value of the equipment on the parent's books is not directly relevant to the decision. What is relevant is the value of the equipment. Thus the parent could sell the equipment at some price to a third party, and it is that value, rather than the historic book value or the valuation placed on the equipment by the host government, that is the relevant price. The parent might also want to take into account that additional tax payments could be due in the form of depreciation recapture in the event the equipment were resold to a third party, so the net receipts from selling the equipment might not be as high as initially assumed.

In focusing upon cash flows in future years from the investment, the manager will look at various joint effects with existing firm operations, alternative techniques for repatriation of cash flows, and the issue of international taxation of the cash flows.

COMMON CASH FLOWS. Income from a proposed project must be reviewed carefully if the firm has the ability to realize some of the revenues regardless of the project. Sometimes, a proposed investment in another country will affect the operations of other units of the firm through vertical integration, such as a mining operation in Chile for a U.S. metal firm, or a sales subsidiary in West Germany for an Italian car manufacturer. The investment also can duplicate the parent operation through horizontal combinations, such as a lamp producer creating a manufacturing outlet in another country. When joint effects occur, the manager evaluates projects by combining total demand for the common product. Then the executives ask themselves, "How much extra business can we create from this foreign operation? For that portion of the business that is taken from an existing operation, what are the savings involved?"

For example, the ability to compete more effectively in the Brazilian home furnishings market might suggest to Frigidaire that the firm locate a refrigerator manufacturing plant there. This plant will have some sales generated from a new market, some sales taken from other competitors who are already there, and some sales that are substitutions of Frigidaire products that are currently imported. The first two components of sales are clearly incremental revenue. The last component, substitution of Frigidaire-Brazil refrigerators for Frigidaire-World refrigerators, might have differential benefits because of different costs of production and importation. However, unless cost savings are present, these sales are not relevant to the project. In the typical case the loss of the sales and profits to Frigidaire-World is a net cost that should be charged to the project.

Often, parents require supervisory fees from subsidiaries as a means of remitting funds from foreign projects. For the project, the relevant cash flow is the after-tax cost of what a real payment for the supervision would be worth in an arm's length transaction. A high fee, created to allow remission of funds from the project to the parent, has no relevance in evaluating the worth of the project per se if it is an accounting or political tool designed for currency remission. For the parent evaluating the cash flow from this project, the supervisory inflow after subtracting any incremental costs is simply one more cash return. On the other hand, taxing and business authorities in the host country might question the propriety of this arrangement unless both sides initially recognize and accept it as a device to permit cash remission.

A variant of the supervisory and/or royalty fee is the **tie-in sale,** in which the subsidiary must buy certain items from the parent. Sometimes this purchase represents an implicit royalty; other times, it is simply a device to insure quality control and/or a low cost to all manufacturing facilities on an integrated, companywide basis (the economy of scale argument for a component of the final product, for example). The conclusion on how to treat this item is the same as for the supervisory and/or royalty fee: It is the value of the product at an arm's length level for the project.

If there is a policy of many small local manufacturing outlets versus centralized manufacturing and there are substantial production economies of scale, individual projects should be charged for the additional costs involved in the diseconomies. Thus while IBM manufactures computers in many nations, its major models tend to be manufactured in one location and shipped throughout the world. Clearly, management perceives total shipping costs of IBM's large computers to be less than the costs associated with diseconomies of a smaller unit production when the machines are manufactured in several locations.

REPATRIATION. For the project, the relevant cash inflow is the return from operation after adjustment for local corporate taxes. From the **parent's** view, however, the crucial variable is the remission of funds to the parent treasury. In the parent appraisal, the cash flows are related to the investment—the supervisory payments after the costs of supervision; royalties, interest, and dividend remission; and loan principal and equity return.

Managers stated in one study that the key factor in a country's remittance policy was the possibility of remittance. Managers of many newer companies have favored parent loans rather than equity to a greater degree than managers of experienced multinationals, although the risk for long-term loans is similar to that of equity. This is because the managers of the newer firms assumed that loans were more easily returnable. Other managers felt that easy availability of equity from the parent was a poor motivator for the local manager compared to a loan obligation with fixed principal repayment.

Many local tax authorities recognize the legitimate concern of parent corporations about remission, but they are also concerned about the development of their own nations. A typical investment contract for a major project might specify the capital structure of the firm, and limit supervisory fees to a certain percentage of gross revenues.

CALCULATION OF CASH FLOWS. Patton Corporation currently exports 80,000 units a year to Country X at a price of \$4.00. The variable cost of producing these units and delivering them is \$2.00 for each unit. There is a proposal that the firm install a manufacturing operation in Palma that would cost \$800,000. In return for an increase in tariffs against other firms, the firm will agree to sell its product at \$3.50, to buy certain raw materials from local suppliers, and to use local managers. Total costs of local labor and materials will be \$1.00 a unit. Patton will turn over the investment at the end of five years to a local investor for the sum of \$1.00. Under this arrangement, the firm's managers believe they can sell about 15,000 units a year. Other materials can be purchased from the parent at \$0.50 a unit, and the parent will receive a direct contribution to overhead after variable costs of \$0.20 for each unit sold. There is a five-year straight-line depreciation of the \$800,000 of equipment. Taxes are 40% of profits in Country X and the parent country has a 50% tax rate with direct credit for Country X's taxes. There is no restriction on cash flow repatriations and the exchange rates are expected to remain constant.

Should they accept the project? The calculations are shown in Exhibit 2. The rate of return on the project is only 3.9%, and the company decides to reject the proposal.

If Patton Corporation executives believe that a major competitor is interested in the project then they must accept a probable loss in sales of the 80,000 units presently sold and, as a result, the basic cash flow of the project, \$259,000 a year for five years, becomes the relevant cash flow. The rate of return in this case is 18.6%.

$$\text{Rate of return on an \$800,000 investment} = \$259{,}000/\text{year} \times 5 \text{ years} = \underline{18.6\%}$$

Perhaps the Minister of Development of the host country states that it would be appropriate if all the cash were left on deposit locally at no interest. At the end of the five-year period the accumulated cash can be remitted to the parent. If the funds are blocked until later years, the only cash flow to the parent during earlier years relates to the profits in the materials produced, \$15,000 a year. Hence the calculations are

	Project	Parent
Investment	\$800,000	\$ 800,000
Cash flow for each year (five years)	\$259,000	\$ 15,000
Terminal cash flow (fifth year)	0	\$1,220,000
Rate of return	18.6%	10.4%

EXHIBIT 2 PROPOSED PROJECT

Cash flow generated by project	
Revenues = 150,000 × $3.50	$525,000
Variable costs = 150,000 × $1.50	−225,000
Operating revenues a year	300,000
Depreciation ($800,000/5)[a]	−160,000
Profit for tax purposes	$140,000
Local taxes @ 40%	−56,000
Profit after taxes	84,000
Depreciation[a]	+160,000
Annual cash flow in Country X	$244,000
Profit on materials sold by parent = (150,000 × $0.20 − 50% of total for taxes)	15,000
Net cash flow to parent with full repatriation	$259,000
Cash flow foregone	
Revenues = 80,000 × $4.00	$320,000
Variable costs = 80,000 × $2.00	−160,000
Extra profits	$160,000
Extra taxes @ 50%	−80,000
Extra cash flow foregone a year	−80,000
Net incremental cash flow	$179,000
Rate of return[b]	
$179,000 a year for five years $800,000 investment	3.9%

[a]Depreciation is a noncash expense, subtracted to compute taxable income, then added back to compute cash flow.

[b]The rate of return is the internal rate of return discussed at the beginning of this section.

Even if a project generates positive cash flows there is no guarantee that the firm will be able to repatriate all the funds. Moreover, alternative channels by which cash is remitted can have tariff and tax implications, so the method of remittance should be part of the planning for the project. These are discussed below; see also "Repatriation."

EFFECT OF A CHANGE IN EXCHANGE RATE. If there is a deterioration in the exchange rate of the local currency and if the analysis is computed in terms of local currency (the peso) and parent currency (the U.S. dollar) the results change.

If the expected deterioration is 5% a year after the first year, then the valuc of the raw material profits decreases if the prices of raw materials purchased from the parent are fixed in local currency, but the relevant cash flow to the parent is dollar cash flow above the manufacturing cost. The example included payment of $0.50 a unit and variable profits of $0.20 before tax. If the local currency deteriorates by 20% over several years, the value of the payment is really only 80% of $0.50, or $0.40. Hence, the unit cash flow contributed assuming production costs continue to be $0.30 a unit is $0.10. Thus, after a 20% decline in exchange rates, the margin has dropped from $0.20 a unit to $0.10 a unit.

The unit profits to the parent from selling raw materials after allowance for the 5% annual deteriorations in the local currency are as follows:

Parent Raw Material Cash Flow

	Year 1	Year 2	Year 3	Year 4	Year 5
Unit payment	$0.50	$0.4750	$0.4513	$0.4287	$0.4073
Cost	(0.30)	(0.30)	(0.30)	(0.30)	
Unit profit	$0.20	$0.1750	$0.1513	$0.1287	$0.1073
Yearly cash flows (150,000 units, 50% tax)	$15,000	$13,125	$11,348	$9,653	$8,048

Using these figures, one can compute the total dollar value of the project's cash flow even although some of the flow is not remitted to the parent.

Total Project Cash Flows in U.S. Dollars

	Year 1	Year 2	Year 3	Year 4	Year 5
Operating cash flows	$244,000	$231,800	$220,210	$209,199	$198,740
Cash to parent on raw materials	15,000	13,125	11,348	9,653	8,048
Total	$259,000	$244,925	$231,558	$218,852	$206,788

Dollar return on $800,000 investment = 14.9%

The decision on the return to use is discussed later in this section. The point of the example is that given the assumptions, the returns do differ considerably.

The effect on the debt-to-equity ratio of the consolidated firm is nil because intercompany loans are eliminated. However, from the standpoint of the debt-bearing capacity of the local firm, local lenders might be more skeptical of a parent's high debt obligation and by placing the parent's debt in a subordinated position this local concern can be dispelled.

TAXATION ISSUES. Foreign income can be taxed on a cash basis or on an accrual basis. On a **cash** basis, foreign income is taxable when it is received in the form of cash for dividends, royalties, and so forth. On an **accrual** basis, income is taxed according to the period in which sales and associated costs are incurred and the right to receive cash is confirmed. The actual cash receipts and expenditures might not have taken place or might have taken place several accounting periods before. Given the complexities associated with accrual systems, there is a tendency for countries to tax foreign income on a cash basis instead of on an accrual basis. However, the result also is a function of how the taxable entity is defined.

A broader definition of the corporate entity reduces the merits of this argument vis-à-vis the multinational. Thus, if Phillips, N.V., is defined as not just a corporation in The Netherlands, but in fact as a worldwide citizen, then taxes should be due on that worldwide income. Sometimes the parent prefers the broad definition for tax purposes; the use of a branch for foreign operations makes it possible for the U.S.

corporation to consolidate branch losses in earlier years, offsetting taxable profits in other operations. At other times, the parent prefers a separate subsidiary in another land when such an arrangement delays or avoids imposition of taxes by the parent's home country. This avoidance is especially valuable when the firm wishes to transfer funds from one nation to another. If the home country taxes profits only when these profits are remitted home, then a tax haven subsidiary that receives funds from a foreign operating subsidiary can reinvest these funds in some other country. Had this intermediate corporation not existed, the withdrawal of profits from the operating subsidiary would have created a homecountry tax liability, reducing the amount that could be reinvested in the other country.

Once the definition of a corporate entity is broadened to include operations in other countries, a question of jurisdiction arises. The policy among nations has been to avoid **dual taxation** upon the same entity. Country X will tax the operations of Patton Corporation in its land, and perhaps withhold taxes on dividends remitted to the home nation. The home country might permit Patton Corporation to receive partial or total credit for the taxes paid to Country X. Typical choices involve the option either (1) to deduct the taxes paid to Country X from gross income taxable at home, or (2) to compute the taxes that would have been due at home had all income been received there, and then to deduct taxes paid in Country X from the home-country tax liability. Patton Corporation managers typically will prefer the latter course; there is a full credit against the home country's taxes for the taxes previously paid as opposed to a simple deduction from taxable income.

Nations also have special tax treaties that alter the amounts that are paid or withheld in those countries. In these situations the subsidiary might not even have to file a tax return in Country X if the operations are kept within well-defined guidelines. For example, the United States presently has special tax treaties with more than 20 nations permitting this nonfiling.

Tax laws are influenced by special policies that are designed to achieve certain goals. A country might wish to sponsor particular types of development by granting major income tax concessions—such as lower tax rates, a moratorium on taxes, or rebates. Taxes can be deferred or reduced by trading companies or export financing corporations.

TWO SPECIAL PROBLEMS: LOCATION AND CURRENCY OF CASH FLOWS

The cash flows of a project, discounted at some rate, are the appropriate means by which to appraise the merits of an investment proposal. In the international area, there are some complexities based on the location of the cash flows and the currency in which they are to be evaluated. Then, too, one must wonder about the appropriate cost of capital for the project, which determines the discount rate. Would the cost of capital differ depending on the currency or the location of the cash flows? To answer this question, it is useful first to recognize some implications of a simple economic world with no barriers to the mobility of capital. The law of one price implies several outcomes discussed below if money is recognized as a homogenous commodity, even though it is denominated in deutsche marks, francs, dollars, or zlotys. After this review of a simple economic world's implications for international investment, a simplifying measure, the terminal rate of return, is shown, which can help managers appraise international investments in some situations.

PARITY RELATIONSHIPS. Three relationships are basic to parity: interest rate parity, the international Fisher effect, and purchasing power parity. The concept of interest rate parity suggests that differences in nominal interest rates among different economies will be offset through capital flows and adjustments simultaneously in prevailing interest rates and the forward rates of currencies; nominal rates that are 4% higher in Country A will be offset by forward market discounts of 4% in Country A's currency for comparable holding periods, assuming free mobility of capital. The international Fisher effect extends the argument that the real interest rate plus inflation rate equal the nominal interest rate from a domestic economy to the world economy by pointing out that currency rates are adjusted through the forward market and through future spot rates to accommodate the differential domestic inflation rates among countries. Purchasing power parity argues that international trade will force adjustment in exchange rates over time as market baskets of goods move away from each other in terms of local currency cost versus foreign currency cost.

It is possible that forecasting exchange rates and differential inflation rates and then attempting to protect oneself in the forward market or the money market are losing games. Such a conclusion depends upon the efficiency of international capital markets and upon a sufficiently large and sophisticated number of arbitrageurs who effectively transform currencies that they regard as homogeneous, neutralizing divergent monetary policies among central banks.

CURRENCY AND LOCATION. Even if one accepts such a calm view of currency levels for the future, one is still left with the problem of setting an appropriate discount rate reflecting the level of risk inherent in the project (see Appendix). If one assumes that investors can efficiently diversify their own (international) portfolios, then nonsystematic risk becomes irrelevant. On the other hand, limitations to full diversification (such as severe international information costs and transaction costs) can make it uneconomical for the investors to diversify on their own and therefore it will be the responsibility of the firm to diversity on its investors' behalf.

The following shows how one measures cash flow based on where the cash is located and the currency used to count it.

	Location of Cash Flow	
Currency of Cash Flow	Parent Country	Subsidiary Country
Parent country	A	B
Local country		C

Some of the studies of U.S. foreign direct investment have implied that the standard of comparison has been A—how many present-value dollars does the U.S. parent receive from the venture? Firms seem to have moved more to a position of B or C. In the case of B, the argument is to use dollars as a counting chip, but not to be concerned about whether the funds can be removed immediately from a country. If a firm plans to be a true multinational, then the fact that there are limitations on repatriations might not be very critical; further investment in the local country might be perfectly in line with the long-run capabilities and interests of the firm. Often what is desired is the possibility to remove the funds, even if it is not planned to do so. A third approach is category C, in which the firm says it will use local currency as the counting measure. In the long run, the firm is committed to that country and to that economy, and does not worry about the dollar equivalent.

The cash can be funds of the parent or funds available locally, but it is a bundle of currencies. For example, many shareholders in U.S. companies are not U.S. consumers. As West Germans or Japanese, they are concerned about a return (perhaps) in their own currency. Even if all the shareholders are U.S. citizens, to the extent that they enjoy Sony Betamaxes, Nissan automobiles, and Chanel perfumes, the bundle of consumption goods with flexible exchange rates means that their return should be a weighted function of where the money will be spent.

The difficulty of determining a discount rate in this case is considerable. Perhaps the non-U.S. investors see their investment as a diversification of their total portfolio remitting from an investment in the U.S. economy, and want the management to think in terms of dollar purchasing power. Maybe the U.S. investors are so divergent in their standards for purchasing imports that no weighting scheme makes sense. Perhaps they do not know what they will purchase in the future individually. Management, even if it were to know the consumption bundles, probably would feel that it has no ability whatsoever to predict exchange rate changes a year in the future, let alone five to 20 years, the life of a typical project. All one needs to recognize is that it is no longer clear what numeraire should be used by a parent in evaluating foreign operations. The easiest assumption is to use the parent's currency, but that is not necessarily the best answer.

If the market fully adjusts, then investors should **not** worry about these currency bundles. However, recent research suggests that the U.S. market is not exactly as fully efficient as some scholars have argued (Modigliani and Cohn, 1979). Certainly the U.S. market for securities, when one considers size, volume of buyers and sellers, transaction costs, and dissemination of information, is more likely to meet the requirements for efficiency than any other developed country's security market, let alone less-developed country's security market. The equilibrating process necessary to drive the security returns and the currency rates to their theoretical economic equilibrium is simply far beyond what most perceive as present in these markets today. The theory might be useful as a norm, but it is not clear that the norm parallels market actions very closely.

Returning to the Patton Corporation example, it is assumed the funds are blocked until the fifth year except for raw material purchases. The cash flows and the related return are

Cash Flows to Parent in U.S. Dollars

	Year 1	Year 2	Year 3	Year 4	Year 5
Cash to parent on raw materials	\$15,000	\$13,125	\$11,348	\$9,653	\$ 8,048
Terminal flow (\$244,000 × 5 years × 0.95^4)					993,698
Total	\$15,000	\$13,125	\$11,348	\$9,653	\$1,001,746

Dollar return on \$800,000 investment = 5.8%

Alternatively, the manager might wish to value the return in terms of local currency, pesos. Since the payments for new materials were assumed to be made in pesos, the local currency values and the associated investment and cash flow create roughly the same value as the return calculated earlier for a constant exchange rate, 18.0%. The flows must be adjusted for the decline in profits to the parent associated with the depreciation of the peso. The local investment is 8 million pesos (assuming an initial exchange rate of 10 pesos to the dollar), local income is 900,000 pesos a year, and the firm generates peso income for the parent as follows:

Total Project Cash Flows in Pesos

	Year 1	Year 2	Year 3	Year 4	Year 5
Exchange rate	10P/US$	10.5P/US$	11.03P/US$	11.58P/US$	12.16P/US$
Raw material cash gain to parent	US$15,000	US$13,125	US$11,348	US$9,653	US$8,048
Raw material cash gain (peso)	150,000	137,813	125,168	111,782	97,864
Operating cash flows	2,440,000	2,440,000	2,440,000	2,440,000	2,440,000
Total	2,590,000	2,577,813	2,565,168	2,551,782	2,537,864

Pesos return on P8 million investment = 18.2%

Thus, depending on the numeraire (peso or dollar) and whether one looks at total project cash flows or the cash flows received by the parent, there are sharply divergent returns associated with this simple investment.

Comparative Rates of Return

	With Peso Depreciation	Constant Peso/Dollar Rate
Total project returns		
in local currency (Peso)	18.2%	18.6%
in US$	14.9%	18.6%
Return to parent in US$ with profit repatriation blocked until fifth year	5.8%	10.4%

From the point of view of the parent company, there are two major problems. First, the currency is blocked. The parent has cash flows that are unused because of restrictions by the host country government. Second, in terms of the currency by the parent, there is a loss in dollar purchasing power.

These problems are acute in this case of a five-year investment horizon. Often the investment by the parent company has a much longer time horizon, in which case the impact of initial controls on repatriation of cash and changes in the relative value of currencies might be evened out over the long run, as long as local prices are allowed to change. If the parent intends to continue expanding a profitable local operation, a repatriation restriction is irrelevant to the evaluation of the project. The expansion of the operations would require that profits be retained and reinvested in the project anyway instead of being remitted to the parent company. On the other hand, a multinational manager with all foreign investments in countries that restrict repatriation should analyze the liquidity of the parent company (e.g., its ability to pay dividends). The other major problem, the change in the relative value of currencies, also acquires a different dimension when a long period of investment is assumed. Some currencies that were considered to be very weak against the U.S. dollar in the 1960s were strong during the 1970s, and very weak again in the early 1980s.

TERMINAL RATE OF RETURN

The sample project has been evaluated in terms of the rate of return of the specific project. However, a firm does not invest in a single project. It invests in a series of projects over time. From the standpoint of the parent (which requires funds for other projects) or the project (where there are currencies blocked by the host country), management needs to focus on the **reinvestment rate** of the cash flows. In many cases reinvestment will be in the project itself. The host country might have created high tariffs on imported goods, allowing the project's output to sell in a protected market. However, the condition attendant to this agreement could be that all domestic demand must be filled at a "reasonable" price. Alternatively, the original capital structure related to the project in the host country might have contained a large debt base linked to the financial cash flows discussed previously. In either case the cash flow from the project might have to be reinvested in the project, both to protect the viability of the project by increasing output to meet domestic demand at a reasonable price and to provide normal funds for expansion given the initial low equity base.

Even if reinvestment in the project is not required because of these considerations, the host country can block repatriation. Accordingly, a reasonable approach is the use of the terminal rate of return (TROR). This approach is useful in any situation in which there are unequal project lives. (A more detailed discussion of the terminal rate of return can be found in Carter, 1974).

The TROR requires the analyst to state the reinvestment rate for cash flow from a project. In the absence of this explicit statement, the rate of return computations implicitly assume that any cash generated during the life of the project is reinvested at the rate of return calculated for the project. The reinvestment rate assumed to compute the TROR can be the firm's cost of capital or a lower rate based on investment of the idle cash in short-term securities. It can change over time, reflecting alternative reinvestment rate assumptions. Whatever the rate, the cash throw-offs from a project are **compounded forward** to some horizon point. The initial investment is compared to this summed horizon value (the sum of each year's cash flows compounded forward to the same point). Then the internal rate of return is computed, which will equate the investment to that compounded horizon value.

Algebraically, a reinvestment rate, r', is assumed. Each period's cash flow is compounded forward to the horizon, n, at this rate. The TROR (r_T) is the rate of return equating the initial investment, Y_0 (< 0), and the sum of compounded horizon values to zero. Thus

$$0 = Y_0 + \frac{Y_1(1 + r')^{n-1}}{(1 + r_T)^1} + \frac{Y_2(1 - r')^{n-2}}{(1 + r_T)^2} + \ldots + \frac{Y_n}{(1 + r_T)^n}$$

$$= Y_0 + \frac{\sum_{i=1}^{n} Y_i(1 + r')^{n-i}}{(1 + r)^n}$$

Perhaps Patton Corporation considers another $800,000 project in Country Y with a stable currency and similar returns of $859,000 a year for five years. The taxation policy is the same, but none of the return is related to purchases of parts from the parent. Hence all of the $259,000 is generated by the project in Country Y. If free repatriation is assumed, the rate of return to the parent is the discount rate, which equates a $300,000 investment with $259,000 a year for five years, or 18.9%.

If currency repatriation is blocked and cash must be kept idle, the rate of return must be based on a $800,000 investment and $1,295,000 (5 × $259,000) received at the end of the fifth year. The return is 10.1%.

If the money can be reinvested locally at 5% after taxes, one can compute a terminal rate of return. This is the return for which an $800,000 investment will provide the amount received after five years from the project's operating cash flowand reinvestment cash flows. This amount is

$259,000 first year invested for 4 years at 5% compounded	=	$ 314,816
$259,000 second year invested for 3 years at 5% compounded	=	299,824
$259,000 third year invested for 2 years at 5% compounded	=	285,548
$259,000 fourth year invested for 1 year at 5% compounded	=	271,950
$259,000 fifth year received at the end of the year	=	259,000
Total at end of fifth year	=	$1,431,138
Terminal rate of return on an $800,000 investment	=	12.3%

The **net terminal value** (NTV) is computed in similar fashion except that the investment is compounded forward at some opportunity (reinvestment) rate and subtracted from the compounded value of the accumulated operating cash flows. However, when the discount rate is related to the cost of capital, this decision rule will provide the same accept-reject signal as a normal net present value evaluation. In the case of the project with low reinvestment rates the results might differ.

The terminal rate of return concept eliminates a major objection to the rate of return analysis (i.e., the ROR assumption of a reinvestment rate that is the same as the project's rate of return). The rate of return seems to be more appealing to corporate executives than net present value, even though the latter is technically superior. Thus, the TROR measure can be welcome in the multinational.

Whatever the method of evaluating cash flows, some cost of capital or required rate of return must be used. Next, therefore, the question of what financing mix a foreign subsidiary should employ is considered; subsequently, the cost of these funds is discussed.

DECIDING UPON A CAPITAL STRUCTURE

PROBLEM OF REPATRIATION. The capital structure of a subsidiary is determined by legal requirements or by the request of the host government, and by the protection afforded the parent if its investment is a loan. These are issues of practical tactics.

One rule is to borrow locally as much as possible. This strategy is followed in order to limit the loss if nationalization takes place, to reduce the foreign exchange loss from currency depreciations in the host country (assuming the loans are denominated in the local currency), and to serve as a motivating device for the local manager (who can be told that the capital costs are dictated by that environment and not by simple parent policy).

The cost of this approach must be considered. Sometimes, the interest rate differential exceeds any sensible expectation about currency realignments. A high local interest rate can compensate for the lender's reluctance to leave money in the local currency if it is likely to depreciate. But the rate charged also can reflect scarcity in the capital markets or the deliberate monetary policy of the host country attempting to encourage the inflow of foreign exchange. Hence the cost of the "insurance" is the difference in cost over the life of the loan for local financing versus alternative external financing proposals. If currency rates are stable and there are no major inflationary effects, borrowing locally at 20% versus externally at 10% means the borrower pays a 10% yearly premium on the amount borrowed to avoid expropriation risk on that part of the investment or to protect against the anger of the local interests in the event that the operation is nationalized with little payment to the investors. However, the small size and lack of depth of many local capital markets and the high cost of dealing with small investors often limit this approach. Moreover, the host government might prefer the multinational that brings in most of the hard currency needed for the project instead of absorbing local funds.

Just as supervisory fees and royalties are sometimes used to minimize disputes over the remission of some funds, many managers term their equity investments in the local operation a loan. Loan repayments are required by the conditions of the financing agreement. Thus, interest and principal payments are expected to have a better chance of approval from the host government than dividend repatriation.

If the host government complains about the amount of parent loans to the subsidiary, these loans can be converted to direct loans against inventory and accounts receivable. This change reduces the security for the local senior lenders, but gives the parent a legitimate basis for lending. A disadvantage of this strategy is that as the business grows, the inventories and accounts receivable are likely to expand, and this expansion requires an increase in debt commitment by the parent at the time when a withdrawal is desired. However, the growing business might be in a better position to substitute local debt for parent debt at this point.

PROBLEM OF TAXATION. A U.S. parent with a favorable outcome from a project might expect to return most of the investment by tax-free loan repayments and then pay a capital gains tax on the sale of the small equity investment in the firm when that sale is made. The Internal Revenue Service might contend that the loan principal is a dividend payment, and is subject to tax. The burden of proof is on the parent to show that these are bone fide loans.

COST OF CAPITAL FOR A FOREIGN SUBSIDIARY

When the parent company is making an investment directly, the parent firm's cost of capital is the appropriate basic cutoff rate or required rate of return. When the project is to be undertaken by a foreign subsidiary, however, the problem is a little more complex.

First, the return to be achieved must reflect not only the cost of funds but also a premium for risk. In principle, this premium can be derived from the capital asset pricing model (see Appendix). In practice, the international manager has to identify the peculiar risks of international business, such as currency, inflation, and political risk. These are discussed individually below.

Second, the international firm consists not just of a single unit but of a parent company and a group of subsidiaries in foreign countries, each of which can obtain funds itself. What cost of capital should be used for investment decisions and performance evaluation in particular foreign subsidiaries? Third, the international firm can obtain funds from a variety of international sources, directly or through subsidiaries, in domestic or foreign currencies. How can one quantify the exchange risk involved in borrowing in foreign currencies? Finally, how should the corporate treasurer treat the cost of financing that is "tied" to a particular investment, such as government-subsidized financing or foreign currency financing used to hedge the exchange risk of foreign investments?

In addition, Appendix A of this volume contains a detailed guide to calculating the exchange rate–adjusted cost of capital. Therefore, the following concentrates on a general discussion of the problems of parent versus subsidiary, of the necessary currency adjustment, and of tied funds sources.

OVERALL COST OF CAPITAL. The international firm consists of several units, each with its own financing sources, and each of which can be legally incorporated in a different country. In many companies, foreign subsidiaries are expected to obtain local financing as far as possible. Some managers have therefore concluded that the cost of capital in a multinational firm must be calculated for each foreign subsidiary and not for the firm as a whole.

But it is easy to see that this approach must be incorrect, because the very feature that distinguishes the multinational firm is that it is integrated worldwide in the sense that it can obtain funds in one country and employ them profitably elsewhere. More specifically, the parent company must be able to evaluate what rate of return should be expected from investments in foreign subsidiaries. The parent must therefore calculate its cost of capital. But this cost of capital cannot be limited to capital obtained domestically in the parent firm's home country, since it will often wish to obtain funds where they are cheaper and more readily available—for example, in the Eurocurrency or Eurobond markets. And what of funds obtained indirectly, by foreign subsidiaries? These, too, must be regarded as part of the parent firm's capital structure, since the firm might in effect only be borrowing through a particular subsidiary in order to obtain low-cost funds. In any case, the parent firm is responsible ultimately for all the debt incurred by the multinational firm, whether borrowed directly or indirectly through a subsidiary. Therefore one must conclude that the cost of capital for the parent firm is the same as the simple overall cost of capital of the international firm, based on all sources of funds at home and abroad.

SUBSIDIARY'S COST OF CAPITAL. What cost of capital should the subsidiary use for capital budgeting purposes? The minimal acceptable rate of return will vary with the riskiness of the country, the subsidiary, and the particular investment being considered. For the moment, however, it is assumed that the investment will not alter the business risk of the firm. Then if the parent company provides all the funds to finance a project abroad, it will use its overall cost of capital as the required rate of return for that project. Thus from the subsidiary's point of view the parent firm's consolidated cost of capital should always be regarded as the cost of funds provided by the parent, and used as the required rate of return for investments of the same risk class as the parent. The form of the funds—debt or equity—is irrelevant.

But what if the subsidiary borrows funds from local sources as well as from the parent? One approach, indeed the usual one, is to take the cost of parent company funds as the subsidiary's cost of equity, and then to combine this with the subsidiary's retained earnings and debt to find a weighted average cost of capital for the subsidiary. This method will yield correct decisions as long as one is careful (1) to include loans from the parent or any other part of the firm as equity and not as debt, (2) to exclude the subsidiary's debt when computing the parent's cost of capital, and (3) to make an adjustment to the cost of subsidiary debt to reflect the fact that such debt alters the firm's debt-to-equity ratio and so can raise the parent's cost of capital.

On the other hand, it is argued above that since the parent company is ultimately responsible for the liabilities of all its subsidiaries, subsidiary debt must be included in the consolidated capital structure and therefore in the overall weighted average cost of capital. In other words, a foreign subsidiary does not have an independent capital structure. This is not to say that the same cost of capital should be applied to different investment decisions; quite the contrary is true, for the marginal cost of capital will be affected by the riskiness of the proposed investment. In either approach, any proposed change in subsidiary debt that alters the firm's capital structure or riskiness will be reflected in the marginal cost of capital of the whole firm. But if additional subsidiary debt raises the cost of capital, it could be that some other source or combination of financing would have been available at lower cost, so that raising local debt was an inappropriate decision in the first place. In other words, calculating the cost of capital based on the subsidiary's capital structure does not properly separate the investment from the financing decision. Employing the overall, worldwide cost of capital enables the financial manager to more readily identify suboptimal financing decisions than does the practice of calculating the cost of capital for each subsidiary's capital structure. It is best to consolidate the obligations to third parties of all units of the firm, parent and subsidiaries, to calculate the global weighted average cost of capital, and to use that cost of capital as the required rate of return for each subsidiary's investment decision.

ADJUSTMENT FOR CURRENCY CHANGES. Since the required rate of return refers to a return in the parent company's currency, the global cost of capital is the minimum return that the subsidiary should earn after translation into home currency.

On the other hand, it is often the case that the management of a foreign subsidiary is expected to make investment decisions on its own. Then it is obviously easier to use the local currency for calculations. Assuming no controls restrict the transferability of funds to the parent, the expected appreciation or depreciation of the local currency can be added to the parent's required rate of return to yield a required rate of return in local currency for the subsidiary:

Required rate of return in local currency = Parent firm's overall required rate of return + Expected annual rate of depreciation of the exchange rate

A more precise calculation is provided in Appendix A.

THE COST OF CAPITAL FOR SUBSIDIZED FUNDS. A large proportion of the financing of foreign operations in international firms is project specific or country specific. The main reasons for this are government restrictions, such as limits on capital outflows or inflows, and government subsidies, such as the provision of low-cost financing for favored purposes.

Where government restrictions or subsidies force financing from a specific source, the cost of that source of financing will probably be different from the free-market case. One way to handle this would be simply to change the firm's weighted average cost of capital to include the cost of this debt in place of some other debt source, and use this revised cost of capital as the required rate of return for that subsidiary or project. However, this approach is less preferable than the alternative method of treating the interest differential as a subsidy or penalty that alters the project's cash flows.

As a result of the subsidy or restriction the firm raises an amount (A) of funds at an interest rate i'. Had the subsidy or restriction not existed, the interest rate on the funds would have been i. Then the subsidy or penalty amounts to $A(i - i')$. This mount should be added to the projected cash flows of the investment for each period, and these adjusted cash flows discounted at the firm's overall cost of capital at market rates.

For example, the firm of MNC International has a global cost of capital of 15% and is considering building a casino in Botswana at a cost of $10 million. The Botswana government offers MNC a five-year loan of $5 million at 10% whereas a similar loan raised directly by MNC would cost 12%. The annual subsidy is thus:

$$\$5 \text{ million} \times (12\% - 10\%) = \$20{,}000$$

This amount should be added to the first five years' expected cash flows, and the total cash flows discounted at a rate of 15%. Assuming expected cash inflows of $3 million during each of the first five years, the five-year net present value of the project is $123,500 and it should be accepted.

THE RISK FACTOR

It seems reasonable to argue that when two similar investment proposals are being considered one should be more critical of the riskier one than of the less risky one. Therefore the riskier the investment being considered, the higher the discount rate that should be applied. If foreign investment is more risky, a higher required rate of return should be applied.

In general, the cost of capital for every investment that is of a different risk class than the firm should have a different required rate of return. This is not inconsistent with the notion of applying the worldwide cost of capital to all investments, for the marginal cost of capital itself will, as a rule, reflect the additonal (or lower) riskiness of the proposed investment. If the investment will make the firm's earnings flow riskier, shareholders and lenders will expect a higher return to compensate them for the additional risk, and the firm's marginal cost of capital will be higher.

BUT WHAT ARE THESE RISKS? The risks of domestic capital budgeting are business and financial risks. There are risks associated with inflation and currency considerations. Finally, there are political risks relating to expropriation and government policies.

BUSINESS RISK. A financial officer evaluates risk associated with a particular line of business. Acquiring an established drugstore chain in a growing metropolitan area normally would be considered as involving less risk than the decision to manufacture a satellite reception disk for consumers. Business risk relates to the particular characteristics of the industry and the firm in question. Cyclical businesses have more business risk than noncyclical businesses. New businesses in an industry generally have greater risk than established firms.

FINANCIAL RISK. The return to the equity holders is related to the business risk plus any financial risk created by the presence of financial obligations senior to the shareholders' claim on the assets of the company. As a greater amount of debt or preferred stock is added to the capital structure, common equity holders require a higher return, since their financial risk is increased by larger principal and interest payments, which increase the probability of financial insolvency. The business risk associated with a firm and an industry has an influence on the capital sturcture. The premier firm in a high-risk industry is unlikely to have the same proportion of AAA debt as a firm in a low-risk industry with many marketable current assets, for example. In addition to these industry characteristics, there are different financial policies followed by the corporate officers. Some nearly identical firms might have relatively high debt (i.e., added financial risk), while others in the same industry and with an equally seasoned business have a more conservative structure, perhaps with no debt.

INFLATION RISK. If there is inflation, consideration must be given to the prospect of increased wages and general operating costs and to the firm's ability to pass on these cost increases in the form of higher prices. The market for the finished product might permit price increases exceeding the net cost increases. Alternatively, allowable price increases might be less than cost increases.

Labor costs might increase at an expected rate of 5% a year and raw materials at 4%; other costs of the firm, such as amortization of research and development costs, might not change if replacement of fixed assets is not contemplated in the near future. Accordingly, the rate of price increase needed to sustain standard profits usually will be much less than the inflation rate associated with many of the costs because the costs apply to a fraction of the revenues, whereas the sales price increase applies to all the revenues. Finally, the terminal value of the project should reflect gains on the eventual sale of assets at the higher inflated price for used equipment, assuming maintenance was adequate.

As a general rule, inflation that is widely accepted is to be built into the cost of debt and equity for the firm. The weighted cost of capital reflects anticipated price changes, and the cash flow assumptions also can accommodate these expectations. To the extent that lenders anticipate price increases, the cost of debt will reflect the cheaper currency in which they are repaid. Equity holders, too, should have a nominal return consistent with inflation and anticipated real returns, and the sensible calculation of the cost of equity should reflect this valuation. Unless the manager has superior forecasting ability, it is unrealistic to add a further increase to the discount rate derived from the cost of capital to adjust for inflation.

The cost of capital should be derived from current and future costs of debt and equity raised in the proportions of the optimal capital structure of the firm. Only current and future costs of funds include the expected inflation rates relevant to future capital projects. The historical cost of funds of the firm, the imbedded cost of capital, measures historical inflationary conditions, not the future inflation expected. Hence with inflationary conditions both the cash flow figures and the cost of capital estimates in capital budgeting should reflect expected inflation rates. Allowing for inflation in the cash flows without adjusting the cost of capital for the effects of inflation would make almost any project appear desirable. The increase in terminal value of the assets alone is bound to produce this result!

Inflation rates in the economic sectors in which the project will operate often will be different from the average for the economy as a whole. However, the overall rate of inflation in the economy is the one that investors will consider in trying to maintain the purchasing power of their money, and it is reflected in the costs of capital. To incorporate the impact of inflation reasonably, the cash flows should reflect the rate of inflation specific to the project, while the cost of capital reflects the inflation rate expected in the economy. The impact of inflation on both cash flow figures and the cost of capital should be considered separately and explicitly.

CURRENCY RISK. One of the main reasons that inflation in another economy is likely to pose substantial problems in capital budgeting decisions is the resulting reaction of the currency exchange rate. With a relatively high inflation rate and goods whose quantity demanded is sensitive to price changes, the country must depreciate its currency for reasons such as purchasing power parity, noted earlier. Relatively high inflation makes the goods less competitive in the world market and forces the country's balance of payments into deficits. However, over the short term, relative rates of inflation and exchange depreciations often differ. In addition, the inflation rate relevant to exchange rate fluctuations is an average of the inflation rates that prevail in different sectors of the economy, whereas a specific investment project will be exposed to only a portion of the various sectors in the economy.

POLITICAL RISK. The two major political risks, typically involving developing countries and/or unstable governments, are related to exchange and expropriation. In addition to the problem of a deteriorating exchange rate discussed earlier, an exchange problem associated with political risk is a block on the currency. There are brokers of varying degrees of legality who engage in the trading of blocked accounts. One way to eliminate blockages in such countries as Greece, Turkey, and the Soviet Union is to arrange swaps between two corporations, each lending to the other in the country where its own funds are restricted. In other situations, a parent can change a high rate of interest on loans to a subsidiary in a country that blocks currency repatriation.

From the standpoint of the corporation, expropriation is defined broadly. Full nationalization of ownership and complete involvement in the operation by the national government is an infrequent extreme example. Generally, expropriation refers to an increased and substantial operating involvement by the host government, which limits the parent corporation's role and reduces cash flows from the operation to the parent. What is expropriated is the owner's right to operate the subsidiary fully.

At the extreme of nationalization, the risk can range from complete uncertainty to a high probability of a takeover. Even given a takeover, there can be substantial variations in possible compensation, ranging from nothing to market value paid immediately. Assessing the probabilities of the various outcomes is very difficult and highly subjective.

The more direct political risk is expropriation. This can be gradual, with increasing demands for participation by locals or by the host government in the profits and ownership of the business. Initially, it might take the form of a high sales tax or the right to buy into the equity of the firm at some price. Often the price is extremely low and related to the book value of the firm. Later, formal plans for takeover can include a five-year phasing of nationals into key operating positions. The more dramatic course is a pure takeover, as, for example, the U.S. copper operations in Chile or the international petroleum corporations in Libya. When the situation warrants, the corporation's officers should consider the worst-case assumption, calculating the maximum loss if expropriation occurred in various years.

Positive approaches to avoid expropriation involve indicating to the host government the firm's interest in the nation on a longer term basis, and accepting an obligation to employ locals and to accommodate various control agreements relating to management, profitability, and investment. There might be arrangements for the government to have a long-run minority or majority position. These contracts indicate the firm's commitment to meet the government in achieving political, developmental, and financial goals for the project. Indirectly, the firm can provide for reinforcing the government's nonfinancial goals by acquiring capital equipment and operating supplies locally; by using locals for unskilled, skilled, and managerial roles; and by spreading equity throughout the local citizenry.

Among the negative approaches is control of the operation by restricting inputs or outputs. By having the local venture provide only one step in the process of selling a product (basic raw material development, or selling imported goods manufactured elsewhere, for example) nationalization of the operation prevents the government from retaining a viable business. Where there is a sizable producing operation that depends on external markets, the control of those external markets, of the transportation to those markets, and/or of intervening processing required to provide the final goods to those markets all restrict the government. A corporation that controls key licenses or patents has leverage upon the government, for operating illegally without these licenses brings sanctions upon the nation.

Finally, there are outside options. First, investment guarantees from OPIC (the Overseas Private Investment Corporation) or another source mean that any expropriation can be recovered to some degree. The determination of value might be very different for the corporation (which views the operation as a going concern) and the insurance agency (which might view it at book value). Such insurance programs have a negative effect on the host governments, for inhospitable investment environments are well noted by these insurance organizations and are transmitted to potential investors who inquire about insurance and risks. Such insurance can eventually be developed through the United Nations or regional insurance banks, for the collective benefits to most developing countries would seem to be considered.

Another strategy, followed by many investors in unstable environments, is to pay whatever price is required for local financing or for unguaranteed outside financing supported by the local investment. In the event of nationalization, the corporation negates any debt obligation, leaving the local lenders to fight with the local government about repayment. Alternatively, as occurred in the Freeport Cuban nickel operation, the major banks can be left to argue with the new government while the corporation goes on its way (home).

Finally, bribes are also possible. The OECD members adopted a voluntary code of behavior in June 1977, stating that firms should not make contributions to political office seekers or pay bribes unless legally permitted. This code of behavior also suggested disclosure of sales and profits by geographic area, and urged firms not to exploit any dominant market positions. The impact of these strictures remains to be seen, but it is likely to be negligible. Like the Code of Ethics for U.S. Congress the problem is enforcement, not standards, and there is no legal implication of the OECD code unless each member nation passes legislation along these lines. Even then, enforcement is hampered unless there is an exchange of information and other cooperation among the nations.

RISK AND DIVERSIFICATION

Consistent with basic capital budgeting theory, higher returns can be obtained only by assuming higher risks. But because of the covariance elements, the portfolio that allows the firm to diversify results earns a surplus return if there are benefits from diversification: The total risk of the diversified firm is lower than the simple sum of the risks of the component projects on their own. In this sense, the corporation can achieve through diversification among projects the same results as the individual investor who diversifies among companies.

Whether or not the corporation can do better than the individual investor depends on the corporation's access to projects in which the individual cannot invest directly. If one believes that the corporation has an advantage over individuals in diversification skills, then the total risk of the corporation for the given level of expected return might be lower than what investors could obtain independently for that expected return. This would be the case because the lower risk is available only to investors in the diversified corporation and not to investors who carve their investments from among the company's projects.

The ability of the corporation to create special diversification opportunities is challenged on two grounds. First, the cost of monitoring and coordinating the broadly diversified firm might exceed any potential benefits from the spreading of risk. Alternatively, some critics discount the existence of benefits from corporate diversification. They argue that the investor can adequately diversify (through investment in a mutual fund). Of course, these two criticisms are not inconsistent with each other. If both are granted, the broadly diversified firm is economically inefficient, for there is a net cost of coordination that is not offset by any diversification benefits unrealizable by individual investors on their own!

The corporation probably can diversify more efficiently than individuals in the multinational setting. In addition to information advantages regarding international opportunities, the major corporation has the ability to use special experience in an industry, to negotiate tax and repatriation agreements, and to marshal a large pool of resources.

CONCLUSION

The standards for international capital budgeting are still uncertain. Most people would agree that cash flows discounted at the appropriate discount rate are the first method of appraisal. Likewise, most would probably agree that the full cash flow, regardless of location, can be discounted in most cases. In a world of freely traded currencies, selection of the numeraire and the discount rate are largely self-cancelling; currencies that are likely to depreciate more heavily will have higher nominal cash flows in later years, but also will involve the use of a higher nominal discount rate, thus leaving the two factors to cancel each other to some degree. However, in areas where the currencies are not freely traded, this cash flow–discount rate correction might not occur. Moreover, these situations also are likely to involve barriers to capital entry and shortages of local currency, meaning that the appropriate discount rate using local capital costs will be significantly higher than if one were to undertake the project with comparable riskiness in a developed country. Beyond this issue of local capital scarcity, the international manager will be wary of various limitations on the mobility of capital and upon the operation of the firm, further adding to the required rate of return. Most international firms, then, probably will use higher costs of capital for a project in an undeveloped country than locals within that country would use. The multinational might have cheaper sources of capital, and its managers could be willing to implicitly subsidize the capital costs of the project. On the other hand, the firm has extra risk from being an outsider. So, one might ask, why do multinational firms invest in less-developed countries? Again, issues such as specialized tax subsidies, the unwillingness of local investors to handle the project under any conditions, substantial externalities vis-à-vis the firm's existing projects, and the ability to generate positive cash flows from operations through the application of special management or technological skills unavailable to the local investor probably are the major factors. Ultimately, as noted, broader issues of strategy and the positioning of the corporation for long-run profit maximization around the world might dominate the calculus of discounted cash flow for a simple project.

APPENDIX: THE CAPITAL ASSET PRICING MODEL AS A TOOL IN CAPITAL BUDGETING

The capital asset pricing model (CAPM) implies that the relevant discount rate for a project is based on the covariance between the return of that project and the return of market portfolio (i.e., some well-diversified portfolio). This covariance is combined with an estimate of the expected market return and the return from a risk-free asset to determine the required return for the project.

Any investor could purchase some combination of the market portfolio and the risk-free asset. The market line connecting these possible combinations, shown in Exhibit 3, provides the trade-offs between risk and return available to an investor.

EXHIBIT 3 THE MARKET PORTFOLIO AND THE MARKET LINE

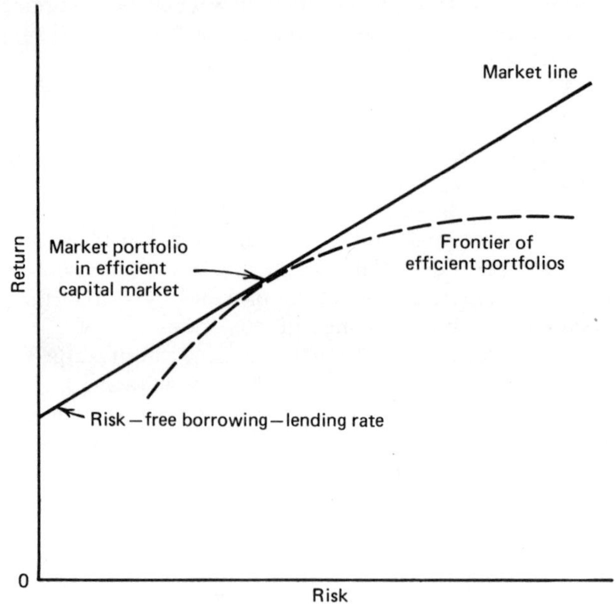

Thus an investor who placed half of his or her funds in the risk-free asset and half in the market portfolio would have an expected return that is half the sum of these two expected returns. Given zero correlation between the risk-free return and the market return, the standard deviation of return (the measure of risk) also would be half the sum of the two standard deviations. Risk and return of other mixtures of the risk-free asset and the market portfolio would fall on the line traced in Exhibit 3.

Using the forecasts of the market return and its variability, the risk-free rate, and the various project returns under different market outcomes, then the minimum required rate of return for a project can be determined. One can compare the return of a portfolio (R_P) to the risk-free return (R_F) and the market return (R_M) through the following formulation.

$$(R_P - R_F) = \alpha + \beta(R_M - R_F)$$

Beta is the measure of the volatility of the security or portfolio (i.e., mutual fund) with respect to the market return. Beta is the covariance of the security with the market divided by the variance of the market return. Alpha is a measure of an excess return for the mutual fund or security above what is required given its volatility. A negative alpha implies that the return of the fund or security over the periods evaluated was not sufficient to compensate investors for its volatility.

For project evaluations, the alpha is removed and one rearranges terms to solve for R_E, the required return on equity in the project. This gives the result *

*Note that σ_{EM}/σ_M^2 represents the covariance between the equity and market returns divided by the variance of the market return.

$$R_E = \beta(R_M - R_F) + R_F$$

or, since

$$\beta = \frac{\sigma_{EM}}{\sigma_M^2}$$

$$R_E = (R_M - R_F) + R_F$$

$$= R_F\,(1 - \frac{\sigma_{EM}}{\sigma_M^2}) + R_M \frac{\sigma_{EM}}{\sigma_M^2}$$

The required project return will be a weighted function of the returns and proportionate financing of debt and equity in the project's financing, or

$$R_{project} = R_E \left(\frac{E}{D + E}\right) + R_D \left(\frac{E}{D + E}\right)$$

where R_E is found as shown in the previous paragraph by using the covariance of the project and the market and an estimated beta.

Even if beta can be estimated from similar projects or the returns of similar firms in the market, if there is any leverage the observed beta will not be the same as the beta for a form or project with different leverage. Then the manager must decide how to compute a cost of capital for a project with leverage that differs from the standard computed above. (For a solution to this problem, see Rodriguez and Carter 1979.)

The theoretical impact of this model is substantial. What makes its application difficult in practical situations is the determination of reasonable forecasts for the market return and the risk-free return in the future. Whatever the estimation problems in the risk-free return evaluation, the biggest question is, What is the market return? When it is in the international setting, is it the return in the home country's security market? Management desires project returns; therefore, some judgment must be made about the market return in different periods. If this figure is used as the estimate of the future market return, then the links between variability in that market return in future years and the equity returns of the projects under review must be determined when the appropriate debt load for the project is included.

REFERENCES

Carter, E. E., *Portfolio Aspects of Corporate Capital Budgeting*, Heath, Lexington, Mass., 1974.

Lewis, C. assisted by K. T. Schlotterback, *America's Stake in International Investments*, Washington, D.C., The Brookings Institution, 1938.

Modigliani, F. and R. Cohn, "Inflation, Rational Valuation, and the Market," *Financial Analysts' Journal* (March–April 1979).

Rodriguez, R. M. and E. E. Carter, *International Financial Management*, Prentice-Hall, Englewood Cliffs, N.J., 1979.

Van Horne, J. C., *Financial Management and Policy*, 5th ed., Dryden Press, Hinsdale, Ill., 1975.

Weston, J. F. and E. F. Brigham, *Managerial Finance*, 5th ed., Dryden Press, Hinsdale, Ill., 1975.

Wilkins, M., *The Maturing of Multinational Enterprise*, Harvard University Press, Boston, 1974.

SECTION 8.6

INTERNATIONAL ACCOUNTING

CONTENTS

SECTION **8.6**

INTERNATIONAL ACCOUNTING

Lee H. Radebaugh

THE ACCOUNTING FUNCTION

Thus far this book has focused primarily on using international capital markets and managing the finance function. Financial managers would be unable to make quality decisions without access to quality information. It is the role of the accounting or controllership function to provide accurate, up-to-date information to financial managers. In addition, the accounting group is responsible for providing information for external users of financial statements, such as investors, creditors, government regulatory agencies, unions, and consumer groups. The accounting group is also integrally involved in planning, budgeting, performance evaluation, pricing decisions, and the control of corporate assets.

Obviously, these functions are performed domestically as well as internationally. However, there are a number of factors that influence the quality of information provided to financial groups, such as different accounting standards and disclosure practices worldwide, foreign currencies that affect the way corporate assets and liabilities are valued, and intracorporate transfer pricing practices. These issues are incorporated in the discussion herein of three key topics: general accounting standards and disclosure practices worldwide, financial accounting and reporting issues, and managerial accounting issues.

GENERAL ACCOUNTING STANDARDS AND DISCLOSURE PRACTICES

DIFFERENCES IN ACCOUNTING STANDARDS. It is a given fact that accounting standards and practices vary, sometimes significantly, from country to country. It is important to realize, however, that there is a difference between requirements for disclosure of information to external users and the basic accounting standards and practices that underlie the financial statements used internally or externally. Accounting standards and practices determine how economic events are recorded in the books and records of a company. Disclosure standards determine how this information is presented to external users of the financial statements, such as the investors and creditors mentioned above. Although the two are separate issues, they are obviously related and are not developed independently of each other.

The fact that accounting standards do vary from country to country puts a lot of pressure on a multinational corporation's information system. It would be impossible to compare investment opportunities in different countries if pro forma financial statements were developed under different assumptions for the recognition of revenues and expenses. Likewise, comparative performance evaluation of subsidiaries and affiliates in different countries would be meaningless if financial statements were not based on the same assumptions. Thus most multinational companies (MNCs) need to develop a uniform international accounting system that identifies each account in the company's chart of accounts, explains how each account is to be valued (historical cost, lower of cost or market, etc.), and demonstrates how each account is to be presented in the financial statements. This is not easy to do, because accounting personnel worldwide must adhere to exactly the same accounting practices if the MNC is to receive accurate, timely, and comparable information. This is helpful for internal purposes as well as for the preparation of information to be disclosed to external users of the financial statements.

In spite of the need for uniform standards and practices for home office use, the MNC must also allow its local affiliates to keep financial records according to local standards in order to satisfy the demands of local capital markets, government regulations, taxing authorities, and the like. These standards could vary significantly, such as in Peru, where consolidation of related companies is not allowed; Sweden, where significant inventory write-downs are allowed; or France and Germany, where tax accounting and book accounting are required to be the same. Thus the MNC is faced with keeping multiple sets of legitimate books to satisfy home office and local affiliate requirements. This is not only costly but confusing, especially if local personnel have trouble reconciling the different sets of books and deciding which ones to use in order to evaluate operational performance.

REASONS FOR DIFFERENCES. Accounting objectives, standards, and practices depend ultimately on the users of the financial statements and the extent of user group influence over the setting of standards. In many developing countries where capital markets are relatively thin and unimportant, most firms tend to be closely held and not really interested in outside equity funds. Thus management determines what information it wants and in what form. Accounting standards are often very primitive in this case, and the accounting profession tends to be fairly inactive and disinterested in developing more sophisticated standards.

In the United States, where there is a broadly based, relatively active capital market, accounting standards are very highly developed by an active profession through the privately funded and independent **Financial Accounting Standards Board** (FASB). The Securities and Exchange Commission (SEC) actively intervenes in behalf of the government, but more in the area of disclosure than the setting of accounting standards and practices.

In most other countries of the world, with the notable exceptions of the United Kingdom, The Netherlands, Australia, and Canada, governments have the greatest influence on the setting of accounting standards. This may be due to an absence of interest on the part of the accounting profession, or because the government is interested in certain standards to aid in fiscal policy and economic development.

Whatever the source of standards, be it the private or public sector, local environment characteristics as well as international influences are instrumental. Hyperinflationary countries such as Brazil and Chile instituted inflation-adjusted accounting standards long before the FASB issued the Statement of Financial Accounting Standards 33 (SFAS 33) for U.S. companies to follow. Educational factors such as the literacy level, specialized training in accounting, availability of management development courses, can also influence the level of sophistication that a country can allow for its accounting system. The legal and political systems of a country can also be influential. The strict adherence to codified legal systems in France and Germany has spawned equally legalistic accounting systems in those countries, as opposed to a more flexible system that one would expect in a common-law country like the United Kingdom. Central command economies like those of Eastern Europe and economies where the government is strongly involved in the ownership and/or control of economic resources (such as Egypt, Peru, and France) find strong government sentiment to standardize accounting principles and practices in order to help direct economic activity, as indicated previously.

International influences come most strongly from former colonial ties. Thus former British and French colonies tend to adopt the accounting systems of their former colonial powers. In a similar fashion countries that have been strongly influenced by the economic strength of U.S. foreign investment, such as Canada and many Latin American countries, have adopted many aspects of the U.S. accounting system. Regional and international groups such as the European Economic Community, the United Nations, and the International Accounting Standards Committee are influencing standards worldwide, but these influences are examined more specifically in "Harmonization of Standards," this section.

DISCLOSURE STANDARDS. Of more immediate concern to the financial manager is the disclosure of information in different capital markets. Obviously U.S. firms that have struggled to comply with disclosure requirements instituted by the Securities and Exchange Commission have an advantage over firms in most other countries due to the stiff requirements of the SEC. A commentary in *The Economist* on a *Financial Times* survey published in 1979 stated: "The Italians generate much hot air but little hard fact: [the] 175-page annual report from Fiat is described as the most useless in the whole survey. The British provide [the] best financial information, but the least data about employees. The Swiss, whose natural reticence provides much of their national income, score predictably low marks. . . . Socially conscious Swedes . . . produce the best profit forecasts."

The point is that disclosure requirements in each national capital market need to be understood and followed. These requirements may necessitate information being prepared in accounting terms different from U.S. **generally accepted accounting principles** (GAAP), and they may necessitate different information than is required in the United States. It has become fairly clear in recent years that the international mobility of capital has had the greatest influence on the harmonization of disclosure practices, and these practices have tended to follow the high standards perfected in the United States. There is no attempt at this point to outline the disclosure requirements in all capital markets for U.S. firms interested in using those markets, but the following issues need to be addressed in each individual market.

1. Can my financial statements be in English, or do they have to be translated into the local language?
2. Can my financial statements be in dollars, or do they have to be translated into local currency units?
3. Can my financial statements be presented according to U.S. GAAP, or do they have to be recast in terms of local GAAP?

One variation of the latter is to present financial statements according to U.S. GAAP but explain the major differences between U.S. and local GAAP and restate a few key numbers, such as net income and total assets or net worth.

HARMONIZATION OF STANDARDS. The efforts to harmonize accounting standards and practices and disclosure requirements are occurring on a regional as well as international basis. On a regional basis, the most ambitious and potentially most effective efforts are taking place in the European Economic Community (EEC). The EEC rules, in some cases, could apply to all firms operating in an EEC country, even firms that are owned by U.S. parent companies. The EEC was originally interested in standardizing accounting principles, but this idea was dropped in favor of the harmonization of minimum standards of reporting. Procedurally, the EEC's commission is empowered to set directives, which are orders to the member states to bring their laws into line with the requirements within a certain period. The EEC tends to move slowly in issuing its directives, which creates impatience among the members, but this process allows wide discussion among countries with very divergent views. The impact of the harmonization process is that countries can no longer set company laws in isolation of EEC deliberations.

In 1978, the fourth directive, which deals with the content, object, and format of accounts, including specific disclosure provisions, was released. That directive requires firms to select among two different balance sheets and four different income statement formats. Although all countries were supposed to have adopted the directive by February 1982, only Denmark had done so as of late 1981. With the possible exception of the United Kingdom, progress has been so slow elsewhere that it appears unlikely that the 1982 deadline will be anywhere close to being met.

What is the implication of the fourth directive to U.S. firms? When the fourth directive goes into effect, multinational companies will have to adhere to the EEC's rules for reporting formats, accounting principles, and footnote disclosures because they will be incorporated into national legislation (see Ernst and Whinney, 1980). Because of numerous differences between the Fourth Directive and U.S. GAAP, EEC subsidiaries of U.S. companies will need to keep two different sets of books.

A proposed Seventh Directive on consolidated accounts is currently being debated, but wide differences of opinion as to how consolidation should take place is hampering any progress there. This proposed Directive has been of concern to non-EEC companies operating in the EEC because it proposes a separate consolidation of all operations that a parent firm has in the EEC. One proposed solution that would satisfy U.S. companies would be to preclude a separate EEC consolidation if: (1) the EEC companies are included in a global consolidation, (2) the global consolidation is prepared in a manner comparable to that prescribed by the Seventh Directive, (3) this is verified by auditors of the global accounts, and (4) these verifications are published by the EEC company as required under the First Directive. United States firms would probably be able to comply with these rules, but Japanese and Swiss companies could be in trouble given their current levels of nondisclosure.

Finally, a proposed Directive on informing and consulting with employees is potentially explosive. From an information standpoint, local management would be required to provide information to employees every six months on issues such as the present and future employment situation, production and investment programs, and the company's economic and financial status. This would be a major departure from information required in the United States and could set a controversial precedent for disclosure worldwide, at least from management's standpoint.

On an international basis, the **United Nations** and the **International Accounting Standards Committee** are two organizations interested in accounting standards. The UN has become involved in accounting standards through the Commission on Transnational Corporations of UNESCO. The commission appointed a group of experts to International Standards of Accounting and Reporting, a committee that has held several hearings and issued draft disclosure requirements but has not been able to agree on final standards. United Nations disclosure concepts tend to focus on the impact of the MNC on the host society, especially in terms of employment and investment. Although the UN is not empowered to enforce its standards, it can attempt to persuade individual countries—especially developing countries—to adopt its standards in local laws. Thus MNCs need to watch the development of UN standards closely and lobby forcefully against potentially damaging disclosure standards.

The last major international effort to affect accounting and disclosure standards is the **International Accounting Standards Committee** (IASC). As of the end of 1981, the IASC had issued 15 standards and had five exposure drafts outstanding. The U.S. approach to IASC standards is acceptance for those standards that are in harmony with U.S. GAAP. The AICPA is the professional accounting body that represents the United States as one of the nine founding members of the IASC. The FASB unofficially responds to IASC exposure drafts, providing input on which final standards are based.

In practice, most IASC standards have been issued after the relevant U.S. standards. In addition, there are few major differences between IASC standards and U.S. GAAP. It would appear that the presence of the United States as a founding member of the IASC has allowed considerable input and influence in the decision-making process. It would be difficult to imagine an IASC standard in substantial conflict with U.S. GAAP. Although most significant countries of the world have representation on the IASC, the committee has no power to enforce its standards. Thus the onus of responsibility falls on each country's representatives. Individual countries could take IASC standards and implement them in home legislation, so it behooves firms to study exposure drafts and provide input to the AICPA where necessary.

FINANCIAL ACCOUNTING ISSUES

As pointed out in the previous section, United States-based MNCs are required to disclose a variety of information to external users of the financial statements at home and abroad. Foreign requirements vary by country, and the SEC and FASB determine guidelines in the United States. Since U.S. firms are required to combine all operations into one set of consolidated financial statements, they need to contend with special problems because of import/export activity and foreign investment. Four of the most important problems deal with accounting for foreign currency transactions, the translation of foreign currency financial statements, preparation of supplementary inflation-adjusted information, and the reporting of foreign geographical segments.

The first two issues dealing with foreign currencies are especially crucial due to a recent change in accounting standards. In December 1981, FASB issued **SFAS 52**,

"**Foreign Currency Translation**," which supercedes **SFAS 8**, the controversial standard issued in 1975. The following discusses requirements of the new standard, which will be effective for fiscal years beginning on or after 15 December 1982, although earlier application is encouraged. A comparison of the new standard with the old one is also made.

ACCOUNTING FOR FOREIGN CURRENCY TRANSACTIONS. United States-based companies can enter into any number of different kinds of transactions involving the flow of money worldwide. The most important of these transactions are the import or export of merchandise, the sale or purchase of services, the payment or receipt of dividends, royalties, and management fees, and borrowing or lending money.

As long as these transactions are recorded in the reporting currency of the company (the U.S. dollar in the case of U.S. corporations), there is no problem in recording these international transactions. However, if the transaction is to be settled in a currency other than that of the reporting currency, then four issues must be resolved: (1) the initial recording of the transaction, (2) the recording of the foreign currency balances at subsequent balance sheet dates, (3) the treatment of any foreign exchange gains and losses, and (4) the recording of the settlement of foreign currency receivables and payables when they come due. (Forward exchange contracts are treated separately herein.)

The procedure to be followed in this situation are spelled out quite explicitly in SFAS 52. Before going into specifics, however, it is important to define the term "functional currency." An entity's functional currency is the currency of the primary economic environment in which the entity operates. In the case of a U.S. exporter, the functional currency is normally the U.S. dollar. In this case, the functional currency is also the reporting currency, since the U.S. exporter generates its financial statements in U.S. dollars. If a U.S. corporation had an independent subsidiary in France that exported goods to Italy, the functional currency of the French subsidiary would probably be the French franc. However, the reporting currency of the U.S. parent would be that of the U.S. dollar, the currency in which consolidated financial statements are prepared. This distinction is made in greater depth in "Translation of Foreign Currency Financial Statements," which follows in this section.

In the case of a U.S. company getting involved in a foreign currency transaction, each asset, liability, revenue, expense, gain, or loss arising from the transaction is to be recorded in the firm's functional currency (probably the U.S. dollar) at the exchange rate in effect at the transaction date. At each subsequent balance sheet date, any balances that are denominated in a currency other than the functional currency of the entity should be recorded at the new balance sheet rate (the current rate). For example, if a U.S. importer is expected to pay a British exporter in pounds sterling for merchandise bought, the liability is denominated in pounds sterling, and its dollar value must be adjusted on each balance sheet to reflect the current exchange rate. The change in dollar value is treated as a foreign exchange gain or loss and is included in the determination of net income in the period in which the rate changes.

The following example assumes that a U.S. importer purchases merchandise from a British exporter on December 1 with payment to be made on January 15 and that the exporter closes its books at the end of December. Exhibit 1 illustrates how the exporter would account for this transaction. It is important to note the following points about Exhibit 1. On December 1, both the asset and liability were recorded at the exchange rate in effect on that date. On December 31, only the liability changed in value. The merchandise took on a dollar value as soon as it was purchased, and that value does not change on subsequent balance sheet dates. The liability, however, is to be settled in pounds (and is thus still denominated in pounds even though it is recorded in dollars), so its dollar equivalent changes whenever the rate changes. For convenience, the dollar value is changed only when a new balance sheet is prepared (in this case with year-end balance). The reduction in dollar value gives rise to a gain in dollars since the importer will be paying fewer dollars to liquidate the debt. The gain goes directly to income in that period when the exchange rate changes, even though the liability has not been settled and the exchange rate could reverse itself. Finally, the settlement of the liability gives rise to another gain since its dollar value has fallen since the last adjustment on December 31.

It is important for the financial manager to understand the **income statement effect** of the rate change. From a cash flow perspective, one would hesitate to recognize a gain or loss until the liability in the example given were liquidated. However, the effect of a rate change shows up long before the settlement date, since gains and losses flow into income whenever financial statements are prepared and exchange rates change.

FORWARD EXCHANGE CONTRACT. A forward contract is a special kind of transaction that is an agreement with the foreign exchange trader of a bank to buy or sell foreign currency at a specific future date at a specified exchange rate (the forward rate). The forward rate is a contractual rate and may or may not equal the spot rate in effect when the contract comes due. The determination of forward rates and the

EXHIBIT 1 FOREIGN CURRENCY TRANSACTION

£1,000,000	Value of the import from Great Britain
\$1.9805 = £1	Exchange rate on December 1
\$1.9407 = £1	Exchange rate on December 31
\$1.9100 = £1	Exchange rate on January 15

DECEMBER 1		
Purchases	1,980,500	
Accounts payable		1,980,500
£1,000,000 @ \$1.9805		
DECEMBER 31		
Accounts payable	39,800	
Foreign exchange gain		39,800
£1,000,000 × (1.9805 − 1.9407)		
JANUARY 15		
Accounts payable	1,940,700	
Foreign exchange gain		30,700
Cash		1,910,000

uses of forward contracts are discussed elsewhere in this volume, but a few general comments on the accounting for forward contracts is appropriate.

There are several different reasons to enter into a forward contract: to **hedge a transaction** such as the import mentioned above, to **speculate** on currency movements, to **hedge a net investment** in a foreign entity, and to **hedge a foreign currency commitment**. In the case of the import described, the importer must deliver foreign currency to the exporter on January 15 and is unsure as to the future spot rate. Therefore, the importer may enter into a forward contract with a bank to deliver dollars in return for pounds on January 15 in order to make payment to the exporter. Thus the importer has a foreign currency receivable from the bank to offset the foreign currency payable to the exporter. Every time the exchange rate changes, the value of the receivable changes, giving rise to a gain or loss that is just the opposite of the gain or loss on the foreign currency account payable, assuming that the size of the contract equals the size of the account payable. This gain or loss on the forward contract receivable is recognized in the income statement immediately, so it offsets the gain or loss on the account payable. The only cost to the importer would be the premium or discount on the forward contract, and that is written off over the life of the contract. Thus the accounting treatment of forward contracts to hedge a foreign currency transaction eliminates the exposure to potential foreign exchange losses.

If a firm enters into a forward contract to speculate on currency changes rather than to hedge an exposure, any gains or losses on that contract are recognized immediately in income. The gain or loss is determined by multiplying the amount of the contract by the difference between the forward rate available on the balance sheet date for the remaining maturity of the contract and the original contracted rate or the forward rate last used to measure a gain or loss.

If a U.S. parent decides to enter into a forward contract or other foreign currency transaction to hedge an investment in a foreign entity, the parent may include any gain or loss on the contract as a separate component of stockholders' equity.

Finally, prior to a transaction a firm may enter into a foreign currency commitment that it may care to hedge with a forward contract. In this case, the premium or discount on the contract as well as any gain or loss due to subsequent rate changes are deferred until the transaction date and included in the measurement of the foreign currency transaction. For example, the U.S. importer might have entered into a commitment with the British exporter in October to receive merchandise on December 1. At the same time, the importing firm might have entered into a forward contract to hedge its commitment. Thus on December 1, any gains or losses and amortization of premium or discount would be added to the cost of the merchandise purchased from the exporter.

It is important to realize that in order for the **separate accounting** for forward contracts against **foreign currency commitments** to hold true, two specifics must be met: (1) the forward contract must be designated as a hedge on a foreign currency commitment, and (2) the foreign currency commitment must be firm. The forward contract may be for an amount equal to the commitment on an after-tax basis, but any foreign exchange gains or losses on an amount in excess of that or for any time period that exceeds the transaction date must be taken into income rather than be deferred.

As can be seen from the above examples, the idea of accounting for forward contracts is to match the recognition of contract gains and losses with those of the independent foreign currency transaction.

TRANSLATION OF FOREIGN CURRENCY FINANCIAL STATEMENTS. The process of translating financial statements from one currency to another occurs for many reasons. The requirements of SFAS 52 exist to assist in consolidation, combination, or the equity method of accounting for foreign operations. There may be other appropriate ways to translate financial statements for other reasons, but they would not be accepted for the purposes listed above.

Consolidation can take place on multiple levels. For example, a U.S. company may have a Swiss subsidiary responsible for European operations that acts as a holding company of those operations. At the same time, the company's operating subsidiary in France may own subsidiaries in former French colonies. Thus the French company would need to consolidate all of its investments into one set of financial statements before sending its results to the Swiss holding company. The Swiss holding company would then need to consolidate all of its European investments before sending financial statements to the U.S. parent, which would then combine all of its worldwide financial statements into one set of consolidated statements. In order for consolidation to occur at each level, financial statements must be translated into a common currency.

Prior Standards. Before SFAS 52, firms were required to translate financial statements into U.S. dollars according to the **temporal method,** or SFAS 8. Under this method, the objective of translation was to produce the same results as if the foreign entity's books of records had been maintained in the parent (reporting) currency. Thus cash, receivables, and payables would be translated at the current rate. Assets and liabilities carried at past exchange prices (basically at historical cost) would be translated at the **historical exchange rate**. Assets and liabilities carried at a current or future exchange price would be translated at the **current exchange rate**. Revenues and expenses would be translated at **average rates**, except for those items related to assets carried at past exchange prices, such as depreciation (fixed assets) and cost of goods sold (inventory). These items would be carried at historical rates. All gains and losses would be taken directly to the income statement in the period of the rate change.

SFAS 8 resulted in an uproar from the business community. In 1978, when the FASB asked for public comments on its first 12 standards, most of the comments it received were related to SFAS 8. Several issues were raised in the comments. The major concern was that immediate recognition of all gains and losses resulted in a distortion of operating results and misleading information, which in turn led to poor economic decisions. Most people felt that gains and losses on foreign currency transactions should be taken directly to the income statement but that gains and losses on translating foreign currency financial statements should somehow be taken out of income.

Another concern was that certain accounts were not being translated properly. Inventory, for example, was translated primarily at historical rates. Thus a rate change in one period might not affect operating profits until the period in which the inventory was sold. This distortion of operating results was perplexing to managers. Many controllers were also concerned about the complexity involved in keeping track of historical costs and historical exchange rates for inventory, an asset which turns over fairly quickly. The preference was to translate inventory at current rates.

Another account that gave rise to concern was long-term debt, which was translated at current rates and thus exposed to foreign exchange losses. Many respondents felt that it was unfair to translate a fixed asset at historical rates and thus have that asset sheltered from any foreign exchange gains or losses, whereas the debt used to acquire the asset was exposed to an exchange gain or loss. The feeling was that the asset should be translated at the current rate in order to match the exposure of the debt, or that the gain or loss on the debt should be somehow taken out of income.

SFAS 8 was carefully thought out, and its principles are internally consistent with the objectives of the standard, which were "to measure and express in dollars and in generally accepted accounting principles the assets, liabilities, revenues, or expenses that are measured or denominated in foreign currency." The change from SFAS 8 to SFAS 52 required a change in objectives in order to end up with a change in standards.

Statement of Financial Accounting Standards 52. The new standard was set to achieve the following **objectives**: to "provide information that is generally compatible with the expected economic effects of a rate change on an enterprise's cash flows and equity" and to "reflect in consolidated statements the financial results and relationships of the individual consolidated entities as measured in their functional currencies in conformity with U.S. generally accepted accounting principles." As was the case with SFAS 8, SFAS 52 provided guidance on what exchange rate (current, historical, or average) is to be used to translate each individual account and how resulting gains and losses are to be recognized in the financial statements. Unlike SFAS 8, which permitted only one way to translate financial statements, SFAS 52 permits the use of two different methods, depending on the circumstances. Before using an example to illustrate the mechanics of translation, how management decides which method to use is examined.

The choice of translation method depends on an understanding of the **functional currency**. As mentioned, the functional currency is that of the primary economic environment where the entity operates. Thus a U.S.-owned French corporation that produces and sells for the French market might consider the French franc as its functional currency, and the currency in which it also keeps its books and records. The functional currency would be translated into the parent company's reporting currency using the current rate method. Briefly, this means that all assets and liabilities would be translated at the current or balance sheet rate, a significant departure from SFAS 8. In addition, all revenues and expenses would be translated at a weighted average exchange rate.

If management decided that the functional currency was something other than the currency of the country where the entity was operating and that in which its books and records were being kept, then those books and records would have to be translated into the functional currency. Normally, this means that management might decide that the reporting currency of the parent (e.g., the U.S. dollar) is the functional currency. In this case, translation would take place under the temporal method of SFAS 8. Once again, the translation process is designed to produce the same results as if the books and records had been maintained in the functional rather than the local currency.

How does management decide whether the functional currency is the local currency in which the books and records are kept or another currency, such as the reporting currency of the parent? Basically, the functional currency would be the local currency if the local operations are relatively self-contained and integrated with the environment. The parent's reporting currency would be considered the functional currency if the foreign entity were considered an extension of and fairly dependent in its dealings with the parent. Since management is responsible for deciding which is the functional currency, several possible suggestions are given in SFAS 52 on how to decide whether the parent or foreign (local) currency is to be selected as the functional currency.

a. Cash flow indicators
   (1) Foreign currency: Cash flows related to the foreign entity's individual assets and liabilities are primarily in the foreign currency and do not directly impact the parent company's cash flows.
   (2) Parent's currency: Cash flows related to the foreign entity's individual assets and liabilities directly impact the parent's cash flows on a current basis and are readily available for remittance to the parent company.
b. Sales price indicators
   (1) Foreign currency: Sales prices for the foreign entity's products are not primarily responsive on a short-term basis to changes in exchange rates but are determined more by local competition or local government regulation.
   (2) Parent's currency: Sales prices for the foreign entity's products are primarily responsive on a short-term basis to changes in exchange rates; for example, sales prices are determined more by worldwide competition or by international prices.
c. Sales market indicators
   (1) Foreign currency: There is an active local sales market for the foreign entity's products, although there also might be significant amounts of exports.
   (2) Parent's currency: The sales market is mostly in the parent's country or sales contracts are denominated in the parent's currency.
d. Expense indicators
   (1) Foreign currency: Labor, materials, and other costs for the foreign entity's products or services are primarily local costs, even though there also might be imports from other countries.
   (2) Parent's currency: Labor, materials, and other costs for the foreign entity's products or services, on a continuing basis, are primarily costs for components obtained from the country in which the parent company is located.
e. Financing indicators
   (1) Foreign currency: Financing is primarily denominated in foreign currency, and funds generated by the foreign entity's operations are sufficient to service existing and normally expected debt obligations.
   (2) Parent's currency: Financing is primarily from the parent or other dollar-denominated obligations, or funds generated by the foreign entity's operations are not sufficient to service existing and normally expected debt obligations without the infusion of additional funds from the parent company. Infusion of additional funds from the parent company for expansion is not a factor, provided funds generated by the foreign entity's expanded operations are expected to be sufficient to service that additional financing.
f. Intercompany transactions and arrangements indicators
   (1) Foreign currency: There is a low volume of intercompany transactions and there is not an extensive interrelationship between the operations of the foreign entity and the parent company. However, the foreign entity's operations may rely on the parent's or affiliates' competitive advantages, such as patents and trademarks.
   (2) Parent's currency: There is a high volume of intercompany transactions and

> there is an extensive interrelationship between the operations of the foreign entity and the parent company. Additionally, the parent's currency generally would be the functional currency if the foreign entity is a device or shell corporation for holding investments, obligations, intangible assets, and the like, that could readily be carried on the parent's or an affiliate's books.

Once the decision is made as to which currency is the functional currency, the translation process can take place. As is shown in subsequent examples, the mechanics of translation are not difficult with which to deal. However, there are a few conceptual problems that need to be resolved. For example, a particular foreign entity might be conducting multiple business activities through branches or divisions, each with a different functional currency requiring a different translation method. The French corporation mentioned earlier may have African subsidiaries that are considered an extension of the French firm. The African operations would be translated into French francs using the temporal method. If the French firm is considered fairly independent of the U.S. parent, then the French statements would be translated into U.S. dollars at the current rate.

Finally, a problem arises for entities operating in **highly inflationary economies**, those in which the cumulative inflation over a three-year period totals approximately 100% or more. The assets of entities in these countries would be highly distorted if they were translated at the current exchange rate, so SFAS 52 requires that the functional currency be the parent currency, resulting in the use of the temporal method.

Before examining another example, the subject of how **gains and losses are treated** must be addressed. When the functional currency is considered to be the local currency, then any gains or losses that arise from translating the financial statements into the parent currency using the current rate method are taken to a separate component of stockholders' equity rather than taken into income. This is a major departure from SFAS 8. If the temporal method is used for cases where the local currency is not considered to be the functional currency, then the foreign exchange gain or loss is taken directly to income. This is the same approach that was used under SFAS 8.

Exhibit 2 shows the difference between the **current rate** and **temporal methods** for translating foreign currency financial statements.

In a simplified way, the foreign exchange gains in Exhibit 2 are derived as a plug figure. In the case of the temporal method, the ending retained earnings balance must be $174,000 in order for assets to equal liabilities and owners' equity. The determination of the foreign exchange gain is as follows:

Retained earnings 12/31/82	$174,000
Less: Net income	– 99,750
Less: Retained earnings 1/1/82	– 62,000
Foreign exchange gain	$ 12,250

That amount is carried directly to the income statement. In the case of the current rate approach, the combined totals of retained earnings and the equity adjustment from translation (the translation gain under SFAS 8) must equal the plug figure to make the two sides balance. The individual balances are computed as follows:

EXHIBIT 2 BALANCE SHEET AND INCOME STATEMENT

BALANCE SHEET
31 DECEMBER 1982

		Temporal Method		Current Rate Method	
	Local Currency	Exchange Rate	U.S. Dollars	Exchange Rate	U.S. Dollars
Assets					
Cash and receivables	100,000	2.05[a]	$ 205,000	2.05	$ 205,000
Inventory	125,000	2.03[b]	253,750	2.05	256,250
Net fixed assets	300,000	1.95[c]	585,000	2.05	615,000
Total	525,000		$1,043,750		$1,076,250
Liabilities and owners' equity					
Current liabilities	115,000	2.05	$ 235,750	2.05	$ 235,750
Long-term debt	100,000	2.05	205,000	2.05	205,000
Capital stock	220,000	1.95	429,000	1.95	429,000
Retained earnings	90,000	—	174,000	—	177,000
Equity adjustment from translation					29,500
Total	525,000		$1,043,750		$1,076,250

Note. Assume that the beginning retained earnings balance was $62,000.

[a]Current or year-end balance sheet rate.

[b]The average rate during the period that the ending inventory was purchased.

[c]The rate when fixed assets were purchased and capital stock was issued.

INCOME STATEMENT
1982

		Temporal Method		Current Rate Method	
	Local Currency	Exchange Rate	U.S. Dollars	Exchange Rate	U.S. Dollars
Sales revenue	700,000	2.00[a]	$1,400,000	2.00	$1,400,000
Cost of sales	(437,500)	2.04[b]	(892,500)	2.00	(875,000)
Depreciation	(45,000)	1.95	(87,750)	2.00	(90,000)
Other expenses	(160,000)	2.00	(320,000)	2.00	(320,000)
Net income before foreign exchange gain (loss)	57,500		$ 99,750		$ 115,000
Foreign exchange gain (loss)	—		12,250		
Net income	57,500		$ 112,000		$ 115,000

[a]Weighted average rate during the year.

[b]Average rate during the period when the merchandise that was sold was initially purchased.

Retained earnings 1/1/82	$ 62,000
Net income	+115,000
Retained earnings 12/31/82	$177,000
Plug figure	$206,500
Less: Retained earnings 12/31/82	−177,000
Equity adjustment from translation	$ 29,500

Obviously these exchange gains and adjustments can be determined more precisely than as a plug figure, but those calculations are beyond the scope of this section.

Ramifications of Statement of Financial Accounting Standards 52. In comparing SFAS 52 with SFAS 8, there are some obvious differences. The new standard allows a great deal of **management flexibility** in choosing the correct method for translating financial statements, thus recognizing that there are inherent differences in foreign operations that may require different methods of translation. Although the new standard may appear to be too flexible to some, it is important to note that once management decides which is the functional currency of a foreign operation, it is not allowed to change unless there is a significant change in the economic facts and circumstances surrounding the original choice.

Another difference is that the objections raised concerning **inventory and long-term debt** are resolved for operations where the functional currency is considered to be the local currency. Thus inventory is translated at the current exchange rate, and fixed assets that are also translated at current rates offset the exposure of long-term debt.

Of great significance is the fact that translation gains and losses for operations where the **functional currency is the local currency** are treated as a separate component of shareholders' equity, thus eliminating these gains and losses from the income statement. This move alone should please many in the corporate world who have felt that these gains and losses caused misleading fluctuations in income.

One of the objectives of the new standard is to provide information compatible with the expected **economic effects** of a rate change on an enterprise's cash flows and equity. The new standard, for firms whose functional currency is the local rather than parent currency, will always place such companies in a net exposed-asset position since net worth is the only section of the balance sheet that is not translated at the current rate. This means that a parent with a subsidiary operating in a country whose currency is strong relative to the parent currency will recognize foreign exchange gains upon translation since the dollar value of the net asset position rises as the exchange rate rises. This is consistent with cash flows since the dollar value of dividends also rises as the exchange rate rises. Under the old standard, a firm could have a net exposed-liability position if the exposed liabilities exceeded the exposed assets. Thus the parent would pick up losses on translation since the dollar value of the net exposed-liability position would rise as the exchange rate rose, even though the parent anticipated a higher dollar dividend flow. This phenomenon is still possible for operations where the functional currency is considered to be the parent rather than the local currency.

In spite of the many things that SFAS 52 does, there are many things that it does not do. The old temporal method is still in effect for firms operating in **highly inflationary countries** and those whose functional currency is considered to be the parent currency. None of the imperfections of the temporal method was modified, so they can come back to haunt a company.

In addition, the current rate method does not totally eliminate the impact of exchange rate changes on the income statement, even though translation gains and losses are taken directly to equity. The reason is because the income statement must still be translated into dollars. If the foreign currency is weakening relative to the dollar, then the dollar equivalent of net income will fall. Many firms experienced this phenomenon in Europe during the recession of 1981. Income in local currency was not rising very much because of the recession, so the strong dollar exacerbated the weak profit picture, resulting in small dollar increases in some cases and dollar declines in others.

Finally, SFAS 8 was very difficult to understand because investors were not really sure how to interpret earnings fluctuations due to foreign exchange gains and losses. The new system may not be any clearer since firms may still have to deal with fluctuating earnings for operations using the temporal method, whereas they also have to explain a new-line item in owners' equity where the current rate method was used.

The key once again may be the **adequate disclosure** of information and explanation of the impact of translation on the financial statements. In terms of the new component to equity, firms are required to disclose the following information in a separate financial statement, in notes to the financial statement, or as part of a statement of changes in equity: (1) beginning and ending amount of cumulative translation adjustments; (2) the aggregate adjustment for the period resulting from translation adjustments and gains and losses from certain hedges and intercompany balances; (3) the amount of income taxes for the period allocated to translation adjustments; (4) the amounts transferred from cumulative translation adjustments and included in determining net income for the period as a result of the sale or complete or substantially complete liquidation of an investment in a foreign entity.

From the standpoint of the financial manager, the method of translating operations does not affect the basic cash flow of the foreign subsidiary. Dividends are declared on local currency, not dollar profits, and they are converted into dollars at the spot rate in effect when the dividend is sent to the parent. However, the method of translation does affect the financial statements, possibly producing an impact on all sorts of investment and credit decisions by management as well as external users. Thus a clear knowledge and understanding of SFAS 52 is important for the international financial executive.

INFLATION-ADJUSTED FINANCIAL STATEMENTS. In September 1979, FASB issued **SFAS 33**, "**Financial Reporting and Changing Prices**." This standard requires firms to disclose as supplementary information the effects of general price level and current cost changes on certain accounts and account balances. Under SFAS 33, firms are required to disclose the following information: (1) information on income from continuing operations adjusted for general price level changes; (2) the purchasing power gain or loss on net monetary items; (3) information on income from continuing operations on a current cost basis (cost of goods sold at current cost and depreciation expense of property, plant, and equipment); (4) the current cost amounts of inventory and property, plant, and equipment; (5) increases and decreases in the current cost amounts of inventory and property, plant, and equipment net of inflation; and (6) certain summary information for the five most recent years. When applying this standard to foreign operations, firms were required to translate foreign currency amounts into U.S. dollars according to SFAS 8 before adjusting the dollar amounts for general price-level changes using a U.S. consumer price index. In the case of current cost adjustments, firms adjust local currency accounts for current cost changes and then translate those amounts into U.S. dollars at the current exchange rate.

The adoption of SFAS 52 has forced the FASB to consider amending SFAS 33 so that it will be consistent with the new translation standard. Thus the board is considering requiring that functional currency amounts first be restated into constant functional currency amounts, using an appropriate measure of the change in a general price level index applicable to the functional currency environment, and then be translated into U.S. dollar equivalent amounts at the average-for-the-year exchange rate. Current cost of goods sold, current cost depreciation, and the increase in current cost amounts would be measured in the functional currency and translated into U.S. dollar equivalent amounts at the average-for-the-year exchange rate. Also, the amount of the translation adjustment would be reported as a separate line item. A noticeable difference is that firms whose functional currency is the local currency would make general price level adjustments according to local inflation before translating the amounts into dollars rather than translating first and then restating for U.S. inflation. Also, an average exchange rate is used for translation rather than a year-end rate. For firms whose functional currency is the parent currency, it appears that there would be little if any change from SFAS 33.

It is difficult to know what, if any, impact the inflation disclosures are having on the finance activities of a firm. Financial analysts seem to be paying more attention to the information than the firms are. Very few firms appear to be using the information to make decisions, unlike Philips, a Dutch company that uses only current cost information, and British companies, which are now allowed to substitute current value statements for their old historical cost statements. The important thing is that U.S. firms will now be looking more closely at the impact of local inflation on local currency financial statements except when the functional currency is the U.S. dollar and, ironically, when the subsidiary is in a highly inflationary country. Then the U.S. dollar rather than the local currency would be considered to be the functional currency. These statements are all very tentative, since the board has not issued a final revision of SFAS 33 as of late 1982.

SEGMENT INFORMATION. A final external financial reporting issue to be mentioned is the requirements for reporting information about foreign operations. "**Financial Reporting for Segments of a Business Enterprise,**" **SFAS 14**, requires that firms disclose, among other things, information about foreign operations and export sales. In order to disclose information about foreign operations, foreign revenues must be at least 10% of consolidated revenues or identifiable assets must be at least 10% of consolidated assets. If this situation holds true, then the foreign segment's revenue from sales to unaffiliated customers, revenue from intracompany sales, operating profit or loss, and identifiable assets must be disclosed.

A firm may choose to lump all of its foreign operations into one segment, or it may disaggregate the data into several segments by individual country or by groups of countries. The decision to aggregate or disaggregate is left up to management. The financial executive needs to be aware of the implications of this disclosure. Greater disclosure may assist the firm in raising capital if it can be shown that investments are in relatively stable areas politically and economically. However, it should be noted that all of the information listed above must be disclosed about each segment, and firms may be hesitant to disclose profit information. One alternative would be to aggregate data in terms of the official disclosures in the footnotes to the financial statements and offer disaggregated sales revenue data in the general business narrative. That would allow firms to provide enough segment information to investors to let them know where the company is operating without disclosing potentially sensitive profit information about each segment.

MANAGERIAL ACCOUNTING ISSUES

PERFORMANCE EVALUATION. Managerial accounting issues cover a broad range of topics, including the capital budgeting issues raised in an earlier section of this volume. An important managerial accounting topic that has financial implications is that of performance evaluation. A number of studies have been conducted in recent years to determine some key aspects of performance evaluation of foreign subsidiaries and foreign subsidiary managers. Most U.S.-based MNCs tend to export their performance evaluation and control systems in order to standardize comparisons worldwide. The most important evaluation criteria, as is the case for domestic operations, are **return on investment (ROI)** and **budgets**. The choice of currency used in evaluations (local currency or parent currency) depends a great deal on the evaluation technique being used. As opposed to using just local currency or just the parent currency, many firms use both currencies. Exhibit 3 lists the results of a recent study of the financial measures used as indicators of performance of multinational chemical companies. Local currency was used for a number of the financial measures, but firms demonstrated a wider acceptance of dollar measures of performance evaluation. However, a number of respondents to the survey indicated that they were beginning to place greater reliance on local currency results, since these results reflect fairly accurately what is going on in the actual environment.

In using any of the financial measures mentioned, there are several issues for a firm to consider, namely, the existence of different accounting standards in each country, the choice of currency for setting budgets and monitoring performance, and the arbitrary nature of intracorporate transfer pricing. Although other issues may enter, these three are central.

DIFFERENT ACCOUNTING STANDARDS. As mentioned, there are numerous differences in accounting standards and reporting practices in countries where a firm might have foreign operations. The local accounting staff may be educated in the local system and used to interpreting financial statements prepared in local GAAP. However, the U.S. MNC must keep a separate set of books according to U.S. GAAP for consolidation purposes. In addition, it will probably require that all reports sent to the headquarters for internal use be prepared according to U.S. GAAP. This enables the firm to compare results worldwide.

CHOICE OF CURRENCY. The choice of currency to set budgets and track performance is complex and includes top management's attitude toward dollar accountability. In Exhibit 4, several possibilities for choice of currency are identified.

The areas in Exhibit 4 that make the most sense are A-1, A-3, P-2, P-3, and E-3. Under cells A-1, P-2, and E-3, the same exchange rate is used to set the budget

EXHIBIT 3 FINANCIAL MEASURES USED AS INDICATORS OF INTERNAL PERFORMANCE EVALUATION

Financial Measures	After Translation in U.S. Dollars (in Percentage)	Before Translation in Local Currency (in Percentage)
Return on investment (assets)	80.0	52.9
Return on equity	48.6	31.4
Residual income	21.4	18.6
Profit	81.4	70.0
Cash flow potential from foreign subsidiary to U.S. operations	65.7	35.7
Budget compared to actual return on investment	45.7	38.6
Budget compared to actual profits	78.6	72.9
Budget compared to actual sales	72.9	72.9
Ratios	34.3	30.0
Others	12.9	11.4

Source. Helen Morsicato, *Currency Translation and Performance Evaluation in Multinationals*, Ann Arbor: University of Michigan Research Press, 1980.

Note. These figures represent the percentage of the total 70 firms that report using each particular measure.

and track performance. In the case of A-1, the exchange rate in effect when the budget was set is used to translate actual results into dollars. Thus management sees the information in dollars, but local managers aren't responsible for exchange rate changes. Area E-3 is very similar in philosophy except that the budget in dollars is updated to reflect the current rate in order to match actual performance translated at the current rate. Option P-2 is slightly different in that management, while not

EXHIBIT 4 POSSIBLE COMBINATIONS OF EXCHANGE RATES IN THE CONTROL PROCESS

Rate Used for Determining Budget \ Rate Used to Track Performance Relative to Budget	Actual at Time of Budget	Projected at Time of Budget	Actual at End of Period
Actual at time of budget	A-1	A-2	A-3
Projected at time of budget	P-1	P-2	P-3
Actual at end of period (through updating)	E-1	E-2	E-3

Source. Donald R. Lessard and Peter Lorange, "Currency Changes and Management Control: Resolving the Centralization and Decentralization Dilemma," *Accounting Review* (July 1977), p. 630.

being held responsible for exchange rate changes, is required to project exchange rates. Top management needs to decide who is responsible for projecting the rate, but there appears to be no attempt to hold anyone responsible for an inaccurate projection.

Possibilities A-3 and P-3 introduce the element of accountability for exchange rate changes. In both cases, a different rate is used to track performance than is used to set the budget. For A-3, management is accountable for the total fluctuation between the rate in effect when the budget was established and the rate in effect when actual performance was recorded. Top management needs to decide where to assign responsibility for exchange fluctuations since A-3 will include operating as well as currency variances. The assumption is that the operating manager is responsible for coping with any currency changes. If that is the case, then the corporate or regional finance staff needs to provide assistance to local management on exposure management techniques. Care must also be taken to ensure that local management does not do something to minimize exchange exposure that might adversely affect operating performance.

For P-3 the same kinds of issues exist as with A-3. The difference is that with P-3 management is required to forecast or project the exchange rate. The currency variance that shows up when the budget is compared with the actual is the difference between what management forecasted the rate to be versus what it actually was. Thus the corporate finance staff needs to provide assistance to local management in projecting the exchange rate.

As pointed out earlier, some companies prefer to use local currency rather than dollar-translated information when setting budgets and monitoring results. This is partly because they feel that the translation process distorts the relationship among accounts that exists in local currency. The introduction of the current rate method in SFAS 52 results in dollar statements that maintain the same relationships that exist in local currency. That may add more credibility to dollar financial statements in performance evaluation.

TRANSFER PRICING. There appears to be a movement toward vertical integration of MNC operations as firms attempt to shore up sources of supply of key materials and components. In addition, the search for cost advantages has led to greater disaggregation of the production process in order to take advantage of the unique comparative advantages that firms have to offer. Thus increasing transfers are found across national borders of semi-finished components and finished goods from one entity to another controlled by a common parent. A key consideration for each government involved as well as the firm itself is, how is the transfer price set?

Because such prices do not occur at arm's length, there is obviously room for manipulation. Governments are concerned because the price attached to a transfer could affect excise taxes (such as border taxes and value-added taxes) as well as corporate income taxes. Companies are concerned because transfer prices affect direct cash flows for payments of goods, taxes, cost structures affecting its competitive position, and evaluation of management performance.

As noted in Exhibit 5, different conditions in each subsidiary country could lead to different transfer pricing decisions. However, this assumes that the firm has the discretion to set arbitrary prices. Tax authorities tend to have the greatest influence prohibiting companies from arbitrarily setting prices. The preference is to have an arm's length price instead. In addition to tax authorities, management itself may prefer an arm's length price for two basic reasons. The first is that it is often difficult

EXHIBIT 5 CONDITIONS IN SUBSIDIARY'S COUNTRY INDUCING HIGH AND LOW TRANSFER PRICES ON FLOWS BETWEEN AFFILIATES AND PARENT

Conditions in Subsidiary's Country Inducing Low Transfer Prices on Flows from Parent and High Transfer Prices on Flows to Parent	Conditions in Subsidiary's Country Inducing High Transfer Prices on Flows from Parent and Low Transfer Prices on Flows to Parent
High *ad valorem* tariffs	Corporate income tax rate higher than in parent's country
Corporation income tax rate lower than in parent's country	Local partners
Significant competition	Pressure from workers to obtain greater share of company profit
Local loans based on financial appearance of subsidiary	Political pressure to nationalize or expropriate high-profit foreign firms
Restrictions on profit or dividend remittances	Political instability
Export subsidiary or tax credit on value of exports	High inflation rate
	Substantial tie-in sales agreements
	Price of final product controlled by government but based on production cost
	Desire to mask profitability of subsidiary operations to keep competitors out

Source. Jeffrey S. Arpan, *Intracorporate Pricing: Non-American Systems and Views*, New York: Praeger, 1972.

to set priorities for transfer prices. For example, goods being shipped to a politically unstable country where there are low corporate income tax rates are subjected to conflicting possibilities. The unstable environment would imply a high transfer price to get goods out, whereas the low tax rate would imply a low transfer price in order to concentrate profits.

The second reason for wanting an arm's length price is performance evaluation. Arbitrary transfer prices affect net income as well as the asset base in ROI calculations. Thus management performance is evaluated in areas where management has no control when arbitrary transfer prices are used. As a result, many firms prefer to use the cost-plus method or some other way of setting arm's length prices on its intracorporate transfers.

CONCLUSION

As financial managers make decisions concerning asset management and funds positioning in the highly volatile and complex international environment, they must rely on the accuracy, reliability, and timeliness of the accounting data supplied by the accounting group. Differences in accounting standards worldwide complicate the recordkeeping process since firms must keep one set of books in accordance with local standards and another set to assist in preparing consolidated financial statements according to parent company external reporting requirements. In addition, comparability of international results for internal purposes is enhanced when common standards are used for preparing internal reports.

Multinational firms are also faced with a variety of specific accounting problems that are a direct result of their international operations. Foreign currency is a big issue as firms need to account for foreign currency transactions and the translation of foreign currency financial statements. As pointed out earlier in the chapter, SFAS 52 adds a new dimension to the issue as firms have the option to translate foreign currency financial statements using the current rate method or the temporal method made popular by SFAS 8, depending on the characteristics of the foreign company whose statements are being translated. Under the current rate method, many of the disadvantages of the temporal method are eliminated, especially since foreign exchange translation gains and losses are to be put in a separate component of shareholder's equity rather than be recognized in income.

Finally, the performance evaluation of subsidiaries and subsidiary management is complicated by transfer pricing decisions and foreign currencies. Under intracorporate transfer pricing, there are a number of international variables that encourage the setting of arbitrary rather than arm's-length prices in order to position funds more effectively. However, these arbitrary prices can injure performance evaluation. Thus management needs to be aware of the effect of intracorporate transfer prices on subsidiary and management performance. Exchange rate changes also need to be taken into consideration in performance evaluation since they can distort the picture which corporate management sees. Thus a decision must be made as to who is accountable for dollar results, and whether or not local currency results are relevant for making decisions.

As can be seen, the same issues that accountants face in a domestic context must be dealt with in an international context. However, variables such as different accounting standards and foreign exchange can create numerous complexities that affect the accuracy, reliability, and timeliness of the accounting data on which the financial group needs to rely.

BIBLIOGRAPHY

American Accounting Association, *Notable Contributions to the Periodical International Accounting Literature—1975–78*, AAA, Sarasota, Florida, 1979.

Arpan, Jeffrey S., and Lee H. Radebaugh, *International Accounting and Multinational Enterprises*, John Wiley & Sons, New York, 1981.

Burton, John C., ed. *The International World of Accounting: Challenges and Opportunities*. The Council of Arthur Young Professors, Reston, Virginia, 1981.

Choi, Frederick D. C., and Gerhard G. Mueller. *Essentials of Multinational Accounting: An Anthology*. University Microfilms International, Ann Arbor, Michigan, 1979.

Daley, Lane A., and Gerhard G. Mueller. "Accounting in the Arena of Global Politics," *Journal of Accounting*, February 1982, pp. 40–53.

Persen, William and Van Lessig. *Evaluating the Financial Performance of Overseas Operations*. Financial Executives Research Foundation, New York, 1979.

Watt, George C., Richard M. Hammer, and Marianne Burge. *Accounting for the Multinational Corporation*. Financial Executives Research Foundation, New York, 1977.

REFERENCES

1. "Behind the Figures," *The Economist*, 24 March 1979, p. 106.
2. Ernst & Whinney International Series, *Fourth Directive European Company Law* (Ernst & Whinney, 1980), p. 2.
3. Statement of Financial Accounting Standards No. 52, *Foreign Currency Translation* (Stamford, Conn.: Financial Accounting Standards Board, December 1981), paragraph 42.

SECTION 8.7

DEFINING AND MEASURING CURRENCY EXPOSURE

CONTENTS

SECTION **8.7**

DEFINING AND MEASURING CURRENCY EXPOSURE

Gilles Puchon

The growing trend of international trade for goods and services around the world has made foreign exchange risk a critical factor to the bottom line of those corporations heavily dependent upon imports and exports. This has become particularly important with the increasing volatility of foreign currency values. For example, the spectacular rebound of the U.S. dollar from a significantly depressed level in 1979 to a strong posture in 1981 exerted undue pressure on U.S. exporters; they are gradually being forced to denominate export prices in the currency of the foreign customer, thereby assuming all exchange risk, in order to maintain their market share. Undoubtedly, the control of foreign exchange risk can be effective only if the exporter is able to manage the fundamental relationships among inflation, foreign exchange, and interest rates. Furthermore, the growing trend of the multinational corporation with subsidiaries dispersed around the world has an added level of complexity in the corporate decision-making process. It pertains to the relationship between the **local currency** of the foreign subsidiary and the **reporting currency** of the parent company. For U.S. multinational corporations, the U.S. Financial Accounting Standards Board has made senior management keenly aware of this local currency and reporting currency relationship by setting international accounting standards, such as the Statement of Financial Accounting Standards 8 (SFAS 8) and its present successor, SFAS 52, for the purpose of performance disclosure to shareholders.

Any attempt to define and measure currency exposure must be fully integrated with management's corporate philosophy, strategic planning process, operating decisions, and financial decisions. Traditionally, a currency exposure has been defined around one or a combination of the concepts of **transaction exposure, translation exposure,** and **economic exposure.** While the following discussion uses SFAS 52 framework to analyze different types of exposures to exchange risk, these concepts are also generally applicable to corporations not subject to U.S. accounting standards.

The author wishes to thank Abraham George for helpful comments. Also see A. George, *Foreign Exchange Management and the Multinational Corporation*, Praeger, New York, 1979.

TRANSACTION EXPOSURE

A transaction exposure arises whenever an entity is committed to a transaction denominated in a currency other than its **functional currency,** which is usually the local currency or the currency in which the entity does a substantial portion of its business. A transaction exposure can be an asset (e.g., export receivable, bank deposit) or a liability (e.g., payable, borrowings), a revenue (e.g., expected future sale) or an expense (e.g., expected purchase of inventory). If a U.S. multinational corporation—XYZ Company—has a subsidiary in West Germany, with the deutsche mark as its functional currency, a transaction exposure will arise whenever this subsidiary holds a receivable denominated in a currency other than the deutsche mark, because it is committed to receive a fixed amount of foreign currency. A change in exchange rate between the foreign currency and the deutsche mark increases or decreases the expected amount of deutsche mark cash proceeds upon collection of the receivable. This increase or decrease of deutsche mark cash received is a foreign currency transaction gain or loss.

A **transaction gain or loss** always creates an increase or decrease of local currency cash flows upon settlement that is generally subject to local tax. In most countries, a transaction gain is taxable at the ordinary income tax rate (or capital gain rate in some instances) and a transaction loss is tax-deductible at the same rate.

In the United States, exposure management practitioners have traditionally recognized a transaction exposure only from the date of booking to the date of settlement and have managed the visible cash gain or loss from an exchange rate change between these two dates. This approach has been designed somewhat around international accounting standards set by the Financial Accounting Standards Board. Both SFAS 8 and its successor, SFAS 52, require that a foreign currency transaction be booked at the exchange rate prevailing at the transaction date and be revalued at each subsequent balance sheet date until it is settled.

For example, the West German subsidiary of XYZ Company makes an export sale for FrF600 on 28 February with a prevailing French franc/deutsche mark cross-rate of 3.00 and does not expect collection until 30 April. The French franc weakened to 3.75 on 31 March and recovered at 3.53 on 30 April. The following are the cash impacts according to U.S. accounting procedures.

Receivable FrF600	Frf/DM Rate	DM Value	Transaction Gain (or Loss) in DM
28 February	3.00	200	—
31 March, first quarter profit and loss	3.75	160	(−40) loss
30 April, second quarter profit and loss	3.53	170	+10 gain
	Realized cash		(−30) loss

Is an entity's **true cash flow impact** accurately reflected in the transaction gain or loss as determined by the accounting rules? Generally, it is not. If the West German subsidiary made a commitment on 1 January to sell for FrF600 with an expected delivery date of 30 April, the cash flow impact would depend upon the rate prevailing on 1 January and that prevailing on 30 April. If the West German subsidiary on 1

January also hedged this sale commitment by entering into a forward contract, the cash flow impact would depend upon the forward premium or discount prevailing on 1 January for maturity on 30 April.

A more comprehensive definition of transaction exposure can, therefore, include **future** (committed or uncommitted) **revenues or expenses** that are not yet embodied in the financial statements but certainly give rise to an increase or decrease of functional currency cash flows. Assuming that the West Germany subsidiary decided not to hedge on 1 January, when the French franc/deutsche mark rate was 2.86, the full cash flow impact would be as follows:

Receivable FrF600	FrF/DM Rate	DM Value	Opportunity Cost/Revenue	Transaction Gain (or Loss)	Net Cash Flow Impact
1 January	2.86	210	—	—	—
28 February	3.00	200	−10	—	—
31 March	3.75	160	—	(−40)	(−50)
30 April	3.53	170	—	+10	+10
Total				(−30)	(−40)

The preceding example clearly shows that the sum of transaction gains or losses as reported at each balance date is only a partial reflection of the net cash flow impact.

When incorporating these concepts of transaction exposure in the longer term strategic planning process, it is critical to distinguish the currency of sale denomination from the currency that functionally determines the price level of goods and services. For example, the West German subsidiary might export its products to France and invoice in French francs. But, if its competitive position in France is such that the market leader is a U.K. exporter that sets the industry price trends in terms of pounds sterling, the West German subsidiary might be forced to follow the leader's pricing strategy. Then, it would have a transaction exposure in pounds sterling and not in French francs.

In order to measure a transaction exposure, the following parameters must be identified:

Local currency
Functional currency (usually the local currency)
Currency of exposure
Amount of exposure (can be expressed in US$ equivalent)
Date of reference or booking
Rate of reference
Local tax rate on foreign currency gain or loss

The French franc receivable of the earlier example can be measured according to the following methodology. (It is assumed that FrF600 was equal to US$100 initially and the West German tax rate is 48%.)

Exposure Measured in US$ Units

Currency of Exposure	Pretax	Aftertax
DM	−100	−48 [−100 × (1 − 0.52)]
FrF	+100	+48 [100 × (1 − 0.52)]

Given that a transaction gain or loss arises only from an increase or decrease of exchange rate between the currency of exposure and the entity's local currency, this cross-rate relationship is reflected in the above methodology by recognizing a transaction exposure in the local currency for the same amount but in opposite sign as that of the currency of exposure. By doing so, the cash flow consequences of a cross-rate change can be easily assessed by simply evaluating the individual rate changes of both the local currency and the currency of exposure vis-à-vis the U.S. dollar.

TRANSLATION EXPOSURE

A **translation exposure** arises from the necessity to express (and measure) a foreign subsidiary's local currency financial statement into the reporting currency for consolidation purposes. Translation of foreign financial statements is necessary whenever a foreign entity keeps its own set of books in local currency, or its functional currency, which might be a foreign currency. Generally, there is no need to translate the parent company's own financial statements as it is presumed to keep its books in the reporting currency (i.e., the U.S. dollar for a U.S. multinational corporation). The question is, at what exchange rate between the local currency (or the functional currency) and the reporting currency should a foreign subsidiary's financial statements be translated? Before 1975, there were no uniform translation procedures for U.S. corporations. In its effort to continually improve the quality of financial reporting, the Financial Accounting Standards Board decided to set a uniform standard for translating foreign financial statements. Consequently, in October 1975, it issued SFAS 8, which adapted the temporal method of translation in order to preserve one single unit of measure (i.e., the U.S. dollar).

In essence, SFAS 8 requires that all balance sheet and income statement accounts carried at historical prices in the local currency be translated at the corresponding historical exchange rates. All accounts carried at current prices must be translated at the current exchange rate. Since the local financial statements must also be prepared in accordance with U.S. generally accepted accounting principles before translation and subsequently upon consolidation, the resulting translation methodology has to be on a temporal basis in order to remain faithful to the historical cost model and related consolidation principles. This has since been modified under SFAS 52 to apply current rates to all assets and liabilities.

A translation exposure can only exist in local or functional currency as its purpose is to capture the relationship between the reporting currency and the local or functional currency. For example, a $100 receivable denominated in French francs on the books of the West German subsidiary not only generates a $100 equivalent long transaction exposure in French francs and a $100 equivalent short transaction exposure in deutsche marks, but also a $100 long translation exposure in deutsche marks.

FrF Receivable on West German Books (in US$)

Currency	Transaction	Translation
DM	− 100	+ 100
FrF	+ 100	

The volume of translation exposure carried by an entity at a given time will be determined by operating practices such as credit policies, inventory management, working capital management, and financial practices such as debt/equity ratios, dividend policies, and intercompany financing techniques. With an increase or decrease of the exchange rate between the local or functional currency and the reporting currency, a translation exposure will generate a foreign exchange gain or loss, of a noncash nature, which is excluded from net income but included in a special equity account of the consolidated balance sheet. From a longer term management viewpoint, it becomes more questionable whether or not translation exposure should be managed. Regardless of the accounting framework for external reporting purposes, the sheer size of translation losses relative to the total corporate performance and net assets is inducing financial management to rationalize the relationship between translation gains or losses and the maximization of return to shareholders. Increasingly, senior management will become more aware of the necessity to set an order of priority between short-term earnings stability and maximization of longer term return on investment and consolidated net worth.

When the local currency is selected to be the **functional currency,** an application of the current rate method and the exclusion of translation gains or losses from net income make it such that earnings per share are not affected in an accounting sense. However, such impairment will have a real cash effect upon dividend payment or liquidation of the firm.

ECONOMIC EXPOSURE

Economic exposure can be evaluated in the context of maximizing stockholders' wealth—the present value of future earnings and net assets left at risk. A proper strategic planning framework that gives full recognition of the financial and operating implications of inflation and foreign exchange can provide senior management greater effectiveness in managing economic exposure in the long run. It might require the integration of operating and financial responsibilities from the policy-making level down to the implementation and performance evaluation levels.

Managing economic exposure in the short run can be extremely difficult because of accounting considerations, sensitivity of the stock market to quarterly earnings for each share, and extreme volatility in the foreign exchange markets.

Economic effects arise throughout the activities of a multinational corporation. For instance,

1. An increasingly strong U.S. dollar vis-à-vis other foreign currencies can result in a loss of market share for U.S. exports as well as for local sales of foreign subsidiaries of U.S. multinationals. A foreign subsidiary's competitive position in the local markets can be such that increasing prices to offset an exchange rate depreciation can result in loss of sales.
2. Credit policies can be such that the longer the credit term granted, the larger the risk for economic loss resulting from exchange depreciation. The more the exchange risk can be passed to or shared with a customer, the less economic risk will be absorbed by the corporation.
3. The more (or less) the corporation can pass increasing costs, due to inflation and foreign exchange, onto a customer the less (or more) the economic risk will be.
4. The lower (or higher) the level of working capital the lower (or higher) the economic risk will be.
5. The more contractual prices can be adjusted for inflation and foreign exchange, the less economic risk will be.
6. The more local earnings are repatriated through dividend payments, the less economic risk will be.
7. The more volatile the foreign exchange and capital markets, the more uncertain the cost of financing will be as measured by the sum of interest expense and debt-related transaction-translation gain or loss.
8. The more inflation differentials deviate from exchange rate adjustments, the greater the economic risk on assets on hand and future cash flows.
9. The more the company's specific price experience deviates from general inflation, the more uncertain economic results will be.
10. The more tax laws ignore the effects of inflation by relying on historical cost statements to assess taxable income the greater the economic risk to the corporation.

One of the most favored approaches to managing economic exposure under SFAS 8 was to include **inventory** as an exposed item even though it was valued on the books at a historical rate. This definition of economic exposure was particularly applicable when the foreign subsidiary financed inventory through local borrowing, making the balance sheet position systematically short. This short position only existed on an accounting basis, while from an economic standpoint, it was more or less offset by inventory. The latter was considered to be a near-monetary item because it became a receivable or cash upon sale. This approach, although still applicable under SFAS 52 with the U.S. dollar as the functional currency, assumes no pricing flexibility from the time the inventory is produced to the time it is sold.

When economic exposure is defined as being merely **after-tax transaction exposure,** it is assumed that maximizing local currency cash flows is tantamount to maximizing U.S. dollar cash flows. A highly profitable subsidiary in terms of generating local cash flows might not be as profitable when the time comes to remit dividends. The inclusion of projected dividend payments in the exposure definition as a general rule is in the right direction of protecting economic risk.

MEASURING THE COST OF DEBT EXPOSURE

Given that exchange rates and inflation affect the cost of capital, financing strategies must minimize costs in real terms. The cost of borrowing is viewed differently at local and parent levels.

Cost of Local Currency–Denominated Debt

Local Level		Parent Level	
	Interest expense		Interest expense
equals:	Nominal cost	plus:	Translation gain/loss
minus:	Local inflation	equals:	Nominal cost
equals:	Real cost	minus:	Parent inflation
		equals:	Real cost

For a **debt denominated in local currency,** the nominal cost of financing is equal to the interest expense at the local level, and its real cost is interest expense adjusted for the local inflation rate. However, from the parent's viewpoint, the nominal cost of financing is equal to local interest expense plus the related translation gain or loss. Since a translation gain or loss fluctuates with exchange rate volatility, the nominal cost of financing becomes uncertain and unpredictable. This risk can be eliminated by hedging the debt-related translation exposure. Over the long run, the nominal cost of financing is equal to the cumulative local interest expense and the cumulative translation gains or losses. However, when the local currency is the functional currency, earnings for each share can be affected by higher (or lower) interest expense without the offset of a translation gain (or loss) flowing through the income statement.

When financing is done through a **nonlocal currency,** the cost of debt is different.

Cost of Nonlocal Currency–Denominated Debt

Local Level		Parent Level	
	Interest expense		Interest expense
plus:	Transaction gain or loss	plus:	Transaction gain or loss
equals:	Nominal cost	plus:	Translation gain or loss
minus:	Local inflation	equals:	Nominal cost
equals:	Real cost	minus:	Parent inflation
		equals:	Real cost

If the foreign subsidiary's debt is denominated in a currency other than the local currency, then the nominal cost of financing will have to also include the debt-related transaction gain or loss.

If the U.S. dollar is chosen as the functional currency, the alternative of borrowing local currency results in the interest expense and translation gains or losses (into the functional currency) being fully reflected in reported earnings.

The nominal cost of financing through **dollar debt** in a foreign subsidiary, as reflected in income statements, includes both interest expense and transaction gains or losses at the subsidiary level. From an economic, corporate standpoint, the nominal cost of a U.S. dollar debt is interest expense, as transaction and translation effects always wash out on a pretax basis.

The management of exposure should be integrated with operating strategies; if the parent company views the cost of debt from a U.S. dollar standpoint, then the financing of inventory with debt must be predicated on the operating management's ability to protect its earning power in terms of U.S. dollar cash flow potential. This can be achieved through proper pricing strategy and/or hedging actions.

STARTING EXPOSURE VERSUS INTRAPERIOD ACTIVITIES

Two types of exposure can be distinguished on the basis of starting positions and anticipated changes in those positions over the planning period. Starting balance sheet exposures relate to assets and liabilities appearing on the balance sheets of the parent and its foreign entities at any given time, including local currency exposures, foreign currency exposures, and dollar exposures. The second type of exposure consists of intraperiod flows that are reflected by the transactions within the planning period. Calculation of the overall exposure is often difficult, because the timing and magnitude of these two types of exposures differ, and because action taken to offset one form of exposure often affects the other.

While corporate practices vary significantly with respect to the type of exposure hedged, one could classify corporations by typical methods in three broad categories. The first group of companies completely ignores intraperiod settlements and develops protection strategies based entirely on exposures as they exist on the present balance sheet or the pro forma balance sheet for the end of the planning period. The second group consists of corporations that disregard balance sheet positions entirely and concentrate on the volume of transactions that are expected to be settled within the planning period. Most corporations fall into the third category, those that hedge certain specific transactions whose timings are known in advance (such as repayment of a debt) while, at the same time, developing overall protection strategies on the basis of balance sheet positions.

Companies that hedge their exposure on the basis of initial balance sheet positions alone can be justified in doing so when their balance sheets are not subject to major changes from one period to another. In other words, use of starting exposures can yield correct results if the anticipated intraperiod transactions do not significantly alter the initial position. This can be illustrated by the following example.

Assuming that currently a company is in a net exposed asset position of DM10,000, it is expected that DM3,000 of receivables will be collected and an equal amount of receivables will be newly booked during the next month, resulting in no change to the DM10,000 position. Also, the dollar/deutsche mark rate currently is 0.40, the anticipated average rate for the next month is 0.39, and the anticipated month-end rate is 0.37.

DM10,000	+3,000 −3,000	DM10,000
0.40	0.39	0.37

Assuming that an average exchange rate is used for translating the appropriate income statement items, the foreign exchange gain or loss at the end of this one-month period can be established as follows:

DM3,000 (0.39 − 0.40)	=	−30	(settled during the month)
DM3,000 (0.37 − 0.39)	=	−60	(newly booked during the month)
DM7,000 (0.37 − 0.40)	=	−210	(stayed on during the month)
Total loss	=	($300)	

Regardless of the transactions that are expected to take place during the month, this company could have viewed its exposure as simply long DM10,000. The expected foreign exchange loss on this balance sheet position can be estimated as

$$\text{DM}10{,}000\ (0.37 - 0.40) = \$300 \text{ loss}$$

The above example clearly illustrates that as long as starting positions are fully hedged, the **unhedged exposure** for any given period depends upon the extent to which the pro forma balance sheet differs from the current balance sheet. However, it is conceivable that while the balance sheet positions of individual foreign entities change from one period to the next, the after-tax net exposure of the company as a whole can remain more or less the same. The role of taxes in determining the real exposure of the company must be closely examined.

Companies that hedge intraperiod transactions alone often try to match the timing of the hedges with that of the transactions. This approach is more appropriate for companies that do most of their business under firm commitments or contractual arrangements whose timings are known in advance. For a great majority of corporations that do not fall into this category, it is impractical to match the timing and duration of the hedges exactly against the numerous transactions that arise from day-to-day business, although utilization of option forward contracts can provide a partial solution.

Corporations that formulate most of their protection strategies on the basis of **balance sheet positions** while hedging certain individual transactions independently do so because some transactions, such as debt repayments and dividend remittances, are individually identifiable in advance and probably of large magnitudes (and hence the senior management gives special attention to them). The major drawback of this approach is that the independent treatment of certain transactions might not be consistent with the overall position of the company. The exposure arising from these individual transactions can be partially offset, or even be completely neutralized, by other exposures elsewhere within the company, and thus there might not have been any need to hedge them individually in the first place.

Regardless of the approach undertaken in exposure management, the overall exposure must be measured fully and correctly. Where balance sheet positions do not alter significantly within a planning period, the overall exposure can be measured on the basis of balance sheet position alone. However, if the **intraperiod transactions** are such that the balance sheets of the various entities within the company undergo significant change, a proper measurement of overall exposure must take those changes into consideration.

Because of the difficulty in handling transactions in the measurement of overall exposure, corporations tend to ignore them and make ad hoc adjustments. The difficulty is a conceptual one—that is, how to account for transactions that represent flows as opposed to stocks. Balance sheet exposures are "stocks" that are easily measurable, while changes in these positions are "flows" that represent intraperiod transactions and are more difficult to measure. However, it is possible to account for the intraperiod transactions in the overall measurement of exposure.

Intraperiod transactions are of three different forms: exposed items on the current balance sheets that are expected to be settled during the planning period (such as a receivable appearing in the current balance sheet that is collected during the planning period); new exposures that are created as a result of future transactions within the planning period and that remain exposed at the end of the planning period (such as a receivable newly recorded during the planning period and not expected to be collected during that period); and new exposures that are created as a result of future transactions within the planning period but are settled during the same planning period (such as a receivable newly recorded during the planning period and also collected during the same period). The foreign exchange gains or losses associated with these different transaction time frames are dependent on the exchange rate at the beginning or the end of the planning period, and are also affected by the exchange rates prevailing during the planning period. In accounting measurements, the convention is to use an average or a weighted average exchange rate to translate revenue and expense items.

One can think of changes in balance sheet positions as debits and credits to current balance sheet items. The transactions that take place during the planning period affect the current balance sheets and are reflected by the debits and credits. An increase in assets is a debit item; an increase in liabilities is a credit item; a decrease in assets is a credit item; a decrease in liabilities is a debit item. The net of debits and credits (the difference between debits and credits) in each currency provides the net change to the current balance sheet positions. The current balance sheet adjusted for this net change gives the pro forma balance sheet.

One can also look at changes in balance sheet positions from a slightly different perspective. If the pro forma balance sheet can be estimated with reasonable accuracy, the anticipated changes in the current balance sheet can be measured directly. The net of all intraperiod transactions in each currency for each entity can be obtained by finding the difference between the current and pro forma balance sheet positions in that currency.

The above simple process yields the total exposure of any entity for a given period. It consists of exposures as indicated by current balance sheets, and those resulting from changes in balance sheet positions as reflected by the difference between current and pro forma balance sheets. Evaluation of these two types of exposures, using appropriate exchange rates, can yield the overall impacts of currency movements.

ILLUSTRATIONS OF DIFFERENT CURRENCY EXPOSURES

Currency exposures can be classified into four categories: (1) foreign currency exposures of the parent, (2) local currency exposures of the foreign subsidiary, (3) third-currency exposures of the foreign subsidiary, and (4) dollar exposures of the foreign subsidiary. The following examples illustrate two different situations in the SFAS 52 environment: (1) those in which the local currency is the functional currency, and (2) those in which the dollar is the functional currency. The objective is to measure the impact of currency movements on the profit and loss statement and the special equity account (translation adjustment account) in different currency situations.

A U.S. corporation has foreign subsidiaries in the United Kingdom and West Germany. For simplicity, only one exposure item in each example is identified. The following exchange rates and tax rates are used in all cases.

Beginning of Period	End of Period
\$/£ = 2.0	\$/£ = 1.5
\$/DM = 0.4	\$/DM = 0.5
\$/SF = 0.3	\$/SF = 0.6

Effective tax rates in the United States, West Germany, and the United Kingdom are assumed to be the same, at 40%.*

LOCAL CURRENCY AS THE FUNCTIONAL CURRENCY

Foreign Currency Exposure of the Parent. Consider DM 300cash of the parent.

Beginning of the Period
U.S. Company Consolidated

Cash (DM300)	\$120	Owner's equity	\$120

End of the Period
U.S. Company Consolidated

Cash (DM300)	\$150	Tax liability	\$12
		Owner's equity	\$138

P&L Consolidated (\$)

FX gain	\$30
Tax liability	(\$12)
Net gain	\$18
Impact on P&L	\$18
Impact on special equity account	NIL

Local Currency Exposure of the Foreign Subsidiary. Consider DM300 cash exposure of the German subsidiary.

Beginning of Period
West German Subsidiary

Cash DM300	Owner's equity DM300

End of Period
West German Subsidiary (DM)

Cash DM300	Owner's equity DM300

*The tables following have been prepared by Multinational Computer Models, Inc., Montclair, New Jersey.

P&L West Germany
No effect

Consolidated ($)	
Cash $120	Owner's equity $120

Consolidated ($)	
Cash $150	Special equity account $30 Owner's equity $120

P&L Consolidated
No effect

Impact on P&L	0
Impact on special equity account	+ $30

Third-Currency Exposure of the Foreign Subsidiary. Consider DM300 cash exposure of the U.K. subsidiary.

Beginning of Period U.K. Subsidiary	
Cash DM300 £60	Owner's equity £60

End of Period U.K. Subsidiary	
Cash DM300 £100	Tax liability £16 Owner's equity £84

P&L U.K. Subsidiary (£)	
Foreign exchange gain	£40
Tax liability	(£16)
Net gain	£24

Consolidated ($)	
Cash $120	Owner's equity $120

Consolidated ($)	
Cash $150	Tax liability $24 Special equity account ($30) Owner's equity $156

P&L Consolidated ($)	
Foreign exchange gain	$60
Tax liability	($24)
Net gain	$36
Impact on P&L	+ $36
Impact on special equity account	− $30

Dollar Exposure of the Foreign Subsidiary. Consider $120 cash of the German subsidiary.

Beginning of Period German Subsidiary	
Cash $120 DM300	Owner's equity DM300

End of Period German Subsidiary	
Cash $120 DM240	Tax credit (DM24)
	Owner's equity DM264

P&L West German Subsidiary	
Foreign exchange loss	(DM60)
Tax credit	DM24
Net Loss	(DM36)

Consolidated ($)	
Cash $120	Owner's equity $120

Consolidated ($)	
Cash $120	Tax credit ($12)
	Special equity account $30
	Owner's equity $102

P&L Consolidated ($)	
Foreign exchange loss	($30)
Tax credit	$12
Net	($18)
Impact on P&L	− $18
Impact on special equity account	+ $30

U.S. DOLLAR AS THE FUNCTIONAL CURRENCY

Foreign Currency Exposure of the Parent. The foreign currency exposure of the parent has the same effects as if the local currency were the functional currency.

Local Currency Exposure of the Foreign Subsidiary. Consider the dollar the functional currency of the West German subsidiary with DM300 cash.

Beginning of Period
West German Subsidiary

Cash DM300 $120	Owner's equity $120

End of Period
West German Subsidiary

Cash DM300 $150	Owner's equity $150

P&L West German Subsidiary ($)

FX gain	$30
Tax	0
Net gain	$30

Consolidated ($)

Cash $120	Owner's equity $120

Consolidated ($)

Cash $150	Owner's equity $150

P&L Consolidated ($)

Foreign exchange gain	$30
Tax	0
Net gain	$30
Impact on P&L	+ $30
Impact on special equity account	0

Third-Currency Exposure of the Foreign Subsidiary. Consider the dollar the functional currency of a U.K. subsidiary with DM300 cash.

Beginning of Period
U.K. Subsidiary

Cash DM300 $120	Owner's equity $120

End of Period
U.K. Subsidiary

Cash DM300 $150	Tax liability $ 24
	Owner's equity $126

P&L U.K. Subsidiary ($)

Foreign exchange gain	$30
Tax liability	($24)
Net gain	$ 6

Consolidated ($)

Cash $120	Owner's equity $120

Consolidated ($)

Cash $150	Tax liability $ 24
	Owner's equity $126

P&L Consolidated ($)

Foreign exchange gain	$30
Tax liability	($24)
Net gain	$ 6
Impact on P&L	+ $6
Impact on special equity account	0

Dollar Exposure of the Foreign Subsidiary. Consider the dollar the functional currency of the West German subsidiary with $120 cash.

Beginning of Period German Subsidiary

Cash $120	Owner's equity $120

End of Period German Subsidiary

Cash $120	Tax credit ($12)
	Owner's equity $132

P&L West German Subsidiary

Foreign exchange gain	0
Tax credit	$12
Net gain	$12

Consolidated ($)

Cash $120	Owner's equity $120

Consolidated ($)

Cash $120	Tax credit ($12)
	Owner's equity $132

P&L Consolidated

FX gain	0
Tax credit	$12
Net gain	$12
Impact on P&L	+ $12
Impact on special equity account	0

CONCLUSION

A multinational corporation needs to integrate the impacts of inflation, foreign exchange rates, and interest rates in the strategic planning process, and develop competitive strategies and day-to-day operating financial decisions in order to effectively deal with problems and take advantage of opportunities presented. On an ongoing basis, the economic impact of foreign exchange rate volatility on the multinational corporation should always be assessed in the context of overall business decisions such as pricing, currency of billing, market structure, competition, and cost/revenue structure.

A foreign exchange risk management program can only be effective when the corporate financial objective and the foreign exchange policy are clearly defined and are fully compatible with management philosophy. The definition and measurement of currency exposure are two of the starting points to the development of a broader financial policy to cope with international financial issues.

SECTION 8.8

CURRENCY EXPOSURE MANAGEMENT

CONTENTS

SECTION 8.8

CURRENCY EXPOSURE MANAGEMENT

Abraham M. George

As a result of the accounting regulations under Statement of Financial Accounting Standards 8 and the recent SFAS 52, U.S. companies have come to recognize the impact that currency movements can have on reported profits. Many have responded by expanding their internal staff and by seeking assistance from financial consulting organizations. The initial reaction to the new environment under floating rates has been somehow to prevent excessive exchange losses that now are reported separately in published financial statements. Many companies began by focusing their attention on the balance sheet exposure and increasing their hedging in the forward exchange market. Companies soon recognized the need to manage the economic exposure of the company while maintaining a happy balance with reported accounting results. Ad hoc policy directives were implemented that, in many cases, resulted in greater losses than would otherwise have occurred. The major problems remain complex but are still quite fundamental: (1) How does a company define and measure exposures that result from both balance sheet positions and transactions, but are interrelated? (2) How does one define and measure economic exposure, and reconcile it with accounting exposure? (3) How does one handle the tax implications on exchange gains and losses? Without resolving these basic issues, a company cannot establish a sound reporting system, much less calculate its after-tax worldwide exposure under any management approach.

Development of a comprehensive **exposure management program** must evolve from a thorough understanding of the implications that currency movements have on the company's financial position. This implies that the management should be able to assess the impact of currency fluctuations on reported income, liquidity, and, ultimately, the economic state of the company. Management should then be in a position to institute timely and well-conceived policy measures to preserve the long-term economic health and profitability of the company.

DEFINING POLICY OBJECTIVES

The absence of well-defined **policies and operating procedures** with respect to exposure management is a major problem of many companies. Clearly defined corporate

---

A substantial part of this section is prepared from the author's book, *Foreign Exchange Management and the Multinational Corporation*, Praeger, New York, 1978.

objectives are a prerequisite to the effective management of currency exposure. Vague **policy goals**, such as "protect the company against exchange losses" or "reduce exchange losses while avoiding unnecessary and expensive coverage," do not suffice. The policy makers should squarely address the issue of managing non-cash flow exposures versus cash flow and economic exposures. Management should state clearly the extent of exchange risk it is willing to incur in each currency, and the role that currency projections should have in deciding protection strategies.

The **management philosophy** with respect to hedging varies from company to company, depending on the risk/cost preference of the management. At one extreme are a few companies that leave most exposures unhedged, in the belief that losses in one period can be offset in a subsequent period when currencies move favorably. This practice is based on a false assumption about a cyclical nature in the movements of currencies over the long term. At the other extreme are those companies that treat the cost of protection as a part of the total cost of doing business abroad, and hedge all exposures fully whenever possible. These firms very often incur not only excessive but sometimes also unnecessary costs. Most companies fall into a third category that bases management decisions on a comparison of potential exchange losses and the cost of protection.

A company can define its **maximum allowable risk** in terms of the total dollar value of all unhedged positions at any given time, or it might specify the maximum ceiling on unhedged positions on a currency-by-currency basis, setting a higher percentage for those currencies that traditionally have been less volatile, or it might set limits within which foreign exchange losses plus the cost of cover must be kept. Policy directives for these constraints can well serve as guidelines for deciding the maximum level of exchange risk a company is prepared to face instead of incurring the cost related to buying protection.

A company's management philosophy with respect to the approach it should adopt in exposure management also must be made known to the managers of foreign exchange. The impact of anticipated long-term currency movements on the overall performance of the company must be thoroughly examined before deciding on the suitability of any given management approach. Exposure management must evolve from an **integrated system of financial functions**, and should give adequate consideration to the operating requirements of individual units. Liquidity positions of subsidiaries, their working capital requirements, and the extent of local financing available are some of the immediate, yet ongoing, factors that influence the choice of the suitable approach to exposure management. The nature of underlying foreign transactions—intracompany versus third-party transactions—the feasibility of adjusting prices to compensate for exchange losses and the limitations placed by the host country on repatriation of earnings all have a direct bearing on the appropriate approach. The long-term objective governing every exposure management decision should be the maximization of the present dollar value of all net cash inflows of the various operating units combined.

CENTRALIZATION AND CONTROL

In the present world, where management decisions are rendered more difficult by differences in countries' tax codes, regulations, and restrictions governing capital flows and borrowing arrangements, and a host of other complexities, the international financial officer responsible for corporate exposure management must constantly choose among several conflicting policy measures. The rationale behind **centralized exchange risk management** is that it facilitates focusing on the problem from an unbiased total corporate viewpoint, and affords greater coordination and control. Moreover, exposure management decisions cannot be made in isolation; they must be fully integrated with other financial policies. The dominant role of the treasury department in coordinating all key financial functions among all individual units within a multinational company places it in a position to formulate and implement exchange risk management policies consistent with corporate objectives.

Regardless of the approach undertaken in exposure management, centralization of foreign exchange management functions is needed for reasons of control, coordination, and avoidance of conflicting actions by different units within the multinational corporation. By expressing all hedges in foreign currencies vis-à-vis a single base currency (U.S. dollars for a U.S. multinational), one is able to net out the numerous cross-currency hedges required to protect exposures of all units. This centralized exposure netting function facilitates the undertaking of protective measures that suit the needs of the entire company.

Under a decentralized approach, each unit is permitted to hedge its own exposure in foreign currencies. Depending upon the management approach, the parent company may hedge the local currency equivalent (in units of the subsidiary's currency) of the same exposure to eliminate translation impact on the special equity account.

For example, given a DM300 asset exposure of a British subsidiary of a U.S. multinational when the dollar/deutsche mark rate is 0.40 and the dollar/pound rate is 2.0 and given further a U.K. tax rate of 40% and a U.S. tax rate of 50%, the cash flow exposure can be hedged by the British subsidiary by selling DM300 forward against the pound sterling. The translation exposure can be hedged by the U.S. parent by an additional £120 forward sale against the U.S. dollar, if desired:

$$\text{DM300} \times \frac{0.40}{2.00} \div [1-0.5]$$

Optimum decision making is unlikely unless financial objectives have been spelled out and communicated, and unless a continuing planning process is institutionalized that renders the goals operational. Exposure managment functions must be coordinated with other financial considerations, such as international cash management and long-term investment decisions. Since policies concerning foreign exchange affect areas beyond corporate finance, participation by key personnel from other departments is highly desirable.

Both policies and specific decisions about exchange risk are often made exclusively by the treasurer in a great majority of companies, with little or no active participation by other members of senior management. This apparent lack of participation by members outside the treasury department creates an internal bias that can have an unfavorable impact upon nonfinancial areas of the business, particularly on marketing and purchasing. The treasurer is, therefore, placed in the unhappy situation of having to justify some actions taken in the interest of the company as a whole, but which might not appear objective from the viewpoint of individual parties.

What is needed is a **systematic procedure** in formulating, executing, and reviewing exchange risk management policies. Apart from an active participation by top management, it appears that a committee approach to decision making is more effective with regard to decisions pertaining to foreign exchange. An exposure management committee should consist of key financial officers of the company and at least one senior member from the accounting, tax, marketing, and purchasing departments. Whenever possible, appropriate senior officers from foreign subsidiaries should be invited to attend some of the policy-setting meetings. The parent company should communicate to its subsidiaries the rational behind those instructions that directly affect them.

The **treasury department** is the center for formulating, coordinating, and executing all exposure management functions. While a committee is ultimately responsible for making policy directives, the treasury department should have sufficient resources to provide the necessary inputs to assist decision making. For example, medium-to-large companies might find it useful to have their own internal economists working within their treasury departments. Such persons can be given the sole responsibility of collecting appropriate macroeconomic data and making exchange rate forecasts. They can, in turn, seek the assistance of outside consulting organizations, while keeping abreast of changing economic and political trends within each country of concern.

Management at subsidiary levels hesitates to execute directives from the parent company if the likely outcome is against its interest. This is so because subsidiaries are evaluated on the basis of return on investment, level of profits, and similar measures. Any action that will affect them unfavorably, regardless of the desirability from a total corporate viewpoint, naturally will not be greeted with enthusiasm. Since foreign subsidiaries have very little say in centralized exposure management, they should not be accountable for their exchange losses or for protection costs incurred as a result of implementing policy directives from corporate headquarters. More important, the performance of foreign subsidiaries should be evaluated in local currency terms, with **proper compensating adjustments** for their own cash losses, and these results should not be biased by exchange conversions into the parent's currency.

The **performance** of the treasury department with respect to exposure management should be evaluated each year. Such evaluations should be consistent with the corporate objectives and policy directives laid down by top managment. In addition to comparing exchange losses that were avoided and the costs incurred in doing so, an evaluation of the past performance must focus on measures taken to reduce or avoid longer term positions in exposed currencies.

LONG-TERM VIEW

Planning for the long term is important in managing foreign exchange risk. A company should have a general idea of the likely changes in its currency positions in the next three to five years as a result of the directions it is taking. Since such a broad, long-term picture of the company is known only to top management, their input in evaluating likely future exposure is essential. Such evaluations must be made in the light of underlying trends in the different economies and currencies, and must give careful attention to changing tax and exchange regulations.

Proper long-term planning should be done to move toward a balanced position wherever possible, but that objective is secondary to other operating goals. A balanced position can be achieved through natural hedges by maintaining opposing positions in currencies that often tend to move in the same direction (such as "snake" currencies). In capital-budgeting decisions, the desirability of financing in currencies that help reduce exposure must be investigated. Since long-term financing decisions affect the exposure of the company for years to come, their importance from an exposure management viewpoint must be emphasized.

COORDINATION OF FINANCIAL FUNCTIONS

Management of short-term credit, long-term debt, liquidity, and working capital in an international context are closely related to foreign exchange management. An **integration** of these financial functions with tax considerations must be one of the goals of every multinational corporation.

When short-term borrowings are contemplated for liquidity reasons, their impact on exposure must also be noted. Subsidiaries establish lines of local credit and draw on them whenever a need arises, seldom considering other sources of short-term financing. Foreign currency financing is rarely contemplated unless there is a clear interest rate advantage. Subsidiaries prefer local currency financing for reasons of convenience, especially because these debts do not involve any foreign exchange implications for them. When strong currency subsidiaries resort to local currency financing this obviously leads to the creation of exposures that are not desirable from the viewpoint of exchange risk management. Centralization of exposure management facilitates coordination of financing and exchange requirements by periodically instructing financial managers at local levels to resort to a particular currency for meeting their short-term requirements. This can be made operational relatively easily by establishing lines of credit in appropriate foreign currencies wherever exchange restrictions do not prevent doing so.

Financing through long-term debt should be undertaken after a careful analysis of exchange implications. In addition to interest rate considerations, the cost of debt must be measured inclusive of potential foreign exchange gains or losses and taxes, all at their present values. Once again the corporate headquarters is in a position to make this analysis and to recommend to local units appropriate financing strategies that are consistent with the interests of the corporation as a whole.

Companies that are organized to pool excess funds of their various units at one central location are able to invest those funds in a manner consistent with interest rate and exchange rate considerations while meeting the liquidity requirements of the various units. Even where there is no formal arrangement for pooling excess funds, the treasury department can still provide short-term investment directives to local units. In addition, excess funds can be transferred from one location to another to meet liquidity requirements or for exposure management reasons, or both.

Neither are working capital management policies independent of foreign exchange considerations. Centralized netting and clearing of intracompany accounts, leading and lagging of receivables and payables, establishment of trade credit terms, and collection policies at local levels could have a direct bearing on exposure management. Managers at the subsidiary level can be asked to implement policy directives from the treasury department that are intended to affect the exposed positions of the company. By properly coordinating these functions in a consistent manner, the foreign exchange objectives of the company can be attained without necessarily creating serious operational problems. In fact, if working capital policies that minimize exchange risk are adopted, they should not cost more in terms of efficiency or lost opportunities than the potential monetary loss they are intended to prevent.

PROTECTIVE MEASURES AGAINST EXCHANGE LOSSES

The **objective** in exposure management is twofold—the minimization of exchange losses as a result of currency movements, and the minimization of protection costs. This dual objective cannot be met without a proper understanding of the different courses of action that might be open to a company in every situation. Among other things, the precise course of action undertaken in a given situation is a function of the protection costs of the available alternatives. The availability of a given strategy, in turn, depends upon institutional constraints and exchange and credit restrictions. The managerial implications of various methods of protection must be thoroughly assessed before a final choice is made.

Broadly speaking, there are **two types of protective measures**: forward exchange contracts and asset liability transactions, such as borrowing and investing, leading and lagging, and prepayments. Some of these measures can be implemented quickly and relatively easily, and hence can be applied in response to immediate or short-term anticipated currency situations. The others, which are more rigid in nature, should form a part of the long-term general policy measures.

GENERAL PROTECTIVE MEASURES. As explained above, **general protective measures** are those implemented on an ongoing basis, as a part of the multinational's normal operations, in order to place the company in a long-term defensive posture. These measures relate to decisions involving long-term borrowings abroad, capital investments in foreign countries, pricing and invoicing intracompany shipments, lagging of payments, and working capital policies. Because of the rather rigid nature of these measures, careful consideration must be given to them prior to their implementation. Decision on these matters must be made only after thinking through their long-term foreign exchange implications.

The long-term outlooks for currencies and the relative tax structures of countries constitute the crucial variables affecting the decisions on general policy measures. For example, it might be quite reasonable to assume that the West German economy will perform better than the British or the Belgian economy in the coming year. Similarly, at present the Dutch economy probably has greater inherent strength than the Italian economy. These economic outlooks should be reflected in the anticipated relative strengths and weaknesses of their currencies. Long-term currency outlooks, when viewed in conjunction with tax implications, provide reasonable insights for rational management decisions.

Long-Term Borrowings and Investments. Most long-term financing decisions are based on interest cost considerations alone. For example, Swiss franc borrowings by multinational corporations since the late 1960s have been motivated by generally low interest rates on such funds. The dollar value of such loans, however, has more than doubled during this period as a result of the appreciation of the Swiss franc. It is crucial that financing decisions take into account not only interest rates but also exchange rate outlooks. Long-term borrowings of weak currencies to finance capital investments in strong-currency countries help a firm to attain the ideal situation of an overall balanced position from **natural** hedges.

Normally, the **financing of new investment projects** in a foreign country requires some capital from the parent company. In developing countries, a continuous outflow of the parent firm's capital to the subsidiary might be required during the initial years of the project because the local capital market of the host country might be more or less closed. If the contribution of the parent firm's capital is to be curtailed to avoid exchange losses from local currency depreciations, the foreign subsidiary must find ways to remit the capital as quickly as possible. Apart from exchange restrictions that are apt to be applied to capital remittances, the foreign subsidiary is likely to encounter obstacles in borrowing locally for the purpose of remittance. Internally generating funds for loan repayments through a reduction in the level of dividends to the parent is not a real alternative to local borrowings, since such a course of action does not lead to a greater reduction in the exposed local currency position of the subsidiary than what would have been accomplished by a full dividend remittance.

Most countries permit equity and debt capital **remittance**, provided the original underlying transaction was registered with the appropriate monetary agencies of the host country. Such remittances are normally permitted in installments, and local borrowings for that purpose are often allowed. Subsidiaries located in weak-currency countries must be instructed to find every available source (not internally generated funds) of borrowing and to make remittances as permitted by local governmental authorities. Accelerated return by the subsidiary of loan capital received from the parent or from strong-currency subsidiaries elsewhere must be encouraged. However, the financial stability of the subsidiary and its ability to finance a loss of capital should not be overlooked. Where the subsidiary's financial position is sound, and no capital projects are immediately outstanding, an accelerated return of capital to the parent might be possible.

As a rule, the parent company should insist that the foreign subsidiary obtain official assurances of repayment of principal and interest whenever a loan is advanced. As a further protection, it is safer to have the parent company's bank lend the required investment to the foreign subsidiary, instead of a direct advance by the parent. Foreign governments are unlikely to bar debt repayments to foreign banks, as they often would fear losing credibility in international financial markets.

Income Remittances. Given the principle that funds should be transferred out of weak-currency countries at an accelerated pace, the foreign subsidiary ought to explore all available **means of remittance**. It is very likely that countries that impose exchange restrictions will be stricter about dividend remittances than about repayment of debt. As a rule, therefore, maximum income remittances must be made consistent with the liquidity position of the subsidiary before debt repayments are considered.

Efforts must continuously be made to accumulate a maximum of claims by the parent company against a subsidiary in a weak-currency country via fees, dividends, royalties, and payments on intracompany sales or purchases. Though such claims are subject to scrutiny by local governmental authorities, a broad credit structure will facilitate transfers of funds when restrictions are placed on a particular type of remittance, thus leaving other opportunities for remittance open.

Certain countries have blocked accounts to retain unremitted income. Local authorities often allow gradual repatriation of such funds through the purchase of local financial instruments and the subsequent sale of these instruments for foreign exchange. Since these facilities are usually limited, prompt action by the subsidiary in applying for and registering such instruments is required. Even though it can involve cumbersome paperwork, subsidiaries in blocked-account countries should pursue these alternative legal means of funds transfer.

Local borrowings for the purpose of income remittance are highly desirable in weak-currency countries, since they create additional liabilities in depreciable currencies while channeling assets to the parent company. To what extent this is possible is determined by the amount of credit available and the terms under which it is procured. In developing countries and in weak-currency countries, there might be credit control measures that will restrict credit availability or entail prohibitive costs. In addition, remitted funds might be subject to rather high withholding taxes.

The decision as to whether a subsidiary should make **accelerated income remittances** out of the proceeds from local borrowings rests on a judgment of timing and the magnitude of anticipated depreciation of the local currency in relation to the interest charged by the bank. The net interest charge on the loan should be less than the likely loss as a result of currency depreciation, and the duration of the loan should exceed the period within which the anticipated depreciation might occur.

Working Capital Policies. Management of working capital and of currency risk are two interrelated functions. On a global basis, allocation of working capital encompasses all the problems and opportunities inherent in management of current assets and current liabilities in a single country, as well as the consideration that the monetary denomination of various balances can be a major factor in minimizing exposure to exchange risk. Proper allocation of cash, receivables, inventory, and payables on a continuous basis can help reduce such risk without having to resort to such specific measures as forward contracts.

Establishing **optimum monetary balances** consistent with liquidity requirements while reducing exchange risks is not an easy task. This requires a proper balance between the monetary assets, which consist of cash, bank deposits, monetary instruments, and accounts and notes receivable, and monetary liabilities, which consist of debts that must be paid in fixed monetary units, accounts and notes payable, and accrued exposures. Even though inventory is not a monetary asset, it is one of the major balance sheet items that generates monetary assets, and hence should be viewed more or less in the same light.

From an exposure management viewpoint the broad **working capital strategy** is to maintain a net asset position in strong-currency countries, and a net liability position in weak-currency countries. On a global basis, it implies maintaining monetary assets in hard currencies and monetary liabilities in soft currencies. Though this ideal goal is difficult to achieve because of exchange and credit restrictions, continuous efforts should be made to move in this direction.

Some companies follow a general policy of holding minimum current assets in their foreign subsidiaries by insuring that all excess funds are transferred to the parent company. Such a policy is not always desirable or possible, especially when local governmental regulations do not permit the foreign subsidiary to hold its excess cash in foreign currency-denominated assets, such as Eurocurrency deposits. The advantage of holding excess cash within the subsidiary (in strong currencies) is that it might facilitate additional borrowing in local currency, thereby creating liabilities in weak currency. These borrowed funds can be used to finance local working capital, or can be converted into dollars and loaned to another unit within the multinational.

Where local **exchange restrictions** prevent maintaining cash balances in foreign currencies, it is often desirable to transmit maximum profits to the parent company or to other subsidiaries operating in countries with strong currencies. Apart from the advantage of reducing assets in weak currencies, the pooling of funds in one central location affords effective coordination of investment of surplus funds.

Cash management policies in weak-currency countries require maintaining minimum local cash balances at all times through sound forecasting and synchronization of cash receipts and disbursements. Cash movements can be accelerated through such techniques as central deposit accounts and wire transfers. If convertibility is restricted, the only available choice might be to invest the excess funds in suitable interest-bearing money market instruments. However, if funds transfers are permitted, the foreign subsidiary should avail itself of all means of remittance, keeping in mind its internal requirements. Interim dividends instead of one year-end dividend should be the practice whereever local authorities permit it. A proper balance between dividend payments and other means of remittance, such as royalties, licenses, technical advice, and management services, should always be maintained, depending on tax considerations and the likely implications of current practices on future payouts.

Some companies use centralized cash depositories for the pooling of excess funds and for the proper investing of these funds. One central authority might specialize in handling the worldwide cash pool, a practice that has the advantage of choosing among various national money market instruments and the Eurocurrency markets for its investments. This central agent is often able to utilize tax advantages of certain types of investments in tax-haven countries. Further, the central pool is in a position to return the necessary funds to any unit that might find itself short of cash and deems it advantageous to utilize the pooled funds. From a tax viewpoint, the ideal location for a centralized cash depository is a tax-haven country, but often a location such as London, New York, or Brussels can be chosen if institutional or legal constraints do not permit the selection of a tax haven.

Since receivables form a major portion of a company's monetary assets, their management takes on an important role. A multinational can significantly reduce its exposure to currency depreciations by reducing the amount of local receivables in weak currencies. As a general rule, strict controls over local currency receivables should be maintained so as to reduce their magnitude. The usual method of minimizing receivables by reducing the length of credit terms might lead to reduced sales, and hence might not be desirable. Similarly, special discounts to speed collections can be more costly than other alternatives available. Factoring is another alternative that should be considered. Borrowing against receivables can be preferable to all other measures, especially if the foreign subsidiary is experiencing liquidity problems or if the interest charges are not excessive. Discounting of commercial bills at a bank or the agencies of a central bank is common practice in many European countries. Many banks offer to purchase commercial bills at low interest rates because they have the facility to rediscount these bills with the central bank or its agencies.

Where intracompany accounts are involved, **centralized netting procedures** provide an effective means of speedily settling accounts. The objective of a centralized clearing center within a multinational is the speedy transfer of funds related to payments for goods and services out of weak-currency countries and to reduce transfer costs. A centralized funds clearing system permits multilateral offsetting of intracompany receivables and payables, thereby minimizing exchange conversions and speeding transfers. It also provides an orderly channel for clearing funds on a worldwide basis and insures that each unit keeps its intracompany transactions on a current basis. The basic principle behind this system is to transfer only net amounts between units according to specified time schedules, each unit purchasing or selling the requisite amounts in advance to hedge the transferable net amounts.

A centralized intracompany netting system is essentially a leading procedure for settling payables that arise from commercial transactions between different units within the multinational company. These procedures should be sufficiently flexible to lag payments when short-term currency expectations call for such an action. (The technique of lagging payments is discussed later in this section.) The basic system can be further modified by incorporating proper denomination of invoices that take advantage of taxes, with a centralized invoicing center coordinating all billing and payment activities.

Inventory management, from an exchange risk viewpoint, is quite complex, and should not take precedence over operating requirements. As a general rule, inventories of raw materials, work in process, and finished goods should be kept at a minimum consistent with normal commercial requirements. The level of inventory cannot be lowered simply to reduce potential exchange risk; inventory management is independent of direct exchange rate considerations unless it requires importation of foreign materials. The variables that normally come into play in deciding the level of inventory are carrying and ordering costs, anticipated demand for finished goods to meet sales requirements, anticipated availability of raw materials, and anticipated costs related to raw materials. In an inflation-prone country, also therefore a likely weak-currency country, it can sometimes be advantageous to keep high levels of inventory if the carrying costs (financing as well as other costs, such as storage costs) are lower. The potential exchange loss that could arise from a depreciation of the local currency is often made up by higher prices on finished goods. Deliberate price adjustments to make up for exchange losses, especially when the inventory is imported, should be pursued whenever possible without jeopardizing commercial viability.

From an exposure management viewpoint, inventory management does not necessarily imply a reduction in the level of inventory in every weak-currency situation. Instead, the emphasis should be on creating offsetting liabilities. It is often possible to finance inventories by short-term local currency borrowing, leaving the monetary assets available for remittance. In other words, the basic principle pertaining to inventory management, from a currency risk viewpoint, is to create additional monetary liabilities to neutralize it, simultaneously reducing other monetary assets through remittances or conversions into hard currencies. This policy, combined with periodic price adjustments on finished goods, can effectively take care of exchange risk problems arising from inventory.

Working capital policies pertaining to **liability management** consist of incurring liabilities in weak currencies and prepaying in strong currencies. Local currency debt financing is generally the rule of thumb in many companies. Although in some instances the company is able to obtain financing relatively cheaply in capital markets outside the host country, management often ignores this option. The basic reason for this general posture is to avoid foreign exchange losses. To some extent this shifts the responsibility for evaluating affiliate financial requirements from parent management, and relies entirely on the local environment. A commitment to a policy of local borrowing to avoid foreign exchange risk can at times be quite costly. In weak-currency countries, short-term funds are often very expensive, though a part of this cost can be recovered through a deterioration of the local currency.

From an exposure management viewpoint, the **cost of insurance** against potential exchange losses through local currency borrowings is the interest rate differential between locally denominated debt and dollar debt. If the foreign affiliate is in a position to borrow a low-interest-bearing foreign currency instead of the dollar, the cost of insurance will not depend only upon the interest rate differential between the local currency debt and the foreign currency debt; it also is affected by the potential exchange loss arising from an appreciation of the borrowed foreign currency.

General policy directives pertaining to liability management should be selective. Long-term currency and interest rate trends must be analyzed in depth before guidelines and policies pertaining to any hard-and-fast rule are established. Only in cases where the trend is currency depreciation and where remittances are hard to make should there be a firm rule of utilizing local debt instead of any other sources of financing. In all other cases, each financing requirement must be evaluated individually, and decisions must be based on a comparison of the costs of alternate means of protection from exchange losses.

Invoicing Policies. Subsidiaries that operate abroad often engage in commercial transactions with other foreign entities of the multinational company, with the parent company in the United States, or with third parties in other countries. In certain cases these foreign transactions of individual subsidiaries are a significant portion of their total sales. Many subsidiaries import raw materials from the parent company or other subsidiaries for local manufacturing processes. The currency denomination of invoices can be a significant element in limiting the extent of currency risk involved in such transactions.

The decision pertaining to the **currency denomination of invoices** on intracompany payments should be based purely on tax considerations. Apart from tax implications, the foreign exchange effect on intracompany payments on a consolidated basis does not depend upon the currency denomination of the invoice. The reason is that the liability in the books of the importing subsidiary is offset by an exactly equal amount of receivables in the same currency in the books of the exporting subsidiary. The dollar loss or gain on the asset is offset by the dollar gain or loss on the liability. However, the tax effects upon gains or losses realized by individual units cannot be ignored.

In an intracompany transaction it makes no sense to have a foreign exchange gain by one subsidiary at the expense of another, unless there are definite **tax advantages**. The currency denomination of the invoice merely determines who will realize the gain or the loss. If the invoice is denominated in the local currency of the exporting company, the latter does not incur any foreign exchange gain or loss, and the importing company must bear the foreign exchange risk. If the invoice is denominated in the currency of the importing company, the situation is reversed. If a third currency, such as dollars, is used, the exchange risk will be shared by both the importer and the exporter. A strategy based simply on realizing a foreign exchange gain by one subsidiary at the expense of another is without merit, since the company as a whole does not stand to gain or lose when the transaction is measured in terms of dollars. The operating performance of individual units is, of course, affected by exchange gains and losses but the consolidated company is not affected when all accounts are translated into dollars. The switching from one currency denomination to another determines who will account for exchange gains or losses at the subsidiary level, and while this can also have implications for liquidity and cash flow, it does not change the total corporate picture, but merely reallocates gains and losses between two interrelated units within the same company. What must be avoided is any external aversive factor, such as an increased tax liability resulting directly from the reallocation of exchange gains or losses.

The objective of properly **selecting the currency denomination of invoices** on intracompany payments is to obtain maximum credits upon exchange losses or to minimize tax liabilities upon exchange gains. As a rule, all shipments from a strong-currency country to a weak-currency country should be invoiced in the currency of the lower tax country. Conversely, all shipments from a weak-currency country should be invoiced in the currency of the country that has the higher tax rate of the two. The validity of this general rule can be illustrated by the following example.

Suppose the British subsidiary of a U.S. company imports from a West German subsidiary. For illustration purposes, a British tax rate of 40% and a West German tax rate of 50% are assumed. The following exchange rates prevail at the time a shipment worth DM3,000 is made by the West German subsidiary: $/DM = 0.40; $/£ = 2.0. Further, the following exchange rates at the time of settlement of the invoice are assumed: $/DM = 0.50; $/£ = 1.50. Contrary to the general rule stated above, it is assumed that the invoice is denominated in deutsche marks.

The initial balance sheets are as follows:

U.K. Subsidiary (£)

Fixed assets £1,000	Payable DM3,000 (£600)
	Owner's equity £400

German Subsidiary (DM)

Receivable DM3,000	Owner's equity DM3,000

Consolidated Balance Sheet ($)

Fixed assets $2,000	Owner's equity $2,000

Assuming that the invoice was denominated in deutsche marks (DM3,000), the West German subsidiary does not incur any exchange loss upon settlement of its claim. However, the British subsidiary will require £1,000 instead of the £600 it had previously allocated to settle the payable. The foreign exchange loss of £400 will receive a tax credit of 40%, or £160. The new balance sheets just prior to settlement of the payable by the British subsidiary appear thus:

U.K. Subsidiary (£)

Tax credit £160	Payable DM3,000 (£1,000)
Fixed assets £1,000	Owner's equity £160

German Subsidiary (DM)

Receivable DM3,000	Owner's equity DM3,000

Consolidated Company ($)

Tax credit $ 240	Special equity account ($500)
Fixed assets $1,500	Owner's equity $2,240

The change in the consolidated owner's equity of $240 ($2,240 – $2,000) indicates the tax credit obtained by the British subsidiary on its foreign exchange loss, which will be reflected also in the consolidated profit and loss statement. The translation loss of $500 shown in the special equity account is a result of the change in dollar value of the fixed assets, which is not applicable to this analysis.

The West German subsidiary invoiced the shipment in its local currency instead of the British pound, as called for by the general rule. Would the multinational as a whole have stood to gain more if the invoice had been denominated in pounds sterling? This question is answered by examining alternative balance sheets for the settlement day under the new assumption.

U.K. Subsidiary (£)

Fixed assets £1,000	Payable £600 Owner's equity £400

German Subsidiary (DM)

Receivable £600 (DM1,800) Tax credit DM600	Owner's equity DM2,400

Consolidated Company ($)

Tax credit $300 Fixed assets $1,500	Special equity account ($500) Owner's equity $2,300

The change in the consolidated owner's equity of $300 ($2,300 – $2,000) indicates the tax credit obtained by the West German subsidiary on its foreign exchange loss of DM1,200. As can be seen, the alternative of denominating the invoice in pounds sterling instead of deutsche marks resulted in a greater tax credit, a difference of $60 ($300 – $240).

The above example shows that denomination of the invoice in the currency of the lower tax country will result in a more favorable tax impact, provided the direction of shipment originates in a strong-currency country and goes to a weak-currency country. In order to implement this general rule, the multinational company should have some expectations about the relative strengths and weaknesses of the currencies of its subsidiaries.

Some companies follow the practice of denominating all intracompany invoices in **U.S. dollars.** There is no particular advantage in doing this between foreign subsidiaries; in fact, it generates accounting difficulties for both foreign units. However, dollar invoicing is certainly applicable to transactions between the parent company and any of its foreign subsidiaries. Once again, the **general rule** holds that all shipments from a strong-currency country to a weak-currency country should be invoiced in the currency of the lower tax country. Similarly, all shipments from a weak-currency country to a strong-currency country should be invoiced in the currency of the country that has the higher tax rate. The above two rules help maximize tax credits or minimize tax liabilities on foreign exchange losses and gains.

Invoices to **third parties** abroad generally follow the conventional rule that they should be denominated in the relatively stronger currency. For example, if the deutsche mark is a stronger currency than Italian lire, the West Germany subsidiary should denominate all its invoices in deutsche marks for its shipments to the Italian importer. Conversely, the Italian subsidiary should denominate its invoices in deutsche marks instead of lire if it exports to West Germany.

For a subsidiary that makes shipments to more than one foreign third-party importer, the above rule might involve denominating invoices to different countries in different currencies. For example, if the French franc is stronger than Italian lire but weaker than West German deutsche marks, the French subsidiary making shipments to an Italian importer should denominate its invoices in the French franc. However, the invoice on shipments to the West German importer should be denominated in deutsche marks.

So far, only the rules pertaining to receivables have been discussed. With respect to payables for the choice of currency in which to make **payments** the rule is simply reversed. The unit that imports from third parties abroad should always try to negotiate payments in the weaker currency. Even though it may be hard to enforce an exposure management strategy on a third party's invoicing policies, many suppliers are willing to oblige the buyer and go along with this suggestion.

It has been shown that the policies with respect to currency denomination of invoices do not depend upon the likely direction of currency movements vis-à-vis the dollar. Instead, these decisions are made on the basis of the relative strength or weakness of the two currencies involved in the transaction. In the case of intracompany transactions, tax rates applicable to the two units also come into the picture.

Since it is operationally difficult to make frequent changes in invoicing procedures of subsidiaries, the parent company should **set guidelines** that form a part of general long-term instructions for all its units. These guidelines should be reviewed at intervals of six months or more, and appropriate instructions consistent with likely currency trends should be conveyed to all units.

It might not always be desirable to preselect the currency of denomination of invoices to third parties, especially when the selected currency is likely to work against the customer's interest. In most cases customers are bound to realize the potential exchange risk facing them, and might prefer other arrangements. In the interest of maintaining customer relations and sales expansion, it might be preferable to follow a moderate exposure management policy that shares some acceptable level of exchange risk with customers.

Transfer Pricing. The mechanism by which profits are transferred through an adjustment of prices on intracompany transactions is termed **"transfer pricing."** The transfer price mechanism can be applied to the sale of goods and services by the parent company to its foreign subsidiaries, or to transactions between strong-currency and weak-currency entities. The parent company, for example, can set prices as high as possible on its intracompany shipments to one of its weak-currency subsidiaries. This will have the simultaneous effect of reducing the profit margin of the subsidiary (assuming that domestic prices are competitive) and increasing that of the parent. The result is a reduction of the taxable income of the subsidiary and the lowering of its ability to pay taxable dividends; however, non-taxed funds are transferred out of the subsidiary in the form of operating charges. While the funds received by the parent, after adjusting for operating costs, are subject to taxes in the parent's location, the transfer pricing mechanism has two clear advantages over most other methods of transferring funds out of subsidiaries. First, the flow of funds is continuous and automatic, corresponding to normal business transactions, and requires no special and deliberate actions. Second, it has a potential tax advantage over other forms of funds repatriation if the combined income and withholding tax rates abroad are higher than the parent company's income tax rates.

The transfer price mechanism can be a major exposure management tool for companies with large intracompany accounts. This is particularly true for oil companies and major manufacturing concerns that ship raw materials and semiprocessed materials to foreign subsidiaries and between subsidiaries.

Whether or not transfer pricing is a useful technique for maximizing corporate profits depends upon its advantages from an overall tax viewpoint and on the foreign exchange implications. However, the practicality of this system is affected by a number of factors. Apart from the question of administering a possibly complex system of unrealistic prices, it tends to obscure the competitive efficiency with which the goods are produced and sold. Further, an arbitrary shift of profits from the purchasing company to the producing company within any single enterprise tends to impair judgment about the true nature of the return on capital. It is also likely to obscure clear evaluation by the central management of the policies and performances of individual subsidiary managements.

Transfer pricing is obviously inappropriate where the parent company has less than full ownership of the subsidiary. It must be remembered that subsidiaries are often audited by impartial or independent accountants, and at times by governmental authorities. Declining profit margins imply lower taxable income for the local government, and the authorities are likely to view such a situation with disfavor. Where exchange controls exist, the authorities are bound to scrutinize intracompany accounts, and might impose restrictions or reallocate income among the different parties within the corporate entity. In addition, the customs authorities are likely to impose higher duty, which might wipe out the potential advantage of transfer pricing.

In spite of the difficulties involved in transfer pricing, it can still be advantageous to incorporate moderate pricing policies. What is needed is a reasonable pricing strategy that is not likely to upset the host country. Such a policy is probably a must with respect to countries that maintain blocked funds. It is important that transfer pricing policies be applied gradually and over a long period, and not exceed a reasonable level. Sudden responses in anticipation of potential adverse currency movements are likely to encounter stiff opposition from governmental authorities in the nations where the foreign subsidiaries are located.

Local and Export Price Adjustment. Many companies respond to actual cash losses from currency movements by increasing the sales prices of their products. This is particularly true of companies that import raw materials or semifinished goods in their manufacturing process. Exchange losses arising from a depreciation of the local currency can be offset partly or fully by raising local prices on finished goods. For companies that operate in countries where there is no forward market to hedge their imports or where the cost of borrowing locally is high, the only offsetting solution might be to raise sales prices.

Increasing prices on goods sold locally or on exports has a positive cash flow impact, provided such increases do not lend to lower sales volume. Local governmental authorities are likely to impose a price freeze soon after major currency devaluations, and hence it might be necessary to institute price adjustments in anticipation of and prior to actual devaluations.

Price adjustments in response to **devaluations** are very similar to adjustments in response to inflation. In order to sustain profits in real terms, it is necessary to increase prices by more than the increase in the general price level, because income taxes can be levied on that part of the increase that the authorities consider profit rather than cost recovery.

Exposure management policies from a **cash flow viewpoint** should institute price adjustments where desirable to offset cash losses due to exchange losses. To the extent that a company is able to adjust prices to neutralize exchange losses, the negative economic impact of currency movements is reduced. Accounting for the economic impacts of exchange rate changes becomes a truly difficult task. It requires not only an evaluation of the potential cash flow impacts but also an adjustment for the potential increase in real revenue from higher prices on inventory. The adjustments needed on a company's sales prices to offset exchange losses depend upon the ratio of imports to total inventory, change in the local currency value of imports, and the potential change in the local price level as a result of devaluations.

Leading and Lagging, and Extension of Trade Credit. Leading and lagging imply speeding up collections on receivables and lagging payments on payables denominated in weak foreign currencies. Leading and lagging techniques are very useful for managing exposures resulting from transactions with third parties as well as for intracompany accounts. Leading policies, such as a prepayment of debt and early declaration of dividends, are normally deliberate and specific, and hence are considered as specific protection policies. The basic principle of leads and lags is to build up debit balances in the weak currency through delayed collections on export receipts and accelerated payments on imports by the weak currency subsidiary. Simultaneously, the strong-currency subsidiary minimizes exchange losses by speeding its sales receipts denominated in weak currencies. This technique has special advantages in intracompany transactions because it helps to increase debit balances in weak currencies and, simultaneously, to increase credit balances in strong currencies within different entities in a multinational enterprise.

It might not always be possible for a weak-currency subsidiary to lead its payables through internally generated funds, especially if it is simultaneously practicing lagging of collections on receivables from abroad. In such cases, the subsidiary should be encouraged to borrow locally to make early payments. Hence, the net cost of lead and lag policies on intracompany accounts will be determined by the cost of borrowing funds locally, the return on funds for the recipient subsidiary, and the relative changes in the currency values. Both the interest costs and the exchange gains and losses should be adjusted for local tax impacts.

The extent to which the cash flows of the two corporate entities are affected will be determined by the currency denomination of the invoice, the respective tax rates, the interest costs, and, most important, the relative movements of the two currencies involved. Hence, the cash flow impact on an intracompany transaction between, for example, the West German and French subsidiaries will be affected by lead-lag policies to the extent of the relative movements of the French franc vis-à-vis the West German mark. However, from an accounting viewpoint, the consolidated U.S. corporation also experiences foreign exchange impacts from a change in the franc/dollar and the deutsche mark/dollar relationships. A calculation of the net impact of asset/liability transactions (which include leads and lags) is illustrated later in this section.

Leading and lagging policies must be implemented on an ongoing basis rather than suddenly, in reaction to imminent changes in currency values. This implies that the treasury department of the parent company appraises the relative strengths and weaknesses of currencies and periodically instructs subsidiaries on leads and lags. Companies that have centralized netting procedures for intracompany accounts should retain the flexibility to control the timing of payment flows between units. A sound lead-lag policy, when implemented in conjunction with invoicing and pricing policies, serves as an ongoing effective protective measure to reduce overall corporate exposure to both short-term and long-term adverse currency movements.

Subsidiaries and the parent company could achieve the objective of lead-lag policies by suitably balancing trade credit terms for intracompany accounts. Shipments to subsidiaries with weak currencies should be made under short payment periods, while longer time is allowed for payments by strong-currency subsidiaries. A formalized routine procedure is likely to control the timing of payments in a manner consistent with the currency outlooks.

It is important to bear in mind that governmental authorities are not likely to view with favor any excessive delays in collections from abroad. Certain countries, such as West Germany, have restrictions on accepting payments earlier than normal into, and delayed payments out of, their countries. Once again, a rational management approach is one that tends to be reasonable as well as consistent over time, and to be based on longer term currency trends rather than anticipating imminent adverse movements.

SPECIFIC PROTECTION MEASURES. In addition to a program of ongoing general protection measures, a company will from time to time be required to implement specific protection measures in anticipation of immediate or short-term adverse currency movements. For example, if it is expected that the Spanish peseta will be devalued at some time in the next few months, the company might want to hedge its net long position in pesetas. Whether or not a company actually hedges its long position will depend upon the expected magnitude of devaluation, the cost of hedging that position, and the availability of hedging facility. Before any protection measure is implemented, the company should evaluate the various alternatives available to it to cover its exposure. The final choice will be determined by the relative costs of alternative protection strategies.

Specific protection measures can be grouped into five classes: **forward contracts, borrowing and investing and/or lending, prepayments, swaps, and other credit measures and payment mechanisms.**

Forward Exchange Contracts. Forward covering through exchange contracts consists of buying or selling a currency to meet a future transaction or to hedge a balance sheet position. An importer can buy in advance, through forward exchange contracts, the amount of foreign currency needed to meet an obligation. Similarly, an exporter who expects to receive a fixed amount of foreign currency (assuming that the exporting firm invoices its customers in their respective local currencies) for a shipment made might want to assure itself that the local currency value of the shipment is also fixed and known in advance, regardless of changes in exchange rates.

It is customary to express the cost of forward cover in annualized percentage terms. For example, assuming that the spot rate is 0.20 and the forward rate for a three-month contract is 0.205, the premium can be expressed as follows:

$$\frac{\text{forward rate} - \text{spot rate}}{\text{spot rate}} \times \frac{12}{\text{months to maturity}} \times 100$$
$$= \frac{0.205 - 0.200}{0.200} \times \frac{12}{3} \times 100$$
$$= 10\% \text{ premium}$$

This cost must be adjusted upward for the cost of any deposit that the bank requires from the company prior to entering into the forward contract. In the case of large companies, no deposit is demanded by the bank, though a ceiling on the size of the transaction might be imposed.

Prior to executing a forward contract, the company must study the prevailing exchange restrictions and tax implications thoroughly. Certain countries are free of exchange restrictions on forward contracts. Others impose various restrictions that normally take the following forms.

1. All forward contracts must be taken through local authorized banks.
2. Contracts are limited to specific commercial transactions.
3. Evidence of underlying commercial transactions must be produced and prior approval must be obtained.
4. The duration of the contract must be limited and must conform to the terms of the commercial transaction.
5. Hedges against balance sheet positions are not permitted.
6. Ceilings are placed on the proportion of the underlying transaction that can be hedged.
7. The parties to the transaction must be disclosed to authorities prior to executing the forward cover.

It is important that the corporate treasurer clearly understands the **implications of hedging** in the forward market. He or she might consider forward exchange contracts for hedging transactions in foreign currencies or for hedging the balance sheet positions of subsidiaries. A distinction between the two must be made because of the cash flow implications. If a forward contract is taken against the parent company's own transactions in foreign currencies, this hedge protects the consolidated company's translation exposure as well as its cash flow exposure. A potential cash flow loss on the commercial transaction of the parent is offset by a potential cash flow gain on the exchange contract. However, if a forward contract is taken against the local currency exposure of one of its foreign subsidiaries, this hedge could result in a potential paper gain or loss on the exposure and a cash flow loss or gain on the contract. Such a forward contract is obviously intended to protect the translation exposure instead of the cash flow exposure of the company. The company should, in such cases, be prepared to incur a cash flow loss on the forward cover in return for the accounting paper gain on the **special equity account.**

The important point to bear in mind is that the forward contract is a potential cash flow transaction, while the underlying exposure might not always be one. Therefore, prior to entering into forward contracts, the company is well advised to consider the cash flow implications and the alternative means of protection available to it.

While the ultimate gain or loss on a forward contract depends upon the exchange rate prevailing on the day of settlement of the contract, the cost of the hedge must be viewed simply as the premium or discount. The exchange gain or loss on a contract, less the premium or discount, is offset by an equivalent loss or gain on the underlying exposure that is being hedged. Hence, the emphasis must be on selecting the alternative means of hedging a given exposure consistent with the management approach, and choosing the strategy that minimizes hedging costs and provides protection from cash flow as well as accounting losses on foreign exchange.

Borrowing and Investing and/or Lending. Borrowing of the local currency in anticipation of a devaluation is a practice that companies attempt whenever possible. Unless the borrowed currency is converted into a strong currency prior to devaluation, there is no advantage in the borrowing. The protection from exchange losses on a company's long position in a weak currency is obtained from an increase in liability in the weak currency and a simultaneous increase in assets in the strong currency. The foreign exchange impact resulting from such an action is determined by the nature of the transaction and the resulting currency movements. The corporate exposure to currency risk is affected by the nature of the underlying transaction, which can take any of the following forms. The corporation borrows locally to pay off a dollar debt to the parent; make a loan to the parent; convert loan proceeds into dollars or into a strong currency, and invest; declare dividends to the parent.

The effects of these and other actions on the company's exposure differ considerably, and therefore must be clearly understood. If a subsidiary borrows locally and pays off a dollar debt, it has the effect of increasing local currency liability in the subsidiary and simultaneously reducing the dollar liability to the parent. If the local currency borrowing is to be used to make a loan payment to the U.S. parent, it has the effect of creating a new liability exposure in the parent company in the currency of the subsidiary.

The foreign subsidiary might instead borrow locally and convert into U.S. dollars in order to make Eurodollar deposits. This results in the following changes of the subsidiary's balance sheet.

Foreign Subsidiary	
+ dollar assets	+ local currency debt

If the local currency borrowing is done to make a dividend payment to the parent, it results in the following changes to the balance sheets.

Foreign Subsidiary	
	+ local currency debt

U.S. Parent	
+ $ cash	

The result is an increase in the local currency exposure of the subsidiary by the full amount of the borrowing. The cash flow exposure is not affected by the above transaction; however, it results in a decrease in the net asset exposure in the currency of the subsidiary by the entire amount of the dividend payment.

In addition to the different types of transactions mentioned, a multinational might undertake fund transfers between foreign subsidiaries. The impact on exposures from such transfers must be properly considered. An analysis of the **role played by taxes** is crucial in deciding on the changes in corporate exposure resulting from specific asset/liability transactions. Each transaction must be systematically analyzed, and its effect on corporate exposure must be calculated carefully prior to implementing an asset/liability transaction to protect against exchange risk.

Prepayments. Prepayments are another form of asset/liability transaction, and hence subject to the same considerations. They are simply leading transactions intended to reduce assets or increase liabilities in weak currencies. These transactions normally take the form of early declaration of dividends, prepayment of debt in foreign currencies, and settlement of other liabilities that are denominated in strong currencies. Just like any other asset/liability transaction, prepayment cost must be measured in terms of the actual interest cost of making prepayments, less interest earned or saved, or in terms of the opportunity cost of funds that were used to make the prepayment, less interest saved or earned from the prepayment. Once again, tax considerations must not be ignored.

Swaps. Swaps are essentially a set of parallel transactions in opposite directions. For example, a U.S. parent might lend local currency to a subsidiary through an intermediary bank under an agreement for repayment of the loan after a stipulated period. The bank receives dollars from the parent that are returned when the subsidiary repays the debt to the bank. The foreign subsidiary gains if the interest rate charged by the bank is less than the return on local investment. The parent gains if the cost of this swap transaction (interest foregone by the parent in making dollar deposits with the bank) is less than the change in the exchange rate of the foreign subsidiary's currency. This type of swap transaction is suitable in situations where the foreign subsidiary is restricted in making any form of direct payments to the parent and requires external funds for its operations. Similar export swaps are also possible wherein the foreign subsidiary repays dollars via export proceeds accumulated over a specified time.

A foreign currency swap is a simultaneous spot and forward transaction, with the forward contract reversing the spot transaction. This technique is useful in cases where a two-way transaction is involved. For example, a parent company might convert dollars in the spot market and make a loan to the foreign subsidiary, and simultaneously hedge the loan repayment by a forward sale of the foreign currency against the dollar. The cost of such a transaction depends on the discount on the forward sales plus the interest rate differential between the two countries.

Forward swaps, one other variation of this type of transaction, involve selling and simultaneously buying forward a given currency for two different maturity dates. The purpose of such a transaction is to provide protection for a potential future exposure from one future date to another. For example, a company might hedge its long currency exposure in deutsche marks for a period starting three months and ending six months from the present date. It would then sell deutsche marks forward for six months and buy deutsche marks forward for three months, thus being covered for the second three-month period. This forward swap mechanism has the advantage of flexibility in exposure management and has the potential for reducing the cost of hedging. For example, if DM10,000 is to be hedged for the above period, the cost will be determined by the two forward rates.

Six-month forward sale	0.4650 × 10,000 =	$4,650
Three-month forward purchase	0.4665 × 10,000 =	4,665
Net cost for hedging three to six months		$ 15

The above cost can be compared with the outright cost of hedging six months. The cost of hedging six months at a forward rate of 0.4650 when the present spot rate is 0.4685 is calculated as follows:

$$\text{cost of hedging} = (.4650 - 0.4685) \times 10{,}000$$
$$= \$35$$

In addition to the possibly higher cost for a single forward sale, it should be noted that exchange gain or loss on a single six-month forward contract will not necessarily offset the exchange loss or gain on the exposure in a future period. The gain or loss on the exposure from three to six months will be determined by the exchange rates prevailing at the end of three months and at the end of six months from the present day, while the gain or loss on the forward contract taken out for a six-month maturity will depend upon the present spot rate and that at the end of six months.

Other Credit Measures and Payment Mechanisms. A weak currency is often selling at a huge discount in the forward market in anticipation of a possible devaluation. The cost of hedging long positions in such currencies is invariably high. Sometimes, it pays to check with corporate officers of banks to see if any other party, especially another multinational corporation, requires funds in such currencies. Another company might be willing to buy a weak currency at a discount for a specified date in the future in exchange for dollars or other currencies it might have in excess. The exchange rate that could be negotiated in an intercompany future transaction could be more attractive than that available in the forward market.

Discounting of export bills in local markets is a technique employed by some companies when exchange restrictions do not prevent spot purchases of foreign currencies. A local bank might discount export bills denominated in the foreign currency at an interest rate higher than the domestic rate. The proceeds are then sold in the spot exchange market for an appropriate strong currency, and can be placed in time deposit until it is advantageous to convert them back into local currency.

A company having more or less **matching** inflow and outflow of a foreign currency over a specified period might be able to establish foreign currency accounts with the permission of the central bank. All inflows over a given period are maintained in such an account, and outflows in the same currency are executed from it as and when required, without the need to convert the inflows immediately into local currency. This technique is helpful in reducing transaction costs, and works as an effective exposure management tool where the local currency is realtively weak.

In addition to all of the above exposure management strategies, a company must continuously explore ways of reducing net long positions in weak currencies. Weak-currency countries are likely to place exchange restrictions that effectively prevent normal outflow of funds. Yet, there are likely to be authorized channels for funds transfer, which can be quite cumbersome and involve a lot of red tape. Prior registration of investments and authorizations for future repatriations are often necessary, but unless these approvals are obtained in advance, any funds remittance abroad might be practically impossible when a need arises. Proper coordination of exposure management functions is required at all levels, and the corporate treasury department should be fully aware of, and be responsive to, the requirements of each situation.

CALCULATIONS OF THE POTENTIAL COST OF AN ASSET/LIABILITY TRANSACTION

As shown, asset/liability transactions can be undertaken to reduce corporate exposure to exchange risk. The foreign exchange gain or loss on these transactions resulting from currency movements exactly offsets the exchange loss or gain on the original exposure. The costs of asset/liability transactions depend mainly on interest rates and tax rates. Prior to implementing any given strategy, the costs of alternative measures must be evaluated.

For the purpose of illustrating the calculations involved in estimating the **cost of an asset/liability transaction,** the following is considered.

The British subsidiary of a U.S. multinational corporation borrows pounds sterling locally for six months and pays off a dollar loan of $100,000 to the U.S. parent. It is assumed that the borrowing cost in the United Kingdom is 12% and that the dollar loan was at 7% interest. The U.K. tax rate is 40% and the U.S. tax rate is 50%. The present spot is 1.85 and the anticipated rate at the end of six months is 1.70. The following calculations are required in estimating the cost of the above transaction:

Interest cost on £54,054 (100,000 ÷ 1.85) for six months = $54{,}054 \times .12 \times \frac{6}{12}$	= £3,243	
Less tax credit of £1,297 (0.40 × £3,243) =	£1,946	
Dollar value of after-tax interest cost at 1.70 =		$3,308
Interest saved on $100,000 loan = $100{,}000 \times .07 \times \frac{6}{12}$	= $3,500	
Less tax of $1,750 (0.50 × $3,500) =		$1,750
Net interest after-tax cost =		$1,558

It should be noted, however, that the above transaction affords an after-tax protection of £32,432 exposure (£54,054 × [1 − 0.40]) for a period of six months. Hence, the after-tax annualized cost is equal to

$$\frac{1{,}558}{£32{,}432 \times 1.85} \times \frac{12}{6} \times 100 = 5.19\%$$

This annualized cost should be compared with the cost of alternative strategies that protect the same after-tax exposure. The cost of the least expensive measure so chosen forms the basis for further management decisions on the extent of cover.

GUIDELINES FOR HEDGING

The decision on whether or not a hedge should be undertaken to protect a given currency position depends primarily upon two factors: (1) the potential exchange loss that is likely to occur, and (2) the cost that will have to be incurred on the hedge. The level of risk as a measured by the potential exchange loss can be compared with the cost of providing protection by the least costly hedge. For any given planning period, the objective in exposure management can be defined as the minimization of the sum of probable exchange losses and the cost of the hedge.

AMOUNT OF FULL HEDGE. Once the after-tax net exposure in a currency is calculated, it is rather simple to calculate the amount of full hedge in that currency. The amount of hedge that will be required for full protection of a given currency position on an after-tax basis depends solely on the tax applicable to exchange gains and losses on the hedge. The net after-tax exposure of the consolidated company, when divided by the factor (one minus the tax rate on the hedge), yields the after-rax amount of the full hedge.

The amount of the full hedge will be greater the higher the tax rates on the hedge. Some companies follow the practice of hedging from lower tax locations in order to reduce the amount of hedge that is required and, hence, the pretax cost of hedging. However, the after-tax cost of hedging is not affected by the differences in tax rates.

For example, an after-tax asset exposure of DM1,000 is given. It is assumed that a multinational has an option of hedging this exposure either from the United States, which has an effective tax rate of 50%, or from a foreign location that has an effective tax rate of 20%. If the hedge is done from the United States, the amount of the full hedge is

$$\frac{\text{DM1,000}}{(1 - 0.50)} = \text{DM2,000}$$

Assuming a discount of US$0.01 on the forward deutsche marks, the pretax cost of a forward sale of DM2,000 will be $20. This cost is normally treated as an expense and is taxed at the corporate tax rate of 50%. The after-tax cost of full hedge undertaken from the United States is therefore $10 ($20 × 0.50).

The amount of full hedge from the foreign location is

$$\frac{\text{DM1,000}}{(1 - 0.20)} = \text{DM1,250}$$

A forward sale of DM1,250 will incur a pretax cost of $12.50 and an after-tax cost of $10 ($12.50 × 0.80). As can be seen, the after-tax cost is identical, regardless of the tax rate applicable to the hedge.

However, it might still be preferable to undertake hedges from lower tax locations for immediate cash flow reasons. A smaller amount of hedge involves a lower immediate cost, and hence a lesser adverse impact upon current liquidity. On the other hand, tax credits affect cash flow only at a later time.

While the policy of undertaking a forward contract from a lower tax location might be preferred in certain cases, precautionary checks must be made prior to doing so. Some countries might disallow a loss on the forward contracts on the ground that the hedge is in connection with a capital asset, arguing that it is unreasonable to allow the loss against the parent company's unrelated income when the corresponding profit is not taken into account. This line of reasoning will not prevent the same revenue authorities from taxing the gains on the hedge even though the corresponding loss was not allowed. Clarifications of tax regulations applicable to each of the multinational's entities must be made by the company treasury department in consultation with the tax department. Further, it must be ascertained that no exchange controls prevent taking hedges from a given country.

DURATION OF HEDGE. Specific protective measures are forward contracts, borrowings in certain currencies for a specified period, prepayment of loans, and other actions that are intended to hedge a position as of a given day in the future. Since the exposure that is being hedged corresponds to the planning period that is chosen, the duration of such hedges should not be less than the planning period. This raises the question of the duration of a planning period.

For the purpose of specific hedging decisions, the ideal planning horizon is three to six months, coinciding with the ends of account periods. A three-month horizon is preferable to a six-month one if pro forma balance sheet positions cannot be estimated accurately. Some companies plan for shorter durations, often based on monthly horizons. The arguments for this practice are that exposures change from month to month, and that currency movements and their expectations change from month to month. However, monthly planning horizons have the following disadvantages.

1. They necessitate monthly reports from each entity, thereby generating more paper work.
2. After-tax calculations are to be made each month.
3. By the time reports arrive from all entities, the reporting month might have expired.
4. They can lead to frequent hedging manipulations each month, especially if exposures change from month to month.
5. Timing of hedges to changes in exposures cannot be matched on a monthly basis, since exposure information has a lag. Information lag could result in hedging exposures that might no longer exist.
6. They can lead to a higher cost, because a hedge against an exposure in a given month might have to be reversed in the subsequent month if the exposure has changed between these two months.
7. Quarterly planning periods have the advantage of netting the ups and downs that are reflected in the monthly figures.

Even though the suggested planning period is three months, it is advisable to enter into forward contracts with not less than six months' maturity. The reason is that forward contracts of or beyond six months' maturity provide greater flexibility, in the sense that there is more time to reverse the contract if sufficient gain has been made on it. As a rule of thumb, a foreign exchange gain of more than 5% on a contract calls for its reexamination, since the market might already have adjusted the exchange rates for the adverse conditions against which the contract was originally intended to protect.

If exposure positions do not change significantly from the end of one quarter to the end of the next, then in theory hedges with a year's maturity can protect the entire exposure for a whole year. This would avoid repeating contracts with shorter maturities several times within a year. When market opportunities exist (e.g., to buy deutsche marks or Swiss francs at $0.38 or to sell sterling at $2.10, as was the case in October 1975) to enter into worthwhile longer term contracts, they should be fully utilized.

In order to facilitate keeping track of forward contracts, it is advisable to enter into contracts with maturity dates on or close to the end of a future planning period. Contracts with random maturity dates will make their management more difficult.

EXTENT OF HEDGE. The purpose of projecting future currency values and their impact on the exposure is to evaluate the degree of risk in maintaining an **unhedged** or **partially hedged position.** The level of risk, when expressed in terms of potential exchange loss, can be compared with the cost of insurance. Such a comparison can lead to more prudent decisions about the extent of hedge for any given currency position.

A fully hedged position that incurs the maximum protection cost implies no exchange risk, while a completely unhedged position carries the full burden of uncertainty. The dual objective of minimizing probable exchange losses and the cost of protection might require a partially hedged position instead of either of the two extreme options. **The extent of hedge** should, therefore, depend upon the decision makers' subjective expectations about future currency values, the probabilities attached to different outlooks, and the related cost of protecting the position.

The two relevant currency forecasts are the most likely outlook and the pessimistic outlook. The anticipated foreign exchange loss under the most likely outlook and the pessimistic outlook for each currency exposure can be compared against the cost of protection by the least costly hedge. Where forward contracts are available, the respective premiums or discounts are good approximations of the cost of protection for the purpose of making hedging decisions, even though less costly protection measures might be available for implementation. Comparison of the potential exchange loss (or gain) and the cost of hedging the entire exposure can yield any of the following cases.

1. The cost of hedge is less than the anticipated loss under the most likely outlook.
2. The cost of hedge is greater than the anticipated loss under the pessimistic outlook.
3. The cost of hedge is less than the anticipated loss under the pessimistic outlook, but greater than under the most likely outlook.

Cases 1 and 2 yield straightforward decisions; case 3 needs further evaluation.

Case	Decision
1	Hedge fully
2	Do not hedge
3	Hedge partially

If the **cost of hedge** is greater than the anticipated loss under the most likely outcome but less than the likely loss under the pessimistic outcome (case 3), the decision pertaining to the extent of hedge needs further thought. Even though the most likely outcome has, by definition, greater probability of occurring than the pessimistic outcome does, a conservative approach to exposure management would require a reduction in the exposed position. The decision in most cases should call for a partial hedge to the extent determined by the subjective probabilities attached to possible outcomes. The unhedged portion of the exposure should be carefully and continuously monitored.

The extent of hedge in case 3 is, therefore, determined subjectively by the financial manager. However, by allocating subjective probabilities to relevant currency forecasts, one can calculate the appropriate amount of partial hedge. A management science approach in determining the extent of hedge is discussed later in the section.

The decision-making processes pertaining to hedging decisions can be simplified by the use of the form shown in Exhibit 1. The information required for the completion of the form is as follows:

1. Currency of exposure.
2. Spot exchange rate as of the day the form is used.
3. Forward exchange rate available on a contract with a maturity date equal to the end of the planning period. A forward contract might not be the least expensive hedge. However, the premium or discount on a forward contract is a good approximation of the cost of hedge.
4. Most likely outcome is based on the forecast exchange rate corresponding to the most likely outlook. The most likely gain or loss should be calculated by using the after-tax exposed figures.

EXHIBIT 1 HEDGING PREPARATION FORM

<table>
<tr><td colspan="10">Planning Period: / / to / /
Type of Exposure: Translation ☐ Cash Flow ☐ Economic ☐</td></tr>
<tr><td colspan="3">Exchange Rate</td><td rowspan="2">Amount of Full Hedge</td><td colspan="2">Most Likely Outcome</td><td colspan="2">Pessimistic Outcome</td><td rowspan="2">Cost of Full Hedge</td><td rowspan="2">Decision</td></tr>
<tr><td>Currency Code</td><td>Spot of / /</td><td>Month Forward</td><td>Rate</td><td>Gain/ Loss</td><td>Rate</td><td>Gain/ Loss</td></tr>
<tr><td></td><td></td><td></td><td></td><td></td><td></td><td></td><td></td><td></td><td></td></tr>
</table>

5. Pessimistic outcome is based on the forecast exchange rate corresponding to the pessimistic outlook.
6. Cost of full hedge is equal to the premium of discount, multiplied by the hedged amount, adjusted for taxes, or is equal to the after-tax interest cost of the asset/liability transaction.
7. The decision on the extent of the hedge should be reached along the lines suggested earlier in the section. The corresponding cost of the hedge based on the decision can also be indicated in this column.

The form shown in Exhibit 1 is an excellent tool for making rational decisions. If exposure management decisions are made by a committee, it can be completed, except for the column pertaining to the decision, by an appropriate financial officer prior to the committee meeting.

The committee can discuss the two outlooks, attach subjective probabilities to them, and compare them against the cost of hedging. This procedure will speed the decision-making process, and is likely to result in rational and sound decisions.

CALCULATION OF THE OPTIMUM EXTENT OF HEDGE. Even though there is some theoretical work about currency forecasts and management of exposure that could aid analytically sophisticated decision makers, there is a gap in the literature concerning the crucial link between exchange rate forecasts and hedging decisions. Various types of decision models that are currently available attempt to recommend more precise courses of action under different potential currency situations. The major emphasis so far has been on the estimation of the expected exchange rates and their variances in order to decide between hedging a given exposed position or leaving it open. More sophisticated approaches that consider the correlation in the movements of currencies have been formulated along the principles of Harry Markowitz's portfolio theory, but they too suffer from serious conceptual problems associated with the estimation of expected exchange rates and the variance of forecasts.

The objectives of exposure management are often defined as maximizing expected gain or minimizing expected loss, and minimizing the variability in expected earnings. In a class of alternative strategies of equal risk, the objective is to choose alternatives with higher expected earnings. Strategies differing in risk and expected earnings can be ranked according to the ratio of the variance to expected earnings, and opportunities with a lower ratio can be chosen. While this approach to exposure management under uncertainty is theoretically illuminating, it is far from operational because of the difficulties in approximating the probability density function of future currency values with any reasonable accuracy.

Choices such as insuring an entire exposure or leaving it fully exposed are clearly either too costly or too risky. In practice, very few managers always have recourse to such extreme courses of action. In most cases protection strategies are influenced by forecasts of exchange rate movements. In the absence of reasonably reliable estimates of expected exchange rates and their variances, management decisions often tend to be ad hoc. What is needed is an approach that integrates an analysis of the uncertainties surrounding the forecasts as well as the costs associated with measures intended to reduce exchange losses.

The degree of flexibility in exposure management is rather limited because exposures in different locations arise in the course of doing business abroad, and hence are more or less given. Management strategies are further limited by credit and exchange restrictions in various countries, and other institutional factors. Therefore, the objective of exposure management should be to minimize potential exchange losses rather than to maximize exchange gains.

Given the difficulty in estimation, exchange rates should not be projected as point estimates but as interval estimates, preferably in the format of most likely, pessimistic, and optimistic outlooks, with corresponding probabilities. Further, the objective of minimizing losses implies that the most likely and pessimistic events are the two relevant forecasts for decision making. The risk associated with a currency forecast is implicitly incorporated in the pessimistic outlook and its corresponding probability. The impacts under the most likely and pessimistic outlooks can be estimated and compared with the cost of protection. One can therefore incorporate risk without estimating the variance of each forecast. An appropriate decision model can be derived to evaluate the level of risk subjectively and to compare it with the cost of protection in every hedging decision.

In the real world, where predictions about future currency movements are difficult, the choice between fully hedging or not hedging at all is often not clear-cut. Instead, a reduction in the exposed position might be more consistent with reducing the level of risk and the cost of protection. The objective can be restated as minimizing the potential exchange loss on the unhedged portion of the exposure as well as minimizing the cost of protection related to the hedged portion of the exposure. The management emphasis is, therefore, shifted to the determination of the extent of hedge, which is a function of the anticipated outcomes from currency movements, the uncertainty as reflected in the relevant probabilities, and cost related to protecting the position.

The first step in determining the extent of the hedge must start from the currency forecast itself. Assuming that one has a long position in a given currency, the relevant forecasts are the most likely and the pessimistic outlooks for that currency. The forecasts should not end there. Two additional questions must be answered: (1) What is the probability of realizing an exchange rate that is less than the present spot rate? (2) What is the probability of realizing an exchange rate that is less than the indifference exchange rate?

The second question introduces a simple concept about the **equilibrium** between the cost of protection and the potential exchange loss. A decision maker would be indifferent about a protection measure if its cost would exactly equal the potential exchange loss on the exposure, provided that loss is known with certainty. The exchange rate (I) corresponding to this indifference condition can be easily calculated from the equation

$$\text{exposure amount} \times (\text{spot rate} - \text{I}) = \text{cost of protection, measured in base currency units.}$$

Therefore

$$\text{I} = \frac{(\text{exposure} \times \text{spot rate}) - \text{cost of protection}}{\text{exposure}}$$

For example, if one assumes that the current spot rate for the deutsche mark is US\$0.42, and the least expensive protection strategy for fully covering DM100,000 is \$1,000, the indifferent exchange rate (I) can be directly calculated as follows:

$$I = \frac{(100{,}000 \times 0.42) - 1{,}000}{100{,}000} = 0.41$$

An approximation of the **indifference exchange rate** would be the forward rate for the duration one is considering. Hence, all of the above calculations can be ignored in those cases where forward rates are available. The second question can, therefore, be restated: What is the probability of realizing an exchange rate that is less than the forward rate?

The decision maker is forced to think about these two relevant probabilities and attach numerical values to them. The interesting point that can be brought out here is that the forecaster would, in most cases, have far less difficulty in providing these two probabilities than in making specific currency projections.

In Exhibit 2 the symbol α is attached to the probability that the future exchange rate would be less than the present spot rate. The symbol β is given to the probability that the future exchange rate would be less than the forward rate (or the indifference exchange rate).

If the exposure is left unhedged, a potential exchange loss could arise from realizing an exchange rate within the range P to S. Since only the interval P to I pertains to rate outlooks that call for a hedge, the expected loss corresponding to this interval is weighted and expressed as a proportion of all weighted outcomes within the entire region of P to S. This procedure yields the appropriate extent of hedge as

$$H = \frac{\beta \times (P - I)}{\beta \times (P - I) + (\alpha - \beta) \times (I - S)}$$

The numerator of the above expression corresponds to outcomes that require hedge, weighted by their probability. The denominator corresponds to all unfavorable outcomes, whether or not they require protection, weighted appropriately by their corresponding probabilities.

In the earlier example, it is assumed that M = 0.40, P = 0.37, α = 0.7, and β = 0.3. An application of the above formula calls for a partial hedge of

$$H = \frac{0.3 \times 100{,}000\,(0.37 - 0.41)}{0.3 \times 100{,}000\,(0.37 - 0.41) + (0.7 - 0.3)\,100{,}000 \times (0.41 - 0.42)} = 75\%$$

EXHIBIT 2

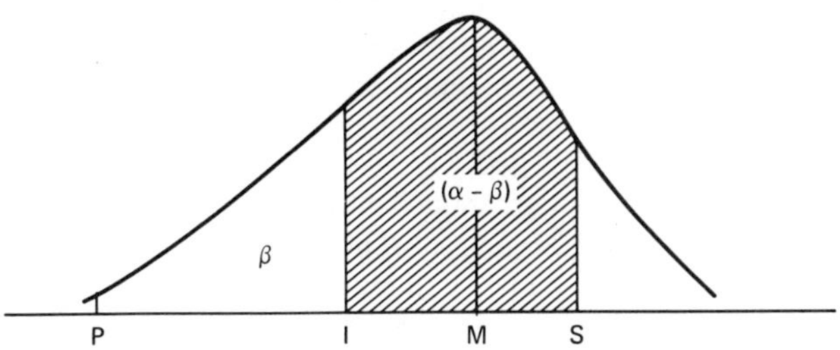

Note. P = pessimistic exchange rate; I = indifference exchange rate; M = most likely exchange rate; S = spot exchange rate.

It is interesting to note that, consistent with the objective of minimizing exchange losses as opposed to maximizing exchange gains, the above formula will call for a 100% hedge if the cost of protection is negative (for example, a premium on a forward sale).

As can be seen, the formula **determining the proportion of hedge** is sensitive to the level of protection cost, the pessimistic and the most likely outlooks, and the probabilities attached to the two relevant intervals within the forecasts. Whenever the decision maker changes expectations, he or she can recalculate the extent of hedge at the prevailing cost of cover, thereby monitoring the adequacy of protection levels.

While shifting the management emphasis to the determination of the extent of hedge, this model has avoided some of the conceptual problems encountered by previous models. It also provides a rational and precise way of reflecting the decision maker's expectations and the current market conditions in hedging decisions. When integrated with the rest of the exposure management functions, this approach can greatly assist in systematically evaluating the currency positions and in taking timely actions.

RECAPITULATION

Implementation of sound protection strategies requires an orderly and planned approach to the foreign exchange problem. It is impossible to achieve the ideal objective of hedging every risky exposure at the right time and for just the right period of time. What must be avoided is frantic action, which often is symptomatic of a lack of planning.

A comprehensive exposure management program for a multinational corporation should take the following sequence.

First, exposure management objectives are decided. This is the responsibility of top management. The objectives decided must be clearly stated in writing, and should be communicated to all units.

Second, exposure management functions are centralized. The treasury department at the corporate headquarters should be made responsible for formulating, coordinating, and implementing all exposure management functions. Depending on the sizes of exposures and the number of currencies involved, there should be sufficient support in terms of personnel and other resources.

An exposure management committee should be formed to make policy decisions and review them periodically. It is suggested that this committee meet once each month to review past policy decisions and to consider any new proposals, but that a complete review of all major issues and their policy decisions be made only once each quarter. Longer term decisions should not be unduly influenced by monthly swings in currency values.

Third, a sound reporting system should be established. Each firm must have a sufficiently detailed exposure reporting system that easily relates to other financial functions of the firm. Most companies communicate their exposure information on a monthly basis through telex, followed by mail confirmation. With the current advances in communication and computer technology, a great deal of time and effort can be saved by the use of international time-sharing computer networks. Several leading banks are now making available such reporting facilities that also serve as excellent management tools. In today's world, where a delay in information processing can cost a great deal, every multinational company is well advised to investigate some of the computer systems available for the management of their foreign exchange exposure.

It is important that subsidiaries be thoroughly briefed about the reporting requirements, and that the information they communicate be audited periodically for accuracy. The entire reporting system must be reviewed at least once a year, so that improvements in content and procedure can be instituted.

Fourth, the decision-making process is formalized. In preparation for every exposure management meeting, the required information must be compiled and circulated among committee members prior to the meeting. It is desirable that monthly meetings be held within one week from the day that exposure information is obtained from all locations.

Implementation of sound protection strategies requires an orderly and planned approach to the foreign exchange problem. Adequate preparation for strategy sessions can go a long way in assisting the decision-making process. Prior to each meeting the following tasks must be completed.

1. Check all exposure reports for any discrepancy.
2. Calculate after-tax exposures of each unit and consolidate them.
3. Compile a detailed list of all existing forward contracts, including the calculation of the effects of reversing them for remaining maturities.
4. Obtain most recent spot rates, and forward rates for different maturities.
5. Obtain information on tax rates, Eurorates, and interest rates prevailing on short-term borrowings and investment in all exposed countries.
6. Obtain information on the lines of credit available and utilized as of that day by each unit.

The form shown in Exhibit 1 is an excellent tool for evaluating exchange risk and for recording the decisions of the exposure management committee. The staff officer responsible for implementing the decisions must be present at every meeting. Speedy implementation is crucial, especially at times of rapid exchange rate movements.

While a thorough examination of the company's exposure is made and an overall management strategy is executed at least once in three months, the two other monthly sessions in each quarter must be utilized for monitoring the positions and for reviewing past decisions in order to decide whether interim actions are necessary. A structured approach to these management functions facilitates smooth functioning in an increasingly complex and crucial area. The ability to anticipate unfavorable events and to prepare for them adequately is critical in deciding whether a company can remain competitive in today's world.

SECTION 8.9

THE MECHANICS OF COVERING FOREIGN EXCHANGE EXPOSURES

CONTENTS

SECTION **8.9**

THE MECHANICS OF COVERING FOREIGN EXCHANGE EXPOSURES

Townsend Walker

The previous section examined different protection strategies and their policy implications. The mix of strategies that is finally chosen by a company may include a variety of specific actions. This section discusses the mechanics of those actions, their purpose, and costs.

ELEMENTS OF EXPOSURE

The corporation in international business is exposed to foreign exchange rate fluctuations because the currency of its income is different from the currency of its expenses. Exchange rates change continually. The rate that generated a profit on a given transaction when it was initiated may easily be different from the exchange rate when the money actually flows. Here are examples of typical exposures.

In May the Charlston Motor Company signs a contract with the government of Tunisia to deliver 50 dump trucks. The trucks will be made in Charlston's Wisconsin plant. They will be delivered in Tunisia in September at which time Charlston will be paid 2 million French francs.

Norris Tools Limited manufactures gardening tools in England's Midlands. The steel is obtained from British Steel; the wooden handles for the tools are bought from a Swedish supplier. Norris agrees to be billed in Swedish kroner since the Swedish supplier offers a better price in its own currency. Orders are placed seven to eight times a year. From the time they are ordered, the handles take a month to arrive, and the invoice is payable within 30 days.

Bailie Industries Limited, a Toronto-based multinational, makes auto accessories in every country of North America and Western Europe. It is company policy that the subsidiaries remit dividends as soon, and as often, as local authorities will allow, but government clearance procedures are notoriously erratic. The result is that the international treasurer in Toronto comes in many mornings to find a telex on the desk stating that lire are sitting in the account in Milan, ready to be converted. A week later a telex from Vienna may advise of schillings being remitted.

In 1975 Parker & Company, a Massachusetts-based electronics firm, borrowed Swiss francs for 10 years at the attractive rate of 5%; the alternative was to borrow dollars at 14%. Parker has been repaying the loan in quarterly installments.

The common elements in all these situations of transaction exposure is that all the companies measure the results of their operations against their home currency. For Charlston, it is U.S. dollars; for Norris, pounds sterling; for Bailie, Canadian dollars; and for Parker, U.S. dollars. The companies all have inflows or outflows of money in foreign currencies. For each corporation there is a time lapse between the day that terms are confirmed and the day that a conversion between foreign currency and home currency takes place. There are three elements in transaction exposure situations—a home currency, a foreign currency, and time.

In the Bailie Industries situation it may seem that time is not a factor; the money is there now. Exposure exists, however, until the conversion to the home currency is actually made. In this instance time has been collapsed. The time between the knowledge of the currency flow and the conversion is hours, as opposed to days or months in the other situations. Norris Tools raises a different time question. From what date does the exposure exist—from the date the order is placed, or when delivery is made? It exists from the date the order is placed because from that date onward Norris is open to the risk that the value of the Swedish kroner will rise in relation to the pound, even though the company has no obligation to pay until the handles are delivered.

What is the risk in the other situations? In Charlston the risk is that the French franc falls in relation to the U.S. dollar; in Bailie, that the currencies of the dividends fall relative to the Canadian dollar; and in Parker, that the Swiss franc rises against the dollar.

Symbols are used to represent these exposure situations and to facilitate finding solutions to them. The symbols consist of balls and arrows of different shades. A ball represents a company, and the shade of the ball represents its currency, the home currency. Arrows are flows of money, and the different shades are different currencies, foreign currencies and the home currency. Unless otherwise indicated, two arrows of the same size represent the same amount of money. Time moves from left to right.

If an arrow is pointing toward the ball, money is coming in—from sales, dividends, bank loans, and so on

An arrow pointing away from the ball means that money is flowing out—as a result of payments to suppliers, repayment of bank loans, and investments

This is an outflow of a foreign currency today

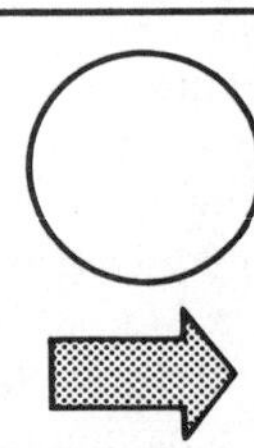

This is an inflow of one foreign currency in one month and an outflow of a different foreign currency in two months

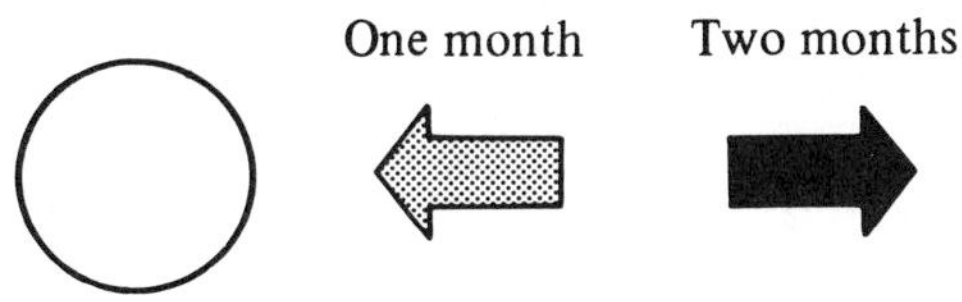

The symbols are used to represent the exposure situations faced by Charlston, Norris, Bailie, and Parker. Since each company is being examined individually, the same shade is used for the home currency and the other shades represent foreign currencies.

Charlston Motor Co.

Assuming the contract is being signed today, Charlston will be receiving French francs in four months. The inflow of foreign currency is shown at four months.

Norris Tools Ltd.

Norris places an order with the Swedish supplier and two months later pays out Swedish kroner; this is shown by the outflow at two months.

Bailie Industries Ltd.

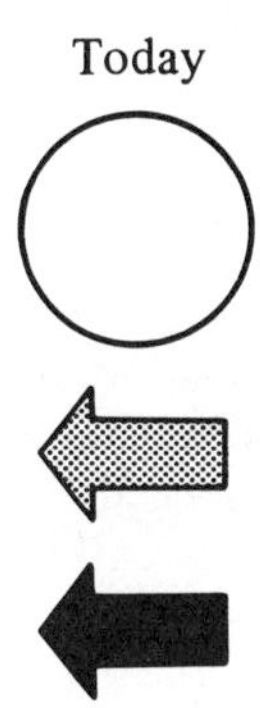

Bailie receives dividends from its subsidiaries, often learning about them the same day they are paid. This is shown by the two arrows of different shades.

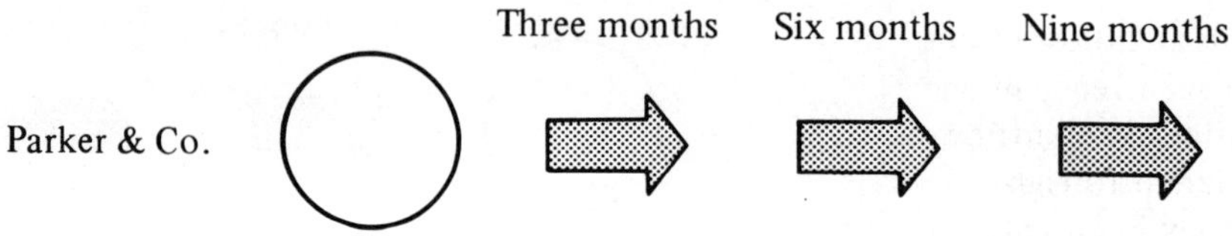

If Parker has just made a loan payment, the following diagram shows what the future looks like for the company, with payments of Swiss francs at quarterly intervals. This is represented by the outflows at months three, six, nine, and so on.

Now the symbolic language can be used to consider other possible exposures.

This situation represents a company selling overseas. The customer is invoiced in the currency of the seller. There is no foreign exchange exposure because the home currency and the currency of the inflow are the same.

This company is an intermediate processing firm in Belgium that buys steel ingots in France and sends specialized steel products back to France. There is no exposure in this particular time period because the foreign currency inflow equals the foreign currency outflow.

This situation is typical of an international trading company. It has inflows and outflows of the same currencies at different times. The company pays for the goods before it receives the proceeds from the resale. There is a time exposure only.

This company makes household products for the European market from its base in Ireland. It imports most of the polyvinyl chloride it uses in the process. This situation represents a payment for the plastic in Dutch guilders and lire receipts from Italian customers. There is a double exposure here. It is possible for both currencies to move in an unfavorable direction for the company.

The three key elements—home currency, foreign currency (or currencies), and time—are all present if a corporation has transaction exposure.

DIFFERENT OPTIONS FOR COVERING

The previous discussion centered upon the foreign exchange exposure created by the daily operations of international companies. This portion considers all the options available to these companies for dealing with exposure and how the options work. Some totally eliminate foreign exchange risk and others lessen the potential impact of an exposure.

An action that eliminates foreign exchange risk is said to cover that risk. An option that totally covers an exposure creates a flow of currency in the opposite direction to the exposure, in the same amount, at the same time.

The options are: (1) techniques for using the foreign exchange and money markets; (2) invoice, sales, and purchasing policies; and (3) trade arrangements. All the options are defined and related to the effect they have on the basic elements of foreign exchange exposure.

SPOT CONTRACT. A spot contract is a foreign exchange contract to buy (or sell) one currency with (or for) another at a given exchange rate for delivery two business days from the date the contract is made. The spot rate is the exchange rate on the spot date. The word "spot" is often used to refer to both the rate and the date. Saturday and Sunday are not business days for foreign exchange in most parts of the world.

Example. On Wednesday, July 25, Bailie Industries Ltd. calls its bank and agrees to buy £1 million with $2.31 million. The exchange rate is £1 = $2.31. Bailie will get the pounds on Friday, July 27, and will give the bank dollars the same day.

Example. On Thursday, July 26, Bailie calls its bank and agrees to sell to the bank DM1. 8 million for $1 million. The exchange rate is $1 = DM1.80. Bailie will give the bank DM1.8 million on Monday, July 30, and the same day will get $1 million from the bank.

A spot contract is represented by two arrows of different shades placed to represent an exchange of currencies two business days ahead; this day is designated t_0.

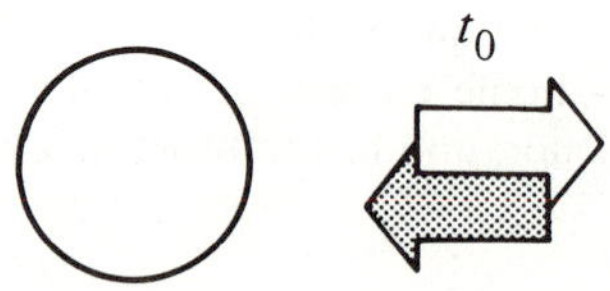

In this example the gray currency is bought with the white currency. Therefore, gray flows in and white flows out.

The spot date, even though it is two business days ahead, marks the starting point in the foreign exchange market. Likewise, the spot rate is the starting price for all transactions. All calculations are made with reference to spot. The prices for transactions that fall on any other day are adjusted for the value of time between that day and the spot date.

If a company has an exposure in two days, it can eliminate that exposure with a spot contract. If the company is obligated to pay pesos in two days, the company enters into a spot contract with its bank to buy pesos. The pesos delivered by the bank to the company in two days will be used to pay its debt. If the company has an exposure in two months, it cannot eliminate that exposure with a spot contract. The company must pay pesos in two months, but under the contract it will receive pesos from the bank in two days. A spot contract itself is not sufficient to offset an exposure in the future; another action is needed to bridge the time gap.

FORWARD CONTRACT. A forward contract is a foreign exchange contract to buy (or sell) one currency with (or for) another at a fixed exchange rate for delivery more than two business days from the date the contract is negotiated. There is no exchange of funds until the future day. Usually forward contracts are made for periods of 1, 2, 3, 6, and 12 months, starting from the spot date. The only difference between the spot contract and forward contract is the time of delivery and consequently the rate of exchange.

The following diagram illustrates the difference between the spot and the forward contract; it assumes a 90-day forward.

	Spot	Forward
Day on which exchange rate is fixed	today	today
Day on which monies are paid and received by the company	Two days from today	92 days from today

Example. On Wednesday, July 25, Norris Tools Ltd. calls its bank and agrees to buy £1 million with $2.3 million for delivery in one month. The exchange rate is £1 = $2.30. Norris will get £1 million on Monday, August 27. (The spot date is July 27; therefore, the one-month date is August 27.) Norris will give the bank dollars the same day. The contracted amounts will be exchanged on August 27 regardless of the exchange rate between pounds and dollars prevailing on that date.

A forward contract is represented by two arrows of different colors placed to represent as exchange of currencies in the future. The only difference between it and the spot contract is the placement along the time horizon (t_{90} is 90 days from the spot date, t_0).

The forward contract itself has the two elements common to most exposure situations—time and currency. A forward contract itself is sufficient to eliminate an exposure in the future. A company knows it must pay pesos in two months; the company executes a forward contract with a bank, and in two months the bank delivers the pesos. The company turns around and pays off its debt. Nothing more is needed; the company has covered its exposure.

BORROWING. Borrowing is an advance of funds by a bank to a company for its temporary use, for which the company pays interest. There is an inflow of funds into the company treasury as a result of the borrowing and an outflow of the same amount plus interest at some future date. The two most common loan arrangements are (1) advances for a fixed period at an interest rate also fixed for the period, and (2) advances for a limited period at an interest rate that will vary with market rates. Eurocurrency advances are typical of the first variety; prime rate borrowing in the United States and overdraft borrowing in Europe are typical of the second type.

Companies borrow money most often to finance their operations. In an exposure situation, borrowing changes the time frame of the foreign exchange risk. Borrowing a foreign currency in which there is a future receivable shifts the risk from the future to the present. The outflow for the loan repayment is offset by the receivable inflow in the future.

Borrowing is represented by an inflow of money on the spot date and an outflow in the future.

Companies borrow money most often to finance their operations. In an exposure situation, borrowing changes the time frame of the foreign exchange risk. Borrowing a foreign currency in which there is a future receivable shifts the risk from the future to the present. The outflow to repay the borrowing is offset by the receivable inflow in the future. The net result of the borrowing is an immediate inflow of foreign currency. Time has been virtually eliminated, but the risk that the foreign currency will change value against the home currency remains. A spot contract is required to convert foreign currency to home currency.

INVESTING. The placement of funds for a period of time for which interest is earned is an investment. There is an outflow of funds from the company on one day as a result of the investment, and there is an inflow of the principal amount plus interest at some future date. The type of placements of greatest interest are short-term money market investments that have a fixed maturity date, such as bank time deposits, certificates of deposit, bankers' acceptances, treasury bills, and commercial paper.

Usually companies invest funds for which they have no current need in their operations. In an exposure situation investing changes the time frame of the foreign exchange risk. In this respect it is like borrowing; however, the two activities differ in the type of exposure they are able to shift in time. If a company invests a foreign currency in which it has a future payable, the risk is moved from the future to the present. The future inflow of the investment offsets the outflow associated with the payable. The net result of the investment is an immediate outflow of the foreign currency. Time exposure has been virtually eliminated; the risk that the foreign currency will change value against the home currency remains.

Investing is represented by an outflow of money on the spot date and an inflow in the future.

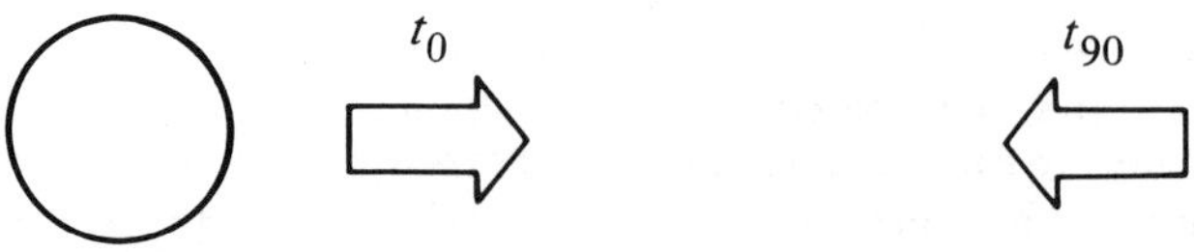

MATCHING. A company matches an exposure by creating an opposite flow in the same currency as the exposure, in the same amount, and at the same time. A company that has a payable of 1 million Dutch guilders in three months will consciously attempt to sell its product in The Netherlands to generate a receivable for 1 million Dutch guilders three months hence. If this is accomplished, the company has completely covered its foreign exchange exposure. Both time and currency elements have been considered.

Given the requirements of a perfect match, it is not easy to accomplish. The product that the company produces must be salable in every country or currency from which its sources come as inputs, or vice versa. Matching also requires the cooperation of the purchasing and sales departments with the treasurer. This technique is most applicable to large, one-time exposure situations where there is time to create the match.

PAIRING. A company pairs an exposure by creating an opposite flow in a currency allied with the currency of the exposure, in the same amount, at the same time. The difference between pairing and matching is the currency in which the flow is created. A candidate for pairing is a third currency that will move with the currency of the exposure. As it appreciates or depreciates against the home currency, so also will the paired currency. For example, Bailie may have an inflow of Dutch guilders in two months and pair with an outflow of Belgian francs. The two currencies are closely linked in trade and their fluctuation controlled by their central banks.

Although pairing may be easier to accomplish than matching and may give the corporate treasurer greater flexibility, it does not cover the risk, as does matching.

Pairing is an attempt to lessen the potential impact of a foreign currency risk by creating a situation where a loss in the initial situation will be offset by a gain in the allied currency. Pairing does create a double exposure, and if the allied currency is poorly chosen, a double loss may result. Pairing of two currencies is most applicable when the currencies are bound by some institutional arrangement, such as the European Monetary System.

LEADING. Leading is advancing the payment or receipt of money. If a company pays a bill immediately that is not due for 60 days, it is leading the payment. Most trade invoices reward the debtor for early payment by giving a discount. In this sense leading a payment is very similar to investing. Money is placed one day and a return is received. In an investment, it is the interest; in leading, it is the discount. Like investing, leading a foreign currency payable due in the future shifts the time frame of the exposure from the future to the present. Likewise, although time has been altered, the currency risk remains.

The arrows can also be used to represent an advance or payment. A firm is due to pay its overseas supplier in 30 days; if it decides to pay earlier, in two days, the change can be represented as follows:

The lower arrow on the right cancels out the original payment at 90 days. The arrow on the left represents the payment that the firm has decided to make in two days. The representation of a lead looks very much like an investment, even though the arrow on the right is not properly a flow.

An analogy also exists between leading a foreign currency receivable and borrowing. If a company asks one of its customers to pay early, it asks the customer to forego the use of the money for the period of the advance. The customer receives a discount from the company for moving up the payment. The company is borrowing from its customer. Like borrowing from a bank, the company has an immediate inflow of currency instead of an inflow in the future. In place of giving a bank interest, the company gives its customer a discount. The time element of the risk has been covered, but the currency risk has not been covered.

The symbolism used for advancing a receivable is:

Leading and **lagging** (the next option) are techniques most often used within multinational companies, rather than between different entities.

LAGGING. Lagging means delaying the payment of receipt of money. If a company pays a bill 30 days late it is lagging its payment. Most creditors charge interest for late payment. If a company pays its foreign currency obligation late, it is effectively borrowing that foreign currency from its supplier and paying interest for it. By doing so, the exposed home company is extending in time its foreign currency risk.

If a company requests that its customer hold off paying foreign currency for an additional 45 days, the company extends its exposure in time. There is a similarity between lagging a foreign currency receivable and investing the foreign currency. In an investment funds flow out, whereas in lagging the funds that should have come in, do not. In both there is a future inflow; in both there is a reward for letting someone else use the money.

NESTING. Nesting is a portfolio approach to currency exposure.* A company that exports only or imports only cannot match or pair; it can, however, use the nesting technique. Using the nesting technique, an exporter bills its customers in a variety of currencies. This means the exporter sells in a number of countries or has some flexibility in billing customers in third currencies. These currencies of invoice are chosen such that the shifting values of each currency with respect to the home currency keeps the whole nest of currencies at a constant value with respect to the home currency.

SUMMARY. The schema that follows classifies the options that have been discussed according to their mode of operation.

Cover			
Time	Time and Currency	Currency	Reduce Impact of Exposure
Lead	Forward	Spot	Nesting
Lag	Match		Pairing
Borrow			
Invest			

Only the forward and matching are self-sufficient options for covering. Leading, lagging, borrowing, and investing must be combined with spot to cover an exposure completely.

THREE BASIC OPTIONS

The three basic options are those that completely cover foreign exchange exposure. The three basic options are (1) forward, (2) borrow-spot-invest, and (3) lead. The mechanical operation of each is described and symbolized for Sloat and Company,

*A good article on the construction of a nest is that by Johnson and Zuber. Although it assumes perfect flexibility in the choice of currencies, the method used is applicable to a limited group of currencies. (See R. Stafford Johnson and Richard A. Zuber, "A Model for Construction Currency Cocktails," *Business Economics*, May 1979, pp. 9–14.)

Inc. Sloat is a U.S. firm that exports calculators to Belgium. The company bills its customers on 90-day terms. Sloat has three options to cover the risk that its foreign currency receivables may decline in value over the next three months.

FORWARD. The forward covers the exposure by creating a matching outflow in the foreign currency in which Sloat has an inflow. The foreign currency receivable is matched in amount and time. The two foreign currency flows offset one another. The foreign currency the exporter receives from its customer is delivered to the bank in 90 days to fulfill the forward contract. Sloat is left with an inflow of its own currency.

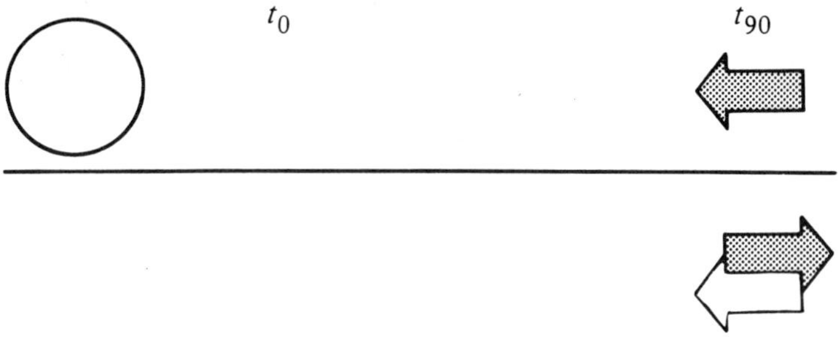

BORROW-SPOT-INVEST. The second option Sloat considers for covering risk is borrow-spot-invest (BSI). Borrowing the foreign currency shifts the time frame of the exposure from 90 days to the spot date. The currency risk is still present, but this is eliminated by a spot contract. Sloat contracts with the bank to sell the foreign currency on the spot date for its home currency. Time is covered and currency is covered, so the exposure is eliminated. Eliminating exposure does not involve only costs; Sloat has its own currency 90 days ahead of schedule. The company has the opportunity of placing its money in a deposit, repaying bank debt, or using the funds for working capital.

The representation of borrow-spot-invest is as follows:

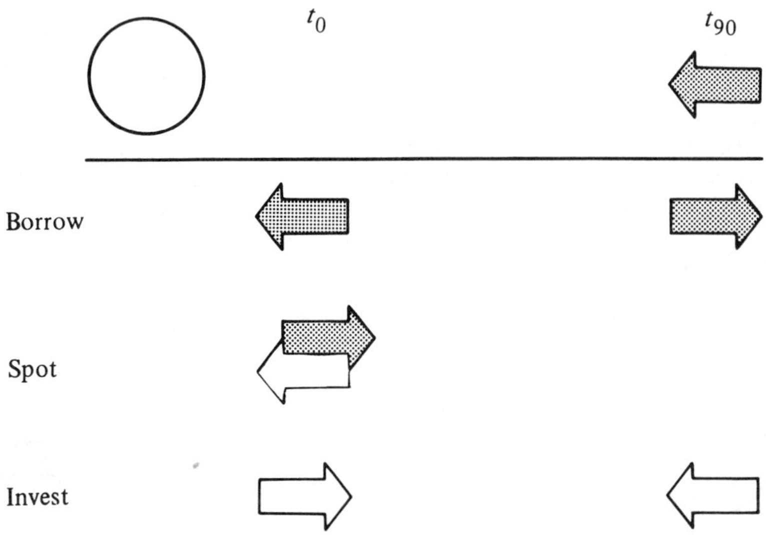

On the spot date, t_0, there is an inflow of gray currency, the loan; that amount of gray is sold for white; that amount of white is invested. All of the inflows and outflows on the spot date cancel one another out. On the future date, t_{90}, the gray currency due from the overseas importer is used to pay off the loan from the bank. There rests an inflow of white currency. This is as it should be. Covering an exposure involves the offset of foreign currency flows and a home currency flow in the same direction as the original exposure.

LEAD. Sloat has a third option, the possibility to lead the payment from its customer. If the customer agrees to the discount Sloat offers, the customer will pay in two days rather than in 90 days, as originally scheduled. Time exposure is covered. Sloat can then call the bank and agree to sell the foreign currency spot for its home currency. The currency exposure is covered. As in the BSI option, the home currency can be invested in money market instruments or utilized in the firm. The lead option is symbolized as

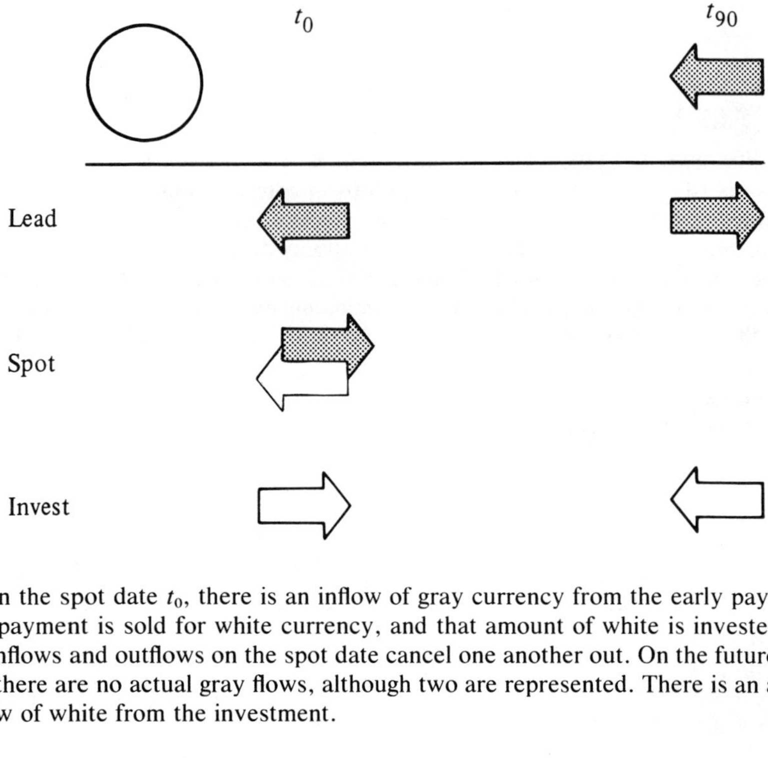

On the spot date t_0, there is an inflow of gray currency from the early payment; that payment is sold for white currency, and that amount of white is invested. All the inflows and outflows on the spot date cancel one another out. On the future date (t_{90}) there are no actual gray flows, although two are represented. There is an actual inflow of white from the investment.

COMPARING THE OPTIONS. The three basic options are illustrated together.

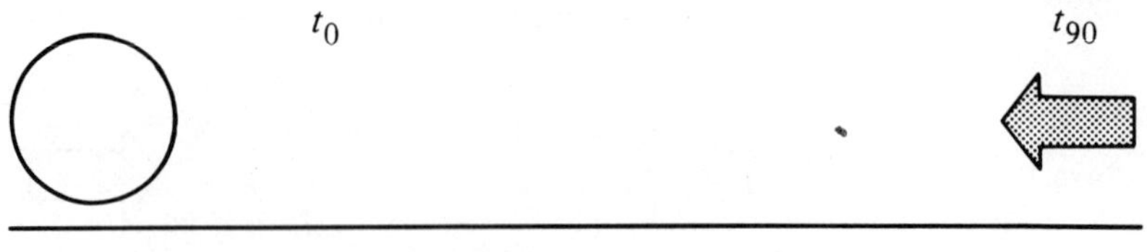

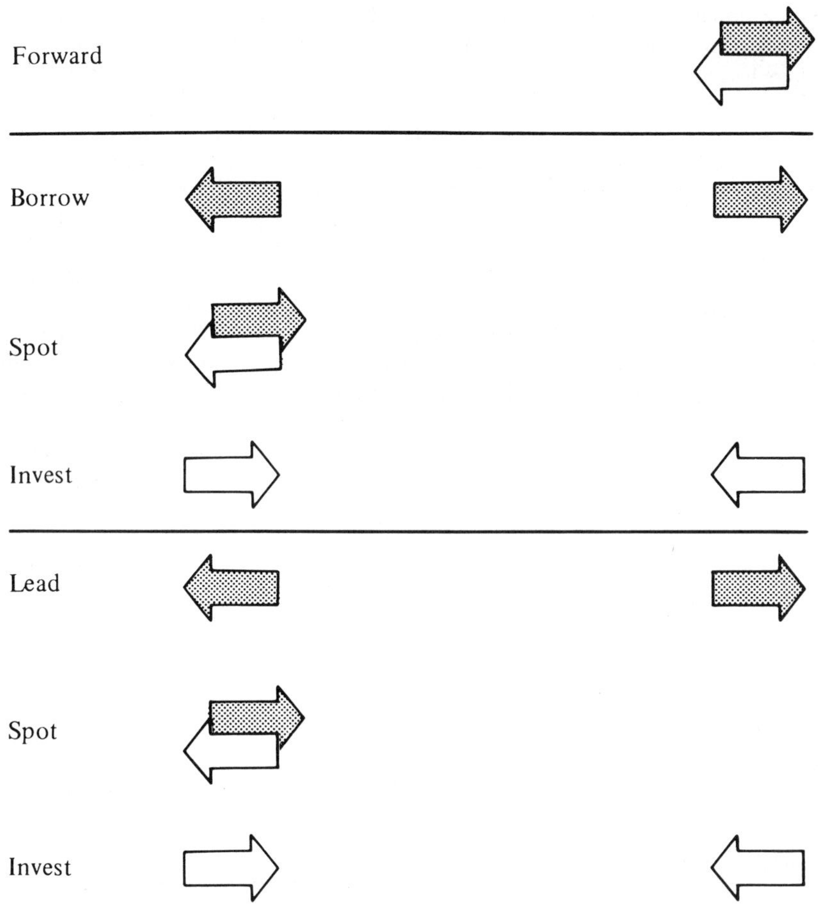

All the basic options completely cover the risk that the foreign currency receivable could decline in value between the present and the future. In all three options the flows of foreign currency cancel on the future date, leaving an inflow of the home currency. The similarity among all three options and how they work is more apparent if one notes that in the BSI and lead options all the flows on the spot date cancel, thus leaving all the options looking very much the same on the future date.

The similarity between the lead and the BSI options is very strong. They differ only in the initial step. In the BSI Sloat borrows from the bank, pays interest, and has an inflow of foreign currency on the spot date. In the lead, Sloat persuades the customer to pay early (borrowing from the customer), pays a discount, and has an inflow of foreign currency on the spot date. The two investment transactions are the same.

COVERING A PAYABLE. Whittemore Trading Ltd. is an importer of chemicals and dyes into Canada. It traditionally imports from West Germany and has carved a niche in the market by specializing in hard-to-get products. Its suppliers bill on 45-day terms, with discounts given for payment within five days. Whittemore faces the risk that its payables in Deutsche marks will become more costly in terms of the

Canadian dollar in the next month and a half. It has available to it the three basic options for covering an exposure. Whittemore can call the bank and contract to purchase foreign currency 45 days forward. The currency that the bank will deliver to the firm will be used the same day to pay off the European suppliers. In fact, Whittemore simply tells the bank to credit the account of its supplier in West Germany. A second way to cover the exposure is to borrow Canadian dollars from the bank, buy Deutsche marks with the borrowed dollars on the spot date, and invest the Deutsche marks for 45 days by depositing them with a bank. (Note that in the case of covering a payable it is the home currency that is borrowed and the foreign currency that is invested. This is the reverse, as one would expect, of what happened when the exposure consisted of a foreign currency receivable.) Borrowing the home currency is not always necessary. If Whittemore is liquid it may use some of its surplus cash, or sell one of its Treasury bills. This would be cheaper than actually borrowing from the bank. The cost is the foregone interest income.

The third alternative for Whittemore Trading is to prepay its supplier and earn the discount. To be able to do this, the firm borrows dollars from the bank and buys Deutsche marks. Again, BSI and lead are the same, with the exception of one step. In BSI the Deutsche marks are invested in the bank for 45 days. In the lead Deutsche marks are invested by being paid to the supplier early, and a discount is earned.

The three options are illustrated together.

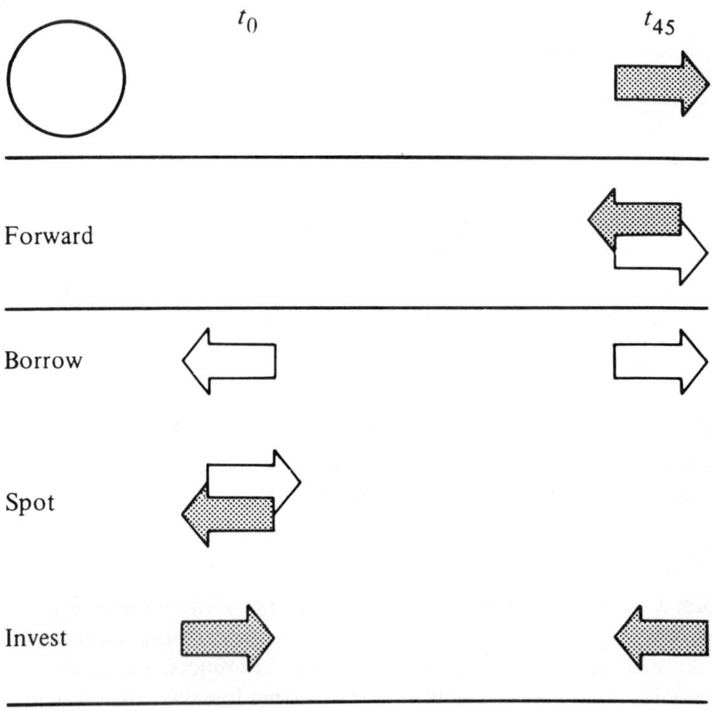

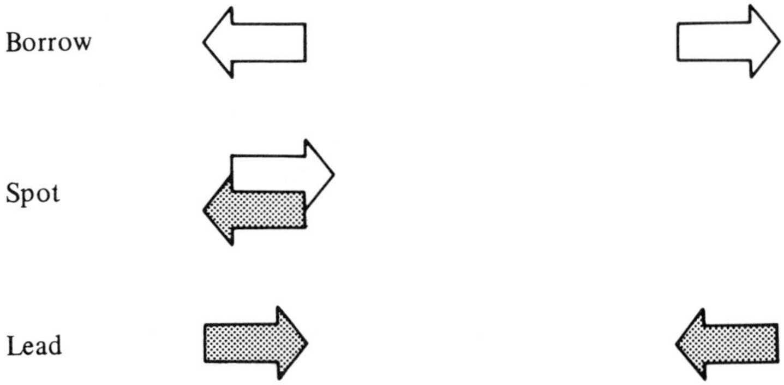

PRICING THE OPTIONS

It is notable that the BSI and lead differ in only one respect, the disposition of the foreign currency. In the BSI it is placed in a deposit with the bank to earn interest; in the lead it is paid to the supplier and a discount is earned. The effect of covering the exposure is to leave the firm with an outflow in its own currency in place of the original outflow of the foreign currency.

Why work at three options when clearly any one of them will eliminate exposure? The reason is that each option has a different cost or earning. (Covering an exposure is not synonymous with an expense; in many situations the result of the transactions is positive.) In a given situation one chooses the option with the least cost; in another situation one chooses the option with the largest earning. The different options produce different earnings and costs because each uses a different combination of money market rates.

Fundamentally there are two different money markets in the world; there is a domestic money market and an external money market for each currency. The external currency market with which most people are familiar is the Eurodollar market. A Eurodollar is a dollar that is deposited in a bank outside the United States. The bank may be a branch of a U.S. bank, as long as it is situated outside of the United States. The dollars may be owned by anyone—U.S. citizens, West Germans, Belgians, or others. The essential characteristics are that the deposits are obligations to pay dollars and are obligations of banking offices outside the United States. The dollar deposit of a French national in a New York bank is not a Eurodollar. Most convertible currencies can be substituted for dollars, producing an external money market. There is a Euromark market, a Eurosterling market, a Europeseta market, a Euro–Swiss franc market, and so on. These different currency markets differ vastly in size.

The second market is the domestic market, also termed "the resident money market." A domestic dollar is one that is deposited in a bank inside the United States. The bank may be the branch of an English bank in the United States. The dollars may be owned by anyone. The same is true for all currencies. There is a resident sterling money market, a resident Dutch guilder money market, and so forth.

The reason for making such a distinction among the markets is that access to them is not universal. The French do not have access to the Euro–French franc market, but the Canadians do, as do the Dutch. The reason that access is not universal is due to exchange control regulations. The second reason for looking at both markets is that the interest rates for the same currency are not the same in the external and domestic markets. The rate for a resident franc deposit for three months is not the same as the rate for an external franc deposit of the same tenor. Rates are different between resident and external markets because of government exchange control. Where strict exchange controls exist there is a greater divergence between external and domestic interest rates. The isolation allows rates in each market to be affected by different forces. A second reason why interest rates differ is because reserve requirements are not levied equally on both types of deposit. A reserve requirement means that the value of an individual's deposit to a bank is worth less because a portion of the deposit must be kept interest-free with the central bank. Therefore, the bank pays interest in accordance with the level of the reserve kept. The schemata following gives an idea of the forces at work.

Domestic Economic Factors	International Factors
Inflation rate Monetary/fiscal policies Stage of the business cycle	Perceptions of inflation rate Perceptions of monetary/fiscal policies Balance of payments Size of the external currency pool

↓

Domestic interest rates

Reserve requirements
Exchange controls

↓ ↙

External interest rates

Liberal Exchange Control Countries

Domestic Economic Factors	International Factors

Domestic interest rates

Reserve requirements

↓

External interest rates

Countries that have strict exchange controls put up a double barrier between the domestic rates and external ones, thereby allowing the international factors to play a much greater role. Where there are liberal exchange controls, the difference between domestic and external interest rates is almost entirely the reserve requirement.

There is no established pattern of difference between external and domestic interest rates. Sometimes external rates are higher than domestic, and other times lower; at times the difference is large, and at other times there is no difference. The best published sources of domestic and external interest rates are the *Financial Times* (London), *Agefi* (Paris), and the *World Financial Markets,* published by Morgan Guaranty Trust Company; banks are also excellent sources. Generally, if a currency is weak on the exchange markets, its external interest rates tend to be higher than the domestic rates. If a currency is strong on the exchange markets, its external interest rates tend to be lower than the domestic rates.

The symbols used for each market are as follows:

Interest earning in the external money market

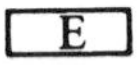

Interest cost in the external money market

Interest earning the domestic money market

Interest earning in the domestic money market

Consequently, the following representation means that an investment is made in the Eurocurrency market. The interest earning is at the rate given in the external money market.

The symbol used to represent the spot rate is $\triangle$. The spot rate represents neither a cost nor an earning itself; it is a price. It is the terms of exchange of one currency for another.

The borrowing shown in the following diagram is made in the country of the money in question, and the interest is payable at the rate given in the domestic money market.

Returning to the situation of Whittemore Trading Ltd., the differences between the costs and the earnings of each option are examined. Whittemore is a Canadian company importing chemicals from West Germany. It has payments due in Deutsche marks at 45-day intervals. The first option Whittemore considers is the BSI. The firm can borrow its own currency from a bank in Canada, buy the foreign currency with the home currency on the spot date, and then invest the foreign currency in a time deposit with a Canadian bank to mature in 45 days. The maturing foreign currency deposit would be used to pay off the obligation to the supplier in West

Germany. By this time Whittemore would have sold the chemicals in Canada and have the money to pay off its loan. Because the trading company would be borrowing Canadian dollars from a Canadian bank, it would pay the rate in the domestic money market. Because the trading company would be investing the foreign currency with a Canadian bank, it would earn interest at a rate given by the external money market of the foreign currency. The transaction can be represented symbolically.

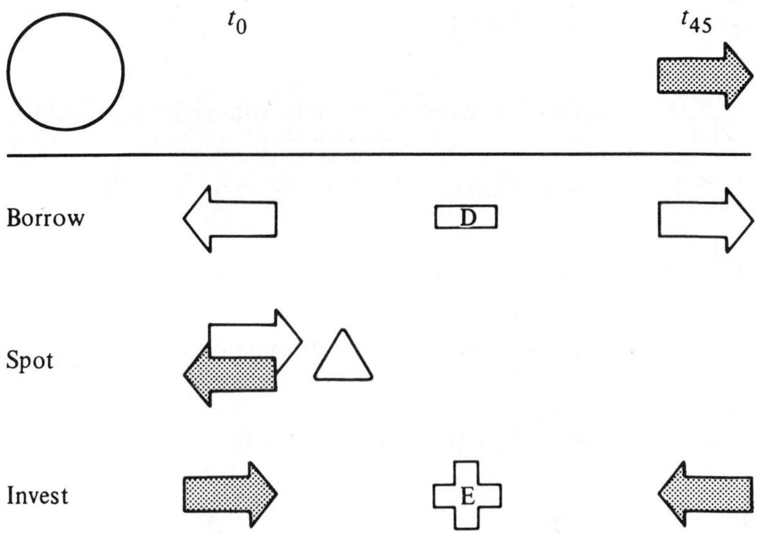

The next option Whittemore examines is the lead. The company has the possibility of paying its supplier early and earning a discount. To do this, the firm would borrow Canadian dollars from a bank in Canada and would then buy the foreign currency with the borrowed dollars on the spot date. The foreign currency would then be paid to the supplier. As in the previous situation, the cost to Whittemore would be determined by rates in its own domestic money market. The earning to the company is the discount it earns. This is determined largely by the value its supplier places on having money early. Objectively, this value would be determined by what the supplier in the foreign country could do with its own currency. This objective value is given by the domestic money market rates in the foreign country. The lead option is symbolized as follows:

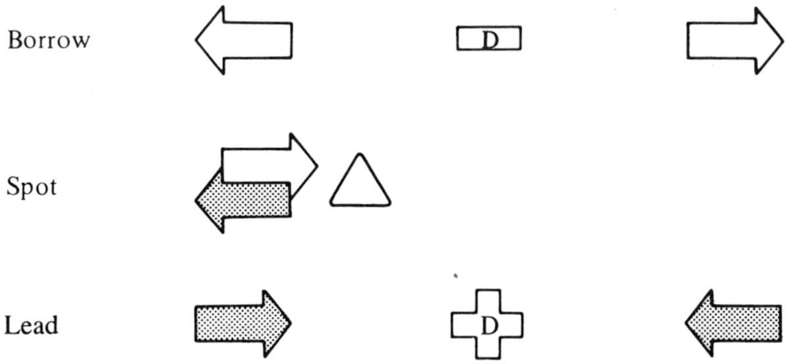

Whittemore also considers the forward contract as an option. The company can call its bank and arrange for delivery of the foreign currency in 45 days. The foreign currency would be paid for with Canadian dollars, the money Whittemore is receiving from domestic sales of the chemicals. The convention for the pricing of the forward transaction is the external money markets of both the currencies involved. This is represented in the following diagram.

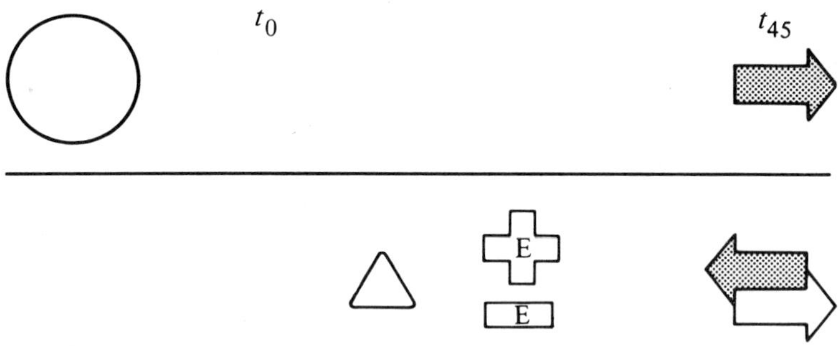

The forward contract is an exchange of currencies in the future; thus it is natural that the pricing of the forward contract should include both elements of exchange and time, the spot price, and interest rates. The fact that external interest rates are used is convention. The placement of the plus and minus signs on the forward should be compared with their placement on the lead and BSI options. In all cases the minus is associated with the currency flowing out in the future, and the plus with the currency flowing in.

The following illustration shows all the options and the way in which they are priced. The reason for putting in the price symbols is (1) to identify what information is needed for comparing the options and (2) later, when the options become more complex, they provide a means for discriminating among options without using numbers.

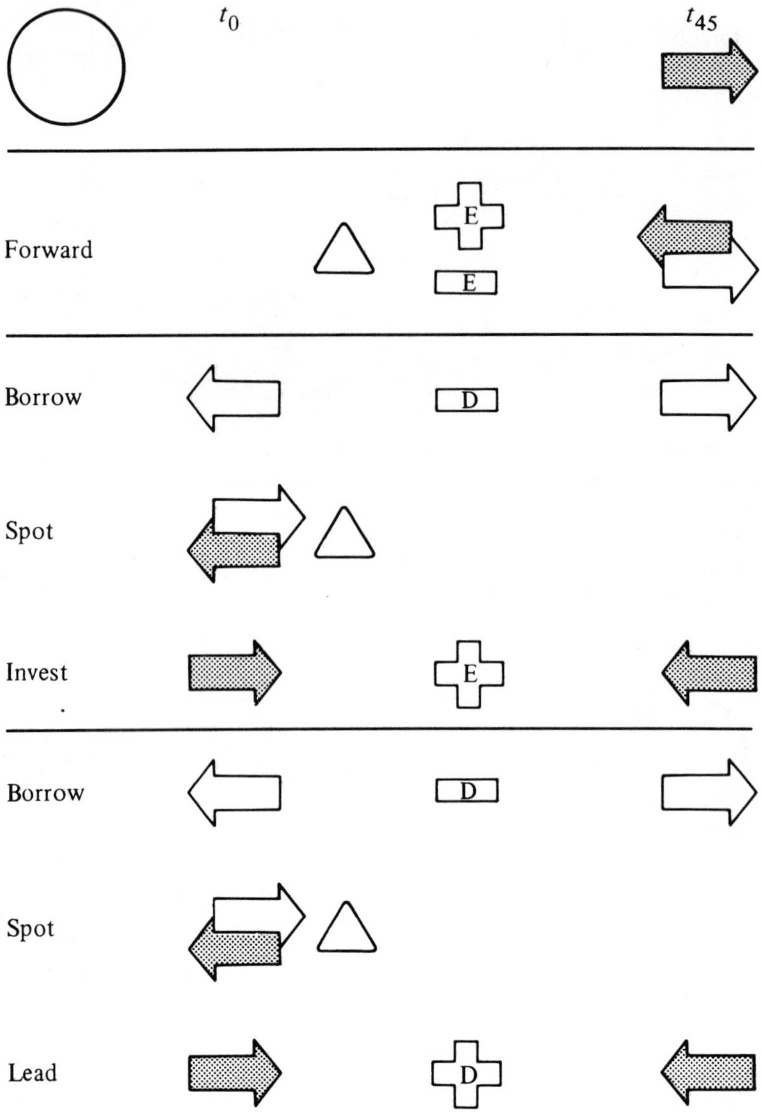

It is evident why it is worthwhile to consider all three options. Because external interest rates differ from domestic interest rates, the cost or earning of each option is different. Whittemore will choose the option with the lowest cost or highest earning.

To make a decision as to which option is the most preferable, Whittemore needs to know only the domestic and external interest rates of the home and foreign currencies. To make a decision on the best option it is not necessary to know the spot rate because it is a common element in all three options. It is necessary to know the spot rate and have an opinion of its evolution in deciding when to execute the best option, but not when deciding which is the best option. The best option at any point in time is an issue that can be analyzed logically, as is done here. The question of when to execute the best option is a matter of judgment about exchange rates.

The following illustration shows the options and their pricing for a receivable exposure.

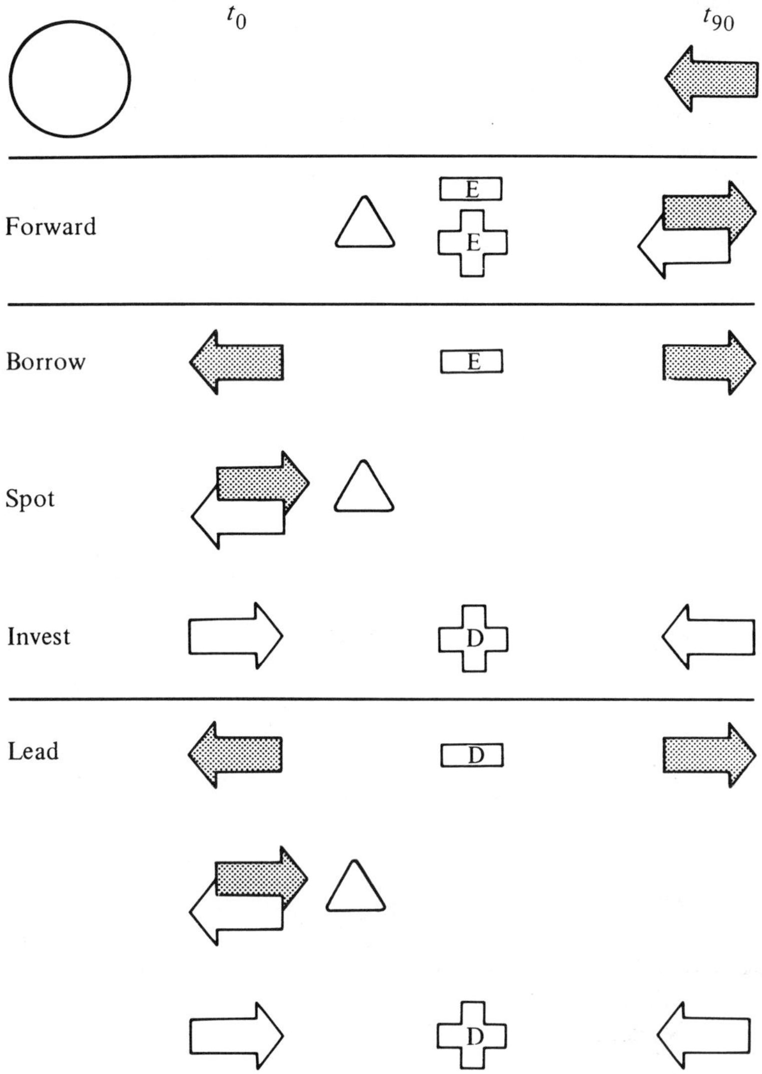

CHOOSING THE BEST OPTION

The three basic options available to the corporate treasurer to cover foreign exchange exposure have been discussed. However, there remains the problem of choosing among the options. The criterion for choice has been mentioned: Choose the option that returns the greatest earnings or the one that has the least cost. It has already been shown that a choice can be made on the basis of interest rates. There are two additional ways to choose among the options. Actual numbers are used to show concretely how a decision is made.

NET INTEREST COST AND EARNING. A decision on the best option can be made on the basis of the net interest cost and earning. Each option involves one interest cost and one interest earning element. The difference between these two gives the net interest cost or earning for the entire option. To show this in practice the situation of Sloat & Company's Dutch subsidiary, Sloat (Holland) N.V. is considered. It exports steam generators to the United States and bills its customers on 180-day terms. The exposure it faces on every order and the basic options for covering it are shown in the following diagram. In addition, the relevant spot rate and interest rates are entered.

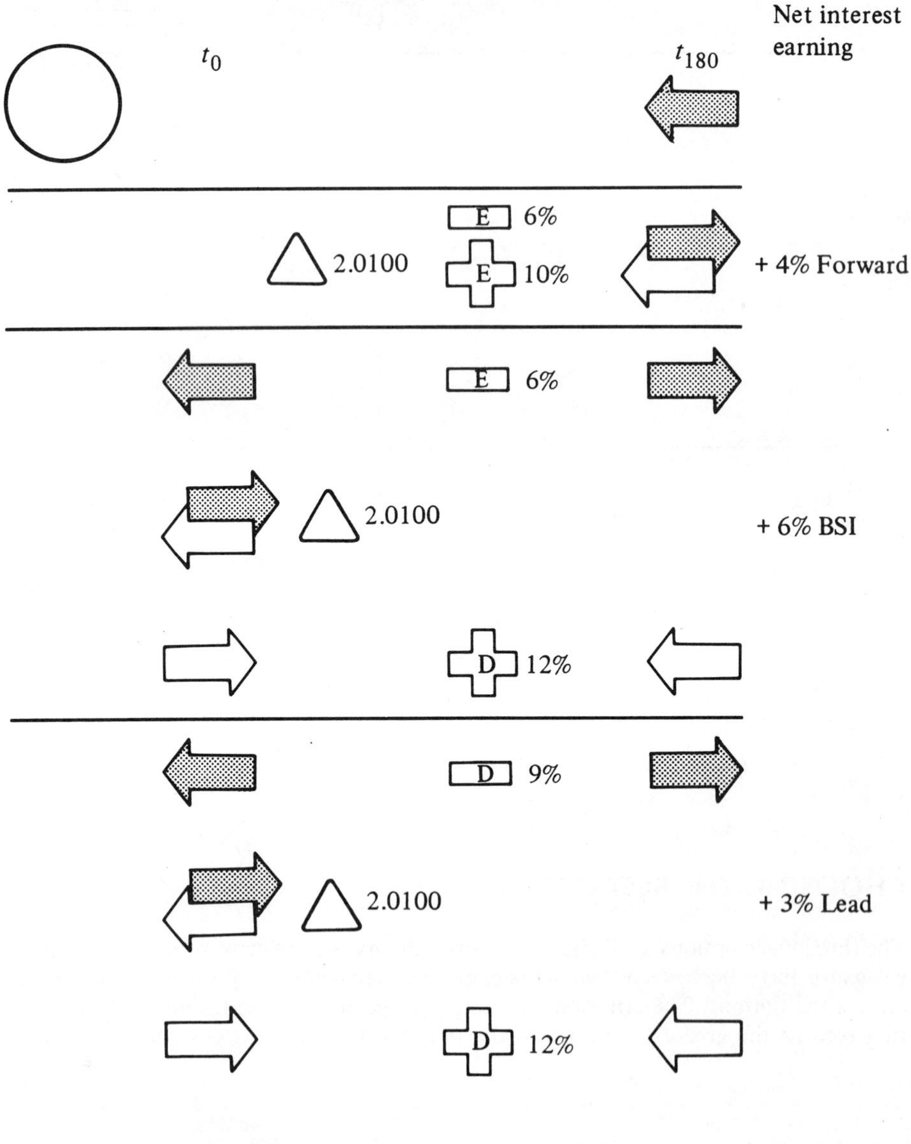

The number 2.0100 is the spot rate; it is the number of white currency units for each unit of gray currency. The net interest earning is shown to the right of each option. It is computed by subtracting the interest cost of the gray currency from the interest earning of the white. The BSI is the best option in this particular situation since the difference between the cost of borrowing and earning from investment is greatest. The foreign currency risk is covered, and the subsidiary has an earning of 6% a year over 180 days. It has borrowed money at 6%, converted it to another currency that is invested at 12%, and covered its exposure. The actual spot rate does not play a role in the choice of the best option.

LOCKED-IN FUTURE RATE. The net interest cost/earning is one way of choosing among options. A second way is the locked-in future rate. This rate combines all the transactions of one option into a single number. This number is in currency units like the spot rate. If the spot rate is three home units to one foreign unit, a locked-in future rate might be 3.23 home units to one foreign unit. The locked-in future rate says that after all of the transactions in an option have been taken into account the foreign currency has been effectively converted to home currency at this rate. The term "future" is used to distinguish it from the spot rate. It is called "locked-in" because the covering options fix, or lock in, the effective rate of conversion between the foreign currency and the home currency. The locked-in future rate is calculated by starting with the spot rate and then adjusting for the net interest rate difference. For the BSI option, the locked-in future rate is 2.0685. This number sums up the borrowing of gray currency at 6%, the conversion of each gray unit to 2.01 white units, and the investment of the whites at 12%.

There is an earning of 6%; this is also indicated by the higher locked-in future rate. It is better to receive 2.0685 whites for each gray than 2.01. The earnings for the forward and lead were less in interest rate terms and so will be less in terms of the locked-in future rate.

The most important use of the locked-in future rate is that it provides the basis for judging whether or not to cover. If it is believed that in 180 days the gray-to-white rate will be 2.08 as opposed to the best option, which is 2.0685, then the company might wait to convert its gray receivable. On the other hand, if the rate in 180 days were forecast to be between 2.02 and 2.00, then the company has much to gain by covering the exposure immediately. To be more precise concerning the judgment, it is assumed that this is February and the receivable is due August 25. If the Sloat subsidiary forecasts that any time in the next six months it will be able to cover its exposure on August 25 at a locked-in future rate of 2.08, then it will wait.

POINTS. The third way of choosing among the options is points. Points are currency amounts that are added to or subtracted from spot rates to show the effect of a combined exchange and money market operation. This result is the locked-in future rate. The points formula is used to convert time costs and earnings, which are expressed in percentage terms, to units of currency. These units of currency can be considered as amounts of interest.

$$\text{points} = \frac{\text{spot} \times (I_h - I_f) \times \text{days}/360}{1 + (I_f \times \text{days}/360)}$$

where

$$I_h = \text{interest rate, home currency}$$
$$I_f = \text{interest rate, foreign currency}$$

Before applying the formula to some concrete examples, the sensitivity of the formula to changes in certain variables is considered.

1. The greater the difference between the interest rates, the greater the number of points, which simply means that a higher interest rate leads to greater interest payment.
2. The more numerous the days, the larger the number of points. The amount of interest paid to the bank is larger if the loan is for one year as opposed to one month.
3. The higher the spot rate, the greater the number of points. Analogously, the larger the amount borrowed, the more that is paid in interest.
4. If the foreign currency interest rate is low and the number of days is small, then the denominator approaches one and its effect fades sharply.

The calculation for the forward in the Sloat example is

$$\frac{2.0100 \times (0.10 - .06) \times 180/360}{1 + (0.06 \times 180/360)} = \frac{0.0402}{1.03} = .0390 = 390 \text{ points}$$

where 390 is the number of points to be added to the spot rate for the locked-in future rate.

The calculation for the BSI is

$$\frac{2.0100 \times (0.12 - 0.06) \times 180/360}{1 + (0.06 \times 180/360)} = \frac{0.0603}{1.03} = 0.0585 = 585 \text{ points}$$

where 585 is the number of points to be added to the spot rate for the locked-in future rate.

The calculation for the lead is

$$\frac{2.0100 \times (0.12 - 0.09) \times 180/360}{1 + (0.09 \times 180/360)} = \frac{0.0301}{1.045} = 0.0289 = 289 \text{ points}$$

where 289 is the number of points to be added to the spot rate for the locked-in future rate.

In making the calculations, the following conventions should be observed: (1) The figures expressed in percentage form should be converted to decimal form (e.g., 4% = 0.04); and (2) the calculations inside the parentheses are performed first. On the top line the two interest rates are subtracted before multiplying by spot and time. On the bottom line the interest rate is multiplied by time before adding 1.

The matrix summarizes the calculations.

Net Interest Cost/Earning

Option	Spot Rate	I_h	I_f		Net	Points	Locked-In Future Rate
Forward	2.0100	+10	−6	=	+4%	390	2.0490
BSI	2.0100	+12	−6	=	+6%	585	2.0685
Lead	2.0100	+12	−9	=	+3%	289	2.0389

The matrix conveys the following information:

1. The BSI is the best option by all criteria—net interest, points, and locked-in future rate. The forward follows, and the lead is the least attractive option.
2. There is an earning if the exposure is covered immediately. By executing the BSI Sloat (Holland) N.V. receives an additional 0.0585 units of its currency for each unit of foreign currency compared with the spot rate.
3. The best locked-in future rate, 2.0685, forms the basis for deciding whether to cover or do nothing. If Sloat thinks that it can get a better rate any time within the next six months, it will wait to cover. Either the spot rate could rise, or the interest rate on its currency increase, or the interest rate on the foreign currency decrease, but these latter two factors will have less of an effect as time goes on.

To become more familiar with the concepts and their practical application, another Sloat subsidiary is considered. The exposure situation, a receivable, the options for covering it, and the relevant rates are shown in the following diagram.

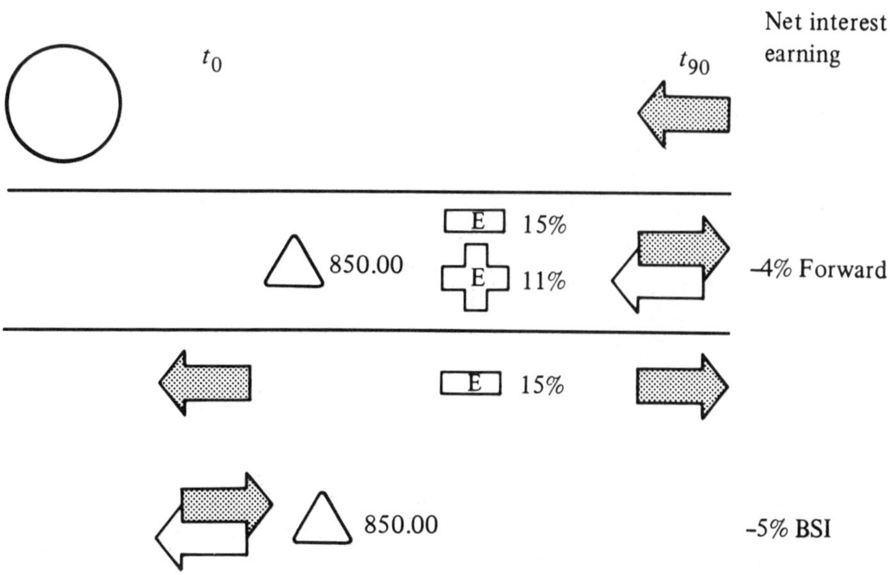

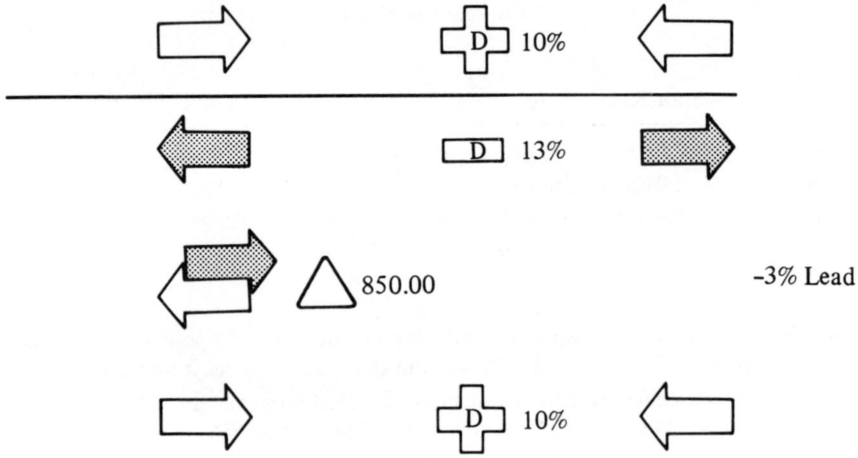

The number 850.00 is the spot rate; it is the number of white currency units for each unit of gray currency. The net interest cost is shown to the right of each option. It is computed by subtracting the interest cost of the gray currency from the interest earning of the white. There is a cost in this case because the interest rate of the gray currency in each option exceeds the interest earning from the white. The best option in this situation is the lead. The lead covers the foreign currency exposure at a cost of 3% a year over 90 days.

The locked-in future rate will be lower than the spot rate because Sloat is incurring a cost in covering this receivable. Because the spot rate is expressed as the number of whites for each gray unit, the company will be worse off by converting a gray receivable to white at a lower rate than at a higher rate. If there is an inflow of 100 grays, the company is worse off if it covers at 840.00 and receives 84,000 whites than if it were able to cover at 850.00 and receive 85,000 whites. The interest cost of the lead is the smallest, and it follows from this that the locked-in future rate for this option should be the highest of the three, followed by the forward and then the BSI. By the same reasoning, the number of points for the lead are the least, followed by the forward and BSI. This follows from the fact that the difference between the spot rate and the locked-in future rate is directly related to the difference in interest rates in a given option. The following matrix shows the results.

Option	Spot Rate	Net Interest Cost/Earning	Points	Locked-in Future Rate
Forward	850.00	−4%	819	841.81
BSI	850.00	−5%	1,024	839.76
Lead	850.00	−3%	617	843.83

If the company believes that sometime within the next 90 days it will be able to cover this exposure at a rate of 865.00, it will certainly wait. This rate represents an improvement over what it can do today. If a rate of 825.00 were forecast, Sloat S.A. would cover with the lead option.

The difference in the receivable situations of the Dutch and Italian subsidiaries is the relative levels of the interest rates. In the Dutch situation the interest rate of the incoming foreign currency is lower than that of the home currency; in the Italian case, the interest rate of the incoming foreign currency is higher than that of the home currency. Lower foreign interest rates mean that covering is done at an earning, whereas higher foreign interest rates mean that covering is done at a cost.

When the exposure involves a payable the association between relative interest rates and the earning from covering is reversed. The following summarizes the relationships.

Interest Rates	Payable	Receivable
$I_{home} > I_{foreign}$	Cost Future rate > Spot	Earning Future rate > Spot
$I_{home} < I_{foreign}$	Earning Future rate < Spot	Cost Future rate < Spot

The spot rate is expressed as the number of home units for each foreign unit (> means greater than; < means less than).

INTEREST COST/EARNINGS (ICE) FORMULA. It has been assumed that the information available for all options is spot rates and interest rates, since this served to illustrate the fundamental determinants of future rates. In the foreign exchange market the information about the forward is conventionally given as a number of points to be added to or subtracted from the spot rate. Points capture in a single number the differential between two external interest rates. Points are this differential in terms of currency units. For the U.S. dollar/Dutch guilder, 329 points less the spot of 2.0180 equals a forward rate of 1.9861. For the Deutsche mark/French franc, 295 points plus the spot of 233.05 equals a forward rate of 236.00.

The interest cost/earnings (ICE) formula is used to convert costs and earnings that are expressed in points (interest amounts) to an annualized percentage. This allows the forward contract that is expressed in points to be compared to other options that are expressed in percentages. The formula expresses the percentage difference between buying (or selling) an amount of currency on the spot date and buying (or selling) that same amount on a forward date. It does so by taking the difference between the spot rate and the forward rate—points—and expressing it as a percentage of the spot rate.

The formula is

$$\text{interest percent (per annum)} = \frac{\text{points}}{\text{spot}} \times \frac{1}{\text{time}} \times 100$$

For the examples mentioned previously, assuming the time period is 91 days,

$$6.45\% = \frac{0.0329}{2.0190} \times \frac{360}{91} \times 100$$

$$5.01\% = \frac{2.95}{233.05} \times \frac{360}{91} \times 100$$

The points have as many decimal places as does the spot rate with which they are associated.

The percentage found in the first case expressed the difference in terms of guilders—the difference between DG2.0190 spot and DG1.9861 in 91 days. From the perspective of a Dutch treasurer, this is how he or she would view a spot transaction versus a one-month transaction. An U.S. treasurer has another point of view. The U.S. treasurer wants to know the difference in dollars between a spot transaction and one in the future. The calculation does not do this. There are two ways of altering the calculation to express the percentage in dollar terms.

1. The exchange rate can be turned around so that it is expressed in dollar terms. If DG2.0190 equals $1 spot, each guilder is worth about 50¢; more precisely, $0.4953 (1 ÷ 2.0190). The forward rate is that of DG1.9861 equals $1, and each guilder is worth $0.5035. The number of points difference is 82. From the point of view of the U.S. treasurer, the percentage in dollar terms is

$$6.55\% = \frac{0.0082}{0.4953} \times \frac{360}{91} \times 100$$

Viewed from New York, the percentage is larger.

2. The formula can be changed (which is less difficult than it appears). The formula that expresses the percentage in dollar terms, even though the exchange rates are expressed in terms of guilders, is

$$\text{interest percent} = \frac{\text{points}}{\text{forward}} \times \frac{1}{\text{time}} \times 100$$

$$6.55\% = \frac{0.0329}{1.9861} \times \frac{360}{91} \times 100$$

This method is easier to work with than the first, although the rationale is less intuitive.

The ICE formula used depends on the perspective of the user.

If spot and points are expressed in home currency units, then

$$\text{ICE-1} = \frac{\text{points}}{\text{spot}} \times \frac{360}{\text{days}} \times 100$$

Home is the United States and the rates are expressed as the number of dollars for each Swiss franc (SF). (Spot SF1 = $0.6135; two-month points are $0.0112.)

$$10.95\% = \frac{0.0112}{0.6135} \times \frac{360}{60} \times 100$$

If spot and points are expressed in foreign currency units, then

$$\text{ICE-2} = \frac{\text{points}}{\text{forward}} \times \frac{360}{\text{days}} \times 100$$

Home is the United States and the rates are expressed as the number of Swiss francs for each dollar. (Spot \$1 = SF1.6300; two-month points are SF0.0292.)

$$10.95\% = \frac{0.0292}{1.6008} \times \frac{360}{60} \times 100$$

The following matrix summarizes the basic information available for calculating the cost/earnings of each option and the formula needed for comparing the options.

Net Interest Cost/Earning

Option	Spot	I_h	I_f	Net	Points	Locked-in Future Rate
Forward	0.2750	ICE formula			13	Spot ± points
BSI	0.2750	10	14	4%	Points formula	Spot ± points
Lead	0.2750	10	12	2%	Points formula	Spot ± points

BRITTAN VALLEY IMPORT CASE. All the techniques discussed can now be applied. Brittan Valley Import Company is located in Laredo, Texas. It is a very large wholesaler of Mexican fruits and vegetables. Orders are paid within one month of the date received. A new delivery totaling 4 million Mexican pesos is due in a couple of days. The treasurer of the company believes that the peso will probably weaken relative to the dollar over the next six months on the order of 4%; this is confirmed in conversations with local bankers. The spot is currently US\$0.04386 for 1 peso. The one-month points are US\$0.00033. They are subtracted from the spot. Brittan Valley can borrow dollars at 12% from its local bank. The bank will accept deposits of Mexican pesos at 23%. The exporter on the other side of the border will give a discount equivalent to 19% a year for payment on delivery. The treasurer examines the three basic options available, chooses the best, and then compares the best option to the forecast about the Mexican peso (pesos, gray; dollars, white).

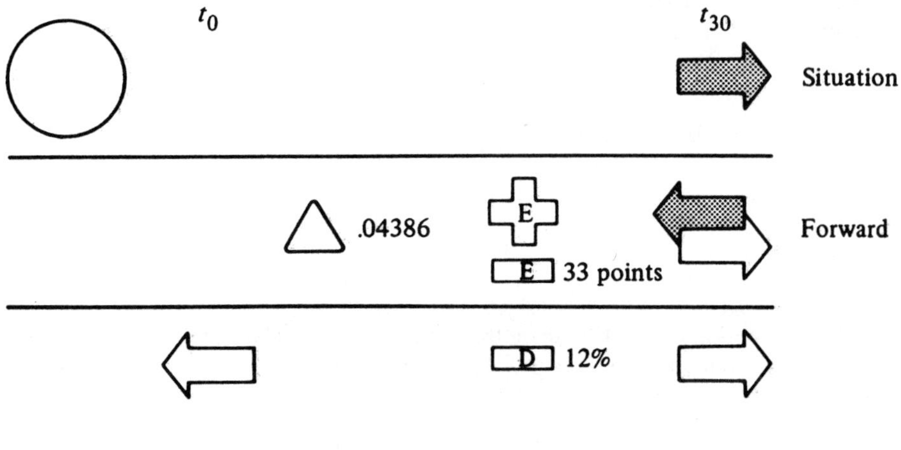

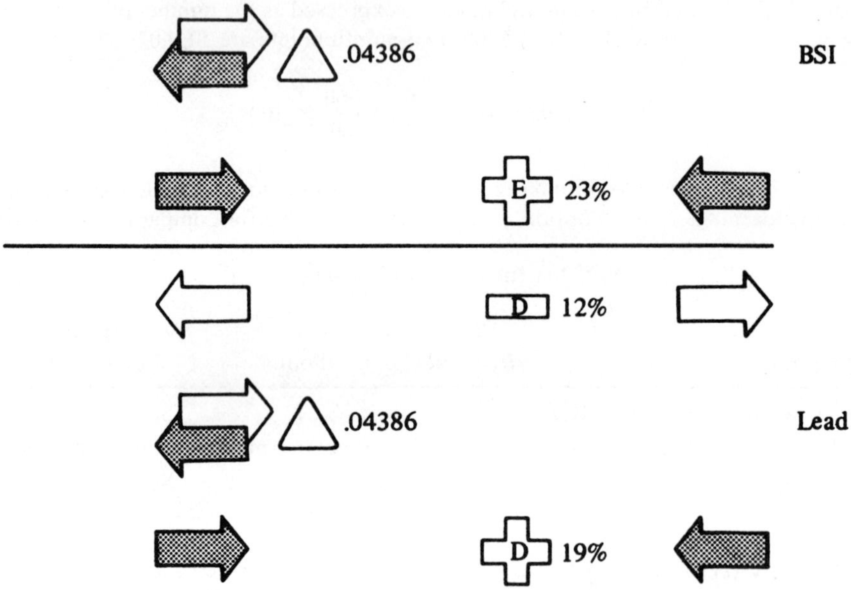

Gray, pesos; white, dollars

Two facts are immediately apparent from this diagram. This exposure can be covered at an earning; the cost of borrowing is less than the earning from investing. The BSI option is more attractive than the lead. The matrix can be filled as follows with the information given.

Net Interest Cost/Earning

Option	Spot	I_h	I_f	Net	Points	Locked-in Future Rate
Forward	0.04386				33	0.04353
BSI	0.04386	12	23	11%		
Lead	0.04386	12	19	7%		

To calculate the interest earnings, ICE-1 is used since the spot and points are expressed in home currency terms. Interest earnings are

$$9.03\% = \frac{0.00033}{0.04386} \times \frac{360}{30} \times 100$$

The best option is the BSI, since the net earnings are 11%. The next steps are to caluclate the points for the BSI and, for completeness, the lead.

$$\text{BSI points} = 0.00039 = \frac{0.04386 \times 0.12 - 0.23) \times 30/360}{1 + (0.23 \times 30/360)}$$

$$\text{Lead points} = 0.00025 = \frac{0.04386 \times (0.12 - 0.19) \times 30/360}{1 + (0.19 \times 30/360)}$$

The points are subtracted from the spot rate because an earnings in a payable situation means that the company pays less of its own currency.

The completed matrix is

Net Interest Cost/Earning

Option	Spot	I_h	I_f	Net	Points	Locked-in Future Rate
Forward	0.04386			+9.03%	33	0.04353
BSI	0.04386	12	23	+11.00%	39	0.04347
Lead	0.04386	12	19	+7.00%	25	0.04361

By all the choice criteria, the BSI option is the best. This option is compared to the forecast. The forecast was that the peso would weaken on the order of 4% over the next six months. On a yearly basis this is 8%. This figure can be compared to the annual earnings of 11% if the exposure is covered. Given the current forecast, Brittan Valley is better off covering its exposure immediately rather than waiting for the exchange rate to move.

WALKING THROUGH AN EXPOSURE SITUATION. The process for analyzing an exposure situation is summarized in the following steps.

1. Identify the exposure.
2. Represent the exposure with symbols.
3. Represent all options that will cover the exposure.
4. Identify the foreign exchange and money markets the options will use.
5. Select the necessary interest and exchange rates.
6. Fill in the matrix with all known interest and exchange rates.
7. Use the formula to convert points to percentages and vice versa.
8. Complete the matrix.
9. Choose the best option.
10. Compare the cost/earning of the best option and the locked-in future rate to the currency forecast.

If the decision is made not to cover immediately, the decision maker is saying that sometime between today and the future date it will be possible to exchange foreign currency for home currency at a price better than the best option currently available.

MULTIPLE EXPOSURES

"Multiple exposures" describes situations where a company has more than one flow in the same foreign currency or has flows in different foreign currencies. In some cases time and money are saved by dealing with more than one exposure at the same time. There are other instances where it is beneficial to deal with each exposure independently.

MORE THAN ONE CURRENCY. A major Dutch trading company has an inflow of dollars in 31 days and at the same time an outflow of the equivalent amount in French francs. There is a temptation to solve both exposures at one time by a dollar-franc forward, or some other option, without any reference to the home currency. However, this strategy does not always yield the best results for the company. The reason is that the best option for covering the dollar inflow may be a dollar-guilder forward, whereas the best option for covering the franc outflow may be a franc-guilder lead. If the options are analyzed only in terms of the dollar and franc the optimal combination is missed.

For this illustration only two options are considered, forward and lead; the principle applies equally to others.

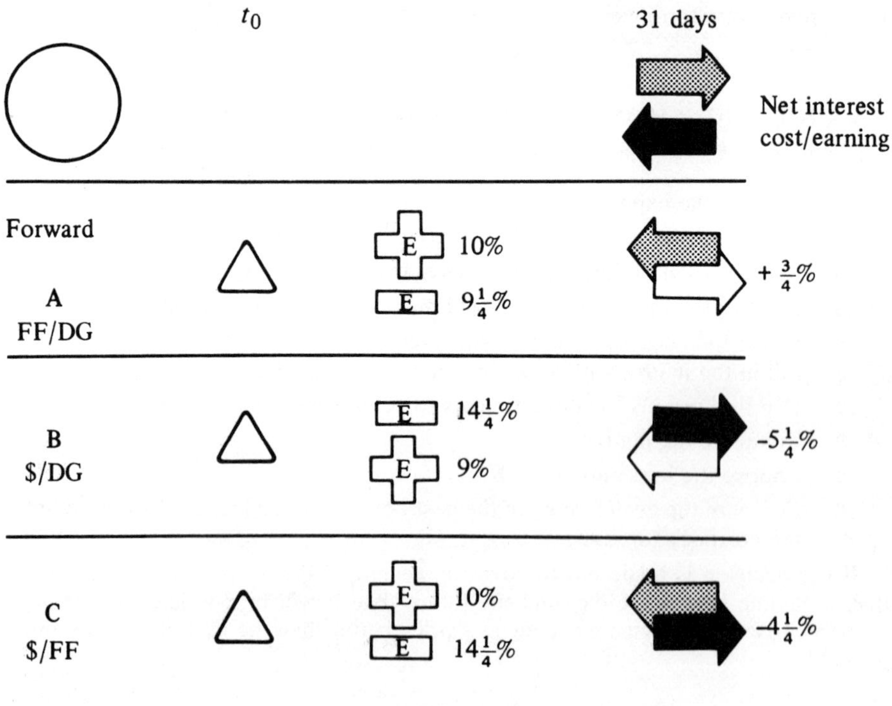

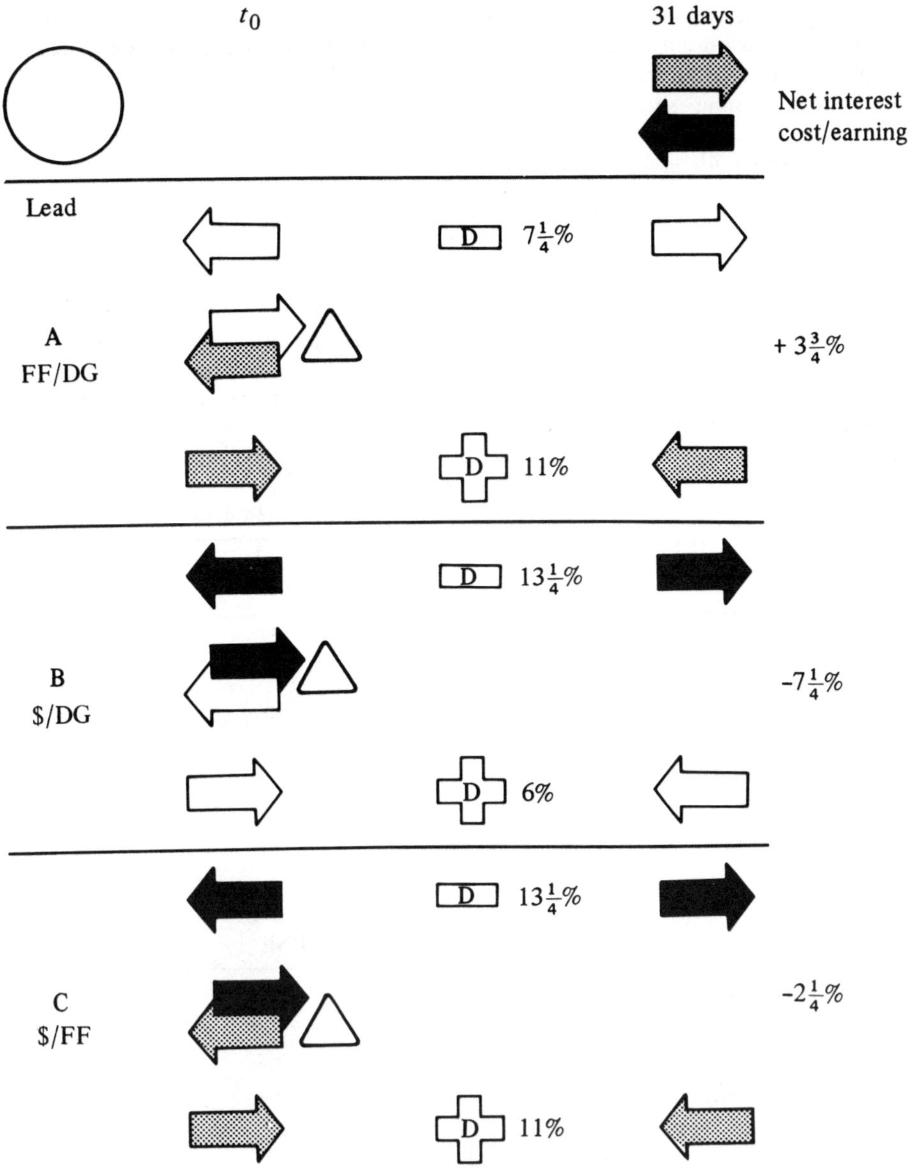

White, Dutch guilders; gray, French francs; black, U.S. dollars

The best way of covering the franc exposure is that of lead A, where there is an earning of 3¾%. The best option for covering the dollar exposure is that of forward B; the cost is 5¼%. The combined cost of covering both exposures is 1½%. This combination is superior to both of the options, forward C and Lead C, which do not go through guilders and deal with francs and dollars directly.

The preceding illustration also points out that if the best option for each exposure is the same, then it is more efficient not to work through the home currency; instead, the dollar-franc option should be used. In the forward the saving is ¼%, the difference between the guilder borrowing and investing rate. In the lead the saving is 1¼%; one bank lending spread is avoided, and again there is the ¼% difference between the guilder rates. In addition to these savings, there is the benefit of not going through both sides of the guilder spot market.

MORE THAN ONE FLOW IN THE SAME CURRENCY. Aspinwall Ltd., a Canadian textile concern, borrowed Swiss francs a number of years ago. It is repaying the loan in quarterly installments of principal and interest. The firm's directors have decided they wish to cover the last four payments all at once. They feel the Canadian dollar is currently at a high point vis-à-vis the franc. The chances of doing better are not very strong. The assistant treasurer is instructed to execute this program as soon as possible. The lead is not a feasible option since the loan agreement with the bank prohibits prepayment.

Aspinwall's assistant treasurer calls the bank for the latest rates.

		Interest Rates	
	Exchange Rates	Domestic Dollars	External Francs
Spot SF/C$	0.7214–.7216		
Three months	148–152	14.375%	5.375%
Six months	268–278	14.375%	5.625%
Nine months	396–406	12.5%	5.5%
Twelve months	512–532	12%	5.5%

A few calculations are made.

	Net Interest Cost	
	Forward	BSI
Three months	8.43%	9.00%
Six months	7.62%	8.75%
Nine months	7.45%	7.00%
Twelve months	7.25%	6.50%

The assistant treasurer reports back to the directors that the three- and six-month installments were covered with forward contracts but the last two quarters were covered with the BSI option. The firm borrows Canadian dollars for two separate periods—nine months and 12 months. It sells the proceeds of both loans spot for Swiss francs and invests the francs in the external market for nine months and for 12 months. When questioned about using a different option to cover the last two quarters, the assistant treasurer points out that it is cheaper because the shapes of the interest-rate yield curves for domestic Canadian dollars and external dollars are different. The following graph is presented.

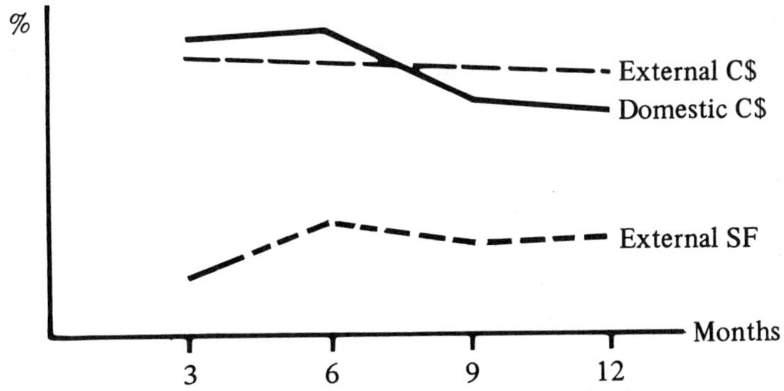

The gap between the interest rates in the two external markets is thinnest for the first two periods; hence the forward is best there. The gap between the interest rates in the franc external and Canadian dollar domestic markets is narrowest in the last two periods; hence the BSI is best there.

Because the shapes of interest-rate yield curves in domestic and external markets are not always the same, each foreign currency exposure in a series should be analyzed independently.

PAYABLE AND RECEIVABLE, SAME CURRENCY, DIFFERENT TIMES. A trading company or an intermediate processing firm imports and pays for goods at one time and sells and receives payment later. The firm of JSW Ltd. imports cotton into Hong Kong for export to Japan and Korea. Most of the trade is denominated in U.S. dollars. A typical cash flow scenario for the Hong Kong firm is illustrated.

It is unlikely that the same option will be the best for both exposures since the relative advantage of the options switches in going from the payable to the receivable. The following options cover JSW's situation.

	31 days	62 days
Forward	+10%	-10%
BSI	+ 9%	- 9%
Lead	+ 8%	- 8%

	6 months	9 months
Forward	-7.62%	+7.45%
BSI	-8.75%	+7.00%

The forward is the best option for covering the payable, but the lead is the best option for covering the receivable. The wide spread between the external interest rates that was desirable in covering the payable is not desirable for covering the receivable. Similarly, the narrow spread between domestic interest rates that makes the lead the best option for covering the receivable makes it the least desirable way to cover the payable exposure.

Payable and Receivable, Same Currency, Same Time. The situation shown below does not constitute an exposure for JSW Ltd. The dates are the same and the amounts are the same also.

The import-export firm can easily allow the inflow to offset the outflow. However, there may be a more worthwhile way for the firm to operate. Earlier it was noted that different options are often appropriate for payable and receivable flows at different times since the relative advantage of the options shifts in going from covering a payable to a receivable, and vice versa.

This idea also applies with even more vigor to payables and receivables that flow at the same time, since the possibility of a change in the shape of the interest rate yield curves is eliminated. An example with the following rates illustrates this point.

	Domestic	External
Hong Kong	5%–5.25%	7%–7.25%
United States	13.75%–14%	14%–14.25%

The forward and lead options are used to illustrate.

Net interest cost/earning

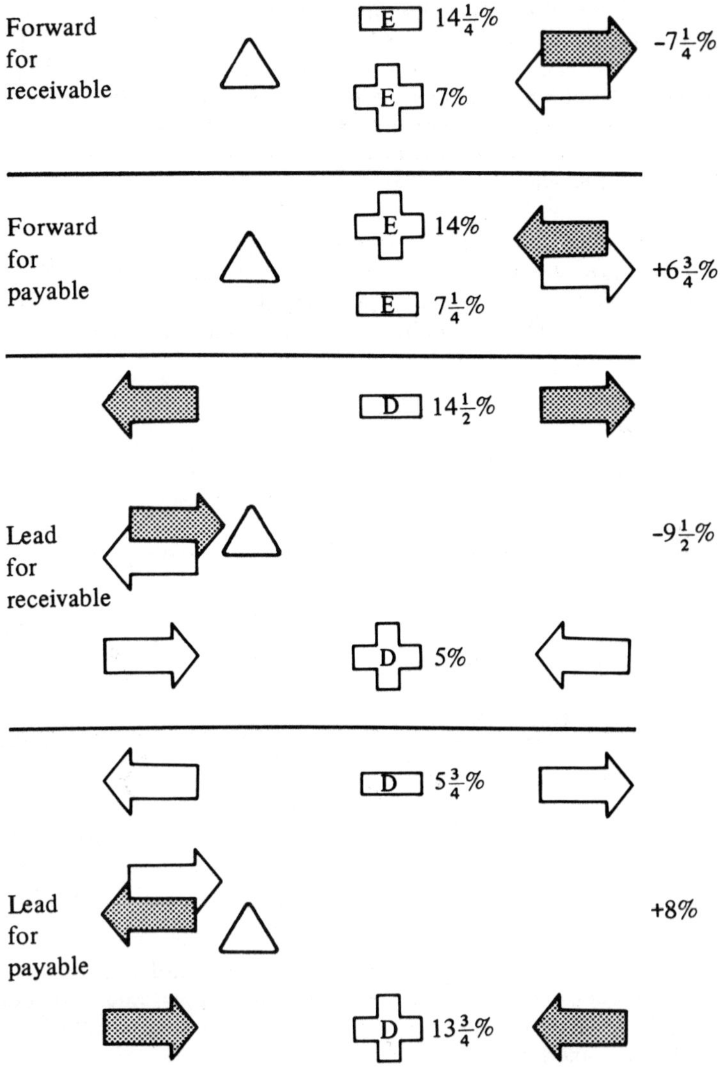

By covering the receivable with the forward and the payable with the lead, JSW Ltd. earns 0.75%. Execution of these options when the two flows cover each other (1) earns the firm US$3,750 on US$2 million over 90 days, (2) decreases the availability of bank credit for other uses, and (3) does not change the debt structure of the firm's balance sheet since current liabilities remain unchanged—accounts payable are reduced by the same amount short-term bank debt is increased.

LEADS AND LAGS

Companies lead and lag payments to change their foreign currency exposure and to finance operations. The lead is one of the basic options for covering an exposure. Other ways to lead will be shown. The lag is an option that eliminates risk when the delay matches a flow in the opposite direction. A West German company puts off paying an invoice in dollars for 30 days because it has a receivable in dollars at that time. A lag extends exposure, however, if there is no matching flow. A payable may be postponed if the company thinks the payable currency will fall against its own. A receivable will be delayed if the company believes the foreign currency will rise in value. The way to determine how much a currency must rise or fall to make the lag worthwhile will be shown.

LEAD. There is more than one way to lead a payable or a receivable. Besides the lead option used previously, another way to lead a future payable is to borrow that currency in the external money market and pay the supplier immediately with the borrowed funds. The loan is repaid by buying the foreign currency forward. This is symbolized as

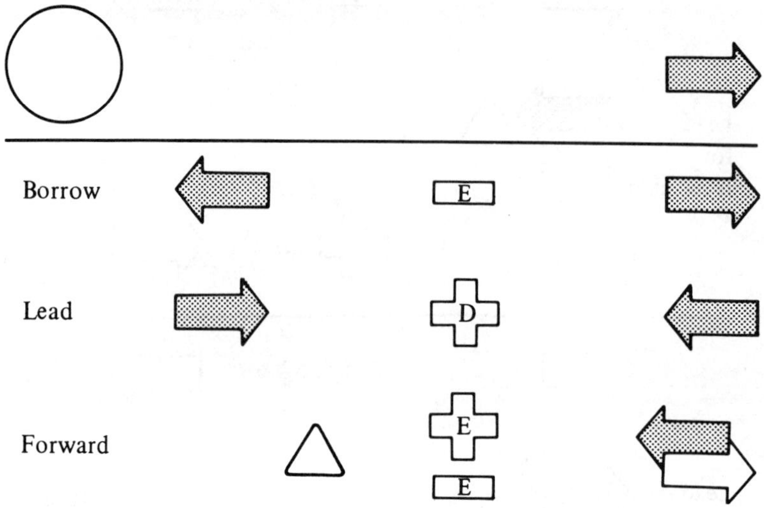

This method of leading is more advantageous than a forward if the external interest rate of the foreign currency is less than the domestic interest rate of that currency. Even if the company has decided not to cover the payable, it is still worthwhile to execute the borrow and lead.

There is an analogous way to lead a receivable—have the customer pay early. Rather than converting to home currency on the spot date, one may invest the foreign currency. The maturing investment is sold forward immediately.

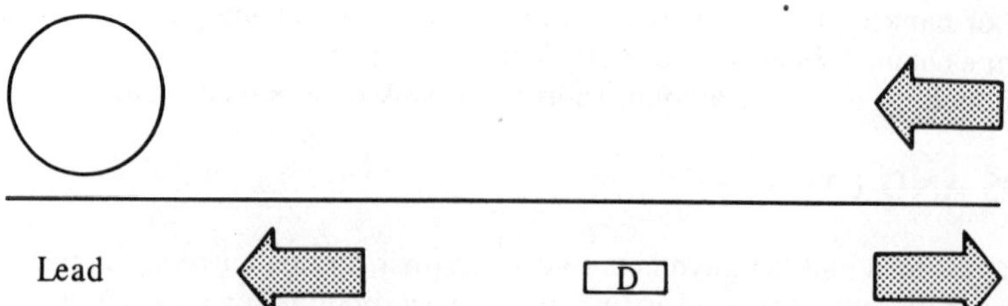

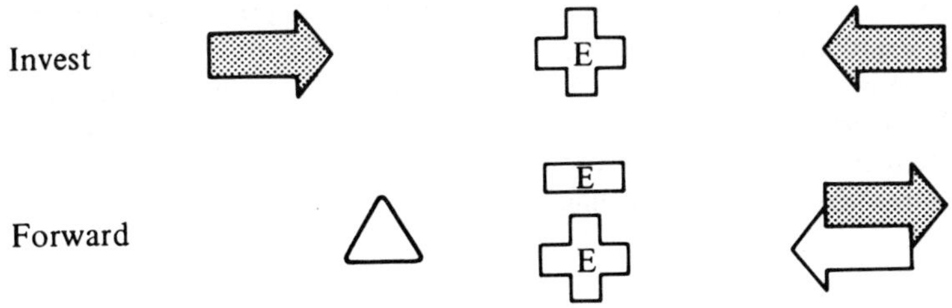

This option is also designed to take advantage of any difference between domestic and external interest rates of the foreign currency. To the extent that there is a positive difference, this option is better than the forward. Again, even if the firm has decided not to cover the receivable, it is worthwhile executing the lead and investment portions of it.

This option is called lead-F. It benefits firms that do not have access to the external market in their own currency. The illustration of the receivable exposure shows an external plus and an external minus for the foreign currency. The plus and minus essentially cancel out, at a cost of 0.25% to 0.5%. (The 0.25% to 0.5% is the spread between the borrowing rate and the investing rate.) The remaining elements are (1) a cost in the domestic money market of the foreign currency and (2) an earning in the external money market of the home currency. No other option produces this comparison if the company cannot access its external money market directly. It is desirable to have the comparison so that the company can choose from all money markets. The purpose of having more than one covering option is to find the best combination from all possibilities. The following chart shows the money market used for each currency in each option.

	Home Currency	Foreign Currency
Forward	External	External
BSI	Domestic	External
Lead	Domestic	Domestic
Lead-F	External	Domestic

With the addition of lead-F all the possible combinations of the money markets are used. If the firm has direct access to its external market, the lead will do the same job as lead-F.

Lead-F can be compared to the other options as follows:

$$\begin{aligned}\text{interest cost/earning} &= \pm \text{ interest rate on borrowing or investment}\\ &\quad \pm \text{ interest rate of lead}\\ &\quad \pm \text{ interest cost/earning of the forward}\\ \text{points} &= \text{forward points} \pm \text{points for lead and borrowing or investment}\end{aligned}$$

LAG. Cranbery Ltd. is an Australian mining company. It wants to delay an upcoming yen payment for another month because it believes the yen will fall against the dollar during that time. A Japanese sister company is expecting those funds, however, and will want to be compensated for the delay. Cranbery is effectively borrowing from its Japanese affiliate for a month. The Australian company will be able to use the funds it does not pay out to buy yen. The treasurer of Cranbery wants to determine whether it is worthwhile to gamble on delaying the payment. Will the expected change in the exchange rate be enough to offset the costs of the lag? The flows for the lag are symbolized in the following diagram.

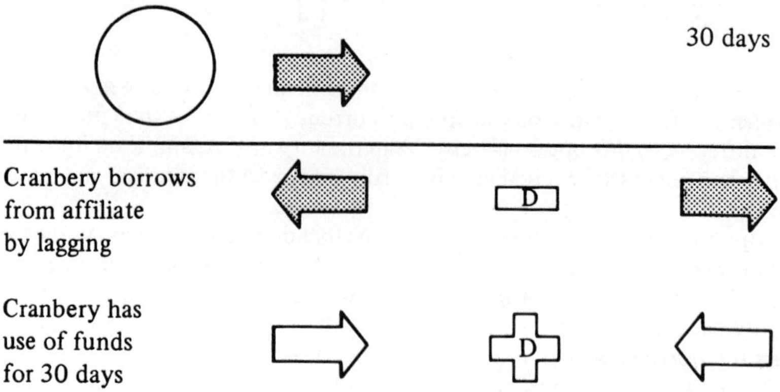

The symbol for the lag is the same as that for borrowing. The Japanese company will charge Cranbery the cost of replacing those funds in the Japanese market; hence there is a symbol for a domestic cost. It is presumed that Cranbery will use the Australian dollars (A$) locally. The earning may be from a money market investment, the postponement of bank borrowing for another month, or it may be used to pay another supplier. Against this cost and earning the treasurer must balance the number of Australian dollars to be paid out today to buy yen against the number expected to be paid out in 30 days. To be as well off in 30 days as today, any cost in delaying the payable must be compensated by an exchange gain. If there is an earning, the company can afford an exchange loss. The treasurer wants to calculate the future break-even exchange rate at which an exchange gain (or loss) compensates a cost (or earning) from delaying payment.

The break-even rate is calculated by converting interest costs and earnings into points.

The points calculation to find the break-even rate is

$$\text{points} = \text{spot} \times (I_h - I_f) \times \frac{\text{days}}{360}$$

The points are then added to or subtracted from spot, depending on whether there is an earning or a cost from lagging the payment. As an example, in the Cranbery situation domestic yen (¥) interest rate is 11% and domestic dollar interest rate is 7%; the spot is ¥/Aus $3.7660 per 1,000 yen.

$$\text{points} = 3.7660 \times (0.07 - 0.11) \times \frac{30}{360} = 126 \text{ points}$$

Since this is a cost to Cranbery the company must recover through an exchange gain and pay out fewer Australian dollars in the future. The yen–Australian dollar rate at which the company covers the transaction must be at least 3.7534 (3.7660 − 0.0126), compared to spot of 3.7660. Cranbery can arrange for the cover any time between the present and 30 days, hoping for something like 3.7400.

Lagging a receivable is very similar to lagging a payable. Now assume that Cranbery has an imminent receivable from New Zealand. Because the affiliate in Wellington is in need of funds Cranbery is willing to delay the inflow of New Zealand dollars.

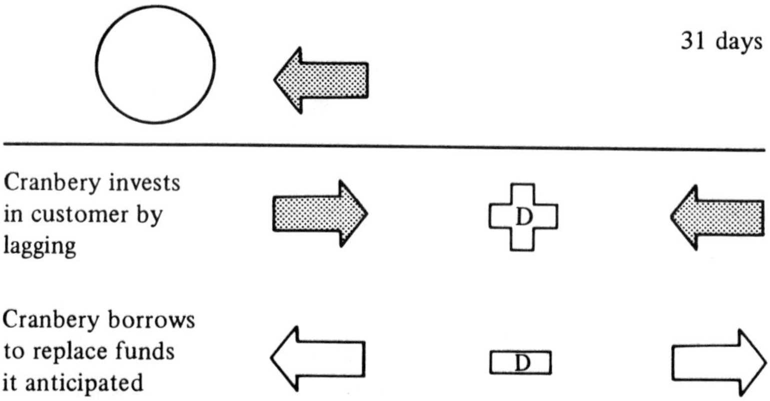

The Australian firm receives its money in 30 days. The New Zealand firm is able to use the funds for working capital or to delay borrowing from the bank for another month. Cranbery expected to receive money and must now forego the use of it. The cost to Cranbery can be either an earning foregone from investment of the funds or the cost of a bank loan. Why might Cranbery agree to the lag if it needs funds for its own operations? The New Zealand affiliate may be near the limit of its bank credit lines, and Cranbery has ample credit facilities.

Before agreeing, the treasurer checks the exchange implications of this lag. If the New Zealand dollar (NZ$) is expected to rise against its Australian counterpart, the treasurer may be willing to suffer a small cost in the delay. If the opposite is expected, Cranbery will want to be compensated through interest earnings. The break-even rate is calculated just as before.

As an example, if the New Zealand dollar interest rate is 13% and the Australian dollar interest rate is 7%, spot is NZ$/Aus $0.8925.

$$\text{points} = 0.8925 \times (0.07 - 0.13) \times \frac{31}{360} = 46 \text{ points}$$

This is an earning for Cranbery Ltd., since the New Zealand firm is paying more than the cost of borrowing. Cranbery can afford to lose a little in the exchange rate and still be as well off in 31 days as the firm is presently. Losing on a receivable means the firm would receive fewer Australian dollars; therefore, the points are subtracted from spot. The break-even rate is 0.8879, below that in which Cranbery would be worse off; above that, it is better off than it is currently.

The conventions for adding and subtracting points to find the break-even rate are

Lag	Receivable Exposure	Payable Exposure
Cost	Add the points	Subtract the points
Earning	Subtract the points	Add the points

With a receivable exposure the objective is to maximize the number of home currency units for each unit of foreign currency. If there is a cost to lag, then the break-even rate must be higher, and must represent more home currency units. If there is an earning through the delay, money gained there can be used to compensate a loss due to a lower exchange rate.

The objective in a payable exposure situation is to pay out the fewest number of home currency units. If there is a cost to the lag, the firm will be just as well off if it pays out even less of its own currency. On the other hand, if the firm earns from the delay, the earning will compensate for a higher exchange rate.

A LAG TO COVER EXPOSURE. Most of the discussion thus far has been devoted to the lag that extends exposure rather than covers it. If the delay of a receivable or payable matches a flow in the opposite direction, the lag covers exposure. But there are cost and earning implications to this way of covering a future exposure. The cost/earning of covering that future exposure is the value of today's flow plus the interest cost and earning from moving it to the future.

Lagging a present flow is not necessarily the best way of covering the future flow. Earning may be greater if the imminent receivable were converted at spot and the future flow were covered by a forward or a BSI. All the options should be considered. The previous discussion examines multiple flows more closely.

THE FORWARD MARKET

A forward rate is composed of a spot rate and points. The points bridge the time gap between spot and the future date. In a sense, the operation implicit in the points carries the spot from the present to the future date. This representation is a 90-day dollar receivable and a sale of dollars and a purchase of lire spot.

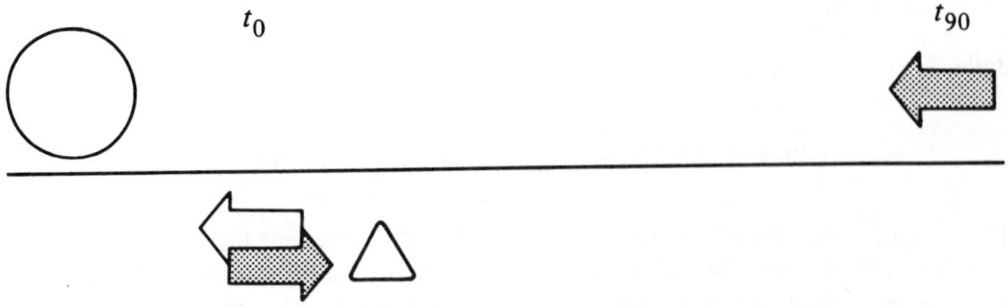

Since the exposure is in the future, another operation is needed, an operation whereby dollars are borrowed and lire are simultaneously invested.

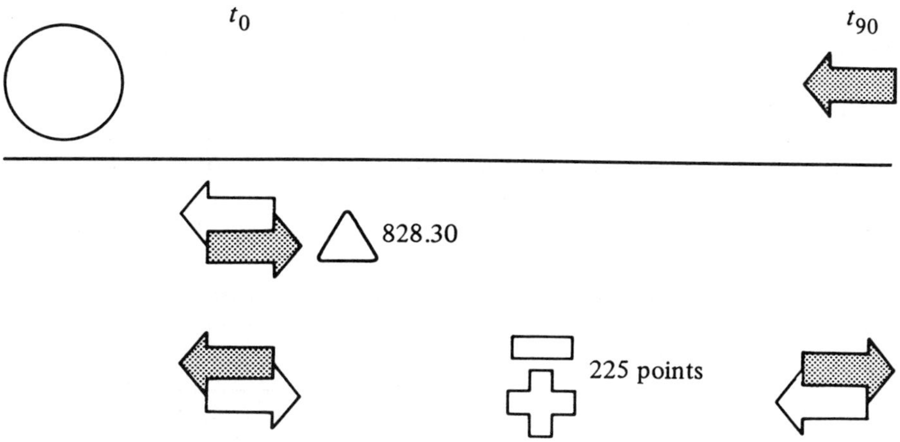

The result is that the flows on the spot day cancel out, leaving a sale of dollars and purchase of lire on a forward date.

The operation in which one currency is borrowed for a period of time and another currency is invested simultaneously in one transaction is a swap. Forward points are also referred to as swap points. The swap is an operation that has all the characteristics of a money market operation but is executed in the foreign exchange market. The points are the mechanism of paying and receiving interest. If one lends the higher rate currency, points are earned. This is arranged by booking the swap as two foreign exchange contracts, one spot and one forward.

Dollar amount the same, lira amount changes:

$$\text{earnings ICE-1} = \frac{\text{points}}{\text{spot}} \times \frac{360}{\text{days}} \times 100$$

$$4.83\% = \frac{10.00}{828.30} \times \frac{360}{90} \times 100$$

Note that the dollar amount is the same on the spot and forward contracts, and the points are earned in lire. The earning arises from buying $1 million for Lit 828.3 million and selling the $1 million back three months later for Lit 830.55 million. That is the compensation for giving up lire that earn a high interest rate and accepting dollars, which earn a lower interest rate, for three months. If the currency on the left of the slash ($/Lit) is held constant, as it is in this case, then the formula ICE-1 is used to calculate the cost/earning of the swap.

There are reasons why the lire amount may be the same on the spot and forward contracts. In that case in the calculation of the cost/earning of the swap formula ICE-2 is used. The reason is that the points are earned in dollars, but the spot rate and the points are in lire.

Dollar amount changes, lira amount the same:

Spot contract — Forward contract

$/Lit 828.30 — $/Lit 838.30

$$\text{earnings ICE-2} = \frac{\text{points}}{\text{forward}} \times \frac{360}{90} \times 100$$

$$4.77\% = \frac{10.00}{838.30} \times \frac{360}{90} \times 100 = \frac{\$11{,}929}{\$1{,}000{,}000} \times \frac{360}{90} \times 100$$

The bank uses the swap, together with the spot, to effect forward operations for its customers. The following illustrations show how.

1. The bank's customer has an exposure, a foreign currency payable (gray).

2. The customer buys the foreign currency forward from the bank with its own currency (white).

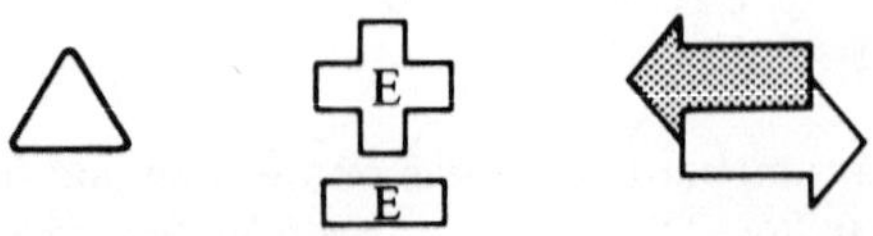

3. The bank has contracted to sell foreign currency and buy the home currency.

Noting the customer's original exposure and the bank's present position, it can be seen that the customer has shifted its exposure to the bank.

4. Banks separate their operations in the spot market and in the forward market. The bank executes a spot contract to cover the currency element and a swap contract to cover the time element of its exposure.

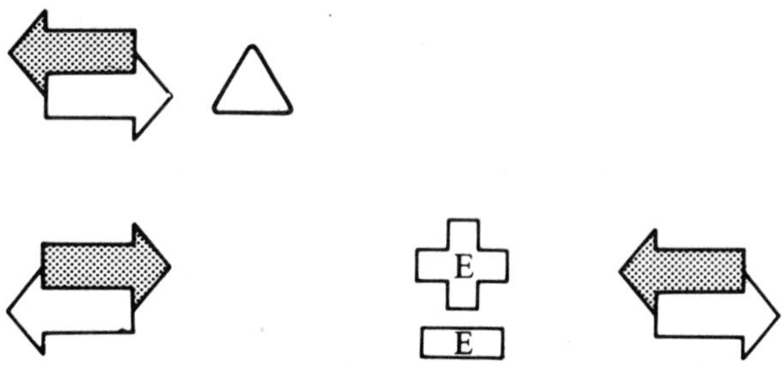

In comparing the pricing of the customer's forward (2) with the bank's coverage of its exposure, it can be seen that the bank passes on to the customer its cost and earnings.

THE DETERMINATION OF FORWARD POINTS. The relationship between points and interest rates is formalized in the points formula. There is a relation specifically between forward points and external interest rates. It was due to convenience, and subsequently by convention, that external currency interest rates have become allied to forward points. External currency markets have a single short-term instrument with standard maturities, the time deposit. Money is placed in a deposit or a deposit is taken (money borrowed) at fixed rates, for fixed periods of time. The standard maturities in the external currency markets are the same as those in the forward market—1, 2, 3, 6, and 12 months. As in the foreign exchange market, time starts on the spot day. External currency deposits have the same degree of risk. The uniformity of the external currency time deposit and its conformity to the conventions of the foreign exchange market make it a convenient standard.

Points and interest rates are both prices of the operations of borrowing and investing. Points refer to a money market operation executed in the foreign exchange market. Interest rates refer to direct acts of borrowing and investing in the money market. Arbitrage is the mechanism that ensures that the points reflect external interest rates, and, in turn, external interest rates reflect the points. Assume it is possible to borrow a currency at 5%, swap it for a second currency at a cost of 4%, and then place the second currency on deposit at 10%. The total cost is 9%; the earnings are 10%. Those with access to the money and exchange markets engage in this activity until either the cost of borrowing rises, the cost of the swap rises, or deposit rates fall. Depending on the depth of the markets, all three occur to varying degrees.

If the cost of the borrowing rises to 5.5% and the cost of the swap rises to 106 points, or 4.25%, and if the rate paid for deposits drops to 9.75%, there is no further incentive to undertake the arbitrage. The cost of the operation is equal to the earnings from it. The profit motive ensures that the forward points reflect precisely the difference between two Eurocurrency interest rates. The equality between the interest rate differential and the forward points is termed "interest rate parity." Another way of expressing this is that in the Eurocurrency markets all interest rates are equal through the forward foreign exchange market.

The line of causation flows both ways; changes in interest rates cause changes in points, and changes in points cause changes in interest rates. The relative importance of the money market and foreign exchange market is different for each currency.

FOREIGN CURRENCY LOANS

The principal reason many companies borrow foreign currency is that it is cheaper than their own. Another reason is that foreign currency may be available when theirs is not. Credit restrictions imposed by central banks often have the effect of drying up the supply of domestic credit, especially for medium-sized enterprises. For those firms and governments that want to borrow very large sums, there are only a few money markets in the world large enough to accommodate them—U.S. dollars, Canadian dollars, Deutsche marks, Swiss francs, and British pounds sterling. The sophistication of some money markets allows the borrower greater flexibility in loan pricing and conditions than it would have in the home currency. Another good reason to borrow foreign currency is to cover a specific foreign currency receivable. As an extension of this idea, a British firm investing in a plant in Austria for sales in that market would borrow schillings to match the continuing flow of its receivables with its interest expenses.

These last two types of foreign currency loan do not involve any risk on the part of the borrower; they cover existing risk. But borrowing foreign currency because it is cheaper or more available or because the terms are more flexible does involve a risk. Foreign currency is converted to home currency immediately. The risk is that the foreign currency might appreciate against the home currency. The borrower has to spend more home currency to buy back the foreign currency at the maturity of the loan than was received when foreign currency was converted to home currency initially.

Why take the risk? The interest saving can be large. In December 1979 there was a 6% saving if Swiss francs were borrowed for five years as opposed to U.S. dollars, and there was an 11% difference between borrowing Swiss francs for one year instead of pounds sterling. On the equivalent of a $1 million loan, this represents a saving of $300,000 in the first case and $110,000 in the second. It would seem worthwhile to take a gamble on the exchange rate. In the first instance the company is betting that the Swiss franc will not appreciate against the dollar by more than 30% in five years and in the second, that the Swiss franc will not appreciate against the pound by more than 11% in one year.

It pays to look more closely at this gamble; the margin for change is not as wide as it appears. Over time, as the Swiss franc appreciates against the dollar, the cost of buying the periodic interest payments increases in dollar terms. The following formula takes this into account. It calculates the percentage of change in the value of a foreign currency loan equivalent to a home currency loan.

$$\text{percent change} = \frac{(I_h - I_f) \times \text{time}}{1 + \left(I_f \times \sum_{k=1}^{N} \frac{k}{N}\right)}$$

for example,

$$26.1\% = \frac{(0.11 - 0.05) \times 5}{1 + \left(0.05 \times \sum_{k=1}^{5} \frac{k}{5}\right)}$$

The first line of the equation is the difference in interest rates over the time period of the loan. The second represents the increasing cost of periodic interest payments in terms of the home currency. As a result, the appreciation of the franc that makes borrowing francs equivalent to borrowing dollars is 26.1% rather than 30%.

Borrowing foreign currency is risky if there are no proceeds of that currency for the repayment. The formula allows an evaluation of that risk and specifies the judgment that must be made about the exchange rate. If spot US$/SF is 1.5665, a 26.1% appreciation of the franc would result in a rate of US$/SF1.1576 in five years. At this rate the Swiss franc loan at 5% borrowed by a U.S. firm for use in the United States would be the equivalent of a U.S. dollar loan at 11% for five years. If the company expects US$/SF to be 1.25, it would borrow francs; if it forecasts US$/SF as 1.05, the company would borrow dollars.

COVERING A FOREIGN CURRENCY LOAN. If a company has borrowed foreign currency but subsequent events indicate that the currency is appreciating more rapidly than forecast, the company can cover the principal and interest exposure.

A firm whose primary motive for borrowing is availability or flexibility of terms may not wish to be open to the exchange risk from the very beginning. When the loan is drawn down (received), the foreign currency is converted spot to the home currency. The repayment of the loan plus interest is covered by a forward. (The BSI and lead options are not applicable since they involve a home currency loan.) The spot and forward transactions together have the same representation as the swap. It is cheaper for the company to approach the initial conversion and forward cover as a single transaction rather than as two separate ones. It avoids entering the spot market on both sides. This illustration of the spot and forward (a spot and a swap) makes that clear.

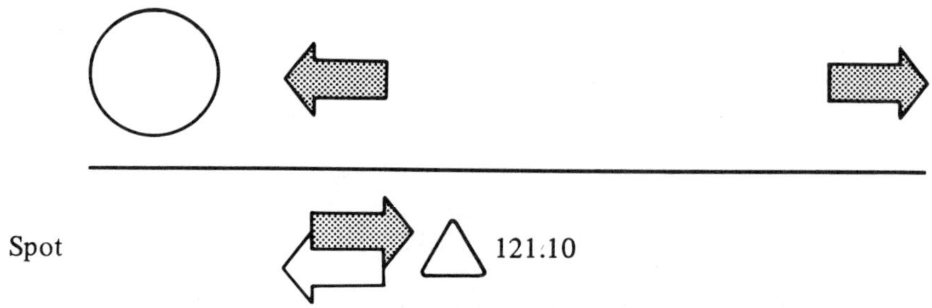

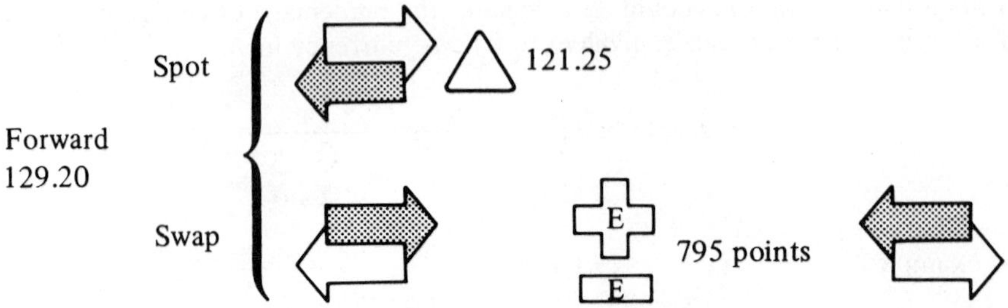

The swap is the only transaction needed. The two spot transactions are superfluous and cost the company money.

The effect of covering the foreign currency loan is to borrow the home currency in the external market. The foreign currency is borrowed in the money market but is then immediately invested in the foreign exchange market through the swap.

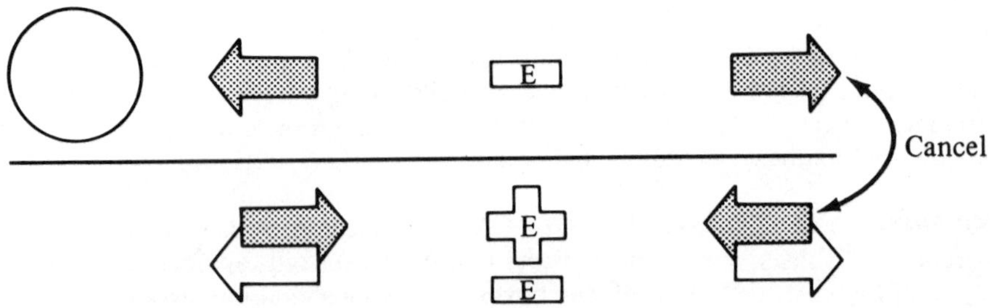

To totally cover the exposure of a foreign currency loan, the interest on the loan is purchased forward also. A loan of SF5 million at 5% has an interest payment of SF253,472.22 at the end of a year. A Dutch company would go to its bank and say that it would like to swap SF5 million spot against one year for guilders (DG) and at the same time buy SF253,472.22 one year forward with guilders. The company sells SF5 million spot at SF/DG 121.25 and buys SF5,253,472.22 forward at SF/DG129.20, a cost of 795 points. The bank combines the future portion of the swap with the forward contract for the interest.

To calculate the cost of the operation of raising home currency by (1) borrowing foreign currency, (2) swapping it for home currency, and (3) buying foreign currency interest forward, three elements must be considered.

1. I_f, the interest rate of the foreign currency
2. The cost/earning of the swap as calculated by ICE-1

$$\text{ICE-1} = \frac{\text{points}}{\text{spot}} \times \frac{360}{\text{days}}$$

3. The cost/earning of buying the foreign currency interest forward as calculated in the following formula

$$I_f \times \frac{\text{points}}{\text{spot}}$$

Combining some terms gives the formula for calculating the total covered cost (TCC) of a foreign currency loan, the cost of borrowing home currency through the money market and the swap.

$$I_h = (I_f \times \frac{\text{forward}}{\text{spot}} \pm \frac{\text{points}}{\text{spot}} \times \frac{360}{\text{days}}) \times 100$$

If read from the left, this equation indicates that the interest rate on home currency raised by a combination money market and exchange transaction is equal to the interest rate on the foreign currency times a factor to account for covering the foreign currency interest forward, plus or minus the cost/earning of the swap.

Example. A Dutch company borrows Swiss francs at 5% for one year. It will convert the francs to guilders for use in Holland. The cost of borrowing the francs and totally covering the exposure gives the effective cost of borrowing guilders.

$$\begin{aligned} \text{SF/DG spot} &= 121.10\text{–}121.25 \\ \text{one year} &= 775\text{–}795 \text{ points} \end{aligned}$$

The interest cost of Dutch guilders is 11.79%.

$$11.79\% = \left(0.05 \times \frac{129.20}{121.25} + \frac{7.95}{121.25} \times \frac{360}{365}\right) \times 100$$

The cost of covering the Swiss franc interest payment adds 0.32% to the cost of borrowing the guilders.

TIME OPTIONS

A number of foreign exchange and money market techniques are grouped together here because they relate to the time element in exposure. The facets of time to be considered are

1. Length, from very short to very long; how to deal with exposures that are before spot and those that are two years after spot, where there is no market.
2. Uncertainty of time. Is the payable due in 30, 35, or 40 days? If the ship delivering the goods is fighting its way to port through stormy seas, no one can pick a definite date for its arrival. Yet, foreign exchange and money market contracts are made for a specific date.

EXPOSURES TODAY, TOMORROW, AND THE DAY AFTER SPOT. The European treasurer of Bailie Industries Ltd. in Toronto often arrives in the morning to find a cable saying that dividends from one of the overseas subsidiaries are available to be remitted immediately. In Hong Kong JSW Ltd. deals in such volume that at least once a month a foreign currency payment slips by and must be paid that day or the next. The spot date is too late. Antigone Shipping buys a foreign currency to provide for the expenses of its ships in foreign ports. From time to time a ship arrives two days earlier than the date on which the currency was bought. Parker & Company decided some months ago not to cover its upcoming Swiss franc loan payment, but rather to wait until the spot day to buy the francs. The payment is now three days away, and the treasurer hears from a reliable source that in the afternoon the Federal Reserve is going to announce a lower discount rate. The measure is intended to spur the U.S. economy but will very likely weaken the dollar, at least temporarily. The treasurer wants to buy immediately.

The problem common to these companies is the need to act quickly and to rearrange funds for short periods of time. The spot date is too late for many of them to act. There are foreign exchange and money market rates for periods of one, two, three, six, and 12 months that start from the spot date. There are also markets for shorter periods of time, closer to the spot date, called "short-date" markets. These exchange and money markets consist of three separate one-day quotes around the spot day and quotes for one and two weeks. These markets differ from those previously discussed because the periods are shorter and because they do not all start on the spot date.

The quote from today to tomorrow is called "**overnight**" (O/N); the present day is the starting day. The quote from tomorrow to spot is called "**tom-next**" (T/N); tomorrow is the starting day. The quote from spot to the day after spot is called "**spot-next**" (S/N); spot is the starting day. The quote from spot to one week is called "**spot-a-week**" (S/W); spot is the starting day. The following diagram illustrates this idea.

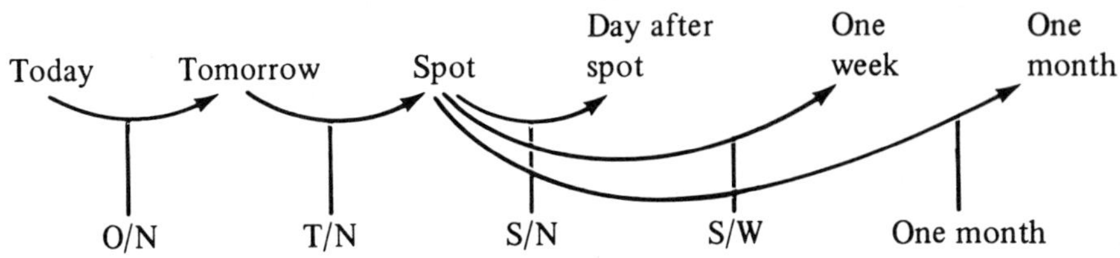

Tom-next and spot-next quotes are available for nearly all traded currencies. For the less active currencies, the tom-next market tends to dry up in the afternoon. Overnight quotes do not exist for all currencies. One governing factor is the time at which banks are required to settle their books for the day. In Zurich it may be 8:00 A.M., in Amsterdam 11:00 A.M., in New York 2:00 P.M., and in London 2:00 P.M. The ability to make an overnight quote also depends on where in the world a bank is in relation to the country of the currency with which it is dealing. A U.S. dollar transaction, no matter where in the world it is made, will involve a movement of funds between two bank accounts in the United States. Likewise, a pounds sterling transaction anywhere gives rise to a transfer of funds in London, and guilders, a transfer between two accounts in The Netherlands, and so on. An overnight U.S. dollar/pounds sterling transaction is made in Brussels at 2:00 P.M. There is one hour to transfer funds in London and six hours to transfer them in New York, because of the time difference. Overnight dollars-yen transactions are quoted in Tokyo, but not in London. Overnight pounds sterling deposits can be made in Paris, but at 9:00 A.M. in New York it is too late. A local bank will be able to provide information on what overnight markets are available in any time zone. Of course, it is always possible for a company to do more if someone is willing to start working very early in the morning.

Covering an exposure the day after spot or one week after spot is exactly the same as covering an exposure one month after spot. The same options are available to corporations. Covering an exposure immediately or the next day involves the same considerations as covering an exposure 30 or 60 days in the future, but some options are not the same. The objective of the options is the same—to find the most efficient combination of external and domestic money markets. The BSI is very similar to the option used to cover future exposures. The combination of a spot and a swap is also used to cover exposures of the same day and the next day. There is no concise terminology; the transactions are sometimes called "spot over tomorrow" or "spot over today." For an exposure the same day or the next, the lead has little practical value. On the other hand, a lag will move the exposure to the spot day, where it can be covered with a spot contract. The basic options for covering an exposure the next day are illustrated.

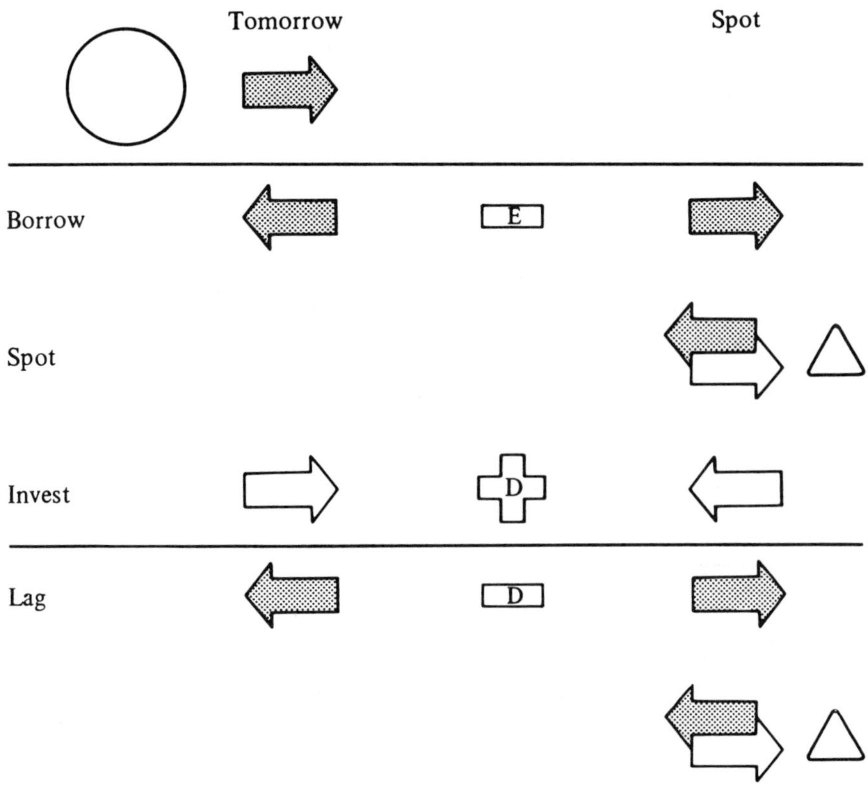

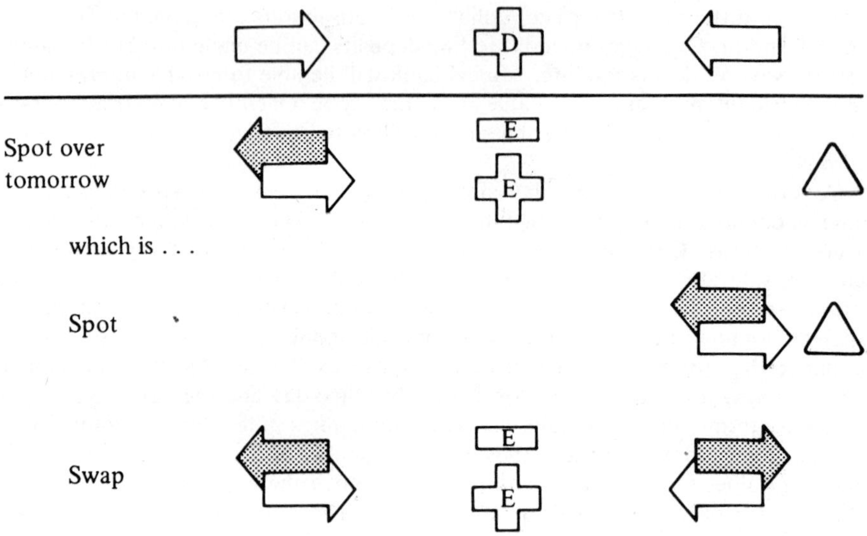

In the BSI, the gray is borrowed from tomorrow to spot. The inflow from the loan covers the payable. The maturing loan is paid off by a purchase of gray on the spot date. The white funds available to buy gray are invested for a day. The maturing white investment is used to pay for the spot purchase.

For the lag, the company puts off paying its gray supplier for a day and is charged the supplier's cost of borrowing for a day. The delayed exposure is covered with a spot contract. The white funds not disbursed are invested for a day.

For a spot-over-tomorrow, just as a bank might put together a spot and a swap to produce a forward, it puts together a spot and a swap to cover an exposure the next day. One price, including both elements, is given to the customer. The white currency is disbursed the next day, and the price of the contract includes an earning for white in the price, just as it includes a cost for the gray.

Comparing the options is the same as with a future exposure.

Example. France is white, the United States is gray, and the spot is US$/FrF4.0120–4.0135. French domestic interest rates are 10%, U.S. dollar domestic interest rates are 15%, external rates are 13%, and the number of points for one day is 4½–3½.

The matrix for comparing the options is as follows:

		I_h	I_f	Net	Locked-in Rate
BSI	4.0135	10	13	−3%	4.0138⅜
Lag	4.0135	10	15	−5%	4.0140⅝
Spot over tomorrow	4.0135			−4.04%	4.0139½

The best option for covering the exposure the next day is the BSI; it is the least costly.

EXPOSURES IN THE FAR FUTURE. Cornie Construction Company has a contract to build a large desalinization plant in Saudi Arabia. The project will take four years from start to finish. Cornie is being paid in Saudi riyals; its expenses are denominated in dollars, yen, Swiss francs, Deutsche marks, pounds sterling, and riyals. Beyond one year the market for Saudi riyals is almost nonexistent. How is Cornie going to deal with its exposure beyond one year?

Antigone Shipping is buying a vessel in Japan. A five-year yen loan from the Japanese export agency will finance the vessel when it is delivered in 12 months. Antigone is somewhat concerned about the yen exposure since most of its revenues are in dollars and the yen is currently at a low point against the dollar. Beyond one year the market for yen is very thin. How is Antigone going to deal with its exposure beyond one year?

The exposures of these two companies cannot be covered since the markets do not extend as far in the future as the exposures. Partial cover is possible. Both Cornie and Antigone can purchase the currencies they require one year in the future and roll the contracts forward to meet the currency obligations. This means that Cornie will buy all the dollars, pounds. Deutsche marks, and other currencies that it needs for the last three years of the contract. Antigone will buy the total principal and interest amount required to pay off the loan. How far ahead the currencies are purchased depends on the companies' views of interest rate movements.

Principal plus interest for Antigone is Y5 billion, payable in semi-annual installments. The company buys this amount one year forward. At the end of one year Antigone rolls forward ¥500 million for six months and ¥4,500 million for another year. At the end of the next year Antigone rolls forward ¥500 million for six months and ¥3,500 million yen for another year. This continues. The exchange risk is covered, but Antigone is forced to carry the interest rate risk. Antigone is not confined to the foreign exchange market; a contract may be more advantageously rolled forward with a borrow-invest or a lead; loan and investment maturities can be mismatched. By the same token it is not necessary to wait until the contract matures; forward-forward transactions can be arranged. Exposures in the far future should not be neglected simply because they cannot be completely covered. The exchange risk can be covered, even though the time exposure cannot be.

CURRENCY SWAPS AND PARALLEL LOANS. A U.S. distiller is increasing the range of its products by buying a company in Scotland. The payback on the investment is estimated to be 10 years. An English electrical supply firm wishes to restructure the liabilities of its U.S. subsidiary to include long-term debt. The company is considering a maturity of 10 to 12 years. Both firms have enough cash in their own currency to carry out the operation but the transactions require a foreign currency. If the dollars are converted to pounds sterling by the distiller and the pounds to dollars by the electrical company, there is an exchange risk. In 10 years there is no guarantee they will get back the amount of their currency they put in. The dollar and pounds sterling exchange and money markets do not extend to these maturities for the large amounts required. Covering the exposure by conventional means is not possible.

The two firms can avail themselves of a currency swap or a parallel loan for 10 years. A currency swap is like any other swap, only longer, and is generally made between two corporations rather than between a bank and a corporation. From the U.S. distiller's point of view, it lends dollars and borrows pounds sterling. From the electrical company's point of view, it borrows dollars and lends pounds sterling. The arrangement is evidenced by exchange of currencies immediately and a reverse exchange in 10 years. The exchange rate on the two contracts is the same. The difference in interest rates between the two currencies is settled by an annual payment rather than by a difference in the prices on the two contracts. The interest rates can be set at the beginning of the transactions for the entire 10 years, or there can be a provision to vary the rates at certain intervals.

Generally the swap is arranged by a bank that acts as a broker between the two parties and collects a fee for the service. Banks also act as intermediaries in the transaction if one company feels uncomfortable assessing the credit risk posed by direct agreement with the other company. The advantages of a currency swap to the companies are that it (1) gives them access to long-term financing, (2) covers the principal exposure resulting from that financing, (3) does not affect the balance sheets of the companies, (4) is generally cheaper than borrowing from a bank or in the bond market, and (5) provides a good return on surplus funds.

The parallel loan accomplishes the same objectives as the currency swap, but not quite as neatly. Under the loan arrangement the U.S. company lends dollars directly to the subsidiary of the British firm in the United States or Canada. Ten years later the subsidiary repays the loan. In the United Kindgom a British firm lends pounds sterling directly to the subsidiary of a U.S. firm. Ten years later the subsidiary repays the loan. Both the U.S. and the British firms loan out their surplus funds, and both of their subsidiaries are funded. Each firm has lent out its own currency and will receive that same amount after 10 years. The interest rates on the loans may be set at the beginning for the entire period or may be reviewed and changed periodically. An additional feature of the parallel loan is a "**top-up**" clause to ensure the equivalence of the two loan amounts as exchange rates change. For example, when the loan agreements were signed, spot £/$2.00 and $10 million equal £5 million. Two years later spot is £/$1.80 and $10 million no longer equals £5 million, but £5,555,556. The British company is obliged to increase its loan to the U.S. subsidiary in the United Kingdom by £555.556. The top-up adjustments are usually triggered by movements of 2% or more in the exchange rate.

The insulation from the effect of exchange rate movements is not as great with the parallel loan as with the currency swap. Also, a parallel loan arrangement has the effect of increasing the size of a company's balance sheet because both the borrowing and investment are reflected.

DATE OF THE EXPOSURE IS UNCERTAIN. Foreign exchange contracts specify delivery of currencies on a definite date, like September 5, not somewhere around September 5. In the Eurocurrency markets most loans are for fixed periods and must be repaid on a definite date. But Cornie Construction has ordered a dozen bulldozers from Switzerland for its project in Saudi Arabia. The ship is scheduled to arrive, be unloaded, and the documents cleared by November 12. The treasurer knows, however, that the port is often jammed and that document clearance can take from two to 12 days. How can the treasurer be certain of the date of payment? If that date is not certain, how can the treasurer be certain of the cost of the Swiss machinery in riyals, the currency in which the company is being paid? There is uncertainty on the income side also because the riyal progress payment depends on the completion of certain stages of the project. At the completion of stage six the West German sub-contractor must be paid. The flow chart indicates that completion day is December 13. Completion on the target day is the exception rather than the rule. For what day should the Deutsche marks be bought? How can a price be locked-in?

The problem of uncertainty is not unique to the construction industry. Firms that utilize large one-of-a-kind machine tools experience delays in delivery time. This is normal given the nature of the equipment. However, when the tools are ordered from a foreign supplier it is difficult to know exactly when to arrange cover.

Option contracts are suited for situations where the date of the exposure is uncertain, but the company wants to lock in the exchange rate. The option contract fixes the price of exchange of two currencies now for delivery during a specified period in the future. The company is able to choose the day in the period it wants delivery. The one option the company does not have is not to take delivery.

PRICING AN OPTION CONTRACT. An option contract is priced so that the customer sells at the lowest rate and buys at the highest rate during the period. For example, rates for a Swiss franc–Saudi riyal (R) transaction are

SF/R spot	2.0900–15
One-month forward rate	2.0840–65
Points	60–50

The points indicate the Swiss franc interest rates are higher than riyal rates. For buyers of Swiss francs this means there is an earning if francs are bought for delivery one month from today rather than today. Cornie Construction wants to buy Swiss francs with riyals sometime during the next month. The two possible rates are SF/R2.0915 and SF/R2.0865. The bank will charge the higher rate because when pricing an option contract it holds onto any earning that could result during the period. The bank acts as if it bought the francs and sold riyals spot and day after day lends the francs and borrows the riyals until Cornie needs them. In this case the bank earns because Swiss franc interest rates are higher than riyal rates. But the bank does not know how long it will be able to earn. Cornie can walk in the next day and ask for the francs. If this happens there is no earning and any benefit the bank gave to Cornie would be a loss to the bank.

The bank also takes the worst-case approach for the seller of the Swiss francs. Given the exchange rates the seller of francs receives fewer riyals in the future than it would today. This is a cost to the seller. A company selling Swiss francs sometime during the next month would be quoted a rate of 2.0840, the lowest rate. The bank charges the customer all foreseeable costs during the option period. The bank acts as if it sold francs and bought riyals spot and then day after day borrows francs and lends riyals until the customer is ready to deliver francs. In this case the bank has a daily cost because franc interest rates are higher than riyal rates. Further, the bank assumes that the customer will not deliver the francs until the last day of the period. If this happens the bank incurs a full month of interest costs.

An option contract may be taken out for one week in the month of May, which is six months away, or for the period March 15 to April 15, which is three months away, or for the months of June, July, and August, which are seven months away. In theory, option periods may be as long as the number of months a particular market extends. Practically, an option period longer than three months may involve additional costs for the customer. Banks are not able to offset customer option contracts by making option contracts with other banks. The risk of changes in interest rates over extended periods requires an additional margin for the risk. Because of the way option contracts are priced, it is advisable to try to narrow the option periods as much as possible.

SECTION 8.10

THE PRACTICE OF CURRENCY EXPOSURE MANAGEMENT

CONTENTS

SECTION 8.10

THE PRACTICE OF CURRENCY EXPOSURE MANAGEMENT

Philip A. Betsch
Kevin P. Wright

Corporate practices in currency exposure management vary significantly with respect to management philosophies, approaches, techniques, and the type of exposures hedged. While every company is unique in the way it conducts business and the environment under which it operates, certain principles of foreign exchange management are common to all. Most importantly, the economic reality of currency movements, as they affect stockholders' earnings and net worth, must be fully recognized by the management in order to formulate appropriate policy directions.

In the following, two approaches to currency exposure management are presented to give readers different perspectives to the subject. It must be pointed out that these approaches are not necessarily applicable to every corporate situation, but can be an additional input to the formulation of a company's own financial management policies and practices.

CURRENCY MANAGEMENT IN THE OVERALL FINANCIAL STRATEGY

When business strategies require a company to produce and sell its products in a foreign currency environment, it exposes itself to currency risk. In real purchasing power terms, an investor must be able to evaluate this risk to net assets and earnings and to develop strategies to minimize potential losses. Consequently, the near-term cash flow effect of transactions in foreign currencies must be separately considered from the long-term effect of business strategies on the net assets left at risk to exchange rate movements and inflation in a foreign country.

Usually, transactions occur in a continuous stream as a normal part of business operations. When these transactions are priced in a foreign currency and originate

---

Philip A. Betsch is grateful to Abraham George for helpful comments; also see George, A., "Comments on Currency Exposure: Taxonomy and Theory," in Levich, R.M. and Wilborg, C.A., (Eds.), *Exchange Risk and Exposure*, Lexington Books, Lexington, Mass. (1979).

in a foreign country, both exchange rates and inflation produce an impact on their real profitability. Currency management, hence, requires capabilities of the firm that include

A basic system to forecast foreign exchange activity tailored to the organization's cash flows

A centralized surveillance function to monitor transactions and coordinate settlements

A high degree of sensitivity throughout the purchasing, billing, and planning departments of each subsidiary to pricing and exchange rates

An internal ability to digest and utilize exchange rate forecasts

Action plans to protect the near-term profit

Actions plans to protect the investment exposure

Normally, both information and strategies derived from these activities are coordinated by a highly centralized group within the corporate treasury department. Most companies elect to maintain a defensive foreign exchange posture, the objective being to minimize currency losses by the least expensive protection plan.

PRICING DECISIONS AND CURRENCY MOVEMENTS

A distinction can be made between **exchange rate exposure** and **real currency exposure:** the former takes into account exposures that are affected by exchange rate changes, while the latter defines positions that are exposed to both exchange rate changes and inflation. Under the assumption of **neutral inflation,** that is, all prices or costs change proportionally, continuous changes in exchange rates in line with the inflation differential between the foreign subsidiary country and the parent company country result in no real currency exposure. However, the assumption of neutral inflation is often restrictive because changes in the cost of doing business deviate from changes in prices that a company can charge for its products.

Corporations are constantly faced with the problem of adjusting prices charged for goods produced and sold during a given period, appropriately reflecting their inflation-induced increased costs. If prices could be increased at the same rate as the increase in costs, the nominal level of profits would also increase at the rate of inflation, thereby keeping the real level of profits constant. This pricing issue gets intertwined with the implications of exchange rate changes when foreign operations or transactions in foriegn currencies are considered.

For every corporate unit, the primary concern is its ability to generate sufficient profits that dividends can be maintained or increased in real terms. For a foreign subsidiary of a U.S. corporation that deals only in its local currency, this would require, in addition to other things, the continuous ability to offset increased costs resulting from inflation in the host country by charging higher prices. This pricing decision is often independent of changes in the exchange rate between the subsidiary's local currency and the dollar. However, the dollar value of the dividends from this subsidiary will depend upon this exchange rate. Unless dividend remittances from this subsidiary have increased by the same proportion as the rate of inflation in the host country, the real dollar value of the dividends will not be constant over time, even if these dividends are entered at exchange rates that have adjusted for the inflation differential between the host country and the parent company's country. By the same token, even if dividend remittances have increased at the rate of inflation in the host country, the real dollar value of these remittances cannot be maintained unless exchange rates have adjusted fully for the inflation differential between the two countries. Therefore, the issue of pricing goods and the management of exchange rates are equally important to the well-being of stockholders.

From the viewpoint of U.S. stockholders, the real currency exposure in a foreign subsidiary that does all its business in its local currency arises from two factors: first, the difference in the percentage change in costs and the percentage change in prices at the subsidiary level, and second, the difference between (1) the percentage change in the dollar rate for the local currency, and (2) the inflation differential between the host country and the United States. The first factor applies to all costs and revenues at the subsidiary level, while the second factor only applies to dividends and other remittances to the parent.

In the case of subsidiaries that do business in currencies other than their own, an additional factor is introduced. For example, in the case of a subsidiary that buys raw materials from abroad while selling the finished goods locally, this new factor can be stated as the difference between first, the percentage change in costs measured in local currency units as a result of (1) higher foreign prices on imported raw materials caused by inflation in the exporting country, and (2) the change in the foreign/local currency exchange rate; second, the percentage change in prices on goods produced from these imported raw materials.

To the extent that prices on finished goods can be adjusted to offset the higher cost on imported raw materials, the real currency exposure is eliminated. From a management viewpoint, what is needed is identification of two elements, the change in the foreign currency cost of imported raw material, and the change in the foreign/local currency exchange rate.

As long as changes in costs are identified in the currency unit of the subsidiary, the prices on finished goods can be adjusted accordingly. If the changes in costs are solely a result of exchange rate changes (a cash flow impact of foreign/local currency exchange rate, and not the local currency/dollar rate), and if these changes in costs cannot be passed on by changes in prices, the economic position of the company is affected. In other words, the cash flow impact of currency movements is an economic exposure to the extent that the level of prices cannot be adjusted by the subsidiary.

TRANSACTION AND TRANSLATION EXPOSURES

Transaction exposures are those that could lead to cash gains or losses upon currency movements. These exposures usually include nonlocal currency accounts receivable and payables, long-term debt, dividends, profit remittances, royalties, technical service fees, administrative charges, and intercompany interest. Translation exposures, on the other hand, are net assets (all assets minus all liabilities measured in local currency units) of each of the foreign subsidiaries.

In many companies, major bulk purchases are usually done on a centralized basis. Whenever possible, these global contracts for the purchase of raw materials and other key items used in the production process are negotiated in the currency of the major market for the finished product. This reduces the vulnerability of the major market to volatile exchange rate movements and inflation, and permits adequate planning time to project cost increases or decreases into marketing strategies. All other user markets participating in this centralized purchase should take financial actions to protect their respective income streams.

The cost of covering the exchange risk at each of the user markets will be reflected in the cost of goods, and finally passed on to the consumer. Hence it becomes strategically imperative to properly rationalize market pricing. In extremely volatile exchange rate markets, it is not desirable to permit market prices to absorb the short-term shock effect of rapid exchange rate movements. A prudent exchange rate policy insulates the impact of large currency movements on transaction exposures at reasonable costs, which in turn can be passed on to the customer.

Since prices cannot be adjusted frequently in most situations, the pricing decision usually requires some expectations about the **impact of inflation** and **exchange rate movements.** The impact of inflation on the cost of goods sold can be identified and incorporated separately into market prices with reasonable accuracy. However, expected currency movements are a different matter. In order to properly plan for the impact of currency movements in the pricing decision, there is a need to budget for the cost of covering transaction exposures and potential exchange losses on uncovered positions.

Frequently, the **cost of covering** the entire transaction exposures is both prohibitive and undesirable. What is required is a well-thought-out plan—one that balances the cost of cover and the exchange risk. Such a plan should lead to a foreign exchange budget within which the cost of cover plus exchange losses on unhedged transaction exposures must be allocated. If realistic targets are determined, then it is up to the foreign exchange manager to implement appropriate tactical measures to limit the currency impact. This in turn permits pricing decisions to incorporate the budgeted impact of currency movements. Actual performance superior to the budgeted figures assures increased profitability.

Protection of translation exposures cannot be ignored; there is a growing tendency on the part of many managers to categorize them as paper exposures. However, these positions are the net assets of stockholders left at risk to inflation and exchange rate movements. Moreoever, several financial ratios are affected by exchange rate gains and losses on translation exposures, which in turn can produce an impact on a number of cash flow items—the cost of borrowings, stock prices, and so forth.

Once again, what is needed is a prudent financial strategy that combines pricing decisions with the dividend policy and currency risk management. Whenever possible, prices must be adjusted to cover partially or fully the impact of local inflation on the net assets. Furthermore, the movements of the exchange rate between the local currency and the base currency (currency preference of majority stockholders) will also determine whether the base currency value of the net assets in the foreign subsidiary can be preserved. A sound earnings retention policy (reciprocal of the dividend pay-out policy) can go a long way in ensuring that the equity in the subsidiary expands at a desirable pace to generate sufficient return on investment. Failure to maintain this equilibrium over a protracted period would result in over- or under-capitalizing the affiliate.

The **overall financial plan** integrates several key objectives, but the issue of permissible translation losses must be achieved within the context of local inflation, return on investment criteria, and the dividend pay-out policy. Once such a plan has been worked out, it is up to the foreign exchange manager to develop appropriate tactical measures to ensure that currency losses on translation positions do not exceed the planned limits.

AN ILLUSTRATION. The following example illustrates a financial plan for a multinational company that integrates foreign exchange management within its general business strategy. Both translation and transaction exposures are separately considered, and decision criteria are developed for each one to meet overall corporate goals.

A French subsidiary imports 50% of its raw materials from the United States and pays for them in dollars. It also exports 10% of its sales to the United States and bills them in dollars. The company management is reviewing the annual business plan of the French affiliate, and is presented with the following financial strategy.

Pro Forma Income Statement
(FrF millions)

Sales	6,250
Cost of Goods Sold	2,500
Operating Contribution	950
Net Income After Taxes	500
Percentage of Net Income of Sales	8.0%

Pro Forma Balance Sheet

Assets		Liabilities	
Current	3,200	Current	1,500
Fixed	950	L.T.	500
Other	350	Parent company—equity	2,500
Total	4,500	Total	4,500

Performance Criteria

ROS	return on sales	8.0%	net income percentage of sales
t	capital turnover	2.5	sales/net equity
D/E	debt equity ratio	0.70	debt/equity
e	earnings retention ratio	0.60	$1 - \dfrac{\text{(net income} - \text{dividend)}}{\text{net income}}$
c	capital formation ratio	1.02	$(e) + (e \times \text{D/E})$
ROI	return on investment	20.0%	$(\text{ROS} \times t)$
g	sustainable earnings growth	20.4%	$(\text{ROI} \times c)$

From past experience, the company has found that at least 60% of the earnings must be retained to maintain a substainable earnings growth rate for the French affiliate for achieving the desired return on investment (ROI). However, this retention ratio might have to be increased in a given year if business conditions, including exchange rate movements and inflation, are likely to have larger than normal adverse impact on profitability.

Exposure Analysis

Transactions exposures

Profit remittance (500 × 40%)	200
Import purchases (2500 × 50%)	1,250
Export sales (6250 × 10%)	(625)
Net transactions—long FrF	825
(Assume that the forward franc is at a discount of 6% against the dollar)	
Budgeted cost of cover	= 825 × 6% = FrF 50
Cost of cover as a percentage of sales	= 50/6250 = 0.8%
Cost of cover as a percentage of equity	= 50/2500 = 2.0%

Translation exposures

Accounting ROI	20%
Less local inflation	(6%)
Real ROI	14%
Less transaction cost/risk as a percentage of equity	(2%)
Net ROI	12%
Earnings retention	= 500 × 60% = FrF 300
Earnings retention as a percentage of equity	= 300/2500 = 12%
Maximum translation loss absorbable	= 12% devaluation of the franc against the dollar.

Exchange Rate and Pricing Strategies

1. Net ROI is 12% unless prices are adjusted for transaction exposure costs and/or losses. Prices are increased by 0.8%, if possible, to offset the impact of currency movements on cash flow, and net ROI is increased to 14% from 12%.
2. The cost of covering transaction exposures plus losses on unhedged transactions must be limited to a maximum of 6% of the transaction exposures.
3. Appropriate tractical measures must be developed to ensure that translation losses do not exceed 12% of the translation exposures.
4. The retention ratio is increased (from 60%) if translation losses exceed 12%, unless revenues from sales are increased by price increases.

A TARGET-ORIENTED APPROACH

For most multinational corporations, foreign exchange management policies are defensive in nature, and rightly so. Often, the objective is to minimize currency exchange losses as reflected in financial statements. Since profitability of the underlying business transaction is greatly determined by the movement of currencies, companies having large volumes of foreign currency transactions must take active approaches to the management of exposures. Such policies call for meeting certain targets in foreign exchange management, just as in other aspects of business.

DEFINING CORPORATE EXPOSURE MANAGEMENT GOALS. Business decisions are more effective when they are made within the context of explicit corporate goals, and currency exposure management decisions are no exception. The key determinant of the style of currency exposure management is the set of goals the corporation has defined for itself in the currency area, goals that cover three important considerations: (1) What is exposed or at risk? (2) What can be done to limit or reduce the exposure? (3) How can one organize to manage risk?

What Is Exposed. **Setting exposure management goals** requires some exposure definition decisions. Exposure to foreign currency fluctuations is a matter of accounting and management sensitivity; that is, there are various ways to measure and evaluate exposures. In a company that is biased toward self-generated financing, for example, it is painful to have the leakage of cash that occurs when intercompany transactions flow at unfavorable exchange rates, while the instability of earnings caused by accounting conventions is of much less concern. Other companies with ongoing financial relationships involving banks or the credit markets might find earnings instability and balance sheet changes equally as painful as cash leakage. The exposure definition that matters to each company is unique to it and goes to the heart of its business operating philosophy. Once again, exposure definitions involve cash flow, earnings, or both.

Cash, intercompany transfers, third-party receivables and payables, and borrowings in foreign currencies are all cash exposures. They are categorized by some shipment exchange rate, borrowing rate, or target rate against which some time later a payment occurs at a different exchange rate. In summary, exposure definition is a top management policy decision because business policy determines management sensitivity to foreign currency exposure.

Exposure Reduction. A company's basic business configuration determines the extent of its currency exposure. For example, exporting extensively from U.S. plants to overseas locations and receiving foreign currency creates transaction exposures for the U.S. producer. It is not likely that the producer will give up the international export business because of exchange rate instability. Manufacturing within the foreign country would alter the transaction exposure but would in turn create an earnings exposure. Top management might question whether the exports need to be denominated in local currency to third-party customers; a change to U.S. dollars billing would reduce exposure but might create marketing problems.

Often subsidiary financial policy aggravates exposure problems. Working capital financing is seldom done in other than the subsidiary's own currency. From an exposure management standpoint for U.S.-based firms this might be a good policy when the dollar is strong but not when it is weak. Similarly, customer receivable financing policies within a subsidiary can influence how much working capital is necessary for operations. Again, customer credit availability will have important marketing implications in addition to exposure management considerations.

Exposure reduction is a necessary but not sufficient element of the corporate exposure management goal. Not all exposure can be reduced without significant business restructuring, which is often an undesirable alternative. Reducing exposure should not be viewed as a static, one-time process; no top management team should be satisfied until it is convinced that exposure as defined for the company has been reduced through structural changes to minimum possible levels.

A strong argument can be made for moving the bulk of the financial impact of currency exposure to a finance subsidiary. The basic thrust of a finance company is financial risk management. Under this approach, the intertwining of exposure reduction and business opportunity decisions is eliminated, leaving each aspect to be managed somewhat independently.

Exposure Management Operations. Exposure management operations deal with the foreign currency risk that remains after exposure reduction processes are complete. It is fair to say that exposure management operations are defensive in character; the objective is to reduce currency risk that arises from doing business internationally. Often one organization's risk can be another organization's opportunity; banks and many other financial institutions often view the exchange market in this light, and even a manufacturer can benefit from having receivables in foreign currency if the dollar is declining, or working capital funding in foreign currency if the dollar is rising. The purpose of exposure management operations is managing the residual risk profitably by meeting corporate exposure management goals. Defensive exposure management operations need not necessarily be money-losing operations or opportunity-foregoing departments. Forward foreign exchange contract positions that are losers or debt positions in high-interest currencies that do not decline in value are hardly effective exposure management results.

In a centralized operation, the primary personnel are currency position managers who monitor the flow of exposure information and marketplace information, and decide whether the exposure needs to be covered or not. Once they have a market position, they then have to decide how long to hold it before returning to an uncovered position once again. These position managers are highly skilled, decisive, well versed in fundamental and technical analysis, with good exchange market contacts to enhance their exchange market views. They usually report to a financial function executive in the treasury area who responds to the resource needs of the trading organization and communicates their market position strategies and profit and loss results to even higher levels of management. By nature, these centralized exposure management activities can position all or part of the company's exposure at any moment and therefore usually have significant minute-to-minute or day-to-day discretionary decision-making power over very large sums. Such operations are usually found at corporate headquarters so that it is easy for senior management of a company to know what the positions of the dealers are for audit and control purposes.

A decentralized approach comprises small operations scattered through subsidiaries with people of mixed skill levels dealing with that organization's particular exposure. Such personnel might have other responsibilities besides foreign exchange and, in fact, might only devote a portion of their working day to currency management. Market information reaching them might be confined only to their own currency situations and there might not be the opportunity for regular marketplace trend discussions. Knowledge of exposure, however, can be much more intimate in a decentralized situation. The senior management in a decentralized situation is sometimes less driven by currency success than by other activities more closely aligned with the mainstream of the business.

If senior management has carefully defined the corporate foreign exchange exposure and has taken the steps to effectively reduce unnecessary currency risk, then it is in a good position to aggressively manage the activities of its foreign exchange managers. Those who run an exposure management operation should have a profit and loss orientation and should be held accountable for the financial implications of hedging operations. Most important, the practice of currency exposure management becomes an operational problem once the corporation has established the basic conditions under which it intends to deal with the foreign exchange market.

ORGANIZING TO MANAGE FOREIGN CURRENCY EXPOSURES

The basic need in managing any activity is information. One cannot manage the unknown. This pertains to both internal corporate data and external information that can affect the results of operations.

INTERNAL EXPOSURE INFORMATION AND FORECASTS. Information about existing and expected transactions has to be reported to the currency exposure management group in a timely and accurate fashion. That is, the group needs to know about transactions soon enough to have a chance at protecting the target rates while those rates still exist in the marketplace, and the amount they protect ought to be reasonably close to what the payment flow actually is when it finally takes place. For example, it is likely that an exporting company knows what it will or is about to export, which will become a payment flow some time later, and an importing subsidiary probably tracks its orders and the lead time for filling them so that it can report what it expects to receive and to pay for some time later.

The flow of internal information starts the development of a currency exposure profile. The exposure management group has little or no interest in how the exposures are formed, just what they will be. In the case of complex currency and subsidiary exposures, however, the use of an exposure presentation model that lays out currency exposure in as simple a form as possible is very important. Such exposure models are assemblers of actual exposures and forecasts, which are easy to read and insure that information does not get lost or buried. Exposure presentation models are available commercially and the timeliness of information flow can be enhanced using the worldwide computer networks in which these models are housed. Exposure presentation models, however, are by nature of a general purpose and might not fit in well with the way in which financial planning information develops within a particular company. In that case, an exposure presentation model properly adapted or developed internally is more suitable. Such models present internal information clearly so that risks can be evaluated and decisions can be meaningfully made.

EXTERNAL MARKET INFORMATION AND FORECASTS. The other crucial element of information necessary for currency decisions is external—the exchange market and all its ramifications. Here it is important to talk about how this information is analyzed for its implications. The analysis of exchange markets is divided into three groups: fundamental and technical are the more straightforward methods, and the third group, that of psychological and conspiracy theories, is more complex.

Fundamental analysis of currency markets is often macroeconomic forecasting. That is, the language of describing and comparing national economies becomes the determining characteristic of exchange rate forecasts. Issues such as differential inflation rates and the relative external strengths or weakness of accounts (trade accounts, current accounts, capital flows) are often examined.

Technical analysts care little for economic fundamentals and their influence on exchange rates, other than for the shock of announcement value of economic news. They look to various statistical or pattern recognition techniques to analyze current exchange market levels and the potential for near-term movement. Their data are the exchange rates themselves—daily highs, lows, closes, fixing values, averages, trends, channels or paths, volumes, accelerations, and decelerations. Efficient market theory postulates that the exchange rate at any point in time embodies all known information. Technical analysts of exchange markets use many of the same tools used by commodity or stock market analysts. Technical analysts concern themselves with the paths or channels in which exchange rates are moving—up, down, or sideways. They care about the rate of movement (momentum) and whether that rate is accelerating or decelerating. At times they analyze how long movements have been taking place against some historical framework or the time duration of previous movements (cycles), to make short-term predictions of currency movements.

Besides fundamental and technical forecasts, there are other theories of how exchange rates are determined, and they can be best described as psychological and conspiracy theories. Psychological determinents are usually fear-motivated (e.g., by the fear of an OPEC (Organization of Petroleum Exporting Countries) price change, or by the fear of an invasion of Poland by the Soviet Union, or by the fear of a socialist government election in France). These examples all represent highly unpredictable events that require decisions about risk management. What position will best fit either outcome? What is the best hedge if the negative event does occur and what is the least costly hedge if the negative event does not occur? Similarly, conspiracy theories might imply the collaborative actions of several major financial institutions in a country against all others—hence the argument that one should always follow a leader.

CORPORATE DEALING ROOM. The next step in organizing to manage foreign currency exposures is the establishment of a **corporate trading** or dealing room. The brain of a dealing room is the trader or trading group, but the heart is a sound, efficient back-office operation. That back office must be able to supply accurate exposure and position information, routinely create and dispose of all confirming documentation from the dealing process, and fulfill all cash flow obligations that arise without involving the dealers. Any problems that regularly take trading people out of the marketplace and into the back-office operations area are counterproductive to the exposure management process.

The position-reporting aspects of back-office operations are essential to dealers. Position-reporting systems can be created internally by a corporation or bought commercially.

Traders are the brain of a dealing room. Whether running outright forward positions, or borrowing or lending Eurocurrency to offset a natural exposure, or simply day trading with limited positions and profitability goals, traders are the front-line decision makers in foreign exchange exposure management. Faced with a very uncertain market providing a price over which they exercise no control, they must decide to commit some amount of the corporation's funds to help accomplish some positive goal. Unfortunately, good intentions do not always lead to good results and traders have just as great an obligation to quickly decide if they have made a mistake. Active positioning is a problem without end, in which yesterday's success counts little for tomorrow, other than from the standpoint of experience.

Corporate goals in the foreign exchange exposure management process greatly influence position taking by traders. If a corporation stresses loss avoidance, for example, and defines what will determine a loss, such as a payment clearing at a lower rate compared to the rate at which it was booked as a receivable, then a dealer will generally cover that exposure immediately upon learning about it should the dealer anticipate any movement toward a weaker value for the currency and away from the booking rate. Even if the goals defined are equally balanced between gain and loss, a dealer might still cover under the conditions mentioned. But that dealer would be relatively quick to take a profit should the spot market show signs of reversing toward a stronger value for the currency.

EXPOSURE MANAGEMENT DECISION MAKING

Exposure management decision making involves the analysis of market situations and market trends in the context of the company's exposure.

MARKET SITUATION ANALYSIS. The exchange market situation is constantly changing; hence market situation analysis is an important element of exposure management decision making. Traders get information and insight into the market by getting involved, committing some funds in a consistant tactical direction, and watching the outcome. Are they trading? Certainly, but the objective is more than simply to make a profit as a bank trader might. The objective is to probe for information through the marketplace that confirms or questions the exposure management strategic plan. Such trading positions, however, can never represent the full extent of a hedge. As a rule of thumb, they might represent less than 10% of the corporation's total exposure at any one time.

Additional **market intelligence** comes from discussions with other market participants. In fact, one of the key tasks of corporate traders is the development of information sources. Market situations can be cast in a technical analytic framework, indicating where exchange rates are currently, compared with where they have moved from. A careful examination of the fundamental factors against where the market is in a technical framework is an interesting way to try to integrate both disciplines in assessing the market situation.

MARKET TREND DEVELOPMENT. A second facet of exposure management decision making is **market trend development**. Market involvement by corporate traders results in mostly running overnight positions rather than only day trading. It is these overnight positions that, when building up or diminishing over a series of days, present an effective hedge of corporate exposure. Again, the key to the recognition of market direction is taking successful overnight positions on a fairly continuous basis, generally in the same direction. Bank trading rooms today do less and less overnight position taking relative to the size of their intraday trading, but that fact should be of little or no concern to the corporate exposure manager. In a corporation, foreign exchange risk is generally measured from some target rate, or the rate at which the exposure was booked. It makes little or no sense to ignore that rate if market trend development is unclear, or likely to jeopardize those target rates. In such a case, the corporate exposure manager knows that the best course of action is to protect those book rates or lock up a profit against them if the manager has allowed the marketplace to move in his or her favor while exposures were not covered. An unprofitable hedge, however, is not a successful hedge. In an active, profit and loss–motivated exposure management program, a hedging decision ought not to be cast in stone. Hedge positions can be offset by forward contracts in the opposite direction, returning the natural position to that of uncovered. It might be possible to lift one side before the other side is liquidated, thereby minimizing cash losses, but taking a contract to offset an existing one is locking up a small loss before it grows large. Hedge positions can be liquidated before maturity if market conditions change and render it sensible to take profits. If one views corporate exposure management as creating profits to offset potential losses on a corporation's natural position or to reduce the cost of cover, it is clear how important profit taking on successful market positions can be.

OPERATIONAL PLANNING AND CONTROL IN FOREIGN EXCHANGE EXPOSURE MANAGEMENT

Because foreign exchange market operations are not in the mainstream of corporate activities and usually involve substantial sums of traded funds, a control or limit system generally prevails. Corporate limits can be large when foreign exchange managers have to take market positions as large or larger than the company's natural position. A good rule of thumb on speculative activity is that a corporation should not take positions it does not need. For example, if one is naturally long in deutsche marks—that is, if one has deutsche marks to sell for U.S. dollars—then even though the deutsche mark is strengthening against the U.S. dollar, all gains from that market development will come from appreciation of the natural position and not from taking on additional market positions in the same direction (by buying deutsche marks). A good back-office operation should provide a clear audit trail if it monitors the flow of dealing confirmations. Such audit control insures that the nonspeculative philosophy of the corporation receives more than lip service by the exposure management group.

Market volatility creates active position switching as traders probe for the market situation and the trend. Artificial limitations on trading volume can be counterproductive to the process of maintaining hedge positions consistent with exchange rate levels.

A foreign exchange exposure management group with a profit and loss orientation needs to report to financial management in the corporation on a regular basis, perhaps weekly in today's environment. Senior management ought to review results at least once a quarter in a profit and loss context. The weekly and quarterly managerial meetings should focus on how well corporate goals are being met, or on operational success or failure. The position-reporting process for such control discussions should be derived from the other reporting and control systems (mentioned under audit considerations and procedures). Since foreign exchange management operations are concerned with successful positioning, not reporting and control, such information should be generated within a corporation's accounting systems, away from the trading process.

PERSONNEL ISSUES IN EXPOSURE MANAGEMENT

The foreign exchange management program in any corporation will only be as good as the people who make market-positioning decisions and the people who control that decision process. Unfortunately, as in any other mainstream corporate activity, there is little substitute for good internally developed skill, hard work, and management support of the foreign exchange management process. Personnel development is a secondary activity to the corporation, but not to the people involved if they are to be successful in reducing currency risk to the company.

Effective traders are directly successful contributors to the corporation's bottom line. Sometimes their compensation does not reflect their contribution, unlike the case in banks and other financial institutions that have separate salary structures for traders in recognition of their unique contributions. With corporations this unique position is more difficult to create. The key necessity is to place corporate exposure management personnel where they can be adequately compensated at the appropriate level within the corporate job hierarchy, or they will simply underperform or be lost to competition.

Successful exposure managers are decisive; the foreign exchange market demands it. Unfortunately, they usually have little or no exposure to the mainstream of the business or to the personnel involved in its management. Foreign exchange management personnel continuously make significant financial decisions in a brief period. It is the obligation of the financial management to be sure that the entreprenurial success of traders can be developed into active mainstream activities.

Exchange markets are 24-hour markets, although no one person can cover them on that basis. Increasing volatility in key currencies requires that the decision-making process be even more accelerated than it has been in the past. Additional vacation or compensatory time—even sabbatical leaves—away from trading are important ways of preventing the burnout of a very valuable internally trained and developed employee.

SECTION **8.11A**

INTERNATIONAL CASH MANAGEMENT

CONTENTS

SECTION 8.11A

INTERNATIONAL CASH MANAGEMENT

Lars H. Thunell
Jack R. Skydel

High rates of inflation and the resulting high and volatile interest rates have increased the importance of **cash management** to the corporate treasurer. Concurrently, the expansion of many businesses into worldwide markets has created a need for international cash management.

Cash management can be examined from two perspectives: an **intracountry** perspective and an **intercountry** perspective. Intracountry cash management deals with the payment systems, banks, investments, and borrowing sources available in a particular country, the United States being only one among several countries in which cash management must be applied. Intercountry cash management deals with cash movements among several countries.

The key conceptual difference between intracountry cash management and intercountry cash management is foreign exchange. Thus **foreign exchange management** must be added to the traditional components of **float management** and **bank account control** in developing a conceptual framework for international cash management. The objective of international cash management is to maximize funds availability at a set level of operating cost and foreign exchange risk, and hence excess cash can be effectively utilized.

OVERVIEW: THE CASH CYCLE

International cash management is most easily viewed within the context of the overall cash cycle (see Exhibit 1). The cash cycle begins on the collection side with a customer transaction. Here the **float management** objective is to accelerate receipts. Once funds are deposited and available for use, the objective is to control balance levels, maximizing cash available to reduce borrowings or increase investments. If the currency of collection is different from the currency of disbursement, a foreign exchange transaction is necessary. The objective in this part of the cash cycle is to identify and manage resulting foreign exchange exposures. On the disbursement side, the objective is to control float.

FLOAT MANAGEMENT. Float is created in business transactions when funds are moved from one party to another. Float is simply the availability of the funds to one

EXHIBIT 1 CASH CYCLE

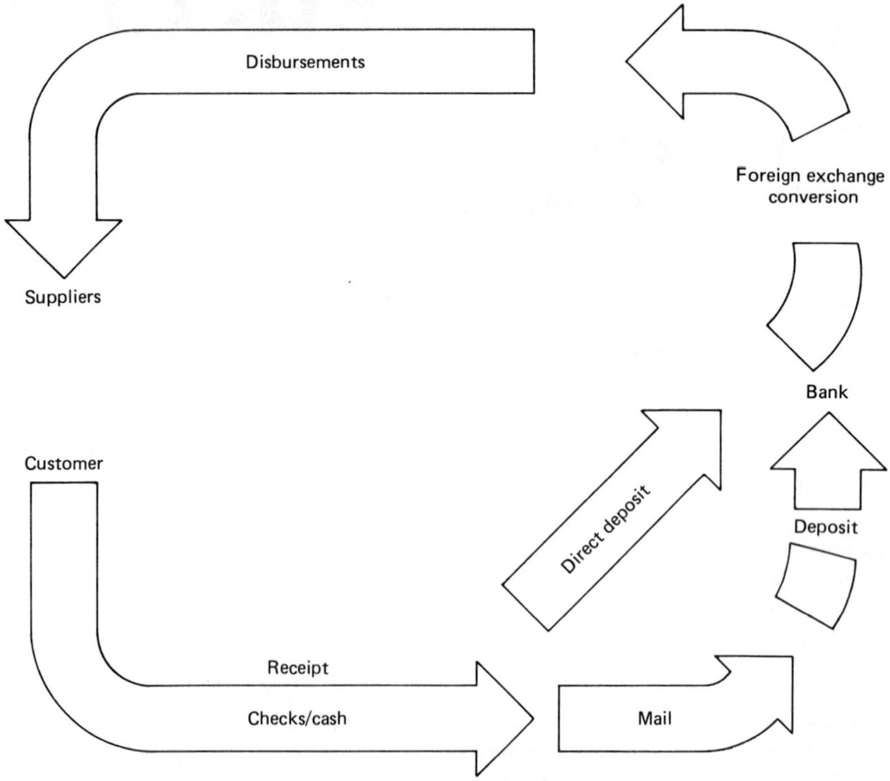

of the parties. In a normal transaction these parties can include the payee, payor, one or several commercial banks, and a central bank, such as the Federal Reserve Bank in the United States.

In analyzing a business transaction, four types of float can be identified: settlement float, transit (or mail) float, processing float, and clearing (or value-dating) float. **Settlement float** is the time between when a payee is requested to remit funds and when remittance is initiated. The float is available to the payee at the expense of the payor. **Transit (mail) float** is the time the payment is in transit. Most often, this is mail time, but it can also be, for example, courier time. **Processing float** is the time a transaction is, literally, in process—for example, the time it takes for a seller to prepare and mail an invoice, or deposit a check that is already received. **Clearing (value-dating) float** is the time between deposit to the bank and when funds are available for use.

Methods for reducing the settlement and transit float vary considerably among countries. The variations depend upon normal country or industry payment practices, and banking systems and practices. For example, in the United States, where direct debiting is not yet prevalent and retail bank giro is nonexistent, cash management efforts have focused on reducing mail float through the use of lockboxes. In Sweden, on the other hand, direct debiting and crediting systems are well developed.

EXHIBIT 2 TYPICAL CUTOFF TIMES FOR CHECK DEPOSITS

Country	Times
United States	Tied to availability schedule
Canada	6:00 P.M. Tied to float analysis
United Kingdom	3:00 P.M.
West Germany	9:00 A.M.
Switzerland	12:00 noon
Belgium	10:00 A.M.
Italy	1:00 P.M.
France	11:00 A.M.

Managing processing float also varies considerably among countries. Exhibit 2 indicates some typical deposit cutoff times for checks. It can be seen, for example, that a seller in West Germany depositing checks at 9:30 A.M. will lose one day of float, while in Belgium or France the float would not be lost. Exhibits 3 and 4 indicate variations in value dating.

BANK ACCOUNT CONTROL. The components of bank account control are (1) bank account architecture; (2) balance information; and (3) bank costs.

Bank accounts should be structured to avoid idle balances. This is accomplished by establishing three types of accounts: collection accounts, a concentration account, and disbursement accounts (Exhibit 5). Collection accounts channel funds into a

EXHIBIT 3 TYPICAL VALUE DATE CONDITIONS

Country	Instrument	Checks Deposited and Other Credits
United Kingdom	Checks	2–4 days
	Direct debit	Same day
	Bank transfer	Same day
West Germany	Checks locally drawn	0–1 day
	Other	1–4 days
	Direct debit	1–2 days
Switzerland	Checks	2 days
	Bank Giro	0–1 day
Belgium	Checks	1 day
	Bank giro	0–1 day
The Netherlands	Checks	1–10 days after posting date
	Bank giro	1 day
Italy	Checks locally drawn	1–2 days
		2–5 days
	Other	
France	Checks drawn on Paris	
	City	1–2 days
	Metropolitan area	2–5 days
	Other	3–5 days

EXHIBIT 4 TYPICAL VALUE DATE CONDITIONS

Country	Instrument	Checks Cleared
United Kingdom	Checks Direct debit Bank transfer	Same day as payment by bank
West Germany	Checks locally drawn Other Direct debit	Same day as payment by bank
Switzerland	Checks Bank giro	Same day as payment or date of issue
Belgium	Checks Bank giro	One business day prior to payment
The Netherlands	Checks Bank giro	One business day prior to payment
Italy	Checks locally drawn Other	Date of issue
France	Checks drawn on Paris City Metropolitan area Other	Date of payment or one business day prior

concentration account; investments or borrowings occur from the concentration account; disbursement accounts are funded from the concentration account.

The method by which the proper bank account architecture is implemented varies widely by country. In the United States, accounts are often with different banks due to prohibitions against interstate banking. Movement of funds from collection accounts to the concentration account can occur by wire transfer or depository transfer check. In many other countries, national banking allows accounts to be with the

EXHIBIT 5 BANK ACCOUNT ARCHITECTURE

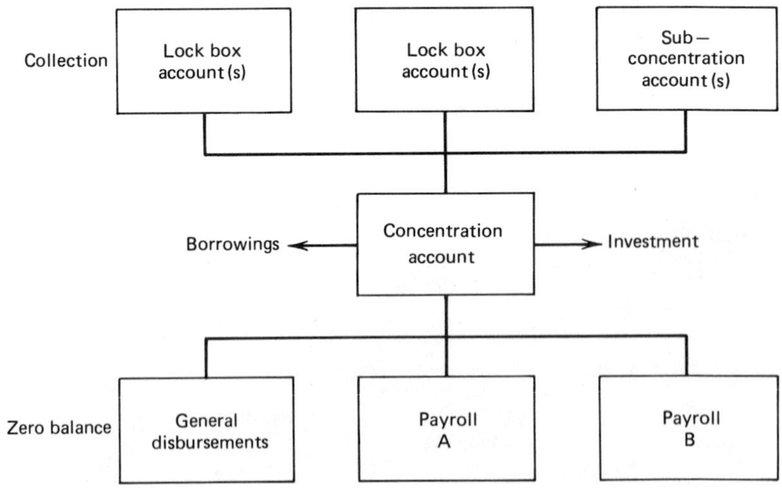

same bank. Money movement then only involves internal accounting. Very sophisticated bank networks, such as those in Canada and Sweden, allow cash to be pooled into one concentration account while maintaining subaccounts at the local operating level. This provides for a centralized pool of cash and decentralized bookkeeping and reconciliation.

A major difference between account management in the United States and other countries is that U.S. bank accounts are normally managed in a credit position. Many other countries connect overdraft facilities with a concentration account and there might never be credit balances. Thus rather than coordinating bank account management with a company's investment program, it must be coordinated with the financing program. For example, separate overnight facilities might be used in place of overdraft facilities or a core financing requirement might allow for longer term borrowings.

Establishing a simple bank account structure is not always entirely feasible. Foreign exchange regulations might force a separation of funds or tax regulations might limit the potential to move funds among subsidiaries. Less sophisticated banks do not always have the operational systems to pool or net accounts.

Given the best possible bank account architecture, **balance information** must be available to control balance levels in the concentration account and to adequately monitor collection and disbursement accounts. Balance reporting as known in the United States is normally not available internationally. In many countries the only ways to obtain balance information are through a daily statement, phoning the bank directly, or requesting a telex. In addition, varying value-dating practices, and particularly back value dating, confound forecasting methods necessary to manage any bank account.

The introduction of U.S.-like balance reporting internationally has been inhibited by local banking systems and practices. Most international banks are not yet selling cash management systems as part of their business and as a result have little interest in supporting a customer's need for balance information. Improved balance information can only be expensive for the banks in the short run by reducing excess balances. Even if a bank is willing to provide timely balance information, it might not have the operating capability. Accounts are often maintained with a bank branch close to where a business is located, rather than the bank's head office. The branch might not have access to Society for Worldwide Interbank Financial Telecommunication (SWIFT), computer terminals, or telex. Communicating through the bank's headquarters is time consuming and information needed to actively control balances becomes outdated. Several banks are trying to overcome these technical difficulties, but so far progress has not been rapid.

The final variable in bank account control is the cost of operating the account network. In the United States, the cost of operating a bank account is a function of item charges, value dating, reserve requirements, and an earnings credit allowance. Monthly bank analysis statements explicitly show the activity of the account and the resulting total cost. These statements can be monitored to insure that agreed-upon terms are being met. There are many variations of bank charging methods, each of which depends upon normal banking practices in the country. Outside the United States there is a greater reliance on the use of value dating as a charging method. This, coupled with the general unavailability of detailed analysis statements from banks, can make controlling or comparing bank costs a difficult task.

One very noticeable difference between the United States and most other countries is the cost of processing a paper item such as a check. The U.S. cost structure favors paper transactions not only in low item costs, but also in value dating. A depository transfer check, the transfer mechanism in many U.S. collection systems, costs much less than a wire and, depending upon availability schedules, can receive same day or next day value. The value-dating conditions in other countries (shown in Exhibit 3) almost universally favor direct debiting or giro over check. Further, the explicit cost for each item associated with a check is generally higher than other transfer methods (see Exhibit 6).

The Federal Reserve Bank of the United States, in its recent move to price services explicitly, has tried to encourage more rapid adoption of automated debiting and crediting. However, the move away from paper in the United States will most likely continue on an evolutionary course.

FOREIGN EXCHANGE MANAGEMENT. Management of cross-border, or inter-country, cash flows involves integrating cash and foreign exchange management. In most cases, cash initially will be mobilized by currency and country. In managing the resulting cash position, whether positive or negative, the **cash manager** can pursue two basic courses of action. First, excess cash can be invested or deficit cash borrowed in the local currency. These actions do not affect a foreign exchange position. Second, the cash position can be adjusted by buying or selling the cash spot on the foreign exchange markets. This action transfers the foreign exchange position.

On the other side, a **foreign exchange manager** can adjust a foreign exchange position by buying or selling currency spot, thus changing the cash position, or by using forward contracts. Until the forward contract matures the cash position would not be affected.

The objectives of a system integrating cash and foreign exchange management are to

Maximize total cash or to minimize total borrowings in all currencies together, avoiding concurrent investment and borrowing unless there are arbitrage opportunities

Minimize foreign exchange exposure levels and insure exposure netting

EXHIBIT 6 TYPICAL BANK CHARGES (in U.S. dollars)

Country	Checks Deposited	Checks Issued
United States	0.04	0.09
Canada	0.04	0.15
United Kingdom	0.06[a]	0.06[a]
West Germany	0.30	0.30
Switzerland	0.05% on turnover	0.05% on turnover
Belgium	Fixed fee	1.00
The Netherlands	1.50	1.50 + 1.25 clearing fee
Italy	0.40	0.40 + .13 stamp duty
France	0.025% on turnover	0.025% on turnover

[a]Or 0.05% of debit turnover.

Minimize fluctuations of foreign exchange exposure levels

Minimize transaction costs

In meeting the objectives of an integrated system, it is important to understand how cross-border flows are generated in the normal course of business. It is necessary also that each operating unit deal with one central point rather than each other (see Exhibit 7). Only a central unit can keep track of net amounts that a unit should pay or receive. The central unit can also

Continuously monitor net open positions and take action

Identify all opportunities for netting exposures between operating units

Provide foreign exchange and investment expertise in support of the operating unit day-to-day activities and in maximizing the foreign exchange profit potential inherent in their business (*e.g.*, cross-border pricing decisions)

Provide centralized foreign exchange reporting

Timing of settlements with the central unit is critical in controlling open foreign exchange positions. Commonly, all units will settle foreign exchange positions at prespecified time intervals. The disadvantage of this system is that, over time, foreign exchange positions can vary significantly. Often these positions will be managed through short-term forward currency contracts timed to mature on settlement day. Funds are delivered and transactions are minimized. However, it can be difficult and

EXHIBIT 7 INTEGRATED CASH MANAGEMENT

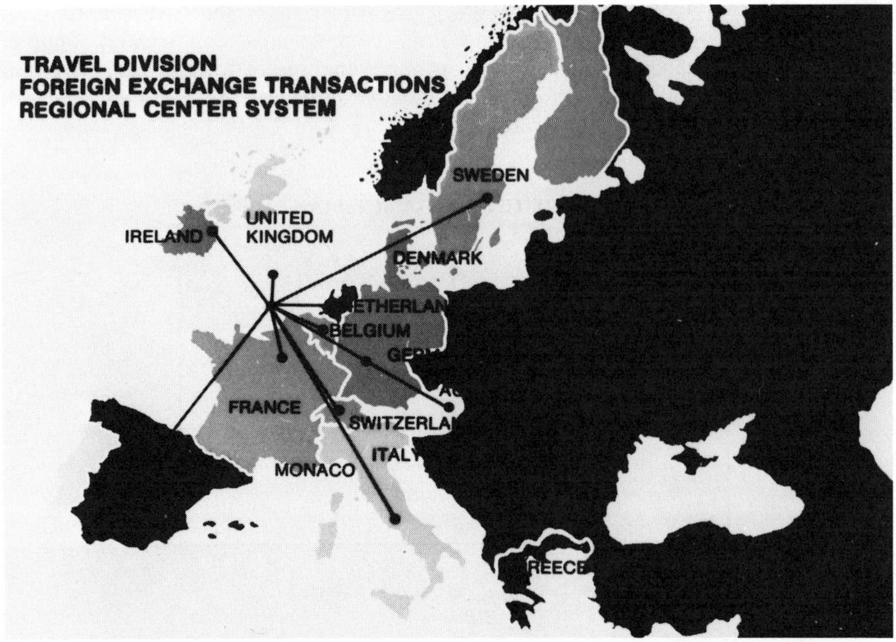

expensive to match settlement dates and forwards exactly. Furthermore, many companies manage forwards at corporate headquarters, increasing coordination problems.

An alternative method of controlling foreign exchange positions is to have settlements occur as a function of exposure level. Spot transactions are used to bring exposure to within an acceptable range. The main advantage of this method is that foreign exchange fluctuations are kept within a set band. Undue risks are avoided (see Exhibit 8). Fluctuations in the cash position within each country are minimized also, reducing borrowing needs or increasing funds available for investment.

Recently, the concept of a centralized netting unit has been taken further. Some companies have established reinvoicing centers or captive finance companies providing for a total integration of cash management, foreign exchange management, and liability management.

CASH MANAGEMENT: A GLOBAL PERSPECTIVE

As corporations continue to expand their operations beyond their resident borders, money and foreign exchange markets remain volatile, government regulations persist, **managing cash resources globally** increases in importance. The high costs of unutilized cash and high risks associated with unmanaged foreign exchange positions have virtually assured attractive rates of return on cash management improvements.

The internationalization on the corporate side is paralleled by a similar development on the banking side. Banks have expanded beyond their resident borders through international mergers and the expansion of major banks. Banks are also focusing more on their international payment systems and cash management services.

Along with a global perspective of cash management comes an expanded concept of the cash manager. The cash manager must have a strong knowledge of the basic business transactions of the corporation. The cash manager must keep abreast of emerging technologies, payment systems, and banking practices in each country. Finally, the cash manager role requires an understanding of foreign exchange and financing, and an ability to integrate day-to-day decisions into the company's overall asset and liability management strategies.

EXHIBIT 8 FOREIGN EXCHANGE MANAGEMENT

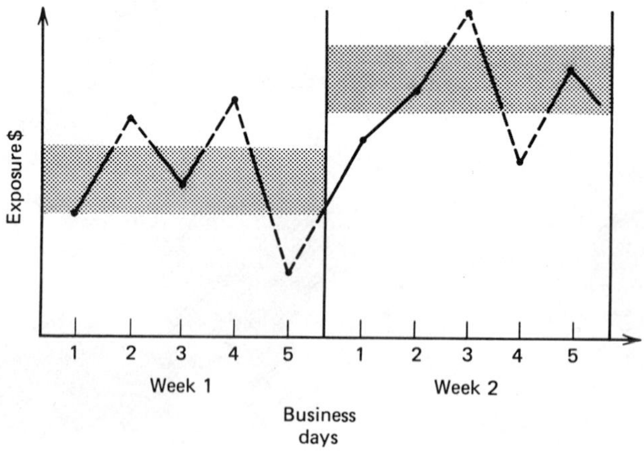

SECTION 8.11B

INTERNATIONAL CASH MANAGEMENT

CONTENTS

SECTION 8.11B

INTERNATIONAL CASH MANAGEMENT

Philip Mees

The word "cash" may mean different things to different people. A retailer may accept cash only, thus no checks or credit cards; a corporation may show cash on its balance sheet and include coins, bills, bank demand deposits, and uncollected checks. When the word "management" is added, corporate financial officers may also think of short-term investments, and with the word "international," foreign exchange exposure comes to mind. This section follows the practice of most banks by defining cash management in a rather narrow sense as the art of managing the movement of money into, through, and out of a company with the objective of maximizing cash availability under control of the company. International cash management, then, is defined as cross-border movement of funds, from and to other companies as well as within the company. Since investment and foreign exchange exposure management have been treated in previous sections they will not be discussed here despite their importance to cash management. It is not possible to manage something without appropriate information; therefore, cash management is divided into two parts: the movement of money and the movement of information relating to the movement of money. Money and information, however, do not always travel along the same track; in fact, it can be argued that disregarding payments in bills and coins, money never moves at all.

Money movements generally arise as a result of a company's operational activities. Cash comes in from customers, is invested, and is used to pay for goods and services bought. This rather elementary cash grows when the company borrows and repays money, when collections and disbursements happen in different locations, and when transactions are effected in different currencies. The number of cash movements to support the company's increasingly complex operations escalates into a mass of internal and external flows that require close supervision for proper payment execution and avoidance of the costs associated with excess cash on bank accounts. This shows why cash management, although an autonomous function in many corporate treasuries, should be an integral part of the overall treasury management of the company. It can have a dramatic impact on the amount of cash available for the company's operations. This is illustrated by the fact that many U.S. companies operate today with almost the same levels of cash they had in 1946, while their sales levels have increased many times.

United States cash managers have achieved such results on the basis of careful analyses of their companies' domestic operations, with particular emphasis on sales, purchasing, and investments. By instituting collection systems that accelerate the receipt of incoming funds and disbursement arrangements that eliminate the need to keep funds in a bank account to cover outstanding checks, they have sharply reduced their needs for working funds. Even more important, their better knowledge of the company's business has enabled them to prepare more reliable cash forecasts, in the process increasing the amounts that could be profitably invested rather than kept on demand accounts.

In the United States, this development has had serious consequences for the banking system, where the level of demand deposits as a percentage of total liabilities is now a fraction of what it was in 1946. However, as the cost of money increased since 1950 traditional levels of demand deposits companies used to keep with their banks became harder to justify. Ever since, companies and banks have worked together to develop increasingly sophisticated cash management methods, the banks motivated principally by strong competitive pressures to increase their corporate service level. The objective of this effort was—and continues to be for every cash manager—the maximization of the company's cash and near-cash assets in order to maximize, in turn, the contribution these assets make to corporate profits.

As with every other corporate activity, cash management begins with planning. The corporate long-term strategic plan and the annual business plan result in the preparation of budgets for each department. One of these, the capital budget, covering the planned capital expenditures for various time horizons, will generally not have an immediate impact on the cash manager. Rather, it underlies the company's long-term financial requirements. But the annual sales forecast and the operating budgets, broken down by month or by quarter, do provide the basis for the statement of anticipated sources and applications of funds to be reduced by the treasury department to the cash budget. Thus, since the entire business of the company ultimately finds expression in cash movements, there is no way a treasurer can do any thorough cash forecasting without corporate plans and budgets as a foundation.

While the operating divisions thus provide the basis for the treasurer's cash forecasts, he or she can, in turn, with a knowledge of the financial systems in various countries, provide valuable input to the divisions. With the treasurer's assistance, foreign exchange exposure on international transactions can be better controlled, special arrangements can be made for collections on large sales, or an unusual financing can facilitate the receipt of a specific contract. Such items all have their influence on the resulting payments. The treasurer can help to avoid problems with local banking practices and regulatory requirements with which an operating division is not necessarily familiar.

Although much more could be said about the treasurer's function in the planning process, attention must now be directed to the problems of the cash manager. First, the handling of cross-border payments by the banking system is traced in detail. Then some specific payment techniques and the credit questions they raise, as well as the principal international payment systems presently in use, are examined. Some typical cash management programs set up by international companies to facilitate their funds flows through these payment systems are also presented. Finally, the discussion is extended beyond the narrow definition of cash management by placing this discipline in a wider financial context, and by sketching what can be done in the future to help international cash managers obtain and work more effectively with the information they need for their function.

THE INTERNATIONAL PAYMENT MECHANISM

Comparing international with domestic money movements in any developed country brings out some interesting differences. A domestic payment, whether by draft, check, or transfer, travels by a well-defined, predictable path involving banks, one or more clearing houses, and final settlement at the central bank. The choices in the total clearing process are usually few, and everyone knows approximately how long it should take. Immediately, the core problem that underlies all cross-border payments arises: **there is no central settlement mechanism**. There is no international central bank. International payments are settled in domestic banking systems. These domestic systems are interconnected more or less efficiently via correspondent relationships between their individual member banks through mutual accounts, financing arrangements, and transaction processing. With international payments there are more factors that can cause uncertainties than with domestic payments: regulations, communication failures, and bank processing delays in all countries involved in the payment. Even if there are no unusual problems, the payment is subject to the laws, customs, and practices of the banking system in each country through which it moves.

For example, an importer in Italy must pay DM10,000 to a West German exporter. The exporter's payment instruction calls for delivery of the funds to an account at Dresdner Bank, Frankfurt. The importer has an account at Credito Italiano, Milan. The payment process is approximately as follows (see also Exhibit 1).

1. The importer issues the payment order and delivers the underlying import documentation to Credito Italiano, with the request to buy the DM10,000 in the foreign exchange market on the importer's behalf.
2. Credito Italiano buys the exchange in the open market (in this case, from Banco di Roma) against payment of the countervalue in lire via the Banca d'Italia and sells it to the importer. Banco di Roma delivers DM10,000 by ordering its correspondent in West Germany, Commerzbank, to make this payment to Credito Italiano's Deutsche mark account at Dresdner Bank, which payment Commerzbank executes via the Bundesbank.
3. Credito Italiano sends an order to Dresdner Bank to pay the DM10,000 to the exporter by crediting the exporter's account and sending the exporter the usual credit advice.

The accounting entries for these transactions appear in Exhibit 2.

The payment seems to have moved from the importer through Credito Italiano and Dresdner Bank to the exporter. However, in reality, between these parties nothing but messages—payment orders and advices—were exchanged. Two real payments did take place, however, almost as a sideline; they are connected with the purchase by Credito Italiano of the foreign exchange that was delivered on its behalf by Banco di Roma to Dresdner Bank (on the basis of a separate payment order). On balance, a lire payment has taken place from one of Credito Italiano's customers to one of Banco di Roma's customers through the Italian central bank; and, in West Germany, a Deutsche mark payment was made by one of the customers of Commerzbank (Banco di Roma) to one of the customers of Dresdner Bank (the exporter) through the Bundesbank. On both sides, the payments are handled through the local

EXHIBIT 1 PAYMENT FROM ITALIAN IMPORTER TO GERMAN EXPORTER IN DEUTSCHE MARKS

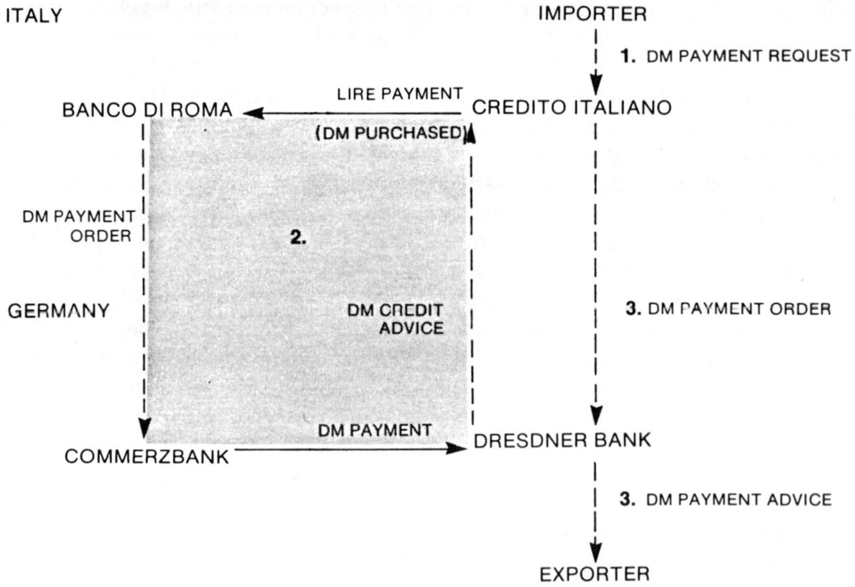

Solid Lines: Money movement through local interbank clearing channels.
Dotted Lines: Information movements.
Shaded Area: Settlement of the related foreign exchange transaction.

domestic banking systems and in accordance with local customs as to foreign exchange approval, processing time, communications systems, value dating, and commissions charged. Every country has its own systems and every bank sets its own standards, which may or may not be negotiable, depending on the bank and the client.

The 14 accounting entries in Exhibit 2 result from one payment between two companies whose banks have a direct correspondent relationship with each other, one of the simplest possible cases. Often, however, the companies' banks do not have a direct relationship and therefore must use another bank in the role of correspondent bank to effect settlement. If then the payment is denominated in a third currency (e.g., U.S. dollars in the Italian–West German example) an even larger number of parties may be involved.

Italy. Importer; local bank of account; international bank.

United States. Correspondents of Italian and West German banks involved directly, and indirectly, in the payment.

West Germany. International bank; local branch of account; exporter.

EXHIBIT 2 TYPICAL INTERNATIONAL PAYMENT; ACCOUNTING ENTRIES

	Debit	Credit
CREDITO ITALIANO		
Dresdner Bank (nostro account)	DM 10,000	
Banca d' Italia (nostro account)		Lit5,000,000
Profit on Foreign Exchange		Lit 25,000
Importer	Lit5,025,000	
Dresdner Bank (nostro account)		DM 10,000
BANCO DI ROMA		
Commerzbank (nostro account)	DM 10,000	
Customer		Lit4,975,000
Profit on Foreign Exchange		Lit 25,000
Banca d' Italia (nostro account)	Lit5,000,000	
Commerzbank (nostro account)		DM 10,000
COMMERZBANK		
Banco di Roma	DM 10,000	
Bundesbank (nostro account)		DM 10,000
DRESDNER BANK		
Bundesbank (nostro account)	DM 10,000	
Credito Italiano		DM 10,000
Credito Italiano	DM 10,000	
Exporter		DM 10,000

Thus, eight banking offices each handle a portion of the payment process, as shown in Exhibit 3.

1. The importer requests the local bank to make a payment of $10,000 to the exporter on the exporter's account at a local branch of Dresdner Bank. Since the Italian local bank has no foreign exchange department, it issues its own payment instructions to Credito Italiano, a large correspondent.
2. Credito Italiano buys the dollars from Banco di Roma, pays this bank the lire countervalue via Banca d'Italia, and receives the dollars on its account at Bank B, New York, from Bank A, through the New York Clearing House.
3. Credito Italiano issues its order to Bank B to pay the $10,000 to Bank C, Dresdner Bank's New York correspondent, and to advise Dresdner of this payment.

4. Dresdner Bank now notifies the exporter, through the local branch, of the arrival of this payment and asks the exporter for instructions as to its application. Assuming that the exporter wants to sell the dollars, Dresdner Bank does so on the exporter's behalf, in this case to Commerzbank. This bank pays the countervalue in deutsche marks, while Dresdner instructs Bank C to pay the $10,000 to Bank D, the New York correspondent of Commerzbank, again, via the New York Clearing House.
5. Dresdner Bank now credits its local branch for the Deutsche mark countervalue and the branch, in turn, credits the exporter.

Thus, four U.S. banks are involved in settling a liability that arose from a transaction in which no U.S. company was ever a party. Since a large majority of international trade is denominated in U.S. dollars, this is not at all an unusual case. All such transactions are paid through the U.S. banking system.

The examples show that no money moves across any national border. Although the ownership of the dollars in the example has changed from Banco di Roma via Credito Italiano and Dresdner Bank to Commerzbank, the actual payments reflecting

EXHIBIT 3 PAYMENT FROM ITALIAN IMPORTER TO GERMAN EXPORTER IN U.S. DOLLARS

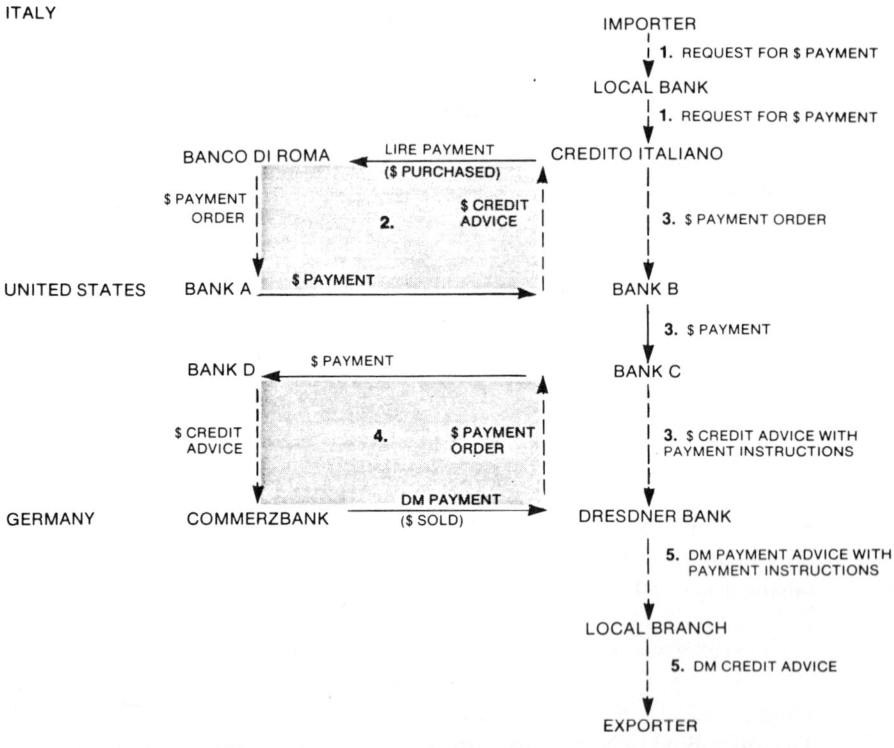

Solid Lines: Money movement through local interbank clearing channels.
Dotted Lines: Information movements.
Shaded Area: Settlement of the related foreign exchange transaction.

these changes were made only between U.S. banks. Similarly, the one lire payment was made in Italy and the one Deutsche mark payment in West Germany. Otherwise, the entire process consists of banks sending each other messages requesting certain bookkeeping entries that reflect the shifting of the extension of credit from one place to another. Whereas the exporter had first extended credit to the importer, the exporter has now become the creditor (depositor) of Dresdner Bank. In the United States, an Italian deposit in one bank was exchanged for a West German deposit in another. In Italy, Credito Italiano's customer deposits decreased and those of Banco di Roma increased. And in all three countries the banks made their accounting entries in their own currencies (disregarding the nostro accounts). Naturally, the exporter could also have elected to receive the dollar proceeds of the sale on a dollar account at his local branch in West Germany. Then the payment would have followed the same path, the only difference being that Dresdner Bank would not have sold the dollars but maintained them in its overall dollar position on behalf of its customer. In principle, therefore, it can be said that money never crosses a border, only messages do.

When the importer makes payment by sending a check instead of by bank transfer the entire process is set in motion by the collection of the check upon receipt by the exporter. Instead of the importer initiating the actual payment, the importer in fact authorizes the exporter to do so by sending the exporter a check drawn on the importer's bank. The exporter thus requests the bank, Dresdner Bank, to collect the check, which means physically sending the item, with payment instructions, to Credito Italiano through the mails. Naturally, this delays the availability of the funds to the exporter while increasing costs with the collection fees charged by Dresdner and Credito. The payment process itself, however, is the same as for a transfer payment, that is, from Credito Italiano through the United States to Dresdner Bank.

In the absence of a central settlement mechanism, the smooth execution of payments depends entirely on the following factors: the efficiency of the banking systems and individual banks involved in the payment; the communications channels used by the banks; the banking customs in each country; and the laws and regulations governing international payments. International businesspeople have long been accustomed to extreme variations in the levels of efficiency of different banking systems in the world. There is no one cause to which to point for these differences. The needs of an economy determine the shape of a country's banking system. To some extent, this results from the political system or from other factors in a country's history. In Scandinavia, for example, international transactions are so large compared to the national economies that, on the one hand, they are very strictly regulated, but on the other, the banks have created highly efficient systems to handle transactions smoothly and quickly. In some countries, where state-owned institutions predominate, the banking system may have developed more through political than through competitive pressure. In many less-developed countries, the banks suffer from such an extreme dearth of trained employees that they often are simply not able to provide service in a modern sense. United States banks have long labored under the organizational separation of their domestic and international departments, and the existence of 14,000 autonomous commercial banks creates its own special problems. The result of these variations in efficiency is that a treasurer is forced to institute widely different cash management methods in different countries.

In recent years, enormous progress has been made in the field of telecommunications. Banks have actively participated in this development. While only a few years ago most routine payment orders and advices were sent by mail, today technology has made the telex less expensive and more reliable. The Society for Worldwide Interbank Financial Telecommunications (SWIFT) has become the preferred communications net between banks. Some banks offer their own private networks for message exchanges with their customers. Soon, banks that do not work with these new networks will prove unable to serve the growing needs of international companies for fast and reliable transaction execution and information.

Banking customs mostly find their origin in the economic and social makeup of a country. For instance, there is the importance of timeliness; in some countries time is simply not as important to people as it is in others. It is only natural that this should result in wide variations in execution speeds and timeliness of information. Also, a tightly organized bank with a strong customer orientation will tend to do better than a bank that is organized to suit its own internal requirements. The custom of overdraft credit extension in Europe requires value dating each transaction posted to the account and this, in turn, has become a source of compensation to banks for the operating services they perform. Conversely, the U.S. policy of not allowing overdrafts, jointly with the prohibition of paying interest on demand deposits has resulted in compensating balance requirements, while value dating in the European sense has been unnecessary.

Finally, most countries have enacted laws designed to protect their currencies and economies against uncontrollable negative influences from abroad. Sometimes, these are simply tracking systems under which transactions can be freely executed but must subsequently be reported to the central bank. At the other end of the scale are the countries where every import or export has to be authorized before the contract is signed and every payment must be made with an individual license of the central bank. This necessarily affects the expectations of a treasurer with regard to the payment traffic with a country. Since most international payments involve converting one currency into another, an additional area of concern to the international cash manager is the regulation of the foreign exchange markets. In a country where the currency is not convertible a bank can usually purchase a foreign currency only from the central bank. It will also have to provide adequate documentation justifying the purchase. Although this often follows a well-defined routine, in some places it causes no end of delays and expenses. But even in the absence of such regulatory difficulties there are wide variations between countries in foreign exchange practices as to pricing, contract duration, and settlement procedures that may severely limit a treasurer's options in this area.

In conclusion, it is evident that lacking a central settlement mechanism, internatinal payments are considerably more complicated than domestic ones. They travel a longer, more segmented path through at least two national banking systems; they strongly depend on relationships between individual banks, on communications systems, and on local customs and regulations. The international cash manager will therefore not only have to be familiar with all these aspects in the countries where his or her company does business but also need the means of tying them together for the proper integration of the overseas financial transactions of the company.

INTERNATIONAL PAYMENT METHODS

The most common international payment instruments are the draft, the check, and the transfer. The discussion that follows specifically identifies some advantages and problems on their different paths through the banking systems; it also briefly touches upon the credit risks to which each exposes various parties.

THE DRAFT. Reduced to its barest essentials, the draft is nothing more than an order of the drawer to the drawee to pay a specific amount of money on a certain date. The cause for this payment order is generally a commercial transaction through which a seller has generated a receivable on a buyer. Since a draft is created by the seller it must be sent to the buyer for acknowledgement, upon which the buyer will instruct the bank to make the required payment. In many cases, instead of sending the draft directly, the seller will ask his or her bank to present the draft to the buyer on the seller's behalf, often through a correspondent bank who acts as agent. This collection process necessarily takes some time because of the intervention of the banks and, for the same reason, it will cost money in the form of collection fees. However, the draft buys a measure of safety for the seller. It protects the claim from going astray and forces the buyer into action, either to make or to refuse payment. It provides the seller with an experienced collection agent who follows the draft during the collection process, issues reminders when the item is outstanding too long, and offers other services to help the seller secure payment. However, these collections require much physical handling and labor-intensive processing by the banks. In addition, in some countries, drafts are subject to stamp duties.

Cost factors become especially important with a time draft, a draft that is not payable at sight but a specified number of days after sight, representing the credit term granted by the seller. The collecting bank first has to present the draft to the buyer for acceptance—signifying the buyer's recognition of liability—and after the credit term, has to present it again for payment. Because of the expense, in some countries sellers do not send the drafts for acceptance but extend credit on open account and draw sight drafts to be presented at the end of the credit term.

Exporters frequently ask their banks to collect drafts with documents attached representing title to the merchandise shipped to a buyer overseas. The key documents are normally the invoice, the bill of lading, and the insurance policy, evidencing, respectively, the transaction, delivery, and insurance in transit. This is called "a documentary collection." As compared with the clean draft discussed above, the seller obtains an additional measure of safety in that he or she preserves control of the title documents until the buyer has honored the draft. Only then can the buyer exchange the documents for the merchandise at the shipping company. Such is theory. In practice, there are some problems—for example, the problem of time. Transportation companies sell two principal things: capacity and speed. On many routes, the merchandise will arrive at the destination before the draft and documents do. The question is whether the transportation company will compromise its product, speed, for the legal requirement of waiting for the presentation of title documents before releasing the goods. Perhaps it is prevented from doing so by local authorities or by lack of storage space. In addition, while there is much international jurisprudence affirming the nature of the ocean bill of lading as a title-giving document, the true value of the airway bill or the trucker's receipt is much less clear—and with shipments by air or truck, the time element is even more important than with ocean-going freight. However, there may still be reasons to use this payment method, such as local practice, regulations by customs or foreign exchange authorities, or requirements by banks financing the transaction.

Finally, a draft can be created pursuant to the requirements of a letter of credit. In this case the seller is instructed to draw the draft on either the issuing or the negotiating bank; the seller receives the money at the time of negotiation of documents complying with the terms and conditions of the letter of credit. Delays can occur if the bank refuses to negotiate the documents because they deviate from the requirements of the letter of credit. Then the draft and documents are sent to the opening bank for approval and subsequent payment, which is similar to a documentary collection. Alternatively, the bank may pay under reserve or cable the opening bank for approval. Letters of credit are governed by well-established rules issued by the International Chamber of Commerce and observed by most international banks. In addition, there is extensive international jurisprudence to guide all parties involved in such transactions.

THE CHECK. A check is simply a draft drawn on a bank, an order to the bank to make a certain payment to a stated beneficiary. However, the bank has no contractual obligation to execute the payment unless it has certified the check or issued its own. For that reason, it is important for the recipient of a check to collect it as quickly as possible and replace it with a credit posted to the recipient's bank account in useable funds. In the United States, an economy built on credit, the collection of increasing numbers of checks drawn on banks all over the country became a major problem around the turn of the century. Long collection times increased the need for borrowed funds on the part of business. For that reason, the Federal Reserve Banks have created a check collection mechanism that can serve as a model for any country in the world as to speed, low cost, and efficiency. Few checks take more than two days to be cleared anywhere in the country. Even Great Britain, another country with a check-based payment system, has been unable to improve on U.S. performance.

As discussed, no such central mechanism exists for international payments. There is no central check collection system. An exporter receiving a check drawn on a bank outside the country can only give it to the local bank with the request to send it to the drawee bank for collection and to credit the exporter's account for the proceeds. The bank then produces a collection form containing payment instructions and sends this, with the check, to the drawee bank. The actual payment follows the process described earlier. Given the fact that this is a low-profit, labor-intensive service, and given the relative levels of efficiency of the mails and of the banks involved in the collection, the entire process may take quite some time, possibly several weeks. Delays might even be aggravated by regulatory problems, such as if the importer did not obtain proper official payment authorization before sending the check. However, in some instances, such as between Canada and the United States, and in many border regions, banks have made special arrangements with each other to facilitate the collection process to the benefit of their customers.

THE TRANSFER. Transfers are payments made pursuant to an order given by a payer directly to the payer's bank to pay a certain amount of money to a beneficiary. (This type of payment was described earlier.) The volume of payments of this type is so large that most international banks have achieved a high degree of automation in the processing of these items. Transfers are, therefore, the fastest, cheapest, and most reliable way of making international payments. These benefits accrue primarily to the beneficiary; the payer is unable to enjoy the disbursement float of a check because his or her account is charged immediately. Whether the banks involved in the transfer will all perform their functions with due speed greatly depends on local practices and regulations, but there is a fundamental difference between transfers and the check payments. With the latter, the bank of the beneficiary has a built-in incentive to accelerate the collection in order to increase its customers' balances. With a transfer there is no such incentive; in fact, it could be argued that the banks have the reverse incentive—after charging a payer's account, the longer they delay the payment, the longer they enjoy free funds. Bank performance on transfers, therefore, is largely determined by competitive conditions and by local standards of customer service, both varying widely from country to country and from bank to bank within a country.

THE CREDIT ASPECT. As has been indicated, many different social and economic customs exist in the world, which can often be explained by historical development. More often than not, local businesspeople are unaware of the backgrounds that influence their own daily actions. An international treasurer has at his or her disposal the full range of payment mechanisms existing in all countries where the company does business. The treasurer's choice of the one to be used in each individual case, however, depends on an awareness of the local situation in question; a little historical research is very helpful in making these decisions.

When the three payment instruments are examined from a credit risk perspective, it is quite clear that the safest one for a seller is the draft drawn under a letter of credit. The seller has a bank's commitment to pay provided the draft is accompanied by certain prescribed documents, which are usually easily provided in the ordinary course of business. The seller therefore obtains payment soon after the merchandise has been shipped. The bank making the payment, upon negotiating the documents, usually does so at the request of a correspondent abroad, the opening bank, which often has an account with the negotiating bank. Depending on the balances in that account, the negotiating bank may run a credit risk on the opening bank by paying the draft and negotiating the documents.

For the buyer and the buyer's bank things look very different. The buyer originally requests his or her bank to open the letter of credit, perhaps several months before the goods are shipped. All that time the opening bank has a contingent claim on the buyer, namely, a claim for reimbursement as soon as the bank has to pay the draft with approved documents. From that time on, until the buyer sees and approves the merchandise, the buyer is exposed to proper performance by the seller, that is, whether he will recieve what he bought. It is important to realize that this is something completely separate from the letter of credit. Banks deal in the documents only; in no way are they a party to the merchandise transaction.

A draft that is sent for collection, with or without documents attached, exposes the seller to the usual risk of payment upon presentation. The buyer might be able to appropriate the merchandise without paying the draft; when distances are great and buyer and seller do not have a standing business relationship this is no imaginary risk. The buyer might also go bankrupt. The seller then has to retrieve the merchandise or find another buyer, which is not easy from a long distance. While attaching documents to the draft may provide the seller with some protection, at least in a legal sense, a clean draft fully exposes the seller to the buyer's payment practices. Finally, the seller also depends on the bank and its correspondents for proper handling of the draft.

The credit risks in checks and transfers are too well known to require space here. They can easily be traced. But these items do highlight an aspect of risk that banks run on each other, caused by the way they deal with each other and often trust each other's judgment. For instance, the opening bank of a letter of credit might pay the draft upon advice from the negotiating bank that the documents comply with the letter of credit; therefore, its account is charged. This can happen several days before the opening bank receives the documents by mail and has a chance to review them. Should its judgment on the correctness of the documents differ from that of the negotiating bank, the possibility of a conflict arises. Also, when a letter of credit is confirmed by a bank, this bank is exposed to the opening bank just as the latter is to the buyer, in the form of a contingent claim. Similarly, with checks, transfers, and many other transactions, banks use each other's services to perform their financial functions in the international economy. They rely on each other's facilities and processing capabilities. There is always the ultimate risk that in the middle of a transaction one of the banks will fail and close its doors, causing severe problems of many kinds.

Generally speaking, the entire international payment mechanism, and therefore all international trade, depends on a smoothly functioning world banking network consisting of a large number of individual banks and a myriad of links connecting these banks with each other. Regardless of political differences or borders, a payment can almost always be made from one country to another. It passes through individual banks under some degree of supervision—and sometimes active intervention—by the central banks in the countries concerned.

INTERBANK PAYMENT AND COMMUNICATION MECHANISMS

Interbank payment and communication mechanisms are those vehicles banks use to facilitate the flow of payments among each other. They include mail, telex, and telegram, as well as clearing systems, modern electronic networks such as SWIFT, and, in some cases, bank-operated private networks. Because of the great variety in speed, efficiency, and cost of these media, and because for many payments there might be a choice of several vehicles, it is important to be aware of their characteristics and their influence on the movement of information.

First, it is important to remember that there is no central international settlement system. All international payments are made in the books of individual banks who cooperate with each other in this function, one of their most vital tasks in the international economy. Since banks are in business to make a profit, they have to reconcile their own interests with those of their customers in choosing the vehicle they use for each payment—a clearing system, or SWIFT, or perhaps the mails. Use of the mails, for instance, might require some labor-intensive typing of forms but might, on the other hand, produce substantial float to the bank. And while a clearing system reduces float, its benefits accrue equally to all participating banks and it reduces internal handling and management costs. Generally speaking, where banks have jointly established vehicles such as clearing houses and SWIFT, they have done so primarily in their own interests, with the motivation to improve customer service not always coming in first place.

MAIL. Despite the widespread availability of electronic communications networks, a surprisingly large number of cross-border payments continues to take place by mail. This includes all checks and drafts, and also many transfers for which time is not critical. It is, therefore, not unusual for a check to take several days to reach its destination, whereupon its collection from a drawee bank in a foreign country might literally take weeks. In order to accelerate the process banks often use private couriers instead of the mails to deliver checks to each other. Although this certainly cuts down the travel float, it does nothing to reduce the banks' processing float, which in the absence of an efficient international check collection mechanism can be substantial. For that reason transfers, especially cable transfers, are much to be preferred. They flow more smoothly from payer, through the banks, to the beneficiary and require less paper being sent around the world. The majority of international clean payments—that is, payments not requiring the handling of documents by banks—are made by transfer. Many small transfers still travel by mail; the larger ones are now handled mostly by telex or SWIFT. Since practically all banks engaged in international transactions have telex machines, telegrams are now seldom used.

TELEX. The telex provides a reasonably reliable network spanning the globe. But it is not one network. It consists of separate, interconnected networks operated by a different company or authority in each country. For that reason, its reliability and capacity depends on the country involved. There have been many cases in which the impossibility of communicating by telex made a large money transfer into or out of a country so difficult that a company put a person on a plane carrying a check for delivery.

In addition, telex messages require much manual handling, with accompanying chances of error. Most banks generate the messages and the necessary test codes by hand—although this can be automated by computer—and there is no uniform format. Although the freedom of format is also one of the advantages of telex, it creates considerable problems at the receiving bank. There the message has to be decoded, read, understood, and processed in the bank's internal systems, again with many chances of error along the way. Since large banks handle thousands of telex payments a day this is a very serious problem for them, from which their customers suffer the consequences in the form of mispostings, delays, and other errors.

SOCIETY FOR WORLDWIDE INTERBANK FINANCIAL TELECOMMUNICATIONS. To reduce the possibility of error and to create additional processing capacity for the growth in world trade the banks in Europe and North America in 1973 founded the Society for Worldwide Interbank Financial Telecommunications (SWIFT). As the name indicates, SWIFT is an interbank communications network carrying messages arising from financial transactions. Its only members are banks who have subscribed to its capital and installed the necessary computer equipment to be connected to the network. The SWIFT network makes use of the latest in computer and communications technology and partly through the principle of redundancy has proved to be a highly dependable facility. Now for the first time there is a common denominator in the international payment system. By 1981 SWIFT had become available in most West European and North American countries, and several Asian and Latin American countries, but not Africa. The SWIFT system requires certain prescribed formats that facilitate the automation of the member banks' processing departments. It has reduced the vexing problem of the multiplicity of formats adopted by banks in different parts of the world for their payment orders. This, coupled with the speed of electronic transmission, enables the banks to execute payments much more cheaply and efficiently than before. Thus even if SWIFT was created by banks for banks from their own desire to improve internal processing efficiencies, member-bank customers are bound to feel the benefits in the form of faster money transfers with fewer errors. It is therefore important for a treasurer to be aware of the existence, reliability, and availability of various alternative facilities for the company's financial transactions in different countries. In the interest of the company a treasurer must also become informed as to which banks are best organized to make optimal use of these facilities.

CLEARING HOUSES. Although clearing houses are generally domestic institutions serving banks in specific localities, the ones in the financial capitals of the world handle many large payments that originate from international transactions. Every international payment is finally settled through domestic payment systems. For example, the New York Clearing House on an average day in 1981 handled about $175 billion in international U.S. dollar transactions alone, in addition to more than $16.5 billion in domestic check clearings.

When there is a clearing house in a city the banks do not make transfer payments or present checks directly to each other. Instead, they accumulate these items and exchange them with each other at a central clearing house. The clearing house calculates the payment each bank has to make or receive in net settlement of its total receivables and payables. The net amounts are subsequently settled through the central bank. This settlement may or may not take place immediately, a factor that is important in the light of the settlement credit risk banks take in dealing with each other, for by not immediately presenting a check that may have been deposited by a customer the previous day but holding it for the clearing the banks incur credit exposure on each other. It is possible that a bank that has a net debit position in the clearing house—more payables than receivables—would not have the funds to settle. Most clearing houses therefore operate under the aegis or with supervision of the central bank and arrangements exist for this bank to assist in the clearing if needed. In some cases, this relationship is more implied than clear-cut; it is then based on the central bank's general function of lender of last resort.

A good illustration of the credit risk implications in a clearing is provided in New York, where the New York Clearing House operates the more traditional check clearing and also, since 1970, the automated Clearing House Interbank Payment System (CHIPS), which was created specifically for international U.S. dollar payments. For the check clearing, the member banks exchange checks at the clearing house several times during the day and night, process these, and post them to customer accounts. Final settlement takes place once a day at 10:00 A.M. at the Federal Reserve Bank of New York after the New York Clearing House has calculated the net amounts for each member bank. It is theoretically possible for a member to fail to settle a net debit position at 10:00 A.M. while, at the other banks, customers have already used the funds that were to be collected for value that day.

CHIPS operates as a separate system from 7:00 A.M. to 4:30 P.M., with final settlement at the Federal Reserve at 6:00 P.M. There are 12 full-member banks and a large number of associate-member banks that are directly connected to CHIPS for sending and receiving payment advices (but most associate-member banks must settle through one of the 12 member banks). Many of the associate members are New York offices of banks domiciled outside the United States. During the day, the banks send and receive payment messages on computer terminals connected to CHIPS and post the items to their customers' accounts. However, since final settlement cannot take place until after closing at 4:30 P.M. (at the latest 6:00 P.M.) all banks operate on the assumption that the incoming funds for which they have received CHIPS advices will indeed be paid to them at the end of the day. The CHIPS rules allow for the reversal of the transactions of a bank that fails to settle a net debit position. Although no formal tie exists to the Federal Reserve Bank of New York it is clear that a reversal of transactions could create such serious problems that as a practical matter Federal Reserve intervention would be the only workable alternative.

This type of indirect dependence by clearing systems on a central bank was underscored by the discussions the banks in London had among themselves on the establishment of a U.S. dollar clearing house in their city. The idea was to exchange dollar items throughout the day and to settle net balances via CHIPS in New York. This meets with several problems. First and foremost there is the credit exposure of the banks on each other, now denominated in dollars. That means that there can be no built-in dependence on the Bank of England, since this bank is not in a position to guarantee availability of a currency other than pounds sterling at all times. The Bank of England would, in turn, be forced to enter into credit arrangements with the Federal Reserve or other U.S. banks to secure its own access to dollars. So far, the Bank of England has been unwilling to do this. Second, the time difference complicates the picture significantly. Because the day in London is five hours ahead of the day in New York, the London bankers would not have certainty of settlement via CHIPS until the following morning. With the huge Eurodollar amounts involved in a London dollar clearing this is seen as a serious obstacle. Finally, the volume of payments in such a clearing would require a common automated system like CHIPS, not yet available. As a result, the dollar clearing that did develop in London is for small items only that do not create significant credit exposure and handling problems.

BANK COMMUNICATION SYSTEMS. Besides the interbank communication and clearing facilities, some banks have also developed their own communication systems, first, for the purpose of carrying messages between their offices and, second, to make the message traffic with companies and correspondent banks easier and cheaper. A client in Europe wishing to send a telex to a New York bank, for instance, may be able to do so by dialing into a local telex number, from which the message is automatically switched to New York. Although this is much less efficient than SWIFT, it offers an alternative and, of course, is useful to non-SWIFT-member banks and companies.

The greatest flexibility, however, is possible with worldwide computer-based communications networks such as the large time-sharing systems. Banks make use of these systems to deliver daily account information to their customers and also to accept payment instructions. In effect, these networks create windows geographically close to the corporate customer through which the customer can communicate financially with the bank on a two-way basis at very low cost and with instant response. For the bank, this makes possible a far-reaching automation of the payment traffic with its customers. While the interbank side is automated, based on SWIFT, the automation has now been extended to the customer side by linking SWIFT via the bank's internal processing system to another network that reaches the corporate customer. The efficiencies of such integrated systems are clear; they reduce slow and error-prone human handling to a minimum.

Reviewing the payment and communication mechanisms presently in use one can conclude that although most of them were originally designed to serve the banks themselves and not their customers, the latter sooner or later reap benefits directly or indirectly. Banks that have integrated SWIFT with their own computer systems are in a better position to give reliable and prompt funds transfer service than those that work with a manual interface or with telex. In developed countries, payment delays are not often caused by the communications facilities; rather they arise from internal inefficiencies in the banks. Large banks in most countries are now making significant progress in improving their automated systems for processing and accounting for the transactions of their customers.

INTERNATIONAL CASH MANAGEMENT PROGRAMS

Well-designed cash management programs follow a few simple ground rules:

1. There is a cash management center that receives and distributes timely information relating to cash movements on a number of bank accounts strategically placed to serve the needs of the company's operating divisions.
2. Information is distributed on the basis of a need to know, which is different from cash requirements.
3. Short payment channels, involving a minimum number of banks, allow for maximum control.
4. Modern communications systems are used.
5. Efficient banks with high standards of customer service are employed.
6. There is a minimal impact on the internal corporate organization, decision-making pattern, and accounting system.

With these ground rules in mind, cash management is divided into four areas: **collection**, **disbursement**, **intercompany payments**, and **control**.

COLLECTION. The cash manager's motto is: "as soon as the customer has initiated payment to us, the money is ours." The cash manager is entitled to use every means in his or her power to gain control over incoming funds as quickly as possible after the payment process is started. The typical method used to achieve this is the establishment of collection accounts close to the customers. In the United States, where most commercial payments are made by check, these collection points are called "lock boxes." The company directs its customers to send their checks to certain post office boxes placed around the country for this purpose, which are opened and emptied each day by local banks on the company's behalf. These banks deposit the checks to collection accounts and collect them from the drawee banks, after which the company concentrates the funds into its main bank, using depository transfer checks or wire transfers. Payment information is sent by the lock-box banks directly to the company's credit department, while the treasury is advised of the total funds credited. Lock boxes are a simple and effective method to cut the float on incoming funds.

Internationally, the objectives of collection are the same, but the technique differs. Each international payment is made in a domestic banking system, namely, in the country of the currency in which the payment is denominated (U.S. dollars are paid in the United States, lire are paid in Italy). International collection systems, therefore, require collection accounts in the countries of the currencies of the payments, not necessarily in the countries of the customers. A West German company with a dollar receivable on a British buyer should receive the funds on a U.S. collection account rather than channeling the dollars to its local bank. This shortens the chain of banks handling the payment and, through the use of the U.S. bank's automated reporting system, makes the relative information available sooner. Through a variety of arrangements such a collection account can be connected to interest-paying short-term investment media. Similarly, lire should be collected in Italy, pesetas in Spain. When a company thus ends up with a variety of collection accounts in different countries it may benefit from the services of a bank to manage the flows through these accounts, to concentrate the funds efficiently, and to manage the foreign exchange exposure. A few banks provide expert specialized services in this field.

As discussed above, check collection between countries is often very slow, while transfers through SWIFT can be very fast. Because of this, unfortunately, the use of checks is increasing, especially by large companies for which the extra disbursement float is important. Accordingly, more receiving companies will have to consider opening lock boxes with their collection banks in order to accelerate the money availability on these check remittances. This service is only slowly becoming available outside the United States, chiefly at the branches of a few major U.S. banks, and its relative usefulness should be carefully evaluated in the light of mail and collection experience. Geographic proximity does not necessarily coincide with shorter mail times, as shown by some preliminary studies done by individual companies. Nevertheless, international lock boxes may well result in faster money availability, especially when courier services are used to collect checks on banks in other countries. But because of the much greater efficiency of transfers, exporters should make every effort to induce their customers to remit by wire transfers (via SWIFT) to a collection account of the same currency.

DISBURSEMENT. In addition to the use of checks, companies make international payments by giving payment instructions to their banks on paper, by telephone, telex, computer tape, or interactive terminal. In many countries, excluding the United States with its check system, the banks will accept instructions on tape to store payment orders for a few days, match the orders to foreign exchange transactions done separately, and execute them on the dates indicated by the customer. The data on the tapes often come directly out of the customer's accounts payable system. In the United States, automation has taken place more on the output side of the banks, supplying account information via electronic means. However, banks use the same electronic networks to accept payment instructions, the processing of which is more and more automated, with the exception of foreign currency payment orders. These are still usually handled in the traditional ways. Companies that have foreign currency collection accounts abroad or foreign currency accounts at their own banks can, of course, make payments directly from those accounts. This will save considerable expense and reduce foreign exchange exposure. All that is required is a test-key arrangement with each bank involved.

INTERCOMPANY PAYMENTS. Payments among companies belonging to the same group should be considered separately because the cash manager can exercise a much greater degree of control over them than over third-party items, provided he or she has the authority and the information to do so. When subsidiary A sends a check to subsidiary B in another country, there is a float benefit to subsidiary A but the corporation as a whole suffers. For many days, the item is out of control for cash and foreign exchange management purposes. Similarily, when a transfer from subsidiary A to subsidiary B takes a week to wind its way through the banking system interest is lost by both companies for those days and the item is also out of control. These problems lead companies to institute arrangements to influence these intercompany funds flows from their headquarters in any of a large variety of ways. Perhaps all that takes place is some consultation on ways to improve the payment methods used. Setting a fixed intercompany payment day for each month improves the possibilities for control. It may be desirable to combine all the foreign exchange conversions in one bank, which then also takes responsibility for the prompt execution of the transfers. Or the company may benefit from a multilateral netting system to eliminate payments that go back and forth among its various units. The particular system used depends on the structure of the company's cash flows, its form of organization, and the savings generated. Several international banks are able to assist companies with the necessary evaluations underlying these systems; only a few banks have the specialized know-how to implement and run them.

Another problem international cash managers face is the control and management of the foreign exchange exposure generated by these intercompany transactions. If foreign exchange exposures are numerous and complex, a captive finance company or a reinvoicing company might be established to take over the intercompany receivables from all units of the group. Besides a foreign exchange exposure management center, such a company also becomes the central collection agent for all group members with its own international collection system. It can centrally finance the entire intercompany receivable portfolio of the group, presumably at better rates than the individual members, and serve in many other capacities in the financial markets on behalf of the group. Offsetting these considerable advantages may be many internal and external arguments involving the company's organizational structure, its management incentive systems, its accounting policy, or legal, tax, and foreign exchange regulatory problems. Finance and reinvoicing companies can certainly be important cash and financial management tools, but they require very careful and detailed feasibility studies.

Finally, the international cash manager should try to maximize the use of excess cash in the foreign subsidiaries of the company. Often one subsidiary will have excess cash in its currency, while another subsidiary is borrowing another currency. Depending on the cash forecasting abilities of both, it might be desirable to arrange an intercompany loan at a rate that benefits both parties. When there are several such situations an international cash pool—perhaps as part of a finance company—can serve as the vehicle to distribute excess liquidity. Companies with excess cash deposit this to the pool; companies with shortages borrow from the pool. Because of their effect on the group foreign exchange exposure these operations should always be centrally managed and a comprehensive information system is an absolute prerequisite. Here also the various laws can create serious complications and not all companies' organizational structures will tolerate such cash pools.

CONTROL. Control problems have received a great deal of attention in U.S. companies and banks. Perhaps control of money movements in the United States is more difficult than in other countries because of the highly fragmented banking system. Also, U.S. banks have traditionally maintained separate international and domestic operating divisions that could pass work between each other only in paper form. Only around 1980 did the most advanced money center banks succeed in electronically integrating these two groups. Finally, U.S. banks routinely provide monthly statements of account; daily statements are usually obtainable but they are always a few days late and may not be free of charge.

Treasurers, therefore, once they had solved their most obvious float problems, started to put pressure on the banks to provide more timely account information. Above all, they wanted balance information but, more and more, they became interested in activity data with full details of each posted item. The banks' answer has been an electronic system with an automated link to the accounting system to deliver the information to the customer via a bank-operated or external time-sharing network. A variety of reports can thus be made available, such as plain account balances, balances plus activity in several levels of detail, averages over a specified period of time, listings of checks paid, securities received and delivered on custody account, and others. Most banks constantly improve these systems and several have the ability to report transactions immediately after they are processed, without waiting for end-of-day posting.

In Europe, the control problem is different. In many countries banks issue daily statements that, because of geographic proximity, reach the customers reasonably promptly. Also, large amounts are routinely advised by telephone and value-dating conventions tend to postpone the use of the money by the customer. Foreign currency conversions, of course, always delay the availability of the local currency equivalent by two days. Finally, the customs of overdraft banking and interest on credit balances mean that prompt information on incoming funds is not critical; the money is immediately productive. Therefore, companies in Europe do not have the same problem keeping track of their accounts as their U.S. colleagues. They have, however, a different control problem: in many countries the banks are accustomed to executing payment orders at their leisure, enjoying the float for a few days. These practices vary widely between countries and also between individual banks. All a company can do is to follow its transactions as closely as possible and to work with banks that will provide the best service. Float, however, is an important source of income for European banks and as long as the payment is in their systems it is out of control for the companies.

Thus automated control systems have arisen in response to specific U.S. requirements. In Europe, companies' efforts are directed to controling the float the banks create for themselves, at the companies' expense.

AN INTERNATIONAL CASH MANAGEMENT PROGRAM

The points made above can be illustrated by reviewing a complex export collection problem and showing how the solution addresses both the cash movement aspects and the distribution of information for control purposes. As an example, ABC Company has subsidiaries in every country in Western Europe, five of which have plants that export directly to third-party buyers all over Europe. Many of these customers regularly place orders with more than one of the five ABC plants. While the accounts receivable are maintained on the books of the exporting plants, the ABC company located in the buyer's country has direct credit and collection responsibility. Head-

EXHIBIT 4 EXPORT CONCENTRATION SYSTEM FOR ABC COMPANY

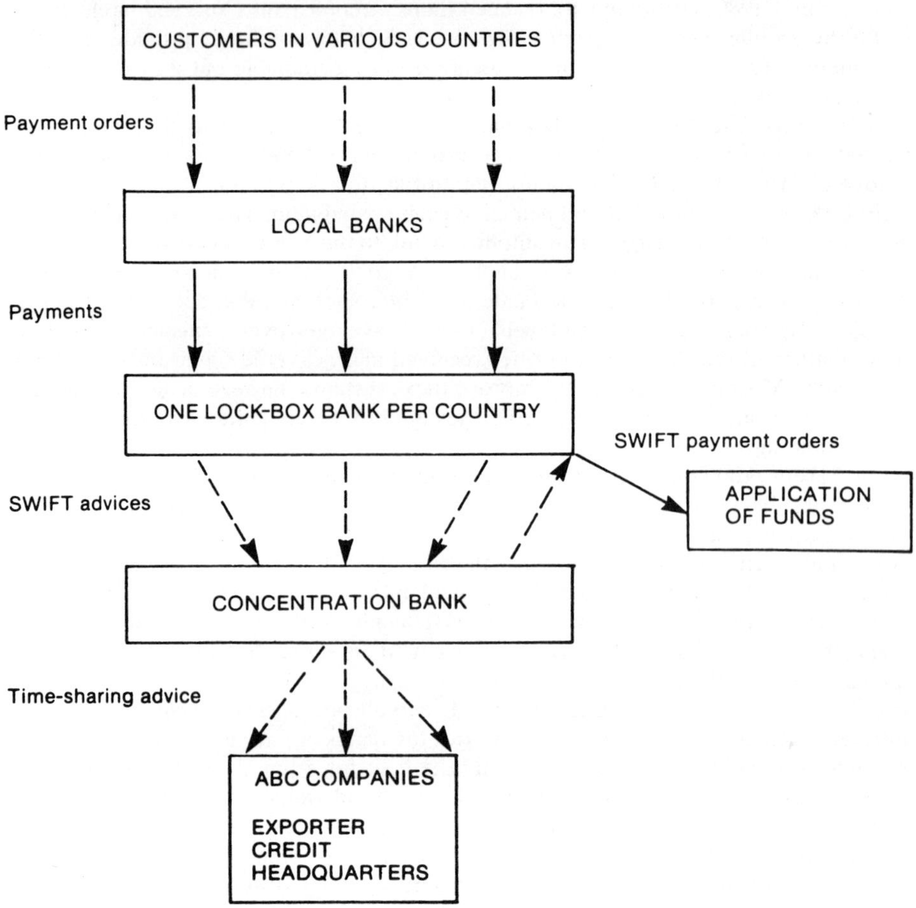

quarters monitors consolidated credit and foreign exchange exposure. Most invoices are denominated in the currencies of the buyers.

A bank was asked to design a system that would (1) maximize the availability of the export proceeds in the currencies designated by the exporting plants; and (2) provide prompt advice of payment to all ABC parties concerned—the exporter, the company responsible for credit and collection, and headquarters. The following collection and concentration system was developed. (See also Exhibit 4.)

1. ABC designated a concentration bank and opened accounts at this bank in all currencies received.
2. The concentration bank opened one lock-box account in each country from which ABC receives the currency. Lock-box banks were chosen for their known internal efficiency and their SWIFT membership.
3. ABC requested its customers to make their local currency payments to the designated lock-box banks via their own local banks.

4. The lock-box banks advised the concentration bank via SWIFT of incoming amounts.
5. The concentration bank sold the incoming amounts to a sale in the foreign exchange market, credited them to a currency account in its books, or deposited them at interest. Processing at the concentration bank is highly automated, requiring minimal intervention by staff.
6. The concentration bank reported the amounts received and their application to the three ABC units concerned via a time-sharing system to which all ABC companies have easy access and which has an automated link to the bank's processing system.

The result was a system with the following advantages.

1. Optimal availability of usable funds through application of the lock-box collection concept coupled with fast communication (SWIFT)
2. Concentration of funds with one bank, which facilitates final application of the money in ABC's cash pool or wire transfers to other banks
3. One central source of payment information that is made available simultaneously to all parties
4. Efficiencies in operations, communications, and auditing because of the use of one concentration bank for all money flows

BEYOND CASH MANAGEMENT

Companies that practice cash management as a discipline and familiarize themselves with the different environments in which they have to work generally succeed in obtaining important improvements in funds availability without too many problems. They bring money flows under more effective control, make use of modern transfer systems, and influence their customers to do the same. They also realize that some float is unavoidable and that there are limits to the demands they can set on their banks, limits that differ from country to country.

At this point, a change takes place in the challenge of the job. The increased control the cash manager has obtained over funds flows brings with it the flow of a large amount of information to his or her desk, ranging from plans, budgets, and forecasts to data from internal systems that monitor accounts payable and receivable, capital expenditures, and short-term investments. From the outside, the banks supply a constant stream of transaction data and information on economic conditions; foreign exchange market and interest rate information comes in from a variety of sources. Somehow, all of this has to be sorted, analyzed, distributed, and acted upon in the treasury department—truly, a formidable challenge that goes well beyond cash management into the problems of managing information to maximize the opportunities for cash management.

The large companies that have solved their cash management problems in a technical sense are now faced with the problem of integrating the data they receive from these many sources into a coordinated information system that (1) facilitates decision making and (2) makes the appropriate information available to other relevant parties. Many of the data originate in computer systems of one kind or another, both internal and external, but are then coordinated manually in the treasury department. Balance and activity figures are used in several reports and forms are filled out by hand for different purposes, often to be reentered into other computer systems. This kind of work, and many tasks like it, can be more efficiently and accurately done if the treasury department collects the data relevant to its function into a data bank maintained on a minicomputer in its department. The necessary reports can then be programmed and much manual work saved.

Contemporary surveys show that leading companies look for ways to gain access to data via electronic means, to employ this in models used as decision-making aids, and to communicate electronically with both their other corporate systems and banks. This requires a new approach to data processing, entirely different from the construction of the typical large-volume processing systems in companies and banks. A treasury information system works with a large variety of different inputs, each in its own format, and has to produce usable output in a highly time-critical environment. The financial markets operate with rigid deadlines for payment orders and investments. Therefore, the system has to be highly flexible and extremely responsive while also allowing for simulations and comparisons of different solutions to a problem.

Most important, however, a treasury information system has to respond to the company's precise, specific requirements as to priorities, organizational and financial structure, methods of doing business, and cash management techniques. Every company is different in these respects. For that reason, treasury information systems must be custom-designed for each company. They are never an off-the-shelf product. A company's needs can grow beyond the standard cash management services of banks to highly individual information requirements. Banks' main line cash management products can, of course, continue to be used but now in the framework of a larger, coordinated system that can be designed only with a thorough understanding of the total function of the treasury department in the company.

What impact will this have on international cash management? To even begin to answer the question one first has to make an inventory of the kinds of information the international cash manager needs and one has to explore techniques for organizing this information. Internal corporate information comes into the treasury from accounting, controllers, international divisions, overseas units, exporting and importing units. These data concern transactions, balances, investments, borrowings, foreign exchange exposure and transactions, credit terms, and so forth. Banks supply transactions and balance data, information on markets, and advice of various kinds. Other sources bring in economic and financial information. The media used by these many sources include mail, wire services, telex, and computer networks accessible via terminal. Few treasurers believe that all of this information is put to optimal use.

A system is needed that receives information into a central file, a library with separate "volumes" containing different kinds of data that are accessible not only individually but in a coordinated way. For instance, in order to monitor cash balances of overseas subsidiaries and to suggest better uses of funds, information on the balances can be combined with cash forecasts, foreign exchange forecasts, interest rates, regulations, and foreign exchange exposure into an optimization model. Such a model can make mathmatically based recommendations, within parameters that reflect policy and other subjective considerations. In the absence of a model, the cash manager can either refrain from any action because there are too many data to consider or use his or her intuition adjusted by opinions of trusted advisers and of colleagues in the company. With a model to convert a multitude of data into logical recommendations the treasurer has a better decision-making tool, one to be used jointly with personal knowledge and personal contacts.

In this way, many treasury functions that are presently very difficult to systematize can be better performed. In some cases, information management is a question of consolidating data; sometimes, decision making is the objective. Always the problem revolves around the need to integrate data from a variety of sources in a variety of formats into a form that is presented as useful information rather than a collection of data. This is the new challenge to the cash manager. When the cash manager has solved immediate cash flow problems he or she has to improve the sources and uses of information, without which one cannot go beyond technical cash management. This development underlines the interrelationships between the different functions in the international treasury department, including foreign exchange exposure, cash movements, investments, bank relations, and current borrowing. For many aspects of these functions the same information is needed and it is the cash manager whose needs will be most urgent on a day-to-day basis.

SECTION 8.12

INTERNATIONAL FINANCIAL MANAGEMENT: THE OVERALL INVESTMENT AND FINANCING PLAN

CONTENTS

SECTION **8.12**

INTERNATIONAL FINANCIAL MANAGEMENT: THE OVERALL INVESTMENT AND FINANCING PLAN

Gunter Dufey

This concluding section is concerned with financing decisions in international companies. The purpose here is to show the **interrelationships of the various aspects of funding decisions,** highlighting the complexities of liability management in international companies. It is designed to serve as a link between the ad hoc decision making and the ex post rationalizations that one finds in the corporate world in contrast to attempts to achieve optimization through formal modeling of business decision situations, a task that requires, by definition, a high degree of abstraction.

From the perspective of international corporate financial management, the **definition of international business** and—by implication—the international firm, is quite comprehensive: It includes all business activities in which management must make financial decisions, taking into account simultaneously (1) the conditions prevailing in **two or more financial markets,** (2) regulatory and institutional **barriers** to the international movement of funds, and (3) the changes in the **exchange rates** of national monies. To illustrate, instead of taking into account one set of national tax rules, one rate of inflation, one set of interest rates, one integrated system of money and capital markets and the assorted institutions, management must now take into account the complex interactions of at least two tax systems, two interest rate structures, and two sets of financial institutions when making decisions. Obviously, this entails additional complications and risks. However—and this represents the other side of the coin—management has available more alternatives and, therefore, better opportunities to attain the firm's objectives: to enhance the value of the business enterprise by minimizing the cost of funds and the risk to the firm.

Thus the range of enterprises for which the practice and theory of international financial management is relevant is much more inclusive than the traditional concepts of the multinational firm (MNF), which is defined typically as a firm having a substantial portion of its activities and assets deployed in different countries. The concept relevant for financial management comprises all firms that are involved in international business, directly or indirectly, to such an extent that the managerial process must take into account the complexities of a **multimarket, multicurrency environment.**

This comprehensive view of the international firm is particularly important when the focus is on a special issue of international financial management, namely, **corporate funding decisions.** If properly viewed, such decisions are relevant for a much larger group of firms than those that conduct business operations abroad through foreign business establishments, typically referred to as MNFs.

THE ALTERNATIVES

From the standpoint of the individual operating unit, for example, a foreign affiliate that is typically in the legal form of a subsidiary and undertakes the asset commitment, two basic alternatives present themselves. First, funds can be obtained from **within** the corporate group. This includes the use of the affiliate's own funds through a reduction of cash or the liquidation of other assets. Alternatively, funds can be obtained from either the parent or one of the sister affiliates who use their own resources. Second, funds can be obtained from outside sources, either directly, from the financial markets, or via the parent and other affiliates. These alternatives are schematically outlined in Exhibit 1.

EXHIBIT 1 FUNDING ALTERNATIVES IN MULTINATIONAL FIRMS

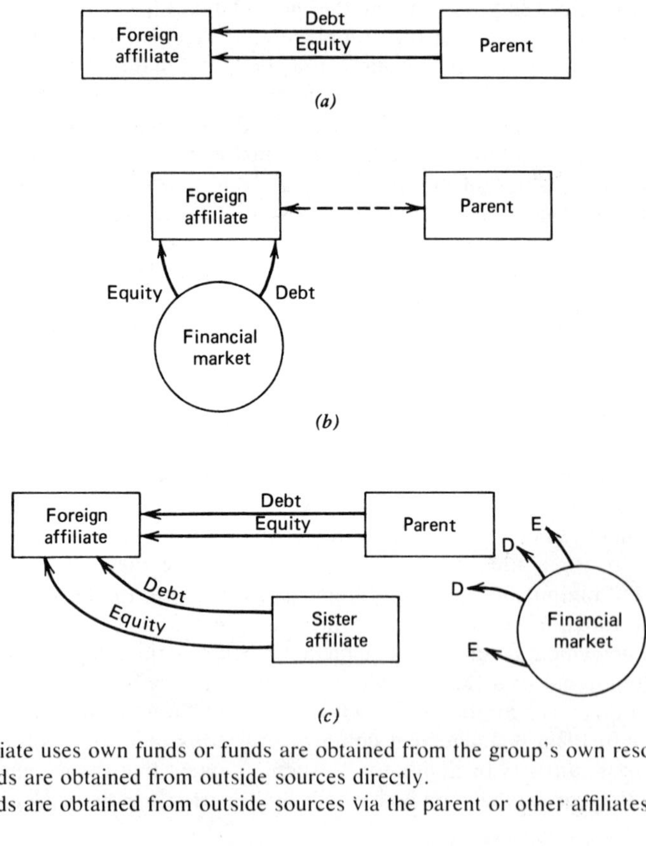

[a]Affiliate uses own funds or funds are obtained from the group's own resources.
[b]Funds are obtained from outside sources directly.
[c]Funds are obtained from outside sources via the parent or other affiliates.

Unless the foreign affiliate uses its own means, a basic decision has to be made in which form to inject the funds into this entity that employs them. And while these decisions are all the same in a formal sense, multinational enterprise financing requires careful **distinction between outside relations and intragroup transactions.** Thus while the labels might look alike, the economic significance of the decision is quite different, except when joint ventures are involved. In this case, complex managerial and financial control issues result that are typical for joint ventures. And while both corporate managements (and academic researchers) are normally unwilling to tackle such problems, strong nationalistic tendencies in many countries make this form of foreign operation much more prevalent than business conditions would suggest.

Limiting the discussion to wholly owned affiliates, it must be pointed out that unlike the case of transactions, the distinction between inside and outside funds is of limited significance. This is because ultimately all funds are outside funds **in an opportunity cost sense;** the alternative use for retained profits is always to repay loans and/or to increase dividends to stockholders. Thus the only difference between the cost of external and internal funds (capital) can be attributed to agency costs (issuing and underwriting fees), restrictive covenants, and/or tax-related costs. To illustrate, a number of countries apply a lower tax rate to distributed earnings than to funds retained within the corporation. In the absence of specific institutional costs or incentives, the cost of internally generated funds in a multinational firm and its affiliates is equal to the cost of capital for the group as a whole.

CAPITAL STRUCTURE DECISIONS

Capital structure decisions are particularly important when financial structure decisions dealing with leverage (or gearing) must be made. To the extent that any priorities can be established among the complex, interrelated steps of a funding decision in an MNF, such strategic considerations probably take first place. Of course, the reason why the debt/equity ratio matters so much is that it determines the financial risk of the enterprise. Because of the contractually fixed nature of payments to debt holders, returns to the owners of equity will fluctuate more in response to given, unanticipated fluctuations of operating returns the higher the proportion of debt relative to equity. Thus a positive partial relationship between the **risk of equity returns** and **leverage ratios** can be documented. Because of nontrivial default costs one can also find that a firm's leverage ratios and enterprise risk are negatively related. The interaction between the tax shield provided by debt and the various costs associated with default provide the theoretical support for an **optimal capital structure.** And to the extent that these factors are influenced by environmental factors such as tax laws and factors affecting the cost and probability of bankruptcy, one finds significant **country factors** in the capital structures of MNFs based in various home countries.

This rationale is often mistakenly applied in the analysis of funding decisions involving individual, wholly owned affiliates. What is usually overlooked is the fact that such wholly owned affiliates of MNFs have a distinct and separate debt/equity ratio only if the parent is prepared to allow the affiliate in question to default on its debt without coming to its rescue. On the other hand, as long as the rest of the MNF group has a **legal** (loan guarantees) or an effective **moral obligation** to prevent the affiliate from defaulting—even if this threatens the survival of the remainder of the group—the individual affiliate has **no independent debt/equity ratio.** Its true leverage ratio is equal to that of the consolidated group.

Since virtually all MNFs feel obliged to their wholly owned (and sometimes even partially owned) affiliates, simply because they cannot afford to lose their financial respectability, the debt/equity ratio of the affiliate is determined by purely institutional factors. Most prominent among such are (1) **statutory laws,** which prescribe a required minimum equity level in many countries; (2) **tax laws,** which often treat interest payments differently than payments on equity (dividends); (3) **exchange control regulations,** which are usually less restrictive when interest payments are concerned; (4) **expropriation risk,** which can be lessened if the parent expects to default on its local debt in the specific case that the lending institutions have also been taken over by the government in question, or the lending institutions are state-owned already.

Thus the debt/equity decision for foreign affiliates is either a **purely legal one**—as opposed to a financial decision—or it involves **strategic questions of ownership** to the extent that third-party investors, local or otherwise, own a part of the affiliate's equity.

When it comes to making debt/equity decisions for the parent, or rather the group as a whole, a very difficult issue arises: Which market's standards will govern its "acceptable" debt/equity ratio? For domestic firms, the answer is usually quite clear. In different national capital markets, certain target debt/equity ratios have been established by market forces for different kinds of firms. These acceptable debt/equity ratios are influenced by the nature of the firm. To illustrate, banks and public utilities, whose operating risk is relatively low, are permitted to have a much higher proportion of debt before the market begins to penalize these enterprises by increasing the required rate of return on equity or the interest on their debt relative to, for example, capital goods producers, whose return on assets is very much subject to the vagaries of the business cycle. The problem for the multinational firm is that different national markets differ quite a bit in terms of standards for acceptable debt/equity ratios, and to the extent that MNFs sell their equity or borrow funds in many countries they must choose a reference market.

Theoretically, this question is largely unsolved because empirical work in finance has not sufficiently progressed to answer the question, "Precisely how are financial assets priced internationally?" That is, which is a more correct approximation of reality, that markets are separated or that they are integrated? In practice, most MNFs do not have to face this problem head on because the great bulk of the equity is usually held by investors of a national market whose standards dominate the applicable debt/equity ratio. However, as more and more companies make an effort to broaden their stockholder base internationally (e.g., by listing their stock on the exchanges of two or more countries) this issue will become more and more acute.

THE CURRENCY DENOMINATION OF DEBT

Next to capital structure decisions, the issue of **debt denomination** is probably the most important strategic aspect of the funding decision. In the absence of specific and identifiable market imperfections, currency decisions cannot be made on the basis of financial market factors alone. They must be coordinated with an analysis of the impact of **currency fluctuations** on the firm's operating cash flows (i.e., **corporate exchange risk**).

The first task here is how to gauge the impact of exchange rate changes on a firm, that is, how to estimate the firm's foreign exchange **exposure.**

The issue has been somewhat confused by the fact that the firm's financial results tend to be invariably compiled by methods based on principles of accrual accounting, which often provide a different picture than the data relevant for business decision making (i.e., expected future net cash flows and their concomitant risk profiles). Thus considerable effort has been devoted in the academic literature, and considerable efforts continue to be expended within corporations, to reconcile differences between the effects of exchange rate changes on an enterprise in terms of accounting data (i.e., **accounting** or **translation exposure**) and the cash flow effects—often referred to as "**economic,**" or **"transaction," exposure.**

The specific differences between accounting and economic exposure are summarized as follows:

1. Accounting data do not capture all commitments of the firm that give rise to exchange risk.
2. Accounting values of assets and liabilities do not reflect the respective contribution to the total expected net cash flow of the firm because of the historical cost principle.
3. Translation rules do not distinguish between the expected and unexpected exchange rates.

From here on, the focus is not on accounting exposure, but on the economic concept of exchange risk. This concept must be compatible with the general economic framework of the firm. Accordingly, this entity exists and has value because the owners and managers expect a positive net cash flow from the exploitation of a competitive advantage. To be precise, at any point in time those responsible for the entrepreneurial function in the firm perceive a certain market opportunity, or a set of market opportunities, that they attempt to exploit by developing and refining an appropriate range of capabilities and skills (i.e., a **competitive advantage**). (Of course, market opportunities and competitive advantages change continually; thus what really exists is a dynamic system of search and adaption.) In order to provide the product or service competitively, the firm requires the set of assets (i.e., working capital, plant and equipment). And since the firm has assets it must fund these assets. Thus for teaching or manufacturing firms at least, the causation clearly runs from expected cash flows accruing to (mostly) real assets to (financial) liabilities.

As far as the concept of economic foreign exchange risk is concerned, this thumbnail sketch of the theory of the firm has a number of important implications.

First, since the purpose of assets is to generate positive net cash flows, asset values depend on their contribution to the **expected cash flow of the firm.** Consequently, the change in the value of an asset caused by exchange rate variations depends on the impact of such changes on the expected net cash flow of the firm. It follows, then, that any analysis of the exchange risk of a firm, or one of its parts, must properly begin with an analysis of the **impact of exchange rate changes on the expected stream of revenues and the expected flow of expenditures** over time. And since foreign exchange rate changes are only one of many reasons why expected net cash flows will not materialize, foreign exchange risk must be defined as the **additional** variability of the expected net cash flow of a firm, the variability that is caused by exchange rate changes.

While there is little new about this concept—it is a straightforward application of conventional ideas from corporate finance and the theory of the firm to exchange risk—it differs considerably from the traditional concept of currency exposure that focuses on the change in value assets and liabilities whose return is contractually fixed.

However, only financial institutions such as banks have the bulk of their assets in claims whose return is contractually set. In contrast, firms whose business is to provide real goods and services have the essential proportion of their investment in assets whose cash flow is **not fixed by contract.**

It must be clearly recognized that without contractual fixing of prices, the return on assets, and with it their value, is affected not only by exchange rate changes but also by price changes caused by exchange rate changes. And since trading and manufacturing firms hold financial assets and liabilities only secondarily (i.e., to support their activities requiring real assets), the key to the analysis of corporate exchange risk is to assess the behavior of cash flows from real (tangible) assets, taking into account both **exchange rate changes** and **concomitant price changes.**

To facilitate the analysis three concepts are introduced that appear relevant and useful to interpret data available within multinational enterprises: (1) **currency of recording;** (2) **currency of denomination**; and (3) **currency of determination.**

An analysis of the exchange risk of the firm begins very often with an inspection of historical data available in corporate accounting records. Such corporate records are always kept in the currency of the country of incorporation. All entries are made in that currency, although the underlying contractual claim might be in another currency. A typical example is foreign currency debt that is recorded in the currency of the borrowing entity, while the obligation in respect to payment of principal and interest is in terms of the foreign currency. The currency of recording, then, is an **accounting** concept.

The currency of denomination is the currency in which various contracts are **stated.** It is a legal concept. The term is self-explanatory and it is straightforward as long as financial claims are involved.

However, when nonfinancial assets are involved, matters get more complex. Inventories serve as a good example—their value is determined not only by changes in the exchange rate, but also by subsequent price changes of the products involved caused by the exchange rate change. But what is true in respect to inventories applies, in fact, to all assets whose cash flow, whether positive or negative, is not contractually fixed. A brief illustration is offered: A firm that requires for its production process raw materials from abroad will find that its stream of expenses for raw materials in terms of local currency go up when the domestic currency depreciates relative to the foreign currency. This is true even if the firm, as a matter of business practice, contracts, invoices, and pays for each **individual** shipment in its domestic currency. If the price increase in terms of local currency compensates completely for the depreciation of that currency, the magnitude of the resulting cash flow, while **denominated** in the importer's home currency, is **determined** by the relative value of the foreign currency.

Of course, other situations can be less extreme. If foreign exporters are unable to maintain prices in terms of their home currency, only a proportion of the importer's expense flow is determined by the foreign currency. And if this proportion is as small as zero (i.e., when exporters must lower their prices to stay competitive with other suppliers of the importer) the currency of denomination and the currency of determination are the same. An analysis of competitive market conditions is necessary to get at the important distinction: currency of denomination versus determination. The underlying concept is, of course, equivalent to the elasticity concept well known in international economics.

The significance of this distinction is that while the currency of denomination is quite frequently subject to management discretion, prices and, therefore, cash flow are determined by **external factors** beyond the control of the firm.

An additional element must be introduced to complete the analysis—the element of **time.** Empirical evidence shows that price changes and exchange rate changes will cancel out over an appropriate time span. This phenomenon has long been recognized in macroeconomics with the **purchasing power parity theory** and the **law of one price.** Looking at individual goods and services one will find that while these relationships hold as a tendency, the adjustment process can take substantial periods of time. To make the implication for the firm clear it can be stated negatively: The firm is subject to economic exchange risk from its operations only to the extent that there is a **time lag** involved in the adjustment of prices to exchange rate changes.

From a practical perspective, the analysis of exchange risk from operations (i.e., the basic activity of the firm) can be captured with three questions.

1. How much **pricing flexibility** does the firm have? That is, can the change in margins offset the effect of the exchange rate change?
2. How **diversified** are markets for inputs and outputs? Or, to add the time element, when can the firm shift markets for its output and sources of supply?
3. Are there any **volume effects** that could compensate for changes in profit margins?

The discussion of economic exposure allows one to draw some conclusions regarding the effects of exchange rate changes on the value of the firm.

First, when properly measured the impact of an exchange rate change on a firm (or a part thereof) depends on the change in **net cash flows** caused by variations in the relevant exchange rates.

Second, this effect is strictly **firm specific**—no general statements can be made that are valid for many firms.

Third, the range of companies that are potentially subject to exchange risk is quite broad, comprising not only firms with foreign investments or foreign markets, but also domestic firms that face extensive foreign competition.

Fourth, international involvement, even on a very extensive scale, does not necessarily subject the firm to exchange risk. For instance, when the firm's cash flows are so diversified that positive and negative effects offset one another, net cash flow and, therefore, the value of the firm is not subject to exchange rate changes. Thus very large international firms with many foreign entities who sell into and purchase from many markets have very often **little real economic exposure.**

Fifth, transactions among wholly owned corporate entities can affect foreign exchange risk **only if relations with outside entities** are affected (e.g., providers of capital denominated in different currencies, tax authorities, foreign exchange control authorities, etc.).

FOREIGN EXCHANGE RATE FORECASTING

Obviously, without changes in exchange rates firms would not be subject to exchange risk. (However, their value might be similarly in jeopardy as a result of real purchasing power risks when rates of inflation differ among countries but exchange rates are fixed, or when international financial transactions become subject to controls and restrictions in order to maintain fixed exchange rates.) It is not surprising that a considerable volume of the literature on corporate foreign exchange risk and corporate foreign exchange policy is concerned with an analysis of foreign exchange rate changes per se. However, the disproportionate emphasis on currency forecasting appears to be misplaced. Obviously, if a firm's management were able to forecast future spot rates with a sufficient degree of accuracy, regular trading and manufacturing activities would become irrelevant. The firm would turn into a pure foreign exchange trading operation, that is, a financial institution with contractual assets and liabilities.

What, then, is the proper role of foreign exchange rate analysis in the context of corporate foreign exchange risk?

In this context it is useful to recognize that the foreign exchange market already provides important information about future spot rates by way of **forward rates.** Here market participants contractually agree to exchange currencies at specific future points in time. Such rates can be taken as indicators of the market's consensus regarding the future trend of exchange rates. The support for this proposition comes from the consideration that speculators could get rich quickly when they became aware of **systematic** deviations of **future spot rates** from **forward rates.**

Foreign exchange market practitioners will point out that forward rates are, in fact, determined by international interest rate differences rather than expectations. While the first part of this statement is undoubtedly true, it leaves unresolved the issue of the determinants for international interest rate differences. But the same speculative considerations apply: When in an uncontrolled market investment opportunities are available that differ only in terms of the currency of denomination, international interest rate differences must reflect expected exchange rate changes. Otherwise one must explain why profit-seeking investors and borrowers would not exploit such profit opportunities and, in doing so, move rates in such ways that the very incentives disappear.

This whole issue can be clarified by stressing the difference between the well-known **interest rate parity theorem,** and an ex ante relationship known as the **external Fisher effect.** The interest rate parity relationship implies that, ex post, all interest rate differentials and forward currency premia discounts are constantly equated by arbitrage. However, interest rate differentials as well as forward premia and discounts change with the **change in expectations.**

How are such expectations formed? Precisely because the opportunities for profits are so tempting, a large number of professionals are constantly trying to beat the market. Foremost among these are the foreign exchange dealers of major banks and their colleagues trading in the international money and bond markets. But they are not the only ones; indeed, one must include all those who undertake economic transactions that affect exchange rates directly or indirectly and are influenced in their decisions by exchange rate expectations that differ from the market's current expectations—as reflected in forward premia and discounts or interest rate differentials respectively.

These **speculators** constantly monitor all available data and pieces of information and process them with informal or formal models with respect to the expected exchange rates. Since those who do not have access to good data or who have poor models get bested in a competitive world by those who do, only the best forecasters survive. Thus the market as a whole, at any point in time, has a very good, indeed the best available ability to arrive at an exchange rate forecast that is quickly incorporated in prices (i.e., international interest rates and differences between spot and forward rates). It is this process of exchange rate and interest rate formation that is the essence of a concept known as **"market efficiency."**

One can conclude, therefore, that when international financial markets are uncontrolled, **forward rates** or **international rate differences** provide the best available indicator as to the prevailing expectation regarding the future course of the exchange rate. One can realistically assume that the same expectations also prevail in markets for real goods and services, including wages. But this means that prices, when contractually fixed, reflect the then-prevailing expectations about price changes and exchange rate changes. As a consequence, what matters is not currency changes per se, but **deviations** from expected rates.

In summary, the market forms expectations about future exchange rate changes that are reflected in prices, wages, and interest rates. But the expectations can be gauged only in situations where organized markets for futures exist. This is true in respect to convertible currencies and interest rates in relatively free financial markets, but only in respect to very few real goods and services.

What must also be clearly recognized is that because expectations are all formed on the basis of current information, data, and models, and as new and surprising things are constantly happening, expectations are subject to change (i.e., actual future spot rates will deviate from expected ones), but it is impossible to know in which direction and by how much.

One must then distinguish among three relevant concepts of exchange rate changes: **absolute changes,** which are of concern to accountants who have the benefit of hindsight; **expected changes,** which are important for those who want to know what the prevailing expectations are; and finally, **unexpected changes,** that is, the source of risk and uncertainty. The other task in the forecasting of currency changes is closely related to the first—to assess the nature of a possible bias. In this respect it is necessary to clearly identify the reasons that give rise to the belief that distortions exist, that is, that interest differentials of forward premia can be expected to overestimate or underestimate systematically the actual exchange rate change. Two possible sources of bias exist. First, it might result from an obvious **market imperfection.** For example, the existence of extensive credit allocation, heavy-handed administrative barriers to international borrowing and lending, and tight exchange controls would provide prima facie evidence for the argument that forward rates deviate systematically from the expected future exchange rate. Likewise, when there is a general expectation that such controls could be imposed, a systematic bias is likely to be evident. In any case, forward rates or interest rate differentials will provide a good starting point for forecasting and for the identification of profit opportunities stemming from **political risks.**

Second, analytically and practically more difficult to deal with is the case that systematic ex ante deviations exist even without such barriers. There are a variety of arguments that support currency premia. Essentially, they all arise from the possibility that **exchange rate changes can be correlated with returns on other assets,** creating a **systematic risk** that cannot be diversified away for speculators. The prevailing view of researchers, however, is that if such a risk premium can be identified ex ante at all, it is probably so small that it can be disregarded for practical purposes.

In order to develop a workable foreign exchange policy, the whole issue can be distilled into two questions.

First, is it reasonable to assume that forward rates and interest rate differentials can be used as **unbiased** estimators of expected future exchange rates?

Second, is it possible to pinpoint specific **sources of bias**? And can the size of the bias be estimated by comparing the interest differential of forward premia to a rate obtained by a forecast, using such indicators as market rates, inflation differentials, balance of payments trends, and the results of statistical forecasting methods?

The answers to these questions have important implications to the management of foreign exchange risk. In the first instance, the problem is how to deal with the **impact of unexpected changes**; in the second instance, management must also take into consideration **whether and how the bias might affect its decisions**.

MANAGING CORPORATE FOREIGN EXCHANGE RISKS

The concept of economic exposure developed above provides the essential stepping-stone toward developing a corporate foreign exchange policy. Since foreign exchange risk stems from changes in net cash flow caused by unexpected exchange rate changes, the essence of a foreign exchange policy must be to avoid or to offset, as far as possible, negative cash flow effects associated with such unexpected exchange rate changes.

Here, the proper structuring of operations suggests itself, involving essentially **strategic business decisions**: appropriate diversification of markets for both output and sources of supplies, building into operations a high degree of flexibility so management can change prices, markets, and sources of supply when an exchange rate change has an unfavorable impact on expected cash flow. The advantage of such policies is that they get at the source of exchange risk. However, the problem is that they all involve substantial **costs**. Typically, products, production processes, and market and supply policies are all established on the basis of fundamental profitability considerations that compel the firm to make various **commitments**, which are either of a contractual or of a strategic nature. The result is a locked-in effect that imposes very often heavy penalties on the firm if prices or business strategy are to be changed quickly. Thus only in extremis will a company resort to operating policies in order to deal with exchange risk.

As an alternative, a firm can use **liability management**. As is shown above, in a financial market where rates are established in an efficient manner, and one that is uncontrolled, no anticipated gain can be had by changing currency denomination and maturities of financial assets. Thus when one neglects relatively minor transactions costs, the expected cost of changing the currency denomination or maturity of debt is zero. Therefore, liability management is the first line of defense to protect the firm's **total** net cash flow from unexpected exchange rate changes.

The principle of using liability management is quite straightforward: The opportunity cost of debt is directly correlated with unexpected exchange rate changes. The discounted cash outflow of foreign currency debt increases or falls relative to home currency debt. Since debt in a profitable firm that has achieved an optimal capital structure is never repaid but only rolled over, it is the change in the **effective interest rate** that causes the cash flow effect. The essence of using liability management to reduce foreign exchange risk is to fund the firm with debt denominated in the currency that causes the changing value of cash flows from operations to be offset by changes in the negative cash flows from effective interest payments.

While the general principle behind this policy is quite simple, the actual implementation requires considerable forecasting ability—not of exchange rates, but of the **behavior of the firm's cash flows in respect to unexpected exchange rate changes**.

Two issues closely related to debt denomination must be settled at the same time: first, how much debt is needed and second, what can be said about the maturity of debt policy?

The answer to the first question flows straight from the general principle established above: The firm needs a volume of debt that provides a change in cash outflows sufficient to offset changes in cash flows from operations. If a firm does not have enough room in its balance sheet, it can use what might be called "phantom debt," that is, **forward contracts**. Such forward contracts are contingent liabilities with implicit interest rates reflecting exchange rate expectations.

As to the second problem, it is necessary to distinguish two aspects of **debt maturity**: (1) the **availability** of funds, and (2) the **duration** of the interest rate. Since foreign exchange policy based on liability management uses the lever of the contractually fixed interest rate, it is the second aspect of maturity that matters here.

The general principle stated above also provides guidance to the maturity decision. The decisive element is the time pattern of changes in cash flows from operations. Adverse effects from exchange rate changes do not last forever; ultimately the firm can raise prices, change markets and sources of supply, and even move production facilities if necessary. All this takes time, and the contractual fixing of prevailing exchange rate expectations incorporated in the interest rate over an appropriate time frame provides the compensating effects. This time pattern of changing cash flows must be matched by a corresponding maturity structure of debt.

Are principles of exchange rate policy altered when the forward rate or interest rate differential cannot be regarded as unbiased predictors?

Where the term structure of exchange rates or interest rates is expected to deviate systematically from the actual expectations because of effective capital and exchange controls, or because of other specific market imperfections, the resulting profit opportunities provide a preference for one currency over the other, since successive currency changes cannot be expected to compensate completely for the interest rate differential. If the firm is in such a situation, two alternatives are possible. First, the currency in which management wishes to denominate its debt for exchange risk purposes happens to also be the cheaper currency. This is the case of congruence. Second, and equally possible, however, is the **conflict** case—the currency in which the debt should be denominated from the point of view of exchange risk management happens to be precisely that in which costs are expected to be higher.

Only the second situation is a challenge for management. As a first approach, management will attempt to avoid the conflict by trying to circumvent capital controls. Often this can be done quite legally through internal funds management. It is important also to remember in this context that a desired debt denomination can be achieved not only directly, but also indirectly; the currency denomination of a liability can be altered with a forward contract.

If the conflict cannot be avoided in this manner, a painful but well-known trade-off has to be made between risk and return, that is, the risk of additional variability due to exchange rate changes and the returns available by funding the firm's operation in the currency that is expected to have an effectively lower cost.

INTRACOMPANY TRANSFERS

The problems encountered in the financial structure decision of a multinational firm and its individual affiliates turn up again when tactical questions of funding international operations are being considered. By their nature MNFs have complicated legal structures, such as that depicted in Exhibit 2.

Of course, Exhibit 2 is a schematic presentation only and in reality an almost infinite number of combinations are possible. For financial management, this raises the question as to which one of the entities should contract with providers of funds. In respect to equity, this is almost invariably the parent company, especially if the firm has a policy of maintaining wholly owned affiliates. With respect to debt, however, there are many possibilities. And unless the answer to the question is, "The same affiliate that needs the funds," another decision must be made right away—how to move the funds through the various corporate entities to their final destination. In turn this decision is directly related to yet another question: In what legal form and in which currency should funds be injected in the affiliate that acquires productive assets?

Having affiliates in many financial markets provides the MNF with opportunities to **minimize the cost of funds** for the corporation by borrowing wherever the effective cost is least. In practice, however, there are serious constraints that limit these opportunities. After all, it is because of the government restrictions, and to a certain extent institutional arrangements, that the cost of funds in various markets will not be equalized through direct arbitrage.

The only real advantage that the MNF has in this respect is that it can somewhat more easily circumvent such restrictions because of its particular structure of centrally coordinated, but legally separate entities. To illustrate, many countries have tight controls on direct lending to borrowers abroad. Theoretically, then, a multi-

EXHIBIT 2 LEGAL STRUCTURE OF A MULTINATIONAL CORPORATION

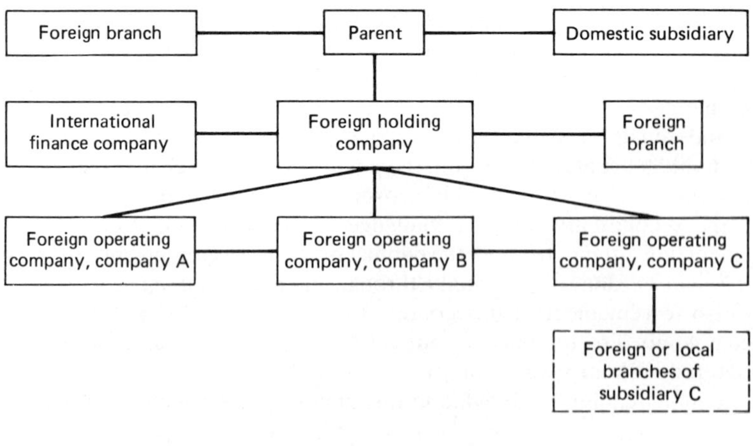

national firm can get around this restriction by having its local affiliate borrow the funds and subsequently transfer them in some form to its parent or sister affiliates. Governments, of course, are aware of such operations, too, and they have usually issued all kinds of rules and regulations to prevent such international **intracorporate transfers of funds**. However, if these regulations were written and administered too tightly, they would strangle international trade and investment. Thus firms usually have some leeway in transferring funds, although their flexibility is much more limited than is usually implied by critics of multinational firms.

In an integrated MNF, where each affiliate has dealings with the others, transfers of funds can usually be effected because most are simply necessary to run the operation, regardless of the existence of restrictions. Thus the question is not one of whether or not to shift funds among the MNF's affiliates, but how much and in which direction. This also highlights the fact that it is often impossible to determine the "correct" arm's length transaction, not only for government but even the corporate controller. To illustrate, economists and accountants still argue about correct cost allocation, transfer prices, and interest charges in multidivision operations that are closely integrated. Interestingly, many financial executives in multinational firms point to the fact that their ability to move funds within the corporate family is severely restricted not only by government, but by the disadvantage of distorting their internal control system.

That MNFs do have some freedom to move funds internationally is simply based on the fact that funds flows can be effected in very many ways, as depicted in Exhibit 3.

Analytically, it is very important to generalize on a point that is made above in respect to the debt/equity ratios: Intracompany transfers of funds do not give rise to any change in the cost of funds or the risk of the multinational firm as such. These transfers have an impact only in terms of taxes, exchange controls, and other regulatory aspects. The cost of funds and financial risk is affected only when there is a change in the kind or amount of **outside sources of funds**. Thus the determinants of such inside transactions are to be found in tax and regulatory matters only.

While all this sounds very complex—and in reality it is complex because of all the environmental factors that impinge upon the decision (tax effects, exchange regulations, financial market regulations and practices, banking relations, etc.)—the basic conceptual framework is quite simple and can be summarized as follows. If an

EXHIBIT 3 FINANCIAL AND REAL FLOWS IN THE MULTINATIONAL FIRM

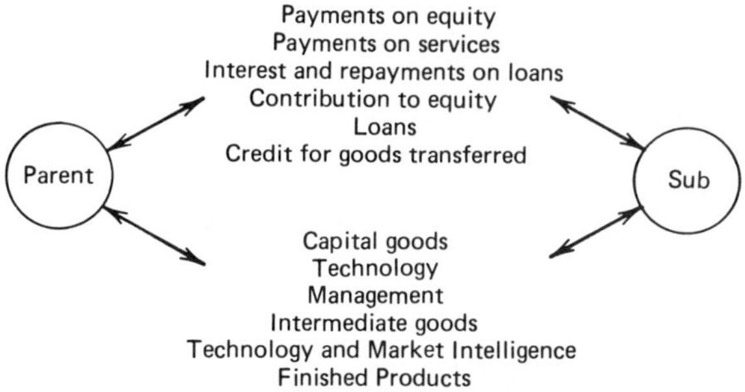

Source: Lessard, D. F., "Transfer Prices, Taxes, and Financial Markets: Implications of Internal Financial Transfers within the Multinational Firm," MIT WP 919-17, April 1977.

MNF requires additional funds, it can raise these funds directly or through any one of its affiliates. The conditions on which the funds are obtained from outside sources (i.e., debt vs. equity, short-term vs. long-term funding, currency of denomination, and restrictive covenants) will have an impact on the basic cost of funds and the financial risk faced by the group as a whole. And it is these relationships that determine the weighted average cost of funds that must be minimized.

CONCLUSIONS

These ideas can be summarized by asking the question, "What does this mean for financial management in general?" First, it means that forecasting efforts should concentrate not on market rates, but instead on how uncertain **deviations** from the forecasted interest or exchange rate **affect the expected net cash flow of the company as a whole**.

Second, the essence of the funding decision is to choose a set of liabilities whose cash flow will **offset**—as much as possible—the fluctuations of cash flow from operations, fluctuations that are caused by unexpected rate changes.

Third, it is the task of financial management to make the best possible tactical decision that the market has to offer on these liabilities, within the strategic funding constraints set by currency denomination, maturity, and capital structure.

Finally, it is necessary to communicate effectively to top management the dimension of the remaining risk so that a **trade-off** decision can be made between those risks that cannot be offset by funding policies and the cost of instituting changes in operations that will reduce the susceptability of operating returns to unexpected exchange rate changes.

BIBLIOGRAPHY

Aliber, R. Z. and C. P. Stickney, "Accounting Measures for Foreign Exchange Exposures: The Long and the Short of It," *Accounting Review*, January (1973).

Brooke, M. Z. and L. Remmers, (Eds.), *The International Firm*, Pitman, London, 1977.

Burns, J. O., "Transfer Pricing Decisions in U.S. Multinational Corporations," *Journal of International Business Studies*, Fall (1980).

Cornell, B., "Inflation, Relative Price Changes, and Exchange Risk," *Financial Management*, Autumn (1980).

Dufey, G., "Corporate Finance and Exchange Rate Variations," *Financial Management*, Summer (1972).

Dufey, G., "International Financial Management," Unpublished manuscript.

Eiteman, D. K. and Stonehill, A. I., *Multinational Business Finance*, 3rd ed., Addison Wesley, Reading, MA, 1982.

Frankel, J., "The Diversifiability of Exchange Risk," *Journal of International Economics*, September (1979).

Giddy, I. H., "The Cost of Capital in the International Firm," *Managerial and Decision Economics*, Autumn (1981).

Kohlhagen, S. W., "The Behavior of Foreign Exchange Markets: A Critical Survey of the Empirical Literature," Monograph 1978–3, Solomon Center for the Study of Financial Institutions, New York University, New York.

Logue, D. E. and G. S. Oldfield, "Managing Foreign Assets When Foreign Exchange Markets Are Efficient," *Financial Management*, Summer (1977).

Mason, R. H., Miller, R. R., and Weigel, D. R., *The Economics of International Business*, 2nd ed., John Wiley & Sons, N.Y. 1981.

Robbins, S. M. and R. B. Stobaugh, "Financing Foreign Affiliates," *Financial Management*, Winter (1972).

Rodriguez, R. M. and E.E. Carter, *International Financial Management*, 2nd ed., Prentice-Hall, Englewood Cliffs, N.J., 1979.

Shapiro, A., "Financial Structure and Cost of Capital in the Multinational Corporation," *Journal of Financial and Quantitative Analysis*, June (1978).

Shapiro, A., "Exchange Rate Changes," *Journal of Finance*, May (1975).

Stonehill, A. et al., "Financial Goals and Debt Ratio Determinants: A Survey of Practice in Five Countries," *Financial Management*, Autumn (1975).

Wright, R. W. and S. Suzuki, "Capital Structure and Financial Risk in Japanese Companies," Proceedings of the Academy of International Business, Honolulu, December 1979.

APPENDIX A

MATHEMATICS OF INTERNATIONAL FINANCE

Ian H. Giddy
and
Ho Sang Kang

THE BALANCE OF PAYMENTS ACCOUNTS

Balance of payments accounting is a **double-entry system** in which one part of a transaction, increasing the external purchasing power of the country, is called a "**source of funds**" and the other part of the transaction, which decreases the external purchasing power of the country, is called a "**use of funds**." In balance of payments accounting uses of funds are **debits** (dr) and sources of funds are **credits** (cr). When a transaction decreases a country's tangible (exports in Exhibit 1) or intangible assets (services rendered), or decreases its foreign financial assets (decrease in investment abroad), or increases its liabilities to foreigners (foreign investment in the United States), it represents a **source of funds**. When a transaction increases a country's tangible (imports) or intangible assets (services bought), or increases its foreign financial assets (increase in investment abroad), or decreases its liabilities to foreigners (decrease in foreign investment in the United States), it represents a **use of funds**.

The following examples show how to use these definitions regarding sources and uses of funds.

Example. A U.S. manufacturing firm exports $1,000 in goods to a customer in France. The French importer pays by drawing on its dollar account with a New York bank. In the U.S. balance of payments accounts this transaction appears as follows:

Decrease in short-term liabilities to foreigners	$1,000 (dr)
Exports	$1,000 (cr)

The exports, a reduction in real assets, provide the United States with a source of funds; however, the French importer reduced its dollar asset, thus reducing U.S. dollar liabilities to foreigners, which represents a use of funds.

EXHIBIT 1 THE BALANCE OF PAYMENTS ACCOUNTS

SOURCES AND USES OF FUNDS	MEASURES OF DEFICIT OR SURPLUS
Exports (+)	
Imports (−)	
	Balance of trade
Receipts for services (+)	
Payments for services (−)	
	Services, net
Gifts from abroad (+)	
Grants to foreign countries (−)	
	Transfers, net
	Current account balance
Direct investment	
In United States (+)	
Abroad (−)	
Portfolio investment	
In United States (+)	
Abroad (−)	
	Balance on long-term capital
	Basic balance
Short-term capital	
Sale of financial assets (+)	
Purchase of financial assets (−)	
	Balance on short-term capital
	Balance on a reserve-transactions basis
	Official reserve
	Decrease (+)
	Increase (−)

Example. In the first example, the U.S. exporter ships the goods using a British shipping service, paying this shipping cost of $85 with a check drawn on its New York account. The entry for this transaction in the U.S. balance of payments would be as follows:

Transportation services	$85 (dr)
Increase in short-term liabilities to foreigners	$85 (cr)

The transportation service bought is an increase in intangible assets, thus representing a use of funds; but because the British shipping service now has dollar deposits, U.S. short-term liabilities to foreigners increase, thus reflecting a source of funds.

Example. A U.S. resident sends a $500 check to a parent in the United Kingdom. In the U.S. balance of payments this transaction appears as follows:

Transfers	$500 (dr)
Increase in short-term liabilities to foreigners	$500 (cr)

The gift that the U.S. resident sent to a U.K. parent represents a use of funds. However, the parent in England now owns U.S. dollar deposits, thus increasing dollar liabilities to foreigners, which is a source of funds.

Example. A U.S. resident buys a $500 bond issued by a British company and pays $500 with a check drawn on a New York bank account. In the U.S. balance of payments this transaction appears as follows:

Increase in long term claims on foreigners	$500 (dr)
Increase in short-term liabilities to foreigners	$500 (cr)

The acquisition of the British bond increases holdings of foreign financial assets, thus reflecting a use of funds. However, the British company now owns U.S. dollar deposits, thus increasing U.S. dollar liabilities to foreigners, which is a source of funds.

A country that accepts the balance of payments accounting procedures described will sum up debits and credits for every interval for which data are collected (usually a year). The net debit (or credit) balance under the "official reserve" heading should match the net credit (or debit) balance on all the other categories combined.

QUOTATIONS AND CALCULATIONS IN SPOT AND FORWARD EXCHANGE

A **spot transaction** involves the purchase of and payment for foreign exchange, with delivery and payment to be completed at once or within one or two business days. A **forward transaction** involves future delivery of one currency in exchange for another currency. This future exchange will take place at a later date at a rate of exchange that has been fixed at the time the contract was consummated.

If the exchange rate is expressed as a **direct quote**, the rate is given as units of home currency needed to buy one unit of the foreign currency. However, if expressed as an **indirect quote**, the exchange rate is given as units of foreign currency available for one unit of home currency. The following example uses a direct quote in a quotation for French francs.

	Bid	Offer
Spot	$0.2112	$0.2113
Six months forward	0.0052	0.0050
Forward outright	$0.2060	$0.2063

Whenever a dealer is asked for a quotation, two prices are provided. One price is the one at which the dealer will buy a currency (**bid**) and the other is the price at which the dealer will sell a currency (**offer**). In the United States, the bid is given before the offer. The amount by which the spot rate of exchange has been adjusted is called the "forward differential." In the above example, because it is less expensive to buy French francs for future delivery, the French franc is said to be at a discount to the U.S. dollar. If one is in doubt as to whether to add or subtract the forward differential, then the **interest differential** can be noted between the two currencies for the appropriate period. If the foreign interest rate is higher than the domestic interest rate, then the forward rate should be cheaper relative to the spot rate (**forward discount**); if lower, then the forward rate should be more expensive to the spot rate (**forward premium**).

Forward quotations are sometimes expressed in terms of an annual percentage deviation from the spot rate. Using the bid in the above example,

$$\begin{aligned}\text{forward discount or premium in annual percentage} &= \frac{0.2060(\$/\text{ FrF}) - 0.2112(\$/\text{FrF})}{0.2112(\$/\text{FrF})} \times \frac{12}{6} \times 100 \\ &= -4.92\%, \text{ or a discount of } 4.92\% \text{ annually}\end{aligned}$$

$$\text{forward premium or discount in annual percentage} = \frac{\text{forward rate} - \text{spot rate}}{\text{spot rate}} \times \frac{12}{n} \times 100$$

where n is the number of months in the forward contract.

THE PURCHASING POWER PARITY THEORY

LAW OF ONE PRICE. The law of one price is a proposition about the relationships among the prices of identical commodities in different countries. In its pure form, it says that the price of a good in one currency will equal the price in another currency, translated at the current exchange rate. Arbitrageurs buy the commodity in the country where the price is lower and sell it in the country where the price is higher as long as the price differential exceeds transportation and other costs. For example, assuming transportation and other costs are negligible, the price of cotton in New York cannot differ significantly from the price in London. This is expressed as

$$P = SP'$$

where S = the spot exchange rate expressed as the number of home currency units required to buy one unit of foreign currency
P = the price of a commodity in the home country
P' = the price of the same commodity in a foreign country

PURCHASING POWER PARITY THEORY: ABSOLUTE VERSION. The purchasing power parity theory is a proposition about the relationship between the commodity price level in the home country and that in a foreign country. Whereas the law of one price deals with individual commodities, the purchasing power parity theory involves **baskets of commodities**. The absolute version states that the price of a representative basket of domestic commodities should not differ significantly from the price of an identical basket of commodities in a foreign country. Thus

$$S = \frac{P}{P'}$$

where S = the spot exchange rate expressed as the number of home currency units required to buy one unit of foreign currency
P = the price level of the home country
P' = the price level of a foreign country

PURCHASING POWER PARITY THEORY: RELATIVE VERSION. The relative version of purchasing power parity deals with the **rate of change** of the exchange rate and of prices in two countries. It says

$$\frac{\dot{S}}{S} = \frac{\dot{P}}{P} - \frac{\dot{P}'}{P'}$$

where the dots refer to rate of change. Multiplying both sides by 100,

$$\frac{\dot{S}}{S} \times 100 = \frac{\dot{P}}{P} \times 100 - \frac{\dot{P}'}{P'} \times 100$$

However, $\dot{P}/P \times 100$ and $\dot{P}'/P' \times 100$ are domestic rate of inflation and foreign rate of inflation in percentage terms, respectively. Thus

$$\hat{S} = \frac{\dot{S}}{S} \times 100 = \pi - \pi'$$

where π = domestic rate of inflation in percentage terms
π' = foreign rate of inflation in percentage terms
$\hat{S}$ = rate of change in the spot exchange rate in percentage terms

The relative version states that the rate of change in the spot exchange rate is equal to the **difference between the rates** of inflation in the home country and the foreign country.

THE FISHER EFFECT

The Fisher effect says that the **nominal interest rate** reflects the **real interest rate** and the **expected rate of inflation**. Investors will acquire and hold monetary assets only if the nominal interest rates are sufficiently high to compensate for the anticipated increases in the commodity price level. For example, if investors anticipate that the commodity price level will increase at 5% a year, the nominal interest rate should exceed the real interest rate by 5% on an annualized basis. For each of two countries,

$$\text{home interest rate} = i = r + \pi \quad (1)$$
$$\text{foreign interest rate} = i' = r' + \pi' \quad (2)$$

where i = nominal interest rate
r = real interest rate
π = expected rate of inflation

and a prime (′) indicates a foreign variable.

Subtracting line 2 from line 1 gives

$$i - i' = (r - r') + (\pi - \pi')$$

Assuming real interest rates are the same in both countries ($r = r'$), then

$$i - i' = \pi - \pi'$$

In other words, where investors can buy any interest-bearing securities, real interest rates tend to be equal across countries, but nominal interest rates will vary by the difference in expected rates of inflation.

It should be noted that equations 1 and 2 are approximations. The actual relationship between i and r should be $i = r + \pi + r\pi$. For moderate rates of inflation, it is customary to ignore the last (cross-product) term.

THE INTERNATIONAL FISHER EFFECT. The international Fisher effect theory says that investors will hold assets denominated in currencies expected to depreciate only if the interest rates on these assets are sufficiently high to compensate for the loss due to the expected change in the exchange rate. If investors anticipate that the price of foreign exchange will increase at 5% a year, domestic interest rates should exceed foreign interest rates by 5% on an annualized basis. Therefore, the international Fisher effect says that the anticipated rate of change in the spot exchange rate equals the difference in nominal interest rates between two countries.

$$\frac{E(S) - S}{S} \times \frac{12}{n} \times 100 = i - i'$$

where S = the spot exchange rate (expressed as the number of home currency units for each unit of foreign currency)
$E(S)$ = the expected future spot exchange rate n months from now (expressed as the number of home currency units for each unit of foreign currency)
i = the nominal interest rate of home (or foreign) country in percentage terms on an annual basis
n = the number of months for the period under consideration

This algebraic expression is an approximation. The actual relationship should be

$$\frac{E(S) - S}{S} \times \frac{12}{n} \times 100 = \frac{i - i'}{1 + i'}$$

The derivation of this actual relationship is very similar to that of the interest rate parity theorem, which is provided following. The only difference is that here $E(S)$ is used instead of the forward exchange rate.

THE INTEREST RATE PARITY THEOREM

When there is a free flow of capital, competition among arbitrageurs ensures that almost all of the time there will be virtually no profit in covered interest arbitrage. The investment yield open to a U.S. covered interest arbitrageur is either

$$1 + i \qquad \text{(deposit in home currency)}$$

or

$$\frac{F}{S}(1 + i') \qquad \text{(deposit in foreign currency)}$$

The nominal interest rate i is earned by the covered interest arbitrageur by keeping \$1.00 on deposit in the United States. Alternatively, the arbitrageur can convert this \$1.00 into a foreign currency (e.g., West German deutsche mark) at a spot exchange rate of $S_{(\$/DM)}$ and invest the funds on deposit in a foreign country (West Germany). Thus at the maturity of the investment the arbitrageur will obtain $(1 + i')/S$ West German deutsche marks. However, the U.S. arbitrageur investing in West Germany must buy dollars forward at rate of $F_{(\$/DM)}$ to stay covered. If the investment opportunity in West Germany yields a slightly higher return than that in the United States, substantial funds will be attracted to West Germany, thereby eliminating the difference in yields between the two investment opportunities. The higher return on the investment in West Germany will be reduced because as funds move into the West German money market, the West German interest rate i' will be reduced, the spot exchange rate $S_{(\$/DM)}$ increased, and the forward exchange rate $F_{(\$/DM)}$ reduced. Then one would expect that the interest rate parity theorem would hold.

$$\frac{F_{(\$/DM)}}{S_{(\$/DM)}}(1 + i_{DM}) = 1 + i_{\$}$$

Dividing both sides by $(1 + i_{DM})$,

$$\frac{F_{(\$/DM)}}{S_{(\$/DM)}} = \frac{1 + i_{\$}}{1 + i_{DM}}$$

Subtracting one from both sides,

$$\frac{F_{(\$/DM)}}{S_{(\$/DM)}} - 1 = \frac{1 + i_{\$}}{1 + i_{DM}} - 1$$

$$\frac{F_{(\$/DM)} - S_{(\$/DM)}}{S_{(\$/DM)}} = \frac{1 + i_{\$} - (1 + i_{DM})}{1 + i_{DM}} = \frac{i_{\$} - i_{DM}}{1 + i_{DM}}$$

$$\frac{F_{(\$/DM)} - S_{(\$/DM)}}{S_{(\$/DM)}} = \frac{i_{\$} - i_{DM}}{1 + i_{DM}} \simeq i_{\$} - i_{DM}$$

Thus the interest rate parity theorem states that the difference in nominal interest rates between two countries should be equal to the forward exchange rate discount or premium.

$$\frac{F - S}{S} \times \frac{12}{n} \times 100 = i - i'$$

where F = the forward exchange rate for contracts due in n months (the domestic currency price of foreign exchange)
S = the spot exchange rate (the domestic currency price of foreign exchange)
i = the nominal interest rate of home (or foreign) country in percentage terms on an annual basis
n = the number of months in the forward contract

TRANSACTION EXPOSURE AND HEDGING

The concepts and calculations involved in hedging an international transaction can best be demonstrated with an example.

A U.S. firm has sold a computer to a British company for £x. The computer has been shipped, and payment is due in n months.

S_t = the spot exchange rate at time t (dollars for each pound sterling)

$\hat{S}_{t+n}$ = the expected spot exchange rate at time $t + n$ (dollars for each pound sterling)

F_{t+n} = the n month forward exchange rate at time t (dollars for each pound sterling)

i = U.S. annual interest rate

i' = U.K. annual interest rate

UNHEDGED POSITION. The U.S. firm will receive in n months, in dollars,

$$x \times \hat{S}_{t+n}.$$

FORWARD MARKET HEDGE. The U.S. firm sells the £x now at the n month forward exchange rate of F_{t+n}. In n months, the firm will receive £x, deliver that sum to the bank, and receive (in dollars),

$$x \times F_{t+n}$$

MONEY MARKET HEDGE. The objective of using the money market for hedging purposes is to generate a gain (or loss) that will compensate for the expected exchange loss (or gain). When the U.S. firm has a net asset position in pounds sterling while expecting a devaluation in that currency, the firm, to counteract that loss, would have to borrow pounds sterling and invest the proceeds in the U.S. money market.

If pounds sterling devalues against the U.S. dollar, the firm has a sterling liability to match its sterling asset, so no net loss is suffered.

The U.S. firm borrows in London

$$\frac{£x}{1 + i'/(12/n)}$$

promising to repay £x in n months. The U.S. firm exchanges the

$$\frac{£x}{1 + i'/(12/n)}$$

for dollars at the current spot exchange rate of S_t, receiving

$$\$\left(\frac{x}{1 + i'/(12/n)} \times S_t\right)$$

The U.S. firm invests this sum in the U.S. money market and will receive at the end of n months

$$\$\left(\frac{x}{1 + i'/(12/n)} \times S_t\right)\left(1 + \frac{i}{12/n}\right) = \$\left(x \times S_t \times \frac{1 + i/(12/n)}{1 + i'/(12/n)}\right)$$

COST OF CAPITAL OF THE INTERNATIONAL FIRM

OVERALL COST OF CAPITAL. The overall cost of capital is the sum of the costs of each financing source, weighted by the proportion of that financing source in the firm's total capital structure. The **weighted average cost of capital** is therefore

$$k = \frac{D}{V}k_d(1 - t) + \frac{E}{V}k_e$$

where k = weighted average cost of capital
k_d = cost of debt
k_e = cost of equity
t = tax rate
D = value of the firm's debt
E = value of the firm's equity
$V = D + E$ = total value of the firm

The weighted average cost of capital concept can be extended to include debt denominated in foreign currencies, debt issued by foreign subsidiaries, retained earnings of foreign subsidiaries, and so forth.

COST OF EQUITY. The cost of equity capital for the parent is given by the formula

$$k_e = \frac{D}{P} + g$$

where k_e = required return on equity
D = expected dividends per share
P = price of a share
g = rate of growth of dividends or capital gains

If the dividends and growth are regarded as inadequate, some people will sell the stock and the price, P, will fall and k_e will rise. Thus, the price adjusts to make k_e equal to the required return on equity.

COST OF RETAINED EARNINGS. The opportunity cost of retained earnings is simply k_e, the rate shareholders could get if they were paid dividends and reinvested them in the same firm. Thus the cost of retained earnings is the same as the cost of common stock.

However, **earnings retained in a foreign subsidiary** are not subject to domestic corporation tax; nor are they subject to withholding taxes or other transfer costs. Therefore, if the parent has a required rate of return on equity of k_e, then earnings retained in a foreign subsidiary will provide an equivalent return if they yield

$$k_{fr} = \frac{(1 - t_f - t_a - w_f)}{(1 - t_f)} k_e$$

where k_{fr} = cost of foreign subsidiary's retained earnings
t_f = foreign tax rate
t_a = additional tax payable (or tax saved) if earnings are repatriated, expressed as a percentage of foreign related earnings
w_f = foreign withholding tax and other costs incurred if earnings are repatriated, expressed as a percentage of foreign earnings

For example, if the subsidiary's tax rate is 40% and that of the parent is 50% (with credit given for foreign taxes paid), and there would be an additional \$5 of withholding tax and other costs if earnings were repatriated, then \$100 of earnings abroad will produce \$60 if retained but only \$45 if repatriated. In this case funds retained abroad are clearly cheaper than parent company retained earnings.

FOREIGN CURRENCY DEBT. The cost of the foreign currency debt of the parent firm equals the after-tax cost of repaying the principal and interest on the debt, calculated in domestic currency. For example, a company borrows in West German deutsche marks for one year at 4%. If during the year the deutsche mark rises against domestic currency by 5%, then the interest cost will be 4% adjusted for the higher cost of West German deutsche marks (i.e., 4% × 1.05 = 4.2%). The repayment of principal costs an additional 5% because of the deutsche mark's appreciation, so the total cost of the debt is 4.2% + 5% = 9.2%. After tax this is 9.2(1 − 0.5) = 4.6%, assuming that the tax rate applicable to exchange gains or losses is equal to the 50% corporate income tax rate.

In general, the **after-tax cost of foreign currency debt** is

$$k_{fd} = \left[(1 + R)\frac{S_1}{S_0} - 1\right](1 - t)$$

where

k_{fd} = effective cost of foreign currency debt
R = nominal cost of foreign currency debt (interest rate, in decimal form)
S_0 = spot exchange rate at time loan is made, expressed in domestic currency units for each foreign currency unit
S_1 = future spot exchange rate at time loan is repaid, expressed in domestic currency units for each foreign currency unit
t = tax rate

What is the effective **cost of a covered foreign loan**? A covered loan will be obtained at the spot exchange rate S_0 and repaid, with interest, at the forward exchange rate F. Thus, in the above formula F is used instead of S_1.

$$k_{fdc} = \left[(1 + R)\frac{F}{S_0} - 1\right](1 - t)$$

where

k_{fdc} = effective cost of covered foreign currency debt
R = nominal interest rate on the 241an, in decimal form
S_0 = spot exchange rate at time loan is made, expressed in domestic currency units for each foreign currency unit
F = forward exchange rate expressed in domestic currency units for each foreign currency unit
t = tax rate

SUBSIDIARY DEBT. The same principles apply to calculating the cost of a foreign subsidiary's debt as for parent debt; that is, the effective cost of a foreign subsidiary's debt must be expressed in parent company currency by adjusting nominal rates for exchange rate changes. Thus one has to convert the subsidiary currency cost to parent company cost.

Subsidiary's Local Debt

$$k_{sl} = \left[[R_l(1 - t_s)]\frac{e_1'}{e_0'}\right]$$

where

k_{sl} = effective cost of local currency debt obtained by a subsidiary

R_l = interest rate charged to the subsidiary on the local currency loan, expressed in decimal form

t_s = tax rate applicable to subsidiary's earnings, expressed in decimal form (This rate is the maximum of either that of the subsidiary or that of the parent company.)

e_0' = spot exchange rate at time loan is made, expressed in parent company currency units for each subsidiary currency unit

e_1' = future spot exchange rate at time loan is repaid, expressed in parent company currency units for each subsidiary currency unit

The after-tax nominal cost of local currency debt obtained by a subsidiary is $R_l(1 - t_s)$. For the parent, this cost must be adjusted for the exchange rate change. Thus one has to convert this local currency cost to parent company currency cost by multiplying $R_l(1 - t_s)$ by e_1'/e_0'.

Under the U.S. foreign *tax credit system*, the tax rate applicable to a subsidiary's earnings is the maximum of either that of the subsidiary or that of the parent company. When the subsidiary tax rate is larger than the parent tax rate, the relevant tax rate is the subsidiary tax rate. However, when the subsidiary tax rate is smaller than the parent tax rate, the correct tax rate that must be used in the above formula is the parent tax rate because the parent has to pay additional tax on the subsidiary's earnings.

Subsidiary's Foreign Currency Debt

$$k_{sf} = \left[(1 + R_f)\frac{e_0}{e_1} - 1\right](1 - t_s)\frac{e_1'}{e_0'}$$

where

k_{sf} = effective cost of foreign currency debt obtained by a subsidiary

R_f = interest rate charged to the subsidiary on the foreign currency loan, expressed in decimal form

t_s = tax rate applicable to subsidiary's earnings (This rate is the maximum of either that of the subsidiary or that of the parent company.)

e_0 = spot exchange rate at time loan is made, expressed in loan currency units for each subsidiary currency unit

e_1 = future spot exchange rate at time loan is repaid, expressed in loan currency units for each subsidiary currency unit

e_0' = spot exchange rate at time loan is made, expressed in parent company currency units for each subsidiary currency unit

e_1' = future spot exchange rate at time loan is repaid, expressed in parent company currency units for each subsidiary currency unit

For example, a West German subsidiary of a U.S. company borrows e_0 Swiss francs (DM1) for one year at 4%. From the subsidiary's viewpoint both the principal and the interest are subject to exchange rate changes. Thus when the loan is due the subsidiary has to pay $e_0(1 + 0.04)$ Swiss francs, but in deutsche marks this amounts to $(e_0/e_1)(1 + 0.04)$. The subsidiary initially borrows DM1, so the cost of repaying the principal and interest on the loan, calculated in the subsidiary currency is

$$(1 + 0.04)\frac{e_0}{e_1} - 1$$

On an after tax basis this is

$$\left[(1 + 0.04)\frac{e_0}{e_1} - 1\right](1 - t_s)$$

Converting this subsidiary currency cost to parent company currency cost, the effective cost of the foreign currency debt issued by the subsidiary is obtained; that is,

$$k_{sf} = \left[(1 + 0.04)\frac{e_0}{e_1} - 1\right](1 - t_s)\frac{e_1'}{e_0'}$$

The formula still applies to the case of covered foreign currency loan, except that the forward exchange rate at the time the loan is made should be used instead of future spot exchange rate. Thus the effective cost of a covered foreign currency loan is

$$k_{sfc} = \left[(1 + R_f)\frac{e_0}{F} - 1\right](1 - t_s)\frac{e_1'}{e_0'}$$

where

k_{sfc} = effective cost of covered foreign currency debt obtained by a subsidiary
F = forward exchange rate at the time the loan is made, expressed in loan currency units for each subsidiary currency unit

INTRACOMPANY LOANS. The effective cost of an intracompany loan is similar to that of a foreign currency loan obtained by a subsidiary, but in this case one has to subtract revenues to the parent and add costs to the parent, taking account of tax effects.

$$k_{si} = \left[(1 + R_i)\frac{e_0}{e_1} - 1\right](1 - t_s)\frac{e_1'}{e_0'} - R_i(1 - t_f) + R_P(1 - t_p)$$

where
k_{si} = effective cost of intracompany loan from parent
R_i = interest rate charged to the subsidiary on the intracompany loan, expressed in decimal form
e_0 = spot exchange rate at time loan is made, expressed in loan currency units for each subsidiary currency unit
e_1 = future spot exchange rate at time loan is repaid, expressed in loan currency units for each subsidiary currency unit

e_0' = spot exchange rate at time loan is made, expressed in parent company currency units for each subsidiary currency unit
e_1' = future spot exchange rate at time loan is repaid, expressed in parent company currency units for each subsidiary currency unit
R_P = interest rate charged to the parent company, expressed in decimal form (parent's cost of funds)
t_p = tax rate applicable to domestic earnings of the parent company
t_f = effective tax rate applicable to foreign-source interest income. This can vary from 0 to t_p, depending on whether the parent company has excess foreign tax credits.

The second term of the above formula, $R_i(1 - t_f)$, is the after-tax revenues to the parent company from the intracompany loan; the third term, $R_P(1 - t_p)$, is the parent's after-tax cost of obtaining the funds. When the intracompany loan is denominated in the parent company currency,

$$e_0 = e_0' \qquad \text{and} \qquad e_1 = e_1'$$

Also, if the loan is covered by the subsidiary, the forward exchange rate should be used instead of the future spot exchange rate. Thus when the loan is denominated in the parent company currency the formula becomes

$$k_{si} = \left[(1 + R_i)\frac{e_0}{e_1} - 1\right](1 - t_s)\frac{e_1}{e_0} - R_i(1 - t_f) + R_p(1 - t_p)$$

and if the loan is covered by the subsidiary it becomes

$$k_{sic} = \left[(1 + R_i)\frac{e_0}{F} - 1\right](1 - t_s)\frac{e_1}{e_0} - R_i(1 - t_f) + R_p(1 - t_p)$$

where

k_{sic} = effective cost of intracompany loan from parent, covered
F = forward exchange rate at time loan is made, expressed in loan currency units for each subsidiary currency unit

SUBSIDIARY'S SWAP LOANS. In a swap transaction, for example, where an arrangement is made between the Bank of Brazil and the U.S. parent of a Brazilian subsidiary, the U.S. parent will lend a given amount in dollars to the Bank of Brazil, depositing dollars in its New York account. The Bank of Brazil in return will make a loan in Brazil of an equivalent number of cruzeiros to the subsidiary. There will be no interest charged on either the dollar or cruzeiro balance.

However, since the swap loan will tie up the parent's dollar funds, an interest charge payable in dollars will be required of the subsidiary on the dollars deposited by the parent. The effective cost of a swap loan is similar to that of an intracompany loan, except that, for the swap: (1) the principal is loaned at a prearranged swap rate, $e_{0(SW)}$, and returned at a prearranged future swap rate, $e_{1(SW)}$; (2) the interest is repaid at uncertain future spot rate, e_1; and (3) there is no tax deductibility of interest for the subsidiary because the dollar deposit in New York made by the parent is not loaned to the subsidiary.

The first term in the effective cost of intracompany loan (which was the cost for the subsidiary, in parent company currency cost) was

$$\left[(1 + R_i)\frac{e_0}{e_1} - 1\right](1 - t_s)\frac{e_1'}{e_0'}$$

Expanding this to separate principal and interest,

$$\left(\frac{e_0}{e_1} + \frac{R_i\, e_0}{e_1} - 1\right)(1 - t_s)\frac{e_1'}{e_0'}$$

↑ Effect on principal ↑ Effect on interest

For the effect on principal of the exchange rate change e_0 and e_1 must be replaced by $e_{0(\mathrm{SW})}$ and $e_{1(\mathrm{SW})}$, respectively. However, for the effect on interest of the exchange rate change e_0 must be replaced by $e_{0(\mathrm{SW})}$ but e_1 must still be used. Also, because there is no tax deductibility of interest, $1 - t_s$ should disappear. Therefore, the above expression reduces to

$$\left(\frac{e_{0(\mathrm{SW})}}{e_{1(\mathrm{SW})}} + \frac{R_i e_{0(\mathrm{SW})}}{e_1} - 1\right)\frac{e_1'}{e_0'}$$

Thus the effective cost of the swap loan is

$$k_{sw} = \left(\frac{e_{0(\mathrm{SW})}}{e_{1(\mathrm{SW})}} + \frac{R_i e_{0(\mathrm{SW})}}{e_1} - 1\right)\frac{e_1'}{e_0'} - R_i(1 - t_f) + R_p(1 - t_p)$$

where

k_{sw} = effective cost of swap loan
R_i = interest charged to the subsidiary on the swap loan, expressed in decimal form
e_0' = spot exchange rate at time loan is made, expressed in parent company currency units for each subsidiary currency unit
e_1' = future spot exchange rate at time loan is repaid, expressed in parent company currency units for each subsidiary currency unit
$e_{0(\mathrm{SW})}$ = swap exchange rate at time loan is made, expressed in loan currency units for each subsidiary currency unit
$e_{1(\mathrm{SW})}$ = swap exchange rate at time loan is repaid, expressed in loan currency units for each subsidiary currency unit
R_p = interest rate charged to the parent company, expressed in decimal form (parent's cost of funds)

t_p = tax rate applicable to domestic earnings of the parent company
t_f = effective tax rate applicable to foreign source interest income. This can vary from 0 to t_p, depending on whether the parent company has excess foreign tax credits.

The cost of several possible forms of debt and equity peculiar to the international firm have been examined. What remains is to combine all the sources into a **weighted average cost of capital** for the international firm. That is, each cost must be multiplied by the proportion of that source in the total financing of the firm, and this summed over all sources. The combination that gives the **minimum total cost** is the optimal capital structure for the firm. When the cost of capital is to be used for capital budgeting purposes, the **marginal cost of new sources** of financing should be used instead of existing costs.

UNITED STATES TAXATION OF FOREIGN SOURCE INCOME

Under the system of taxing worldwide income, the U.S. government avoids double taxation by allowing a certain amount of credit for taxes already paid on this income in foreign countries. Basically, there are two approaches in calculating the U.S. tax obligation: the direct and the indirect foreign tax credit systems.

DIRECT FOREIGN TAX CREDIT. "Direct tax" denotes a foreign income tax imposed directly on the U.S. taxpayer. This includes the foreign **income tax** paid by the foreign branch of a U.S. corporation and foreign **withholding taxes** deducted from the dividend paid to a U.S. corporation by a foreign corporation.

Case 1

Earnings of foreign branch	\$ 100
Foreign income tax at 45%	45
Included in U.S. income	100
U.S. tax at 48%	48
Less foreign tax credit	45
Net U.S. tax payable	\$ 3

Case 2

Dividend from foreign corporation	\$100
Foreign withholding tax at 10%	10
Net amount received	90
Included in U.S. income	100
U.S. tax at 48%	48
Less foreign tax credit	10
Net U.S. tax payable	38

INDIRECT OR DEEMED–PAID FOREIGN TAX CREDIT. If a U.S. corporation holds at least 10% of the voting power of a foreign corporation, the U.S. corporation can claim a foreign tax credit for income taxes paid by the foreign corporation. Therefore, a U.S. parent company receiving a dividend from a foreign subsidiary can claim a foreign tax credit not only for dividend withholding taxes but also a part of the foreign subsidiary's tax on its earnings.

For example, a U.S. parent company has two wholly owned European subsidiaries. The West German subsidiary has an income before taxes of $80 million. The West German subsidiary declares a 100% dividend, which means that the 15% West German withholding tax has to be paid on the full amount of after tax earnings. The West German corporate income tax rate is 36% on paid-out earnings. The Belgian subsidiary has a before-tax profit of $260 million, but it declares a dividend of 50%. The Belgian corporate and withholding tax rates are 48% and 15%, respectively. The earnings and pay-outs of the subsidiaries, according to U.S. definitions, are given in Exhibit 2. Exhibit 3 shows the calculation of the applicable U.S. corporate tax.

EUROPEAN MONETARY SYSTEM

Until March 1979 the European Monetary System was known as the "joint float" or "snake" agreement, which had started in 1972. In March 1979 the old joint float became the European Monetary System (EMS). The **European Currency Unit** (ECU), which is a weighted average of EMS exchange rates, is used as the unit of account in the EMS. There are two different limits on exchange rate movements. The parity grid system places restrictions on the extent to which each EMS currency can rise or fall in relation to every other EMS currency. The divergence indicator system sets limits within which each currency is permitted to vary with respect to the ECU. (The discussion of this topic draws heavily on Burtle, 1981.)

PARITY GRID SYSTEM. For each currency the parity is a previously set exchange rate. On each working day a percentage change can be calculated between the spot and the initial parity. Under the parity grid system the differences from parity are not permitted to vary more than the 2.25 percentage points band (except for Italy, where by special agreement six percentage points are permitted).

EXHIBIT 2 EARNINGS AND PAY-OUTS OF EUROPEAN SUBSIDIARIES (in millions of U.S. dollars)

	West Germany	Belgium
Before-tax earnings	$80	$260
Income tax rate	36%	48%
Income taxes	28.8	124.8
After-tax profit	51.2	135.2
Dividend pay-out ratio	1	0.5
Dividends	51.2	67.6
Dividend withholding tax rate	15%	15%
Withholding tax	7.68	10.14
Dividends received by parent	$43.52	$ 57.46

EXHIBIT 3 CALCULATION OF APPLICABLE U.S. CORPORATE TAX

	German Subsidiary	Belgian Subsidiary
Dividends received by parent	$43.52	$57.46
Adding withholding tax	$ 7.68	$10.14
Dividend pay-out ratio times foreign income tax paid	1 × 28.8 = 28.8	0.5 × 124.8 = 62.4
Taxable income	$80	$130
U.S. tax obligation	0.48 × 80 = 38.4	0.48 × 130 = 62.4
Less tax credit		
Income tax[a]	28.8	62.4
Withholding tax	7.68 36.48	10.14 72.54
U.S. taxes (or tax credit)	$ 1.92	($10.14)
U.S. tax payable (excess tax credit)		1.92 − 10.14 = ($8.22)

[a]The income tax credit is the dividend pay-out ratio times foreign income tax paid.

If the Danish krone is about 2.5% above the parity against the dollar and the Belgian franc is about 0.8% below its parity against the dollar, then the range in differences from parity is 3.3 (i.e., 2.5 + 0.8) percentage points, which exceed the 2.25 percentage point limit set in the parity grid system. Under these circumstances Denmark would sell kroner to bring down its exchange rate, while Belgium would buy Belgian francs to push up its exchange rate until differences from parity are within the 2.25 percentage point limit. In practice, however, the parity grid system is operated without reference to the dollar. For example, if the parity of West German deutsche marks against Dutch guilders is 1.10537, the West German deutsche mark is permitted to move as high as 1.1305 or as low as 1.080775 under the parity grid system.

DIVERGENCE INDICATOR SYSTEM. Divergence indicators are deviations in currency values from the European Currency Unit, which is a weighted average value. Exhibit 4 shows how to calculate the value of the ECU as of 13 March 1979.

EXHIBIT 4 VALUE OF THE EUROPEAN CURRENCY UNIT (ECU) IN U.S. CENTS (13 March 1979)

Currency	Value of ECU Currencies	×	Number of Currency Units in ECU Basket	=	Value of Currency Unit in ECU Basket
West German deutsche mark	53.7600¢	×	0.828	=	44.51¢
French franc	23.3400¢	×	1.15	=	26.84¢
British pound	204.7000¢	×	0.0885	=	18.12¢
Netherlandian guilder	49.8000¢	×	0.286	=	14.24¢
Belgian franc	3.3940¢	×	3.80	=	12.90¢
Italian lire	0.1182¢	×	109.0	=	12.88¢
Danish krone	19.2100¢	×	0.217	=	4.17¢
Irish pound	204.7000¢	×	0.00759	=	1.55¢
Value of the ECU				=	135.21¢

It is possible to calculate the value of the overall ECU in each EMS currency. Exhibit 5 shows how the market value of the ECU is calculated in Danish kroner.

To calculate the divergence indicator, the market value of the ECU in Danish kroner is compared to its parity value. In the above example the divergence indicator is −0.66%, since the market value is 0.66% below the parity value. Parity values and maximum permitted divergence indicators for EMS currencies are as shown in Exhibit 6.

SPECIAL DRAWING RIGHTS

In 1969, the special drawing rights (SDRs) plan authorized the **International Monetary Fund** (IMF) to create a special asset that would be accepted among IMF members in exchange for dollars and other currencies. Each participating country received an amount of SDRs in proportion to its IMF quota. Originally each SDR was valued at the equivalent of $1.00 worth of gold in 1969. Given the devaluation of the dollar relative to gold afterward, the value of the SDR was raised accordingly. In July 1974, however, the IMF decided to fix the value of the SDR for each business day in terms of a cocktail of currencies, based upon exchange rates of 16 major world currencies. In 1980 the basket of currencies was revised to include only the five major currencies. Effective 1 January 1981, the units of local currencies in the basket are as follows (International Monetary Fund, 1981).

U.S. dollar	0.540
West German deutsche mark	0.460

EXHIBIT 5 DIVERGENCE INDICATOR FOR THE DANISH KRONE (13 March 1979)

Currency	Value of Each Currency in U.S. Cents	Value of Each Currency in Danish Kroner	×	Number of Currency Units in ECU Basket	=	Value of Currency Unit in ECU Basket in Danish Kroner
West German deutsche mark	53.7600¢	2.798500	×	0.82800	=	2.3172
French franc	23.3400	1.215000	×	1.15000	=	1.3973
British pound	204.7000	10.655900	×	0.08850	=	0.9430
Netherlandian guilder	49.8000	2.592400	×	0.28600	=	0.7414
Belgian franc	3.3940	0.176700	×	3.80000	=	0.6715
Italian lire	0.1182	0.006153	×	109.00000	=	0.6707
Danish krone	19.2100	1.000000	×	0.21700	=	0.2170
Irish pound	204.7000	10.655900	×	0.00759	=	0.0809
	Market value of ECU in Danish kroner				=	7.0390
	Parity value of ECU in Danish kroner				=	7.08592
	Market value above or below parity value				=	−0.66%
	Maximum permitted divergence				=	±1.63%

EXHIBIT 6 PARITIES AND MAXIMUM PERMITTED DIVERGENCE INDICATORS IN THE EUROPEAN MONETARY SYSTEM

Currency	Parity (Units per ECU)	Maximum Divergence Indicator (%)
German mark	2.510640	1.13%
French franc	5.798310	1.35
Netherlandian guilder	2.720770	1.51
Belgian franc	39.458200	1.53
Italian lire	1148.150000	4.07
Danish krone	7.085920	1.63
Irish pound	0.662638	1.67

British pound	0.071
French franc	0.740
Japanese yen	34.000

Exhibit 7 shows how to calculate the value of the SDR for a particular day.

The exchange rates used in this example are New York foreign exchange selling rates quoted by a major New York bank. In practice, however, the IMF uses the middle rates between the buying and selling rates at noon on the London exchange market as determined by the Bank of England.

CURRENCY COMBINATION AND CURRENCY OPTION BONDS

CURRENCY COMBINATION BONDS. Various currency combination bonds have been developed by combining several currencies according to some weighting process. The amount of each currency in the currency cocktail generally remains fixed, but the value of the cocktail changes as the component currencies depreciate or appreciate relative to each other. The fluctuations of any one currency are reflected in changes in the value of the cocktail in proportion to its weight in the cocktail.

EXHIBIT 7 CALCULATION OF THE VALUE OF THE SPECIAL DRAWING RIGHT ON 30 NOVEMBER 1981

Currency	Exchange Rate (U.S. dollars per unit of local currency)	×	Number of Units of Local Currency per SDR	=	Value of Local Currency in One SDR (U.S. dollars)
U.S. dollar	1.000000	×	0.540	=	$0.540
West German deutsche mark	0.452200	×	0.460	=	0.208
British pound	1.960500	×	0.071	=	0.139
French franc	0.17900	×	0.740	=	0.132
Japanese yen	0.004674	×	34.000	=	0.159
			Value of the SDR	=	$1.178

Examples of currency combination bonds are European Composite Units (EURCOs), European Economic Community–European Units of Account (EEC-EUAs), SDRs, and ARCRUs.

The EURCO, often referred to as the "Eurococktail," is a basket of the currencies of the nine member countries of the European Economic Community (EEC). The weights in the EURCO reflect the relative gross national products of the nine countries.

The European unit of account agreed upon by the EEC members in 1975, EEC-EUA, is identical in concept to the EURCO. However, the EEC-EUA gives slightly different weights to the component currencies. The following hypothetical example shows how the value of the EEC-EUA changes as the component currencies fluctuate. In the top half of Exhibit 8 the calculation of the value of the EEC-EUA as of 10 March 1982 is shown. By 10 May 1982 the British pound is assumed to depreciate by 10%, from \$1.8190/£1 to \$1.6371/ £1. During the same period, however, the French franc is assumed to appreciate by 10%, from \$0.1658/FrF1 to \$0.1824/FrF1. In the bottom half of Exhibit 8 the value of the EEC-EUA as of 10 May 1982 is calculated assuming that all the other currencies stay at the level of 10 March 1982. The change in the value of the EEC-EUA during the two-month period is \$0.0030, or 0.29% of the value as of 10 March 1982. Although the British pound and the French franc have fluctuated by 10%, the value of the EEC-EUA has changed only by 0.29%. Therefore, currency combination bonds can be used as a means of stabilizing the purchasing power of coupons when individual currencies are expected to fluctuate widely.

The SDR (Special Drawing Rights) is a cocktail of five major world currencies. Effective 1 January 1981, the units of local currencies in the cocktail are as follows:

U.S. dollar	0.540
West German deutsche mark	0.460
British pound	0.071
French franc	0.740
Japanese yen	34.000

The ARCRU (Arab Currency Unit) was created by Hambros Bank of London. It was intended to appeal to potential investors from Arab countries.

Subscription to currency combination bonds and the payment of interest and principal cannot be made in the denomination unit of the cocktail bonds because no such composite currency is available for private transaction purposes. Thus the payment currency is generally fixed in the debenture agreement. Borrowers and lenders are indifferent to the payment currency because there is no advantage in choosing any particular currency as the payment currency.

CURRENCY OPTION BONDS. Currency option bonds are among the more innovative creations of the Eurobond market. The lender can, prior to each coupon date, choose the currency in which interest payments are to be made. The currencies of choice and the exchange rates among the currencies are set at the time of bond offering.

For example, a U.S. investor bought a **dollar-sterling currency option bond** that offered payment in U.S. dollars or sterling pounds and the exchange rate was \$1.50/

EXHIBIT 8 CALCULATION OF THE VALUE OF THE EUROPEAN ECONOMIC COMMUNITY–EUROPEAN UNIT OF ACCOUNT (EEC-EUA)

Currency	Exchange Rate (U.S. dollars per unit of local currency) on 10 March 1982	×	Number of Units of Local Currency per EEC-EUA	=	Value of Local Currency in One EEC-EUA (U.S. dollars)
West German deutsche mark	$0.424800	×	0.8280	=	$0.3517
British pound	1.819000	×	0.0885	=	0.1610
French franc	0.165800	×	1.1500	=	0.1907
Italian lire	0.000786	×	109.0000	=	0.0857
Belgian franc	0.022900	×	3.8000	=	0.0870
Danish krone	0.126100	×	0.2170	=	0.0274
Irish pound	1.492500	×	0.0076	=	0.0113
Netherlandian guilder	0.387400	×	0.2860	=	0.1108
The value of the EEC-EUA on 10 March 1982				=	$1.0256

	Exchange Rate (U.S. dollars per unit of local currency) on 10 May 1982	×	Number of Units of Local Currency per EEC-EUA	=	Value of Local Currency in One EEC-EUA (U.S. dollars)
West German deutsche mark	$0.424800		0.8280	=	$0.3517
British pound	1.637100[a]		0.0885	=	0.1449
French franc	0.182400[a]		1.1500	=	0.2098
Italian lire	0.000786		109.0000	=	0.0857
Belgian franc	0.022900		3.8000	=	0.0870
Danish krone	0.126100		0.2170	=	0.0274
Irish pound	1.492500		0.0076	=	0.0113
Netherlandian guilder	0.387400		0.2860	=	0.1108
The value of the EEC-EUA on 10 May 1982				=	$1.0286
The value of the EEC-EUA on 10 March 1982				=	$1.0256
Change in the value of the EEC-EUA				=	$0.0030

[a] This example assumes that the dollar value of the British pound falls by 10% and the French franc rises by 10% since March 10. All other currencies are assumed to remain unchanged.

£1.00. If the principal was $1,000 and the interest rate was 10%, then initially the borrower would pay $100, or £66.67 in interest. However, if the actual exchange rate became $2.00/£1.00, the U.S. investor would choose pounds sterling as the currency of the coupon. The investor would receive £66.67 in interest and convert that sum to dollars at a rate of $2.00/£1.00, obtaining $133.34 in interest. This $133.34 is larger than the original $100.00 that would have been obtained in the case of no exchange rate changes. If the actual exchange rate became $1.00/£1.00, the U.S. investor would choose U.S. dollars rather than pounds sterling, receiving $100.00 in interest. Thus in the case of appreciation of pounds sterling relative to U.S. dollars, the currency option bond is better than a straight Eurodollar bond that pays 10% interest. In the case of appreciation of U.S. dollars relative to pounds sterling, the currency option bond is as good as the straight Eurodollar bond.

Most currency option bonds involve only two currencies. However, currency option bonds with more than two currencies also exist. The European Currency Unit bond is one such example; it includes the West German deutsche mark, French franc, Belgian franc, Luxembourgian franc, Netherlandian guilder, and Italian lire.

The investors in currency option bonds make some gain unless all currencies included in the bond depreciate against the desired currency. When all currencies in the bond depreciate against the desired currency, the investor loses in the same proportion as the currency that has depreciated the least.

Given the advantages of currency option bonds to lenders, lenders are expected to pay a price in the form of a lower interest rate. In other words, the foregone interest is the price for a currency option clause.

FOREIGN EXCHANGE FUTURES

Foreign exchange futures are contracts for delivery of a certain amount of foreign currency at some future date. The dollar price for the foreign currency is agreed on the day the contract is bought or sold. Like the forward market, no money changes hands at the time the contract is entered, and as with forward contracts, gains or losses are incurred as a result of subsequent currency fluctuations. In both markets, the total gain or loss will equal the difference between the futures price (or forward rate) and the spot exchange rate on the date of maturity of the contract, multiplied by the amount of the contract.

The **difference between the forward and futures markets** is that in the forward market, a profit (or loss) is realized on the maturity date, while in the futures market **all profits and losses must be settled on a daily basis.** This procedure, called "marking to the market," requires that funds change hands each day. The funds are added to or subtracted from a mandatory margin account that traders are required to maintain. In contrast, in the forward market no money changes hands until delivery occurs.

The other chief feature of the futures market is that futures are traded through organized exchanges or clearing houses, such as the International Monetary Market in Chicago. Trading in standardized currency contracts is conducted by open auction on the floor of the exchange. The trading watches individual buyers and sellers to set prices; however in executing each sale and purchase the clearing house of the exchange takes the opposite side of each position. The fact that losses are realized and settled every trading day limits the risk of default to the clearing house.

The exchanges specify the characteristics for contracts in order to make them standardized and tradable. For example, one British pound contract on the International Monetary Market (IMM) has the following specifications.

Contract size:	£25,000
Delivery instrument:	Sterling deposited in a designated bank
Delivery months:	March, June, September, December
Price increments:	\$0.0005 or \$12.50 a contract
Daily price limits:	\$0.0500 (\$1,250 a contract) above or below the previous day's settlement price

Foreign currency futures prices are, as the example suggests, quoted in terms of dollars for each unit of foreign currency. The fourth (or fifth for some currencies) decimal point to the right is called a "point"; thus the minimum fluctuation for the pound is five points, or $0.0005. The various currencies traded on the IMM and their minimum fluctuations are as follows:

Currency	Units for each contract	Decimal equivalent of minimum fluctuation	Dollar value
British pound	25,000	× $0.0005	= $12.50
West German deutsche mark	125,000	× $0.0001	= $12.50
Swiss franc	125,000	× $0.0001	= $12.50
Canadian dollar	100,000	× $0.0001	= $10.00
Mexican peso	1,000,000	× $0.00001	= $10.00
Japanese yen	12,500,000	× $0.000001	= $12.50
Dutch guilder	125,000	× $0.0001	= $12.50
French franc	250,000	× $0.00005	= $12.50

Quotations of currency futures prices are quoted daily in financial newspapers. For example, the quotations for the British pound on two successive days were as follows:

British Pound—£25,000, in Dollars a Pound

Date	Opening Price	High Price	Low Price	Settling Price	Change from Previous Day	Open Interest
Wednesday						
June	1.8395	1.8425	1.8315	1.8365	−0.0065	14,614
September	1.8455	1.8470	1.8360	1.8410	−0.0065	1,815
December	1.8505	1.8505	1.8440	1.8450	−0.0070	110
March	—	—	—	1.8480	−0.0060	6
Thursday						
June	1.8380	1.8385	1.8345	1.8380	+0.0015	14,275
September	1.8445	1.8450	1.8405	1.8435	+0.0025	1,792
December	1.8480	1.8480	1.8450	1.8475	+0.0025	114
March	—	—	—	1.8510	+0.0030	6

From these figures the gain or loss from buying a June pounds sterling contract can be calculated at the settling price on Wednesday and the selling price on Thursday.

Wednesday price:	$1.8365
Thursday price:	$1.8380
Difference in points:	+15 (i.e., +$0.0015)

Since every five-point fluctuation in a pounds sterling contract is worth $12.50, the profit, ignoring commission fees, is therefore $12.50 × 3 = $37.50.

The quotations above also allow the calculation of the cost of a futures swap. A futures swap is the simultaneous buying and selling of two futures contracts on two different dates. This is useful to lock in a borrowing or investing rate in a foreign currency; indeed this technique is used in a topic below, "Hedging Eurocurrency Interest Rates." For example, one can buy pounds sterling in September and then resell it in December. The swap cost based on Thursday's closing prices is

December contract	\$1.8475
September contract	\$1.8435
Difference	+\$0.0040

This difference is commonly expressed as an annualized percentage, as follows:

$$\text{Foreign currency swap rate} = \frac{\text{dollar/foreign exchange rate for last date} - \text{dollar/foreign exchange rate for first date}}{\text{dollar/foreign exchange rate for first date}} \times \frac{360}{\text{number of days}} \times 100$$

$$= \frac{1.8475 - 1.8435}{1.8435} \times \frac{360}{91} \times 100 = +0.86\%$$

The computation gives a positive swap rate to reflect the fact that if one buys pounds sterling in September for later resale into dollars in December, more dollars will come back than are paid.

RELATION BETWEEN FUTURES PRICES AND FORWARD EXCHANGE RATES. Futures prices should normally equal forward exchange rates. If they do not, arbitrage will restore equality. For example, if the forward exchange rates for December delivery of pounds sterling were \$1.8440 to \$1.8450 and the futures price \$1.8475, then a dealer with access to both markets could make a profit by buying pounds sterling in the forward market at \$1.8450 and selling a futures contract for delivery on the same day at \$1.8475, netting 25 points, or \$62.50 a contract. Transactions like this one will bid the futures price down, or the forward rate up, or both, until approximate equality is restored.

$$\text{Futures price of a currency} = \text{Forward exchange rate}$$

But wait! There is a difference between the two contracts, as observed earlier, in that the gains or losses on a futures contract are settled day-by-day, instead of in a lump sum at the maturity of the contract. Therefore, if one is rather sure of a speculative gain, because the futures price (and the forward rate) are observed to be below the forecasted spot rate, then the futures contract would be preferred because the gain would probably be realized earlier. If the market as a whole expected this, then the futures price would be bid up above the forward rate. Thus if

$$E(S_{t+n}) > {}_tP_n$$

then

$$ {}_tP_n > {}_tF_n $$

where $E(S_{t+n})$ is the expected future spot exchange rate in dollars for each foreign currency unit and ${}_tP_n$ is the futures price and ${}_tF_n$ is the forward rate at t for delivery n days later.

Conversely, if futures prices and forward rates are expected to fall, a deferred loss would be preferred. Thus if

$$ E(S_{t+n}) < {}_tP_n $$

then

$$ {}_tP_n < {}_tF_n $$

From these two relationships it follows that if

$$ E(S_{t+n}) = {}_tP_n $$

then

$$ {}_tP_n = {}_tF_n $$

A further qualification is that day-by-day futures market gains (or losses) will have to be invested (or borrowed) at uncertain future interest rates. This Cox-Ingersoll-Ross effect could cause futures prices to deviate from forward rates. However, Cornell and Reinganum (1981) looked at actual rates for the British pound, Canadian dollar, West German deutsche mark, Swiss franc, and Japanese yen and found that forward rates and futures prices do not differ significantly from each other.

FOREIGN EXCHANGE OPTIONS

Foreign exchange options are instruments that allow traders and corporations to gain from advantageous currency surprises while limiting the risk of adverse currency movements. As such, they can be a useful tool in exchange risk management. They can also be useful in dealing with certain kinds of business risk—when an overseas deal falls through, for example, or when a bid on a contract is accepted—that is, whenever a firm is uncertain whether a foreign currency cash inflow or outflow will materialize.

DEFINITIONS. A foreign exchange option is a contract conveying **the right to buy or sell a designated quantity of a foreign currency** at a specified price (exchange rate) during a stipulated period under stated conditions.

The terminal date of the contract is called the "**expiration date**" (or "maturity date"). If the option can be exercised before the expiration date, it is called an "**American option**"; if only on the expiration date, a "**European option**."

The party retaining the option is the **option buyer**; the party giving the option is the **option seller** (or **writer**). The exchange rate at which the option can be exercised is called the "**exercise price**." The buyer of the option must pay the seller some amount (the **option price**, or the **premium**) for the rights involved.

A **call option in foreign exchange** is the right to **buy** a specified number of foreign currency units from the option seller at a specified exercise price (in dollars) up to and including the exercise date. A **put option** is the right to **sell** the foreign currency to the option seller at a specified dollar price, up to the expiration date. Since the right to buy West German deutsche marks at a known exchange rate is also the right to sell dollars in exchange for West German deutsche marks at the same exchange rate, it is evident that a foreign exchange put option is simply a call option seen from the other currency's viewpoint.

The important feature of a foreign exchange option is that the holder of the option has the **right**, but not the obligation, to exercise it. The holder will only exercise it if the currency moves in a favorable direction. Thus once an option has been purchased one cannot lose—unlike a forward contract in which one is obliged to exchange the currencies and therefore will lose if the movement is unfavorable.

As an example an option on pounds sterling, for £12,500, is used. Every options contract specifies the **amount**, the **exercise price**, and the **expiration date**. In Exhibit 9 sterling is now $1.78 and the exercise price is $1.85. The option expires in (it is assumed) December. The price or premium for a call option might be, for example, $0.03 a pound (i.e., $375.00). Since the spot rate is below the exercise price, a **call option** will only be "in the money" if sterling rises above $1.85. But a **put option** is already "in the money"—it is worth at least $0.07. As the spot rate moves, so does the option's value.

To understand how options can be used for hedging, one can use diagrams such as Exhibit 9, that show the **net profit** from various basic options strategies, assuming positions are held until expiration. The horizontal axis shows the possible **actual spot price** of sterling at the expiration date.

The holder of a call option will exercise the contract only if the spot exceeds the exercise price. If sterling is below $1.85, only the premium has been lost. If the spot exceeds the exercise price by more than the premium, one has made money. The higher the spot, the greater the profit.

For someone **selling a call**, the profit picture is the mirror image of that of the option buyer. The seller gets the premium, but if the spot rises above the exercise price the option will be exercised. The seller will have to buy sterling at (for example) $1.90 and sell at the prearranged exercise price of $1.85. The net loss is $0.05 − $0.03 = $0.02.

A **put** is the **right to sell** pounds sterling at the exercise price, so the option holder gains in proportion to the amount the pound falls **below** the exercise price (less the premium paid).

Again, the seller of a put gets the premium, but loses if sterling falls below the exercise price (less the premium). The put seller's profit picture is thus the upside-down mirror image of the put buyer's profit.

SOME LIMITS ON FOREIGN EXCHANGE OPTION PRICES. The actual price of a foreign exchange option will depend on a number of factors (to be discussed later) including the future volatility of the exchange rate. Before discussing such elusive features of option pricing, however, some basic characteristics of—and boundaries

EXHIBIT 9 BASIC FOREIGN EXCHANGE OPTIONS STRATEGIES

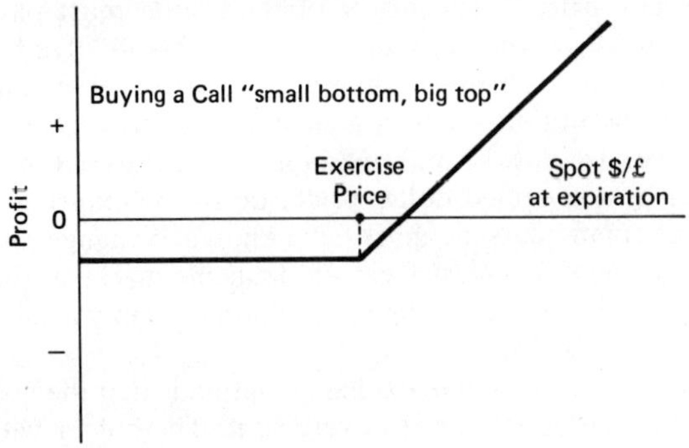

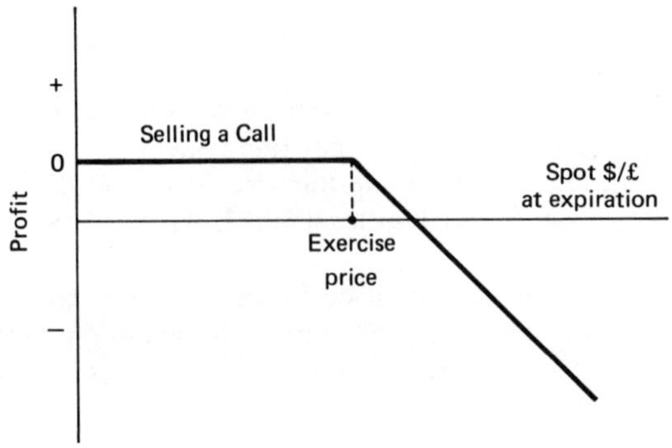

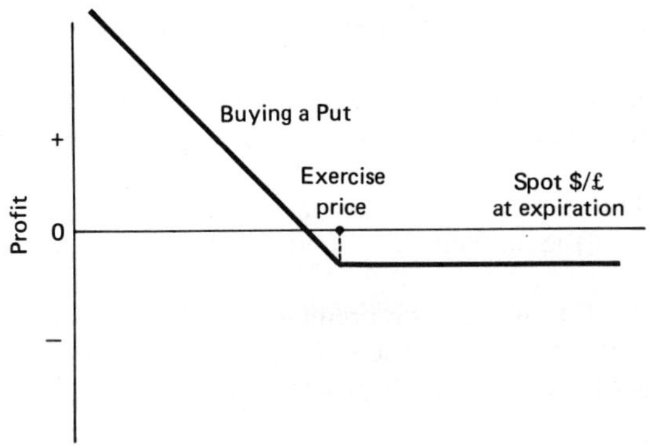

on—the prices of foreign exchange options should be identified. Formal proofs (in the case of stock options) can be found in Smith (1976).

Only call options are discussed at this point. It is simpler to do so; later it will be shown that there are well-defined relationships between calls and puts in foreign exchange so that anything said about calls can be translated into statements about puts.

The following limits give clues to the basic factors determining relative option prices, which are summarized in subsequent discussion.

1. Option prices are never negative. From the definition of an option, exercise is voluntary, so nobody would sell an option for less than zero.
2. At any date before the maturity date a U.S. call option must sell for at least the difference between the spot exchange rate and the exercise price. In other words, if $S > E$, then $C(E) \geq S - E$ where S is the spot exchange rate and $C(E)$ is the dollar price of a call option on one unit of foreign currency with an exercise price of E. Both S and E are expressed in dollars for each unit of foreign currency. Sometimes $S - E$ is called the "intrinsic value" of the call option. An option with a positive intrinsic value is said to be "in the money."
3. A U.S. call option price must always exceed the difference between any forward exchange rate, F, and the exercise price, E, discounted to the present at the interest rate, r. That is,

$$C(E) \geq \frac{F - E}{(1 + r)^t}$$

   where F is the forward exchange rate (in dollars for each unit of foreign currency) for any maturity between the present date and the expiration date. The reason is clarified by the assumption that $C(E) < (F - E)/(1 + r)^t$. Then one could buy the call, costing $C(E)$, and enter a forward exchange contract to sell the foreign currency forward for F dollars. These two enable the investor to exercise the call at the maturity date of the forward, buying at E and selling at F, and lock in a profit whose present value is greater than investment cost. Since risk-free profit opportunities like this are arbitraged away, such cannot be the case.
4. A U.S. call with a longer time to maturity than another call will be priced at least as high as the call with the shorter term to maturity.
5. If two foreign exchange options differ only in exercise price, then the one with the lower exercise price must be priced at least as high as the option with the higher exercise price. If $E_1 < E_2$, then $C(E_1) \geq C(E_2)$. Logically, the lower the exercise price, the more profit one will make for a given rise in the currency.

INFLUENCES ON FOREIGN EXCHANGE OPTION PRICES. A gain can be made by the holder of a call option any time the exchange rate (in dollars for each foreign currency unit) exceeds the exercise price. The bigger the excess, the bigger the gain. Similarly, a gain will be made by the holder of a put option if the option is exercised at any rate below the exercise price. Thus the value of a foreign exchange option is related to that of the **currency itself**, although the relationship is not strictly linear.

Clearly the value of a call option also depends on the **exercise price**, for if the spot rate at expiration is below the exercise price, the option is worthless (for a call option). In general the **lower the exercise price relative to the current spot rate**, the more valuable the call option is.

It also seems reasonable to suppose that the **longer the option has to run** before expiration, the more chance there is of the spot rate exceeding its current level, and therefore the greater the chance that the option can be exercised (or sold) at a profit. Moreover, this chance will be greater the greater the **volatility** of the currency's exchange rate. It follows that the price of the option is higher the more time remains before expiration and the greater the volatility of changes in the exchange rate.

Finally, option prices tend to be higher the higher the **riskless rate of interest.**

PRICING A CALL OPTION: THE BLACK–SCHOLES FORMULA. The most widely used and practical method of combining the above influences to come up with an estimate of the appropriate price of an option is the **Black-Scholes option valuation formula.** Although used primarily in connection with stock options, the formula can readily be used to estimate the value of a foreign exchange option, and prehaps to identify situations where options are overpriced (or even underpriced). The method originally appeared in Black and Scholes (1973). An intuitive explanation can be found in Sharpe (1978). The formula is valid only for call options. Once one knows how to price a call option, however, the put-call–forward exchange parity relationship can be employed (to be described later) to price any put option.

The formula for the currency call option value at an exercise price of E is

$$C(E) = SN(d_1) - \frac{E}{e^{\rho t}}N(d_2) \tag{3}$$

and

$$d_1 = \frac{\ln(S/E) + (\rho + 0.5\sigma^2)t}{\sigma\sqrt{t}} \tag{4}$$

$$d_2 = d_1 - \sigma\sqrt{t} \tag{5}$$

where S = spot exchange rate, in dollars for each unit of foreign currency
E = exercise price of the option
e = 2.71828
t = time before expiration (in years)
ρ = risk-free interest rate (e.g., Treasury bill rate with maturity t) expressed on a continuous compounding basis. This is equal to $\ln(1 + r)$ where r is the simple annual interest rate, expressed as a decimal.
ln = the natural logarithm
σ = standard deviation of the continuously compounded annual rate of change of the exchange rate, which can be measured historically by calculating the standard deviation of $\ln(S_t/S_{t-1})$ for (monthly) data, and multiplying by $\sqrt{12}$ (or $\sqrt{n}$ where n is the number of periods a year)
$N(d)$ = probability that a deviation less than d will occur in a normal distribution with a mean of zero and a standard deviation of 1. Given d, this can be

found from a standard normal probabilities table such as Exhibit 10. A more tedious, but also more accurate, approximation can be obtained from the following formula.

$$N(d) = 1 - 0.5(1 + .04986734d + .0211410061d^2 + .0032776263d^3 + .0000380036d^4 + .0000488906d^5 + .000005383d^6)^{-16} \quad (6)$$

EXHIBIT 10 STANDARD NORMAL PROBABILITIES: VALUES OF $N(d)$ FOR SELECTED VALUES OF d

d	$N(d)$	d	$N(d)$	d	$N(d)$
		−1.00	.1587	1.00	.8413
−2.95	.0016	− .95	.1711	1.05	.8531
−2.90	.0019	− .90	.1841	1.10	.8643
−2.85	.0022	− .85	.1977	1.15	.8749
−2.80	.0026	− .80	.2119	1.20	.8849
−2.75	.0030	− .75	.2266	1.25	.8944
−2.70	.0035	− .70	.2420	1.30	.9032
−2.65	.0040	− .65	.2578	1.35	.9115
−2.60	.0047	− .60	.2743	1.40	.9192
−2.55	.0054	− .55	.2912	1.45	.9265
−2.50	.0062	− .50	.3085	1.50	.9332
−2.45	.0071	− .45	.3264	1.55	.9394
−2.40	.0082	− .40	.3446	1.60	.9452
−2.35	.0094	− .35	.3632	1.65	.9505
−2.30	.0107	− .30	.3821	1.70	.9554
−2.25	.0122	− .25	.4013	1.75	.9599
−2.20	.0139	− .20	.4207	1.80	.9641
−2.15	.0158	− .15	.4404	1.85	.9678
−2.10	.0179	− .10	.4602	1.90	.9713
−2.05	.0202	− .05	.4801	1.95	.9744
−2.00	.0228	.00	.5000	2.00	.9773
−1.95	.0256	.05	.5199	2.05	.9798
−1.90	.0287	.10	.5398	2.10	.9821
−1.85	.0322	.15	.5596	2.15	.9842
−1.80	.0359	.20	.5793	2.20	.9861
−1.75	.0401	.25	.5987	2.25	.9878
−1.70	.0446	.30	.6179	2.30	.9893
−1.65	.0495	.35	.6368	2.35	.9906
−1.60	.0548	.40	.6554	2.40	.9918
−1.55	.0606	.45	.6736	2.45	.9929
−1.50	.0668	.50	.6915	2.50	.9938
−1.45	.0735	.55	.7088	2.55	.9946
−1.40	.0808	.60	.7257	2.60	.9953
−1.35	.0885	.65	.7422	2.65	.9960
−1.30	.0968	.70	.7580	2.70	.9965
−1.25	.1057	.75	.7734	2.75	.9970
−1.20	.1151	.80	.7881	2.80	.9974
−1.15	.1251	.85	.8023	2.85	.9978
−1.10	.1357	.90	.8159	2.90	.9981
−1.05	.1469	.95	.8289	2.95	.9984

The use of this formula is not as complicated as it might seem. A step-by-step example is given below. However, it does depend on a number of assumptions, the most serious of which in the case of currency options is that changes in the currency's value follow a "log normal" distribution with constant variance. While this might be a practical approximation of the truth, several studies have found that in practice the distribution of exchange rate changes is more long-tailed than the log normal distribution. This means that the measure of volatility, σ, could be somewhat questionable.

Example. To estimate a currency option's price using the Black-Scholes formula, all one needs is

- A hand calculator or computer that can calculate a standard deviation and that can give the logarithm of a number (or a log table)
- A table of standard normal probabilities such as Exhibit 10 or formula 6
- The Black-Scholes formula (equation 3), together with equations 4 and 5
- A series of past spot exchange rates
- Paper and pencil

For example, an assistant international treasurer of a corporation has a possible (but not certain) payment of $1 million to make in pounds sterling at the end of three months. The treasurer wishes to consider the use of a call option (the right to buy sterling) at two different exercise prices: $1.92 or $1.94. The present spot rate is $1.90. The three-month Treasury bill rate is 12% annually. What would options at these two exercise prices cost? First, the option with an exercise price of $1.92 is considered.

Step 1. What data are there to plug into the formula?

Spot rate: $S = 1.90$

Exercise price: $E = 1.92$

Time remaining: $t = 0.25$ (three months, or a fourth of a year)

Interest rate: $\rho = 0.1133\%$, this is found by taking the natural logarithm of $(1 + 0.12)$

Step 2. What is the standard deviation of $\ln(S_t/S_{t-1})$?

The following historical data are the end-of-month spot exchange rates from the IFS International Monetary Fund's *International Financial Statistics* for the past couple of years.

Month	Spot Rate	$\ln(S_t/S_{t-1})$
January	2.2683	
February	2.2787	.00457
March	2.1668	−.05035
April	2.2660	.04476
May	2.3300	.02785
June	2.3620	.01364

Month	Spot Rate	$\ln(S_t/S_{t-1})$
July	2.3380	−.01021
August	2.3926	.02308
September	2.3883	−.00180
October	2.4383	.02072
November	2.3595	−.03285
December	2.3850	.01075
January	2.3860	.00042
February	2.2045	−.07912
March	2.2442	.01785
April	2.1404	−.04736
May	2.0695	−.03369
June	1.9428	−.06318
July	1.8560	−.04571
August	1.8370	−.01029
September	1.8005	−.02007
October	1.8450	.02441
November	1.9700	.06555
December	1.9080	−.03198
	Average =	−.00752
	Standard deviation (SD) =	.0362733

And σ = (SD) $\times \sqrt{12}$
Thus σ = .1256544

Step 3. Formulas 4 and 5 give the values of d_1 and d_2:

$$d_1 = \frac{\ln(1.90/1.92) + [.1133 + 0.5(.1256544)^2].25}{.1256544\sqrt{.25}}$$

$$= .31558$$

$$d_2 = d_1 - .1256544\sqrt{.25}$$

$$= .25275$$

Step 4. Exhibit 10 can be used to find the approximate corresponding values of $N(d_1)$ and $N(d_2)$.

$$N(d_1) = N(.31558) = .6179$$

$$N(d_2) = N(.25275) = .5987$$

Or, more accurate numbers can be calculated from formula 6.

$$N(d_1) = .6238 \quad \text{and} \quad N(d_2) = .5998$$

Step 5. Formula 3 can be used to find the value of this option:

$$\text{Option with \$1.92 exercise price} = C(1.92)$$
$$= 1.90 \times .6238 - \frac{1.92}{e^{.1133 \times .25}} \times .5998$$
$$= \$0.0657$$

Thus a three-month call option on pounds sterling with an exercise price at about 1% above the spot rate would be priced at about 3% of the spot rate.

In a similar fashion, starting with Step 3, one can calculate the value of a call option on sterling with an exercise price of $1.94. Doing this gives

$$\text{Option with \$1.94 exercise price} = C(1.94) = \$0.0549$$

Thus when the exercise price is further from the immediate spot price, the option is cheaper.

As noted above, this method depends on a number of assumptions, among which the **estimate of the standard deviation** is particularly important. In the example, historical data were used, which meant that one had to choose **which** series to use. How recent should the data be? How frequent should the observations be? The daily data could have been used instead; for example, based on daily pounds sterling exchange rates for December 1981, the estimated standard deviation is .104 (instead of .126), giving option prices of $0.058 and $0.047 for the $1.92 and $1.94 exercise prices, respectively. Thus when the estimated standard deviation is lower, the option price is also lower.

Exhibit 11 gives some estimated standard deviations based on monthly and daily data for three major currencies. According to these estimates, the Swiss franc is the most risky currency and would produce the highest-priced options.

The estimated standard deviations from Exhibit 11 can be used to plug into formula 3 to find option values for these currencies. Alternatively, the reader could save trouble by using another table, Exhibit 12, in which estimates have already been made of the option price based on various exercise prices (relative to the spot price), interest rates, and standard deviations. The option prices and spot rates are expressed as a percentage of the exercise price. For example, based upon the following information, one can determine the price of a call option on West German deutsche marks.

EXHIBIT 11 TYPICAL STANDARD DEVIATIONS OF EXCHANGE RATE CHANGES

Currency	Monthly Data, 1981–82	Daily Data, December 1981
British pound sterling	.126	.104
West German deutsche mark	.130	.084
Japanese yen	.132	.087
Swiss franc	.155	.107

EXHIBIT 12 TYPICAL OPTION PRICES FOR CALL OPTION ON FOREIGN CURRENCIES BASED ON BLACK-SCHOLES MODEL
(option price shown as percentage of exercise price)

Annual Standard Deviation	5%			10%			15%			20%			25%		
Annual Interest Rate	5%	10%	15%	5%	10%	15%	5%	10%	15%	5%	10%	15%	5%	10%	15%
Spot Rate as Percentage of Exercise Price															
THREE-MONTH OPTIONS															
90%	0.00005	0.003	0.002	0.06	0.10	0.17	0.36	0.49	0.65	0.89	1.10	1.32	1.56	1.81	2.08
92	0.0015	0.007	0.02	0.17	0.27	0.42	0.65	0.86	1.10	1.33	1.61	1.91	2.11	2.43	2.76
94	0.02	0.07	0.17	0.41	0.62	0.89	1.10	1.40	1.75	1.91	2.27	2.65	2.78	3.17	3.58
96	0.15	0.36	0.70	0.86	1.22	1.65	1.73	2.15	2.61	2.65	3.09	3.56	3.59	4.05	4.52
98	0.64	1.16	1.85	1.59	2.13	2.74	2.57	3.11	3.68	3.54	4.08	4.64	4.52	5.05	5.60
100	1.71	2.58	3.52	2.64	3.37	4.14	3.62	4.28	4.97	4.60	5.23	5.87	5.58	6.19	6.80
102	3.33	4.39	5.45	4.01	4.88	5.78	4.88	5.65	6.44	5.81	6.53	7.25	6.77	7.45	8.13
104	5.23	6.35	7.43	5.61	6.60	7.59	6.32	7.20	8.07	7.17	7.97	8.77	8.08	8.83	9.57
SIX-MONTH OPTIONS															
90%	0.012	0.07	0.27	0.42	0.77	1.27	1.27	1.81	2.46	2.33	2.98	3.70	3.49	4.20	4.96
92	0.066	0.27	0.78	0.76	1.30	2.03	1.82	2.51	3.32	3.01	3.77	4.62	4.25	5.06	5.92
94	0.25	0.76	1.73	1.28	2.05	3.03	1.51	3.37	4.35	3.79	4.69	5.66	5.10	6.02	6.98
96	0.71	1.70	3.14	2.01	3.04	4.27	3.35	4.38	5.53	4.70	5.73	6.82	6.05	7.07	8.13
98	1.59	3.08	4.87	2.97	4.26	5.71	4.34	5.55	6.85	5.72	6.88	8.09	7.00	8.22	9.37
100	2.92	4.80	6.78	4.16	5.68	7.33	5.49	6.87	8.32	6.86	8.14	9.47	8.22	9.45	10.70
102	4.59	6.69	8.75	5.55	7.29	9.09	6.79	8.32	9.90	8.10	9.51	10.95	9.45	10.78	12.11
104	6.46	8.66	10.75	7.13	9.03	10.93	8.21	9.88	11.57	9.45	10.97	12.51	10.76	12.17	13.60

Spot rate: $S = 0.432$ (\$/DM)
Exercise price: $E = 0.450$ (\$/DM)
Time remaining: Three months
Interest rate: 10% (annually)
Standard deviation: 13.0% (from Exhibit 11, based on monthly data)
Spot rate as percentage of exercise price: $0.432/0.450 \times 100 = 96\%$

Using Exhibit 12, one finds the option price between 1.22 (based on a 10% standard deviation) and 2.15 (based on a 15% standard deviation) as a percentage of the exercise price. Therefore, the price of a call option on West German deutsche marks under the stated conditions would be between $0.0122 \times 0.45 = \$0.0055$ for each deutsche mark and $0.0215 \times 0.45 = \$0.0097$ for each deutsche mark. Interpolating, the option price would be \$0.008 a deutsche mark.

ARBITRAGE RELATIONSHIPS BETWEEN OPTIONS AND FORWARD EXCHANGE. Although an **option** is a contract that **need not be exercised,** while a **forward exchange contract must be completed** (or reversed), the two kinds of contracts are linked in interesting ways. The basic relationships between forward exchange rates and option premiums stem from the fact that various combinations of options, forward contracts, deposits, and borrowings can duplicate one another.

The options being discussed are hypothetical European options because they are not exercised before the expiration date. However, most of what follows applies to U.S. as well as to European options, because U.S. options on foreign exchange are highly unlikely to be actually exercised before the expiration date—they are always more valuable "alive" than "dead." The following are some important arbitrage relationships.

Relationship 1. A combination of buying a call and selling a put at the same exercise price E is equivalent to buying a currency forward at exchange rate E. Of course, one will have paid for the call and gained from the put; this is a net cost or gain that has been ignored. The next relationship takes this into account explicitly.

Relationship 2. For any exercise price E, the difference between the price of a put and a call at E, $P(E) - C(E)$, equals the difference between E and the forward exchange rate F, discounted to the present at the interest rate r. In other words,

$$C(E) - P(E) = \frac{F - E}{(1 + r)^t} \tag{7}$$

This is the put-call–forward exchange parity (PCFP) theory.

If 7 is not true, a profit can be made. How?

If

$$C(E) - P(E) < \frac{F - E}{(1 + r)^t}$$

then the first step is to buy a call at E; second, to sell a put at E; third, to sell the foreign currency forward at F.

If

$$C(E) - P(E) > \frac{(F - E)}{(1 + r)^t}$$

then the first step is to sell a call at E; second, to buy a put at E; third, to buy the foreign currency forward at F.

Relationship 3. The prices of a call option and a put option with an exercise price at the forward exchange rate are equal. That is

$$C(F) = P(F) \tag{8}$$

The reason can be found in equation 7. If the exercise price is equal to the forward rate (i.e., $F = E$), then the right-hand side of equation 7 is zero; that is, $C(E) - P(E) = 0$. Therefore, $C(E) = P(E)$ when $F = E$.

Relationship 4. The price of a foreign exchange put option in one currency is the same as that of a call option in the other currency at the same exercise price, E; that is,

$$C(E) = SEP'\left(\frac{1}{E}\right) \tag{9}$$

and

$$P(E) = SEC'\left(\frac{1}{E}\right) \tag{10}$$

where a prime designates something in the foreign currency.

This could be called "international put-call equivalence" (IPCE). An option to buy currency B with currency A at price E is identical to an option to sell currency A in exchange for currency B at price E. Thus what is termed a "call" in one currency is a put in the other, and vice versa. The price of a call is $C(E)$. In the other currency, regarded in terms of local currency units, the price of the corresponding put for one unit of foreign currency is $P'(1/E)$. Therefore, the price for a put on E units of foreign currency is $EP'(1/E)$. Since this is the same as the original call, they must be priced identically when translated at the current spot exchange rate, S. (If this doesn't hold, arbitrage!)

PRICING A PUT OPTION IN FOREIGN EXCHANGE. The procedure for finding out the price of an option using the Black-Scholes formula applies only to a call option. However, now a relationship between the price of a call option and that of a put option are evident through the forward exchange market, the PCFP.

$$C(E) - P(E) = \frac{F - E}{(1 + r)^t} \tag{11}$$

where F is the forward exchange rate for delivery on the expiration date of the options. Solving for $P(E)$,

$$P(E) = C(E) + \frac{E - F}{(1 + r)^t} \tag{12}$$

Therefore, by plugging the call option price, $C(E)$, which can be found using the Black-Scholes formula, into equation 12, one can determine the put option price, $P(E)$.

EQUIVALENT POSITIONS. From relationships 1 through 4 above, especially the put-call–forward exchange parity, one can also deduce that investors can achieve virtually identical profit and risk positions in various ways. These can be related to a well-known relationship in the foreign exchange and money markets—the interest rate parity theorem (IRPT)—to show **triangular equivalence** relationships between (1) borrowing and investing positions; (2) forward exchange positions; and (3) put and call options positions.

The following are examples of such triangular equivalent positions. For ease of exposition the examples use the U.S. dollar as the home currency and the pound sterling as the foreign currency.

A Long Position in a Foreign Currency

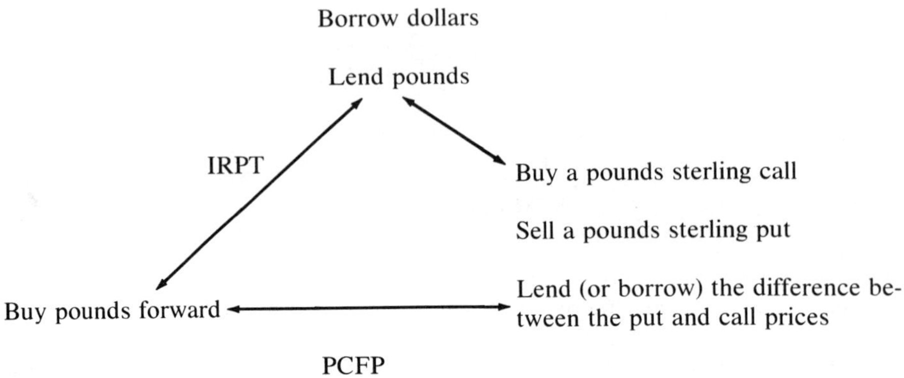

This is the fundamental triangular equivalence relationship. The following come from rearrangements or reversals of these.

A Short Position in a Foreign Currency

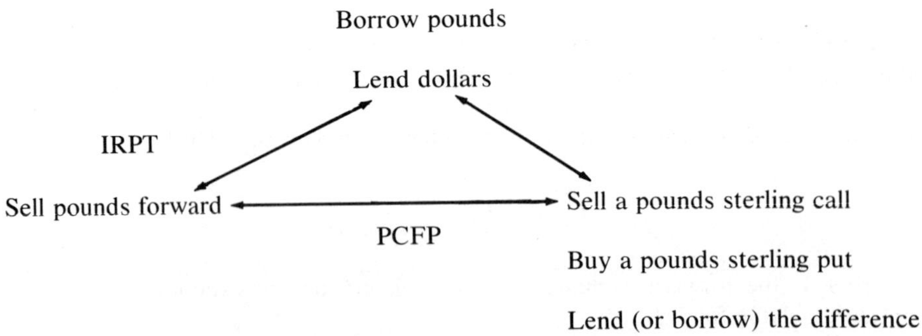

This is exactly the same as the first diagram, seen from the pounds sterling point of view. (Remember that, from the IPCE above, a call to buy pounds sterling is the same as a put to sell dollars for sterling.)

A Hedged Long Position in a Foreign Currency

Borrow dollars

Lend pounds

Sell pounds forward

(equals zero profit: IRPT)

Buy pounds forward ⟷ Buy a pounds sterling call

Sell pounds forward

(equals a zero net position)

Buy a pounds sterling call

Sell a pounds sterling put

Lend (or borrow) the difference

Sell pounds forward

(equals zero profit: PCFP)

The above equivalence triangle is obtained by simply adding a forward sale of sterling to each of the three positions in the first diagram.

A Hedged Short Position in a Foreign Currency

Borrow pounds

Lend dollars

Buy pounds sterling forward

(equals zero profit: IRPT)

Sell pounds forward ⟷ Sell a pounds sterling call

Buy pounds forward

(equals zero net position)

Sell a pounds sterling call

Buy a pounds sterling put

Lend (or borrow) the difference

Buy pounds forward

(equals a zero net profit: PCFP)

This equivalence triangle is obtained by adding a forward purchase of sterling to the positions in the second diagram.

Replicating a Call in a Foreign Currency

Borrow dollars

Lend pounds

Buy a pounds sterling put

Buy pounds forward ⟷ Buy a pounds sterling call

Buy a pounds sterling put

All that has been done here is to add a long put to each position in the first diagram.

Replicating a Put in a Foreign Currency

Borrow pounds

Lend dollars

Buy a pounds sterling call

Sell pounds sterling forward ⟷ Buy a pounds sterling put

Buy a pounds sterling call

To conclude this topic, it is evident that one does not require a complete set of put and call markets in all currencies in order to achieve the full range of investment and hedging strategies. The creative banker or foreign exchange manager can use the arbitrage and equivalence relationships to create almost any risk-return position in foreign currencies that one might desire.

THE TERM STRUCTURE OF INTEREST RATES AND INTEREST RATE FUTURES

TERM STRUCTURE OF INTEREST RATES. The relationship between yield and maturity on securities differing only in length of time to maturity is known as the **term structure of interest rates.** The term structure can be studied graphically by plotting yield and maturity for equivalently graded securities at a moment in time.

To illustrate a basic equilibrium relationship among interest rates in different maturity ranges, suppose there are currently two alternatives: a one-year security and a two-year security.

	Time t → Time $t+1$	Time $t+1$ →
Alternative 1. One-year security	${}_tR_1$	$\exp({}_{t+1}R_1)$
Alternative 2. Two-year security	${}_tR_2$	${}_tR_2$

Time t Time $t + 1$

In this diagram ${}_tR_n$ represents the **actual** rate of interest at time t on a security with maturity n, and $\text{Exp}({}_{t+1}R_1)$ is the **expected** value of the future interest rate that will prevail at time $t + 1$ on a security with maturity 1. Investors will select the strategy that offers the greatest expected return over the two periods. Therefore, the equilibrium will occur when the two alternatives give them the same return.

$$(1 + {}_tR_2)^2 = (1 + {}_tR_1)\,[1 + \text{Exp}({}_{t+1}R_1)] \tag{13}$$

expected future interest rate

In effect, the long-term interest rate can be thought of as the **geometric average** of present and expected future short-term interest rates.

Dividing both sides of equation 13 by $(1 + {}_tR_1)$ one obtains

$$\frac{(1 + {}_tR_2)^2}{1 + {}_tR_1} = 1 + \text{Exp}({}_{t+1}R_1) \tag{14}$$

In addition, given ${}_tR_2$ and ${}_tR_1$, a **forward interest rate** can be defined as the implicit rate that equalizes yields on long-term and successive short-term investments.

$$(1 + {}_tR_2)^2 = (1 + {}_tR_1)(1 + {}_{t+1}r_{1t}) \tag{15}$$

forward interest rate

where ${}_{t+1}r_{1t}$ is a forward rate, as of time t, for a one-period loan beginning at time $t + 1$. As before, one can solve for ${}_{t+1}r_{1t}$ by dividing both sides by $(1 + {}_tR_1)$; the result will be the same as equation 14.

According to the **expectations theory** of the term structure of interest rates, the implied forward rate represents the market's forecast (i.e., the expected future short-term interest rate).

$${}_{t+1}r_{1t} = \text{Exp}({}_{t+1}R_1) \tag{16}$$

More generally, a security that matures n periods from now can be compared to an alternative strategy of investing in a sequence of n one-period securities. In equilibrium then the following relationship should hold.

$$(1 + {}_tR_n)^n = (1 + {}_tR_1)(1 + {}_{t+1}r_{1t}) \ldots (1 + {}_{t+n-1}r_{1t})$$

where ${}_tR_n$ represents the actual rate of interest at time t on a security with maturity n, and ${}_{t+1}r_{1t}$ and ${}_{t+n-1}r_{1t}$ are forward rates for one-period loans beginning at times $t + 1$ and $t + n - 1$, implied in the term structure at time t. The formula for deriving the one-period forward rate beginning at time $t + n$, implied in the term structure at time t, is

$$1 + {}_{t+n}r_{1t} = \frac{(1 + {}_tR_{n+1})^{n+1}}{(1 + {}_tR_n)^n}$$

or

$$_{t+n}r_{1t} = \frac{(1 + {}_tR_{n+1})^{n+1}}{(1 + {}_tR_n)^n} - 1 \tag{18}$$

More generally, the formula for deriving the k period forward rate beginning at time $t + n$, implied in the term structure at time t, is

$$(1 + {}_{t+n}r_{kt})^k = \frac{(1 + {}_tR_{n+k})^{n+k}}{(1 + {}_tR_n)^n}$$

or

$$_{t+n}r_{kt} = \left[\frac{(1 + {}_tR_{n+k})^{n+k}}{(1 + {}_tR_n)^n}\right]^{1/k} - 1 \tag{19}$$

The forward interest rate is not merely an abstract concept—indeed, any investor can **lock in** the forward interest rate $_{t+n}r_{kt}$ by **borrowing** for n periods (at $_tR_n$) and investing the funds for $n + k$ periods (at $_tR_{n+k}$). Alternatively, the investor can lock in a future interest rate by buying a futures contract in the interest rate futures market.

INTEREST RATE FUTURES. Any anticipated future commitment in the money markets exposes both borrowers and lenders to the **risk of interest rate** changes from the present until the time when the borrowing or lending occurs. To minimize these risks, money market participants can **hedge** in the interest rate futures market. A hedger knows that he or she will be participating as a borrower or lender in the **"cash" market** at some specific time. The investor uses the futures market to provide forward price protection for anticipated money market transactions.

A financial manager who anticipates having funds to **lend** in the short-term money markets at a known time in the future can hedge against the risk that interest rates might drop by the time of actual lending. Such an investor can hedge this risk by buying a futures contract immediately at a specified rate for delivery at a specified future time. If interest rates fall by the delivery date, the contract will appreciate in value. The appreciation in value on the futures contract can offset the lender's "opportunity loss" from the actual decline in interest rates. Thus for investors anticipating loanable funds to be available in the future, the appropriate futures market hedge is a long hedge.

Borrowers in the money markets also can use interest rate futures to protect themselves against increases in interest rates by selling an interest rate contract for future delivery. If interest rates rise by the delivery date, the value of the futures contract will drop. The financial manager can buy back the contract for a lower price, thus making a gain. The gain from the futures contract can offset the increase in the cash borrowing costs. Thus for borrowers anticipating actual borrowing in the future the appropriate futures market hedge is a short hedge.

As is the case with the foreign exchange futures market, in the interest rate futures market the clearing house of the exchange takes the opposite side of each position. Moreover, the exchange requires "marking to the market," which means that all profits and losses must be settled on a daily basis. If the value of a Treasury bill contract increases during the course of a day, the holder receives cash; if it falls, the holder must pay the loss. This happens every day for every change in price up to the final day of the contract. On the maturity date, the futures price must equal the cash (spot) price of the Treasury bill. Hence, the payment required on the maturity date to buy the underlying Treasury bill is simply its spot price at that time.

Yields and Prices of Treasury Bill Futures. The International Monetary Market of the Chicago Mercantile Exchange provides a futures market in U.S. Treasury bills (T bills). The IMM has established a method of quoting T bill yields for futures contracts that is unique in futures trading. The IMM system is essentially an index based on the difference between the actual T bill yield and 100.00. Thus a T bill yield of 7.00% would be quoted on the IMM at 93.00. When a person expects interest rates to go up, he or she would be a seller of the T bill futures since the dollar price of the bill would drop as interest rates went up. On the other hand, if a person expected interest rates to fall, that person would be a buyer of the T bill futures since the dollar price of the bill would rise as interest rates went down.

Dealers in Treasury bills normally quote T bill prices on a **discount basis**—that is, the T bill yield is the difference between the **face value** of a bill and its **market value,** as a percentage of the bill's face value on an annualized basis. Hence, the calculation of the **discount yield for T bill futures** expresses the interest rate as an annualized percentage of the maturity value of the Treasury bill (i.e., as a percentage of the face value of $1 million). Bond equivalent yields, in contrast, are expressed as a percentage of the initial value of the instrument.

The actual **price of a T bill futures contract** and **bond equivalent yield** (to compare with other interest rates) can be calculated from the quoted T bill yield as follows:

Step 1. Treasury bill yields equal 100 minus the IMM index. Given the IMM index on 90-day bill futures is 93.5, find the T bill yield.

$$\begin{aligned}\text{T bill yield} &= 100 - 93.5\\ &= 6.5\%\end{aligned}$$

Step 2. Given the T bill yield, find the T bill futures price.

$$\text{T bill futures price} = \text{T bill face value} - \frac{(\text{days to maturity} \times \text{T bill yield} \times \text{T bill face value})}{360}$$

Given a T bill yield of 6.5%,

$$\begin{aligned}\text{T bill futures price} &= \$1{,}000{,}000 - \frac{(90 \times 0.065 \times \$1{,}000{,}000)}{360}\\ &= \$983{,}750\end{aligned}$$

Step 3. Given the T bill futures price, find the bond-equivalent yield.

$$\text{Bond equivalent yield} = \frac{(\text{T bill face value} - \text{T bill futures price}) \times 365}{\text{days to maturity} \times \text{T bill futures price}}$$

Given a T bill futures price of $983,750,

$$\text{Bond-equivalent yield} = \frac{(\$1{,}000{,}000 - \$983{,}750) \times 365}{90 \times \$983{,}750}$$
$$= 6.7\%$$

The following example shows how a borrower who plans in December to sell $1 million in 90-day commercial paper in March could protect himself or herself against higher future interest costs by taking a short position in the 90-day Treasury bill futures market.

In this example, it is assumed that the commercial paper rate is always 0.5% (50 basis points) below the T bill rate. Then the borrower can lock in a borrowing rate equal to the T bill yield, less 0.5%.

Example

Cash Market		Futures Market	
December			
Anticipated selling $1 million commercial paper in March		Sold one March T bill contract at 6.5% (IMM index 93.5)	
		Face value (one contract):	$1,000,000
		Value:	$ 983,750
March			
Sold $1 million commercial paper at 7.5%		Bought (offset) one March T bill contract at 8% (IMM index 92.0)	
Revenue:	$981,250		
Interest cost:	18,750		
Less hedge profit:	(3,750)	Value:	$980,000
Effective cost:	$ 15,000	Profit from futures:	$ 3,750
Effective interest rate:	6%		

In the example, the interest cost is calculated as 7.5%/4 = 1.875%, because the borrowing is for 90 days; 1.875% of $1 million is $18,750, the interest cost. Reducing the net interest cost to $15,000 is equivalent to a 90-day interest rate of 1.5%, or 6% on an annual basis.

Note, however, that the borrower can be sure of locking in the cost **only** if the correlation between commercial paper and T bill rates is perfect. The risk that this relationship might not be perfect is called **"basis risk."** Because of basis risk, it is best to hedge with a futures instrument as similar as possible to the anticipated borrowing or investing instrument.

Eurodollar Futures. While the organized futures markets were initially limited to contracts for government debt instruments, they have now broadened to trading in other securities, including domestic and offshore bank deposits. Deposits outside the United States that are denominated in dollars are Eurodollar deposits. These bear an interest rate closely related to the domestic deposit rate.

Eurodollar futures on the IMM are contracts for delivery of a $1 million time deposit in one of several major banks in London at some specified future date. The Eurodollar futures price is actually an **index** that is calculated as 100 minus the yield (in annual percentage terms). The yield for Eurodollar **time deposits** is calculated as an **add-on yield** (i.e., as a percentage of the initial value—$1 million—rather than as a percentage of the maturity value of the instrument). (The latter is a discount yield, and is used for T bill yield calculations.) Typical quotations are presented as follows:

Three-Month Eurodollar Time Deposit Futures
(on $1 million; points of 100%; add-on)

Delivery Month	Opening Price	High Price	Low Price	Settlement Price	Points Change	Add-on Yield
June	85.40	85.52	85.17	85.24	+8	14.76
September	85.36	85.47	85.22	85.30	+10	14.70
December	85.35	85.43	85.22	85.22	+2	14.78
March	85.30	85.35	85.22	85.22	−1	14.78

Comparing the fifth and seventh columns, one can see that the add-on yield is simply 100 minus the settlement price, the closing price at the end of the trading day.

Eurodollar futures can be particularly useful for banks, borrowers, or investors that wish to lock in a future interest rate in the Eurodollar market. The following is an example of how a bank could hedge against a rise in the cost of funds in the Eurodollar market. The example is adapted from the Chicago International Monetary Market's *Inside Eurodollar Futures*.

> If the bank were in a positive-sloping yield curve environment, the typical transaction would be to take a three-month deposit and make a six-month loan. The objective would be to profit from the difference between short rates and long rates. But there is a risk that rates could rise by the time of the rollover and the bank might wish to hedge itself against such a rate rise.
>
> OBJECTIVE
>
> On 12 June, the September Eurodollar contract was priced at an index of 82.20 (100 minus 17.80%) and the bank wishes to hedge the last three months' deposit from 16 September to 16 December.
>
> RATES
>
> Eurodollar quotations 12 June:
>
> From spot (16 June):

To three months (16 September—92 days):	17.00%
To six months (16 December—183 days):	17.8125%
Interest received on loan for 183 days at 17.8125%:	$90,546
Cost of funds for 92 days at 17%:	$43,444
Available to pay last 91 days interest:	$47,102

> ACTION

1. On 12 June, the bank sells one September contract at 82.20 (17.80%), borrows three-month Eurodollars (cash) at 17.00%, and invests for six months at 17.8125%.
2. On 14 September the bank borrows three-month Eurodollars in the interbank market at 20.00%, and reverses out (buys) one September contract at 80.00 (20.00%).

RESULTS

12 June, one September contract is sold at:	82.20 (17.80%)
14 September, one September contract is bought at:	80.00 (20.00%)
Profit on the contract: +220 basis points	2.20 (2.20%)

Each basis point is worth $25

Total profit on hedge: 220 × $25 × 1 contract = $5,500

OBSERVATIONS

The cost of the three-month rollover of the time deposit has increased from 17.00% to 20.00% for the last 91 days. Thus the cost of the last rollover is $50,560. However, the effective cost of the last rollover is $45,060 because the bank has now made a profit of $5,500 from the futures contract ($50,560 − $5,500 = $45,060). Subtracting this effective cost of $45,060 from the previously determined amount available to pay interest for the last rollover of $47,102, one gets $47,102 − $45,060 = $2,042 as a profit from the whole operation.

Hedging Eurocurrency Interest Rates. Hedging Eurocurrency interest rates—for example, hedging against a rise in the Eurosterling interest rate—can also be accomplished by means of futures contracts. This can be done by using a Eurodollar deposit futures contract (to lock in the future dollar interest rate) together with two foreign currency futures contracts (to lock in the exchange rates at which the currency is initially bought and subsequently sold).

The locked-in foreign currency (Eurocurrency) interest rate can readily be computed as follows:

$$\text{Locked-in Eurocurrency interest rate} = \text{Eurodollar futures contract yield (add-on basis)} - \text{Foreign currency swap rate (positive or negative)}$$

More explicitly, the method of calculation involves three steps:

1. Eurodollar futures contract yield = 100 − Eurodollar futures contract price index

2.
$$\text{Foreign currency swap rate} = \frac{\text{dollar/foreign exchange rate for last date} - \text{dollar/foreign exchange rate for first date}}{\text{dollar/foreign exchange rate for first date}} \times \frac{360}{\text{number of days}} \times 100$$

3. Subtracting the result of step 2 from result of step 1 to give the locked-in foreign currency interest rate.

The following example shows how a Eurosterling hedge can be created. The example also is adapted from *Inside Eurodollar Futures*.

First, using step 2, as explained above, the annualized foreign currency swap rate is determined.

RATE ASSUMPTIONS	
Dollar/sterling rate to sell British pounds for 16 December:	1.9900
Dollar/sterling rate to buy British pounds for 16 September:	1.9800
The difference or premium:	+0.0100

$$\frac{0.0100}{1.9800} \times \frac{360}{91} \times 100 = 2.00\% \text{ annualized premium}$$

Having calculated the annual premium, a customer calls a Eurocurrency banker in June for a price to borrow Eurosterling from 16 September to 16 December. In June the banker would

Buy September British pounds:	1.9800
Sell December British pounds:	1.9900
Annualized premium on currency swap:	+2.00%
Sell September Eurodollar contract at 83.85:	−16.15%
Net cost of Eurosterling in September is fixed at:	14.15%

The banker has now, in June, locked in the funding cost at 14.15%.

The reason is as follows. The currency swap (buying sterling at 1.9800 and selling at 1.9900) locks in a 2.00% premium for the exchange of dollars into sterling (in September) and repayment into dollars (in December). Therefore, to have sterling available at a known cost all the banker has to do is to borrow dollars from September to December at a known cost. The Eurodollar futures contract locks in the dollar cost of funds at 16.15%. The net cost is therefore 16.15% − 2% = 14.15%.

Relationships between Add-On Yield, Discount Yield, and Bond Equivalent Yield. Futures yields can be expressed in three different ways. The **discount yield** is the interest rate as a percentage of the maturity value of the investment. The **add-on yield** is a percentage of the initial value of the instrument. Both are annualized on the basis of a 360-day year. The **bond equivalent yield** is the add-on yield, but calculated on the basis of a 365-day year. Each can be converted into one another as follows:

$$\text{Add-on yield} = \frac{\text{discount yield} \times \dfrac{\text{days to maturity}}{360}}{100 - \text{discount yield} \times \dfrac{\text{days to maturity}}{360}} \times \frac{360}{\text{days to maturity}} \times 100$$

$$\text{Discount yield} = \frac{\text{add-on yield} \times \dfrac{\text{days to maturity}}{360}}{100 + \text{add-on yield} \times \dfrac{\text{days to maturity}}{360}} \times \frac{360}{\text{days to maturity}} \times 100$$

$$\text{Bond equivalent yield} = \text{add-on yield} \times \frac{365}{360}$$

$$= \left(\frac{\text{discount yield} \times \dfrac{\text{days to maturity}}{360}}{100 - \text{discount yield} \times \dfrac{\text{days to maturity}}{360}} \right) \times \frac{365}{\text{days to maturity}} \times 100$$

$$\text{Add-on yield} = \text{bond equivalent yield} \times \frac{360}{365}$$

$$\text{Discount yield} = \frac{\text{bond equivalent yield} \times \dfrac{\text{days to maturity}}{365}}{100 + \text{bond equivalent yield} \times \dfrac{\text{days to maturity}}{365}} \times \frac{360}{\text{days to maturity}} \times 100$$

Example. Given a three-month Eurodollar time deposit yield (add-on) of 6.7%, find the discount yield and bond equivalent yield.

$$\text{Discount yield} = \frac{6.7 \times \dfrac{90}{360}}{100 + 6.7 \times \dfrac{90}{360}} \times \frac{360}{90} \times 100$$

$$= 6.5896\%$$

$$\text{Bond equivalent yield} = 6.7 \times \frac{365}{360}$$

$$= 6.793\%$$

LINK BETWEEN FUTURES MARKET YIELDS AND IMPLIED FORWARD INTEREST RATES. The link between futures yields and forward interest rates can best be shown with an example using one-year and two-year Treasury bills.

For example, as of December 1981, there are two investment alternatives: to buy a two-year T bill, or to buy a one-year T bill and a December 1982 T bill (one-year) futures contract.

Alternative 1	← R_2 →	← R_2 →	
Alternative 2	← R_1 →	← R_{fut} →	
December 1981	December 1982		December 1983

In the above diagram R_1 and R_2 are the yields as of December 1981 on a one-year T bill and a two-year T bill, and R_{fut} is the yield on a December 1982 T bill futures contract.

The overall return for alternative 1 is $(1 + R_2)(1 + R_2) = (1 + R_2)^2$ and that for alternative 2 is $(1 + R_1)(1 + R_{fut})$. Both alternatives are risk-free, ignoring reinvestment of interest. Therefore, the returns on both should be equal.

$$(1 + R_2)^2 = (1 + R_1)(1 + R_{fut}) \tag{20}$$

What causes this to hold? If the left-hand side of equation 20 is greater than the right-hand side, investors will buy two-year T bills and sell one-year T bills and December 1982 T bill futures contracts. This causes two-year yields to fall and one-year yields and futures yields to rise until equality is established. Similarly, if the left-hand side of equation 20 is smaller than the right-hand side, demand will shift to the shorter term investment plus T bill futures contract, thereby establishing the equality between the two investment alternatives. Thus to see whether the futures market is in equilibrium with the cash market equation 20 should be tested to see if it holds. Or dividing by $(1 + R_1)$ and subtracting 1, equation 21 could be tested.

$$R_{fut} = \frac{(1 + R_2)^2}{(1 + R_1)} - 1 \tag{21}$$

But from equation 19, the right-hand side of equation 21 is simply the forward interest rate, r_{for}, as the forward interest rate is defined such that $(1 + R_2)^2 = (1 + R_1)(1 + r_{for})$. Therefore, one can say that equilibrium between futures market and the term structure of interest rates holds when

$$R_{fut} = r_{for}$$

That is, the forward interest rate must equal the futures interest rate.

If by any chance the equality does not hold, portfolio managers can profit by rearranging T bill portfolios in accordance with the following rules.

1. If the forward interest rate exceeds the futures interest rate, one should buy longer term T bills, sell shorter term T bills, and sell T bill futures.
2. If the futures interest rate exceeds the forward interest rate, one should sell longer term T bills, buy shorter term T bills, and buy T bill futures.

Evaluating Arbitrage Opportunities in the Cash and Futures Markets. While the previous discussion describes the basic theoretical relationship between futures and forward interest rates, it differs from real-world practice in one important respect. That is, to take advantage of arbitrage opportunities when the forward rate differs from the futures rate, the arbitrageur must **borrow** funds—usually at a rate above the T bill rate.

In this case it is not enough for the forward and futures rates simply to differ. The differential should be enough to compensate for the arbitrageur's higher borrowing cost. The rules therefore change a bit.

The following summarizes the **two basic arbitrage rules** for someone who does not already have a cash position in T bills; the explanations follow.

Rule 1. If

$$\underset{\substack{\uparrow\\ \text{1-year}\\ \text{futures}\\ \text{yield}}}{R_{\text{fut}}} < (1 + \underset{\substack{\uparrow\\ \text{2-year}\\ \text{T-note}\\ \text{yield}}}{R_2})^2/(1 + \underset{\substack{\uparrow\\ \text{1-year}\\ \text{borrowing}\\ \text{cost}}}{R_1^{\text{bor}}}) - 1 \tag{22}$$

then buy a two-year T note, borrow for one year, and sell the T bill futures for delivery in one year.

This decision rule involves using the two-year T note to deliver on the futures contract in one year's time. The proceeds from the T bill delivery will be used to pay off the loan. For this to be profitable, the long-term yield must exceed the compounded cash and futures yields.

$$(1 + R_2)^2 > (1 + R_1^{\text{bor}})(1 + R_{\text{fut}}) \tag{23}$$

where, as before, R_1^{bor} is the arbitrageur's one-year borrowing rate.

Dividing both sides by $(1 + R_1^{\text{bor}})$ and subtracting 1 gives

$$R_{\text{fut}} < \frac{(1 + R_2)^2}{(1 + R_1^{\text{bor}})} - 1 \tag{24}$$

If this condition is fulfilled, the first rule should be followed. Note that if the borrowing rate R_1^{bor} is equal to the T bill rate, the right-hand side simply becomes the definition of forward interest rate, r_{for}, and the previous rules hold: if $R_{\text{fut}} < r_{\text{for}}$, do it!

A little bit of manipulation will enable one to discover how much of a gap between the futures and forward rate is necessary for arbitrage to be profitable. Changing signs in equation 22 and adding r_{for} to both sides of the inequality gives

$$r_{\text{for}} - R_{\text{fut}} > \frac{(1 + R_2)^2\,(R_1^{\text{bor}} - R_1)}{(1 + R_1)(1 + R_1^{\text{bor}})} \tag{25}$$

The other basic arbitrage rule is the reverse strategy.

Rule 2. If

$$\underset{\substack{\uparrow\\ \text{1-year}\\ \text{futures}\\ \text{yield}}}{R_{\text{fut}}} > (1 + \underset{\substack{\uparrow\\ \text{2-year}\\ \text{borrowing}\\ \text{cost}}}{R_2^{\text{bor}}})^2/(1 + \underset{\substack{\uparrow\\ \text{1-year}\\ \text{T bill}\\ \text{yield}}}{R_1}) - 1 \tag{26}$$

then one should borrow for two years, buy one-year T bills, and buy T bill futures for delivery in one year.

The method here is to borrow for two years but invest for only one year; the second year's investment yield is locked in by buying a T bill futures contract. This will only be profitable if the combined borrowing cost (R_2^{bor} for two years) is less than the compounded investment yield, cash and futures.

$$(1 + R_2^{bor})^2 < (1 + R_1)(1 + R_{fut}) \tag{27}$$

remembering that R_2^{bor} is the arbitrageur's two-year borrowing rate.

Dividing both sides by $(1 + R_1)$ and subtracting 1 gives

$$R_{fut} > \frac{(1 + R_2^{bor})^2}{1 + R_1} - 1 \tag{28}$$

Once more, the equivalence to the previous rule should be noted: If the borrowing rate equals the T bill rate, the right-hand side becomes the forward interest rate.

More manipulation will enable one to see again how big the future rate–forward rate gap has to be for arbitrage under the second rule to be profitable. Subtracting r_{for} from both sides of equation 26 gives

$$R_{fut} - r_{for} > \frac{(1 + R_2^{bor})^2 - (1 + R_2)^2}{1 + R_1}$$

REFERENCES

Black, F. and M. Scholes, "The Pricing of Options and Corporate Liabilities," *Journal of Political Economy,* May–June (1973).

Burtle, J. L., "The International Monetary System," In Altman, E. I. (Ed.), *Financial Handbook,* Wiley, New York, 1981.

Chicago International Monetary Market, *Inside Eurodollar Futures*

Cornell, and Reingunum, "Forward and Futures Prices: Evidence from the Foreign Exchange Markets," *Journal of Finance,* December (1981).

International Monetary Fund, *Annual Report,* Author, Washington, D.C., 1981.

Sharpe, *Investments,* Prentice-Hall, Englewood Cliffs, N.J., 1978.

Smith, "Option Pricing: A Review," *Journal of Financial Economics,* January–March (1976).

APPENDIX B

SOURCES OF INFORMATION

The following is a list of periodicals containing articles, surveys, or data on financial and business conditions in various countries. The list was compiled by Steve Zamarripa under the supervision of Professor Ian Giddy at Columbia University. Every effort was made to be accurate; however, it was not possible to verify the continued publication of all periodicals listed.

GENERAL PUBLICATIONS

Title	Publisher	Frequency
World Business Perspectives	The Conference Board Inc.	monthly
Wharton Magazine	Trustees of the University of Pennsylvania	
World Economy	Trade Policy Research Centre	quarterly
World Development	Pergamon Press Ltd.	quarterly
World Review of Economic Studies	Society for Economic Analysis Ltd.	quarterly
Public Finance	The Hague	quarterly
Public Financial Quarterly	Sage Publications Inc.	quarterly
OECD Observer	Organization for Economic Cooperation and Development	bimonthly
Financial Market Trends	Organization for Economic Cooperation and Development	quarterly
Main Economic Indicators	Organization for Economic Cooperation and Development	monthly
Lloyds Bank Review	Lloyds Bank Ltd.	quarterly
Journal of Money Credit and Banking	Ohio State University Press	quarterly
Journal of Commercial Bank Lending	Robert Morris Associates	monthly
Journal of Comparative Economics	Academic Press	quarterly

Journal of Banking and Finance	North Holland Publishing, University of Bergamo	quarterly
Journal of Business, Finance and Accounting	Basil Blackwell	quarterly
International Economic Scoreboard	The Conference Board	bimonthly
International Finance	Chase Manhattan Bank	biweekly
International Currency Review	International Currency Review	quarterly
World Economic and Social Indicators	The World Bank	quarterly
International Economic Review	Wharton School of Finance and Commerce	quarterly
Borrowing in International Capital Markets	The World Bank	semiannually
Harvard Business Review	Harvard Business Press	bimonthly
The Eastern Economist	Eastern Economist	weekly
World Report	First National Bank of Chicago	monthly
Business Week	McGraw-Hill Publications	weekly
Business & Finance	Belenos Publications Ltd.	weekly
The Banker	Financial Times of London	monthly
Bankers Magazine	Warren, Gorham and Lamont Inc.	bimonthly
Federal Reserve Bank of New York Quarterly Review	Federal Reserve Bank of New York	quarterly
Economic Review	Federal Reserve Bank of San Francisco	monthly
	Institutional Investor Systems Inc.	monthly
Business International Money Report	Business International Corp.	weekly
International Business Week	McGraw-Hill Publications	weekly
Columbia Journal of World Business	Columbia University Graduate School of Business	quarterly
Surveyor	American Bureau of Shipping	quarterly
F & S International Annual	Predicasts Inc.	annually
Barclay's Country Reports	Barclay's Bank	irregularly
Barron's National Business & Financial Weekly	Dow Jones & Co.	weekly
Business Economics	National Association of Business Economists	quarterly

Capital Investments of the World	Chase Manhattan Bank	triennially
Conference Board of World Business Perspectives	The Conference Board	bimonthly
Weekly Economic Package	Chemical Bank	irregularly
Economic Forecast Summary	Chemical Bank	monthly
Monthly Economic Newsletter	Citibank	monthly
Survey of Current Business	U.S. Department of Commerce	monthly
Economic World	Economic Salon Ltd.	monthly
Economic Outlook 1982	London Business School	monthly
Economic Report of the President and Annual Report of the Council of Economic Advisors	Superintendent of Documents, U.S. Government Printing Office	annually
World Outlook	Economist Intelligence Unit	annually
Financial World	Macro Communications Inc.	bimonthly
Financial Weekly	Fleet Financial Publishing	weekly
First Chicago Report	First National Bank of Chicago	monthly
Forbes	Forbes Inc.	bimonthly
Fortune	Time Inc.	bi-weekly
IDB News	Inter-American Development Bank	monthly
Finance & Development	International Monetary Fund	quarterly
Institutional Investor Forecast Issue	Institutional Investor Systems Inc.	annually
Journal of International Business Studies	Academy of International Business	triannually
Morgan Guaranty Survey	Morgan Guaranty Trust Co.	monthly
Newsweek	Newsweek Inc.	weekly
The Guardian	The Guardian	daily
New York Times	New York Times Inc.	daily
Overseas Business Report	Superintendent of Documents, U.S. Department of Commerce	irregularly
OECD Economic Outlook	Organization for Economic Cooperation and Development Publications Center	semiannually

OECD Economic Survey of Member Countries	Organization for Economic Cooperation and Development Publications Center	22 times yearly
Quarterly Economic Report	Security Pacific National Bank	quarterly
Financial Post Survey of Markets	Maclean-Hunter Ltd.	annually
Time	Time Inc.	weekly
U.S. News & World Report	U.S. News & World Report Inc.	weekly
Value Line Investment Survey	Arnold Bernhard & Co. Inc.	weekly
Wall Street Transcript	Wall Street Transcript Inc.	weekly
World Development Report	The World Bank	annually
World Business weekly	Financial Times	weekly
Public Affairs Information Service	Public Affairs Information Service Inc.	annually
ABA Banking Journal	Simmons-Boardman Corp.	monthly
American Economic Review	American Economic Association	five times yearly
Aramco World Magazine	Arabian American Oil Company	bimonthly
Bank News	Bank News Inc.	monthly
Bankers Monthly	Bankers Monthly Inc.	monthly
World Financial Markets	Morgan Guaranty Trust Co.	monthly
Barclay's Review	Barclay's Bank Ltd.	quarterly
Bulletin for International Fiscal Documentation	International Bureau of Fiscal Documentation	monthly
Business Economics	Secretary-Treasurer, National Association of Business Economics	quarterly
Business	Georgia State University	bimonthly
Cashflow Magazine	Coordinated Capital Resources Inc.	bimonthly
Challenge	M.E. Sharpe Inc.	bimonthly
Atlantic Economic Journal	Atlantic Economic Surveys	quarterly
Points under Pressure	Business International Corp.	research report
World Trade Strategies in a Decade of Change	Business International Corp.	research report
Worldwide Economic Indicators	Business International Corp.	annually

New Directions in Multinational Corporate Organization	Business International Corp.	research report
Sources of World Financial and Banking Information	Greenwood Press	annually
Subject Index to Sources of Comparative International Statistics	CBD Research	annually
A Subject Guide to Data on Industrial, Business, Social, Educational, Financial and Other Topics for the United States and Internationally	Gale Research	irregularly
Worldcasts Regional	Predicasts	quarterly
World Bank Atlas	The World Bank	annually
World Debt Tables: External Debt of LDCs	The World Bank	annually
International Financial Statistics	International Monetary Fund	monthly (with annual)
Monthly Bulletin of Statistics	United Nations	monthly
National Accounts Statistics	Organization for Economic Cooperation and Development	annually
Statistical Yearbook	United Nations	annually
World Energy Supplies	United Nations	annually
Handbook of Economic Statistics	Central Intelligence Agency	annually
World Development Report	The World Bank	annually
World Trade Annual	Walker Inc.	annually
Yearbook of International Trade Statistics	United Nations	annually
Yearbook of National Account Statistics	United Nations	annually
Yearbook of World Energy Statistics	United Nations	annually
Main Economic Indicators	Organization for Economic Cooperation and Development	monthly
Economic Forum	Economic Forum Institute	semiannually
Financial Market Trends	Organization for Economic Cooperation and Development	five times yearly
Financial Planner	International Association of Financial Planners Inc.	monthly

Financial Planning Today	Panel Publishers	bimonthly
Financier	Financial Edit Ltd.	monthly
Institutional Investor	Institutional Investor Systems Inc.	monthly
Inter-American Economic Affairs	Inter-American Affairs Press	quarterly
Intereconomics	HWWA Institut für Wirtschaftsforschung	bimonthly
International Business	World Trade Associates, Inc.	bimonthly
International Monetary Fund Staff Papers	International Monetary Fund	quarterly
Investors Chronicle and Financial World	Bracken House	weekly
Journal of Comparative Economics	Academic Press Inc.	quarterly
Journal of Political Economy	University of Chicago Press	bimonthly
Journal of Retail Banking	Consumer Bankers Association	quarterly
London Business School Journal	London Graduate School of Business	semiannually
Magazine of Bank Administration	Bank Administration Institute	monthly
Managerial Finance	MCB (Managerial Finance) Ltd.	triennially
Mergers and Acquisitions	Information for Industry Inc.	quarterly
Midland Bank Review	Midland Bank Ltd.	quarterly
Multinational Business	Economist Intelligence Unit Ltd.	quarterly
OPEC Bulletin	Organization of Petroleum Exporting Countries	monthly
OPEC Review	Organization of Petroleum Exporting Countries	quarterly
Petroleum Economist	Petroleum Press Ltd.	monthly
Price Waterhouse Review	Price Waterhouse and Co.	quarterly
Public Finance	Technische Universität Berlin	triennially
Public Finance Quarterly	Sage Publishing Inc.	quarterly
Sloan Management Review	Alfred P. Sloan School of Management, Massachusetts Institute of Technology	quarterly
U.S./Arab Commerce	U.S. Arab Chambers of Commerce	bimonthly

World Economy	Elsevier Scientific Publishing Co.	quarterly
IDB Newsletter	Inter-American Development Bank	quarterly
Meeting of the Board of Governors Report	Inter-American Development Bank	annually
International Bank for Reconstruction and Development Report	The World Bank	annually
International Development Association Report	The World Bank	annually
IMF Monograph Series	International Monetary Fund	irregularly
Federal Reserve Bank of Chicago International Letter	Federal Reserve Bank of Chicago	biweekly
Foreign Exchange Yearbook	Halsted Press	annually
Bankers Monthly	Rand McNally & Co.	monthly
Banque: Revue du Banquier, de son Personnel, et de sa Clientell	Congress d'Organisation Bancaire	monthly
Polk's World Bank Directory	R.L. Polk Ltd.	semiannually
World Banking	Investors Chronicle	annually
Balance of Payments Yearbook	International Monetary Fund	annually
Bank of London and South America Review	Lloyds Bank Ltd.	monthly
Barclay's Overseas Review	Barclay's Bank	monthly
Breve	National Foreign Trade Council	weekly
Business Asia	Business International Corp.	weekly
Business Europe	Business International Corp.	weekly
Business International	Business International Corp.	weekly
Business Latin America	Business International Corp.	weekly
Economic Week	Citibank	weekly
The Economist	Economist Newspaper Ltd.	weekly
Euromoney	Euromoney Publications	monthly
Exchange Restrictions	International Monetary Fund	annually
European Interest Rates	William & Glyn's Bank	monthly

Finance and Development	International Monetary Fund	quarterly
Financing Foreign Operations	Business International Corp.	monthly
Foreign Information Service	Citibank	monthly
Foreign Money Quotation List	Deak and Co.	monthly
Forex Service	International Reports Inc.	monthly
IMF Survey	International Monetary Fund	bimonthly
Information Guides for Doing Business Abroad	Price Waterhouse and Co.	irregularly
International Bond Letter	Crédit Suisse White Weld	monthly
International Business Series	Ernst and Ernst	irregularly
International Foreign Exchange Guide	International Reports Inc.	irregularly
International Reports	Internationsl Reports Inc.	weekly
Investing, Licensing and Trading Conditions Abroad	Business International Corp.	irregularly
London Financial Times	Financial Times Ltd.	daily
Main Economic Indicators	Organization for Economic Cooperation and Development	monthly
Management Monographs	Business International Corp.	irregularly
Money International	Citibank	monthly
Noticias	National Foreign Trade Council, Inc.	weekly
Pacific-Asia Report	National Foreign Trade Council, Inc.	biweekly
Rates of Change in Economic Data for Ten Industrial Countries	Federal Reserve Bank of St. Louis	semiannually
Research Reports	Business International Corp.	irregularly
Rundt's Weekly Intelligence	S. J. Rundt and Associates	weekly
Selected Interest and Exchange Rates	Federal Reserve Board	weekly
Statistical Bulletin	The Conference Board	monthly
The Week in Eurobonds	Kidder, Peabody	weekly
Wall Street Journal	Dow Jones & Company Inc.	daily

World Financial Markets	Morgan Guaranty Trust Co.	monthly
CEI Currency Manager	Claremont Economics Institute	monthly

UNITED STATES AND CANADA

United States

Business Review	Economic Department, Wells Fargo Bank	monthly
United States Banker	Cleworth Publishing Inc.	monthly
Schroder Report	J Henry Schroder Bank & Trust Co.	weekly
Business Statistics	Department of Commerce	weekly
Chartbook on Prices, Wages and Productivity	Department of Labor	monthly
Economic Indicators	Council of Economic Advisers	monthly
Federal Budget Trends	Federal Reserve Board	quarterly
Federal Reserve Bulletin	Federal Reserve Board	monthly
Federal Reserve Statistical Release	Federal Reserve Board	weekly
Monetary Trends	Federal Reserve Board	monthly
Monthly Chart Book	Federal Reserve Board	monthly
Morgan Guaranty Survey	Morgan Guaranty Trust Co.	monthly
National Economic Trends	Federal Reserve Bank of St. Louis	monthly
Survey of Current Business	Department of Commerce	monthly
U.S. Balance of Payments Trends	Federal Reserve Bank of St. Louis	quarterly
U.S. Financial Data	Federal Reserve Bank of St. Louis	weekly
Foreign Economic Trends and Their Implications for the U.S. Department of Commerce	Superintendent of Documents, U.S. Dept of Commerce	irregularly
Economic Outlook USA	Survey Research Center, University of Michigan	quarterly
Economic Perspectives	Federal Reserve Bank of Chicago	bimonthly
Economic Review	Federal Reserve Bank of Atlanta	bimonthly
Economic Review	Federal Feserve Bank of Kansas City	monthly
Quarterly Review	Federal Reserve Bank if New York	quarterly

Business Review	Federal Reserve Bank of Philadelphia	bimonthly
Economic Review	Federal Reserve Bank of Richmond	bimonthly
Financial Review	James M. Kelly School of Business Administration	quarterly
International Economic Indicators	Superintendent of Documents, U.S. Government Printing Office	quarterly
Journal of Commerce Bank Lending	Robert Morris Associates	monthly
Journal of Contemporary Business	Graduate School of Business Administration, University of Washington	quarterly
Journal of Economics and Business	School of Business Administration, Temple University	triennially
Journal of Portfolio Management	Institutional Investor Systems Inc.	quarterly
Legal Economics	American Bar Association	bimonthly
Venture	Venture Magazine Inc.	monthly
NCUA Quarterly	National Credit Union Administration	quarterly
New York Clearing House Association Statement of Members	New York Clearing House Association	weekly
Banking Journal	American Bankers Association	monthly
American Banker	American Banker	daily
American Institute of Banking Bulletin	American Institute of Banking	quarterly
Bankers Monthly	Rand McNally & Co.	monthly
Commerical and Financial Chronicle		weekly
Girard Letter	Girard Trust Co.	quarterly
Investment Banking	Investment Bankers Association of America	monthly
Trust Belletin	Trust Division of American Bankers	monthly
Money Review	Bank of Virginia Co.	biweekly
FDIC Annual Report	Federal DepositInsurance Corporation	annually
Insider's Chronicle	New York National News Service Inc.	weekly
Bankers Blue Book	Rand McNally & Co.	semiannually

U.S. Comptroller of the Currency, Annual Report	U.S. Government Printing Office	annually
Financial Reporting Trends	Ernst & Ernst	annually
Index to Bank Letters, Bulletins and Reviews	Kio Press	quarterly
American Banking and Industry Blue Book	Associated Marketing Directories Inc.	annually
Journal of Bank Research	Bank Administration Institute	quarterly
United States Banker	Cleworth Publishing Co.	biweekly
Federal Reserve Chartbook	Federal Reserve Board	quarterly
United States Investor/Eastern Banker	Frank P. Bennett & Co.	weekly
FDIC, Assets and Liabilities: Commercial and Mutual Savings Banks	Federal Deposit Insurance Corp.	semiannually
FDIC, Bank Operating Statistics	Federal Deposit Insurance Corp.	annually
National Fact Book of Mutual Savings Banking	National Association of Mutual Savings Banks	annually
Annual Statistical Digest	Federal Reserve Board	annually
Moody's Bank and Finance Manual	Moody's Investors Service	annually
Moody's Manual of Investments	Moody's Investors Service	annually
Export-Import Bank of the U.S. Annual Report	Export-Import Bank of the U.S.	annually
Fact Book	Federal Reserve Bank of Chicago	biennially
Weekly Review of Periodicals	Federal Reserve Board	weekly

Canada

Bank of Canada Review	Bank of Canada	monthly
Bond and Money Market Letter	McLeod, Young, Weir	weekly
Business and Economics	Toronto Dominion Bank	occasionally
Business Review	Bank of Montreal	monthly
Canada's Business Climate	Toronto Dominion Bank	quarterly
Canadian Economic Comment	Royal Trust Co.	occasionally
Canadian Foreign Exchange Review	Nesbett, Thomson, and Co.	monthly

Canadian Statistical Review	Information Canada	monthly
Capital Markets and the Economy	Barns Brothers and Denton	weekly
Economic Review	Dominion Securities Harris	monthly
Government Finance	Dominion Securities Harris	monthly
Market Startegy	Dominion Securities Harris	quarterly
Money Market Review	Dominion Securities Harris	biweekly
Monthly Letter	Royal Bank of Canada	monthly
Monthly Review	Bank of Nova Scotia	monthly
Canadian Business Magazine	Canadian Business Media Ltd.	monthly
Survey of Business Attitudes and Investment Spending Attitudes	The Conference Board in Canada	quarterly
Datafacts	The Conference Board in Canada	quarterly
Executive Bulletin	The Conference Board in Canada	irregularly
Canadian Journal of Economics	University of Toronto	quarterly
Governmental Finance	Municipal Finance Officers Association of the U.S. & Canada	quarterly
Canadian Banker & I.C.B. Review	Journal of Canadian Bankers Association	semiannually
Canadian Business	Canadian Business Media Limited	monthly
Canadian Business Review	The Conference Board in Canada	quarterly
Business Quarterly	Canada's Managers Journal	quarterly
Banque Canadienne Nationale Report	Banque Canadienne Nationale	annually
Report of the Canadian Imperial Bank of Commerce	Canadian Imperial Bank	annually
Report of the Dominion Bank, Toronto	Dominion Bank	annually
Annual Report of the Royal Bank of Canada	The Royal Bank of Canada	annually
Credit Union in Canada	Bank of Canada	annually
Bank of Canada Statistical Summary	Bank of Canada	annually
Canadian Business Trends	The Conference Board in Canada	monthly

Canadian Imperial Bank of Commerce Commercial Letter	Canadian Imperial Bank of Commerce	monthly
Canadian Statistical Review	Dominion Bureau of Statistics	annually

PACIFIC BASIN AND ASIA

Afghanistan

Annual Report	Da Afghanistan Bank	annually
Quarterly Economic Review of Afghanistan	The Economist Intelligence Unit Ltd.	quarterly

Australia

ANZ Quarterly Survey	Australia and New Zealand Banking Group	quarterly
Business Conditions in Australia	Bank of New South Wales	quarterly
Business Indicators	ANZ Banking Group	monthly
Economic Review	Commercial Bank of Australia Ltd.	quarterly
National Bank Monthly Summary	National Bank of Australasia	quarterly
Review	Bank of New South Wales	quarterly
Round-up of Economic Statistics	Government Publishing Service	monthly
Statistical Bulletin	Reserve Bank of Australia	monthly
Treasury Information Bulletin	Government Publishing Service	monthly
Monthly Review of Business Statistics	Bureau of Statistics	monthly
The Quarterly Economic Review of Australia	The Economist Intelligence Unit Ltd.	quarterly
Australian Economic Review	Institute of Applied Economic and Social Research	quarterly
Australian Journal of Statistics	Australian Government Department of Statistics	triennially
Australian Stock Exchange Journal	Australian Stock Exchange Journal Ltd.	monthly
Bankers Magazine of Australasia	Bankers Institute of Australasia	monthly
Economic Activity	University of Western Australia	quarterly

Economic Record	Brown, Prior, Anderson Ltd.	quarterly
Report and Financial Statement	Reserve Bank of Australia	annually
Banking and Currency	Bureau of Census and Statistics	annually
Commonwealth Bank of Australia Balance Sheet	Commonwealth Bank of Australia	semiannually
Institute of Bankers of New South Wales Journal	Institute of Bankers of New South Wales	quarterly

Bangladesh

Annual Report	Bangladesh Bank	annually
Bangladesh Economic Survey	Ministry of Finance	annually
Political Economy	Bangladesh Economic Association	annually
Quarterly Economic Review of Bankgladesh	The Economist Intelligence Unit Ltd.	quarterly

Brunei

Bulletin Trimestriel	Banque de la Republique du Brunei	triennially
Quarterly Economic Review of Brunei	The Economist Intelligence Unit Ltd.	quarterly

Burma

Bulletin of Statistics	Union Bank of Burma	quarterly
Quarterly Economic Review of Burma	The Economist Intelligence Unit Ltd.	quarterly
Union Bank of Burma Report	Union Bank of Burma	annually

Fiji

Annual Report	Fiji Governmental Savings Bank	annually
Fiji Bank Bulletin	Fiji Bank Ltd.	monthly
Quarterly Economic Review of Fiji	The Economist Intelligence Unit Ltd.	quarterly

Hong Kong

Fortnightly Quotation Sheet	Forex Group of Companies	biweekly
Hong Kong Economic Papers	Union Press	semiannually
Quarterly Economic Review of Hong Kong	The Economist Intelligence Unit Ltd.	quarterly
Market Letter	Forex Group of Companies	weekly

India

Indian Journal of Economics	University of Allahabad	monthly
Reserve Bank of India Bulletin	Reserve Bank of India	monthly (with weekly supplement)
Monthly Abstract of Statistics	Central Statistical Organization	monthly
Quarterly Economic Review of India	The Economist Intelligence Unit Ltd.	quarterly
Fortnightly Business Letter	United Commercial Bank	fortnightly
Imperial Bank of India, Report	Imperial Bank of India	semiannually
Report to the Board of Directors to the State Bank of India and Reserve Bank of India	State Bank of Hyderabad	annually
Central Bank of India Statement of Accounts and Report	Central Bank of India	annually
Monthly Notes	Central Bank of India	monthly
Indian Institute of Bankers Journal	Indian Institute of Bankers	quarterly
Reserve Bank of India Bulletin	Reserve Bank of India	monthly
Functions and Working	Reserve Bank of India	quarterly
Statistical Tables Relating to Banks in India	Reserve Bank of India	annually
Deposit Insurance Corporation Annual Report	Deposit Insurance Corp.	annually

Indonesia

Bank of Indonesia Bulletin	Bank of Indonesia	quarterly
Bank Negara Indonesia Report	Bank Negara Indonesia	annually
Bulletin for Indonesia Economic Studies	Australian National University	triennially
Quarterly Economic Review of Indonesia	The Economist Intelligence Unit Ltd.	quarterly
Report of the Governor for the Financial Year	Bank of Indonesia	annually

Japan

Quarterly Economic Review of Japan	The Economist Intelligence Unit Ltd.	quarterly
Japan Statistical Yearbook	Bureau of Statistics	annually

Monthly Economic Review	Bank of Japan	monthly
Monthly Finance Review	Ministry of Finance	monthly
Weekly Review	Bank of Tokyo	weekly
Japan Economic Yearbook	The Oriental Economist	annually
Business Japan	Nihon Kogyo Shimbum	monthly
Japan Banking Briefs	Fuji Bank Ltd.	monthly
Fuji Bank Bulletin	Fuji Bank Ltd.	monthly
Survey of Japanese Finance and Industry	Industrial Bank of Japan Ltd.	quarterly
NRI Quarterly Economic Review	Nomura Research Institute	quarterly
Sumitimo Bank Review	Sumitomo Bank Ltd.	monthly
Economic Eye	Keizai Koho Center	irregularly
Japan Quarterly	Asahi Shimbun	quarterly
Japanese Economic Studies	M.E. Sharpe Inc.	quarterly
Sumitomo Quarterly	Sumitomo Quarterly Publications Committee	quarterly
Nihon Ginkó Policy Board Report	Nihon Ginkó	annually
Industrial and Financial Statistics	Nippon Kogyo Ginkó	semiannually
Nippon Kohyo Ginkó Report	Nippon Kogyo Ginkō	semiannually
Tokyō Ginkō Report	Tokyō Ginkō	semiannually
Keio Business Review	Society of Business & Commerce, Keio University	annually
Economic Survey, Japan	Organization for Economic Cooperation and Development	annually
Asian Affairs	Asia Kyokai	quarterly
Economic World	Economic Salon Ltd.	monthly
Hitotsubashi Journal of Economics	Hitotsubashi University	irregularly
Japan Business News	Japan Business News Publishing Inc.	semimonthly
Japan Economic Journal	Nihon Keizae Shimbun Ltd.	weekly
Economic Bulletin	Economic Research Institution	irregularly
Kobe University Economic Review	Kobe University	annually
The Nikko Monthly Bulletin	Nikko Securities	monthly
Osaka Economic Papers	Department of Economics, Osaka University	quarterly
Economics Statistics Monthly	Nihon Ginkō	monthly

Economic Survey of Japan	M.I.T.I.	annually
Focus Japan	Japan External Trade Organization	monthly
Tokyo Financial Review	Bank of Tokyo	monthly
Mitsuibishi Bank Review	Mitsubishi Bank	monthly
Economic Statistics Monthly	Bank of Japan	monthly
Monthly Statistics of Japan	Prime Minister's Office, Statistical Bureau	monthly
LTCB Newsletter (Long Term Credit Bank of Japan)	Bank of Japan Ltd.	monthly
Economic Review	Kyoto University	semiannually

Kampuchea (Cambodia)

Quarterly Economic Review of Cambodia	The Economist Intelligence Unit Ltd.	quarterly

Laos

Quarterly Economic Review of Laos	The Economist Intelligence Unit Ltd.	quarterly

Malaysia

Bank Negara Malaysia Statistical Supplement	Bank Negara Malaysia	monthly
Bulletin Trimestriel	Banque de la Republique du Brunei	triennially
Quarterly Economic Review of Malaysia	The Economist Intelligence Unit Ltd.	quarterly
UMBC Economic Review	United Malayan Banking Corp.	monthly

Mauritius

Bank of Mauritius Annual Report	Bank of Mauritius	annually
Development Bank of Mauritus Report and Accounts	Development Bank of Mauritus	annually

Nepal

Nepal Rastra Bank Quarterly Economic Bulletin	Nepal Rastra Bank	quarterly
Quarterly Economic Review of Nepal	The Economist Intelligence Unit Ltd.	quarterly

New Zealand

Annual Report of Board of Directors and Statement of Accounts	Reserve Bank of New Zealand	annually

Bank of New Zealand Annual Report	Bank of New Zealand	annually
New Zealand Economic Bulletin	New Zealand Embassy	monthly
New Zealand News Review	Reserve Bank of New Zealand	biweekly
Quarterly Economic Review of New Zealand	The Economist Intelligence Unit Ltd.	quarterly
Reports and Accounts	Australia and New Zealand Banking Corporation	annually
Reserve Bank of New Zealand Bulletin	Reserve Bank of New Zealand	monthly
Reserve Bank of New Zealand Economic Review	Bank of New Zealand	monthly

North Korea

Quarterly Economic Review of North Korea	The Economist Intelligence Unit Ltd.	quarterly

Pakistan

Bulletin, State Bank of Pakistan	Public Relations Department, State Bank of Pakistan	monthly
Pakistan Economist	Economist Publications Ltd.	weekly
Quarterly Economic Review of Pakistan	The Economist Intelligence Unit Ltd.	quarterly
Report of the Central Board of Directors	State Bank of Pakistan	annually

Papua New Guinea

Quarterly Economic Review of New Guinea	The Economist Intelligence Unit Ltd.	quarterly

People's Republic of China

Business China	Business International Corp.	bimonthly
China Economic Report	Research Institute/ International Currency Review	quarterly
China Business Review	National Council for U.S./ China Trade	bimonthly
Central Bank Weekly	Central Bank of China	weekly
Report of Financial and Price Statistics	Central Bank of China	weekly
Bank of China Annual Report	Bank of China	annually

Bank of China Bulletin	Bank of China	quarterly
Shanghai Bankers' Association Joint Reserve Board Annual Report	Shanghai Bankers' Association	annually
Quarterly Economic Review of China	The Economist Intelligence Unit Ltd.	quarterly

Philippines

Central Bank Review	Central Bank of the Philippines	weekly
Central Bank Economic Indicators	Central Bank of the Philippines	semiannually
Central Bank of the Philippines Report	Central Bank of the Philippines	annually
Journal of Philippine Statistics	National Census & Statistical Office	quarterly
NEDA Development Digest	National Economic and Development Authority	biweekly
NEDA Economic Indicators	National Economic and Development Authority	monthly
Philippine Development	National Economic and Development Authority	bimonthly
Philippine Economic & Industrial Journal	Philippine Economic & Industrial Association	bimonthly
Philippine Financial Statistics	Central Bank	quarterly
Philippine Prospect	Department of Public Information	biweekly
Quarterly Economic Review of the Philippines	The Economist Intelligence Unit Ltd.	quarterly
Statistical Bulletin	Central Bank of the Philippines	quarterly

Singapore

Quarterly Economic Review of Singapore	The Economist Intelligence Unit Ltd.	quarterly
Singapore Banking and Finance	Singapore Bankers Association	annually
Singapore Business	Times Periodicals Pte. Ltd.	monthly

South Korea

Hanguk Sanop Unhaeng Report	Hanguk Sanop Unhaeng	annually
Hanguk Unhaeng Economic Statistical Yearbook	Hanguk Unhaeng	annually
Hanguk Unhaeng Quarterly Economic Review	Hanguk Unhaeng	quarterly

Hanguk Unhaeng Report	Central Bank of Korea	annually
Monthly Review	Korea Exchange Bank	monthly
Quarterly Economic Review	Bank of Korea	quarterly
Quarterly Economic Review of South Korea	The Economist Intelligence Unit Ltd.	quarterly

Sri Lanka (Ceylon)

Bank of Ceylon Report & Facts	Bank of Ceylon	annually
Central Bank of Ceylon Bulletin	Central Bank of Ceylon	monthly
Quarterly Economic Review of Sri Lanka	The Economist Intelligence Unit Ltd.	quarterly
Report to the Monetary Board to the Ministry of Finance	Central Bank of Sri Lanka	annually
Review	Bank of Ceylon	monthly

Taiwan

Bank of Communications, Taipei Annual Report	Bank of Communications	annually
Business Taiwan	Business & Industry Taiwan	weekly
Economic Review	Bank of China	bimonthly
Free China Review	Kwang Hwa Publishing	monthly
Monthly Economic Survey	International Commercial Bank of China	monthly
Quarterly Economic Review of Taiwan	The Economist Intelligence Unit Ltd.	quarterly
T'ai-wan Yin Haug Report	T'ai-wan Yin Haug	annually

Thailand

Bangkok Monthly Review	Bangkok Bank Ltd.	monthly
Bank of Thailand Economic Report	Bank of Thailand	annually
Bank of Thailand Monthly Bulletin	Bank of Thailand	monthly
Bank of Thailand Monthly Report	Bank of Thailand	monthly
Bank of Thailand Statistical Bulletin	Bank of Thailand	monthly
Business Review	Business Review Co.	monthly
Investor	Investor Inc.	monthly
Quarterly Economic Review of Thailand	The Economist Intelligence Unit Ltd.	quarterly

Turkey

Quarterly Economic Review of Turkey	The Economist Intelligence Unit Ltd.	quarterly
Report of the Board of Directors and Committee of Auditors	Turkiye Cumburiyet Merdez Bankase	annually
Turkiye Cumhuriyet Merkez Bankasi Bulten	Turkiye Cumhuriyet Merdez Bankase	annually

Vietnam

Ngán Háng Quôc-Gia Viêt-Nam Kinh-tê Tâp-san: Bulletin Économique	Ngân Hâng Quôc-Gia Viêt-Nam	annually
Quarterly Economic Review of Vietnam	The Economist Intelligence Unit Ltd.	quarterly

Pacific Basin in General

ASEAN Business Quarterly	Asia Research Pte. Ltd.	quarterly
Asian Business	Far East Trade Press Ltd.	monthly
Asian Development Bank Annual Report	Asian Development Bank	annually
Asian Economics	Research Institute of Asian Economics	quarterly
Asian Finance	Asian Finance Publications Ltd.	monthly
Asian Monetary Monitor	Asian Monetary Monitor Ltd.	bimonthly
Asian Outlook	Asian Peoples' Anti Communist League	monthly
Asian Wall Street Journal	Dow Jones & Company Inc.	weekly
Economic Bulletin for Asia and the Pacific	United Nations	semiannually
Oriental Economist	The Oriental Economist	monthly
Pacific Basin Quarterly	The Pacific Basin Institute	quarterly

LATIN AMERICA AND THE CARIBBEAN

Argentina

Argentina Economic Report	Hollandsche Bank-Unie	monthly
Argentine Republic	Secretaria de Industria y Commercio	semiannually
Boletin Estadístico	Banco Central de la Republica Argentina	monthly

Business Trends	Consejo Tecnico de Inversiones	weekly
Desarrolo Económico	Instituto de Desarrollo Economico y Social	quarterly
Economic Information on Argentina	Ministry of Economy, Treasury, and Finance	monthly
Economic Report	Ministry of Economics	semiannually
Economic Review	Banco Central de la Republica Argentina	quarterly
Indicadores de Coyuntura	Fundacion de Investigaciones Economicas Latinoamericanas	monthly
Investigaciones Económicas	Universidad de Litoral	quarterly
Mimoria Anual	Banco Central de la Republica Argentina	annually
Mimoria y Balance General	Banco de la Nacion Argentina	quarterly
Newsletter Argentina	First National Bank of Boston	weekly
Panorama de la Económia Argentina	Associacion de Dirigentes de Ventas de Buenos Aires	quarterly
Quarterly Economic Review of Argentina	The Economist Intelligence Unit Ltd.	quarterly
Revista de Ciencias Económicas	Colegio de Graduados en Ciencias Economicas	quarterly
Revista del Banco de la Nacion Argentina	Banco de la Nacion Argentina	quarterly
Sintesis Informativa	Banco de la Provincia de Buenos Aires	
Véritas	Véritas	monthly

Bahamas

Annual Report & Accounts	Central Bank of the Bahamas	annually
Economic Report	Central Bank of the Bahamas	quarterly
Quarterly Economic Review of the Bahamas	The Economist Intelligence Unit Ltd.	quarterly

Barbados

Annual Report	Central Bank of Barbados	annually
Economic and Financial Statistics	Central Bank of Barbados	monthly
Quarterly Economic Review of Barbados	The Economist Intelligence Unit Ltd.	quarterly

Belize

Annual Report	Central Bank of Belize	annually
Quarterly Economic Review of Belize	The Economist Intelligence Unit Ltd.	quarterly

Bermuda

Quarterly Economic Review of Bermuda	The Economist Intelligence Unit Ltd.	quarterly

Bolivia

Estadistica Bancaria	Superintendencia de Bancos	monthly
Estudios Económicos y Estadisticas	Banco Central de Bolivia	annually
Quarterly Economic Review of Bolivia	The Economist Intelligence Unit Ltd.	quarterly

Brazil

Anuario Estatistica do Brasil	Departamento de Divulgacao Estatistica	annually
APEC: Analise e Perspectiva Económica	APEC Editora S.A.	biweekly
Brazilian Economy: Trends and Perspectives	Banco Lar Brasileiro	quarterly
Brazilian Performance	Banco de Investimento do Brasil	periodically
Newsletter Brazil	First National Bank of Boston	weekly
Revista Brasileira de Económia	Instituto Brasiliero de Económia de Fudacao Getulio Vargas	quarterly
Boletim Mensal de Banco Central do Brasil	Banco Central do Brasil	monthly
Brazilian Business	American Chamber of Commerce for Brazil	monthly
Boletim	Banco Central do Brasil	quarterly
Annual Report	Banco de Brasil	annually
Ministerio da Industria e do Comercio Realatorio das Actividades	Ministerio da Industria	annually
Boletim Estatistico	Conselho Nacional de Estatistica	quarterly
Brazilian Economic Studies	Instituto de Planejamento Económico e Social	monthly
Conjuntura	Instituto Brasileiro de Económia	monthly

IPEA Boletim Económico	Instituto de Planejamento Económia e Social	bimonthly
Brazil Economic Report	Hollandsche Bank-Unie	monthly
The Quarterly Economic Review of Brazil	The Economist Intelligence Unit Ltd.	quarterly

Chile

Annual Report Presented to the Banking Superintendent	Banco Central de Chile	annually
Balanza de Pagos de Chile	Banco Central de Chile	annually
Boletin Estadistico	Superintendencia de Bancos	monthly
Boletin Mensual	Banco Central de Chile	monthly
Chile Economic News	Corporacion de Fomento de la Produccion	monthly
Informe Económico Anual	Oficina de Planificacion Nacional	annually
Memoria Anual del Banco Central de Chile	Superintendencia de Bancos	annually
Panorama Económico	Universidad de Santiego	irregularly
Quarterly Economic Review of Chile	The Economist Intelligence Unit Ltd.	quarterly

Colombia

Annual Report by the Manager to the Board of Directors	Banco de la Republica	annually
Boletin	Superintendencia Bancaria	monthly
Colombia Today	Colombia Information Service	monthly
Colombian Newsletter	Banco Comercial Antioqueno	monthly
Condensed Statement	Banco de la Republica	monthly
Informe Anual	Banco de la Republica	annually
Quarterly Economic Review of Colombia	The Economist Intelligence Unit Ltd.	quarterly
Revista del Banco de la Republica	Banco de la Republica	monthly

Costa Rica

Balances de Situaciones y Estado de Ganancias y Perdidas	Banco Nacional de Costa Rica	annually
Boletin Estadistico	Banco Central de Costa Rica	bimonthly
Memoria Anual	Banco Central de Costa Rica	annually

Quarterly Economic Review of Costa Rice	The Economist Intelligence Unit Ltd.	quarterly
Revista	Banco Central de Costa Rica	quarterly

Cuba

Boletin Informativo	Consejo Nacional de Economia	monthly
Cuba Economica Financiera	Consejo Nacional de Economia	monthly
Memoria	Banco Nacional de Cuba	annually
Quarterly Economic Review of Cuba	The Economist Intelligence Unit Ltd.	quarterly
Revista	Banco Nacional de Cuba	monthly

Dominican Republic

Boletin Mensual de Banco Central de la Republica Dominicano	Banco Central de la Republica Dominicano	monthly
Memoria Anual	Banco Central de la Republica Dominicano	annually
Quarterly Economic Review of the Dominican Republic	The Economist Intelligence Unit Ltd.	quarterly

Ecuador

Boletin	Banco Central de Ecuador	quarterly
Comercio Exterior Ecuatoriano	Banco Central de Ecuador	monthly
Informacion Estadistica	Banco Central de Ecuador	quarterly
Memoria	Banco Central de Ecuador	annually
Memoria	Superintendencia de Bancos	irregularly
Memoria del Gente General	Banco Central de Ecuador	annually
Quarterly Economic Review of Ecuador	The Economist Intelligence Unit Ltd.	quarterly

El Salvador

Informes y Proyectos	Banco Central de Reserva de El Salvador	annually
Quarterly Economic Review of El Salvador	The Economist Intelligence Unit Ltd.	quarterly
Revista	Banco Central de El Salvador	bimonthly

Guatemala

Boletin Estadistico	Banco Central de Guatemala	quarterly

Boletin Estadistico	Banco de Guatemala	monthly
Memoria Anual	Banco Agricola Mercantil de Guatemala	annually
Quarterly Economic Review of Guatemala	The Economist Intelligence Unit Ltd.	quarterly

Guyana

Quarterly Economic Review of Guyana	The Economist Intelligence Unit Ltd.	quarterly

Haiti

Annual Report of the Fiscal Department	Banque Nationale de la Republique d' Haiti	annually
Quarterly Economic Review of Haiti	The Economist Intelligence Unit Ltd.	quarterly
Rapport	Banque Nationale de la Republique d' Haiti	annually

Honduras

Boletin Estadistico	Banco Central de Honduras	semiannually
Boletin Mensual	Banco Central de Honduras	monthly
Memoria	Banco Central de Honduras	annually
Quarterly Economic Review of Honduras	The Economist Intelligence Unit Ltd.	quarterly

Jamaica

Quarterly Economic Review of Jamaica	The Economist Intelligence Unit Ltd.	quarterly

Mexico

Business Trends	Publicaciones Ejecutivas de Mexico	weekly
Comercio Exterior	Banco Nacional de Comercio Exterior	monthly
Review of the Economic Situation of Mexico	Banco Nacional de Mexico	monthly
Review of Economic Conditions in Mexico	Banamex	quarterly
El Trimestre Economico	Fondo de Cultura Economica Mexico	quarterly
Lloyd's Mexican Economic Report	Allen W. Lloyd Associates, S.A.	monthly
Economic Panorama Bancomer	Bancomer S.A.	monthly

Informe Anual Asamblea General Ordinaria de Accionistas	Banco de Mexico	annually
Boletin Estadistico	Comision Nacional Bancaria	annually
Los Bancos y El Mercado de Valores	Comision Nacional de Valores	annually
Nacional Financiera Informe Anual	Nacional Financiera	annually
Technical Assistance Report	International Labor Office	irregularly
Investigacion Economica	Universidad Nacional Autonoma de Mexico	quarterly
Direccion General de Estudios Económicos	Oficina de Barometros Económicos	triennially
Revista de Estadistica	Departamento Autonomo de Prensa y Publicidad	monthly
Dualismo	Centro de Estudios Económico y Sociales de la Universidad Vercurzana	semiannually
Economic Panorama	Banco de Comercio System	bimonthly
Revista de Económica y Estadistica	Secretaria de la Económia Nacional	monthly
Revista Hacienda y Finanzas	Secretaria de la Económia Nacional	monthly
The Quarterly Economic Review of Mexico	The Economist Intelligence Unit Ltd.	quarterly

Nicaragua

Boletin de la Superintendencia de Bancos y de Otras Instituciones	Banco Central de Nicaragua	monthly
Informe Anual	Banco Central de Nicaragua	annually
Quarterly Economic Review of Nicagagua	The Economist Intelligence Unit Ltd.	quarterly

Panama

Memoria	Banco Nacional de Panama	annually
Quarterly Economic Review of Panama	The Economist Intelligence Unit Ltd.	quarterly

Paraguay

Boletin Estadistico del Banco Central de Paraguay	Banco Central de Paraguay	monthly
Paraguay Económico	Banco Paraguayo de Datos	monthly
Quarterly Economic Review of Paraguay	The Economist Intelligence Unit Ltd.	quarterly

Peru		
Boletin	Banco Central de Peru	quarterly
Boletin Mensual	Banco Central de Reserva del Peru	monthly
Quarterly Economic Review of Peru	The Economist Intelligence Unit Ltd.	quarterly
Puerto Rico		
Annual Report	Governmental Development Bank of Puerto Rico	annually
Economy & Finance, Puerto Rico	Department of Treasury	annually
Quarterly Economic Review of Puerto Rico	The Economist Intelligence Unit Ltd.	quarterly
Suriname		
Quarterly Economic Report of Suriname	The Economist Intelligence Unit Ltd.	quarterly
Summary Contents of the Annual Report	Centrale Bank van Suriname	annually
Trinidad and Tobago		
Quarterly Economic Review of Trinidad and Tobago	The Economist Intelligence Unit Ltd.	quarterly
Uruguay		
Incicadores de la Actividad Economico Financiera	Banco Central de Uruguay	annually
Quarterly Economic Review of Uruguay	The Economist Intelligence Unit Ltd.	quarterly
Venezuela		
Quarterly Economic Review of Venezuela	The Economist Intelligence Unit Ltd.	quarterly
Boletin Mensual	Banco Central de Venezuela	monthly
Venezuela Up-to-Date	Institute of Scientific Research	monthly
Revista de Contral Fiscal	Contraloria General de la Republica de Venezuela	quarterly
Informe Anual	Banco Agricola y Pecuario	annually
Memoria	Banco Central de Venezuela	annually
Revista	Banco Agricola y Pecuario	quarterly
Boletin	Camara de Comercio	monthly

Revista	Banco Central de Venezuela	annually
Informe Económico	Banco Central de Venezuela	monthly
Memoria y Cuenta	Corporacion Venezolana de Fomento	annually
Report	Corporacion Venezolana de Fomento	annually
Estudios Preliminares Sobre Industrias	Corporacion Venezolana de Fomento	irregularly
Cuadernos C.V.F.	Corporacion Venezolana de Fomento	bimonthly
Cuadernos de Informacion Económica	Corporacion Venezolana de Fomento	bimonthly
Venezuela Economic Report	Hollandsche Bank-Unie	quarterly
Technical Assistance Report	International Labor Office	irregularly
Orientacion Económica	Instituto Venezolano de Analisis Económico y Social	quarterly
Boletin Mensual de Estadistica Fiscal	Direccion de Económia y Finanzas	quarterly
Revista de Fomento	Ministerio de Fomento	monthly
Data on Petroleum and Economy of Venezuela	Comptroller's Department	annually
Informe de las Actividades Realizadas	Consejo de Economia Nacional	annually

West Indies

Quarterly Economic Review of the West Indies	The Economist Intelligence Unit Ltd.	quarterly

Windward and Leeward Islands

Quarterly Economic Review of the Windward & Leeward Islands	The Economist Intelligence Unit Ltd.	quarterly

Latin America and the Caribbean in General

America Latina en los Anos Ochenta	Servicios de Informacion CEPAL	monthly
Annual Meeting of the Board of Directors	Caribbean Development Bank	annually
Annual Report	Caribbean Development Bank	annually
Caribbean Business News	IPC Business Press Ltd.	monthly
Caribbean Monthly Bulletin	Institute of Caribbean Studies	monthly

CEPAL Comision Económico para America Latina	United Nations Economic Commission for Latin America	quarterly
CNBS Comision National Banacaria y de Segurus	Republica de El Salvador	monthly
CTC Reporter	United Nations	quarterly
Decada del Desarrollo Latinoamericano	United Nations	monthly
Economic Survey of Latin America	United Nations	annually
Revista	Federacion Lationamericana de Bancos	quarterly
Revista de Económia Latinoamerica	Nuevo Orden Económico International	quarterly
Revista de Económia Politica	Centro de Estudios Constitucionales	quarterly
Revista de la Integracion y el Desarrollo de Centroamerica	Banco Centroamericano de Integracion Ecónomia	quarterly

MIDDLE EAST AND AFRICA

Abu Dhabi

Quarterly Economic Review of Abu Dhabi	The Economist Intelligence Unit Ltd.	quarterly

Algeria

Quarterly Economic Review of Algeria	The Economist Intelligence Unit Ltd.	quarterly
Technical Assistance Reports	International Labor Office	irregularly

Angola

Boletim Mensal de Estatistica	Direccao dos Servicos de Estatistica	monthly
Commerce Exterieur	Direccao dos Servicos de Estatistica	annually
Quarterly Economic Review of Angola	The Economist Intelligence Unit Ltd.	quarterly
Relatorio-Sinteseda Actividade dos Organismos-e Servicos	Secretaria Provincial deFormento Rual	annually

Bahrain

Quarterly Economic Review of Bahrain	The Economist Intelligence Unit Ltd.	quarterly

Benin

Quarterly Economic Review of Benin	The Economist Intelligence Unit Ltd.	quarterly

Botswana

Annual Report	Bank of Botswana	annually
Annual Report	National Development Bank of Botswana	annually
Quarterly Economic Review of Botswana	The Economist Intelligence Unit Ltd.	quarterly

Burundi

Quarterly Economic Review of Burundi	The Economist Intelligence Unit Ltd.	quarterly

Cameroon

Annual Report and Accounts	Cameroon Development Corporation	annually
Direction de la Statistique et de la Compatabilite Nationale	Cameroon Development Corporation	annually
Quarterly Economic Review of Cameroon	The Economist Intelligence Unit Ltd.	quarterly

Cape Verde

Quarterly Economic Review of Cape Verde	The Economist Intelligence Unit Ltd.	quarterly

Central African Republic

Annual Report	Central Bank of the Central African Republic	annually
Quarterly Economic Review of the Central African Republic	The Economist Intelligence Unit Ltd.	quarterly
Rapport d'Activite	Banque des Etats de l'Afrique Centrale	annually

Chad

Quarterly Economic Review of Chad	The Economist Intelligence Unit Ltd.	quarterly

Comoros

Quarterly Economic Review of Comoros	The Economist Intelligence Unit Ltd.	quarterly

Congo (Brazzaville)

Quarterly Economic Review of Congo (Brazzaville)	The Economist Intelligence Unit Ltd.	quarterly

Rapports	Banque du Congo Belge	annually
Rapports et Bilan	Banque Belgo-Cangolaise	annually
Reports Presented to the Shareholders at Their Annual General Meeting, Balance Sheet and Profit and Loss Account	Banque du Congo	annually

Dijibouti

Quarterly Economic Review of Dijibouti	The Economist Intelligence Unit Ltd.	quarterly

Dubai

Quarterly Economic Review of Dubai	The Economist Intelligence Unit Ltd.	quarterly

Egypt

Economic Bulletin	al-Bank al-Ahli al-Misri	quarterly
Economic Review	al-Bank al-Markazi al-Misri	quarterly
Economic Review	Central Bank of Egypt	semiannually
Etudes Financieres	Banque Belge et Internationale en Egypte	monthly
General Statistics	al-Bank al-Ahli al-Misri	annually
Quarterly Economic Review of Egypt	The Economist Intelligence Unit Ltd.	quarterly
Report of the Board of Directors	Central Bank of Egypt	annually
Revue Economique Trimestrielle	Banque de Port-Said	quarterly
Serie de Conferences	Institut des Etudes Bancaires	annually

Ethiopia

National Bank of Ethiopia Annual Report	National Bank of Ethiopia	annually
National Bank of Ethiopia Quarterly Bulletin	National Bank of Ethiopia	quarterly
National Bank of Ethiopia Quarterly Review	National Bank of Ethiopia	quarterly
Quarterly Economic Review of Ethiopia	The Economist Intelligence Unit Ltd.	quarterly
Ya' Ityopya negd Bank Annual Report	Ya' Ityopya negd Bank	annually

Gabon

Quarterly Economic Review of Gabon	The Economist Intelligence Unit Ltd.	quarterly

Gambia

Central Bank of Gambia Annual Report	Central Bank of Gambia	annually
Bulletin	Central Bank of Gambia	quarterly
Quarterly Economic Review of Gambia	The Economist Intelligence Unit Ltd.	quarterly

Ghana

Quarterly Economic Review of Ghana	The Economist Intelligence Unit Ltd.	quarterly

Guinea

Quarterly Economic Review of Guinea	The Economist Intelligence Unit Ltd.	quarterly

Guinea Bissan

Quarterly Economic Review of Guinea Bissan	The Economist Intelligence Unit Ltd.	quarterly

Iran

Bulletin	Bank Markazi Iran	bimonthly
Bulletin	Bank Melli Iran	irregularly
Quarterly Economic Review of Iran	The Economist Intelligence Unit Ltd.	quarterly

Iraq

al-Nashra al-Fasliyah	al-Masrif al-Sinai al-Iraqi	annually
al-Tagrir al-Sanawi	al-Masrif al-Sinai al-Iraqi	annually
Report	al-Bank al-Markazi al-Iraqi	annually

Israel

Bank Leumi Economic Review	Bank Leumi Le-Israel	quarterly
Bank of Israel Bank Statistics	Examiner of Banks, Bank of Israel	monthly
Business Review & Economic News from Israel	Israel Discount Bank Ltd.	quarterly
Economic Review	Bank of Israel	quarterly
Israel Business and Investors' Report	A.G. Publications Ltd.	monthly
Israel Economic Bulletin	Ministry of Trade & Industry	fortnightly
Israel Economic Report	Hollandsche Bank-Unie N.V.	monthly
Israel Economist	Economist Ltd.	monthly
Israel Industry & Commerce	Ministry of Commerce & Industry	bimonthly

Jerusalem Post Economic Annual	Jerusalem Post	annually
Jerusalem Quarterly	MidEast Institute	quarterly
Monthly Foreign Trade Statistics	ha-Lishkah ha-Merkazit le-Statistikah	monthly
Quarterly Economic Review of Israel	The Economist Intelligence Unit Ltd.	quarterly
Recent Economic Development	Bank of Israel, Research Department	semiannually
Review of Economic Conditions in Israel	Bank Leumi le-Israel	quarterly
Yarnon le-Statistikah Shel Sehar Huts	ha-Lishkah ha-Merkazit le-Statistikah	monthly

Ivory Coast

Quarterly Economic Review of the Ivory Coast	The Economist Intelligence Unit Ltd.	quarterly

Jordan

Annual Report	Central Bank of Jordan	annually
Monthly Statistical Review	Central Bank of Jordan	monthly
Quarterly Economic Review of Jordan	The Economist Intelligence Unit Ltd.	quarterly

Kenya

Annual Report	Central Bank of Kenya	annually
Economic Review	Central Bank of Kenya	monthly
Quarterly Economic Review of Kenya	The Economist Intelligence Unit Ltd.	quarterly

Kuwait

Annual Report	Central Bank of Kuwait	annually
Economic Report	Central Bank of Kuwait	annually
Final Accounts	Ministry of Finance	annually
Kuwait Economist	Economist Ltd.	monthly
Quarterly Economic Review of Kuwait	The Economist Intelligence Unit Ltd.	quarterly
Quarterly Statistical Bulletin	Central Bank of Kuwait	quarterly
Technical Assistance Report	International Labor Office	irregularly

Lebanon

Quarterly Economic Review of Lebanon	The Economist Intelligence Unit Ltd.	quarterly
Rapport	Masrif Lubnan	annually

Lesotho

Quarterly Economic Review of Lesotho	The Economist Intelligence Unit Ltd.	quarterly

Liberia

Annual Report	Ministry of Planning and Economic Affairs	annually
Annual Report	National Bank of Liberia	annually
Annual Report of the Liberian Development Corp.	Liberian Development Corporation	annually
Economic Survey of Liberia	Ministry of Planning and Economic Affairs	annually
Liberian Economic and Management Review	University of Liberia	semiannually
Public Sector Accounts of Liberia	Ministry of Planning and Economic Affairs	annually
Quarterly Economic Review of Liberia	The Economist Intelligence Unit Ltd.	quarterly
Statistical Bulletin	National Bank of Liberia	monthly
Technical Assistance Report	International Labor Office	irregularly

Libya

Annual Report of the Board of Directors	Central Bank of Libya	annually
Economic Bulletin	Central Bank of Libya	quarterly
Quarterly Economic Review of Libya	The Economist Intelligence Unit Ltd.	quarterly
Technical Assistance Report	International Labor Office	irregularly

Madagascar

Quarterly Economic Review of Madagascar	The Economist Intelligence Unit Ltd.	quarterly

Malawi

Quarterly Economic Review of Malawi	The Economist Intelligence Unit Ltd.	quarterly
Report and Accounts	Reserve Bank of Malawi	annually

Mali

Quarterly Economic Review of Mali	The Economist Intelligence Unit Ltd.	quarterly

Mauritania

Quarterly Economic Review of Mauritania	The Economist Intelligence Unit Ltd.	quarterly

Mauritius		
Quarterly Economic Review of Mauritius	The Economist Intelligence Unit Ltd.	quarterly
Morocco		
Economic News from Morocco	U.S. Embassy	monthly
Etudes et Statistiques	Bank al-Maghrib	monthly
Monthly Bulletin of Information	Banque Marocaine du Commerce Extrieur	monthly
Quarterly Economic Review of Morocco	The Economist Intelligence Unit Ltd.	quarterly
Rapport	Bank al-Maghrib	annually
Technical Assistance Report	International Labor Office	irregularly
Mozambique		
Quarterly Economic Review of Mozambique	The Economist Intelligence Unit Ltd.	quarterly
Namibia		
The Quarterly Economic Review of Namibia	The Economist Intelligence Unit Ltd.	quarterly
Nepal		
Quarterly Economic Review of Nepal	The Economist Intelligence Unit Ltd.	quarterly
Niger		
Quarterly Economic Review of Niger	The Economist Intelligence Unit Ltd.	quarterly
Nigeria		
Annual Economic Review of Nigeria	Standard Bank Group Ltd.	annually
Annual Report	Federal Office of Statistics	annually
Digest of Statistics	Federal Office of Statistics	quarterly
Economic and Financial Review	Central Bank of Nigeria	quarterly
Federal Loans Board Report	Lagos, Federal Government Printer	annually
Nigerian Journal of Economic and Social Studies	Nigerian Economic Society	quarterly
Nigerian Trade Journal	Department of Commerce and Industry	quarterly
Quarterly Economic Review of Nigeria	The Economist Intelligence Unit Ltd.	quarterly

Oman

Quarterly Economic Review of Oman	The Economist Intelligence Unit Ltd.	quarterly

Qatar

Quarterly Economic Review of Qatar	The Economist Intelligence Unit Ltd.	quarterly

Rwanda

Quarterly Economic Review of Rwanda	The Economist Intelligence Unit Ltd.	quarterly

Sao Tome

Quarterly Economic Review of Sao Tome	The Economist Intelligence Unit Ltd.	quarterly

Saudi Arabia

National Economic Review	Saudi Arabian Ministry of Finance	annually
Quarterly Economic Review of Saudi Arabia	The Economist Intelligence Unit Ltd.	quarterly
Saudi Arabia Development Plan	U.S. Department of Commerce	every five years
Statistical Study	Saudi Arabian Monetary Agency	annually

Senegal

Quarterly Economic Review of Senegal	The Economist Intelligence Unit Ltd.	quarterly

Seychelles

Quarterly Economic Review of Seychelles	The Economist Intelligence Unit Ltd.	quarterly

Sierra Leone

Quarterly Economic Review of Sierra Leone	The Economist Intelligence Unit Ltd.	quarterly

Somalia

Bolletin	Banca Nazionale Somala	monthly
Quarterly Economic Review of Somalia	The Economist Intelligence Unit Ltd.	quarterly

South Africa

Quarterly Bulletin	South Africa Reserve Bank	quarterly
Short-Term Economic Indicators	Department of Statistics	monthly
Finance and Trade Review	Volkskas Ltd.	semiannually

Financial Mail	Financial Mail Ltd.	weekly
South African Journal of Economics	Economic Society of South Africa	quarterly
Annual Report	Registrar of Banks	annually
Report of Annual Accounts	South African Reserve Bank	annually
Report on the Ordinary General Meeting	South African Reserve Bank	annually
Economic Report	South African Reserve Bank	annually
Standard and Chartered Review	Standard & Chartered Banking Group Ltd.	monthly
Standard Bank Review	Standard Bank Review Ltd.	monthly
State of South Africa: Economic, Financial, and Statistical Yearbook for the Republic of South Africa	De-Gama Publications	annually
Quarterly Economic Review of South Africa	The Economist Intelligence Unit Ltd.	quarterly

Sudan

Bulletin	Bank al-Sudan	quarterly
Quarterly Economic Review of Sudan	The Economist Intelligence Unit Ltd.	quarterly
Report	Bank al-Sudan	annually

Swaziland

Annual Report and Financial Statements	Swaziland Development and Savings Bank	annually
Quarterly Economic Review of Swaziland	The Economist Intelligence Unit Ltd.	quarterly

Syria

Quarterly Economic Review of Syria	The Economist Intelligence Unit Ltd.	quarterly
Syrie et Monde Arabe	Office Arabe de Presse et de Documentation	monthly

Tanzania

Economic Bulletin	Central Bank of Tanzania	quarterly
Quarterly Economic Review of Tanzania	The Economist Intelligence Unit Ltd.	quarterly

Togo

Quarterly Economic Review of Togo	The Economist Intelligence Unit Ltd.	quarterly

Tunisia

Annual Report	al-Bank al-Markazi al-Tunisi	annually
Quarterly Economic Review of Tunisia	The Economist Intelligence Unit Ltd.	quarterly
Revue Economique Trimestrielle	Banque de Port-Said	triennially

Uganda

Quarterly Economic Review of Uganda	The Economist Intelligence Unit Ltd.	quarterly

United Arab Emirates

Bulletin	United Arab Emirates Currency Board	semiannually
Quarterly Economic Review of the United Arab Emirates	The Economist Intelligence Unit Ltd.	quarterly

Upper Volta

Quarterly Economic Review of Upper Volta	The Economist Intelligence Unit Ltd.	quarterly

Yemen, Arab Republic of

Quarterly Economic Review of the Arab Republic of Yemen	The Economist Intelligence Unit Ltd.	quarterly

Yemen, People's Democratic Republic of

Quarterly Economic Review of the People's Democratic Republic of Yemen	The Economist Intelligence Unit Ltd.	quarterly

Zaire

Rapports et Bilan	Banque Belgo-Zairoise	annually
Rapport Annuel	Banque du Zaire	annually
Bulletin Trimestriel	Banque du Zaire	triennially
Bulletin Mensual de la Statistique	Banque du Zaire	monthly
The Quarterly Economic Review of Zaire	The Economist Intelligence Unit Ltd.	quarterly

Zambia

Quarterly Economic Review of Zambia	The Economist Intelligence Unit Ltd.	quarterly
Report and Statement of Accounts	Bank of Zambia	annually

Zimbabwe

Quarterly Economic Review of Zimbabwe	The Economist Intelligence Unit Ltd.	quarterly
Zimbabwe Journal of Economics	A.M. Hawkins, JAC Gridlestone and J.M. Robertson	quarterly

Middle East and Africa in General

Africa	Africa Journal Ltd.	monthly
African Business	IC Magazines Ltd.	monthly
African Report	African American Institute Inc.	bimonthly
Annual Report of the Arab Bank	Arab Bank Ltd.	annually
Eastern African Economic Review	Eastern African Literature Bureau	semiannually
Middle East and African Economist	Middle East and African Economist	monthly
Middle East Economic Digest	MEED Ltd.	weekly
Report of the Board of Directors	African Development Bank	annually
Report of the Board of Directors, Balance Sheet, and Profit and Loss Account	Arab Bank Ltd.	annually
Review of African Political Economy	Merlin Press	

EUROPE

Albania

Quarterly Economic Review of Albania	The Economist Intelligence Unit Ltd.	quarterly

Austria

Austria and the ERP	Federal Chancellory	quarterly
Austrian Economic News	Bundeskammer der Gewerblichen Wirtschaft	monthly
Austria's Monetary Situation	Oesterreichische National Bank	monthly
Economic Bulletin	Oesterreichische Landerbank	monthly
Economic Letter	Creditanstalt Bankverein	monthly

Economic Survey	Organization for Economic Cooperation and Development	annually
Quarterly Economic Review of Austria	The Economist Intelligence Unit Ltd.	quarterly
Wirtschaftsberichte	Creditanstalt Bankverein	bimonthly

Belgium

Annual Report	Banque de Bruxelles	annually
Annual Report	Societe General de Banque	annually
Bulletin	Banque Nationale de Belgique	monthly
Bulletin	Societe Generale de Banque	monthly
Bulletin de Conjoncture	Banque de Bruxelles: Service des Etudes Economiques	monthly
Bulletin Financier	Banque de Bruxelles	weekly
Bulletin de Statistique	Ministere des Affaires Economiques	monthly
Conjoncture Boursiere	Societe Generale de Banque	monthly
Notes Mensuelles sur la Situation Economique	Conseil Central de l'Economie	monthly
Quarterly Economic Review of Belgium	The Economist Intelligence Unit Ltd.	quarterly
Rapports	Banque de la Societe Generale de Belgique	annually
Report from Brussels	Banque de Bruxelles	monthly
Statistiques Industrielles	Institut National de Statistique	bimonthly
Weekly Bulletin	Kredietbank	weekly

Bulgaria

Bulletin Mensuel Statistique	B'lgarska Narodna Sofia	monthly
Economic News of Bulgaria	Bulgarian Chamber of Commerce	monthly
Quarterly Economic Review of Bulgaria	The Economist Intelligence Unit Ltd.	quarterly
Rapport	Banque Nationale de Bulgarie	annually

Cyprus

Quarterly Economic Review of Cyprus	The Economist Intelligence Unit Ltd.	quarterly

Czechoslovakia

Annual Report of the National Bank of Czechoslovakia	Narodni Banka Ceskoslovenska	annually
Bulletin	Narodni Banka Ceskoslovenska	monthly
Bulletin	Statni Banka Ceskoslovenska	annually
Czechoslovak Economic Digest	Pragopress	irregularly
Czechoslovak Foreign Trade	Rapid	monthly
Jahresrechnungen Comptes Annels	Narodni Banka Ceskoslovenska	annually
Quarterly Economic Review of Czechoslovakia	The Economist Intelligence Unit Ltd.	quarterly
Tydenik pro Finance Obchod Prumysl a Zemedelstvi	Hospodarsky Rozheld	weekly

Denmark

Beretning om de Danske Bankers Virksomhed	Banktilsynet	annually
Compte Rendu	Danmarks Nationalbank	annually
Copenhagen, Aktieselskabet Kjobenhavns Handelsbank	Kjobenhavns Handelsbank	monthly
Denmark Quarterly Review	Kjobenhavns Handelsbank	quarterly
Monetary Review	Danmarks Nationalbank	weekly
Quarterly Economic Review of Denmark	The Economist Intelligence Unit Ltd.	quarterly

Finland

Economic Review	Kansallis-Osake-Pankki	quarterly
Ekonomiska Samfundets Tidskrift	Union Bank of Finland	quarterly
Monthly Bulletin	Suomen Pankin	monthly
Monthly Review	Bank of Finland	monthly
Quarterly Economic Review of Finland	The Economist Intelligence Unit Ltd.	quarterly
Report	Pohjoismai den Yhdyspankki	annually
Unitas	Union Bank of Finland	quarterly

France

Quarterly Economic Review of France	The Economist Intelligence Unit Ltd.	quarterly

Le Nouvel Economiste	Classemeit des Premieres Societes Françaises et Europeennes	weekly
Bulletin Mensuel de Statistique	INSEE	monthly
Bulletin Trimestriel	Banque de France	quarterly
Conjoncture	Societe General	monthly
France	Ambassade de France	monthly
Situation Hebdomadaire	Banque de France	weekly
Statistique Mensuelles	Conseil National du Credit	monthly
Statistiques Trimestrielles	Conseil National du Credit	quarterly
Assemblee Generale Ordinaire Rapports et Resolutions	Banque de Paris et des Pays-Bas	annually
Rapports de Conseil d'Administration et des Comissaires des Comptes	Banque Nationale de Credit	annually
Report of the Board of Directors and Auditors	Banque Nationale pour le Commerce et l'Industrie	annually
Commission de Controle des Banques Rapport	Commission de Controle des Banques	annually
Rapport Annual	Conseil National du Credit	annually
Revue Economique	Banque Nationale de Paris	annually
Entreprise	Entreprise	bimonthly
L'Expansion	L'Expansion	monthly

Germany, East

Quarterly Economic Review of East Germany	The Economist Intelligence Unit Ltd.	quarterly

Germany, West

Quarterly Economic Review of West Germany	The Economist Intelligence Unit Ltd.	quarterly
Economics	Institute for Scientific Cooperation	biannually
German Economic Review	Bayerische Hypothekin-und Wechsel-Bank	weekly
Monthly Report	Devtsche Bundesbank	monthly
Report from Germany	Merck, Finck and Co.	monthly
Report	Deutsche Bundesbank	annually
Statistische Beihefte Series 1: Banking Statistics; Series 2: Securities Statistics; Series 3: Balance of Payments; Series 4: Seasonally Adjusted Data	Deutsche Bundesbank	monthly

Kredit and Kapital	Duncker und Humblot	quarterly
Business in Germany	Bayerische Staatsbank	monthly
Wirtschaftsbericht	Bayerische Staatsbank	semimonthly
Das Geld-und Kreditwesen in Berlin	Landeszentralbank in Berlin	monthly
Geschaftsbericht	Landeszentralbank von Rheinland-Pflaz	annually
Annual Report	Reichsbank	annually
Geschaftsbericht	Bayerische Staatsbank	annually
Wirtschaftliche Mitteilungen	Deutschebank und Disconto Gesellschaft	monthly
Monthly Report	Deutsche Bundesbank	monthly
Ergebnisse der Bankenstatistik für Berlin	Landeszentralbank in Berlin (West)	monthly
Economic Surveys	Organization for Economic Cooperation and Development	annually
Wirtschaftlicher Informationsbrief	Bayerische Staatsbank	weekly
Weekly Report for the Institute of Business Research	Institut fur Konjunkturforschung	weekly
Economic Report from Germany	Deutsches Industrieinstitut	weekly
Bulletin of the Hamburg World Economic Archives	Hamburgisches welt-Wirtschafts Archiv	semimonthly
Finanzbericht	Bundesministerium der Finanzen	annually

Greece

Annual Report	National Mortgage Bank of Greece	annually
Argotike Trapeza tes Hellados	Argotike Trapeza tes Hellados	annually
Greek Economic Review	Society for Economic Research, Papazisis Press	quarterly
Quarterly Economic Review of Greece	The Economist Intelligence Unit Ltd.	quarterly
Report	Ethnike Trapeza tes Hellados	annually
Report (Trapeza tes Hellados)	Bank of Greece	annually
Report of the Chairman of the Board	Trapeza Emporike tes Hellados	annually
Report to the Governors	Ethnike Trapeza tes Hellados	annually

Review	Ethnike Trapeza tes Hellados	quarterly
Statistical Bulletin (Trapeza tes Hellados)	Bank of Greece	annually

Hungary

Act a Juridica Academiae Scientiarum Hungaricae	Akademiai Kiado	semiannually
Banque Nationale di Hongrie Rapport	Banque Nationale di Hongrie	annually
Figyelo Economic Weekly	Hirlapkiado Vallalat	weekly
Hungarian Economy	Kultura	quarterly
Hungaropress	Hungarian Chamber of Commerce	fortnightly
Monthly Report of the National Bank of Hungary	Magyar Nemzeit Banque	monthly
Quarterly Economic Review of Hungary	The Economist Intelligence Unit Ltd.	quarterly
Report Submitted by the Annual Meeting of the General Assembly of the National Bank of Hungary	Magyar Nemzeit Banque	annually
Weekly Bulletin	Budapress	weekly

Iceland

Quarterly Economic Review of Iceland	The Economist Intelligence Unit Ltd.	quarterly
Seolabanki Islands Report	Seolabanki	annually
Seolabanki Islands Statistical Bulletin	Seolabanki	monthly

Ireland

Business and Finance	Belenos Publications Ltd.	weekly
Central Bank of Ireland Report	Central Bank of Ireland	annually
Economic and Social Review	Economic and Social Studies Association	quarterly
Irish Banking Review	Irish Banks Ltd.	quarterly
Journal of the Institute of Bankers of Ireland	Institute of Bankers of Ireland	quarterly
Quarterly Bulletin	Central Bank of Ireland	quarterly
Quarterly Economic Review of Northern Ireland	The Economist Intelligence Unit Ltd.	quarterly
Quarterly Economic Review of the Republic of Ireland	The Economist Intelligence Unit Ltd.	quarterly

Italy

Quarterly Economic Review of Italy	The Economist Intelligence Unit Ltd.	quarterly
Bollettino	Banco d'Italia	quarterly
Bollettino Mensile di Statistica	Istituto Centrale di Statistica	monthly
Congiuntura Italiana	Istituto Nazionale per lo Studio della Congiuntura	
Indicatori Mensili	Instituto Centrale di Statistica	monthly
Italian Economic Survey	Association of Italian Joint Stock Companies	bimonthly
Italian Economic Situation	Credito Italiano	bimonthly
Italian Trends	Banca Nazionale del Lavoro	monthly
Supplemento al Bollettino	Banca d'Italia	weekly
Review of Economic Conditions in Italy	Banco di Roma	quarterly
Quarterly Bulletin of the Italian Economy	CARIPLO (Cassa di Risparmio dalle Provincia Lombarde)	quarterly
Revista di Politica Economica	Servizio Italiano Publicazioni Internazionali	monthly
Economic News from Italy	Elite Publishing Corp.	weekly
Quarterly Review	Banco Nazionale del Lavoro	quarterly
Economia Internazionale	Istituto di Economia Interazionale	quarterly
Relazione del Consiglio d'Administrazione	Banca Commerciale Italiana	annually
Abridged Version of the Report for the Year 1982	Banca d'Italia	annually
Assemblea Generale Ordinaria dei Partecipauti Anno	Banca d'Italia	annually
Review of Economic Conditions in Italy	Banco di Roma	bimonthly
Azienda Bancaria Sezione Credito Fondiario e Sezione Autonoma Opere Pubbliche	Instituto Bancario San Paolo di Torino	annually
Report	Instituto per la Reconstruzione Industriale	annually

Luxemburg

Quarterly Economic Review of Luxemburg	The Economist Intelligence Unit Ltd.	quarterly

Malta

Quarterly Economic Review of Malta	The Economist Intelligence Unit Ltd.	quarterly

Netherlands, The

A.B.N. Economic Review	Algemene Bank Nederland	bimonthly
Amsterdamsche Bank-Incasso Bank Review	Amsterdamsche BankIncasso Bank	quarterly
Annual Report	Algemene Bank Nederland	annually
Business Comments	Algemene Bank Nederland	bimonthly
De Economist	H.E. Stenfert Krose	quarterly
Economic Quarterly Review	Amsterdam-Rotterdam Bank	quarterly
Economic Review	Economic Research Department	irregularly
Economisch Kwartaaloverzicht	Amsterdam-Rotterdam Bank	quarterly
Financial Statement	Algemene Bank Nederland	annually
Financieeleconomisch Bureau	Twentsche Bank	weekly
Netherlands Economic Bulletin	Economic Information Service	biweekly
Quarterly Economic Review of the Netherlands	The Economist Intelligence Unit Ltd.	quarterly

Norway

DNC Monthly Survey of Norwegian Trade, Industry, and Finance	Dennorske Creditbank Statistics Department	monthly
Economic Bulletin	Norges Bank	quarterly
Economic News from Norway	Bergens Privatbank	monthly
Monthly Survey	Norske Creditbank	monthly
News Bulletin and Statistical Appendix	Norwegian Information Service	irregularly
Norges Bank Balance Sheet	Norges Bank	monthly
Norges Bank Economic Bulletin	Norges Bank	quarterly
Norwegian Commercial Banks: Financial Review	Economic Research Institute of the Commercial Banks of Norway	monthly
Økonomisky Revy	Bank of Norway	monthly
Quarterly Economic Review of Norway	The Economist Intelligence Unit Ltd.	quarterly
Statistisk Arbok	Central Bureau of Statistics	annually

Utdrag av Norges Bank Boker	Norges Bank	monthly

Poland

Bank i Kredyt Styczen	Bank i Kredyt	monthly
Narodowy Bank Polski Information Bulletin	Narodowy Bank Polski	annually
Narodowy Bank Polski Wiadomosci	Narodowy Bank Polski	monthly
Quarterly Economic Review of Poland	The Economist Intelligence Unit Ltd.	quarterly

Portugal

Boletim Informativo	Banco Totta y Acores	monthly
Boletim Trimestral	Banco de Portugal	triennially
Economia	Executive Secretary, Rivista Economia	triennially
Letter	Banco Totta y Acores	bimonthly
Quarterly Economic Review of Portugal	The Economist Intelligence Unit Ltd.	quarterly
Report to the Board of Directors	Banco de Portugal	annually

Rumania

Banque Commerciale Roumaine Rapports du Conseil d' Administration et des Conseurs a l'Assemblee General Ordinarie	Banque Commerciale Roumaine	annually
Quarterly Economic Review of Rumania	The Economist Intelligence Unit Ltd.	quarterly
Report of the Board of Administration and the Report of the Council of Auditors	Banca Nationala a Romaniei	annually
Report to the Advisor to the National Bank of Rumania	Banca Nationale a Romaniei	annually
Rumanian Foreign Trade	Chamber of Commerce of Rumania	quarterly
Statistica Societatilor Anonime din Romania	Institutul Central de Statistica	annually

Soviet Union

ASTE Bulletin	University of Pennsylvania Association for the Study of Soviet-Type Economics	quarterly

Bulletin	American-Russian Chamber of Commerce	monthly
Bulletins on Soviet Economic Development	Department of Economics and Institutions of the USSR	quarterly
Ecotass (Soviet Union Economic and Commercial News Weekly)	INDREBA	weekly
Ekonomicheskaya Gazeta	Pravda Publishing House	weekly
Finansy: Kredit SSSR	Ministerstvo Finansov	monthly
Moscow Narodny Bank Monthly Review	Moscow Narodny Bank Ltd.	monthly
Quarterly Bulletin for Soviet Russian Economies	Moscow Narodny Bank Ltd.	quarterly
Quarterly Economic Review of the USSR	The Economist Intelligence Unit Ltd.	quarterly
Soviet Export	KORP	bimonthly
Trade Information from the USSR	American-Russian Chamber of Commerce	monthly
Ukranian Quarterly	Ukranian Congress Committee of America Inc.	quarterly

Spain

Banco Central	Servicio de Estudios Económicos	monthly
Boletin Estadistico	Banco de Espana	monthly
Boletin Informative	Banco Central	monthly
Boletin Oficial de Banca y Seguros	Direccion General de Banca, Bolsa y Inversiones	monthly
Memoria	Banco Central	annually
Memoria	Banco de Credito Industrial	annually
Memoria Presentada por el Consejo de Administracion	Banco de Vizcaya	annually
Memoria y *Balance*	Banco Hispano Americano	annually
Moneda y Credito Revista de Económia	Martin/Martin	monthly
Noticiario Económico	Banco de Vizcaya	monthly
Quarterly Economic Review of Spain	The Economist Intelligence Unit Ltd.	quarterly
Report for the Financial Year	Banco Espanõl de Credito	annually
Revista Financiera	Banco de Vizcaya	annually

Sweden

Current Business in Sweden	Svenska Handelsbanken	quarterly

Economic Survey	Gotabanken	occasionally
Monthly Economic Survey	National Central Bureau of Statistics	monthly
Monthly Report	Skandinaviska Enskilda, Banken	monthly
News from Sweden	Swedish Information Service	monthly
Quarterly Economic Review of Sweden	The Economist Intelligence Unit Ltd.	quarterly
Quarterly Review	Skandinaviska Enskilda, Banken	quarterly
Annual Report	Svenska Handelsbanken	annually
Annual Report	Sverig es Riksbank	annually
Banking Statistics	Bankinspektionen	monthly
Skrifter	Svenska Bankforeningen	annually
Statistical Yearbook	Sverig es Riksbank	annually
Sweden's Economy	Svenska Handelsbanken	annually
Swedish Economy	National Institution of Economic Research	quarterly

Switzerland

Quarterly Economic Review of Switzerland	The Economist Intelligence Unit Ltd.	quarterly
Bulletin	Crédit Suisse	monthly
Business Facts and Figures	Union Bank of Switzerland	monthly
Economic Suryey of Switzerland	Union Bank of Switzerland	annually
Foreign Exchange News	Union Bank of Switzerland	biweekly
Prospects: Business News Survey	Swiss Bank Corporation	quarterly
Switzerland in Figures	Union Bank of Switzerland	annually
Schweizerische Nationalbank	Bank of Switzerland	monthly
Swiss Economic News	Swiss Office for Development of Trade	monthly
Monatsbericht	Swiss National Bank	monthly
Harry Browne's Complete Guide to Swiss Banks	McGraw-Hill	published
Rapport	Schweizerische Bankiervereinigung	annually
Swiss Facts and Figures	Union of Banques Suisses	quarterly
L'Economie Suisse	Union de Banques Suisses	annually
Bulletin	Swiss Bank Corporation	irregularly
Le Mois Economique et Financier	Swiss Bank Corporation	quarterly

The Swiss Economy	Crédit Suisse	annually
Economic Survey, Switzerland	Organization for Economic Cooperation and Development	annually

United Kingdom

Quarterly Economic Review of the United Kingdom	The Economist Intelligence Unit Ltd.	quarterly
Barclay's Review	Barclay's Bank	quarterly
Economic Progress Report	Information Division of the Treasury	monthly
Lloyd's Bank Review	Lloyd's Bank	quarterly
Midland Bank Review	Midland Bank Ltd.	quarterly
Monthly Digest of Statistics	Central Statistical Office	monthly
Monthly Newsletter	National Westminister Bank	monthly
Quarterly Bulletin	Bank of England	quarterly
Survey of Current Affairs	British Information Services	monthly
United Kingdom Indicators	British Information Services	monthly
Bank of England Quarterly Review	Bank of England	quarterly
British Business	Department of Industry and Trade	weekly
Scottish Bankers Magazine	Institute of Bankers in Scotland	quarterly
Scottish Journal of Political Economy	Longman Group Ltd.	triennially
Standard Bank Review	Standard Bank Investment Corporation Ltd.	monthly
Journal of Institute of Bankers	Institute of Bankers	bimonthly
Scottish Economic Bulletin	Scottish Economic and Planning Department	semiannually
Three Banks Review	Royal Bank of Scotland	quarterly
Statistical Summary	Bank of England	annually
Report	Bank of England	annually
Reports and Accounts	Bank of England	annually
The Banker	London Financial News Ltd.	monthly
Bankers Magazine	The Banker's Magazine	monthly
The London Banker's Yearbook	Thomas Skinner & Co.	annually
Quarterly Review	National Westminister Bank	quarterly
Economics	Cambridge University	irregularly
British Affairs	British Information Service	quarterly

Business Forecast	Charterhouse Group Ltd.	quarterly
District Bank Review	District Bank Ltd.	quarterly
Economic Trends	Great Britain Central Statistical Office	monthly
Financial Times	The Financial Times Ltd.	daily
National Institute Economic Review	National Institute of Economic and Social Research	monthly
Review of British Industry	The Financial Times Ltd.	annually

Yugoslavia

l'Activité Economique en Yougoslavie	Narodna Banka Kraljevine Yugoslavye	monthly
Annual Report	Narodna Banka Jugoslavyi	annually
Bulletin Trimestriel	Narodna Banka Kraljevine Yugoslavye	quarterly
Economic Analysis	Yugoslav Association of Econometrics and Management Sciences	quarterly
Economic Review	Economic Daily Privredni Pregled	monthly
Economic Surveys of Yugoslavia	Organization for Economic Cooperation and Development	annually
Narodna Banka Kraljevine Yugoslavye Annual Report	Narodna Banka Kraljevine Yugoslavye	annually
Privileged Agrarian Bank Limited Report	Privileged Agrarian Bank Ltd.	annually
Quarterly Economic Review of Yugoslavia	The Economist Intelligence Unit Ltd.	quarterly
Statisticki Bilten	Savezni Zarod as Statistiken	irregularly
Yugoslavia Export	Yugoslaviapublic Publiciti Office	monthly

Europe in General

Bulletin of European Communities	European Community Information System	
Eastern Economist	Eastern Economist Ltd.	weekly
Eastern European Quarterly	Eastern European Quarterly	quarterly
Economic Bulletin for Europe	United Nations	biannually
European Free Trade Association Bulletin	European Free Trade Association	bimonthly
European Economy	Commission of the European Communities	quarterly

Journal of Economics	Central Banks of Finland, Iceland, Norway, Sweden, and the Joint Committee of Nordic Social Science Research Council	quarterly
Kredietbank	Inter-Alpha Group of Banks	weekly
Report from Europe	Chemical Bank	bimonthly
Rumanian Foreign Trade	Chamber of Commerce	quarterly
Skandinaviska Enskilda Banken Quarterly Review	Skandinaviska Enskilda Banken	quarterly

GLOSSARY

Absolute purchasing power parity (PPP). Requires that the exchange rate equalize the price of a market basket of goods in the two countries. Since the composition of market baskets and price indexes varies substantially across countries, and because many goods are nontraded or are subject to tariffs, it is unlikely that absolute PPP will hold in the real world.

Act of state doctrine. Under law, a foreign branch is in some respects treated as a separate entity, arising from the fact that it operates in a different jurisdiction from the parent company. The act of state doctrine obliges a domestic court to give effect to the laws and other acts of a recognized foreign government, such as exchange controls or deposit freezes.

Ad valorem tariff. A tariff that is calculated as a percentage of the value of the goods entering the country.

All-current (closing-rate) method. A foreign currency translation method under which all foreign currency items are translated at current exchange rates.

American option. An option that can be exercised on or before the fixed expiration date.

Appreciation. A gradual increase in the value of a currency, usually occurring over several days or weeks as the result of market forces of supply and demand.

Arbitrage. "Riskless" transactions to take advantage of a price differential or a yield differential in excess of transaction costs.

Arm's length standard. The principle under which intracompany pricing of goods and services is determined by the prices that would be charged to unrelated parties. This standard has been incorporated into U.S. tax law (Section 482).

Articles of Agreement. Specify the powers and responsibilities vested in the International Monetary Fund by members of that international organization.

Asian Currency Unit. A trading department of a bank in Singapore that has received a license from the monetary authorities in Singapore to deal in external currency deposits.

Balance of payments. A financial statement prepared for a given country summarizing the flows of goods, services, and funds between the residents of that country and the residents of the rest of the world during a certain period of time. The balance of payments is prepared using the concept of double-entry bookkeeping, where the total of debits equals the total of credits.

Balance of trade. The net of imports and exports of goods and services reported in the balance of payments.

Compiled by Ian H. Giddy with the assistance of Mary Townswick.

Bankers' acceptances. Drafts drawn on a bank and accepted by the bank, meaning that the bank will honor them at maturity. The maturity date is determined from that date of the acceptance or drawing of the draft plus the period of time indicated in the draft.

Bank for International Settlement. A bank for European central banks formed in 1930 to promote cooperation among its members. It serves as the agent for the European Monetary Cooperative Fund and it also collects data on the size of the Eurocurrency market and central bank intervention in the foreign exchange market.

Bankhaus Herstatt. A West German bank that failed in the mid-1970s, due to mismanaged foreign exchange trading. Its failure increased the awareness of authorities of the lack of foreign exchange market regulation.

Bank rate. Often the key interest rate in the banking system of certain countries (such as the United Kingdom). It is the rate at which the central bank of a country lends to its own money market institutions.

Basic balance. The net of the following accounts in the balance of payments: exports and imports of goods and services, unilateral transfers, and long-term capital flows.

Basis. The difference between cash and futures prices, or the difference between yields on different (but similar) financial instruments.

Bearer instrument. A negotiable instrument payable on demand to the individual who holds the instrument. Title passes by delivery without endorsement.

Bill of lading. A receipt from a carrier for goods shipped and a contract by the carrier for delivery of those goods. Bills of lading are usually negotiable; that is, they are made out to the order of someone.

Bloc arrangement. A system (such as the European Monetary System) where the currencies of several countries float jointly against other currencies.

Bretton Woods Conference. A meeting of representatives of non-Communist countries in Bretton Woods, New Hampshire, in 1944. The participants agreed on the characteristics of the international monetary system that prevailed through 1971, which was a fixed exchange rate system.

Bridge financing. Medium-term financing, usually at fluctuating interest rates, that customarily takes the form of renewable overdrafts or discounting facilities. It is used as a continuing source of funds while the borrower obtains medium- or long-term fixed-rate financing, usually from sources other than commercial banks.

Buffer Stock Facility. A lending program administered by the International Monetary Fund to finance contributions by member nations with payments difficulties to buffer stock agreements.

Call option. The right to buy a fixed amount of foreign exchange at a specified price within a specified time.

Capital asset pricing model. A theoretical model that relates the return on an asset to its risk. The risk is defined as the contribution of the asset to the volatility of the portfolio.

Capital mobility. The extent to which private capital is free to respond to investment opportunities abroad. This mobility requires well-developed exchange and financial markets, freedom from official restrictions on foreign investment, and confidence that future government policies will not prevent the repatriation of invested funds.

CD futures. Bank certificates of deposits traded for future delivery at some prearranged yield on an organized futures exchange.

Central bank. The institution with the primary responsibility to control the growth of its country's money stock. It might also have regulatory powers over commercial banks and sometimes over other financial institutions, and it usually serves as the fiscal agent for the government.

Certificate of deposit (CD). A placement of funds for a certain period of time with a bank, for which the depositor receives a confirmation making the deposit receipt a negotiable instrument. Investment bankers create a secondary market where CDs can be purchased and sold prior to maturity. Investors usually accept a smaller interest rate on CDs than on regular time deposits because the investment is more liquid.

Charting. Interpreting foreign exchange market activity and predicting future movements, usually over a short period, from graphic depictions of prices and volumes. It is a primary tool of technical analysts.

Clearing house. An institution through which futures contracts are cleared, in which the clearing house assumes the role of being the buyer to each seller and seller to each buyer, collecting losses and paying profits. It deals only with approved members.

Clearing House Interbank Payments System (CHIPS). An automated clearing facility operated by the New York Clearing House Association that processes international transfers among its members. It moves dollars among 100 New York financial institutions—mostly major U.S. banks, branches of foreign banks, and Edge Act subsidiaries of out-of-state banks.

Commodity Futures Trading Commission (CFTC). The federal agency with authority to oversee futures trading.

Compensatory Financing Facility. A lending program administered by the International Monetary Fund to finance short-term imbalances in members' international payments caused by temporary shortfalls of exports.

Compound tariff. A tariff that has both ad valorem and specific components.

Compressibility ratio. A ratio that assesses a country's liquidity position. It is the ratio of vital imports and debt service payments to exports, capital inflows, and aid receipts.

Conditionality. The International Monetary Fund's practice of requiring members to adopt changes in their domestic economic policies as a condition for receiving balance of payments loans from the fund.

Confirmed irrevocable letter of credit. A type of credit issued by the importer's bank and confirmed by a bank in the exporter's country. The importer's bank commits itself irrevocably to pay the exporter's draft and the confirming bank (the exporter's bank) adds to this commitment by assuming the responsibility to pay the exporter's draft, provided that all conditions stated in the letter of credit are met.

Consignment. An arrangement under which the exporter ships and delivers the product to the importer and receives payment only after the importer sells the product.

Consolidated financial statement. A financial statement that is the result of the line-by-line combination of the assets, liabilities, revenues, and expenses of a parent company and its principal subsidiaries. Reciprocal accounts stemming from intercompany transactions are typically eliminated.

Consortium. A syndicate of banks that pool their resources in order to offer larger loans, greater capability in international banking, different types of international activity, and various currency resources.

Controlled foreign corporation. A foreign corporation of which more than 50% of the total voting power of the stock is owned by U.S. shareholders. A U.S. shareholder is any U.S. corporation, individual, or other entity owning, directly or indirectly, 10% or more of the total voting power. These shareholders are liable for taxes on certain undistributed earnings of the controlled foreign corporation.

Convertible bond. A fixed-interest security that is convertible into the borrower's common stock under stipulated conditions. The difference between the price of ordinary shares at the time of the issue of the bonds and the rate at which they can be converted is the convertible premium. The attractiveness of convertible bonds lies in the possibility of a rise in the price of the common stock or an appreciation in the currency in which the stock is quoted during the bond's life.

Correspondent bank. A bank, located in one geographic area, that accepts deposits from a bank in another region and provides services on behalf of this other bank. Internationally, many banks maintain one account with a correspondent bank in each major country so as to be able to make payments in all major currencies. Correspondent banks are usually established on a reciprocal basis, with the two banks maintaining local currency accounts with each other.

Cost, insurance, freight (CIF) price. A standard price quotation by an exporter, covering the cost of goods, any marine insurance, and all transportation charges to the foreign port of entry.

Cost of capital. The weighted rate of return expected by the various parties financing the firm. Bondholders expect a return equivalent to the market interest rate on debt, while equity holders expect a return that is a function of dividends received and capital gains as the stock appreciates in value, adjusted for risk. The cost of capital is traditionally used as a hurdle rate that projects must yield in order to be accepted by the firm.

Cost-plus method of transfer pricing. A method of pricing used in transactions between entities that are owned or controlled by the same interests. The arm's length price is the cost of producing the product, plus a markup based on the seller's similar transactions with unrelated parties.

Cost-plus loan pricing. The interest rate on a loan is expressed as a function of some publicly known cost-of-funds measure, such as LIBOR (London interbank offered rate).

Countervailing duty. Taxes imposed on imports to offset the effects of the foreign subsidies.

Country risk. A broad spectrum of risk, including political as well as economic risk, caused by potential conflict between corporate goals and the national aspirations of host countries. The essential element in country risk is some form of government action preventing the fulfillment of a contract or agreement.

Covered interest arbitrage. Borrowing one currency, converting the proceeds into another currency, where it is invested, and simultaneously selling this other currency forward against the initial currency. Covered interest arbitrage takes advantage of—and in practice quickly eliminates—any temporary discrepancies between the forward rate and the interest rate differential of two currencies.

Covered interest differential. The deviation from interest rate parity, sometimes incorrectly called the "implicit" premium.

Covering. Protecting the value of the future proceeds of an international trade transaction, usually by buying or selling the proceeds in the forward market.

Crawling peg system. An exchange rate system in which the exchange rate is adjusted frequently and deliberately, perhaps every few weeks, usually to reflect prevailing rates of inflation. In Brazil, for example, where a crawling peg system has been in use for some time, the cruzeiro devalues about 10 times a year.

Credit risk. In lending operations, the likelihood that a borrower will not be able to repay the principal or pay the interest.

Credit Tranche Facility. The primary lending program administered by the International Monetary Fund to finance the short-term payments imbalances of member nations.

Cross-default provision. A provision in a loan agreement that allows the lender to declare the loan immediately payable and to terminate any further extension of credit if the borrower defaults on any other debt.

Cross-rate. The exchange rate between currencies B and C if the rates between currencies A and B and A and C are already known. Unless broken, the cross-rate should be consistent with the other rates.

Currency area. Countries whose reserve holdings are denominated primarily in the currency of another or whose currencies are more or less formally linked to another and whose exchange control regulations parallel those in the dominant currency.

Currency band. A band within which a currency is allowed to fluctuate on both sides of its official parity. The central bank of the country concerned intervenes in order to maintain the value of the currency within the permissible range.

Currency basket. A method for determining the value of a financial asset or currency as a weighted average of market exchange rates. The weights in this average are often defined to be specific quantities of currencies, hence the term "currency basket." A basket can contain two or more currency components, but the number of currencies included is usually limited by practical considerations.

Current exchange rate. The exchange rate ruling at the balance sheet date or during the income statement period.

Current/noncurrent method. A foreign currency translation method under which current balance sheet items denominated in foreign currencies are translated at current exchange rates and long-term items are translated at historical rates.

Debenture bonds. General, unsecured obligations of an issuing firm, which are claims only on the general assets of the corporation.

Debt-service ratio. A common ratio used to assess a country's creditworthiness. It is the ratio of a country's debt-service payments to exports.

Deemed tax. The amount of the total income tax paid abroad that can be subtracted from the U.S. tax a corporation must pay. It is calculated by multiplying the tax paid abroad by the proportion of after-tax income that is remitted as dividends.

Deferred payment. A type of payment under a letter of credit in which the exporter ships the goods to the importer but does not get paid immediately. The payment is made by the opening bank at a specified time when all conditions stipulated in the letter of credit are met.

Demand deposit. Funds in a current account (a checking account) that can be withdrawn at any time without notice, depending on local regulations. Demand deposits might or might not be interest-bearing deposits.

Depreciation. A gradual decline in the value of a currency, usually occurring over several days or weeks, because of market forces of supply and demand.

Devaluation. An official government act that produces a substantial decline in exchange rates, usually immediately.

Direct exporting. Shipping goods to a country without using any of its domestic intermediaries. Channels that use foreign agents or distributors or the manufacturer's own foreign sales facilities, for example, are direct.

Direct quotation. A rate of exchange quoted in units of foreign currency for each unit of the domestic currency.

Discount. The amount by which a currency is cheaper for future delivery than for immediate or spot delivery is a forward market discount. If sterling is selling for US$2.3940 on the spot market but at US$2.3920 for delivery in three months, then it is selling at a 20-point discount.

Discounting. Where a sale is to be settled by a bill of exchange, the seller can discount it that is, give it to a financial institution in exchange for immediate payment of an amount less than the face value to reflect the interest cause of payment before the receivable settlement date.

Divergence indicator. Signals the divergence of a European Monetary System member's economic policies from those of its neighbors. Divergence is measured by fluctuations in the market value (in terms of each member currency) of the European Currency Unit relative to its central or par value.

Divergence threshhold. The critical value of each European Monetary System member's divergence indicator that, when reached, establishes the presumption that domestic economic policies will be adjusted.

Domestic International Sales Corporation (DISC). A corporation that can defer from U.S. taxation approximately 25% of the total income from the manufacture and sale of the goods it exports. To qualify as a DISC, a corporation must receive at least 95% of its gross income from exports and at least 95% of its assets must be export assets.

Doomsday tax. The U.S. tax code provides that when a foreign affiliate is set up in a tax-haven country to siphon income from a higher tax area, income from the tax-haven country is subject to U.S. tax whether or not it is remitted to the United States. The proceeds from liquidating a tax-haven company can also be subject to tax, called the "doomsday" tax.

Double hedging. A technique used to hedge by purchase of foreign contracts whereby the volume of forward contracts purchased exceeds the exposed position, ostensibly because the profits on the forward contracts are taxed.

Double taxation. By double taxation is meant that taxes are paid twice—once abroad (where the income was earned) and a second time in the U.S., as the company is a U.S. company. A principle of U.S. tax law is that double taxation should be avoided. If a U.S. company has already paid taxes abroad, it should only pay enough taxes in the U.S. to bring the overall rate up to the U.S. rate.

Draft. A written order to pay a specified amount of money at a specified time to a given person or to the bearer.

Economic exposure. The effect of currency changes on the parent currency value of the future cash flows generated by a company's foreign operations.

Edge Act corporation. A subsidiary of a U.S. commercial bank that obtains income by operating in foreign countries. It is given powers not held by domestic U.S. banks to operate in ways similar to the practices of the foreign banks. The subsidiary might have a U.S. office, but such an office could handle only international banking, including accepting deposits arising from international transactions.

Effective exchange rate. A rate measuring the overall nominal value of a currency in the foreign exchange market. It is calculated by forming a weighted average of bilateral exchange rates, using a weighting scheme that reflects the importance of each country's trade with the home country.

Entrepôt financial centers. World financial centers that play the role of bringing foreign lenders and foreign borrowers together. The countries in which these centers are located might or might not be capital exporters or importers, but they are channels through which international funds pass.

Eurobanks. Financial intermediaries that simultaneously bid for time deposits and make loans in a currency or currencies other than that of the country in which they are located.

Eurobond. A long-term bond underwritten by an international syndicate of banks and marketed internationally in countries other than the country of the currency in which it is denominated. The issue is thus not subject to national restrictions.

Eurocurrency. A currency held in the form of time deposits in financial institutions outside the home country of the currency.

Eurodollars. Dollars held in the form of time deposits in banks outside the United States. These banks can be foreign-owned or overseas branches of U.S. banks.

European Currency Unit (ECU). A currency basket composed of specific quantities of the currencies of European Monetary System members. The ECU is used as part of the system's divergence indicator and provides a unit of account used to value members' exchange reserve assets.

European Economic Community (EEC). The Common Market, composed of 10 countries: Belgium, Denmark, France, Ireland, Italy, Luxemburg, The Netherlands, the United Kingdom, West Germany, and Greece. These countries have formed a customs union with a common external tariff and are working to achieve greater economic and political intergration.

European Free Trade Association (EFTA). Common regulations for tariffs and trade established in 1959 by Austria, Denmark, Norway, Portugal, Sweden, Switzerland, and the United Kingdom.

European Monetary System. A structure of agreements governing the exchange market activities of participating members of the European Economic Community. These agreements currently require members to closely manage the exchange values of their currencies relative to other members. Ultimately, the agreements envision the creation of a European Monetary Fund and movement toward monetary unification.

European option. An option that can be exercised only on the fixed expiration date.

European Unit of Account (EUA). An artificial currency unit that originally changed in value only when all 17 of the currencies of the member countries of the European Payments Union changed in value, two-thirds of them in the same direction.

Exchange controls. Restrictions on the convertibility of a currency or on the movements of funds in that currency, imposed by the central bank or local authorities.

Exchange rate. The bilateral exchange ratio that is quoted by foreign exchange traders or reported in a newspaper. It expresses the number of units of one currency that must be offered in exchange for a unit of another currency.

Exchange rate overshooting. Occurs when exchange rate changes are in excess of some given standard of volatility.

Exchange risk. The risk assumed by a party to an international transaction in which the party could incur an exchange loss as a result of currency movements. An exchange loss on an international transaction can be either from receiving a smaller amount in home currency or from paying a higher amount in home currency at the maturity of the transaction than was expected at the outset.

Exercise price. The exchange rate at which a foreign exchange option can be exercised.

Export finance vehicle. A vehicle company set up to buy the export receivables of affiliated companies. Export finance companies perform exposure and/or liquidity management functions.

Export-Import Bank. An independent agency of the U.S. government that was established in 1934 to stimulate U.S. foreign trade. The Exim Bank supports commercial banks that are financing exports and provides direct financing, loan guarantees, and insurance to foreign buyers purchasing U.S. goods.

Extended Facility. A longer term lending program of the International Monetary Fund for the use of member nations with serious balance of payments problems that are not expected to reverse themselves in the near future.

Factoring. A financing method in which the borrower assigns the customer receivables as collateral to a firm (called a factor), who normally assumes responsibility for collection.

FASB 8. A regulation of the Financial Accounting Standards Board, in effect from 1976 to 1981, that required companies to translate their foreign-affiliate financial statements using the temporal method. Foreign currency gains or losses were reported on the income statement as ordinary income.

FASB 52. A regulation of the Financial Accounting Standards Board, in effect as of December 1981, which revises standards for translating foreign currency financial statements. Financial results must be measured in the functional currency of the foreign entity (except in cases of high inflation). Translation is done using the all-current method, with transaction losses showing up on the parent's income statement and translation losses on the parent's balance sheet.

Federal funds. Money deposited with the U.S. Federal Reserve Bank, the U.S. Central Bank. This money is available immediately. Purchases of U.S. Treasury bills and other money market instruments in the domestic U.S. dollar money market can be made only with federal funds.

Federal funds market. Strictly speaking, the market for loans of funds that are deposited with the U.S. Federal Reserve. It has come to include the market for all loans of immediately available funds that can be used to satisfy reserve requirements.

Filter rule. A rule for buying and selling currencies based on the premise that once a movement in a currency's exchange rate has surpassed a given percentage movement, it will continue to move in the same direction.

Financial Accounting Standards Board (FASB). The private organization in the United States responsible for establishing the standards for financial accounting and reporting.

Fisher effect. The theory that interest rates in any country rise by approximately the same percentage as the rate of inflation, so if the basic rate of interest is 3% a year when there is no inflation, and if inflation then occurs and continues at the rate of 5% a year, the basic rate of interest will rise to approximately 8% a year.

Fixed exchange rate system. A system in which the values of various countries' currencies are tied to one major currency (such as the U.S. dollar), gold, or special drawing rights. The term should not be taken literally because fluctuations within a range of 1% or 2% on either side of the fixed rate are usually permitted in such a system.

Floating exchange rate system. A system in which the values of various currencies relative to each other are established by the forces of supply and demand in the market without intervention by the governments involved.

Floating-rate notes. Short-term, floating interest-rate securities. The interest rate is pegged to LIBOR, and is adjusted semiannually. These securities are attractive during periods of rising interest rates when issues of straight bonds are subject to capital depreciation.

Foreign bond. A long-term security issued by a borrower in the national market of another country. Underwritten by a syndicate from one country alone and sold on that country's capital market, the bond is denominated in the currency of the country in which it is sold.

Foreign Corrupt Practices Act of 1977. Federal legislation designed to avoid improper corporate payments abroad. Under the act corporate violators can be fined up to $1 million and others are liable for fines up to $10,000—not payable by the company—and five years in prison.

Foreign Credit Insurance Corporation (FCIA). A private association of leading U.S. insurance companies, affiliated with the Export-Import Bank, that provides short- and medium-term credit insurance to exporters, enabling them to obtain or offer better financing in certain cases.

Foreign currency translation. The process of expressing in the reporting currency of the enterprise those amounts that are denominated or measured in a foreign currency.

Foreign exchange broker. An individual who introduces the two parties in a currency or deposit transaction to each other. The parties could be a buyer and a seller of foreign currencies or a borrower and a lender of a given currency. The broker charges a fee for this service. Brokers seldom take a position for themselves; they only arrange for transactions among other parties.

Foreign exchange option. A contract conveying the right to buy or sell a designated quantity of a foreign currency at a specified price during a stipulated period under stated conditions. The term is sometimes incorrectly used to mean an optional date forward contract.

Foreign exchange trader. An agent who stands ready to buy and sell currencies out of inventory and expects to earn a profit for the costs and risks incurred. The foreign exchange trader is an intermediary who smooths transactions between businesspersons in different countries, as they might arrive at the market at irregular and unpredictable times.

Forward contract. An agreement to exchange at a specified future date currencies of different countries at a specified contractual rate (the forward rate).

Forward exchange market. This market involves contracts for exchange of currency at some date in the future. The standard maturities for contracts available are, one, two, three, six, and 12 months, although contracts for any maturity can be negotiated.

Forward forward swap (or forward swap). A pair of forward exchange deals involving a forward purchase and a forward sale of a currency, simultaneously entered into, but of different maturities.

Fourth directive. A European Economic Community accounting standard that deals with the content, object, and format of accounts, including specific disclosure provisions. The directive is an order to member states to bring their laws into line with its requirements.

Free alongside (FAS) quotation. An exporter's price quotation that includes delivery of goods alongside a designated vehicle, with the importer responsible for all subsequent movement of the goods.

Fronting loan. A parent-to-affiliate loan channeled through a financial intermediary, usually a large international bank. This type of loan reduces political risk since government authorities are more likely to allow the local affiliate to repay a loan to a large international bank than to the parent company, given a situation of political turmoil or blocked funds.

Functional currency. The currency of the primary economic environment in which a firm operates. Normally it is the currency of the environment in which an entity primarily generates and expends cash.

Futures contract. A highly standardized foreign exchange contract written against the exchange clearing house for a fixed number of foreign currency units and for delivery on a fixed date. Because of the high level of standardization, futures contracts can be traded readily in a secondary market.

General Resources Account. The lending program through which the International Monetary Fund provides short-term balance of payments financing to its members.

Gold standard. A monetary agreement under which national currencies are backed by gold and the gold is utilized for international payments.

Grossing up. Obtaining the U.S. taxable income by adding the deemed tax to gross dividends remitted from the foreign subsidiary. The U.S. tax rate is applied to this sum, and tax credits for the deemed tax and the withholding tax are subtracted to obtain the net U.S. tax.

Group of Ten. Ten major industrial countries (West Germany, France, Belgium, The Netherlands, Italy, the United Kingdom, Sweden, Canada, Japan, and the United States) that pledged in 1962 to stand ready to lend their currencies to the International Monetary Fund under what was termed the "General Arrangements to Borrow." The Group of Ten took the lead in subsequent changes in the international monetary system.

Hard currency. A strong, freely convertible currency. A strong currency is one that is not expected to devalue in the foreseeable future.

Historical exchange rate. The foreign currency exchange rate in effect on the date when an asset or liability was acquired, or at the date of a subsequent change in the accounting valuation of the asset or liability.

Hot money. Speculative bank deposits that are moved around the international money markets to take advantage of currency and interest rate movements.

Imputation system. Resident stockholders are allowed to credit a portion of the tax paid at the corporate level against the taxes imposed at the stockholder level.

Indicator rules. Publicly announced rules that link adjustments in the par values of exchange rates to movements in economic statistics. Par values adjust automatically under this exchange rate management policy, while official intervention holds market rates in the neighborhood of the par value.

Indirect exporting. Exporting in which the manufacturer relies on export middle-persons in the target country.

Indirect quotation. A rate of exchange quoted in units of domestic currency for each unit of foreign currency.

Interest equalization tax. A form of foreign exchange control established by the U.S. government that required U.S. residents to pay a special tax on any purchase of foreign securities. It was in effect from 1963 until the end of 1973.

Interest rate parity. The process that ensures that forward margins equal the interest rate differentials on equivalent securities in the two financial centers involved.

International Accounting Standards Committee (IASC). A private international organization concerned over setting standards for financial accounting and reporting and composed of accounting bodies representing various nations.

International Banking Act of 1978. Federal legislation designed to remove many of the competitive advantages that foreign banks had over their domestic U.S. counterparts. The Federal Reserve Bank, for example, is now authorized to impose reserve requirements on foreign banks and there are restrictions on their ability to take deposits nationwide.

International banking facilities (IBFs). Free monetary zones in the United States that can be established by U.S. depository institutions, Edge and Agreement corporations, and by U.S. branches and agencies of foreign banks. The IBFs accepting foreign deposits are exempted from reserve requirements and interest rate restrictions, and can make loans to foreign borrowers.

International finance subsidiary. A corporation that is wholly owned by a U.S. parent company and is incorporated in the United States, usually in Delaware. Its purpose is to facilitate the parent company's financing of its international operations. If less than 20% of the subsidiary's gross income is received from U.S. sources, interest paid by the subsidiary to its foreign bondholders is not subject to U.S. withholding tax.

International Fisher effect. The theory that the higher interest income (agio) received from investment in a country that has inflation will approximately equal the loss in value from the depreciation of the currency of that country.

International licensing. The transfer of industrial property rights (patents, trademarks, and/or proprietary know-how) from a licenser in one country to a licensee in a second country. These rights are usually not sold outright, but granted for a specified period of time in return for a royalty compensation.

International Monetary Fund. An international institution created to provide a forum in which nations can jointly examine each other's economic policies, discuss the operation of the international monetary system, and negotiate revisions in international monetary relations. The objectives of the Fund include supervising the exchange market intervention of member nations, providing the financing needed by members to overcome short-term payments imbalances, and encouraging monetary cooperation and international trade among nations.

International Monetary Market. A centralized auction market in Chicago where currency and financial futures contracts are traded.

Joint venture. A business venture in which two or more parties, often a foreign firm and a local firm, government agency, or individual, have equity interests.

Lag. To defer payment of a debt. A firm with a subsidiary in a hard currency country that has capital inflow controls will often encourage the subsidiary to lag its payments in order to take advantage of a possible revaluation of the hard currency.

Law of comparative advantage. According to this law, a country will specialize in producing and will export those goods that it can produce cheaply relative to the costs of producing them in foreign countries. It will import those goods that it can produce only at relatively high cost.

Lead. To prepay a debt. A company with a subsidiary in a soft-currency country that has capital outflow controls will often encourage the subsidiary to prepay any money due to the home office to avoid the risk of the soft currency depreciating relative to the home currency.

Letter of credit. A letter issued by a bank, usually at the request of an importer, indicating that the opening bank or another will honor drafts if they are accompanied by specified documents under specified conditions.

Liquidity risk. The uncertainty involved in holding assets that trade a small volume for each unit of time.

Lombard rate. The rate of interest charged on a "Lombard loan"; that is, an advance against the collateral of specific listed securities in Europe.

London dollar CDs. Negotiable certificates of deposit issued by all major Eurobanks. Denominations range from $10,000 to several million dollars and maturities range from a call basis to over five years.

London interbank offered rate (LIBOR). The interest rate at which prime banks offer dollar deposits to other prime banks in London. This rate is often used as the basis for pricing Eurodollar and other Eurocurrency loans. The lender and the borrower agree to a markup over the LIBOR, and the total of LIBOR plus the markup is the effective interest rate for the loan.

Long position. To have greater inflows than outflows of a given currency. In foreign exchange operations, long positions arise when the amount purchased of a given currency is greater than the amount sold. In money market operations, a long position arises from investing a given currency for a shorter period of time than it is borrowed.

Managed float (dirty float). A floating exchange rate system in which some government intervention still takes place. A government could announce that it will let its currency float, but it might secretly allow its central bank to intervene in the exchange market to avoid too much appreciation or depreciation.

Margin. A performance bond used as a safeguard to both the buyer and seller of a futures contract and to the brokerage firm carrying the account. It indicates that there will be adequate funds available in the customer's account to make settlement when open futures positions are liquidated.

Market maker. An institution that stands willing to buy or sell an asset at some price, or an institution that deals so frequently and in such volume in an asset that it makes it possible for others to buy or sell that asset at almost any time.

Matching. A process whereby a company balances its long positions in a given currency (assets, revenues, or cash inflows) with its offsetting short positions in that currency (liabilities, expenses, or cash outflows). The remaining (unmatched) position is the net exposure in the currency.

Merchant bank. A specialist bank that, apart from carrying out a banking business, also acts as an advisor to companies, including assisting with the flotation of new issues of shares on the stock market.

Momentum analysis. A technique used to predict short-term exchange rate changes. Momentum models study the direction and impetus behind past exchange rate movements to predict future movements.

Monetary-nonmonetary method. A foreign currency translation method in which nonmonetary assets and liabilities are translated at their historical exchange rates and monetary items are translated at current exchange rates.

Money market. A financial market for short-term securities; a market in which short-term borrowings and investments are made. Negotiable certificates of deposit, acceptances, and commercial paper are some of the instruments commonly used in the money market.

Most-favored-nation clause. In international business treaties, a provision against tariff discrimination between two or more nations. It provides that each participant will automatically extend to other signatories all tariff reductions that are offered to nonmember nations.

Multiple currency pegging. An exchange rate management policy under which the weighted average exchange value of a currency is held within a specified neighborhood of a par value through official intervention in the exchange market.

Multiple-rate methods. Accounting methods for translating foreign currency financial statements that use a combination of historical and current exchange rates, based on the parent company's perspective. Foreign-based operations are viewed as extensions of the parent company rather than independent entities.

New York Futures Exchange. A centralized auction market where currency and financial futures contracts are traded.

Offshore finance subsidiary. A foreign corporation that is wholly owned, directly or indirectly, by a direct investor in a separate country. An offshore finance subsidiary is usually located in a tax-haven country since its purpose is to enable a multinational corporation to finance its international operations without being subject to domestic withholding taxes on remittances to foreign investors.

Option premium. The price paid to the seller of a foreign exchange option for the rights involved.

Optional date forward contract (or forward option contract). A forward exchange contract in which the rate is fixed but the maturity is open, within a specified range of dates.

Organization for Economic Cooperation and Development (OECD). An organization that provides for intergovernmental discussion among 24 industrialized countries in the fields of economic and social policy. It also collects and publishes data and makes short-term economic forecasts of its member countries.

Parallel loan (back-to-back loan). An arrangement in which two business firms in separate countries borrow each other's currency for a specific period of time. At an agreed terminal date they return the borrowed currencies. Such a swap creates a covered hedge against exchange loss since each company, on its own books, borrows the same currency it repays.

Parity grid. The matrix of bilateral par values for the currencies of members of the European Monetary System. This grid establishes the intervention prices between which each member government is obliged to maintain the exchange value of currency in terms of every other group currency.

Points. The number of units, often expressed in terms of the last two or three significant digits, of an exchange rate. It is customary to state that a currency has appreciated or depreciated by some points from a previous exchange rate. Forward exchange-rate quotes are often expressed in terms of so many points premium or discount above or below the spot rate.

Premium. The amount by which a currency is more expensive currently than for future delivery at a given time. If Swiss francs are selling at U.S.$0.2320 in the spot market but at U.S.$0.2325 for delivery in three months, then they are selling at a five-point premium for this period.

Primary and secondary financial statements. A system under which two different sets of financial statements are prepared. Primary statements are those provided for domestic readers. Secondary statements are prepared for foreign readers and reflect the language, currency, accounting principles, and auditing standards of the foreign country.

Put option. The right to sell a fixed amount of foreign exchange at a specified price within a specified time.

Quota. A restriction on the quantity of an item that can be imported into, or exported from, a country during a specified period of time.

Real effective exchange rate. A rate calculated by dividing the home country's nominal effective exchange rate by an index of the ratio of average foreign prices to home prices. This rate attempts to measure the overall competitiveness of home-country goods in international markets.

Real exchange rate. The value of a currency in terms of real purchasing power determined by comparing the price of a hypothetical market basket of goods in two different countries, translated into the same currency at the prevailing exchange rate. It is useful for measuring the price competitiveness of domestic goods in international markets and also for calculating the real value of investment projects.

Recapture provision. Some companies used to reduce their taxes by switching from a branch to an affiliate status. At the time of heavy start-up costs they would operate as a branch, and since these losses were consolidated with the parent company earnings, tax savings would result. When the foreign operation began to make profits, it would be changed to affiliate status. The recapture provision in the U.S. Tax Reform Act of 1976 declares that such tax savings can be claimed by the Internal Revenue Service.

Regulation D. A Federal Reserve System regulation that classifed deposits held for less than 30 days at its member banks as demand deposits, subject to reserve requirements. This regulation was modified in 1980, when a new type of time deposit, with a minimum maturity of 14 days, was defined.

Regulation Q. A regulation of the Federal Reserve System that established a ceiling on interest rates on time deposits in the United States. Member banks were forbidden to pay interest on deposits with maturities of less than 30 days. This regulation played a significant role in the growth of the Eurodollar market.

Relative purchasing power parity. Requires that the percentage change in the exchange rate equal the differential percentage change in the price of a market basket of goods in the two countries.

Repurchase agreement. A contract in which the seller of an asset agrees to buy back an asset sold on a specific date. This technique is frequently used when a bank, for regulatory reasons, cannot accept a deposit from a customer and pay interest on it. In such a case, the bank can sell a security to its customer and agree in writing to repurchase this security on the date the customer wants to have the money back.

Revaluation. An official government act that produces a substantial increase in an exchange rate, usually overnight.

Rollover. A short swap designed to employ or borrow foreign currency balances. In a rollover applied to a currency that trades on a two-day spot basis, for example, a trader can sell a currency for delivery in one business day and buy that currency back for delivery in two business days.

Rollover Ratio. A ratio used to assess a country's creditworthiness. It is the reciprocal of the average maturity of a country's external debt.

Second Amendment. Ratified in 1978, this amendment to the Articles of Agreement of the International Monetary Fund allows members more flexibility in the management of exchange rates than under the Bretton Woods system of adjustably pegged exchange rates. This amendment also increases the supervisory responsibilities of the IMF and makes the special drawing rights more attractive as reserve assets.

Securities and Exchange Commission. The government body responsible for regulating the financial reporting practices of most publicly owned corporations in connection with the buying and selling of stocks and bonds.

Short position. A greater outflow than inflow of a given currency. In foreign exchange operations, short positions arise when the amount of a given currency sold is greater than the amount purchased. In money market operations, a short position arises from borrowing a given currency for a shorter period of time than it is invested.

Sight draft. A bill of exchange that is due when presented.

Single-rate method. An accounting method used to translate foreign currency financial statements. The foreign entities are viewed from a local rather than a parent company perspective, so all foreign currency items are translated at a constant rate, the current rate.

Smithsonian Agreement. Specified the first stage of the multilateral exchange rate realignments that immediately preceded the collapse of the Bretton Woods system of international monetary relations.

Society for Worldwide Interbank Financial Transfers (SWIFT). A standardized electronic message transfer service designed to send and confirm instructions concerning funds transfers associated with international payments.

Soft currency. A weak currency whose convertibility is, or is expected to become, restricted.

Space arbitrage. The simultaneous purchase and sale of a currency in two different markets to take advantage of different exchange rates in those markets and to profit from the difference.

Special drawing rights (SDRs). Monetary accounts held at the International Monetary Fund for payments among governments. The rights can be transferred to other countries in exchange for convertible currencies, either voluntarily or for convertible currencies supplied by countries designated by the IMF. At first, SDRs had a fixed value in gold, but later their value was determined by a weighted basket of major currencies.

Specific tariff. A tariff that is calculated as a fixed amount for each unit imported, such a $0.01 a pound duty on condensed milk.

Split-rate taxation system. The statutory rate of taxation on distributed corporate earnings is lower than that on retained earnings. Japan and West Germany have this type of system.

Spot foreign exchange market. A market involving an exchange of bank drafts denominated in different currencies. A spot contract implies an immediate exchange.

Spot rate. The current rate of exchange quoted between two currencies. The spot rate is usually quoted as a bid rate and an offer rate.

Spread. The difference between the buying and selling rates.

Straight bonds. Nonconvertible Eurobond issues with fixed interest rates and fixed maturities.

Subsidiary. Any organization that has more than 50% of its voting stock owned by another firm.

Supplementary Financing Facility. A lending program administered by the International Monetary Fund to provide member nations with the additional resources necessary to deal with serious balance of payments problems that are not available through the Credit Tranche Facility.

Surety bond. A guarantee that a person or corporation will perform an obligation due to another person or corporation. It is issued by a surety, which is a specialized surety company, or an insurance company.

Surveillance. Generally refers to the occasional reviews of members' economic policies conducted by the International Monetary Fund to insure that nations do not abuse their rights and responsibilities in the choice of an exchange market policy under the Second Amendment.

Swap contract. A simultaneous purchase and sale of foreign currency for two different value dates. The swap can be viewed as a simultaneous borrowing and lending operation. It is a single transaction between two parties and since the rates (for simultaneous buying and selling) are set in advance, the trader is not exposed to changes in the foreign exchange rate.

Swap lines. Lines of credit extended from one government to another that can be drawn on to provide the foreign currencies needed for official intervention in the exchange market. These lines of credit, once drawn, provide very short term financing of imbalances in international payments. Swap lines are also referred to as "reciprocal currency arrangements."

Swap network. In the United States, the swap network is a set of short-term reciprocal currency agreements of $30 billion that the Federal Reserve maintains with 14 foreign central banks and the Bank for International Settlements. Each agreement allows the Federal Reserve and the foreign banks short-term access to the other's currency up to a specified limit.

Tariff. A schedule of taxes that a government imposes on imports or exports.

Tax haven. A country that imposes little or no tax or withholding on the profits from transactions carried on from that country, especially on income from interest and dividends.

Technical methods. Methods of predicting exchange rate changes, based on the belief that the forces of supply and demand are reflected in patterns of price and volume of trading. Technical analysts examine these patterns in order to predict future movements.

Temporal method. A foreign currency translation method under which the translation rate adopted must preserve the accounting principles used to value assets and liabilities in the original financial statements. Items stated at historical cost are translated at historical exchange rates; the current exchange rate is used for items stated at replacement cost, market value, or expected future value.

Terms of trade. The ratio of export prices to import prices expressed in the same currency.

Time arbitrage. The simultaneous purchase and sale of a currency for different maturity dates to take advantage of exchange rate differentials over time.

Transaction exposure. The exposure inherent in a foreign currency transaction, both commercial (trade receivables and payables) and financial (dividend and loan payments).

Translation (or accounting) exposure. Foreign currency assets, liabilities, revenues, and expenses that are consolidated at current exchange rates into parent currency–denominated group financial statements.

Value-added tax (VAT). A sales tax applied to the value of a product at each point in its manufacture, based on the selling price of the good. Each firm can credit against the tax the amount of VAT passed on to it by other suppliers and manufacturers.

Value compensation. The normal settlement arrangement for a foreign exchange transaction, in which payments are made in both currencies on the same date.

Value date. The contracted date on which the foreign exchange is to be delivered or received. For forward transactions, the value date and the maturity date are synonymous.

Value today. A special spot foreign exchange transaction in which delivery and payment are made on the same day as the contract, instead of the normal one or two business day lag.

Value tomorrow. A special spot foreign exchange transaction in which delivery and payment are made on the next business day after the contract.

Vertical integration. A method of diversification in which a corporation purchases a supplier or a customer. This is a common route when a company moves abroad, as it seeks to ensure its supply network as well as its outlets.

Voluntary export restraint. A country that is threatened with import restrictions on the part of a major trading partner might voluntarily limit its exports of a particular product to that importing country.

Warrant. A call option to buy a stated number of shares of stock at a specified price.

Withholding tax. A tax collected by the source originating the income, in contrast to one paid by the recipient of the income after the funds are received. For example, a withholding tax on interest payments to foreigners means that the tax proceeds are deducted from the interest payment made to the lender and collected by the borrower on behalf of the government.

Yankee bonds. Dollar bonds issued in New York by foreigners. They are underwritten by an international syndicate managed by U.S. banks and placed in the United States. These bonds are subject to U.S. law and must be registered with the Securities and Exchange Commission.

Yield curve. A diagram of interest rates prevailing on a class of securities that are alike in every respect except term to maturity. A yield curve can be sloping either upward or downward.

Yield to maturity. The value of a bond defined as the present value of the future stream of income payments plus the present value of the principal payment at maturity, both discounted at the appropriate rate of interest for bonds of that maturity and quality.

INDEX